ENCYCLOPEDIA of GERONTOLOGY

Age, Aging, and the Aged

Volume I

A–K

ENCYCLOPEDIA of GERONTOLOGY

Age, Aging, and the Aged

Volume I

A–K

Editor-in-Chief

James E. Birren

Center on Aging
University of California, Los Angeles

ACADEMIC PRESS

San Diego   New York   Boston   London   Sydney   Tokyo   Toronto

This book is printed on acid-free paper. ∞

Academic Press, Inc.
525 B Street, Suite 1900, San Diego, California 92101-4495, USA
http://www.apnet.com

Academic Press Limited
24-28 Oval Road, London NW1 7DX, UK
http://www.hbuk.co.uk/ap/

Library of Congress Cataloging-in-Publication Data

Encyclopedia of gerontology / edited by James E. Birren.
          p.   cm.
     Includes index.
     ISBN 0-12-226860-1 (set : alk. paper). -- ISBN 0-12-226861-X
(v. 1 : alk. paper). -- ISBN 0-12-226862-8 (v. 2 : alk. paper)
     1. Geriatrics--Encyclopedias.   2. Gerontology--Encyclopedias.
I. Birren, James E.
     [DNLM: 1. Geriatrics--encyclopedias.   WT 13 E563 1996]
RC952.5.E58   1996
612.6'7'03--dc20
DNLM/DLC
for Library of Congress   95-47195
                                                     CIP

PRINTED IN THE UNITED STATES OF AMERICA
96 97 98 99 00 01 EB 9 8 7 6 5 4 3 2 1

Contents

VOLUME 2

x

Contents

About the Editor-in-Chief

James E. Birren's many awards include the 1996 American Society on Aging President's Award, the Brookdale Foundation Award for Gerontological Research, the Sandoz prize for Gerontological Research, and the award for outstanding contribution to gerontology by the Canadian Association of Gerontology. Dr. Birren is currently Associate Director of the Center on Aging at the University of California, Los Angeles, and serves as an adjunct professor in medicine, psychiatry, and biobehavioral sciences. He is also Professor Emeritus of gerontology and psychology at the University of Southern California. Dr. Birren's previous positions include serving as Chief of the Section on Aging of the National Institute of Mental Health, founding Executive Director and Dean of the Ethel Percy Andrus Gerontology Center of USC, founding Director of the Anna and Harry Borun Center for Gerontological Research at UCLA, and President of the Gerontological Society of America, the Western Gerontological Society, and the Division on Adult Development and Aging of the American Psychological Association. Author of more than 250 scholarly publications, Dr. Birren's research interests include how speed of behavior changes with age, the causes and consequences of slowed information processing in the older nervous system, the effect of age on decision-making processes, and the role of expertise in skilled occupations. He has served as a delegate to several White House Conferences on Aging and continues to develop national priorities for research and education related to issues of aging.

About the Editorial Advisory Board

Victor W. Marshall is Professor of Behavioral Science at the University of Toronto and Director of its Centre for Studies of Aging. He served from 1990 to 1995 as Network Director of CARNET, the Canadian Aging Research Network, a Canadian federally funded, nationwide Network of Centres of Excellence. Professor Marshall is a fellow of the Gerontological Society of America and a founding member of the Canadian Association on Gerontology. He was Editor-in-Chief of *The Canadian Journal on Aging* for five years and is now on the editorial boards of the *Journal of Aging and Health* and *Ageing and Society*. More than 100 publications report his work from a broad social science perspective rooted in sociological training. Professor Marshall's work has covered such diverse aspects of aging as the family, long-term care, public policy, and death and dying, but it currently focuses on social theory of aging, independence and aging, and aging in relation to work and the life course. He directs a large multidisciplinary research program in the latter area funded by the Canadian government.

Thomas R. Cole's book *The Journal of Life: A Cultural History of Aging in America* (Cambridge, 1992) was nominated for a Pulitzer Prize. Another of his works, *The Oxford Book of Aging* (1994), for which he was Senior Editor, was noted as one of the most memorable books of 1995 by the *New Yorker*. Dr. Cole is Professor and Graduate Program Director at the Institute for Medical Humanities, University of Texas Medical Branch in Galveston, and a Fellow of the Gerontological Society. He has served as Chair of the Gerontological Society of America's Humanities and Arts Committee and on the editorial boards of *The Gerontologist, Generations,* and *Journal of Aging and Health*. Dr. Cole has published many articles and books on the history of aging and humanistic gerontology.

Alvar Svanborg was awarded the Thureus Prize for Research by the University of Uppsala, 1980; the Brookdale Foreign Award for distinguished contributions in gerontology, 1985; the Harold Hatch Award from Mount Sinai School of Medicine, New York, 1986; the Sandoz Prize for Gerontological Research, 1987; and the Third Age Award, XIV International Congress of Gerontology, Acapulco, Mexico, 1989. Dr. Svanborg is a Beth Fowler Vitoux and George E. Vitoux Distinguished Professor of Geriatric Medicine, Professor of Medicine, and Chief, Section of Geriatric Medicine, Clinical Director of Research in Gerontology, University of Illinois, Chicago. He has served as Scientific Advisor to the Swedish National Board of Health and Welfare, 1968–1988; Expert to the Supreme National Swedish Insurance Court, 1969–1988; and Swedish delegate at the United Nations World Assembly on Aging, 1982. Dr. Svanborg has been a consultant to the World Health Organization since 1970 and Special Advisor to the Director of the World Health Organization since 1984, in addition to serving as President of the Federation of Gerontology of the Nordic Countries from 1973–1988. Dr. Svanborg has been an advisor to the United States government, the Greek government, Hungarian authorities, the Israeli government, and the Polish government. He obtained his specialist license in internal medicine and cardiology in 1954 and in geriatric medicine in 1966. His research work has been focused in medical biochemistry, clinical physiology, internal medicine, medical gerontology, geriatrics, and long-term care medicine.

Edward J. Masoro was the recipient of the 1989 Allied-Signal Achievement Award in Aging Research. In 1990, he received the Geriatric Leadership Academic Award from the National Institute on Aging and the Robert W. Kleemeier Award from the Geron-

tological Society of America. In 1991, he received a medal of honor from the University of Pisa for Achievements in Gerontology, and in 1993, Dr. Masoro received the Distinguished Service Award from the Association of Chairmen of Departments of Physiology. In addition, he received the 1995 Irving Wright Award of Distinction of the American Federation for Aging Research and the 1995 Glenn Foundation Award. He served as President of the Gerontological Society of America from 1994–1995, as Chairman of the Aging Review Committee of the National Institute on Aging (NIA), and as Chairman of the Board of Scientific Counselors of the NIA. Dr. Masoro has held faculty positions at Queen's University (Canada), Tufts University School of Medicine, University of Washington, and Medical College of Pennsylvania. From 1973 through May of 1991, he served as Chairman of the Department of Physiology at the University of Texas Health Science Center at San Antonio. He currently continues his duties as Professor Emeritus in the Department of Physiology and is the Director of the newly created Aging Research and Education Center. Since 1975, Dr. Masoro's research has focused on the influence of food restriction on aging. He has served or is serving in an editorial role for 10 journals, and in January of 1992, he became the Editor of the *Journal of Gerontology: Biological Sciences.*

K. Warner Schaie has received the Kleemeier Award for Distinguished Research Contributions from the Gerontological Society of America and the Distinguished Scientific Contributions Award from the American Psychological Association. Dr. Schaie is the Evan Pugh Professor of Human Development and Psychology and Director of the Gerontology Center at the Pennsylvania State University. He also holds an appointment as Affiliate Professor of Psychiatry and Behavioral Science at the University of Washington. A fellow of the Gerontological Society and the American Psychological Association, Professor Schaie has served as president of the American Psychological Association Division of Adult Development and Aging and as Editor of the *Journal of Geronotology: Psychological Sciences*. Author of more than 250 scholarly publications of the psychology of aging, Dr. Schaie's interests include the life course of adult intelligence, its antecedents and modifiability, and methodological issues in the developmental sciences.

Preface

The study of aging has come to be one of the more important areas of interest because of its implications for the well-being of individuals and society. In 1900, persons over 65 years of age were the smallest portion of developed societies. Today they are emerging as the largest. This massive age shift occurring in population is affecting all institutions from universities to our places of work. It is little wonder that the growth of information about the processes of aging has been exponential in recent years.

The contents of this encyclopedia show that the growth of information ranges from the images of older persons held by the public and the media through the molecular and biological processes of aging, individual health and well-being, and what psychology and the social sciences have found out about the individual and group processes of aging. Throughout the world there is recognition that gerontology is timely and needed to answer questions being raised about the aging of individuals and societies. To assemble the expanding knowledge and make it easily accessible this encyclopedia was developed.

An international editorial group had the task of deciding on the content to be included and identifying prospective writers for the mature as well as for the emerging topics within the scope of gerontology. The subject of gerontology is broad, many fields of study are involved, and terminology differs. The topics in these volumes are arranged alphabetically, but readers are encouraged to use the index at the end of the encyclopedia in addition to searching the texts directly since the same or related topics may be treated under different headings. Readers are urged to explore the comprehensive index to access the rich array of information about aging that has been assembled in this *Encyclopedia of Gerontology*.

James E. Birren

How to Use the Encyclopedia

The *Encyclopedia of Gerontology: Age, Aging, and the Aged* is intended for use by both students and research professionals. Articles have been chosen to reflect major disciplines in the study of gerontology and adult development and aging, common topics of research by professionals in this realm, and areas of public interest and concern. Coverage includes five major areas: the biology of aging, the psychology of aging, aging and the social sciences, health sciences, and the humanities and aging. Each article serves as a comprehensive overview of a given area, providing both breadth of coverage for students and depth of coverage for research professionals. We have designed the encyclopedia with the following features for maximum accessibility for all readers.

Articles in the encyclopedia are arranged alphabetically by subject. Complete tables of contents appear in both volumes. Here, one will find broad discipline-related titles such as "Demography" and "Pharmacology," research topics such as "Dementia" and "Creativity," and areas of public interest and concern such as "Abuse and Neglect of Elders" and "Ethics and Euthanasia."

The Index is located in Volume 2. Because the reader's topic of interest may be listed under a broader article title, we encourage use of the Index for access to a subject area, rather than use of the Table of Contents alone. For instance, Alzheimer's Disease is covered within the article "Dementia," and osteoporosis is covered in the article "Bone and Osteoporo-

sis." Because a topic of study in gerontology is often applicable to more than one article, the Index provides a complete listing of where a subject is covered and in what context.

Each article contains an outline, a glossary, cross references, and a bibliography. The outline allows a quick scan of the major areas discussed within each article. The glossary contains terms that may be unfamiliar to the reader, with each term defined *in the context of its use in that article*. Thus, a term may appear in the glossary for another article defined in a slightly different manner or with a subtle nuance specific to that article. For clarity, we have allowed these differences in definition to remain so that the terms are defined relative to the context of each article.

Each article has been cross referenced to other articles in the encyclopedia. Cross references are found at the first or predominant mention of a subject area covered elsewhere in the encyclopedia. We encourage readers to use the cross references to locate other encyclopedia articles that will provide more detailed information about a subject.

The bibliography lists recent secondary sources to aid the reader in locating more detailed or technical information. Review articles and research articles that are considered of primary importance to the understanding of a given subject area are also listed. Bibliographies are not intended to provide a full reference listing of all material covered in the context of a given article, but are provided as guides to further reading.

A

Abuse and Neglect of Elders

Lynn McDonald

University of Toronto

Formal Caregivers Professionals and semiprofessionals, such as social workers, physicians, lawyers, home-care providers, and nurses, who care for older persons in a wide variety of settings.

Informal Caregivers Family members or close family associates who care for the older person, either in the older person's own home or the caregiver's home.

Neglect Intentional or unintentional harmful behavior on the part of an informal or formal caregiver in whom the older person has placed his or her trust. Unintentional neglect is a failure to fulfill a caregiving responsibility, but the caregiver does not intend to harm the older person; intentional neglect occurs when the caregiver consciously and purposely fails to meet the needs of the older person, resulting in psychological, physical, or material injury to the older person.

Self-abuse An act of commission on the part of the older person that may result in physical, psychological, or material injury. The causes of the problem are considered to be the same as for self-neglect, and the same question may be raised as to the appropriateness of including self-abuse as part of elder abuse, because a trusted other is not involved

Self-neglect An act of omission on the part of the older person, such as the failure to take care of personal needs, which may result in psychological, physical, or material injury. The problem can often be attributed to the older persons' diminished physical or mental capabilities to care for themselves. There is some question as to whether self-neglect should be included in a consideration of elder neglect and abuse, because no abusive caregivers are involved.

ELDER ABUSE, also called mistreatment or maltreatment, is harmful behavior directed towards older persons by family members or professional caregivers whom the older person loves or trusts or upon whom they depend for assistance. The destructive behavior can cause physical, psychological, and material injury to the older person resulting in unnecessary distress and suffering. Physical abuse includes any act of commission that involves the intentional infliction of physical discomfort, pain, or injury. Examples of physical abuse include such behaviors as restraining, slapping, kicking, cutting, or burning, all of which lead to bodily harm. Medical maltreatment and sexual abuse are frequently considered to be instances of physical abuse. Psychological abuse, sometimes referred to as verbal or emotional abuse, involves the intentional infliction of mental anguish or the provocation of fear of violence or isolation in the older person. Psychological abuse can take various forms, such as name-calling, humiliation, intimidation, or threats of placement in a nursing home. Material abuse, often referred to as financial abuse, involves the intentional, illegal, or improper exploitation of the older person's material property or financial resources by the abuser. Material abuse can include fraud, theft, or use of money or property without the older person's consent. Acts such as theft, physical assault, rape, and burglary by a person *outside* of a trusting relationship with the older person usually would not be classified as elder abuse but rather as crimes. Crimes against the elderly include some, but not all, forms of elder abuse.

I. THE EXTENT AND SOCIAL CONTEXT OF ELDER ABUSE

A. Prevalence and Incidence

1. Elder Abuse in Domestic Settings

Although many studies have documented the existence and nature of elder abuse and neglect, only a few have collected data on the prevalence (number of occurrences in a lifetime) and the incidence (number of new occurrences within a specific time) of the problem among the noninstitutionalized elderly. Reliable data have been difficult to obtain because definitions of elder abuse and neglect vary, methodologies used to deal with the highly sensitive topic differ, and samples studied do not fully or accurately represent older people. In light of these difficulties, it is not easy to interpret reported prevalence rates, which vary from as low as 3% in Norway and the United States, 4% in Canada, and 5% in Finland, to as high as 17% in Sweden.

In the United States, a study carried out in the greater Boston area in 1985–1986 based on a representative sample of 2,020 persons, all 65 years of age or older, found that 3.2% had experienced some type of abuse. About 2% of the sample were physically abused, 1.1% chronically verbally abused, and about .4% were neglected. Material abuse was not considered in this investigation, resulting in a generally lower prevalence rate reported in other studies. This survey showed that spouse abuse was more prevalent (58%) than abuse by adult children (24%); it showed that equal numbers of men and women were victims, and that economic circumstances and age were not related to the risk of abuse.

Variations of the American prevalence study were carried out in both Canada and Great Britain. The 1989 national Canadian study of 2008 randomly selected older persons, found that about 4% of the sample reported some type of abuse. Approximately 2.5% of the sample experienced material abuse, 1.4% experienced chronic verbal aggression, and .5% suffered physical abuse. About .4% reported neglect. Both physical abuse and chronic verbal aggression were perpetrated by spouses, whereas material abuse

tended to be perpetrated by both relatives and nonrelatives. As in the American study, men and women were equally represented as victims.

Reports based on a subsample of 593 elders, from a British national survey of 2130 persons in 1992, showed that 5% of the sample were verbally abused by a family member, 2% were physically abused, and 2% were financially abused. More women than men were verbally abused, and a slightly higher proportion of men reported physical and financial abuse.

The results of these national prevalence studies cannot be directly compared because of differences in their methods and procedures; all three investigations indicate, however, that most older people are not victims of abuse and neglect. The prevalence rates of 5% or less are relatively low, but they may also be misleading. Although these studies represent the best prevalence studies currently available, they all suffer from flaws in design and implementation; they are subject to cultural and contextual differences and, more than likely, provide low estimates because the cognitively impaired have been excluded from at least two of the investigations.

Incidence rates for elder abuse are still virtually unknown in most countries. However, attempts at estimates have been made by the National Aging Resource Center on Elder Abuse in the United States. In 1986, 117,000 substantiated reports in domestic settings were made, as compared to 128,000 in 1987, 140,000 in 1988, 211,000 in 1990, and 227,000 in 1991. These nationwide figures have to be interpreted with some caution, because of the wide variation in the definitions and criteria for reporting abuse and the possibility of duplication in reporting. It is obvious that the incidence rate is rising, but this could be a function of more awareness of the problem or better reporting procedures. There is no way of knowing whether the problem is getting better or worse, because there are no accurate figures on the amount of abuse now or in the past.

2. Elder Abuse in the Institution

Institutional abuse is the mistreatment of older persons living in facilities such as nursing homes, hospitals, or long-term care institutions; it is perpetrated by the formal caregiving staff and sometimes by other patients or visitors. Elder abuse and neglect by formal caregivers falls into the same categories as that committed by informal caregivers, but the victims are likely to be more vulnerable to abuse, by virtue of the fact that they require the protective environment of the facility. Some researchers have added violations of basic rights to the list of abuses that can occur in institutions. Such violations include denying elderly people the right to make personal decisions or the right to privacy. [*See* CAREGIVING AND CARING; HOUSING.]

Institutional abuse has been researched much less than domestic abuse, possibly because so few older persons live in institutions (only about 5% of older persons live in nursing homes in the United States). There is enough anecdotal evidence, however, from both North America and Europe, to suggest that abusive behavior is a widespread, regular aspect of institutional life. There have been reports of material abuse including the theft of patient's funds and fraudulent therapy and pharmaceutical charges; physical abuse including such medical maltreatment as inappropriate chemical and physical restraint; and psychological abuse including social isolation.

The most rigorous study of abuse in nursing homes was carried out in the United States. In a random survey of 577 nurses and nursing home aides made in 1989, staff were asked to report on abuse perpetrated by others and to report on their own abusive actions. Only physical and psychological abuse were considered. The researchers found that, overall, 36% of the sample had seen at least one incident of physical abuse in the preceding year. The most frequent type of physical abuse observed by the staff was the excessive restraint of patients. A total of 81% of the surveyed staff had witnessed at least one psychologically abusive incident in the preceding year. The most frequent type of psychological abuse observed by the staff was yelling at a patient in anger (70%). Ten percent of the nurses reported that *they themselves* had committed one or more physically abusive acts, the most common being the excessive use of restraints (6%). Forty percent of the nurses admitted to psychological abuse, the most common form being yelling at a patient (33%).

Few theories have been proposed to explain abuse of the elderly in institutions. As in the analysis of domestic abuse, several North American scholars have identified a number of factors that they believe contribute to the abuse of elderly residents by staff in nursing homes. These factors include the lack of comprehensive and consistent policies with respect to

the infirm elderly; the fact that the long-term care system is characterized by built-in financial incentives that contribute to poor quality care; the poor enforcement of nursing home standards; the lack of highly qualified and well-trained staff; the powerlessness and vulnerability of the elderly residents, and the tendency of staff to avenge patient aggression.

One U.S. researcher has developed a model of the potential causes of elder abuse in nursing homes. This model includes factors related to the socioeconomic environment of the institution, such as the supply of nursing home beds and local unemployment rates; the characteristics of the facility, such as ownership status, size, staff–patient ratios, and staff turnover rates; staff characteristics, such as age, education, gender, and degree of burnout; and resident characteristics, such as health of the patients, their degree of social isolation, and gender.

In a partial test of this model, the researchers found evidence that the maltreatment of nursing home patients appeared to some extent to be a response to highly stressful working conditions, rather than a consequence of the characteristics of the nursing home, such as the size or ownership status of the institution. Staff who were burned out and who experienced aggression from patients were more at risk of becoming abusive towards their elderly patients.

B. Characteristics of Victims and Perpetrators

The first wave of research on elder abuse, beginning in the late 1970s, concluded that the typical victim was over 75 years of age, a female with debilitating physical and psychological impairments, and dependent upon a family caregiver, usually a daughter. Research at the end of the 1980s, based on sounder methodologies, cast some doubt on these observations and indicated that the situation was far more complex than originally presumed. The focus shifted from the classification of the victim to the classification of the perpetrator, and to profiles of different combinations of victims, perpetrators, and types of abuse. Today mounting research evidence emphasizes the interactive aspects of elder abuse and supports distinctions between patient-directed, patient-generated, and mutual abuse. A decade of research can be distilled to four major observations. First, victims of psychological and physical abuse usually have reasonably good physical health but suffer from psychological problems. Their abusers have a history of psychiatric illness or substance abuse, live with the victim, and depend on them for financial resources. Second, patients with dementia, who exhibit disruptive behavior and who live with family caregivers, are more likely to be victims of physical abuse. [See DEMENTIA.] Their abusive caregivers may suffer from low self-esteem and clinical depression. Third, victims of financial abuse are usually unmarried, have relatively poor health, and are socially isolated. Their abusers often have financial problems stemming from a history of substance abuse. Fourth, victims of neglect tend to be very old, with cognitive and physical incapacities. Their dependency on their caregivers serves as a source of stress.

II. THEORETICAL EXPLANATIONS

Much of the literature on elder abuse does not make an important distinction between theoretical explanations and the individual factors related to abuse. A theory provides a general, systematic explanation for observed facts; in the elder abuse literature, particular factors, such as stress or dependency, are often treated as complete theoretical explanations even though they are only factors and could be incorporated in any of a number of theories. The specific relationships between the various factors and elder abuse form propositions upon which theories are built. Over the course of the brief history of elder abuse, different accounts of the relationships among the factors have led to at least four distinct theoretical perspectives. Their variations are of particular import, as each theory determines what actions should be taken to ameliorate the abuse and neglect.

A. The Situational Model

Probably the first and most widely accepted perspective is the situational model, which has its roots in the mainstream perspectives on child abuse and family violence. The basic premise of the situational model is that stressful situations cause the caregiver to abuse the older person, who is usually viewed as the source of the stress. This approach suggests that mistreatment is an irrational response to stressful situations. The situational variables that this theory links to abuse include factors related to the caregiver and the

elder as well as social and economic conditions. Interventions grounded in this perspective attend to reducing the stress of the caregiver. One major flaw of this perspective is that it fails to account for the fact that many caregivers, who experience the same stresses as abusers, do not mistreat their elderly. The perspective has also been criticized for being dangerously close to blaming the victim, because it identifies the older person as the source of the stress.

B. Social Exchange Theory

Social exchange theory is based on the assumptions that social interaction involves an exchange of rewards and punishments between people, and that all people seek to maximize rewards and minimize punishments. In most relationships, people have different degrees of access to resources and different capabilities to provide services to others, which makes some people more powerful than others. In the social exchange perspective it is argued that, as people age, they become more powerless, vulnerable, and dependent on their caregivers; these characteristics make them at risk for abuse. There are many problems with this perspective, not the least of which is its basic ageist assumption: people do not automatically become dependent and vulnerable as they age. Indeed, several researchers have argued that the dependency may lie elsewhere. A number of investigations have found the abuser to be dependent on the older person; the *abuser's* sense of powerlessness leads to maltreatment. Interventions prompted by a social exchange analysis would first have to identify the dependent party. If the older person were assessed to be dependent, then services aimed at increasing independence would be in order, whereas a dependent adult child might need help from mental health services or require vocational training or job placement in order to become self-reliant.

C. The Symbolic Interaction Approach

This approach also has its roots in the family violence literature and focuses on the interactive processes between the elder and the caregiver. This perspective attends not only to the behaviors of the elder and the caregiver but also to both parties' symbolic interpretations of such behavior. This analysis of elder abuse focuses on the different meanings that people attribute to violence and the consequences these meanings have in certain situations. Social learning, or modeling, is part of this perspective: the theory holds that abusers learn how to be violent from witnessing or suffering from violence, and the victims, in suffering abuse, learn to be more accepting of it. Interventions based on this approach would focus on changing family values and norms regarding abuse and would attempt to empower the older person. The difficulty with this approach is that it does not consider the social or economic factors that might influence the abusive process; neither does it account for the fact that not all caregivers who were abused as children abuse their elders.

D. Feminist Models

The existing prevalence studies indicate that spouse abuse is an important component of elder abuse. Most scholars have assumed that this is a form of wife abuse "grown old," and as such, it has been explained by a wide variety of feminist scholars as one consequence of family patriarchy, which is identified as the main source of violence against women in society. A patriarchy is seen as having two basic elements: a structure in which men have more power than women, and an ideology that legitimizes this power. The family is considered to be the most fundamental unit of patriarchy in society, and traditional sex-role expectations for wives provide ideological support for the less powerful position of women in the household hierarchy. This power imbalance makes women vulnerable and open to abuse whether they are young or old. Feminist interventions generally include consciousness raising and mutual problem solving within a caring and equal relationship. The shortcoming of this approach is that, to date, there is little empirical evidence to support the claims of the theory. And, it is at best, a partial account of elder abuse, because older men are just as likely as older women to be abused.

The application of feminist theories to all forms of spouse abuse is a hotly debated issue. The small but growing body of research on gay and lesbian domestic violence has seriously thrown into question gender-based theories of partner violence. The real culprit, it is argued, is the power imbalance between the partners. Feminist theories then, might be extended to explain both female and male spouse abuse if developed in these terms. In addition, there is also evidence

to suggest that not all spouse abuse "grows old"; new spouse abuse can appear for the first time in old age.

Overall, most scholars have realized that there is a broad diversity in the manifestations of elder abuse and neglect and have abandoned their search for a comprehensive, all-inclusive explanation of the phenomena. In the future, new theories of elder abuse may explain different dimensions of elder abuse and neglect, and theoreticians will probably cast their net wider, including gerontological theories alongside the family violence theories that have been, so far, the mainstay of the elder abuse literature. As a consequence, practitioners will have a wider array of interventions at their disposal, which will facilitate the provision of more effective care for mistreated elders.

III. RISK FACTORS FOR ABUSE

More extensive research has been carried out on the specific factors hypothesized to be associated with elder abuse and neglect. The emphasis on risk factors undoubtedly follows from the demand for protocols for screening those at risk, for assessing the nature of the abuse and neglect, and for choosing appropriate interventions. These factors have become the backbone of these protocols, many of which have been developed for both domestic and institutional abuse. The principal factors that have been associated with abuse include the personality traits of the abuser, the intergenerational transfer of violence, dependency, stress, social isolation, and social structural factors such as ageism.

A. Personality Traits of the Abuser

This factor, also referred to as intraindividual dynamics or the psychopathology of the abuser, is based on observations from a number of studies that discovered an inordinately high proportion of abusers had histories of psychiatric illnesses and problems with drugs and alcohol. As in the family violence literature, there is much controversy surrounding this hypothesis, mainly because psychopathology has not been directly and *causally* linked to abuse. In the field of aging, it is troublesome to regard caregivers as mentally unstable, given the burgeoning gerontological literature that portrays family members as willing, responsible, and concerned. Others have criticized this approach because it overlooks the role of structural factors, such as poverty or ageism, and it rules out the use of resources to intervene at the societal level. The only conclusion that can be drawn at this time is that the role of perpetrator psychopathology in elder abuse and neglect is unresolved and requires further exploration.

B. The Intergenerational Transmission of Violence

There is some evidence to suggest that children learn through observation and participation that violence is an acceptable response to stress. Having learned violent behavior, a significant number of children are violent towards their own children and their spouses in adulthood. This transmission of violent behavior may be reinforced by a family subculture that accepts and condones violence. Although this is a popular hypothesis in the literature on family violence, very few elder abuse studies have actually found evidence to support the idea that children who were mistreated by their parents went on to abuse the parents in later life. In fact, several studies have clearly found no basis for the relationship. It appears then, that further research is required to test this hypothesis.

C. Dependency

There are two contrasting views in the literature about dependency. According to one view, it is hypothesized that, because of physical or cognitive incapacities, the older person becomes increasingly dependent upon the caregiver for psychological, physical, and material support. This dependency is a heavy burden for the caregiver and can result in resentment and caregiver stress. A lack of resources and inadequate support services for the caregiver may then exacerbate the situation to the point where abuse of the elderly can occur. The alternative view is that abuse is not caused by the dependency of the older person, but is a consequence of the dependency of the abuser upon the older person. Several research studies have shown that abusers were dependent upon their older victims for financial and emotional support and for housing and transportation. In this situation, abuse can occur as a result of perceived powerlessness on the part of the adult child. Either way, it is the imbalance in power that is the potential risk factor leading to abuse.

Critics of the dependency hypothesis point out that not all dependent relationships among elders and caregivers result in elder abuse and neglect, and that there must also be some triggering event or crisis that precipitates the abuse. In short, although dependency may be a significant factor in abuse, it is not clear how it operates to produce abuse.

D. Stress

The responsibility of providing long hours of physical and emotional care to a frail elderly person can be overwhelming. Since the early 1980s, several studies have shown that abusers often know too little about the aging process and sometimes hold unrealistic expectations of the capabilities of an older person. The abuser is frequently overburdened by attempts to meet the needs of both their own family and those of the older person and becomes exhausted, frustrated, and sometimes resentful in the process. Research has shown that situations such as these can become abusive.

Earlier investigators found that the stress of caregiving for older persons who suffer from physical and cognitive impairments was more likely to result in neglect than in physical aggression. The most recent studies of patients with dementias, such as Alzheimer's disease, have shown that the link between cognitive impairment and abuse is precipitated by the interactive, day-to-day problems that arise between the patient and the caregiver. As an example, in patient–caregiver dyads where the caregiver was assessed as being clinically depressed, the risk for severe physical violence was three times greater than for those dyads where the caregiver was not depressed. In this study, those Alzheimer's victims living with their family but without the presence of a spouse were three times more likely to be severely abused than patients in other living arrangements. Another study found that the disruptive behaviors of the patient and the low self-esteem of the caregivers with whom the older person lived were associated with abuse. Although these newer investigations suffer from methodological inadequacies and require more extensive confirmation, the interactional nature of the relationship between stress and abuse is quickly becoming obvious.

E. Social Isolation

Research in the field of family violence has consistently discovered some degree of social isolation in almost all violent situations. Similarly, several elder abuse researchers have found that abused elders were significantly more likely to have had fewer contacts with friends and family members than were non-abused elders. This finding was interpreted to mean that there is less likelihood for family violence when an older person has strong and active family and social ties. The presence of involved family and friends might not only deter violent behavior but could also provide additional support to modify the weary caregiver's sense of burden and stress. As with other instances of family violence, it is not clear whether social isolation is the cause of the abuse or the result of the abuse. Some researchers have speculated that in controlling the behavior of the victim, the abuser may limit the social contacts of the abused. At the same time, the mistreated older person may not interact with others because of shame or fear, thereby augmenting the degree of isolation. A third finding in the research is that social isolation is not associated with abuse.

F. Structural Factors

Research has been preoccupied with the abused and the abuser at the expense of exploring the wider implications of age, gender, race, ethnicity, and class, all of which influence people's positions in the social structure and their opportunities in life. For example, older people can be subject to discriminatory attitudes and actions that are based on negative perceptions about their chronological age. Experts have proposed that such ageist attitudes towards older people may contribute to the development of elder abuse. Misconceptions and distortions about aging dehumanize older persons, making it easier for them to be victimized, and for the abusers to feel little or no remorse. At the same time, elderly people may even view the maltreatment as deserved, as they too may have adopted society's negative attitudes. The feminist models also supply an account of the structural factors: gender determines a set of positions in society that facilitate, and even justify, the abuse of women. Other crucial factors that are known to influence the aging process, such as race, ethnicity, and socioeconomic status, are only now attracting modest attention. As would be expected, the few investigations that do exist show that elder abuse is viewed quite differently by different cultures. [See AGEISM AND DISCRIMINATION.]

IV. RESPONSES TO ABUSE AND NEGLECT

A. Adult Protection Legislation

Many jurisdictions in North America have introduced special adult protection legislation at the state or provincial level in response to the problem of elder abuse and neglect. This legislation generally falls into three categories: (a) adult abuse legislation, with mandatory reporting; (b) elder abuse legislation, with mandatory reporting; (c) adult or elder abuse legislation with no mandatory reporting. Adult abuse legislation applies to persons over the age of 18, but is often restricted to those suffering from physical and cognitive impairments. Elder abuse legislation is directed specifically to older persons, usually defined as individuals over the age of 60 or 65. This age distinction has been criticized by a number of scholars as a form of ageism: the definition implies that age is synonymous with incapacity. Although all fifty states of the United States have legislation authorizing the state to protect and provide services to vulnerable or incapacitated adults, other countries have been slower to enact special legislation. In Canada only four provinces have enacted adult protection legislation, and Britain has no provisions at all.

Mandatory reporting, the legal obligation to report cases of elder abuse, occurs in the majority of jurisdictions in the United States, but the obligation is usually imposed only on certain individuals, such as nurses, doctors, the police, and social workers. The purpose of the legislation is to act as a deterrent to elder abuse and neglect and also to provide a mechanism for collecting data and monitoring prevalence and incidence rates. The legislation frequently grants the reporting individual immunity from civil and criminal liability in order to encourage individuals to report. Failure to comply with mandatory reporting laws can result in fines, civil liability for damages, reports to professional licensing boards, and short jail terms.

I. The Child Welfare Model

When protection legislation was first introduced in North America beginning as early as 1973, most jurisdictions borrowed the existing child welfare legislation, which called for the mandatory reporting of suspected cases of abuse. At the time, the transfer seemed plausible because the legislation was conveniently in place, and an argument could be made for similarities between older persons and children. These similarities were, and are today, superficial and misleading but, nevertheless, adult protection legislation has been largely determined by child protection principles. The principles, transposed to the context of elder abuse, ultimately portray the older people as frail, incompetent, and incapable of looking after themselves.

2. Mandatory Reporting

a. Effectiveness   The research studies on mandatory reporting (all done in North America) have cast doubts on the contribution the process can make to the prevention of elder abuse and neglect. Several studies have shown that cases reported under mandatory reporting provisions were already known to the authorities. Such findings imply that there is no significant increase in the reporting of abuse and neglect under mandatory reporting provisions. In contrast, several studies have shown the number of cases reported to be up, but so too is the number of unsubstantiated cases. Other studies have shown that the statutes failed to ensure the consistent collection of information that would aid in the tracking of the types and extent of abuse and neglect. There is confusing research as to what types of cases mandatory reporting is likely to uncover. Several studies have found that mandatory reporting is more likely to be associated with cases of neglect and self-neglect; however, others established that reporting is more likely to be associated with cases of physical abuse. The few studies that examined the relationship between mandatory reporting and institutionalization of the older victim indicated that mandatory reporting could result in increased rates of institutionalization of the abused, although contact with protective services was the more plausible explanation. Finally, the passage of a mandatory reporting law does not mean that those who are required to report will be aware of the law or be motivated to comply. A small number of researchers investigating the reporting behaviors of physicians found few referrals came from physicians; many physicians did not know about the laws, and many perceived reporting as more costly than beneficial. The general conclusion in the research literature is that the effectiveness of mandatory reporting systems in the various states needs further investigation as to their effectiveness.

b. Drawbacks   Although mandatory reporting may have been well intentioned, albeit hastily implemented, the wisdom of transposing it to the context of elder abuse and neglect continues to be questioned. Critics, who concentrate on the requirement of mandatory reporting, argue that the legislation implies elders are incompetent and unable themselves to make reports; they are, in essence, infantilized by such laws. These laws may in turn serve to reinforce and to encourage ageism in society. Furthermore, many scholars believe that mandatory reporting provisions violate older people's civil rights and freedoms, by taking away the control they have over their lives. Some critics strongly question the whole purpose of the legislation, because of the support it gives to the perpetrator psychopathology hypothesis. Lastly, questions have been raised about the capacity of the state to offer better alternatives once the abuse has been identified. In the United States, concerns have been voiced that there are not enough health and social services currently available for the elderly, and that mandatory reporting represents just one more strain on the system.

B. Programs

A program provides a blueprint for service delivery, establishes resources, and coordinates the delivery of service through government or private and public agencies. Three major programs have emerged in response to elder abuse: the statutory adult protection service programs, programs based on the domestic violence model, and advocacy programs for the elderly. A fourth model, now developing rapidly, could be identified as the integrated model. It is not useful to categorize the various services, as each program ultimately makes use of them all.

1. Adult Protection Programs

The adult protection legislation in the United States provides the legal framework for protective services for vulnerable adults. The mandated services are provided in approximately three-quarters of the states by special adult protection units in state social service departments, and, in most of the remaining states, by state units on aging. As would be expected, there are great variations in state responses, depending on the financial commitment of the state and other organizational and political factors.

The legislation confers a wide range of powers of intervention, which varies from state to state. The usual procedures for the state-designated units are to receive reports of suspected cases of abuse, to screen the cases for potential seriousness, to conduct an investigation if mistreatment is suspected, to develop a care plan that will resolve the abuse, and then to transfer the case to other community agencies for case management and the delivery of services. The protective services program represents a mixture of legal, health, and social services that allows for the widest array of interventions and for considerable coordination and interdisciplinary teamwork. Many adult protection workers have had specialized training in the substantive area of elder abuse and neglect. New and innovative learning initiatives are increasing: for example, the creation of a special student training unit within adult protective services was recently instituted for the first time in the United States with considerable success.

Recognizing that not all clients will voluntarily accept protective services, the protection workers may use guardianship or conservatorship to ensure that the older person receives the necessary services. Some states have created special court procedures to secure court orders for protective services, to place the client in a nursing home, to provide emergency treatment when the client is in danger, and to enter a client's home against the client's wishes. Proponents of these wide-ranging interventions argue that the rights of the older person are always safeguarded; the goal is to enhance the individual's level of functioning while protecting them from injury. They maintain that little can be done for the victim who refuses services (about 36–40% of elders refuse service); therefore only mandated interventions ensure that the victim receives at least the minimum help. As well, such interventions will be limited by prudence: few practitioners are willing to risk intervention unless they are on solid legal ground.

Those against an enforcement-oriented approach to service provision dispute these claims. At the outset, they observe that the vagueness of the legislation in many jurisdictions places adult protection workers in a quandary the moment they try to decide whether abuse has occurred. It is almost impossible to use legal powers to force oneself into an older person's home and at the same time respect the person's basic rights; the protection worker can easily come into conflict

with both the older person and the abuser. In addition, adult protection workers have been accused of being "trigger happy" in placing older persons in nursing homes and of treating older people as if they were children—an unavoidable occupational hazard given the child welfare roots of the adult protection programs.

2. Domestic Violence Programs

The domestic violence model for program delivery is an adaptation of the programs that have been instituted to combat woman abuse. This approach is gaining momentum in North America, because it does not violate people's civil rights, nor does it discriminate on the basis of age. The domestic violence response to elder abuse involves crisis-intervention services, such as telephone hotlines, a strengthened role for police in the laying of charges, court orders for protection, the use of legal clinics, emergency and secondary sheltering, support groups for both the abused and the abuser, and individual and family therapy, and the use of a whole range of health, social, and legal services. An integral component of domestic violence services is public education and especially the education of the abused about their rights. Almost all of these services have been adapted specifically for elder abuse victims, and sometimes for their abusers. For example, existing shelters have been modified to accommodate older abused women, and new shelters have been established to accommodate both men and women. Along with shelters, there are support groups for victims, hotlines for abused elders, special legal clinics, and family and individual counseling programs. An example of each type of service can be found in North America; however, most attempts at service delivery have been scant and sporadic, and have shown little evidence of coordination. Whether the model is effective in helping the older victim is still a moot question.

The domestic abuse model is not without its critics, who quickly point out that the flaws in the model equally apply to elder abuse. Problems with police response, restraining orders, poorly managed shelters, and the shortage of follow-up services are but a few of the issues. Gerontologists have also cautioned against the singular use of crisis intervention, because older person's problems tend to be multiple and interrelated, take a long time to solve, and need to be monitored closely. They also have drawn attention to the inadequacy of the model when applied to cases of neglect. Police intervention or education about rights are inappropriate in the face of family or self-neglect.

3. Advocacy Programs

Advocacy includes all actions performed on behalf of an individual or group in order to ensure that their needs are met and their rights are respected. Like the domestic violence model, this approach recognizes that the older person is an adult in a potentially dangerous situation. Advocates for the abused use the least restrictive and intrusive interventions in the older person's situation. A distinction can be made between legal advocacy and social advocacy: legal advocacy involves lawyers and occurs in the courts, and social advocacy uses nonlegal mechanisms. Advocacy programs can be formal or informal. Formal advocacy is usually performed by professionals, who are paid for their services within the context of a structured program, and informal advocates can be anyone from a family member to a community volunteer. In practice, advocates advise clients of their rights and the alternative services available, and they can assist them in carrying out agreed-upon plans. The most important feature of the advocacy model is the advocate's independence from the formal delivery system; this distance allows the advocate to establish a positive relationship with the older person. Formal and informal advocacy programs are used in a number of states and provinces; they operate in the community or in institutions and nursing homes. Although advocacy may appear to be nonintrusive, some social scientists have suggested that, in practice, it can be quite intrusive, especially if the advocate is immune from liability and is not accountable.

4. The Integrated Model

An observable trend at the community level has been the development of multidisciplinary teams made up of workers from a broad array of agencies that represent all of the programs described above. These community-based teams or committees provide consultations on atypical and difficult cases of abuse, help to resolve agency disagreements, and provide services,

such as legal and medical consultations not readily available in the community. Initial assessments of this approach have been very positive: service providers become familiar with one another, resources are organized and dispersed in a single initiative, and more comprehensive care plans are produced. The main drawback is that the committees spend more time per case than professionals acting alone.

C. Services

It is evident from the literature that the services already available to older persons provide the bulk of the resources used in response to elder abuse, regardless of what approach is utilized, and that new or uniquely designed services are not always required. Most elder abuse practitioners face difficulties in accessing limited resources, especially in critical emergency situations, and they must deal with the challenges of coordination and collaboration in the existing patchwork of services.

BIBLIOGRAPHY

Bennett, G., & Kingston, P. (1993). *Elder abuse: Concepts, theories, and interventions.* London: Chapman & Hall.

Eastman, M. (1994). *Old age abuse: A new perspective* (2nd ed.). London: Chapman & Hall.

MacLean, M. (Ed.). (1995). *Abuse and neglect of older Canadians: Strategies for change.* Toronto: Thompson Educational Publishing, Inc.

McDonald, P. L., Hornick, J. P., Robertson, G. B., & Wallace, J. E. (1991). *Elder abuse and neglect in Canada.* Toronto: Butterworths Canada, Ltd.

Pillemer, K., & Finkelhor, D. (1988). The prevalence of elder abuse: A random sample survey. *Gerontologist, 28(1),* 51–57.

Podnieks, E. (1992). National survey on abuse of the elderly in Canada. *Journal of Elder Abuse & Neglect, 4(1/2),* 5–58.

Ogg, J. (1993). Researching elder abuse in Britain. *Journal of Elder Abuse & Neglect, 5(2),* 37–54.

Wolf, R. S. (1992). Victimization of the elderly: Elder abuse and neglect. *Reviews in Clinical Gerontology, 2,* 269–276.

Wolf, R. S. (1994). Elder abuse: A family tragedy. *Ageing International,* March, 60–64.

Wolf, R. S. (1994). What's new in elder abuse programming? Four Bright Ideas. *Gerontologist, 34(1),* 126–129.

Wolf, R. S., & Pillemer, K. (1989). *Helping elderly victims: The reality of elder abuse.* New York: Columbia University Press.

Accidents: Falls

Brian E. Maki and Geoff R. Fernie

Sunnybrook Health Science Centre, University of Toronto

Hip Fracture The breaking of the proximal femur (i.e., the portion of the thigh bone nearest to the pelvis).

Post Fall Syndrome A severe fear of falling that may occur as a result of experiencing a fall. Behavior is characterized by a tendency to stagger, to clutch and grab at objects, and to show hesitancy or alarm when asked to walk without assistance.

Transient Ischemic Attack A momentary reduction in blood flow to the brain that can result in dizziness, unsteadiness, or loss of balance. Often used to refer specifically to blockage of the vertebral or basilar arteries of the brain; however, temporary limitations of the blood supply to the brain may also occur due to drop in blood pressure when standing up (postural hypotension) or irregularities in heart output (cardiac arrhythmia).

An **ACCIDENTAL FALL** can be defined as any occasion on which the body drops unintentionally to the floor or ground or to some other lower level (e.g., a bed or chair). In most cases, the faller is initially standing upright; however, falls may also occur from a seated or supine position. It is difficult to obtain accurate information about the incidence, circumstances, and causes of falls, because many falls are unwitnessed and the fallers themselves are often unable to give a reliable account of what happened. A few studies have used video cameras to record small numbers of actual naturally occurring falls. However, the majority of studies have relied on information reported by the faller during follow-up interviews; therefore, many results described in the literature must be viewed with a degree of caution.

I. THE FALLING PROBLEM

A. Incidence of Falls

Although the incidence of falls in young and middle-aged adults is not well established, it is well known that falling is very common in the elderly. Studies have consistently shown that 30–60% of individuals aged 65 and older will experience one or more falls in a given year. These incidence rates are remarkably high, particularly when one considers that most studies are likely to underreport the true incidence of falls. Incidence rates appear to be higher in institutional settings, females experience more falls than males, and the frequency of falling increases with age.

B. Injuries Resulting from Falls

Even though the majority of falls do not result in serious physical injury, the societal costs associated with fall-related injuries are enormous. For Americans aged 75 and older, falls are the leading cause of fatal injury, accounting for twice as many deaths as motor vehicle accidents. Approximately 20–30% of falls result in soft-tissue injuries (contusions, lacerations) that require medical attention, and approximately 5–10% result in bone fracture. The fracture injuries most commonly occur at the upper and lower extremities, but fractures of the vertebra, ribs, pelvis, skull, and face are also reported. Females are more likely to suffer fractures than males, likely due, in large part, to the much higher incidence of osteoporosis in females. [*See* Bone and Osteoporosis.] Hip fractures (proximal femur) are, by far, the most serious fall injury, in terms of measurable health-care costs. In the United States alone, there are an estimated 250,000 hip fractures each year, and the vast majority of these occur as a result of falls in persons aged 65 and older. The average acute-care hospital stay for hip fracture is 21 days (longer than for any other diagnosis) and the associated annual health-care costs are estimated to be $9 billion. In many cases, the hip fracture is "the beginning of the end." In nearly 30% of cases, death occurs within 1 year of the fracture, usually due to complications such as pneumonia, thrombosis, or fat embolism. Even if the faller does survive, there is often a severe loss of mobility and independence.

C. Other Medical Consequences of Falls

If the faller is alone and is unable to get up or to somehow summon help, he or she may lie on the floor for a prolonged period of time. Potential medical consequences include dehydration, hypothermia, and pneumonia. One study found that 50% of fallers who lay on the floor for more than 1 hour died within 6 months of the fall. An indirect consequence of falling relates to the restriction of activity that often follows the fall, which can lead to deconditioning and associated complications in the cardiovascular and respiratory systems.

D. Psychosocial Consequences of Falls

It is only recently that the psychosocial consequences of falling have received due recognition. The "postfall syndrome" has been described as an extreme fear of falling, characterized by a tendency to stagger, to clutch at objects, and to show hesitancy or alarm when asked to walk without assistance. Although such a severe reaction may be relatively uncommon, a general fear of falling and loss of self-efficacy and confidence in one's ability to balance is very widespread, occurring in up to 60% of individuals over the age of 65. Fear of falling is a common consequence of experiencing a fall, but up to 50% of cases involve individuals who do not have a recent history of falling. The health-care costs associated with fear of falling are very difficult to estimate; however, it is clear that this fear commonly leads to anxiety, social withdrawal, and self-imposed restrictions on physical activity. Moreover, the restrictions on activity can trigger the start of a debilitating, downward spiral in which inactivity leads to deterioration in strength, flexibility, and motor control, which in turn lead to further unsteadiness and loss of confidence, culminating in loss of mobility, independence, and quality of life. Falls are cited as a contributing factor in 40% of admissions to nursing homes.

II. BIOMECHANICS OF FALLS

A. Precipitating Events

During upright stance, equilibrium requires the center of mass of the body to be positioned over the base of support defined by the feet. In a small proportion of falls, a transient physiological event (e.g., transient ischemic attack) may disrupt the posture control mechanisms responsible for maintaining equilibrium. Changes in sensory conditions may also disrupt the posture control system (e.g., moving visual fields due to crowds or escalators; changes in room lighting). In the majority of cases, however, a fall is precipitated by (a) a mechanical perturbation, (i.e., a change in the forces acting on the body) *and* (b) a failure of the posture control system to compensate for this perturbation. Two general types of mechanical perturbation can occur. The perturbation may cause the center of mass to be displaced beyond the existing base of support (e.g., a push or a collision). Alternatively, during movements such as walking, the perturbation may somehow prevent the base of support from being realigned underneath the moving center of mass (e.g., a slip or a trip). It is important to note that the change in forces acting on the body can arise not only from external sources, such as a push or a collision, but also from the self-induced displacements of the body that occur during movements such as walking, bending, reaching, turning, rising, and so on.

B. Balance Recovery

Compensatory postural reactions rely upon the use of sensory information (visual, vestibular, and somatosensory) in order to detect unexpected perturbations. The earliest compensatory reactions occur automatically, within a tenth of a second, and act to generate muscle torque at the ankle and/or hip joints in order to restore the center of mass to a position over the base of support ("feet-in-place" response). Very early and rapid movements of the feet (compensatory stepping) or arms (to grasp objects for support) also occur automatically and play a very important role in preventing a fall. Arm movements may also serve a protective role, to absorb energy should impact with the ground occur.

C. Impact

If the recovery mechanisms are unable to compensate for the perturbation in the available time, impact with the floor or ground will occur. The energy of the falling body is more than sufficient to cause a fracture unless adequate energy absorption occurs (i.e., through postural reactions, protective arm movements, or the cushioning provided by soft tissue or padding). Although forward falls tend to occur most frequently, backward and lateral falls are also very common. Hip fractures are most likely to occur as a result of lateral falls onto the hip or side of the leg, whereas fracture of the upper extremity tends to occur in falls where the arm is used to absorb the impact, regardless of the fall direction.

III. CIRCUMSTANCES OF FALLS

A. Where Do Falls Occur?

Falls can and do occur virtually anywhere, and it is a truism that falls are most likely to occur wherever the individuals spend the majority of their time. Thus, for example, falls in the home occur most commonly in the bedroom and bathroom. Certain areas of the home or institution can be considered to represent a higher risk because of specific environmental hazards such as slippery surfaces (e.g., wet floor tiles in kitchen and bathroom, wet or icy walkways or stairs), trip hazards (e.g., mats at entrances), or poor lighting.

Elevators seem to be a particular problem in some buildings, due to risks of tripping over the threshold or being hit by the automated door. About 5–10% of falls in the elderly occur on stairs. These deserve special mention because of the heightened risk of injury. Even though the elderly use stairs much less than younger adults, persons over 65 account for 85% of the deaths resulting from stairway falls. Head injuries, relatively rare in level-surface falls, comprise approximately 30% of the injuries due to stairway falls.

B. When Do Falls Occur?

There is little consistent evidence that falls are more likely to occur at any specific time of the day or day of the week. Reports of seasonal variation in falls or fall-related injuries are likely due, in large part, to weather-related factors. Some studies have demonstrated an increased incidence of hip fractures during the winter (northern hemisphere); however, it is not clear whether this is linked to an increased risk of slipping on ice or snow, effects of hypothermia on motor coordination, effects of fewer daylight hours, or other factors.

C. Activities and Movements Associated with Falling

Over 50% of falls are reported to occur during walking, and about half of these falls are attributed to trips. About 20–25% of falls during walking have been attributed to slips, and the remainder of these falls likely involve collisions (bumping into something), pushes (e.g., aggressive behavior, jostling in a crowd, swinging doors, gusts of wind), or missteps (i.e., failure to place the feet appropriately when stepping). Other activities and movements commonly associated with falling included transferring to or from a chair or bed, turning, bending, or reaching.

IV. CAUSAL FACTORS

A. The Multifactorial Nature of Falls

One approach to understanding falls has been to attribute the cause to either "intrinsic" or "extrinsic" factors. Intrinsic factors pertain to the individual and include such factors as balance control, motor control, and cognitive status, all of which may be dependent on age, medical condition, and medication use. Extrinsic factors pertain to the environment (e.g., floor surface, lighting, furniture, handrails). Most falls involve a complex interaction of both intrinsic and extrinsic factors.

There are two fundamental biomechanical factors that determine whether a fall occurs: (a) the characteristics of the perturbation, and (b) the efficacy of the compensatory postural reactions. Both of these biomechanical determinants are influenced by both intrinsic and extrinsic factors. Environmental hazards, such as slippery floor surfaces or obstacles, lead to increased opportunity for perturbations to occur, yet the ability to avoid these hazards is dependent on intrinsic factors such as cognition, sensory function, and motor control. At the same time, the ability to compensate for the perturbation is strongly dependent on the intrinsic balancing abilities of the individual, but the efficacy of the stabilizing postural reaction is also influenced by the environment (e.g., unobstructed floor space to move the feet, availability of handrails or other objects to grasp, and visual cues).

The relative importance of the different causal factors is very dependent on age, health status, and mobility. In relatively young, healthy, and mobile individuals who have relatively subtle balance impairments, falls may result if activities that significantly challenge postural stability are continued without slowing down or otherwise making allowance for these impairments. The stability of older individuals who have significant health or mobility problems may be challenged by much less provocative activities and less hazardous surroundings. Individuals with acute or chronic medical conditions may also be more likely to experience falls resulting from transient physiological events.

B. Control of Postural Balance

Postural control deteriorates with aging, and the impairment tends to be greatest in the individuals who fall. Compensatory reactions tend to be slower and may show inappropriate sequencing of muscle activation, resulting in increased postural sway and decreased ability to recover balance without stepping or grasping a handrail. The loss of stability appears to be most pronounced in the lateral direction. This lateral instability is evident in the earliest feet-in-place

reactions, and may also impact on the control of compensatory stepping reactions. Elderly individuals are more likely to take multiple steps in order to recover their balance, and the later steps often appear to be directed so as to recover lateral stability. Another element of postural control involves the anticipatory or predictive postural adjustments that normally precede volitional movement and act to minimize the destabilizing effect of the movement. Elderly individuals may lack these anticipatory postural adjustments or show changes in the relative timing of the postural and voluntary muscle activity.

The deterioration in postural control that occurs in aging could be due to (a) decreased sensitivity in the visual, vestibular, and proprioceptive sensory systems; (b) impaired ability of neural centers to integrate sensory information and generate appropriate stabilizing motor commands; (c) reduced speed of neural processing and signal conduction; (d) impaired ability of the central nervous system (CNS) to adapt to changes in task demands or environmental conditions; and (e) reduction in muscle strength and range of motion. Falling risk may increase due to any of these normal age-related changes, and clinical or subclinical neurological pathologies or use of alcohol or medications may exacerbate the instability.

C. Control of Gait and Volitional Movement

Whereas the age-related changes in postural control described above pertain to the ability to correct for postural perturbations, age-related changes in the control of gait and volitional movement may increase the likelihood that perturbations will be experienced. For example, impaired control of gait may increase the likelihood of slipping or tripping over obstacles. It is well known that aging tends to bring a reduction in walking speed, due primarily to a decrease in stride length, and age-related increases in stride width and double-support time (the proportion of time spent with both feet on the ground) may also occur. Even though these gait changes ostensibly act to increase stability, they are often cited as risk factors for falling. Recent evidence suggests that some of these changes may, in fact, be adaptations related to fear of falling, and that risk of falling is more closely associated with other factors, such as stride-to-stride variability in the control of the gait. In addition, decreased toe clearance during swing may increase the risk of tripping, increased foot velocity at heel contact may increase the risk of slipping, and slowed reaction time or impaired vision (or use of bifocal lenses) may impact on the ability to avoid obstacles and hazards. Impaired ability to sense foot position and pressure on the sole of the foot may affect the ability to adapt the gait to accommodate changing ground conditions (i.e., surface irregularities, slipperiness, floor compliance). Control of gait and volitional movement may be further affected by impairment of visual perception, gaze stability, and spatial orientation. [*See* BALANCE, POSTURE, AND GAIT.]

D. Cognitive and Behavioral Factors

Cognition and alertness play an important role in preventing falls, in terms of avoiding environmental hazards. In addition, selection of activities and behaviors is an important factor. Some elderly individuals may be at greater risk of falling because they fail to recognize age-related decreases in their physical abilities and continue to pursue high-risk activities, without slowing down or taking other precautions. On the opposite side of the coin are the activity restrictions that often accompany fear of falling. These restrictions may be disproportionate to any decline in physical ability, but may ultimately cause such a decline, due to inactivity. There is a delicate balance between the need to preserve an active and independent lifestyle and the goal of preventing falls and fall-related injuries.

E. Medical Risk Factors

In addition to normal age-related changes in balance and motor control, aging brings an increased incidence of specific medical conditions that may also heighten falling liability. Furthermore, there is evidence that falling risk increases with the number of chronic medical problems.

Visual impairment, due to cataracts, macular degeneration, glaucoma, or nutritional deficiency, are common in the elderly, and may affect ability to interact safely with the environment. [*See* VISION.] In addition, postural control may be affected, particularly because the elderly seem to rely heavily on visual feedback in maintaining balance. Control of balance, gait, and volitional movement may be affected by neurological disorders such as Parkinson's disease,

normal pressure hydrocephalus, hemiplegia (due to stroke), peripheral neuropathy (secondary to diabetes, pernicious anemia, or nutritional deficiencies), and Alzheimer's disease and other dementias. Cognition and alertness will also be affected by disorders such as dementia and depression. [*See* DEMENTIA; DEPRESSION.] Abnormalities of the feet, such as bunions, are very common and can have a pronounced effect on the ability to balance and ambulate safely. Arthritis, particularly in the knee, can affect the ability to ambulate, climb stairs, and rise from chairs safely. [*See* ARTHRITIS.] Osteoporosis (decrease in bone mass) and osteomalacia (decrease in bone mineralization) are very common in elderly females, and are associated with an increased risk of fall-related fractures.

Other medical factors can lead to transient physiological disturbances that momentarily disrupt the posture-control mechanisms, causing dizziness, imbalance, or syncope (fainting). These would include conditions that affect brain metabolism, such as hypoglycemia, as well as conditions that disrupt the blood flow to the brain. The latter would include cardiac arrhythmias, orthostatic hypotension (drop in blood pressure due to change in posture), postprandial hypotension (drop in blood pressure after eating), transient ischemic attack (decrease in blood flow to the brain due to occlusion of the vertebral and basilar arteries), and transient visual disturbance (due to ocular ischemia). The so-called drop attack (characterized by the legs giving way, without loss of consciousness, and subsequent inability to get up) is thought to be a particular form of vertebrobasilar insufficiency. Dizziness and instability can also be caused by diseases that attack the vestibular balance organs: labyrinthitis or vestibular neuritis (ear infections), Meniere's disease (fluid buildup in the inner ear), or acoustic-nerve tumor. Finally, acute illness such as stroke, myocardial infarction, congestive heart failure, gastrointestinal bleeding, infection, or seizure can also disrupt the neural control of balance and movement.

Medication use can increase falling risk through a number of mechanisms. Psychotropic medications, such as antidepressants and sedative-hypnotics (long-acting benzodiazepines), can disrupt cognitive alertness and the control of balance and movement through effects on the CNS. Antidepressants are also thought to promote postural hypotension, as are diuretics and other antihypertensive medications; however, the evidence supporting an increased risk of falling due to this effect is inconsistent. Certain anti-psychotics may induce tardive dyskinesia or Parkinsonism, drugs such as aspirin, aminoglycosides, and diuretics may have toxic effects on the vestibular organs, and use of alcohol is well known to affect the control of balance and gait. Falling risk may increase because of interactions between multiple medications (as well as alcohol) and because prescribed drug dosages are often inappropriate, failing to recognize age-related increase in sensitivity and decrease in ability to process and clear the drugs.

F. Environmental Factors

The main environmental factors that affect the risk of falling are flooring and footwear, furniture, handrails, lighting, and stairways. It is clear that the flooring and footwear should provide adequate friction to prevent slipping, but it is also important that excessive friction that might cause the foot to "catch" should be avoided. Unexpected transitions in frictional properties (e.g., from carpet to polished tiles) appear to contribute to the risk of slipping, and even slightly raised edges of carpets and tiles can cause trips. The compliance of the flooring and footwear is also important. It appears that excessive cushioning can impair balance by interfering with the ability to sense foot position and pressure, and thick carpeting may also increase the likelihood of catching the toe and tripping. Unsecured area rugs are a prime risk factor for slipping, and the loose edges of rugs and mats increase the risk of tripping. Other trip hazards include electrical cords and obstacles such as low tables and footrests. Seating that lacks armrests may allow individuals to fall out of the chair and may also contribute to instability during ingress and egress. The stability of the furniture itself is also important, as furniture is often grasped for support when moving around the room. Handrails and grab-bars are also important stability aids, but are often lacking or inadequate. Lighting is particularly important in view of the visual deficits that can occur in the elderly. Insufficient intensity, pooling of light, and glare increase the risk that falls will occur. Stairway falls have been attributed to inadequate lighting, poor visibility of tread edges, and visual distractions (e.g., mirrors and paintings), as well as absent or inadequate handrails, obstacles placed on the steps, step-to-step variation in step di-

mensions, inadequate tread size, and loose carpeting on treads. [See GERONTECHNOLOGY.]

V. PREVENTATIVE MEASURES

A. Identifying the High-Risk Individual

In order for fall-prevention interventions to be cost-effective and practicable, it is desirable to identify and target the high-risk individual. Ideally, it would be possible to identify this individual at an early stage of impairment, so as to prevent serious injury, as well as the onset of the fear of falling and activity restriction spiral. Sophisticated screening tools are not needed to identify individuals who already have a well-documented history of falling, because past falling is, in fact, one of the best predictors of future falling. A number of screening batteries have been proposed, and the specific tests that are included depend on the target population (e.g., community dwellers versus nursing home); however, most include some form of balance and gait assessment. Clinical balance assessments may involve rating the steadiness of the subject in performing different types of movements and activities. More sophisticated balance tests are based on biomechanical or electromyographic measurements of postural sway, anticipatory postural adjustments preceding volitional movement, or compensatory reactions to perturbations (applied, most commonly, using moving platforms). These may require more expensive equipment, but have shown greater success in predicting falling risk, in comparison to the clinical tests. In performing any balance test, it is important to recognize that fear of falling can seriously confound balancing performance (i.e., some individuals may do poorly because of their anxiety more so than any real deterioration in postural control). Questionnaires that assess balance confidence and self-efficacy may be helpful in identifying these individuals.

B. Reducing the Individual's Risk of Falling

A clinical approach to the fall-prone patient should involve a thorough medical examination to identify and treat any underlying medical factors. Medication use and visual deficits are two risk factors that are often most amenable to alteration. Individuals who perform poorly on balance tests, in the absence of overt pathology, can be targeted for balance or gait training programs. The martial art of Tai Chi has shown promise as an inexpensive and enjoyable method of improving balance, as well as strength, flexibility, and cardiovascular function. Conversely, generalized aerobic exercise or strength training programs may not necessarily be effective in improving balance. For individuals who have a fear of falling, it is important to establish whether this fear is justified (i.e., whether true balance deficits exist) before embarking on therapy to increase balance confidence. Walking aids can be prescribed, not only to improve mechanical stability, but also as a means of augmenting sensory feedback and improving confidence. Risks due to inappropriate footwear can be reduced by avoiding high heels, high-friction crepe soles, smooth leather soles, or excessive cushioning. Education is an important component of any prevention program, as many individuals are unaware of the risk factors for falling and the preventative measures that can be taken. Finally, it may be feasible to "fall-proof" the homes or rooms of high-risk individuals, by eliminating obvious environmental hazards.

C. Preventing Injuries and Other Adverse Consequences of Falls

In conjunction with reducing the risk of falling, interventions can also be aimed at reducing the risk of injury or other adverse consequences of falls. One way to reduce the risk of fractures is to provide some form of padding. Padded garments to protect the hips have been developed; however, there is often a reluctance to wear these types of garments. An alternate approach is to pad the floor, by means of carpeting. Although overly thick carpets may increase instability, a relatively thin carpet can absorb a surprisingly large amount of energy during the impact of the body with the floor. Another approach is to train individuals to fall in a way that minimizes the risk of injury (e.g., rolling with the fall). Finally, the increased risk of fracture due to osteoporosis can be tackled by means of calcium supplements, low-protein diet, and, possibly, estrogen therapy. The complications associated with the "long lie" following the fall can be reduced by providing emergency response systems, and by teaching individuals maneuvers to aid in getting up. In institutions, use of patient restraints can be avoided

by using bed alarms to signal when a high-risk individual is attempting to get out of bed.

D. Making the Environment Safer

A number of safety principles should be implemented in the design of new buildings. Not only should slippery floor surfaces be avoided wherever possible, but also abrupt transitions in frictional properties (e.g., from carpet to polished tiles) should be minimized. Wherever possible, these transitions should be "flagged" by tying them to visual cues such as doorways. Potentially misleading visual cues, such as floor tile patterns that might be misperceived as steps, should be avoided. Lighting should be uniform and adequately high in intensity. Windows and skylights should be placed so as to minimize glare; polarized or tinted glass may also help to prevent glare. Stairways should have uniform step dimensions, treads that are of adequate size to support the foot, tread edges that are highly visible, and handrails that are visible, graspable, and securely mounted.

Comprehensive checklists have been developed to aid in "fall-proofing" existing environments. The following steps are usually recommended. Carpet edges (including stair treads) should be tacked down; area rugs and mats should be avoided where possible (or secured to the floor, otherwise); nonskid or nonglare wax should be used on hard flooring surfaces; nonskid strips should be placed in the bathtub; and loose electrical cords and other trip hazards should be eliminated. Canopies, blinds, and drapes can help to minimize contrast between naturally and artificially illuminated areas, and also to reduce glare. Finally, all stairs should be equipped with suitable handrails, and grab bars should be installed in bathrooms.

BIBLIOGRAPHY

Black, S. E., Maki, B. E., & Fernie, G. R. (1993). Aging, imbalance and falls. In H. Barber & J. Sharpe (Eds.). *Vestibulo-ocular reflex, nystagmus and vertigo* (pp. 317–335). New York: Raven Press.

Holliday, P. J., Cott, C. A., & Torresin, W. D. (1992). Preventing accidental falls by the elderly. In J. Rothman & R. Levine (Eds.), *Prevention practice: Strategies for physical therapy and occupational therapy,* (pp. 234–257). Philadelphia: W. B. Saunders.

Kellog International Work Group on the Prevention of Falls by the Elderly. (1987). The prevention of falls in later life. *Danish Medical Bulletin, 34* (suppl. 4), 1–24.

Radebaugh, T. S., Hadley, E., & Suzman, R., (Eds.). (1985). *Falls in the elderly: Biologic and behavioral aspects.* Philadelphia: Saunders.

Tideiksaar, R. (1989). *Falling in old age: Its prevention and treatment.* New York: Springer.

Velas, B., Toupet, M., Rubenstein, L., Albarede J. L., & Christen, Y. (Eds.). (1992). *Falls, balance and gait disorders in the elderly.* Paris: Elsevier.

Weindruch, R., Hadley, E. C., & Ory, M. G., (Eds.). (1991). *Reducing frailty and falls in older persons.* Springfield, IL: Charles C. Thomas.

Accidents: Traffic

Patricia F. Waller

University of Michigan

Blood Alcohol Concentration (BAC) Refers to the percentage of alcohol in the blood, as determined by objective measure of breath, blood, urine, or other bodily fluid.

General Estimates System (GES) A national probability sample of police-reported crashes of all levels of severity.

Intelligent Transportation Systems (ITS) Previously known as IVHS, or Intelligent Vehicle/Highway Systems, sometimes referred to as "Smart Cars/Smart Highways"; refers to the application of communications and other technologies to the transportation system to increase efficiency and safety.

Nationwide Personal Transportation Survey (NPTS) A nationwide survey of a representative sample of households to collect data on the frequency, purpose, and mode of personal transportation, as well as other information on users of the transportation system.

Traffic Accident Damage (TAD) Scale A measure of the location of impact to the vehicle and the degree of vehicle crush occurring in a crash.

Mobility is important at all ages, including the elderly, and in our society it usually involves the use of a personal vehicle. Older drivers, as a group, have higher crash rates based on mileage driven. Their crash risk begins to rise after age 55 and increases at an accelerating rate, so that drivers over age 80 have the highest crash rates of any group. Because of these differences among different-aged elderly, some have made distinctions among older drivers, defining age 55 through 64 as young-old, age 65 through 74 as middle-old, age 75 through 84 as old-old, and age 85 and older as very old. Older drivers are also more vulnerable to serious and fatal injury once a crash occurs, and the crashes of older drivers differ from those of younger drivers in important ways. There is great variation in performance both among elderly drivers and within the same older driver from one time to another. There are not good measures to predict which older drivers will do well and which will not. Although chronological age can serve as an indicator that may suggest further scrutiny, it is not a good predictor of performance for individual drivers. With an aging population, more drivers will not qualify for licensure, but their transportation needs will not cease. Any measures implemented to restrict the mobility of older persons must be substantiated by sound evidence, which is not available currently. As our population ages, the issue of mobility and safety of older citizens will become more critical.

I. CHANGING DEMOGRAPHICS

The two major changes in the demographics of the population that have implications for the elderly in traffic are the dramatic increase in the proportion of the population that is older and the changes in the role of women in traffic.

A. The Elderly

In the United States, as in most of the Western world, the age distribution of the population is changing, with a disproportionate increase in the elderly and a corresponding decrease in the young. These changes have profound implications for transportation of the elderly. Because there will be a relatively smaller younger population, it will become more important that older persons be able to meet their own mobility needs for as long as possible. [*See* DEMOGRAPHY.]

In our society mobility is important at all ages, because it is almost always an essential part of access to life's necessities—health care, shopping, employment, recreation, education, visits with family and friends. There is some evidence that mobility may be an important factor in maintaining good health in the elderly. With increasing concerns about rising health-care costs, assuring transportation for the elderly could prove a cost-beneficial investment.

B. Women

Women are increasing their rate of licensure, accounting for almost half of all licensed drivers. They purchase about half of all new cars sold, are increasing their average annual mileage, and increasing their proportion of the total driving that occurs. Although men still account for the majority of miles driven, the increase of women in the labor force, the increase of single-parent homes headed by women, the increase in women's economic independence, and the increase in their vehicle ownership represent major changes from the past, ones that have implications for aging and traffic crash risk.

II. AGING AND TRAFFIC INJURY

Older people are more likely to be seriously or fatally injured in the event of a traffic crash. This greater vulnerability is not because older drivers have more severe crashes. The Traffic Accident Damage (TAD) scale is a measure of the location and degree of vehicle crush and has been shown to be strongly related to driver injury. The TAD ranges from 0–7, with 7 being the most vehicle crush. Figure 1 illustrates the relationship between age and driver fatality, taking TAD into consideration. It can be seen that the oldest groups experience the highest rates of fatality, given a crash of specified severity.

Although it has long been recognized that older people are more vulnerable to injury, the increase in vulnerability actually begins in the early twenties and increases steadily. Nonfatal injury is also greater with increasing age, and for injured victims who are hospitalized and recover, the length of hospital stay increases with increasing age. Thus, the elderly traffic injury victim represents a more costly problem in terms of health care.

III. AGING AND DRIVING PERFORMANCE

A. Mode of Travel

Older people are heavily dependent upon the private vehicle, and this dependence is increasing. In 1990, between 75 and 95% of all trips made by older persons were made by private automobile. Rates were higher for the "young old" (in this case, age 60–64) and gradually decreased with increasing age. However, even for the "very old" (85 and older), more than three-fourths of their trips were made by private vehicle. Walking is the second most frequent trip mode, but it is a poor second. Walking has actually decreased in relation to other modes.

B. Driver Licensure

The loss of licensure for the elderly is viewed in many ways as a loss of independence and even identity. Most elderly people in the United States today are drivers. Figure 2 shows that, based on the Nationwide Personal Transportation Survey (NPTS), a national survey of a representative sample of households, between 1983 and 1990 licensure rates increased for all ages, but the elderly increased the most.

C. Driving Exposure

During the same time period, average annual mileage increased for all ages, including the elderly. Because

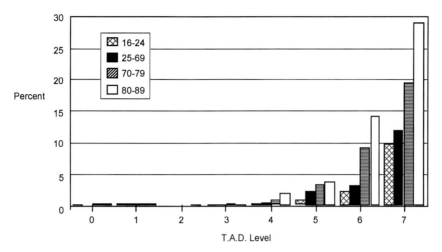

Figure 1 Proportion of fatal injuries by driver age and crash severity Traffic Accident Damage (TAD) scale. (From Massie & Campbell, 1993.)

the elderly increased their licensure at higher rates than other ages, their actual proportion of total driving increased even more than indicated by increases in average mileage rates for individual drivers.

Measures of miles driven do not reflect the quality of driving exposure, that is, the times, places, and conditions under which driving occurs. Older drivers reduce their nighttime driving, and, with increasing age, they also restrict their driving to lower speed roads (eliminating interstate and freeway driving), low traffic volumes, and good weather.

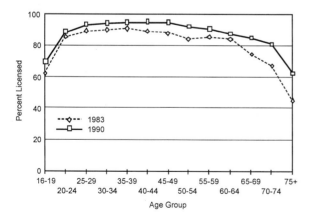

Figure 2 Proportion of population licensed by age, 1983 versus 1990, from National Personal Transportation Surveys. (From Massie & Campbell, 1993.)

IV. AGING AND CRASH RISK

Crash risk may be calculated in several ways, including risk per number of licensed drivers, risk per miles driven, and risk per population.

A. Crash Risk per Licensed Driver

Based on crashes per 100 licensed drivers, older drivers appear to be safer than any other age group. In 1993, drivers age 55–64, 65–74, and 75 and over had 7, 6, and 8 crashes per 100 licensed drivers, respectively, versus 12 for all licensed drivers. Highest rates were for drivers under age 20. The low crash rates for older drivers are cited as the basis for lower motor vehicle insurance rates for the elderly.

B. Crash Risk per Miles Driven

Older drivers drive much less than other licensed drivers, and when crash risk is based on miles driven, crash risk begins to rise slightly in the late fifties and increases at an accelerating rate thereafter. Figure 3 shows the relationship between crash risk and driver age, by gender. This increase occurs *even though the evidence indicates that, as a group, older drivers try to restrict themselves to the safest times and places.* The crashes of older drivers are not

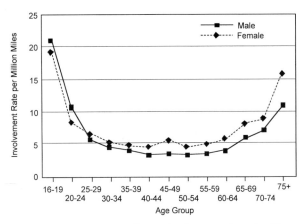

Figure 3 Crash rates per million miles, by age and gender. (From Massie & Campbell, 1993.)

characterized by deliberate high-risk behaviors, such as alcohol use or speeding, but rather appear to be more errors of omission, such as failing to yield right-of-way.

C. Crash Fatality Rates by Population

A third way to measure risk is by fatality rates based on population groups. Traffic deaths account for a very small proportion of total deaths above age 50, and hence may be considered of little consequence for this age group. However, as shown in Figure 4, when traffic fatalities are considered independently of

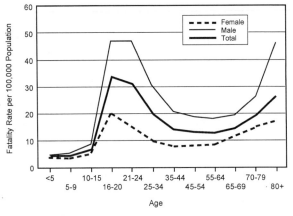

Figure 4 Population death rates from motor vehicle crashes, by age and gender, U.S.A., 1991. (From National Highway Traffic Safety Administration, 1993).

other causes of death, population rates show marked increases among the elderly.

D. Crash Culpability

Not only do crash rates based on mileage increase with increasing age, but also the probability of the older driver being found at fault increases. Older drivers are much more likely than younger drivers to be involved in multivehicle crashes, and in as much as 80% of such cases, the older driver is found to be at fault.

V. AGING, ALCOHOL, AND DRIVING

The evidence for increased crash risk when alcohol is used has been clearly established. It is less well recognized that older people are differentially impaired by alcohol. The first major study establishing relative risk of crash as a function of blood alcohol concentration (BAC) found that older persons with BACs at or above 0.10% had much higher crash risk than other drivers at the same BAC. Although alcohol is not currently a major factor in older driver crashes, when it is used by older drivers, their performance is more impaired.

This same study found that women may be more impaired by alcohol than are men. The crash risk for men at a 0.08% BAC was about twice what it was at 0 BAC, but for women the risk was ninefold, or four and half times that for men. In this early study, gender differences were attributed to differences in driving experience. However, more recent studies report similar findings. Although women still drive less than men, they are sufficiently experienced that they should be well past the steep portion of the learning curve, so that differential experience no longer appears to be a plausible explanation for differences in crash risk.

Laboratory studies of tasks unrelated to driving also indicate that the performance of women may be more impaired than men at a given BAC. These differences are important because they have serious implications for older women drivers over the next decades. Age interacts with BAC to affect performance, and if women are more impaired by alcohol than men, then an increase in older women drivers who drink may result in unprecedented problems on the road. [*See* ALCOHOL AND DRUGS.]

VI. COHORT DIFFERENCES

The need to address the older driver is recognized, but it is often assumed that the issue is primarily one of increasing numbers. If we learn more about older drivers today, we can use that information to develop programs for the future. However, future older drivers may differ from current ones in important ways.

A. Driving Experience

Although for most drivers, driving is a greatly over-learned task, many older drivers acquired their skill on very different roadways and may not be highly skilled in certain kinds of driving. As driving experience on modern highways increases, the relative over-involvement in crashes per mile driven for older drivers, although still high, is decreasing over time. Older drivers today are much more experienced than older drivers 20 years ago. If this trend continues, it would be anticipated that future older drivers will further decrease their relative elevated risk.

B. Alcohol Use

Although alcohol is not a major factor in older driver crashes today, future older drivers may differ in this regard. Drivers currently in their sixties and older, grew up during Prohibition or the Great Depression or both, a time when per capita alcohol consumption was much lower than it is today, and alcohol-related health problems were reduced. Since then, alcohol consumption patterns have changed.

The baby boom generation is characterized by attitudes and behaviors that differ from those of their predecessors, particularly in the case of women. The older members of this generation are moving into their fifties, so that age-related changes in driving are likely to appear over the next decade. Alcohol use by women in this generation is much greater than was true for their elders at this age.

Against this backdrop is the recent drop in alcohol-related driving. Since the early 1980s, public attitudes toward drunken driving have become much more negative. Alcohol-related crashes have decreased, not only as a proportion of total crashes but also in absolute numbers.

How these differential trends in alcohol use will affect future cohorts of older drivers remains to be seen.

VII. MEDICAL CONDITIONS AND THE OLDER DRIVER

Impaired vision is probably the most widely recognized medical problem for older drivers. With increasing age, almost all drivers suffer some loss of vision, and eye disease becomes more prevalent. Because of the obvious relationship between vision and driving, and because of the relative ease of measuring certain kinds of visual functioning, all states include vision requirements for original driver licensure, and most states require it for license renewal. It is difficult to show a strong relationship between vision and driving performance as measured by crashes, but more complex measures of vision that have been developed recently show promise of utility. [*See* VISION.]

The data on dementia and driving are mixed. Although there is no question that dementia affects driving performance, whether the early stages are associated with greater crash risk is not definitely established. Drivers suffering from dementia are more likely to become lost than to crash. [*See* DEMENTIA.]

Other medical conditions more prevalent among the elderly, such as heart disease and diabetes mellitus, may also affect driving performance, but they have not been shown conclusively to increase crash risk.

VIII. THE AGING COMMERCIAL DRIVER

Driving commercially poses special problems for an aging driving population. Heavy truck traffic has increased more rapidly than passenger vehicle traffic, a trend that will continue. With the aging population, major trucking companies are having difficulty finding qualified drivers. Although the crash risk for drivers in general begins to rise after around age 55, for commercial drivers, who cannot restrict their schedules to the safest times and places, this increase begins earlier and rises more steeply. In collisions between heavy trucks and passenger vehicles, over 90% of the fatalities occur to occupants of the passenger vehicles. Other forms of commercial driving that utilize older drivers include the transport of rental vehicles and the operation of school buses. The issue of the older commercial driver will almost certainly become an increasing problem.

IX. AGING AND PEDESTRIAN CASUALTIES

The elderly are underrepresented in pedestrian casualties overall (both injured and killed) but overrepresented in pedestrian fatalities. Thus the elderly are less likely than other pedestrians to be involved in a crash, but once they are hit, they are more likely to die. Figure 5 shows pedestrian fatalities by age and gender. It can be seen that, for both men and women, the numbers increase with increasing age. It should be noted that these are raw numbers and are not based on population. If population were taken into account, the increase for the elderly would be even more dramatic.

The most hazardous situation for the elderly pedestrian is negotiating intersections, especially in urban areas. The standard (and legal) timing of pedestrian crossing signals is not adequate for many older pedestrians to reach the opposite curb before traffic is allowed to enter. The average walking velocity of younger pedestrians is about one and a half times that of older pedestrians, with many elderly even slower.

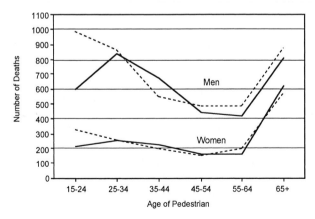

Figure 5 Pedestrian fatalities by age and gender, 1982–1984 (dashed line), 1989–1991 (solid line).

At busy high-risk intersections, the implementation of interventions, such as lengthening the time of the crossing signal, improved roadway markings, pedestrian signals on median islands, larger speed limit signs and increased enforcement of speed limits, and safety education at senior citizen centers, has resulted in marked decreases in pedestrian casualties.

X. THE POTENTIAL OF TECHNOLOGY

With the completion of the Interstate Highway System, the United States is embarking on a new era in transportation. Known as Intelligent Transportation Systems (ITS), and sometimes referred to as "Smart Cars, Smart Highways," ITS applies communications and other technologies to increase the efficiency of our current highways. Vehicles will communicate with the highway (and vice versa) and with each other. A major purpose of ITS is to simplify the driving task and to increase safety. Information will be provided to the driver on traffic problems ahead, including potential alternative routing. Drivers could also obtain a local yellow pages, with detailed information on restaurants, motels, and other facilities available in the next town. They can be alerted of an impending hazard, such as a vehicle in their blind spot or a vehicle rapidly decelerating ahead. These and other technologies are being developed and tested.

In ITS, the older driver is of special concern. It is not known to what extent additional information will be beneficial or will lead to information overload, complicating the task for drivers who need greater simplification, not increased complexity. Whether, and to what extent, short-term training with new technology could assist in the use of new driver aids also is not known. Nevertheless, if new technology is designed, taking into account the abilities and limitations of older users, it holds promise of extending the self-sufficiency of many elderly drivers.

XI. ALTERNATIVE TRANSPORTATION FOR THE ELDERLY

Although driving performance of older people may be improved through such measures as physical therapy, perceptual therapy, driver education, and traffic engineering improvements, eventually most older people will no longer qualify for driver licensure. Yet their transportation needs will not cease. Maintenance of contact with others is associated with better health and well-being, and the elderly still must have access to health care, shopping, recreation, and other activities.

Older persons disqualified for driving must be channeled into alternative means of transportation. In most areas of the country, traditional public transport is prohibitively expensive, but every community has a surprising amount of paratransit, that is, transit that falls between fixed route buses or light rail and the personal vehicle. Paratransit is usually earmarked for specific limited purposes, such as transporting employees of a large organization to and from work, transporting patients to medical care, or providing other special services. Although it would require addressing complex legal, institutional, and political barriers, at a local level this paratransit can be coordinated so that existing resources can be used much more effectively to meet the needs of our growing population of elderly and at minimal cost.

BIBLIOGRAPHY

Barr, R. A., & Eberhard, J. W. (1991). Safety and mobility of elderly drivers, Part I. *Human Factors, 33,* (5). 497–603.

Eberhard, J. W., & Barr, R. A. (1992). Safety and mobility of elderly drivers, Part II. *Human Factors, 34*(1). 1–123.

Evans, L. (1991). *Traffic safety and the driver.* New York: Van Nostrand.

Massie, D. L., & Campbell, K. L. (1993). *Analysis of accident rates by age, gender, and time of day based on the 1990 Nationwide Personal Transportation Survey.* Ann Arbor, MI: University of Michigan Transportation Research Institute.

National Highway Traffic Safety Administration. (1993). *Fatal accident reporting system 1991.* Washington, DC: U.S. Department of Transportation.

National Research Council (U.S.). Transportation Research Board, Committee for the Study on Improving Mobility and Safety for Older Persons. (1988). *Transportation in an Aging Society: Improving Mobility and Safety for Older Persons,* vols. 1 and 2. Transportation Research Board, Washington, DC:

Retchin, S. M. (Ed.). (1993). Medical considerations in the older driver. In *Clinics in geriatric medicine,* (Vol. 9 (2), pp. 279–490).

Transportation Research Board. (1994). *Driver performance data book update: Older drivers and IVHS.* (Transportation Research Circular 419). Washington, DC: National Research Council.

Waller, P. F., & Blow, F. C. (1995). Women, alcohol, and driving. In M. Galanter (Ed.), *Recent developments in alcoholism (Vol. 12, pp. 103–123). Alcoholism and Women.* New York: Plenum Press.

Achievement

Dean Keith Simonton

University of California at Davis

Career Age The number of years an individual has been active within a given domain of achievement. Also called professional age.

Equal-Odds Rule The empirical generalization that the ratio of successful works to total output stays more or less constant across an individual's career.

Last-Works Effects The tendency for creative products conceived toward the end of life to exhibit qualitative and quantitative changes. These changes suggest a resurgence and transformation of creativity in the final years.

ACHIEVEMENT is a generic concept that can cover a tremendous range of human activities. These activities may have little in common and may require rather distinctive biological, psychological, and sociological conditions. To offer some obvious examples, the Nobel laureate in physics may have little in common with the Olympic athlete, just as the founder of a successful business enterprise may share nothing at all with a movie star. However, close examination of these and other cases does reveal that all instances of achievement tend to feature the same four characteristics.

First, achievements are behaviors or products that make an individual stand out from the majority of individuals who are active in the same endeavor. Not every author wins the Nobel Prize for literature; not every tennis player becomes a singles champion at Wimbledon; not every entrepreneur manages to build from scratch a Fortune 500 company. As these instances show, some individuals may attain distinction by offering something unique to the world, such as an artistic masterpiece, whereas others may make a name for themselves by performing some well-defined task better than any competitors, such as sprinting 100 meters faster than anyone else in the world.

Second, achievements are behaviors or products that reflect favorably on the skill or talent of the person under view. Only a tiny percentage of the population have the mental or physical capacity to make a serious bid for a major honor, award, or prize. It is for this reason that lottery winners are not credited with achievements; the skill needed to purchase a lottery ticket is of a very ordinary kind that everybody possesses.

Third, we usually associate achievement with motivational characteristics, such as effort, persistence, drive, and determination. As a consequence, individuals who enjoy a certain natural talent at some task but who make no attempt to develop further their native skills are most likely to be called "underachievers." So important is this third characteristic of achievement behaviors that we will sometimes label an activity an achievement even when it requires far more motivation than ability or skill [*See* ACTIVITIES.]. For instance, many of the achievements listed in the *Guinness Book of Records* are of this variety. Someone who holds the world record for the number of days spent sitting atop a pole is going to earn admiration more for persistence than for talent. Nevertheless, those achievements that seem to require *both* ability *and* effort seem to elicit the most widespread and profound esteem.

Copyright © 1996 by Academic Press, Inc.
All rights of reproduction in any form reserved.

Fourth, the word achievement is normally assigned to behaviors or products that have positive social value. Accordingly, notorious assassinations or infamous crimes are seldom considered accomplishments. Unfortunately, this component of the concept is not always easy to evaluate. Not only may value judgments vary from culture to culture, but these assessments may also vary from individual to individual within the same culture. In some nations, assassination for political or religious reasons may be actually encouraged. And for some pacifists, a general's victories on the battlefield may constitute criminal acts of institutionalized homicide. Nevertheless, nothing prevents us from adopting a relativistic conception of societal norms. If an activity tends to earn praise from the majority of those living within a given sociocultural system, it can be counted as a notable accomplishment.

In this article, the focus shall be on those achievements that exemplify all of the central characteristics. The key question then becomes how this level of achievement varies as a function of a person's age. At what point can it be safely inferred that a particular individual is "over the hill" or "past his or her prime"? Does there exist an age beyond which one should not anticipate further accomplishments of the kind witnessed earlier in the career? To address this question, I will first review the empirical findings on this subject. Next I examine some of the possible theoretical interpretations of those results.

I. EMPIRICAL FINDINGS

The scientific study of the relation between age and achievement is one of the oldest research topics in the history of the behavioral sciences. The earliest such investigation was conducted in 1835 by Adolph Quetelet, who examined how the production of notable plays varied as a function of the dramatist's age. This was the first study to demonstrate how creative productivity often declines in the later years of life. However, the first truly thorough research on this subject was conducted by Harvey C. Lehman, especially as summarized in the 1953 book *Age and Achievement*. Lehman investigated virtually every possible domain of achievement, including both creativity and leadership. He also attempted to introduce much more systematic and rigorous methods in his quest for the typical age curves for various intellectual, aesthetic, political, and economic endeavors. Although subsequent investigators have identified several methodological flaws in Lehman's work, many of the central results have been replicated in studies that use more advanced analytical techniques. In particular, the literature supports the conclusion that significant achievement tends to decline after a career peak, which most often occurs around midlife. In addition, the specific nature of this decent will vary according to many other factors, such as the specific domain of achievement. These and other complications will become apparent below, where I examine the longitudinal changes in three broad domains: leadership, creativity, and entertainment.

A. Leadership

Of all categories of achievement, leaders may occupy the highest place. Political, military, economic, and religious leaders all define the world in which one inescapably lives. A nation's material and emotional well-being closely depends on the politicians who write its laws, the generals who defend its boundaries, the entrepreneurs who introduce new products and create new industries, and the religious figures who guide a people's moral and spiritual life. It should not be surprising, then, that of all forms of achievement, leaders tend to be the most prominent. The average person on the street may not know who most recently received the Nobel Prize for literature or for physics, but few would not be able to identify the individual who serves as the nation's current head of state. Even the historical reputation of leaders tend to exceed that of individuals active in different domains of attainment.

Given the significance of leadership, the relation between age and achievement assumes great practical importance. When is a person too old too occupy such a critical position in society? This question is best addressed by looking separately at political, military, religious, and economic leadership.

1. Politicians
When speaking of the relation between age and political achievement, leadership can be assessed in many different ways. The most common definition in research is simply to note the age at which individuals are most likely to ascend to a particular political posi-

tion. At what age do individuals become president, prime minister, senator, governor, member of parliament, secretary of state, ambassador, and so forth? This research shows that leaders in such established political roles enter during their more mature years, most commonly in their fifties or sixties. Moreover, it is not rare to see status quo political leaders who are even older. At the same time, it is clear that the age distributions tend to vary according to the nature of the political position. Among politicians in the United States, Senate legislators tend to be older than those in the House of Representatives, whereas among chief executives, presidents tend to be older than state governors. Of course, some of these contrasts can be attributed to differences mandated by law. Nonetheless, this cannot entirely explain the age differences, because the most typical age ranges tend to be older than those set down by law. For example, most presidents exceed the minimum by about 20 years. In fact, successful presidential candidates tend to be close to 55 years old, whereas most losing candidates tend to be either much younger (as low as 36) or much older (as high as 85).

So far we have considered only established political roles. Other political leaders achieve distinction by heading revolts, rebellions, or revolutions against the established government. These revolutionaries and rebels are far more prone to be much younger than their contemporaries who occupy status quo positions. For example, among politicians of the twentieth century it was rare for a status quo politician to attain power before the age of 40. In contrast, almost half of eminent revolutionaries were younger than 35 at the onset of their involvement, and almost 80% were younger than 45 years old. Interestingly, as a political system matures, the average age of its leadership tends to increase as well. This trend is seen in the history of the United States since its inception at the end of the eighteenth century. Members of Congress in the twentieth century are about a decade older than those at the beginning of the nineteenth century. Furthermore, the average ages of those serving as Speaker of the House have increased from the forties to the seventies. These upward trends cannot be entirely attributed to shifts in mean life span. In fact, for some political positions the trends go in the opposite direction. The governors of the American colonies were actually about 20 years older than the governors of the various states of the Union after the Revolution.

Colonial governors, as subordinates of the British crown, had to represent more strongly the status quo. Hence, the same principle applies. Youth challenges the powers that be, and maturity defends those institutional powers.

These findings all focus on the age at which individuals fill certain leadership roles. Although this is certainly a reasonable criterion of achievement—given the difficulty of attaining these positions—it is not the sole criterion that one can use. Indeed, a more critical gauge of achievement would be some indicator of the leaders' actual performance during their tenure in office. For example, one investigation looked at the relationship between the age at which a U.S. president is inaugurated and his subsequent performance as an executive, legislator, and diplomat. Absolutely no relationship was found. Older chief executives are no better or worse than those much younger, and there exists no peak age for maximum success.

Nevertheless, it is necessary to point out a serious methodological problem with many of these studies. For most political offices in democratic systems the length of tenure is rather restricted. In the U.S. presidency, for instance, only one chief executive has served more than eight years, and many have served four or less. This is too little time to calculate longitudinal trends. What is required is an analysis of leaders who have served throughout their adult lives. The only political institution where this is feasible is hereditary monarchy. Because monarchs may then ascend to the throne at a young age and may remain enthroned until death, these leaders allow us to scrutinize changes in performance over three decades or more. One empirical inquiry that examined a large sample of long-tenured monarchs in fact discovered a tendency for performance to peak when the figure was around 42 years old. After that peak, there was a gradual decline in the monarchs' ability to expand or maintain their political power and influence. Thus, age decrements can be found when the observations are truly longitudinal in nature.

2. Commanders

The study of military leadership presents some of the same problems seen in the study of politicians. For example, a careful distinction must be made between the age at which an individual is most likely to occupy the role of general or admiral and the individual's performance in that role. Thus, one early investigation looked at the age at which commanders led armies in historic battles, without noting whether the battle was won or lost. As a result, the information obtained was very limited in its implications. Another difficulty is even more severe than that seen in the study of political leaders. Although military careers can last a long time, the central function of those careers, namely fighting wars, usually has a much shorter duration. It is rare for a major war to last for more than five years, and a very large proportion may go on for only a year or two. Seldom can a commander's tactical success be traced over a long period of time. As a consequence, there is no other choice but to examine cross-sectional rather than longitudinal data. Is the age of two opposing commanders in a battle a predictor of who will be mostly likely to emerge the victor? The answer is affirmative. For instance, one empirical study looked at the winners and losers in 326 land battles. The older a general was in comparison to his opponent, the less likely he was to take the offensive by attacking first. In other words, older commanders tend to adopt more conservative, defensive tactics. This age trend is important because taking the initiative on the battlefield is a key predictor of tactical victory. In addition, there was evidence of a curvilinear relationship between age and military success. The commanders who were closest to the peak age of 45 years were most likely to be those with the most career victories and the longest winning streaks. Altogether these findings suggest that military achievement, at least as defined by battlefield victory, may decline in the later years of a commander's life.

3. Entrepreneurs

Economic leaders are extremely important to the material well-being of any capitalist society. After all, these are the leaders, the business people, who market the new products and create the new jobs that are essential to a high standard of living. Yet research on these figures is relatively limited. Most studies indicate that entrepreneurial leadership may peak somewhat late in life. Typically, the most distinguished leaders first reach the high point of their financial power in their late fifties. Moreover, these individuals do not actually attain wide recognition for their economic accomplishments until somewhere in their sixties. Thus, this form of achievement may require somewhat more maturity and experience in the business world. At the same time, these age curves are not easy to

interpret. The income and influence of entrepreneurs are largely based on decisions made earlier in their careers. The seeds of the wealth of an Andrew Carnegie, John D. Rockefeller, Henry Ford, or other corporate giant were often planted in their thirties. It takes time for the risky investments of youth to make an impact on an industry. Even so, these entrepreneurs usually manage to continue their money-making abilities until quite late in their lives. Only in rapidly changing markets might they find themselves suffering from younger competitors. In this sense, economic leadership is similar to what tends to hold for diplomats and other forms of political leadership in which accumulated expertise is at a premium.

4. Religious Leaders

The life span development of those who lead religious movements and institutions follow a pattern that closely parallels what has been observed for political leaders. On the one hand, some figures attain distinction by becoming the head of some established religious group, whether a church, denomination, or sect. These status quo religious leaders tend to be quite advanced in years. The history of the Roman Catholic papacy provides a typical illustration. Almost all popes were older than 50 years old at the time they were elected, and around two-thirds were well over 65. Furthermore, the optimal age range for becoming pope lies roughly between 80 and 90. On the other hand, the founders of new world faiths are often much younger. It is extremely rare for a founder to be older than 60, and most tend to be between 35 and 38, and many are much younger than that optimum interval. To offer examples from the history of Christianity, John Wesley founded Methodism at age 35; Martin Luther launched the Protestant movement at 34. Ignatius Loyola wrote the *Spiritual Exercises* at 30. John Calvin wrote the *Institutes* at 27. Joseph Smith began Mormonism at 25. George Fox founded the Quaker faith at 23. Jesus himself was probably around 30 at the height of his mission. Similar statistics hold outside the Christian faith. For example, Buddha was probably in his mid-thirties when he began teaching the fruits of his enlightenment. Of all the world's major faiths, Islam had the oldest founder, and even he, Mohammed, was only 40 when be became the Prophet. Facts such as these support the conclusion made by G. Stanley Hall that "men in their prime conceived the great religions, the old made them prevail." Curiously, when exceptions to this rule seem to appear, the underlying principle persists upon closer examination. Thus, Popes Innocent III and Leo X, for instance, entered the pontificate in their late thirties. Yet both were extreme activists, the first in the political sphere, the second in the cultural.

B. Creativity

The subject of the relationship between age and creative productivity has already been treated at length in the article on creativity in this encyclopedia. Therefore, here I summarize only the central findings. There are six of them [See CREATIVITY.]

1. Typical Age Curve

Plotting the number of contributions individuals make as a function of their age creates a single-peaked, inverted-U curve. More specifically, the output of works first increases up to a certain optimum, after which productivity gradually declines. By the eightieth year of life, the decrement in output is about 50% of the level reached at the career peak. Although this might seem a substantial drop, I must note two extenuating facts. First, even a creator who is well advanced in years can expect to maintain a respectable level of creative productivity. Second, the output rate seen by individuals in their seventies is about the same as that seen by those in their twenties. In this sense, septuagenarians can hold their own against the youngest members of their discipline.

2. Interdisciplinary Differences

The typical age curve varies substantially according to the specific domain of creative achievement. In some fields the peaks may appear relatively early in life, and the postpeak declines can be relatively rapid. This is the situation for lyric poetry and abstract mathematics, for example. In other fields, however, the productive optima usually occur much later in life, even as late as the fifties. Such delayed peaks are common in history and philosophy. Furthermore, those creative domains that feature later productive maxima also tend to exhibit gradual, even negligible, declines. Thus, in these late, and slowly maturing disciplines, aging has minimal impact on creative achievement. Moreover, even in those disciplines characterized by early peaks and rapid declines, the output rate does drop to zero. In fact, the typical creator in these domains will at least maintain a level of productivity by age 80 that will equal about 10% of that observed at the career peak.

3. Career versus Chronological Age

Although most researchers tend to view the longitudinal changes in terms of chronological age, this practice is not really correct. Instead, the curves expressing changes in creative productivity are better defined according to career or professional age. Those who begin their careers earlier in life will tend to exhibit earlier peaks as well. By the same token, those whose careers get a very late start will normally enjoy later peaks. This means that it sometimes happens that late bloomers will actually attain their career high points in the last one or two decades of life. In addition, it is perfectly possible for a person to exhibit *two* career peaks. This can happen when an individual already successful in one field decides to make a midlife career change, and thus develops a second successful career in later life.

4. Individual Differences

One should not overlook the fact that individual differences in creative achievement are quite substantial. Not all creators are created equal, but rather some produce considerably more creative ideas than their less accomplished colleagues. In most disciplines the top 10% who are the most productive are usually responsible for 50% of all contributions in the field, whereas the bottom 50% who are the least productive all together account for only about 15% of the total achievement. As a consequence, this cross-sectional variation explains more variance in output than do the longitudinal changes attributed to career age. Accordingly, highly prolific creators in their seventies or eighties will equal or even exceed the output levels of other, less productive creators in their thirties or forties.

5. Equal-Odds Rule

There are two ways to count output across the career. On the one hand, one can simply tabulate the total number of works produced, regardless of whether the pieces are successful or not. For example, one might count the number of scientific papers produced per decade without regard for whether these papers made any contribution to the field. On the other hand, one might restrict the counts to merely those creations that can be considered genuine achievements. For instance, we could tabulate on those scientific papers that receive a specified number of citations in the publications of other scientists working in the same discipline. The first kind of measure gauges quantity, or pure productivity, whereas the second kind of measure assesses quality or real creativity. Obviously, if the standpoint is one of achievement, the exclusive quality measures are superior to the inclusive quantity measures. This distinction also has interesting repercussions for understanding how aging affects creative achievement. In the first place, the age curves for quantity and quality are essentially the same. Those periods in an individual's life in which the most works are produced are also those in which the most influential products are most likely to emerge. Furthermore, by calculating the proportion of successful works to total output, one finds that the quality ratio fluctuates more or less randomly throughout the career. This means that older members of a creative enterprise will have roughly the same success rate as those members at their supposed creative prime. In other words, even though the elder creators may be producing fewer masterpieces, they are also generating fewer neglected works. This "equal-odds rule" suggests that from the perspective of the quality ratio, one cannot realistically speak of an age decrement at all. Age is simply unrelated to the probability of success.

6. Last-Works Effects

I can advance a step beyond the last point. Highly creative individuals will frequently undergo a resurgence of creative activity towards the end of life. This upsurge in total output, as the equal-odds rule maintains, will correspond to an increased production of important works. More importantly, as death draws near the creativity of these individuals will often undergo a qualitative transformation that renders their final works quite distinct. In the visual arts, for example, it is not uncommon for master painters to enter into a phase in which their works exhibit a notable "late style." In addition, creators will often devote considerable effort to the production of a single piece that successfully serves as an artistic "last testament" or "career capstone." In classical music, for instance, this creative shift has been called the "swan-song phenomenon." What makes these achievements especially significant is that they often appear when the individual's health has been undergoing chronic and

debilitating deterioration, including blindness, deafness, arthritis, and other infirmities. Thus the age curves notwithstanding, the aging process need not prevent exceptional creators from maintaining their creative powers right to the end.

C. Entertainment

In this final category are placed several miscellaneous forms of achievement that cannot be classified as either leadership or creativity. Because the number of potential domains is extremely diverse, we will only review three representative areas of accomplishment. These concern sports, chess, and film.

I. Athletes

Among all the principal domains of achievement, accomplishments in sports are almost exclusively the province of youth. Sports championships, such as the Olympics, are predominantly populated by athletes in their twenties. Indeed, for some events, like female gold medalists in swimming, it is the teenagers who are most likely to prevail. Moreover, the various age optima for athletic competitions tend to be quite stable over long periods of time. For instance, the mean age of Olympic gold medalists in track-and-field events has stayed relatively constant since the first Olympics were held. In addition, the variation around these means is usually rather small. For most athletic activities, the top athletes will be no more than 5 years apart in their ages.

On the other hand, it is also true that the ages of peak achievement tend to vary systematically according to the particular sport. In swimming and track, for example, there appears a fairly consistent tendency for the longer events to be won by older athletes, the differences sometimes exceeding 5 years. More importantly, the age optima are even greater for those competing in sports where skill is more important than either speed, strength, or stamina. Thus, champions in shooting, golfing, bowling, and billiards are most frequently in their early thirties. Even so, there exists no regular sport in which the championships are most commonly held by athletes in their forties or older. So, the main generalization stands: Older adults cannot be expected to compete at the same level as younger athletes.

However, this last remark should not blind us to another fundamental truth. There always exist substantial individual differences in athletic performance, differences that tend to be relatively stable across time. Consequently, a top athlete past his or her prime may still be competitive to lesser athletes who are at their prime. When focusing on those who receive the gold medals or most valuable player awards, one tends to forget that there are older competitors that came in third or fourth in the event, match, or ballot. The classic illustration is the baseball pitcher Nolan Ryan who went from a record-breaking player in his late twenties to a still highly competitive player in his late thirties. In fact, he was still breaking records shortly before injury forced his long-delayed retirement.

2. Chess Masters

The previous section observed that those sports that place the most emphasis on skill are most likely to be those with older champions. This tendency may lead one to ask, What about those competitive activities in which the skill is entirely mental rather than physical? For example, because card and board games do not require any extraordinary proficiency in eye–hand coordination, one might anticipate that championship players can do so at older ages than is typical in sports. There is indeed evidence that this expectation fits the facts. For instance, Arpad Elo devised an objective measure of the performance of chess masters, which he then used to gauge how expected performance changed over the career course. The average age for peak competitiveness was around age 36, and the range of maximal to near maximal performance was between the late twenties and the late forties. Furthermore, a player at about age 63 could expect to play as well as a player at around age 21. Hence, the assets of youth are much less conspicuous for a competitive activity that is almost entirely intellectual in nature.

Finally, what was said of athletes holds equally well for chess grandmasters. The strongest players in the later stages of their careers are superior to lesser players in their prime. Individual differences in skill are so pronounced as to often overwhelm longitudinal changes in competitive ability. A prime example is a player like Emanuel Lasker who became world champion in 1894 and successfully defended his title when he was 53 years old. Significantly, even in his sixties Lasker was able to pull off some classic victories in chess competition.

3. Movie Stars

The final domain of achievement in entertainment concerns actors and actresses in film. Acting may seem far removed from the preceding two domains, yet in certain respects they are actually comparable. In the first place, the movie business is extremely competitive, so that only a small percentage of aspiring actors and actresses can expect to attain star status. Second, like chess, acting largely represents an intellectual skill that is acquired and developed. Third, like athletics, success in films requires certain physical attributes, even if these characteristics are not usually of the same kind demanded in sports. In particular, it is rare for an actor or actress to rise to stardom without emanating an unusual amount of physical attractiveness. Whether we call them handsome or beautiful, most project in their performances a certain amount of sex appeal. This latter attribute raises an intriguing question: Might not the relation between age and achievement within this domain vary according to gender? After all, the sexual attractiveness of men and women may change in different ways as a function of the aging process. Indeed, where women might quickly lose sex appeal, men might actually gain as their appearance grows more masculine and "distinguished." Only if the skill component of great acting predominated would one expect the accomplishments of actress and actors to follow the same life course.

Research on this question supports the conclusion that gender contrasts are in fact quite conspicuous. For example, one inquiry looked at the ages of the actors and actresses who were the top moneymakers. The curves for the two sexes were dramatically different. The women began to make big money earlier, around the late teens, reached the peak of their careers in the late twenties, and were largely finished as box-office attractions by their late thirties. The men, in contrast, did not really take off until the early twenties, attained their peaks in the early thirties, and, most significantly, continued to enjoy some box-office success until they attained the late sixties. Curiously, largely the same age curves appeared for stars who turned in best performances as judged by movie critics. The best performance of an actress most often appears in the late twenties, that of an actor in the early thirties. Furthermore, whereas women have little chance of such an accomplishment beyond age 40, the prospects for actors remain good into the sixties. Hence, physical attractiveness may be far more crucial than performance skill in determining the achievements of movie stars. Not only must women be younger than men to maximize success, but also women must experience a more precipitous drop in their opportunities for stardom. Admittedly, these curves represent only statistical averages, and accordingly, exceptions do exist. Katherine Hepburn is a classic illustration of a woman whose achievements as an actress survived the deterioration of her physical beauty. Nonetheless, for the vast majority of movie stars, the aging process harms the careers of women much more than those of men.

II. THEORETICAL EXPLANATIONS

The previous section emphasized the empirical findings on the connection between age and achievement. No attempt was made to discuss the theoretical explanations for these diverse results. This deficiency is rectified in the next section. The available substantive interpretations may be grouped into three categories: biological, psychological, and sociological.

A. Biological Processes

It is perhaps too common to explain any age decrements in achievement in terms of the adverse effects of the aging process on individual health. Older persons almost invariably experience marked declines in physical vigor. Aging also brings about a slowing down of mental functioning due to changes in the central nervous system. In addition, it may take increasingly longer to overcome the disabilities resulting from injuries and infections. No doubt these biological consequences of aging take their toll on an individual's capacity for achievement. Yet these interpretations are incomplete. For example, a purely biological explanation cannot accout for why career age is more predictive of creative productivity than is chronological age. Those who get a late start on their careers may actually be attaining their career peaks when they are well advanced in years. Nor can the physical repercussions of aging help us to understand the basis for interdisciplinary contrasts in creative output. It takes far more physical exertion to write a novel than to write poetry, and yet novelists peak much later in life than do poets. In all, one must realize that biological interpretations have to be applied with extreme caution. Otherwise, one may overlook the fine details regarding the relation between aging and achievement.

Nonetheless, in some domains biological processes can carry most of the explanatory weight. This is most evident in sports. As pointed out, the optimal ages for top performance in various athletic competitions have remained rather stable for at least a century. The age at which an individual is most likely to become an Olympic champion depends almost entirely on the nature of the athletic event and the gender of the participants. All the medical advances of the twentieth century have not significantly modified these age curves. This temporal stability suggests that there are fundamental physiological bases for the age curves. Sprinters will be younger than long-distance runners for purely physical reasons.

Biological explanations may take another form as well. According to sociobiologists, some patterns of human interaction are the products of standard evolutionary processes. Since the beginning of our species, individuals have been engaged in the business of optimizing their reproductive success, and this preoccupation has favored the dominance of certain types of social behaviors. For example, if individuals select mates according to fertility, then the attractiveness of men and women should exhibit very different age curves. Where women are maximally fertile in the twenties and early thirties, men maintain their ferility until much later in life. This contrast may help explain the dramatic difference between the career trajectories of actors and actresses. Because a woman's fertility declines so precipitously, her sex appeal on the silver screen suffers a drastic drop as well, until the actress no longer will be seen as a box-office attraction.

Of course, this sociobiological principle alone cannot explain why the actors get a slower start than do the actresses. After all, young men can prove to be quite fertile. However, here one can evoke another explanatory principle from sociobiological theory, namely that the sexual attractiveness of men is influenced by their success in life's competition. Attractive males are supposedly "survivors" who have endured the tests and have emerged victorious, as evinced by their control over power and resources. By this account, then, an older male holds the edge over the younger male. This would not only explain why actors peak later than actresses, but also why the decline is so much more gradual. Men in their sixties can display an attractiveness only enjoyed by women in their twenties. Incidentally, this same phenomenon may also account for why status quo political and religious leaders tend to be older. Social animals increase their reproductive success by selecting the best individuals to lead their group. These are going to be the individuals with the most experience and success. As a consequence, whereas successful actresses tend to be much younger than successful actors, women leaders tend to rise to power at about the same ages as men do.

Considerably more research must be undertaken before one can have full confidence in sociobiological explanations. Even so, these accounts indicate that the impact of biological processes can be far more subtle and complex than simply attributing achievement decrements to the infirmities of age.

B. Psychological Processes

Many have proposed that the linkage between aging and achievement reflects more fundamental changes in the psychological processes that underlie the attainment and maintenance of success. Perhaps the single-most common explanation is a possible age decrement in intellectual functioning in the later years of life. Particularly provocative is the distinction between two varieties of intelligence, namely "crystallized" and "fluid." Crystallized intelligence concerns knowledge, information, and expertise, whereas fluid intelligence concerns flexible problem-solving ability. Whereas the first may increase or at least stay relatively constant across the life span, the second may exhibit fairly sharp declines in the later years of life. This contrast in developmental trends may help to understand the interfield differences in career trajectories, because each domain of achievement probably requires a different optimal mix of crystallized and fluid intelligences. For instance, a diplomat, historian, or head of an established church probably needs more crystallized than fluid intelligence, and thus their career peaks appear in advanced maturity. On the other hand, revolutionaries, poets, and founders of new faiths may need more fluid than crystallized intelligence, thereby pushing the career optima toward more youthful ages. [See DECISION MAKING AND EVERYDAY PROBLEM SOLVING; LEARNING.]

However, motivational factors may also play a role, perhaps even the most important part. For example, one investigator has proposed that achievement is a function of two components: experience and enthusiasm. Although experience continuously increases with age, according to this theory, enthusiasm first peaks sometime in the early thirties and thereafter decreases. The career optimum then appears where the sum of these two curves maximizes, which occurs around the late thirties. Yet different domains may require a characteristic mix of experience and enthusiasm. Revolution and poetry, for instance, may require greater zeal, whereas diplomacy and history may demand more wisdom. The career peaks will appear at different ages accordingly.

The foregoing explanations operated under an age-decrement assumption. Either intellectual ability or enthusiasm underwent an age-related decline in the processes that underlie achievement. Nonetheless, other psychological explanations do not presume the occurrence of such inexorable age decrements. For example, some researchers have proposed psychoeconomic theories that presume that achievement operates in a manner similar to business investment. Achieving individuals are trying to optimize their long-term assets, and to do so they must invest in their "human capital." The utility of these investments may diminish in the latter part of any life for the simple reason that an individual is less likely to be around to reap the profits. Nonetheless, this choice to redirect effort may be reversed if at any time the person perceives an altered cost–benefit ratio. Such calculations may result from modified family circumstances, career changes, and more optimistic perceptions of probable life spans. The important point is that the achievement potential of individuals may not necessarily decline just because the observed levels of achievement may appear to fall off. At different stages of their lives people must adjust their priorities according to considerations that are unrelated to inherent capabilities.

C. Sociological Processes

One must not ignore the often extremely powerful impact of larger societal forces on the relationship between age and achievement. Sometimes these influences may take a rather explicit form. Political institutions, in particular, will often possess constitutions or bylaws that specify the acceptable ages at which certain positions of authority may be occupied. The U.S. Constitution, for instance, states that an individual must be at least 25 to serve as a member of the House of Representatives, 30 to serve as senator, and 35 as president of the United States. This means that the age curves are automatically truncated at the lower end, and that the occupants of the various federal positions will exhibit a certain amount of age stratification. Although other political systems have been successfully governed by very young heads of state, such a possibility is constitutionally prohibited in the U.S. system. Of course, the legal restrictions can just as well go in the other direction. For many years, and in many places, organizations both private and public practiced mandatory retirement. We will never know how many potential achievements never saw the light of day because individuals at age 65 suddenly found themselves denied the resources to continue their work.

These institutional constraints cannot tell the whole story, however. Other social realities have a part to play as well. The U.S. presidency provides another illustration. Why is it that successful presidential candidates tend to be in their mid-fifties, whereas unsuccessful candidates tend to either younger or older? One could argue that this age function reflects a fundamental necessity of presidential politics. In order to get elected to the White House, one must build a political base, a foundation that relies most heavily on a candidate's own cohort. Those who are much younger than 50 probably have not yet managed to construct the necessary broad support. Furthermore, those who are much older than 50 will likely see their political base erode as members of their cohort retire or die, and as younger politicians recruit support from the younger generations. Hence, the

career trajectory here may represent nothing more than the pragmatics of coalition formation. A candidate's intrinsic capacity for leadership may have relatively little impact on this process.

Although these examples all focus on leadership, social influences may determine the career trajectories for other forms of achievement as well. For instance, the optimal age for creativity in scientific disciplines tends to increase as a discipline matures. It takes more time for individuals to acquire the necessary expertise, and it requires more time to work out the implications of any given idea. Moreover, I have by no means discussed all the sociological processes that affect the location of the age peak and the magnitude of the postpeak decline. It should suffice to say that the amount of achievement that one can legitimately expect of older achievers is a complex function of biological, psychological, and sociological factors. Under the right combination of these factors, the amount of achievement that one can anticipate from even octogenarians is truly substantial.

BIBLIOGRAPHY

Baltes, P. B., & Baltes, M. M. (Eds.). (1990). *Successful aging.* Cambridge, UK: Cambridge University Press.
Brontë, L. (1993). *The longevity factor.* New York: HarperCollins.
Perlmutter, M. (Ed.). (1990). *Late life potential.* Washington, DC: Gerontological Society of America.
Simonton, D. K. (1994). *Greatness.* New York: Guilford Press.

Activities

John R. Kelly

University of Illinois

The "Active Old"   Those in later life who are relatively able and have the resources to engage consistently in activity.

Activities   The purposive activities undertaken for a variety of purposes. This analysis focuses on those other than maintenance and employment.

Constriction   A pattern of social and geographical narrowing of activity sometimes associated with aging.

Continuity Theory   The maintenance of consistent patterns of life, including self-definitions, strategies, and values as well as activities.

Core Activities   The immediate and accessible activities that engage the most time and continue through the life course.

ACTIVITIES in the inclusive sense of what people do, include a wide variety of forms, contexts, and associations. The common view of older adults is that they become less active with age. More precise research, however, shows that some kinds of activity do not decline, whereas those that do require particular personal, economic, and social resources. For those with adequate income and viable health, activity outside the home characterizes older persons with the highest levels of life satisfaction and lowest levels of morbidity and institutionalization. For the most part,

older persons continue most of the same kinds of activity in much the same places and with most of the same associates as in midlife and preretirement years. The pattern of constriction is selective and may reflect choices as well as decrements. The "core" of immediate, informal, and easy-access activities continues for both the "active old" and those in the transition to frailty. Activities have a range of meanings, both personal and social. Older persons do not abandon all activity that requires developing skills and meeting challenges. Rather, there is a rhythm of engagement and disengagement that fits age-related opportunities and limitations. Continuity theory, then, points to who people are and to what they do in later life. Patterns of later-life activity and meaning offer guidelines for programming and marketing as well as warnings against inaccurate stereotypes.

I. WHAT IS ACTIVITY?

Activities are what people do. The range is almost infinite. Some activity is demanding and some relaxing; some social and some solitary; some physical and some mental; some ordinary and everyday and some rare and extraordinary. From one perspective, we are what we do. We become who we are in the context of activity. At any age, then, activities are not trivial. We work, we love, we learn, and we play. We do all sorts of things for all sorts of reasons. This chapter, however, focuses on activities other than those associated with paid work and household and family maintenance.

A. Age and Activity Participation

What do older people do? There are two generalizations that are both true, but seem conflicting. The first is that older adults go on doing most of the same activities they have done before. The second is that there are reductions in participation rates in many kinds of activity that are indexed by age. Later-life activity is characterized by both continuity and constriction. Furthermore, there are no "activities of the old" despite common stereotypes. There is no eruption of "old folks" activities, such as knitting, bingo, or World War I singalongs. For the most part, older persons continue most of the activities that contributed to their lives previously, especially those that are relatively accessible and that are part of the daily round of life. On the other hand, the lower rates of participation are found largely for activities that did not have high rates for midlife adults, such as competitive sports, strenuous outdoor activity, and demanding kinds of travel.

This pattern reflects current understandings of nonwork activity in the lives of adults. Such activities are part of an overall pattern of life with roles and their responsibilities and expectations, cultural values and lifestyles, gender and sexual orientations, social class and access to resources, and socialization histories. Although individuals may have distinctive activity patterns, they are developed in and out of particular life histories and circumstances. There is no basis for expecting that at some magic age all those factors disappear to be replaced by the number of years elapsed since birth. In fact, age is not even a powerful predictor of those abilities and resources that are required for most activities. Furthermore, when required to, individuals are able to adapt to changes in ways that permit continued engagement in valued activities.

Two community studies produced generally consistent results in identifying the kinds of activities most subject to reduction in later life and those with sustained levels of participation. Chad Gordon and associates investigated leisure and the life span in Houston, Texas. Overall, age was correlated with lower rates of activity. When types of activity were distinguished, however, significant differences were identified. Later-life adults had the lowest levels of drinking and dancing, going to movies, sports and exercise, outdoor activities, and, more moderately, travel, reading, and cultural participation. There was no age-related re-

duction, however, for television viewing, informal discussion, spectator sports, cultural consumption, entertaining, community organizations including church, and home embellishment. For men, there was an increase in cooking for pleasure and an increase for both men and women in solitary activities. In general, the age-related reductions were for activities requiring physical exertion or prowess and getting to relatively inaccessible environments. On the other hand, activities around the home and with familiar companions remained fairly consistent in later years up to frailty and acute limitations.

A study of adults in Peoria, Illinois, yielded similar results. Exercise and sport and outdoor recreation declined for each age category from 40 on. Both, however, began with relatively low rates of regular participation. On the other hand, social activities, cultural consumption, and community organizations demonstrated no age-related rate declines. Family leisure was lower only for widows age 75 and above and travel and home-based activity lower only for men and women age 75 and older. Again, the lower rates are related to physical demands and distance. Also, in general, those age 65–74 could be labeled the "active old," because many kinds of activity have no decline until the over-75 years, which are more likely to entail the limitations and losses of frailty. Table I displays the results of a national study of over 18,000 households and also demonstrates that age indicates participation in some kinds of activities, but not others. [See LEISURE.]

B. Explanation of Activity Participation Patterns

There are, of course, significant factors other than age that differentiate participation rates. Males are more likely than females to engage in team sports and to visit bars and clubs. Females have higher rates in cultural production and consumption. Education is highly correlated to cultural activities. And there are anomalies by age: golf, for example, is a sport with relatively low age-related rate declines. What is more significant, however, is that age is not a good index of activities that can be done in or from the home, such as walking and gardening, and those that can be self-paced, such as exercise at home. Also, social activities, including those outside the home, have continued high rates of engagement in later life. In gen-

Table I Activity Participation Rates by Age: Percent in 1990[a]

Activity	Age			
	18–34	35–49	55–64	65+
Bowling	24	17	9	6
Golf	12	12	11	6
Tennis	10	7	4	2
Downhill skiing	7	4	2	1
Cross-country skiing	3	3	1	1
Waterskiing	7	4	1	1
Swimming	32	27	14	8
Fishing, freshwater	15	14	11	7
Hunting	8	7	5	2
Hiking	8	8	5	3
Camping	13	13	7	4
Exercise walking	25	28	28	20
Jogging or running	12	7	2	2
Aerobics	9	8	3	2
Ice skating	5	4	1	1
Bicycling	15	13	7	3
Sailing	3	2	2	1
Basketball	9	3	2	1
Softball	11	6	3	1
Volleyball	10	6	2	1
Fitness program at home	19	16	12	8
Indoor flowers and plants	19	24	23	18
Outdoor gardening	23	32	31	29
Cooking for fun	26	29	23	14
Cocktail parties	10	11	9	6
Dinner parties	25	30	26	18
Casino gambling	13	15	16	13
Movies	45	38	24	17
Theater or concerts	33	30	25	21

[a] Source: 1990 Study of Media and Markets, Simmons Market Research Bureau.

eral, it is important to differentiate the kinds of activities that have age-related rate losses rather than refer to an overall pattern of withdrawal or disengagement. Older adults go on doing what is accessible, possible, and found to yield positive meanings and outcomes. Older people find ways to go on doing most of what is most important to them.

In 1961 Cumming and Henry proposed that there is a functional pattern of "disengagement" by older adults. This withdrawal accompanies the loss of sa-

lient roles and is alleged to reflect the choices of older persons. Clearly, however, such a withdrawal is not universal or general. Rather, it is selective. Many older persons would seem to remain quite involved in activities that are both possible and considered worthwhile or that can be adapted to current abilities. Gardening and golf are examples of activities that can be more self-paced. Concerts and dinner parties provide ways of continuing valued associations and experiences.

Baltes and Baltes proposed that rather than disengagement, later-life activity engagement may be characterized by "selective optimization with compensation." This approach is based on the presupposition that older persons are social actors who are still in the process of constructing lives with meaning. They go on learning, negotiating with both opportunities and limitations, defining their possibilities, making existential decisions for both the present and the future, redefining themselves in the process, and even resisting forces that might be arbitrarily limiting. They select rather than merely succumb to loss. They strive to optimize their lives rather than allow age to define life for them. They adapt to changed conditions and abilities rather than allow themselves to be forced out of meaningful engagement. Of course, some have developed lifestyles and identities that contain central elements of existential decisiveness and resistance. Others are more passive and acquiescent. But the activity patterns of older persons are more likely to be consistent with previous patterns of negotiating life than quite different.

Disengagement, however, is one theme of activity choices through the life span. Relaxation and even escape characterize some preferences for the young and those in middle life. They have times when separation from the demands of central roles, undemanding entertainment, and even being alone are sought and valued. There is a balance between engagement and disengagement in any lifestyle, a balance that may change through the life course as roles change. One possibility is that in later life, when paid work demands may be lessened, activities may be valued that involve interaction with others and even demands on skills and energy.

In general, then, there are age-related declines in participation in some kinds of activities, but not in others. Age, especially when measured in broad categories of 10–15 years, may index changes in abilities and resources for a percentage of those in that bracket.

There are still tennis players and backpackers over 65 and even over 75, but not as many. Age itself determines nothing, but it does index the probability of some measureable decrements. On the other hand, there are other kinds of activities for which age seems largely irrelevant. Many are social and involve family and friends. Others may also involve high levels of skill, especially those that do not demand concentrated energy and strength. They may continue previous commitments to demanding activities that are central both to social integration and identities. Even limitations in geographical mobility, social roles, customary companions, and physical attributes do not eliminate all activity that incorporate long-held competencies and values.

II. WHY IS ACTIVITY IMPORTANT?

There is now a wide range of research indicating that activity engagement is a significant factor in later-life success. Some physical health outcomes require regular moderate exercise. Mental health outcomes most often point to the quality of social relationships. Life satisfaction measures, both global and specific, refer to engagement in activity that is regular, outside the home, and involves other people.

A. Activity and Life Satisfaction

Reviews of the relationship of activity engagement to measures of subjective well-being are predominantly, if not universally, positive. The most powerful designs are longitudinal in following the same people over time. The Duke study reported by Erdman Palmore separates out factors of income, health, and other resources and conditions. The factors that characterize those most satisfied with later life are group and physical activity for both men and women and solitary activity for women.

The simplest model for analysis would be that those who do the most are most satisfied, that there would be a significant correlation between the number of activities and the life satisfaction measures. In fact, such correlations have been inconsistent or weak. Rather, as suggested in the previous analysis, the kind of activity or the quality of the experience seem to count for more than sheer numbers. Rather, too wide a range of activities could indicate a lack of commit-

ment to one or a few found especially satisfying. For example, comparative analysis suggests that differences in samples, activity lists, and other details can produce correlations that are significant, accounting for between 1 and 10% of the variance in subjective well-being.

Different studies have employed different sets of activities. Some focus on physical or educational activity, already seen to be somewhat exceptional in later-life patterns. The author has included a wider range of activities and found that activity engagement accounts for over 6% of satisfaction when all other factors are accounted for. A meta-analysis included only social activity and analyzed over 500 pieces of data. Social activity was found to account for up to 9% of the variance in net life satisfaction when controlling for covariates. For those over 65, social activities contributed more than for younger adults. This is consistent with the findings of the persistence of social activity in later years. [See LIFE SATISFACTION.]

B. Activity and Health

It is no surprise that there is a consistent correlation found between engagement in physical activity such as exercise and sport and various measures of physical health. Of course, correlation is not causation. However, measures of relative health, especially those of the cardiovascular system, have been improved by entering and continuing a physical exercise program. The physical health relationship, then, is supported by both correlational and experimental research. Although those in good health may be most able to engage in physical activity, it is reasonable to suppose that regular activity through the life span would be a contributing factor.

Nor is it surprising that positive measures of mental health and negative measures of mental illness are also tied to activity. Most activity outside the home involves other people. Even physical exercise such as walking or aerobics usually has a social dimension. The rough generalization is that anything that gets older people out of the home and with other people contributes to mental health. On the other hand, loneliness and social separation are associated with various kinds of mental distress. This points up the significance of social activity for older persons. Furthermore, there is now considerable evidence that the quality of such relationships is more important than the quantity. Just being with others is not the key, but rather mutual activity in which the relationships are expressed, developed, and enhanced. In the later transition to frailty, social activity may be mixed with caregiving and various modes of assistance in central relationships.

What may be more surprising is the connection between activity and more esoteric measures of health. In the national health interviews, activity engagement was found to be correlated to various aspects of health and also to lower rates of institutionalization and mortality rates for each age category. In a recent Yale study of health and aging, regular physical and social activity marked those least likely to be hospitalized or to die. One summary of the wide range of studies, designs, and measures is that doing something is more healthy than not.

C. What Kinds of Activity Make a Difference?

Doing some things is better than others.

First, regular physical activity, preferably at least three times a week and continued throughout the year, is required to secure the health benefits listed above. The problem is that all studies of physical activities indicate that regularity and persistence is just what a vast majority of older persons do not accomplish. Especially when such activity requires special locales or programs, only a small minority even begin programs and most who begin drop out. There seem to be two kinds of remedies. The first is to emphasize activity that is more accessible and self-paced. At the present, walking is the only growing physical activity for older adults and golf the only sport with high retention rates. Rather than promote special programs that are likely to have both high thresholds of entrance and low retention, health promotion efforts can focus on activity that begins at home, includes others who are readily available, and is relatively cost free. The main difficulty with walking is climatic, snow and ice are not good surfaces for older adults. The second approach is based on psychological studies of persistence in exercise. Studies of older adults have found that a sense of self-efficacy, of control with direct feedback of results, enhances persistence in exercise. Program and even equipment design can maximize this sense of doing something that gets results, preferably in a social context of mutual reinforcement.

Second, some kinds of activities appear to charac-

terize those with the highest levels of later-life satisfaction. Longitudinal research at Duke University identified physical and social activity outside the residence for both women and men. Other research indicates that for those age 40–54, travel and cultural activities were most important to satisfaction. Social and sport or exercise were of moderate importance. For those age 55 through 64, social, cultural, and travel activities contributed most with sport or exercise and family activities also salient. For those 65 through 74, social and travel activities were significant with cultural activities also contributing. For those age 75 and older, home-based and family activities had the highest correlations with subjective well-being, with cultural activity including reading and community organizations (usually church) also significant. The age-related pattern of progression is worth noting. The range of activities that differentiate the most satisfied is constricted in later years. Travel loses its importance to home-based activities. Cultural activity is weighted more toward reading at home and less toward attending concerts and other events.

Nonetheless, the weight of research identifies the salience of activity that has two themes: getting older persons into stimulating environments as with travel and into regular contact with other persons. Only in the later years, because of frailty and loss of independence, does the locale become reduced to home and more familiar locales. There is another and more specific dimension, however.

The third aspect of identifying the kinds of activity that contribute most is based on research into activity that challenges skills and requires developed and sustained competencies. Mihaly Csikszentmihalyi calls the experience of such activity "flow." It is the experience of a meeting of challenge and skill in the activity that leads to a high level of involvement and immersion. When challenge exceeds ability the result is anxiety. When skill exceeds the demands, the result is boredom. The flow experience, on the other hand, draws the participant back into the activity, focuses attention, produces excitement, and calls on high levels of mental and/or physical ability. Such "high-investment" activities also tend to produce communities of common action and the more long-term commitments that Robert Stebbins calls "amateurism" or "serious leisure." There are several lines of research that identify older persons engaged in such activity as those who are most often happy, healthy, and looking forward to the future.

Life at any age is, after all, more than a matter of filling in time and meeting the expectations of others. At best, it involves taking action that gives a sense of competence, worth, and ability. Older persons do not graduate from this perspective. Simply filling time and being entertained does not tend to produce high levels of satisfaction with the self or with life. Furthermore, we are social beings who forge meaningful bonds with those engaged in common significant action. That action may take place at work, in the household, or in the community. It may be purposeful and outcome-oriented, "productive," or focused on the experience, leisure, or play. What seems to be most important is that the rhythm or balance of life at any age incorporates some activity that is demanding, involving, and supports a sense of worth and ability.

One problem related to this perspective is that of resources. Activities that require skill development over time are often those that also require costly equipment, special environments, and other resources that come with a price. Furthermore, they are most often developed by persons with a history of discretionary income and educational experience. Such resources are unevenly distributed through the population. As a consequence, the promotion of high investment activity for older adults may take on something of an elitist flavor. Gender, social class, educational history, and even age itself may be factors that limit opportunity for such activities. Furthermore, market-sector providers tend to target the more affluent market segments for many of the most exciting and cost-intensive activity venues. Adventure travel and "ecotourism" tend to come at a high price.

Activity, then, is important because it is central to a satisfying and healthy later life. It is important to recognize, however, that the kind of activity makes a difference. In the overall balance of engagement, there need to be activities that are challenging and involve interaction with others in common action. Furthermore, in later periods of the aging process, such activity may be constricted in both context and form. Adaptation to later-life limitations, then, involves adjustment to what is possible and the development of viable opportunities. Developmental and challenging activity may have to be reformulated and brought closer to home.

III. CONTEXTS OF ACTIVITIES

Activities may be constricted in location and social context through the years. The overall pattern of ac-

tivity engagement, however, begins largely in the residence at any age.

A. The Home: The Activity Center

To begin with, the activity that takes the most time in contemporary culture is television in its several forms. On average, older adults watch over three hours of television a day, less than teens and up to an hour more than those in the paid workforce. Television is in almost all homes, now with cable and video in most. The home electronic entertainment center is always available, low cost, and varied. It sometimes takes precedence over other possibilities. It is always the residual possibility, there when all else fails to attract or become realized. In the future, the variety offered by this home center will become more varied, more targeted to different population segments, and increasingly sophisticated and selective. There is no reason to assume that electronic entertainment will take a lesser place in later-life activity.

Television, however, is only the beginning of home-based activity. Reading for pleasure is a major activity at home that is retained in later years. Various kinds of home enhancement and maintenance, indoors and out, are also significant. Gardening and yard maintenance and improvement are important, although seasonal in northern climates. Decorating as well as raising plants are indoor and year-round activities. Some cooking is a creative activity that goes far beyond just providing adequate nourishment. There is a mix of necessity, role expectation, and intrinsic meaning in some activity around the home and yard that may be satisfying in later life. Necessity gives a sense of worth because of its worklike character. Doing more than is required, however, with higher standards of quality and innovation may add a sense of personal efficacy and investment.

Many hobbies are also home-based. Traditional handcrafts for both men and women usually have a history of family provision in preindustrial epochs, but now are done primarily for personal satisfaction. Many women's crafts are related to decorating and clothing. Men's more often have a "shop" nature, such as woodworking, or a mechanical character, such as restoring old cars. In some cases the hobbies and crafts may also be connected with organizations that promote the craft and provide opportunities for learning and display. Although the participation figures for each individual craft do not seem large, the totals for all such activities include up to half of older adults.

Perhaps most important is home-centered social interaction. Considerable informal socializing is with other household members. Somewhat less is with regular associates, family, and friends seen on a frequent and even regularly scheduled basis. Furthermore, there are more formal events, such as entertaining, dinner parties, and other invitation occasions. Such socializing is often second only to television in the amount of time allocated, even not counting brief interludes of communication and interaction that are interspersed through the day and evening.

One problem with considerable research on activity at any age is the preoccupation with formal and organized activities. Such a focus tends to overlook most of what most people do most days. Much of home-based activity unfolds in a more or less regular pattern through the day and does not require specific decisions or arrangements. Nevertheless, including that omnipresent entertainer television, it usually fills most waking hours. Special designated events are the punctuation in the ordinary round of life. Furthermore, as women and men move through the active aging years toward frailty, accessible and informal home-based activities become more and more significant, not only to time allocation but also to life satisfaction.

On the other hand, it is also important to recall that regular engagement in activity outside the home has been found to distinguish those with the highest levels of life satisfaction. Filling the daily round with activity that provides pleasure and meaning is not insignificant. It is the basis for any further extension into more challenging and involving activity. Those who have little at home except television, who lack regular opportunities for interaction, communication, and sharing are deprived of this fundamental context of activity. Nonetheless, however well time is filled, easy access often means low demand. Some home-based activity is challenging, requires skills developed over years of learning, and can be quite central to a sense of worth and competence. But some is more entertainment than purposeful activity. The issue is more what the activity calls upon and its level of involvement than where it is located.

B. Organized Recreation

The stereotype of "old folks" activity shows a seated circle doing something routine and undemanding, sometimes even childlike in nature. Usually there is a young leader pretending to show enthusiasm for old songs or crocheting look-alike potholders. Although there may be such limited and segregated programs, they have little to do with noninstitutionalized older adults. To begin with, relatively few adults over 65 years of age participate in age-segregated activities at all or with regularity.

The 1984 National Health Interview Survey finds that less than 10% of older adults attend senior center or other such programs regularly. There is consistent evidence that no more than 15% join any "senior" programs. Such programs may serve important functions for their particular constituencies. Most research finds that participants in senior centers are disproportionately female with limited incomes, often those with quite restricted resources. They also tend to be those with reduced social resources, the widowed, or unmarried. Centers also offer a variety of support services that are especially designed for the same constituency and their needs for health and management assistance at below-market prices.

For the majority of older adults, however, if they are involved in one community organization, it is most likely to be religious. Church, temple, synagogue, and mosque are age-integrated rather than segregated. Even though such institutions reflect their communities as well as historic class constituencies, they tend to involve a full spectrum of ages, usually in programs that are age-inclusive. They offer intergenerational contact and activity, even though some also have age-designated groups. For many, they are a context of continuity with many roles and responsibilities that are retained through life transitions and traumas. Religious organizations provide a context of meaning and affirming rituals as well as a familiar context of association, which is probably why regular participation is associated with higher levels of life satisfaction. Churches also offer opportunities for service, again in a familiar context that does not require broaching new environments or assuming new self-definitions.

There is also a wide range of other organizations that provide contexts for companionship, routines and rituals, regular activities, social acceptance and identities, and service to others. Programs develop service opportunities for the retired. Community recreation agencies schedule activities for those out of the paid workforce, sometimes with specific age designations. There are organizations focused on one of the arts, a craft, or some form of continuing education or discussion. There are others that combine some ritual with social interaction in traditional "fraternal" organizations. And these are only those that are formally organized. There are also many self-organized groups that play cards, attend concerts, have lunch or coffee, discuss books, or share a hobby on a regular basis. Such groups provide a high degree of familiarity and communicative interaction when members have shared years of personal history. They may even become quasi-families for older persons who have lost other intimates.

Organized activity is often based on a particular kind of activity, frequently with some extrinsic purpose. In a small town there may be a group that makes quilts to support a local school or hospital program. Public recreation offerings usually include some low-impact exercise directed primarily toward older participants and with a health-maintenance orientation. There are hundreds if not thousands of different kinds of "support groups" for those coping with particular illnesses, conditions, or traumatic events. The activity or common need draws people together, but the group that is formed may take on a life of its own in providing caring and sharing for regular members.

One thing is clear. It is a great mistake to concentrate only on age-designated programs and organizations when trying to understand the community involvement of older adults. Rather, the entire spectrum of organized activity is relevant. In fact, age-segregated activity is a very small proportion of the entire organizational context of activity. The vastly larger set of organizational contexts are those that continue from earlier life periods. "Senior" programs are on the margins of the entire pattern.

There is an exception, however. Especially in sunbelt areas, there are hundreds of recreation-oriented retirement communities. These communities sell housing of various types and price levels by promising activity amenities and programs. When they are new, they attract relatively active retirees who come ready to make new friends, engage in physical activity such as golf and swimming, and join in the organized activity of the community. Residents may actually increase their participation levels in response to the offerings, the social environment, and their own expectations. In time, of course, the first cohort in such communities will age. More residents will be widowed. More will suffer health and physical decrements. The activity

levels in more demanding away-from-home activities tend to decline until the community reaches a plateau of multicohort stability with a diversity of ages and conditions. It is important to recognize, however, that a combination of accessible facilities and a culture of activity together can create a high overall level of activity that defies age limitations and stereotypes.

C. The Market Sector: The New Targets

Customary attention to organized activity through community programs and organizations should not be allowed to obscure the significance of market-sector activity opportunities. Especially in the last decade or so, business has discovered the later-life market. As more older persons enter retirement with relatively good health and incomes well-above maintenance, older adults have become target market segments for almost anything.

The centrality of home electronics has already been introduced. Thus far, little special marketing has been aimed at older adults. There has been some attention to simplified control systems with more manipulable controls, but the targets are not simply age-related. With the proliferation of cable television channels, there may be some age-targeted programming other than daytime religion. For the most part, however, television still programs toward younger viewers.

Advertising, on the other hand, is changing. More television ads depict active older persons in attempts to attract consumers of vitamins, over-the-counter medicines, cars, travel, and other products for conditions associated with age. The most obvious change is in tourism advertising. The former almost-total depiction of the young and vigorous in travel ads has given way to more of a mix. Preretirement adults at the height of their earning power but without child-care requirements along with the young-old retirees are now recognized as the travel market with perhaps the greatest spending potential. Furthermore, more than the young, they are assumed to be willing to pay for service convenience, safety, and comfort in ways that increase the profit potential. Travel packages are, after àll, more profitable than unpackaged travel with locally obtained lodging, meals, and entertainment.

Within the community, there are also a multiplicity of market-sector offerings directed toward older adults. Sport and exercise centers schedule programs for the retired. Travel agents arrange bus tours as well as the more exotic airborne destinations. Shopping malls are designed not only for retail selling space, but also to become local destinations where people meet, walk, browse, snack, eat, and are entertained. As the population ages, such planning and marketing are likely to increase. The retiree lunch special may replace the business lunch in some locations.

As introduced in the previous section, one major market segment is the second-home and retirement community. Again, especially in locations that offer longer outdoor climates and particular amenities such as proximity to water, multimillion dollar communities are developed for older markets. They are aimed at the affluent, tend to be upscale in price, and compete for a limited market segment. Many are models of planning with enhanced natural environments, activity facilities, and appropriate housing. The profit is in the real estate part of the business with the activity provisions used as attraction factors. They are targeted so strictly toward upscale markets, however, that there has often been a saturation with consequent business failures and bankruptcies.

The market sector has a built-in bias. The activity opportunities provided are those that are relatively cost-intensive. They offer travel packages and cruises combined with profit-enhancing gambling and subsidized shopping stops, rather than accessible walkways and informal meeting places. Businesses must yield a return on investment and target the market segments most able to pay. They tend to develop environments for short-term profit rather than long-term conservation. Nevertheless, the full picture of activity contexts cannot ignore the market providers. Also, insofar as involvement in travel, environmentally based activity, and cultural engagement mark the most satisfied older adults, then the offerings of these businesses are of considerable significance for those able to afford their goods and services.

D. The Social Character of Activity

A focus on the great variety of activities engaged in by older persons should not be allowed to obscure the profoundly social nature of many of them. Watching television is, of course, primarily the consumption of entertainment and frequently involves little or no social exchange. The preponderence of other activity, however, is social. In fact, the activity itself is often largely a context for interaction and communication.

Social interaction itself, especially when it is informal and interspersed into the daily routine, is the center of many activities.

Research on later life indicates that social interaction retains its importance in terms of frequency and salience until limited by losses in mobility and communicative ability. Often the card game or the lunch gathering is primarily a justification for meeting. Even activities that call for the development of skill and long-term commitment become the centers of communities of common action. Around all kinds of activities—collecting, exploring, or learning—the participants form subcultures with symbols of membership, media focused on the organization built around the activity, special vocabularies, sharing of histories and experiences, and face-to-face gatherings for mutual activity. In many cases, such activity associates become primarily communities, friends, and companions in relationships nurtured over many years.

The real context of much activity, then, is social. The activity, environment, or organization is there to provide a container for the real action and meaning, the expression and development of social relationships.

IV. MEANINGS OF ACTIVITY

There is no single meaning associated with each kind of activity. Rather, the form of an activity combines with factors such as social context, role carryover, environment, life-course responsibilities and commitments, self-definitions, and values to shape the meaning of an activity. Nevertheless, several lines of research have identified a number of consistencies in the meanings of activity.

A. The Dialectics of Activity

These meanings are not simple or hierarchical. Rather, there are fundamental dialectics expressed in activity. One is between engagement and disengagement. In some activities individuals seek to become involved in action and interaction, to seek out stimuli and excitement, to respond to challenge with action. There is, however, the other side of the dialectic. There are also times and places when individuals seek to disengage, to escape from demand, to avoid high levels of stimulation. Most people at any age attempt to arrive at a satisfactory balance between the two dimensions of challenge and escape, of involvement and separation. For older adults, a central issue is whether the balance tends to tilt away from challenge and toward disengagement. Furthermore, do social expectations and opportunity structures bias activity patterns away from more demanding and stimulating activities? This dialectic is in part a reformulation of the old debate between disengagement and activity in aging. The reformulation accepts the reality of some kinds of withdrawal and constriction of activity, but insists that there is always the significant other side of engagement with activity that involves the self in meaningful action that demonstrates competence and integrates the self with others in common action and communication.

The second dialectic is between the personal and the social. As already indicated, one basic dimension of activity that becomes more salient for older adults is social involvement. Activities often are primarily vehicles for social engagement, for expressing and developing meaningful relationships. The other side of the dialectic, however, is the personal or existential. Personal expression and development do not disappear with age. Rather, lives with the highest levels of satisfaction involve both existential activity in which the self demonstrates continued ability and worth as well as activities that create community. Both existential self-creating activity and social integration require something more than waiting to be entertained. Both are forms of action in the context of a variety of activities that include challenge and/or community.

The dialectic is not just between different kinds of activities. Certainly the contrast between watching television and playing in a string quartet is self-evident. However, an activity may have multiple dimensions. For example, swimming may be relaxed play in and near the water or disciplined lap counting. Furthermore, the water may be a locale for both relaxed social exchange or for the integrated action of a competitive game. Even television watching may be detached viewing or the vicarious engagement of an athletic contest involving a team with which the viewer closely identifies. The point is for aging to retain the tension in the dialectic so that no significant dimensions are surrendered. Life should not become mono-dimensional in any period of life. Engagement needs to be balanced by disengagement, social involvement with solitude, and demand with security.

B. The Meanings of Activities

The forms and contexts of activities are not irrelevant, however. Howard Tinsley developed a line of research that identifies the central meanings found in a variety of common activities. Unlike most research on activity meanings, he and his colleagues have studied older adults. The dimensions of activity engagement identified include the following:

Meaning Dimension	Examples of Activities
1. Intellectual stimulation	puzzles, reading
2. Catharsis	swimming, jogging, sports
3. Expressive compensation	fishing, gardening, boating
4. Hedonistic companionship	parties, social events
5. Supportive companionship	picnicking, visiting
6. Secure solitude	collecting
7. Routine, temporary indulgence	games, cards
8. Moderate security	golf, bowling, music
9. Expressive aestheticism	chess, cooking, arts, crafts

Other approaches have yielded different sets and categories of meaning. Such a connection of activities with meaning does not include the significance of the physical environment or the social context. Tennis with friends may be primarily social, with grandchildren more nurturing and playful, and with peers highly competitive. Tournament bass fishing is highly organized, technologized, and competitive, whereas fly fishing on the Salmon River may be more a tranquil escape into the natural setting.

What is the appropriate balance for older adults? That would seem to become a more or less individual matter depending on self-definitions, abilities, resources, and values. The obvious danger, however, is that of a withdrawal from activities that challenge abilities and involve other persons, a retreat into private entertainment.

A list of the various outcomes of activity can be divided into personal and social outcomes:

1. Personal: enjoyment of an environment, escape from demand, physical exercise, creativity, relaxation, stimulus seeking, self-development, achievement and challenge, filling time, intellectual aestheticism, reflection and meditation
2. Social: interaction and contact, new relationships, sexual involvement, family interaction, recognition and status, social power, altruism and service

There is no final or complete list of possible outcomes. In fact, most activities offer varied combinations of such outcomes in configurations that change from one occasion to another. The presence or absence of a particular companion or opponent, unanticipated weather changes, moods and emotional predispositions, interruptions and interference, and other situational factors alter the meanings of an event or episode. Furthermore, activity may be primarily mental or imaginative as well as physical, meditative as well as communicative, environmentally aware as well as detached, focused on the immediate experience or on goals, planned or spontaneous, grounded in reality or in fantasy, exploratory or routine.

In any activity, however, there is more than the form of the action. There is meaning, partly brought to the situation and partly developed within it. And as individuals work out patterns of activity commitment, they seek and find salient meanings. Why? is always a central question leading to the what of the activity itself.

C. Domains and Dimensions of Activity

Life, then, has a kind of rhythm of engagement and disengagement. That rhythm may change with age as roles are gained and lost and as resources and abilities are altered. A more complete understanding of the meanings of activity in the aging process is needed. The current opposition of disengagement to activity separates what is in reality a process over time involving multiple factors. Personal history with its class, gender, and ethnic shaping of opportunity structures brings older persons to where they are. Both the self and the conditions of life are constantly changing, sometimes abruptly and unexpectedly. It is relatively simple to point to common age-indexed declines in some kinds of activities. It is also relatively simple to correlate higher activity levels with measures of satisfaction, health, and success. To follow and understand the processes of retention and loss, of adaptation and reconstitution in a variety of social contexts is much more complex.

An institutional social analysis usually identifies productive activity with the domain of work, expression with leisure, learning with education, and bonding with the family. The roles associated with those domains shift through the life course with the transitions of school graduation, marriage, childbearing, launching, unemployment, divorce, and retirement. It

is evident that no universal or linear scheme of role transitions can encompass the variations of the contemporary life course for men and women. Nevertheless, the "Third Age" tends to be described in terms of role loss—paid work and retirement, marriage and widowhood, leisure activity and health decrements.

As long as life domains are specialized in meaning, then aging takes on an inevitable negative cast. The developmental task is coping with loss. The author, however, has found that dimensions of meaning are not limited to one domain. To a measurable degree, commitment, satisfaction, productivity, social bonding, development and learning, and involvement are found in all three of the domains of paid work, family and community relationships, and leisure. Insofar as this is true for an individual, then the balance or rhythm of such meanings may be reconstituted in later life when roles are altered. A sense of productivity and worth may be found in nonwork activities. Disengagement is only one meaning of leisure activity.

V. SUMMARY AND EXPLANATORY THEORY

Activities may be "what people do" with an incalculable variety in forms, settings, aims, and outcomes. Nevertheless, there are several clear patterns of activity in later life.

1. Most older adults perceive themselves to have a "full" day. They are not sitting around with nothing to do. Most older adults are relatively satisfied with their lives.

2. There is, however, a pattern of constriction in which the range of activities is reduced. This reduction is selective and concentrated on activities that require more strenuous physical exertion or travel. "Disengagement" is not general. Rather, the pattern is better described as selective optimization with compensation. There is a dialectic between engagement and disengagement both within and among activities.

3. The pattern of continuity is centered around a "core" of home-based activities that are accessible and everyday. This core tends to expand to fill in time formerly occupied by roles now left behind.

4. Those most satisfied with their lives, however, are most often engaged in regular activities outside the home that provide challenge and relationships

with family and friends. Such activities have both developmental and social dimensions.

5. Such activity does not, for the most part, take place in age-segregated settings.

6. Significant activities usually continue those proven satisfying in earlier years, although older adults do still select, replace, and even inaugurate new activities. Continued activity engagement reinforces identities, established competencies, self-image, values, and relationships.

7. As a consequence, those activities most likely attract older adults build on familiarity, reputations of quality, established abilities and identities, communities of action and interaction, and histories of satisfaction.

8. Conversely, activities that require older persons to redefine themselves as "old" or in any way incompetent or inferior are unlikely to be attractive.

The spectrum of activities engaged in by older adults is nearly as vast and diverse as for those who are younger. There are no "old folks" activities as such. A selection of activities, however, both informal and organized, is revised to accommodate the changes in roles and resources that are part of later life. Time, energy, and other resources are reallocated to create a revised balance of meanings and outcomes.

A. Explanatory Theory

Rather than a general pattern of disengagement, older adults as social actors negotiating the final years of their life journeys adapt to altered opportunities and resources. Their aims, however, are not likely to change radically. They continue to choose activities they have found satisfying in the past. They continue to want to associate regularly with persons with whom they have meaningful relationships of a high quality. Activities, then, are selected within the realm of current possibility to maintain a sense of a self of ability and worth and a community of relationships of communication, caring, and sharing. There are changes and adjustments. Baltes and Baltes call this process "selective optimization with compensation."

The pattern sought may be understood in terms of certain dialectical processes. It includes both meaningful engagement, even the challenge to utilize skills and competencies developed over time. Such activity has been termed *high investment* or *serious* leisure. In

such activity older persons who have lost paid work and often some family roles are able to demonstrate to themselves and others that they are still persons of ability. They maintain a sense of a competent identity. In the activity context, they also retain former associations that have been significant. Regular engagement in such activity distinguishes those most satisfied with their later lives.

The other side of the activity dialectic, however, is disengagement. There are some kinds of activities no longer possible or satisfying due to decrements in resources. Some require intimidating travel, difficult physical exercise, or high financial costs. Other activity contexts are abandoned when significant companions are lost or the opportunity structure changes. This disengagement, however, involves compensation in which activities are adapted to make retention possible. Activities in which demands and pace can be controlled are most likely to be adaptable to aging conditions. The point is that disengagement is selective, not total.

Two underlying concepts seem valuable in understanding this process. The first is Sharon Kaufman's concept of the "ageless self." Older persons, however much they may be conscious of age in general and of their own mortality, do not radically redefine themselves at some critical age as "old." Rather, they tend to define themselves as the same persons who have made it that far on the journey of life. They recognize changes, but those changes impact fundamentally the same person. As a result, they tend to value most those activities that yield a continuation of selfhood. Identities are more continuous than disjunctive, more adjusted than basically revised. In some cases activities can be maintained with relatively little compensation. In others, activities are substituted as with volunteering for paid work roles.

The second concept is Robert Atchley's continuity theory. Accepting that many aspects of life may change with age, continuity theory proposes that the fundamental styles of coping with change are relatively consistent. The values, worldviews, coping mechanisms, self-definitions, and even social worlds of older adults are largely maintained. Activities, therefore, are selected to support and express such continuity. Sometimes the activities themselves, with symbolic meanings central to one's selfhood, may be held tenaciously. Sometimes their meanings can be continued only with adaptation or a shift to more accessible activities. There is, however, in the lives of older persons a connection between certain skills and associations and a profound sense of who one is. Continuity theory is based on more than just a continuation of activities. Much more it calls for a continuation of meanings in the midst of change. The retention of types of abilities and their demonstration provides a sense of personal continuity. The retention of salient social roles and contexts yields a social context of continuity of selfhood validated by others. Activity contexts may provide such continuity even through major traumas and losses.

B. Implications

For resource allocation and public policy, there can be no presumption that older adults will withdraw from activity and that they need little consideration. To the contrary, retention of engagement is critical to the quality of later life. Not only satisfaction, but also elements of physical and mental health are clearly supported by continued involvement in meaningful activity. Such activity, however, is relatively seldom age segregated. Rather, older persons are more likely to seek to maintain continuity of selfhood and of associations. Although there may be some constrictions in terms of resources, there is no radical disjunction of abilities or interests at any designated age. Rather, public policy should be one of inclusion, maximized access, and support of every kind of activity. Especially those activities that offer some challenge of abilities, sense of worth, and meaningful social integration contribute most to the quality of later life. Continuity is more than theory; it can be the basis of relevant public policy.

For programming and marketing, any appeal that requires older persons to redefine themselves, especially in a negative or demeaning way, should be avoided. Rather, the aim should be to build on satis-factions of the past, to maximize continuities of activity and social context. Uprooting activity from familiar physical and social environments to "senior centers" is clearly counterproductive. Rather, it should be assumed that the time of older adults seems fairly full and that to attract them to any program every effort should be made to project an image of high quality. Timetables, access, and the pacing of activities can be adjusted to older clienteles without labeling the offering in terms of age or social segregation. Rather, marketing activities to older adults, from either the public or market sector, should stress abilities, personal development, learning, excitement, and social integration.

For the aging person, perhaps the first implication is not to accept any negative redefinitions from any source. Later life may offer new possibilities for meaningful activity as resources are gained and some role limitations reduced. Maintaining activity is central to successful aging. Such activity contributes most when it has a connection with past satisfaction, employs developed abilities, and facilitates social bonding in meaningful relationships. Both selection and compensation may be necessary in the aging process. However, the key is the retention and even reconstitution of involvement that supports a sense of a self that is able and of value to others.

BIBLIOGRAPHY

Baltes, P. B., & Baltes, M. M. (Eds.). (1990). *Successful aging: Perspectives from the behavioral sciences.* New York: Cambridge University Press.
Csikszentmihaly, M. (1990). *Flow: The psychology of optimal experience.* New York: HarperCollins.
Kelly, J. R. (Ed.) (1993). *Activity and aging: staying involved in later life.* Newbury Park, CA: Sage.
MacNeil, R., & Teague, M. (Eds.). (1987). *Aging and leisure: Vitality in later life.* Englewood Cliffs, NJ: Prentice-Hall.

Adaptation

Susan Krauss Whitbourne and Erin L. Cassidy

University of Massachusetts at Amherst

Competence Adaptation Model A model that regards optimal adaptation as a match between the individual's functional abilities and the degree of stimulation and challenge presented in the environment.

Coping The process through which the individual reduces stress.

Ego Integrity Erikson's eighth stage of ego development, corresponding to the individual's sense of wholeness, honesty, and completion regarding the life that has been lived.

Identity The individual's sense of self, incorporating various physical, psychological, and social characteristics of the individual, and the continuity of the self over time.

Identity Accommodation Changing one's identity in response to identity-relevant experiences.

Identity Assimilation The interpretation of life events relevant to the self in terms of the cognitive and affective schemas that are incorporated in identity.

Life Span Construct A model proposing that adults plan and evaluate their life events in terms of an underlying set of assumptions, expectations, and ideas about what their lives could be.

ADAPTATION is the readjustment of self or identity to the changing roles, operations, and structures of the environment. Adaptation is manifest in attitudes and behavior and is influenced by past and current life experiences.

I. BACKGROUND CONSIDERATIONS

The search for the key to satisfactory adjustment in old age is the basis of a significant body of work within the fields of psychological and social gerontology. Some of the earliest research on personality and social development in later life addressed the enormously complex issue of trying to identify the "best" or most "successful" way for the individual to age. These empirical attempts involved the description of different personality types who varied in their approach to the aging process, from "disengaged" to "active." Whether it was beneficial for the older individual to take a passive or an active approach to the aging process served as the touchstone for considerable controversy and debate among gerontologists. A now discredited view of psychological aging, the "disengagement theory" proposed that the elderly become increasingly oriented toward internal preoccupations as they face the inevitability of death, and that this movement inward was psychologically adaptive. Despite the theory's lack of support, there still persisted the idea in the gerontological literature that with age, individuals become more preoccupied with their own psychological concerns and less oriented toward other people. However, the research on which this idea is based was seriously flawed. Furthermore, the notion of a radical alteration in personality in response to the aging process is not substantiated by research. Instead, it is becoming recognized that the challenges to the individual's personality presented by the aging processes are adapted to according to the individual's personality style. Successful adaptation to the aging process is seen, in these terms, as involving the ability to maintain a consistent view of the self over time. In addition, the individual must accommodate the physical changes brought about by aging, whatever changes there are in health, and to the impending closeness of death. These accommodations are facilitated by the use of coping strategies that enhance the individual's emotional state and present the individual with viable ways of making practical changes that can compensate for whatever losses occur in physical and mental functioning.

Contemporary researchers are still directing their efforts to this search for the "optimal" path of adaptation to the demands and challenges presented by the aging process. Currently, researchers invoke paradigms involving perceived control, the sense of self or identity, and ways of coping, representing a shift from typologies to process-oriented models of adaptation. It is now recognized that adaptation in later adulthood reflects multidimensional influences of biological, psychological, and social processes that have operated throughout the individual's life course.

II. ADAPTATION TO STRESS

The adaptational demands presented to the older individual can be seen as challenges to the individual's ability to cope. An overall framework for studying the adaptation of older adults to stress is provided by a cognitive model of coping, in which stress is defined in terms of the individual's perception that a situation is threatening because it overwhelms the individual's ability to meet the situation's demands. Some of the adaptational demands in later life that have been studied with regard to coping include bereavement, poor health, caregiving, fears of aging, risks to personal safety, threats to self-esteem, and uncertainty of life beyond death.

The importance of successful adaptation to these demands of later life can be seen from research investigating the effects of inadequate coping strategies on health status in the elderly. For example, one group of investigators examined the relationship between stress, social support, coping, and immune function in a sample of older adult women. The respondents were classified as either having experienced major stressors in the past year or as being free of major stress. Those women who had been highly stressed had poorer immune functioning than women who had not experienced stressors, and a significant proportion of the variation in immune system markers was accounted for by psychosocial variables indicative of social support. Coping difficulties and lack of social support were also found to be predictive of hospital readmissions for a sample of elderly cardiac patients. The subjective experience of stress, particularly on a daily basis, was also related to prescription drug misuse among another sample of elders. Thus, coping strategies can significantly influence the outcome of an older adult's attempt to adapt to the demands of aging.

In a cognitive model of stress and coping, Lazarus and Folkman have identified two major coping strategies: problem-focused and emotion-focused coping. In problem-focused coping, the individual attempts to reduce stress by changing a feature of the situation or the self. Problem-focused coping strategies include confrontation and planful problem solving. Emotion-focused coping is used when individuals attempt to change the way they view a stressful situation. Some emotion-focused coping strategies include wishful thinking, distancing, and positive reappraisal. Which of these coping strategies is more adaptive varies according to the situation, and there is no one generally accepted successful way to reduce stress. However, observations of the reactions of elders to stress lead to general characterizations of unsuccessful and successful coping strategies in later life.

Passive, emotion-focused coping strategies appear to characterize the reactions of elders who are less successful in managing stress. These strategies include self-blame, wishful thinking, avoidance, fantasy, and escape into drugs and alcohol. Unfortunately, people tend to attribute mild, short-term symptoms to aging, leading them to adopt more passive coping strategies, and these strategies ultimately can reduce health status even further.

By contrast, successful elders use more active coping strategies, including sport and physical recreation, interacting with others for social support, and keeping busy by participating in social groups and learning new skills. Successful copers see themselves as in control of their experiences, view themselves positively, and take a confrontive, optimistic, and self-reliant approach to stressors. In cases of chronic illness, they accept restrictions, but still look for new possibilities in life. An active, problem-focused coping style seems then to be positively associated with handling adversity in later life. However, this style of coping does not necessarily involve close self-scrutiny, introspection, or an intensive process of life review. A positive orientation to one's past life based on involvement with family and a focus on past successes may help the older adult view the future more positively. For some individuals, prayer may prove beneficial, and for those individuals who tend to rely on external sources of control in their lives, dependency and reliance on other people may form the basis for successful coping. Intelligence may also play a role in helping older individuals manage their everyday needs.

There are significant ethnic and cultural variations in coping strategies that researchers have only recently begun to investigate. Compared to Whites African-American elderly are in some ways better prepared to cope with stress. They have had a lifetime of using social support during times of stress and developed flexible ways to seek help. Furthermore, a lifetime of poverty and adversity makes some African Americans better able to handle uncertainty. Friends appear to provide an important source of coping for elderly African Americans more so than is the case for Whites, who rely more heavily on relatives. Older, high-income Whites may actually be at greatest risk for not having social support during times of stress.

The ability to cope with stress has also been investigated among rural elders, who show some distinctly adaptive strategies. They are more likely to seek information or advice about health problems, and use problem-focused coping to deal with economic stresses. Men in particular are more likely to use cognitive strategies such as redefinition of the problem and logical analysis most frequently in dealing with stress, particularly that associated with social relationships, and a strategy of resigned acceptance in dealing with family stresses.

Another strategy for adapting to stress involves the process of social comparison, a mechanism that can be utilized to assess one's position in terms of the stereotypes regarding age-related changes. For example, in one investigation it was reported that older

women who more often employed positive social comparison were found to have higher ratings of mental health, regardless of how poor their physical health actually was. In this sense, the stereotypical view of the changes that come with aging can serve to function in the adaptation process. This view of aging can provide a set of "normative" experiences and losses to which individuals can compare and accept their own experiences. Also, such stereotyped views of aging provide a buffer to protect one's sense of well-being because one's actual experiences will, by comparison, appear more successful and adaptive. The result of social comparison is that older adults are able to maintain or even expand their degree of life satisfaction even as they experience real age-related changes in functioning.

Religion provides another context for coping with physical and cognitive aging changes. Through involvement in community religious activities, the individual can access important social network resources as well as receive verification of their role as contributing members of society. Beliefs in the values and teaching of one's religion can also provide the individual with a source of inner strength and sense of purpose in life. The sense of burden that elders may feel in attempting to cope with their own health problems or those of family members can be alleviated when viewing these demands in terms of fulfilling a higher purpose in life. [See RELIGION AND SPIRITUALITY.]

It appears that successful agers find ways to adapt their coping strategies to reduce the stressors they encounter in their daily lives. They also take advantage of the principle, "Use it or lose it!" They discover ways to compensate for physical and psychological changes associated with the normal aging process that can potentially interfere with the ability to perform daily activities and to cope successfully with environmental stressors. Some of these compensatory activities include regular and consistent involvement in physical exercise, the seeking of intellectual stimulation, and the willingness to take advantage of commercially available prostheses, such as proper hearing aids and eyeglasses. Going beyond the concept of coping, which implies a responsiveness to externally produced events, some elders seek new levels of personal growth and development through constant searching for new opportunities to learn and stay involved in the world around them. Furthermore, elderly adults with a lifetime of experiences with stress have developed unique strengths to aid them in this coping with the aging process.

III. ADAPTATION TO THE ENVIRONMENT

The quality of the physical and social environment must also be considered in understanding adaptation to changes associated with later life. Theoretical models relating the individual's adaptation to the quality of the environment point to the need for a match or "fit" between the characteristics of the individual and the demands of the environment. One approach to the person–environment interaction is provided in the competence adaptation model. In this model, optimal adaptation is theorized to occur when the individual's functional abilities are matched to the degree of stimulation and challenge presented in the environment. Another aspect of person–environment fit involves the matching of the individual's motives and needs with the "press" of the environment. An individual with a high need for autonomy, according to this model, would be optimally adjusted in an environment that promotes and supports the independence of the individual. To the extent that the environment fosters dependence, the individual's adaptive ability will be reduced. In other words, using one's personal resources proactively will result in greater well-being than passively reacting to the demands of the environment. This dynamic interplay can refer to adaptation on the emotional or physical level. Furthermore, without stimulation or reinforcement for independent, autonomous behavior, it is also likely that the individual will enter a downward spiral of accelerated deterioration and dependence.

IV. ADAPTATION TO PHYSICAL AND COGNITIVE CHANGES

Physical and cognitive changes associated with aging place demands on the ability to adapt to the physical and social environment. When age-related changes create difficulties in physical mobility, social interaction, and everyday decision making, the individual's quality of adaptation to the environment will be re-duced. This reduced adaptive ability creates more problems in daily life, as the individual finds it more difficult to go about his or her daily routines. Equally important is the effect of the individual's lowered adaptability on feelings of competence. Psychologists have long argued that feelings of competence play a major role in the self-concept and identity. To the extent that the aging individual is and feels less able to handle daily tasks, he or she will begin to develop a set of negative changes in identity, including a lowered sense of self-esteem and self-efficacy. Furthermore, this loss of competence invades the individual's sense of stability and continuity over time, as the individual is forced to redefine the self as less capable than in earlier years. The overlay of negative social attitudes toward the aging process further contributes to the potential erosion of the individual's identity as a competent and worthwhile individual. All of these changes may be reflected in a variety of psychological symptoms and a further reduction of competence, as the individual begins to live out a fatalistic self-fulfilling prophecy in which he or she simply gives in to the inevitability of the aging process.

Countering the downward spiral is the natural spirit that many elders have as they approach the aging process, in which they regard the changes with age as a challenge not unlike the many others they have faced in their long lives. Rather than become demoralized by the awareness of a progressive deficit in functioning, they seek ways to reverse or at least slow down this manifestation of the aging process and spontaneously compensate for loss of functioning in one area by building strengths in others. Although these behaviors promote their adaptation to the environment and maintain their sense of identity and self-efficacy, individuals who take this active approach to the aging process run the risk of becoming demoralized and frustrated when they are faced with changes that they cannot overcome. They are particularly vulnerable to rapid-onset diseases that negate their prior efforts to remain healthy and active. [See IDENTITY.]

V. ADAPTATION TO CHANGES IN SOCIAL ROLES

In Western society, great value is placed on the individual's economic productivity, which traditionally is linked to a man's financial worth. Increasingly, the role of provider is being assumed by women as well as men. Due to the social and cultural emphasis on economic worth, retirement presents the potential for an individual to feel devalued and stripped of social importance. Furthermore, given the assumption that autonomy and independence are desirable qualities, the reliance of older individuals on the government or private pension plans for subsistence can challenge their sense of well-being as contributors to society. Added to these difficulties are views of the elderly as financial burdens. Discussions within the news media regarding the national debt portray elders as a drain on the budget due to the vast funding needs of Medicare and Social Security programs. These negative attitudes can affect not only people's expectations about the process of aging, but also the self-perception and affective experiences of older individuals themselves.

Individuals may be expected to vary, however, in the extent to which they incorporate society's negative views about the elderly into their identities and sense of well-being, particularly with regard to the economic and psychological transitions to retirement. For older adults socialized in the importance of the work ethic, loss of their occupation through retirement will be a major blow to their sense of well-being. They will feel useless and regard their lives as devoid of meaning. Other individuals, however, may be able to draw upon their previous identities within the world of work, defining themselves as retired "x's," where "x" represents the individual's primary past occupation. Development of involvement in leisure and recreational activities prior to retirement may also moderate the individual's response to retirement. An individual who maintains an active lifestyle can adjust more readily to the disappearance of work from daily routines than an individual whose work completely determined the activities of daily life. [See Leisure; Retirement; Work and Employment.]

Changes within the context of the family represent another challenge to adaptation for the aging individual. Married couples experience a number of changes associated with the aging process that can pose significant threats to the later-life relationship and ultimately each individual's sense of well-being. The task of caring for a married elder who becomes infirmed due to physical changes or Alzheimer's disease typically falls on the spouse, and can be a source of unending stress and burden. Another set of challenges pertains to the area of sexuality. There are many common stereotypes and misconceptions regarding the potential for enjoyment in the later years. Older couples can sometimes be affected by these negative, and usually inaccurate, beliefs. For example, some individuals might think that it is abnormal, or even morally wrong, to maintain an active sexual life into their later years. But for most couples, sexual intimacy does continue over the years of marriage. Even if this intimacy does not consist of sexual intercourse, the expression of affection and loyalty can become very important in the later years. In this regard, it is worth noting that though older couples still view sexual intimacy as important, they also place a greater value on qualities that develop over time, such as security and level of commitment to each other. [See Sexuality, Sensuality, and Intimacy.]

The exit and reentry of grown children increasingly has become an adaptational challenge due to economic changes affecting the job options for young adults. Changes caused by the movement of children into and out of the home not only affect the physical space and privacy of the older couple, but their intimate relationships as well. The return of adult children can require the older couple to reestablish interaction patterns within the household more characteristic of their middle adult years, leading to an exacerbation of potential stresses existing at that time.

Traditionally, households have one person that retires, but here again, patterns are changing so that there are increasing numbers of households in which both the husband and wife are employed. In this case, the couple may choose to retire at different times or plan their retirement together. Choosing to retire in an unsynchronized fashion can have a major impact on intimacy because each partner in the relationship faces role changes at different times, making the adjustment to a new lifestyle as a couple potentially more challenging. After retirement, the daily lives of both members in the relationship change drastically. Time once occupied by the requirements of work no longer presents restrictions, and other activites must be found to take their place. As a result of this transition, couples find that they are able to spend a considerably greater amount of time on the growth of their relationship, perhaps narrowing down their interactions increasingly to each other and a few close friends. This increased time together may have favorable effects. Couples who remain together can become more accepting, tolerant, and respectful of their partners, and behave in ways that are more affectionate and loving. The increase in free time may lead some couples to spend some of that time interacting with friends, an activity that can bolster marital satisfaction through strengthening the partners' identity as a couple.

There can be benefits, then, as well as challenges, as the married couple ages. Personal differences, which for many years may have been held in abeyance due to the competing demands of children and work, often come back into focus at this time. In learning to interact as a dyad once again, the couple is often faced with developing new ways to communicate and make decisions. By identifying and working out solutions to marital difficulties, the couple can often maintain a satisfying relationship as well as developing an even greater level of enjoyment from the partnership. This is an especially challenging task in the postretirement years, because the couple will not only be working on their relationship together, but learning to restructure their own personal time as well.

VI. THE ROLE OF IDENTITY

The process of adaptation may also be seen as involving psychosocial factors relating to the quality of the individual's investment in relationships, understanding of one's place in the life course, and resolution of issues related to mortality. These factors are best understood in the context of Erikson's eight-stage psychosocial model of the life cycle in which it is assumed that change occurs systematically throughout adulthood. Erikson proposed that after adolescence, with its often tumultuous search for identity, adults pass through three psychosocial crisis stages. The stages corresponding to the early and middle adult years focus on the establishment of close interpersonal relationships (intimacy vs. isolation), and the passing on to the future of one's creative products (generativity vs. stagnation). In the final stage (ego integrity vs. despair), the individual must resolve conflicted feelings about the past, adapt to the changes associated with the aging process, and come to grips with the inevitability of death. Erikson's ideas, although difficult to operationalize, have provided a major intellectual inspiration to workers in the field of personality development in adulthood and old age.

In Erikson's model, each psychosocial crisis is theorized to offer an opportunity for the development of a new function or facet of the ego. However, the crisis involving identity has special significance as it establishes the most important functions of the ego: self-definition and self-awareness. Following the development of identity, according to Erikson, additional functions of the ego evolve, including love, care, and wisdom. In old age, according to Erikson, the individual engages in a process of reviewing past experiences and incorporating those into a cohesive and positive identity. The sense of identity that emerges from this process, which Erikson called "existential" identity, plays an important role in adaptation to the changes experienced in later life and the ability to meet death without fear. For some elders, this process might involve a reassessment of their goals and expectations to meet future needs, and for others it might mean taking time to examine their sense of self and to conform their identity to the life that they have actually lived.

The role of psychosocial factors may perhaps best be understood in terms of the mediating effects of identity on adaptation throughout the life course. The life span construct has been proposed as a mechanism for linking identity development in adulthood with the processes involved in adapting to life experiences. This construct is theorized to be a translation of the content of adult identity into a subjective model of age-appropriate and expectable events and themes. The life span construct was a central component in a conceptual model proposed by Whitbourne to suggest a mechanism for linking identity development in adulthood with the processes involved in coping with stressful life events. This construct is theorized to be a translation of the content of adult identity into a subjective model of age-appropriate and expectable events and themes.

Briefly, the life span construct model proposes that adults plan and evaluate their life events in terms of an underlying set of assumptions, expectations, and ideas about what their lives could be. For example, if an individual's identity is largely defined in terms of involvement in the family, then family-related events would be expected to form the basis of the life span construct. To the extent that these themes are age-linked, it is hypothesized that these age-related expectations reflect the prevailing society's age norms and structure. Themes related to gender-related expectations would also be reflected in the life span construct, as these expectations often pertain to the ages at which it is considered normative for women and men to have experienced certain events.

Derived from the life span construct model are the concepts of the "scenario" and the "life story." The scenario is the individual's projection into future events based on personal and social norms regarding age and gender as these are reflected in the individual's sense of identity. For example, a 51-year-old woman may include in her scenario the expectation that by the age of 60 years, she will have become a grandmother. Events in the past are hypothesized to be woven into a life story, the individual's autobiography that is continually constructed and reconstructed throughout life. Although the life story is theorized to change in a way that is responsive to actual life events, it is theorized to evolve in a way that enhances and maintains the individual's identity.

Essential to the model is the assumption that the life-span construct underlies many general and specific evaluations that individuals make of their life experiences, but that this evaluation is rarely conducted at the conscious level of awareness. The individual's sense of satisfaction or dissatisfaction with her life would, it is theorized, reflect the extent to which the life story enhances the life-span construct and the scenario includes future possibilities that appear achievable. To maintain a positive sense of identity, it is proposed that individuals use the processes of identity assimilation and accommodation. These terms, which are derived from Piaget's concepts of cognitive assimilation and accommodation, are defined in terms of denial of life events inconsistent with a person's inferred life span construct (assimilation) or willingness to report these life events, particularly those with a highly negative content (accommodation). A person may use identity assimilation to reinterpret an event into the life story in a way that does not detract from the individual's sense of identity in that domain. Returning to the previous example, if at age 72 years, the woman has not become a grandmother due to the divorce of her daughter before she had her own children, her life story may resolve this discrepancy through assimilation by attributing the change in her own family's circumstances to the de-

mise of "family values" in contemporary society. By contrast, identity accommodation involves incorporating the reality of an event that was inconsistent with the scenario in a way that causes the individual to change the life-span construct. In the example of the 72-year-old woman, identity accommodation would be said to occur if she blamed herself for failing to raise her daughter "right."

Although identity assimilation and accommodation are regarded as processes rather than personality traits, there may be some value in conceptualizing them as personal styles. Some individuals may be more likely to use assimilation and others accommodation when confronting events that have a bearing on their life-span constructs. This approach may be particularly helpful in conceptualizing the life-span construct in older adults whose life stories are longer and more elaborated than their scenarios, and hence may be more influenced by the processes of identity assimilation and accommodation. Having had a lifetime of experiences that either confirm or challenge the life-span construct, it might be expected that older adults tend to rely increasingly on one or another process. Which is more adaptive is an empirical question. Erikson's theory would argue that accommodation is a more adaptive process, or at least a balance between assimilation and accommodation in which the reality of past failures is integrated into the individual's sense of self. However, given the potentially adaptive value of denial in coping with life events, an argument could be made that assimilation serves a more positive protective function in preserving the older adult's identity.

In keeping with the assumption that the life span construct operates below the level of conscious awareness, the measure designed to assess the life span construct of an individual involves a projective type of format. This measure, the "life drawing," is a free-hand drawing of an individual's personal time line or life events, with the only reference point being a horizontal line at the bottom of the page marked "age and/or year." Respondents are instructed to write or draw in a time-line fashion their life events (past, present, and future) along this time line. In the original research using this measure on men and women ranging from their early twenties to sixties, age differences were established on measures derived from the life drawing on the dimensions of temporal dominance. The life drawings were also used to assess the theoretically relevant processes of identity assimilation and accommodation. The processes of identity assimilation and accommodation were investigated in a group of hospitalized psychiatric patients ranging in age from the twenties to sixties. By comparing the life drawings with hospital records, which provided objective documentation of the respondents' life histories, it was possible to determine whether respondents were using identity assimilation, in which they denied the reality of their hospitalizations, or identity accommodation, in which they integrated into their life span constructs the reality of their disorders. The life drawing, then, has proven to be a useful measure in these preliminary investigations of theoretically derived concepts based on the life span construct.

In subsequent research on a sample of elderly community-dwelling women, it was possible to test predictions that dimensions of the life span construct would be related to adaptation in later adulthood. For this purpose, new measures were derived from the life drawing and a larger sample of older adults used than in previous studies. Furthermore, the similarity of cohort- and gender-based age expectations in an age- and gender-homogenous group made it possible to control for contextual variables that might impact the life span construct. Thus, all women in the sample would have been exposed to the cultural norms of the 1920s and 1930s, when they were in their teenage and early adult years, a time when their life span constructs would be emerging. Cohort or period influences, such as the changing expectations regarding women's roles in society, should be similar for all respondents. With these influences minimized, the relationships could be explored among temporal and content-related measures derived from the life drawing, well-being, a sense of control over one's personal destiny, and affective dimensions of time perspective. Based on Erikson's theory, it was expected that a positive sense of adaptation would be related to a life drawing with the individual as the protagonist and an orientation toward past life events. It was also predicted that a belief that one has controlled her own destiny should relate to a positive sense of well-being. The findings indicated that the individuals willing and able to provide complete data had a positive bias in their orientations to their life drawings. Qualitative impressions from the life drawings added weight to this interpretation, with at least 15 women spontaneously providing "advice" on how they managed to

cope with their lives by focusing on the positive, maintaining "faith," and using denial when dealing with stress. Other similar statements reflected the importance of hard work and persistence, and the ability to enjoy life one day at a time. These observations, interestingly, reflect the moderating effects of "self-complexity." According to this view, the more ways in which an individual can define herself as competent, the more likely it is that she can buffer herself against failure or loss in any of those domains.

In terms of the theoretical concepts of identity assimilation and accommodation, it would appear that the women who maintained a positive view of their lives by focusing on these coping methods tended to use assimilation more than accommodation. Although it is not possible to determine with certainty the nature of the actual life events to which these women referred, the fact that they professed the value of maintaining a positive attitude despite losses would suggest an outward adherence to the mechanism of identity assimilation in producing their life stories. Also apparent in these statements was a major theme in the life drawings concerning the role of family. As observed in the quantitative findings, family events figured prominently in the life drawings, and a focus on family was modestly related to positive affect statements. In inspecting the life drawings, this importance of family was evident in the number of family members who were drawn in conjunction with particular events (usually as stick figures) or whose entry and exit into the woman's life provided a demarcation point in her own life span construct. One of the most striking of these instances was a drawing that was almost exclusively composed of stick figures. There appeared to be several generations represented in this drawing, all of whom were centered around a church. For these women, their place in the progression of generations appeared to be a central feature of their life span constructs.

These examples suggest that positive affect toward one's life is related to a lack of preoccupation with the past, involvement with family, and a turning outward rather than inward. In contrast, a focus on the past and involvement in one's own personal losses rather than involvement with family was a feature of the less positively oriented drawings. These findings counter what we will examine next in relation to adaptation: the role of reminiscence, life review, and development of a sense of ego integrity.

VII. EGO INTEGRITY AND ADAPTATION IN OLD AGE

In addition to the development of an existential identity in later adulthood, Erikson proposed that the end of life brings with it concerns regarding ego integrity—the achievement of a sense of wholeness and completion in one's life and self. According to Erikson, the optimally adjusted older adult is one who has achieved a state of ego integrity and can look at the past without regrets and the future without fear. Such an individual has a positive attitude toward life, accepts life for what it was, a sense of accomplishment, and a feeling that if life could be lived over again, it would be done so without major changes. This sense of accomplishment and completion allows the individual to face death and not see it as a premature ending or even to be dreaded. By contrast, older adults who feel that they did not fulfill their potential or who have a weak and fragmented sense of self are in a state of despair. Such individuals constantly regret past decisions and wish they could live their lives over again. They fear death because it will occur before they have corrected their past errors.

At the intersection of identity and ego integrity are very different sets of reactions to the aging process. The individual characterized by despair views each physical, cognitive, and social loss as a constant reminder of impending death. This individual will be constantly subjected to new threats, and will need to resort to identity assimilation as a way of protecting the self from these threats. Conversely, the individual who has achieved ego integrity does not fear aging or the future, and is able to respond to aging changes in a more balanced manner.

The state of ego integrity is one that is not easily achieved. It is highly dependent upon many factors, and particularly the individual's past history of adaptation. However, even in individuals who have successfully adapted to prior life crises, the sheer number of losses and changes in old age present a far greater challenge. A stable but flexible identity as well as a sense of acceptance of the life that has been lived appear to be the major factors involved in successful adaptation to the aging process. In reconciling this theoretical approach with the observations based on the life drawing research, it appears that there are multiple paths to adapting to the changes associated with the aging process. For some older adults who are more philosophically inclined, a critical examination of the self in relation to past experiences may provide the impetus for movement into a final stage of self-integration. Other older adults may adapt successfully by taking a more active approach—engaging in activities that maintain their physical and cognitive functioning but giving little thought to the larger implications of the aging process for the sense of self. Finally, there are those elders whose involvement in issues external to the self, such as family, religion, or other formal and informal roles, helps maintain their sense of optimism and purpose in life. In helping older individuals achieve a state of optimal adjustment, it may be of primary importance to remember that there are multiple paths to successful adaptation, reflecting the continuity of the individual's lifelong personality patterns, social context, and adaptational demands.

BIBLIOGRAPHY

Berkman, B., Millar, S., Holmes, W., & Bonander, E. (1991). Predicting elderly cardiac patients at risk for readmission. Special Issue: Applied social work research in health and social work. *Social Work in Health Care, 16*(1), 21–38.

Brubaker, T. H., & Roberto, K. A. (1993). Family life education for the later years. *Family Relations, 42*, 212–221.

Carstensen, L. L. (1992). Social and emotional patterns in adulthood: Support for socioemotional selectivity theory. *Psychology and Aging, 7*, 331–338.

Erikson, E. H. (1963). *Childhood and society* (2nd ed.). New York: Norton.

Erikson, E. H., Erikson, J., & Kivnick, H. Q. (1986). *Vital involvement in old age.* New York: W. W. Norton.

Folkman, S., Bernstein, L., & Lazarus, R. S. (1987). Stress processes and the misuse of drugs in older adults. *Psychology and Aging, 2*, 366–374.

Heidrich, S. M., & Ryff, C. D. (1993). The role of social comparison processes in the psychological adaptation of elderly adults. *Journal of Gerontology: Psychological Sciences, 48*, 127–136.

Lawton, M. P., & Nahemow, L. (1973). Ecology and the aging process. In C. Eisdorfer & M. P. Lawton (Eds.), *The psychology of adult development and aging.* Washington, DC: American Psychological Association.

Lazarus, R. S., & Folkman, S. (1984). *Stress, appraisal, and coping.* New York: Springer.

McCrae, R. R., & Costa, P. T., Jr. (1990). *Personality in adulthood.* New York: Guilford.

McNaughton, M. E., Smith, L. W., Patterson, T. L., & Grant, I. (1990). Stress, social support, coping resources, and immune status in elderly women. *Journal of Nervous and Mental disease, 178*, 460–461.

O'Brien, S. J., & Conger, P. R. (1991). No time to look back:

Approaching the finish line of life's course. *International Journal of Aging and Human Development, 33*(1), 75–87.

Poon, L. W., Martin, P., Clayton, G. M., Messner, S. A., Noble, C. A. & Johnson, M. A. (1992). The influences of cognitive resources on adaptation and old age. *International Journal of Aging and Human Development, 34*, 31–46.

Reich, J. W., & Zautra, A. J. (1991). Experimental and measurement approaches to internal control in at-risk older adults. *Journal of Social Issues, 47*, 143–158.

Whitbourne, S. K. (1985). The psychological construction of the life span. In J. E. Birren & K. W. Schaie (Ed.), *Handbook of the psychology of aging* (pp. 594–618). New York: Van Nostrand Reinhold.

Whitbourne, S. K. (1986). *Adult development.* New York: Praeger.

Whitbourne, S. K. (1987). Personality development in adulthood and old age: Relationships among identity style, health, and well-being. In K. W. Schaie (Ed.), *Annual review of gerontology and geriatrics* (pp. 189–216). New York: Springer.

Whitbourne, S. K., & Dannefer, W. D. (1985–86). The life drawing as a measure of time perspective in adulthood. *International Journal of Aging and Human Development, 22*, 147–155.

Whitbourne, S. K., & Powers, C. B. (1994). Older women's constructs of their lives: A quantitative and qualitative exploration. *International Journal of Aging and Human Development, 38*, 293–306.

Whitbourne, S. K., & Sherry, M. S. (1991). Subjective perceptions of the life span in chronic mental patients. *International Journal of Aging and Human Development, 33*, 65–73.

Wright, L. K. (1991). The impact of Alzheimer's disease on the marital relationship. *The Gerontologist, 31*, 224–237.

Adult Education

Ronald J. Manheimer

University of North Carolina at Asheville

Expressive Motive Motivation to learn about a subject as an end in itself.
Instrumental Motive Motivation to learn about a subject as a means to another end.
Lifelong Learning The view that education plays a continuing, although changing, role throughout the life course.

ADULT EDUCATION includes both formal (for credit) and informal (noncredit) learning, intentionally undertaken by adults in the context of an educational setting. Older adult education has evolved as a subcategory of adult education and as an extension of gerontological concern for late-life development. In the last 20 years, older adult education has come to span programs offered through colleges and universities, churches and synagogues, senior centers, libraries, department stores, public schools, nursing homes, and adult day centers. Programs cover a spectrum from life enrichment (liberal arts focused) to skills enhancement and job retraining.

I. HISTORICAL PERSPECTIVES

A. Adult Education from Colonial America to the Twentieth Century

Adult education opportunities in the United States date back to the 1700s when coffee houses functioned as adult educational institutions, mainly for disseminating political propaganda. Many of the coffee houses in New York City provided writing and reading materials for their customers.

The earliest leaders of our country believed that democracy depended on the educability of the citizenry. Through widespread educational efforts, the public decision-making process could be improved. Benjamin Franklin, a great believer in this theory, established one of the first adult education activities in the colonial United States, called Junto, a weekly study group of 12 people who met to discuss community and social issues, which led to formation of the first local lending libraries.

Almost 100 years later, a lecture series, the Lyceum (in ancient tradition, an association providing public lectures, concerts, and entertainments) was established to introduce adult citizens, residing in small towns and rural areas, to scholarly knowledge. These lectures were an attempt to raise the educational levels of participants who had not completed an elementary level education. Approximately 50 years later, the Methodist Episcopal Church established the Chautauqua movement to introduce religious studies, liberal arts education, and the performing arts. Basically nondenominational, it drew audiences from all over to the summer assembly tent performances. Similar "tent chautauquas" were held across the country. The New York Chautauqua village today attracts large numbers of older people.

B. Emergence of Older Adult Education: Two Sources

Although the expression "lifelong learning" had been in use for many years, only recently has that concept been applied to older adult learners. As gerontology became an established field, it influenced the adult education movement, and educators began to consider older adults as potential students of lifelong education.

Until the early 1950s a cultural bias toward youth had a detrimental effect upon the growth of educational programs for older adults. Yet, in 1949, a Committee on Education for Aging was established under the Department of Adult Education of the National Education Association (NEA). In 1951, this committee became a part of the Adult Education Association of the United States. For the first time in U.S. history, this committee developed a descriptive book on educational programming for older adult learners, *Education for Later Maturity: A Handbook*.

The 1960s and early 1970s saw adult education influenced by the burgeoning field of gerontology. For example, as an outgrowth of the 1971 White House Conference on Aging, the Administration on Aging awarded a 2-year grant to the American Association of Community and Junior Colleges to explore ways for community colleges to highlight the needs of older persons and contribute to their quality of life. In addition, several community colleges tapped new funds made available through Title I of the Higher Education Act of 1965 and Title III of the Older Americans Act of 1965 to hire coordinators or part-time program directors to design and implement courses for seniors.

Still, the prevailing thinking in this period was to focus on providing seniors with knowledge and skills to cope successfully with the problematic aspects of growing older. According to David A. Peterson, "educational programs emphasized the crisis of adjustment to retirement and the need for outside assistance to overcome the trauma of role change." This approach corresponds to what Harry R. Moody characterized as the "social service" model of older adult education in which aging is regarded as a problem that education can help to ameliorate.

During the 1950s and 1960s only a few educational administrators considered offering educational programs for older adults. The few programs in operation were experimental in nature with no research base. In the early 1960s, gerontological researchers devoted considerable energy to examining links between aging, intelligence, and memory. [*See* MEMORY.] The combined emphasis on the youth culture and research on age-related cognitive declines continued to have a

negative impact upon attitudes toward older adult educational programs.

The 1971 White House Conference on Aging highlighted the value of education for older adults. Independent of federal legislation, a multitude of new educational programs for seniors arose in senior centers, community colleges, universities, community schools, and churches and synagogues. These programs expanded greatly in the mid-1970s and 1980s. During this period, funding from the National Endowment for the Arts (NEA) and the National Endowment for the Humanities (NEH) helped support numerous educational programs for older adults.

C. Older Adult Education and the Concept of the Third Age

The concept of the Third Age has had moderate impact on older adult education in the United States. The phrase derives from the French *L'Université du Troisième Age* (University of the Third Age or, U3A) first proposed by its founder, Pierre Vellas, in 1973. Vellas recognized the combined vitality and longevity of many older persons in France and thought that French universities should promote a combination of instruction for seniors, research emphasizing the well elderly, and opportunities for personal development. U3A programs have spread through Europe, Britain, Australia, Canada, and to some degree to the United States.

British sociologist Peter Laslett, who helped to establish the U3A movement in Great Britain, gave a precise socioeconomic meaning to the Third Age. Laslett observed that, until quite recently in the twentieth century, only a fortunate few, the wealthy and healthy, had a Third Age. For the rest, the Fourth Age (a period of frailty and disability) came before they had a chance to enjoy the Third. New characteristics associated with retirement that emerged in the 1950s—better health, economic security through pensions, and improved societal and self-image of the older person—created a unique period for which people could plan. Hence, the Third Age is a product of demographic expansion of retirement-age individuals, economic security through national public policy, improvement in health care and access to care, and changing attitudes of and toward older adults. The Third Age, said Laslett, "is an attribute of a population, indeed of a nation, as well as of particular men and women." [*See* RETIREMENT.]

Laslett thought that the newfound period of relative leisure must be met with opportunities for people of all classes to deepen their sense of culture and to participate in educational programs that would enable them to appreciate art, history, philosophy, music, and other subjects that were valuable to experience simply for the sake of learning itself. Without educational engagement, the Third Age would, said Laslett, "turn out to be indolence indefinite."

II. OLDER PERSONS' CAPACITY TO LEARN

A. Research on Cognitive and Intellectual Functioning

Parallel to the emergence of older adult education as meriting the attention of adult educators and gerontologists (and revisions in thinking about the needs and goals of older learners) were changes in appraisal of cognitive functioning among older persons. Although focus on the decline of older persons' intellectual powers characterized early research, more recent research findings pointed to stability in cognitive functioning over time. While recognizing decrements in some areas, they also emphasized older learners' relatively undiminished capacities and fascinating shifts in the type of intellectual abilities that may come with aging. Maintaining intellectual functioning and capacity is one purpose of education in later life.

K. Warner Schaie questioned the assumption that older people tend to function less well intellectually than younger people. He contended that all older adults do not exhibit intellectual decline. Sociologists Matilda White Riley and John Riley undertook a series of studies on intellectual functioning that showed improvement with age under certain conditions. They found continuity in intellectual functioning where life situations continued to be stimulating and challenging, people had opportunity to use their skills, and access to educational opportunities.

Psychologist Labouvie-Vief pointed out that the early phase of geropsychology was heavily influenced by the prevailing decrement model of aging. Research presumed that physical and mental processes manifested "primary, inherent, universal, and irreversible

biological concomitants of aging." But as a developmental model began to influence the direction of research, geropsychologists began to more carefully differentiate gains and losses in cognitive functioning. Hence, psychologists applied the distinction between two forms of intelligence: crystallized (derived from experience) and fluid (more biologically determined). Although the latter may show marked signs of decline with aging, the former shows less decline and longer stability. Later, the distinction between "competence" and "performance" was used to indicate differences in intellectual functioning. [*See* THEORIES OF AGING: BIOLOGICAL; THEORIES OF AGING: PSYCHOLOGICAL.]

Labouvie-Vief developed a "trade-off view" of cognitive development as a process in which some forms of intellectual integration are dissolved while new forms of integration occur, particularly around adaptations in relation to "pragmatic necessities."

B. Uniqueness of Older Learners

By the mid-1960s small inroads were made in removing the educational bias toward the young while attitudes toward older adults began to change. For example, social workers trained during the 1940s and 1950s had been instructed to discourage reminiscing among older people because it was viewed as a form of pathology—the person denying or having lost contact with the present. However, between the late 1950s and early 1970s this view changed dramatically. The work of psychiatrist Robert Butler and developmental psychologist Erik Erikson helped service providers and educators to recognize a universal "life review" process and a quest for personal integration occurring normally among the elderly. It was deemed that this process could serve as the basis for therapies and educational programs by building on older persons' life experiences and histories.

Some researchers and educators went even further. They described elements of wisdom and creativity in the life review process. Not only were older adults still capable of learning and expressing themselves, because of their treasure house of past experience, they could be ideal students and could make excellent teachers. [*See* LIFE REVIEW; REMINISCENCE.]

If later life is regarded as a unique developmental stage with its own special tasks and opportunities, then education in the later years may be regarded as distinct from adult education. For example, Moody has argued that, unique to old age, some older learners are capable of understanding philosophical and spiritual matters that only a lifetime of experience could make possible. Just when does a person reach that threshold of unique insight? Again, it is probably not a matter of chronology but of maturity.

Other researchers such as Clayton and Birren have focused on the search for wisdom in later life as a unique characteristic of older persons. Old age, being the last stage in the life course, may be viewed as an attempt to explore the meaning of one's experiences and to integrate an understanding of these experiences acquired throughout a lifetime. Many gerontologists and adult educators believe that self-actualization should be the ultimate goal of every older adult educational program.

C. Compensation and Learning Styles

Paul Baltes is an important theorist whose research on cognitive functioning and intelligence in later life further supported the value of education. Baltes and his colleagues at the Max Planck Institute for Neurological Research in Berlin distinguished between two types of mental activity: (a) the biologically shaped "hardware of the mind," which operates the speed and accuracy of memory, sensory input, ability to make distinctions and comparisons, and ability to put things into categories (also termed "cognitive mechanics"); and (b) the "software of the mind," more a product of culture, upbringing, and environment, and including reading and writing skills, language comprehension, professional skills, self-knowledge, and coping skills (which Baltes calls "cognitive pragmatics").

Baltes and associates found that although older persons' memory capacity would increase if they participated in memory training techniques, they would still not reach the level of younger persons who received the same training. They concluded that the hardware of the mind does show a decline with age. But when it came to real-life problem-solving tests— for example, counseling a threatened suicide or advising a 15-year-old girl who wanted to get married— they found no major differences between those 30–70 years of age. In fact, those above 60 were as likely to be among the top 20% of "wisdom performers" as younger adults.

Paul Baltes's work asserts that there are qualitative differences in how some older people think—with declines in some areas offset by advances in others. Most recent research findings suggest that chronological age is not the key determinant of cognitive ability and that attempts at formulating a general theory of older learners may be a misguided effort. Although there clearly are declines in memory and intellectual functioning associated with aging, these declines vary widely with individuals, whereas certain capabilities seem enhanced with age. Baltes coined the phrase *selective optimization with compensation* to describe how older people learn to delimit while maximizing their learning goals in order to offset declining skills.

III. MOTIVES OF OLDER LEARNERS

A. Instrumental–Expressive Continuum

A considerable amount of research has centered around the dichotomous pair of terms *expressive* and *instrumental* to characterize learner motives. Learning for its own sake has been classified as expressive, whereas learning directed toward some further outcome or external objective is said to be instrumental. The distinction in motives has aided educational administrators to plan appropriate curricula. But some confusion persists about the distinction. Learning French, for example, might be desirable in and of itself for the person who enjoys learning languages or wants to read Molière in the original. But for the person who hopes to command some mastery of the language for the 2-month visit to Provence, the motivation is instrumental. Similarly, the popularity of computer courses among seniors may stem, on the one hand, from the pleasure of gaining facility with a new technology or keeping up with the grandchildren, to a desire to acquire skill with Lotus 1-2-3 in order to computerize household bookkeeping or land a part-time job.

B. Problem of Determining Motives

Other difficulties in classifying the motives of older learners stem from this dual perspective: the intrinsic character of the educational activity and the learner's goals. For example, numerous studies have shown that "intellectual stimulation," a seemingly expressive orientation, is the most important value of education for those enrolled in liberal arts-focused Learning in

Retirement Institutes (LRIs), Elderhostel programs, Shepherd's Centers, and similar programs. But the term *intellectual stimulation* may mean for some the chance to increase appreciation of literature, philosophy, or history, whereas for others it suggests a desire to glean information that will help the individual keep up to date with current social and cultural issues.

Studies of older persons' motives for enrolling in formal and informal education programs have yielded a wide disparity of results. Some surveys have concluded that people are more likely to be instrumentally oriented and others have found expressive motives to be predominant. This, in part, may be a function of when the studies were conducted, what population was studied, and which categories or taxonomy were assumed. For example, studies conducted at senior centers in the early 1970s are likely to yield instrumental orientations because the types of programs offered tended to deal with coping issues and hobbies. By contrast, studies of participation in Elderhostel, which began to attract a sizable enrollment in the late 1970s, tend to yield the opposite results, as most people elect these courses for intellectual and personal enhancement. Researchers Wirtz and Charner point out that the hypothesized instrumental–expressive continuum may force participants into artificial categories. Hence, inconsistent findings may be the result of utilizing scales that lack psychometric validity.

C. Life Tasks, Needs, and Wants

Lowy and O'Connor probably had the most useful idea for reviewing motivation among seniors. They constructed a matrix that combined instrumental and expressive orientations with "need categories" (e.g., coping, contributive, influencing) developed by McClusky to produce a holistic overview that would integrate a wide range and mix of learner goals and orientations.

A major problem of studying seniors' motivations for educational programs, as pointed out by Jeffrey Leptak in his literature review, is that most of the research is quantitative. Although methodologically correct from a social science perspective, the use of preference rankings falls short of providing deeper insight into how older participants think about their own motives. Cognitive interest and intellectual stimulation are abstractions distant from the older per-

sons' actual fascination with a particular subject matter.

Review of seniors' educational motives shows that, like adult learners in general, seniors exhibit a wide diversity of needs, interests, and wants that may be conditioned by socioeconomic and educational backgrounds, the institutional setting where programs are offered, and the existence or availability of opportunities. Theories of the motives of older learners are useful as hypotheses for planners, but they should not become constraints.

IV. OLDER ADULT EDUCATION AND PUBLIC POLICY

The history of older adult education has been influenced by changes in government policies. The first major development came with the creation of the Older Americans Act (OAA) in 1965, which established the Administration on Aging and provided needed funding for gerontological training and research at colleges and universities. The act opened the door for new educational opportunities for older adults and extended educational gerontology, workforce training, and multidisciplinary graduate programs as well as research in addressing the needs of older adults learners.

The 1971 White House Conference on Aging advanced recommendations that paved the road for educational programming for older adults. Education received special attention at the conference, where recommendations called for increased funding and manpower to provide older adult educational programs in the private and public sector.

Congress enacted the Older Americans Comprehensive Services Amendments of 1973 to strengthen the OAA. Under this act the Administration on Aging was reorganized under the U.S. Department of Health, Education, and Welfare (HEW) and the Federal Council on the Aging was created, as well as the National Information and Resource Clearinghouse for the Aging. Grants were given to state governments for special library and education programs for older adults. Research in the field of aging and grants for training personnel to work with older adults were encouraged.

A. State and Local Levels

In addition to federal policies concerning older adult education, many states established guidelines to allow or require a waiver or reduction of tuition fees for older adults enrolled at a state-supported institution of higher education. Thirty-eight states have enacted some type of statutes.

The private sector also became involved in the educational pursuits of older adults during the 1970s. An initiative was taken to design projects that would enable older adults to become involved in new careers, to further their knowledge so that they might continue to contribute to society. Private-sector programs established to meet the needs of the aging included those of the American Association of Retired Persons (AARP), National Retired Teachers Association, National Association of Retired Federal Employees, National Association for the Spanish-Speaking Elderly, National Center on the Black Aged, Inc., The National Council on the Aging, Inc., National Council of Senior Citizens, National Farmers Union, and the National Indian Council on Aging.

The Edna McConnell Clark Foundation funded many research projects to determine the best utilization of sevices for older adults. One of their projects included a grant to the American Association of Community and Junior Colleges to extend career opportunities to older adults by assisting them to prepare for further careers before and after retirement.

B. Nongovernmental Organizations

Federal, state, and local policies have partially shaped funding streams and institutional missions in promotion of older adult education. To some extent, these policies have served to motivate or catalyze a variety of institutional developments. But the bulk of new initiatives have occurred independent of governmental policies or foundation support. The following section reviews this broader scope of organizations serving older learners and how these have changed during the last few decades.

V. PROGRAM MODELS AND CURRICULA

A. Colleges and Universities

1. Community Colleges

In 1989, the League for Innovation in the Community College and the AARP conducted a national survey of League member institutions (community colleges). From the approximately 600 community colleges responding to the survey, researchers Doucette and Ventura-Merkel found (a) most older adult educational programs came under organizational units such as community services, adult education, or short courses; (b) the majority of the colleges conducted noncredit courses with fees ranging between \$25–\$50 per course; (c) some colleges allowed students 60 and older to audit credit courses with fees waived; (d) half of the League colleges had a special program or center for older adults or both at their college; (e) three-fourths of the colleges reported offering noncredit classes to older adults; and (f) full-term credit courses were often taught at off-campus sites.

Catherine Ventura-Merkel, then Senior Education Specialist in the Special Projects Section of AARP, and Don Doucette, then Associate Director of the League for Innovation in the Community College, reported that the types of courses being offered in the community colleges were traditional classes in exercise and nutrition, avocational arts, crafts, hobbies, and trips, and financial management programs on retirement and estate planning.

The courses least likely to be offered were in fact the ones demographers and other analysts contended are most needed by the older adult population. These courses include skills training for second and third occupations, personal development courses, and health-care programs. Ventura-Merkel and Doucette concluded that only a small number of community colleges were offering programs and services for older adults. The colleges that did offer programs were mostly designed for retired groups of seniors.

2. Elderhostel

Founded in 1975 by Martin Knowlton as a short-term residential college program for people over 60, Elderhostel originally operated under the auspices of the Center for Continuing Education at the University of New Hampshire in Durham. The first Elderhostel programs in 1975 were run by a small group of colleges and universities in New Hampshire with 220 older adults participating in course offerings. In 1977, Elderhostel became an independent, nonprofit organization with the full support of the university. A national office was established in Boston to coordinate all Elderhostel activities. In 1979, a computerized national mailing list system was installed, and the national office began registering participants for any Elderhostel program anywhere in the country by phone or mail.

Since 1986 Elderhostel has grown at a rate of 15–25% (though leveling off in the 1990s). The program operates in more than 1800 sites in the United States and Canada and in 45 countries worldwide. The enrollment averages over 300,000 annually. The sponsoring institutions are largely 4-year colleges and universities, but environmental study centers, scientific research stations, and conference centers also serve as program hosts. In 1993 Elderhostel began offering a social action component for people who wished to travel to a site and become affiliated with a local community service project where they could both serve and learn. In 1994, Elderhostel lowered the age requirement to 55.

3. Learning in Retirement Institutes

An LRI is an organization of retirement-age learners dedicated to meeting the educational needs of its members. LRIs generally fall into one of two general program categories: institution-driven (designed by professional staff and taught by the regular higher education faculty) or member-driven (designed and taught by the members with the cooperative sponsorship of a higher education institution). Members may also take an active role in governing the organization, with elected directors and officers.

Of an estimated 200 LRIs, over 160 are members of an umbrella organization, Elderhostel Institute Network (EIN), a subsidiary of Elderhostel. Several national conferences were devoted to the institute concept, and the number of LRIs has increased dramatically since the mid-1980s.

The LRI programs include core courses and classes in the humanities and liberal arts. Literature, history, public affairs, and music and art appreciation have proven to be the most popular among participants. Often the core curriculum is supplemented by classes in computer science, foreign languages, fine arts, and writing. Recreational and physical fitness programs are also offered.

4. Certificate Programs

Some older adults require educational courses that prepare them for retraining and second and third careers. Certification programs provide this type of training. Some colleges and universities have estab-

lished special programs to make the older learner's transition back into the educational environment more appealing as well as preparing them for new careers or new job challenges. One such program is Kingsborough Community College's "My Turn." This special tuition-free college education program has waived all admission requirements with the exception that students must be residents of New York state and 65 years of age by the first day of class. Many students are working toward a GED (General Equivalency Diploma), and others are working toward an associate's degree.

Another such program is at the University of Massachusetts, Boston, campus where qualified students over 60 prepare to serve as professionals in the fields of gerontology. Not all have high school degrees and only one-third have college degrees. The university has sought diversity in the backgrounds as well as the ages and ethnicities of students. Upon completion of the program students receive a state certificate in gerontology. Graduates of the program have found job opportunities in government agencies serving the aging, nursing homes, working for political candidates, and administering programs for the aging.

B. Senior Centers

During the 1970s the multiservice senior center concept began to flourish. Activities and services available at these centers included hot meals and nutritional education, health education, employment services, transportation assistance, social work services, educational activities, creative arts programs, recreation, leadership, and volunteer opportunities.

The recreation–education component of senior center programming varies with availability of community resources and interests of participants. Some of the more common activities include arts and crafts, nature studies, science and outdoor life, drama, physical activity, music, dance, table games, special social activities, literary activities, excursions, hobby or special interest groups, speakers, lectures, movies, forums, round tables, and community service projects. One popular educational program used by senior centers since 1975 is Discovery through the Humanities, a NEH-funded series based on large-print anthologies and audiotapes, made available by the National Council on the Aging for reading and discussion groups.

C. Older Adult Service and Information System

The Older Adult Service and Information System (OASIS) is a consortium between business and not-for-profit organizations designed to challenge and enrich the lives of adults 55 and older. Educational, cultural, health, and volunteer outreach programs are offered at the OASIS Centers to provide participants an opportunity to remain independent and active in community affairs. The May Department Stores Company, the major national sponsor, provides OASIS with dedicated meeting and activity space in many of its stores. Initial support for the program was provided by the Administration on Aging.

The national office establishes program quality requirements and overall management and operations guidelines. Currently there are 29 OASIS Centers operating from coast to coast with over 130,000 members. Each center has permanent and specially designed space for offices, student lounges, and meeting rooms. Courses are offered in areas of visual arts, music, drama, creative writing, contemporary issues, history, science, exercise, and health. Many courses are held in collaboration with local medical, cultural, and educational institutions.

Volunteer outreach is an important component of the OASIS program. Many participants are trained in the Older Adult Peer Leadership (OAPL) program, to teach classes in the community, and to work in intergenerational programs helping young children. In 1990, more than 2000 volunteers gave over 110,000 hours of their time to run the OASIS sites.

D. Shepherd's Centers

A nonprofit community organization sponsored by a coalition of religious congregations, Shepherd's Centers are committed to the delivery of services and programs for older adults. In 1972, the first Shepherd's Center was founded by Dr. Elbert C. Cole in Kansas City, Missouri. Twenty-three churches and synagogues joined in an interfaith effort to provide a ministry by, with, and for older adults. In 1972 the original center began with only six volunteers. Today, over 90 Shepherd's Centers in 25 states comprise a network of 15,000 volunteers serving over 175,000 older adults. The services and programs of the Shepherd's Center are designed to empower older adults

to lead creative, productive, meaningful, and interdependent lives.

One of the many programs offered by the Shepherd's Centers is the Adventures in Learning program, which utilizes older adults as teachers, students, planners, and participants. Classes are normally held weekly, bimonthly, or monthly. The purpose of the educational program is to provide an environment where older adults may share their knowledge, talents, skills, and new interests with their peers. A committee of volunteers makes the program decisions regarding curriculum, faculty, marketing, and evaluating. This committee is composed of faculty and students with background experience in education, public relations, administration, the arts, health, and clerical services. Most of the teachers are older adults who volunteer their time, knowledge, and skills.

E. Other Models

The great diversity of older adult education programs also encompasses computer literacy and the use of public libraries. SENIORNET, based in San Francisco, has encouraged establishment of numerous computer centers and labs across the country where older adults learn to use computers and take advantage of inexpensive access to the computer centers if they do not own their own machines. Public libraries have become a focal point in many communities for library-sponsored educational programs for seniors that range from humanities reading and discussion groups to practical information and skills training.

VI. PARTICIPATION RATES AND FUTURE TRENDS

The percentage of people over 55 who were formally enrolled in courses tripled between 1969 and 1981. Although accurate national data are not available on seniors' participation in both formal and informal (noncredit) programs, continued expansion is reflected in AARP's *Directory of Learning Opportunities for Older Persons*, which has doubled in size over the last 10 years. In 1981, an estimated 4% of people over age 65 were enrolled in adult education, and 5.7% of those 55 and over. A rate of 6–7% is estimated for the 1990s. This does not include noncredit offerings such as Elderhostel, LRIs, and so on.

The future of older adult education is both promising and perplexing. Even with the relatively flat growth of the older adult population during the 1990s, certain types of programs have multiplied across the country. LRI programs based in colleges and universities are growing at a rapid pace (the vast majority established since 1989) though they often exist at the margins of power and resource allocations. Shepherd's Center Adventures in Learning programs, OASIS centers, and SENIORNET sites have also shown remarkable expansion. With the exception of senior centers, most development has taken place outside the network of aging organizations, perhaps because primarily the well elderly are served by these programs and the aging network is more focused on service delivery to the frail and at-risk.

Demand for programs is a function of prior education. Median years of schooling for people 65+ was 8.3 years (17% finished high school) in 1950. Today it is 12.1 years (55% high school completion) and rising. In 1950, only 3.4% of those over 65 had college education. Today, close to 12% are college grads, and that number will rise dramatically with the movement of baby boomers toward retirement.

The growth of older learner programs, not unlike adult education in general, is somewhat unpredictable because it is not the result of a coordinated national effort, government policy, or public expenditure of money. Umbrella organizations like the EIN and Shepherd's Centers of America conduct workshops and offer support services to groups that want to establish programs. In 1992, the American Society on Aging (ASA) formed an Older Adult Education Network membership group and introduced a valuable newsletter, and NCOA has its Arts and Humanities Committee. Still, older adult education seems to be driven more by the changing demographics of an aging society than by the intention of any particular group.

Many senior education programs are taking on intergenerational and volunteer community service projects, suggesting that participants hold a broad view of self-actualization. Being of sevice to members of other generations and taking leadership positions in community organizations points to a different concept of personal fulfillment—communal belonging. This is particularly critical in light of societal concerns about justice between generations as reflected in national health-care policy debates and perceived conflicts over scarce funds for at-risk youth and the at-risk elderly.

How will other social institutions respond to the new generation of retirees who have unprecedented goals, expectations, resources, and creative and contributory powers? Lessons can be learned from educational organizations trying to meet the new seniors' wants and needs.

BIBLIOGRAPHY

Beckman, B. M., & Ventura-Merkel, C. (1992). *Community college programs for older adults: A resource directory of guidelines, comprehensive programming models, and selected programs.* Laguna Hill, CA: League for Innovation in the Community College and the American Association of Retired Persons.

Fischer, R. B., Blazey, M. L., & Lipman, H. T. (1992). *Students of the Third Age—university college programs for retired adults.* New York: Macmillan Publishing Company.

Greenberg, R. M. (1993). *Education for older adult learning, a selected, annotated bibliography.* Westport, CT: Greenwood Press.

Laslett, P. (1991). *A fresh map of life, the emergence of the third age.* Cambridge, MA: Harvard University Press.

Lowy, L., & O'Connor, D. (1986). *Why education in the later years?* Lexington, MA: Lexington Books.

Manheimer, R. J., Snodgrass, D., & Moskow-McKenzie, D. (1995). *Older adult education: A guide to research, policy, and programs.* Westport, CT: Greenwood Press.

Moskow-McKenzie, D., & Manheimer, R. J. (1994). *A guide to developing educational programs for older adults.* Asheville, NC: UNCA University Publications.

Peterson, D. A. (1983). *Facilitating education of older learners.* San Francisco, CA: Jossey-Bass.

Peterson, D. A., Thornton, J. E., & Birren, J. E. (Eds.). (1986). *Education and Aging.* Englewood Cliffs, NJ: Prentice-Hall.

Sherron, R. H., & Lumsden, D. B. (Eds.). (1990). *Introduction to educational gerontology* (3rd ed.). New York: Hemisphere Publishing Co.

Ageism and Discrimination

Thomas G. McGowan

Rhodes College

Social Dislocation   The loss or redefinition of social roles resulting in lowered social status and decreased social participation.
Social Organization   The structure of institutions and their interrelationships.
Stereotype   A belief, usually negative, based on a nonexistent or exceptional characteristic categorically attributed to all members of a particular group.
Stereotyping   The social psychological process of ignoring personal attributes (i.e., personality, character) and labeling individuals according to stereotypes based on group affiliation.

AGEISM is defined as the negative stereotyping and systematic devaluation of people solely because of their age. Robert Butler introduced the term in 1969 and in doing so provided a general conceptual basis for the study of age-based discrimination and related problems. Ageism is a complex phenomenon with historical, cultural, social, psychological, and ideological dimensions. In ageist cultures advanced biological aging is negatively defined and used as a basis for devaluing the social status of elders. This process of devaluation takes the form of interpersonal (micro) and institutional (macro) discrimination, examples of which include job discrimination, media stereotyping, intergenerational segregation, avoidance of contact, and condescending or abusive interpersonal treat-

ment. The emergence of ageist cultures is attributed to historical factors such as technological development, industrialization, economic competition, and changes in societal attitudes. Like other forms of discrimination, ageism involves a social psychological process by which personal attributes are ignored and individuals are labeled according to negative stereotypes based on group affiliation. In American society elders are stereotyped as rigid, physically unattractive, senile, unproductive, sickly, cranky, impoverished, and sexless. Gerontological research shows that these stereotypes are spurious—they are based on myths and are contradicted by empirical facts. The persistence of ageism is attributed to its roots in basic values, such as the glorification of youth, individualism, economic competition, and the reduction of human worth to economic utility. These values create a cultural environment in which the drawbacks of aging are emphasized, the benefits of aging are ignored, and individual elders are blamed for problems they have not created (for example, being unemployed due to job discrimination). The alleviation of ageism will require a broad social and cultural critique that goes beyond the bounds of traditional gerontology and its theoretical foundation in positivism and functionalism, perspectives that are incapable of supporting the rigorous analysis of value-laden topics such as ageism.

I. HISTORICAL EMERGENCE OF AGEISM

A. Industrialization and Social Organization

The multidisciplinary literature on aging explains the emergence of ageism largely in terms of changes in social organization resulting from industrialization and the growth of a market-based economy. During the nineteenth century advances in technology, public health, and medicine reduced infant mortality and increased life expectancy in the United States. Meanwhile, changing social patterns resulting from industrialization led to a decline in birth rates. Coupled with immigration restrictions introduced early in this century, these changes altered the age composition of the overall American population. Since 1900 the proportion of elders comprising the American population thus increased dramatically, giving rise to the emergence of an historically unprecedented demographic group—the elderly. This development created new demands on society and government and helped to redefine the meaning of old age in America.

According to some, industrialization was the most crucial factor in the historical emergence of ageism. The social status of elders is based on the organization of institutions such as the family, economy, and political system. In preindustrial, agricultural societies elders typically occupied positions of high social status due to their control of crucial resources, such as information, land, and political and familial authority. Industrialization fundamentally altered the organization of social institutions and with it the social position of elders. The advantage historically held by elders owing to many years of work experience was lost as methods of production became industrialized and machine operation requiring little skill and training became prevalent. The elders' superior experience was no longer an asset in a world distinguished by rapid social and technological change. Older people found their skills unwanted and encountered discrimination in the workplace. Elders seeking to keep their jobs or find new ones were brought into direct competition with young adults, who were considered by manufacturers to be better suited for the repetitive, unskilled tasks typical of factory production.

In the burgeoning market-based society of the late nineteenth and early twentieth centuries elders lost their traditional economic roles and thus the material basis for their social and cultural devaluation was laid. Workplace competition between young and old created intergenerational conflict that contributed to, and was itself promoted by, ageist stereotypes and existing discrimination. Job competition between old and young created the need for legislative regulation of employment rights based on age, reforms that inevitably favored the young at the expense of the old.

B. Cultural, Ideological, and Social Psychological Factors

Contributing to the historical rise of ageism was a shift in societal attitudes. Social historians argue that negative attitudes toward the elderly were widespread as early as the middle of the nineteenth century, and by the late nineteenth century the cultural characterization of elders had shifted from favorable to unfavorable. The rise in ageist attitudes coincided with rapid industrial and economic expansion and served the interests of business owners interested in having a young, poorly paid, malleable workforce. Some researchers contend that the emergence of ageist attitudes was ideological in nature for it legitimized age discrimination in the workplace. In a broad sense, negative attitudes served the ideological purpose of advancing the interests of dominant groups by devaluing the worthiness of elders and undermining the legitimacy of their political claims and social interests.

The rise in negative societal attitudes toward the elderly had a cultural as well as ideological component. Ageist attitudes are grounded in deeply rooted cultural beliefs and patterns, such as the glorification of youth, the conceptualization of the individual as a freestanding autonomous subject, the ideal of unfettered socioeconomic competition, and the reduction of human worth to economic calculus. These cultural values are implicit in common expressions such as "put up or shut up," "if you can't stand the heat get out of the kitchen," and "only the strong survive." Such beliefs and patterns penalize elders and encourage the reductionist perception of age-related social problems. For example, the tendency is to view problems experienced by elders as "individual problems" and to ignore their basis in historical, cultural, and social structures.

The tendency to blame the victim is an important component of ageism and other types of discrimination. If an elder is unhappy with a new living situation, cultural stereotypes encourage us to attribute the unhappiness to the elder's stubbornness or rigidity. This occurs in spite of the fact that the unhappiness may be perfectly justified given the circumstances. If an elder is bored, stereotypes dictate that it is the elder's personal problem for, after all, elders are noncreative and sluggish. Regardless of the root causes of social conditions, be they historical, cultural, or economic, the tendency is to hold the individual elder personally responsible for their problems. This tendency is related to the general difficulty that many of us have understanding people and situations in terms of the broader contexts that structure them.

The culturally rooted tendency to blame the victim is related to a key component of ageism—stereotyping. Stereotyping is a social psychological process in which negative attributes that may in fact exist in the case of a small percentage of group members are generalized and used to categorize all members of the group. For example, the fact that a small percentage of elders are frail and dependent is taken as a general attribute of being elderly. Thus, in spite of the fact that the majority of elders are not frail, "frailty" becomes a defining characteristic of being old. The personal characteristics of individual elders are then ignored and elders are labeled according to this negative stereotype based on their group affiliation. Stereotyping is discriminatory because it denies self-hood and devalues the ontological uniqueness of the individual. Stereotyping also provides a social psychological rationale for other types of discrimination, such as interpersonal avoidance and job discrimination.

When individual elders experience problems such as job loss, illness, or unmet housing needs, they are *individually* blamed for their distress. Yet the blaming process involves stereotyping and the *denial* of individual characteristics. The social situation of elders is thus paradoxical. Individual qualities are ignored as elders are perceptually lumped together under a general, derogatory category, yet individual elders are blamed for the fact that they are affected by problems they have not created.

The problems of negative attitudes and stereotyping are exacerbated by the power of electronic mass media. Elders are underrepresented in television, radio, and film productions and rarely appear in advertisements. When elders do appear in television programs, for example, their characterization is usually negative. Ironically, watching television is the single-most time-consuming leisure activity among elders in the United States, making them high-level consumers of images that devalue them through exclusion or negative characterization. [*See* LEISURE.]

II. SOCIAL DISLOCATION

A. Loss of Social Status

The foregoing description of the historical emergence of ageism, generally referred to as the modernization theory of ageism, illustrates how changes in social organization, combined with the cultural and ideological propagation of negative attitudes, created a brave new world for elders. Being old in the modern world is distinguished by greater quantity (increased life expectancy) and lower quality (social devaluation and discrimination). Modernization resulted in the social dislocation of elders—a process in which traditional social roles were lost and the social status of elders decreased as a result of fundamental changes in the organization of social institutions. For example, modernization altered the structure of the American family and the position of elders within it. The economic importance of the family declined as the economic base shifted from agricultural to industrial production. Family size was reduced, mobility increased, and the tendency for elders to live in residences aside from those of their children became common. Opportunities for intergenerational contact and involvement were thus reduced or redefined in terms other than those to which the elders were accustomed and from which they traditionally benefited. In a broad sense, the social status of elders was undermined as their traditional control of authority, information, and economic assets was lost. [*See* MODERNIZATION AND AGING.]

The general process of modernization thus fundamentally altered the position of elders in society. The process of social dislocation restricts elders' participation in mainstream social activity by redefining their economic and social roles. This occurs through job discrimination and through the age segregation of social relations. Decreased access to jobs denies elders the roles of worker and income earner and the personal, social, and economic benefits of such roles. Age segregation and the widespread avoidance of contact with elders also restricts elders' social participation. The most obvious example of this is the age-based organization of housing. Elders are encouraged to live among themselves in congregate or institutionalized settings, physically separated from neighborhoods and communities. Although this may increase interaction among elders in particular settings, it isolates them from the general community and restricts their intergenerational contact and social participation. Intergenerational relations are increasingly limited to market relations and to formal social relations such as those existing between social service providers and elders. The decline of opportunities for informal intergenerational contact results in the cultural marginalization of elders by situating them at the periphery of mainstream social activity. Young people are increasingly socialized without the benefit of having had a substantive intergenerational relationship. Youths thus have little experience to draw upon when they do come into contact with elders, increasing the likelihood that such contact will largely be oriented in terms of negative stereotypes internalized through socialization.

Social dislocation has important implications for elders at the social psychological level. Because people of all ages understand themselves largely in terms of their involvement and social relations with others, work and social activity are key elements in sustaining social psychological well-being. The loss of social and economic roles restricts access to self-affirming social experiences, thus threatening self-esteem. The ageist organization of society simply confirms through experience the cultural message that elders are worthless, burdensome, and expendable. It is no wonder that many elders have come to perceive themselves in terms of the negative cultural stereotypes that pervade society. This is a particularly disturbing aspect of ageism for it means that elders have become contributors to their own devaluation. Social dislocation diminishes social status, threatens self-esteem, and places elders at risk for a variety of health-related problems, both physical and social psychological.

B. Subculture and Minority Group Theory

The social dislocation of elders has led some researchers to argue that the elderly exist in a subculture distinct from that of mainstream society. This argument is partly based on the fact that elders living in congregate settings tend to hold common values, interests, and behavioral patterns distinct from those of mainstream or popular culture. Gerontologists have debated, however, whether it is theoretically valid to conceptualize the existence of the elderly in terms of a subculture. A related theoretical development conceptualizes the elderly as a minority group. Minority group theory argues that elders share a common

experience of social victimization through interpersonal and institutional discrimination. This view is consistent with Butler's initial conceptualization of ageism, in which explicit parallels between age-based discrimination and other forms of discrimination, such as racism and sexism, are made. However, minority group theory is undermined by the fact that, beyond the common variable of age, elders comprise an extremely heterogeneous social group consisting of people from different races, ethnic groups, socioeconomic strata, religions, and political parties. This diversity is reflected in the fact that in spite of their age-specific interests, elders have yet to form a coherent voting block that would allow them to influence national elections and political decision making in general. The political power of elders is instead manifested through specific, lobbying organizations consisting of subgroups of elders. [*See* POLITICAL ATTITUDES AND BEHAVIOR.]

Regardless of whether the elderly constitute a subculture or a minority group, it is clear that people of advanced age share unique and difficult conditions as members of modern society. In addition to managing losses brought on through natural, biological processes (for example, death of spouse, increased risk of illness), elders must contend with discrimination in virtually all aspects of society. These difficulties may be compounded when the effects of race, class, and gender are taken into account.

Practitioners and members of the aging network have created and implemented an extensive number of social support services designed to ensure a socially just living standard for elders. However, obstacles restrict the full utilization of these services, and the most needy are often among those who are unable to take advantage of available services. Empirical research documenting the nature and pervasiveness of ageism has contributed to the development of applied projects and social reforms aimed at its amelioration. The Age Discrimination and Employment Act outlaws age-based workplace discrimination, and retirement is no longer mandatory for federal government employees. In spite of these efforts, however, ageism remains a defining feature of our culture. For example, many employers admit to discrimination against elders, and unemployed elders report great difficulty finding employment. [*See* WORK AND EMPLOYMENT.] Although many elders enjoy a relatively good living standard in economic terms, elders are stigmatized by negative stereotypes and face the prospect of financial disaster in the event of long-term illness.

III. AGEISM AND GERONTOLOGY

A. Ageism and the Development of Gerontology

Today ageism is an important gerontological topic. However, this was not always the case. Despite the fact that ageism was culturally pervasive by 1900 (and some social historians argue, much earlier), gerontological research during the first half of the twentieth century focused primarily on senescence and the social and economic issues created by an aging population. The gerontological literature during this period is dominated by a concern over the "problem of aging." Aging was considered a social problem not because elders were being discriminated against but because an aging population meant increased demands on society and government, such as health care, housing, and other social services. It also meant intergenerational competition in the workplace. In short, an aging population was a problem because it meant sharing resources and providing services across a broader spectrum of society, something undesirable to those in positions of power and control.

Instead of viewing the unprecedented emergence of an elderly population as an historical accomplishment ripe with possibility, gerontologists instead conceptualized it as a social problem. This may be explained by the fact that from the time gerontology was founded (approximately 1903), its development followed a conservative course well within the boundaries of dominant culture. Like other fledgling social sciences, gerontology initially perceived itself as a positive science modeled on the methodology of biomedicine, thereby attaining credibility and material support. The biomedical modeling of gerontology gave priority to empirical, methodological, and practical concerns, discouraging the conceptualization of research problems along philosophical lines. This retarded the theoretical development of the discipline, systematically precluding the study of value-laden topics and questions concerning the "meaning" of aging. The limited degree of theoretical development that did take place followed functionalist social theory, a conservative theoretical perspective itself derived from biological

science. Functionalist theory conceptualizes society as an organism consisting of mutually dependent institutions. The emergence of an elderly population was thus conceptualized within gerontology in terms of its effect on existing institutions. The "problem of aging" was therefore not conceptualized from the perspective of the elderly but from the perspective of government agencies and other dominant social groups. Without the theoretical capacity to conceptualize the problems of aging from the perspective of the elderly, the social problem of ageism could not be "discovered." It is therefore not surprising that it took more than 60 years for gerontologists to explicitly conceptualize the problem of ageism and to treat it as a legitimate research topic.

B. Disengagement and Activity Theory

Although social dislocation was not explicitly conceptualized as a form of discrimination until the late 1960s, there were earlier attempts to make sense of the phenomenon. The most ambitious effort along these lines was the development of disengagement theory. Introduced in 1961, disengagement theory conceptualized social dislocation as a natural and positively functional social process. The social dislocation or disengagement of elders from social roles and institutions was explained as a mutually beneficial process stemming from biological and psychological decline. According to the theory, disengagement benefits elders by relieving them of the stressful demands of performing work and social roles, roles that, due to the elders' biological decline, had become difficult to perform. The primary social benefit of disengagement, the theory argued, was that it created social and economic opportunities for younger adults and filled social positions with the most capable and highest functioning individuals.

Disengagement theory stimulated a widespread and long-standing debate in gerontology, particularly concerning its claims that disengagement is (a) the natural outcome of innate processes and (b) serves a positive social function. True to its theoretical grounding in functionalism, disengagement theory conceptualized social dislocation from the perspective of dominant social institutions and used an essentially biological argument to justify its theoretical claims. These and other features of disengagement theory were subjected to numerous critiques, and its antithesis, activity theory was eventually put forth. Activity theory argues that activity limits imposed by biological decline are minimal for most elders until the period immediately preceding death. Where disengagement is evident it is explained largely in terms of socially created obstacles to roles and social activity. The primary difference between the two theories is that activity theory departs from functionalism by considering historical, social, and cultural factors that structure and limit the social engagement of elders. In short, activity theory counters disengagement theory's naturalistic and biological explanation of social dislocation with a sociocultural explanation. However, activity theory implicitly defines human worth in terms of established cultural values, specifically, activity and productivity. Like disengagement theory, it fails to explore the philosophical meaning of human worth and the fact that elders, in spite of their activity level, deserve a social place within the cultural mainstream.

Given the positivist and functionalist tradition in gerontology it is not surprising that the first comprehensive attempt to make sense of the social dislocation of elders conceptualized it as a natural process based on inherent and inevitable biological and psychological processes. Positivism presupposes a closed-ended history, implying that the existing social order, the *is*, is the natural and hence correct form of social organization. From this perspective, the social dislocation of elders, already a cultural and social reality, could not be conceptualized as anything other than the normal outcome of a natural process. Empirical data indicating the contentment of some elders in their roleless social positions were interpreted by theorists as evidence of the benefits of disengagement. This interpretation ignored the fact that these were the feelings of elders who had disengaged within an *ageist* society. Considering this, the contentment or life satisfaction expressed by elders could be interpreted as a product of the fact that it is less stressful to conform to the dominant social order than it is to actively oppose it.

The identification of ageism as a social problem required a basic theoretical shift within gerontology. Specifically, the acknowledgment of ageism as a gerontological topic required the ability to conceptualize the problem of aging from the perspective of those who had aged. This presupposed the theoretical transcendence of functionalism and a shift toward humanist theories capable of supporting the empirical study of explicitly value-laden topics. It is not surprising that the study of ageism became an explicit gerontological topic only after the social sciences and American society experienced a revolt against the functionalist paradigm. In addition to legitimating the study of ageism, the importance of Butler's introduction of the concept was that it legitimated the conceptual and empirical study of the *meaning* of aging as it was being experienced by elders themselves. Butler's conceptualization of ageism thus had symbolic as well as practical importance for gerontologists—it signaled a shift in the conceptualization of the *problem of aging* from the perspective of researchers and policy makers to the perspective of people who encounter ageism on a routine basis.

C. Conceptualizing Ageism

Like most gerontological topics, the study of ageism is cross-disciplinary, and its conceptualization and empirical study differ according to the orientation of the researcher. Psychologists, for example, emphasize the attitudinal component of ageism, whereas sociologists tend to focus on the importance of social dislocation. However, regardless of disciplinary orientation, the study of ageism is culture bound and is therefore implicitly influenced by cultural factors. This should be kept in mind when designing projects or interpreting research findings. The researcher who believes that cultural influences can be transcended methodologically is mistaken. Only through the rigorous theoretical scrutiny of concepts can one effectively address the problems presented by studying ageism from within the bounds of an ageist culture. Even when a responsible theoretical effort is made, the passing of time may reveal ageist assumptions that may only be apparent from the vantage point of history.

The study of ageism has been hampered by gerontology's widely acknowledged theoretical shallowness. This weakness is especially problematic in the case of ageism because ageism is a complex phenomenon with historical, cultural, social, psychological, and ideological dimensions. Since Butler provided a general conceptual definition of ageism, little has been done to specify the interrelationship of these various dimensions or to develop a general theory of ageism. This has resulted in the production of many research efforts that, in spite of their methodological soundness, have contributed little to our understanding of ageism and its amelioration.

The empirical study of ageism has been dominated by psychological research focused primarily on the description, documentation, and analysis of negative attitudes. These studies evidence that (a) negative attitudes against elders are widespread; (b) elders often view themselves negatively and may hold negative attitudes toward young people; and (c) in some cases providing factual knowledge to young adults will change their attitudes toward elders. The significance of this type of research is that it serves as a basis for the development of antiageist applied projects and interventions. These types of programs seek to combat ageism through consciousness raising and the manipulation of attitudes. However, the conceptualization of ageism as an attitudinal problem severely limits the potential impact of such programs by implicitly reducing the complex phenomenon of ageism to only one of its many dimensions. The fact that attitudes comprise only one dimension of ageism suggests that the attitude-manipulation strategy holds little promise for ameliorating ageism.

In contrast to the attitude-based intervention strategies are the increasing number of intergenerational programs involving direct, mutually beneficial contact *experiences* between elders and nonelders. These programs not only combat negative attitudes but serve to relocate elders in socially meaningful roles. Such programs therefore address the problem of social dislocation as well as negative stereotyping. They also provide rare intergenerational contact experiences for nonelders, allowing them to develop their understanding of aging and to practice intergenerational interaction.

Conceptual reductionism—the emphasis of one dimension of a concept to the exclusion of others—not only limits the potential effectiveness of applied, antiageist programs, it also invites misconception and misunderstanding of basic research findings. An example of this may be found in the literature on age integration, which describes how social dislocation may be addressed by organizing homogeneous, elderly communities. Research shows that elders living in communities or apartment buildings with high concentrations of elders are likely to report high levels of life satisfaction. Gerontologists attribute this to the fact that living in an environment consisting of people with similar life experiences provides a feeling of community, support, and social acceptance generally not found by elders in society. Depending on the type of situation, elders may have greater access to recreational and social activities, new opportunities to form relationships, and access to new social roles. The high life satisfaction of age-congregated living is attributed to the social integration that they provide. [*See* LIFE SATISFACTION.]

The interpretation of this research, however, will differ according to the way the meaning of ageism is conceptualized. From a functionalist perspective, the logic of socially integrating elders by segregating them from mainstream society appears conceptually sound. Indeed, the empirical measurement of high life satisfaction among elders may be cited as evidence of the strategy's viability. However, from a humanist perspective, the elders' high level of life satisfaction may be interpreted as a by-product of ageism. Many African-American college students, for example, prefer to attend traditionally black colleges and universities because the homogeneity of these campuses allows them to relax and avoid expending energy concerning themselves with actions and incidents that might be perceived as inappropriate from the perspective of the dominant culture. Perhaps elders residing in age-congregated communities are expressing a similar sentiment. Living among themselves they do not have to contend as often with the ageist behavior of nonelders that would otherwise devalue them and undermine their self-esteem.

The creation of homogeneous elderly communities is a strategy that avoids the deeper social issue of ageism by applying a reductionist conceptual definition of integration. It may be more accurate to describe the conceptual meaning of integration as it is applied in such cases as a process of *intragration,* for it refers to interaction and social relations within a single group (elders) and not to the building of relations between or among members of different groups. This approach may in fact reinforce ageism by confirming in practice the cultural stereotypes that distinguish elders as different and not suited for mainstream social participation.

Like disengagement theory, the "integration through segregation" strategy of dealing with social dislocation implicitly assumes that social dislocation is a natural fact that requires an adaptive response on behalf of elders. In the case of disengagement theory, elders are supposed to adapt by accepting new roles of low social status. In the case of integration through segregation, elders are expected to create subcommunities in which they can enjoy a separate but equal "socially meaningful" existence relative to that experienced in the dominant culture. Underlying both of these examples is the flawed functionalist assumption that ageism is a natural or necessary fact—some*thing* other than the historical, cultural, and social construct it in fact is. Would elders prefer segregated living if mainstream society and the cultural environment were nonageist? Integration through age segregation implicitly accepts ageism as a social fact to which elders must adapt.

In spite of the general condition of conceptual reductionism in the study of ageism, examples of theoretically comprehensive research do exist. Among these the contributions of Gerald Gruman are perhaps most instructive, distinguishesd as they are by his emphasis on cultural factors, historical detail, and theoretical rigor. The anthro-gerontological classic *Number our Days* by Barbara Myerhoff and Edmund Sherman's *Reminiscence and the Self in Old Age* are also good examples of nonreductionist gerontological research. These works conceptualize aging from the experiential perspective of elders and do so by way of an integrative, historically conscious and culturally astute theoretical orientation.

IV. THEORETICAL CONSIDERATIONS

A. Personhood and the Anthropological Dimension of Ageism

The gerontological study of ageism is strong regarding the empirical analysis of macrolevel forces but weak regarding the theoretical and empirical analysis of interpersonal and microlevel phenomena. Too little is known about the *meaning* of aging and ageism, and this contributes to reductionism at the conceptual and applied levels of analysis. Developing a theoretical understanding of the meaning of aging allows one to begin conceptualizing ageism in a manner that reflects the interests and experiences of elders, clearing the way for the design of interventions that speak directly to their concerns.

Since Butler's introduction of the concept of ageism, research has increasingly reflected the interests of elders. However, these interests are often evident only at the general level of research design and not at the conceptual level. The result is the production

of well-intentioned interventions that miss the mark due to conceptual reductionism. This is precisely the problem with the attitudinal approach to ageism. An important theoretical step toward advancing the study of ageism is to reconceptualize the phenomenon in terms of the experiences and understanding of those who encounter it as a defining factor in their lives. In the words of Betty Friedan, we must break through the *mystique of age* to study the *personhood of age*.

In a manner similar to her analysis in *The Feminine Mystique,* Friedan argues that the reality of aging, and ageism, is distorted by the internalized images that we have of aging. Like the typical woman of several decades ago, elders today live in a culture that defines the reality of their condition in a way that contrasts sharply with their actual lived experience. The woman of the 1950s was supposed to be content serving others in her role as wife, mother, and housekeeper. When she experienced a lack of meaning in her life it was her psychological wellness rather than the legitimacy of gender stereotypes that was called into question. However, when women began to accept the validity of the meaning of what they actually experienced, in spite of its divergence from cultural stereotypes, they were able to see the stereotypes as mystifying and distortive—as a *mystique*.

Elders must contend with cultural stereotypes that not only devalue them socially but that teach them to devalue themselves. The self-devaluation of elders is frequently observed in field situations involving direct contact. Many elders are quick to interject self-deprecating comments such as "Why do you want to interview me, my life wasn't important," or "I am an old has-been, I have nothing interesting to say." These people are repeating the cultural mantra of ageism taught to them by the media and confirmed in their interpersonal experiences.

Personhood refers to the experiential reality of the elder's condition and daily existence. Focusing on personhood shifts the focus—of elder and gerontologist alike—away from the mystifying and distorting attitudes that confuse self and social understanding toward a clearer and more valid understanding of the meaning of aging and ageism. The study of personhood gives voice to the experiences of elders providing a basis for the development of a nonageist cultural understanding of aging and ageism.

Ageism is unique in that, unlike other types of discrimination (for example, racism or sexism), age discrimination is perpetrated and propagated by people who will someday be old. People participating in ageism are thus contributing to their own eventual victimization. This speaks to the fact that young and middle-aged adults do not live in conscious awareness of their aging or their ageist behavior.

Much has been written about biological and psychological developmental stages, but too little is understood about the existential meaning of the experience of aging. The denial and dread of aging has been observed by a number of gerontologists, but little effort has been spent exploring the philosophical questions posed by the phenomenon. Developing a theoretical understanding of the meaning of aging is a precondition for advancing the theoretical and empirical study of this and other phenomena directly related to ageism.

Our lack of cultural understanding regarding the meaning of aging may be likened to the anthropologist's understanding of the "other." Like the anthropologist, our understanding of the "other" (in this case, the elderly), is prestructured by our cultural situation (in this case, ageism). The understanding of the "other" grows as the anthropologist increasingly shares the cultural world of the "other" through shared experience. Understanding is gained through participation in common practices that presuppose culturally embedded meanings. The understanding attained by the anthropologist through shared experience is thus a practical understanding.

Short of arguing that elders exist in a subculture, it is nevertheless true that their cultural situation vis-à-vis nonelders, particularly youth, is unique. The world of meaning and practice in which elders were socialized no longer exists. A gulf of understanding thus separates youth from elders in the sense that both were socialized differently with regard to historical meanings, cultural values, social norms, and routine practices. Elders are accused of "not keeping up with the times" and for, in many cases, preferring their "world out of time" to the present. Few realize that changing with the times presupposes a process of self-rejection involving the discrediting of the practices and meanings that shaped the self through socialization—a process not easily justified. In premodern societies the culture and social norms changed extremely slowly. Consequently, there was little difference, if any, between the socialization of elders and the socialization of youth decades later. In rapidly changing

modern state societies the opposite is the case. Elders and youth are socialized into dramatically different social realities. Elders are thus victimized by rapid social change in the sense that their social status is, in many respects, that of a cultural outsider. This means that in modern (or postmodern, as some prefer) societies, understanding elders has essentially become an anthropological task. Overcoming ageism will require, in large part, the cultivation of the anthropological ability to understand elders in terms of the ontological conditions of their existence, both past and present. The development of such an ability presupposes intergenerational relationships involving shared practices and the systematic creation of social settings and contexts conducive to such relationships.

In addition to the importance of personhood and the anthropological task of understanding elders, researchers must theoretically account for the ideological component of ageism. An ideology is an action-oriented belief system that promotes the organization of institutions in a manner that favors the interests of particular social groups. Although age-based discrimination is often unintentional, deliberate discrimination does occur, and when it does it serves to advance the interests of nonelderly groups by devaluing the claims and interests of elders. For example, social historians have shown that ageism is particularly acute during periods of economic scarcity and intense competition. The cultivation of understanding through the creation of intergenerational institutions must contend with ideological forces that promote the maintenance of the status quo. To state it bluntly, certain groups have an interest in maintaining ageism.

Finally, ageism must also be theoretically understood as a moral issue. Indeed, the introduction of the concept by Butler, as well as the commitment of many gerontologists and practitioners to ameliorate ageism, may be viewed as a humanist attempt to alleviate a morally repugnant social phenomenon. The humanist conceptualization of ageism argues that the social status and quality of life of elders should not be devalued as a result of economic, social, or technological developments. Elders are to be considered dignified human beings worthy of respect and social place.

A growing number of gerontologists agree that a more philosophical and theoretically rigorous understanding of ageism is needed in order to advance its empirical study and cultural amelioration. Developing such an understanding will require the assistance of the real experts on ageism, the elders who experience it every day of their lives. It is the burden of gerontology to develop theoretical and methodological strategies for tapping into this expert knowledge and experiential understanding. By directly sharing the personal experiences of elders through intergenerational experience, nonelders may begin to understand the meaning of aging and ageism. Without such understanding there exists little hope of advancing the study of ageism or ameliorating ageism through applied interventions.

BIBLIOGRAPHY

Allport, G. W. (1954). *The nature of prejudice.* New York: Doubleday.

Amir, Y. (1969). Contact hypothesis in ethnic relations. *Psychological Bulletin, 71,* 319–342.

Butler, R. N. (1969). Ageism: Another form of bigotry. *The Gerontologist, 9,* 243–246.

Cohen, L. (1994). Old age: cultural and critical perspectives. *Annual Review of Anthropology, 23,* 137–58.

Estes, C. L., Binney, E. A., & Culbertson, R. A. (1992). The gerontological imagination. *International Journal of Aging and Human Development, 35, 1,* 49–65.

Gruman, G. J. (1978). Cultural origins of present-day "age-ism": The modernization of the life cycle. In S. F. Spicker, K. M. Woodward, & D. D. Van Tassel (Eds.), pp. 359–394. *Aging and the elderly: Humanistic perspectives in gerontology.* Atlantic Highlands, NJ: Humanities Press.

Myerhoff, B. (1990). *Number our days.* New York: Touchstone.

Palmore, E. (1990). *Ageism.* New York: Springer.

Reinharz, S., & Rowles, G. D. (Eds.). (1988). *Qualitative gerontology.* New York: Springer.

Sherman, E. (1991). *Reminiscence and the self in old age.* New York: Springer.

Winch, P. (1990). *The idea of a social science and its relation to philosophy* (2nd ed.). Atlantic Highlands, NJ: Humanities Press.

Age Stratification

Matilda White Riley

National Institute on Aging

Age Age refers to both people and their surrounding social structures. For people, age marks how much of the lifetime has so far been lived. In social structures, age denotes criteria both for performing in roles and for entering and leaving them. It operates in complex ways to locate people of every age in society.

Age-Related Roles Positions in social structures (e.g., schools, nursing homes) where age (or some substitute for age—reading readiness, frailty) is used as a criterion for permitting (or proscribing) role occupancy, entry, or exit, or for defining role expectations or sanctions for performance.

Age Strata The rough divisions by age of people from younger to older within a society or group. Age strata reflect socially significant aspects of people and are only partly defined by biology.

Aging Aging consists of interacting biological, psychological, and social processes that start with birth (or conception) and end with death. The term is widely used to refer to the biopsychosocial changes in the later stages of the life course.

Cohort A set of people born at approximately the same period of time, or entering together into a particular system, such as a hospital, school, or community of scientists. Members of a cohort thus experience a common slice of history. Through "cohort succession" (or "cohort flow"), new members are continually born into a society (or entering a group), move up through the age strata as they grow older, eventually die, and are replaced by members of oncoming cohorts.

Structural Lag When people grow up and grow old in antiquated social structures that provide inadequate opportunities or incentives, the mismatch is known as "structural lag." In aging research, the concept is useful for understanding the failure of firms, families, and other social structures to provide rewarding roles for the large numbers of comparatively healthy people who are living longer and growing older in new ways.

At any given time, every society—like most social groups—is roughly divided into strata (or categories) of people who differ in age and who participate in social structures appropriate for particular ages. As a conceptual scheme, **AGE STRATIFICATION** is used in gerontology for studying the characteristics and behavior of older people at particular periods of time, and for understanding their roles (or places) in the community, the workplace, the family, and other social institutions. This heuristic scheme and the concrete phenomena it represents point to potentials for enhancing the situations of older people in the future. The strata of people and the age-related roles, as described in this scheme, are among the bases of social organization that shape sociocultural, psychological, and biological life and the historical course of humankind.

I. OVERVIEW

What are the places of older people in society? What traces remain today of the *gerontocracy* of preliterate

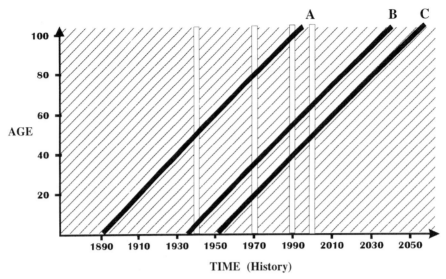

Figure I   The aging and society framework.

societies where power and deference were often accorded to elders because of their wisdom and experience? What tendencies toward *juvenocracy* (Robert Merton's term) are creeping in when, for example, large cohorts of younger people dominate all strata in the science establishment? or the political system? How long will older people be relatively subservient to the power and influence of the middle-aged? Why are older people often treated as incapable and dependent, when in fact most are capable and strive for independence? What are the facts about differences and similarities between older people and younger people—in health, intellectual functioning, ability to cope with problems, and many other respects? In what respects are older people similar to younger people? What accounts for the differences and similarities? How do individuals experience, adapt, or contribute to societal patterns?

To begin to answer such questions requires a conceptual scheme that simplifies, selects, and defines key components, and shows the relationships among them.

A. Conceptual Framework

Age stratification provides such a scheme for use in interpreting or designing particular studies. However, it is only part of a larger conceptual framework that is diagrammed in Figure 1. We can start with the many diagonal bars as representing cohorts of people. Each cohort consists of people born in the same time period, who are aging—that is, moving across time and upward with age. [*See* COHORT STUDIES.] (Called the "aging and society paradigm," this conceptual framework, foreshadowed by Karl Mannheim and S. N. Eisenstadt in 1952, has been developing for three decades and continues to develop in the work of Matilda Riley, Anne Foner, and many colleagues.)

It is within this larger framework that the vertical bars locate both the roles and the people in the age-stratification scheme. At any given time (such as 1990), each vertical bar represents the age-related role opportunities and normative expectations provided in the various structures, (e.g., in schools for the young, in work organizations for those in the middle years, in nursing homes for the old, in families for all ages, etc.). In addition, each vertical bar directs attention to the people alive at that time, arranged in strata from the youngest at the bottom to the oldest at the top.

In referring to the age strata of people, these vertical bars have a special feature: each bar produces a cross-section slice through all the diagonals—that is, a slice through the coexisting cohorts of people. That means that those in the several strata differ not only in age, but also in the cohorts to which they belong and the associated historical experiences. This feature of age stratification has far-reaching implications for the people involved and for society as a whole.

Cross-section slices also have dynamic implications for both people and roles as we imagine the vertical bars moving through time. Comparison of two or more selected verticals (like A, B, and C) reflects changes in age-related roles as, with the passage of time the society undergoes structural alterations in the economy, in science and the arts, in moral values, in political or religious life, in public health, and so forth. And while the roles in the surrounding structures are changing, the people in the age strata are also changing. Those who will be old 20 years from now are not the same people who are currently old: the currently old will be replaced by oncoming cohorts of new people, with experiences very different from their predecessors.

In short, the full aging and society framework includes the interplay between two "dynamisms" (or sets of processes): (a) the changing patterns of human lives in successive cohorts and (b) changes in society and its age-related roles and structures. Within this larger compass, age stratification can be thought of as taking snapshots of these dynamisms as they portray age strata of people and age-appropriate roles at successive periods of time.

For any given study, parts of the scheme can be selected as useful. The focus can be either macrolevel (on the total society); mesolevel (on groups and structures, of which roles are the smallest unit); or microlevel (on individuals, as active participants within the strata).

Also to be noted is the fact that many terms in the conceptual framework are often used loosely in popular discourse, or given conflicting definitions by the several disciplinary schools that contribute to gerontology. Yet, clear definition and standardization of terms are essential to scientific advance in the study of age.

B. Age versus Other Bases of Social Stratification

The character of age stratification becomes clearer when contrasted with other forms of stratification. Despite many common elements, age stratification is strikingly unique because the underlying processes of aging and cohort succession are among the few social processes that are universal as long as the society endures. These processes are also inevitable, although they can be modified: as through evolutionary changes in the organism, interventions in the aging process, or infusion of new people through immigration.

1. Enduring Characteristics
Certain other important forms of stratification are based on human characteristics such as sex, race, or ethnic background, which, unlike age, do not ordinarily change as members of a cohort grow older. Within age strata, however, such characteristics produce subdivisions as, for example, older Blacks differ substantially from older Whites, and differences by gender are so pronounced that age differences must often be analyzed separately for males and for females.

2. Class
Age strata are also significantly subdivided by social class. Because class stratification, based on economic and educational criteria, has dominated much of the sociological literature, age stratification is often mistakenly confused with class stratification. Nevertheless, each form is separate and distinct, although there are common elements. As with age strata, solidarities are likely to form within classes or conflicts to break out between classes, and members of a cohort can be mobile from one class to another. However, unlike growing older, which can never turn back, class mobility can move either up or down. And unlike age mobility, class mobility is neither inevitable nor universal. Age strata of people are found in every society; but the association between age-related roles and the differing rewards provided by social classes varies with deeply rooted political, economic, and moral institutions of particular societies.

3. Ideology
Questions are often raised about whether age *should* be replaced by other bases of stratification. There are controversies over whether opportunities or rewards in particular structures, such as health-care systems, should be allocated on the basis of *need*, rather than age. Other controversies contend that *achievement*, rather than age, should control tenure in a job, for example; or that *functional capacity* should serve as the basis for promotions. Such issues, inherent in age stratification, require judgments often involving entrenched values rather than simple empirical results from research on age.

C. Pervasive Themes

In examining details of age stratification as a conceptual scheme, six central themes are noteworthy:

1. **Dual focus** on both people and roles in social structures. Of course, the two are separable only in the abstract: In reality one cannot exist without the other. Conceptual attention is optimally focused on both and on their interdependence, as they influence each other through complex processes and mechanisms (see section IV). [*See* COHORT STUDIES.] But conceptual attention to each one separately is essential for understanding how people change—or fail to change—in special ways that differ from the ways in which schools, firms, nursing homes, or other social structures are changing.

2. **Dynamics** are inherent in every component of age stratification. Driven by the universal processes of aging and cohort flow, the age strata cannot even be imagined as people "standing still" while social change is occurring around them.

3. **Age interconnectedness** permeates age stratification. Older people must be understood in relation to other people of all ages, and age structuring of roles for particular ages implicates age criteria for other ages also.

4. **Diversity** characterizes every aspect of both people and roles. For example, older people range widely from the frail to the robust, and their varied roles accord both extreme affluence and dire need. To speak of "the" old people or to use averages in describing them statistically obscures the underlying heterogeneity. Nevertheless, for highlighting features of age that transcend the complexities, average or modal patterns are often useful.

5. **Alterability** allows room for interventions aimed to prevent or reverse such possible decrements of old age as economic deprivation, chronic ill health, memory loss, low self-esteem, and withdrawal from active participation in social and economic roles. Unlike their relatively unchanging genetic background, people's lives in all their aspects are responsive to changes in society. A major use of the age-stratification scheme is to identify potentials for enhancing the situations of older people in the future.

6. The **broad reach** of age stratification extends across biological, psychological, and social disciplines, as aging is itself a "biopsychosocial" process. Moreover, although most examples cited here refer to the contemporary United States, the conceptual framework is being used to identify its universal features through studies of societies and cultures throughout the world and across historical (and anticipated future) time.

II. AGE STRATA OF PEOPLE

Focusing first on people as we imagine them apart from roles, age stratification is important for recognizing age differences and similarities among them at given periods of time, and for examining current interactions and relationships among those who differ or are similar in age.

A. Age Composition of the Population

1. Numbers of People in the Age Strata

Figure 2 shows at a glance the demographic divisions of the population into age categories. When given further meaning in the age-stratification scheme, these categories form the basis for age strata (the cross-section "slices" from Figure 1). A single age pyramid, as for 1955, shows the numbers of people in each stratum and the position of older strata in the population as a whole. The contours of the pyramid, with more people at the base than at the apex, reflect historical increases in the annual number of births as well as increases in mortality with age. The subdivision by sex begins to indicate the diversity within strata: at the youngest ages males slightly outnumber females, but at the oldest ages this ratio is reversed.

By comparing two or more pyramids, as between 1955 and (estimated for) 2010, changes over time in age composition become apparent. Between these dates, the baby boom cohorts have moved from the bottom to the middle, and as they replace the previous incumbents of the middle strata, they change the shape of the pyramid. Most striking of all are the increased sizes of the oldest strata—even requiring the addition of a still older stratum, the "90+." These added strata reflect the unprecedented increases in longevity over this century. The presence of more females than males in the middle-aged and older strata has yielded the popular description of the elderly as a "population of women." (In order to focus on age composition, the overall growth of the population in every

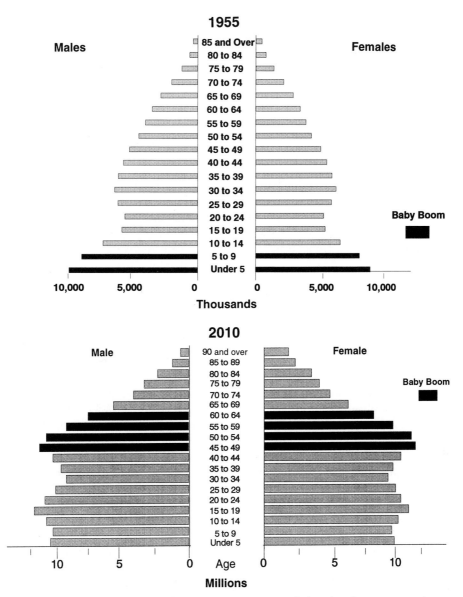

Figure 2 Age composition of the population: Age pyramids for selected years 1955 and Thousands 2010. (From Taeuber, C. M. (1992). *Sixty-five Plus in America*. (Current Population Reports P23-178RV). Washington, DC: U.S. Bureau of the Census.

age stratum is not shown in the chart for 2010— different scales are used in the two pyramids.) [*See* DEMOGRAPHY.]

2. Age Differences

Essential as such demographic data are, however, they only begin to tell the age-stratification story. The rigid chronological boundaries separating one stratum from the next cannot show (for either age pyramid) the wide heterogeneity in physical and mental characteristics, attitudes, and social behaviors (at age 65, e.g., some people resemble those at age 45, while others resemble those at age 85). Moreover, the bare facts in the pyramids can scarcely hint at the countless differences (as well as similarities) between older and younger people. For example, current age differences are widely reported on the average in such physiological functions as nerve conduction velocity, heart output, maximum breathing capacity, and multiple rather than simple diseases; and in such behavioral functions as sensation and perception, complex sensorimotor responses, and ease of learning and remembering. Socially, many older people are constrained by invidious "ageist" attitudes (in health care, e.g., as compared with younger people with identical symptoms, they are more likely to be given a poor prognosis for recovery, and to be given palliative rather than interventionist treatment). Certainly no age pyramid can uncover the potential capacities of old people (or children) that had remained hidden until uncovered through scientific experiments in prevention or rehabilitation.

B. Age Strata versus Aging

A central point to remember is that all such age differences across strata are "current," pertaining to the particular times at which they were observed. When this caveat is overlooked, inferences drawn from current differences can lead to a serious "cross-section fallacy": that is, erroneously interpreting cross-section age differences as if they described the process of aging.

How such fallacies occur is suggested by referring back to Figure 1 as it contrasts age differences in strata (the verticals) with differences associated with aging (the diagonals). Each diagonal traces a cohort of the *same* people as they age over many decades of time. For example, in cohort B those 55 years old in 1990 were born in 1935 in the aftermath of the Great Depression and the prelude to World War II; these people will not reach 75 until the year 2010, when the surrounding structures will predictably be quite different. By contrast, each vertical shows for a single period of time (such as 1990) a cross-section of *different* people, who are entirely unlike in age, in the cohorts to which they belong, and the structures in which they are currently participating.

Yet, absurd as it seems, misinterpretations of ross-section differences in strata to mean differences in aging abound. Some early studies even compared old people in nursing homes with their young doctors, and assumed that the differences described the aging process! More sophisticated studies, falling

into this trap, have perpetuated false stereotypes of universal and inevitable decline because of aging. Of course, everyone dies, and certain biological declines usually precede death in human beings, as they do in animals. Yet some putative stereotypes, like the early belief that intelligence declines after age 20, have been corrected: they arose simply because those in the younger strata, members of more recent cohorts, were better educated than were their predecessors. Other stereotypes have been traced, not to biological aging, but to diminished social contacts, loss of employment, reduced sense of personal control, or inadequate health care. A number of stereotypes of inevitable aging decline are being challenged through experiments demonstrating that certain decrements of old age can often be restored or reversed through social interventions (the theme of alterability). [See AGEISM AND DISCRIMINATION.]

The danger of such fallacies underscores the differing implications of research findings on age strata and those on aging processes—each useful in its own right. Moreover, the reminder that different age strata contain members of different cohorts emphasizes that the older people being studied today are not the same people who will be old in the future.

C. Age Stratification of People

As an aid to probing the complex significance of cross-section patterns, Figure 3 shows the conceptual components of the age-stratification scheme. As one part of the scheme, the diagram locates the age strata of people in the two small boxes at the left. These boxes, which require meticulous definition, direct attention to the people of particular ages (cf. their demographic base in Figure 2 above) and to their behaviors (acts) and capacities.

I. People, Acts, and Capacities

In studies of any particular society or group, age may be viewed either as a property of individuals, or as a collective property of particular age strata that differ from one another in size and composition (by gender, ethnicity, etc.). Members of different strata differ in past experiences undergone or future experiences anticipated, and they vary widely in ways of acting or thinking. They also vary in the capacity or motivation

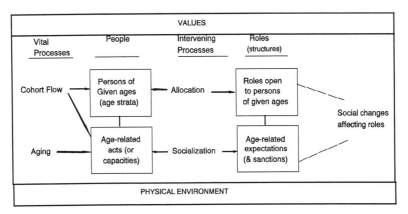

Figure 3 Components of Age Stratification.

to perform. For example, some older people may be less responsive than younger people to technical retraining for various reasons, perhaps because they have forgotten the strategy for learning or because they start with a generally poorer educational background. In addition, capacity and motivation are markedly contingent on role opportunities (to be described in section III).

2. Sources of Age Strata

Shown at the left of Figure 3 are the underlying processes of cohort flow and aging that impinge directly on people to form the age strata at given periods of time. As new cohorts of people are born and begin their journey through life, they continuously replace the cohorts that preceded them through the successive life stages. This process of cohort flow (or cohort succession) yields the numbers and kinds of people in each of the strata at any particular moment. Meanwhile, the biopsychosocial process of aging produces changes within cohorts as they move from one stratum to the next, affecting their capacity and performance at every age. (Multidisciplinary implications of the aging process are explicated in the work on behavioral medicine, as by David Hamburg). To repeat: the age strata of people are cross-section slices through various cohorts at differing stages of the life course.

D. Age Relationships

Cross-section views of age strata are useful for understanding not only age differences, but also the rela-

tionships among people within and across age strata. Some studies focus on interpersonal networks according to the relative ages of a person's role partners (such as spouse, friends, parents, or offspring). Other studies focus on age-based movements or groups, such as those espousing certain political or ethical ideologies. [*See* Network Analysis.]

Studies of relationships across or within age strata often report strong mutual support (as between generations in a family, or among age peers in Alzheimer's support groups). But relationships that are hostile can sometimes erupt into open conflict, as when parents and offspring contend over ownership of property, or when young newcomers to the political scene rebel against the power of their elders. Such conflict can be a source of change in families and societies, an aspect of the dynamic theme that is intrinsic to the age stratification of people.

III. AGE-RELATED ROLES IN SOCIAL STRUCTURES

Age strata of people take on full meaning only when viewed in their relationship to the surrounding social roles with their built-in age criteria (as foreshadowed back in 1942 by the work of sociologist Talcott Parsons and anthropologist Robert Linton). It is these roles that help to shape the thoughts and actions of people as role incumbents, and are in turn further shaped by incumbents who often modify existing roles or create new ones.

A. Age Structuring of Roles

The details of the age-stratification scheme (Figure 3) call attention to the meanings of age-related roles. The two boxes at the right (which correspond to the people in the age strata and their acts and capacities—pictured at the left) refer to these roles. The upper box indicates the numbers and kinds of roles open (or closed) to people of particular ages (e.g., the number of jobs open to workers under age 20 or over age 60), and the lower box indicates the associated age-related expectations, resources, and sanctions (punishments and rewards) for performance.

1. Age Criteria for Entry, Exit, and Performance

Just as age divides the population into strata, age is built into social structures in the form of "criteria" for occupying, entering, or relinquishing certain roles. Age criteria also govern how roles are performed: they define role expectations as to appropriate behavior and control the facilities and rewards (or punishments) for performance.

Age criteria operate in complex and subtle ways. Sometimes chronological age is used *directly* as a criterion stated in laws, regulations, or contracts. For example, until a certain age a person cannot marry, leave school, drive, drink alcohol, vote, or become president. Beyond a certain age, a person may be entitled to national health insurance or special tax advantages, or may be required to retire. Age also operates *indirectly* as a criterion through association with other factors. For example, biological stage limits motherhood, educational requirements affect the minimum age of entry into certain jobs, or the requirement of rapid reaction time or extreme physical exertion tend to exclude the aged from certain occupations.

Another important distinction is between "normative" and "factual" age criteria. Many criteria are normative: they indicate what people of given ages *ought to* do or think. For example, role expectations differ for an infant son and a son in his teens, or for a young worker and the worker nearing the end of her career. Normative criteria reflect the underlying values of a particular society or subgroup. Other criteria reflect *factual* regularities or average patterns of "what everyone does or thinks" in particular age strata. For example, a person may be judged as "too old" to become a foster parent, or to enter medical school, or to participate in certain sporting activities.

Of course, the existence of age criteria does not imply passive compliance with expectations. Any role incumbent is an active participant, and may have the motivation and capacity to challenge existing age-based criteria. In turn, the age-related expectations, supports, facilities for performance, rewards, and punishments are contributed by other people (role partners or "agents"), such as nursing aides for the role of elderly patient, or bureaucrats for the role of pension recipient. At the same time, persons are not only influenced by roles, but can themselves exert influence. Nursing home residents often resist succumbing to the expected dependency, and by being independent may reshape the role itself by altering the expectations and responses of their caregivers.

2. Underlying Processes

How does this age structuring of roles come about? What enables many age-related roles to persist despite the succession of incumbents? What brings about changes in roles? Within the age-stratification scheme, two sets of processes affecting roles and role criteria are indicated by the arrows in Figure 3: those connecting roles with people in the age strata (center of the diagram), and those emanating from broad social changes (at the far right).

a. Intervening Processes Affecting roles as well as people are the dual processes of *allocation* and *socialization.* As new cohorts of people are continually replacing their predecessors in the age strata, and as role structures change, allocation is a set of mechanisms for the continual assignment and reassignment of people to the appropriate age-related roles. Allocative processes are in part initiated by individual role incumbents themselves, and in part they operate through various agencies such as personnel managers or college admission directors and through such allocative devices as pension plans, certificates of birth or death, high school diplomas, professional licenses, lists of available jobs, or insurance rules for hospital admissions. Socialization involves learning and relearning by incumbents as they move into new roles (such as college student, army inductee, or fast-food jobs for retirees). Socialization also involves a complementary set of processes for teaching individuals in each age stratum how to perform new roles, to adjust to changing roles, or to relinquish old ones. In short, allocation helps to balance the numbers and kinds of people at particular ages with the roles open at these ages; and socialization helps to balance the training of new recruits to meet the role expectations that these recruits themselves are often pressing to change.

In the age-stratification scheme these two processes are given special meaning: both operate at every age, and both are reciprocal, with people being acted upon and also taking an active part themselves (note the two-directional arrows in the diagram). For example, just as the young mother takes an active part in socializing her baby, the baby in turn takes an active part in socializing the mother. Or, just as older workers receive retraining from corporations, they also influence the character of the retraining programs.

b. Social Change Processes Quite apart from the influence of incumbent people, role structures have been undergoing manifold changes of their own, ranging from movement of many jobs overseas, growth of the service sector, development of federal and private pension plans, to reorganization of families (e.g., grandparents become surrogate parents). Such structural alterations follow change principles that involve the entire social fabric (suggested at the far right of Figure 3); and the sources of shifts in numbers and kinds of age-related roles and their built-in age criteria are myriad. Many of these shifts can be traced to broad social, economic, scientific, and other historical changes (including changes in values and in the physical environment); to deliberate interventions from governments, leaders, or pressure groups; or to changes in one structure that affect related structures. Because of the importance of age-related roles for both individuals and society, the underlying processes are receiving fresh attention in gerontology (and are the special focus of the Program on Age and Structural Change—PASC—at the National Institute on Aging).

B. Organization of Age-Related Roles

No role stands by itself. All roles in families, offices, nursing homes, and other social structures are intricately interconnected across the society as a whole and in complexes of roles available to particular age strata.

1. Societal Interconnectedness
At any given time, the roles related to all the varied ages in a society coexist, fit together or fail to fit, and can affect each other. In a school, for example, the

definition of the role of 1st grader affects and is affected by the role of 4th grader; in a factory, the role of beginning worker affects and is affected by the role of manager (typically defined as older in age or seniority). Over time, all these interconnected roles either remain stable or they change together (synchronically). If the performance expectations for 1st graders are changed, the expectations for 4th graders will be changed concomitantly.

2. Role Complexes
Within strata, age as a criterion can link together complexes of roles that are otherwise differentiated. Thus old age places some women simultaneously in the roles of grandparent, widow, caregiver, volunteer worker, and resident in a retirement community; or middle age brings together the roles of parent, offspring, spouse, and worker. However, the specific age boundaries of such multiple roles often differ. Even a century ago, when few people lived long enough for clearly defined retirement, historians tell of older people "stepping down" at quite different ages from public office, from private authority in family and kin group, and from work.

3. Role Contradictions
Many age-related role complexes involve conflicting expectations. For example, the role of spouse may be in conflict with the role of parent; work roles often interfere with child-care roles; teenagers as peer group members may be expected to spend evenings in sexual adventures, but in the filial role be expected by their parents to study. In another example, elderly persons in their role as patients may be expected by their surgeons to make prompt recoveries, but as family members expected by their caregivers to be cautious and dependent. Such role conflicts can produce strains and tensions and can result in adaptations ranging from revolt, to innovative role changes, to complete withdrawal from the scene.

4. Role Inequalities
Moreover, role complexes often involve differences in rewards, creating age-based inequalities that are even more potentially disruptive of both human lives and the social order—particularly when perceived as inequities. In contemporary society, the middle-aged have long been advantaged in such respects as income, power, and the sheer number of roles available. By

the same token, however, they have been disadvantaged in lack of time to spend with families or in leisure opportunities for new learning or new adventure. Because of recent increases in old-age entitlements, however, it is the aged (though still suffering from lack of esteem) who are often denigrated as "greedy geezers." The push for "intergenerational equity" in support of children as well as older people is just one symptom of the pressures toward structural change inherent in age-related role inequalities. Like the conflicts potentially emanating from hostile relationships among people, contradictions and inequalities in roles also contribute to the dynamic theme that is intrinsic to age stratification.

IV. AGE DYNAMICS

The foregoing analyses of people and roles (sections II and III) show that dynamic forces are pervasive in the age-stratification scheme. Viewed in cross section at particular periods of time, they implicate three sets of dynamic processes and mechanisms:

1. Underlying the age strata of people are the biological, psychological, and social processes of aging and cohort succession, and the age structuring of roles reflects broad societal and cultural changes.
2. Endemic in the age strata of people are potential conflicts, and stresses are engendered in age-related roles by contradictory expectations and inequalities of rewards.
3. Processes of allocation and socialization continually modulate the relations between people and roles at the various ages. However, this modulation is only partially successful, and major lags or imbalances persist between the capacities of people and role opportunities for them in the society.

Deeper understanding of these three sets of processes now requires the encompassing aging and society paradigm (outlined in section I), with its dialectical interplay between the transcendent "dynamisms" of changing lives and changing role structures. [See Co-HORT STUDIES.] This larger view of the interconnections between people and roles across time, rather than synchronically in cross section, provides new insights into the age-stratification scheme and its persistent imbalances.

A. Imbalances between People and Roles

Throughout the industrialized world today there is a "mismatch" (to use George Maddox's term) between the strengths and capacities of the increasing numbers of older people, and the inadequate role opportunities to utilize, reward, and sustain these strengths. While nearly three decades have been added over this one century to the average length of life, and while people grow older in new and diverse ways, many surrounding social structures have lagged behind: they are still geared to the needs of the much younger population of a century ago. This current mismatch in the age-stratification scheme, when viewed over time as "structural lag," derives from two general principles from the aging and society paradigm: the principles of "interdependent dynamisms" and of "asynchrony" between these dynamisms.

I. Interdependent Dynamisms
As the first principle, there is a continuing interplay between two dynamisms (or sets of processes): changing lives of people and changing social structures with their age-related roles. (Here we speak of modal patterns that transcend the wide diversity of both lives and structures.) These two dynamisms, though discrete, are interdependent: each influences the other. In one direction of the interplay, as schools, families, hospitals, firms, and other structures change over historical time, people's lives are continually being shaped and reshaped. For example, restructuring of work roles, by producing early retirement, changes the entire life-course pattern as many persons move from work into retirement. In the other direction, as the patterns of many individual lives are modified through alterations in the aging process and differences between successive cohorts, reciprocal pressures are generated for still further changes in social structures and roles. For example, because of today's structural lag, increasingly capable and potentially productive older people press in varied ways to alter the nature of retirement described many years ago by Ernest Burgess as a "roleless role."

2. Asynchrony
The second principle explains that this interplay between structures and lives does not run smoothly.

Some form of lag is inevitable because of the asynchrony, or difference of timing, between the two dynamisms.

This difference in timing can be seen by referring back to the criss-crossing lines in Figure 1. On the one hand, changes in the pattern of lives are revealed by comparison of information about selected diagonal lines, such as A, B, and C. (As indicated earlier, the diagonals denote successive cohorts of individuals who, over their lives, move across time and upward in age from birth to death.) On the other hand, changes in structure are detected through comparison of vertical lines. (The vertical lines denote social structures and roles through which, at particular time periods, the several cohorts of people are passing and replacing each other.) Thus aging individuals are continually moving along the diagonal axes of the life course—but change in social structures is moving along its own axis of historical time, which has no clear rhythm or periodicity.

Because these two sets of lines are continually criss-crossing each other in different directions, only in theory can they be perfectly synchronized. It is this asynchrony that produces a recurring mismatch between them—a lag of one dynamism behind the other. Unlike the current lag of structures behind lives, under other circumstances lives can lag behind structures, as when the abilities or training of workers is inadequate for the technologically advanced jobs available. Because of the persistent asynchrony, some form of lag by either structures or people is endemic in the age-stratification scheme.

B. Potentials for Alterability

Because both people and roles are alterable, these universal pressures are to an extent modifiable either through naturally occurring changes or deliberate intervention. Assessing possible directions of alterability provides a knowledge base for the gerontological aim of enhancing older people's future opportunities to lead healthy and productive lives (a value judgment which, like all such judgments, is subject to social and cultural diversity and change).

I. Feasibility
The potential for interventions that could affect today's structural lag has been widely demonstrated. Research experiments with structural changes have found, for example, that even at the oldest ages health can be enhanced if independence, rather than dependence, is fostered in nursing homes; leg muscle strength can be greatly improved by training regimens, and (save for the minority with mental disease) old people's performance on intelligence tests can be restored, through structures providing appropriate training, to their levels of 20 years earlier. Recent studies have shown marked improvements in older people's functioning through medical interventions (such as knee and hip replacements or cataract surgery); through safety devices in design of housing, transportation, and arrangement of furniture and rugs within the house; and through social supports in families and communities. Such accumulating evidence elaborates the pattern of age stratification by identifying specific structural potentials for alterability in people's lives.

2. Possible Directions for Future Change
In exploring possible directions of future change, one useful approach contrasts two extreme types of age stratification: *age differentiation* versus *age integration*. (These are "ideal types" in Max Weber's sense, as idealized selections from reality. Either type can be imagined as defining a vertical line in Figure 1).

Societies of the extreme age-differentiated type are characterized by three often-studied "boxes": retirement or leisure for older people; work and family roles for the long span of the middle years; and roles in schools, vocational centers, and universities for the young. In the real world, this age-differentiated type embodies many features of today's society: the convenience and familiarity of age as the basis for structuring, but also the rigidity and the inequities of age constraints. By contrast, in the extreme age-integrated type of societies, the age barriers are lowered or removed. Roles in all structures—education, work, and leisure—are more open to people of every age. This ideal type provides a scenario for anticipating possible outcomes of interventions to reduce, or perhaps to exacerbate, the problems of structural lag; and for considering the basic values implicated in such outcomes.

The age-integrated type, when used as a research tool for exploring individual and social implications, would remove age criteria as barriers. It points to entirely new definitions and meanings. It also raises new questions. For people, age integration would provide flexibility, optimizing potentials for interspersing periods of work with periods of education and of leisure. But would such age flexibility mean unfettered freedom from constraints? Would it intensify an emphasis on "me" over "we?" Would it forestall any balance between rights and responsibilities? For social structures, age integration would mean that people of all ages are brought together throughout society—but with what implications? Would integration foster confrontation, aggression, even conflict between young and old? Would it disturb the comfort of homophily and the self-esteem engendered by having age peers as reference points? Or, might age integration encourage sharing by the young in the wisdom and experience of the old? and by the old in the vigor and adventurous spirit of the young? Might integration across all ages press toward social order, civility, a new sense of community? Such questions are under continuing research attention.

Whatever direction the pattern of age stratification takes in the future, it is clear that certain pressures to reduce the structural lag, though latent, are already underway. The themes of diversity, age interconnectedness, and alterability merge with the dynamic theme to foreshadow changes in the age strata of people and the age structuring of roles. In the future, as in the past, any such changes in age stratification will involve alterations throughout the deeply rooted economic, political, cultural, and moral institutions of society and the underlying culture and values.

V. CONCLUSION

In sum, the age-stratification scheme is a useful tool for understanding the place, potentials, and problems of older people in the society, the community, the family, the workplace, and other social institutions. It plays its part in developing a knowledge base for prolonging the productive and healthy middle years of life, and preventing such possible decrements of old age as economic deprivation, chronic ill health, memory loss, low self-esteem, and withdrawal from active participation in social and economic roles.

Beneath the many complexities and diversities of age stratification, the power of age in understanding both human lives and social change can be writ large in three statements:

1. Age is a universal feature of both people and roles in every society. Even in age-homogeneous groups, it operates as an important basis of relationships.
2. Age stratification takes widely diverse patterns and forms, as evidenced by variations across time and space.
3. Age underlies a fundamental principle: the certainty of change, beginning either with people or with roles. As Pitirim Sorokin demonstrated back in 1947, "immanent change" characterizes all of human history.

BIBLIOGRAPHY

Abeles, R. P., Gift, H., & Ory, M. G. (Eds.). (1994). *Aging and quality of life*. New York: Springer.

Hayflick, L. H. (1994). *How and why we age*. New York: Ballantine.

Kertzer, D. I., & Schaie, K. W. (Eds.). (1989). *Age structuring in comparative perspective*. Hillsdale, NJ: Erlbaum.

Maddox, G. L. (1994). Social and behavioural research on ageing: An agenda for the United States. *Ageing and Society (14)*, 97–107.

Riley, M. W. (1994). Aging and society: Past, present, and future. *The Gerontologist, 34 (4)*, 436–446.

Riley, M. W., Kahn, R. L., & Foner, A. (Eds.). (1994). *Age and structural lag: Society's failure to provide meaningful opportunities in work, family, and leisure*. New York: Wiley.

Taeuber, C. (1992 rev. 1993). *Sixty-five plus in America*. Washington, DC: U.S. Bureau of the Census.

Alcohol and Drugs

Edith S. Lisansky Gomberg

University of Michigan

Alcohol-Related Problems Medical, legal, occupational, family, and social problems.

Illegal or Controlled Substance Schedule I drugs, defined as manifesting a high potential for abuse and no currently acceptable medical use, including heroin, LSD, and marijuana.

Medications Any drug substance, prescribed or over-the-counter, taken for therapeutic purposes. This includes prescribed use of psychoactive drugs.

Pharmacodynamics Physiological and psychological response to drugs; there are gerontological changes in drug response.

Pharmacokinetics The time course of absorption, tissue distribution, metabolism, and excretion of drugs and their metabolites from the body.

A **DRUG** is defined as any substance (not food), natural or synthetic, which by its chemical nature alters an organism's structure or function. Drugs may be found in nature or they may be produced in the laboratory. They may also be classified in terms of their chemical composition or, in the case of psychoactive drugs (e.g., alcohol, opiates, nicotine, etc.), in terms of their central nervous system action. A major classification is in terms of social acceptability; drugs vary from widely accepted (caffeine) to illicit substances, which often appear as "street drugs" (heroin). *Drug abuse and drug dependence* may be defined as deviant usage. Diagnosis is usually made in terms of the American Psychiatric Association standards set forth in the *Diagnostic and Statistical Manual IV.*

I. INTRODUCTION

There are several classes of drugs to be reviewed here. First, there is the use by older people of medications in general and psychoactive medications (anxiolytics, stimulants, etc.) in particular; these are likely to be prescribed, although there is a "street" supply from nonmedical sources. Second, there is the use of over-the-counter (OTC) drugs that need no prescription and may be bought in any pharmacy. Third, there is nicotine used by Americans of all age groups and by the elderly. Fourth, are the controlled substances, banned by law. The best known controlled substances are marijuana, heroin, and cocaine; associated with crime and violence, these drugs get the most media attention. Fifth, there is the use and abuse of the legal drug, alcohol.

A major area of study is the biological change over the life span that occurs in the body's response to different drugs. *Pharmacokinetics* involves the study of the time course of absorption, tissue distribution, metabolism and excretion of drugs and their metabolites from the body, and the relationship of drug disposition to the duration and intensity of drug effects.

Studying the effects of age on pharmacokinetics produces information about the mechanism of altered pharmacodynamics in the elderly. *Pharmacodynamics* is the physiological and psychological response to drugs. Pharmacodynamics is concerned with the greater or lesser response of *older* people to particular drugs, independent of pharmacokinetic effects. Different psychoactive drugs, for example, may produce different pharmacodynamic effects in the elderly (e.g., the response of older persons to some of the benzodiazepines appears to be an enhanced response).

A. Age Changes

1. Pharmacokinetics
Although there do not appear to be significant age changes in drug absorption, with aging there are changes in body composition that influence drug distribution. There are age changes in drug elimination, particularly a decline in renal function.

2. Pharmacodynamics
Age changes in sensitivity to some drugs and increased sensitivity to drugs acting on the central nervous system (CNS) are observed; the susceptibility to adverse drug reactions appears to be increased.

3. Adverse Drug Reactions
Adverse drug reactions (ADRs) in the elderly can result from multiple drug therapy, drug overuse or misuse, slowing of drug metabolism or elimination, or to age-related chronic diseases, alcohol intake, and food–drug incompatibilities. ADRs in the elderly are more severe than among younger patients. Risk factors include being female, living alone, multiple diseases, multiple drug intake, and poor nutritional status. [*See* PHARMACOLOGY.]

II. MEDICATIONS

The increase in acute and chronic illnesses that appears in older populations produces greater healthcare expenditure and more medications for this subgroup of the population. Older people constitute approximately 12% of the general population, but estimates are that they receive a third of all prescriptions. Older people also buy and use a disproportionately larger number of OTC drugs. A list of the most widely

used prescribed drugs includes general medications and psychoactive drugs; cardiovascular medication, diuretics, antibiotics, and analgesics are among the most frequently used drugs as are psychoactive drugs, such as sedative-hypnotics including benzodiazepines, and psychotherapeutic drugs, which include antidepressants and stimulants.

Although some treatment facilities report sizable patient intake of older persons with drug-associated problems and dependence on psychoactive drugs, this issue has never evoked much interest. It may well be that in the minds of legislators and the public, keeping older people sedated is an acceptable idea. Older persons frequently associate their intake of psychoactive drugs with problems like insomnia or depression, and almost half of those taking such drugs report that they could not perform their daily activities without the medication. The issue of prescribed psychoactive drug use and misuse among the elderly is complex and has psychological, societal, and policy components.

There are several questions related to the use of prescribed psychoactive medication. Nursing home use of such drugs is a problem, and it is questioned whether such medication is used for the benefit of the patients or for the benefit of staff to facilitate patient caregiving. Age differences in drug problems are reflected in the contrast of drug-associated emergency room (ER) use: younger patients are likely to present in ERs with emergencies relating to controlled substances like cocaine; older persons are more likely to present in ERs with problems associated with misuse of a psychoactive drug, usually prescribed. There are also gender differences. Up to age 65, women are prescribed and use more psychoactive drugs. From age 65 on, the differences become complicated, and data suggest that antidepressants are more widely prescribed for older men than for older women. This may be related to older men's utilization of medical resources, or possibly to a gender difference in psychiatric problems among older people. For older (white) men, the decline in power with aging is reflected in suicide rates. Although suicide rates remain low and stable with aging women, they rise with age among older men.

National surveys of elderly persons living in the community show a widespread usage of psychoactive drugs, and it has been noted by several investigators that older people receive a disproportionately high percentage of psychoactive drug prescriptions. The question of abuse, misuse, and dependence is raised infrequently, usually as a caveat that a given drug (e.g., a sedative) should not be used continually for more than 2 weeks. In spite of that caution, approximately half the older persons queried in research studies report that they could not perform their regular daily activities without the medication. Societal concerns about older persons' use of substances seem to focus on alcohol.

The elderly have more health problems than younger people and therefore are more likely to be taking multiple prescriptions. Such multiple drug therapy means an increased risk of adverse drug reactions. Studies involving hospital patient monitoring have suggested a number of drugs of concern: dioxin, diuretics, aspirin, psychotropics, cytotoxins, and nonsteroidal anti-inflammatory drugs (NSAIDs). Adverse drug reactions may be a consequence of multiple drug therapy, drug interactions, changes in older persons' drug metabolism or elimination, noncompliance with prescribed drug use, incompatible food–drug combinations, or alcohol intake combined with medication use. It is estimated that the incidence of adverse drug reactions is two to three times more frequent among the elderly than among younger patients. To compound the difficulties, adverse drug reactions among older people are more severe, and there are those investigators who believe that drugs should be prescribed at lower initial doses for older patients. There are also investigators who believe that medications are overprescribed for the elderly and that some restraint in prescription would be helpful.

Data from the Drug Abuse Warning Network (reports from urban ERs) indicate that older people are most likely to present with problems relating to non-barbiturate sedatives, tranquilizers, barbiturate sedatives, and antidepressants. On all of these, the percentage of women appearing in ERs is greater than the percentage of men.

Several classifications have been made of different usage of psychoactive drugs. One such classification distinguishes appropriate use, unintentional misuse, and purposeful misuse. Another differentiation is of benzodiazepine use: first, there is a *low* or therapeutic dose, the usual prescription pattern, and no withdrawal symptomatology when use ceases. There is also high-dose therapeutic use, which is again prescribed but usually produces withdrawal symptoms when use ceases. Second, there is intake involved in multiple-drug use, frequently involving alcohol; here the aim is to achieve a "high" or some form of self-prescribed relief.

A problem relating to medical practice and prescription drugs is the question of noncompliance. Noncompliance is seen as a major problem, including the following:

1. Nonuse—not obtaining the prescribed drug, perhaps because of cost.
2. Partial use—ceasing before course is complete, perhaps because of side effects, or combinations of prescribed drug with OTC drug not prescribed.
3. Incorrect dosage—more or less than prescribed.
4. Improper timing or sequencing of medication.
5. Shared medications.

A survey by the largest organization of older persons, the American Association of Retired Persons (AARP), found that 40% of the respondents experienced side effects; half of those said that side effects had not been discussed by health-care personnel. Although noncompliance is often attributed to cognitive limitations of older persons, a question has been raised as to whether the noncompliance is more likely to be linked to limited financial resources, a denial mechanism, issues of autonomy, and the quality of communication between patient and physician. Although it has been suggested that older people have the "right" to make decisions about their drug intake, the extended life expectancy is related to pharmaceutical advances. What is needed is a balanced view in which patient and physician can arrive at a modus operandi and a rationale for medication intake.

III. OVER-THE-COUNTER DRUGS

The most commonly used nonprescription drugs are analgesics, nutritional supplements like vitamins, laxatives, and antacids. Nonnarcotic analgesics are the most commonly reported drugs of purchase by older persons both in the United States and in other countries. When the question is raised whether the elderly use more OTC medications than other age groups, there is disagreement. Some investigators believe that older people purchase and use disproportionately more OTC medication than other age groups; other investigators believe that elderly people do not use such OTC medications excessively.

The Food and Drug Administration has suggested that there be special labeling on prescribed drugs for persons over 65. The general response to the suggestion of special age-related labeling on OTC drugs has been negative, and consensus among investigators is that labeling by specific medical condition is preferable. It is of interest to note that more information is available to OTC drug consumers on packaging and package inserts than to consumers of prescribed drugs.

The question of home remedies and folk remedies may be raised here. Although herbal teas and chicken soup are not in the same category as drugs or medication, such folk remedies are widely used and probably more often by poor people. Perhaps studies of American eating habits could include such investigation. One suspects that self-medication with home remedies is the first line of health defense with most people.

IV. NICOTINE

Men are more likely to be smokers than women, although the percentage gap between the sexes has narrowed considerably in the last 20 years. The Public Health Service has tracked the marked increase in female smoking during and after World War II and by the 1960s, lung cancer deaths among women began to rise. Since 1985, lung cancer has passed breast cancer as the chief cause of cancer death among women.

A survey of people 65 and older in Massachusetts showed that those *less* likely to be current smokers included respondents living alone or with their children, those who reported their health as poor or fair, and "the frail elderly."

The relationship between smoking and a variety of diseases is well documented. A review of studies of the metabolism of drugs in older persons concluded that the effects of aging, nicotine, and alcohol are confounded.

V. ILLEGAL SUBSTANCES

The occasional social use of drugs like marijuana, hashish, and even cocaine probably does occur among older individuals, and there are apparently users of illicit drugs (e.g., heroin) who began drug use earlier in life and have survived into old age. One of the widely held beliefs about opiate addicts was that they did *not* survive to old age, that they either died or "matured out." There is, however, a small number of elderly heroin-dependent people who have managed to maintain their habits and live beyond their sixties. In the mid-1970s, people over 60 years of age constituted .005% of the methadone maintenance population in New York City; ten years later, the proportion had risen to 2%. These are not drug-dependent people whose habit is of recent onset; they are long-term heroin addicts who have survived. Interestingly enough, the Michigan Department of Public Health reported that for treatment admissions in 1992–1993, for those 60 and over, heroin was the primary substance of abuse for 3%.

Study of the New York City methadone-maintained survivors showed a number of variables relevant to survival: the survivors had long-lived parents, they avoided violence, and were careful about the use of clean needles. They were able to hold some drugs in reserve, used other drugs—particularly alcohol—moderately, and were generally in reasonable health when compared with same aged people in the general population.

The use of banned substances is associated with younger rather than older persons. In Michigan, treatment admissions for those under 60 show twice the percentage of younger patients whose primary substance of abuse is heroin: 6% compared to 3%. The contrast is even sharper for those whose primary substance of abuse is cocaine or crack: 18% of those under 60 and 2% of those 60 and older. Data from the criminal justice system suggest a triadic relationship: youth, criminal activity, and illegal drugs. For older persons, the criminal justice system has traditionally been involved with the homeless skid row man. In recent years, however, arrests for public intoxication have diminished, and the homeless population has become more heterogeneous.

VI. ALCOHOL

Alcoholic beverages are legal and socially accepted. As such, they are used infrequently or moderately, they may be consumed in large quantities, or they may produce alcohol abuse, alcoholism, or dependence for some users. We will examine briefly the moderate social use of alcoholic beverages by older persons and then move to alcohol-related problems as manifested in abuse or dependence.

To what extent is alcohol used by older persons? It has been generally accepted that moderate drinking declines with age, but some data challenge this. Perhaps there is a historic shift so that the older cohort of the 1990s behaves differently with alcoholic beverages than the older cohort of the 1950s or 1960s. There are National Health Interview Survey (NHIS) results that suggest an increase in alcohol intake among men 65 and older, and a small increase among the same aged women. A few community-based longitudinal studies have shown an increase over time; a Framingham, Massachusetts, study showed a large increase for women. Drinking is tied to laws and social customs, and there has been a trend in recent decades toward greater acceptability. Many small communities with local prohibition laws have shifted to acceptance, and women's drinking in particular is likely to be affected by social acceptability. Older people as well as younger people are affected by changing mores.

How much of a health risk is alcohol for older persons? It is certainly true that the older population is more likely to manifest both acute and chronic illness; it is also true that this population takes more medication than younger groups. The question of age changes in hepatic blood flow and the capacity of the liver to metabolize drugs is relevant. Older people show a decrease in body water content that produces higher peak serum ethanol levels for the same amount of alcohol, which would produce lower peak levels for younger people. There are other relevant age changes, and the increased vulnerability of the brain with aging raises questions about symptomatic behavior like confusion, depression, and dementia as they may relate to alcohol intake. The general consensus, however, is that *light* drinking is not particularly harmful to older persons, provided they are reasonably healthy and take no medications that interact with alcohol; one drink a day is considered prudent.

VII. DRINKING PROBLEMS

Although there may be a larger number of older adults with psychoactive medication problems, they are not likely to appear in substance abuse services. It is much more likely that older adults who drink heavily or frequently and who manifest alcohol-related health and other problems will appear, voluntarily or not, at such services. In Michigan, treatment admissions of patients under 60 years of age include 62% for whom alcohol is the primary substance of abuse; for people 60 and older, alcohol is the primary substance of abuse for 86%. In a study done at a veterans' hospital 65% of the younger alcoholic men and 80% of the older alcoholic men in the study group chose alcohol as "substance of first choice."

The literature on elderly alcoholism is limited, and samples are drawn from hospitals, arrest records, outpatient clinics, and housing for older people, and from community and national surveys. The issue of how patients are screened is also relevant. Although standard screening instruments are widely used, there is a question about the meaningfulness of some of the criteria for diagnosis of alcoholism. Losing time from work may be irrelevant, falls and medical problems may be more relevant. Caution is needed: Surveys show a relatively low percentage of problem drinkers among those 60 and over but the size of the problem may be larger. A recent study examined the records of all hospital inpatient Medicare Part A beneficiaries, 65 and older, and reported a high prevalence of alcohol-related hospitalizations. The highest rate of such hospitalization occurs in the 45–64-years-old age group (94.8 per 10,000 population) and the second highest rate was in the 65-and-over age group (65.1 per 10,000 population). The alcohol-related disorders included alcohol abuse and dependence, and alcoholic liver disease, psychoses, cardiomyopathy, gastritis, and polyneuropathy.

There is a vast literature on neuropsychological or cognitive loss which is a by-product of heavy or problem drinking. Such psychological deficits have been explored in terms of functions impaired, gender differences, and the relationship of age to cognitive impairment. The latter produced a "premature aging hypothesis," which posited premature senescence brought on by heavy drinking; evidence about this hypothesis has been mixed. Cognitive impairment may focus on specific functions: short-term memory, nonverbal abstracting, the ability to process new information, and so forth. There is a question about the reversibility of the cognitive loss, and it is generally believed that older problem drinkers may regain loss function, given time, although the process is slow.

One of the most interesting phenomena of elderly problem drinking is the subtyping: *early onset versus late onset.* Some authors have defined late onset as the beginning of problem drinking around age 40; this means that a group of problem drinkers are divided into those who began problem drinking in their twenties or younger and a group that began around age 40. There is a good deal of literature that indicates that the younger-onset group will show more positive family history, more comorbid diagnoses of antisocial personality, and poorer prognosis. If we are, however, to associate *onset and old age,* it would be better to differentiate problem drinkers at 65 or 70 into early onset and *recent* onset. That a group of late- or recent-onset problem drinkers exists has been verified by a number of reports that suggest that about one-third of older problem drinkers studied qualify as recent onset. There is an interesting question whether such recent or late onset is associated with experienced stress; several investigators studying stress and drinking have come up with support for stress-as-etiology and others with stress-as-irrelevant data. Stress may be a complex phenomenon that impacts differently depending on gender, general health, socioeconomic status, life experience, and so on.

There are drinking-related factors, and it seems a reasonable hypothesis that problem drinking is more likely to occur in someone who has had a history of intermittent heavy drinking. There are changes in role and status with old age and different coping mechanisms and ability to adapt among older people. There are also shifts in the social environment, particularly for the elderly who move to a different location.

By and large, *the patterns of drinking and alcohol-related problems* do not seem remarkably different for older and younger problem drinkers. Older alcoholics are less likely to get into fights and less likely to have work-associated problems. They may have more alcohol-related health problems, more accidents, more concern about income, and possibly more likelihood of binge drinking.

Information about *elderly female alcoholics* is sparse, but a recent report compares such men and women in their sixties. The women report more marital disruption than the men and that is consistent with other age group gender comparisons; marital disruption in this age group, however, is less likely to be divorce or separation for the women, of whom 51% were widowed (compared with 18% of the men). There is a striking difference in reported age at onset: more than a third of the women report onset in the last 10 years and only 4% of the men do. Another significant gender difference is heavy or problem drinking by a significant other; as occurs in all age groups' gender comparison, more women report the spouse as heavy or problem drinker than do men. Also, true of all age group gender comparison is that women are more likely to drink at home and less likely than men to drink in public places. Effects of alcohol as reported by the women show more negative effects (e.g., feel miserable) than do the men, the men report significantly more often that they "get along better with people" when drinking, and there are no gender differences in aggression as a result of drinking. A final gender comparison: women are significantly more likely to report dependence and tolerance in psychoactive drug use (e.g., minor tranquilizers) than are men. Again, this gender difference appears throughout the life course.

VIII. THE ROLE OF ETHNICITY

An early study, conducted in an ER of a Florida hospital, gave some figures for admissions 60 and older: 3.5% were Hispanic elderly, 6.2% were black elderly, 20.3% were white elderly.

A study of aging and ethnicity, containing material from the United States General Accounting Office, 1992, shows the following: for the 65 and older groups, a third of Whites are defined as "poor"; for Hispanics that proportion is 69%; for Blacks 100%. Clearly *older* minority group members have benefited little from affirmative action programs designed to help people through school or business. Such programs have clearly helped younger African Americans (*New York Times,* June 24, 1995).

This relates to an interesting contrast within the Black–White comparison in relation to drinking: when low-income black men are compared with low-income white men, they report significantly *more* drinking consequences and drinking problems. When affluent black men are compared with affluent white men, the difference in drinking problems is diminished to insignificance. Comparisons of Black–White drinking problems must therefore include not only age and gender but income as well: Significant interactions have been observed of social class, race, *drinking* consequences, and total alcohol-related problems. [*See* RACIAL AND ETHNIC DIVERSITY.]

Researchers have reported a comparison of elderly alcoholic men in treatment. There were 142 white patients, mean age 64, and 27 black patients, mean age 62. Some interesting differences were found:

1. The black patients (although drawn from the same clinical sources) showed significantly less educational achievement, occupational status, income, and current employment status. This is the age group that has benefited little from recent affirmative action programs.

2. Compared on drinking behaviors and patterns, it appeared that the black alcoholics drank larger quantities, preferred high-alcohol-content beverages, and were significantly more likely to engage in drinking in public places.

3. The black alcoholics had used or abused drugs other than alcohol to a greater extent than reported by the white alcoholics; and though both groups were elderly, the black men reported earlier age introduction to and use of "street" drugs. One may raise the question of availability of such drugs in the community.

4. Health consequences were reported more often by the black elderly alcoholics than the white and a regression model for health consequences showed that the variables of greatest relevance were educational achievement, lifetime daily drinking average, drinking in public, and dependence on drugs other than alcohol.

An array of social, community, and institutional consequences of the heavy drinking was reviewed, and on the job and with the police, the black men reported more trouble; they also reported more rejection from friends. A regression model for social, community, and institutional consequences found the variables of greatest relevance to be educational achievement, lifetime daily drinking average, drinking in public, and race.

The triple stigma of being black, elderly, and alcoholic presents formidable challenges in finding these people, motivating them, and working at rehabilitation.

Questions have been raised about the prevalence of heavy drinking or alcohol abuse in *retirement communities*. There are no controlled studies, (e.g., a comparison of the drinking of retirees who move to retirement communities and those who stay in their own homes). It may very well be that moving to a different state, an excess of free time, and social facilitation may play a role for some elderly drinking, but that has yet to be demonstrated.

A half century ago, there was much research interest in *the chronic drunkenness offender*. A disproportionately high percentage of arrests for drunkenness and public intoxication was noted among men 60 years of age and older. Two major changes have occurred in what used to be called skid row: first, a Supreme Court decision which permits arrests for antisocial behavior (e.g., disorderly conduct) but not for intoxication per se; second, the character and locale of the homeless population has changed. The homeless population now includes many former mental hospital patients and may be found in many different locales (airports, train terminals, etc.). In some inner cities, there has also been a drift of African Americans and Native Americans toward the old skid row neighborhoods. At present, it is more likely that the elderly homeless alcoholic will be referred to a detoxification center, but little progress has been made in measures to help the rehabilitation process.

The question of whether those older persons who live alone are more likely to be heavy drinkers is not resolved. Older women are more likely to live alone than older men, and the rate of problem drinking is considerably lower for those women than for older men. There are certainly older alcoholics who live alone, but a review of their histories may show a lifetime of alcohol abuse and an alienation of family; living alone is therefore a consequence rather than a cause of the abusive drinking. Study of this question must take into consideration the gerontological fact of differences in subgroups of the U.S. population: the elderly person living with family members is more characteristic of some ethnic groups than others and is clearly related to socioeconomic status, family location and relationships, state of health, marital status, and so on.

IX. TREATMENT AND PREVENTION

A great deal has been written about the elderly alcohol abuser, but there are really three major questions:

First, how do older alcohol abusers get into treatment? Second, what kinds of problems in diagnosis and management do such patients present and are there unique patterns in their clinical histories? Third, having made the diagnosis of alcohol abuse with or without accompanying comorbid symptoms, what are the most effective ways to proceed in treatment?

Older patients may be referred or brought to a substance abuse facility by family members, ER personnel, policemen, physicians, social agencies, or law enforcement agencies. A major basis for referral is the presence of alcohol-related health problems. One Canadian program notes that clients rarely enter a program to deal with their addiction but rather for help with other problems (e.g., accommodations, health care and the like).

The manner in which an elderly patient enters a substance abuse facility is very much a matter of his or her social networks and support systems. It may be concerned family or friends who bring in a client, but it is at least as often police or medical authorities bringing a patient who has long since destroyed family contacts.

There is, however, the question of maintaining contact. We have been studying elderly persons, diagnosable by the *Diagnostic and Statistical Manual IV* (*DSM-IV*) as alcoholics or alcohol abusers. The subjects came from hospitals, Alcoholics Anonymous, community advertising, general hospital wards, senior citizen housing, and community centers. Interviews were conducted with 104 unremitted alcoholic men currently in treatment and with 67 men, diagnosable as alcoholic but not in treatment. The groups were demographically similar and differed only in the fact that significantly more of the not-in-treatment group was retired. The most striking differences between the two groups of men occurs when they are asked for self-description about their drinking (e.g., asked if they could stop drinking without a struggle after one or two drinks). Fifty-four percent of the men in treatment answered no compared with 24% of the not-in-treatment group. Examined for the nine symptomatic behaviors necessary for a diagnosis of alcohol abuse of alcoholism (*DSM-IV*), the men in treatment responded positively significantly more often than the not-in-treatment men. Drinking patterns were quite similar, but the men in treatment reported significantly more

alcohol-related health problems. Finally, there was a striking difference in help-seeking behavior. In summary, older alcoholic men in treatment show greater severity of alcoholism (*DSM-IV*) and are more likely to self-describe as problem drinkers or alcoholics. They are more likely to engage in help-seeking behaviors that may include the use of the ER in a local hospital, a chapter of the Alcoholics Anonymous, seeking out a friend or relative or a physician, and so forth.

Finally, are there more effective ways of working with the elderly alcohol-dependent person? One question that has arisen is the efficacy of elder-specific programs (e.g., group therapy with a group made up of elderly patients). Reports are mixed, but as with other special populations, if feasible, it is probably wise to offer an elder-specific group. Working with elderly patients is not remarkably different from working with other age groups, but the counselor must be patient because the tempo may be slower. A nonconfrontational therapist who encourages reminiscence as well as discussion about current problems is recommended.

A note on prevention: Because we are not really on firm ground in describing the antecedents or etiology of alcohol problems among the elderly, effective prevention programs must wait upon more knowledge of etiology. Although there is disagreement among researchers about the role of stress in facilitating heavy or problem drinking among the elderly, it is wise to develop aid programs for those who are recently widowed, recently retired, or even recently removed from one residence to another.

BIBLIOGRAPHY

Adams, W. L., Barboriak, J. J., & Timm, A. A. (1993). Alcohol-related hospitalizations of elderly people. *Journal of the American Medical Association, 23,* 1222.

Beresford, T. P., & Gomberg, E. S. L. (1995). *Alcohol and aging.* New York: Oxford University Press.

DesJarlais, D. C., Joseph, H., & Courtwright, D. T. (1985). Old age and addiction: A study of elderly patients in methadone maintenance treatment. In E. Gotteil, K. A. Druly, T. E. Sokolda, & H. M. Waxman (Eds.), *The combined problems of alcoholism, drug addiction and aging.* Springfield, IL: Charles C. Thomas.

Dufour, M. C., Archer, L., & Gordis, E. (1992). Alcohol and the elderly. *Clinics in Geriatric Medicine, 6,* 127.

Gomberg, E. S. L. (1982). The young male alcoholic: A pilot study. *Journal of Studies on Alcohol, 43,* 683.

Gomberg, E. S. L. (1990). Drugs, alcohol and aging. In L. T. Kozlowski, H. M. Annis, H. D. Chappell, et al. (Eds.), *Research advances in alcohol and drug problems* (vol. 19, p. 171). New York: Plenum Press.

Gomberg, E. S. L. (1995). Older women and alcohol: Use and abuse. In M. Galanter (Ed.), *Recent development in alcoholism: Volume 12. Women and alcoholism* (p. 81). New York: Plenum Press.

Hartford, J. T., & Samorajski, T. (Eds.). (1984). *Alcoholism in the elderly: Social and biomedical issues.* New York: Raven Press.

Maddox, G., Robins, L. N., & Rosenberg, N. (Eds.). (1984). *Nature and extent of alcohol problems among the elderly.* (Research Monograph 14, N.I.A.A.A., DHHS Publ. No. (ADM) 84-1321). Washington, DC: U.S. Government Printing Office.

Michigan Department of Public Health. (1994). *Substance abuse services for older adult.* (OA 089/10M/9-94/NOG). Lansing, MI: Author.

Allergic Reactivity in the Elderly

Truman O. Anderson

University of Illinois

B Lymphocytes Cells of the lymphocyte lineage that migrate from the bone marrow, mature in the gut-associated lymphoid tissue (GALT), and are subsequently responsible for synthesis and release of specific antibody immunoglobulins. These soluble proteins are structurally configured to react with the foreign antigen that incites their production. The immunoglobulins constitute the humoral arm of the immune response.

Interleukins (IL) A general term for cytokines, a special class of soluble leukocyte products that serve important intercellular communication and regulatory roles and thus profoundly influence the character of the immune response.

Immunoglobulins (Ig) The soluble protein products secreted by activated, B cell-derived plasma cells that carry combining sites specifically reactive with the inducing antigen or allergen. Immunoglobulins are produced in five variant forms designated IgM, IgD, IgA, IgG, and IgE. Antigen or allergen-Ig union presages foreign antigen removal and destruction by a variety of mechanisms.

Isotype Switch The mechanism by which B cells "switch" from producing immunoglobulin M (IgM) to produce IgE, or IgG, or IgA molecules that continue to carry the structural (epitope) regions reactive with the inciting allergen, but combine it with a different Fc segment. This switch changes the nature of the secondary reaction characteristics of the Ig.

T Lymphocytes Cells of the lymphocyte lineage that migrate from the bone marrow to the thymus gland where they mature and are programmed to subsequently carry out one of a number of vital effector or regulatory roles in the operation of the immune system. These roles include functions such as controlling B cell activation or effecting specific delayed hypersensitivity responses.

THE IMMUNE SYSTEM has evolved to protect against infections and to eliminate any other foreign material from the body. Ordinarily it accomplishes this without causing significant physiologic or structural damage to tissues of the individual host. When an infection is persistent, however, or when the foreign material is difficult to eliminate, the stimulus to the immune system is intensified. Also, if the individual is genetically prone to respond immunologically to even very low concentrations of foreign material such as inhaled plant pollen, an allergic or hypersensitivity state develops. These intensifications of the usual immune reactions lead to associated or concomitant forms of tissue damage in the host that are manifest clinically. It is our purpose here to look at such reactions in the elderly and how they are influenced by the aging process.

I. BACKGROUND

In immunologic parlance, allergies or hypersensitivity states are disorders in which immune responses, sometimes directed against otherwise harmless substances, result in inflammation and consequent tissue damage. Common clinical examples of such unfortunate hypersensitivities include hay fever, allergic asthma, hives, eczema, anaphylactic reactions to insect stings, serum sickness, farmers lung, and contact dermatitis.

Under the right circumstances, hypersensitivity reactions can develop in anyone, but there are some individuals in whom there appears to be a genetic predisposition to develop allergic responses—particularly of the immediate type. Such persons are said to be atopic. Although classic allergic reactions most often first appear in the young, they can occur at any age and although they may persist for years, they tend to wane or even disappear in the elderly. The involution of allergic reactivity in particular and immune responses in general in the aged is our focus.

Immunological reactions are ordinarily protective and are designed to prevent or to overcome infection by viruses, bacteria, fungi, or other micro-organisms. When the system is operating vigorously, it may also play a key role in suppressing the formation and growth of tumors. Thus, an intact immune system is crucial for our survival in a biologically hostile and competitive world. [See IMMUNE SYSTEM.]

It is an old clinical observation that the elderly often die of infections or of tumors that they are simply unable to overcome. In the era prior to the advent of antibiotics, pneumococcal pneumonia used to be called "the old man's friend," because it was so often the gentle terminal event in an otherwise long and relatively healthy life. An elderly patient with an extensive multilobar pneumonia would often develop only a modest fever of perhaps 100° F to 101° F, an elevation of the white blood count of 8000 to 10,000 with a slight "left shift," (i.e. the appearance of a few immature white cells in the blood). Clinically, the patient would not seem severely ill. Shortly thereafter he would die. Given the same extent of pneumonia, a young adult would develop a fever of 105° F to 106° F, a white blood count elevation to 35,000, and show many young band cells in the blood. He would feel very ill, but he would live. It was apparent that the intensity, the vigor of the systemic responses to infection in the young adult and in the elderly individual were dramatically different. Clearly, very old people did not handle infections well. The suspicion arose

decades ago that this might be because the capacity to mount an immune response becomes progressively impaired as the individual ages. And indeed it does.

To understand not only why resistance to infection is impaired, but why hypersensitivity or allergic responses involute in the aged, it is necessary to describe how hypersensitivity states develop in the first place. To this end, it may be useful to review some basic features and to list the major reactive elements of the immune system.

II. BASIC ELEMENTS AND FUNCTIONS OF THE IMMUNE SYSTEM

Immunologic responses exhibit two singular characteristics. The first of these is that the reactions are specific (i.e., a given immunologic reaction is directed only against the foreign antigen or allergen that elicited the response—although there may be some cross-reaction with allergens that are structurally related). The second is that the system is able to distinguish self from nonself. Except under rare circumstances, such as those that obtain in autoimmune disease, the immune system simply does not react against the body's own tissues. This makes good biologic sense, because the central objective for the immune reaction is to remove from the body macromolecules and life-forms that are foreign to its own makeup and are potentially harmful.

Immunological specificity resides in the receptors or recognition structures on the surface of T and B lymphocytes. The capacity to discriminate self from nonself is largely a function of the T lymphocytes. As T cells from the bone marrow pass through the thymus gland, those with receptors having a strong affinity for self-antigens and hence might react with the body's own tissues are eliminated. Others are restricted to react to foreign antigens only in conjunction with self-defining structures called the class I or class II major histocompatibility complexes (MHCs). Thymic screening and programming of T lymphocytes is a complex and incompletely understood process, but it is central to direction and control of immune responses throughout the life of the individual.

The gut-associated lymphoid tissue (GALT) is probably to B cells what the thymus is to T cells in terms of the environment it provides for B cell maturation.

Although an intact, fully functional immune system is generally very adept at discriminating self from nonself, it does not readily distinguish between foreign substances that are potentially harmful and those that are chemically or biologically innocuous. To illustrate, in allergy-prone individuals the immune system may not only react to, neutralize, and remove life-threatening bacterial toxins in the course of an infection (an eminently useful response), but may also react vigorously to inhaled, harmless animal dander protein or to plant pollen. This latter kind of immunologic reaction may result in severe allergic rhinitis or asthma—a biologic response that is misdirected, probably not protective, and carries with it more harm than good.

The varied and complex functions of the immune system are subserved by a number of cellular elements and by many soluble biologically active effector macromolecules. These include enzymes and other regulatory proteins that possess stimulatory and inhibitory properties. Chief among the cellular components are T and B lymphocytes, macrophages, polymorphonuclear leukocytes, mast cells, and basophils. Among the soluble, secreted regulatory or effector molecules are the macrophage or lymphocyte-derived cytokines or interleukins (ILs) and the proteins of the serum complement cascade.

T lymphocytes and their subsets of CD4 or T helper and CD8 or T suppressor cells are extraordinarily versatile. They serve vital regulatory roles by influencing B cell functions as well as themselves effecting cell-mediated cytotoxicity and delayed hypersensitivity responses. These latter two reactions are particularly important in destroying parasites, fungi, and intracellular bacteria as well as virus-infected cells and tumor cells. B lymphocytes (and their derivative plasma cells) are responsible for antibody-mediated immune reactions.

B cells produce and release soluble antibody proteins that are tailored to the tasks of neutralizing toxins and extracellular viruses as well as facilitating phagocytosis (cellular engulfment) and destruction of bacteria. Antibodies are structurally configured to conform to and react with the surface structure of the foreign allergen or antigen. A useful analogy often used is that antibodies fit the antigen much like a key fits a lock. Antibodies are made in five immunoglo-bulin (Ig) isotypes, IgM, IgG, IgA, IgD, and IgE. These proteins are alike in that they react specifically with the antigen or allergen that elicited their production, but differ in their secondary properties, properties that are manifest after they combine with the inciting antigen. The structures and special reaction characteristics of the immunoglobulins are shown schematically in Figure 1.

Most B cells initially carry and manufacture IgM antibodies. In the face of many kinds of allergen exposure or under conditions of persistent antigenic stimulation, B cells may undergo a process called class switching. They "switch" from making IgM antibodies to making IgG or IgA or IgE antibodies of the same antigenic or allergenic specificity. The class switch is induced and controlled by T helper (CD4) cells through their formation and release of certain of the ILs or cytokines. Class switching is achieved by retention of the Fab segment carrying the site specifically reactive with the inciting allergen, eliminating the original Fc segment and replacing it with the Fc portion of the new isotype. This results in the production of antibodies whose secondary reaction characteristics, manifest after combination with the inciting allergen, are different from those of the original IgM isotype.

As described below, B cells are ordinarily activated and induced to form antibodies by T cells that have themselves been activated by prior contact with processed foreign antigen or allergen. Thus this process of B cell activation is termed T cell dependent. On rare occasions B cells may encounter what are termed thymus or T cell-independent antigens. These include lectins, polymeric proteins, and a good number of polysaccharides with structures that are able to activate B cells directly by cross-linking B cell surface receptors with little or no T cell help. T-independent response produces mostly IgM, confirming that T helper cell lymphokines are required for class switching.

Immunologically mediated defense and hypersensitivity reactions also depend upon macrophages, phagocytic polymorphonuclear leukocytes, and metabolically active mast cells and basophils. The latter two cell types manufacture, store, and release a host of effector molecules. Acting in concert with the proteins of the serum complement cascade, the ILs, and other regulatory cytokines, these elements comprise a very intricate system that underpins immunologically triggered and directed inflammatory responses. With-

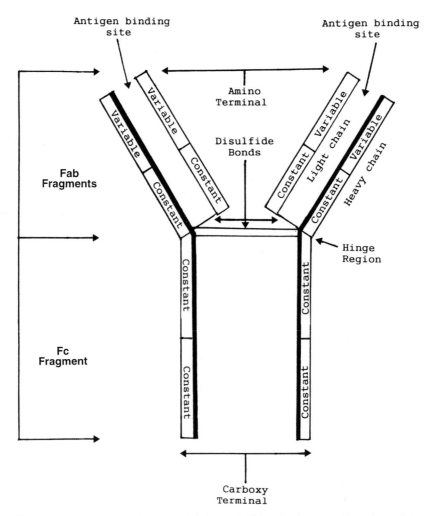

Figure 1 Basic structure of immunoglobulin antibody molecules. Variable regions of the light and the heavy chains constitute the epitope or antigen-combining site. Constant regions of the heavy chain in the Fc fragment hold structures responsible for the secondary reaction attributes of the particular antibody isotype (i.e., complement fixation and binding to cell surface receptors). Immunoglobulins differ in whether they are monomeric, dimeric, or pentameric expressions of this basic structure and in the differing chain lengths and nature of the receptors on the Fc segment of the heavy chains.

out these reactive capacities, humans could not resist infections or tumors and could not long survive.

III. RESPONSE TO ALLERGENS—SENSITIZATION

How then do allergic or hypersensitivity states develop? The series of steps that follow and the atten-dant explanations identify the mechanisms that operate in the genesis and expression of the four classic hypersensitivity states as classified by Gell and Coombs. Sensitization to an airborne pollen will serve to illustrate the typical reaction sequence.

Pollen grains are breathed in through the nose and impinge on the nasal mucous membrane. The pollen is partially solubilized and a major sensitizing antigen is absorbed into the underlying tissues. Here the pollen antigen or allergen encounters and is engulfed by a macrophage. Within this remarkable cell, the allergen is dissembled into polypeptide fragments. In association with a structure termed the class II major histocompatability complex (MHC-II), these fragments are externalized and presented on the surface of the macrophage. By the time this allergen processing is complete, the macrophage has most likely migrated to the environment of a regional lymph node.

Next, the macrophage displaying the allergen fragment or MHC-II complex is perused by a series of helper T cells (CD4 cells). Then a particular T helper cell bearing a T cell receptor (TCR) with a structural configuration complementary to that of the pollen fragment locates and locks on to the pollen MHC-II complex through its receptor. At some point in this process, the pollen fragment is confirmed as foreign, and the T cell is activated.

This antigen-processing activity just described as a function of macrophages can also be carried out by B cells—particularly those whose surface receptors fit the foreign antigen or allergen especially well. The B cell may internalize the antigen, process it, couple it with the MHC-II complex, and present it to the appropriate T helper cell, much as does the macrophage.

The activated T helper cell undergoes clonal proliferation and differentiation. The derivative T helper cells produce and release a number of soluble substances called lymphokines, which activate those B cells that carry surface receptors akin to those on the T cell (i.e., those that are also structurally complementary and specifically reactive with the allergen). In addition, some of the activated T helper cells differentiate into effector cells that are destined to bring about delayed hypersensitivity (DH) reactions on subsequent contact with the inciting allergen (below). Some become memory T cells, cells poised for rapid mass reaction if they later again encounter the same antigen. This is termed a secondary or recall response and is more rapid than the initial or primary response.

The activated B cells in turn proliferate and differentiate into plasma cells that produce and excrete large amounts of antibody specifically reactive with the allergen. Almost invariably, several lineages of plasma cells develop, each of which manufacture and release antibodies of differing isotypes. Thus stimulation by a single allergen, such as an airborne pollen,

results in the production of IgG as well as IgE antibodies and also in the induction of a condition of delayed hypersensitivity mediated by special T helper cells.

There is one other variant of the allergic response that needs to be mentioned. Rarely, when some individuals are treated with a drug such as an antibiotic like penicillin, the drug or some metabolite of it may bind to the surface membrane of a cell (e.g., a red cell). In this attached configuration, the drug may prompt an antibody response with its own structure acting as the "foreign" determinant. The resulting antibodies will subsequently seek out and combine with any of the individual's red cells carrying the penicillin or penicillin metabolite. The combination between the antibody and penicillin determinant on the red cell may activate the complement system and the red cell may be lysed or ruptured.

IV. MANIFESTATIONS OF HYPERSENSITIVITY STATES

Once initial contacts with an allergen have occurred and the foregoing reactions have ensued, the individual is said to have been "sensitized." The diversity of these responses to initial stimulation with a single allergen accounts for the different hypersensitivity reactions that result on subsequent contact with the allergen. These four kinds of reactions may be described as follows.

Type I or the immediate type of hypersensitivity, mediated by IgE antibody, is what most people recognize as classic allergies. IgE antibodies, formed after initial sensitizing contact with the pollen or other allergen, attach themselves by their Fc piece to the surface of submucosal mast cells and circulating basophils. When the pollen or other sensitizing allergen again gains access to the tissues, it reacts with the mast cell-bound IgE antibodies, cross-linking them and triggering the degranulation of the cells. This degranulation releases a series of biologically active mediators into the tissues, including histamine, leucotrienes, prostaglandins, and eosinophil chemotactic factor. These compounds cause an acute inflammatory response in the upper and/or the lower airways with vasodilation, itching, local tissue swelling, increased mucous gland secretion, smooth muscle contraction and eosinophilic infiltration. This is the mechanism behind hay fever or allergic rhinitis, allergic asthma, and the life-threatening anaphylactic reactions to bee or wasp stings or to penicillin administration in pencillin-allergic individuals.

Type II or cytotoxic hypersensitivity may be expressed in three forms. Each of the reaction sequences requires antibody. If the sensitizing foreign material is a drug or a drug metabolite that has been incorporated into a cell membrane, perhaps the membrane of a red blood cell, antibodies (most often of the IgG isotype) attach to the bound drug and attract and activate the serum complement system. This results in lysis of the red cells. If this process is sufficiently widespread, it can produce a serious hemolytic anemia. Alternatively, antibody attached to a membrane-fixed determinant may attract and secondarily bind through its Fc receptor to what are termed natural killer cells (NK cells). These cells can, by a process not yet completely understood, also bring about lysis of the antibody-coated target cell. Finally, if the allergen–antibody-coated cell is not too large, it may be opsonized and destroyed by engulfment by a phagocytic cell, which also hooks on through a receptor on the Fc fragment of the antibody. It is worth noting that this same type of hypersensitivity reaction in its three variant forms is thought to operate in destroying tissue in a number of autoimmune states. In autoimmune diseases, the membrane-bound target is not a foreign drug or allergen, but is presumably a normal cell constituent mistakenly viewed as foreign by the immune system.

Type III or immune complex hypersensitivity is the immune reaction responsible for a number of clinical conditions, including hypersensitivity lung diseases, serum sickness, and immune complex kidney disease. Antigen exposure in this disorder is usually intense and protracted. This leads to a quantitatively impressive antibody response because the sensitizing antigen or allergen is often cleared from the body with difficulty. The allergen and the antibodies combine and then fix complement, which results in an inflammatory reaction. Vascular walls are damaged in the process and their permeability is increased. As a result of this initial damage, the deposition of the immune complexes in the vascular walls and tissues may then worsen and perpetuate the inflammatory cycle by attracting polymorphonuclear leukocytes that further accentuate local tissue damage. When such complexes deposit in renal glomeruli, kidney disease results. The presence of immune complexes in the circulation is not an uncommon event. Ordinarily they are rapidly removed by circulating red cells (picked up by red blood cell complement receptor) or by phagocytosis. It is when the complexes are formed in the presence of antigen excess that they deposit in tissues and tissue damage ensues.

The mechanism of Type IV hypersensitivity (also termed tuberculin, contact, or delayed hypersensitivity) is antibody independent and is mediated by T cells alone. The very descriptive term *delayed* hypersensitivity is employed because the reaction becomes manifest and reaches its peak only after about 48 hours following reexposure to the sensitizing antigen. A subset of T cells of the CD4 type especially programmed to secrete cytokines IL 2 and Interferon N (IFN) gamma appear to be responsible for precipitating the Type IV inflammatory reaction and the consequent tissue damage. If it is sufficiently intense, a local delayed hypersensitivity reaction can result in vascular occlusion and tissue necrosis. Delayed hypersensitivity underlies the disease contact dermatitis, as in the reaction to poison ivy, and under such circumstances is clearly deleterious. Paradoxically, as noted earlier, this same hypersensitivity state is an absolutely crucial feature of the complex immune response, which serves to contain virus infections and to control mycotic and intracellular microbial infections such as tuberculosis. This is also the reaction responsible for the diagnostically useful tuberculin skin test.

V. INVOLUTION OF HYPERSENSITIVITY STATES WITH AGING

Again, the vigor of immune responses, including allergic or hypersensitivity reactions, diminishes in the elderly. The nature of the impairment has been studied extensively over the past two decades, and we now know some of the bases for immunologic senescence. These changes are best understood in light of the mechanisms producing the hypersensitivity reactions just described.

Although there are some variations in published reports, the overall number of immunocompetent cells and their various subsets does not appear to change much with advancing age except very near the end of the individual's life. This phenomenon has been well documented in the Baltimore Longitudinal Study of

Aging. In the majority of the subjects, the absolute peripheral blood lymphocyte count remained within the normal range into advanced age. However, a marked lymphopenia was found in men in the 3 years preceding their deaths. Although in most studies in humans, B cell and macrophage numbers appear to be maintained, and the total number of T cells may remain nearly constant, there seems to be an increase in the proportion of immature T cells in the elderly.

This release of immature T cells into the peripheral blood of the elderly may reflect changes in the thymus, the organ that consistently shows the most dramatic changes as humans grow older. This key structure, so important in the development and management of T cell activity, begins to involute at puberty and continues to do so until middle age. After the age of 50, the thymus contains less than 10% of its previous immunologically active cell mass—most of which is replaced by adipose tissue. As this process progresses, there is a concomitant decline in the synthesis and release of regulatory thymic hormones. These hormones are no longer even detectable after the age of 60 years. Some level of thymic activity, however imperfect, is probably maintained in the elderly because T precursor cells continue to leave the bone marrow and home in on the thymus. It appears that the positive and negative selection, the maturation, and programming of the T cells in the thymic environment is impaired. This also may be a key factor that contributes to the increasing autoimmune activity seen in the aged.

Given the extensive involutional changes in the thymus, it is perhaps not surprising that the T cells more than B cells are the most directly and profoundly affected in the aging process. The extant, long-lived peripheral T cell population in the blood, the lymph nodes, and the spleen may also develop functional deficits over time. These are manifest in important ways. Cell-mediated immunity and delayed hypersensitivity, both manifestations of direct T cell effector activity, may be seriously compromised. It has been demonstrated that a group of individuals over 80 who became nonreactive or hyporesponsive in tests for delayed hypersensitivity showed a higher mortality over a 2-year period than did a comparable group who were not hyporesponsive. The loss of delayed hypersensitivity and impairment of specifically directed cytotoxic cell-mediated immunity opens the door for reactivation of latent viral, mycotic, or tubercular infections.

Furthermore, perhaps reflecting the repeated immunologic stimulation that accrues over the years, the elderly show increasing numbers of T cells committed to memory function.

T cells from the aged when placed in culture show a marked decrease in their ability to proliferate when exposed to phytohemagglutin (PHA) or concanavalin A, two potent mitogens (compounds that stimulate cell division). Among old T cells, only about half are able to respond to such stimulation. Furthermore, when they do respond, old T cells show an impairment in calcium uptake, a decrease in enzyme induction, a decrease in protein synthesis, and a decrease in nuclear response to intracellular signals.

All these deficits in the efficiency of intracellular processes diminish the replicative capacity of the T cells. They also substantially decrease the T cell's ability to form and release those soluble regulatory substances so crucial to the T cell role in arousing and controlling the overall immune response.

In this regard, the decline in IL2 production has been extensively studied and the mechansim of the failure defined in some detail. Deficiency in IL2 production has broad ramifications. It affects not only T cells, but B cells and antibody production as well. Deficits in T cell synthesis and release of other ILs, of B cell differentiation factor, and of B cell growth factor decreases the effectiveness of intercellular communication and thus of immunoregulation.

Witness to this failure in immunoregulation in the aged is the decrease in B cell capacity to mount a vigorous specific antibody response to T cell-dependent allergenic or antigenic stimulation. It appears that the B cell response to T cell-independent antigens may be less compromised. The levels of such natural antibodies as isoagglutinins against blood group antigens also decline in the aged. Oddly, other elements of the B cell population show increases in the production of autoantibodies. Fortunately, although old people show an increase in autoantibody activity, they do not often show a concomitant increase in autoimmune diseases.

Defects in regulatory function are also manifest in the proliferation of single B cell lineages in the elderly, which synthesize and release large amounts of monoclonal "antibody" of obscure specificity. These latter immunoglobulins are produced in such quantity that they are manifest as "M" peaks on serum electrophoresis. They appear to be produced by a B cell clone that has escaped normal T cell suppressor or other dampening regulatory influences. Among 90-year-olds, as many as 15 to 20% may show M peaks. Such monoclonal "gammopathies" not infrequently presage the onset of fatal lymphoproliferative malignancies in the elderly.

Macrophages seem to withstand the aging process relatively well, but are not entirely spared. Their number seems not to diminish much with time, and they appear to retain phagocytic and antigen processing and presentation processes fairly well. Importantly, however, their capacity to produce ILs and other soluble factors may be impaired as the individual ages.

It appears to be relatively well established that classic allergic or immediate (Type I) hypersensitivity reactions are far less frequent in old age. The reasons appear to be several. Serum IgE concentrations are significantly lower in the elderly than in the young, and the differences are most marked in males. The specific IgE response to administration of diphtheria toxoid has been found to be lower in the aged, and the intensity of the immediate skin test "weal and flare" reaction is reduced in old people. It is suggested that these findings are not only because of a decrease in the ability to make IgE, but are also a reflection of impaired mast cell function.

Some particularly elegant work has shown a decrease in the production and the response to IL4, the cytokine that is key to controlling the synthesis and release of IgE. As previously noted, this Ig isotype is responsible for immediate hypersensitivity reactions or classic allergies. The impressive decline in IgE explains the disappearance or the diminished intensity of allergic rhinitis and allergic asthma in patients who are up in years. Severe IgE-mediated reactions such as anaphylaxis can occur in the elderly, but they are rare. The involution of the atopic state ranks among the few comforts of growing older.

Serious impairment of immune responses including those in the realm of allergic or hypersensitivity states carries ominous portent. Thus, assessment of the condition of the immune system in the elderly can provide important prognostic insights.

BIBLIOGRAPHY

Barbee, R. A., Lebowitz, M. D., Thomson, H. C., & Burrows, B. (1976). Immediate skin reactivity in a general population sample. *Annals of Internal Medicine, 84,* 129.

Bender, B. S., Nagel, J. E., Adler, W. H., & Andres, R. (1986). Absolute peripheral blood lymphocyte count and subsequent mortality of elderly men. The Baltimore Longitudinal Study of Aging. *Journal of the American Geriatric Society, 34,* 649.

Chang, M. P., Makinodan, T., Peterson, W. J., & Strehler, B. L. (1982). Role of T cells and adherent cells in age-related decline in murine interleukin 2 production. *Journal of Immunology, 129,* 2426.

Cheung, H. T., Twu, J. S., & Richardson, A. (1983). Mechanism of the age-related decline in lymphocyte proliferation: Role of IL-2 production and protein synthesis. *Experimental Gerontology, 18,* 451.

Coombs, R. R. A., & Gell, P. G. H. (1975). Classification of allergic reactions responsible for clinical hypersensitivity and disease. In P. G. H. Gell, R. R. A. Coombs, P. J. Lochman, (Eds.), *Clinical aspects of immunology* (3rd ed., pp. 761–781). Oxford: Blackwell Scientific Publications.

Delespesse, G., DeMaubeuger, J., Kennes, B., Nicaise, R., & Govaerts, A. (1977). IgE mediated hypersensitivity in aging. *Clinical Allergy, 7,* 155.

Kennes, B., Brohee, D., & Meve, P. (1983). Lymphocyte activation in human aging: V. Acquisition of response to T cell growth factor and production of growth factors by mitogen stimulated lymphoytes. *Mechanisms of Aging and Development, 23,* 103.

Lerner, A., Philosophe, B., & Miller, R. A. (1988). Defective calcium influx and preserved inositol phosphate generation in T cells from old mice. *Aging: Immunology and Infectious Disease, 1,* 149.

Palma-Carlos, A. G. (1976). Allergic diseases in the aged. *Allergie und Immunologie, 4,* 187.

Roberts-Thomson, I. C., Whittingham, S., Youngchiayud, U., & Mackay, I. R. (1974). Aging, immune response, and mortality. *Lancet, 2,* 368.

Somers, H., & Kuhns, W. J. (1972). Blood group antibodies in old age. *Proceedings of Social Experimental Biology and Medicine, 141,* 1104.

Tollefsbol, T. O., & Cohen, H. J. (1986). Expression of intracellular biochemical defects of lymphocytes in aging: Proposal of general aging mechanism which is not cell specific. *Experimental Gerontology, 21,* 129.

Vercelli, D. (1993). Regulation of immunoglobulin E synthesis in young and aged humans. In H. J. Zeitz (Ed.), *Immunology and allergy clinics of North America. Immunologic problems in the aged* (Vol. 13, pp. 751). Philadelphia: W.B. Saunders.

Wu, W., Pahlavani, M., Cheung, H. T., & Richardson, A. (1986). The effect of aging on the expression of interleukin 2 messenger ribonucleic acid. *Cell Immunology, 100,* 224.

Arthritis

Elizabeth M. Badley and Linda M. Rothman

Wellesley Hospital Research Institute, Toronto, Ontario, Canada

Arthritis   Conditions involving joint inflammation.
Musculoskeletal   System of the body comprising the bones, cartilage, ligaments, tendons, and joints.
Nonsteroidal Anti-Inflammatory Drugs (NSAIDs) Drugs used to treat inflammation, which is one of the main symptoms of arthritis.

ARTHRITIS is a major cause of morbidity and disability, particularly in older people. Although, strictly speaking the term *arthritis* means inflammation of the joints, this word is commonly used to encompass disorders of the joints, ligaments, tendons, and other components of the musculoskeletal system. Arthritis and rheumatism comprise more than half of the conditions included in the larger classification of musculoskeletal disorders (MSD). Other conditions in the larger family of MSDs are back disorders not associated with arthritis, and metabolic bone disorders such as osteoporosis. These are not covered in this review. Rheumatic disorders is another collective term for conditions affecting the musculoskeletal system.

I. BACKGROUND

The signs and symptoms of arthritis and related conditions are pain, stiffness, swelling, muscle weakness, and limitation of movement of the joints. In aggregate,

these are the most frequent constellation of symptoms that affect older people. The greatest impact in the population is in terms of morbidity and disability. Arthritis is associated with a high use of ambulatory health services and medication, although it is not a major cause of hospitalization or mortality. Traditionally, the burden of arthritis in the population has been underestimated as a result of its low mortality rate and its insidious onset. In a survey in Ontario, Canada, the prevalence of arthritis was 18.5% in the general population, with the prevalence increasing almost linearly with age from 6.3% in the 16–24 age group to 51.2% for those aged 75 and older. Arthritis has been ranked first in prevalence in women ages 45+ and in men 65+ years compared to other chronic conditions. Surveys carried out in the United States provide similar results.

Despite the fact that the frequency of arthritis increases with age, such that for many conditions the majority of those affected are over the age of 60, there are few studies that describe the epidemiology, natural history, and response to therapy in the older segments of the population. Arthritis in the elderly presents special diagnostic challenges to the clinician. The different types of arthritis have an array of symptoms and signs that may appear quite similar. The complaints are often vague and ill defined, and are associated with insidious decline in overall function. Older people may also fail to seek care for symptoms because these conditions are considered by many to be a normal part of aging. Musculoskeletal symptoms can also be caused by other conditions, and multiple conditions in the same patient may complicate both diagnosis and management. Pain is the most common symp-

Table I Clinical Aspects of Common Rheumatologic Disorders in the Elderly[a]

Disorder	Osteoarthritis	Rheumatoid arthritis	Polymyalgia rheumatica	Gout	Pseudogout
Gradual onset	+++	+++	+++	0	+
Joint swelling or effusion	+++	++++	+	++++	++++
Joint pain	++++	++++	+	++++	++++
Symmetrical involvement	+	+++	++++	+	+
Muscle pain	+	+	+++	+	+
Radiographic abnormalities	++++	+++	0	+	+++
Synovial fluid crystals	+	+	0	+++	+++
Elevated sedimentation rate	+	+++	++++	+	+
Anemia	0	++	+++	0	0
Positive antinuclear antibody	0	+	+	0	0
Positive rheumatoid factor	0	+++	+	0	0

[a]0, does not occur; +, occurs occasionally; ++, occurs frequently; +++, almost always occurs; ++++, difficult to make diagnosis without it.

Source: Clinical Aspects of Common Rheumatologic Disorders in the Elderly. Adapted from Table 8–5 in Kane, R. L., Ouslander, J. G., Abrass, I. T., Essentials of Clinical Geriatrics. McGraw–Hill Book Company; 1984.

tom in rheumatic disease patients consulting a physician, and this may be misinterpreted because of the presence of other conditions, including depression. Unfortunately, there are no simple diagnostic tests to facilitate a diagnosis of arthritis.

There are over 100 different types of arthritis and related conditions, so it is not possible to review all of them here. In this chapter, we describe the clinical characteristics, epidemiology, and management of selected types of arthritis, indicating, whenever possible, any special considerations that might apply to the older population. A comparison of the major clinical findings of five common types of arthritis in the elderly is provided in Table I. The chapter concludes with a discussion of the overall impact of arthritis in seniors, and general management strategies to reduce the impact of arthritis in the elderly population.

II. TYPES OF ARTHRITIS IN THE ELDERLY

A. Osteoarthritis

1. Clinical Features

In addition to being the largest single cause of arthritis in humans, osteoarthritis (OA) is a major source of health problems in dogs, horses, and many other ani-mals. Skeletal remains going back to prehistory show signs of osteoarthritis. Despite its high frequency in the population and its importance as a cause of suffering, it is less well studied than many of the other rheumatic disorders. [See RHEUMATIC DISEASES.] Current understanding suggests that OA may be a heterogeneous group of conditions sharing common pathologic features, many of which are visible as the typical changes on X rays. These include joint space narrowing due to loss of articular cartilage and the remodeling of bone, particularly beneath the joint, resulting in patchy thickening (sclerosis) of bones, and subchondral cysts, which are areas of bone loss beneath the cartilage. Remodeling of bone at the joint margins may result in the formation of bony spurs called osteophytes. Figure 1 illustrates the typical changes that can occur with OA. The most common symptom of OA is pain, most often related to joint use, which can also occur at rest and at night. Stiffening or gelling of joints in the morning and after any extended period of inactivity such as sitting, usually occurs, but is relieved within minutes rather than hours with activity. The range of movement of the joints is often restricted, with pain at the end of the range.

OA may affect many joints of the body, most typi-

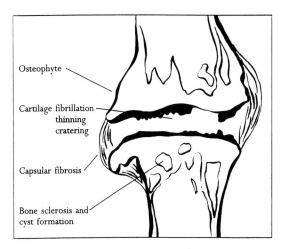

Figure I Pathological features of osteoarthritis. (From Figure 1, Hutton, C. W., Practical problems: Osteoarthritis—Clinical features and management. In R. Butler, M. Jayson, F. McKenna, & D. Scott (Eds.), Reports on Rheumatic Diseases. Chesterfield: Arthritis and Rheumatism Council, 1995: No. 5, Series 3.)

cally the knees, hips, hands, and the spine. The joints most commonly involved in OA are shown in Figure 2. In all joint sites except the hip, OA is more common in women than in men. Diagnosis of OA is difficult for a variety of reasons. There is no clear

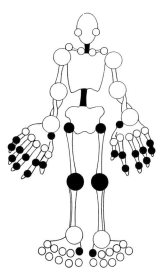

Figure 2 Black shading indicates those joints most often affected in osteoarthritis. (From Figure 1, Cooke, T. D. V., & Dwosh, I. L., (1986). Clinical features of osteoarthritis in the elderly. *Clinics in Rheumatic Diseases, 12*(1), 155–172.)

disease marker, and although there is agreement that pathological, radiological, and clinical components contribute to the diagnosis of OA, there is no consistent correlation between these different manifestations of the disease. At any one time, only a proportion of joints with obvious OA on X rays (approximately 50%) will be clinically troublesome. It is unknown why so many people with radiographic evidence of OA have no symptoms or disability.

OA can occur without any obvious predispositions, or it can apparently result from a previous injury or disease of a joint that may have occurred many years earlier. There have been attempts to classify the different syndromes of OA based on the pattern of joints affected. An important distinguishing feature of OA is that the shoulders, elbows, wrists, and ankles are seldom affected in primary OA, as they are in inflammatory arthritis such as rheumatoid arthritis (see below). Although not primarily inflammatory, patients with OA may have episodes of inflammatory osteoarthritis with swelling and warmth of the affected joint. OA is slow to evolve, and often has periods of relative stability lasting many years. Rapid progression can occur, and spontaneous improvement is a rare but well-described phenomenon.

2. Epidemiology and Risk Factors

OA is the most frequently occurring type of arthritis in the population. Very little data exist measuring the incidence of OA in the population, as there are problems in defining the disease onset and a lack of longitudinal data. Prevalence data indicate the OA increases with age, with age being the most powerful risk factor for the disease. The prevalence of osteoarthritis in the population aged 65 years and older ranges from 33% for symptomatic OA to more than 80% for OA defined by radiographic changes. It has been estimated that due to the aging of the population in Canada, the number of people with OA-associated disability will almost double between 1986 and 2020. In the United States, it has been estimated that the number of people with activity limitation associated with arthritis would increase by 45% between the years of 1985 and 2000.

Risk factors for osteoarthritis are those related to a generalized susceptibility to the disease, and to mechanical factors resulting in abnormal biomechanical loading of joints. Susceptibility to OA has been found to be related to increased age, obesity, heredity, and female sex. There are marked racial differences in prevalence and distribution. Factors that have been found to be negatively associated with OA include the presence of osteoporosis (especially at the hip joint) and cigarette smoking. [See BONE AND OSTEO-POROSIS.] Trauma to the joint, joint incongruency, and occupational or leisure physical activities that involve repetitive use of particular joint groups resulting in abnormal biomechanical loading of joints are associated with the development of OA. Low socioeconomic status has also been associated with increased rates of arthritis in general, as well as for many other chronic diseases. Although there exists some secular and geographic variability in the rates of osteoarthritis this has not, to date, been adequately explained.

3. Management

The treatment of OA is largely symptomatic. OA is still widely thought to be a degenerative disease caused by aging and excessive use of the joints (a "wear-and-tear" disease). Evidence to the contrary is extensive but old concepts of OA are still prevalent in the medical community as well as in the public domain. OA is easily dismissed as "one of those things"; an inevitable part of the aging process about which nothing can be done. Furthermore, patients and caregivers may believe that it is best to be inactive to protect joints—a strategy that can have disastrous consequences.

The objectives of management are relief of symptoms to minimize disability and impact on quality of life and to limit progression of the disease. The outcome of OA is very heterogeneous. An obvious management goal is to reduce the risk of progression and prevent phases of rapid worsening, although this assumes an understanding of what factors control the outcome. Mechanical factors almost certainly play a part; instability and malalignment of joint probably accelerate OA and should be corrected where possible. Pain, loss of motion of the joints, and muscle weakness will all contribute to the development of disability.

Ideally, a hierarchical cumulative approach to management of OA should be used. All patients with OA should receive input regarding education, counselling, and dietary advice if overweight. For those with more severe OA, teaching about joint protection may be required and it is important to assess level of function and handicap. Shoe alterations and walking aids can help alleviate problems of biomechanic ori-

gin, and assistive devices may be needed to assist with activities of daily living. Simple analgesics, either on a regular or an on-demand basis, are the mainstay for treatment of pain, and short courses of Nonsteroidal anti-inflammatory drugs (NSAIDs) may be needed for control of more severe symptoms. Finally, other options for the minority of patients who present with very severe symptoms include intra-articular steroids, joint lavage, debridement, medical synovectomy, and major surgical procedures such as joint replacement.

The causes of the symptoms are poorly understood. In view of this it is not surprising that there is still debate about the value of drugs and many other treatment modalities. NSAIDs are widely prescribed. Their use in the older population has recently been brought into question. Changes in the metabolism of older people, particularly kidney and liver function, may lead to potentially serious or even lethal side effects when drugs are taken in full doses. As a general principle, it is recommended that elderly patients receive a reduced dose. Adverse events, such as gastrointestinal bleeding, may be silent or asymptomatic and may eventually cause a major medical emergency. It has also been suggested that some types of NSAIDs may even accelerate the progression of OA, because of their affect on prostaglandin metabolism in the joints. It is important, therefore, to carefully weigh the benefits of the use of NSAIDs with the potential risks.

Studies have demonstrated that for OA of the knee, simple analgesics such as acetaminophen, codeine, and low-dose salicylates can result in clinically important relief of symptoms similar to NSAIDs. Local applications that include NSAIDs have been developed. These and other rubs have been shown to be beneficial in some cases. Nonpharmacologic methods of pain relief, such as acupuncture, may also help, although these techniques have not been well studied for this disorder.

In advanced cases surgery may be indicated. The techniques include realignment of joints by osteotomy and partial or total joint replacement. Total hip and total knee replacements are well established and frequently result in dramatic relief of pain and improvement of function. Indications for surgery are uncontrolled pain, particularly pain at rest and pain at night, and increasing disability. Joint replacement protheses have a limited life (around 20 years), but this is not a contraindication in the older individual.

B. Crystal-Induced Types of Arthritis

These are a family of types of arthritis which have in common the finding of microscopic crystals in the tissues or synovial fluid of the joint. The crystals are believed to play a role in the inflammatory process of the disease.

C. Gout

I. Clinical Features

The most common type of crystal arthritis is gout. Gout occurs as uric acid crystallizes in the joints, causing intense inflammation. The joint is typically, hot, red, and swollen and the pain is extreme. Attacks of gout may be associated with the taking of diuretic therapy, particularly in women. Gout attacks frequently affect the lower extremities, classically the big toe. Any joint may be affected, and particularly in older women gout attacks may be located in the distal finger joints previously damaged by osteoarthritis. In the elderly, gouty arthritis is more difficult to diagnose as it is often less acute than in younger patients and may be mistaken for OA. This can be further complicated as occasionally gout and OA coexist, even in the same joints.

2. Epidemiology and Risk Factors

Gout is the most common cause of inflammatory arthritis in men over the age of 40, with a peak incidence in the fifth decade. The peak incidence for females is over the age of 60. It is difficult to determine incidence and prevalence rates of the disease, as the course of the disease is characterized by exacerbations and remissions. There is also a tendency for misdiagnosis by both patients and clinicians. Estimated prevalence rates are 5–28/1000 for males, and 1–6/1000 for females in the United States. It has been estimated that gout is probably the second most common form of inflammatory arthritis in the United States. It occurs worldwide, and regional differences may reflect racial predisposition, although this has not been proven. Gout frequently results in occupational limitations, increased use of medical services, and significant short-term disability, making the disease a significant public health problem.

The epidemiology of gout appears to be changing. Studies of temporal trends have indicated increases in prevalence over the last few decades in several countries with high standards of living. The sex ratio has also changed with the ratio of males to females with gout previously being 20:1, but recent figures now are 2–7:1. It has been suggested that these changes may be attributed to the use of drugs, increased longevity, and changes in lifestyle.

Risk factors for gout are varied. The plasma urate concentration is directly related to the risk of developing gout. The risk of developing gout is similar in males and females for particular urate concentrations, and the lower prevalence of gout in females is likely indicative of lower urate concentrations. Urate concentrations are highly age dependent, with levels increasing with age. There appears to be a genetic predisposition to the disease, as gout is associated with inherited enzyme abnormalities, and inherited urate under-excretion. Environmental factors are also important, as gout is associated with diet, drugs, and toxins (e.g., lead).

3. Management

Treatment of an acute episode of gout is with an appropriate NSAID, particularly one with serum uric acid-lowering properties. If there are three or more attacks in one year, treatment includes allopurinol with or without colchicine. For patients with severe or frequent attacks of gout and tophi (deposition of uric acid in locations under the skin), long-term therapy (hypouricemic therapy) can be given to lower the level of uric acid in the blood so as to reverse the deposition of urate and prevent further attacks.

D. Calcium Phyrophosphate Deposition Arthropathy

I. Clinical Features

Inflammation in calcium phyrophosphate deposition arthropathy (CPPD) is induced by the presence of crystals of calcium pyrophosphate (CPP) in the joints. At least 50% of the attacks are in the knees, but the shoulders, wrists, and ankles may also be affected. Although not as painful or intense as gout, the syndrome is just as common. It is often seen in people with preexisting OA.

2. Epidemiology and Risk Factors

CPPD arthropathy occurs most often in aging females. The mean age of onset is between 65–75 years. It is estimated that it affects 10–15% in those aged 65–75, and 30–60% in those over 85 years. CPPD has been reported throughout the world. There appears to be familial aggregation, but no genetic associations have been identified to date. CPPD arthropathy appears to be associated with aging of the articular cartilage, although so far the nature of this association has not been clarified.

3. Management

The aims of treatment are to reduce symptoms, to identify and treat any triggering illness, and to rapidly mobilize the patients as inflammation settles. Rapid mobilization is important as older patients are prone to complications from prolonged immobility. In many cases joint aspiration to remove synovial fluid from the joint may be the only treatment required. An intra-articular steroid injection may be appropriate for a joint that does not settle after the first aspiration. Analgesic and anti-inflammatory drugs may provide additional benefit when used with caution in these elderly patients. Management of CPPD arthropathy includes controlling chronic inflammation with NSAIDs and reducing adverse mechanical stress (see section IV). Surgery such as total joint replacement may be necessary in the presence of advanced joint degeneration.

E. Rheumatoid Arthritis

1. Clinical Features

Rheumatoid arthritis (RA) is one of the most common autoimmune diseases. It typically begins as symmetrical pain and swelling of the small joints of the hands and feet. A major symptom of RA is stiffness in the morning that can last for several hours. The disease is typically accompanied by fatigue, anorexia, and weight loss. Table II compares the characteristics of RA and OA.

The peak onset of RA is in midlife, although onset late in life is not rare. Older RA patients fall into two categories: patients who have suffered from chronic RA for many years or even decades, and patients with recent or new onset of disease. Patients with established disease may still have active disease, or may be burnt out but still have symptoms because of secondary degenerative changes in joints previously damaged by RA. Rehabilitation and nondrug modalities make an important contribution to the clinical

management of RA. One of the major advances in the care of older patients with significant deformity as a result of RA has been the evolution of orthopedic surgery, especially total joint replacement. There is every reason to believe that in the long run the outcome of surgery in older patients is at least as good, if not better, as for younger patients.

RA with onset in the older patient may differ from the disease in the younger adult. Extra-articular manifestations of the disease (such as vasculitis) occur less often in the late-onset patient. Late-onset RA may include a seronegative benign synovitis similar to polymyalgia rheumatica (see below). The course of RA is unpredictable. The majority of patients will experience intermittent periods of active disease alternating with periods of relative or complete remission. A minority may have complete remission, but a small group of patients will have severe, unrelenting, progressive disease. Irreversible joint deformities may also characterize the physical findings of people with long duration and greater severity of disease. These may lead to difficulties in walking and with activities of daily living (ADLs) and result in significant functional disablement.

2. Epidemiology and Risk Factors

The prevalence of RA has been estimated at between 1–2% for the general population, with the prevalence increasing with age in both men and women. A U.S. National Health Examination Survey (1960–1962), found a prevalence of RA of over 10% of the population over the age of 65. The sex ratio of RA also varies with age. The disease affects mainly females under the age of 60, but over age 60 the relative proportion of males increases to approach a much more equal sex ratio. Previously, the peak onset of RA was between ages 35–55, but it appears that this peak age has been increasing. This may imply a change in the characteristics of the disease. Other changes over time include a decrease in the incidence of RA in U.S. and European populations. The reasons for this are unclear.

In addition to age-related predisposing factors, sex hormones may play a role in predisposition to RA. There is evidence of nulliparous women having increased risk, as pregnancy is associated with remissions of the disease and postpartum periods with exacerbations, symptomatic onset occurs at menopause, and oral contraceptives decrease the risk of RA. Other

Table II Clinical Features of Osteoarthritis versus Inflammatory Arthritides[a]

Clinical features	Osteoarthritis	Inflammatory arthritides
Duration of stiffness	Minutes	Hours
Pain	Usually with activity	Occurs even at rest and at night
Fatigue	Unusual	Common
Swelling	Common, but little synovial reaction	Very common with synovial proliferation and thickening
Erythema and warmth	Unusual	Common

[a]Osteoarthritis may also be inflammatory.

Source: Clinical features of Osteoarthritis versus Inflammatory Arthritides. From Table 8–6 in Kane, R. L., Ouslander, J. G., Abrass, I. T., Essentials of Clinical Geriatrics. McGraw–Hill Book Company; 1984.

factors that have been found to be positively associated with the disease include low socioeconomic status and low education and psychological stress. Although climate, geography, and altitude do not appear to affect the prevalence of RA, there is evidence that the occurrence of RA varies between populations. Prevalence rates have been found to be particularly low in oriental populations, and high in adult Native American populations. The reasons for this variability have not been well defined.

3. Management

Treatment of RA is similar in outline to that of other forms of arthritis, although the content may be different. The mainstay of treatment for RA in the elderly is medication, which is similar to that in the younger patient, with the caveat that adverse drug reactions may be more likely. Classically, physicians have followed the pyramid approach when selecting drug treatment in RA. Simpler, safer, and less potent drugs (NSAIDs) are used first, and more powerful, possibly dangerous drugs are reserved for later phases or resistant cases. However, it is increasingly suggested that the optimal approach to treatment should include early use of the powerful drugs, the so-called slow-acting antirheumatic drugs (SAARD). The drugs include potentially disease-modifying and immunosuppressive agents, and as their name suggests, there is a delay, of up to 6 months depending on the drug, before their benefits are felt. These drugs carry a greater risk of serious adverse effects, and their use needs to be carefully monitored under the supervision

of a physician experienced in the treatment of RA. Corticosteroids may also have a place in treatment, either systemically in low doses (although there is a risk of complications including an increased risk of osteoporosis) or injected into inflamed joints to reduce inflammation. For more details about the drugs available and the complex subject of the treatment of RA, readers are referred to medical or patient information texts. The latter are available from arthritis organizations, such as the Arthritis Foundation in the United States and The Arthritis Society in Canada.

Surgical treatment for RA patients often is recommended to relieve unresolved pain, loss of function, and deformity. The major goals of various orthopedic procedures are to relieve symptoms and to improve function. Joint replacement of the hips and knees, tendon repair, and carpal tunnel release are some of the more frequently employed measures in the elderly. Age itself is not a contraindication for surgery, nor a predictor of poor results. RA is an important cause of disability. The general principles of the management of disabling arthritis are reviewed below.

F. Polymyalgia Rheumatica

1. Clinical Features

Polymyalgia rheumatica (PMR) is a clinical syndrome of middle-aged and elderly people characterized by pain and stiffness in the neck, shoulder, and pelvic girdles, often accompanied by constitutional symptoms such as fever, fatigue, anorexia, and weight loss. Stiffness is the predominant feature and is particularly severe after rest and may prevent the patient from getting out of bed in the morning. Muscular pain is often diffuse and is accentuated by movement. Pain at night is common.

2. Epidemiology and Risk Factors

PMR is a condition of the older patient. It is seldom diagnosed under the age of 50. The mean onset of PMR is approximately 70 years, with a range of about 50–90 years. Women are affected two to three times more often than men. It is difficult to determine prevalence and incidence rates of the disease, as there is lack of specificity of signs and symptoms. The annual incidence rate has been estimated at 50/100,000 for persons over the age of 50.

There may be a genetic predisposition to the disease, as there appears to be familial aggregation. Environmental factors may also be important, as there is clustering of cases in time and place. The greatest majority of patients are Caucasian, and the disease appears to be more common in the northern United States and Canada, as compared to the southern states.

3. Management

Of the forms of arthritis affecting the elderly, PMR is one of the more difficult to diagnose and one of the most important to identify. The response to small doses of corticosteroid treatment may be dramatic. This treatment is usually required for at least 2 years. PMR may be confused with late-onset RA in elderly patients. A certain percentage of patients with PMR will also suffer from temporal arteritis, frequently with involvement of the ophthalmic arteries. If the latter condition is allowed to go untreated it carries a serious threat of permanent blindness, which can be averted through the use of large doses of corticosteroids. Unfortunately there is no specific test for PMR.

III. IMPACT OF ARTHRITIS IN THE ELDERLY POPULATION

The greatest impact of arthritis in the population is in terms of morbidity and disability, with the major burden of this group of conditions resting within the elderly population. Arthritis is the most frequently cited cause of activity limitations for men and women age 45+ compared to other chronic conditions, with the prevalence of arthritis disability being generally higher in females. According to data from the U.S. national Longitudinal Study on Aging (1984), community-dwelling elderly (ages 70+) who report arthritis represent the greatest proportion of individuals with physical limitations (68%), limitations in ADLs (75%), and instrumental ADLs (70%), such as shopping, managing money, and housework.

RA and other inflammatory arthropathies are commonly viewed as the most likely types of arthritis to lead to disability. Data from population surveys suggest, however, that the most frequent cause of arthritis-related disability is OA. Although a smaller proportion of people with OA than RA experience disability, because of its much higher overall prevalence (10% of OA in the general population versus 1% of RA), OA is the most frequent cause of disabling arthritis. Population data indicate that there are +7 people with OA and severe disability for every 1 person with severe disability and RA.

Disabling arthritis is likely to have an impact on all aspects of life. Table III presents a picture of the scope of the impact on individuals aged 65 years or older with arthritis-related disability. The data are from the 1986 Canadian Health and Activity Limitation Survey (HALS). Although the data cannot be broken down into types of arthritis, it is important to remember that the majority of people with disabling arthritis in this age group will have OA, which is predominant in the aging population.

For people with arthritis-associated disability, there may be an impact on mobility, which is the ability to move around effectively in the environment. Virtually all people in this age group had some trouble with mobility such as walking, standing, or climbing stairs (93%). Thirty-four percent were unable to leave their residence independently. There may be a loss of physical independence, with the need to rely on the help of other people. Three-quarters of those with arthritis disability experienced some dependence due to disability, and half were dependent on help weekly or more often. Against this backdrop it should be noted that over one-third of those with arthritis disability lived alone. There is also an effect on occupation, including work, leisure, and obligations in the home. Over 80% of people never attended sporting events, concerts, plays, or movies, 46% never participated in

Table III Indicators of the Effect of Arthritis on the Lives of Those with Arthritis Associated Disability over the Age of 65 in Canada

Indicator of effect on daily life	Persons with disability affected over the age of 65 (%)
Mobility	
At least some trouble with mobility[a]	92.5
Trouble or unable to climb stairs	69.2
Trouble or unable to walk 400 yards	70.5
Trouble or unable to stand >20 min	68.0
Cannot leave residence or only with attendant	33.8
Physical Independence	
Some dependence because of disability[b]	74.1
Dependent on help weekly or more often[b]	51.5
Trouble or unable to bend to pick up object	52.3
Trouble or unable to cut toe or fingernails	48.6
Trouble or unable to get in or out of bed	20.1
Trouble or unable to dress	17.2
Social Integration	
Lives alone	32.8
Never visits relatives or friends	19.8
Occupation	
Never attends sporting events, concerts, plays, or movies	83.3
Never participates in hobbies, arts, crafts	46.0
Never participates in social activities	20.1
Socioeconomic self-sufficiency	
Income <$20,000	63.4
Out-of-pocket expenses because of disability[c]	35.6
Base population >age 65 (thousands)	266195

[a]Has trouble with or is unable to do one or more of the following: walk 400 yards without resting, walk up or down a flight of stairs, carry an object of 10 lbs for 30 ft, move from one room to another, stand for more than 20 min.

[b]Dependence, help because of health problem. Occasional: heavy household chores; looking after personal finances (e.g., banking, paying bills). Weekly or more frequent: shopping for groceries or other necessities; everyday housework. Daily: personal care (e.g., washing, grooming, dressing, feeding); moving about within own residence; preparing meals.

[c]Out-of-pocket expenses for medication, special aids or supplies, health and medical services not covered by insurance, modifications to residence, transportation, personal services (e.g., attendant, housekeeping services, etc.).

hobbies, arts, or crafts, and 20% never participated in social activities. Social integration may be affected as well as relationships with other people. Finally, there may be reduced economic self-sufficiency, not only through reduced earning power, but also as a result of the extra expenses incurred because of the disease. Sixty-four percent of seniors with arthritis disability had an income of less than $20,000, and 36% incurred extra expenses as a result of their disability.

IV. MANAGEMENT OF ARTHRITIS IMPACT

The principles for management of the painful and disabling consequences of arthritis are similar for all types of arthritis. Ideally, arthritis is treated early to prevent its progression to impairment and disability. The medical management of specific types of arthritis has been previously discussed. More generally, a family physician or general practitioner (or in some cases nurse practitioners) may manage the arthritis problem if it is straightforward, or can act as a gatekeeper for referral to other services. Unfortunately, research suggests that due to inadequate training regarding musculoskeletal conditions, primary-care management of arthritis can frequently be suboptimal. The medical specialist particularly concerned with the treatment of people with arthritis is the rheumatologist. The corresponding surgical specialty is orthopedics. Specialist care is desirable for conditions such as RA, at least to establish an appropriate management strategy. This type of care usually includes a complete diagnostic workup, and advice regarding the appropriate drug regime together with appropriate monitoring of the patient for medication side effects. Tertiary care services may also be provided in some centers by rheumatologists who specialize in some of the rarer arthritis disorders. Appropriate and timely referral to orthopedic survey is also important, particularly in view of the potential for total joint replacements and other types of surgery to control pain and restore function.

Physical therapy and occupational therapy are also important in the management of arthritis, although there has been little research to date investigating the efficacy of therapy interventions. Physical therapy strategies include exercises that aim to maintain or increase range of joint motion, to correct or prevent muscle weakness or wasting (which may also lead to instability of joints), and to help correct malalignment of joints or abnormal use of joints or both. Hydrotherapy (exercise in water) can have advantages particularly for people with severe arthritis, as the buoyancy of the water helps reduce the stress on the joints. Although the use of exercise as a mode of treatment for arthritis is a topic that has been relatively neglected in the literature, there is some evidence that exercise can reduce pain, suppress need for medication, and help maintain function. There is also some suggestion that cartilage repair occurs with a regular program of exercise.

It is important to encourage moderate levels of general physical activity within the limits of severe fatigue. Brief periods of several days of enforced rest may be followed by loss of muscle strength, with the risk of a permanent decline in functional ability, including ability to walk. Even in the presence of active RA with constitutional manifestations, it is important that elderly persons maintain a certain level of physical activity to maintain function.

Occupational therapists are involved in the care of people with arthritis, by constructing splints to stabilize joints and reduce pain and by providing input regarding environmental modifications to facilitate the performance of ADLs. Occupational therapists also conduct functional evaluations that are essential for treatment planning for older patients. Being able to transfer from a chair to a standing position, walk short distances, and get on and off a toilet independently may make the difference between living independently and requiring physical assistance or even institutionalization. Occupational therapists also offer education regarding joint protection and energy conservation techniques, which may help to reduce and improve joint alignment and prevent muscle fatigue.

Both occupational therapists and physical therapists may provide input regarding assistive devices and environmental modifications. The availability and use of assistive devices can make an important contribution to maintaining independence in people with arthritis disability. Assistive devices may be useful, for example, to help put on shoes and stockings or to open jars. Other devices include raised chair or toilet seats to facilitate rising from sitting, and bath seats to assist bathing. Adapted shoes are also particularly important in lower limb arthritis. Extra depth shoes and orthoses may accommodate the anatomical changes of aging and help to cushion the heel to absorb impact loading. Simple walking aids such as a cane can also reduce joint loading and reduce pain. Finally, adaptations to the physical environment in the home, such as handrails in the bathroom and on stairs may be important in preserving independence. [See GERONTECHNOLOGY.]

Education is another important management strategy that may be offered at many different levels. Physicians, therapists, and trained laypeople may all be involved in educating people about their arthritis. Education is important to promote the patient's, their relative's, and their caregiver's understanding of the condition so they know what they can do to adapt and cope with pain and the disabilities that may result from arthritis. Education can cover a variety of topics. Currently, education focuses on providing advice about activity and exercise, pain management techniques and the use of simple aids (such as canes), and joint protection. Educational and community support interventions have been found to have a positive impact on many aspects of health status, including knowledge, pain, compliance with medication, emotional and social well-being, and disability. Programs that include and emphasize problem solving, coping, self-efficacy, and endurance exercise have proven more effective than traditional programs that emphasize pathophysiology, range of movement, and joint protection.

All the previous management strategies outlined above focus on the individual and what they can do within their immediate environment to manage their arthritis. The broad social environment can also make an important contribution to reducing the impact of arthritis on individuals. The social environment encompasses the attitudes of others, both within the family and in the community in general, cultural background and values, and expectations. Increased public awareness of arthritis could result in changes that would greatly enhance an individual's quality of life, by providing a more accepting and adaptable environment that would ultimately facilitate function of older people with arthritis.

ACKNOWLEDGMENTS

We thank Mary Bell, MD, MSc, FRCP(C) for her assistance in reviewing this manuscript. Funding for the authors is provided by the Ontario Ministry of Health through their Health-System Linked research unit grant scheme, National Health Research and Development Program (Seniors' Independence Research Program), and The Arthritis Society (Canada).

BIBLIOGRAPHY

Kane, R. L., Ouslander, J. G., & Abrass, I. B. (1984). *Essentials of clinical geriatrics*. New York: McGraw-Hill Book Company.
Kean, W. F. (Ed.). (1986). *Clinics in rheumatic diseases, arthritis in the elderly* (Vol. 12, No. 1). London: W.B. Saunders.
Klippel, J. E., & Dieppe, P. A. (Ed.). (1994). *Rheumatology*. London: Mosby-Year Book Europe Limited.
Schumacher, H. R. (Ed.). (1993). *Primer on the rheumatic diseases* (10th ed.). Atlanta: Arthritis Foundation.

Atherosclerosis

Michael T. Crow, Claudio Bilato, and Edward G. Lakatta

National Institute on Aging

Advanced Glycation End Products Proteins or lipids that have been irreversibly modified by nonenzymatic glycation and oxidation.

Arteriosclerosis The thickening of the medial layer and stiffening of arterial blood vessels.

Atherosclerosis An inflammatory-fibroproliferative disease of the inner layer of larger arteries that underlies almost all coronary heart disease as well as many other cardiovascular diseases.

Fatty Streak One of the earliest recognized stages in the development of atherosclerosis, characterized by the presence of foam cells, lipid-laden macrophages and vascular smooth muscle cells.

Fibroatheroma An advanced stage of atherosclerosis characterized by elevated, opaque, and hard lesions.

Fibrous/Complicated Plaque An advanced stage of atherosclerosis characterized by endothelial layer ulcerations, cyclic thrombus and collagen deposition, and gradual lumenal reduction.

Nuclear Factor-κB (NF-κB) A DNA-binding complex composed of c-rel proteins, p50, or p65 required for the increased transcription of a number of genes whose products are involved in attraction, transmigration, and differentiation of monocytes to form the fatty streak.

Preatheroma An intermediate stage of atherosclerosis development characterized by the elaboration of extracellular matrix components and resulting in alternating layers of macrophages, T cells, and smooth muscle cells recruited by the tunica media.

Relative Risk (Ratio) The ratio of the risk value in the presence and absence of the variable under examination.

Tunica Intima (or Intima) The region of the blood vessel between the lumen and internal elastic lamina, containing the endothelium, continuous basal lamina, and, depending on species, age, and underlying pathology, interstitial matrix or vascular smooth muscle cells.

Tunica Media (or Media) The region of blood vessel between the internal and external elastic laminae, containing vascular smooth muscle cells specialized for contraction.

In the United States, cardiovascular diseases (CVD) linked to **ATHEROSCLEROSIS** account for more than 25% of deaths in the population below age 65, but they become by far the leading causes of mortality among individuals over 65 (51% in men and 56% in women). In this article, we first review the epidemiological data that demonstrate that aging is itself an independent risk factor for the development of CVD and address the question of whether and how the major risk factors for CVD (e.g., hypertension, lipids, and smoking) apply to the elderly. This is followed by a description of the development and progression of atherosclerotic lesions and a summary of experimental observations, mostly in animals, of age-associated changes in the structural organization and responsiveness of cells within the vessel. Finally, we

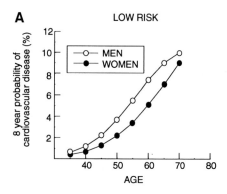

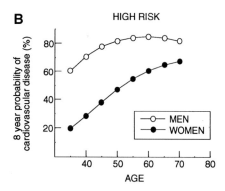

Figure 1   Probability of cardiovascular disease (CVD) as a function of age in men and women at low (A) and high (B) risk. Data replotted from the Framingham Study.

discuss the relationship between the accumulation of age-associated protein–lipid modifications and the increased incidence and severity of atherosclerosis in the elderly, focusing on the role of advanced glycation end products.

I. IS AGING A RISK FACTOR FOR CARDIOVASCULAR DISEASE?

The central question in the study of aging and atherosclerosis is whether the increased incidence of cardiovascular disease (CVD) mortality in the elderly is the result of the prolonged exposure to standard risk factors or a reflection of a change in the biology of the organism intrinsic to the aging process. Epidemiological data compiled from the Framingham study suggest that the latter is likely to be true and that aging is an independent risk factor for the development of CVD. Figure 1A is a graph of the probability for developing

CVD in men and women ages 35–70 who are at low risk. Low risk refers to individuals with no known risk factors and is defined as having a systolic blood pressure (BP) less than 105 mm Hg, a serum cholesterol of less than 185 mg/dl, and no evidence of glucose intolerance, cigarette smoking, electrocardiogram (ECG) abnormalities, or left ventricular hypertrophy. The graph shows that the probability of contracting CVD rises steeply with age in men, increasing approximately 15-fold over the period between 35 and 70 years of age. For women over the same age interval, the probability increases approximately 22-fold. These data show that age affects the risk for developing CVD even in the absence of any of the currently accepted risk factors and can, therefore, be considered as an independent risk factor for the development of CVD. [*See* CARDIOVASCULAR SYSTEM.]

This conclusion is further supported by experimental data that show that the response of animals to a defined atherogenic stimulus differs depending on age. One such study was performed in New Zealand white rabbits in which inflammatory-fibroproliferative lesions similar to that of atherosclerosis in humans can be induced after switching to a hyperlipidemic diet enriched with cholesterol. When the diet was administered for a defined period (18 months) to both young (4 months) and middle-aged (46 months) rabbits, the incidence of vascular lesions as well as their severity was greater in the older animals. Untreated animals at any age exhibited no atheromatous lesions, although older animals did exhibit a markedly thickened intima. In the young rabbits, cholesterol–lipid feeding resulted in the appearance only of fatty streaks. In the older rabbits, on the other hand, not only were the number of atheromatous lesions greater than in the young, but the majority of these were also fibroatheromas, representing a more advanced state of atherosclerotic plaque development.

II. IS THERE AN INTERACTION BETWEEN AGE AND OTHER RISK FACTORS FOR CARDIOVASCULAR DISEASE?

A. Multiple Risk Factors

If aging itself is a risk factor for developing CVD, do the major risk factors for CVD apply to the elderly as they do in the younger population? Figure 1B shows the data from the Framingham Heart Study on the age-dependent probability in men and women with high risk for developing CVD. High-risk individuals were defined as having a systolic BP equal to or greater than 195 mmHg, a total serum cholesterol of greater than 335 mg/dl, glucose intolerance, smoking, and ECG abnormalities. For high-risk men, the age trend is much less steep than for low-risk men, indicating that multiple CV risk factors blunt the effect of age. The effect of aging in high-risk women, however, is still readily evident, probably due to the much lower probability values for premenopausal women compared to age-matched men. A comparison of Figures 1A and B indicates that the relative effect of multiple risk factors (the relative risk ratio) is less pronounced in elderly individuals than in young adults. In women, for example, there is an approximate 50-fold increase in the probability for developing CVD associated with high risk at age 35 but only a 7.5-fold increase at age 70. In men, the blunting of the relative effects of multiple risk factors is even greater. This blunting in both men and women is likely due to (a) the heterogeneity of elderly populations with respect to health status and to (b) the selective removal with time of those at greatest risk. Although relative risk ratios may be blunted with aging, it is important not to lose sight of the fact that the absolute increment in risk in older individuals far exceeds that in the young. The individual effects on the elderly of three major risk factors for CVD—hypertension, cholesterol, and cigarette smoking—are considered next.

B. Hypertension

The mean systolic BP of most Western populations rises with age in both men and women. The linear increase in systolic BP and the rise in pulse pressure during aging may be the result of the progressive stiffening and diminishing compliance of the vasculature that is well documented to occur during aging. These changes in vascular stiffness may, in turn, be secondary to the thickening of the tunica media of large and medium-sized arteries and to changes in the composition and nature of the extracellular matrix (ECM) of the vessel wall that occur with advancing age (see next section).

In contrast to that observed for the effects of multiple risk factors, both the Framingham Heart Study and the European Working Party on High Blood Pressure in the Elderly (EWPHE) study have demonstrated that the relative effect (i.e., the risk ratio) of high BP on the incidence of coronary heart disease (CHD) does not change with age. Less clear are the data on the effectiveness of treating hypertension in the elderly. The Systolic Hypertension in the Elderly Program (SHEP), the Hypertension Detection and Follow-up Program (HDFP), and the EWPHE studies have all reported mixed results. The SHEP study reported a significant reduction of 36% in CV events and stroke in patients on antihypertensive therapy, but no significant effect on CV mortality or the number of cardiac deaths. A nonstatistically significant reduction in all-cause deaths was reported by HDFP and EWPHE, although EWPHE did demonstrate a significant beneficial effect of therapy on CV mortality. More recent data from a large clinical trial conclude that treating hypertension in the elderly can significantly decrease the risk of death from CVD. The consensus, therefore, is that antihypertensive therapy in the elderly can decrease the risk of CVD death and can significantly reduce CV events such as stroke that affect the quality of life in the elderly.

C. Cholesterol

Despite considerable evidence that hypercholesterolemia is strongly associated with higher risk of atherosclerosis-related diseases in middle age, an association between high levels of cholesterol and CHD in older individuals remains controversial. A significant association between total cholesterol (TC) and CHD in the elderly was reported by both the Honolulu Heart Program and the Baltimore Longitudinal Study on Aging (BLSA). In the Framingham Heart Study, on the other hand, TC was significantly associated with CHD risk only in older women with TC greater than 306 mg/dl; in other subgroups, no significant effect of TC was observed. Likewise, a preliminary report from one cohort of the Established Population for the Epidemiological Study in the Elderly (EPESE) indicated that TC was not associated with a significantly higher rate of mortality or hospitalization for CVD and CHD. This study also reported that there also was no significant association between levels of cholesterol within high-density lipoproteins (HDL-C) and mortality, a conclusion contradicted by two well-designed studies. The first, an update of the Framingham Heart Study, showed that partitioning TC into low- and high-density subgroups (LDL-C and HDL-C, respectively) restored the predictive power of cholesterol for CHD incidence. The second study is a more extensive and complete analysis of the EPESE communities involving data from all four cohorts. This study showed that there was a strong relationship between HDL-C levels and mortality from CHD in individuals 71 years and older. The relative risk of death from CHD for those with low HDL-C levels (<35 mg/dl) was 2.5 compared to those with normal to high HLD-C (>60 mg/dl). Taken together and conservatively interpreted, it can be concluded that although HDL-C remains an independent risk factor for CHD in the elderly, the association between TC and atherosclerosis-related disease and mortality becomes weaker with age. [See CHOLESTEROL AND CELL PLASMA MEMBRANES.]

Unequivocal proof of the predictive power of lipids and lipoproteins for CHD would involve testing the effectiveness of hypercholesterolemic therapy on CHD and/or other atherosclerosis-related disease morbidity and mortality. To date, no specific clinical trial for the treatment of hypercholesterolemia in elderly populations has been reported. Recently, however, a randomized study (the Scandinavian Simvastatin Survival Study Group) among individuals with CHD between the ages of 35 and 70 demonstrated that treatment with simvastasin (a cholesterol-lowering drug) significantly decreased CHD mortality as well as major coronary events, including the subgroup older than 60 years.

Elevated levels of lipoprotein a (Lp[a]) (>30 mg/dl) are also associated with myocardial infarction, stroke, and other atherosclerotic-related CVD. Most of these studies have been performed on populations below 60 years, and recent cross-sectional observations have suggested that the clinical relevance of Lp(a) as a risk factor is less marked in the elderly (Dubbo study). However, a recent report demonstrating a close relationship between Lp(a) levels and atherothrombotic disease in Japanese older than 75 years is likely to rekindle interest in the impact of Lp(a) in the elderly as are recent reports that Lp(a) inhibits the plasminogen cascade and the activation of transforming growth factor $\beta1$ (TGF$\beta1$), an important inhibitor of smooth muscle cell (SMC) proliferation and migration (see below).

D. Cigarette Smoking

In younger populations, cigarette consumption represents not only one of the more potent risk factors for the development of atherosclerosis, but also one that, if eliminated, clearly decreases the risk for developing atherosclerosis. Although the mechanism(s) for its deleterious effects are unclear, the clear reversibility of its effects suggests that it may be involved in acute events leading to CV crisis.

Controversy surrounds the role of cigarette smoking as a predictor of CVD in the elderly. For example, no relationship between cigarette smoking and CHD or mortality from it was reported in the Framingham Heart Study among the elderly free of clinical heart disease. An increased risk of CHD due to cigarette smoking, however, was confirmed in the Honolulu Heart Program and the EPESE. In the latter study, the relative risk due to cigarette smoking was 2.0 for men and 2.6 for women, and former smokers had rates of CV mortality similar to those who never smoked, regardless of the age of cessation. In conclusion, even if its predictive power may be less, the deleterious effects of cigarette smoking and the immediate benefits of quitting extend into old age.

III. THE PATHOGENESIS AND PROGRESSION OF ATHEROSCLEROSIS

Atherosclerosis could be characterized as an excessive inflammatory-fibroproliferative response to a chronic insult. The nature of the "insult" remains unknown, but is likely to start with the retention and subsequent modification (primarily by oxidation) of LDLs in the vessel wall. In the initial stages of atherosclerosis, endothelial cell function is altered so that circulating leukocytes adhere to the endothelial surface and transmigrate into the subendothelial space or intima. Within the intima, the monocyte differentiate into macrophages, which actively take up cholesterol retained by the ECM to become foam cells. These events are driven by the expression of genes for adhesion molecules, such as VCAM-1, ICAM-1, and ELAM-1, by chemoattractants, such as monocyte chemoattractant protein-1 (MCP-1), and by differentiation factors, such as macrophage colony-stimulating factor (M-CSF), the expression of which are all activated by incubation of endothelial cells with oxidized LDL and mediated through the nuclear transcription factor, NF-κB. Together with T cells and lipid-containing vascular SMCs (VSMCs) that are already in the intima, this early focal accumulation is known as the *fatty streak*. Fatty streaks tend to occur in areas of the vessel close to ramifications and bifurcations of the vessel, often at sites where intimal VSMCs accumulate. Fatty streak formation is thought to be reversible and can be found in a high percentage of coronary arteries at autopsy, even those from young children.

Further development of the atherosclerotic plaque involves the recruitment of VSMCs, their loss of differentiative function, and the assumption of a "synthetic" phenotype in which organized contractile filaments are replaced by an extensive endoplasmic reticulum (ER) and a large Golgi complex. SMCs now acquire the ability to proliferate, to degrade and synthesize ECM components, and to produce, secrete, and respond to a variety of growth factors and cytokines. The involvement of VSMCs and the elaboration of ECM components results in alternating layers of macrophages, T cells, and SMCs. The lesion at this stage is an intermediate or transitional lesion also known as a *preatheroma*. Cholesterol derived from LDL-C or the lysis of foam cells initially accumulates as small pools in the ECM, but as these pools grow, they coalesce into a central core of extracellular lipid covered by a cap of VSMCs, macrophages, and ECM and are known as *fibroatheroma*. The lesions at this stage appear firm and elevated, with an opaque surface that bulges into the lumen of the vessel. Beginning at this stage, a central necrotic core is present in the lesion.

Although developing atheromata are covered by intact endothelial layers throughout most stages of lesion development, the progression toward more advanced and complicated stages involves ulcerations of the endothelium due to its injury and loss. This results in cyclic thrombus formation and accelerated collagen deposition to form a fibrous cap. There is a gradual reduction in the arterial luminal diameter and the lesions become increasingly more sclerotic and less cellular. This loss in cellularity is likely due to a previous imbalance in cell proliferation and programmed cell death (apoptosis) in the cells of the lesions. At the shoulders of the plaque, the fibrous cap is thinner and contains numerous macrophages. These can release proteases and cause enzymatic degradation of the ECM, leading to fissuring, ruptures,

and tears. These events can result in intraplaque hemorrhage, occlusive thrombus formation, and ultimately, to the sudden onset of an acute vascular syndrome.

Although lesions in various stages of development can be seen postmortem within the same artery, the natural history of lesion development described above parallels the chronological development and aging. Surprisingly, the arteries of individuals in the first and second decades of life already contain fatty streaks, which tend to form in areas of eccentric intimal thickening but lack any SMCs. Preatheromas do not appear until late in the second decade and fibroatheromas can be seen as early as the third decade of life. With advancing age, the lipid content of the lesions decline while sequential events of mural thrombus followed by plaque reorganization and the deposition of collagen and other ECM components results in lesions that contain multiple layers of collagen that vary in age and that progressively reduce the arterial lumen. Although the early stages of plaque development (i.e., fatty streak and preatheroma) are, under some circumstances, reversible, later stages are not.

IV. THE BIOLOGY OF THE AGING VASCULATURE

A. Age-Associated Changes in the Vessel Wall

With advancing age, the cellular and structural architecture of the vessel wall is altered. Structurally, collagen density and content increase, whereas elastin organization appears disorganized. These changes result in an increase in the passive stiffness of the vessel and are likely to contribute to the "hardening" of arteries (arteriosclerosis) with old age. The cellular changes involve hypertrophy of medial VSMCs and an infiltration of the intima with VSMCs and monocytes. The net result of these modifications is a thicker and more dilated vessel with an increasingly cellular intima. Given the important role played by VSMCs in the atherosclerotic lesion development and the predisposition for atherosclerotic lesions to form and develop at areas of intimal thickening, these changes are likely to be a contributing factor in the accelerated formation and maturation of lesions in the elderly.

There are a number of reports of changes in endothelial and VSCM function and responsiveness with age. Aging is associated with a large increase in endothelial permeability that could favor the entry and trapping of plasma macromolecules and accelerate the atherosclerotic process. The ability of endothelial cells to produce prostacyclin, which inhibits platelet aggregation and the release of PDGF by endothelial cells, decrease with age as does the production of nitric oxide (NO) by endothelial cells and the NO responsiveness of VSMCs. On the other hand, production of endothelin-1, which stimulates VSMC proliferation and migration, increases with age.

When VSMCs are placed in cell culture, they also show an age-dependent variation in cell cycle distribution, with older VSMCs having a higher percentage of their population in DNA synthesis, indicating that they are replicating faster. This growth advantage has been linked to a resistance in the growth inhibitory effects of TGFβ1. VSMCs established from older rats produce TGFβ1, but express fewer binding sites on their cell surfaces and degrade it more rapidly than VSCMs from younger animals. The role that TGFβ1 and cell responsiveness to TGFβ1 plays in atherogenesis is unclear, but it is of interest to note that Lp(a), which has been implicated as a risk factor for CVD (see above), inhibits the activation of TGFβ1 both in vitro and in vivo, possibly removing an important inhibitory influence on SMC migration and proliferation.

The hypothesis that arterial vessels from older animals show an exaggerated response to injury is supported not only by animal studies referred to earlier in which a defined atherogenic stimulus elicited a greater atherogenic response in older animals. It is also supported by observations made in the rat showing that the degree of myointimal thickening resulting from endothelial injury (produced by gentle denudation without disruption of the media) is substantially greater in old compared to young animals. This difference in responsivity is maintained when arterial segments from young and old animals are transplanted into old and young hosts respectively, indicating that the changes in responsiveness are an intrinsic property of the vessels.

B. The Role of Advanced Glycation End Products

Advanced glycation end products (AGEs) are proteins and lipids that have been irreversibly modified by nonenzymatic glycation and oxidation. Although initially identified and implicated in the vascular complications associated with diabetes mellitus, AGEs also accumulate in the plasma and on long-lived proteins in the vessel wall of aged individuals and animals. A role for AGEs in the development and progression of atherosclerotic lesions is indicated by the following observations and experiments:

1. The biological effects of AGEs are mediated through a specific cell surface receptor, termed RAGE (receptor for AGE). Activation of this receptor on cultured endothelial or VSMCs leads to alterations in gene expression that could influence multiple steps in progression and pathogenesis of vascular lesions. Many of the changes in gene expression are similar to that seen with oxidized LDL and involve increased oxidant stress to the cell.

2. RAGE expression in the vessel wall is dramatically increased following either acute vascular injury, such as that inflicted by a balloon catheterization, or in response to chronic vascular disease, such as that associated with the development of atherosclerotic plaques. In both cases, expression is confined to virtually all cell types in intima cell layer (e.g., endothelia, SMCs, and monocytes). In keeping with this pattern of expression, RAGE is also expressed in the intima that develops in many large vessels with aging and may, in fact, participate in the changes in the vessel architecture accompanying aging and predisposing the vessel to disease.

3. AGEs can be found in the microenvironment of developing atherosclerotic lesions. Reminiscent of the situation for the oxidation of lipoproteins, this same microenvironment may promote AGE formation.

4. Infusion of AGEs exacerbate atheromatous lesion formation in lipid-fed animals and accelerates fibrous plaque formation in these animals.

Although only a few of the changes in gene expression that result from RAGE activation have been characterized, it is clear that one of the consequences of the AGE–RAGE interaction is increased VSMC migration and monocyte infiltration, both of which are prelesional events for atherogenesis. This interaction may thus accelerate the development of the atherosclerotic lesion, thereby contributing to the increased severity of this disease with advancing age. [See GLYCATION.]

BIBLIOGRAPHY

Cooper, L. T., Cooke, J. P., & Dzau, V. J. (1994). The vasculopathy of aging. *Journal of Gerontology 49,* B191.

Corti, M. C., Guralnik, J. M., Salive, M. E., Harris, T., Field, T. S., Wallace, R. B., Berkman, L. F., Seeman, T. E., Glynn, R. J., Hennekens, C. H., & Havlik, R. J. (1995). HDL cholesterol predicts coronary heart disease mortality in older persons. *Journal of the American Medical Association, 274,* 539.

Crow, M. T., Boluyt, M. O., & Lakatta, E. G. (1995). The molecular and cellular biology of aging in the cardiovascular system. In N. Holbrook, G. R. Martin, R. A. Lockshin (Eds.), *Cellular aging and cell death.* New York: J. Wiley and Sons (p. 81)

Han, D. K. M., Haudenschild, C. C., Hong, M. K., Tnkl, B. T., Leon, M. B., & Liua, G. (1995). Evidence for apoptosis in human atherogenesis and in a rat vascular injury model. *American Journal of Pathology, 147,* 267–277.

Harris, T., Cook, E. F., Kannel, W. B., & Goldman, L. (1988). Proportional hazard analysis of risk factors for coronary heart disease in individuals aged 65 and older: The Framingham heart study. *Journal of the American Geriatric Society, 36,* 1023.

Kannel, W. B., & Gordon, T. (1980). Cardiovascular risk factors in the aged: The Framingham study. In S. G. Haynes & J. A. Ross (Eds.), *Proceedings of the Second Conference on the Epidemiology of Aging.* (NIH publication 80-969) (p. 65). Bethesda, MD.

Ross, R. (1993). The pathogenesis of atherosclerosis: A perspective for the 1990s. *Nature, 362,* 801.

Schmidt, A. M., Hori, O., Brett, J., Yan, S-D., Wautier, J-L., Stern, D. (1994). Cellular receptor for advanced glycation endproducts. Implications for induction of oxidant stress and cellular dysfunction in the pathogenesis of vascular lesions. *Arteriosclerosis Thrombosis 14,* 1521.

Spagnoli, L. G., Orlandi, A., Mauriello, A., Santeusanio, G., de Angelis, C., Lucreziotti, R., & Ramacci, M. T. (1991). Aging and atherosclerosis in the rabbit. Distribution, prevalence, and morphology of atherosclerotic lesions. *Atherosclerosis, 89,* 11.

Attention

David J. Madden

Duke University Medical Center

Philip A. Allen

Cleveland State University

Automatic Processing Performance of a task without the involvement of attention.

Capacity The information-processing resources available for the performance of a cognitive task.

Controlled Processing Performance of a task that involves attention.

Event-Related Brain Potential (ERP) The change in electrical activity, measured at the scalp, associated with stimulus presentation or response selection.

Positron Emission Tomography (PET) A method for obtaining three-dimensional images of metabolic activity and blood flow in the brain, as measured from the decay of radionuclides that are either injected or inhaled.

Reaction Time (RT) The time between the onset of a stimulus and the subject's response, frequently used as a variable in the study of attention.

Regional Cerebral Blood Flow (rCBF) The rate of blood flow within a specific region of the brain.

Selectivity The discrimination of relevant and irrelevant information.

Vigilance The preparation for specific stimulus events.

Visual Search A laboratory task frequently used to study attention, in which subjects decide, on each trial, whether one or more target items (usually letters or digits) are present in a visual display.

ATTENTION comprises several components: the resources available for task performance (capacity), the discrimination of relevant and irrelevant information (selectivity), and the preparation for specific stimulus events (vigilance). Attentional capacity has been investigated in the context of consistent versus varied stimulus–response mapping, dual-task performance, and the statistical control of mediating variables. The investigation of selective attention has involved providing specific stimulus dimensions for identifying task-relevant information. Studies of vigilance have measured subjects' ability to monitor sources of information for extended periods of time. Although an age-related decline in the capacity aspect of attention has been observed relatively consistently, the selectivity and vigilance components of attention appear to be more resistant to age-related change.

I. CATEGORIES OF ATTENTION

Attention is one of the most actively investigated aspects of cognitive functioning. Unlike many of the theoretical constructs associated with experimental cognitive psychology, however, attention is also part of our everyday vocabulary, and outside of the laboratory our nontechnical understanding of attention is frequently quite serviceable. People know when they are attending to something and when they are not. What is not evident from everyday experience, however, is how attention can be measured empirically. That is, independent of self-report, what would serve as a demonstration that someone is attending? A complex set of theoretical and methodological issues has arisen during the course of research in this area. Although significant progress has been made, many of the theoretical issues remain unresolved, and it is not always possible to distinguish empirically the different theoretical models of attention that investigators have proposed. In considering the potential changes in attention associated with aging, it is important to realize that although age differences exist as empirical findings, the measures of attention with which they are associated are subject to varying theoretical interpretations independent of the age issue.

The empirical studies of attentional processes have addressed the performance of specific cognitive tasks. To avoid defining a new form of attention for each task, and to facilitate the comparison of results across tasks, it has been useful to categorize different forms of attention. Two researchers have proposed that there are three important components of attention: capacity, selectivity, and vigilance. Capacity refers to the limited processing resources available for task performance. The selectivity component refers to attention as the control of processing some stimuli rather than others. The vigilance component represents the preparatory or orienting aspect of attention, as in monitoring a particular location for the appearance of a specified event. It is not likely that these components are separable in an absolute sense, or that they have completely different representations in the central nervous system (CNS), but the categories do provide a useful framework for summarizing empirical research on attention, as well as the age differences that have been observed.

II. ADULT AGE DIFFERENCES IN CAPACITY

A. Capacity as Effort

Everyday usage of the term *attention* frequently carries the connotation of effort, as when, for example, one reports a difficulty in "paying attention." Similarly, some tasks are more attention-demanding than others, in the sense of requiring additional effort or cognitive resources. Contemporary treatments of attention have also emphasized this *limited capacity* dimension and have proposed that task performance is the result of the momentary relation between capacity supplied and capacity demanded.

How can attentional capacity be measured empirically? One type of cognitive task that has been frequently used to study attention is *visual search*, in which one or more target items (e.g., letters, numbers, words) are compared to one or more items presented in a visual display. In a particular search task, for example, the subject's goal might be to respond *yes* or *no* with regard to whether any item from the target set is present in the display. A frequently used index of attentional demands is the *comparison load effect:* the increase in either reaction time (RT) or error rate associated with increases in the number of items to be compared. A particularly important variable is the consistency of the relation of stimuli to responses. In a consistent mapping (CM) condition, the same response is always assigned to a particular target; in a varied mapping (VM) condition, individual items are used as both targets and distractors across the trial sequence. Researchers have reported that extensive practice (several thousand trials) under CM conditions appeared to eliminate the attentional demands of visual search and classification tasks. After CM practice, for example, search RT and error rate were virtually independent of the number of targets in the search set (e.g., a search for six targets would be as efficient as search for two targets). Shiffrin and Schneider referred to this attention-free form of performance as *automatic processing*. Under VM conditions, in contrast, search RT always increased with the number of items in the search set, indicating that attention-dependent, *controlled processing*, was required.

Other researchers have examined age differences under CM and VM conditions in a variety of search and classification tasks. The general conclusion of these experiments is that an age-related decline exists in the ability to develop automatic processing. That is, young adults are more adept than older adults in using the structure of the task to reduce attention demands. These authors propose that two different variables determine the magnitude of age differences in automatic process development in search tasks. The first is the unitization of the target set items. With CM practice, subjects become able to combine the features of the target set so that several items can be searched for as efficiently as one item. This is the variable responsible for the reduction in target set size effects. The second variable is the development of differential strength of target and distractor items, which refers to the degree to which a display item will elicit a *target present* response. This is the variable involved in the reduction of display size effects in visual search. Target set unitization is relatively preserved as a function of age, whereas target strengthening is vulnerable to age-related decline. In one study, the effects of target set size, after 2600–5000 CM trials in letter–digit search and semantic category search, were minimal for both young and older adults, whereas display size continued to have a more pronounced effect for the older adults. Another study included various transfer conditions following CM and VM training in a semantic category visual search task and found that the greatest age difference occurred in the transfer condition that assessed the combined effects of target and distractor learning. Older adults appeared to have differentiated the targets and distractors to a lesser extent, over CM practice, than young adults, and as a result the older adults were actually less disrupted by a reversal of target and distractor items.

Measures of attentional capacity using CM–VM effects are based on a detailed theoretical framework of automatic and controlled information processing, and this theory is controversial. As a more theory-independent approach, investigators have used the speed–accuracy relation as a measure of attentional capacity. In the majority of RT experiments, subjects are instructed to respond as quickly as they can while still being correct. This type of instruction represents only one segment of the complete function relating accuracy to speed. When this function is examined empirically, by requiring subjects to adopt a range of speed–accuracy emphases, the result is an S-shaped curve containing plateaus at the lower left (fast but inaccurate) and upper right (slow but accurate) ends, connected by a linear function representing increasing accuracy as a function of increasing RT. The slope of the linear segment has been interpreted as an index of attentional capacity, in terms of the rate of gain of information. Several studies of adult age differences in the speed–accuracy relation have indicated that the rate of gain of information, as reflected in the speed–accuracy slope, is slower for older adults than for young adults, consistent with an age-related decline in attentional capacity.

The analyses of the speed–accuracy relation and the investigation of CM–VM effects are both limited in that the index of attentional capacity is derived from subjects' performance of a single task. Thus, both the speed–accuracy slope and the comparison load RT slope are essentially measures of the rate of information transmission within a single task. The limitation of this approach is that a wide range of information transmission rates has been reported for various tasks, which is not consistent with the concept of a general capacity limitation. In addition, RT may increase across task conditions for reasons (such as an increase in the number of response alternatives) that do not necessarily reflect changes in attentional capacity.

As an alternative, there has been considerable interest in dual-task measures of attentional capacity. In this approach, subjects perform two tasks concurrently. Assuming that the attentional capacity available for task performance is limited, the pattern of interference between the tasks (i.e., competition for processing resources) may be informative regarding the capacity limit. Two widely used forms of dual-task assessment are the concurrent task paradigm and the secondary task paradigm. In the concurrent task paradigm, dual-task and single-task conditions are compared. In one version of this paradigm, a choice RT task is performed during the retention interval of a short-term memory task (e.g., subjects are given seven digits to remember, then perform the RT task, and finally recall the digits). The attentional capacity demands of the RT task are assessed by comparing RT task performance on memory-load trials and no-load trials. In the secondary task paradigm, subjects are instructed to devote most of their attention to the primary task (usually a version of choice RT), while monitoring the occurrence of a secondary task stimulus (e.g., a tone), which also requires a response. The attentional demands of the primary task are reflected in the pattern of RT changes that occur in the secondary task.

Many dual-task investigations of age differences have been conducted, and the results are generally consistent with an age-related decline in attentional capacity. Several studies have addressed the elementary cognitive operations involved in the identification and comparison of visually presented letters. In one version of the secondary task technique, the primary task was visual search (i.e., a choice response regarding which one of two target letters was present in a visual display of several letters) and the secondary task was tone detection. Relative to a single-task tone detection baseline, the secondary task RT during visual search was disproportionately greater for older adults than for young adults.

Secondary-task studies have also used letter matching (i.e., *same–different* judgments regarding letter pairs) as the primary task and tone detection as the secondary task. In these experiments the primary task stimuli were presented sequentially, rather than simultaneously. The tone stimuli could thus be located prior to the occurrence of the second letter (to assess encoding of the first letter) and after the occurrence of the second letter (to assess comparison and retrieval processes). In all of the experiments, the increase in secondary task RT, relative to a baseline, was differentially greater for older adults, but in some instances only the absolute increase in secondary task RT, rather than the more stringent proportional difference measure was assessed. When the complexity of the *same* response was varied (i.e., matches based on physical shape, name, or category similarity), the age-related increase in secondary task RT was significant for both encoding and comparison–response processes in each match condition, but was particularly pronounced for the comparison–retrieval processes associated with category matches.

Practice may be an important variable moderating age differences in dual-task performance. In experiment one, subjects completed more than 7000 trials of single-task visual search (3584 trials each of CM and VM conditions). Following practice, subjects performed a VM memory search task concurrently with CM and VM visual search. The addition of the memory search task disrupted the VM visual search performance of both age groups. Over the course of 1152 dual-task trials, however, young adults were able to improve their dual-task CM visual search performance to their previous single-task level, presumably as the result of automatic (attention-free) processing of the CM stimuli. The VM memory search task continued to disrupt the older adults' CM search performance, however, and they were not able to achieve their previous single-task levels.

Dual-task methodology has also been applied to studies of higher order cognitive processes. These experiments are also consistent with the concept of an age-related reduction in attentional capacity. Concurrent task studies of verbal reasoning, silent reading, speaking, and maze completion have reported that the decrement in performance from single-task to dual-task conditions was relatively greater for older adults, and the age difference increased as a function of the level of difficulty within the cognitive tasks. Several dual-task experiments that have focused specifically on memory retrieval have demonstrated that the attentional demands of retrieval of information from both short-term and long-term memory are greater for older adults than for young adults.

Although the results of the dual-task studies consistently suggest the existence of an age-related decline in attentional capacity, there are many interpretive problems associated with dual-task methodology. A problem relevant to the interpretation of age differences is that it is difficult to separate the effects of a secondary task from the effects of allocation strategy. That is, if young and older adults were equivalent in available attentional capacity, but the older adults chose to emphasize performance in the primary task at the expense of the secondary task, then an apparent age-related decline in secondary task performance would result. It has been proposed that this issue could be addressed by examining empirically the relation between primary task and secondary task performance, when subjects are instructed to devote a specific proportion of attention to one task versus the other. The resulting function, referred to as a Performance Operating Characteristic (POC), represents a strategy-independent measure of attentional capacity. Researchers in one study reported that, in a POC analysis of relatively simple visual discrimination tasks, no age-related decline in the ability to divide attention was evident. In a later study, however, a POC analysis of a more memory-dependent task (recall of letters vs. digits from a briefly presented display) indicated an age-related decline in attentional capacity.

Another problem with dual-task measures is that there may be no unique characteristic of the dual-task paradigm that reveals the effects of attentional capacity. The changes in secondary task RT may reflect the overall difficulty of the task rather than specifical attentional demands. McDowd and Craik varied task difficulty (in terms of the number or depth of cognitive operations required) independently of the single- and dual-task dimension. Although an age-related decrement in dual-task performance was evident, it could not be distinguished statistically from task difficulty. It thus appeared that the requirement to divide attention in the dual-task conditions was essentially another method of increasing the overall complexity of the perceptual-motor task.

The issue of distinguishing dual-task effects from task complexity is not unique to the investigation of attention. A prominent theoretical framework for interpreting age differences in cognitive performance holds that virtually all cognitive aging effects can be characterized as a form of generalized age-related slowing. That is, aging is associated with a generalized decline in the speed of cognitive processing, presumably as a result of age-related changes in the integrity of the CNS. [see BRAIN AND CENTRAL NERVOUS SYSTEM.] When RT is the dependent variable, any increase in task complexity, as defined by young adults' RT, would be expressed as an increase in the absolute magnitude of age differences. A widely used method of examining generalized slowing was introduced in 1965. This method (also known as *the method of systematic relations*) involves an analysis of the mean RTs obtained at the task condition level, rather than at the individual subject level. It was reported that there was a highly linear relation between the task condition mean RTs of older adults and the corresponding means of young adults, which implies that the overall complexity of the task, rather than the processing requirements of specific task conditions, is the determinant of the magnitude of the age differences. Although this generalized slowing methodology has been applied widely in the analysis of age differences in RT tasks, there is considerable debate regarding whether the methodology is adequate for distinguishing between generalized and task-specific age-related slowing.

B. Capacity as Speed

A particularly important issue in the analysis of attentional capacity is that even if subjects' performance in dual-task paradigms is assumed to represent the effects of limited processing resources or effort, there is no independent assessment of this form of attention, and as a result the measurement of attention can be criticized as being circular. According to this perspective, although age differences in dual-task performance can be obtained reliably, the conclusion that these differences are capacity-related is not justified without an independent measure of attentional capacity. One alternative is to consider processing speed as a form of capacity. Thus, if an independent measure

of processing speed can be obtained, the relation between this measure (i.e., attentional capacity) and age differences in cognitive performance can be assessed. Salthouse has used regression analyses to develop this approach in two directions. First, a measure of processing speed is used as a mediator variable in hierarchical regression analyses of the relation between age and cognitive task performance. The amount of age-related variance in task performance is estimated both before and after the speed variable is entered into the regression equation. As a result, the degree of attenuation in the age-related variance introduced by the speed variable can be estimated. This attenuation represents the relative influence of processing speed in determining the observed age differences in performance. For example, in psychometric tests involving integrative reasoning, geometric analogies, mental paper folding, and cube assembly, the degree of age-related decline (in terms of the proportion of variance in the dependent variable related to age) ranged from .169 to .305. The measure of processing speed was a composite of tests measuring simple perceptual comparisons, such as the Digit Symbol Substitution subtest of the Wechsler Adult Intelligence Scale. Entering the processing speed measure before age in the regression equation led to a greater than 85% reduction in the variance attributable to age. This result, replicated in several studies, suggests that capacity, in the sense of the processing speed of elementary perceptual operations, is an important determinant of age-related changes in cognitive performance. This substantial influence of speed as a mediator holds for paired-associate and free-recall measures of memory as well as measures of reasoning and spatial abilities. The mediation is more pronounced for perceptually based measures of speed than for motorically based ones.

The second type of regression procedure that has been used to develop the concept of capacity as speed is path analysis. In this approach, the observed relations among variables are examined for their fit to a prespecified model. The path analysis yields path coefficients, which are standardized regression coefficients expressing the amount of standard deviation change in one variable as a function of one standard deviation change in another variable. As a result, whether the influence of one variable on a second variable is direct or mediated by a third variable can be determined. In the hierarchical regression approach discussed previously, the concern was with the degree to which the introduction of a variable (processing speed) attenuated age-related variance. Path analysis allows the development of a model of the direct and indirect (i.e., mediated) relations among variables. One study found that path analyses disconfirmed two extreme models in which either all, or none, of the age-related variance in cognitive performance was attributable to age-related reduction in processing capacity. The relation between age and cognitive performance contained both indirect (i.e., mediated by capacity) and direct paths. The capacity-mediated effects were smaller in magnitude than the direct effects, those representing the combined influence of variables other than capacity. In another study, however, involving more knowledge-dependent criterion tasks (e.g., solving anagrams, listing words with specified beginnings or endings), the indirect effects of age (i.e., mediated by perceptual speed and vocabulary) were greater than the direct effects.

C. Quality of Internal Representations

Measures of processing speed appear to be useful as an independent, empirical anchor for the operational definition of attentional capacity in the performance of cognitive tasks. Ultimately, however, changes in processing speed represent changes in the CNS. The question is whether age-related slowing should be considered a "disciplinary primitive" that cannot be further decomposed, or whether the causes of age-related slowing can be determined. One researcher proposed that the older CNS may be "noisier" than that of a young system, in the sense of having either less distinct neural signals or higher levels of background noise. When performing a cognitive task, older adults would consequently need additional time to achieve a signal-to-noise ratio comparable to that of young adults. Experiments that have attempted to influence the level of neural noise by the manipulation of stimulus quality, however, have yielded inconsistent results.

Other researchers have investigated a related concept, *internal noise*, in a series of short-term memory and perceptual matching tasks. These authors have found that the internal representation of the stimuli is noisier for older adults than for young adults. The representation of order information in a recognition memory task, for example, exhibited an age-related increase in variability. In a task requiring subjects to match the color of letter pairs, older adults were more disrupted than young adults by an irrelevant dimension, the similarity in shape of the letters, as would be predicted by an age-related increase in neural noise.

The concept of neural noise is potentially useful as an explanation for age-related slowing, but at present the noise concept is limited by the reliance on indirect measures. When behavioral measures are used to infer the properties of the CNS, a complex set of assumptions are often required to interpret the behavioral data in neurophysiological terms. In addition, it is not always clear that different predictions would be made by a generalized slowing theory. A slowing of all the processes involved in stimulus registration may lead to a degraded representation to the same extent as would a noisy CNS. Finally, it is difficult to empirically distinguish the effects of external noise, such as stimulus discriminability, from those of internal noise.

D. Neurophysiological Measures of Processing Speed and Capacity

Neurophysiological measures provide, by definition, direct indices of CNS functioning. Two classes of measures are particularly relevant to the investigation of age-related changes in attention: (a) event-related brain potentials (ERPs) measured by electroencephalogram (EEG) and (b) changes in regional cerebral blood flow (rCBF) measured by positron emission tomography (PET). The two types of measures are complementary in that ERPs provide relatively fine-grained information regarding the time course of stimulus processing but poor spatial localization of the brain activity, whereas PET measures of rCBF can be localized to within a few millimeters but must average brain activity occurring over at least 1 minute.

The ERP is a change in electrical activity, measured at the scalp, in association with stimulus presentation or response preparation and execution. The ERP represents synchronous changes in the EEG that are time-locked to the presentation or the execution of a response. It consists of a series of positive and negative deflections in the electrical polarity in the EEG, which are referred to as the components of the ERP. One frequently investigated component of the ERP is the P300, which is a positive change in polarity possessing a peak in amplitude approximately 300 ms following the onset of a simple stimulus. The latency of the P300 appears to reflect stimulus encoding and categorization processes; it is relatively independent of response processes. Experiments in which both RT and P300 measures are obtained simultaneously, have indicated that age differences in RT may primarily represent response-dependent processes. Similarly, other studies have found that although the function relating RT to memory-set size in a memory scanning task is typically steeper for older adults than for young adults, the function relating P300 latency to memory-set size is comparable for the two age groups. Thus, the attentional capacity limitations that have been suggested on the basis of processing-speed analyses may primarily represent processes associated with response selection and execution. These processes would still be central, in the sense of occurring in the brain rather than in the effector organs, but some stimulus encoding processes (represented by P300 latency) would be less vulnerable to age-related slowing. It has been proposed that the neural structures implicated in the control of voluntary movement are more vulnerable to aging than other structures.

PET is a relatively new imaging modality that was developed specifically to measure brain metabolic activity and rCBF. The metabolic and rCBF changes are measured from the decay of radionuclides that are either injected or inhaled. Although a three-dimensional image of activity is generated, the activity must be integrated over time. The integration period varies from 1–45 min, depending on the type of radionuclide used. (The most widely used technique yields PET images of rCBF after a 1-min integration period.) The metabolic and rCBF measures can be obtained either while subjects are in a resting state or during the performance of a cognitive task. In the latter case, the pattern of metabolic or rCBF values obtained during performance of a control task can be subtracted from the values obtained during performance of an activation task, yielding a PET image of task-specific change. PET research conducted with young adults has implicated the existence of two neural systems mediating attentional functioning: (a) one in frontal cortical areas involved in the division of attention among relevant stimuli; and (b) one in occipital and parietal cortical areas involved in the use of specific stimulus dimensions for selective attending. It is possible that these two neural systems correspond to the capacity and selectivity components of attention that have been defined on the basis of behavioral measures. The PET methodology is thus a potentially valuable

source of information regarding age-related changes in the functional neuroanatomy of attention. The available data are mixed; age-related reductions in metabolic activity and rCBF have been reported in regions of frontal cortex, which is consistent with an age-related decline in attentional capacity. The majority of PET investigations of aging have used resting state conditions, however, and age comparisons have yet to be developed in PET activation paradigms focusing specifically on attentional processes.

III. ADULT AGE DIFFERENCES IN SELECTIVITY

A. Selection of Relevant Information

The second component of attention, selectivity, is more theoretically tractable than the concept of attentional capacity. Whereas the concept of capacity is associated with complex issues of definition and measurement, selective attention can be defined operationally as the selection of relevant information. That is, perceptual tasks in the laboratory (as well as in the real world) typically involve both relevant and irrelevant sources of information, and an important function of attention is to direct processing to the information relevant to completing the task at hand. This approach to the investigation of attention derives from the *perceptual filter* theory of Broadbent and has been applied frequently to the issue of age differences. As was the case in investigations of attentional capacity, research on selective attention has used visual search and classification paradigms extensively. [See PERCEPTION.]

In the 1960s, researchers conducted a series of investigations of age differences in selective attention. Increasing either the number of response categories, the number of stimuli comprising a category, or the number of items in the target display, typically led to a greater RT increase for older adults than for young adults. They concluded that the age differences in this type of task could be characterized as a decrement in "ignoring irrelevant or redundant information."

Other reports of an age-related decline in the efficiency of selective attention have appeared. Researchers have reported that age-related slowing in a visual search task was more pronounced in a conjunction search condition than in a feature search condition.

In the former case, the nontargets comprise target features (e.g., search for a red X target among red O and green X nontargets), whereas in the latter case the target and nontargets do not share features (e.g., search for a red X target among green O nontargets). The age differences associated with this conjunction search condition was interpreted in terms of the attentional demands of avoiding "illusory conjunctions" of nontarget features.

Two points are important for evaluating age differences in selective attention. First, age-related changes in the sensory processes of vision are likely to contribute to age differences in cognitive tasks using visual stimuli. It is well established that an age-related decline occurs in several aspects of optical function, such as increased opacity of the ocular media, reduced accommodative ability, and increased density of the lens. When a display contains both target and nontarget items, older adults' visual search performance is also disproportionately impaired when the target item is presented outside of the foveal region. These changes would have a direct influence on the ability to discriminate relevant and irrelevant information, by requiring additional time and eye movements to resolve the features of individual display items. Researchers have monitored eye movements during visual search and found that age differences in search performance were eliminated when the number of eye movements was partialled statistically. From other results, however, it appears that when eye movements, acuity, and retinal illuminance variables are controlled, an age-related decline in visual search performance remains. Thus, an age-related decline exists beyond the level of the retina.

Second, when those experiments are considered that provide subjects with explicit sources of relevant and irrelevant information within a task, there is substantial evidence for the preservation of selective attention abilities in older adults. In one study, for example, the feature search condition provided a single visual feature, either *red* or *angular*, that was sufficient to distinguish target and nontarget items. If the data are viewed as an improvement in search performance associated with feature search, rather than a decrement in performance associated with conjunction search, the results suggest an age constancy of selective attention, because this improvement was at least as great for older adults as for young adults. Several other forms of distinguishing target and nontarget

items, such as familiar sequencing of the stimuli and partitioning letter–digit categories, lead to equivalent changes in RT for young and older adults.

In one particularly effective method of designating relevant information, a cue, presented prior to or simultaneously with the display, indicates the spatial location of the target. When, for example, a visual display contains a number of items that could each potentially be the target, subjects' performance is typically improved by the presentation of a cue that designates the spatial location of the target. In general, the magnitude of spatial cuing effects have been found to be at least as great for older adults as for young adults, consistent with the preservation of selective attention.

B. Allocation of Selective Attention

Even if the ability to use selective attention does not change qualitatively with age, the age-related slowing that is evident across a range of attention-demanding tasks (section III.B) leads to the expectation that the time required to allocate selective attention effectively would increase with age. Under some conditions (e.g., increased display encoding demands) this expectation has been confirmed. Several experiments investigating the time course of spatial cuing, however, have indicated a substantial degree of age constancy in the time course of allocation. The RT to a visual display typically decreases as the interval by which the cue precedes the display increases, up to some asymptotic point. Although with complex displays older adults may require a longer cue-display interval than young adults to use the cue effectively, it has been found that the decrease in RT across an increasing cue-display interval exhibits a similar pattern for young and older adults. Other forms of cuing have also exhibited an age constancy in time course. When the cue indicates the nature of the response to be made rather than a spatial location, or specifies which aspects of the target should be processed (e.g., respond to a letter's color rather than its identity), the time course of cuing has been found to be comparable for young and older adults.

Models of attentional allocation suggest that the width of attentional focus can vary, in the sense of being either relatively focused on detailed information or relatively distributed across less detailed information. Experiments that have varied the width of subjects' attentional focus across horizontal displays of letters have found that the RT effects were similar for young and older adults. The differences exhibited by the older adults did not appear to be specifically attentional, but instead related to the retinal eccentricity of the target. The relative emphasis, across trials, on focused versus distributed attention also appears to be similar for young and older adults. Studies estimating the proportion of trials on which subjects use focused attention have indicated that this proportion does not vary with age.

C. Inhibitory Processing and Selective Attention

We have discussed selective attention in terms of the discrimination of relevant and irrelevant information. In other contexts it has been emphasized that this goal can be achieved not only by selecting relevant information but also by suppressing or inhibiting irrelevant information. Two researchers, for example, have developed an influential theory in which it is proposed that an age-related decline in the ability to inhibit irrelevant information underlies age differences in cognitive performance. These researchers proposed that the performance of cognitive tasks, especially those involving language comprehension, involve working-memory processes (i.e., limited capacity storage and comparison operations). Essential to these comprehension processes is the use of inhibitory mechanisms that prevent the intrusion of irrelevant information in working memory. The existence of an age-related decline in inhibitory processes is suggested by several forms of evidence from text comprehension and memory tasks.

The experimental paradigm that is most frequently used to investigate inhibitory processes is negative priming. In one version of this paradigm, the display contains two letters, one in red and one in green; the subject's task is to name the target (red) letter as quickly as possible. The critical result is that, across a series of trials, subjects are slower to name the target when it had been a distractor (i.e., green) letter on the immediately preceding trial. That is, subjects are "negatively primed" by the distractor on the preceding trial, suggesting that naming the target is accompanied by an active suppression of the distractor. In several naming tasks involving letters, pictures, and words, the magnitude of negative priming has been found to be greater for young adults than for older

adults, indicating an age-related reduction in the inhibition of the distractor letter. This result apears to be inconsistent with the preservation of selective attention that has been obtained in studies of spatial cuing (section III.A,B). Older adults have been found to exhibit significant negative priming, however, when the current target is located in the display position that had recently contained a distractor. In a revised model of age-related changes in inhibitory processes, those processes underlying the inhibition of distractor identity are subject to age-related decline, whereas the inhibition of distractor location is relatively preserved as a function of age.

The distinction between identity and spatial location information is useful for integrating the negative priming results with those obtained in selective-attention paradigms. Results inconsistent with the revised version of the inhibitory processing model, however, have also appeared. One group investigated a series of RT tasks, and the results were generally not indicative of an age-related decline in inhibitory processing. Although older adults exhibited more difficulty than young adults in stopping an overt response and in adopting new rules in a categorization task, the two age groups did not differ in the magnitude of identity-based negative priming, spatial cuing, and response compatibility effects.

IV. ADULT AGE DIFFERENCES IN VIGILANCE

Like selectivity, the vigilance component of attention is amenable to operational definition in laboratory tasks. Vigilance, also referred to as sustained attention, represents the ability to detect stimulus change. In our everyday perceptual experience, preparing to respond to an expected event is a common occurence. Several variants of this type of perceptual task have been developed. Whereas studies of the capacity and selectivity aspects of attention often involve search and classification tasks, vigilance experiments have been concerned with simple stimulus detection as well as more complex identification processes. Comparatively few studies of age differences in vigilance have been conducted. The most frequently investigated vigilance task is the Mackworth Clock Test, in which the pointer of a clock-like device moves in discrete steps (like the second hand of a clock), but occasionally moves two steps rather than one. The subject's task is to detect the occasional change in the movement of the pointer, over the course of an hour. Initial investigations of age differences in the clock test indicated that detection accuracy was comparable for young and older adults during the first 15 min of monitoring, but that there was a relatively greater decline in the older adults' performance over three additional 15-min periods of monitoring. Later investigations of this task, however, found that although both detection accuracy and speed declined over the monitoring period, this decline did not vary significantly as a function of age. Reanalyses of the data from the earlier studies indicated that the age differences that had appeared may have been a statistical artifact.

Recent studies have obtained an age-related decline in vigilance in more complex tasks, such as detecting, in a series of briefly presented red squares, a target square that was slightly smaller than the nontarget squares. Researchers have found that, in complex visual-discrimination tasks, an age-related decrement in vigilance was magnified by either stimulus degradation or increasing event rate. This age difference was not attenuated by 20 sessions of specific practice in the vigilance task. Thus, when the complexity of the task is increased, the vigilance component of attention is vulnerable to age-related decline.

V. CONCLUSION

Age-related changes in attention are a complex mosaic of stability and change. With capacity-demanding tasks (i.e., tasks requiring cognitive effort or processing resources), an age-related decline has been frequently observed. The theoretical issue of whether this decline represents an age-related change in atten-

tional capacity, processing speed, or response selection processes, however, is unresolved. In tasks that provide subjects with a specific distinction between relevant and irrelevant information, the efficiency of attending selectively to the relevant information has been often found to be similar for young and older adults, although an age-related decline in inhibiting irrelevant information has been observed under some conditions. Simple forms of vigilance performance appear to be resistant to significant age-related decline; it is more difficult for older adults to be vigilant in complex visual-discrimination tasks. Current research focuses on estimating the magnitude of age differences in the context of specific models of attentional processes.

ACKNOWLEDGMENTS

Preparation of this chapter was supported by Research Grant R01 AG02163 from the National Institute on Aging.

BIBLIOGRAPHY

Hartley, A. A. (1992). Attention. *In* F. I. M. Craik & T. A. Salthouse (Eds.), pp. 3–49 *Handbook of aging and cognition* Hillsdale, NJ: Erlbaum.

Kausler, D. H. (1991). *Experimental psychology, cognition, and human aging* (2nd ed.) New York: Springer-Verlag.

Madden, D. J., & Plude, D. J. (1993). Selective preservation of selective attention. In J. Cerella, J. Rybash, W. Hoyer, & M. L. Commons pp. 273–300. (Eds.), *Adult information processing: Limits on loss* San Diego: Academic Press.

McDowd, J. M., & Birren, J. E. (1990). Aging and attentional processes. *In* J. E. Birren & K. W. Schaie, (Eds.), pp. 222–233 *Handbook of the psychology of aging,* (3rd ed.) San Diego: Academic Press.

Salthouse, T. A. (1991). *Theoretical perspectives on cognitive aging.* Hillsdale, NJ: Erlbaum.

Autonomic Nervous System

Stephen Borst

Veterans Administration Medical Center, Gainesville, Florida, and University of Florida

ANS Autonomic nervous system.

Adrenergic Having the properties of epinephrine. Drugs that produce effects similar to those of epinephrine are said to be adrenergic, as are nerve endings that release norepinephrine (NE) and the cell surface receptors that bind NE and epinephrine.

Baroreceptor Reflex A mechanism for minute-to-minute regulation of blood pressure (BP). Baroreceptors located in arteries of the upper body respond to a reduction in BP by signaling the brain to activate the sympathetic nervous system, thereby raising the arterial pressure.

Catecholamines Any of various amines that function as hormones and neurotransmitters in the autonomic nervous system, most notably epinephrine, norepinephrine (NE), and dopamine (DA). The British names for epinephrine and NE are adrenaline and noradrenaline.

Cholinergic Having the properties of acetylcholine; refers to drugs that mimic acetylcholine (ACh), nerve endings that release ACh and the cell surface receptors in tissues that respond to ACh.

Neurotransmitter A chemical substance that is re-leased from nerve endings when the nerve fires. The neurotransmitter diffuses across the small space of the synapse and binds to a receptor located on an adjacent cell, where it produces its physiologic effect.

PNS Parasympathetic nervous system.

Postural Hypotension Reduced arterial pressure in the upper body after rapidly standing upright.

Renin–Angiotensin System A mechanism for longer term regulation of blood pressure (BP). A fall in arterial pressure causes release of renin from the juxtaglomerular apparatus of the kidney. The enzymatic action of renin causes the formation of angiotensin II, which raises systemic BP by causing vasoconstriction and renal retention of water and salt.

SNS Sympathetic nervous system.

The **AUTONOMIC NERVOUS SYSTEM** (ANS) controls the vegetative or visceral functions of the body, including heart rate, blood pressure (BP), the motility and secretion of the digestive system, the urinary bladder, aspects of sexual function, and many other responses. Some of the major responses elicited by the ANS are listed in Table I. The responses of the ANS are involuntary. In contrast, the somatic nervous system controls voluntary responses or skeletal muscle. Somatic impulses arise in the motor region of the cerebral cortex. Autonomic impulses arise in the spinal cord, brain stem, and hypothalamus. Autonomic impulses also receive higher control from a region of the cerebral cortex known as the limbic cortex.

There are two separate arms of the ANS: the sympathetic nervous system (SNS) and the parasympathetic nervous system (PNS). The ANS and PNS are

Table I Autonomic Responses

	Sympathetic response	Parasympathetic	Predominant tone
Heart			
S-A node	β_1 increased heart rate	Decreased heart rate	Parasympathetic
Conducting system	β_1 increased automaticity	Decreased automaticity	Parasympathetic
Ventricles	β_1 increased force		
Blood vessels			
Arterioles	α_1 constriction		Sympathetic
Arteries	β_2 dilatation	—	
Veins	α_2 constriction		
Eye			
Ciliary muscle		Contraction for near vision	
Iris	α_1 pupillary dilatation	Pupillary constriction	Parasympathetic
Lung			
Smooth muscle	β_2 relaxation	Constriction	—
Secretions	α_1 decrease; β_2 increase	Increase	
Salivary glands			
Fluid and electrolytes		Increased secretion	—
Proteins	β increased secretion		
Sweat glands			
Palms and soles	α_1 stimulation	—	—
General sweating	Cholinergic stimulation		
Gastrointestinal tract	Decrease motility	Increased motility	—
	Contract sphincters	Relax sphincters	
Liver glucose secretion	α_1, β_2 stimulation	—	—
Adrenal medulla	Catecholamine secretion	—	—

distinct in details of their anatomy and biochemistry. They are also partially opposing in the nature of the physiological responses that they provoke. Activation of the SNS produces a state of arousal and readiness. The PNS generally governs digestive and secretory functions.

I. GENERAL DESCRIPTION OF THE AUTONOMIC NERVOUS SYSTEM

A. Anatomy of the ANS

The motor neurons of the somatic nervous system arise in the spinal column, and their axons pass directly to skeletal muscle without synapsing. In contrast, the outgoing fibers of the ANS also have their cell bodies in the spinal column, but before reaching the target organ, they synapse in one of the peripheral autonomic ganglia. Thus the autonomic pathway from the spinal cord to target tissue consists of two neurons; one preganglionic and one postganglionic.

Sympathetic fibers emerge from the thoracic and lumbar regions of the cord and pass into one of the sympathetic chain ganglia, which are located close to the spine. Some fibers synapse in the chain ganglion. This results in the spreading of the impulse to other fibers both higher and lower in the chain. Other fibers pass through the chain ganglia uninterrupted and synapse in one of the two major peripheral sympathetic ganglia, the celiac ganglion or the hypogastric plexus. In general, the spreading of sympathetic impulses leads to a diffuse activation. Often, many sympathetic responses are elicited together. This is ideal for a system that produces the fight or flight state of arousal that readies the body for action. BP and heart rate are elevated; glucose is released into the blood; the pupils dilate and digestion is inhibited. One more feature of the SNS aids in its diffuse activation. Sympathetic fibers innervating the medulla of the adrenal gland stimulate release of epinephrine and norepinephrine (NE) into the systemic circulation. The action of these two hormones is to stimulate simultaneously all of the tissues that are innervated by the

SNS and in addition some tissues that are not innervated.

The organization of the PNS is simpler than that of the SNS. Parasympathetic neurons emerge with the cranial nerves or from the sacral region of the spinal cord. They pass most of the way to their targets before synapsing in ganglia that are located close to or are imbedded within the target organs. The postganglionic neurons are often very short. The anatomy of the PNS is designed for discrete activation. Parasympathetic responses are often evoked singly.

B. Pharmacology of the ANS

There are three major types of synapse in the ANS; the adrenergic synapse located in the target organs innervated by the SNS, the cholinergic synapse in the target organs innervated by the PNS, and the cholinergic synapse located in the ganglia for both the SNS and PNS. Consideration of the effects of age on the postsynaptic receptors located in these synapses is important for two reasons. First, changes in the receptors or postreceptor biochemical events play an important role in the impairment of some autonomic responses with age. Second, these receptors are the major targets for drugs affecting the ANS. Thus the response to many drugs may also be altered with age.

Acetylcholine (ACh) is the neurotransmitter at both the autonomic ganglia and parasympathetic effector sites (target organs). However, the postsynaptic receptors are different at these two sites. The ganglionic synapse is called nicotinic, and the PNS effector synapse is called muscarinic, based on the ability of the postsynaptic receptors to preferentially bind either nicotine or muscarine. NE is the neurotransmitter at sympathetic effector sites. [See NEUROTRANSMITTERS AND NEUROTROPHIC FACTORS.] The postsynaptic receptor may be either an α- or β-adrenergic receptor, based on the preferential binding of certain drugs. Many clinically useful drugs have been synthesized to specifically stimulate or block α-adrenergic, β-adrenergic, and muscarinic cholinergic receptors. In some cases, the response to these drugs is altered in senescence and will be discussed below. Drugs that interact with the nicotinic cholinergic receptors in the autonomic ganglia do not see widespread clinical use. These drugs produce a lot of side effects, as they affect both the SNS and PNS.

C. Autonomic Responses, Principle of Predominant Tone

As mentioned above, the SNS and PNS often innervate the same tissues. The responses of the two arms of the ANS are opposing in some cases, but not in all. When both the SNS and PNS innervate the same tissue, one system may be more active at rest than the other. In such a case, either the SNS or PNS is said to exert a predominant tone. The major examples of predominant tone are listed in Table 1. The terms *resting tone* and *intrinsic tone* are synonymous with *predominant tone*.

An example of predominant tone is seen in the control of heart rate. Activation of the SNS increases heart rate and activation of the PNS decreases heart rate. At rest, the PNS is active and the SNS is inactive. ACh is released in the heart and NE is not. As a result, the heart beats slower at rest than it might if there were no autonomic innervation. When the subject is exercising, the situation is reversed. The sympathetic drive is higher and the heart rate increases dramatically. Thus the predominant tone to the heart is parasympathetic at rest and sympathetic during exercise.

Predominant tone is important in considering the actions of agonists (receptor stimulators) and antagonists (receptor blockers). Agonists mimic the effects of the neurotransmitter, directly stimulating the receptor, and thus agonists will always produce a response. In contrast, antagonists are effective only when an agonist or neurotransmitter is present whose action can be blocked. As a result, antagonists may have little effect on tissues where there is no predominant tone. Atropine (a muscarinic blocker) blocks the action of ACh in lowering heart rate. Propranolol (a β-adrenergic blocker) blocks the action of NE in elevating heart rate. Atropine markedly elevates heart rate in a resting subject. Propranolol has little effect on heart rate in the same individual. [See CARDIOVASCULAR SYSTEM.]

II. ANATOMIC CHANGES IN THE ANS WITH AGE

A number of global changes occur with age in the human nervous system. These affect the ANS, as well as other parts of the nervous system. The weight and volume of the nervous system reaches a maximum at puberty and later begins a progressive decline beginning in middle age. Some areas are relatively spared, such as the parietal lobes and brain stem. In the peripheral nerves, there is a loss in fiber number and a loss of myelination. The number of neurons is reduced with age, although the extent of loss has been difficult to assess in humans. The remaining neurons have a reduced cell volume and fewer dendrites. The most reliable marker that has been identified for aging of the nervous system is the accumulation of the fatty brown pigment lipofuscin within the neuron. Lipofuscin is absent in the neurons of newborns. Its accumulation increases progressively until senescence, when 60–70% of neurons contain inclusions.

The density of autonomic innervation has been difficult to study in humans, and we have to rely mainly on animal data. One human study found that sympathetic innervation of the posterior tibial artery is reduced with age. Animal studies are not in complete agreement, but suggest the sympathetic innervation decreases in some tissues with age. For example, arteries are more affected than are veins.

III. FUNCTIONAL CHANGES IN THE ANS WITH AGE

A. Sympathetic Nervous System

1. Circulating Catecholamines

Circulating NE is increased in humans with age and epinephrine is unchanged. Most of the NE that circulates in the blood derives from adrenergic nerve terminals. In contrast, all of the epinephrine derives from the adrenal medulla. NE released into the synapse may either be degraded, reabsorbed by the same nerve terminal that released it, or it may spill out of the synapse and eneter the systemic circulation. The possible explanations for increased NE levels in the elderly include (a) reduced clearance across the capillary bed and (b) increased release from sympathetic nerve terminals and from the adrenal glands. Most evidence points to the conclusion that increased NE release is the reason for elevated NE.

Circulating epinephrine and NE increase in response to a variety of stimuli including exercise, standing upright, and a mental stress test. The increase in NE is exaggerated in the elderly, but the increase in epinephrine is not. Because the epinephrine derives from the adrenal medulla and the NE mainly from

adrenergic nerve terminals, one can conclude that under a variety of conditions, NE release resulting from sympathetic nerve activity is increased in the elderly.

There are two reasons for the increase in the release of NE in sympathetic nerve terminals. First, sympathetic responses are impaired as a result of age in a number of important target tissues. It is thought that greater release of NE occurs in an attempt to get an adequate response from these failing target tissues. The second reason concerns the loss of sensitivity in the baroreceptors. When pressure increases in the carotid artery and some other vessels, those vessels expand, activating the baroreceptors, which in turn act to reduce sympathetic outflow. Reduced sympathetic outflow reduces heart rate and peripheral resistance, thereby correcting the original increase in pressure. In older individuals, the vessels are more rigid and do not stretch as much in response to pressure. Thus decreased baroreceptor sensitivity contributes to elevated NE and may also contribute to hypertension in the elderly.

2. β-adrenergic and α-adrenergic Responses

In the heart, NE released from sympathetic nerves stimulates β-adrenergic receptors. These receptors mediate increases in heart rate and in the force of contraction. The impairment of these responses with age results in a reduced ability to increase heart rate during exercise. Because cardiac output is a limiting factor in exercise, exercise capacity is also impaired. β-adrenergic stimulation of the heart is also required for the postural hemodynamic response, which is called into play when BP drops in the upper body, such as after standing up rapidly. Thus decreased β-adrenergic responsiveness in the elderly contributes to postural hypotension, or an inability to maintain BP after standing up. The number of β receptors is not actually reduced in the aging heart, but the coupling of the receptor to biochemical events inside the cell is reduced.

β-adrenergic dilatation of blood vessels is impaired with age. The dorsal veins in the human hand constrict in response to the α-agonist phenylephrine. This response is unchanged with age. To measure β-adrenergic vasodilatation, the veins are first constricted with phenylephrine and then dilated with the β-agonist isoproterenol. The response to isoproterenol is reduced with age both in terms of maximum response and sensitivity. The inherent ability of the vessel to relax is not impaired with age, as evidenced by the fact that dilation in response to papaverine and nitroprusside are unchanged with age. What is impaired specifically is β-adrenergic triggering of vasodilatation.

β agonists are useful in treating asthma because of their ability to open the airways by causing a relaxation of bronchial smooth muscle. Adrenergic fibers are associated directly with submucosal glands of the lung and bronchial arteries, but not bronchial smooth muscle. β agonists act indirectly by opposing the parasympathetic constriction of bronchial smooth muscle. Adrenergic fibers innervate parasympathetic ganglia and cause bronchodilation by inhibiting cholinergic output. Animal studies show that there is a reduced β responsiveness in aging.

α-adrenergic responses are impaired with aging in some, but not all cases. In human arteries, $\alpha 1$-stimulated constriction is unchanged with age. In human veins, the α constriction is reduced with age. Both the α-adrenergic stimulation of the heart and the α-adrenergic constriction of veins contribute to the postural hemodynamic response. Because both responses are impaired with age, the elderly experience postural hypotension, that is, difficulty in maintaining BP after standing.

There is evidence both in animal and human studies that the SNS has a protective role against autoimmune disease. In mice, the chemical destruction of sympathetic nerve endings exacerbates various experimental models of autoimmune disease. The β-adrenergic agonist isoproterenol has a protective effect against these same models of autoimmunity. Thus it is possible, although not proven, that reduced adrenergic responsiveness is involved in the increased incidence of autoimmune disease in the elderly.

B. Parasympathetic Nervous System

The parasympathetic input, or vagal tone, to the heart is reduced with age. This is due to a decrease in the intrinsic sinus rate in the elderly and the resulting reduced need to "brake" the heart. The reduced vagal tone can be seen in the response to atropine, a blocker of the muscarinic receptor present in parasympathetic nerve endings. Atropine produces a smaller increase in heart rate in the elderly than in young subjects. There is also direct evidence in animal studies that parasympathetic responsiveness of the heart is re-

duced with age. Bradycardia, or slowing of the heart, in response to cholinergic agonists is reduced with age.

Bronchial smooth muscle is also innervated by the vagus nerve and contracts in response to cholinergic stimulation. Animal studies have shown that this response is exaggerated in senescence. The mechanism is a decrease in the content of acetylcholinesterase, the enzyme that terminates the action of the neurotransmitter ACh. As a result, ACh released into the synapse has a more prolonged action.

Gastrointestinal (GI) function is impaired in the elderly, and certain aspects suggest autonomic dysfunction. In humans, there is difficulty in swallowing, increased gastric emptying time, increased intestinal transit time, constipation, and reduced absorption of calcium and fat. The rat model has shown reduced transport of water, sugars, and amino acids. The density of innervation of the enteric nerve plexus is reduced in senescence. Reduced parasympathetic responses in the GI tract result in reduced secretions and motility. These changes contribute to a number of problems that are more common in the elderly, including achalasia and pseudo-obstruction. Achalasia is a disorder of swallowing involving a failure of the lower esophageal sphincter to relax. This relaxation is mediated by a parasympathetic discharge of the vagus nerve, which is impaired with aging. Pseudo-obstruction is dilation of the large bowel in the absence of an obstruction and occurs almost entirely in the elderly. [See GASTROINTESTINAL SYSTEM: FUNCTION AND DYSFUNCTION.]

The PNS controls salivary excretion of fluid and electrolytes. Xerostomia, or dry mouth, is common in the elderly. However, parasympathetic responses in the salivary glands are unchanged with age and do not play a role in xerostomia.

IV. CHANGING ROLE OF THE ANS IN CARDIOVASCULAR RESPONSES

A. Control of Blood Pressure

Falls and the attendant risk of hip fracture are an important problem in the elderly. Postural hypotension, which is caused in part by autonomic dysregulation in the elderly, plays a major role in the risk of falling. Postural hypotension may be defined as drop in systolic pressure of 20-mm mercury, which is sustained for at least 1 min after standing. Postural hypotension occurs in approximately 30% of the population aged 65 or more. A drop in pressure of this magnitude is not alone sufficient to directly cause a fall through syncope (fainting). However, note that the drop in pressure may be considerably greater on a given occasion. When postural hypotension is combined with other factors, a fall may easily result. These other factors include impaired vision and impaired gait due to, among other things, impaired proprioception (positional sense), especially in the ankles. [See ACCIDENTS: FALLS; BALANCE, POSTURE, AND GAIT.]

The causes of postural hypotension in the elderly include an impaired postural hemodynamic response, volume depletion, and the presence of certain drugs. The causes of impaired postural hemodynamic response are mainly autonomic. These include a diminished baroreceptor reflex, the loss of α-mediated constriction of veins, and the loss of β stimulation of the heart.

Postprandial hypotension is a common problem in the elderly. Lowest dip in BP occurs about 1 hour after eating. Carbohydrate meals produce the greatest drop. The mechanism is the inability to compensate for vasodilatation in the GI tract. The clinical significance of postprandial hypotension is unclear. It may precipitate strokes and myocardial infarction. Postprandial hypotension is also a factor in producing postural hypotension.

B. Exercise Performance

The increase in cardiac output that occurs during exercise is mediated by the SNS. There is an increase in heart rate, an increase in the force of contraction, and an increase in stroke volume. Shunting of blood to the skeletal muscle is accomplished by vasodilatation in the muscle vasculature and vasoconstriction in other tissues. The vasoconstriction is sympathetic and so is a component of the vasodilatation. In the elderly, two key sympathetic responses are impaired, namely β-adrenergic stimulation of the heart and β-adrenergic dilation of arteries supplying skeletal muscle. The increase in cardiac output that occurs during exercise is rate-limiting for the amount of exercise that can be performed before lactic acid accumulation begins. As a result, autonomic dysfunction in the elderly may limit their exercise capacity. The decline in exercise capacity that occurs with age also involves other fac-

tors, such as reduced cardiac reserve, peripheral circulatory factors, and reduced muscle mass. [See MOTOR CONTROL; NEUROMUSCULAR SYSTEM.]

V. AUTONOMIC DYSFUNCTION IN DISEASES COMMON IN THE ELDERLY

Primary autonomic failure is a disorder of degeneration of the postganglionic neurons of the SNS. Symptoms are postural hypotension, impaired thermoregulation due to inability to sweat, low circulating catecholamines, impotence, GI and urinary dysfunction. Symptoms are most severe in the elderly.

Multiple system atrophy (or Shy-Drager syndrome) is a disease of preganglionic neurons of the SNS. There is degeneration in the sympathetic centers of the brain and in the lateral horn of the thoracic segments of the spinal column. With Shy-Drager syndrome, most of the same autonomic symptoms are seen as with primary autonomic failure, but there are often motor deficits as well. Circulating catecholamines are normal at rest, but fail to increase properly in response to a stimulus, such as rapid standing.

In Parkinson's disease, there are often signs of autonomic dysfunction. Postural hypotension is often seen as a side effect of medication with l-dopa. The addition of a peripheral decarboxylase inhibitor, such as carbidopa, can eliminate this problem by confining the actions of l-dopa to the central nervous system and thus preventing the action of l-dopa on the autonomic ganglia. Other signs of autonomic dysfunction result from the disease process itself. Parkinson's disease is often accompanied by lesions of the spinal column similar to those that cause motor difficulties in Shy-Drager syndrome. The impotence associated with Parkinsonism may have a basis in autonomic dysfunction. Abnormalities in thermoregulation are due to lack of sweating. Accidental hypothermia is a risk due to absence of shivering.

VI. ALTERED AUTONOMIC RESPONSES TO DRUGS COMMONLY PRESCRIBED IN THE ELDERLY

Treatment of hypertension in the elderly is a double-edged sword. Effective lowering of BP often brings increased incidence of postural hypotension, a contributor to falls. α blockers often induce postural hypotension in the elderly and this may limit their use for hypertension and prostatic outflow obstruction. β-receptor stimulation of the heart, which occurs during the postural response, is already diminished in normal aging. Thus, with the introduction of an α-blocker, both the α-adrenergic and β-adrenergic arms of the postural response are now impaired. β-blockers and diuretics also increase the likelihood of postural hypotension. Calcium channel blockers and angiotensin-converting enzyme inhibitors carry less risk.

The elderly have an increased susceptibility to adverse effects of tricyclic antidepressants. Tricyclics such as amitryptyline exert their antidepressive effects by inhibiting neuronal reuptake of NE. These compounds also have α-blocking effects and anticholinergic effects. As a result of underlying autonomic dysfunction, the elderly are more susceptible to these side effects. Because tricyclics block α receptors, they cause sinus tachycardia in the elderly due to vasodilatation and postural hypotension for the reasons described above. The anticholinergic side effects of tricyclics include xerostomia (dry mouth), blurred vision, constipation, and urinary retention. The xerostomia is caused by an inhibition of parasympathetic stimulation of salivary fluid and electrolyte secretion. The blurred vision is caused by impaired contraction of ciliary muscle of the eye, which is involved in accommodation for near vision. Newer antidepressants such as Prozac work by a different mechanism. They inhibit the neuronal reuptake of serotonin rather than NE. Whether the side effects of these drugs present a special problem in the elderly remains to be seen.

BIBLIOGRAPHY

Amenta, F. (Ed.). (1993). *Aging and the autonomic nervous system*. Boca Raton, FL: CRC Press.
Bannister, R. (Ed.). (1988). *Autonomic failure: A textbook of clinical disorders of the autonomic nervous system*, (2nd ed.). Oxford: Oxford University Press.
Borst, S. E., & Lowenthal, D. T. (1991). Cardiovascular drugs in the elderly. In A. Brest (Ed.), *Cardiovascular clinics: Geriatric pharmacology* (pp. 161–173). Philadelphia: F. A. Davis Co.
Guyton, A. C. (1991). *Textbook of medical physiology* (8th ed), (pp. 667–678). Philadelphia: W.B. Saunders Co.
Hockman, C. H. (1987). *Essentials of autonomic function*. Springfield, IL: Charles C. Springer.
Loewy, A. D., & Spyer, M. K., (Ed.). (1990). *Central regulation of autonomic functions*. New York: Oxford University Press.

Balance, Posture, and Gait

Marjorie Woollacott

University of Oregon

Adaptive Postural Control Modifying sensory or motor response strategies in response to changing task and environmental demands.

Anticipatory Posture Control Pretuning sensory and motor processes in expectation of postural demands based on previous experience.

Cognitive Processes Higher level neural processes such as attention, motivation, and planning. It is difficult to make a clear distinction between higher level perceptual or motor processing and cognitive processing, because there is a gradual transition and overlap between processing levels.

Postural and Balance Control Regulating the body's position in space for the dual purposes of stability and orientation. Stability is the ability to maintain the position of the center of body mass (COM) within specific boundaries, or stability limits. Orientation is the ability to maintain an appropriate relationship between the body and the environment or task.

Sensory Strategies Organizing sensory information from visual, somatosensory, and vestibular systems for postural control.

Research on **BALANCE, POSTURE, AND GAIT** in older adults has become a priority in the health-care field because data indicate that falls are a major threat to independence in older adults and an important contributor to fatalities. For example, it has been shown that nearly one-third of adults over the age of 75 experience at least one fall per year, and 6% of these adults sustain fractures as a result. Research on balance and gait in the older adult has focused on (a) identifying the contributions of primary aging versus secondary effects due to pathology or a sedentary lifestyle to deterioration in balance and gait; (b) determining if there are specific neural and musculoskeletal subsystems that show a decline with aging; and (c) creating effective measures for the prevention and the rehabilitation of decline in balance function with aging. Several approaches have been used in the past to study and assess balance and locomotor skills in the elderly from both a research and clinical perspective. Traditionally, balance control was studied from a reflex perspective, and global methods of measuring balance were used. More recently a systems approach to the study of balance in the older adult has been used. This approach has the advantage of allowing clinicians and researchers to assess whether there is a decline in identified subsystems contributing to balance and gait.

I. INTRODUCTION

A. Models of Aging and Posture and Gait Control

A large number of research studies examining age-related changes in sensory and motor systems underlying balance and gait function have indicated that there is a deterioration in these systems in many older adults. However, there is not yet agreement in the scientific community on the causes for these changes in the neural systems underlying balance and gait. For

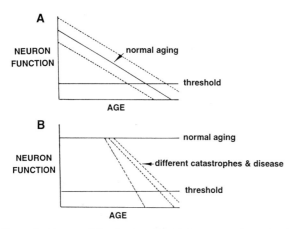

Figure 1 Two models of aging. Model A suggests that aging is associated with an inevitable decline in neuronal function in all systems. Model B suggests that neuronal function remains optimal with aging unless specific catastrophes or diseases affect areas of the brain. (From Woollacott, M., 1989. Aging, posture control, and movement preparation. In M. H. Woollacott, & A. Shumway-Cook (Eds.), *Development of posture and gait across the lifespan* (p. 156). Columbia, SC: University of South Carolina Press.)

example, two different models of aging have been proposed to explain declines in balance and gait function. One model predicts that the process of aging causes a linear decline in neuron function within all nervous subsystems, and that, as neuron numbers decline in specific subsystems, various disease states will manifest. However, a second model predicts that neural function will remain at a relatively high level throughout life, unless there is a catastrophe or disease that affects a specific part of the nervous system. Thus pathology could result in a rapid decline in a specific neural function; however, other neural subsystems would remain unaffected. These models are shown in Figure 1.

It is important to determine which of these models more accurately predicts age-related changes in balance and gait function because each one leads to very different conclusions regarding the *inevitability* of functional decline with aging. For example, because the first model predicts that deterioration in neuronal function is inevitable, this could result in expectations by the older adult and clinicians that they will show losses in balance and gait with age. However, because the second model predicts optimal neural function if optimal experiential factors exist and pathology is not present, it is assumed that balance and gait function will remain high throughout life. The older adult and

clinicians will thus focus on preventive health care and rehabilitation strategies aimed at maintaining function at normal young adult levels.

1. Primary and Secondary Factors Associated with Aging

It has been hypothesized that there are both primary and secondary factors associated with age-related declines in motor abilities. Primary factors, such as genetics, would lead to an inevitable decline in neuronal function within a particular subsystem. For example, certain diseases that affect basal ganglia function, and therefore motor abilities, are genetically based.

Secondary factors or experiential factors include such things as nutrition, exercise, insults, and pathologies. Later in this chapter, I will discuss research on exercise programs, which have been shown to improve balance and gait function. [*See* DIET AND NUTRITION.]

2. Variability in Older Adults' Balance and Gait Abilities

A review of the literature on age-related changes in balance and gait function shows an interesting inconsistency in the findings from different laboratories, which may indicate a large amount of variability in the performance of different older adults. Some studies show no change in posture or locomotor function with age, whereas others show a severe decline in these abilities. One possible explanation for this discrepancy in the research literature is that there are many different definitions researchers use in classifying an individual as an older adult. Certain laboratories define all individuals over 65 years of age as older adults, whereas other laboratories attempt to exclude any individuals with pathology from their research. One study examining the effects of aging on gait, found that mean walking speed in subjects ($N = 71$, ages 60–99 years) was lower than that found in any previous study. This may occur because no criteria were used to exclude individuals with pathology. A second study also examining age-related changes in gait, screened 1,187 individuals (65 years and over) to select 32 who were free of disorders of the musculoskeletal, neurological, or cardiovascular systems, or any previous history of falls. As might be expected the results of this research indicated that there were no significant age-related changes in their parameters measuring the variability of gait. The researchers thus concluded that it is pathology rather than aging, per se, that contributes to increased variability in gait in older adults. These types of results suggest that there is considerable variability across subjects in this population, and that it is impossible to make generalized assumptions about declining physical capabilities in this group.

II. BALANCE CONTROL IN OLDER ADULTS

A. Early Studies

Balance control may be defined as the maintenance of a person's center of mass (COM) within their stability limits, which are defined as their base of support. Balance control thus indicates the ability to regulate one's static upright posture or to recover from unexpected threats to balance, such as the balance threat that occurs when standing on a bus that starts to move.

In addition to static balance control, an adult must also be able to maintain balance during many other daily activities, such as walking. Maintaining balance during walking requires the integration of postural adjustments into the step cycle in order to allow safe forward movement. In this dynamic task the COM is not maintained within the base support, but moves along the medial border of the support foot. This integration of balance control into voluntary activities is essential to the accomplishment of most goal-oriented tasks and requires the ability to respond to constantly changing environmental and task demands.

Classically, the assessment and treatment of balance function in the older adult has been centered around global measures of balance abilities, such as the measurement of total body sway. A study examining the degree to which sway during quiet stance changed across the life span, found that subjects at both ends of the age spectrum (6–14 years and 50–80 years) showed significantly more sway during quiet stance than did young adults.

Other research using a measure of both the amplitude and velocity of global body sway to assess the balance skill of institutionalized older adults, indicated that sway velocity is correlated with frequency of balance loss. Older adults who fell more than once per year showed higher velocities of sway when standing quietly, when compared to those who did not fall.

Some of the earlier studies regarding balance function in the older adult often assumed that one could find a single cause of instability in an individual, such as peripheral neuropathy or postural hypotension. In addition, clinicians typically assessed balance function using a reflex model of balance control, limiting tests to evaluation of tendon reflexes, righting reflexes, and vestibulo-ocular reflexes, and predicting that with aging more "primitive" reflexes would be released from inhibition. However, more recent research has indicated that a reflex framework of motor control is limited, because many other motor processes contribute to motor function.

It has become clear that for any given individual there are complex interactions between intrinsic factors related to the level of function of different nervous or musculoskeletal subsystems and also extrinsic environmental factors. It is important to study these interactions in order to clearly understand the factors that contribute to falls in the older adult. In one study researchers observed a group of community-dwelling older adults for 1 year and documented all falls. The study concluded that reductions in physical activity, reduced proximal muscle strength, and reduced stability during quiet stance were all strongly linked with an increased risk of falling. They also showed a significant association between falls and arthritis of the knees, stroke, impairment of gait, hypotension, and the use of psychotropic drugs. The study concluded that multiple risk factors, many of which are remediable, are associated with most falls in older adults.

Though this approach has significantly improved our understanding of factors contributing to balance deterioration in the older adult, it is limited by the use of relatively broad categories to classify intrinsic factors related to falls, such as "loss of stability while standing." Such categories do not allow the identification of problems in specific subsystems that may be constraining balance abilities.

B. Systems Approach to Age-Related Changes in Balance

Researchers have begun to use a new method for testing balance control in older adults. This approach, often called a systems approach, attempts to identify the relative contribution of deterioration in specific neural and musculoskeletal subsystems to a decline in balance function. The systems model of balance control has the advantage of being able to aid the clinician in evaluating the degree to which a decrease in the function of individual subsystems contributes to deterioration in balance and gait in the older adult. According to the systems model, balance is considered to emerge from complex interactions among several factors, including a variety of neural subsystems, the musculoskeletal systems of the individual, and the task and environmental situations in which the individual is balancing and moving. The postural control system is usually identified as the neural and musculoskeletal subsystems that contribute to balance function.

In assessing balance function in the older adult from a systems model one would evaluate both the neural components (motor systems, sensory or perceptual systems, adaptive systems, cognitive systems) and the musculoskeletal components (muscle strength, range of motion of ankle, knee, and hip joints, and the vertical alignment of the body) that contribute to balance. The next section includes a review of research on changes in balance control in the older adult, using a systems perspective.

1. Musculoskeletal

Many research studies have examined the extent to which postural components of the musculoskeletal system change with age. For example, it has been shown that strength of the leg muscle can show a reduction of 40% in older (80 years) compared to young adults (30 years). Research has shown that older adults with a history of falls (nursing home residents) show an even greater reduction in muscle strength, with ankle-dorsiflexor strength being 14% of that of nonfallers. In addition, spinal flexibility is reduced in the older adult, causing a rounded or forward flexion of the posture alignment, and arthritis may cause a decrease in the range of joint motion in the ankle, hip, and knee joints.

2. Neuromuscular Response Patterns

When older adults are faced with an unexpected threat to standing balance, such as the sudden start or stop of a bus or a subway car on which they are standing, are they capable of responding to that threat in as efficient a manner as a young adult?

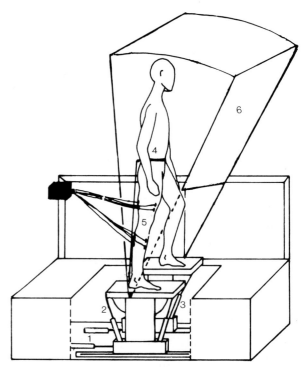

Figure 2 Experimental paradigm. Subject stands on hydraulically activated platform that moves unexpectedly forward or backward (1–3, hydraulic cylinders). A belt attached to the hips measures sway (4). Surface electrodes (5) measure muscle responses. A visual surround (6) can be rotated with the subject's sway to minimize sway-related visual inputs. (From Woollacott, M. H., Shumway-Cook, A., & Nashner, L. M., 1986. Aging and posture control: Changes in sensory organization and muscular coordination. *International Journal of Aging and Human Development, 23,* 100.)

In order to answer this question research has been performed to simulate this situation and to examine the characteristics of postural muscle response patterns that are activated in response to the unexpected forward or backward movement of a platform on which the subject is standing (Figure 2). When the balance of a young adult is disturbed by this type of movement, there is typically sway focused at the ankle joint, and muscle responses that return balance to normal are activated first in the stretched ankle muscle and radiate upward to the muscles of the thigh and hip.

Research comparing the response characteristics of older adults (61–78 years) and younger adults (19–38 years) has shown that the postural muscle response organization was generally similar between the two groups, with responses being activated first in the

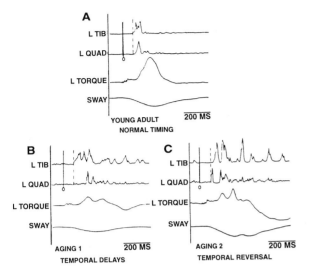

Figure 3 Changes in temporal structure of muscle response synergies in the elderly. Normally coordinated muscle response pattern in a young adult (A) compared to a pattern of temporal delay (B) and temporal reversal (C). (From Woollacott, M. H., Shumway-Cook, A., & Nashner, L. M., 1986. Aging and posture control: Changes in sensory organization and muscular coordination. *International Journal of Aging and Human Development*, 23, 335.)

stretched ankle muscle and radiating upward to the muscles of the thigh.

However, the two groups also showed four specific differences in response characteristics.

1. Onset latencies for the postural muscles (ankle dorsiflexors) were significantly slower for the older adults compared to the younger adults when platform movements caused backward sway (example shown in Figure 3A and B).

2. For almost half of the older adults, there was an occasional disorganization of the muscle response pattern, with proximal (thigh) muscles being activated before distal (ankle) muscles (example shown in Figure 3C). It is interesting that this type of response organization is typical of certain patients with central nervous system (CNS) lesions.

3. The older adults coactivated the antagonist and agonist muscles of a joint together significantly more frequently than the younger adults, possibly to stiffen the joints as an alternate way to increase joint stability.

4. Older adults also tended to use a strategy of balancing that involved hip movements rather than simple ankle movements to control sway. It has been

suggested that some falls in the older adult may be caused by a drop in the use of the classical ankle balance strategy and a shift toward the use of a hip balance strategy, as a result of pathological conditions such as peripheral sensory neuropathy. [*See* NEUROMUSCULAR SYSTEM.]

3. Sensory Contributions

In order to balance effectively in a variety of environments, it is necessary to utilize information from three sensory systems: the visual, somatosensory (proprioceptive, cutaneous, and joint receptors), and vestibular systems. This information must be combined appropriately to accurately represent the body's position in space. Each sensory system contributes a different frame of reference for balance orientation. There are different sensory strategies that can be used in balance control, each involving a different weighting by the higher nervous system centers of the visual, somatosensory, and vestibular inputs. In order to remain balanced in changing task conditions one must also be able to appropriately select the most effective sensory input for the specific task. Older adults have been shown to have deficits in specific sensory systems, which could contribute to a difficulty in organizing sensory inputs appropriately for changing task conditions.

For example, studies indicate that cutaneous vibratory sensation thresholds at the knee are increased in the frail elderly (70–90 years) compared to young adults. They noted that many of the older adults had difficulty perceiving stimulation at the ankle joint, and thus they did not include information about ankle thresholds in the study. These problems could be due to problems with peripheral neuropathy in their population.

Research on age-related changes in the visual system indicate that less light is transmitted through the retina with increasing age. Also, age-related reductions in visual contrast sensitivity cause problems in contour and depth perception, which are critical for postural control. These types of visual deterioration could result from cataracts, macular degeneration, and ischemic retinal or brain disease.

Studies on vestibular system changes in the older adult indicate that there is a 40% reduction in hair cells in the semicircular canals and the utricle and saccule, along with a similar reduction in myelinated fibers of the vestibular nerve. However, it has also been pointed out that a 75-year-old showed almost a normal number of nerve fibers in the vestibular nerve. This again points out that age-related degeneration of specific systems is not inevitable, but may be related to pathology. A partial deterioration in vestibular function can result in dizziness, which may also lead to loss of balance in the older adult. Deterioration of otolith function can lead to positional vertigo.

Older adults may not have a balance problem with deterioration in any one of these sensory systems, because the other systems contribute redundant information on balance and are usually available to compensate for this loss. However, balance problems could become apparent when walking in dimly lit areas or on unusual support surfaces like ramps, thick carpets, or grass. Multisensory deficits may also occur in older adults. In this case the ability to compensate for loss of sensory information with alternative senses is difficult or impossible.

4. Adaptation

As mentioned above, older adults may show problems with adapting their use of sensory inputs to varying task and environmental situations. For example, if an older adult has peripheral neuropathy and thus does not rely on somatosensory inputs, he or she may overly rely on visual inputs, even when they are inappropriate. For example, older adults may have difficulty balancing when crossing a busy intersection because visual cues from moving cars and pedestrians may create the illusion of self-sway, and the resulting postural response could cause balance loss.

How can the ability of older adults to balance under changing environmental conditions be tested? A technique called moving platform posturography allows the researcher to measure the balance of a subject under a combination of sensory conditions, including one in which the support surface rotates with the person's sway, distorting ankle joint somatosensory inputs, and another in which the visual enclosure around the subject also rotates in the anteroposterior direction with sway, again distorting visual inputs related to sway.

Studies have examined the ability of elderly people to adapt senses to changing conditions using posturography testing. It is of interest that there were not significant differences in amount of body sway for healthy active older adults versus young adults except

in conditions where both ankle joint inputs and visual inputs were distorted or absent (conditions 5 and 6). In these conditions half of the older adults lost stability and needed an assistant's aid to balance. However, most of the older adults maintained stability on the second trial of these conditions, indicating the ability to adapt to changing sensory conditions, with some practice.

In order to determine if the above types of changes in postural control with aging were indicative of normal aging or, alternatively, were due to borderline pathology, the older adults in one of the studies (who considered themselves healthy and active) were given a neurological exam. The results of the exam were correlated with their performance on the balance tasks. It is of interest that the neurologist noted borderline neural impairment such as diminished deep tendon reflexes, mild peripheral nerve deficits, distal weakness in tibialis anterior and gastrocnemius, and abnormal nystagmus in many of the older adults. These results suggest that borderline pathology may contribute significantly to balance dysfunction in the older adult.

In another study, the performance of older adults with balance problems (symptomatic) was compared to that of healthy older adults (asymptomatic) and young adults (young). As seen in Figure 4, the older adults with balance problems showed significantly more falls on conditions 5 and 6 (both visual and ankle joint inputs were distorted or absent) than did the young and healthy older adults.

C. Anticipatory Postural Adjustments

Postural adjustments may be used in a reactive manner, as described above, or in an anticipatory manner, in order to stabilize the body in advance for instability caused by a voluntary movement. One cause of falls in the older adult could be an inability to activate these anticipatory responses before voluntary movements, such as lifting a heavy object, resulting in loss of balance during the subsequent movement. Studies have shown that it is in dynamic situations such as walking, lifting, and carrying objects that a majority of falls in the older adult occur.

In the young adult, the same postural muscle response patterns that are activated during stance balance control are activated in an anticipatory manner before making a voluntary movement while standing.

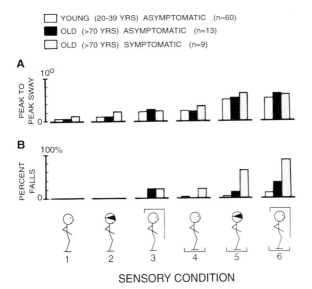

YOUNG (20-39 YRS) ASYMPTOMATIC .(n=60)
OLD (>70 YRS) ASYMPTOMATIC (n=13)
OLD (>70 YRS) SYMPTOMATIC (n=9)

A 10° PEAK TO PEAK SWAY 0

B 100% PERCENT FALLS 0

1 2 3 4 5 6

SENSORY CONDITION

Figure 4 A comparison of number of falls in the six sensory conditions in young, elderly nonfallers, and elderly fallers. (From Horak, F., Shupert, C., & Mirka, A., 1989. Components of postural dyscontrol in the elderly: A review. *Neurobiology of Aging, 10,* 732.)

For example, when asked to pull on a handle, first the gastrocnemius muscle of the calf is activated, followed by the hamstrings muscle of the thigh, and then the prime mover muscle, which is the biceps muscle of the upper arm. Thus the responses are activated starting with the muscles closest to the base of support and the response then moves upward to the proximal muscles. A research study examined age-related changes in the ability of older adults to activate these postural muscle-response synergies in an anticipatory manner. The study showed that older (mean age 71 years) adults showed significantly longer muscle onset latencies for postural muscles when compared to young adults (mean age 26 years), when the participants were asked to push or pull on a handle in a reaction time (RT) task. Figure 5 shows the postural versus voluntary muscle RTs for each subject in the young versus older adult group. Note that there was both an increase in postural muscle RT and the prime mover voluntary muscle RT. It was also noted that muscle response latencies were much more variable in the older compared to the young adults, and the organization of postural muscles responses was also significantly different. It is not clear whether these differences in postural response organization are due to nervous system deficits or to the use of an alternate strategy to compensate for other constraints within the nervous and musculoskeletal system.

A systems model of balance control would predict that this slowing in voluntary RT in the older adult could be caused either by the need for advance stabilization by the already delayed and possibly weaker postural muscles and/or to slowing in the voluntary control system itself. Because the absolute differences in onset times between the young and the older adults were larger for the voluntary muscles than the postural muscles, there may be a slowing in both systems in the older adult.

D. Cognitive Systems

It is possible that, with aging, a person's capacities to balance may be reduced compared to their abilities at a young age, but they may balance normally as long as they can focus attention on the task. When they have to focus on many tasks at the same time, however, they may find that their capacity to perform well both the postural task and the other tasks is reduced. For example, if an older adult is walking quickly along a busy street while carrying many packages and talking to a friend, if his balance is threatened, it may be more difficult to recover than if the person were walking alone in a quiet environment.

Recently, a significant amount of research has been performed to determine the extent to which older adults may have problems with balance when attention is distracted. Research has shown that older adults with a history of falls sway significantly more than young adults and healthy older adults when they were asked to perform a secondary task (a sentence-completion task) compared to a control (no task condition) while standing quietly. This effect of the secondary task was increased further when subjects were asked to stand on a compliant surface, which increased postural demands. It has been suggested that healthy young and older adults could allocate attentional resources to postural control in a flexible and dynamic way, whereas older adults who had experienced falls had more difficulty allocating attention to postural demands. [*See* ATTENTION.]

A second cognitive factor, fear of falling, may also affect balance performance. Fear of falling has been found to affect balance during a spontaneous sway

SIMPLE REACTION TIME

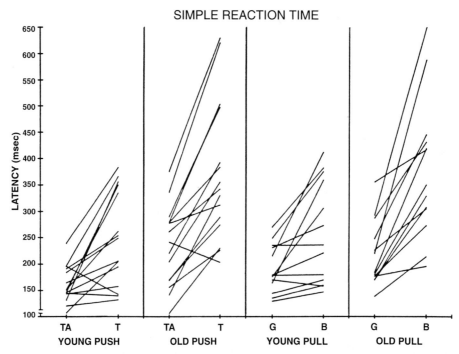

Figure 5 Individual values of postural and prime mover (voluntary) muscle onset latencies in young versus older adults for a simple reaction time task in which the standing subject pushed or pulled on a handle at chest height. (From Inglin, B., & Woollacott, M. H., 1988. Age-related changes in anticipatory postural adjustments associated with arm movements. *Journal of Gerontology, 43*, M109.)

test and one-leg stance test, though it is not clear whether subjects with a fear of falling have a true deterioration in postural control mechanisms, or whether the fear of falling affects the balance performance in an artifactual manner.

E. Balance Retraining Research

The above research suggests that there is a significant deterioration in balance abilities in many older adults, and that decreases in level of function of specific neural and/or musculoskeletal systems contributes to this deterioration. A number of laboratories are now focusing on exploring whether this deterioration in balance function can be reversed with training. Research concerning balance training has included a variety of training paradigms related to such areas as aerobic capacity, strength increases, and sensory balance training.

Research has also focused on general aerobic exercise as a way of improving stability in the older adult.

In one study, subjects participated in an exercise program of stretching, walking, RT maneuvers, and static and active balance exercises performed for 1 h three times a week for 16 weeks. No significant differences were found in balance abilities after training between the exercise and control groups when measured on one- and two-legged balance tests with eyes open and eyes closed. This lack of improvement with training may have been due to a lack of focus on training a specific subsystem related to balance control, causing the training effects on any single system to be insignificant.

Other researchers have studied the efficiency of a second type of training program, which focuses on muscle strength training to improve balance in frail nursing home residents. A study using high-resistance weight training of the quadriceps, hamstrings, and adductor muscle groups found highly significant gains in muscle strength in all subjects. Changes in balance control were not measured directly, but it was noted that subjects increased walking velocity, and two sub-

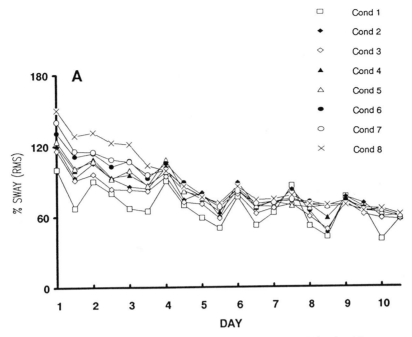

Figure 6 Percent reduction in body sway (root mean square: RMS) for the eight sensory conditions during the training period for one subject (From Woollacott, M., & Moore, S., Hu, M. H., 1993. Improvements in balance in the elderly through training in sensory organization abilities. In G. E. Stelmach & V. Homberg (Eds.), *Sensorimotor impairments in the elderly* (p. 384). Kluwer: Dordrecht.)

jects no longer used canes to walk by the end of the training period.

Another study used a balance training protocol that focused on improving the use of different sensory inputs and the integration of these inputs for balance control in older adults from 65–87 years old. Subjects were asked to balance under eight different sensory conditions in which visual and somatosensory inputs were gradually reduced or distorted. Figure 6 shows the changes in sway of one subject under the eight conditions for the 10 days of training. Significant reductions were found in the amount of sway in the training group between the first and the last day of training in the five most difficult training conditions. In addition, performance remained above control levels for at least 4 weeks after the training ended, and it transferred to a second balance task, that of standing on one leg with eyes open and closed. In addition, increased balance abilities were accompanied by specific changes in muscle response characteristics to platform perturbations. These included significantly less coactivation of antagonist muscles after training, indi-

cating that subjects were using more refined balance strategies.

III. WALKING CHARACTERISTICS IN OLDER ADULTS

Many of the same issues that were addressed above in relation to questions concerning the inevitability of balance deterioration in aging also apply to the research on age-related changes in gait. Earlier clinical studies on gait disorders often included patients with such problems as gait apraxia, hypokinetic-hypertonic syndrome, and *marche à petit pas*, and thus considered the characteristics associated with these types of pathology as associated with the normal aging process. They often called these disorders "senile gait." More recently a careful survey on 50 patients with previously undiagnosed gait disorders showed that a causal diagnosis could be made in 84% of the older adults. Myelopathy, Parkinsonism, frontal gait disorder (normal-pressure hydrocephalus, multiple strokes), cerebeller degeneration, and sensory imbalance were typical disorders that had been previously undiagnosed. Thus, as with balance disorders, gait disorders may not be a pure age-related phenomenon.

A. Changes in Velocity and Stride Length

The characteristics of gait patterns can be reported in many ways. One common way to measure gait patterns is to use a stopwatch to measure walking speed. From early observations using simple techniques such as this, it has been consistently reported that there is a decrease in walking speed with age. One of the first investigations on age-related changes in gait patterns described the earliest stage of gait pattern change (between 60–72 years of age) as consisting of a slower walking velocity, smaller displacement amplitudes of the joints, and a shorter stride length.

Another early approach involved observations of pedestrians walking in New York City. Walking cadence and velocity were measured using a marked distance on the sidewalk. As age increased, there was a decrease in walking velocity, step length, and step rate. These changes were similar to the first stage of change in gait in the above report. This approach has the advantages of being performed in a setting where gait characteristics will be more natural. However, this approach has limitations including a lack of knowledge of the subjects' health status, and lack of control over the goal of the walking behavior. To overcome these limitations laboratory studies have been performed.

One study examined the relationship between age (young adults: 21–47 years; older adults: 66–84 years) and the variability of gait. To separate an age effect from pathology researchers excluded older adults with any disorder likely to affect gait or balance, including all musculoskeletal, neurological, or cardiovascular disorders, bilateral visual impairment, or glaucoma, a history of falls or dizzy spells during the last year, use of a walking aid, and women who typically wore high heels. After screening, only 32 of the 1187 older adults (66–84 years old) were used in the study. Stride time, double-support time, step length, and stride width were compared for each group using an electronically equipped walkway. Step length of the older adult was shorter than that of the young adult, but the coefficient of variation (median/

range) of the step length was similar for the two groups, indicating that older adults were not more variable than younger adults. No significant differences between age groups in the stride width or double-support time measurements were found and thus it was concluded that the variability of gait patterns of healthy older adults is not different from young adults.

B. Kinematic Analysis

Though information on age-related changes in walking speed and stride length is useful, it does not allow the determination of age-related changes in the movement of body segments that may cause the reductions in speed and stride length. Kinematic (video, film, or optoelectronic) analysis of gait has been used by investigators to investigate age-related changes in body motion during gait.

In one study, subjects from 20–87 years of age were photographed while they were walking at preferred and fast speeds. Twenty kinematic measures were made from the resulting photographs. In men, gait cycle duration and stance duration increased after 65 years of age, whereas stride width increased after 74 years of age. Out-toeing and gait variability (rhythmicity of repeated strides) increased while peak heel elevation decreased after 80 years of age. There were also age-related changes in floor clearance patterns for the foot, decreases in knee flexion amplitude, and decreases in ankle extension amplitude at push-off. For women, similar changes were seen, except that a decreased stride length was noted after 50 years, along with a slower walking speed, and faster cadence. It is interesting to note that for women there was a significant influence of habitual use of high heels on the gait characteristics.

Note that while some studies find age-related changes in most of the variables they investigate, other studies do not. This may be dependent upon whether the subject population is carefully selected to be pathology free. The sum of research findings suggest that pure age-related changes in gait kinematics are relatively minor in comparison with effects due to borderline pathology.

C. Kinetic Analysis

Kinematic analysis of gait allows the description of locomotion movement patterns, but it does not give information regarding force generation by the subject. In order to determine if there were changes in characteristics of force generation in older (62–78 years) versus young (21–28 years) adults, researchers compared the kinetic data of walking trials for the two groups, using an inverse dynamics model. They noted that older adults generated significantly less power by the plantar flexors at push-off, and absorbed significantly less energy by the quadriceps femoris muscle during the late stance and early swing phase of gait. They suggested that a reduction in plantar flexor power during push-off could cause a shorter step length, a more flat-footed heel strike, and increased double-support stance duration, all of which have been observed consistently in other studies on gait characteristics in older adults. One cause of a weaker push-off could be a reduction in ankle plantar flexor muscle strength, which has, in fact, been noted in many other studies. In addition, high push-off power is known to act upwards and forward, and is thus destabilizing. Thus it is also possible that this change is adaptive to give a more stable gait pattern.

D. Neuromuscular Analysis

How do the above changes in kinetics and kinematics relate to changes in muscle response patterns underlying gait? In studies comparing patterns of muscle activity in younger (aged 19–38 years) and older (aged 64–86 years) women during normal gait, average electromyographic (EMG) activity levels in gastrocnemius, tibialis anterior, biceps femoris, rectus femoris, and peroneus longus muscles were higher in the older age group than in the younger group. Changes in muscle response characteristics at specific points in the step cycle have also been noted. Thus, at heel strike, the activity of peroneus longus and gastrocnemius was elevated in the older women, compared to the younger women. It has been suggested that this elevated activity could be a result of a strategy to increase coactivation of agonist and antagonist muscles, thus increasing the stiffness of the joint and improving stability during the stance phase of gait. This strategy is often used by subjects who are not skilled in a task, or who require increased control of the task.

Studies have also examined the effects of changes in sensory systems on gait patterns in the older adult. One study examined the effect of changing the visual environment on gait characteristics during stair de-

scent in older women (55–70 years). Stair descent was tested under the following conditions: stairs painted black, stairs paint black with the subject wearing a headband with a light-scattering plastic shield (called the blurred condition), and stairs painted black with a white stripe added at the edge of every tread. Motion analysis of the subjects' stair climbing performance showed significantly slower cadence, larger foot clearance, and more posterior foot placement when the older adults were asked to walk under the blurred condition as compared to the other two conditions. It was also noted that foot clearance was larger than that observed previously in studies with young adults.

E. Changes in Adaptive Control

An important aspect of locomotor control is the ability to use visual information to change gait characteristics in order to avoid upcoming obstacles. One study performed experiments that asked whether one contributing factor to poor walking performance in older adults might be a reduced ability to sample the visual environment during walking. In this experiment older and young adults were asked to wear opaque liquid crystal eyeglasses with a switch that could be pressed by the subject to make the glasses transparent whenever the subject wished to sample the environment. Participants walked across a floor that was either unmarked or had regularly marked footprints, on which the participants were supposed to walk. When asked to walk on the footprints, the young subjects sampled frequently and for short intervals, whereas the older subjects sampled less often but for longer periods. This resulted in the older adults monitoring the terrain much more than the young adults.

Another study was performed in which young and older adults were asked to walk along a walkway, and when cued by a light at specific points along the walkway, to either lengthen or shorten their stride to match the position of the light. This tested the ability of older adults to modulate the step cycle to avoid an object. Researchers found that the older adults had more difficulty than the younger adults in modulating their step length when the visual cue was given only one step duration ahead. Young adults succeeded 80% of the time, whereas older adults succeeded 60% of the time when they were required to lengthen the step and only 38% of the time when required to shorten the step. However, both young and older adults performed equally well when the visual cue was given two steps in advance. It has been suggested that balance difficulties contribute to the problems that older adults had in shortening their step. This requirement of older adults to make modifications to gait patterns more than one step before meeting an obstacle may contribute to their need for increased visual monitoring of the environment during walking.

Because it has been shown that older adults show a decreased floor clearance for the swing leg, this could cause problems in stepping over objects, and thus result in trips. Therefore kinematics of gait of healthy young and older adults were analyzed while they stepped over obstacles of varying heights (0 vs. approximately 1, 2, and 6 in.). The smaller heights corresponded to typical floor and door thresholds and the larger ones to curb-stone, or a toy, or a pet that might be found at home. No age-related change in foot clearance over an obstacle was found. However, 4 of 24 older adults compared to 0 younger adults stepped on an obstacle during the experiment. Because the trials with obstacle contact were found equally throughout the test period, it has been predicted that inattention, rather than fatigue, was probably the cause of these incidents. It has also been found that older adults use a more conservative strategy while crossing the obstacles. This consists of a slower crossing speed, shorter step length, and a placement of the last heel strike before the obstacle closer to the obstacle.

Age-related differences in gait characteristics while crossing obstacles may be in part causes by decreased joint range of motion in the legs of the older adults. Thus age-related changes in cognition and range of joint motion might be two factors causing changes in older adults' gait characteristics during obstacle crossing.

F. Factors Influencing Changes in Gait Characteristics

Though there are small but significant differences in the gait characteristics of healthy older adults compared to younger adults, studies have shown that older adults with a history of falls have significantly different gait characteristics than those without falls. It has been noted that older women fallers were able to stand for significantly shorter times with feet in tandem position than nonfallers, and also showed increased step width during gait. These changes could be caused by undiagnosed pathology in these subjects. However, it is also possible that, as a result of many falls, older adults develop a fear of falling, which also contributes to changes in gait patterns.

The results of many studies indicate that one reason older adults walk less quickly than young adults is that they consciously choose a more conservative or safe walking style. This suggests that fear of falling may contribute to changes in gait in the older adult. For example, one study found that preferred walking speed, anxiety level, and depression are significant predictors of fear of falling in older adults.

IV. SUMMARY

The above research examined age-related changes in various neural and musculoskeletal systems contributing to balance and gait. Studies on age-related changes in balance control have shown changes in the neuromuscular response characteristics, including decreased muscle strength, a slowing of response latencies, occasional disruption in response organization, and an increased coactivation of agonist and antagonist muscles when responding to threats to balance. In addition, older adults showed more problems than young adults when balancing under conditions in which sensory inputs were reduced or absent.

Similarly, in research on gait, studies have reported a reduction in walking speed and in stride length, with an increased double-support phase. This was accompanied by increases in coactivation of muscles around the ankle joint. Older adults also show less power generated by the plantarflexor muscles at push-off, which could cause the reduced stride length. The reason for the weaker push-off could be reduced muscle strength.

However, it is of interest that in many of the studies showing these changes in posture and gait, a large percentage of the older adults were within the range of younger adults on the various parameters tested. It was often a small number of older adults that contributed to the significant changes observed, indicating a high amount of heterogeneity in the older adult population.

BIBLIOGRAPHY

Alexander, N. B. (1994). Postural control in older adults. *Journal of the American Geriatric Society, 42,* 93–108.

Craik, R. (1989). Changes in locomotion in the aging adult. In M. H. Woollacott & A. Shumway-Cook (Eds.), *Development of posture and gait across the life span*. Columbia, SC: University of South Carolina Press.

Horak, F. B., Shupert, C. L., & Mirka, A. (1989). Components of postural dyscontrol in the elderly. *Neurobiology of Aging, 10*, 727–738.

Hu, M. H., & Woollacott, M. (1994). Characteristic patterns of gait in older persons. In B. S. Spivack, (Ed.), *Mobility and gait* New York: Marcel Dekker, Inc.

Woollacott, M. H., & Hu, M. H. (1993). Improvements in balance in the elderly through training in sensory organization abilities. In G. E. Stelmach & V. Homberg, (Eds.), *Sensorimotor impairment in the elderly*. Dordrecht: Kluwer Academic Publishers.

Behavioral Genetics

C. S. Bergeman

University of Notre Dame

Robert Plomin

Institute of Psychiatry
University of London

Behavioral Genetics The study of genetic and environmental factors that create behavioral differences among individuals.
Heritability A statistic that describes the proportion of phenotypic variance that is due to genetic variance.

One of the most important questions in gerontology concerns the origins of individual differences in the aging process. Gerontological **BEHAVIORAL GENETICS** consists of a theory and method that can be applied to the study of both the genetic and environmental sources of differences among elderly individuals. The present chapter includes a brief overview of the theory and methods, as well as a description of emerging studies focusing on behavioral genetics and aging. In addition, recent research assessing genetic and environmental influences on longevity, cognitive functioning, personality, and psychopathology in later life is reported. The chapter concludes with suggestions for future research in this rapidly developing field.

I. WHY PEOPLE AGE DIFFERENTLY

Age-related diseases and physiological changes that are regarded as a part of "normal aging" do not affect all people in the same way, nor do all individuals experience the same changes as they reach the same age. In fact, older people are thought to be more diverse than younger people in health, psychological functioning, and dimensions of social interaction. In other words, the heterogeneity noted among age peers increases over the life course, and the members of a cohort are said to "fan out" as they age, becoming more dissimilar for any given characteristic. The need to explain this functional heterogeneity is a major objective of research in gerontological behavioral genetics.

A. Behavioral Genetics

Behavioral genetics is a theory of the etiology of individual differences in a population. This theory applies to individual differences in behavioral characteristics and says little about the average differences between groups (i.e., differences between males and females or between members of different cultures). Thus, behavioral genetic methodologies can answer questions such as why some elderly individuals function better than others, but the approach is less relevant to group questions such as why women live longer than men. Although the focus of research in this area is often on genetic influences on behavior, the theory is also useful for describing environmental sources of variance, and is a powerful tool for exploring the environmental influences contributing to individual differences in behavior. Thus, the label of behavioral genetics is misleading, because the theory and methods are as informative about environmental influences on behavior as they are about genetic factors.

It is important at the onset to emphasize that there are no "genes for behavior." Genes are blueprints for the assembly and regulation of proteins, which are the building blocks of our bodies. Each gene codes for a specific sequence of amino acids that the body assembles to form a protein. The proteins then interact with other physiological intermediaries (i.e., other proteins—hormones or neurotransmitters) or environmental factors. Therefore, when talking about genetic influences on behavior, we are referring to indirect and complex paths between genes and behavior via proteins and physiological systems. Although the information coded in our DNA can ultimately influence behavior in certain directions, it is important to keep in mind that the paths are indirect, and genetic influences are indeed just influences—propensities, or tendencies, that may nudge development in one direction rather than another. It is also important to avoid the mistaken notion that genetic influences are immutable. Genes do not determine one's destiny; they do not turn on at conception and run "full throttle" until death. Thus, even though research has indicated that genetic differences among individuals can contribute to phenotypic differences, the phrase "genetic influence" does not imply that the environment is not necessary for development, nor does it imply genetic determinism in the sense of a direct relationship between genes and their effect on behavior. [*See* DNA AND GENE EXPRESSION.]

B. Estimating Genetic and Environmental Influences

Heritability is a descriptive statistic that is defined as the proportion of phenotypic variance in a population that is due to genetic variance, which can be partitioned into two types—additive and nonadditive. *Additive genetic variance* is the extent to which genotypic values add up linearly in their effect on the phenotype, whereas *nonadditive genetic variance* represents genetic influences due to dominance (interactions between alleles at a single locus), as well as the variance due to the higher order interactions called epistasis. Environmental differences among individuals can also lead to phenotypic differences between them, and behavioral genetic research offers some of the best evidence for the importance of environmental influences on development. The environmental component of variance can be separated into *shared environmental*

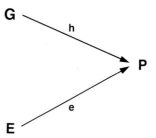

Figure 1 Path diagram of the basic behavioral genetic model, in which G is the genotypic value, E is the environmental value, and P is the observed phenotypic deviation; *h* is the square root of heritability and is defined as the proportion of the standard deviation of the phenotype that is caused by variation in the genotype; *e* is the environmentally influenced phenotypic variation.

influences, which are any environmental influences that contribute to phenotypic similarity among family members, and *nonshared environment*, which is defined as any environmental influence that makes family members different from one another.

A major development in behavioral genetics over the past two decades is the testing of explicit models, rather than the simple examination of correlations. Model-fitting techniques are especially useful when combination designs, which yield many different familial correlations, are employed. Although model-fitting techniques are somewhat complex, they are mentioned because most of the current research is reported in terms of model-fitting analyses.

Behavioral genetic model-fitting techniques are based on path analysis, a method first described by Sewell Wright in 1921. The path diagram in Figure 1 represents the basic proposition that phenotypic variance can be due to genetic and environmental variance. Thus, variability in genotypes (G) and environments (E) cause variability in the phenotype (P). That is, $P = G + E$, and G and E are assumed to be uncorrelated. The path labeled *h* is the square root of heritability (h^2), and is defined as the proportion of the standard deviation of the phenotype that is caused by variation in the genotype. The path *e* represents the environmentally induced phenotypic variation.

Figure 2 represents a simple path diagram for twins or siblings. If looking at twins, P1 represents the score of one member of the twin pair on the behavior of interest, and P2 refers to the score of the other twin. G and Es refer to genotypic and shared environmental

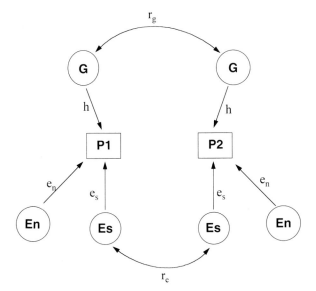

Figure 2 Simple path diagram for twins or siblings. P1 and P2 are the observed variables for members of a twin pair; G is the genotypic value; En is the nonshared environmental deviation; Es is the shared rearing environmental deviation; h, e_s and e_n are the path coefficients that signify heritability, shared environment, and nonshared environment, respectively; r_g is the coefficient of genetic relationship of the twin or sibling pair; r_e reflects whether the twins are reared together or apart.

variables, respectively. The model assumes that r_g (the genetic correlation) is 1.0 for identical or monozygotic (MZ) twins and 0.5 for fraternal or dizygotic (DZ) twins if the genetic influences operate in an additive manner, and 1.0 for MZ and 0.25 for DZ twins if the genetic influences operate in a nonadditive way. r_e (the environmental correlation) is specified as 1.0 if the twins are reared together (T), and 0.0 if the twins are reared apart (A). En represents nonshared environmental influences which do not contribute to twin similarity.

To illustrate, the intraclass twin correlations for a questionnaire measure of emotionality in the Swedish Adoption/Twin Study of Aging (SATSA) are as follows: rMZA = .33; rMZT = .37; rDZA = .09, and rDZT = .17. The pattern of correlations indicate genetic influence because on average the MZ twin correlations are higher than the DZ twin correlations. The correlations also suggest some influence of shared rearing environment, because twins reared together are slightly more similar than twins reared apart. Quantitative genetic model-fitting analyses provide a

powerful tool for assessing genetic and environmental influences on behavior because they estimate the parameters simultaneously, and provide both standard errors for the parameter estimates and a chi-square goodness-of-fit index. Results of model-fitting analyses for this emotionality measure using LISREL indicate that 28% of the variance is due to genetic influences, 12% to shared rearing environment, and the balance to nonshared environmental factors.

C. Developmental Behavioral Genetics

Developmental behavioral genetics merges developmental psychology with behavioral genetic theories and methodologies, permitting the exploration of the origins of change as well as continuity in development. One of the most basic developmental questions is whether the relative importance of genetic variance (heritability) differs with age. This "differential heritability" is most often assessed cross-sectionally by comparing (within studies) subjects of different ages or by comparing results across studies focusing on different age groups. Reviews of behavioral genetic research indicate major differences in the results of behavioral genetic analyses in infancy, childhood, adolescence, adulthood, and old age. Because most of this work is cross-sectional, it addresses the question of whether the relative contribution of genetic and environmental influences differs in various age groups. The answer appears to be yes.

Because cross-sectional research can only provide information about *age differences*, not *age changes*, the results of comparisons of individuals in different age groups may not reflect the developmental process occurring as individuals age, but may instead reflect cohort effects. For example, the environmental changes across generations shown to be significant by researchers interested in life-span development can affect the etiology of individual differences. That is, characteristics associated with specific cohorts or variables related to historical change can contribute to different estimates of genetic and environmental influence on behavior. This occurs because heritability is a population-specific parameter, and quantitative genetic parameters change when genetic and environmental sources of variation change.

More interesting are longitudinal behavioral genetic studies focusing on the etiology of individual differences in age-to-age continuity and change. One common misconception is to equate *genetic* with *stable,* but longitudinally stable characteristics are not necessarily hereditary, nor are genetically influenced characteristics necessarily stable over time. In other words, the effects of a given set of genes may be exerted continuously during development, or new genetic effects may come into play at certain developmental stages. Similarly, the effects of the environment may be stable and uniform over time, or the quality of the environment may fluctuate across the life span.

Using longitudinal designs, it is possible to assess the extent to which genetic or environmental effects at one age are related to genetic and environmental effects at another. The age-to-age genetic and environmental correlations (r_g and r_e, respectively) describe the extent to which genetic and environmental influences are temporally stable. A genetic correlation of 1.0 means that the genetic effects correlate perfectly between the two ages, and a genetic correlation of 0.0 implies that a completely different set of genetic factors affects individual differences of the trait at the two ages. Loosely interpreted, the genetic correlation indicates the extent to which there is overlap in the genetic effects operating at two or more occasions, regardless of their relative contribution to phenotypic variance. Thus, r_g can be substantial even though the heritability is low and vice versa. Environmental correlations can be conceptualized in a similar way.

II. BEHAVIORAL GENETIC STUDIES OF AGING

Ten years ago, only one study specifically designed to address issues of genetic and environmental influences on biobehavioral aging had been reported—the New York State Psychiatric Study of Aging Twins—which was started by Franz Kallmann and Gerhard Sander in 1946 to study hereditary aspects of aging and longevity. Since that time, there has been a growth in the number of behavioral genetic studies of aging, and much research is still in the early stages.

Three general designs are used—family studies, adoption studies, and twin studies. If heredity is important for a particular behavior, pairs of individuals who are similar genetically should be similar for the trait of interest. If heredity is not important, differences in genetic similarity should not affect the resem-

blance of these pairs of individuals. This concept is the basic premise behind family designs such as the Seattle Longitudinal Study (SLS). The family portion of the SLS was initiated in 1990 by including the adult offspring and siblings of the original sample. An important contribution of the family design to our understanding of the etiology of individual differences in later life is to estimate the extent to which individual differences are due to familial factors—whether genetic or environmental—and to provide an upper-limit estimate of genetic and shared family environmental influence. Family studies are particularly valuable because first-degree relatives represent the population to which we wish to generalize the results of behavioral genetic investigations.

In addition, the SLS capitalizes on the "instant longitudinal design," in this case using parents and offspring from young adulthood to middle age, and siblings from young adulthood to old age. The long-term longitudinal nature of the SLS also provides a unique opportunity to study relatives tested at roughly the same age; differences in same-age comparisons of sibling resemblance and parent–offspring resemblance as a function of year of birth provides a novel test of cohort effects.

The *adoption design* severs the relationship between shared environment and shared heredity. Genetically related individuals adopted apart (and reared in uncorrelated environments) will resemble each other only for genetic reasons. Genetically unrelated individuals adopted together into the same family will only resemble each other for reasons of shared environment. An interesting example is the SATSA, which includes a large sample of identical twins reared apart (99 pairs). Resemblance between these pairs (expressed as a correlation) can be attributed to heredity, because unlike identical twins reared together, resemblance is not due to shared environment. SATSA is a combined twin–adoption design, and it includes information from 351 pairs of twins reared apart as well as a matched control group of 407 pairs of twins reared together. A variety of scales measuring different phenotypic traits have been collected longitudinally at 3-year intervals from 1984 to 1993.

One of the most common behavioral genetic designs is the comparison between resemblance of identical and fraternal twins, referred to as the *twin method*. MZ twins are genetically identical and share 100% of all genetic influences, whereas DZ or frater-

Table I Behavioral Genetic Studies of Later Life

Study	Sample[a]	Age range[b]	Primary measures	Design
New York State Psychiatric Study of Aging	120 Pairs 75 MZ 45 DZ	60 +	Cognitive functioning; longevity	Longitudinal twin study
Swedish Adoption/Twin Study of Aging	724 Pairs 99 MZA 166 MZT 238 DZA 221 DZT	26–87	Personality, health & well-being, cognitive functioning, environment	Longitudinal adoption/ twin study
Minnesota Twin study of Adult Development and Aging	220 Pairs 93 MZ[b] 67 DZ[b]	27–88	Cognitive functioning, lifestyle, activities, health	Cross-sectional twin study
Seattle Longitudinal Family Study	Probands 531 Offspring 304 Sibling	39–91 22–74 22–89	Cognitive functioning; family environment	Family study
Kinki University Adult Twin Study	97 Pairs	50–78	Cognitive functioning, health	Cross-sectional twin study
OCTO-Twin	351 Pairs	79–98	Cognitive functioning & decline, personality, health	Twin study
Black Elderly Twin Study	700 Pairs (expected)	65 +	Physical functioning	Twin study

[a] For longitudinal studies, sample size and age are provided for the sample at the first point of measure. MZ, monozygotic; DZ, dizygotic; MZA, MZ raised apart; MZT, MZ raised together, DZA, DZ raised apart, DZT, DZ raised together.

[b] Number of pairs tested to date.

nal twins share 50% of genetic influences that operate additively. The New York State Psychiatric Study of Aging Twins is an example of the twin design, and most of the gerontological behavioral genetic studies currently being developed use the twin method. See Table I for a brief overview of these studies.

III. GENETIC AND ENVIRONMENTAL INFLUENCES ON DEVELOPMENT IN LATER LIFE

A. Longevity and Health

The concept of a familial contribution to longevity is certainly not a new one. Over a century ago Oliver Wendell Holmes offered the following advice, "Those wishing long lives should advertise for a couple of parents, both belonging to long-lived families." Genealogical studies have consistently established a significant, but modest, familial component to the hu-

man life span. Because familial resemblance includes both genetic and environmental influences, family studies alone do not provide conclusive evidence of a genetic component to longevity. The best evidence of a heredity component to the life span comes from twin and adoption studies. For example, in the Danish Twin Register, a modest heritability estimate of about 25% was assessed for the length of the life span, with no differences in heritability by gender. The twin correlations were consistent with a nonadditive pattern of genetic variance, and most of the environmental variance was of the nonshared variety.

One possible explanation for the modest relationship between parents and offspring for longevity is that what children inherit from their parents is not longevity per se, but rather frailty. That is, children may inherit a set of susceptibilities, or risk factors, that alters their chances of death at different ages. For example, the results of a Danish adoption study indicated that premature death (death prior to age 50) of biological parents related to a twofold increase in mortality of adoptees. In other words, the premature death of adoptees was related to their biological, but not adoptive, parents. In addition, the Prospective Study of Adult Development contrasted the health of 65-year-old men with long-lived and short-lived parents and grandparents to test the belief that individuals with long-lived ancestors are more physically vigorous and better adapted psychologically in old age. Results supported the contention of a relationship between familial longevity and better general health in late midlife, but the anticipated relation with psychological adjustment was not supported. [See LONGEVITY AND LONG-LIVED POPULATIONS.]

B. Cognitive Functioning

Cognitive abilities are among the most heritable dimensions of behavior, with genetic factors consistently accounting for about 50% of the variability in studies of childhood, adolescence, and young adulthood. Much less is known about the etiology of cognitive functioning in middle age and later life, but with the development of studies focusing on gerontological behavioral genetics, this picture is changing. Two rival hypotheses have been proposed regarding the heritability of cognitive functioning in later life. One view is that important environmental effects on cognitive functioning may not be realized until adulthood, especially the types of knowledge that relate to sociocultural experience. As the relative importance of the environment increases, it is speculated that heritability will decrease with age. Conversely, it has been suggested that heritability increases with age because self-selection of experiences reflects inherited abilities, interests, and dispositions. In this way, experience is thought not only to reflect, but to reinforce underlying genetic differences among individuals.

A study of the etiology of individual differences in IQ in the SATSA indicated that 80% of the variability for 60-year-old (average age) twins was due to genetic differences. This estimate is higher than the 50% estimate that is typically observed in studies of adolescents and young adults. It was originally speculated that the higher heritability estimates could be related to specific characteristics of the Swedish sample, but these results have been replicated in studies using middle-aged and older subjects in U.S. and Norwegian samples. The greater heritability in older samples than in younger samples is consistent with predictions from

developmental behavioral genetics that suggest that when heritability changes with development, it increases, and with the second hypothesis described above. It should be noted, however, that these results are based on cross-sectional comparisons of individuals of different ages. Results of longitudinal analyses in early childhood support the suggestion that heritability increases for IQ scores, at least up until the early school years. Whether the heritability of cognitive abilities continues to increase during adolescence is less clear, and very little is known about adulthood and old age from a longitudinal behavioral genetic perspective.

A longitudinal study of the twins in the SATSA measured over a 3-year interval indicated a very high stability for general IQ ($r = .92$) between the two occasions of measurement. Longitudinal behavioral genetic analyses indicated that nearly 90% of the phenotypic correlation was due to genetic mediation. In other words, the results indicate that genetic effects contribute to continuity rather than change. The genetic correlation (r_g) for IQ was .99, suggesting almost complete overlap in the genetic influences at the measurement occasions. Of course, 3 years is a relatively short interval of time in an older person's life; longer intervals of time may show more evidence for genetic change.

Research on specific cognitive abilities also implicates substantial genetic involvement. Results from the Minnesota Twin Study of Adult Development and Aging (MTSADA), a study that assessed multiple tests of memory, found heritability estimates of 56–64% for word recall, immediate and delayed text recall, and figure memory. Estimates from the SATSA ranged from 38% for a memory factor to 58% for verbal abilities and perceptual speed. One interesting point that has come out of this research is the etiology of fluid and crystallized intelligence. *Fluid intelligence* is often defined as basic information-processing abilities that are influenced by biological, genetic, or health factors, such as tests of speed and accuracy, spatial rotation, block design, and visual or motor memory. *Crystallized intelligence,* on the other hand, is defined as abilities that are based on cultural knowledge (e.g., tests of information, language comprehension) and is thought to be environmentally and culturally influenced. Results of research in specific cognitive abilities has indicated little evidence for a differential heritability for specific cognitive abilities that have been associated with fluid versus crystallized intelligence.

Consistent with studies of younger adults, specific cognitive abilities show lower heritability than general IQ in older samples. It has been speculated that the genetic influences on the cognitive domain are more general than specific. An interesting analysis from the SATSA looked at the relationship between the factor loading of the specific scale on the principal component and estimates of heritability and found that the factor loadings were correlated with the heritability of the tests. The authors speculated that the more a trait taps into general cognitive ability, the more heritable it is.

In another interesting study, the MTSADA researchers looked at the relationship between memory and cognitive functioning, lifestyle, and personality factors. They were interested in the general observation that there are large individual differences in memory ability among older individuals. In addition, older individuals who are high in verbal ability maintain a high level of intellectual activity, have larger working memory capacity, maintain a high level of general or physical activity, and manifest little test anxiety. The researchers specifically focused on the etiology of the relationship between measures of memory capacity and measures of social class (occupation, education, and vocabulary), processing speed (reaction time, digit symbol), intellectual activity, and physical activity. The results indicated that genetic influences on memory are largely mediated by processing speed and social class, whereas environmental influences on memory are mediated to some extent by physical activity. Thus, the authors suggested that interventions for a decline in memory functioning might best be targeted at lifestyle variables such as physical activity.

C. Personality

Results of research in childhood, adolescence, and young adulthood indicate that genetic influence for self-reported personality is significant, ranging from 30 to 50%. Shared environment is of little importance in individual differences in personality, meaning that growing up in the same family does not make two individuals similar to one another. Nonetheless, most of the variance is environmental, even for the most heritable personality traits, but it is of the nonshared type. [See PERSONALITY.]

Heritability for personality in later life is only slightly lower than results reported earlier in the life span. For example, research from the SATSA indicated that 31, 41, 40, and 29% of the variance in neuroticism, extraversion, openness to experience, and conscientiousness, respectively, was due to genetic differences between individuals. There was little evidence for the importance of shared rearing environment. The exception was agreeableness, which indicated that shared environment, not shared genes, was important in the familial resemblance for this trait. As expected, nonshared environment accounted for the largest portion of the variance in all five traits. It is interesting to note that although personality traits are quite stable across the life span, they are only moderately heritable. This finding provides support for the assertion that characteristics need not be highly heritable in order to be stable.

Behavioral genetic research has also assessed characteristics of personality that may be particularly relevant in later life. One example is locus of control (LOC), which refers to the extent to which one's generalized expectations for reinforcement are internal or external. Internal locus of control refers to the belief that outcomes are contingent on one's own behavior, whereas external locus of control refers to the belief that outcomes are determined by chance or other outside forces. Research in childhood and adolescence has assumed that control is learned from one's family and social environments, and that beliefs about control are modifiable by principles of social learning theory. In later life, locus of control has been associated with both physical health and psychological well-being. As a result, interventions directed at increasing personal control have been applied.

Analyses in the SATSA have considered the extent to which genetic and environmental influences are important in the development of responsibility, life direction, and luck—three subscales typical of measures of LOC. Results indicated that genetic influences are most important for self-attributions concerning responsibility and life direction, accounting for 30% of the variance. However, the familial similarity for the perceived role of luck in determining life's outcomes is largely due to shared rearing environmental influences.

D. Psychopathology

I. Dementia

Dementia is a global term for any neurological disorder whose primary symptomology is the deterioration of mental functioning. Alzheimer's disease (AD) is arguably the most severe and devastating of all of the different types of dementia, accounting for about 50% of all cases of severe dementia. Many epidemiological studies have been carried out in order to identify risk factors for AD. Apart from increased age, the other variables that has been consistently identified is a family history of the disorder.

Recent twin studies suggest some genetic influence for the typical late-onset AD. The only twin study of a less common form of dementia called vascular dementia found no genetic influence for this type of dementia. Most exciting is the finding, replicated in numerous studies, that a gene (apolipoprotein E) involved in cholesterol transport in the blood is associated with late-onset AD. Individuals with one form of this gene have four times the risk for late-onset AD as do individuals with the other form of this gene. Additionally, a rare form of AD was shown to be linked to another gene for early-onset cases with simple patterns of inheritance. [*See* DEMENTIA.]

2. Depression

Depression in older adults is extremely common, perhaps as many as a third of older adults are seriously depressed. Throughout the life span, research is not yet sufficient to draw clear conclusions about the extent of genetic influence on depression. Twin studies suggest some genetic influence on clinically relevant depression, perhaps greater genetic influence on major depressive disorder, and even greater genetic influence on manic depression. However, very little is known about the genetic and environmental origins of depression in later life.

SATSA results suggest only modest genetic influence on self-reported depressive symptoms, although there is some evidence that genetic factors might increase in importance after 60 years of age, perhaps due to genetic influences on frailty or vitality. Unlike most personality measures, shared rearing environment accounted for more variance than genetic factors. Research from the Southern California Twin Project on twins and families of a wide age range found genetic influence on negative affect, but shared environmental influence on positive affect. The Camberwell Collaborative Depression Study of adults varying widely in age showed familial resemblance for depression. The morbidity risk for depression was about 25% for first-degree relatives of depressed probands as compared to about 10% in the population. A particularly interesting aspect of this study concerned life events. The frequency of stressful life events was greater among the relatives of depressives than in the general population, even when negative events associated with the probands were discounted. These results suggest that both the liability for depression and the propensity to experience stressful life events are familial. The authors conclude that stressful life events may be associated with depression because individuals are prone to hazard, and not just susceptible to stress.

Such data suggest that the relationship between life stress and depression may be more complex than was previously thought. The surprising finding that experiencing (or reporting) life events is familial is explored further in the next section. [*See* DEPRESSION.]

E. Life Events, Social Support, and Family Environment

A new area of interest in behavioral genetics is to consider the possibility of genetic influence on measures that are presumably measures of the environment. This line of research is based on the supposition that measures of the environment are often indirect measures of the behavior of individuals. Rather than thinking in terms of genetic influences on the environment per se, genetic influences on experiences are most likely due to genetically influenced characteristics of individuals.

Life events is a category of environmental measures used in more than a thousand studies, with reports suggesting that life events happen (or are perceived to happen) to some people more than others. Model-fitting analyses in the SATSA demonstrated significant genetic influence on individual differences in reports of the occurrence of life events. This implies that "bad luck" is related to genetically influenced attributes of individuals, and that events of the type traditionally reported do not just happen capriciously. To test this hypothesis, it was predicted that controllable life events, which may be related to aspects of an individual's personality or mood state, should be more heritable than uncontrollable ones. As predicted, controllable events showed greater genetic influence ($h^2 = .43$) than uncontrollable events ($h^2 = .18$) in the sample of Swedish twins. These results were confirmed in a sample of young and middle-aged adults from the Virginia Twin Registry. [See LIFE EVENTS.]

Recent research from the SATSA and from the Virginia Twin Registry has also indicated that measures of social support are heritable. This may not be surprising given that genetically influenced characteristics such as personality may affect how individuals construct their social environments, and how they feel about and behave toward others. In addition, others may respond to individuals on the basis of genetically influenced characteristics. It is also possible that genetic influences are detected because most of these measures rely on self-reported perceptions of the environment and genetic effects could accrue because these perceptions filter through a person's memories, feelings, and personality.

Multivariate genetic analyses have explored the etiology of the association between measures of social support and psychological well-being in later life. Results consistently indicate that both genetic and environmental influences are important in the etiology of this relationship. That is, the genetic influences that contribute to the perceived adequacy of the support network also contribute to depressive symptoms and life satisfaction. Nonshared environmental influences also mediate this phenotypic relationship. The process by which this occurs awaits longitudinal analyses. However, some research has suggested that genetic and environmental effects that contribute to perceptions of social support may act as a buffer for psychological well-being. [See SOCIAL NETWORKS, SUPPORT, AND INTEGRATION.]

Similar types of analyses have also focused on the etiology of measures of family environments. Results indicate that measures of family environment, whether retrospective to the rearing environment or involving the current family environment, show at least some genetic influence. What was even more surprising was that across a variety of studies, measures of warmth consistently show greater genetic influence than measures of control. Studies of this type establish a need to reformulate our thinking about the environment as being something "out there" that impinges on the organism in a unidirectional manner. One area for future research is to begin to identify

those genetically influenced characteristics of individuals that are responsible for the genetic variance found in these "environmental" measures. Likely candidates include cognitive functioning and personality traits.

IV. FUTURE RESEARCH DIRECTIONS

Results of behavioral genetic research of the second half of the life span indicate the need to consider both genetic and environmental sources of individual differences in the aging process. Behavioral genetics provide a theory that can go beyond the simple nature–nurture comparisons to consider different types of genetic (additive and nonadditive) and environmental (shared and nonshared) influences, the developmental interface between nature and nurture, and the etiology of age-to-age continuity and change.

Concerning this latter point, several gerontological behavioral genetic studies are ongoing. However, additional longitudinal research is still needed in this area. Results of cross-sectional studies of genetic and environmental influences on behavior have indicated that there may be some important etiological differences at various points in the life span. One thing that researchers in the field of gerontology have learned, however, is that one cannot indiscriminately infer that the causes of age differences are the same factors that contribute to age-to-age change. Additionally, the etiology of continuity and change for one trait of interest is not necessarily related to another; thus, the assessment of whether genetic influences are stable needs to be tested empirically for each phenotype of interest. It has also been suggested that gerontological research should concentrate on understanding transition periods in later life, especially those that have functional significance. In other words, future research may focus on the etiology of functional changes in older adults as they move from optimal functioning to normal functioning, or from normal functioning to disease states or pathological functioning. Through the use of longitudinal behavioral genetic designs (e.g., longitudinal analyses of phenotypic relationships in genetically related individuals), it is possible to disentangle the dynamic pattern of genetic and environmental influences on development in later life.

Most knowledge about the genetics of individual differences in aging comes from quantitative genetic research on twins and adoptees. However, this is the dawn of a new age; the stunning advances in molecular genetics will increasingly be used to identify specific genes responsible for the nearly ubiquitous genetic influence seen for behavior. The best example to date is the association between the gene for apolipoprotein E and late-onset dementia. The allure of molecular genetics, however, should not detract from the need for more quantitative genetics research that can guide the search for genes. Such quantitative genetic research is likely to be most helpful in understanding nurture rather than nature, and especially the interface between them.

Genetic influences are likely to be significant and substantial for many dimensions of variability in later life. Understanding the etiology of differences among individuals may be critically important for improving the quality of later life. At the very least, it is crucial to begin to understand the causal factors underlying individual differences in functioning and adjustment late in the life span, because that is the path that will lead to primary prevention and identification of potential intervention strategies. Because people are so different, one cannot expect to find one single intervention, or prevention strategy, that will work for all elderly individuals. Behavioral genetic research on individual differences in aging takes an important first step in the direction of understanding the etiology of these individual differences.

BIBLIOGRAPHY

Bouchard, R. J., Jr., & Propping, P. (Eds.). (1993). *Twins as a tool of behavioral genetics.* New York: John Wiley & Sons.

Hayflick, L. (1994). *How and why we age.* New York: Ballantine.

McGuffin, P., Owen, M. J., O'Donovan, M. C., Thapar, A., & Gottesman, I. I. (1994). *Seminars in psychiatric genetics.* London: Gaskell.

Pedersen, N. (1996). Gerontological behavioral genetics. In J. E. Birren & K. W. Schaie, (Eds.), *Handbook of the psychology of aging.* (4th ed.) (pp. 59–77). San Diego: Academic Press.

Plomin, R. (1994). *Genetics and experience: The interplay between nature and nurture.* Thousand Oaks, CA: Sage.

Plomin, R., DeFries, J. E., & McClearn, G. E. (1990). *Behavioral genetics: A primer.* New York: W. H. Freeman.

Plomin, R., & McClearn, G. E. (Eds.). (1993). *Nature, nurture, and psychology.* Washington, DC: American Psychological Assoc.

Bereavement and Loss

Dale A. Lund

University of Utah

Bereavement Both the situation and the long-term process of adjusting to the death of someone to whom a person feels close.

Grief The affective or emotional responses that people often experience during the early phases of the bereavement process.

Mourning The commonly accepted or culturally patterned ways people behave and express themselves during the bereavement adjustment process.

Resiliency The ability to bounce back or recover from stressful and difficult losses and bereavement experiences.

BEREAVEMENT refers to both the situation and the long-term process of adjusting to the death of someone to whom a person feels close. The term also has been used in reference to losses other than death, such as the loss of a home or personal belongings because of fire or a natural disaster. It is more common, however, to use the term bereavement in situations following the death of a friend or relative, or even an animal companion. Other terms associated with the bereavement process include grief and mourning. These terms are distinguishable from bereavement in that they refer to specific aspects of the broader process. Grief is characterized by the affective or emotional responses that people often experience

during the early phases of the bereavement process. These feelings frequently include disbelief, confusion, shock, numbness, sadness, and sometimes anger and guilt. Feeling abandoned, lonely, or depressed and being preoccupied with thoughts of the deceased person and the events surrounding the death are often components of grief.

Not all persons experience these feelings, and the degree of intensity varies in those who do, but it is common for bereaved persons to feel a wide range of emotions that come and go quickly and can reappear over many months or even years. Culture plays a role in shaping how people experience and express bereavement. Most professionals use the term *mourning* to refer to the commonly accepted or culturally patterned ways people behave and express themselves during the adjustment process. Mourning refers to such behaviors as crying, missing work, altering daily routines, attending funerals, cremations, and burials, following standards for dress and appearance, and participating in other rituals that are influenced by the surrounding culture.

I. VARIETY OF BEREAVEMENT EXPERIENCES

Throughout our lives we experience many kinds of losses that require us to make adjustments. As infants, we become temporarily separated from parents and siblings. We leave the familiar surroundings of the home to attend school. As children, we lose toys, clothes, pets, and valued belongings. We, or our friends, move away to new neighborhoods. Children lose relationships with teachers, clubs, organizations, and peers, as they advance from elementary grades through high school and college. Over the life course we lose more friendships and relationships from job relocations, deaths, and retirement. With divorce rates near 50% in the United States, millions are experiencing the loss of marital relationships, parents, and family life. Some people also will lose hair, hearing, sight, muscle tone, independence, and mobility. In short, if we are fortunate to live long lives we will experience many significant losses. Each loss has the potential of disrupting patterns of behavior, requiring adjustments, but also, adding to the course of our development. Bereavement can accompany these losses, if what was lost was highly valued by the individual.

It is important to acknowledge the numerous and diverse losses that we experience because each one can contribute to a better understanding of how people manage and cope with other bereavement situations. For example, we might better understand and help older bereaved spouses if we know more about how they experienced relocation, physical, and relationship losses earlier in their lives. Similarly, we need to appreciate the uniqueness of each loss or bereavement experience. Although sadness might be a grief response common to both relocation and the death of a spouse, it is unlikely that anger or guilt would be equally present in both situations.

As stated previously, bereavement is most commonly used in reference to losses due to death. In the field of gerontology, with an emphasis on older adults, some of the most common death-related losses are the deaths of parents, spouses, siblings, and friends. Much of the information in this report is based on spousal bereavement in later life because more gerontological research has focused on this loss. At younger ages we are most likely to experience the death of a parent, older relative, or school classmate. Some experts have described the death of a parent as the loss of our past, the death of a spouse or sibling as the loss of the present, and the death of a child as a loss of part of our future. Again, we have learned that our early and consistent experiences with death-related losses can shape our attitudes and ways of coping well into later life. For example, the young boy who is told to be strong and not to cry after his father's death might easily grow up to be the unexpressive and isolated widower in late life.

Although statistics cannot capture the full essence of the bereavement process they are very helpful in documenting the commonality and expectedness of the experience. Government reports have indicated that over 2 million people die each year in the United States. Over 400,000 of the deaths are children and youth under the age of 25. Also, each year there are at least 800,000 new widows and widowers.

The death of a spouse is an increasingly common experience among aging adults, particularly women. The 1990 Census revealed that only 1% of the population between ages 18 and 54 were widowed, but 34% of those 65 and over and 67% of those 85 and over were widowed. A gender difference becomes increasingly apparent in the later years of life. After age 65, nearly 49% of the women but only 14% of men were widowed. In the 85+ category, 80% of women and 43% of men were widowed. These high percentages actually underestimate the number of persons who experience the death of a spouse because they do not include those who remarried.

II. MULTIDIMENSIONAL NATURE OF BEREAVEMENT

Bereavement is an important topic because the adjustment process can impact virtually every aspect of a person's life. This multidimensional nature of bereavement means that the coping process can affect emotions, spirituality, identity, social interactions and relationships, sexuality and intimacy, work productivity, financial stability, health, and even death. Patterns of interaction in family life are radically altered when someone dies. Family meals, and other daily rituals related to getting ready for work, school, or church are affected by the absence of the deceased family member. In the case of spousal bereavement the survivor often changes her or his self-concept to an "uncoupled identity" because she or he now carries out their daily life alone rather than as part of a couple. Bereaved persons may lose their appetite and motivation to remain physically active, so nutrition, exercise, and physical well-being can be essential parts of the coping process.

The multidimensional nature of bereavement is evident in the topics that professionals from different disciplines choose for special attention. Sociologists often examine bereavement's impact on family life, interactions, life satisfaction, and the role of culture and socioeconomic characteristics in shaping these bereavement outcomes. Finding differences among men and women, rich and poor, and diverse ethnic groups are common concerns for sociologists. Psychologists frequently examine the emotions of grief, depression, morale, and identity and how previous relationships and personality of the bereaved influence their coping strategies. Social workers are likely to assess family functioning and the need for and effectiveness of specific community services. Nurses and other health professionals are often concerned about the mental and physical well-being of bereaved persons. Economists are usually interested in the financial stability of bereaved persons and families. Because many women in the United States do not have the same level of retirement and other financial benefits as men, they are much more likely to suffer economically during widowhood. Each discipline and professional group adds a unique focus to examining bereavement experiences, and collectively, we better understand the many ways that bereavement can affect our lives.

Another way to appreciate the multidimensional nature of bereavement is to recognize that bereavement takes place in a context. Although there are many common reactions and feelings that most people experience during the course of bereavement, there also are many unique experiences that may not be widely shared. For example, some bereaved persons feel intense guilt and anger, whereas others feel relief and a sense of celebration. Some are overwhelmed with sadness and immobilized by depression, whereas others confront the loss as a challenge and opportunity for growth. In order to understand why one person manages very well and another never seems to adjust to the loss, it is necessary to examine the multidimensional nature of the context in which bereavement occurs. Previous life experiences, personality traits, social support received from others, circumstances surrounding the death, and a person's competency in managing the many tasks of daily living are some of the many factors that comprise the context of bereavement. Health professionals and clinicians who work with bereaved persons are better able to provide assistance when they know more about the specific aspects of each individual's bereavement context. What helps one person may not be of much value to another.

III. SOURCES OF KNOWLEDGE ABOUT BEREAVEMENT

Although the subject of death has received considerable thought and discussion for thousands of years, much less attention has been devoted to the subject of how death affects those who are left to grieve. The last 50 years, however, has seen a steady increase in interest and writing about bereavement. Academic disciplines, especially psychology, sociology, social work, nursing, and other behavioral and health professions have contributed attention and knowledge to the subject through the development of theory and research. Clinicians who work directly with the bereaved have added their knowledge about ways to help those having greatest difficulty. Religious leaders and members of various clergy have shared their experiences regarding spiritual aspects of the bereavement process. Local bookstores are now replete with numerous autobiographical reports written by bereaved persons who have had experiences that they want to share. Four sources of knowledge—theory and research, clinical reports, religious, and autobiographical accounts—each make unique contributions to our understanding of bereavement. These different sources of knowledge, however, have unique advantages and limitations that need to be recognized because they can lead to different and competing conclusions. [See DEATH AND DYING.]

Bereaved persons frequently turn to their clergy or their religious beliefs for comfort and guidance. Most religions have a set of beliefs regarding the questions of ultimate meaning. What is the purpose of life? Does God or a supernatural being have a plan for each specific person? Is there special meaning in the death of the loved one? Because most religions offer answers to these and other questions, religiously oriented people can find predictability, structure, and meaning to help them during the upheaval of bereavement. We have learned from research, however, that religion and spirituality are only part of the bereavement context and that the long-term adjustment process involves much more than a religious code to follow. Research has not confirmed that religious beliefs and practices are universally helpful to bereaved persons, but we do know that many people turn to their spiritual views as a source of knowledge. [See RELIGION AND SPIRITUALITY.]

Autobiographical books on grief and bereavement

are abundant because bereaved persons want to know how others have managed, if their experiences are unique or common, and how they can cope better with their loss. These personal accounts can be useful because they offer detailed descriptions of feelings, problems, and solutions that worked for the authors. Some bereaved persons, for example, might find comfort in knowing that their feelings of anger and guilt were shared by the author and benefited by following some of the suggestions in the book. Much caution should be exercised, however, because the author's credentials are most likely in journalism rather than bereavement.

Books, articles, and reports written by therapists, counselors, and other clinicians also provide valuable knowledge about bereavement. Like autobiographical accounts, clinical reports offer detailed personal descriptions of the bereavement process and usually offer suggestions for helping to alleviate problems. These in-depth reports about individuals' bereavement experiences are not only interesting but they help to organize experiences of more people, identify serious adjustment difficulties, and inform other professionals and bereaved persons of specific intervention strategies and their consequences. Knowledge that comes from clinical practice, however, must be interpreted in a way that recognizes the uniqueness of the clients or patients. Those who receive counseling or professional clinical services are likely to differ in some important ways from those who never seek help. Bereaved persons who receive these services are more likely to be experiencing the greatest difficulty in adjusting, have less social support available to them, have financial resources adequate to pay for the services, and have a tendency to rely on others for help. If we based our knowledge about bereavement solely on information from clinical clients we would not know about the experience of the majority of bereaved persons. It is equally important to know how people manage their grief on their own and to what extent they want and need help even though they do not seek professional assistance.

Research and theory have been much slower in adding to our knowledge about bereavement, but their contributions have been essential. Sigmund Freud was one of the earliest to theorize about bereavement. In the early 1900s Freud practiced and wrote extensively about psychoanalytic theory and applied it to understanding the feelings and thoughts that follow separation or loss of attachment. His work was followed by other theorists, and eventually systematic research studies were completed. Erich Lindemann also used a psychoanalytic framework to guide perhaps the first bereavement study in 1944. His study interviewed over 100 relatives of 13 people killed in a fire at the Boston Coconut Grove night club. Research and theory related to bereavement has steadily increased since these early beginnings. We now have numerous theories and research findings that both support and challenge what we initially believed to be true about bereavement.

Knowledge that is based on theory and research has given us information on a broader range of bereaved persons. By collecting data from people who have not sought professional help, and represent varied cultures and social classes, we have learned much more about what is common and what is unique during bereavement. Systematic research studies, using well-developed and standardized scales, representative samples of bereaved persons, and nonbereaved control groups have revealed findings that are inconsistent with and challenge some of the previous views based upon the other sources of knowledge. These research findings are presented in more detail later in this report under the section on the "Course of Adjustment." One of the most prominent research findings is that although bereavement is a highly stressful experience and some people report, "never getting over it," the majority of bereaved persons are very resilient. They find personal and social resources to meet their needs and manage their adjustment process. Research also has not been able to confirm that people go through specific stages as suggested by many clinicians and some theorists. The process is much more varied and complex than the uniform course depicted in the stage theories. Also, research has documented that not all people need to equally express their emotions outwardly to others in order to avoid a buildup of problems that will come out even worse later. Many people who appear in control and able to manage their early grief very well tend to be doing very well years later. In short, all four of the sources of knowledge have added to a fuller and more useful understanding of bereavement.

IV. COURSE OF ADJUSTMENT

A. Perspectives, Theories, and Models

Because the bereavement process is multidimensional, and professionals from different disciplines are educated to emphasize specific aspects of human behavior, we have numerous perspectives, theories, and models that provide divergent views about bereavement. Perspectives, theories, and models differ in their degree of specificity and complexity, but they essentially provide a framework or set of guidelines to help describe, interpret, explain, and understand behavior, in this case grief and bereavement. They help to focus attention on specific parts of the bereavement context. They provide clarity and orderliness. If the perspectives, theories, and models are adequate and relatively accurate, they can be applied to predicting bereavement adjustments and guiding the development of interventions to help those in greatest need. The following section briefly summarizes some of the most prominent theories about grief and bereavement.

1. Psychoanalytic Theories

Most of the variations in psychoanalytic theory applied to bereavement emphasize the importance of recognizing the conscious and subconscious ties or attachments that the bereaved person formed with the deceased. According to this view the bereaved person must express rather than repress all of the feelings associated with the detachment or loss. Anger, guilt, fear, and love, when expressed by the bereaved, help lead to normal instead of abnormal grief. These theories also stress the importance of early childhood relationships and separations because these first experiences remain throughout life. When children have traumatic losses in early life they often form ambivalent relationships later, repress their anxieties, and have greater difficulty with grief and bereavement. Separation anxiety is seen as an instinctive reaction to loss, but it's essential that the bereaved person withdraws from the deceased and forms new attachments.

Sigmund Freud, Erich Lindemann, John Bowlby, Colin Murray Parkes, and Peter Marris are the most prominent contributors to psychoanalytic theory and bereavement. Although each theorist has his own unique interpretations, they have generally agreed that grief is largely an intrapsychic process that each bereaved person must cognitively resolve in order to avoid delayed, distorted, or abnormal grief. Some of the abnormal reactions include social withdrawal, hypochondriacal symptoms, psychosomatic illnesses, and hyperactivity. Normal grief is thought to be marked by distress and impaired functioning, but re-

covery is expected. The bereaved person usually has a period of upset, protest, and anxiety because of the separation. He or she is likely to search for the deceased in familiar settings. Despair and depression can follow because the deceased does not return. A reorganization phase occurs when the griever accepts the reality of the loss, resolves the feelings of guilt and anger, restructures his or her life, and returns to normal functioning. These theories suggest that bereavement follows a relatively ordered progression of phases and that unresolved grief occurs when the sequence is disrupted or distorted.

2. Stress, Appraisal, and Coping Theories

Theories of stress, appraisal, and coping have been applied to bereavement because the death of a spouse, parent, child, and sibling are generally considered to be among the most stressful events that happen. Stress exists when the demands on the individual exceed the resources readily available to meet the demands. The death of a loved one, particularly when the deceased was an important part of the daily life of the bereaved, creates stress in many ways for the survivor. Daily life is radically changed because the bereaved can no longer rely on the deceased for ongoing companionship, conversation, security, guidance, comfort, love, sharing, listening, and instrumental assistance, such as financial support, transportation, and caregiving. Bereavement requires the survivor to change and adjust to an environment where the deceased is absent.

When bereavement occurs each person must cognitively appraise his or her situation, usually consistent with their previously established patterns of dealing with stress. Cognitive appraisal means that people consciously assess their loss, try to make sense out of it, and determine the consequences. The degree of stress and subsequent adjustment difficulties are largely dependent on the bereaved person's appraisal of the situation and the coping strategies that they use.

The most common types of appraisal are pain, threat, challenge, and relief. Those who see primarily the pain often focus their attention on the damage already done and expend much of their energy in anger, sadness, and depression, and their coping strategy often involves withdrawal, self-blame, and feeling overwhelmed. Those who see their loss as a threat are aware of the stress but are uncertain about their ability to deal with it. The death of their loved one means that they see other losses that are likely to follow. Their coping strategies usually include fear and worry about future threats to their lives. Rather than focusing their energy in broader ways to make their adjustment easier, they often engage in wishful thinking. The bereaved who see the loss as a challenge recognize the stress and the need to adapt. They assess their strengths, limitations, and needs and pursue a course of action that will allow them to learn and possibly grow from the experience. Having pride, self-confidence, motivation, and some skills in doing the many tasks of daily living help the bereaved to define the situation as a challenge and follow a more problem-focused approach to adjustment. Richard Lazarus, Susan Folkman, Leonard Pearlin, and many others have advanced the theory and research on stress, appraisal, and coping wherein the perspective continues to make very important contributions to understanding bereavement.

3. Stage and Task Models

Ever since Elizabeth Kubler-Ross proposed the well-known stage model of the dying process, it has been applied to many discussions of how people deal with problems and life crises. The dying person was seen to pass through a naturally occurring sequence of experiences beginning with denial and progressing through anger, bargaining, depression, and eventually culminating in acceptance. Because bereaved persons and many professionals became familiar with the stage model developed by Kubler-Ross and they could see many similar emotions, thoughts, and issues expressed during the course of bereavement, it only seemed natural to apply the sequential and progressive stages to bereavement.

Although research has identified and confirmed that bereaved persons experience many of the same kinds of emotions, thoughts, and behaviors presented in the stage models, the overall bereavement process appears to be much less orderly, sequential, and uniform than these models suggest. For example, some bereaved persons report many years after the loss that they sometimes feel the sadness, pain, and regret that they experienced in the first several weeks. The stage models have contributed to our knowledge about bereavement because they have helped to identify parts of the complex process and provided a foundation for further study.

Similar to the stage models and building on some of the concepts from other theories is the idea that

adaptation requires the bereaved person to accomplish or complete specific tasks. William Worden's "tasks of mourning" approach is an example. His work is based on the assumption that grief is work, requiring both emotional and physical energy to complete. He suggests that it is important for the bereaved to eventually accept the reality of the loss, to experience the pain of grief, to adapt emotionally and socially to an environment in which the deceased is missing, and to psychologically relocate the deceased person in their life and move forward. Although many other specific tasks can be added to his model, it does provide another useful approach to be used in helping bereaved persons. The task-oriented approach highlights the importance of being active and learning new skills rather than simply being passive and allowing time to pass and heal the wounds of grief.

4. Other Theories

Many other theories from social, behavioral, and health sciences have been used to understand some aspects of grief and bereavement, but most of them have not been systematically tested in research. Some of the theories have received only limited attention even though they have considerable promise in explaining and predicting bereavement behaviors and helping bereaved persons through the process. For example, family and systems theories, symbolic interactionism, the health belief model, and the theory of reasoned action have much to add but have not been extensively used.

Family and systems theories are relevant to bereavement because bereaved people are members of nuclear and extended families and their lives take place within functioning systems. People do not live in total isolation from families, groups, and organizations, and their experiences within these units are important parts of the broader bereavement context. An 80-year-old widow is impacted by how other family members grieve the death of her husband, who also may have been a father, grandfather, uncle, or brother. Just like individuals, families grieve. Some family members provide strength and support to one another and other families create more conflict and tension during bereavement. Systems theory recognizes that people are parts of larger systems, and individual lives consist of various functioning parts as well. Anger and depression following bereavement can easily carry over from the home to the workplace and many other social settings thereby impacting and further complicating other relationships.

Symbolic interaction theory that comes from the discipline of sociology has much to offer the topic of bereavement. The theory emphasizes the importance of social interactions with others and how they shape a person's self-concept or identity, which in turn influence behavior. Bereavement losses have the potential of altering a person's interactions and self-concepts and ultimately bereavement adjustments. From the field of health education the health belief model and theory of reasoned action are examples of conceptual frameworks relevant to bereavement. Both are applicable to examining the way bereaved persons make decisions and what they take into account to decide a course of action. Bereavement can very easily lead to neglect of one's own health. These approaches suggest that a broad range of factors, including messages in the media, can influence bereavement behaviors by identifying healthy behaviors to pursue and stressing the likelihood of positive outcomes that will follow. Grief requires energy, for example, so good nutrition and some regular exercise might assist with making other bereavement adjustments.

Finally, the most prominent theories in the field of gerontology have relevancy to understanding bereavement, but they have not received much attention. Disengagement, activity, continuity, and age-stratification theories have contributions to make, and it is hoped that in the future they will be examined and tested in research. Disengagement theory would suggest that those who were already gradually withdrawing from society would have less difficulty during bereavement than those who have not yet begun the process of withdrawal. The bereavement experience would not seem as abrupt to them. Activity theory would argue in favor of maintaining relatively high levels of physical activity during bereavement because it will help create greater life satisfaction and well-being. Continuity theory would suggest that the best course of action during bereavement would be to continue doing most of the things that one had always enjoyed. Age-stratification theory could be used to better understand why age might influence bereavement adjustments and that people in different age cohorts have different needs during stressful life transitions. In short, theory helps to inform and guide research and considerably more of both theory and

research is needed to improve the knowledge about grief and bereavement.

B. Research on the Bereavement Process

Research on bereavement has considerably increased in the last 15 years. Some studies have waited many weeks and months to interview bereaved persons, and others have obtained information only days after the death occurred. Some have followed bereaved persons for several years to examine long-term outcomes, but most studies have obtained information at only one point in time, providing only a limited picture of the process. Only few projects have included nonbereaved control groups even though it is valuable to be able to compare the thoughts, feelings, and behaviors of bereaved persons with those who are not experiencing death-related bereavement. Research has included more women than men, more adults than children, and more Caucasians than racial and ethnic minorities. Even with these and other limitations, research has improved the understanding of grief and bereavement. It is not possible to review all or even most of these findings, but five of the most important general conclusions are presented here.

First, bereavement is very stressful, but many people manage their losses with considerable resiliency. In the case of spousal bereavement, the majority of research participants report that their loss situation is the worst and most stressful thing that has ever happened to them. The death of a child also creates stress and is particularly difficult because children are expected to live longer than their parents. Among adults, it is disturbing when both of their parents are deceased because it means that their own generation in the family is now the most senior. The death of a spouse, parent, or child almost always brings out thoughts of mortality and death among the survivors. In our culture thoughts about the inevitability of death are usually troubling because we have not openly discussed death. Some researchers have attempted to identify how many people continue for several years having major difficulties that interfere with their daily lives. It has been estimated that between 15 and 25% will need some kind of professional help with their bereavement adjustments.

Apparently, even though bereavement is extremely stressful it is somewhat surprising to know that so many people are resilient and able to restructure their lives in ways that allow them to find enjoyment again. Knowing this helps direct attention to those 15–25% who are most distressed and unable to manage their bereavement losses alone. This issue is discussed in greater detail in the next section, which presents information on the predictors of bereavement adjustments.

Second, there is considerable diversity among and within bereaved persons. Not all people experience the same feelings, thoughts, and actions as they move through the process. For example, a 65-year-old widow described herself in the following way 4 weeks after her husband's death: "I am a very lonely person. Lousy, all washed out, despondent, feel deserted, angry, hurt, hopeless, alone, mixed-up, cannot concentrate, very emotional, very tired, cry a lot, hateful, very bitter, misfit, nobody, very miserable, very much of a loner." This same woman described herself in much the same troubled way two years into the bereavement process. She added that she was concerned about herself and really hurt inside. She noted that she was sick of living alone and didn't care about life. In contrast, another 69-year-old widow described herself at 6 months after her husband's death as being "independent, excited about keeping busy, enjoying the company of others, and working in my yard and doing handiwork." This diversity in bereavement reactions also is found within each individual. It is not unusual to find a person simultaneously experiencing a full range of feelings and behaviors. For example, a bereaved person can feel angry, guilty, and lonely, yet at the same time feel personal strength and pride in how he or she is coping. A 70-year-old woman described herself at length as being busy, enjoying many different activities, and doing things with other people, but her final self-descriptive comment was that she still feels lonely. It is common for bereaved persons to experience simultaneously both positive and negative feelings.

Third, a theme emerging from recent studies is that of being more cautious in using the term *normal* to describe grief or bereavement. Because of the great deal of diversity the same individual may experience and express herself or himself in a variety of ways during bereavement. What would have been considered outside the realm of "normal" grief several years ago may now be considered a normal part of the process. For example, talking to a deceased spouse would once have been defined as abnormal or even pathological, but recent research findings show that this is actually a very common practice among bereaved spouses—and it is now often encouraged as a therapeutic technique.

Rather than applying rigid labels such as normal or abnormal, it is more appropriate to use terms such as *common* or *uncommon* to describe bereavement feelings and behaviors. A bereaved person is far less stigmatized by being told that she or he is experiencing some uncommon feelings than by being told, "You are abnormal."

Fourth, recent studies have revealed that the bereavement process is more like a roller-coaster ride than an orderly progression of stages with clear time frames associated with each stage. The bereavement roller coaster is characterized by the rapidly changing emotions of grief; meeting the challenges of learning new skills; recognizing personal weaknesses and limitations; developing new patterns of behavior; experiencing fatigue, loneliness, and helplessness; and forming new friendships and relationships.

Researchers have been unable to identify clear time markers associated with these many ups and downs. In fact, the highs and lows can occur within minutes, days, months, or years. Fortunately, most bereaved persons experience a roller-coaster ride that becomes more manageable over time, with fewer abrupt highs and lows. This gradual improvement may never lead to an end or resolution, however, because many bereaved spouses report: "You never get over it—you learn to live with it."

Fifth, loneliness and problems associated with managing the tasks of daily living are two of the most common and difficult adjustments for older adults. These problems are even more difficult for the spousally bereaved because their daily lives are closely connected with their spouses and they frequently become dependent on each other for conversation, love, and sharing of tasks. Loneliness is problematic because it involves missing, sadness, and a void that does not go away simply by being with or among other people. Many bereaved report feeling lonely but not being alone. In the case of experiencing the death of a parent, child, or sibling who may live many miles away, the bereaved often describe how lonely they feel when they realize they can no longer call their loved one on the phone or hear their voice again. [See LONELINESS.]

Unfortunately, most older adults have not learned to do many of the tasks of daily life that are important to their health, well-being, and happiness. Many men have not learned how to prepare meals, wash clothes, and clean house. Similarly, many older women have not learned how to do home repairs, maintain an automobile, and manage finances. Research has shown that these deficiencies further complicate the bereavement process. It is hoped that future cohorts of men and women will be better prepared and skilled in a much broader range of tasks of daily living.

C. Predictors of Bereavement Adjustments

One often hears people say that the passage of time will heal the wound. This statement is problematic and inaccurate because it implies that little or no effort is required to cope with the situation. Simply allowing time to pass is supposed to bring about successful adjustment. Although it is a fact that most bereaved persons experience less difficulty and more positive adjustments over time, it is important to recognize that it is what people do with their time that determines the outcomes. Successful adjustments require active rather than passive coping strategies.

Many bereaved persons have told others that it is most helpful to take one day at a time and to remain active, busy, and socially connected with other people. Being physically and socially active during the process can help to reduce the feelings of despair, helplessness, loneliness, and being overwhelmed that often contribute to a long-term strategy of waiting—often in vain—for time to bring about healing. In addition to these active coping strategies, recent studies have documented the importance of having social support from others and opportunities for self-expression available, especially in the early months of bereavement. Some of the most difficult and stressful bereavement experiences occur in the first few months when grief issues are especially intense. [See ACTIVITIES; SOCIAL NETWORKS, SUPPORT, AND INTEGRATION.]

Researchers have also learned that how a person copes with loss early in the process appears to be one of the best predictors of long-term coping. Those who report having effective coping experiences in the first couple of months usually cope better than others a few years later. Bereaved persons therefore are likely to benefit most from social support that they receive early in the process and from opportunities to express how they feel at this time. Some of the most appreciated and helpful support comes from those who allow

the bereaved to openly express anger, sadness, and other emotions without passing along advice and counsel. It is important for bereaved persons to know that their reactions are common and that others respect their feelings and care about their well-being. Self-help groups for bereaved persons provide good opportunities for self-expression, particularly for those who do not already have someone in whom they can confide.

The importance of internal coping resources is supported by research that has focused on the role of self-esteem and self-efficacy. Both concepts represent personal coping resources that individuals develop throughout their lives. Self-esteem refers to the positive or negative judgments or evaluations that one makes about self-worth. Self-efficacy refers to one's ability to meet the changing demands of everyday life and feeling confident to do so.

The way people feel about themselves and how skilled they are in managing the many tasks of daily living—maintaining a household, paying bills, driving a car, knowing how to access resources, and so on—will influence how effectively they adjust to the loss of a loved one. People who develop positive self-esteem and competencies such as social, interpersonal, and instrumental skills are likely to have more favorable bereavement outcomes than those who develop negative self-images and lack self-efficacy.

Self-esteem and self-efficacy are highly interrelated because people who have confidence and pride in themselves are usually more motivated to learn new skills, and the process of becoming more competent in daily life itself creates more positive self-esteem. Bereaved persons with these positive characteristics are likely to cope quite well because they will not be content with a passive approach to coping. Conversely, bereaved people who never developed these personal coping resources are likely to experience long-term difficulties because they are more inclined to believe that they deserve to remain depressed, lonely, and incapacitated. These people tend to feel overwhelmed and take few constructive actions on their own behalf. [See SELF-ESTEEM.]

The predictors of adjustment to bereavement are similar for both men and women and for young and older adults. Age and gender are not the most influential factors in the course of bereavement. What is of greater importance is to develop positive feelings about oneself early in life, continue to enhance these views over the life course, and develop skills that help one to meet the changing circumstances and demands of daily living. People with these traits are more likely than others to adjust well to nearly any major life stress or transition. Human development is a lifelong process. In the case of late-life bereavement, the developmental process is challenged. During this transition period, the bereaved person can remain physically, psychologically, and socially disrupted or can emerge with a sense of growth from learning new skills, becoming more independent, and developing a clearer self-identity.

V. INTERVENTIONS

Although it is tempting to conclude that most bereaved persons will need help with their adjustment process, this is not the case. Research has shown that many bereaved persons do not want or need intervention services. This point is important to recognize, because it is frequently assumed by clinicians and service providers that most older bereaved persons are depressed, socially isolated, and incapacitated by their loss. The research evidence does not support this assumption, although certainly some bereaved persons are depressed, isolated, and incapacitated. The tasks for those developing intervention services are many, and among their first should be an attempt to reach those who are at greatest risk—to seek them out rather than simply announcing the existence of the service—and encourage their participation by explaining how and why the service will be helpful. It is absolutely critical to recognize that many, perhaps most, of the potential population of bereaved persons will not want to participate. This can be discouraging to those who are committed to the value of their services, but their motivation to continue their efforts will probably be less adversely affected if they anticipate the lack of enthusiasm among many potential clients. For example, only 44% of the bereaved spouses who completed a study by the author said that they would have liked the opportunity to attend self-help groups. In a later study, only 27% of those assigned to self-help groups actually agreed to participate.

Interventions need to be available early in the bereavement process and continue over relatively long periods of time. There is a good deal of research evidence that the first several months (usually 1 to 4 months) are the most difficult and that early adjustments will influence outcomes much later. Also, because bereavement may last for many years and some people may not be ready for early interventions, it would be most helpful to have services available over long periods of time. This does not mean that the same people need to continue receiving services for many years, although some will have this need: rather, bereaved persons need to have an opportunity to participate when they are ready.

Because the impact of bereavement is multidimensional, it is imperative that interventions offer comprehensive and diverse services. It is unlikely that any one intervention will be capable of providing all that is needed, but each intervention should clearly identify which needs are being targeted in relation to the overall multidimensional process so that there is an awareness of what help is not being provided. For example, the death of a spouse in later life can impact emotions, psychosocial functioning, health, family life, interpersonal relationships, work, recreation, and financial situations; those designing interventions that provide primarily an opportunity for self-expression (such as self-help groups) should recognize that some dimensions are not likely to be addressed. Ideally, all communities would have available a variety of interventions or services so that each person's unique skills, resources, and circumstances could be matched to the most appropriate set of services. Although this is unlikely, we can at least strive to offer interventions with the broadest scope of impact. Therefore, whenever possible, it would be worthwhile to impact several dimensions simultaneously by providing opportunities for self-expression and the enhancement of self-esteem; by teaching new skills to complete the tasks of daily living; by enhancing and mobilizing already existing social support networks; by providing education and assistance regarding health, nutrition, and exercise; and by encouraging social participation.

Various intervention formats and professionals are needed to ensure that appropriate services are available. Not all people experience bereavement in the same way; similarly, not all people will use or benefit from the same interventions. In terms of format, some people will only want to have a one-on-one type of intervention. This might be because they feel the uniqueness of their situation can be dealt with more effectively one-to-one because they are reluctant to express personal and sensitive feelings in group situations. Others have reported that they particularly enjoyed being in a self-help group because they learned from others, recognized some commonalities in their situations, and enjoyed the socializing and friendships that developed.

Many people have skills and expertise that are well suited for helping the bereaved. Phyllis Silverman, who developed the widow-to-widow program, has shown that widows are quite capable of assisting each other. An experienced widow can reveal to the new widow that they have been there and that they know how it feels to grieve. Also, there are important contributions that can be made by researchers, gerontologists, psychologists, psychiatrists, physicians, social workers, nurses, occupational therapists, art therapists, counselors, clergy, and many other professionals, including social scientists, lawyers, accountants, educators, and direct service providers. Again, because bereavement has a multidimensional impact, interventions can be developed by many different professional and trained team members. Other bereaved persons can provide a sharing of experiences while trained persons assist with legal, financial, health, spiritual, and educational issues. A multidimensional team approach is highly recommended because it will increase the likelihood of developing interventions that address the diversity of needs and lead to greater success.

It should be understood that bereavement is a common and natural experience that we all share. Unfortunately, many people are not well prepared for the pain, threats, and challenges that it presents. Because bereavement occurs in broader contexts, we do not all have the same personal and social resources available, or have the same experiences and needs. What appears to help one person may have an entirely different impact on someone else. The best way to be prepared to help bereaved persons is to be educated about the process, assess the context in which it occurs, become familiar with a wide range of helping resources, and be patient, a good listener, and nonjudgmental.

BIBLIOGRAPHY

Aiken, L. R. (1994). *Dying, death and bereavement* (3rd ed.). Boston: Allyn & Bacon.

Cleiren, M. (1993). *Bereavement and adaptation.* Washington, DC: Hemisphere/Taylor & Francis.

De Spelder, L. A., & Strickland, A. L. (1992). *The last dance* (3rd ed). Mountain View, CA: Mayfield.

Irish, D. P., Lundquist, K. F., & Nelsen, V. J. (1993). *Ethnic variations in dying, death, and grief.* Washington, DC: Taylor & Francis.

Kutcher, A. H. (1990). *For the bereaved: The road to recovery.* Philadelphia: Charles Press.

Lund, D. A. (1989). *Older bereaved spouses.* Washington, DC: Hemisphere/Taylor & Francis.

Parkes, C. M. (1987). *Bereavement: Studies of grief in adult life* (2nd ed.). Madison, WI: International Universities Press.

Stroebe, M. S., Stroebe, W., & Hansson, R. O. (1993). *Handbook of bereavement.* New York: Cambridge University Press.

Worden, J. W. (1991) *Grief counseling and grief therapy* (2nd ed.). New York: Springer.

Bioenergetics

Jon J. Ramsey and Joseph W. Kemnitz

University of Wisconsin, Madison

Basal Metabolic Rate (BMR) Metabolic rate calculated from oxygen consumption measured in a resting, postabsorptive individual at thermoneutrality.

Calorimetry A technique for determining energy expenditure by measuring heat production (direct calorimetry) or measuring oxygen consumption and carbon dioxide production (indirect respiration calorimetry).

Dietary Restriction Reduction of energy intake without malnutrition by restricting dietary intake through the use of a specially formulated nutrient-dense diet.

Doubly Labeled Water Method A technique used to determine production of carbon dioxide in free-living individuals by measuring differences in the rate of loss of the stable isotopes oxygen-18 and deuterium from individuals dosed with $^2H_2^{18}O$.

Energy Balance The mathematical difference between total energy intake and total energy expenditure. A positive energy balance is indicative of weight gain (energy storage) and a negative energy balance is indicative of weight loss (energy depletion).

Free Radicals Highly reactive atoms or molecules containing unpaired electrons that may damage membranes, structural proteins, enzymes, nucleic acids, or other cellular components.

Glycation Theory A theory that proposes that nonenzymatic attachment of glucose molecules to proteins and nucleic acids is a mediator of aging.

Thermic Effect of Meals (TEM) The energy expenditure associated with the digestion, absorption, and assimilation of food into body stores.

Total Energy Expenditure The sum total of energy expenditure from basal metabolic rate, TEM, and all forms of activity.

BIOENERGETICS is a broad subject covering all phases of energy metabolism from the molecular and cellular level to the whole animal. The study of bioenergetics and aging is a particularly interesting field because energy metabolism and the process of aging appear to be closely linked. Aging is generally associated with a decrease in both energy intake and energy expenditure. These decreases are also associated with an age-related shift in body composition toward a decrease in lean body mass (LBM) and an increase in percent body fat. Many of the diseases and physiological problems associated with old age are closely tied to these alterations in energy metabolism. Experimental manipulation of components of energy metabolism have also been shown to have dramatic effects on life span and age-related changes in physiological parameters. Specifically, dietary energy restriction has been shown to greatly increase life span in animal models, and increased energy expenditure through physical exercise slows the decline in many physiological parameters. An understanding of bioenergetics is crucial to the overall understanding of the process of aging.

I. BACKGROUND

Changes in many aspects of energy metabolism are among the most consistent and noticeable characteristics of aging. It is interesting to note that dietary energy restriction is the only experimental treatment that has been consistently shown to decrease or delay the physiological processes and diseases associated with aging (i.e., to "slow aging") and to extend ultimate life span. This finding indicates a close association between energy utilization and the fundamental processes of aging. Clearly, an understanding of bioenergetics is important to understand many of the physiological and biochemical changes with aging. Although age-related changes in the various components of bioenergetics show some differences between species, this discussion will focus on the results of aging and human energetics with occasional reference to animal experiments.

Aging is often associated with shifts in energy balance, with obesity being a particular problem in midlife and wasting a problem for many who survive to advanced age. Changes in body weight (BW) and body composition are a function of total body energy balance (the difference in energy intake and energy expenditure). BW gain requires a positive energy balance, whereas BW loss is accompanied by a negative energy balance. The factors in the energy balance equation, therefore, are energy intake, energy storage, and energy expenditure.

Energy intake is simply the caloric content of the food eaten by the individual, assuming complete absorption. Energy consumption is a function of the total amount of diet consumed and the chemical composition of the diet. Energy intake is controlled by both psychological and physiological factors, which will be discussed later in this overview. In most cases, energy intake declines with advancing age. [See DIET AND NUTRITION.]

Energy storage or body composition refers to the chemical form in which excess energy is stored in the body. Excess energy may be stored as fat, protein, or carbohydrates. The majority of the body's energy is stored as either fat (which contains the most calories per gram of tissue) in adipose tissue or as protein in muscle with a limited amount stored as carbohydrate in the form of glycogen. Aging is accompanied by a decrease in total body mass, and a shift in body composition towards a decrease in body protein and an increase in percent body fat.

Energy expenditure is the final component of energy balance. Energy expenditure in turn is composed of three parts: basal metabolic rate (BMR) or resting energy expenditure, the thermic effect of meals (TEM), and activity.

BMR is defined by the measurement of resting, postabsorptive energy expenditure in individuals at thermoneutrality. BMR is typically responsible for 50–80% of total energy expenditure. The processes that contribute to resting oxygen consumption and energy expenditure include activity in the Na^+/K^+-ATPase pathway, mitochondrial proton leak, protein turnover, ionic calcium movements, triacylglycerol turnover, and other substrate cycles. The major contributors to resting oxygen consumption are the Na^+/K^+-ATPase activity and mitochondrial proton leak, which are each responsible for 20–30% of resting metabolic rate, and protein turnover, which is responsible for approximately 20% of resting metabolic rate.

The digestion, absorption, and assimilation of food is associated with an energy expenditure called TEM. TEM is responsible for approximately 10% of total energy expenditure but will vary depending on meal size and composition.

Physical activity is the most variable component of total energy expenditure, being responsible for 10–40% of total energy expenditure. Activity includes all of the energy-consuming processes not comprising BMR or heat increment.

Aging tends to result in a decrease in all of the components of energy expenditure. The age-related decline in resting metabolic rate expressed on a total body mass basis has been firmly substantiated. The exact effect of age on TEM and level of physical activity is still the subject of some debate, but several researchers have reported decreases in both processes with aging.

Understanding the mechanisms underlying changes in energy expenditure is obviously very important to an overall understanding of the initiation and progression of age-related physiological changes and diseases. Two experimental treatments, dietary energy restriction and exercise, have potential to offer insight into the processes of aging. Dietary energy restriction is the only experimental procedure that has been shown to consistently increase ultimate life span. Exercise, on the other hand, has been shown to decrease age-related changes in many processes, but additional research is needed to determine if exercise consistently increases the length of life.

II. ENERGY INTAKE

Aging is generally associated with a decrease in energy intake. Decreases in energy intake have the potential to cause several problems. First, a decrease in energy intake is often not matched with a proportionate change in energy expenditure, which can lead to negative energy balance and loss of body mass. This can be extremely damaging to an individual already in a compromised body composition and lead to an increased risk of morbidity and mortality. Second, a decrease in energy intake is usually associated with a decreased intake of other nutrients, resulting in increased risk of malnutrition-related illnesses. Several studies have shown that a significant portion of the elderly population are deficient in at least one major nutrient. Matching energy intake to energy expenditure is clearly an important concern in the elderly. Previous attempts to characterize energy requirements in the elderly have suffered from the fact that they have relied on dietary recall to determine energy intakes, a procedure that often results in underestimation of actual food intakes. These studies have also been criticized for their small sample sizes or extrapolation of results from younger individuals to the elderly. Alternatively, energy expenditure can be used as an indirect measure of food intake. Continued research is needed, however, that will accurately determine total energy expenditure in elderly people. The use of the doubly labeled water method for determining energy expenditure offers a chance to measure energy expenditure in free-living individuals and should increase the reliability of energy requirement recommendations.

Decreases in energy intake appear to be associated with several other changes that occur with the aging process. Impairment of taste and smell sensation occur with increasing age. Taste and smell are two major determinants of the palatability of foods, and a decrease in either or both of these senses will clearly cause a decrease in flavor intensity of foods. Decreased palatability of familiar foods probably contributes to the decrease in energy intake with aging. Depression

and some forms of medication are common causes of decreased appetite and food intake in the elderly. Problems with oral health, poor dentition, and gum disease also contribute to depression of food intake in the elderly. Additionally, aging is associated with decreased saliva production and swallowing problems that can make eating difficult. [See DEPRESSION.]

A variety of hormonal and neural changes that occur with aging also may play a role in decreasing energy intake. Endogenous opioid peptides have been proposed to play a role in increasing food intake, especially of foods high in fat content. The activity of this opioid system, however, decreases with age. Studies with rats have shown a diminished response in older animals to opioid agonists or antagonists when compared to younger animals. Old animals have also been shown to have lower levels of opioid peptides in the hypothalamus. Although the role of opioid peptides in food intake has not been completely delineated, low activity of this system may contribute to age-related declines in food intake. Aging has also been shown to result in increased activity of the gastrointestinal peptide and cholecystokinin (CCK) systems. CCK has been shown to inhibit eating to a greater extent in old compared to young mice. CCK also has prolonged action in old mice, and elderly humans have higher CCK levels than younger individuals. Slowing gastric emptying is another action of CCK and other gastrointestinal peptides, such as gastric inhibitory peptide. Similarly, studies in the elderly have shown decreased solid and liquid emptying of the stomach when compared to young individuals. Slow rates of passage through the gastrointestinal tract are correlated with decreased food intakes, so this may also contribute to depression of food intake with aging. Testosterone and estradiol are two other hormones that influence food intake and decrease with aging. Estradiol has been shown to inhibit food intake, and testosterone withdrawal is associated with decreased food intake. Men exhibit a greater decrease in food intake during later life than women, which is consistent with the changes in circulating gonadal hormones at that time. [See ENDOCRINE FUNCTION AND DYSFUNCTION.]

Health concerns associated with continued weight loss and negative energy balance in the elderly require interventions that may stimulate increased energy intake. Exercise may be one of these methods that stimulates increased energy intake in older individuals.

Studies relating exercise activity to energy intake have not been conclusive with some reporting no change in exercise-associated intake and others reporting an increase in intake with exercise. It appears that food intake following regular exercise is probably dependent on body composition and intensity of exercise. Studies with lean and obese individuals have shown that exercise increases food intake in lean individuals, whereas food intake in obese individuals does not change. Other studies have also suggested that moderate or intense activity is needed to increase energy intake with light activity having little or no effect. This result has been confirmed in experiments with elderly individuals which have noticed increases in energy intake with moderate exercise and no change in intake with light exercise. Encouraging elderly individuals to participate in exercise programs has the potential to increase energy intake along with the many cardiovascular and bone-strengthening benefits of exercise.

III. BODY COMPOSITION, NUTRIENT METABOLISM, AND AGING

Aging is associated with very clear changes in body composition. In general, aging results in a decrease in total body mass along with a decrease in lean body mass (LBM) and total body protein while increasing percent body fat.

Progressive loss of body protein due to a large decline in skeletal muscle mass is a well-established component of the aging process. In young adults, skeletal muscle comprises nearly half of body weight, while at 70 years of age skeletal muscle comprises only a quarter of total body weight. The changes in body protein with aging are almost exclusively a function of decreases in skeletal muscle mass, because nonmuscle LBM is not markedly affected by aging. This decrease in skeletal muscle mass decreases the overall motor function of the muscles and may limit the individual's ability to respond to stresses requiring mobilization of body protein stores.

The aging process results in several changes that probably contribute to the loss of muscle mass. First, aging is associated with a decrease in physical activity reducing biomechanical forces on skeletal muscle needed for maintenance or growth of muscle mass. Exercise, especially strength training, can reverse the decline in muscle mass in the elderly. Changes in levels of anabolic hormones also contribute to the age-related decline in muscle mass. Spontaneous and stimulated growth hormone (GH) secretions are decreased with age. Related to decreased secretion of growth hormone, circulating levels of insulinlike growth factor-1 (IGF-I) and insulinlike growth factor binding protein-3 (IGFBP-3) also decrease with age. Deficiencies in GH and IGF-I are both associated with reduced protein synthesis and loss of LBM. Decreases in testosterone and estrogen levels probably also play a role in the depletion of LBM. Insulin-mediated suppression of body protein breakdown, unlike other actions of insulin, does not appear to decrease with age. Overall, a decrease in physical activity and decreased levels of anabolic hormones appear to be the likely causes of loss of lean body mass with aging. [See NEUROMUSCULAR SYSTEM.]

In addition to hormone- and activity-mediated effects on whole body protein loss, aging may be associated with alterations in muscle damage and protein turnover. It has been demonstrated that exercise results in a severalfold increase in muscle ultrastructure damage in older individuals compared to younger subjects. This information has been used to support the idea that older exercising individuals may require a greater protein intake than the recommended daily allowance. Skeletal muscle protein turnover decreases with age and results in a decreased contribution of skeletal muscle protein turnover to whole body protein turnover. Whole body protein turnover measurements, however, are mixed and suggest no major difference between young and old individuals.

Changes in body protein content are accompanied by an increase in percent body fat in elderly individuals. Total body fat can increase by greater than 50% between 20–30 and 70–80 years of age. Coupled with a concomitant decrease in muscle mass, this can result in a dramatic increase in percent body fat.

The increase in body fat, however, is probably not a function of diet because aging tends to be associated with a decrease in both rate and amount of dietary fat absorbed. In fact, a significant percentage of individuals over 62 years of age have been shown to have steatorrhea, indicating malabsorption of dietary fat.

Several factors contribute to increases in percent body fat in the elderly. First, a decrease in physical activity may result in a positive energy balance and increased storage of energy in adipose tissue instead of increasing muscle mass. Second, aging is associated with a decrease in catecholamine activity and hormone-induced lipolysis in adipocytes. In women, fat accumulation also appears to be associated with hormonal changes with menopause, because estrogen and progesterone treatment tend to prevent increases in abdominal fat accumulation. Overall, aging is associated with the inability to match energy intake with energy expenditure. Decreases in energy expenditure and adipocyte lipolysis together appear to be major contributors to age-related increases in body fat. [See ENDOCRINE FUNCTION AND DYSFUNCTION.]

Although the contribution of carbohydrate storage to body composition is minimal, changes in carbohydrate metabolism play an extremely important role in the aging process. Aging is associated with an overall deterioration in glucose tolerance due to increased peripheral tissue insulin resistance. Fasting and postprandial glucose levels have been shown to steadily increase after approximately 30 years of age. The postprandial increase in glucose levels is a dramatic difference between young and old individuals, but moderate elevations of glucose levels over a long time period may be responsible for many of the glucose-related problems with aging. Pancreatic β-cell function is reduced in older individuals as shown by a decreased release of insulin in response to glucose. Insulin resistance and high plasma glucose levels increase the risk of many age-associated problems including nonenzymatic glycation of proteins and amino acids. In addition to hyperglycemic problems, hyperinsulinemia in the elderly causes elevation of plasma lipids, vascular problems, and may contribute to hypertension.

IV. ENERGY EXPENDITURE

As discussed previously, aging is associated with changes in all of the components of energy expenditure. Decreases in BMR, TEM, and activity are all important contributors to the overall etiology of aging.

BMR is a function of the varying oxygen requirements of the different tissues. Research has suggested that internal organs are responsible for approximately 60% of resting energy expenditure. Adipose tissue is responsible for approximately 5% of resting energy expenditure, and skeletal muscle consumes the re-

maining 35–40% of resting energy expenditure. These values show that LBM is responsible for approximately 95% of BMR. A change in LBM can therefore have a substantial influence on BMR. Aging is associated with a substantial decrease in LBM and a major decrease in BMR.

The age-related decline in BMR is one of the most firmly established characteristics of aging. BMR decreases between approximately 13–20% as individuals age from their thirties to eighties. This change in BMR appears to be nonlinear with accelerated decreases occuring at approximately 40 to 50 years of age. Gender influences both the onset of accelerated decreases in resting energy expenditure and the magnitude of these decreases. The decline in BMR begins at approximately 40 years of age in men but does not begin until after menopause, or approximately 50 years of age, in women. Men also have a decrease in BMR close to 20%, whereas the magnitude of the decrease in women is substantially less at approximately 13%.

The primary reason for decreases in BMR in both genders is the decrease in LBM. Some research groups have even suggested that decrease in lean tissue mass entirely explains the decrease in BMR with age. Experimental results suggesting the BMR expressed on a body water basis remain constant with age have been used to support this idea. Sufficient research results exist, however, to suggest that decreased LBM, although a major contributor to decreases in BMR, is probably not the only process involved.

Many of the cellular processes contributing to resting oxygen consumption have the potential to be involved in reduction of BMR in the elderly. Some research groups have shown that the Na^+/K^+-ATPase activity decreases with age. It has been suggested that this decrease in Na^+/K^+-ATPase activity may be responsible for approximately 3% of the decrease in BMR with aging. Decreases in skeletal muscle protein turnover have also been suggested to contribute to decreases in resting energy expenditure. Direct measurements of mitochondrial proton leak and aging, however, have not been published. Previous research showing changes in mitochondrial membrane composition and damage to mitochondrial membranes and DNA with aging suggests that changes in mitochondrial membrane proton permeability may be another factor involved in decreased resting energy expenditure in the elderly.

In addition to decreases in BMR, the aging process is generally considered to decrease TEM and physical activity. Most experiments show a decrease in the energy expenditure of meal ingestion with age. Diet composition, meal size, and activity all contribute to age-associated differences in TEM. Some studies with high-protein meals have found no difference in TEM between young and old individuals, but studies with glucose meals have found older individuals may have as much as 25% lower energy expenditures than younger subjects. Problems with glucose metabolism and insulin resistance probably explain the differences in TEM between the different types of diets.

Exercise has also been shown in many studies to increase the thermic effect of a meal. It has been suggested, therefore, that decreased activity in the elderly may explain their decrease in TEM. It has also been proposed that decreased intakes in elderly individuals contribute to low TEM with age because TEM changes proportionately with meal size.

A decrease in physical activity is another characteristic of the aging process. Low physical activity is a major contributor to decreased total energy expenditure with aging. Studies have shown that total hours of activity and intensity of activity decrease with aging. Studies have also shown that the ratio of thermic effect of eating to BMR decreases with age, demonstrating that decreases in activity are often of greater magnitude than the decrease in BMR.

The effect of exercise on BMR has not been firmly established. Results indicate either an increase in BMR or no change with exercise training. The discrepancies in research findings are probably due to differences in methodology or intensity of exercise. Nonetheless, some experiments have reported that strenuous exercise training may result in an increase in BMR by as much as 10%. Exercise slows the age-related loss in fat-free mass (FFM) and may increase BMR through this increase in FFM. [*See* METABOLISM: CARBOHYDRATE, LIPID, AND PROTEIN.]

V. RESTRICTED ENERGY INTAKES AND EXERCISE

Restriction of energy intake is an experimental tool that has been found to increase life span by as much as 50% in rodent models. The process involves limitation of dietary intake by at least 30% of normal ad libitum intake values. Restricted animals are also fed a specially formulated nutrient-dense diet to ensure dietary restriction does not cause nutritional deficiencies. Most investigators using rodents have employed an early-onset paradigm to evaluate the effects of dietary restriction, imposing restriction around the time of weaning. This results in severe stunting of the animals. Recently, there has been increased attention to the adult-onset model of dietary restriction, in which restriction is not begun until adult stature has been achieved. Apart from the effects on growth, the early-onset and adult-onset approaches appear to lead to qualitatively similar outcomes.

Dietary restriction affects such a wide range of physiological systems that it is clear that its actions must be through a fundamental aging process. This broad action of dietary restriction, however, has made it very difficult to pinpoint the mechanism through which dietary restriction exerts its action. Dietary restriction decreases the incidence of leukemia, pituitary tumors, lymphomas, atherosclerosis, diabetes mellitus, and other age-associated diseases. Dietary restriction also decreases serum glucose, insulin, and other physiological parameters.

The mechanism of action of energy restriction on the aging process still remains to be determined. It is clear, however, that overall energy restriction rather than restriction of a specific macronutrient is responsible for its life-prolonging effect. Experiments using low-protein or low-fat diets without restricting energy have failed to produce the dramatic life-prolonging results observed with energy restriction. Potential mechanisms for the action of energy-restricted diets on aging are discussed below.

Energy-restricted diets have been used to test a variety of theories about aging. One idea is that many of the problems with aging are simply caused by increases in body fat. Dietary restriction results in a decrease in body fat and fat cell number, but the failure of experiments to show a strong correlation between body fat and length of life suggests that decreasing body fat is not the primary mechanism of dietary restriction.

A second theory is that dietary restriction slows processes of growth and development and that this in turn slows the aging process. Food restriction does generally decrease DNA and protein synthesis. Energy restriction also results in a decrease in the release of reproductive and mitogenic hormones, including insulin, thyroid-stimulating hormone, GH, estrogen, and prolactin. This results in the observation of decreased mitogenesis rates in tissues. Energy restriction, however, has similar life-prolonging effects if initiated at weaning or adulthood, which suggests that growth suppression is probably not the primary mode of action.

Another proposed theory suggests that metabolic rate and oxygen consumption are important determinates of aging. This theory holds that continued damage to cells by reactive oxygen intermediates leads to the symptoms of aging. Reduction in metabolic rate and oxygen consumption would then result in a slowing of the aging process. In support of this idea, long-lived animals do tend to have lower metabolic rates per unit of body mass than short-lived animals. Dietary restriction experiments, however, have produced mixed results, with some studies reporting a decrease in oxygen consumption and others reporting no change. Age of onset of dietary restriction and the manner in which metabolic rate is expressed may explain these discrepancies. Experiments with dietary restriction imposed at weaning have reported no decrease in oxygen consumption per unit of LBM, whereas adult-onset dietary restriction experiments have found decreases in oxygen consumption compared to control animals expressed per animal, per LBM, and per body mass raised to the .75 or .67 power. Experiments reporting no change in metabolic rate with dietary restriction, however, have largely been limited to expression of metabolic rate per LBM. Overall, dietary restriction initiated in adult animals appears to decrease oxygen consumption and this reduction of metabolic rate may play a role in the action of adult dietary restriction.

Free radical production and damage have been proposed as possible causes for many of the symptoms of aging. Under normal conditions, 1–3% of respired oxygen is converted to superoxide radicals at the mitochondria. Coupled with an age-related decrease in free radical defense systems such as superoxide dismutase, catalase and peroxidase, it is easy to see that free radical damage could greatly accumulate with age. Energy restriction, however, has been shown to decrease free radical damage and lipid peroxidation in liver microsomal and mitochondrial membranes. Dietary restriction has also been shown to increase superoxide dismutase and catalase activity and mRNA concentrations by as much as 50%. Inhibition of free radical damage has the potential to be an important contributor to the actions of energy restriction.

Nonenzymatic glycation of proteins and amino acids has also been proposed to be a cause of many of the aspects of aging. Decreases in plasma glucose levels are an established outcome of dietary energy restriction. This would be expected to be associated with a decrease in glycation. Several experiments have also shown that caloric restriction decreases protein glycation. This process also has the potential to be a major contributor to the overall actions of dietary restriction on aging.

It has also been suggested that energy restriction slows down age-related changes in membrane composition, and this may be responsible for many of the effects of this intervention. Dietary restriction appears to decrease age-related increases in cholesterol and to increase membrane fluidity. The membrane composition modifications may change hormonal stimulation and other processes that could contribute to effects of energy restriction on aging.

Energy restriction experiments have shown remarkable results in all animal species studied but have suffered from the fact that no experiments have been attempted on long-lived primate species. Recently, long-term dietary restriction studies have been started with monkeys and have produced very promising results. After more than two years of dietary restriction, restricted monkeys have shown a decrease in blood glucose and insulin and increased insulin sensitivity compared to control animals. Dietary restriction was also shown to result in a slight decrease in glycosylated hemoglobin. This information is encouraging because it appears that many of the results noticed with rodent experiments are also present in long-lived primate species.

Physical exercise is another intervention that has the potential to slow many of the age-related changes in energy metabolism. Physical activity exerts a significant influence on energy intake and total energy expenditure. Several studies have demonstrated that routine exercise increases BMR. Studies with older individuals have also shown that physically active individuals have a higher BMR than sedentary individuals. Similarly, physically active individuals have a lower depression in BMR with advancing age than do sedentary individuals. Physical activity, especially weight training, may increase BMR by increasing

LBM. Experiments have also shown, however, that endurance exercise may increase BMR independently of changes in FFM. Exercise has also been shown to increase food intake and increase the thermic effect of a meal, reversing typical age-related changes. Exercise together with increases in BMR and TEM should result in an increase in total energy expenditure. Care must be taken, however, to ensure that the intensity of an exercise program is not so great as to decrease normal daily activity and thus fail to increase total energy expenditure. Exercise programs that maximize energy expenditure have the potential to slow body composition changes with aging along with improving insulin sensitivity and reducing blood pressure. Some rodent experiments, however, have shown that exercise increases median but not overall length of life. Further research is needed, however, to determine the effect of long-term exercise programs, and exercise in conjunction with moderate dietary restriction, on the length of life.

VI. CONCLUSIONS

The aging process results in changes in nearly all areas of energy metabolism. Energy intake, heat increment, and energy expenditure are all reduced with age. The magnitudes of these changes are generally not proportional, resulting in a negative energy balance with advanced age. In addition to decreases in body mass, aging is associated with a decrease in LBM and a corresponding increase in percent body fat. The aging process is also associated with an overall decrease in all areas of energy expenditure. Decreases in BMR with age have been well established, although most

researchers have also noticed decreases in TEM and activity in the elderly. Additional research is greatly needed to determine the mechanism for most of these age-related changes in energy metabolism.

Dietary energy restriction and exercise are two interventions that offer promise to slow the aging process and offer insight into major processes responsible for age-related physiological problems and diseases. Dietary energy restriction is the only experimental procedure that has consistently been shown to dramatically increase the length of life in warm-blooded animals. Recent research with long-lived primate species suggests that dietary restriction may have similar effects in primates as in other animals. Continued research is needed to determine the primary mechanisms of action through which energy restriction slows the aging process. Exercise also appears to slow many of the age-related changes in energy metabolism, but the effect of long-term exercise programs on the length of life remains to be determined.

BIBLIOGRAPHY

Kemnitz, J. W., Weindruch, R., Roecker, E. B., Crawford, K., Kaufman, P. L. A., & Ershler, W. B. (1993). Dietary restriction of adult rhesus monkeys: Design, methodology, and preliminary findings from the first year of study. *Journal of Gerontology, 48 (1),* B17–B26.

Masoro, E. J. (1993). Dietary restriction and aging. *Journal of the American Geriatrics Society, 41 (9),* 994–999.

Poehlman, E. T. (1993). Regulation of energy expenditure in aging humans. *Journal of the American Geriatrics Society, 41,* 552–559.

Weindruch, R. (in press). Caloric restriction and the puzzle of aging. *Scientific American,* January.

Young, V. R. (1992). Energy requirements in the elderly. *Nutrition reviews, 50 (4),* 95–101.

Body: Composition, Weight, Height, and Build

Alice S. Ryan and Dariush Elahi

University of Maryland at Baltimore

Body Mass Index (BMI) A rough estimate of body fat.
Fat Ether-extractable lipid.
Fat-Free Mass Body weight minus fat mass.
Lean Body Mass Body mass minus ether-extractable fat, includes stroma of adipose tissue.
Visceral Fat (intra-abdominal adipose tissue) Portion of the internal fat in the abdominal cavity lining the intestinal tract.
Waist–Hip Circumference Ratio (WHR) A measure of abdominal fat distribution.

The **COMPOSITION OF THE HUMAN BODY** changes during the entire aging process from development to maturation and during the advancing years (55 and above). The sum of the body components, body weight, also fluctuates during an individual's life span and can influence body build. Taken together with the events during a person's life, it is possible that during the aging process, various disease states can develop. This coexisting phenomena whereby body composition, aging, and disease intertwine provide complex interactions for study. This chapter describes the components of body weight and the various methods currently employed for the determination of body composition. A description of the age-related changes in body composition and how some changes are related to disease will follow.

I. BODY WEIGHT AND ITS CONSTITUENTS

This chapter describes the components of body weight (BW) and the various methods currently employed for the determination of body composition. A description of the age-related changes in body composition and how some changes are related to disease will follow.

BW is composed of the sum of a variety of tissues, the largest component being body water, which comprises approximately 60% of body weight. Body water can be further divided into intracellular (40%) and extracellular (20%) components. As an example, a young man's BW may be composed of 60% water, 7% skeleton, 18% protein, and 15% fat. These separate entities differ among individuals and change by gender during the aging process. Furthermore, an excessive increase or loss of various body components are associated with disease. In order to document these alterations and their health consequences, various methods have been developed to assess these changes in body composition.

Body weight is easily and accurately measurable. Recommended BWs as a function of height are based on various tables and provide some aid in assessing obesity. These tables are based on the impact of weight

Table I Comparison of the Weight-for-Height Tables from Actuarial Data: Non-Age-Corrected Metropolitan Life Insurance Company and Age-Specific Gerontology Research Center Recommendations

Height (ft and in)	Metropolitan 1983 weights[a] (25–59 yr)		Gerontology Research Center[a] (Age-specific weight range for men and women)				
	Men	Women	20–29 yr	29–39 yr	39–49 yr	50–59 yr	60–69 yr
4 10		100–131	84–111	92–119	99–127	107–135	115–142
4 11		101–134	87–115	95–123	103–131	111–139	119–147
5 0		103–137	90–119	98–127	106–135	114–143	123–152
5 1	123–145	105–140	93–123	101–131	110–140	118–148	127–157
5 2	125–148	108–144	96–127	105–136	113–144	122–153	131–163
5 3	127–151	111–148	99–131	108–140	117–149	126–158	135–168
5 4	129–155	114–152	102–135	112–145	121–154	130–163	140–173
5 5	131–159	117–156	106–140	115–149	125–159	134–168	144–179
5 6	133–163	120–160	109–144	119–154	129–164	138–174	148–184
5 7	135–167	123–164	112–148	122–159	133–169	143–179	153–190
5 8	137–171	126–167	116–153	126–163	137–174	147–184	158–196
5 9	139–175	129–170	119–157	130–168	141–179	151–190	162–201
5 10	141–179	132–173	122–162	134–173	145–184	156–195	167–207
5 11	144–183	135–176	126–167	137–178	149–190	160–201	172–213
6 0	147–187		129–171	141–183	153–195	165–207	177–219
6 1	150–192		133–176	145–188	157–200	169–213	182–225
6 2	153–197		137–181	149–194	162–206	174–219	187–232
6 3	157–202		141–186	153–199	166–212	179–225	192–238
6 4			144–191	157–205	171–218	184–231	197–244

[a] Values in this table are for height without shoes and weight without clothes.

on total mortality and do not consider specific disease states. Overweight is defined as 20% over the weight-for-height recommendations according to the various Metropolitan Life Insurance Company tables. Separate tables are provided for men and women. These tables have not been uniformly accepted because of possible sample bias and the necessity of choosing body frame. Furthermore, the tables published in 1942, 1959, and 1983 have increasing desirable optimal weights; some investigators prefer the use of the 1959 table. The recommended weights are applicable only to healthy individuals and not to those whose medical conditions affect BW. Thus, BW recommendations for older individuals are difficult. The Gerontology Research Center (GRC) of the National Institute of Aging has developed age-specific weight for height ranges that are applicable to both genders (Table I) and that have also been recommended by the National Research Council and the U.S. Department of Agriculture (USDA). This table better represents the changes in BW with age and allows for increases in weight by decade from 20 to 69 years. The increased weight allowance in the age-specific table is close to 10 lbs per decade.

Another estimate of obesity, which also uses both height and weight but combines these measurements into one value, is the Quetelet Index or body mass index (BMI). This measurement takes into account the height of an individual because it would be expected that weight should increase as a function of height. This index is calculated as weight divided by height squared (kg/m^2). Normal standards for BMI are in the range of 20–27 kg/m^2 for women and 20–25 kg/m^2 for men. Persons with a BMI between 25 and 30 kg/m^2 are defined as overweight, whereas those with a BMI greater than 30 are considered obese. Age-adjusted BMI and the acceptable range for normal weight from the GRC-recommended table is presented in Table II. Another parameter calculated from height and weight is body surface area, which like

Table II Computation of Body Mass Index from the Age-Specific Gerontology Research Center Recommendations

Age range	Lower limit (kg/m²)	Average (kg/m²)	Upper limit (kg/m²)
20–29	17.6	20.4	23.3
30–39	19.2	22.1	25.0
40–49	20.8	23.7	26.6
50–59	22.4	25.3	28.2
60–69	24.0	26.9	29.8

BMI gives an estimate of obesity but does not determine the components of BW. The reduction in height that occurs with aging (compression of vertebral disks) does not significantly affect any of the estimates of BW described above. Various methods have been developed that provide good estimates of body composition that are more predictive of risk conditions than weight and height alone.

II. MEASUREMENT OF BODY COMPOSITION

Direct measurement of body composition is obtained only from cadaver analysis. Results from these studies provide normative weight data on tissues and organs and are highly accurate. However, because this method cannot be used during an individual's life span, indirect methods have been developed to accurately assess body composition; they can be used repeatedly in clinical and research settings across the age span. The constituents of body composition and the currently available tools for their measurement will be discussed below.

A. Total Body Composition

Numerous methods exist for the measurement of total body fat and regional adiposity. In a two-compartment model for the measurement of body composition, BW is divided into fat (F) and fat-free mass (FFM), (BW = F + FFM). FFM is further divided into five fat-free components, namely water, osseous and cellular mineral, protein, and glycogen. Most indirect measurements of total body fat are based on compositional differences between the estimated weight of lean and fat tissues and their respective densities. Although FFM and lean body mass (LBM) are often used interchangeably, they are slightly different. Excluded in the estimated mass of fat is the soluble fat component, (i.e., the ether-soluble fraction of the adipose tissue and fat stored in nonadipose tissue sites). Thus, FFM includes the water and protein fractions of adipose tissue. LBM equals BW minus weight of adipose tissue. LBM does not include the weight of water and protein fractions of adipose tissue. The methods that are currently used to make measurements using the two-compartment model are hydrodensitometry, isotope dilution, and total body potassium. Methods such as bioelectrical impedance, total body electrical conductivity, and urinary 3-methylhistidine and urinary creatinine are other alternatives. A three-compartment model of body composition composed of fat, FFM, and bone mineral content is assessed by either dual-photon or dual-energy X-ray absorptiometry (DXA). For determination of the multielemental body compartments, neutron activation analysis (NAA), prompt gamma neutron activation analysis (PGNA), delayed-gamma-neutron activation analysis (DGNA), and inelastic neutron scattering can be used. Regional adiposity and muscle mass are estimated with computed tomography (CT), magnetic resonance imaging (MRI), or sonography. A brief description of these various techniques follows. Several review papers discuss each method in great detail, and textbooks on this topic are available.

1. Hydrodensitometry

Hydrodensitometry or underwater weighing, considered for many years the "gold standard" for measuring body fat, is based upon the Archimedes principle whereby the volume of a mass = volume of liquid displaced by that solid. Thus, BW in the air and water are measured to determine body density (D_b). Percent fat is determined with the equations described by anthropometry pioneers Siri and Brozek as

Siri: percent fat = $4.95/D_b - 4.5$

Brozek et al.: percent fat = $4.570/D_b - 4.142$.

Fat mass and FFM are then calculated. Residual lung volume must be determined prior to or during underwater weighing using either the helium or nitrogen dilution methods. Fat and FFM values in adults are assumed to have reference values (0.9007 g/ml and 1.10 g/ml, respectively), which may not be accurate in women, athletes, or the elderly. Furthermore, this technique assumes adequate subject hydration, a fasted state, and a 100-ml volume of intestinal gas.

2. Isotope Dilution

The measurement of total body water (TBW) is made with the isotope dilution method. The method of TBW is based on the assumption that the ratio of water weight to FFM equals 0.732. Therefore, FFM is calculated as body water/0.732 and Fat mass = BW − FFM. Body water may be estimated with the dilution of labeled water using heavy isotopes of hydrogen (deuterium, D_2O) and/or oxygen ($H_2^{18}O$, $D_2^{18}O$) or radioactive water using tritiated hydrogen (^3H_2O), usually administered orally. Measurement of TBW relies on the relationship that $C_1V_1 = C_2V_2$, where C_1 equals the concentration of the ingested isotope, V_1 equals the volume of the ingested isotope, C_2 equals the concentration of the isotope in the body after equilibration (as in plasma, saliva or urine), and V_2 equals the volume to be determined or TBW. The concentration of the tracer is measured both before and after its equilibration in the body compartment and volume is mathematically determined. The assumptions of this technique are (a) C_2 is completely at equilibrium in each body compartment at the time of measurement, (b) the isotope has not been incorporated with any body constituent other than the tracer (water), and (c) between administration of the tracer and its measurement, there has been a stable state with respect to influx and efflux of the tracee into the water compartments of the body. TBW is overestimated by about 4% for D_2O and ^2H_2O due to the exchange with hydrogen in labile nonaqueous compounds such that the tracer may be lost as the hydrogen breaks off and becomes part of another cellular compartment. With ^{18}O, the stable oxygen of water exchanges with the oxygen of bicarbonate in the blood, and thus $H_2^{18}O$ has an error of about 1%. Stable oxygen is very costly and the supply is rather limited. Furthermore, all methods require skilled personnel and sophisticated measuring techniques and equipment. Tritiated water (^3H_2O) also involves radiation exposure.

3. Total Body Potassium

Total body potassium (TBK) is used to estimate LBM because the ratio of potassium (K) to LBM is relatively constant. From cadaver and in vivo studies, the ratio of K/LBM is generally accepted to be 68.1 Meq K/kg LBM in men and 64.2 Meq K/kg LBM in women. In this method ^{40}K, a naturally occurring radioisotope, is detected by a sensitive gamma ray detector placed close to the subject in a heavily shielded room. TBK is then mathematically determined from the measured ^{40}K. Although this method has an accuracy of approximately 3–4%, is nontraumatic, and noninvasive, it is very expensive and technical. It should also be noted that measurement of ^{40}K may be erroneous in potassium-depleted states.

4. Anthropometry

Anthropometry values, such as those obtained by skinfold thickness and limb circumferences, can be used in multiple-regression equations to predict body density and to calculate body fatness and FFM. Skinfold thicknesses can be taken in several sites, such as bicep, tricep, suprailiac, subscapular, thigh, and abdomen. The measurement of skinfold thickness is based on two assumptions: (a) the thickness of the subcutaneous adipose tissue reflects a constant proportion of the total body fat, and (b) the sites selected for measurement represent the average thickness of the subcutaneous adipose tissue. The validity of using skinfold equations to predict body composition is restricted to populations from whom these equations were derived. Other contributing factors to error in this technique include the biological variation in fat in other depots such as intermuscular, intramuscular, and fat surrounding organs and the gastrointestinal tract. For additional information on anthropometry a comprehensive manual provides details for measurement procedures and standardized techniques for more than forty anthropometric measurements.

5. Bioelectrical Impedance and Total Body Electrical Conductivity

Both BIA and TOBEC are based upon the assumption that fat acts as an insulator and FFM conducts electrical current. Body fluids and cell membranes are responsible for conductance and capacitance (low impedance) respectively, whereas bone, fat, and triglyceride are nonconductive and have high impedance. BIA is based upon the principle that the impedance of a geometrical system is related to conductor length and configuration, its cross-sectional area, and signal frequency. The impedance of the flow can be described as $Z = aL^2/V$, where Z is impedance in ohms, a is volume resistivity in ohm (cm), L is conductor length in centimeters, and V is volume in liters. Impedance can be partitioned into its components, resistance (R) and reactance (Xc): $Z^2 = R^2 + Xc^2$. Electrodes are placed at the wrists and ankles, a small current is introduced, and the resistance to the current is measured. Appropriate regression equations are used to predict FFM and hence fat mass from BW. Misplacement of electrodes can introduce error.

With TOBEC, the differences in electrical conductivity and dielectric properties of the fat-free and fat tissues are used to determine body composition. While the subject lies on a carriage that moves through a coil, the change in impedance and amplitude for the signal when the coil induces the current to the body is measured and provides a measurement of FFM. This instrument requires a large amount of space and is expensive but is quick and affords great ease to the subject. An important assumption for both BIA and TOBEC is a balanced hydration state such that either dehydration or fluid overload reduces the accuracy of FFM.

6. Dual-Photon Absorptiometry and DXA

Both dual-photon absorptiometry (DPA) and DXA allow separation of body mass into bone mineral, fat tissue, and fat-free soft tissue, a three-compartment model. For DPA, a whole-body scanner frame, a NaI(Tl) (sodium iodide) detector, and the radionuclide source, 153 Gd (gadolinium) with energies of 44 and 100 keV, distinguish between bone and soft tissue. DXA has essentially replaced DPA has an X-ray source with two photon energies of 38 and 70 keV. This is a more stable source of radiation, and unlike the 153 Gd source does not have to be changed because of radionuclide decay. Furthermore, DXA has greater precision and accuracy than DPA. A measure of the soft-tissue attenuation at the two energy levels is referred to as the Rst. The Rst correlates inversely with the proportion of soft tissue as fat. The ease that DXA affords the subject makes it an attractive alternative for body composition assessment in the elderly or those who may fear submergence in the water with hydrodensitometry. Furthermore, DXA directly determines bone mineral content, and because bone mass declines with age, this method may provide greater accuracy in body composition determination in the aged population. Radiation ex-

posure, albeit small, and the high cost of the instrument are considerations that may limit the use of this method. In addition, body thickness may also affect mineral and fat estimates. The small scanning width of the current instruments may be too small for obese subjects to fit within, thereby underestimating bone mineral, fat tissue, and fat-free tissue in these subjects.

7. Urinary 3-methlyhistidine and Creatinine Excretion

Muscle mass analysis can be determined by techniques such as urinary 3-methlyhistidine (3-MH) excretion and urinary creatinine excretion. Creatinine and 3-MH are end products of muscle metabolism that cannot be further metabolized. They are excreted quantitatively in the urine and are directly proportional to muscle mass. High-performance liquid chromotography is conducted to determine a peak value of absorption of these products. Day-to-day variability, complete and accurate urine collections, and the need to comply to a meat-free diet prior to analysis are requirements of these methods that limit the accuracy of this technique.

8. Neutron Activation Analysis

Neutron activation analysis (NAA) is the only technique available for the measurement of the multi-elemental composition the body. In general, a moderated beam of fast neutrons is delivered to the subject. Unstable isotopes are created and are reverted to a stable condition by emission of one or more gamma rays of characteristic energy. The induced radioactivity is measured in a whole body counter. The energy level identifies the element, and the level of activity indicates its abundance. Neutron activation can be used for determination of Ca, Cl, K, P, N, Mg, and Na. Specifically, a method known as prompt gamma neutron activation (PGNA) analysis measures total body nitrogen. Nitrogen (^{14}N) is excited to ^{15}N and gamma rays. Delayed gamma neutron activation (DGNA) analysis allows the measurement of total body mineral through the excitation of ^{48}Ca to ^{49}Ca and gamma rays. Using appropriate equations, total body fat can be calculated with the estimation of total body protein by PGNA, bone mineral by DGNA, and body water by isotope dilution. Another system, inelastic neutron scattering, can provide an estimate of total body carbon. A miniature deuterium-tritium accelerator generates fast neutrons that result in gamma rays produced from ^{12}C. The model assumes that total body carbon is distributed to a certain percent in fat, protein, glycogen, and bone ash. Using the measurement of total body carbon, nitrogen, and calcium, total body fat can be estimated. Although NAA can provide valuable information, it is very costly, requires a high radiation dose and highly skilled investigators, and presently there are few facilities in the world where it can be performed.

A modification of this method uses simultaneous measurements of the ratio of body carbon-to-oxygen with large $Bi_4Ge_3O_{18}$ (bismuth-germanium-oxygen, BGO) crystal detectors. The signal-to-background ratio for the carbon detection is vastly improved (sixfold) compared to the NaI(Tl) detectors, and the method also allows for the measurement of regional body fat. The basis for this modification is the large differences in carbon and oxygen content betwen fat and lean tissue. The technical aspects of this modification have been published, and its accuracy has been validated against hydrodensitometry in humans. Additional advantages include a significant reduction in radiation exposure (much less than a chest X ray) and cost of operation (by more than two-thirds). The validation report from the Body Composition Laboratory at USDA Human Nutrition Research Center on Aging at Tufts University is in press (J. J. Kehayias).

B. Regional Assessment

1. Computerized Tomography

Regional adiposity and skeletal muscle mass can be determined with CT. This approach relates small differences in X-ray attenuation to differences in the physical density of tissues. The scanner computer constructs a two-dimensional image of the underlying anatomy in the scan area. The cross-sectional area of adipose, bone, and muscle can be determined for each image. Because thickness is known, relative surface area or volume can be calculated. Furthermore, CT scans of the abdominal region, typically performed at the L4-L5 region, assess both subcutaneous and intra-abdominal (visceral) adipose tissue and are highly accurate. This method is also used for measurement of muscle mass in the thigh, calf, or other regions of interest. Because of the relatively large exposure to ionizing radiation (compared to DXA), routine whole-body scans and multiple scans in the same individual limit the use of CT. Also, the cost and availabil-

ity of modern CT scanners prohibit routine use. Recently, researchers have lowered the radiation dose and have applied multiple scan slices across the total body in order to estimate total body fat.

2. Magnetic Resonance Imaging

MRI also quantitates total fat mass and discriminates differences in regional fat and muscle tissue. MRI is based on the principle that atomic nuclei behave like magnets. An external magnetic field is applied across a part of the body. Each nucleus or magnetic moment attempts to align with the external magnetic field. A radio frequency wave is used simultaneously to rotate the nuclei $90°$ to the magnetic field. The absorbed energy from the activated nuclei is released when the radio frequency is shut off. This radio signal is used to develop an image and thus a clear determination of adipose and muscle tissue. In contrast to CT, MRI does not use ionizing radiation. Its restricted availability and high cost also limit its use in body composition assessment. Similar to CT, MRI can quantify intra-abdominal adipose tissue and subcutaneous fat of the abdomen as well as appendicular muscle mass.

3. Sonography

To determine abdominal fat using ultrasound the patient lies in a recumbent position and subcutaneous thickness and intra-abdominal fat are measured next to the umbilicus in the xypho-umbilical line. Either a 5-mHz or a 7.5-mHz transducer is used to measure subcutaneous fat thickness, whereas intra-abdominal fat is measured using a 3.5-mHz transducer. Using images on the screen, the thickness of subcutaneous fat is measured with calipers placed at the skin-fat and fat-muscle interfaces, and that of visceral fat at the internal face of muscle and the anterior wall of the aorta. Ultrasound measurements for the determination of intra-abdominal fat is a relatively new technique. Both subcutaneous and visceral fat by ultrasound are significantly correlated with that determined by CT in obese women across the age span. Sonography requires a skilled operator, but because it is safe, noninvasive, does not involve radiation exposure, and the imager is widely available, it could potentially substitute for CT or MRI if these methods are unavailable.

4. Anthropometrics

The regional distribution of body fat can be estimated by the simple ratio of waist circumference to hip circumference (WHR). A WHR of >0.8 is generally considered to be upper body obese and one below as lower body obese. WHR correlates with CT and MRI analysis of abdominal tissue. Other simple measures of regional obesity can be made with circumferences from other parts of the body as well as depths, breadth, and skinfold measurements. For example, the measurement of abdominal sagittal diameter is an indicator of central obesity. Several researchers have developed predictive equations with the use of CT as the criterion method to estimate intra-abdominal adipose tissue. These equations utilize simple anthropometry, DXA measures, and the combination of the two to estimate intra-abdominal adipose tissue.

III. CHANGES IN BODY COMPOSITION DURING AGING

Weight, BMI, and the components of body composition are altered in the aging process. In healthy people BW increases gradually from early adulthood until the fifth to sixth decade, after which weight tends to plateau. The National Health and Nutrition Examination Surveys (NHANES) have examined the prevalence and trends of overweight U.S. adults from 1960 to 1991. The results of their surveys indicate that the prevalence of being overweight has increased during this time period in both men and women in three races (non-Hispanic, Mexican-American, and African-American) (Table III). Currently, approximately one-third of all adults in the United States are estimated to be overweight. Moreover, BMI levels and BW increased 1 kg/m² (approximately 3.5 kg) from 1988 to 1991. BMI computed from the weight for height table (Table I) indicate that average BMIs for the third and fourth decades are 20.4 kg/m² and 22.1 kg/m² and increase by 1.6 kg/m² each decade thereafter (Table II).

Not only does an increase in BW accompanied by a loss of height occur with age, but the various components of the body change during the aging process. Skeletal muscle, bone mass, and body water decline and fat mass increases.

Peak FFM in males is reached in the mid-thirties and then progressively declines. In females, FFM remains relatively stable until approximately age 50, upon which the decline in FFM occurs at a slower rate than males. A number of studies have demonstrated an average loss of FFM of approximately 16% between the ages of 25 and 70 years. The loss of muscle mass with age results in reductions in muscular strength and aerobic fitness in older individuals. Accompanying this loss of FFM, there is a concomitant increase in percent fat. A 30-year-old male's body fat averages approximately 18%, which increases to 26% by age 70. The comparable increase from 24 years to 70 years in women is 24 to 36%.

The components of FFM (i.e., water, protein, and mineral) vary such that changes in total body protein and total body nitrogen with age are documented. These losses confirm the muscle loss with aging. The loss of muscle mass is strongly associated with a loss of body water. Total body water accounts for approximately 80% of FFM at birth. In young adults, TBW comprises approximately 72% of FFM. Thus, a loss of body water occurs until maturity but remains relatively constant throughout adulthood and middle age. Total body water on average is lower in females than males. Losses of body water occur after age 70 in females and somewhat earlier in males with a nadir at this age (70–80 years). It is unclear whether the loss in TBW is due to a decrease in intracellular water, extracellular water, or a combination of the two, but most studies agree that TBW is decreased in elderly subjects and even more so in the very old. The decline in TBW suggests a change in the hydration of the fat-free compartment (increased with normal aging), although definitive conclusions are lacking.

In addition to the losses of LBM and TBW with age, the loss of bone mass is consistently documented. Peak bone mineral mass is reached at age 30–35 years followed by a progressive decline. Bone mass is related to BW, FFM, and fat mass. By age 70, spinal bone mineral density (BMD) is diminished by approximately 20% in women, slightly less than the 25% loss observed in the femoral neck. Men lose BMD at a rate that is two-thirds that of women in the spine and a quarter in the femur, which may explain the reduced fracture risk and rate in males. Relative risk is also site specific, and regional adiposity specifically in the hip may be protective against fracture. Furthermore, the rate of bone loss varies with site and may be greater in areas with more travecular bone than those areas of predominantly compact bone. Total body mineral may decline at a slower rate than the decline observed in specific sites. A more dramatic loss of bone mass occurs during menopause. The loss

Table III Age-Adjusted and Age-Specific Prevalence of Overweight; U.S. Population 20–74 Years of Age[a]

Population group	Prevalence of overweight by study (%)			
	NHES I (1960–1962)[b]	NHANES I (1971–1974)	NHANES II (1976–1980)	NHANES III Phase 1 (1988–1991)
Age 20–74 years	24.3	25.0	25.4	33.3
Race/Sex				
White				
Men	23.0	23.8	24.2	32.0
Women	23.6	24.0	24.4	33.5
Black				
Men	22.1	23.9	26.2	31.8
Women	41.6	43.1	44.5	49.2
Sex/Age, years				
Men				
20–74	22.8	23.7	24.1	31.7
20–29	18.4	15.7	15.1	20.2
30–39	21.8	28.4	24.4	27.4
40–49	25.5	30.2	32.4	37.0
50–59	28.8	27.1	28.2	42.1
60–74	23.0	21.6	26.8	40.9
Women				
20–74	25.7	26.0	26.5	34.9
20–29	10.1	12.6	14.7	20.2
30–39	21.9	22.9	23.8	34.3
40–49	26.8	29.7	29.0	37.6
50–59	35.0	35.5	36.5	52.0
60–74	45.6	39.0	37.3	41.3

[a] Pregnant women excluded. NHES indicates National Health Examination Survey; NHANES, National Health and Nutrition Examination Survey.

[b] A total of 0.9 kg was subtracted from measured weight to adjust for weight of clothing.

of bone mineral with age would contradict the assumption of a constant mineral concentration in the FFM across different ages, especially in women. This could impact the density of FFM, although this is currently controversial and additional research is needed. Many factors influence both peak bone mass and its loss, including nutritional state, physical activity levels, disease (e.g., hyperparathyroidism, etc.), genetics, certain drugs (glucocorticoids, anticonvulsants), alcoholism, smoking, immobilization, and hormonal status. [See BONE AND OSTEOPOROSIS.]

Changes also occur in the amount and location of body fat deposition with age. Body fat tends to accumulate in the abdominal region with increases in both subcutaneous and visceral fat. This change is somewhat greater in males than females. Thus, there is an age-related redistribution of fat to the central and intra-abdominal region. Visceral adiposity has been implicated as a causative factor in metabolic disorders.

IV. BODY COMPOSITION AND RELATIONSHIP TO DISEASE

The significant changes in BW, height, and composition that occur in the aging process affect health and can promote an increase in propensity to disease. Furthermore, mortality and morbidity are related to these changes. Mortality rate is lowest within an optimal weight range. Research suggests that the weight gain observed in aging should be maintained into very old age and that relative high body weights in the elderly population are associated with the lowest mortality.

In contrast, a very low BMI is associated with a higher mortality. Thus, those underweight (low BMI) and those overweight (high BMI) have the highest mortality. The health implications of being overweight and obesity generally support a higher relative risk in the aged. Specifically, the increase in obesity is associated with increased prevalence of cardiovascular (CV) disease, hyperlipidemia, hypertension, insulin resistance, and diabetes.

The risk of CV disease is higher in the overweight and obese. Numerous studies have shown that increased BW associated with aging as well as fat distribution are accountable for abnormal lipid concentrations, thus increasing the risk for CV disease. The relative risk of hypercholesterolemia (defined as a level of 250 mg/dl or higher) in adults aged 20–25 years is 1.5-fold higher in overweight than nonoverweight individuals. Between the ages 20–44, the relative risk is 2.1 times higher in overweight versus nonoverweight adults. In the age range 45–75 years, being overweight is not associated with increased risk of hypercholesterolemia. The risk is higher in overweight black men, compared to overweight white men, white women, and black women. [See Cardiovascular System.]

The NHANES surveys demonstrate that the relative risk of hypertension, defined as systolic blood pressure of 160 mmHg or higher and diastolic blood pressure of 95 mmHg or higher in adults aged 20–75 years, is threefold higher in overweight than nonoverweight individuals. Between the ages of 20–44 years and 45–75 years, the relative risk of hypertension in overweight individuals is 5.6 times and 1.9 times higher than nonoverweight adults, respectively.

Compared to white men, the prevalence of diabetes in adults aged 20–75 years is 30, 70, and 100% higher in white women, black men, and black women, respectively. The relative risk of diabetes in adults aged 20–75 years is three-fold higher in the overweight versus the nonoverweight. Between the ages of 20–44 years and 45–74 years, the relative risk is 3.8 and 2.1 times higher in overweight than nonoverweight adults, respectively.

In addition to the quantity of fat in the body, the location of fat plays a dominant role in determining whether obesity is detrimental and its influence on risk factors for disease. This is illustrated with the measurement of WHR such that a high WHR is significantly correlated to CV disease, noninsulin-dependent diabetes mellitus, and hypertension. This regional obesity with preferential deposition of body fat in the trunk region is independently associated with CV disease and related mortality. In contrast, fat deposition in the periphery does not show an increased risk for heart disease. In addition, upper body obesity is associated with glucose intolerance, hyperinsulinemia, and insulin resistance. More precise measures of upper obesity, including intra-abdominal adipose tissue by CT or MRI, are associated with insulin resistance and an atherogenic profile.

Other changes in body composition, such as the loss of BMD, are related to disease states. This age-related decline in bone mass results in a decrease in bone mass and strength that may lead to an increase in fractures in the vertebral bodies, proximal femur, and distal radius, a disease otherwise known as osteoporosis. To illustrate, the risk of hip fracture triples with each 10% decrease in femur BMD. Because men have higher bone mass than women throughout the life span, and BMD declines at a slower rate in males than females, the incidence of osteoporosis is lower in males.

The age-related changes in BW and body composition are associated with a number of diseases. These changes, which can be documented by a variety of methods currently available depending upon the resources and the population being studied, are influenced by nutrition, activity, genetics, and economic and social concerns.

BIBLIOGRAPHY

Anonymous (1983). Metropolitan height and weight tables. *Statistical Bulletin, 4,* 2–9.

Bjorntorp, P., & Brodoff, B. N. (Eds.). (1992). *Obesity.* New York: J. P. Lippincott.

Bray, G. A. (Ed.). (1989). *The medical clinics of North America: Obesity* vol. 73(1). Philadelphia: W. B. Saunders Company.

Brownell, K. D., & Fairburn, C. G. (Eds.). (1995). *Eating disorders and obesity.* New York: Guilford Publications.

Ellis, K. J., & Eastman, J. D. (Eds.). (1993). *Human body composition: In vivo methods, models, and assessment.* New York: Plenum Press.

Forbes, G. B. (1987). *Human body composition: Growth, aging, nutrition, and activity.* New York: Springer-Verlag.

Kuczmarski, R. J., Flegal, K. M., Campbell, S. M., & Johnson, C. L. (1994). Increasing prevalence of overweight among US adults. *Journal of the American Medical Association, 272,* 205–211.

Lohman, T. G., Roche, A. F., & Martorell, R. (Eds.). (1988). *Anthropometric standardization reference manual.* Champaign, IL. Human Kinetics Books.

Bone and Osteoporosis

Dike N. Kalu and Richard L. Bauer

University of Texas Health Science Center at San Antonio

Bone Densitometry Determination of bone mass by measurement of the differential absorption of an X-ray beam by bone and soft tissue.

Bone Loss A decrease in bone mass from the peak bone mass level due to a variety of factors, including menopause.

Bone Mass Amount of bone an individual has.

Bone Remodeling Breakdown and reformation of bone; occurs throughout life.

Cancellous Bone Bone type consisting of interconnecting spicules and plates or trabeculae; also called trabecular or spongy bone.

Colony-Stimulating Factors (CSFs) Secreted by marrow cells and regulate the development of hematopoietic progenitor cells.

Compact Bone Bone type that appears visually as a homogeneous dense tissue.

Growth Factors Polypeptides secreted by cells; act in autocrine–paracrine fashion.

Osteopetrosis A disorder characterized by dense bone due to a failure of osteoclastic bone resorption.

Osteoporosis A disorder of bone characterized by a diminished quantity of bone and increased susceptibility to fracture.

Peak Bone Mass The maximum amount of bone acquired by an individual.

The tremendous interest in bone research relates largely to the need to develop effective strategies for preventing and managing the age-related **BONE LOSS** that leads to **OSTEOPOROSIS** in an increasing number of elderly people. This number will continue to rise, especially in the Western world where people are living longer, unless successful antiosteoporosis programs are implemented. With our incomplete understanding of the pathogenesis of bone loss and a cure for osteoporosis still elusive, the momentum of research on bone and osteoporosis will most certainly spill into the next century. This chapter is in two parts. The first part focuses on the basic biology of bone and serves as a background for the second part, which deals with osteoporosis.

I. BONE

A. Bone Function and the Skeletal System

The endoskeleton of mammals, including humans, often persists for millions of years as fossil bones that serve as poignant reminders of life lived long ago. The stability of the endoskeleton has left the impression in the minds of many that bone is a static, inert, permanent structure. This is not true. Mature bone is, in fact, a very dynamic tissue that is constantly being broken down and re-formed by a process known as bone remodeling. Because of its rigidity, the skeleton serves to support and maintain the shape of the body, protects vital organs and tissues within the cavities of the cranium, thorax, vertebral column, and long bones, and aids locomotion by transmitting the force of muscular contraction from one part of the body to another. The structure of bone is ideally suited to its mechanical functions. Bone is a specialized connective tissue composed of an extracellular organic matrix impregnated with an inorganic component. The combination of mineral and organic material accounts for the great strength of bone and its ability to withstand stress.

Bone serves as a reservoir of ions and contains 99% of the calcium in our body. It is a calcium bank from which calcium can be drawn when dietary sources are deficient. Thus, bone plays an important role in maintaining optimum concentration of extracellular calcium, which is critical to the regulation of diverse physiological processes, including muscle contraction, neuromuscular excitability, cardiac rhythmicity, membrane permeability, exocytotic secretion of macromolecules, blood clotting, mitotic activity, and many enzyme reactions. In addition to being the storehouse for calcium, bone is home to marrow within which blood cells are formed. Marrow is also a source of hemopoietic progenitors of osteoclasts, stromal cell progenitors of osteoblasts, and of growth factors and cytokines that act locally within the bone microenvironment to regulate bone remodeling. Accordingly, marrow cells and cytokines have been implicated in the etiology of the imbalance in the opposing activities of bone-resorbing and bone-forming cells that impair remodeling and lead to osteoporosis.

B. Organization of the Skeleton

Architecturally, the skeleton is organized in two parts: the appendicular skeleton consists of bones of the limbs, and the axial skeleton includes the vertebral column, the ribs, the sternum, and the bones of the cranium. Although bone is a hemopoietic organ in growing individuals, following maturity the appendicular skeleton converts to a mostly fatty marrow and is no longer an important site for hemopoiesis, whereas hemopoiesis continues throughout life within the bones of the axial skeleton. Bone turnover is generally higher in bones containing hemopoietic marrow than in those containing fatty marrow.

Macroscopically, bone is of two types: cancellous and cortical bone. Cancellous bone consists of thin interconnecting spicules and plates or trabeculae and is also called trabecular or spongy bone. In between the spicules are cavities filled with marrow. Cancellous bone is present as a component of the axial and appendicular skeleton particularly in vertebral bodies and the ends of long bones. In contrast to cancellous bone, human compact bone appears visually as a homogeneous, dense tissue, but microscopically it is riddled with small channels containing blood vessels. Compact bone makes up about 80% of skeletal mass and is found in the bones of the appendicular skeleton, especially in the diaphyses of long bones as well as around all bones. In reality, different bones contain different proportions of cancellous and cortical bones. For example, ulna and vertebra contain about 10 and 40% cancellous bone, and 90 and 60% cortical bone, respectively. The medullary cavities of long bones contain marrow that is contiguous with marrow in the lattices of cancellous bone compartments.

Because of its extensive lattice structure, only 15–25% of cancellous bone volume consists of calcified tissue. The rest is mainly marrow and blood vessels. Consequently, cancellous bone tissue has a large surface-to-volume ratio and is in close proximity to blood. Because the surface of cancellous bone is lined by a large number of cells, it is very metabolically active and sensitive to factors that decrease or augment bone mass. In contrast, calcified bone accounts for 80–90% of compact bone. Therefore, compact bone has a small surface-to-volume ratio; it is less metabolically active than cancellous bone, and it is mainly responsible for the mechanical and protective functions of bone.

C. Bone Composition

Bone consists of inorganic and organic components. The inorganic component accounts for about 65% of the dry weight of bone, and consists primarily of calcium phosphate crystals similar to crystalline hydroxyapatite, some amorphous calcium phosphate salts, and small amounts of other ionic species, such as Na^+, Mg^{2+}, Cl^-, F^-, CO_3^{2+}, and citrate. Organic compounds make up the remaining 35% of the dry weight of bone. About 90% of the organic component is collagen, a common extracellular matrix protein composed of three polypeptides that form an extremely stable triple helical molecule. Bone contains mainly type I collagen, which is a heteropolymer of two $\alpha 1$ and one $\alpha 2$ chains. Hydroxyproline and the pyridinium cross-links of collagen, pyridinoline, and deoxypyridinoline, are released from bone matrix during bone resorption and are measured in urine as indices of bone resorption. Pyridinium cross-links are more specific for bone collagen than urine hydroxyproline, which also derives from extraosseous collagen. During bone formation, carboxyterminal propeptide of type I procollagen is released from bone and is measured in blood as a specific index of bone formation.

The remaining 10% of the organic matrix of bone consists of noncollagen proteins. About 25% of these are adsorbed to bone matrix from circulating proteins, such as serum albumin and platelet-derived growth factor. The other noncollagen proteins present in bone matrix are proteoglycans, proteins that facilitate cell attachment (such as fibronectin and osteopontin), growth related proteins (such as transforming growth factor-β and insulin-like growth factors I and II [IGF-I, IGF-II]), and vitamin K-dependent γ-carboxylated (gla) proteins (such as osteocalcin [bone-gla-protein] and matrix-gla-protein, which have calcium-binding properties). Osteocalcin is present mainly in bone and is measured in biological fluids as a specific marker of the rate of bone turnover and perhaps of bone formation.

D. Bone Cells

1. Osteoblasts

There are three principal types of bone cells: osteoblasts, osteocytes, and osteoclasts. The osteoblastic lineage is composed of mature osteoblasts, osteocytes, and lining cells that are found on trabecular and intracortical bone surfaces. Mature osteoblasts are mononucleated cells that contain large amounts of alkaline phosphatase. They have basophilic cytoplasm and the fine structure of cells actively involved in protein synthesis and secretion, such as extensive rough endoplasmic reticulum and well-developed Golgi apparatus. Osteoblasts synthesize and secrete bone collagen and most of the bone matrix proteins previously described. They also participate in activities that lead to the mineralization of bone collagen matrix to form calcified bone through mechanisms that are not completely defined. Osteoblasts derive from mesenchymal and stromal cells in bone and marrow and most likely from the same progenitors as colony-forming units for fibroblasts (CFU-F). CFU-F formed in cultures of bone marrow contain cells that have phenotypic characteristics of osteoblasts, such as staining positively for alkaline phosphatase and forming bone nodules in the presence of β-glycerophosphate.

2. Osteocytes

Osteoblasts that are no longer actively secreting bone matrix eventually become encased in calcified bone formed by new osteoblasts. The enclosed osteoblasts lose much of their prominent rough endoplasmic reticulum and become osteocytes, which are the most abundant bone cell type. Not all osteoblasts survive as osteocytes. Those that survive reside in lacunae and develop long protoplasmic extensions that lie in small canals known as canaliculi. The latter are probably used for transporting nutrients within bone. Functions that have been proposed but not substantiated for osteocytes in bone biology include osteocytic osteolysis, mineral exchange, and repair of microdamage. In addition, recent reports indicate that osteocytes act as mechanosensors that respond to deformation from skeletal loading and relay the information through their protoplasmic extensions; the net effect is appropriate adjustments in bone resorption and formation by osteoclasts and osteoblasts. The network arrangement of osteocytes and their extensive labyrinth of canalicular system are ideally suited for a strain transduction function that is involved in adaptive modeling and remodeling of bone. Osteocytes make contact, by means of their canalicular system, not only with neighboring osteocytes but also with the lining cells that separate calcified bone from the extracellular fluid. It has been postulated that parathyroid hormone acts on these lining cells to regulate the supply of calcium from bone fluid to the extracellular fluid by a mechanism that does not involve bone resorption.

3. Osteoclasts

The third major bone cell type is the osteoclast. Osteoclasts are large multinucleated cells with as many as 10–100 nuclei. They are commonly found on bone surfaces that are undergoing remodeling, and their function is to resorb bone. Osteoclasts are motile and can move around a circumscribed region resorbing calcified bone. A useful though nonspecific marker of osteoclasts is tartrate-resistant acid phosphatase. The enzyme is also found in macrophage polykaryons, which have the same lineage as osteoclasts. Unlike macrophage polykaryons, part of the cell membrane of osteoclasts consists of protoplasmic infoldings that are in intimate contact with bone. Resorption of bone is restricted to this ruffled border located in grooves called Howship's lacunae. To initiate bone resorption, osteoclasts secrete, in the region of the ruffled border, lysosomal enzymes and hydrogen ions the generation of which is catalyzed by carbonic anhydrase type II. The hydrogen ions provide optimum pH for lysosomal enzymes that facilitate organic matrix degradation during bone resorption. Inability of osteoclasts to produce carbonic anhydrase or to form a ruffled border as in c-src oncogene-deficient mice, results in inability to resorb bone and osteopetrosis.

Several observations indicate that osteoblasts, which are best known for their bone-forming function, also play a supporting role in osteoclastic bone resorption. First, osteoblasts, but not osteoclasts, contain receptors for parathyroid hormone and 1,25 (OH)$_2$vitamin D, the main systemic hormones that stimulate bone resorption. Second, these systemic hormones can successfully stimulate osteoclasts to resorb bone only if osteoblasts are present. These observations are consistent with the notion that parathyroid hormone and 1,25(OH)$_2$vitamin D stimulate osteoblasts to produce a soluble factor that, in turn, stimulates osteoclasts to resorb bone. The nature of this coupling factor(s) remains unknown. Osteoclasts are hematopoietic in origin. They appear to arise from a CFU for the granulocyte-macrophage series (CFU-GM), and to be formed from the fusion of mononuclear precursor cells that are present in bone marrow and the circulation.

E. Bone Growth, Modeling, and Remodeling

The amount of bone in the skeleton and the ultimate fate of bone are determined by growth, modeling, and remodeling of bone. In the case of the long bones, their mass is determined by their linear growth and circumferential expansion. Linear bone growth occurs at the growth plate present at the ends of long bones between the epiphysis and diaphysis. Cartilage cells called chondrocytes are present at the proliferative zone of the growth plate and synthesize an organic matrix that is subsequently calcified. The calcified matrix is partially resorbed by osteoclasts leaving a remnant of cartilage on which osteoblasts deposit woven bone to form the trabeculae of the primary spongiosa. As the trabeculae mature, they undergo further remodeling, and the woven bone is resorbed and replaced by lamella bone. This is the secondary spongiosa. Continuous activity of the cartilage cells in the growth plate leads to continuous addition of new bone between the epiphysis and diaphysis and the

elongation of bone. When maturity is attained, these activities cease as the growth plate disappears and the epiphysis fuses with the diaphysis and abrogates linear bone growth. In contrast, circumferential growth of long bones continues throughout life by the addition of new lamellar bone beneath the periosteum through the process of membranous ossification.

During the growing period bones undergo varying degrees of modeling, which is the process that determines their size and shape. Bone modeling involves resorption drifts that progressively remove bone from one surface and formation drifts that add bone to other surfaces. Modeling is regulated by mechanical influences and local and systemic factors and can add new cortical bone to bone cross sections. Like longitudinal bone growth, bone modeling is no longer effective after the attainment of skeletal maturity. In contrast, mature bone continues to be resorbed and reformed throughout life by osteoclasts and osteoblasts through the process known as bone remodeling.

Bone remodeling has several functions. It replaces primary spongiosa with calcified lamellar bone during longitudinal bone growth. It maintains the mechanical competence of mature bone by renewing its components and by preventing or removing areas of fatigue and microdamage within bone. It determines the net amount of bone present at any time, and it provides calcium to the extracellular fluid. Remodeling is initiated by the appearance in bone of osteoclasts at the site to be remodeled, such as the cortical-endosteal surface, trabecular-endosteal surface, or from the surfaces of the channels that course throughout the interior of cortical bone. The osteoclasts resorb a quantum of bone. After a brief period the cavity formed by osteoclasts is lined by osteoblasts that refill the cavity with new bone. Newly formed resorption cavities and those in the process of being refilled with bone are termed basic multicellular units (BMUs). When the refilling is complete, the resultant new bone is the bone structural unit (BSU), Haversian system, or osteon. Thus, bone remodeling occurs in an orderly sequence involving an activation and initiation phase, resorption phase and formation phase, with a reversal phase between resorption and formation. Activation involves the recruitment of mononuclear preosteoclasts to the site to be resorbed where they mature and fuse into osteoclasts. In humans, the resorption phase lasts for about 21 days, and the formation phase is completed in several months. In young adults, the coupling of formation to resorption is balanced and there is no net loss of bone as a result of remodeling.

The rate of bone remodeling is modulated by a wide variety of factors, including mechanical factors, gender, hormones, calcium homeostatic challenge, and drugs. Furthermore, defects in bone remodeling occur with aging and can be expressed in several ways: The resorption cavities could become too large; there could be too many of them, and their refilling with new bone could be delayed, slowed, or incomplete. Any of these or their combination can result in less bone. Currently, it is not clear what initiates the activation of BMUs, and what controls their birthrate, number, and life span during a remodeling remains an enigma. Furthermore, it is not known how osteoclasts or their precursors are attracted to bone sites destined to be resorbed, and the signals for terminating osteoclastic bone resorption and initiating osteoblastic bone formation are equally unclear. The clarification of these uncertainties about bone remodeling is crucial and remains the subject of intense research, because the bone loss that occurs with aging in humans likely results from defects in bone remodeling. These defects may be secondary to alterations in the secretion and activities of systemic hormones and growth factors that regulate bone remodeling, such as parathyroid hormone (PTH), thyroxine and growth hormone, which accelerate it, and estrogen and calcitonin, which probably retard it. Of the systemic hormones, the best studied, with regard to age-related bone loss, are PTH, calcitonin, $1,25(OH)_2$vitamin D, and estrogen.

1. Systemic Hormones

a. PTH The chief cells of the parathyroids secrete PTH, a peptide with important actions on bone formation, bone resorption, and the regulation of calcium and phosphorus homeostasis. PTH increases calcium release from bone, enhances renal distal tubular reabsorption of calcium, and stimulates the formation of $1,25(OH)_2$vitamin D by inducing the renal synthesis of 1α-hydroxylase. It also inhibits renal proximal tubular reabsorption of phosphate and thereby promotes phosphaturia. When PTH is given by constant infusion, it is catabolic and stimulates osteoclastic bone resorption by increasing the recruitment and differentiation of hematopoietic precursors to form osteoclasts and by promoting the activity of preformed osteoclasts. PTH binds to its receptor on os-

teoblasts and stimulates the release of putative signal factor(s) that in turn stimulates osteoclastic activity. When PTH is given by intermittent injections it is anabolic and a powerful stimulator of osteoblastic bone formation. It appears to mediate this effect, in part, by increasing the number of marrow progenitors of osteoblasts while decreasing the number of marrow progenitors of osteoclasts. Some investigators have suggested that the bone anabolic action of PTH is mediated in part by IGF-1, which has been shown in vitro to be released by osteoblast-like cells exposed to PTH. This view is not supported by recent findings.

b. $1,25(OH)_2$vitamin D $1,25(OH)_2$vitamin D is a secosteroid formed in the kidney by the hydroxylation of 25-hydroxyvitamin D at the 1α position. It acts directly on intestine cells to stimulate calcium and phosphate absorption; it has some actions on bone that are similar to those of PTH, and it promotes osteoclastic bone resorption by stimulating the recruitment and differentiated functions of osteoclasts. Osteoblasts, but not osteoclasts, contain receptors for $1,25(OH)_2$vitamin D, and like PTH, $1,25(OH)_2$vitamin D appears to stimulate osteoclastic bone resorption indirectly via osteoblasts. In addition, $1,25(OH)_2$vitamin D is obligatorily required for normal calcification of bone. However, its actions on bone formation beyond increasing plasma calcium and phosphate, the building blocks of bone, are not well understood. $1,25(OH)_2$vitamin D stimulates osteoblasts to synthesize osteocalcin, which has been suggested to play a signaling role in the bone remodeling cascade.

c. Calcitonin The parafollicular cells of the thyroid gland synthesize and secrete calcitonin, a hypocalcemic and hypophosphatemic peptide hormone whose actions on bone and on osteoclasts are largely opposite to those of PTH and $1,25(OH)_2$vitamin D. Exposure to calcitonin causes contraction of the cytoplasm and the ruffled border of osteoclasts, disaggregation of mature osteoclasts to mononuclear cells, and inhibition of bone resorption. These effects are mediated directly by the binding of calcitonin to its specific receptors on osteoclasts. Exogenously administered calcitonin can, therefore, modulate bone remodeling through its inhibitory actions on osteoclastic bone resorption. However, the physiological significance of calcitonin in humans is unclear, because excessive secretion or deficiency of the hormone is not associated with marked alterations in calcium or skeletal metabolism.

A wide variety of other systemic hormones have important actions on bone metabolism. These include growth hormone, insulin, thyroid hormones, glucocorticoids, and the sex steroids, androgens and estrogens. The sex steroids are of particular interest because their deficiency, as occurs during aging, results in accelerated bone loss in humans. Recent studies indicate that these sex steroids interact with growth factors and cytokines to regulate bone remodeling. [See ENDOCRINE FUNCTION AND DYSFUNCTION.]

F. Growth Factors and Cytokines

A major advance in bone research in the last two decades is the realization that bone and marrow contain a plethora of growth factors that most likely act locally within the bone microenvironment to regulate bone remodeling. Examples of these local factors are IGF-I and II, transforming growth factor-β family (TGFs), fibroblast growth factor (FGF), platelet-derived growth factor (PDGF), bone morphogenetic proteins (BMPs), and prostaglandins (PGs). Except for PGs the growth factors are all polypeptides. The TGFs and IGFs will be described briefly to illustrate the possible role of growth factors in the coordination of bone remodeling.

a. TGF-β Three isoforms of TGF, TGF-β_1, TGF-β_2, and TGF-β_3 have been recognized. The isoforms share considerable sequence identity, bind to the same receptors, and have similar actions. TGF-β is produced by immune cells and by osteoblasts, and it is stored in high amounts in bone matrix where it is present in a latent form. Activated TGF-β has notable skeletal actions. It enhances osteoblastic bone formation by stimulating osteoblast proliferation and activity, and it inhibits the actions of osteoclasts by suppressing their activity and formation from mononuclear precursors. Because of its dual antagonistic actions on bone cells, it has been proposed that TGF-β released from bone undergoing resorption serves as the signal factor that terminates bone resorption and initiates bone formation during bone remodeling.

b. IGFs Another candidate coupling factor for bone remodeling is IGF. There are two forms, IGF-I and IGF-II. Both have similar skeletal actions, with IGF-I being much more potent and better studied. IGF-I was first recognized as a systemic hormone produced by the liver under the stimulatory influence of growth hormone (GH) to mediate the bone anabolic actions of GH. It is now known that IGF-I is also produced by a wide variety of other organs and tissues where it may act locally as an autocrine–paracrine growth factor. One such tissue is bone, where IGF-I is known to be produced by osteoblasts. IGF-I stimulates collagen matrix synthesis and bone formation by increasing the number and activity of osteoblasts. The latter and other IGF-producing cells synthesize and secrete IGF-binding proteins (IGFBP) as well. Six identified as IGFBP-1-6 have been characterized. By binding to IGFs the BPs may act to prolong the half-life of IGFs, modulate their activity, or serve to present IGFs to specific target cells. There is substantial evidence that IGF-I not only stimulates osteoblastogenesis but also enhances osteoclastogenesis. Consequently, IGF-I present in bone matrix may, like TGF-β, be released during bone remodeling to couple formation to resorption. Bone cells also produce IGF-II, which is much more abundant than IGF-I in human bone matrix and may be the major skeletal IGF in humans. In addition to growth factors, cytokines, which are best known for their hematopoietic and immune system connection, play important roles in the regulation of bone remodeling. The best studied, especially with regard to age-related bone loss, are interleukin-1 (IL-1), TNF-α, GM-CSF, IL-6, and IL-4. They are all polypeptides.

c. IL-1 IL-1 exists in two forms, IL-1α and IL-1β. The isoforms have about 30% sequence homology, bind to the same receptor, and have similar actions. IL-1 is produced by many cell types and has diverse biological actions. In bone, it stimulates osteoclastic resorption by enhancing the proliferation and differentiation of osteoclast progenitors, increasing the fusion of the progenitors to form multinucleated osteoclasts and by increasing the activity of mature osteoclasts. The effect on mature osteoclasts depends, at least in part, on PG synthesis and on the presence of osteoblasts or stromal cells. IL-1 may be responsible for local bone destruction that occurs in chronic inflammatory diseases and for hypercalcemia associated with squamous cell carcinomas.

IL-1, TNF-α (tumor necrosis factor), and GM-CSF

have been proposed to contribute to the increased bone resorption that occurs in postmenopausal women. This view derives, in part, from reports that peripheral blood mononuclear cells (PBMC) isolated from ovariectomized women secrete more of these cytokines constitutively than PBMC from similar women treated with estrogen. However, it is not clear why in these reports increased production of IL-1 occurred constitutively in cells that normally require activation to secrete IL-1.

d. Interleukin 6 Another cytokine whose skeletal action has received much attention is interleukin-6 (IL-6). IL-6 is produced by many cell types, including marrow stromal cells. It stimulates the formation of osteoclasts from precursors, and probably also enhances the activity of mature osteoclasts. IL-6 is present at high levels in the marrow and blood of patients with Paget's disease of bone, and it has been implicated in the increased bone resorption that occurs in this disease. Estrogen exerts a tonic inhibition on IL-6 secretion by marrow stromal cells, and the secretion of the cytokine increases following overiectomy. Marrow from ovariectomized animals produces more osteoclast-like cells in ex vivo cultures than marrow from control animals, and the increased osteoclastogenesis is prevented by pretreatment with IL-6 antibody. Consequently, it has been proposed that IL-6 is responsible for the increased osteoclastic bone resorption that causes bone loss in ovarian hormone-deficient states. However, the investigation of the role of interleukins in bone loss due to ovarian hormone deficiency has produced conflicting results that remain a subject of immense controversy.

e. Other cytokines Other hematopoietic factors that have important actions on bone include IL-4 and M(macrophage)-CSF. Transgenic mice made to overproduce IL-4 (*lck*-IL-4-mice) develop severe osteopenia similar to human involutional osteoporosis. The bones of the *lck*-IL-4-mice were characterized by marked cortical and trabecular thinning accompanied by profound decrease in osteoblastic activity with insignificant effect on osteoclastogenesis. It remains unclear whether IL-4 acts to decrease the activity of mature osteoblasts, which are known to have IL-4 receptors and/or to inhibit the recruitment and differentiation of osteoblast progenitors. In contrast to IL-4 overproduction, deficiency of M-CSF due to a point

mutation in the gene for M-CSF results in failure of osteoclastic bone resorption, the occlusion of bone marrow with unresorbed bone and osteopetrosis as occurs in op/op mice. When these mice are treated with M-CSF the osteopetrosis is cured, underlining the importance of M-CSF in the regulation of osteoclastogenesis.

Based on the type of information outlined above, there is a growing consensus that cytokines and local growth factors in bone and its microenvironment act through autocrine and paracrine mechanisms and interact with systemic hormones to regulate bone remodeling and maintain bone balance. Current studies to uncover the nature of these complex interactions are the key to a clear understanding of the aberrations in bone remodeling that underlie diverse bone diseases. However, some have cautioned that much of the information on the actions of cytokines and growth factors on bone remodeling is based mostly on in vitro findings. One of the challenges of the future is to substantiate the validity of these in vitro findings for animals and humans. Knowledge derived from these studies will likely pave the way for designing effective therapeutic strategies for managing bone diseases, the most common of which is osteoporosis.

II. OSTEOPOROSIS

Osteoporosis is an age-related disorder characterized by diminished bone mass. Although usually asymptomatic, it predisposes one to fractures, particularly of the wrist, spine, and hip, if the thinned and weakened bone is sufficiently traumatized. Like many chronic diseases, osteoporosis has a multifactorial etiology.

A. Fracture Risk

I. Epidemiology
Fractures of the hip, distal forearm, and spine are most often associated with osteoporosis, although fractures occur at other sites as well. The lifetime cumulative incidence of wrist and hip fractures in women is 15%. Vertebral fractures have a lifetime cumulative incidence of 25%. The results of fracture include pain, disability, and death. Of the three common osteoporotic fractures, hip fractures cause the greatest morbidity and mortality. There is a 15–20% higher mor-

tality rate in the first year after a hip fracture than in age-matched controls. Some of the increased mortality is attributable to underlying diseases (e.g., dementia and frailty), which predispose one to falls and fractures. However, 20% of ambulatory patients who suffer a fracture are nonambulatory 1 year later.

The incidence of osteoporotic fracture increases exponentially with age. Hip fractures are rare before age 50, but exceed 30 fractures per 1000 women per year over age 80. Women are twice as likely to suffer a hip fracture as are men. These age and sex differences are ascribable to age and sex-related differences in bone mass. Bone mass increases from birth and reaches a peak near the end of the third decade of life. After peaking there is an age-related loss of about 0.5% per year. Women start with 20–30% less bone than men and also have a period of accelerated bone loss associated with menopause.

Both cross-sectional and longitudinal studies indicate that bone mass is a predictor of future fractures. Ethnic groups with greater bone mass have a lower risk of fracture, and case control studies examining hip and vertebral fracture patients have documented lower bone mass among fracture patients than among controls. In one longitudinal study, a doubling of hip fracture risk occurred with each 0.1 g/cm^2 decrease in radial bone mass. Low bone mass, and therefore, high fracture risk, is most prevalent in the elderly. Low bone mass in old age is due to failure to develop a substantial bone mass during adolescence and early adulthood or to the excessive loss of bone thereafter.

2. Skeletal Growth and Achievement of Peak Bone Density

Genetic and environmental factors play important roles in bone growth and development during adolescence and early adulthood. Clear differences in fracture rates and in bone density exist between ethnic and racial groups. Whites, particularly those of Scandinavian origin, have high fracture rates and have been found to have a relatively low bone mass. By comparison, African Americans have only one-third to one-half the risk of fractures of Whites and have bone masses that are about 10% greater. These population studies cannot exclude the possibility that other risk factors that differ between ethnic groups (e.g., risk of falls, body weight, diet, and exercise) may account for the observed differences in fracture rates. Inhabitants of Japan have a relatively low bone mass,

but low fracture rates, suggesting that factors other than bone mass may affect fracture rates.

Studies in twins indicate greater correlation of bone mass among identical than nonidentical twins. This association appears to be independent of body weight, which is also a heritable trait. The concordance of bone mass between twins tends to decrease as the age of the twins increases, which suggests that environmental factors, cumulative with age, may modify the genetic determinants of bone mass. Genetic variation of the vitamin D receptor is being studied as one potential source of heritable differences in bone mass. In some populations, homozygosity for one vitamin D receptor genotype accounts for up to 20% of the variation in bone density between individuals. Failure to find these same effects in other populations may indicate that environmental factors, such as diet, may ameliorate the effects of this genotype. Preliminary studies have found less bone loss in homozygotes receiving calcium supplements.

Obesity, which is also a largely inherited trait, is consistently identified as a strong predictor of bone density and as protective against fractures. In case control studies, each 10-pound increase in weight is associated with a decrease of about 13% in the risk of fracture. The relationship between body weight and fracture may be the result of several factors. First, the skeleton of a heavier person may be exposed to greater weight bearing and respond by developing greater bone mass. Second, obese persons have higher serum estrogen and androgen concentrations than do their nonobese counterparts, and this may protect against bone loss. Third, it is postulated that falling may be less traumatic if the impact is cushioned by fat.

Peak bone density is increased by high calcium intake and by exercise during adolescence. In a randomized study of twins, in which one of each pair of twins was assigned to receive a calcium supplement, bone density increased in the calcium-treated twins. Similarly, weight-bearing exercise in adolescence appears to optimize peak bone density.

3. Age-Related Bone Loss

After achieving peak bone mass sometime in early adulthood, normal women lose little bone until menopause. In women, the rapid loss of bone that occurs with cessation of ovarian function continues at a rate twice that for men of equal age even 10 years after menopause, and estrogens have been found to slow bone loss in 70-year-old women. In contrast, men have no apparent "menopausal" bone loss, and testosterone supplements appear to have no effect on bone loss in older men with normal gonadal function. Postmenopausal women, particularly heavy women, with increased concentrations of nonovarian sex steroids (e.g., dehydroepiandosterone) also have lower rates of bone loss.

A variety of medications affect urinary calcium loss, alter bone mass, or accelerate osteoporosis. These include heparin, aluminum-containing antacids, cytotoxic agents, antiseizure medication, and thyroid supplements. The drugs most clearly identified with osteoporosis are adrenal corticosteroids. Long-term use of adrenal steroids accelerates trabecular bone loss and is associated with both vertebral and hip fractures.

Cross-sectional studies have found lower bone mass and a higher risk of Colles', hip, and vertebral fractures in smoking women. Estrogen metabolism appears to differ in smokers and nonsmokers; however, it is unknown whether the observed differences are due to other characteristics that differ between smokers and nonsmokers (e.g., body weight). No studies have examined the effects of smoking cessation on bone mass.

Alcohol abuse is associated with an increased risk of hip fracture in men. Bone mass is decreased in alcoholics, although other factors, such as an increased propensity to falls, may also contribute to increased fracture risk due to alcohol abuse. [See ALCOHOL AND DRUGS.]

Periods of inactivity, such as prolonged bed rest, lead to rapid bone loss of as much as 1% per week, which is 50 times the usual age-related loss. In cross-sectional studies, bone mass is associated with lean body mass and muscle strength, and the age-related decrease in lean muscle mass is paralleled by a decrease in bone mass.

Exercise, particularly weight-bearing exercise, appears to increase bone mass. For example, the dominant arm of lifelong tennis players has substantially more bone mass than the nondominant arm. Several controlled, but not randomized, studies have demonstrated that weight-bearing exercise increases bone mass. Among postmenopausal women, exercises that require weight bearing of the upper extremities for 15 minutes three times weekly over 5 months increased bone mass of the distal radius by 3.8%.

Other studies have found that combinations of walking, stair climbing, jogging, and standing exercises increased lumbar spine bone mass by 4–7% over control groups. However, cessation of the activity eventually leads to loss of the excess accumulated bone.

4. Falls

Trauma, usually from falls, is a necessary prerequisite for fracture, and in contrast to diminished bone mass, may itself be sufficient to cause fracture. It is estimated that the kinetic energy involved in falling directly onto the hip is several times greater than that required to fracture the trochanter. Fortunately, muscle and fat padding over the hip, and reflex movement of the arm and lower extremity that partly break the fall usually diminish this kinetic energy sufficiently to prevent fracture. Less than 5% of falls result in fractures, and less than 1% result in hip fractures. The incidence of falls increases with age, with about 25% of ambulatory women over age 70 falling at least once each year. In older patients, defensive reflexes are often diminished, and the force of the fall applied directly to bone is therefore increased. As these patients frequently have diminished bone mass, fractures occur. [See ACCIDENTS: FALLS.]

B. Clinical Evaluation

1. Risk Factors

As noted above, several risk factors have been identified that predict fracture risk. In cross-sectional studies, such clinical predictors have a limited ability to predict bone density. One study has described the ability to identify fewer than half of the persons in the bottom third of bone mass. A prospective study reported only in abstract form found that clinical parameters were not significant predictors of future spine fractures in a 5-year follow-up study of 1104 women. In contrast, measurement of bone density was highly predictive. It should be noted that the inability of risk factors to predict bone mass does not preclude their importance. For example, adrenal steroids cause osteoporosis and fractures, and the history of steroid use is a useful indicator to identify persons with an increased risk of fractures.

2. Secondary Osteoporosis

Age and menopause-related bone loss are the most common causes of osteoporosis; however, other disorders may present as diminished bone mass or fracture. In a series of 300 patients referred to an osteoporosis clinic, the most common causes of low bone mass were (1) adrenal corticosteroid use (26); (2) hypovitaminosis D (10); (3) gastrointestinal disorders leading to disrupted calcium or vitamin D absorption (9); (4) chemotherapy (8); (5) rheumatoid arthritis (8); (6) hypothyroidism (7); (7) malignancy (7); (8) poliomyelitis (4); (9) alcohol abuse (4); (10) prolonged bed rest (1); (11) antiseizure medications (1). The causes of diminished bone mass in these conditions are various, including disorders of vitamin D and calcium absorption (adrenal corticosteroids, hypovitaminosis, gastrointestinal disorders, antiseizure medications); inhibitors of bone formation (adrenal corticosteroids, chemotherapy, alcohol abuse); accelerated bone loss due to inactivity (rheumatoid arthritis, poliomyelitis, prolonged bed rest); or direct effects on bone (malignancy).

3. Measuring Bone Density

Characteristic radiolographic changes of spinal osteoporosis include collapsed vertebrae, ballooned disks, and demineralization of vertebral bodies characterized by apparent accentuation of the end plates and a radiodensity similar to that of lung tissue. Using these criteria for diagnosis of osteoporosis in women over age 75, spinal radiographs were abnormal in only 50% of patients with a hip fracture, but were abnormal in 27% of controls without fractures. In women 65–75 years of age, radiographs were abnormal in 35% of fracture patients, and were positive in 18% of controls without fracture.

Bone absorbs energy as radiation passes through it, and the amount of attenuation is a direct measure of bone mass. Single- and dual-energy densitometers are commercially available for quantifying bone mass. Single-energy densitometers have a radiation source with a single energy peak. Absorption of this energy wave is in part dependent on the amount of soft tissue overlying bone, and, as a consequence, this test measures bone mass accurately only at peripheral sites (e.g., the mid and distal radius). Longitudinal studies indicate that measurement of bone at the wrist can predict future fractures. Fracture risk doubles for each 0.1 g/cm^2 decrease in radial bone mass. Although 38% of women 80 years of age or older have bone densities below 0.6 gm/cm^2, 47% of fractures occur in this group.

Dual-energy densitometry utilizes an X-ray beam with two energy levels. Differences in absorption of the two energy beams by soft tissue and bone allow for measurement of bone in the hip and spine, independent of soft tissue densities. The radiation dose from dual-X-ray densitometry is small. Reliability of the measurement is excellent, with reported test–retest coefficient of variation of about 1–2% for the hip and 2–3% for the spine. Inaccurate readings may occur in patients with significant degenerative joint disease of the spine or with overlying calcifications. Longitudinal studies indicate that measurement of axial bone density with dual-X-ray densitometry is significantly superior to other techniques.

C. Treatment Strategies

1. Postmenopausal Estrogen Replacement

Menopause is characterized by progressive ovarian failure accompanied by a period of accelerated bone loss. The causes of this bone loss are uncertain. However, estrogen receptors have been identified in bone, and the effect of estrogens may be to suppress bone resorption directly. In addition, estrogen appears to facilitate intestinal calcium absorption. Early menopause with onset prior to age 50 has been identified as a risk factor for fracture in several case control studies. Surgical menopause with oophorectomy, because of its more profound depletion of estrogen, appears to be an even stronger predictor of fracture than early natural menopause.

Case control studies have reported that treatment of postmenopausal women with estrogen can decrease fracture risk by 40–70%. Controlled studies have also demonstrated beneficial effects of postmenopausal estrogens on bone mass and fracture incidence. In postoophorectomy women, there is no decrease in cortical bone mass after 10 years of treatment with conjugated estrogens (2.0 mg daily) and progesterone (10 mg daily). Control patients, in contrast, had more than an 11% loss of bone mass. The beneficial effect of estrogen was greatest if initiated within 3 years of surgery. There is considerable debate about the effectiveness of estrogens started more than 7–10 years after the onset of menopause. The optimum dose of conjugated estrogens for prevention of bone loss is 0.625 mg daily.

Other factors besides effect on bone mass and fractures may influence the decision to initiate estrogen therapy. In several case control and longitudinal cohort studies, estrogens have been demonstrated to increase endometrial cancer risk by four- to eightfold. Concurrent use of progesterone appears to decrease the risk of endometrial carcinoma and may have an additional favorable effect on bone mass.

Estrogens also appear to have a beneficial effect on cardiovascular disease, reducing mortality from this disease by an estimated 40%. This effect is thought to be secondary to a rise in high-density lipoproteins (HDL) and a decrease in low-density lipoproteins (LDL) and perhaps due to changes in platelet aggregation that prevent intracoronary thrombus formation. These lipid changes occur principally because of direct effects of estrogen on liver protein synthesis, and are maximized by absorption of the estrogen compounds from the gut. Unfortunately, the addition of progesterone, which has been found to prevent endometrial carcinoma, may partially negate estrogen's beneficial effects on lipids, because at least some progesterone compounds decrease HDLs. For medroxyprogesterone this effect is dose-dependent. The effect of the combination therapy on cardiovascular disease morbidity and mortality is unknown.

The effect of estrogen and progesterone replacement therapy on breast cancer risk is controversial. Several recent reports indicate a 10% increase in breast cancer incidence in estrogen-treated women. This increase was restricted to long-term users of estradiol, but not to users of conjugated estrogens that are commonly prescribed in the United States. There was also some indication that the combination of estrogens and progestins further increased breast cancer risk. Other reports indicate no increased risk. Given the frequency of breast cancer, even a modest increase in risk would have a substantial effect on overall mortality. Women treated with estrogen–progesterone combinations often have cyclic bleeding. This is frequently an undesirable side effect and a common reason for discontinuing therapy.

2. Calcium

Calcium is the main mineral constituent of bone, yet controversy remains about its effectiveness in preventing and ameliorating osteoporosis. Calcium balance studies suggest that the minimum daily requirement of premenopausal women is greater than 800 mg daily. However, national surveys indicate that few

American women over age 40 consume this much calcium.

Randomized controlled trials assessing the effects of calcium on bone mass in postmenopausal women have yielded varying results in different populations. In populations with low calcium intakes of the United States bone mass increased when the diet was supplemented with 750 mg of calcium daily. European populations in which average calcium intakes approached 1000 mg daily showed no beneficial effect of calcium supplementation. The effect in postmenopausal women may also vary at different skeletal sites. One study found no effect of calcium at the distal radius but showed a significant increase in bone at the proximal radius. Persons with preexisting vertebral fractures appear to have a larger beneficial effect from taking calcium supplements than do persons without such fractures. In trials comparing calcium to estrogen supplementation, calcium is clearly inferior to estrogens in suppressing bone loss.

Increased calcium intake during adolescence may increase peak bone mass. Cross-sectional studies among adolescents as well as perimenopausal women indicate that higher calcium intake, as measured crudely by frequency of milk consumption at meals, predicts bone mass. Intervention studies of supplementary calcium in adolescence also have found that calcium supplementation may modestly increase bone mass.

A consensus conference convened by the National Institutes of Health has recommended minimum intakes of calcium to maintain bone mass. In premenopausal women the recommended calcium intake is 1000 mg daily. Estrogen enhances calcium absorption, and calcium excretion rates are greater after menopause. The recommended minimum daily requirement after menopause is 1500 mg daily.

3. Vitamin D

Vitamin D deficiency causes rickets in children and osteomalacia in adults. Both are characterized by poor calcification of the bone protein matrix leading to a reduced bone mass indistinguishable from senile osteoporosis except by bone biopsy. Vitamin D is available through dietary sources, principally dairy products that are supplemented with vitamin D, or from sunlight exposure. [See DIET AND NUTRITION.]

Several authors have noted lower serum vitamin D concentrations in patients with osteoporotic fractures than in controls. Low-grade osteomalacia has been described by some authors in 25% of U.S. patients with hip fractures. In some, but not all, case control studies, fracture patients have lower concentrations of vitamin D than for age-matched controls. Results of vitamin D therapy in clinical trials have also been inconsistent. In a randomized controlled trial there was no effect of calcitriol $(1,25(OH)_2D3)$ on bone mass of the spine, distal radius, or mean total body calcium in 86 postmenopausal women with an average dose of 0.4 mg/day. In contrast, a similar study found an increase in bone from a larger dose (0.8 mg/day) in a study of 27 postmenopausal women with osteoporotic fractures. Bone resorption decreased, and spinal fracture rates improved with treatment; however, therapy was often complicated by decreased renal function and hypercalcemia. In populations with low serum concentrations of vitamin D, such as the elderly and nursing home residents, vitamin D supplements of 400 to 800 units have shown a dramatic decrease in hip fracture rates. Variability of responses in other trials may reflect relative differences in vitamin D concentrations in the study populations.

4. Fluoride

Early studies in miners exposed to fluoride found marked increases in bone mass. Several ecological studies have noted lower hip fracture rates in areas where the fluoride content of the water exceeded 2 parts per million. As early as 1982, a nonrandomized, but controlled study showed potential beneficial effects of fluoride on vertebral fracture rates. Subsequent studies have noted frequent side effects from fluoride treatment including synovitis, fasciitis, stress fractures in the lower extremities, osteomalacia, and nausea and vomiting. The stress fractures are thought to be secondary to abnormalities in the cross-bridging of hydroxyapatite crystals in fluoride-treated individuals. Two randomized controlled trials have found no beneficial effect on fracture rates in the spine and a high incidence of these stress fractures. The usual dose of fluoride in these trials exceeded 50 mg. Subsequent analyses of these trials examining persons taking lower doses have noted fewer side effects, an increase in bone density, and a decrease in fractures. These result suggest that fluoride may have a role in osteoporosis treatment, although the appropriate dosage is yet to be decided.

5. Calcitonin

Calcitonin is a naturally occurring hormone secreted by the thyroid parafollicular cells that modulates osteoclast-mediated bone resorption. Although calcitonin has not been demonstrated to be deficient in osteoporotic persons, randomized trials have found that exogenous calcitonin administered intranasally or by injection decreases the rate of bone loss in postmenopausal women. In randomized trials with calcitonin, there was a two-thirds reduction in vertebral fractures, and in a large case control study, lower hip fracture rates were found in calcitonin-treated individuals.

6. Bisphosphonates

Bisphosphonates are analogs of pyrophosphate. They inhibit calcium phosphate crystallization and dissolution in vitro and inhibit bone resorption by osteoclasts in a dose-dependent fashion in vivo. Bisphosphonate therapy has been found to result in a net gain of bone mass of about 4% and a decrease in vertebral fracture rates in postmenopausal women as compared to untreated controls. Bisphosphonates attach to the bone matrix and have very long half-lives. They are commonly used for treatment of Paget's disease, a disorder characterized by rapid turnover of bone. Bone resorption is diminished in bisphosphonate-treated osteoporotic patients without significant disruption of bone formation. This results in net bone accumulation.

BIBLIOGRAPHY

Aloia, J. F., Vaswani, A., Yeh, J. K., Ross, P. L., Flaster, E., & Dilmanian, F. A. (1994). Calcium supplementation with and without hormone replacement therapy to prevent postmenopausal bone loss. *Annals of Internal Medicine, 120,* 97–103.

Dawson Hughes, B., Dallal, G. E., Krall, E. A., Harris, S., Sokoll, L. J., & Falconer, G. (1992). Effect on vitamin D supplementation on wintertime and overall bone loss in healthy postmenopausal women. *Annals of Internal Medicine, 115,* 505–512.

Favus, M. J. (Ed.). (1993). *Primer on the metabolic bone diseases and disorders of mineral metabolism* (2nd ed.). New York: Raven Press.

Heaney, R. P. (1993). Bone mass, nutrition, and other lifestyle factors. *American Journal of Medicine, 95,* 29S–33S.

Horowitz, M. C. (1993). Cytokines and estrogen in bone: anti-osteoporotic effects. *Science, 260,* 626–627.

Jee, W. S. S., (1991). Introduction to skeletal function: Structural and metabolic aspects. In F. Bronner & R. V. Worrell (Ed.), *Basic Science Primer in Orthopaedics*, (pp. 3–34). Williams & Wilkins.

Kanis, J. A., Melton, L. J. III, Christiansen, C., Johnston, C. C., & Khaltaev, N. (1994). The diagnosis of osteoporosis. *Journal of Bone Mineral Research, 9,* 1137–1141.

Mohan, S., & Baylink, D. J. (1991). Bone growth factors. *Clinical Orthopedic Related Research, 263,* 30–48.

Morrison, N. A., Chang Qi, J., Tokita, A., Kelly, P. J., Crofts, L., & Nguyen, T. V., Sambrook, P. N., & Eisman, J. A. (1994). Predictor of bone density from vitamin D receptor alleles. *Nature, 367,* 284–287.

Mundy, G. R. (1993). Cytokines and growth factors in the regulation of bone remodeling. *Journal of Bone and Mineral Research, 8*(suppl. 2), S505–S510.

Parfitt, A. M. (1995). Problems in the application of in vitro systems to the study of human bone remodeling. *Calcified Tissue International, 56* (suppl. 1), 55–57.

Brain and Central Nervous System

William Bondareff

University of Southern California Medical School

Astroglia A population of nonneuronal cells with numerous, branching processes that provide mechanical and functional support to central nervous system neurons.

Hippocampus A region of the brain located in the medial part of the temporal lobe and concerned with memory.

Locus Ceruleus A group of pigmented neurons in the roof of the pons that is the principle source of the noradrenergic innervation of cerebral cortex.

Nucleus Basalis of Meynert A collection of neurons in the orbital frontal part of the brain that is a major provider of cholinergic innervation for the cerebral cortex.

Synapse Point of junctional contact between neurons where electrochemical signal is transmitted.

Although age-related changes in the human **BRAIN** are readily demonstrated, it is always difficult, and in most cases impossible, to know how much of those changes are due to aging per se. Elderly humans are afflicted acutely with numerous age-related diseases and suffer the cumulative affects of numerous other chronic illnesses. They are affected by neuroactive medications used to treat their acute diseases and by the cumulative effects of other neuroactive substances, such as alcohol and caffeine. The effects of an increasingly hostile environment are often not easily differentiated from those due to the effects of aging on the structure and chemistry of the brain.

Age-related changes in brain functions are also readily demonstrated, and at least some of these appear to reflect the process of aging rather than environmental change. Age-related changes include changes in secondary memory, reaction time, visuospatial memory, complex attention, language fluency, and problem solving. Neurobiological substrata of these cognitive changes are unknown and their elucidation is the raison d'être of gerontological research.

I. GROSS ANATOMY OF THE AGING BRAIN

Structural changes due to aging in the brain have been characterized on three organizational levels. At the level of gross structure, changes in brain weight, based on measurements made after death, are significant. Although the amount is uncertain because of postmortem changes in fluid compartments, the loss is nonetheless probably in the order of 10%. Changes in brain volume are probably most reliably assessed on the basis of imaging—computed tomography (CT) or magnetic resonance imaging (MRI). Imaging shows the cerebrospinal fluid volume to be relatively constant in young adults to about age 40; then it begins to increase, especially after age 60. The brain, which occupies more than 90% of the cranial cavity between ages 20 and 50, occupies progressively less after age 50. In older adults, then, there is a significant decrease in brain-to-cranium volume and an increase in cerebrospinal fluid volume of about the same magnitude. Regional decrements in brain volume have been reported in frontal and temporal lobes, cerebral cortex, basal ganglia, corpus callosum, and hippocampus.

II. MICROSCOPIC ANATOMY OF THE AGING BRAIN

A. Neuronal Death

At a microscopic level, decrements in numbers of neurons with age are well documented but not without controversy. Neuronal loss does not occur uniformly throughout the brain but occurs in selected areas, and is often difficult to evaluate because of technical limitations. These include methodological limitations of microscopic morphometry, uncertainties in differentiating neuroglia and neurons, transient neuronal atrophy as a result of which some neurons cannot be seen with a conventional light microscope. Nonetheless, in humans deceases of 15 to 57% are reported in cerebral cortex from selected gyri of the frontal, temporal, parietal, and occipital lobes, and comparable decrements are reported for locus ceruleus, substantia nigra, cerebellar Purkinje cells, and hippocampal pyramidal neurons. Neuronal loss can be regionally specific, as in the hippocampus where significant loss is reported in area CA4 and the subiculum, but not in the dentate, CA1, or CA2. Neuronal loss in the human nucleus basalis of Meynert is less certain and still less certain in other regions, although seemingly reliable decrements are reported in rodents. Decreases in the number of synapses and perhaps in the number of dendrites are other morphometric indicators of neuronal malfunction in the aged brain. Like neuronal loss, they too may be better documented in laboratory animals than in the human brain.

B. Neuronal Injury

The metabolic failure of neurons and neuronal systems in old age need not require actual loss of neurons, neurites, or synapses. Neuronal atrophy and hypertrophy have both been reported as characteristics of aged neurons. Neuronal atrophy in the nucleus basalis of Meynert has been described in some rodents. In other rodent strains and in old humans these cholinergic neurons appear to hypertrophy. Neuronal atrophy in the infundibular nucleus in older men and postmenopausal women has been ascribed to the loss of steroid negative feedback. Other indications of compromised neuronal function might include the accumulation of lipofuscin and neuromelanin. Although there is no convincing evidence that the accumulation of these substances is neurotoxic, the accumulation of lipofuscin has the appearance of crowding out organelles involved in synthesis and transport, and neuromelanins can bind potential toxins such as 1-methyl-4-phenylpyridine.

III. AGE CHANGES IN NEUROTRANSMITTERS

Morphometric changes (see above) indicate changes in the aged human brain in neurotransmitters and in interneuronal communication. There is, for example, a well-documented central cholinergic deficit in animals. In humans, deficits in choline acetyl transferase activity are reported in hippocampus, entorhinal cortex, frontal cortex, and cerebellum, and a decreased density of cholinergic fibers in amygdala has been found in older adults. Relatively little is known about cholinergic receptors, especially nicotinic receptors in the aged brain. However, muscarinic receptors appear to be decreased in the human brain, and significant decrements are reported in cerebral cortex and striatum and hippocampus in old rodents. Changes in noradrenergic and seratonergic transmission are not well defined. Norepinephrine is reportedly reduced in the aged human brain, and dopamine may be reduced in the caudate nucleus. However, in more adequately controlled studies, norepinephrine and dopamine turnover are reportedly unchanged, whereas seratonin turnover is increased in old rats. Reduced regional seratonin concentrations with no accompanying decrease in 5-hydroxy indoleacetic acid levels have been found in aged human brains. These are believed to result from decreased metabolism of the indolamine precursor, coupled with a compensatory increased metabolic activity in surviving terminals that maintains functionally normal levels of the transmitter in nerve terminals. Glutamergic function appears to be relatively stable in old age.

IV. AGE CHANGES IN THE NEURONAL MICROENVIRONMENT

Although they remain unexplored in the elderly human brain, changes in the extracellular neuronal microenvironment with age, which are primarily known from animal studies, can reasonably be predicted to effect neuronal aging in humans. [*See* MODELS OF AGING: VERTEBRATES.] Their functionally important relationships with age changes in neurotransmission are outlined in Figure 1. The neuronal microenvironment consists, primarily, of vascular elements and extracellular space, all of which appear to change with age. A decreased extracellular space, demonstrated in the brains of old rats, may serve to limit the diffusion of metabolites and, perhaps, transmitter substances in the aged brain. Age changes in the extracellular space have barely been investigated in the human brain. Changes in the cerebral vasculature are legion, but changes in the human brain microvasculature

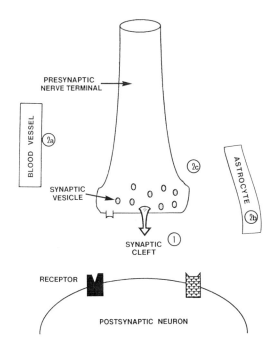

Figure I Age changes in the brain include (1) selective decrease in the amount of neurotransmitter substance available for neurotransmission and decrease in certain receptors; and (2) changes in the neuronal microenvironment, such as endogenous changes in the cerebrovasculature (a), astroglia (b), and extracellular space (c) that compromise neuronal nutrition and interfere with the interaction between transmitter substances and receptors.

with age are poorly understood. Changes due to aging in cardiovascular tissues add to changes due to degenerative diseases in the same manner as age changes add to changes resulting from neurodegenerative diseases. Aging, thereby, accelerates vascular degenerative diseases with the result that systolic blood pressure and low-density lipoprotein (LDL) cholesterol increase with age and older persons are at increased risk for cerebroischemic vascular disease. Changes of vascular tissues due to aging include the decreased production of endogenous vasodilatory agents and alterations in the structure and distribution of collagen, elastin, and glycosaminoglycans. The effects of these changes on the aged brain are unknown, but likely sequelae of such changes would include interference with neurotransmission and myriad disturbances in neuronal metabolism.

It can be anticipated that age changes in the microvasculature might affect electrolytes mediating neuronal electrochemical activity. Although no changes in Na^+/Ca^{2+} exchange activity and Ca^{2+} permeability were found in a study of human frontal cortex, studies of rodent brain do reveal age changes in inositoltriphosphate receptor Ca^{2+}-release channels and calcium-mediated after-hyperpolarization. Adenylate cyclase activity, oxidative phosphorylation, mitochondrial electron transport mechanisms, and DNA metabolism all appear impaired in old rodent brains. Changes such as these, if not reflective of programmed changes in the neuronal genome, may reflect age changes in the neuronal microenvironment. It is unknown whether such changes, whatever their origin, are of sufficient severity to abolish such dynamic neuronal functions as those involved in synaptic plasticity.

The role of astroglia in the process of aging remains unclear. Astrocytic end feet contribute to the neuronal microenvironment in that they help separate neuronal and extracellular (vascular channels and extracellular space) elements. They contribute to the isolation of synaptic complexes, such as represented by cerebellar glomeruli. They can occupy space resulting from the loss of neurons and segregate pathological materials, such as degenerating extracellular neurofibrillary tangles. Astrocytes express apolipoprotein E and probably produce neurotrophic factors. They may play a role in neuronal metabolism and assist the plastic neuronal response to injury by facilitating nutrient transport. Hypertrophy of the astrocytic compartment with no accompanying increase in the number of astrocytes in old age has been demonstrated in rats, but it is not known how this might aid or inhibit processes associated with aging.

V. NEURONAL PLASTICITY IN THE AGED BRAIN

Axons are regenerated more slowly in old animals, but neurons in aged brains retain the capacity for synaptic plasticity. They react to the effects of trauma or metabolic insult by replacing lost synapses with new ones, although the regenerative process may be delayed in old animals. As long as there is accurate replacement of lost connections, neuronal plasticity appears to be a continuous dynamic process underlying the capacity to form and destroy circuits continually as new material is learned or forgotten. However, aberrant axonal sprouting or erroneous replacement of synapses can also lead to faulty circuitry and environmentally nonadaptive behavior. It is unclear how much of this neuronal plasticity depends upon the presence of nerve growth factors (NGF), as NGF has been shown to improve performance on spatial memory tests when injected into the region of the nucleus basalis of Meynert in aged rats. The expression of NGF appears to be preserved in old age.

VI. NEUROPATHOLOGY OF AGING

A number of changes characteristic of specific neuropathological disorders are found in the aged human brain, but in smaller number or attenuated form. Atrophic changes in gross structure such as ventriculomegaly and sulcal widening, which are characteristic of neurodegenerative diseases often associated with dementia, are found in nondemented, apparently normal elderly persons. Although some persons showing MRI signs of cortical atrophy may be cognitively impaired, some may not be, and there is no convincing evidence that such findings herald the later development of a progressive dementing disorder. The demonstration by MRI of numerous, voluminous lesions in the periventricular white matter is, similarly, usually associated with neuropathology, although the presence of lesions of lesser number and amount is a common finding in old people who show no significant cognitive impairment, are not demented, and may never develop a dementing disease. [See DEMENTIA.]

Microscopic neuropathological changes often found in the aged human brain include senile plaques, β-amyloid (BA) deposits, neurofibrillary tangles, and granulovacuolar degeneration complexes. These may be more numerous in the hippocampus, but they occur throughout the brain in old age in smaller numbers. Again, their presence may be associated with impaired cognition or psychopathology, but in many cases there is no apparent pathology and no abiding evidence that such lesions represent an early stage or attenuated form of a progressive dementia such as Alzheimer's disease.

Neurofibrillary tangles and senile plaques, when they are found in nonimpaired, apparently normal older adults, may be indicators of *pathological aging*. This refers to the presence of abnormal findings that hasten or intensify the process of what is conventionally termed *normal aging*. The concept of pathological aging is illustrated by a recent study of demented older adults in whose brains it was possible to demonstrate cytoplasmic structures containing ubiquitin-bound protein. These microscopic-size structures, called Lewy bodies, are characteristic findings in Parkinson's disease and a non-Alzheimer's disease dementia. They were found in the cerebral cortex unaccompanied by plaques and tangles in very few cases in which dementia was mild. They occurred more frequently in addition to abundant senile plaques and neurofibrillary tangles with more severe dementia. It can be assumed that the presence of abnormal aging will intensify the affects of a neurodegenerative disease and vice versa.

Senile plaques consist of dystrophic neurites and BA protein. The dystrophic neurites contain an abnormal form of tau protein that is aggregated so as to form paired helical filaments (PHF). These PHFs are further aggregated to form the neurofibrillary tangles occasionally found within pyramidal neurons or found extracellularly in the hippocampus in nondemented older adults. They are rarely found in the cerebral cortex in older, cognitively normal adults. Normal tau protein is not aggregated in PHFs but bound to tubulin in microtubules that are, thereby, stabilized and able to participate in intraneuronal transport. Abnormal tau protein, presumably because it is hyperphosporylated, is unable to bind with tubulin, which destabilizes microtubules and disrupts transport systems. There is evidence of slowed septal-hippocampal axonal transport of glycoproteins in old rats, but the underlying mechanism is unknown. It is not known if the presence of abnormal tau protein in the hippocampus or other parts of the aged human brain plays any role in the delay of intraneuronal transport or in the dysfunctional cognition that occurs typically in older adults.

A second abnormal protein, βA, which is found in the core of senile plaques and in diffusely distributed extracellular collections, has been shown to be cytotoxic to cells *in vitro* under some conditions that are not fully defined. As it occurs in the aged brain in the extracellular space, often closely associated with blood vessels, it may interfere with the transport of ions, transmitter substances, and metabolites through synaptic clefts and the perineuronal extracellular space. It seems unlikely that the overexpression of amyloid precursor protein, from which abnormal βA protein is derived, results in the accumulation of βA in apparently normal older adults in small amounts, or in large amounts in Alzheimer's disease. It seems unlikely, also, that the formation of abnormal tau protein results from the overexpression of tau protein-related genes. The accumulation of both abnormal proteins in apparently normal old persons and in victims of Alzheimer's disease appears to be posttranslational.

BIBLIOGRAPHY

Bondareff, W. (1985). The neural basis of aging. In J. E. Birren & K. W. Schaie, (Eds.), *Handbook of the psychology of aging.* New York: Van Nostrand Reinhold.

Coffee, C. E., & Cummings, J. L. (eds.). (1954). *Textbook of geriatric neuropsychiatry.* Washington, DC: American Psychiatric Press.

Cotman, C. W. (1990). Synaptic plasticity, neurotrophic factors, and transplantation in the aged brain. In (E. L. Schneider & J. W. Rowe (Eds.), *Handbook of the biology of aging* San Diego: Academic Press.

Finch, C. E. (1993). Neuron atrophy during aging: Programmed or sporadic? *TINS 16,* 104.

Goldman, J. E., Calingasan, N. B. and Gibson, G. E. (1994). Aging and the brain. *Current Opinion in Neurology, 7,* 287.

Gottfries, C. G. (1990). Neurochemical aspects of aging and diseases with cognitive impairment. *Journal of Neuroscience Research 27,* 541.

Cancer and the Elderly

Michael L. Freedman

New York University Medical Center

Apoptosis Cell suicide in a genetically programmed manner.

Cancer A transformation of a single normal cell, which then divides to form a clone of malignant cells. Cancer cells grow autonomously, are not regulated by normal controls, and do not die appropriately. These cells are abnormal and spread throughout the body, thereby killing the person.

Cancer Treatment Therapies to cure or palliate cancer.

Carcinogenesis Cause of cancer.

Cell Transformation The change of a cell to a different form. If unregulated, this can lead to cancer.

Malignancy A disease that will kill the host.

Neoplasm "New growth," a term used to describe a tumor.

Oncogenes Normal genes (proto-oncogenes) that mutate and in their new form cause cancer.

CANCER is probably the most dreaded disease of elderly people. As greater advances are made in the prevention of atherosclerotic disease (heart attacks and strokes), cancer has become an increasingly common cause of death in elderly people. It is estimated that around the year 2000, cancer will be the number one cause of death in the elderly. This discussion will review the causes and biology of cancer; possible ways of preventing it; clinical descriptions of some of the common cancers; how to screen for cancer, and treatment options.

Cancer is one of the most chronic diseases of old age. As more people are treated successfully to prolong their life, greater numbers are living with cancer. It is important for all professionals dealing with the elderly to understand what the disease is and how to deal with it. In the past, the elderly were denied treatment because they were considered "too old." We now know that in many instances the elderly do as well or better with cancer treatments than the young.

I. DEFINITION AND CLASSIFICATION OF CANCER

Cancer may be defined by listing the four characteristics that describe how cancer cells behave differently from normal cells.

1. Cancer usually begins from a single cell that proliferates to form a clone of malignant cells.
2. Cancer cells grow autonomously, are not regulated by the normal controls, and do not die appropriately.
3. Cancer cells do not differentiate in a normal coordinated manner and do not look the same as the normal cells surrounding them.
4. Cancer cells develop the capacity for

discontinuous growth and spread to other parts of the body (metastases).

Normal cells can express these properties at certain appropriate times, such as wound repair or embryogenesis. In cancer, however, the characteristic is excessive and inappropriate to the organism. Cancer is also called malignant neoplasm. This implies that the growth is a new growth (neoplasm), and that if unchecked it will kill the host (malignant).

Cancer traditionally was classified as either being a carcinoma or a sarcoma. It was thought for many years that a neoplasm arose from normal cells of either epithelial (carcinoma) or mesenchymal (sarcoma) origin. However, in recent years, evidence has accumulated that most neoplasms arise from immature cells that then differentiate along normal cell lines. It is still useful to define cancer cells as being either a carcinoma or a sarcoma, but physicians now realize that a carcinoma of the lung does not arise *from* lung cells but rather *differentiates in the direction of lung cells*. Thus, a neoplasm is usually named by what the cells resemble and where they arise. A cancer of the lung implies that the cells resemble lung cells and arise in that organ. An osteosarcoma resembles bone cells and is found in bone.

The traditional classification of neoplasms is into benign and malignant types. These characteristics are determined by the predicted behavior of the tumor rather than by the microscopic morphology. In recent years the tendency has been to restrict the term *malignant* only to tumors that metastasize. Because some malignancies are very slow growing and late to metastasize, new terms are used to describe their propensity: *borderline, intermediate,* or *undetermined.*

Microscopic grading is another way of classifying tumors in an attempt to predict if the neoplasm is slow growing (rarely metastasizing and highly curable) or fast growing (often metastasizing and rarely curable). The criteria used included cellularity, pleomorphism, mitotic activity, type of margins, amount of matrix formation, and the presence of inflammation necroses and hemorrhage. Most often the three-grade system is used: grade 1 (well-differentiated); grade 2 (moderately differentiated); and grade 3 (poorly differentiated or undifferentiated). The lower the grade the more likely the person with the tumor is to survive.

Finally, in terms of classification, there are some lesions that predispose the person to develop cancer, usually a carcinoma. Because cancer is a multistep process, what is seen microscopically are the various steps before a full-blown malignancy develops. These have been called dysplasia, atypical hyperplasia, atypical proliferation, and carcinoma *in situ.* Because these terms have been used in a confusing manner, it is probably safer to designate these lesions as intraepithelial neoplasia. Using this term plus a grading system to indicate varying degrees of severity is probably the most reasonable way of directing therapy.

II. EPIDEMIOLOGY OF CANCER

Cancer occurrence in a period of time for a given population is expressed in various ways (Table I). The incidence rate is a direct measure of the probability of developing cancer and is usually expressed per year. Incidence rates may be crude (all ages) or age-specific. Because cancer is very age-dependent, age-specific rates are usually more informative. When comparing population groups with different age distributions (such as the United States vs. China), the incidence rate should be age adjusted by multiplying each age-specific rate by the percent of individuals in a population with the same ages and then summing these to produce a single value. For etiological studies incidence rates tend to be more informative than mortality rates, as they identify all diagnosed cases.

In contrast, the prevalence rate is usually not used to study etiology, but is useful to plan health services, as it measures the burden of disease in the population. The mortality (death) rate gives us information as to which cancers are most lethal. Because this rate is

Table I Measures of Cancer Frequency

Incidence	*Number of persons developing cancer in a unit of time* total population living at that time
Prevalence	*Number of persons with a cancer at a given point in time* total population living at that time
Mortality (death) rate	*Number of persons dying of cancer in a unit of time* total population living at that time
Case-fatality rate	*Number of deaths from cancer* × 100% number of persons developing cancer

Table II Estimated New Cases and Case-Fatality Rates of Major Cancers in the United States in 1992 (NCI SEER Program)[a]

	Number of cases	Case-fatality rate (%)
All sites	1,130,000	46
Lung	168,000	87
Colon and rectum	156,000	37
Breast (excluding intraepithelial neoplasia)	181,000	26
Prostate	132,000	26
Urinary tract	78,000	25
Uterus (excluding cervical intraepithelial neoplasia)	45,000	22
Oral cavity and pharynx	30,300	26
Skin	32,000	27
Pancreas	28,300	89
Leukemia	28,200	65
Ovary	21,000	62
All other sites	229,600	58

[a]NCI SEER; National Cancer Institute Surveillance, Epidemiology, and End Results.

derived from death certificates, it may often be inaccurate. However, it is useful to evaluate the impact of cancer prevention and treatment on the general population. The case-fatality rate is a measure of the severity of the disease and is usually expressed as a percentage. This number is least useful in chronic cases as it is expressed per unit of time. In chronic cases, it is more useful to express the survival rate per 5 or 10 years. [See EPIDEMIOLOGY.]

A. Patterns of Cancer Occurrence

Cancer is currently the number two killer in the United States, second to heart disease. It is responsible for over 22% of all deaths and with the decline in heart rate death, will probably become the number one cause of death around the year 2000. Cancer is currently the leading cause of death for women age 35–74.

Because cancer is mostly a geriatric illness, as the population ages, more and more people will die of this disease. Most epithelial cancers are rare under the age of 30, but then the incidence rises with age. In the population over age 80, cancer is the number one cause of death. Table II shows the major forms

Table III Average Annual Age-Adjusted Incidence Rates per 100,000 People for Common Cancers by Racial and Ethnic Groups for U.S. Males 1975–1985 (NCI SEER Program)

Type of cancer	Whites	Blacks	Hispanics
All sites	404.1	490.2	265.5
Lung	82.1	119.6	32.2
Colon and rectum	60.3	55.6	29.7
Prostate	77.3	112.8	71.5
Urinary tract	40.5	24.7	19.6

of cancer and the estimated number of new cases and the case-fatality rates using NCI SEER data for 1992. These are all marked ethnic variations in cancer incidence as well as differences between men and women.

Table III shows the marked differences between men in age-adjusted incidence rates for men of selected cancer sites between Whites, Blacks, and Hispanics in the United States. In Table IV, similar data are shown for women. These differences suggest that there are genetic factors in the development of cancer. There are also differences in socioeconomic classes. Overall, the lower the socioeconomic class, the higher the cancer rate. This might reflect differences in the use of tobacco, nutritional status, and exposure to carcinogens. This may also explain some of the differences for Black, White, and Hispanic cancer incidence.

Clusters of cancer have occurred in various geographic regions and in people of similar occupations. These types of studies have been useful in identifying potential environmental risks.

Table IV Average-Annual Age-Adjusted Incidence Rates per 100,000 People for Common Cancers and Racial and Ethnic Groups for U.S. Females 1975–1985 (NCI SEER Program)

Type of cancer	Whites	Blacks	Hispanics
All sites	316.1	296.6	220.4
Lung	29.7	31.2	15.6
Colon and rectum	45.1	45.8	7.6
Breast	91.5	76.4	50.9
Cervix	8.8	19.7	17.1
Uterus	27.1	14.8	11.2
Urinary tract	12.4	10.1	7.5

III. POSSIBLE CAUSES OF CANCER

A. Tobacco

The epidemiologic approach has made it possible to identify lifestyles and other environmental exposures as causes of cancer. Tobacco smoking is the number one risk identified to date. Smoking has long been linked to cancer of the lung, larynx, pharynx, esophagus, bladder, and pancreas. In recent years, evidence has been found that smokers are also prone to cancer of the kidney, uterine cervix, stomach, nose, and leukemia. It is estimated that smoking cigarettes accounts for 40% of cancer deaths in men and 20% in women, with lung cancer being the most common. For smokers of two packs or more per day, the risk of lung cancer is 20 times that of nonsmokers. In addition, smokeless tobacco and passive exposure to smoking also increases the risk of developing cancer.

B. Alcohol

Consumption of alcohol potentiates the effect of smoking of cancers of the mouth, pharynx, esophagus, and larynx and is estimated to account for 3% of cancer deaths. Alcohol might also potentiate other carcinogens.

C. Environmental Pollutants

The workplace also exposes people to various carcinogens, and it is estimated that 5% of all cancer deaths result from this. Asbestos is the major occupational carcinogen, as it causes both lung cancer and the rarer mesotheliomas. Smoking is synergistic with asbestos as smokers exposed to asbestos have a far greater chance of developing cancer than nonsmokers. Other examples of occupational risks include benzene-causing leukemia, radiation-induced cancers, aromatic amines and bladder cancers, inorganic arsenic and lung, skin, and liver angiosarcoma, and vinyl chloride and angiosarcoma.

It has been difficult to ascertain how important environmental pollution is in causing cancer. It is regarded as relatively uncommon, and only 2% of cancer deaths are caused by environmental pollution. Certainly smokers are at greater risk to develop cancer than nonsmokers exposed to the same atmosphere. Some of the risks identified include asbestos; airborne arsenic; cooking oil vapors in wok cooking in China; and effluents from coal-heating stoves.

D. Radiation

Ionizing radiation is another well-studied carcinogen. It has long been known that radiologists, survivors of the atomic bomb in Japan, and patients receiving radiation therapy are at increased risk to develop cancer. Nearly all sites of the body are vulnerable, with the most sensitive being bone marrow, breast, and thyroid. It is not clear how much, if any risk comes from diagnostic X-rays or background atmospheric radiation over long periods of time.

Ultraviolet radiation from the sun is the major risk factor to develop all skin cancers (squamous cell, basal cell, and melanoma). Skin cancers usually develop on sun-exposed areas and are more common in people who work outdoors and who have fair skin. Very high rates of skin cancers occur in people who have genetic illnesses exacerbated by sunlight (xeroderma pigmentosum and albinism). The offending UV radiation appears to be in the UV-B spectral range (290–320 nm). It is believed that depletion of the ozone layer has led to greater amounts of UV-B radiation reaching the earth's surface.

An estimated 2% of cancers arise from exposure to pharmaceutical medications. There is evidence that conjugated estrogens taken after menopause increase risk to develop endometrial cancer of the uterus, and possibly breast cancer. Estrogens have also been implicated in causing vaginal and cervical cancer in daughters of women treated with this hormone during pregnancy. The combination of estrogens and progesterone in postmenopausal women seems to decrease the risk of cancer of the uterus.

Other medications causing cancer include alkylating agents inducing nonlymphocytic leukemia and immunosuppression drugs causing non-Hodgkin's lymphoma.

Drugs are not always a negative; there is new suggestive evidence that nonsteroidal anti-inflammatory drugs (NSAIDS) protect against cancer of the colon.

E. Viruses

Viruses have been implicated in causing some cancers throughout the world. In the United States an estimated 5% of all cancers are related to viruses. Epstein-Barr virus (EBV) probably causes endemic Burkitt's lymphoma in Africa and nasopharyngeal carcinoma in China. Hepatitis B virus (HBV) in Asia and China is associated with hepatocellular carcinoma; human T-lymphotropic virus type I (HTLV-1) is linked to adult T-cell leukemia in Japan and the Caribbean. Human immunodeficiency virus (HIV), which causes acquired immunodeficiency syndrome (AIDS), is associated with Kopasi's sarcoma in homosexual men. It is now thought that a second carrier virus other than HIV is the responsible agent for this malignancy. Human papillomavirus is associated with cancer of the cervix and is sexually transmitted. Other potential virus-induced cancers include childhood leukemia and Hodgkin's disease (possibly EBV).

F. Diet and Nutrition

Although this area seems to be very important in the high incidence of cancer in Western countries, the specific dietary components that either cause or protect against cancer remain unknown. High dietary fat intakes have been implicated as risk factors in colon and breast cancer. High-fiber diets seem to protect against cancer of the colon. Vitamins and other micronutrients may also be protective, such as carotenoids against cancer of the lung; vitamin C against gastric cancer; indole compounds in cruciferous vegetables against colon cancer; allyl sulfide in onions and garlic against gastric cancer; vitamin D and calcium against colon and breast cancer; selenium and vitamin E against gastric cancer. In addition, certain dietary factors may cause cancer, such as aflatoxin (a metabolite of the fungus aspergillus flavius) contaminating foods such as peanuts are linked to liver cancer; salted foods are related to gastric cancer; and nitrosamines are related to nasopharyngeal carcinoma. [See DIET AND NUTRITION.]

G. Genetic Susceptibility

Genetic factors seem to play some role in the development of cancer, but determining how much is related to genes as opposed to environmental and ethnic differences is difficult. For example, nasopharyngeal cancer in Chinese could result from a genetic predisposition or a propensity to eating salted fish with high

nitrosamine levels. In any event, genetic factors are very important in skin cancer. The darker the skin, the less likely is one to develop skin cancer. An example of how complicated this area is may be seen by looking at cancer of the lung. Most smokers do not develop cancer of the lung, but if a person has the genetic makeup to rapidly oxidize certain drugs, the risk of developing smoking-related cancer of the lung is much higher. This could be the result of metabolizing various compounds to active carcinogens. In any event, there are approximately 200 single-gene disorders linked to neoplasia. However, these make up a very small fraction of cancers and include rare conditions such as Werner's syndrome, Bloom's syndrome, Peutz-Jeghers syndrome, and the various hereditary immunodeficiency states.

IV. PRINCIPLES OF CARCINOGENESIS

Classically, carcinogenesis was viewed as a two-stage process: initiation (genetic) and promotion (epigenetic). However, this is too simplistic, and it is now realized that there may be six or more independent genetic mutational events. The newer theory of carcinogenesis is that it is a multistage process driven by both genetic damage (initiation) and other cellular changes (promotion). Tumor initiation betgins in cells through genetic mutations that may be caused by chemical carcinogens, viruses, and physical agents. These mutated cells respond differently to their environment and have a selective growth advantage. The newly initiated tumor may be less responsive to negative growth factors, terminal cell differentiation, or programmed cell death (apoptosis). The initiated tumor cells will expand (clonal expansion) if there is physical disruption of the cells' normal microenvironment outside of genetic damage. This stage, promotion, also occurs from chemicals, viruses, and physical agents and results in further selective clonal expansion and proliferation of the initiated cells. The tumor-promotion stage, although it results in proliferation, also will cause further genetic mutation either by increasing cell proliferation or by the nature of the promoting agent (virus, chemical, physical) itself.

As the cells continue to proliferate with repeated genetic changes, such as activation of proto-oncogens, inactivation of tumor suppressor genes, and inactivation of antimetastatic genes, the tumor will transform into a malignancy. This multistage theory of carcinogenesis helps explain why the elderly are so susceptible to cancer. Time is an important element in carcinogenesis, as it takes multiple "hits" to change a cell into a malignancy. The hits are both genetic and epigenetic, which explains why one may also need multiple risk factors. Thus, the elderly person has been exposed for years to various potential chemical, physical, and viral carcinogens.

V. CANCER PREVENTION

A. Dietary Changes

Animal studies support a cancer-promoting role for fat, and in humans epidemiological data strongly suggest that dietary fat intake may be associated with incidence and mortality of cancers of the breast, colon, rectum, and prostate. There is also some data implicating fat in cancers of the ovaries, uterus, pancreas, and lung, but the evidence is not as strong. There is still a debate if it is total dietary fat, specific fats, or total calories that are involved in carcinogenesis. In any event, cancers of breast, colon, and prostate are highest in North America and Western Europe and lowest in Asia, which is directly related to the intake of total fat in the diet even when adjusted for total calories.

Increased saturated fat intake is associated with an increased incidence of breast, colon, and prostate cancer. High total polyunsaturated fats seem to increase the incidence of breast and prostate cancer. High fiber intake reduces cancer incidence particularly for colon cancer. In countries where there is a high olive oil intake (a monounsaturated fat), breast cancer is less. Certain fats such as the longer chain, highly polyunsaturated omega-3 fatty acids, such as is found in fish, offer protection against cancer. For example, Eskimos who consume large amounts of fat from fish are at low risk to develop cancer, including breast cancer.

When migrant group studies are done, it shows that as the diet switches to the new country in terms of fat intake, the cancer rate also increases to that of the new country. For example, major increases in breast, prostate, and endometrial cancer incidence occurred among four immigrant groups to Hawaii: Chinese, Japanese, Filipinos, and Europeans. When studies were done over time in Japan, it was found that from 1957 to 1973 the fat in the diet doubled as did the total number of breast cancer deaths.

High fat intake also seems to be associated with colorectal cancer. Most studies support the role of saturated fat in carcinogenesis rather than polyunsaturated fat or monounsaturated fats. There have been other studies that implicate high beef intake and other animal proteins. In the other cancers such as prostate, ovary, pancreas, and lung, there may also be a connection with fat. However, these studies had methodological problems and are far from conclusive.

Most experimental animal studies have suggested that dietary fat acts as a cancer promoter, but there is now some evidence that it may be an initiator also. It may be that fat acts by changing cell membrane characteristics or by changing the neuroendocrine system. With cancer of the colon, it has been postulated that fat influences the metabolic activity of fecal microflora and the concentration of sterol substrates in the colon. As a consequence, secondary bile acids, which are carcinogens, form in the colon.

The problem with the fat hypothesis is that the dangers of fat may result from eating patterns of childhood. Similarly, it is not clear if modification of the diet in adulthood or in the later years is of benefit. Furthermore, it is difficult to separate dietary fat from calories. Diets high in fat tend to be associated with obesity. Obesity would conceivably be the risk for breast and endometrial cancer by raising estrogen levels. Caloric intake is inversely related to physical activity, and obese people usually do not exercise as much. Regular exercise appears to lower the risk for cancer, particularly colon cancer.

B. Fiber

A diet low in dietary fiber is associated with high cancer rates. Burkitt was the first to suggest that in Africa the low rate of colon cancer resulted from high fiber intake and large stool bulk. Nonstarch polysaccharides, as found in fruits and vegetables, are the type of fiber that seems to correlate best with low cancer incidence.

C. Micronutrients

Because fruits and vegetables are high in micronutrients, it may be that it is not just fiber but these micronutrients that protect against cancer. Cancer of the lung seems to be lower in populations that have a high beta carotene intake; other carotenoids may also be involved. Vitamin C may protect against certain cancers such as gastric cancer by blocking formulation of nitrosamines. Indole compounds found in cruciferous vegetables may decrease colon cancer, and allyl sulfide in garlic and onions may lower the risk of gastric cancer. It has been suggested that high calcium and vitamin D intake protect against colon and breast cancer. Selenium appears to protect against gastric and esophageal carcinomas. Vitamin E and folic acid also may play roles in protecting against cancer. There are also concerns that various food additives and contaminants are carcinogenic.

D. Hormones

Taking exogenous hormones may increase the incidence of certain cancers. Estrogens have been implicated in uterine cancer and possibly in breast and ovary cancer. Testosterone is involved in cancer of the prostate. Certainly in people taking hormonal replacement, screening procedures for the cancers is essential.

E. Alcohol

High alcohol intake is associated with cancers of the oral cavity, pharynx, esophagus, and larynx, particularly in people who smoke. A smaller risk seems to exist between alcohol and liver, rectal, pancreatic, and breast cancers. A safe recommendation is to limit the intake of alcohol to moderate amounts, such as 1–2 drinks per day.

F. Tobacco

Tobacco smoking is the most modifiable carcinogenic risk. Smoking is firmly linked to cancer of the lung, larynx, mouth, pharynx, esophagus, bladder, and pancreas. It also seems that smokers are more likely to develop cancer of the kidney, cervix, nose, stomach, and leukemia. The antismoking campaign in the United States and other countries is directly aimed at this problem.

Cancer prevention, in summary, currently emphasizes cessation of smoking; limiting alcohol intake; modifying diet to include avoidance of obesity, de-

creasing fat intake, increasing fiber, particularly fruits and vegetables (to a minimum of six servings a day); and avoidance of food additives and contaminants. Whether or not additional micronutrients should be added to our diet is currently being studied.

VI. MOLECULAR BIOLOGY OF CANCER

A. Gene Regulation

The human genome contains 50,000 to 100,000 genes. Each cell in the body contains the same genetic material, but only a few genes are expressed in each cell that determine its phenotype. A gene consists of deoxyribonucleic acid (DNA). The gene will transcribe a ribonucleic acid (RNA). In the nucleolus the RNA transcribed is ribosomal RNA (rRNA) and in the nucleoplasm the RNA transcribed is messenger RNA (mRNA) and transfer RNA (tRNA). The DNA gene acts as a template to form RNA.

Through a process called translation the cell forms protein. In this process, mRNA serves as the information source, the ribosomes move along the mRNA adding amino acids carried by specific tRNAs to the growing peptide. At the end of this process, the newly formed protein is released and undergoes posttranslational modifications necessary for function of the protein. Both transcription and translation are exquisitely controlled by a large array of cellular factors, which in turn are products of gene regulation, transcription, and translation. These factors regulate gene expression and ultimately determine what the cell will manufacture, how it will grow and function, and how long it will live. If these controls are disturbed, the cell will not grow and differentiate normally; the ultimate disarray is cancer.

Spontaneous human cancers arise from a series of somatic genetic cellular changes caused by abnormal deletions, rearrangements, or point mutations. These DNA changes result in failure to regulate transcription and thereby disorder translation. The cell, therefore, becomes cancerous.

B. Oncogenes

Oncogenes are damaged versions of normal genes (proto-oncogenes) that control cell growth and differentiation. It is important to realize that a proto-oncogene is a normal gene, and only through pathological processes does it become an oncogene. Cancer is a multistep process in which multiple genetic alterations must occur usually over many years. Thus, only after a long span of time will cell differentiation, division, and growth be changed. In human cancers, inherited mutations are relatively rare. Most oncogenes are acquired in the form of chromosomal translocations, deletions, amplifications, inversions, or point mutations. Oncogenes may act as transformers of cells, and therefore act as positive regulators of growth. Oncogenes may also arise from normal genes that suppress tumor growth (recessive oncogenes). In this situation, the alteration results in lack of uncontrolled cell division and growth.

Oncogenes have been identified by studying transforming retroviruses and common sites of retroviral insertion, study of the transforming genes in DNA tumor viruses, DNA-mediated gene transfer in cell culture, identification of genes at translocation breakpoints in human cancer, and isolation of tumor-suppression genes in chromosomal deletions.

Tumor-suppression genes (antioncogenes), particularly the p53 gene, have been implicated as playing a central role in tumor formation. P53 is located on chromosome p17, and alterations of this gene locus are found in a large percentage and wide variety of tumors. Change in P53 is the most common alteration in human cancer. Normal p53 gene activity seems to suppress tumor growth and inactivation of its activity (such as by viruses) allow uncontrolled division and growth.

Recent work has shown that most genes whose alterations or deregulation lead to cancer are involved in cell division, and cell division is controlled by signal transduction. To achieve coordinated growth, differentiation, and adaptation, cells have to have complex pathways from outside the cell to inside. These pathways initiate and amplify signals (signal transduction) from outside the cell to specific targets within the cells, such as the nucleus and cytoskeleton. These signals start at the extracellular cell membrane where all surface receptors interact with ligands (growth factors) that are soluble or on other nearby cells. Growth factors, therefore, initiate the signal that tells the cells to proliferate and grow by entering the cell cycle.

C. Apoptosis and Cancer

Up until 3 years ago, scientists believed that most cells died by necrosis, where a cell is damaged and releases its contents suddenly. Now it is known that much of cell death is more gentle and genetically programmed by the process called apoptosis. In apoptosis, when the cell is damaged, the DNA initiates cell destruction, or suicide, and the cell is slowly broken into small packages that are removed by phagocytic cells and there is no inflammation. In cancer not only does proliferation occur, but apoptosis is blocked, resulting in accumulation of abnormal cells.

Traditionally, cancer therapies such as radiation and chemotherapy were directed to induce necrosis of the cancer cells. Scientists are now beginning to investigate mechanisms of restoring and inducing apoptosis in cancer cells. Several approaches are being taken; one is to introduce apoptosis signals, allowing the cancer cells to die while rescuing the normal cells; another is to reintroduce into the cancer a normal gene involved in setting off apoptosis, such as the normal P53 gene; a third method is to shut off proliferation genes (such as mutated Ras), which by itself inhibits apoptosis. If the mutated Ras gene is shut down, apoptosis will start up again and cancer cells will die.

D. Cancer Metastases

The reason that cancer kills people is that the tumor both invades and metastasizes. Approximately 30% of patients newly diagnosed with a cancer have detectable metastatic disease. About another 30% have occult metastases (micrometastases) that will become evident in time. Thus, 60% of cancer patients will have multiple metastases and will ultimately fail therapy and die of the cancer. The formation of metastases begins early in the growth of the primary tumor and increases with time.

Cancers can have very different metastatic potential, which depends upon their histologic type and intrinsic aggressiveness. It appears that metastasis occurs soon after the primary tumor vascularizes. Metastasis is a separate process from tumor formation. The genetic changes that lead to tumor formation do not by themselves cause erosion and metastases (see Table V). Invasion involves substances such as proteases, adhesion receptors, and motility cytokines. Metastases also involve these.

E. The Cell Cycle

In every population of cells there are three types of cells. The first group consists of cycling cells that con-

Table V Progression of Cancer and the Positive and Negative Influences on Its Growth and Spread

	Growth	Spread
Positive influences	Activated oncogenes Growth factors (cytokines)	Proteases Adhesion receptors Motility cytokines Angiogenesis
Result	Uncontrolled proliferation	Invasion and metastases
Negative influences	Tumor-suppression genes Growth inhibitors	Metastatic suppression genes Protease inhibitors Immunologic rejection
Result	Decreased or no growth	No invasion or metastases

tinuously proliferate by going from one mitosis to the next. The second is composed of terminally divided cells that will die without ever dividing again. In the third group the cells are not dividing, but can reenter the cell cycle if the appropriate stimulus is supplied. This is termed G0.

The cell cycle itself has four different phases: G1, S-phase, G2, and mitosis (Table VI). For a cell to go from G0 to G1, multiple genes must be expressed (i.e., C-MYC and C-FOS). Then during G1 as the cell begins to grow, in order to progress, other genes are activated (e.g., ornithine decarboxylase; C-MYB). The critical point in G1 is called the restriction point, and to pass through this point insulinlike growth factor (IGF-1) and the GFI receptor gene must be activated. G1 cyclins are also produced either before or after IGF-1, and these proteins are necessary to allow the cell to carry on DNA synthesis or enter the S phase. During the S phase, all of the DNA synthesis genes are activated, including the DNA polymerases. Tumor suppression genes (antioncogenes) such as P53 seem to work at this step, either before DNA synthetic genes are activated or between appearance of IGF-1 receptor and the transcription of the DNA synthesis genes. After the chromosomes are replicated, the cell enters the G2 phase where the genes necessary for mitosis (or meiosis) are activated. During this phase, products such as $P34^{cdc2}$, cyclins A and B, and C-Mos are produced. The cell then enters the M phase and the cell divides. All of the genes that are activated

Table VI The Cell Cycle and Associated Production of Selected Gene Products

Phase of cell cycle	Activity of cell	Examples of genes activated
G_0	Resting	As enters G1 C-MYC and C-FOS and others
G_1	Growth to prepare for DNA synthesis	Ornithine decarboxylase C-MYB Insulinlike growth factor 1 (ILGF-1) ILGF-1 Receptor G1 Cyclins
S	DNA synthesis Chromosomal duplication	DNA polymerases All other DNA synthesis genes
G_2	Growth to prepare for mitosis (or meiosis)	$P34^{cdc2}$ Cyclins A and B C-MOS
M	Mitosis or meiosis	

during the cell cycle are proto-oncogenes. Mutations in these genes can lead to abnormal growth and then would be termed an oncogene. The suppressor factors are then the antioncogenes. In addition, genes coding for growth factors (cytokines) are also proto-oncogenes and their mutations are oncogenes.

F. Growth Factors (Cytokines)

Growth factors are proteins that regulate cell and function by binding to specific receptor molecules in the cell membranes and thereby stimulating receptor-mediated activation of intracellular signal transduction pathways. These pathways are activated beginning with stimulation of tyrosine kinase to phosphorylate other proteins. These are both stimulatory and inhibitory growth factors.

Many oncogenes are analogues of cellular proto-oncogenes that code for growth factors, their receptors, or pathways mediated by tyrosine kinase activation. Some viral oncogenes have been shown to be derived from animal cell proto-oncogenes and work via these growth factor and receptor pathways. Expression of viral oncogenes is sufficient to induce malignant transformation in certain cells. Many other oncogenes have been found that apparently are not viral in original that work at these sites of growth factors and receptors and signal transduction.

G. Chromosome Abnormalities

Cancer is often associated with specific chromosomal abnormalities. Many of the genes involved in consistent chromosomal rearrangements have been identified. Some of the resultant alterations in gene structure and function have been found. It is clear that as a rule, multiple genetic changes are usually required to transform a cell from its normal to a malignant state. The simplest chromosomal change is a gain or loss of a whole chromosome. Structural changes are translocations (exchange of material between two or more chromosomes), deletions (loss of DNA from a chromosome), and inversions (a single chromosome is broken in two places and the central portion is inverted). Translocations are the most common chromosomal abnormalities found in human cancer, but some deletions have also been described. In some cancers, the chromosome appears normal, but there is extra genetic material (amplification) or a point mutation.

Many proto-oncogenes are located in the chromosomal bands that are involved in consistent translocations. Because of the translocation, the proto-oncogene is either not in the right place, or is altered so that it functions as an oncogene.

At present, chromosomal analysis helps to define the type of malignancy as specific cancers have specific chromosomal abnormalities. In the future, researchers hope to be able to type a tumor to make a genetic diagnosis and direct therapy towards the specific genetic defect. [See DNA AND GENE EXPRESSION.]

H. Molecular Markers

At present, diagnosis of cancer depends mainly on histological examination of tissue. The problem is that a cancer can be missed in a tissue sample or it can be misread. The hope for the future is that molecular biology tests will be available to identify the genetic and cellular alterations of each specific cancer. At present, there are a few cancer antigens that can be identified in blood (such as carcinoembryonic antigen in colon cancer and prostate-specific antigen in prostate cancer), but these tests are relatively crude compared to the potential of molecular biology. Both of these processes also depend upon the factors that originally caused the tumor. Negative factors such as metastatic suppressor gene product protease inhibitors and immunologic rejection will determine if and how fast the cancer will spread. Thus, a cancer may invade and metastasize if there is an imbalance of motility and proteolysis either from excess of positive factors or loss of negative factors (decreased metastatic suppressors, decreased protease inhibitors, or loss of immunologic surveillance). The same factors that are needed for tumor invasion and metastases are required for angiogenesis. A tumor metastasizes only when it begins to lay down new blood vessels.

In considering why cancer is such a common cause of death in the elderly, an understanding of the effect of age on all of these steps is necessary. At present, complete knowledge as to how age effects tumor growth or spread is lacking.

VII. COMMON CANCERS IN THE ELDERLY

A. Lung Cancer

Lung cancer is the leading cause of death in the United States for both men and women. It accounts for 35%

of male and 19% of female cancer deaths. In contrast to other major cancers, lung cancer mortality has increased sharply in the last 50 years, and now averages 50 deaths annually per 100,000 people. Half of all lung cancers occurs in people age 65 and older. At age 50 in men, the incidence of cancer is 100 per 100,000, whereas at age 70 it is 500 per 100,000. For smokers, the risk of lung cancer continues to rise with increasing age. However, for men over 80 and women over 75, the incidence of lung cancers decreases in the general population, reflecting lower smoking prevalence.

Cigarette smoking causes 80–90% of all lung cancer. There is a direct relationship between the total number of cigarettes smoked in a lifetime and development of cancer. In addition, passive exposure to cigarette smoke is a health risk.

The positive aspect of this is that it is never too late to stop smoking. Elderly people who stop smoking will have a lung cancer risk reduction to as high a degree as young people. It is pivotal for health-care workers to advise all people to stop smoking.

Tobacco smoke contains at least 20 carcinogens that can act as either initiators or promoters of cancer. Asbestos exposure increases the risk of cancer 3–5-fold in nonsmokers and 80–90-fold in smokers. A family history of lung cancer also raises the risk of developing lung cancer about 2.5-fold. There are also numerous other substances such as nickel, chromium, arsenic, polyvinyl chloride, isopropyl oil, and various hydrocarbons that have weaker causal links to lung cancer. Ionizing radiation, particularly in miners, acts synergistically with cigarette smoking.

There are four main subtypes of lung cancer: squamous cell, small cell, adenocarcinoma, and large cell. Small cell lung carcinoma (SCLC) is the most lethal and aggressive of all lung cancers, and often the others are described collectively as nonsmall cell lung carcinoma (NSCLC). Most lung cancers are linked to cigarette smoking; however, SCLC and squamous cell have a 20–25 times greater risk in smokers than in nonsmokers. Adenocarcinoma and large cell are about three times the risk in smokers.

SCLC arises from primitive basal epithelial cells of neuroectodermal origin, the Kulchitsky cell. One characteristic of this type of cancer cell is that it sometimes secretes peptide hormones such as adrenocorticotropic hormone (ACTH) or antidiuretic hormone (ADH). The cell of origin progresses through metapla-

sia, atypia, and finally, carcinoma. The cancer grows as a submucosal infiltrate and often causes extrinsic airway compressions with postobstructive pneumonia. SCLC grows rapidly, metastasizes early, and is rarely surgically curable. It is the most common lung cancer to cause superior vena canal syndrome and recurrent laryngeal nerve paralysis (hoarseness).

Squamous cell lung cancer is also highly linked to cigarette smoking. This type of cancer arises from respiratory epithelial injury with replacement of columnar epithelial cells with metaplastic squamous epithelium. The process continues with progression through atypia to carcinoma. It arises in large central airways and often presents with cough, hemoptysis (coughing of blood), and postobstructive pneumonia. This is the slowest growing of lung cancers and is the most likely to be surgically curable.

Adenocarcinoma and large-cell lung cancers typically present in peripheral locations outside of the airways. Adenocarcinoma is associated with pre-existing lung scars. Bronchio-alveolar carcinoma is an uncommon variant of adenocarcinoma, and is not linked to cigarette smoking. It has the best prognosis of all lung cancers. Both adenocarcinoma and large-cell have much better prognosis than SCLC.

With increasing age, the relative proportion of squamous cell cancer increases whereas adenocarcinoma decreases. In people under 55, about 30% of lung cancers are squamous cell, whereas over age 70 close to 50% are. This implies that surgical cure rates would potentially be greater in elderly people.

Lung cancer is usually symptomatic at the time of diagnosis. It may present as cough, wheezing, chest pain, shortness of breath, pneumonia, or coughing up of blood. Many patients with lung cancer will have systemic symptoms such as loss of appetite, weight loss, fatigue, and weakness. In SCLC, patients can have sodium problems due to increased ADH secretion by the tumor or Cushing's syndrome from ACTH secretion. When there are metastases, the patient can have a wide variety of symptoms referable to where the tumor is, such as bone pain, abdominal pain, or confusion. It is important in older people to investigate these nonspecific symptoms and not to just attribute them to "old age" or to comorbid conditions.

B. Colorectal Cancer

Colorectal cancer is the second most common malignancy in the United States. This cancer occurs mainly in older people, and only about 10% is found in people under 50 years. Age is the leading risk factor for colorectal cancer and doubles each decade after age 50 until age 80.

Another major risk factor is the presence of colonic adenomatous polyps. About 5% of adenomas become malignant, with villous adenomas being more likely than tubular adenomas to turn malignant. The larger the adenomas (more than 1 cm), the more likely it is to become cancerous. Also, the more polyps that are present, the more likely there is to be cancer.

If there is one cancer of the colon, there is a greater likelihood to develop a second. Patients with familial polyps are at greater risk to develop colorectal cancer.

Inflammatory bowel disease also predisposes one to cancer of the colon. About 3–5% of patients with ulcerative colitis will develop cancer. The risk of developing cancer increases with duration of the disease and the extent of bowel involvements. Granulomatous colitis also carries an increased risk of cancer, even though it is less than ulcerative colitis.

It is now believed that lifestyle is very important in developing colorectal cancer. A high-fiber, low-fat diet seems to be protective. Beer drinking and sedentary lifestyles have been also suggested as possible risks. Strangely enough, cigarette smoking seems to be protective.

Most colorectal cancers can be classified into five morphological types: adenocarcinoma, mucinous (colloid) adenocarcinoma, signet-ring adenocarcinoma, scirrhous, and carcinoma simplex. The more differentiated the tumor is histologically the better is the prognosis.

Anatomic staging has been very useful in carcinoma of the large bowel, as this is a late metastasizing tumor. The Duke's staging system is the one most commonly used (Table VII). This system prognosticates how the patient is likely to do. Age does not affect prognosis, nor does age affect treatment outcomes. Thus, in older people it seems important to screen for cancer of the colon with digital rectal exams; checking the stools for blood; and in patients with family histories or blood in the stool or a history of polyps to do examination of the colon. It is not yet definitively clear what combination of screening tests should be used.

Prompt recognition of cancer of the colon is very important. If the cancer is in the left side of the colon,

Table VII Duke's Classification of the Stages of Colorectal Cancer

Stage	Localization of cancer	Prognosis (% cure rate)
A	Confined to mucosa or muscularis	80–90
B1	Infiltration through intestinal wall into outer muscle	70
B2	Infiltration through outer muscle	60
C	In regional lymph nodes or immediately adjacent organs	35–50
D	Spread to distant sites	0

it will present with crampy abdominal pain, signs of obstruction, or bleeding. Rectal cancers bleed and the patient complains of constipation, a sense of incomplete evacuation and urgency. Cancers of the right side of the colon can present with abdominal pain, but often presents as iron-deficiency anemia (weakness). This has led many centers to use a complete blood test and serum ferritin as screening tests in the elderly and to examine the colon with barium enema and sigmoidoscopy or colonoscopy in all patients with iron deficiency.

C. Breast Cancer

Breast cancer is the most common invasive malignancy in women and increases in incidence with advancing age. Over 50,000 women more than 65 years of age are diagnosed annually in the United States out of 180,000 new cases developing breast cancer. Lung cancer since 1985 has exceeded breast cancer as a cause of death in women, indicating that therapy for breast cancer has been much more successful than lung cancer. The incidence of breast cancer continues to rise.

Breast cancer is characterized by a long duration and a marked heterogeneity among and within patients. In general, breast cancer is one of the slower growing tumors with a long preclinical (nondetectable) phase. Even when the cancer is apparent and metastasized, the life span of the patient may be for many years. In spite of this, some patients have a more aggressive form of the disease and die rapidly. As a general rule, older patients have more estrogen receptors (better differentiated tumors) and fewer cells in the S-phase of growth or slower growth. These factors should indicate a better prognosis, but elderly women often present with more extensive disease and metastases. Thus, one cannot prognosticate in an individual patient on the basis of age alone. Overall, histologic type, location, and stage are the same at all ages.

A unifying hypothesis to explain breast cancer with age is the theory that most breast cancers arise in the premenstrual period when the breast is proliferating under the cyclic influences of gonadotropins, estrogen, progesterone, and prolactin. It is during this period that the initiation and promotion of neoplasia is likely to occur. Because overall most breast cancer grows slowly, it will take many years to show up, and will do so in the postmenopausal years. The better differentiated tumors (estrogen and progesterone receptor positive), have fewer cells in the S-phase, will take many years to grow, and are the ones that will show up in older ages. Conversely, the faster growing tumors will become clinically apparent in the premenopausal years.

The risk of a woman in the United States to develop breast cancer during her lifetime is 11%, and 3–4% will die from this disease. Overall, 70% of breast cancer patients do not have any identifiable risks. The risk factors that have been implicated include family history, early menarche, late menopause, not having children, first pregnancy over the age of 30, possibly high-fat diet and high alcohol intake, and exposure to ionizing radiation.

Recently, multiple mutations on chromosome 19 (BRCA) have been identified in families with breast and ovarian cancer. This accounts only for 10–20% of breast cancer cases.

The role of hormonal use is still not clear. In both young women taking oral contraceptives and postmenopausal women taking estrogens, there may be a very slight increased risk to develop breast cancer. However, this is not definitive, and in any event, seems to be a very small, if any, risk.

Breast cancer is classified histologically as either ductal or lobular, corresponding to the ducts and lobules of the normal breast. It is believed that in spite of this most tumors arise in the terminal duct sections of the breast. Breast cancer can present as an intraepithelial neoplasm (carcinoma in situ) and is either lobular or ductal. Of the invasive carcinomas, about 75% are ductal, 10% lobular, 9% medullary,

3% minimally invasive ductal, and the remainder are a variety of histological types. Lobular tumors tend to be multicentric and bilateral. A poor prognostic finding is inflammatory breast cancer in which tumor cells block lymphatic channels in the breast. Paget's disease refers to a neoplastic eczemoid change of the nipple. Its prognosis is determined by the underlying neoplasm.

Noninvasive carcinomas are almost cured by mastectomy, as they rarely metastasize. Ductal carcinoma in situ can be palpable or more likely is found in mammography as microcalcifications. It is often unilateral and unifocal but occasionally can be extensive throughout the breast. It is usually found in older women. In contrast, lobular carcinoma *in situ* is invisible on mammography as it does not calcify, is usually multicentric and often bilateral, and is found in younger women.

Clinical staging is based upon the size and extension of the tumor, spread to lymph nodes and metastatic sites (Table VIII). The chances of cure worsens with the higher stages and the absolute number of involved lymph nodes. Also, the larger the tumor the worse the prognosis. Tumors with a high content of estrogen and progesterone receptors relapse slightly less, are more receptive to hormonal manipulation, and therefore patients with this tend to live longer. Younger women also do worse than older women, and obesity is a risk for worse prognosis.

Breast cancer usually is found as a painless mass, often first felt by the woman. At the time of discovery, the average size of the lesion is 2.5 cm, and 50% of invasive lesions have already spread to the axillary nodes on the same side (Stage II or greater). In contrast, the average size of the breast cancer found on mammography is 0.5 cm and is much less likely to have spread. Mammography, however, has a 10% false negative rate, and any mass should be biopsied if there is any doubt to its benign nature.

At the time of initial diagnosis, even many early breast cancers have already spread within the breast or have metastasized (metastases too small to be felt). This is why in many cases the patient, after removal of the tumor, is given radiation to the breast (if lumpectomy was chosen rather than mastectomy) and adjuvant chemotherapy to eradicate micrometastases. Tamixofen (an antiestrogen to the breast) is useful particularly in the elderly woman with estrogen receptor positive tissues.

Table VIII Stages of Breast Cancer

Stage	Tumor (cm)	Tumor in nodes	Metastases
0	in situ	None	None
I	≤2	None	None
IIA	2–5 or	None	None
	≤2	Movable same side axillary	None
IIB	>5	None	None
	2–5	Movable same side axillary	None
IIIA	≤5	Fixed same side axillary	None
			None
	>5	Movable or fixed same side axillary	None
IIIB	Extends to chest wall or skin	None or any same side axillary or internal mammary	None
	Any size or extension	Internal mammary	None
IV	Any size or extension	None or spread to any lymph node	Present

D. Cancer of the Prostate

Prostate cancer is the most common cancer of men and is second only to lung cancer as a cause of cancer death. It is responsible for over 3% of all deaths in men over age 55. The age-specific mortality rate is double in African-American men as compared to Whites. In 1992, more than 134,000 men were diagnosed with prostate cancer, and over 32,000 died. More than one-half of men diagnosed with prostate cancer die within 10 years. Cancer of the prostate is the most common malignancy in human beings if one looks at autopsy data. Over 40% of men over the age of 75 have cancer in their prostate glands, but over a lifetime only 23% of these men will develop clinical disease, and only 7% of them will die of the disease. Thus, there is a great difference between having histologic evidence of the disease and actual clinical problems from it.

The incidence and mortality from prostate cancer in the United States has climbed steadily since 1970, particularly in Blacks. In African Americans, cancer of the prostate is more often diagnosed in later stages, is more likely to be poorly differentiated, and survival time is shorter than in Whites. In contrast, black Africans have a low incidence of the disease. The incidence of cancer of the prostate is low in Asia, but rises in Asian immigrants to the United States. American Eskimos have a low risk for prostate cancer as compared to Americans in general or to Native American groups.

The explanation for these epidemiological differences have been contributed to levels of testosterone and diet. African Americans have higher testosterone levels than Whites or African Blacks. The dietary factors that are suspected include quantity and type of fat, low selenium, low carotene, and high protein. It appears that unsaturated fat is a greater risk than saturated fats. Omega-2 fatty acids found in seafood, as eaten by the Eskimos, may be protective. Other possible risks include industrial pollutants, high cadmium, and genetic factors.

Cancer of the prostate may be described as either clinically important (threatening the life or well-being of the patient), or clinically unimportant (latent and no threat to the person harboring it). However, time is critical in determining if a cancer that is clinically unimportant becomes important. Thus, many men will have a latent cancer which, if given enough time, will go through the multistep process necessary to develop into a clinically important malignancy. The latent cancers are usually small, well differentiated, noninvasive, and there is a normal serum prostatic-specific antigen (PSA) that does not rise. The clinically important cancers are larger, poorly differentiated, invasive, and the serum PSA is high and keeps rising.

In many elderly men, if there is a life expectancy of less than 10 years, or if the patient has a disease that is likely to be fatal in the near future, one does not have to rush to treat the patient.

The most common type of cancer in the prostate is adenocarcinoma, accounting for almost 98% of all

Table IX Staging of Cancer of the Prostate

Stage	Characteristics
A1	Well differentiated, found in biopsy, not clinically apparent
A2	More diffuse pattern, but not clinically apparent
B1	Palpable nodule, one lobe only, less than 1.5 cm in diameter
B2	Larger than 1.5 cm
C1	Invades tissues around prostate
C2	Invades seminal vesicles
D1	Involves regional lymph nodes
D2	Metastatic

cancers. They may be well, moderately, or poorly differentiated. They are usually staged as shown in Table IX. A Stage C or D cancer is definitely life-threatening. A Stage B cancer progression is usually watched to see whether or not it is clinically important.

Most patients with Stage A disease are asymptomatic at the time of diagnosis. As the tumor grows, it may lead to obstructive symptoms of the bladder or urethra, such as frequency of urination, nocturia, hesitancy, and narrow urinary stream. As the disease spreads locally, it may lead to constipation and lymphedema of the legs. It usually metastasizes to bone, and the patient may present with low back pain, which can be mistaken for arthritis.

Cancer of the prostate is often diagnosed after a nodule is felt on rectal examination of the prostate gland, followed by ultrasonography and needle biopsy. Now that the prostatic-specific test (PSA) is in wide use, many men are found to have mild elevations (4–10 mg/ml), which is nonspecific as benignly enlarged prostate will give these readings. In addition, the test is not all that sensitive, as about 10% of men with normal PSA levels have carcinoma of the prostate. Only about 25% of men with PSA of 4–10 mg/ml will have cancer, but about 65% of men with a PSA of greater than 10 mg/ml will have cancer of the prostate. Thus, the sensitivity and specificity of the test is not as good as one would like using 4 mg/ml as a cutoff. Using the 10 mg/ml cutoff, the detection of patients with cancer is 25% of Stage A, 35% of Stage B, 50% of Stage C, and 65% of Stage D. [*See* PROSTATE.]

E. Cancer of the Bladder

Over 50,000 new cases of cancer of the bladder are diagnosed early in the United States, with about 10,000 people dying of it. The older one gets, the more likely they are to develop bladder cancer, and the survival rate is lower with advancing age.

Cancer of the bladder is more common in men, and is related to occupational exposure to aryl-amines such as found in workers in the organic chemical, dye, rubber, and paint industries. The strongest association is found in cigarette smokers. Other associations are in people with chronic inflammation of the bladder. There have been fears that artificial sweeteners (cyclamate and saccharin) may induce bladder cancer, but to date, this has not been shown in human beings.

In the United States, approximately 95% of all bladder cancers are transitional cell carcinomas. About 3% are squamous cell, and the rest are adenocarcinomas. Most bladder tumors are papillary transitional cell carcinomas. They are classified by into three grades. Grade 1 is well differentiated with limited atypia and mitoses. Grade 3 lesions have a marked increase in cell layers and cell size with marked pleomorphism and mitoses. Grade 2 is intermediate. It is believed that cancer of the bladder arises by damage to the bladder endothelium by carcinogens, infections, stones, or other foreign bodies (such as indwelling catheters). This will lead to hyperplastic growth and immature cells. This will progress (multiple hits) through metaplasia to carcinoma in situ, and finally invasive carcinoma.

Staging of cancer of the bladder is shown in Table X. The lower the stage and grade, the better is the

Table X Staging for Cancer of the Bladder

Stage	Characteristics
0	Tumor limited to mucosa, carcinoma in situ
A	Extension into submucosa
B1	Extension less than halfway through muscularis
B2	Extension more than halfway through muscularis
C	Involves perivesical fat
D1	Invades lymph nodes below sacrum
D2	Involved lymph nodes above aortic bifurcation or distant metastases

Table XI Staging of Cancer of the Kidney

Stage	Characteristics
I	Tumor confined to kidney
II	Involved perinephric fat only
III	Involves renal vein, or regional nodes, or both
IV	Distant metastases or extension beyond perinephric fat

prognosis. Cancer of the bladder tends to occur as multiple lesions and to recur.

Most patients with cancer of the bladder present with painless hematuria. If any red cells are persistently found on urinalysis, cystoscopy is indicated. Less frequently the patient will complain of dysuria and frequency. Advanced cancer is rare as a presenting symptom, as most people will go to a doctor when blood is noted in the urine.

F. Cancer of the Kidney

Over 25,000 cases of cancer of the kidney are diagnosed yearly with close to 11,000 deaths. This represents about 3% of cancer deaths and is more common in men than women. Cancer of the kidney is most common from ages 50–70.

The risk factors to develop cancer of the kidney include cigarette smoking, obesity, and analgesic abuse. Other environmental factors include asbestos, cadmium exposure, and working in the leather industries. Patients with end-stage kidney disease who develop cysts are also at increased risk.

The most common histologic type of kidney cancer is adenocarcinoma. Tumor grading is not used frequently in this type of malignancy. Staging is shown in Table XI. In more than one-half of patients, metastatic disease is present at time of diagnosis.

Cancer of the kidney clearly presents as gross hematuria, pain, and flank mass, but this is found in only about 20% of cases. Many times the disease can be noted by painless microscopic hematuria or is found when the patient presents with systemic symptoms such as anemia, fever, weight loss, and fatigue. Rarely, the patient may have polycythemia. Early disease can only be detected by evaluating any microscopic hematuria. [*See* RENAL AND URINARY TRACT FUNCTION.]

G. Ovarian Cancer

Ovarian cancer is the eighth most common cancer of women in the United States, but it is the fourth leading cause of cancer death. More women die from ovarian cancer than from cervical and endometrial death combined. Approximately 21,000 new patients are diagnosed every year and 13,000 women die. Cancer of the ovary increases with age and peaks at age 80. Approximately 1% of female deaths are from cancers of the ovary.

Ovarian cancer is usually found in industrialized nations with the notable exception of Japan. Japanese Americans have a higher incidence of ovarian cancer than Japanese in Japan, but it is still lower than in the white population. In the United States, ovarian cancer is most common in white women. Risk factors include a low number of pregnancies (each pregnancy lowers the risk by about 10%); use of anticonvulsant drugs, history of breast cancer, and exposure to asbestos and talc. Birth control pills lower the risk to develop ovarian cancer.

Most cancer of the ovary is of the epithelial type and in women over 65 accounts for 95% of the cases. Cancer of the ovary spreads early by surface shedding, lymphatic spread, and less commonly, blood-borne metastases. Over 50% of women presenting with this cancer have disease spread outside of the pelvis (Stage III or IV). Table XII shows the staging used for ovarian cancer. Older women will present with a Stage III or IV disease about 65% of the time.

Ovarian cancer is usually asymptomatic until it

Table XII Staging of Ovarian Cancer

Stage	Characteristics
I	Limited to ovaries
IA	One ovary; no ascites
IB	Both ovaries, no ascites
IC	With ascites on cells in the peritoneum
II	One or both ovaries with pelvic extension
IIA	Involves uterus or fallopian tubes
IIB	Involves other pelvic structures
IIC	With ascites or cells in peritoneum
III	1 or 2 ovaries; intraperitoneal metastases or positive retroperitoneal nodes Extension to small bowel or omentum
IV	Distant metastases

spreads. By the time the woman notices pain, abdominal swelling, vaginal bleeding, or GI distress, the disease is widespread. The only way to identify early disease is by pelvic examination and finding an adnexal mass. Any adnexal enlargement in a postmenopausal woman should be considered a malignancy until proven otherwise. Ultrasound is useful in detecting ovarian masses, but is considered too expensive to use for routine screening.

H. Cancer of the Uterus

Cancer of the uterine cervix can and does occur in elderly women. However, the peak age occurrence is between ages 48–55. Hopefully, vigorous annual screening of young women (Pap smears) will result in fewer and fewer cases in older ages. At present it is still recommended that Pap smears be done in elderly women who have not been adequately screened up to the age of 65. Up to 60% of women over the age of 65 have not had a Pap smear taken.

Cancer of the endometrium is the most common of all gynecologic cancers. The peak age to develop this cancer is 60–64. It is a relatively easy cancer to detect; it spreads late and Pap smears will detect about 50% of them. The key to detecting gynecologic cancers in older women is an annual pelvic exam.

I. Other Cancers

Cancer does arise in any organ of the body, including the skin and hematopoietic tissues. In all of these systems, the same principles apply, that to develop cancer there are multiple hits resulting in greater degrees of undifferentiation and spread. As a general rule, therefore, given the time necessary to develop a malignancy, the elderly are more likely to have almost any malignancy.

The original histologic grading and clinical staging for malignancy was done in Hodgkin's disease, and then the other lymphomas. These principles are now applied to all cancers and have proven useful in predicting care rates and in devising therapeutic regimens.

Unfortunately, cure rates in many malignancies are still very low. Cancer of the pancreas, stomach, esophagus, brain, liver, multiple myeloma, and acute leukemia all carry very poor prognoses. As a general rule, in the elderly cancer presents in a more advanced form, is more likely to have metastasized, and the patient is less likely to be able to tolerate as much therapy.

VIII. SCREENING FOR CANCER

The goal of screening for cancer is to detect disease at an early point and to be able to institute curative therapy at that time. Any screening procedure must meet certain criteria to be used; it must be safe, inexpensive, easy to do, have high sensitivity and specificity. The illness being screened should be common and a cure must be available.

There are four benefits sought in any cancer-screening program. The primary benefit is to find disease that would be fatal if left untreated. The second benefit is that disease found early requires less harmful therapy. Third is that it is cheaper to society if cancer is found early, and finally, the people who test negative are reassured. However, any screening program also has many disadvantages. In many cancers that are detected the prognosis is not changed so that the morbidity to the patient is actually longer. Second, screening detects findings that if left alone, would not have harmed the patient. The third disadvantage is that false-positive tests lead the physician to order many other tests causing considerable anxiety to the patient. The fourth problem is that many of the diagnostic tests can in themselves be harmful. The fifth disadvantage is cost to society, and finally, false-negative tests will falsely reassure the patient.

Taking all of this into consideration, extensive cancer screening is usually reserved for cervix, breast, and colon. Although there are advocates for screening for cancer of the prostate and lung, these are not universally accepted. The current recommendations for screening are shown in Table XIII. These are in flux as most screening programs have not shown a reduction in the mortality or morbidity of the cancer being studied. At the present time, however, most people are following these suggestions.

IX. PRINCIPLES OF CANCER THERAPY

The mainstays of cancer therapies are surgery, radiation, and chemotherapy. In recent years, newer methods of therapy are bone marrow transplantation, use

Table XIII Screening Recommendations for Cancer

Site	Recommendations
Cervix	Annual Pap smear after age 18; after three negative smears, perhaps every 3 years at discretion of physician
Breast	Breast self-exam monthly; physician exam yearly; mammography every 1–2 years after age 40; mammography yearly after age 50 questionable if mammography necessary after age 80
Colorectal	Yearly exam after age 40; yearly fecal occult blood after age 50; Sigmoidoscopy every 3–5 years after age 50; colonoscopy or barium enema in people with personal history or family history of colon or rectal cancer or polyps or ulcerative colitis
Lung	Chest X-rays not recommended, but may be used in the elderly at high risk
Prostate	Digital exam prostate yearly; prostatic-specific antigen very controversial

of cytokines, immunotherapy, hormones, and antihormones, and gene therapy. The elderly are candidates for cancer therapy; indeed, all too often they are denied therapy because either the doctor, the patient, or their family are misguided as to the benefits of treatment. In many instances the elderly do better with therapy than the young.

A. Surgery

Surgery is the oldest treatment for cancer, and until recently was the only therapy that could cure cancer patients. Surgical treatment has changed drastically in the past 20 years. Advances in surgical techniques and a better understanding of the patterns of spread of individual cancers have led to more successful operations. The development of alternate and adjunct treatment strategies has led to less extensive surgery.

Age is not an independent risk factor for surgery. The determinants of surgical risk include the status of the heart, lungs, kidneys, brain, liver hematopoietic, and endocrine systems as well as the nutritional status and presence of diseases such as diabetes. An elderly patient who is healthy can withstand surgery as well as a young person using newer methods of anesthesia and postoperative monitoring.

Surgery can be used for six different reasons:

1. Removal of primary cancer
2. Reduce bulk of residual disease
3. Resection of metastatic disease with curative intent
4. Surgery for treatment of an emergency situation in cancer, such as bleeding or infection
5. Palliation
6. Reconstruction and rehabilitation

B. Radiation Therapy

Radiation therapy may be used as either primary therapy or as an adjunct to surgery or chemotherapy. Primary radiation therapy is often used in the elderly with multiple diseases who are poor surgical risks, as there is no appreciable acute mortality from irradiation. Associated medical conditions do not contraindicate curative treatments. Other advantages of radiation in the frail elderly are preservation of function in the organ from which the cancer originates, and that curative treatment can be delivered even when the anatomic boundaries of the tumor are not amenable to surgery.

The disadvantages of radiation therapy include the disturbing side effects, the length of time of treatment (up to 2 months), and the development of secondary malignancies. Secondary malignancies are of less concern in the very old.

Newer methods and equipment have made radiation therapy much more tolerable. Certainly secondary or adjuvant radiotherapy with limited surgery and chemotherapy are very attractive to older people. Limited surgery followed by local radiation treatment decreases the morbidity of either treatment alone. Likewise, radiation as an adjunct with chemotherapy allows the physician to decrease the dose of either treatment alone, and thus avoid some of the side effects.

C. Chemotherapy

It has been thought that changes in pharmacokinetics of drugs with age may limit the ability to deliver curative doses of chemotherapy to the elderly. However, there are still relatively few studies that have shown this. It is widely accepted that CCNU and methotrexate doses should be reduced in the elderly, and bleomycin toxicity is greater with advancing age. Usually, the limiting factor in delivering chemotherapy is bone marrow reserve, which is decreased in the elderly. However, the wide availability of blood products and growth factors to stimulate bone marrow (such as erythropoietin and colony-stimulating factors) have greatly improved the situation. Bone marrow transplantation has not been well studied in older people. Bone marrow may be harvested from the patient and retransfused into them after chemotherapy is given (autologous transplantation). Allogenic transplantation from a different donor so far has not been used in the elderly and is limited mainly to young people.

Chemotherapy is often dreaded by older people because of its systemic symptoms. There is no evidence that the elderly tolerate this form of treatment any worse than the young, nor is there data showing it does not work as well. Many more studies are needed to assess the true value of chemotherapy in the elderly.

D. Hormonal Therapy

Certain tumors are responsive to hormonal manipulation, notably cancer of the breast and cancer of the prostate. The antiestrogen tomoxifen has been particularly useful in postmenopausal women with cancer of the breast to palliate metastatic disease and perhaps to prevent development of further disease. Other hormonal therapy, such as oophorectomy, adrenalectomy, and megesterol therapy have been useful. In cancer of the prostate, orchiectomy, estrogen therapy, the use of luteinizing hormone-releasing hormone (LHRH) agonists to lower testosterone, and alpha 5 reductase inhibitors to block the reduction of testos-terone to dihydrotestosterone have been useful in palliation.

E. Biological Therapy

The use of red blood cell, platelet, and at times granulocyte transfusions have greatly helped patients overcome the severe effects of anemia, bleeding from thrombocytopenia, and infections from granulocytopenia. Clotting factors are available for people who need them. Now there are numerous growth factors such as erythropoietin to stimulate red cell production; granulocyte macrophage colony-stimulating factor (GM-CSF) to stimulate production of both granulocytes and macrophages; granulocyte-stimulating factor (G-CSF) to stimulate granulocyte production; macrophage colony-stimulating factor (M-CSF) to increase production of macrophages; and interleukin-3, which increases neutrophils and eosinophiles and sometimes basophiles and platelets. Studies are in progress using combinations of these factors to enable the cancer patient to receive more curative therapies.

Immunotherapy is also being widely studied in cancer therapy. Immune cells secrete two types of soluble proteins: antibodies and cytokines. Both of these have the ability to destroy tumor cells. Specific tumor antibodies may be directed against the person's own cancer and are being studied as a means of therapy. The cytokines, which are actually hormones produced in the immune system, are potentially very useful. Studies have shown that use of interferons and interleukin-2 are promising in some cancers. Nonspecific immunotherapy to increase the immune system has been widely tried with bacillus Calmette Guerin (BCG), a modified form of the tubercle bacillus. This has not been very successful, but it is hoped that more specific immunotherapy with monoclonal antibodies and specific cytokines will be of greater value.

F. Gene Therapy

The goals of gene therapy are to introduce a gene into a patient's body to target and repair malfunctioning cells with minimal side effects. There are three strategies of gene therapy. Dysfunctional genes may be replaced and altered to become functional or augmented with a healthy gene at a different locus in the cell. At present, gene augmentation is the most feasible.

In order to be able to perform gene therapy, the defect in the disease must be understood and a normal functional gene has to be cloned. To date, the most effective way to get a gene into a cell has been using a virus vector. Human cancer, as discussed previously, is often associated with aberrant gene expression or mutations in specific genes (oncogenes). The hope is that the effects of the abnormal gene can be overcome. Other strategies for gene therapy are to insert a gene that would be lethal to the cancer cell; insert a gene making the cell sensitive to chemotherapy; insert an antisense oncogene into the cancer cell; or to introduce a gene to trigger apoptosis. An antisense oncogene is transcribed in reverse order to the oncogene so that the complementary mRNAs hybridize and the oncogene activity is stopped, as there is no translation.

X. SUPPORTIVE CARE AND QUALITY OF LIFE

In caring for cancer patients, it is clear that there are numerous problems that must be addressed. Often the patient will die, has considerable pain, is not eating and is nauseated and vomiting, and is depressed. Any cancer program must deal with these in order to achieve any quality of life.

A. Pain

Numerous studies have shown that 30–50% of patients undergoing cancer therapy and 60–90% of patients with advanced disease have pain. Patients with cancer are managed most effectively with a multidisciplinary approach. The goal is to allow the patient sufficient relief of pain in order to be able to tolerate therapy. For terminally ill patients, the goal is to allow them to function at a level they choose and to die free of pain.

Drug therapy should be effective in virtually all patients. With mild to moderate pain, nonopiate drugs are used. If they do not work, one switches to codeine, oxycodone, or propoxyphene. For moderate to severe pain, the stronger opiates are used. To date, the most effective drug seems to be morphine. Now

that it is in oral form, it is quite easy to take. Meperidine should not be used, as it causes CNS irritability. The newer availability of fentanyl transdermal patches, a strong opioid analgesic, has been a very useful albeit an expensive addition to treat chronic pain. At terminal stages morphine may be used as an intravenous drip regulated by the patient.

In addition to analgesic, other drugs may be used to treat associated depression, sedation, nausea, and constipation. When using narcotics, it is essential to use the drugs "around the clock"—in other words, to prevent pain and not to give it just when the pain occurs. Even if it means waking the patient, it is important to keep the blood level of the drug at a level to prevent pain. Combinations of drugs to potentiate the opiates are very useful. All possible approaches should be tried such as acupuncture, injection of painful sites, physical therapy, nitrous oxide, hypnotism, and biofeedback. If need be, surgical procedures such as cordotomy or local blocks of nerves should be done. The goal is to eliminate pain.

B. Nausea and Vomiting

New advances in the last 10 years have decreased the problem of nausea and vomiting in the cancer patient. The phenothiazines were the only drugs available to control nausea and vomiting until almost 10 years ago. Metoclopramide, a dopamine central and peripheral receptor antagonist, was the first new drug introduced, and now there are other drugs and combinations of drugs that may be used. The substituted benzamides that block serotonin receptors (specifically the type 3 or 5-HT3 receptors) are becoming available. At present edansetron is available in the United States. Other useful drugs include butyrophenones (haloperidol); phenothiazines (prochlorperazene); corticosteroids, benzodiazepines, and cannabinoids.

C. Nutritional Support

Control of nausea and vomiting help to allow the patient to eat and drink. It is essential to offer the patient high-calorie and high-nutrient food supplements, to use intravenous therapy when necessary, even at home, and to consider the use of gastrostomy tube feedings if wanted. Tube feedings may be stopped if and when the patient can eat or no longer chooses this therapy.

D. Psychological and Social Supports

The case of patients with cancer require a multidisciplinary team. Various supportive care and continuing-care programs have been developed to manage dying patients both in the hospital and at home. The focus of treatment shifts to symptom control and palliative comfort care. Home-care services, home and hospital-based teams, and home and hospital-based hospice care are readily available to cancer care patient and the family. Both the patient and the family need help, supportive psychotherapy, and preparation for death. The team is available 24 hours a day. Nurses, social workers, and physicians work together with the pa-tient and family to achieve comfort and a dignified death.

BIBLIOGRAPHY

Brocklehurst, J. C., Tallis, R. C., & Fillit, H. M. (1992). *Textbook of geriatric medicine and gerontology* (4th ed.). Edinburgh: Churchill Livingstone.

Cohen, H. J. (Ed.). (1987). Cancer I general aspects and Cancer II: Specific neoplasms. *Clinics in Geriatric Medicine* (Vols. 3:3, 3:4; pp. 419–824). August 1987, November 1987. Philadelphia: W. B. Saunders Company.

DeVita, V., Jr., Hellman, S., & Rosenberg, S. A. (Ed.). (1993). *Cancer principles and practice of oncology* (4th ed.). Philadelphia: JB Lippincott & Co.

Hazzard, W. R., Andres, R., Bierman, E. L., & Blurs, J. P. (Eds.). (1990). *Principles of geriatric medicine and gerontology* (4th ed.). New York: McGraw Hill, Inc.

Kelley, W. N. (Ed.). (1993). *Textbook of internal medicine* (2nd ed.). Philadelphia: JB Lippincott & Co.

Cardiovascular System

Alvar Svanborg

University of Illinois at Chicago

Bundle of His A small band of atypical cardiac muscle fibers that originates in the atrioventricular node in the interatrial septum, passes through the atrioventricular junction, and then runs beneath the endocardium of the right ventricle on the membranous part of the interventricular septum. It divides at the upper end of the muscular part of the interventricular septum into right and left branches that descend in the septal wall of the right and left ventricle, respectively, to be distributed to those two chambers. This bundle propagates the atrial-contraction rhythm to the ventricles, and its interruption produces heart block.

Concentric Hypertrophy Hypertrophy of the heart. The wall becomes thicker at a largely unchanged inner radius.

Eccentric Hypertrophy The increase of wall thickness of the heart is balanced by some adaptive increase also of diastolic lumina.

Echocardiography A method of graphically recording the position and motion of the heart walls or the internal structures of the heart and neighboring tissue by the echo obtained from beams of ultrasonic waves directed through the chest wall. Called also ultrasonic cardiography.

Endothelium The layer of epithelial cells that lines the cavities of the heart and the blood and lymph vessels, and the serous cavities of the body.

Laser-Doppler *Laser*: (light amplification by stimulated emission of radiation) A device that transforms light of various frequencies into an extremely intense, small, and nearly nondivergent beam of monochromatic radiation in the visible region with all waves in phase. Capable of mobilizing immense heat and power when focused at close range, it is used as a tool in surgical procedures, in diagnosis, and in physiologic studies. *Doppler effect*: The relationship of the apparent frequency of waves, as of sound, light, and radio waves, to the relative motion of the source of the waves and the observer, the frequency increasing as the two approach each other and decreasing as they move apart.

Myocardium The middle and thickest layer of the heart wall, the main component of the cardiac muscle.

Myosin The most abundant form of protein (2/3) in muscle. Along with actin, it is responsible for the contraction and relaxation of muscle and is the main constituent of the thick filaments of muscle fibers.

Sarcoplasm The interfibrillary matter of the striated muscles; the substance in which the fibrillae of the muscle fiber are embedded.

Windkessel Phenomenon Old German expression used to describe the wall compliance of aorta and large conduit arteries, largely like the effect of an air-filled container (Windkessel) coupled to a pump tube circulatory system, transforming the rhythmic cardiac output into a more even, although still pulsatile, blood supply to tissues.

Studies of aging of the **CARDIOVASCULAR SYS-TEM** have only recently been possible in humans through the development of noninvasive techniques that can be applied without risks and used in systematic, longitudinal population studies. This has allowed improved understanding of how to distinguish manifestations of aging from symptoms of morbidity and, consequently, a widening of knowledge about aging also at ages when morbidity becomes common. This article will exemplify findings about aging in the last part of life and possibilities for a postponement of functional or morphological decline.

I. INTRODUCTION

The cardiovascular (CV) system is one of the organ systems for which it is difficult to clearly differentiate the morphological and functional manifestations of aging from symptoms of morbidity. This is especially the case at ages when aging really takes its toll. Many of the most common heart and vascular diseases in humans occur at ages when aging per se simultaneously influences morphology and function.

There are primarily two reasons why the understanding of aging of the CV system separately from disease has markedly advanced during recent years. Developments of noninvasive techniques have allowed more detailed and repeated examinations not only in animals, but also in humans. For the CV system, examples are echocardiography (EKG) and laser-Doppler measurements. In spite of these technical advancements, a prerequisite for an improvement of the knowledge on aging distinguished from disease in older persons is longitudinal follow-ups of populations or samples representative for a population, or at least for a definable part of a population. Abnormal conditions can remain relatively silent and go underdiagnosed over long periods even when this condition might have certain consequences for the circulatory system.

Many attempts have recently been made to combine longitudinal population studies with advanced studies of the circulatory system through noninvasive and harmless examinations. Examples are the Framingham and Baltimore longitudinal studies in the United States and the longitudinal study of 70-year-olds in Gothenburg, Sweden. Gains in knowledge about aging have also been made through studies in animals with a shorter life span than humans, and for which genetic and environmental influence could be better evaluated. In the United States, the National Institute of Aging offers inbred strains of rats up to very old age. For a review of the literature concerning CV aging, refer to Folkow and Svanborg (1993), where we have discussed most of the information presented here in more detail and have listed appropriate references. For an overview refer to Fleg (1986) and Lakatta (1990).

In the same way as for many other organs, the aging-related changes in morphology and function of the CV system vary not only between individuals within the same species, but also between cells, organs, and organ systems in a given individual. The dominating morphological change in the human body during aging is organ atrophy due to a decrease in cell mass and a decline in the body water. At ages above 65–70, the average person shows a decline in all body fractions even though the decline in body fat is slower than the decline in cell mass and body water, at least in the age interval 70–80. This decline in body cell mass results in a lower metabolic demand on the circulation, and the drying of tissues caused by a declining proportion of body water would obviously have impact on organ distensibility or compliance, as illustrated by an early-in-life starting decline of the elasticity of the lens in the eye, running parallel to a decline in hydration.

At the cellular level, cross-bridge connections between proteins as well as reported changes in the intracellular handling of calcium seem to contribute to changes in compliance of heart and vessel walls. The changes in body water have been reported to occur mainly extracellularly, but certain changes might occur also intracellularly. At the organ level (e.g., in the heart), the proportion of muscle tissue in relation to connective tissue components delines, which in itself should influence tissue compliance. Also within the connective tissues, changes producing increased stiffness have been reported, implying (e.g., a fragmentation of the elastin filaments and a faster decline in proportion of the more elastic of the collagen fibers). Some of these processes leading to increased organ stiffness are presumably influenced by exogenous factors, as illustrated by observations that high blood glucose concentration might trigger formation of cross-links between proteins, and that physical activity might delay rate of decline of the more elastic collagen fibers. As will be further emphasized below, the changes in distensibility and compliance of the heart and vessels are of central importance for the understanding of aging-related morphological and functional changes related to aging.

II. MORPHOLOGICAL ALTERATIONS

The structural geometry of the heart and vessels varies during the adult period of human life not only because of aging and morbidity, but also because of other factors. Increased demand on the heart caused by, for example, extensive physical training, increased blood volume during pregnancy, or increased metabolic demand because of, for example, hyperfunction of the thyroid gland, usually results in an eccentric hypertrophy, implying a thickening of the left chamber wall with some adaptive increase also of the chamber volume. These changes are generally reversible. The other main form of morphological change is the concentric hypertrophy characteristic for, for example, long-standing blood pressure increase, or at considerable hypertension even after shorter periods. In those situations the wall thickness increases at a generally unchanged inner chamber diameter. Various combinations of eccentric and concentric hypertrophy occur when both preload and afterload are changing. During aging there are changes in both preload and afterload because of changes in tissue compliance, changes in myocardial contractile strength, and so on, which will affect the cardiac structure.

The changes in structure and volume of the human heart are dominated by both concentric and eccentric hypertrophies of primarily the left ventricle and a widening of the left atrium. In apparently healthy older persons, there are signs of a small increase of diastolic lumina during rest associated with a modest increase in myocardial mass (i.e., some concentric hypertrophy). One reason for these structural changes is obviously the changes in vascular compliance leading to augmented peripheral resistance and a pulse pressure elevation, and a higher end-systolic afterload. But available information indicates that of greater importance for the structural and functional changes are the alterations of the compliance of the heart, leading to a decline in the filling of the heart and to an eccentric hypertrophy, widening of diastolic lumina

associated with a modest increase in myocardial mass, and certain impairment of the diastolic function.

The aging-related changes in tissue compliance influence also the dynamics of the heart valves, which become thicker, fibrotic, and sometimes with calcium deposits. These changes often prolong the closure time and constitute a hinder for a tight closure. To what extent changes in the valves between the left atrium and ventricle might be the main reason for the marked increase in the volume of the left atrium during aging is not clearly demonstrated.

In a clinical perspective, these changes in the heart volume and structure are important. Heart volume estimations through X-ray show an increase in heart volume in relation to body surface area from age 30–40 to 65–70 of approximately 100–150 ml. At ages above 70, however, no further significant volume expansion in relation to body surface area has been documented, which might imply that at these higher ages, the decline in cell mass, and organ atrophy in general, dominates over functionally induced heart volume alterations. At least in the later phases of life, muscle cells in general show a decline in number; and this is also the case for the myocardium. The myocardium is, however, able to compensate in volume for this declining cell number through hypertrophy. Several studies on autopsy material have reported that the heart weight in relation to the body weight is increasing with age even up to the ninth and tenth decades. The older the age, however, the more difficult it is to differentiate between aging and morbidity, and detailed longitudinal studies are almost always a prerequisite for the identification of changes caused by aging per se.

These gross anatomical changes occurring with increasing age have obvious and important consequences for diagnostic and therapeutic criteria. Chest X ray with estimation or measurement of the heart size is one of the most common examinations. The awareness of aging-related changes versus, often rather similar, changes indicating morbidity is indeed essential.

Microscopically, the myocardial muscle cells are commonly somewhat larger and fewer, and with an accumulation of lipofuscin in the paranuclear sarcoplasma, often associated with basophilic degeneration, and occasional focal amyloid deposits. An accumulation of fat cells between the myocytes and increased amounts of subepicardial fat is a common

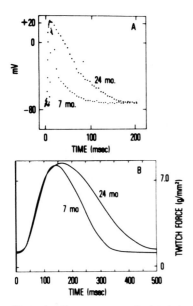

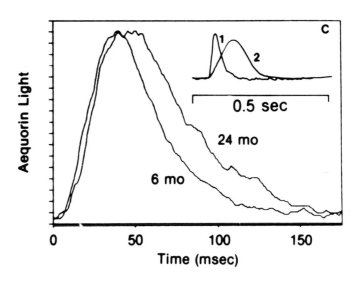

Figure 1 Computer resynthesis of simultaneous measurements of transmembrane action potentials (A) and contraction–relaxation events in ventricular papillary muscles from adult (7 mo) and senescent (24 mo) rat hearts. (B) Changes in aequorin luminescence in cardiac muscles from adult (6 mo) and senescent (24 mo) rats, reflecting age-related alterations of intracellular free calcium during contraction–relaxation cycle. (C) Principal time relationships between luminescence and contraction curves. Note prolongations of "plateau" phases and of repolarization, relaxation, and calcium decay phases in senescent myocardium. (From Orchard & Lakatta, 1985. *Journal of General Physiology, 86*, 637.)

finding. It is not clear that these cellular and interstitial alterations influence myocardial function.

III. MYOCARDIAL FUNCTION

Most studies at the cellular level have been performed on animals. Modest changes have been reported in mitochondria and enzymes, suggesting a decline in oxidation, energy storage, and transformation that might be significant for the function at least during increased demands on function. No changes in resting membrane potentials have been reported, but on excitation, the action potentials usually show some prolongation of the depolarized phase and repolarization events in association with prolongations of the refractory periods. There is also a shift toward slower myosin isoforms. The most characteristic change in the aging myocardial cell function is a prolonged decay time from the peak contraction (Figure 1). The sarcoplasmic reuptake of intracellular free calcium ions, and perhaps also transmembrane calcium expulsion, proceeds at a slower rate in the aging myocardium,

and the rate of cell relaxation is slower (for review see Lakatta, 1987). In addition, in humans the end-systolic afterload is often increased, which implies not only some prolongation of the systolic isometric and ejection phases but also, and perhaps particularly so, a prolongation of the relaxation phase, interfering with the diastolic filling. In a classical study by Strandell during the 1960s no difference between young and old were found in pulmonary wedge pressure at rest, but pressure rose more in the old during exercise, which might at least partly be due to the reduction in diastolic compliance of the old heart. More recent results by Lakatta's group might, however, indicate that a less vigorous myocardium with attenuated increased sympathetic inotropic activation may play a role.

Furthermore, the receptor-mediated cardiac response to catecholamines is also attenuated in the hearts of older people, probably due to insufficient function of the messenger system from the receptor into the cell. This combination of intrinsic and extrinsic impacts on contractility explains why the contraction strength and relaxation speed is lower and responds less effectively on demand in the older heart than in the heart of a young person.

IV. NEUROCONDUCTIVE SYSTEM

The intrinsic rhythmic activity induced in the small sinus node situated in the wall of the right atrium has been reported to change in two ways during aging: the number of pace-making Purkinje cells declines, and the shell around the node becomes thicker. It is not known how many of the pace-making cells are needed to secure normal rhythmic activity. It is believed that both the decline in cell number and the fibrosis of the shell negatively influences the pace making and the spread of excitation over to the atrioventricular (AV)-node. The AV-node is reported to maintain its cell population. Fleg et al. have suggested that there are age-related transmission changes involving the AV node connections with the bundle of His. The further spread of excitations through the bundle of His might also be impaired because of loss of Purkinje fibers, particularly in the left bundle.

The resting heart rhythm is not changed during aging per se, even though the phasic variations in heart rate accompanying respiration gradually decrease. The ability to speed up the heart rate is, on the other hand, markedly impaired. A young person has the ability to speed up the heart rate to about 180–200 beats per minute, which is reduced to 140–160 beats per minute at the age of 70–75 years. Studies by Saltin indicate that the ability to increase the heart rate is stable for a given age and cannot be influenced by, for example, physical training, although the cardiac output at a given heart rate can improve.

Examples on the clinical relevance of these manifestations of aging of the neuroconductive system are that a lengthening of the P-R (distance from the P-wave on EKG to the R-wave) interval and a first degree AV block is not uncommon in apparently healthy older persons. Sudden death probably related to cardiac arrhythmia is fairly common in very old people who otherwise lack symptoms of definable abnormalities that might cause heart arrhythmias. It seems to be reasonable to assume that aging of the neuroconductive system of the heart sometimes can lead to a natural death, thus caused by aging in itself.

V. VASCULAR SYSTEM

Structural changes occur also in the vascular walls during aging. A thickening of the vascular wall occurs especially in smaller arteries and arterioles. The hemodynamics of the consecutive vascular sections are specialized, and aging-related changes vary from one section to the other. The smooth muscle function of these specialized sectors of the vascular tree with all its "branches" seem to be influenced by aging in slightly different ways. The vascular smooth muscles in the aorta and large arteries are most commonly studied and tend to show some reduction of their maximal contractile strength with age as a response to such stimuli as cathecolamines. Both contractile and relaxation responses to, for example, potassium and calcium ions have been reported to be affected. Endothelial cells, and their cooperation with smooth muscles, are also reported to be influenced by aging. Several studies indicate that their ability to respond with release of vasodilator nitrous oxide declines with age, whereas the dilator response to drugs like papaverine or nitrodilators are reported to be essentially uninfluenced by aging.

Human aging is associated with stiffening of the aortic valves, the aorta, and more peripheral arteries, plus widening and elongation of the aorta, which has obvious consequences for the blood pressure. Age-related changes in compliance of the vessel walls are apparently mainly due to aging-related changes, including fragmentation of the elastic filaments, and an increase of collagen tissue with less elastic collagen fibers, as already described. To what extent these changes are caused by intrinsic aging-related processes, or consequences of the long-lasting wear and tear to which human arteries are exposed is not clear. Many clinical reports indicate that systolic hypertension might be even more serious for older people than diastolic pressure increase. High systolic peaks may imply accentuations of arterial wall stress and further wall changes and damage. The well-known aging-related reduction of the aortic-arterial Windkessel function may be one of the most serious changes that affect the human CV system. A slight adaptive thickening of the media of resistance vessels may also occur during aging, reducing the wall compliance and lowering maximal flow capacity also in that part of the vascular tree. Little seems to be known concerning possible effects of aging on the capillary exchange vessels in the various systemic circuits. Available information indicates, however, that both morphology and flow capacity are relatively uninfluenced by aging.

VI. SYSTEMIC VEINS

Similar to other parts of the CV system, the morphological changes in the veins during aging are dominated by a reduction in wall compliance and a decline in smooth muscle strength and speed of contraction. Ordinarily, the majority of the blood is to be found in the systemic veins. Especially in humans with their ability for erect vertical position, vasoconstrictor control of venous smooth muscle tone is of dominant importance for the circulation in general. In general, the alpha-1 receptor-mediated sympathetic function appears to be relatively well preserved during aging. Age-dependent decline in beta and alpha-2-mediated functions might, however, together reduce the efficiency of the sympathetic nervous control of the venous system in the old person. A widening of veins, commonly occurring in older peo-

ple, causes valvular insufficiency and often tendency to edema, primarily in the legs.

VII. PULMONARY VASCULAR BED

Although all blood has to be directed to flow back through the lungs from the right to the left heart, the blood pressure is low in the pulmonary circuit and the walls of the vessels are thin. In a similar way as in other circuits, the vessel walls become thicker and with lower compliance. The pulse amplitude increases also, which becomes especially prominent during exercise. The reduction of pulmonary Windkessel compliance elevates the end-systolic afterload for the right ventricle. In the same way as for the left side, the right ventricle also shows evidence of slight or moderate diastolic dysfunction.

VIII. BLOOD PRESSURE

Several population studies from industrialized countries show an increase in both systolic blood pressure

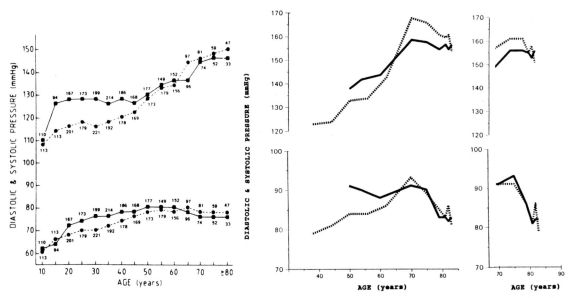

Figure 2 (A) Systolic and diastolic blood pressures in 5-year age classes of a representative Belgian population sample (*n* = 4,202). (From Staessen et al., 1990, *Journal of Hypertension, 8*, 393.) (B) Similar data from a representative Swedish population ("H 70 study" in Göteborg, Sweden) from the age of 38 years in women and 50 years in men. Note gradual decline of diastolic pressure above age 70 years. This pressure decline was evident also when the same individuals were followed longitudinally over a 12-year period (*far right*), implying that it is a truly age-related change of pressure profile. (From Landahl et al., 1986, *Hypertension, 8*, 1044.

Table I Arterial Blood Pressure[a] in Three Age
Cohorts of 70-Year-Olds (without
Drugs 2D, 2E, or 2F)[b]

	Women			
	1	2	3	
SBP	168	166	160	$p < 0.000$
DBP	93	90	85	$p < 0.000$
	Men			
	1	2	3	
SBP	159	160	157	$p < 0.361$
DBP	96	92	84	$p < 0.000$

[a] SBP, systolic blood pressure; DBP, diastolic
blood pressure.
[b] 2D, 2E, 2F = At that time available blood pres-
sure-lowering drugs and diuretics.

(SBP) and diastolic blood pressure (DBP) in adults, at least during the age interval of 20–70 years. Women start with lower pressure than men. The rate of increase with increasing age is, however, faster in females; and some studies indicate that women reach a higher both SBP and DBP after age 55–60 years than men (Figure 2). In some populations followed longitudinally, a decline in BP has been observed at ages above 70–75 years, as illustrated in the right part of Figure 2. The maximal height of the DBP seems to occur at a lower age in males (50 years) than in females (70 years). These gender differences cannot be explained by sex differences in selective mortality as they occur in samples followed longitudinally.

There are, however, also reports, usually from less-developed countries, where very little or no age-related increase in BP has been observed at cross-sectional age comparisons. In those countries longevity is usually low, which limits the possibility for comparison. The possible influence of environmental and lifestyle factors must obviously also be considered, illustrated by a report from a 20-year follow-up study from age 35–40 to 55–60 in 144 Italian nuns and 133 "control" laywomen of the same ethnic background. The control women showed principally the same age-related increase as those shown in Figure 2, although no significant change was observed in the nuns. It is clearly demonstrated that body weight, physical activity level, smoking habits, and so on influence BP. Comparison of Japanese men living in Japan, Hawaii, or California showed that those in

Japan had the lowest and those in California the highest BP, but when BP was adjusted for body weight these differences disappeared. Comparison of BP at age 70 between different age cohorts showed that, for example, in Gothenburg, Sweden, those born in 1901 or 1902 had significantly higher BP than those born 5 years later, and that those born 10 years later had even lower BP (Table I).

The complex sympathico-hormonal and parasympathetic control of the CV system is a part of the overall neuroendocrine system, and alterations caused by aging are discussed in other contexts of this book. It is, however, important to emphasize that the CV response to psychosocial stimuli can be altered in the old person. Intense emotional stimulation may produce greater pressure loads and neurogenic cardiac activation than, for example, physical exercise in many older persons. The pressure load on the heart may become particularly high. At the same time, tachycardia may shorten the nutritional perfusion time for the myocardium as most of the cellular perfusion takes place during diastole, and diastole shortens when the heart rate increases. It seems reasonable to assume, on the other hand, that most older persons have experiences that might help them to overcome the most dangerous stress reactions, and too much social isolation might imply a lack of "training" to withstand emotional events that are a part of ordinary life.

BIBLIOGRAPHY

Fleg, J. I. (1986). Alterations in cardiovascular structure and function with advancing age. *American Journal of Cardiology, 57*, 33.

Fleg, J. I., Das, D. N., Wright J., & Lakatta, E. G. (1990). Age-associated changes in the components of atrioventricular conduction in apparently healthy volunteers. *Journal of Gerontological Medical Sciences, 45*, 95.

Folkow, B., & Svanborg, A. (1993). Physiology of cardiovascular aging. *Physiological Reviews, 73*, 725.

Lakatta, E. G. (1987). Why cardiovascular function may decline with age. *Geriatrics, 42*, 84.

Roberts, J., & Goldberg, P. B. (1979). Changes in responsiveness of the heart to drugs during aging. *Federation Procedures, 38*, 1927.

Strandell, T. (1964). Circulatory studies on healthy old men. *Acta Medica Scandinavia, 414*, (suppl. 1), 1.

Saltin, B. (1986). The aging endurance athlete (p. 59). In J. R. Sutton & R. M. Brock (Eds.), *Sports medicine for the mature athlete*, Indianapolis, IN: Benchmark Press.

Caregiving and Caring

Carol J. Whitlatch and Linda S. Noelker

The Benjamin Rose Institute

Care Receiver A person who requires day-to-day assistance due to an illness or accident.

Community-Dwelling Adult An adult who lives in a private home rather than in an institutional setting.

Formal Caregiver Typically a paid professional associated with a service organization or independent contractor who provides or manages care for an ill or impaired person. Volunteers associated with a service organization are also considered formal caregivers.

Informal Caregiver A family member or friend, typically unpaid, who provides or manages care for an ill or impaired person.

Long-Term Care Assistance provided over an extended period of time due to chronic illness or disability either at home or in an institution.

CAREGIVING is broadly defined as the act of providing assistance or care to a family member, friend, or client that enables the care recipient to maintain an optimal level of independence. This assistance can be instrumental or hands-on, affective, financial, or otherwise of value or necessity to the care recipient. Caregiving varies in its intensity and duration, with care provided ranging from 1 hour per day, to one entire weekend per year, or to 24 hours a day for years at a time. Although providing care can be stressful to both caregivers and care recipients, the effects on caregivers can be long-term, lasting for many years after their care responsibilities have ended.

I. PREVALENCE OF CAREGIVING IN THE UNITED STATES

It is estimated that 15% of U.S. adults care for a seriously ill or disabled family member. Research on caregivers, whether formal or informal, paid or unpaid, has grown dramatically in both quality and quantity over the past decades. With increasing sophistication in both methodology and theory, caregiving research in the 1990s is characterized by its continued advances in theory, methodology, and application. To appreciate the growing significance of caregiving research in the twenty-first century, it is important to understand caregiving's prevalence and impact as well as current conceptual frameworks that evolve from empirical findings and public awareness of caregiving and policy. A thorough integration, expansion, and application of the theoretical underpinnings of caregiving research will promote further advances in the caregiving literature. Moreover, it provides a perspective from which theory can facilitate efforts in determining the appropriate points for effective intervention.

A. Background

The growing percentage of adults aged 65 and older in the United States, and particularly those over the age of 85, has had a dramatic effect on the prevalence of caregiving over the past decades. In 1980, 11% of the population was 65 years of age or older, whereas in 1993 this percentage had increased to nearly 13%. Moreover, it is projected that by the years 2000 and 2050, 13% and 20%, respectively, of the U.S. population will be at least 65 years old. [*See* DEMOGRAPHY].

Of the nearly 32.5 million older adults living in the United States, it is estimated that 7 million require assistance with personal care or instrumental tasks such as bathing, dressing, meals, and housekeeping. By and large, the families of these impaired older adults provide the majority of assistance with hands-on care as well as emotional and financial support. Specifically, 71% of all long-term care is provided in the community, and 85% of all in-home care is provided by family members and friends. However, only 14% of home care is provided by paid professionals. This low percent may reflect the disproportionate reimbursement for home care as compared to institutional care.

Between 2.6 and 13.3 million informal caregivers assist community-dwelling disabled elderly, with a more accurate estimate between 5 to 8 million caregivers. This estimate is based on the 7 to 8 million community-dwelling elderly with at least one functional disability or with Alzheimer's disease (AD) or another type of degenerative dementia. An additional 1.69 million informal caregivers continue to provide some level of assistance to their relative once they become institutionalized.

B. Types of Care Provided

Empirical research documents the wide variety of predictors of care provision depending on characteristics of both the caregiver and care recipient. One pivotal factor is the elder's type of functional impairment and the nature of their debilitating disease. Cognitively impaired adults differ in their care needs as compared to physically impaired but cognitively intact adults. For example, caregivers of adults with physical impairments (e.g., stroke, traumatic brain injury, multiple sclerosis) report providing substantial assistance with self-care activities such as bathing, eating, dressing, and walking. In addition to assisting with self-care activities, caregivers of adults with cognitive impairments (e.g., AD, degenerative dementia) report spending a great deal of time and energy dealing with their relative's problem behaviors, such as agitation, memory deficits, wandering, and inappropriate behaviors. [*See* DEMENTIA.]

Caregiving tasks also vary depending upon the care recipient's level of impairment and stage of illness. For example, persons in the initial stages of dementia exhibit more deficits in memory and personality than in self-care tasks. As the disease progresses, cognitive functioning further deteriorates leading to deficits in self-care activities. With most dementing illnesses, physical difficulties occur later in the disease progression, and it is unlikely that the care recipient's mental or physical condition will improve. Conversely, with conditions such as traumatic brain injury or stroke, care recipients can be bedridden from the start, with only minor deficits in cognitive functioning. For persons with nondementing illnesses, the progression and outcome of their condition is less certain, and they can experience periods of remission or stability punctuated by acute episodes.

Household income, social network characteristics, and access to community services also affect care provision. It is often assumed that caregivers use formal services only after they have exhausted all sources of informal assistance. Although this is true for many families, access to services is also linked to factors unrelated to social network characteristics. For example, income level is associated with use of formal services because most community-based long-term care is paid out-of-pocket. Thus, income and network characteristics are interrelated and instrumental to the accessibility of services.

II. PROVIDERS OF CARE

A. Informal Caregivers

The care received by millions of older adults comes from a wide variety of sources. Although informal care is the most preferred and frequently used source of assistance for older adults, formal care services also provide a great deal of support, especially for the millions of older adults who live alone or who have no family or friends available to provide assistance. Older adults who have a choice, however, prefer that family and friends help them once assistance becomes necessary.

I. Primary versus Secondary Caregivers

When it becomes clear that an older family member requires some form of structured assistance, families go through a period of reorganization as they restructure their lives. Frequently, one individual, whether by choice or convenience, becomes the primary caregiver. The job of the primary caregiver, although rarely specified, is to be the direct provider of the elder's care. The stressful nature of providing care causes many primary caregivers to seek assistance from other family members, friends, or service providers. However, it is understood, though not necessarily made explicit, that the primary caregiver is the main person in charge of the care.

A naturally occurring hierarchy seems to exist within families that often leads to a designated primary caregiver. If a care recipient is married, his or her spouse will most likely become the primary caregiver. Adult daughters are also likely candidates. Approximately 23% of family caregivers are wives, 13% are husbands, 29% are adult daughters, and 9% are sons. In addition, the quality of the caregiver's relationship with the care recipient is associated with who will provide care. Family members with contentious or antagonistic relationships with the care recipient are less likely to provide care than those relatives who are more compatible. Unfortunately, when the caregiver and care recipient are not compatible, it is common for both to experience heightened distress.

The health of family members, their proximity to the care recipient, and the demands of their everyday life are additional factors that influence whether or not a family member will become the primary caregiver. These factors also influence the level of involvement family members have in the provision of care. Family members in poor health or at risk for worsening health are less likely to become caregivers. About one-third of primary caregivers assume the role because they live closer to the care recipient than other family members. Employed relatives or those with multiple and/or competing family demands are also less likely to be caregivers. However, even under these demanding and stressful conditions, family members are still more likely than service providers to care for impaired older persons. [See HOME CARE AND CARE GIVING.]

Secondary caregivers typically are defined as individuals who provide unpaid supplemental or intermittent assistance, in contrast to the primary caregiver who has major responsibility for meeting the care recipient's needs and provides the largest amount of care. Most elderly have more than one informal caregiver, although informal caregiving networks tend to be relatively small, averaging two in number.

Spouse caregivers, found in approximately one-third of informal caregiving networks, have the smallest networks and provide the most hours of help per day. Larger informal networks are more common among female care recipients or those who live with an informal caregiver. In these instances, the primary caregiver is often an adult daughter (or daughter-in-law) whose spouse, children, and/or siblings serve as secondary caregivers. Most caregiving networks include adult children or children-in-law; however, about 25% include extended kin and unrelated helpers as the primary caregivers.

Secondary caregivers typically supplement the help provided by primary caregivers, particularly in the areas of household tasks, personal care, and socialization. In contrast, assistance with money management and medical care appears to remain the responsibility of one caregiver. Secondary caregivers also supply important assistance to the primary caregiver as well as the care recipient. They are a prominent source of companionship and emotional support for the primary caregiver as well as a source of respite or relief from caregiving responsibilities. In total, informal caregiving networks supply an average of 7 hours of help daily to community-residing impaired older persons.

Recent studies suggest there is remarkable stability in the composition of informal caregiving networks, even over a 10-year period. Most care recipients retain the same primary caregiver and, when a change is made, it is when an informal caregiver of the next generation assumes caregiving responsibilities. Frequently, the death or health deterioration of a spouse caregiver results in an adult child taking up the primary caregiver's role.

The literature on primary and secondary caregivers has a number of limitations. These include varied definitions of "primary" caregiver across studies and differences in reports about the caregiver's primacy. Additional limitations include the type and amount of assistance rendered in relation to who serves as the respondent, and possible variation in primary caregiver status depending on the type of assistance provided. Recently, research has utilized more global models that give attention to the full range of informal and formal helpers and examine the nature of the ties between these helpers. Research is also moving to include a wider variety of assistance areas for both the care recipient and primary caregiver, and panel designs that speak to change over time in network structure and functioning.

2. In-Home versus Institutional Care

Until recently, the tasks and responsibilities of caregivers were thought to end once a care recipient was placed in an institutional setting. Current research indicates that caregivers continue to remain very active in the lives of their impaired family members once institutionalization becomes necessary. Family caregivers visit often and frequently travel great distances in order to spend time with their relatives. Caregivers of nursing home residents often perform many of the same tasks they did while caring at home, including assistance with eating, personal care, and walking. In fact, a large majority of caregivers remain very active in the lives of their placed relatives for many years after the initial placement has occurred.

With continued involvement in the care of their impaired relative comes the potential for additional distress. Once their family member is institutionalized, caregivers must restructure and redefine their lives and adjust to their new role. Recent research indicates that the stresses of caregiving are not alleviated by placement. Although these caregivers are relieved of the day-to-day demands of in-home care, many continue to feel distress. In fact, although some caregivers are less distressed, many exhibit symptoms well above their preplacement levels of distress. It appears that placement alters rather than eliminates the stresses of caregiving.

3. Consequences of Caregiving

There is substantial empirical evidence indicating that the stress of providing in-home care over the long term affects a caregiver's mental and physical health. Caregivers are more depressed than age-matched controls, exhibit deficits in physical health and depressed immunologic functioning as a result of caregiving, and use prescription drugs for depression, anxiety, and insomnia two to three times more often than the rest of the population.

Caregivers also report financial strain as a result of providing care over the long term. Whether living at home or in an institution, the cost of providing care to a disabled or demented family member can be exorbitant. In some areas of the United States the cost of caring for an adult with AD has been estimated at $47,000 per year. Compared to their same-age peers in the general population, caregivers are more likely to report adjusted family incomes below the poverty line. Adding to this financial strain is the fact that the responsibilities of caregiving often lead to changes in work status. Caregivers often lose time from work, chose to retire early, or give up work entirely while they are helping their impaired relative.

Characteristics of the care recipient's illness are also related to compromised health for caregivers. For persons with disabilities, the severity of the care recipient's illness has been found to be the most important predictor of caregiver stress. This finding is similar for caregivers of persons with stroke, dementia, cancer, and other debilitating illnesses. When the impaired persons' behaviors become unpredictable and ambiguous, caregiver distress is often further compromised. Thus behaviors such as acting out, wandering, and agitation are associated with increased caregiver distress. Lastly, cognitive impairment during the early stages of a disease appear to be more stressful to caregivers than the cognitive impairment of the later stages.

B. Formal Care

Older persons disproportionately utilize acute and long-term health-care services, whether home- and community-based or institutional (hospital and nursing home). Consequently, they and their informal caregivers are more widely affected by legislation that has significantly changed reimbursement for health care and led to corresponding changes in health-care provision. In 1983, the implementation of the Medicare hospital prospective payment system dramatically altered admission and discharge patterns, effectively transferring 21 million hospital days to home and community. The "sicker and quicker" discharge of older persons from the hospital was viewed as placing a heavier burden on informal caregivers as well as spurring the growth of hospital-based and proprietary home-care agencies.

The passage of the OBRA Act in 1987 led to increased requirements for the training of nursing home staff and changes in resident care planning and review, which were designed to improve the quality of resident care. OBRA also addressed the pressing issue of the frequent impoverishment of community-dwelling spouses of nursing home residents. Specifically, OBRA mandated policy that allowed the community-dwelling spouse to retain the equity in their home and one half of their other assets in order to facilitate their continued ability to live independently. The extent to which these changes actually resulted in improved care, more positive attitudes toward nursing homes, and decreased spousal impoverishment is not known.

Lastly, recent legislative efforts to reform U.S. health care have prompted provider-initiated reengineering of hospital and other health-care organizations. Current trends indicate a move toward managed care systems in which flat fees are paid by insurers on a per capita basis to keep enrollees healthy. This system has been shown to limit the frequency and amount of service use and simultaneously contain health-care costs. As yet, it is unclear how these dramatic changes in reimbursement and the organization of health-care systems will affect older persons' patterns of formal service use and their outcomes, alter the role of family caregivers, and affect attitudes toward and patterns of nursing home use. [See HEALTH CARE AND SERVICES.]

I. Prevalence of Community-Based and Institutional Service Use

Findings from the 1987 National Medical Expenditure Survey indicate that only 36% of the 5.6 million Americans aged 65 and over with functional disabilities use community-based services (e.g., home health care, homemaker, day programs, telephone monitoring, special transportation, and senior centers offering congregate meals and other services). The majority of this care (75%) is paid by the individual, while the public sector covers the cost for the remaining one-fourth of the users.

About 20% of disabled older persons rely exclusively on formal services, whereas 16% combine informal with formal care, 35% exclusively use informal care, and 29% have no assistance. Home care is the most widely reported service used, although studies involving the older population in general suggest services offered by senior centers are more commonly utilized. The most frequently used type of help by disabled elderly is housekeeping and meals; in fact, housekeeping is also the most widely used form of

assistance by elderly without chronic disabilities. Among disabled older persons receiving community-based services, over two-thirds use entirely home-based services. This sizable group of home-based service users is comprised largely of the most severely impaired older adults. Another one-fourth of older adults rely exclusively on out-of-home services at senior centers, day programs, and congregate meal sites. A small minority (about 10%) combine in-home with out-of-home services.

Long-term residential care services are used by only 5% of the elderly at any given time. However, 25–35% of older Americans can expect to spend some time during their later life in a nursing home. In addition to problems related to combining a residence with a treatment setting and generally unfavorable attitudes toward institutionalization, the high cost of nursing home care dissuades many elderly and their families from its use. The high cost of this care modality has led to the growth of preadmission screening programs to reduce state Medicaid expenditures for long-term residential care and to the implementation of alternative comprehensive community-based care programs frequently targeted to Medicaid-eligible elderly.

Assisted living is another alternative to skilled residential care that is becoming increasingly popular with moderately impaired older persons and their families. This service arrangement maximizes the older persons' lifestyle choices in less restrictive housing environments that also provide supportive services. Typically, these services include housekeeping, transportation, and meals, although some facilities also provide supervision of medications and limited personal care.

2. Conceptualizations of Formal Service Use

The stressful nature of caregiving has led many researchers to examine the impact of service use on caregiver well-being. The most widely applied conceptual framework for service utilization by the elderly is a behavioral model developed by Andersen and colleagues to predict the use of physician and other health-care services. The Andersen Model, which includes both individual and social factors, views service use as a function of three categories of predictors: predisposing, enabling, and need characteristics. Predisposing factors typically include sociodemographics (e.g., age, race, and health beliefs) that exist prior to the illness or need for service and can be related to the individual's propensity to use service. Enabling characteristics are resources that facilitate service use. These can be individual, family, or community characteristics such as level of education, household income, and the availability of nursing home beds. Need characteristics often precipitate service use and represent illness conditions, symptoms, and functional losses. Research findings generally support the prominence of need factors as the most powerful predictor category; however, the model typically explains little variance in the elderly's use of health-care services.

Bass and Noelker have expanded the Andersen Model to include predisposing, enabling, and need characteristics of both the older individual and the primary caregiver. Chronically ill or disabled older persons receive most care from family members and other informal caregivers who, in turn, influence the older person's use of formal assistance. This can occur directly when the family caregiver seeks out a service on behalf of the impaired person, or indirectly when the caregiver's needs influence the decision to provide formal help. This approach also reflects the impact that an older person's illness and disability has on the family system and the methods by which the family manages the treatment of the ill member. Research findings lend support to the significance of caregiver characteristics, particularly care-related strains, as predictors of the elderly's use of home health care.

More recently, social support models have been adapted and applied to explain the elderly's use of both informal and formal assistance. This approach is premised on the recognition that the exclusion of formal service use from models of social support weakens the full effects that assistance from others has on the individual's adjustment to negative life events. Moreover, these models incorporate the reality that informal and formal helpers often perform similar functions for chronically ill older persons, including emotional support and instrumental help with personal care and household tasks.

3. Predictors of Service Use by Older Persons and Their Caregivers

Many of the same predictors explain the elderly's use of community-based and nursing home care. These include advanced age, gender (female), cultural background (Euro-American), marital status (unmarried), living arrangements (alone), and level of functional disability. Additionally, the absence of a willing, able, and proximate informal caregiver is a major factor in nursing home placement. This is particularly salient when the older individual has a neurological condition such as a stroke. Generally, family members control the timing of nursing home entry and physicians exert a major influence on the decision, particularly when it follows the older person's hospitalization.

Recent research utilizing the Andersen Model has examined predictors of mixed helping networks for the elderly. Formal and informal help are more commonly used when the elderly person is of more advanced age, living alone, more functionally impaired, the informal caregiver(s) is a more distant kin member or unrelated, and more financial resources are available to purchase services. However, even in mixed helping networks, the amount of formal assistance remains very limited compared to the amount provided by informal helpers.

A similar research approach has been used with a focus on race as a predictor of mixed helping networks and change over time in network composition. Interestingly, race has been found to have little explanatory power once other important factors, namely, functional status and health change were controlled. Consistent with findings from most studies, women and those living alone are more likely to have mixed networks, Whites disproportionately tend to use nursing home care, and married elderly tend not to use formal helpers. Although African-American elderly are less often married, their larger households and greater variety of informal helpers are thought to counterbalance the absence of a spouse caregiver.

Over the last 20 years, services targeted to informal caregivers have been developed and become more widely available based on the demonstrated stressful effects of long-term caregiving. These services include respite care, peer- and professionally led support groups, education programs in care-related skills, training in problem-solving skills and behavioral techniques for patient management, and counseling and psychotherapy. Evaluations of these interventions have yielded mixed results, and many have been compromised by sampling and other methodological limitations. Current work is directed toward determining the most efficient intervention for specific types of caregivers, the most effective timing of these interventions, and the most appropriate duration of use.

One difficulty commonly encountered in evaluations of caregiver interventions is enrolling sufficient numbers of caregivers in study samples, even when the service is provided free of charge. Various explanations offered for the apparent underutilization of care-related services include unfamiliarity with the service, lack of perceived need, reliance on informal helpers for care-related assistance, absence of culturally relevant services, and barriers to the service system and the delivery of services. To date, relatively little empirical attention has been given to the prevalence, sources, and predictors of care-related service use. Existing evidence suggests that the different types of care-related services have different predictors. In general, however, the predictors of caregiver service use are kinship tie (adult child), living with the care recipient, being employed, more perceived care-related stress, and more informal and formal assistance provided to the care recipient.

C. Heterogeneity within Caregivers

Caregiving research has made significant advances in clarifying the ambiguities surrounding the different experiences of caregivers in relationship to gender, kinship tie, age, and cultural or ethnic identity. Advanced research designs and methodological techniques have led to a better understanding of the interrelationships among the sociodemographic characteristics of caregivers.

I. Gender Differences

By and large, studies of caregiving families indicate that women are more likely than men to take on the role of caregiver. Similarly, women caregivers, whether employed or not, spend more time providing care than do male caregivers. The tasks undertaken by women caregivers also differ from the tasks of their male peers. Women are more likely to provide personal care assistance, whereas men are more likely to take on more instrumental tasks such as decision making and financial management.

Research findings typically indicate that caregiving women report greater distress than men, regardless of the care recipient's diagnosis and level of impairment. This finding is consistent regardless of caregiver employment status. It is also evident regardless of whether the older adult has a diagnosis of cancer, dementia, stroke, head injury, physical impairment, or mental illness.

One explanation for these gender differences draws upon studies of health and well-being in the general population indicating that women commonly score higher than men on indicators of stress. Alternately, women may be more comfortable than men expressing feelings of stress. It has also been suggested that the nurturant role developed by men in later life may be rewarding or act as a form of repayment for the care they received in the past, which in turn helps to counteract the otherwise negative effects of caregiving.

2. Kinship Ties

When a family member requires assistance, it is most likely the wife or daughter of the impaired relative who will become their caregiver. Among men, husbands are most likely to be caregivers; sons and sons-in-law are much less likely to take on the role. In fact, it is more common for an older woman to be cared for by her daughter-in-law than by her own son.

There is evidence that caregivers differ in their levels of distress depending upon the type of kinship tie they have to the care recipient. Typically, caregiving wives report higher levels of emotional distress than husbands. Differences between adult daughter and wife caregivers are also common, although some studies find daughters to be more distressed whereas other studies report the reverse. In addition, there are exceptions to these findings where no differences are found by kinship tie.

3. Age

The effects of caregiver age are nearly impossible to disentangle from the effects of other caregiver and care recipient characteristics. Some studies find that age and kinship tie are confounded with spouse caregivers, who are significantly older than other groups of caregivers. Other studies suggest that caregiver age is confounded with ethnic group and marital status. In addition, there is conflicting evidence about the relationship between caregiver age and distress; some studies find older caregivers to be the most distressed, whereas other studies find younger caregivers to be the most stressed. However, among employed caregivers, especially those with both child- and adult-care responsibilities, younger caregivers are more likely to experience greater distress as well as absenteeism, interruptions at work, and difficulty in combining work and family.

A related issue concerns older generations caring for younger generations. It is common for elderly parents to care for their disabled adult or chronically ill children or grandchildren. Within the African-American community, increasing numbers of midlife and older women have primary responsibility for their grandchildren and great-grandchildren. Typically, a family crisis precipitates grandparent caregiving. Most often the older generation's child, whether as a teenager, young adult, or at midlife, is unable to care for his or her own children. The conditions under which grandparents in general, and grandmothers in particular, become caregivers often reflect the broader context within which these "older" caregivers live. Yet, the circumstances that lead to a parent's inability to care for their own child are often compounded for grandparents. Low or nonexistent rates of child support, low income, inferior family leave policies, inadequate support as well as their own physical health problems often place grandparent caregivers at risk for developing further difficulties. Differences in this phenomenon are evident by cultural group with 12% of African-American children living with grandparents compared to 5.8% Hispanic, and 3.6% white.

4. Ethnic or Cultural Differences

Until recently, little was known about the experience of caregivers with diverse cultural and ethnic identities. Advances in cross-cultural research have demonstrated the diversity among caregivers throughout the world, including differences between developing and developed countries, urban and rural settings, and different class or caste structures.

Within the United States, recent research focusing on ethnic diversity among caregivers indicates both similarities and differences among caregivers. Some work suggests that for family members caring for relatives with a variety of disabilities, there is no clear relationship between the caregivers' ethnicity and the amount of stress they experience. Yet, no matter what the ethnic background or identity of a caregiver, it is clear that across all ethnic groups family care is the most preferred and relied upon source of assistance. Extensive and supportive kin networks have been documented in Americans of all ethnic backgrounds, including Mexican Americans, African Americans, Asian Americans, and Euro-Americans (e.g., Jewish, Greek, Italian, Polish, Irish, etc.).

Currently, most research focuses on the differences between Euro- and non-Euro-American caregivers paying little attention to the great heterogeneity within different ethnic groups. For example, Euro-American caregivers are frequently compared to Asian, Hispanic, or African-American caregivers. Growing evidence indicates differences between these groups are less pronounced than differences within the groups. In addition, it has been suggested that group differences may be more related to the length of time since immigration than to specific ethnic background. As a result, there has been a call to shift efforts away from intergroup study and instead to focus attention on intragroup differences. [*See* RACIAL AND ETHNIC DIVERSITY.]

III. THEORIES OF CAREGIVING

The following sections present a brief overview of theories related to family caregiving. These theories, although not exhaustive, represent the conceptual developments that have influenced a great portion of the caregiving research over the past decades. This overview and integration is presented to foster expansion of the theoretical foundation of caregiving research. These theories, conceived by researchers from a range of disciplines, incorporate the personal, social, and temporal contexts of caregiving.

A. Social Functioning

1. Social Competence and Breakdown

The Social Competence and Breakdown Theory draws upon Symbolic Interactionism (SI). SI is one of many sociologically based theories of human interaction that has been recently adapted to explain development across the life span. SI emphasizes the dynamic interactions and processes that naturally occur in everyday relationships. To illustrate, individuals gain a sense of self through the interpretation of others' responses to their own behavior. In turn, the individual can change his or her behavior to influence the interpretation and response (e.g., approval, criticism) of others.

Drawing upon SI and other theoretical perspectives, Social Competence and Breakdown Theory, presented by Kuypers and Bengtson, posits that the negative consequences of aging (e.g., illness, loss) can lead to a breakdown in the social competence of the elderly. The authors suggest that the subsequent "negative spiral" can occur for older adults. An elderly individual, whose self-concept may already be vulnerable because of role loss or negative stereotypes about the elderly (e.g., ageism), experiences a health-related crisis. This crisis leads to labeling of the older person as dependent by a health professional, family, or others in the social environment. The attribution and acceptance of a definition of dependent results in atrophy of previous competency skills and the individual adopts the self-concept of sick, inadequate, or incompetent. This self-labeling leads to further vulnerability, and the negative cycle escalates, with further adverse consequences to social and psychological competence.

More recently, Bengtson and Kuypers have adapted this model to problems facing the aging family. Expanding upon this conceptualization, they posit that the sudden and unexpected dependency of an aged family member can lead to caregiving problems that test the competence of the family as well as the individual. A thorough understanding of the nature of individual-familial-environmental interactions affecting competence can facilitate the identification of interventions that may improve family functioning and reduce the sense of helplessness felt by many caregivers.

2. Models Linking Formal and Informal Support: Hierarchical Compensation, Task-Specific, Supplementation, and Substitution

Several models have been proposed for conceptualizing the relationship between informal (unpaid) and formal (paid) helpers. First, Cantor's widely recognized Hierarchical Compensatory Model has been subsequently enlarged into the social care system. Its key premise is that the elderly's preferences for informal caregivers reflect a normative pattern in the intimacy or closeness of social relationships. Thus, caregiving activities are expected to be performed by the closest available and capable family member with spouses as first choice, followed by children, other kin, friends or neighbors, and formal helpers. In cases of more severe functional impairment, greater need for assistance, limited availability of informal helpers, more fluidity, and overlap between informal and formal helpers is likely to occur.

A second conceptualization of the relationship between informal and formal helpers is Litwak's Task-specific Model. In this model the appropriate source of help is determined by the type of assistance task. Informal helpers are best suited to assisting with non-technical tasks and those that cannot be scheduled (toileting, transferring), and formal helpers can best manage specialized tasks that can be scheduled. As a result, the allocation of tasks between informal and formal tasks reflects a clear division of labor with "dual specialization" or task segregation occurring between the two types of helpers. This arrangement minimizes the likelihood of conflict and other negative outcomes occurring between the two types of helpers.

An alternative perspective gave rise to the Supplementation Model of Edelman and Hughes, which posits that task sharing mainly occurs between the elderly's informal and formal helpers. Because most assistance needed by chronically ill and disabled elderly is routine help with personal care and daily activities, rather than technical and specialized care, supplementation by formal helpers alleviates the time-consuming and potentially exhausting demands on informal caregivers.

In contrast, it has been hypothesized that, given the option, formal care would be used by families to substitute for informal care. Greene's Substitution Model gives pause to planners and policy makers who advocate expanded reimbursement for community-based services because it is widely recognized that the public sector cannot assume the full cost of long-term care for disabled persons. However, little empirical evidence exists that families abrogate their role as the primary source of assistance to older impaired relatives if service availability is expanded. Families who have the financial resources and choose to purchase care from agencies or independent providers typically remain involved as care managers.

Each of these conceptual approaches provides a plausible description of the relationship between informal and formal helpers. Although each one notes empirical support for its perspective, this support is inconsistent and limited by several factors. Some of these include investigation of a limited range of assistance tasks, a focus on sources of help with hypothetical tasks, and a lack of attention to change over time in the inclusion and involvement of informal and formal helpers. Furthermore, a great many networks do not include formal helpers over the entire course of caregiving and remain independent of the formal sector of community-based and residential care. Other studies indicate when paid assistance is sought, it is primarily for help with household chores.

3. Gender Theory

The application of gender theories of caregiving has increased in recent years. This body of work has been greatly informed by feminist scholarship and has its roots in the Gender Socialization Framework and Social Role Perspective. Gender Socialization proposes that gender roles are internalized as stable personality traits and result from gender differences in socialization during childhood. In contrast, a Social Role Perspective explains gender differences in behaviors as the result of a person's current and continuous construction of social realities and the related role demands of these realities. Using a Gender Socialization Framework to understand gender differences in caregiving and caring, one would expect early role socialization and personality factors to be linked to greater involvement of women in care tasks. In contrast, a Social Role Perspective would posit that women are more involved than men in caring activities because women have fewer alternative roles as a result of their limited access to diverse social resources.

More recent work within feminist scholarship has moved away from these two views of gender, focusing instead on issues related to inequity and identity. This redirection is due in part to the fact that women, by default, perform more care tasks and, in turn, are more distressed than men. Moreover, distinct stressors affect caregivers, typically women, who provide care both on the job and at home. These women have double caregiving duties that increase their vulnerability to stress. They begin their days fulfilling domestic caregiving responsibilities at home, go to work where they render care to nonfamily members, and return home to resume domestic obligations. Thus, because women bear the burden of caregiving in Western society, they are more vulnerable to caregiving's negative effects.

Feminist scholars agree that caring is devalued in Western society, whether in the home or workplace. How to rectify this devaluation remains intensely controversial. Indeed, many feminist scholars insist that the reformulation of basic issues helps to reveal the meaning and nature of caregiving. As a result, recent feminist study has emphasized the integration rather than separation of two spheres of caring: motivation and orientation. The excessive focus on the motiva-

tion for caring presumes that with the right motivation, caring is not problematic. On the other hand, viewed as an orientation, caring is seen as something inherent to the everyday experience of women especially. Instead, scholars suggest that caring is work, as well as an integrated core of human activity. Moreover, because it can be unbounded, difficult to define, and hard to control, caring is best seen not as an identity but as work.

Researchers Fisher and Tronto proposed that the caring process consists of four components: caring about, taking care of, caregiving, and care receiving. Caring about is the attention paid to the world that focuses on continuity, maintenance, and repair. This attention does not necessarily require that action be taken. Rather, caring about something is a necessary precursor if action related to maintenance or repair is to occur. Taking care of involves the responsibilities and activities we take on that "keep our world going." Caregiving is the hands-on work of maintenance and repair that requires more commitment of time and resources than taking care of. Care receiving is the response to caregiving by those toward whom care is directed.

The social context of caring also is emphasized within feminist theory. The contexts range from the household and community, marketplace, and bureaucracy to the relationship between caregiver and recipient, payment, and location of work. Many care activities that were previously provided at home have been transferred to the waged labor force. A great majority of these service workers are women, who are paid to do tasks that are closely related to the tasks they leave at home. This illustrates the link between care at home and care in the service community.

In general, feminist scholars do not promote the view of caring as a universal element of women's identity, or as a human quality, separate from the cultural and structural circumstances that create it. To feminist scholars, caring is a process that maintains and repairs our world and, in turn, should be highly valued within our world.

B. Family Functioning

I. Caregiving Systems and Dyads

The study of caregiving systems has its roots in family systems theory and research. Early work in this area focused on intra- and intergenerational family dynamics, including dyadic relationships. Drawing from this perspective researchers present a variety of paradigms. Research focusing on dyadic interactions, has led to a rethinking of the unit of analysis in caregiving research. Rather than focusing on the caregiver alone, in dyadic research the unit of analysis is the relationship.

Other researchers have presented an interdisciplinary approach for understanding the developmental processes of both caregiver and recipient. This dyadic conceptualization is based on the view that illness is not singularly experienced and proposes diverse patient–family outcomes. The family is examined as a unit because its members are so closely involved in the management of illness and are the main source of aid for ailing elders. In this model, caregiver and care recipient outcomes are seen both separately and together and either as positive or negative. A caregiver can have a positive outcome, whereas the care recipient does not, and vice versa. As well, both can prosper (i.e., have positive outcomes) or decline (i.e., negative outcomes). The results of this work, which focuses on heart-disease caregiving, indicates that diverse patterns of dyadic mental health outcomes exist. In addition, the results indicating that increased caregiver age is related to poor dyadic caregiver outcomes underscores the importance of the life stage of members of the caregiving dyad. A model such as this, which clarifies how families as a whole react to serious illness, will be useful in determining dyadic patterns that are either productive or ineffective.

2. Circumplex Model of Family Functioning

The Circumplex Model of family functioning, proposed by Olson, Spenkle, and Russel, posits that family cohesion and adaptability determine the family's ability to accomplish developmental tasks and cope with stressors (such as long-term illness). Cohesion is the degree of bonding within a family group, whereas adaptability represents the degree of flexibility demonstrated by the family. For optimal family functioning and effectiveness, families should be balanced on both these factors. To illustrate, too much cohesion or closeness leads to enmeshment, whereas too little results in a disengaged family system. Similarly, too much adaptability leads to chaos, whereas too little leads to a rigid family system.

For a family dealing with long-term disability or illness, the Circumplex Model suggests that poor adaptation is a result of an imbalance of cohesion and adaptability. Although the model does not suggest specific therapeutic techniques for correcting an imbalance, the authors suggest that it is therapeutically useful to share the assessment with the family. Throughout the counseling process, clinicians can use the model to assess the family's progress and reorganization. By involving the family in developing treatment goals that correct the imbalance in cohesion and adaptability, families can learn to function more effectively in both the short- and long-term.

3. Double ABCX Model

The Double ABCX Model of illness adaptation of McCubbin and Patterson, which draws upon Hill's ABCX family crisis model, proposes that an event such as an illness (A), invokes a family's resources (B), and depending upon how the family interprets the event (C), a crisis or noncrisis is produced (X). Thus, a family's ability to invoke resources (e.g., community, family, and personal) and coping responses is related to how family process shapes the course and ease of a family's adjustment and adaptation over time.

The emphasis on family resources and coping responses is critical to further adapting the ABCX Model to the potential crisis of family caregiving. Families with adequate resources and coping responses may not reach a crisis. This is not to say that families who use community services or have access to other assistance have reached a crisis. Rather, the appropriate and timely use and acceptance of services and assistance may act to protect the family against further stress and potential crisis. In the future, it may prove useful for researchers to use the ABCX Model in order to focus their efforts on the study of well-adapted family caregivers.

4. Boundary Ambiguity in Family Functioning

Pauline Boss and her associates have proposed the conceptualization of boundary ambiguity, that is, the ambiguity a family experiences when they are not clear which of its members is psychologically in or out of the family system. This ambiguity occurs when family members are uncertain who is in or out of the family, or when there is a lack of clarity about who is responsible for specific roles and tasks within the family system. Boundary ambiguity can block the family reorganization necessary to accommodate the chronic stress of caregiving.

Boundary ambiguity occurs when a care recipient is emotionally or cognitively unavailable, as is often the case with demented family members. When this loss is only partial, that is, the care recipient is available physically but not emotionally or cognitively, caregivers often have difficulty grieving. As a result, families are unable to accept and grieve the loss of their family member, and unable to restructure and reorganize the family and its roles.

Recent cross-sectional work by Boss and her colleagues suggests that boundary ambiguity mediates the link between care recipient functioning (i.e., problem behaviors) and a caregiver's sense of mastery and level of depression. Their results suggest that changes in the care recipient can create an ambiguous situation for families resulting in a loss of mastery and increased depression. These cross-sectional findings reflect the complexity of the caregiver's perception of their experience and point to the importance of using multidimensional indicators of care recipient and caregiver characteristics and well-being, and of replicating the study with a longitudinal design.

C. Individual Functioning

1. Stress Processes in Caregiving

Pearlin and his colleagues have presented the Stress Process Model of Family Caregiving, which has its roots in sociological and psychological theories of stress and coping. Building upon these theories, Pearlin and colleagues have conceptualized the caregiving experience as a "career," thus allowing a framework for identifying continuities and discontinuities in the lives of family caregivers. This framework proposes that transitions occur in the caregiving career as individuals provide long-term care for chronically ill or demented family members. The stages in the caregiving career include (a) role acquisition, where the individual becomes incumbent in their duties and responsibilities; (b) role enactment, which consists of the in-home care period and its continuation over time; (c) the transition to institutional care, when in-home care is no longer possible and is replaced by full-time institutional care; (d) death of the care recipient, which includes a period of bereavement and grief; and (e) social reintegration, or the aftermath of care, when the caregiver works towards becoming reintegrated into his or her social environment.

Within the Stress Process Model the experience of caregiving is conceptualized as a chronic stressor which, as with other chronic stressors, proliferate and reconfigure over time. The model integrates multiple domains that interact to produce various caregiving outcomes or consequences. The four domains include background characteristics, primary and secondary stressors, mediators of stress, and outcomes. Over the years, Pearlin and his associates have tested and reorganized this model so that it more accurately depicts the process of caregiving.

Background characteristics (e.g., age, gender, ethnicity, education, etc.) are expected to exert their influence throughout the caregiving process, whereas primary stressors are the objective and subjective indicators of the needs and demands of the care recipient. Primary objective stressors include the care recipient's cognitive status, personal and instrumental care needs (i.e., activities of daily living: eating, bathing, walking, etc.), and problem behaviors (e.g., agitation, wandering, acting out, etc.). Primary subjective stressors reflect specific adversities endemic to the experience of caregiving. These stressors include role overload, which taps the burnout and fatigue of caregiving, role captivity, which taps the feelings of entrapment and confinement of the caregiving role, and relational deprivation, which reflects the loss caregiver's feel as their relationship with the care recipient becomes more distant and unfamiliar.

Secondary stressors are the products of primary stressors. These stressors are viewed as secondary, not because they are less potent than primary stressors, but because they are an outgrowth of the ongoing process of caregiving. Secondary role strains are found in the roles and activities that occur external to but are still influenced by the caregiving situation. Work conflict, family conflict, and financial strain are secondary role strains central to the experience of caregiving. Secondary intrapsychic strains underscore dimensions of self-concept. These include loss of self, a sense of competency as a caregiver, mastery, self-esteem, and the feeling of personal gain or enrichment.

Over time, as the care recipient's condition worsens, primary and secondary stressors are expected to proliferate, thus leading to negative caregiver outcomes such as depression, anger, anxiety, and compromised physical health. Mediating conditions act to limit this proliferation by lessening the negative effects of the multiple domains of stress. These mediators include coping (e.g., management of the situation, of the meaning of the situation, or of stress symptoms; positive comparisons and reduced expectations) and social support (formal, informal, instrumental, and emotional).

Taken together, primary and secondary stressors and mediating conditions reveal the dynamic and complex nature of caregiving. Clear specification of the interrelatedness of these domains allows the precise delineation of their influences on caregiving outcomes. Moreover, this model provides a framework for the development and empirical testing of caregiver interventions designed to contain the proliferation of caregiving stressors.

IV. THEORY BUILDING: INTEGRATION AND EXPANSION OF CURRENT THEORIES

The increased prevalence of caregiving is a relatively recent phenomenon, stemming from major social and demographic changes occurring throughout this century. These changes include an unprecedented number of older Americans, particularly the oldest old, who are most in need of assistance; smaller and more diversely structured families; medical technology that prolongs life without restoring functioning; and new roles for women that take many outside the home and family. The outcome of these changes anticipated by planners and policy makers was viewed as a potential "social problem": with the burgeoning number of elderly in need of long-term care, families would be less willing or able to assume this responsibility. In turn, it was expected that there would be increasing economic pressures on the public sector due to escalating expenditures for long-term care.

As a result, research on family caregiving became a priority for federal funders in the 1970s and 1980s. Many of the early investigations were primarily descriptive surveys, designed to provide information about the prevalence, nature, and negative consequences of family caregiving. Reports from a significant number of caregivers in the study samples lent support to the perspective that caregiving had adverse effects on health and personal well-being, employment, financial status, and family relationships. Consequently, later studies commonly applied conceptual models that reinforced a focus on caregiving as a

problem or source of stress, such as Lazarus and Folkman's theory of stress and coping and McCubbin and Olsen's theory of family crisis and problem solving. As demonstrated earlier in our discussion of theoretical approaches to caregiving, more recent research evidences growing diversity in the application of behavioral and social science theories to the caregiving experience and outcomes.

Drawing upon overlapping components and empirical findings from the theories described earlier, we propose a theoretical model that directs attention to specific points for intervention in the caregiving process. This model draws heavily upon the work of Pearlin and colleagues, who have developed and refined the Stress Process Model of Family Caregiving, thus highlighting the importance of multidimensional models, longitudinal designs, and the interrelatedness of research informing intervention as well as the reverse.

As described earlier, the Stress Process Model includes primary objective and subjective stressors, secondary role and intrapsychic strains, and consequences of caregiving. From previous research we know that specific components within the Stress Process Model are related and that different types of social support work to alleviate many of the negative effects between stressors. For example, Figure 1 demonstrates the empirically known relationships that exist between stressors and how social support acts to buffer these negative interactions (see thick arrows in Figure 1). Recent work suggests that instrumental social support, both formal and informal, as well as the emotional support provided to the caregiver by friends and family, acts to moderate or buffer the deleterious effects of stress at specific points within this model. The thick arrows of Figure 1 show that formal support lessens the negative effects of a care recipient's functional loss on a caregiver's feeling of role overload (i.e., the feeling of burnout or fatigue from caregiving). On the other hand, informal support lessens the negative effects of a care recipient's problematic behavior on a caregiver's feeling of role overload.

Figure 1 also reflects the empirically studied relationships between role overload and work conflict, and between work conflict and caregiver depression. Role overload is associated with increased work conflict which, in turn, is associated with increased depression. Here we see the differential buffering effects of infor-

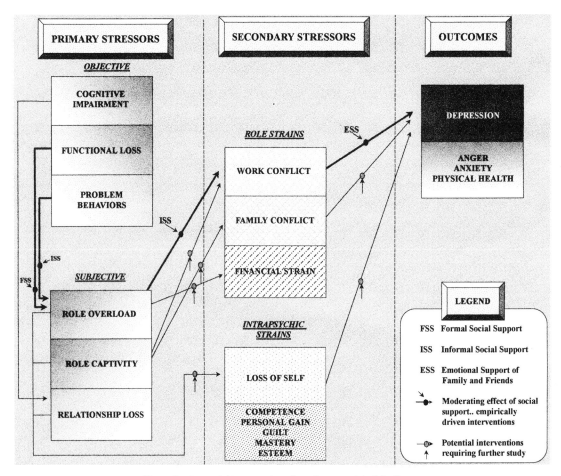

Figure 1   Potential interventions based on empirical findings.

mal and emotional social support on work conflict and depression. Informal support lessens the negative effect of caregiver overload on caregiver work conflict, whereas emotional support helps to moderate the negative effects of caregiver work conflict on depression. Based on empirical findings, there are many points in the stress process where social support can alleviate different types of caregiver distress.

Additional research suggests efficacious points at which social support may act to intervene in order to moderate the negative effects of stressors. The thin lines seen in Figure 1 reflect the results of recent research suggesting specific relationships exist between a variety of stressors. Currently, however, little is known about how social support acts to buffer these potentially negative effects. For example, research has found that care recipient cognitive impairment leads

to a sense of relationship loss for the caregiver. In other words, caregivers of demented relatives report that they feel they have lost the relationship they once had with their impaired relative. Unfortunately, there is no evidence that this loss can be lessened by social support.

We also know that subjective primary stressors (i.e., role overload, role captivity, and relationship loss) are related to a caregiver's loss of self. In turn, loss of self is associated with increased levels of caregiver depression. Given that social support ameliorates the deleterious effects of comparable components of the stress model, it is likely that social support could similarly lessen the negative effect of subjective primary stressors on the caregiver's loss of self, and, in turn lessen the negative effect of loss of self on depression.

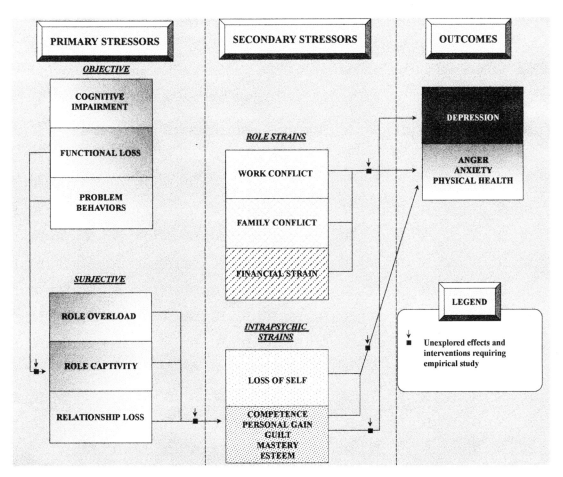

Figure 2 Previously unexplored interventions.

We also know very little about how a care recipient's functional losses and problem behaviors affect caregivers' feelings of role captivity (see Figure 2). As well, no research examines the relationship between primary subjective stressors (i.e., role overload, role captivity, and relationship loss) and intrapsychic strains. Considering the potential utility of social support in ameliorating the deleterious effects of similar pathways, there are many opportunities for future research and potential intervention. Drawing upon previous research, Figure 2 demonstrates that informal social support may act to buffer the potentially negative relationship between problem behaviors and role captivity. Formal social support might alleviate the negative effects of functional loss on role captivity. The negative effects of primary subjective stressors (e.g., caregiver role overload, role captivity, and rela-

tionship loss) may be countered by informal social support. Similarly, the effects of secondary intrapsychic (i.e., caregiver competency, gain, guilt, etc.) or role strains might be lessened by emotional support.

These examples illustrate the potential utility of interventions based on related empirical findings. Yet there are numerous pathways within the stress process model that are currently unexplored. For example, little is known about the precursors to caregiving outcomes such as anger, anxiety, and declining physical health. Research that documents the interrelationships among these factors over time, as well as the impact of social support in moderating the effects of these relationships, will help to inform intervention techniques.

The conceptualization of caregiving as a dynamic process containing multiple domains and developmental transitions is imperative to the advancement of caregiving theory, methodology, and intervention. After the initial onset of caregiving, the care recipient experiences a continued and long-term period of progressive decline to which the caregiver must constantly adapt. Once in-home care becomes unmanageable and placement becomes a reality, caregivers go through another transition as they adapt to their new role in the institutional setting. With the death of the care recipient comes another transition for the caregiver. And although bereavement may appear to be the final stage of adjustment and signal the end of their caregiving career, it is not uncommon for caregivers to take on the responsibility of providing care to another family member at some later point in their lives.

As the stressors of the caregiving process proliferate and intensify, so do their negative consequences. Given the increasing prevalence of caregiving and the heterogeneity among caregivers, it is no wonder that so great an effort has been made to understand the process that drives it. Scholarly work within the literature is rich with a greater understanding of the process of caregiving. Recent advances in theory, methodology, and intervention have propelled the literature forward and laid the foundation for further debate, critical thinking, and innovative intervention. Research and interventions that are clearly grounded in theory and informed by the successes and failures of applied work will contribute greatly to the understanding of the process of caregiving and caring.

BIBLIOGRAPHY

Abel, E. K., & Nelson, M. K. (1990). *Circles of care: Work and identity in women's lives.* Albany, NY: State University of New York Press.

Aneshensel, C. S., Pearlin, L. I., Mullan, J. T., Zarit, S. H., & Whitlatch, C. J. (1995). *Profiles in caregiving: The unexpected career.* San Diego: Academic Press.

Biegel, D. E., Sales, E., & Schulz, R. (1991). *Family caregiving in chronic illness.* Newbury Park, CA: Sage.

Kahana, E., Biegel, D. E., & Wykle, M. L. (Eds.). (1994). *Family caregiving across the lifespan.* Thousand Oaks, CA: Sage.

Minkler, M., & Roe, K. M. (1993). *Grandmothers as caregivers.* Newbury Park, CA: Sage.

Neal, M. B., Chapman, N. J., Ingersoll-Dayton, B., & Emlen, A. C. (1993). *Balancing work and caregiving for children, adults, and elders.* Newbury Park, CA: Sage.

Pearlin, L. I., Aneshensel, C. S., Mullan, J. T., & Whitlatch, C. J. (1995). Caregiving and its social support. In L. K. George & R. H. Binstock (Eds.), *Handbook of aging and the social sciences* (4th ed.) San Diego: Academic Press.

Cell Death

Richard A. Lockshin
St. John's University

Zahra Zakeri
Queens College

Apoptosis Death of a cell through a characteristic pattern including most or all of the following: cell shrinkage, margination of chromatin, fragmentation, destruction of DNA by digestion at nucleosome bridges, and noninflammatory phagocytosis.

Bcl-2 An oncogene, named after the cancer in which it was discovered, B-cell lymphoma-2. A B cell is a type of immunocompetent cell. *Bcl*-2 acts by preventing cell death rather than by stimulating cell division.

Fas, Fas Ligand Fas is a protein expressed by several cells, and fas ligand (FasL) is a cell surface protein similar to tumor necrosis factor. When T cells are activated, they express FasL, inducing apoptosis. Failure of this interaction has been associated with autoimmune diseases and excess proliferation of T cells.

Immunocompetent Cells Any of several related cells of the immune system, which variously retain memory of foreign proteins that have been encountered, communicate this information to other cells, synthesize antibodies against these proteins, or actively destroy infected, invading, or damaged cells.

Necrosis Death of a cell by loss of control of energy resources and ion balance, resulting in cell swelling and rupture, producing an inflammatory response.

Nucleosome Organized grouping of basic proteins (histones) around which DNA wraps. There is approximately one nucleosome for every 180 base pairs of DNA.

Oncogene Gene involved in cell growth and division, often associated with mechanisms regulating mitosis. The term *oncogene* (cancer gene) refers to the fact that these normal cellular genes have been captured by viruses, leading to their uncontrolled expression and consequent loss of regulation of growth in infected cells.

Phagocytosis Consumption of one cell by another. The consuming cell is termed a *phagocyte*. Some cells (macrophages) are designed to destroy other cells, and are considered professional phagocytes. Others may consume a dead neighboring cell and are considered to be amateur phagocytes.

Programmed Cell Death Death of a cell by a mechanism involving an identified sequence of steps to its death, often in nontoxic circumstances, and frequently requiring activation of specific genes. In appearance, the collapse is usually but not always apoptotic.

The term **CELL DEATH** has three meanings. It refers to a limited potential for division of normal cells in culture, disappearance of cells during the normal lifespan of an individual, and the highly controlled suicide of cells. An age-related decline in function of the immune system may reflect the first meaning, the limited life span of cultured cells. The second is poorly defined but presumably results from cell suicide, otherwise described as programmed cell death or apoptosis, which is often controlled by specific genes that protect or destroy cells. This controlled cell death is important in the development of the nervous system and in the differentiation and death of cells in the immune system. Failure of programmed cell death or apoptosis can lead to cancer and autoimmune disease, and excessive cell death can result in immune failure, neurodegeneration, or loss of cells in an infarct. Future therapies are likely to attempt to regulate programmed cell death and apoptosis.

I. DEFINITION OF THE TERM *CELL DEATH*

Cell death, particularly in the context of aging, has at least three meanings for different audiences. First and most familiar to nonresearch audiences, is loss of cells as an individual ages through pathology or perhaps reasons that cannot be attributed to any specific abnormality other than the passage of time. For the gerontologist, this loss is most critical in the immune system, because it leads to substantial increase in susceptibility to infection; in the central nervous system (CNS), because lost neurons are currently irreplaceable, and in the skeletal muscle, because these cells are likewise irreplaceable. In a less absolute sense, cirrhotic loss of cells in the liver is not followed by regeneration, and this loss also therefore becomes life threatening.

The second major sense of the term *cell death* is reference to the failure of most normal vertebrate cells to reproduce indefinitely in culture, also described as limited life span of cells in culture. Although they cease mitosis, they may continue to survive for several months in a postmitotic state. Thus this definition tends to be a bit imprecise as an understanding of when the cells actually die, and the relation of cessation of mitosis to actual death remain incomplete.

The third sense of cell death is physiological cell death, variously referred to as active cell death, programmed cell death, or apoptosis. The latter two terms are slightly different but are often considered to be synonymous. Programmed cell death was first described in 1964 in an embryological or developmental context and referred specifically to the identification of a sequence in which a cell destined for death could be observed to mature metabolically toward its fate long before it was committed to that fate. When it was later recognized that programmed cell death could often be prevented by inhibiting protein synthesis, the implied assumption of a genetic control be-

came more explicit, and the first clear identification of a genetics of cell death, in the ascarid worm *Caenorhabditis*, brought the research into the field of molecular biology.

II. LIMITED LIFE SPAN OF CELLS IN CULTURE

During the late 1950s and early 1960s, Harry Eagle developed a culture medium that marked the beginning of an era of well-documented maintenance of cells *in vitro*, and it finally became possible to analyze the potential of cells to reproduce and differentiate without the influence of other cells or fluctuating hormones and growth factors or circulation. In 1961, Hayflick and Moorhead reported that, although they had tried all logical parameters, they were unable to maintain normal diploid human cells, as opposed to cancerous cells, in indefinite culture. The medium was adequate to the extent that it supported vigorous growth of younger cells, but no strain of cells survived longer than 50 ± 10 population doublings. (In their terms, a population doubling was regrowth following a 1:2 subdivision of the culture.) This limitation appeared to be consistent among numerous newly started cell lines. Furthermore, cell lines started from fetal or infant tissue survived longer than lines started from elderly individuals, and cell lines started from short-lived animals survived fewer population doublings than lines from long-lived animals. They therefore postulated that there was an intrinsic limit to the life span of normal cells in culture, and that this limit might contribute to the inability of individuals to survive indefinitely. This laboratory contributed the cell lines to the research community. Of these lines, the WI-38 line (for Wistar Institute, where the culture was established) became a national resource material, as did another line, MRC-10 (Medical Research Council, from England). The research that generated from laboratories using these and similar lines of cells has profoundly influenced gerontology. The major principles that have been developed as of 1995 are as follows:

1. When vertebrate cells are cultured, all normal lines of cells show intrinsic life spans. Transition to immortality is typically a sign that the culture has become equivalent to malignant cells.

2. The number of divisions that cells can undergo decreases with the age at which the explant is taken. In genetic diseases often considered to be cases of premature senescence, such as progeria and Werner's syndrome, cells cultured from affected individuals often show extremely restricted potential for reproducing. In these specific cases, however, the primary defect may specifically affect the fibroblastic cell types that are usually cultured, and the argument may therefore be tautological.

3. The potential for reproduction of fibroblasts such as WI-38 or MRC-10 cells vastly exceeds the number of fibroblasts that can reasonably be expected to be produced in a normal life span. Therefore, it is unlikely that any individual suffers specifically from a lack of fibroblasts. For erythroblasts (the progenitors of red blood cells) and the precursors of thymocytes and peripheral lymphocytes, however, serial transplantation experiments suggest that the limit may be reached if the tissue is transplanted through only a few generations. It is possible, therefore, that the notable decline in function of the immune system, which renders many elderly individuals incapable of resisting infection, is at least partly traceable to their inability to produce immunologically competent cells. [See IMMUNE SYSTEM.]

4. Failure of the cells to continue to divide does not mean that they have died. In many instances, cells that have ceased to divide can be maintained for many months in culture. The fibroblastic cells that have become postmitotic have differentiated into a different type of cell. This differentiation has attracted the attention of many top researchers. The decision to opt out of mitosis involves several components, including active suppression of mitosis, inactivation of genes that normally initiate a cell division, and the loss of expendable DNA at the tips of chromosomes. (Because of the mechanics of reproduction of DNA, the last little tip at the end of the chromosome is lost with each cell cycle. Organisms compensate for this problem by starting life with a long stretch of meaningless, or noncoding, DNA, called a telomere. When cells use up this telomeric DNA, they lose the ability to divide. Cancerous cells achieve immortality in part by activating an enzyme called telomerase, which can restore the missing piece.) [See DNA AND GENE EXPRESSION.]

5. Cells in culture that have ceased to divide finally die by an independent process that is thought by many to be equivalent to apoptosis. These cells may signal their fate by activation of specific genes, one of which is called *terminin*, and which may be seen in many dying cells.

III. CELL DEATH *IN VIVO*

In spite of the elaborate and frequently exciting cell biology generated by the study of cells maintained in culture, most losses of cells in the body are not related to failure of stem cells to continue to divide but are either accidental necrotic deaths, as when cells distal to a clogged artery die from asphyxiation, or the deliberate suicide of cells under stress or deprived of supporting growth factors or hormones. These two types of death, necrosis and physiological cell death, comprise the bulk of the losses considered to be important manifestations of aging.

A. Programmed Cell Death

The term *physiological cell death* is a more general description for two terms that are commonly used in the literature: *programmed cell death*, which implies a specific causal sequence, and *apoptosis*, which refers to the mechanics and morphology of the death of the cell. Programmed cell death has an obvious morphology or morphologies and specifically differs from necrosis, in which cells, deprived of energy for any reason, ultimately lose control of ion and solute migration across the cell and mitochondrial membranes, imbibe water and calcium, and lyse.

B. Apoptosis

The morphologies vary somewhat including a graded series of changes, but they tend to group into two major types: one in which the cytoplasm is heavily consumed by autophagic (lysosomal) activity; and a second, common to many vertebrate cells, in which cytoplasmic changes are relatively modest, but nuclear changes are early and dramatic, including coalescence and margination of chromatin, followed by shrinkage of the cell and degradation of DNA in a characteristic manner. DNA is cut between proteins called nucleosomes that bind to it at regular intervals, so that when the cut DNA is separated by size in a process called electrophoresis, the different size classes of DNA line

Table I Characteristics of Different Types of Cell Death

Characteristics of Necrosis

- Proximate cause of failure is insufficient energy to maintain ionic pumps.
- Cause of failure usually involves masses of cells rather than individual cells.
- Calcium enters mitochondria and precipitates. Mitochondria swell and lyse.
- Cell loses osmotic control, swells, and lyses, releasing intracellular products.
- Inflammatory response ensues and cell is destroyed and consumed by phagocytes.
- In general, there is no evidence that the cell has time to respond to the challenge or makes any effective response.

Characteristics of Programmed Cell Death

- Stage at which cell is deteriorating but death is reversible
- Often best illustrated by developmental or metamorphic events
- Blocked, at least temporarily, by inhibition of mRNA or protein synthesis
- Cell condenses; nucleus condenses at varying times
- Consumption of cell by autophagocytosis or by phagocytosis

Characteristics of Apoptosis

- Early nuclear condensation and margination of chromatin
- Fragmentation of nuclei into several pieces
- Fragmentation of DNA as detected by electrophoresis or in situ end labeling
- Typically, condensation of cytoplasm with no activation of lysosomes
- Alteration of cell surface proteins
- Phagocytosis by nonprofessional phagocytic cells (neighboring cells)

up in a distinct ladder-like pattern. (In an uncontrolled degradation of DNA such as that seen in necrosis, the DNA is cut at random intervals, and the electrophoretic pattern is that of a smear.) The latter, nonlysosomal, type of physiological cell death technically fits the definition of apoptosis. These points are illustrated in Table I and Figure 1.

IV. PROGRAMMED CELL DEATH

The concept of genetic programming of cell death was inherent in the recognition that specific regions of embryonic cell death differed among species, for instance that there were patches of cell death in the interdigital regions of the foot palettes of chick embryos, but not in the corresponding regions of foot palettes of web-footed birds such as ducks. Similarly, certain teratological abnormalities traceable to single genes were thought to derive from abnormalities of cell death. However, the humble ascarid worm *Caenorhabditis elegans* contributed the first unequivocal documentation for a genetics of cell death. In this organism, the origin and fate of each cell is known, and approximately 15% of the cells in the embryo are born only to die shortly thereafter. Several laboratories through assiduous efforts demonstrated that a small number of genes controlled the death of these cells. These genes function at several levels: two classes of genes are necessary, along different pathways, for cells to die, and one class prevents the death of these cells. A fourth set specifies which cells are supposed to die, and others regulate the phagocytosis and digestion of the corpses. The sequence is illustrated in Figure 2. A similar sequence is likely to exist in *Drosophila*, where a gene responsible for controlling

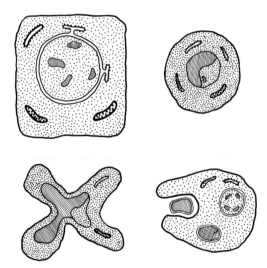

Figure I Schematic of changes occurring during apoptosis. In the upper left, a normal cell displays a round nucleus with occasional chromatin patches, an endoplasmic reticulum budding off the nucleus, and mitochondria. During early phases of apoptosis (upper right) the cell rounds and shrinks, while the chromatin aggregates against the nuclear membrane. Other organelles remain intact. The apoptotic cell then fragments into small membrane-bound particles (lower left), which may or may not include portions of the nucleus. Finally (lower right), in cells within the body, the fragments are engulfed by macrophages or by neighboring cells.

Figure 2 Sequence of control of cell death in *Caenorhabditis*. In order for cells to die by apoptosis, they must contain members of two classes of cell death genes, one of which appears to be a protease. All or most cells are capable of activating these genes, but the death program is suppressed by a cell death prevention gene that is similar to a mammalian oncogene. During development, the cell death prevention gene is turned off in specific cells, allowing the programmed developmental deaths of unique cells. Cells that die are finally phagocytosed by other cells, requiring genes for recognition of the dead cell, nucleases, and perhaps other enzymes.

numerous embryonic cell deaths has been found to exist.

These genes have homologs among mammals. Most notable are the following: the cell death prevention gene *ced-9* is homologous to a mammalian gene, *bcl-2* (B cell lymphoma-2), which prevents the death of B lymphocytes. These surviving lymphocytes may eventually turn malignant. One of the genes necessary for the death of the *Caenorhabditis* cells is homologous to a specific protease, which is itself required in several experimental forms of cell death. Also in mammals, a gene known to be important in preventing the expansion of tumors, *p53*, acts in a manner similar to that of the cell death genes. Most interesting, in both mammalian cells in culture and in *Caenorhabditis* the anticell death genes *bcl-2* and *ced-9* may under some circumstances by experimentally exchanged, and variants of the cell death-inducing protease family may likewise be exchanged. Thus it is fair to assume that the mechanisms of cell death have been highly conserved in evolution and that similar processes operate in mammalian cells. As is described in sections V and VI below, many other genes may be up-regulated in different instances of cell death. However, since causality has not been established and our understanding remained fluid in 1995, excessive attention to many of these genes was not considered appropriate. [*See* MODELS OF AGING: VERTEBRATES.]

V. APOPTOSIS

A. Degradation of the Nucleus

The common morphology of dying cells is not yet fully explained. Although there are several well-understood

mechanisms that can explain the swelling and bursting of a necrotic cell, it is more difficult to explain the shrinkage and changes of nuclear morphology that are common to cells dying by apoptosis. Characteristically, the earliest changes are a rapid coalescence of chromatin and its collection along the nuclear membrane. These are frequently associated with degradation of DNA at specific points (Figure 3) by an enzyme that may be already resident in the nucleus, suggesting therefore that changed conditions in the cell or in the

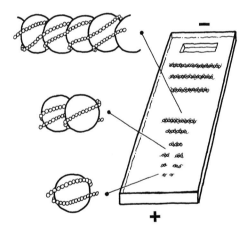

Figure 3 Origin of the hallmark DNA ladder. In normal eukaryotic cells, DNA helices are wound around aggregates of basic proteins (histones). These aggregates are consistent in size and are termed *nucleosomes*. The DNA in the gap between each nucleosome is more readily digested by certain nucleases than are the approximately 180 base pairs of DNA directly on the nucleosome, breaking the DNA into discrete units differing in size by approximately 180 base pairs. When DNA is electrophoresed or driven by an electric current through an agarose gel, the smaller pieces move more rapidly. Thus, in apoptosis, a distinct "ladder" of DNA is formed. In necrotic cell death, digestion of DNA is far less organized and a smear rather than a ladder is formed.

nucleus allow the enzyme to attack the DNA. Other evidence, however, argues against the idea that cleavage of DNA to nucleosomal fragments is a critical step in apoptosis. Several laboratories have detected damage to DNA prior to its degradation to nucleosomal size, including its release from the nuclear membrane by a possibly proteolytic cleavage. Other research indicates that the morphology and the degradation of DNA may be dissociated, whereas arguments and data from several sources suggest that damage to DNA does not immediately kill the cell. Thus, although the specific destruction of the nucleus may be a hallmark of apoptotic cell death, its origin and significance remain mysterious.

B. Cell Shrinkage

The second salient characteristic of apoptosis is shrinkage and condensation of the cell, while organelles and cell membrane remain intact. It is not easy to explain this process. In order for a cell to shrink, it must extrude water. Because other cells in the vicinity, unaffected by apoptosis, remain of normal size, the osmotic tension of the extracellular fluid presumably has not changed. Therefore, only three mechanisms are available for it to lose water. It must decrease intracellular solute; it must develop a contractile force sufficient to extrude water against osmotic pressure, or it must actively extrude solute, with water following. It might decrease intracellular solute by crosslinking, polymerizing, or precipitating proteins. The cytoskeleton provides the only known means of contractile force in the cell, and it is doubtful that it can generate the force necessary. One can get an estimate by assuming the cell to be a cube with a striated muscle shortening one dimension. Because most muscles can generate a force of approximately 5 kg/cm^2, and it would take a force of approximately 2 kg/cm^2 to maintain a volume reduction to half the original cell size, a cell would need a density of cytoskeleton approximately half the density of myofilaments in a striated muscle, with the contractile force of the muscle, to account for the collapse of the cell. Although this force is of the right order of magnitude, it does not appear to be the most logical explanation for the collapse of the cell.

An alternate explanation is cross-linking or precipitation of proteins. There is currently no evidence that the highly condensed proteins are precipitated or insoluble. Proteins cross-linked by transglutaminase are common in many apoptotic bodies, suggesting that cross-linking may play a role in the shrinkage of the cell.

C. Phagocytosis (Cell Surface Proteins)

Because one characteristic of an apoptotic cell, at least one found in an organism as opposed to one in culture, is that it is phagocytosed by a phagocyte or, more frequently, by a neighboring cell that previously was not considered to be phagocytic, the surface of the attacked cell must carry some markers that identify it as apoptotic. Some of these markers have been identified. Some represent glycoproteins known previously to have been on the surface but now more exposed or exposed in different orientation because of the rearrangement of the cell membrane. Others may identify specific cells as apoptotic and ripe for consumption. Loss of sialic acid from membrane carbohydrates, appearance of phosphatidyl serine on the cell surface, and binding of cell surface receptors all play roles in phagocytosis in specific instances. This targeting is sufficiently effective that the growth of tumors expressing it can be forced to regress by appropriate manipulation of the gene. Another example is fas ligand (FasL), a cell surface protein related to tumor necrosis factor and expressed primarily in activated T cells. Fas is produced by several types of cells. Binding of fas to its ligand induces apoptosis, and failure of the interaction may lead to autoimmune diseases and other immunoproliferative disorders.

VI. HOW A CELL DIES

The mechanism by which a cell dies a physiological death is not yet well understood. Signaling mechanisms frequently involve growth stimuli or sudden withdrawal of growth stimuli in otherwise congenial environments, and the first responses of cells about to undergo apoptosis are related to those of cells about to reinitiate mitosis. In cells that are subject to many influences, several laboratories have documented that the paths to apoptosis are typically at least partially independent, recalling the dual sets of genes required for cell death in *Caenorhabditis*. Typically, energy resources in a doomed cell remain adequate, and cell and mitochondrial membranes remain intact, until substantial damage has been done to the cell; the irreversibility of death, which tends to be coincident with massive morphological and biochemical damage, is established at a later time than the commitment to the death pathway. These several observations led to the conclusion that cell growth and cell death are tightly linked. For instance, many of the genes activated in growing or dividing cells are proto-oncogenes. Proto-oncogenes are important in the initiation of cell growth or cell division. They owe their names to the fact that they are occasionally captured by viruses. In the virus, they are separated from the controlling genes that typically reside next to them on normal chromosomes, and they therefore cause uncontrolled growth or cancer. One of these proto-oncogenes, c-myc, is also activated in many forms of cell death. C-myc is well enough known that the exact structure of the gene has been established, and only very limited areas of the gene, a few base pairs in length, actually control the oncogenicity. This precise region of the gene is also influential in apoptosis, suggesting that the product of the gene can stimulate the growth of the cell under some circumstances and can stimulate cell death in other circumstances. A general image of how cell death occurs may be that numerous factors are required for a cell to complete the complex process of growth or mitosis and that, if any of the factors are unavailable, the cell will die.

VII. CELL DEATH IN AGING

Organisms do not die from programmed cell death or apoptosis. Although the limited life span of cells in culture suggests that a decrease in cell division may contribute to decreased function in immunodefense and maintenance of the epidermis, erythroblasts and intestinal crypt cells do not approach their mitotic potential in a normal life span. For postmitotic cells such as neurons and muscle, the consequences of physiological cell death are more important, and because in tumors cell death is a major factor determining the expansion of the malignancy, interest in cell death is high. The most important areas relating gerontology and aging are the following.

A. Malignancy

Several lines of evidence indicate that cell death is a factor in malignancy. In many tumors, the rate of cell death is a better indicator of malignant potential than is the rate of cell division. Dietary restriction, the only known means of extending life span in mammals, may increase the rate of apoptosis. The bcl-2 oncogene acts by inhibiting cell death, and other genes such as Apo-1 regulate the rate of apoptosis in a tumor. These observations by themselves argue that study of cell death should be of interest to oncologists. Another consideration is that most chemotherapeutic techniques attempt to kill mitotic cells. In doing so, they necessarily damage other normal but highly mitotic tissues, such as intestinal epithelium, lymphocyte stem cells, and epidermis, as well as cells with high metabolic demands, such as liver and neurons. A chemotherapeutic approach attempting to induce apoptosis in tumor cells promises to be far less toxic, or minimally to deflect toxicity from normal mitotic cells. [See CANCER AND THE ELDERLY.]

B. Gradual Cell Loss

Perhaps the most important suggestion is one derived from a current sense of the biology of apoptosis. As mentioned in the previous section, there is a curious relationship between growth stimuli and responses and apoptosis. Several laboratories have detected homologies between receptors for growth factors and receptors that, when activated by binding a product, trigger cell death. Similarly, as many cells respond to stimuli that will lead to their death, genes normally associated with growth responses, including those required for cell division, are up-regulated. One or more of these genes, such as several cell cycle genes (which are up-regulated during specific phases of cell division) and oncogenes (genes frequently normally used in cell division, which by uncontrolled regulation can cause cancer or cancerlike transformations) are activated in an aberrant manner, and restriction of the activity of these genes may prevent the death of the cell. One interpretation of these results is that the dysregulation is itself a signal, and that cells are programmed to self-destruct if all growth-regulating stimuli impinging on the cell are not completely consistent with the ability of the cell to respond. Particularly among cells that can still undergo mitosis, such a response would be a powerful defense for the organism against potential malignancy. There is at least one claim that the rate of apoptosis declines with age. A low rate of apoptosis could preserve cells but could also heighten the risk of cancer.

C. Deliberate Self-Destruction in the Immune System

As is described above, cell death in the differentiating immune system is delicately balanced to ensure a wide variety of immunocompetent cells, resting in reserve against a nearly infinite variety of possible antigens, without either attacking self or, by multiplying, draining resources when not needed. The complexity of the controls and stimuli needed to maintain a primary T- or B-lymphocyte is very great, involving a delicate balance of interactions between antigens presented to the cell at specific stages in the differentiation of the immunologically competent cell and the ability of the differentiating and stem cells to recognize those antigens. The complexity may be required to assure the destruction of cells that may form antibodies against one's own body. Other functionally important exploitations of the ability of cells to die are self-destruction of a cell infected by viruses to limit replication of the virus, and self-destruction of a cell that, by virtue of damage to its DNA (mutation) threatens to become cancerous. Among the several steps that cells take toward carcinogenicity, loss of sensitivity to signals to die is an early and ominous one. Nevertheless, the salubrious loss of cells in such circumstances likely contributes to the gradual deterioration of immunocompetence with aging. In a chronic viral infection, for instance, huge numbers of immunocompetent cells may be generated, but a slight imbalance between generation and loss will lead to such a gradual deterioration. Such an imbalance may be seen, for instance, in the progression of acquired immunodeficiency syndrome (AIDS) by gradual loss of specific immunocompetent cells over a 10-year course (representing a net imbalance of 0.03% per day between loss and replacement) or in the difference between immunologically competent centenarians and their less fortunate cohorts. Similarly, an imbalance of 0.004% between the birth and death of hundreds of millions of cells per day could reduce the number of immunocompetent cells by half by the end of an average lifetime. What is startling is that the balance is so precise. As we learn to understand how these controls trigger cell death, we are likely to develop cell death-based therapies either to maintain immunocompetent cells or to prevent autoimmunity, both complications of aging.

D. Loss of Postmitotic Cells

Loss of postmitotic cells, especially in the CNS, remains a threatening aspect of aging. Many of these losses appear not to be necrotic, derived from circulatory failures, but rather a physiological death of a cell strained beyond its limit. It has become evident, for instance, that loss of cells even in stroke may be by apoptosis, suggesting that cells undergo a prolonged period of agony during which they might conceivably be rescued. A major molecular product generated in senile dementia of Alzheimer type (SDAT), an oxidized form of the β-amyloid accumulated in the disease, is toxic to neurons and, in culture at least, they display such signs of apoptosis as up-regulation of specific oncogenes and protection by experimental activation of the antiapoptosis gene bcl-2. Therapeutic considerations remain theoretical. It is likely that the cells that eventually die do so after having passed a considerable period of agony, since postmitotic cells are frequently more resistant to apoptosis than are rapidly replaced cells. Such an explanation would account for the late onset of cell loss in SDAT as well as for other losses less directly attributable to disease. One presumes that the agonizing cell is identifiable before it succumbs and, as in programmed cell death, passes through a reversible phase. Here a therapeutic goal is to identify the agonizing cell, identify what aspect of its support is inadequate, and to intervene to stabilize it before it dies. [See BRAIN AND CENTRAL NERVOUS SYSTEM; DEMENTIA.]

BIBLIOGRAPHY

Barr, P. J., & Tomei, L. D. (1994). Apoptosis and its role in human disease. BioTechnology, 12, 487–493.

Bright, J., & Khar, A. (1994). Apoptosis: Programmed cell death in health and disease. Bioscience Reports, 14, 67–82.

Bursch, W., Oberhammer, F., & Schulte-Hermann, R., (1992): Cell death by apoptosis and its protective role against disease. Trends in Pharmacological Science, 13, 245–251.

Cohen, J. J., (1993). Apoptosis. Immunology Today, 14, 126–130.

Kerr, J. F. R., Wyllie, A. H., & Currie, A. R. (1972). Apoptosis: A basic biological phenomenon with wide-ranging implications in tissue kinetics. British Journal of Cancer, 26, 239–257.

Kerr, J. F. R., Winterford, C. M., & Harmon, B. V. (1994).

Apoptosis: Its significance in cancer and cancer therapy. *Cancer, 73,* 2013–2026.

Koli, K., Keski-Oja, J. (1992). Cellular senescence. *Annals of Medicine, 24,* 313–318.

Lockshin, R. A., Zakeri, Z. F. (1990). Programmed cell death: New thoughts and relevance to aging. *Journal of Gerontology, 45,* B135–B140.

Monti, D., Troiano, L., Tropea, F., Grassilli, E., Cossarizza, A., Barozzi, D., Pelloni, M. C., Tamassia, M. G., Bellomo, G., & Franceschi, C. (1992). Apoptosis—Programmed cell death: A role in the aging process. *American Journal of Clinical Nutrition, 55* (Suppl.), 1208S–1214S.

Nuñez, G., & Clarke, M. F. (1994). The *bcl*-2 family of proteins: Regulators of cell death and survival. *Trends in Cell Biology, 4,* 399–403.

Raff, M. C. (1992). Social controls on cell survival and cell death. *Nature, 356,* 397–400.

Reed, J. C. (1994). *Bcl*-2 and the regulation of programmed cell death. *Journal of Cell Biology, 124,* 1–6.

Tenniswood, M. P., Guenette, R. S., Lakins, J., Mooibroek, M., Wong, P., & Welsh, J-E. (1992). Active cell death in hormone-dependent tissues. *Cancer and Metastasis Reviews, 11,* 197–220.

White, E. (1993). Death-defying acts: A meeting review on apoptosis. *Genes and Development, 7,* 2277–2284.

Wyllie, A. H. (1987). Apoptosis: Cell death in tissue regulation. *Journal of Pathology, 153,* 313–316.

Wyllie, A. H. (1993). Apoptosis (The 1992 Frank Rose Memorial Lecture). *British Journal of Cancer, 67,* 205–208.

Wyllie, A. H. (1994). Apoptosis: Death gets a brake. *Nature, 369,* 272–273.

Zakeri, Z., & Lockshin, R. A. (1994). Physiological cell death during development and its relationship to aging. *Annals of the New York Academy of Sciences, 719,* 212–229.

Cholesterol and Cell Plasma Membranes

Thomas N. Tulenko, David Lapotofsky, Robert H. Cox,* and R. Preston Mason

Medical College of Pennsylvania
*University of Pennsylvania

Membrane Fluidity The ease with which lateral mobility of membrane proteins or lipids is permitted along the membrane phospholipid bilayer. Compounds that alter membrane fluidity either increase or decrease lateral mobility of these molecules.

Arterial Vasospasm Inappropriate vasoconstriction resulting in the reduction and impairment of blood flow. Vasospastic events result in poor tissue oxygenation and therefore poor tissue function due to impaired blood flow.

Phenotypic Modulation In vascular smooth muscle cells, the predominant phenotypic state is the "contractile" phenotype characterized by robust contractile ability, with reduced protein (matrix) secretion, and little to no replicative ability. In vascular disease, phenotypic modulation occurs in which the smooth muscle cells shift to the "synthetic phenotype," which is characterized by marked proliferative activity, augmented protein (matrix) secretion, and reduced contractile ability.

The **PLASMA MEMBRANE** is a lipid bilayer structure separating the intracellular from the extracellular compartments. It provides an important barrier pro-

tecting the cell from a variety of molecules present in abundance in the extracellular space. Communication between the cell and its extracellular signals occurs largely through proteins imbedded in the bilayer. These integral membrane proteins are held in the bilayer by virtue of a registration of their hydrophobic amino acids with the hydrocarbon core of the membrane bilayer. In this way, the bilayer serves as a two-dimensional solvent system for these signal proteins, which include ion channel proteins, molecular pumps, exchange proteins, and a wide range of cell surface receptors. The ability of these signal proteins to function properly depends on the composition, dynamics, and structure of the membrane "solvent" features. Changes in bilayer composition have been shown to alter the activity of numerous membrane proteins, many of which play crucial roles in regulating cell function. Age-related alterations in bilayer lipid composition and dynamics have been described for the plasma membrane in several cell types. Common to most studies is an increase in the cholesterol content of the bilayer. Why this change occurs and the degree to which it disturbs cell function with age needs to be more carefully addressed. This article discusses how cholesterol fits into cell membranes and the molecular interactions it has with the other membrane lipids and how these interactions alter membrane dynamics, structure, and function. In particular, we have focused this discussion on cholesterol's potential involvement in disturbing plasma membranes in cells of the vascular wall and in the central nervous system

(CNS), which may contribute to the genesis of cellular defects of two particular diseases that are of special concern in the elderly, atherosclerotic heart disease and Alzheimer's disease (AD).

I. BACKGROUND

A. Membrane Lipid Composition and Physical Characteristics

Many scientists regard the cell plasma membrane merely as the thin black line typically drawn around the cell to delineate the inside of the cell from the outside. Indeed, one of the principle roles of the plasma membrane is to serve as a barrier to keep the cell contents inside and the extracellular contents outside. The membrane bilayer itself is largely resistant to permeation by both charged and most uncharged molecules, as well as a wide variety of extracellular signals. However, the movement of materials and information across this barrier is essential to cell function and is accomplished almost exclusively by membrane proteins that serve transport, diffusion, receptor, and phagocytic processes. Membrane proteins are complex macromolecular assemblies imbedded in the membrane lipid bilayer. These transmembrane pathways have been heavily studied and well described. Lost in the interest and activity surrounding the structure–function relations of membrane proteins is the lipid bilayer itself, and the effect that changing the lipid components (i.e., phospholipids and cholesterol) has on the qualitative characteristics of the bilayer. This is a vital issue because the lipid bilayer serves also as a two-dimensional solvent system in which the various membrane proteins are inserted. The proteins are held in the lipid bilayer by virtue of a hydrophobic registration of their lipophilic amino acid residues, with the hydrocarbon core fatty acyl chains. It stands to reason that changes in the composition of the membrane may alter qualitative aspects of the bulk lipid phase and therefore may well have marked effects on functional aspects of the transmembrane proteins. Recent studies described in this article suggest that defects in the bilayer characteristics may have pathogenic roles in important diseases of growing significance to the elderly.

The plasma membrane, like all other membranes in nature is composed of a bilayer of various phospholipids, which include phosphatidylcholine (PC), phosphatidylethanolamine (PE), phosphatidylserine (PS), phosphatidylinositol (PI), phosphatidic acid (PA), and sphingomyelin (SP), as well as various glycolipids. At neutral pH, the phosphorus head group is polar, whereas the fatty acyl chains remain neutral. Thus, phospholipids have amphipathic properties and, as such, they spontaneously assemble into lipid bilayers in aqueous media with the polar head groups oriented toward the aqueous phase and the nonpolar fatty acyl chains orienting toward each other, thereby excluding water. In addition, nearly all eukaryotic, but not prokaryotic membranes also require sterols. In mammals, this sterol requirement is exclusively for the 3-hydroxy form of unesterified (free) cholesterol. In mammalian plasma membranes the most abundant phospholipids by mass are PC, PE, PS, and SP, and to a much lesser degree PA and PI. The level of SP correlates well with the amount of cholesterol. SP and cholesterol have been suggested to form noncovalent bonds, and SP levels in membranes appear to be driven, at least in part, by the cholesterol content, to the extent that SP levels may even serve to "protect" cholesterol content in the plasma membrane. Perhaps the greatest variability in membrane lipids is seen in the cholesterol content. The cholesterol to phospholipid mole ratio (FC:PL) ranges from below 0.1:1 (10 mol percent) in most intracellular membranes to over 1:1 (100 mol percent) in plasma membranes of Schwann cells and red blood cells (RBCs). At a 0.5 FC/PL mole ratio (50 mol percent) approximately one molecule of cholesterol is present for every two molecules of phospholipid. In most mammalian cell plasma membranes, cholesterol is the single most abundant membrane lipid where the FC/PL mole ratio is approximately 0.3–0.5.

The rationale for phospholipids in the bilayer is straightforward; they are ideally suited to forming the thin, pliable barrier enclosing cells. Furthermore, the intrinsic motion of their fatty acyl chains provides a fluid hydrocarbon core permitting conformational changes in membrane proteins as well as lateral movement of membrane constituents. Thus, without exception, all membranes are composed of phospholipids. As for the rationale for specific classes of phospholipids, the problem becomes more complex, because specific functions for the individual phospholipid classes need to be identified. In this regard, the phospholipids subserving signaling functions are the easiest to explain. The importance of membrane PI in the IP₃/DAG second messenger pathway is well established, as is membrane SP and its hydrolytic products sphingosine and ceramide in the regulation of cell function, in large part through their effects on protein kinase C (PKC) activity.

However, the role of membrane cholesterol in plasma membranes, unlike phospholipids, is less straightfoward. To begin with, although free cholesterol is an absolute requirement in mammalian membranes, it is not a requirement for membranes of lower life forms. Indeed, prokaryotes have no sterols in their membranes. So why eukaryotes need a membrane sterol, and why mammals in particular choose cholesterol for their membrane is odd, and perhaps unfortunate because cholesterol's requirement for membrane and hormone synthesis is countered by its potential lethality in the bloodstream. Free cholesterol is highly insoluble in aqueous media so it readily partitions into phospholipid bilayers. In fact, this is its exclusive intracellular location. In mammals 3-hydroxycholesterol is the only membrane cholesterol species. The presence of the 3-hydroxy group confers a specific orientation of the molecule in the bilayer such that the polar hydroxyl group orients this end of the sterol ring near the surface of the bilayer in the polar phosphorus-head group region. The hydrophobic ring structure partitions into the fatty acyl chain region of the phospholipid leaflet where it occupies a position spanning approximately 6 to 15 Å out from the center of the bilayer. The sterol ring is a planar, conformationally inflexible ring structure, and in this position in the bilayer it can greatly hinder the intrinsic motion of the fatty acyl chains, thereby ordering the bilayer and reducing membrane fluidity in native membranes. In addition, kinks in the phospholipid fatty acyl chains are thought to create transient free volume elements or open space regions in the membrane bilayer during acyl chain motion. These free volume elements likely provide pathways for the movement of small molecules like glucose that can diffuse across lipid bilayers, a process that is reduced by increasing the cholesterol content of the bilayer. They may also provide the space or "breathing room" for protein conformational changes necessary for membrane proteins to mediate transport of materials and/or information from one side of the bilayer to the other. The fractional free volume is therefore reduced by cholesterol in proportion to its concentration in the membrane.

In this way, altering membrane cholesterol levels may well hinder activity of some membrane proteins. The functional significance of cholesterol in membranes likely relates, in part, to its ability to "set" the level of fluidity and fractional free volume. More recently, membrane cholesterol content has also been shown to greatly affect membrane bilayer width, a parameter function with considerable potential consequences to the activity of various membrane proteins. As described below, there is a direct, linear, and highly significant relationship between membrane cholesterol and bilayer thickness. This structural effect of cholesterol on membranes is another interesting and important function of this sterol, and one that is likely integrated into the membrane cholesterol regulatory scheme.

The asymmetrical distribution of cholesterol in cells is another intriguing aspect of this sterol. Several lines of evidence suggest that the greatest fraction of cell cholesterol is located in the plasma membrane where the FC/PL mole ratio is usually around 0.5. This is much higher than is thought to exist in mitochondrial, lysosomal, Golgi, endoplasmic reticulum (ER), or nuclear membranes. In fact, free cholesterol is often used as a marker for the plasma membrane. Using the cholesterol oxidase assay in a fibroblast cell line, Evonne Lange has estimated that over 90% of the cell's cholesterol is in the plasma membrane. However, the cholesterol oxidase technique is not without its shortcomings, and this value may be an overestimate. Nonetheless, current wisdom holds that the plasma membrane is highly enriched with cholesterol relative to the subcellular membranes. Why this asymmetry exists is not clear, but it may be necessary to provide a suitable barrier function of the plasma membrane lipid bilayer. Because cholesterol reduces the fractional free volume of the bilayer, it limits bilayer permeability to small molecules that would otherwise diffuse across it more readily. Lastly, because cholesterol impacts on bilayer structure, it may also provide suitable structural conditions for proper function of the membrane proteins.

B. Regulation of Membrane Cholesterol

Generally, lipid–protein interactions are regarded as either direct (i.e., a certain lipid species may be required for a protein to function properly) or indirect (as through membrane microviscosity). Both of these interactions have been demonstrated for membrane cholesterol. For any given cell line, the plasma membrane seems to be relatively fixed with regard to its phospholipid profile and cholesterol composition, but significant differences between cell lines are common. Thus, each cell line seems to know what its plasma membrane phospholipid and cholesterol composition ought to be and strives to maintain its unique profile. This suggests that the plasma membrane lipid composition is carefully regulated, presumably at the genomic level. Although this all makes good sense, it is difficult to understand this regulation because membranes are self-assembled structures. Nonetheless, phospholipid profiles can be generated, at least in part, through their differential synthesis and assembly into Golgi membranes destined for the plasma membrane. Further cell-specific refinement of the phospholipid profile is accomplished through the synthesis and regulation of various phospholipid-active enzymes, such as the various cellular phospholipases and flipases. However, these pathways do not explain the regulation of cholesterol content of the plasma membrane. Nearly all cells have the capacity to synthesize cholesterol, a pathway that is largely held in check in mammals by an abundance of cholesterol that comes to the cell from the outside, primarily by lipoproteins. Cholesterol appears to gain access to the membrane bilayer primarily by aqueous diffusion, as this route has been established for the movement of cholesterol between phospholipid surfaces, between low-density lipoproteins (LDL) and smooth muscle plasma membranes, and between subcellular membranes. Membrane cholesterol levels are determined by the relative rates of cholesterol absorption into and desorption out of the bilayer. In the steady state, these rates must be equal. In nonsteroidogenic and nonproliferating cells, the supply of this sterol to cells is almost exclusively through plasma LDL, the level of which is greatly affected by dietary and hepatic factors. Under normal conditions, removal of cholesterol from the membrane is accomplished by high-density lipoprotein (HDL) from the outside ("reverse cholesterol transport"), a largely unregulated process for cholesterol removal from peripheral cells. Thus, because the extracellular routes for cholesterol to the plasma membrane are unregulated, membrane cholesterol is likely regulated from inside the cell, presumably by the cholesterol esterification/deesterification pathways (ACAT and CEH). Because these enzymes have only recently been purified through cloning techniques, this regulatory pathway has yet to be defined, and our understanding of the details of how cellular-free cholesterol levels, and therefore also membrane cholesterol, are controlled is meager at best. It is clear, however, that cells are good at regulating their membrane cholesterol levels. For example, in arterial smooth muscle cells (SMC) in culture, enrichment of the cells with cholesterol using cholesterol donor liposomes increases the membrane FC/PL mole ratio. When the cholesterol-enriched SMC are then left in culture without the liposomes, the SMC membrane cholesterol content gradually returns back to control levels over 4–5 days. This return is accompanied by an increase in cell cholesteryl esters, consistent with regulation by the ACAT/CEH pathway.

II. ISOLATING PLASMA MEMBRANES FOR STUDY

In any discussion of plasma membrane composition or characteristics, a comment on membrane isolation is essential because the limitations of the technique are important to understand. A major technical problem impeding our understanding of the composition, dynamics, and structure of the membrane lipid bilayer has been the extreme difficulty in isolating and studying it in pure form. On the one hand, "membrane function" can most easily be studied using transport techniques (i.e., measuring the movement of ions and molecules into [influx] and out of [efflux] cells). However, this type of transport is mediated mostly by large, complex, amphipathic proteins, and the degree to which the lipid characteristics of the bilayer contributes to this process is hard to delineate. For this, the plasma membrane must be isolated, and herein lies the problem. The standard and by far most common approach to isolate plasma membranes is to fractionate the cells osmotically or mechanically, followed by differential ultracentrifugation. This can be applied to intact tissue, dispersed cells, and cells in culture. Differential ultracentrifugation yields a membrane fraction (i.e., microsomes) containing varying degrees of purity relative to internal subcellular membranes. Unfortunately, "pure plasma membranes" are impossible to obtain. Contaminating the microsomal membrane fraction are the other "light" membranes such as Golgi and ER membranes. Even with further fractionation, such as gradient ultracentrifugation of the microsomal membrane preparation, contamination is reduced, but not eliminated. Compounding purification by ultracentrifugation, yield is disproportionately reduced as purity is increased. Lastly, even with extreme care and refined procedures, lipid exchange between membrane fractions during the sample preparation cannot be avoided. Hence, what was pure plasma membrane to the cell becomes something less in the test tube. Notwithstanding these difficulties, "relatively" pure plasma membranes can be prepared and studied, so long as one appreciates that the ideal pure plasma membrane is only a theoretical endpoint. For this reason, the differential distribution of membrane markers is important to demonstrate in any membrane preparation, without which it is impossible to estimate the degree of purification.

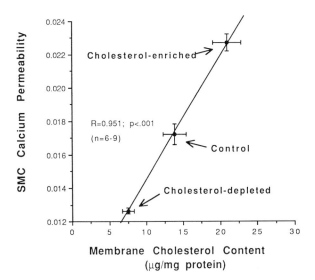

Figure 1 Effects of altering membrane cholesterol content on the permeability of the cell to calcium. SMC, smooth muscle cell. A marked decrease in calcium permeability is seen with decreases in membrane cholesterol content, whereas a marked increase in membrane calcium permeability is seen with increases in membrane cholesterol content. Membrane cholesterol content is expressed as the mass of cell-free cholesterol per milligram cell protein.

III. ALTERATIONS IN MEMBRANE CHOLESTEROL: COMPENSATORY VERSUS PATHOLOGICAL

A. Compensatory Alterations

Because changes in membrane cholesterol, in either direction, disturb lipid bilayer dynamics and structure, it seems reasonable to suspect that this would also alter membrane and cell function. There is abundant evidence supporting this notion using in vitro systems. For example, in cultured arterial SMCs in early passage, increasing membrane cholesterol content, as a single, isolated and independent variable, increases passive membrane permeability to calcium as illustrated in Figure 1. In these studies, alterations in membrane cholesterol were accomplished by incubating SMC monolayers overnight with either cholesterol donor liposomes (FC:PL ≈ 2:1) or cholesterol acceptor liposomes (FC:PL = 0:1). It is clear that when membrane cholesterol increased above control levels, calcium permeability increased, and when membrane cholesterol levels were decreased below control levels, calcium permeability also decreased. Moreover, following the shift from either high or low cholesterol levels, if the SMC were placed in cholesterol-neutral medium, the membrane cholesterol alteration reversed back to control levels, as did passive calcium permeability. Because calcium is an important cell second messenger, these studies suggest that

changes in membrane cholesterol levels are likely to have marked influences on cell function.

However, in vivo, it is not always apparent whether changes in membrane cholesterol are pathological or compensatory. This is particularly true in studies of age-related alterations. Several studies have demonstrated an increase in cholesterol content with age including neuronal, cardiac, and arterial SMCs. Figure 2A illustrates an increase in the FC/PL mole ratio with age in SMC membranes isolated from the aorta of Fisher 344 rats. In these studies, cholesterol enrichment was evident only in the senescent period. Figure 2B illustrates marked alterations in membrane phospholipids from the same samples. These changes in membrane lipid composition with age are accompanied by changes in K$^+$ permeability as illustrated in Figure 2C, which demonstrates an age-dependent suppression of K$^+$ efflux through the Ca-dependent K$^+$ channel with adrenergic stimulation. As with free cholesterol (FC) content, this is particularly evident in the senescent period. Studies like this are therefore consistent with the conclusion that, at least in arterial smooth muscle, aging is associated with a remodeling of the membrane bilayer. Remodeling of this type (i.e.,

A

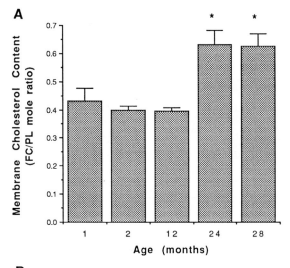

B

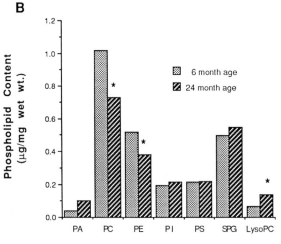

C

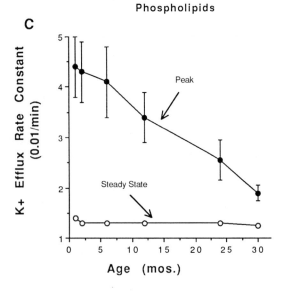

an increase in cholesterol and ridigizing phospholipids [PC]) would be expected to reduce membrane fluidity, and this has been reported in other cell lines by other investigators. However, these changes in smooth muscle membrane lipid composition, lipid dynamics, and membrane function with age are apparently not associated with equivalent changes in tissue function, because contractile properties, passive stiffness, collagen, and elastin synthesis do not appear to be altered with age, at least in this animal model of aging (Fisher 344 rat). We conclude from this that these age-related changes in membrane lipids were either unrelated to cell function, or that they constituted a physiologic compensatory response to aging so as to protect cell and tissue function.

Changes in membrane lipid composition in neuronal cells as a function of age has been previously reported. Specifically, an increase in cholesterol content (i.e., increased FC/PL mole ratio) has been reported for cortical gray matter, whole brain lipid extracts, as well as in platelets and lymphocytes derived from aged human subjects. In neuronal microsomes, in vitro manipulation of membrane cholesterol content alters the binding activity of various neurotrans-

Figure 2 (A) Age-dependent alterations in membrane cholesterol content in aortic smooth muscle isolated from Fisher 344 rats at various ages. There is nearly a 50% increase in membrane cholesterol content in the senescent period (24–30 months). Between 9–18 animals were studied in each age group. (**B**) Alterations in membrane phospholipids with age in aortic smooth muscle isolated from Fisher 344 rats. For simplicity, only the 6- and 24-month ages are illustrated. Note significant reductions in phosphatidylcholine (PC) and phosphatidylethanolamine (PE) at 24 months while lysophosphatidyl-choline (lysoPC) is increased. The significance of these alterations is not clear in that tissue functional parameters (vasoconstriction and stiffness) were not altered at these ages. Between 9–18 animals were studied. PA, phosphatidic acid; PI, phosphatidylinositol; PS, phosphatidylinositol; PS, phosphatidylserine; SP, sphigomyelino). (C) Age-dependent decrease in K⁺ efflux induced by activation with norepinephrine (NE, 1 μM) in rings of aortic smooth muscle obtained from Fisher 344 rats at various ages. Solid circles indicate peak activation K⁺ efflux values and open circles indicate steady-state K⁺ efflux values. Currents mediated by K⁺ efflux tend to stabilize the cell membrane. In arterial smooth muscle, activation of this current by NE prevents membrane depolarization, which would be expected to limit vasoconstriction. Whether this decrease in K⁺ efflux over age alters vasoconstriction to NE is unlikely as force generation to NE was unaffected by age in these experiments. For this reason, these changes are likely compensatory rather than pathological.

mitters to their respective receptors. In addition, changes in synaptic membrane signal transduction have also been observed that correlate with increases in membrane cholesterol content. In many cases, the effect of cholesterol enrichment may be reversed with membrane-fluidizing agents, including S-adenosyl-methionine, but the degree to which fluidizing the membrane alters membrane structural parameters has not been determined. Metabolic alterations leading to changes in membrane cholesterol can only be speculated. LDL receptors are expressed on neural cells. Apoprotein E, one of the LDL receptor's two ligands, is synthesized in astrocytes. This suggests that LDL, the cholesterol-rich lipoprotein in humans, may have an important role in cholesterol metabolism in the CNS. Although this relationship has been clearly established for peripheral cells, the relationship between plasma cholesterol levels and neuronal membrane cholesterol content has yet to be defined. However, age-related changes in cell and membrane cholesterol content have been described in several neuronal tissues, but the degree to which these alterations in membrane cholesterol content reflect compensatory or pathological processes is not clear.

B. Disease-Related Alterations in the Elderly: Alzheimer's Disease

Unlike the alterations in membrane composition and function noted above, which occurred in the absence of alterations in tissue function, notable alterations in certain neuronal membrane bilayers have been seen in conditions clearly associated with functional deficits. A good example of such a potential pathogenic alteration is seen in Alzheimer's disease (AD), a major neurological disorder in the elderly. AD is a neurodegenerative disorder associated with aging that is characterized by progressive loss of higher intellectual function in the absence of focal neurologic defects. A characteristic neuropathological lesion in the cerebral cortex of patients with AD is the neuritic plaque composed primarily of a 42-amino acid peptide, referred to as beta amyloid (βA4). The number of neuritic plaques generally correlate with the degree of dementia in AD. The mechanism underlying the elevated formation of βA4 is not well understood, however. [See DEMENTIA.]

The βA4 peptide is derived from a large, membrane-bound amyloid precursor protein (APP) that is broadly expressed throughout the cerebral cortex. Proteolysis experiments indicate that the cleavage site on APP that releases the βA4 peptide fragment is the carboxy terminal end of βA4. The site is normally imbedded in the membrane bilayer, and hence, formation of the βA4 peptide fragment is prevented. It is possible that the basis for abnormal APP cleavage that leads to βA4 formation may be related to fundamental changes in membrane lipid composition and structure that could lead to exposure of the βA4 cleavage site.

Alterations in the lipid composition of neuronal membranes in AD has been characterized by various methods, including ^{31}P nuclear magnetic resonance (MRI) thin layer chromatography, and elemental analysis. These studies have demonstrated marked changes in phospholipid composition, including certain metabolites of phospholipid degradation. In addition, biochemical analyses indicate that the cholesterol content of neuronal membranes isolated from an affected cerebral cortical region of AD brain tissue is significantly lower than in corresponding age-matched control and Parkinson's disease samples. The effect of changes in neuronal lipid composition on the structure of plasma membrane lipid bilayers has been directly determined with the use of small angle X-ray diffraction. The results of this analysis showed a reproducible reduction in the overall width of reconstituted AD membrane lipid bilayers relative to age-matched controls. We suggest that this thinning of the membrane bilayer may increase the probability for proteolytic cleavage and release of the βA4 fragment from APP. Interestingly, there was no evidence for changes in lipid composition or structure in neuronal membranes reconstituted from unaffected regions of the AD brain (i.e., cerebellum) relative to control subjects. Furthermore, this reduction in membrane lipid bilayer width could be reversed by adding cholesterol back to the AD samples. Thus, abnormal cleavage of APP may be attributed to basic changes in the architecture of the neuronal plasma membrane bilayer secondary to reduced cholesterol content. Why membrane cholesterol content in these membranes is decreased is not clear and constitutes a clear direction for future studies. Of note is the recent discovery of the expression of an apo E isoforms (E_4) in AD patients, the presence of which appears to predict risk and severity for developing AD. However, any link between dysregulation of apo E and altered cortical membrane cholesterol and structure in these subjects has yet to be demonstrated.

C. Disease-Related Alterations in the Elderly: Atherosclerosis

Another disorder of increasing prevalence with age is heart disease and stroke. Here a link between defects in membrane cholesterol and cell function may also be important. In industrialized cultures, nearly one-half of all causes of death can be attributed to arterial wall disease in which the gradual buildup of fatty lesions and plaque on the luminal surface of large arteries encroaches on organ blood flow. This very gradual, silent process converts in a matter of moments to the acute life-threatening crisis of myocardial infarction or stroke when plaque rupture occurs triggering thrombotic occlusion and ischemia of downstream tissues. [See ATHEROSCLEROSIS.]

Although cardiovascular mortality is clearly linked with elevated serum cholesterol levels, the cellular basis for atherogenesis is very poorly understood. Moreover, just how molecular cholesterol per se fits into the pathophysiology of atherosclerosis has been a total mystery. However, there is a growing belief that serum hypercholesterolemia and/or defects of lipoprotein metabolism lead to the abnormal retention of LDL in the arterial wall. Once there in concentrations greater than can be cleared effectively by the monocyte–macrophage pathway, several biological events likely occur that lead to plaque development and the eventual demise of the arterial lumen and organ blood flow. Recent studies shed new light on the cellular basis of atherogenesis and clearly point to defects in membrane cholesterol levels as a potentially important element in the early pathogenic alterations of arterial wall cells in this disease. Studies from our laboratories have shown that enrichment of arterial SMC plasma membranes with cholesterol augments vasoconstrictor activity by increasing calcium permeability and cytosolic calcium levels. Although these studies were performed in vitro, more recent studies have demonstrated very similar findings in rabbits fed a cholesterol-enriched diet for up to 10 weeks. In these studies, atherosclerotic lesions developed in the aorta, and aortic wall segments were isolated and studied for their vasoconstrictor activity and calcium permeability. Again, basal and stimulated calcium permeability and cytosolic calcium levels were elevated. This

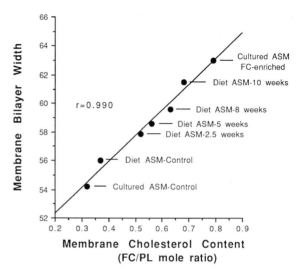

Figure 3 The effects of membrane cholesterol enrichment on membrane bilayer width as determined using small angle X-ray diffraction. Membranes were freshly isolated from smooth muscle cells (SMC) dispersed from the rabbit aorta. Note that the increase in membrane cholesterol tracked with the duration of cholesterol feeding as well as with membrane width. This correlation of membrane width with membrane cholesterol content was preserved for SMC enriched in culture with cholesterol donor liposomes as well as in SMC freshly isolated from rabbits fed cholesterol for up to 10 weeks.

change in calcium handling was accompanied by an increase in vasoconstrictor activity to adrenergic stimulation and stimulation with serotonin. We concluded from these studies that the augmented vasoconstrictor activity was caused by the elevated cell calcium levels in SMC, and this defect may explain the common occurrence of vasospastic syndromes in atherosclerotic vessels. Based on our previous studies, we speculated the increase in SMC calcium permeability was secondary to an increase in SMC plasma membrane cholesterol content. This notion was strongly supported in studies in SMC freshly dispersed from the aorta of cholesterol-fed animals. We found that the cholesterol content of the SMC plasma membrane increased as a function of time on a high-cholesterol diet. Using small angle X-ray diffraction analysis, we also found that the membrane bilayer width increased over the cholesterol feeding period, and this increase in membrane width correlated very highly with membrane cholesterol content, as illustrated in Figure 3. This relationship between membrane width and membrane cholesterol content was preserved regardless of cell origin (i.e., cultured vs. freshly dispersed SMC) or method of enrichment with cholesterol (in vitro with liposomes or in vivo by cholesterol feeding to animals). Moreover, this increase in bilayer width and cholesterol content was apparent prior to the appearance of visible lesions, suggesting that the enrichment of SMC plasma membranes in dietary atherosclerosis is an early event in the genesis of atherosclerotic lesions. That "excess" membrane cholesterol is causally linked to these changes in SMC during atherogenesis is strongly inferred by our recent observation that they are all reversed back to normal levels following reversal of membrane cholesterol content by incubation of the cells overnight with the human cholesterol acceptor lipoprotein HDL.

In comparing the membrane and cell alterations that result from acute cholesterol enrichment of SMC in culture with membrane and cell alterations that are seen in SMC isolated from atherosclerotic aorta, we have concluded that the phenotypic alterations in SMC that are seen in atherogenesis may actually be induced by enrichment of the SMC plasma membrane. These membrane alterations common to acute cholesterol enrichment in vitro and chronic cholesterol feeding (in vivo) include elevated membrane cholesterol levels, decreased membrane fluidity, increased membrane width, increased membrane calcium permeability, decreased membrane Na$^+$/K$^+$ ATPase activity, and an increase in unstimulated and stimulated cytosolic calcium levels. The cellular phenotypic alterations induced by cholesterol in vitro that are common to in vivo hypercholesterolemia include increased cytosolic calcium levels, increased contractile function, increased proliferation rate, and increased mitogen secretion. The ability of human HDL to reverse all these membrane and cell functional alterations strongly supports the hypothesis that they are all driven by enrichment of the SMC plasma membrane with cholesterol. It is clear that excess membrane cholesterol may have broad cellular consequences owing to its ability to induce phenotypic modulation in SMC. Whether it is also responsible for the increased synthesis of extracellular matrix typical to atherosclerotic lesions is currently under investigation.

In summary, these findings have led us to speculate that enrichment of the SMC plasma membrane with cholesterol contributes to the changes in SMC metabolic activity seen in atherogenesis. Thus, the development of excess membrane cholesterol in SMC secondary to retention of LDL in the aterial wall may play a pivotal and early role in the genesis of the cellular defects responsible for this important human disease.

IV. SUMMARY

It has been known for some time that cholesterol is a major lipid constituent of cell plasma membranes. Although its role there has been regarded largely along the lines of setting membrane fluidity, it is becoming increasingly clear that it also has important membrane structural effects. Changes in membrane cholesterol composition have been demonstrated to induce significant alterations in the activity of various membrane proteins, and therefore also in cell function, including alterations in the phenotypic state, at least in SMC. However, in age-related alterations, it is not clear whether the alterations in membrane cholesterol reflect compensatory alterations or pathologic alterations. In the case of AD and atherosclerotic vessel disease, two major disorders of prevalence in the elderly, cholesterol may well be playing a pathogenic role. However, in other situations, changes in membrane cholesterol appear to be part of a compensatory response to aging designed to actually protect or preserve cell and tissue function. Thus, molecular cholesterol appears to play a vital role in regulating the healthful activities of cells by its ability to modulate characteristics of plasma membrane that permit optimum performance to the wide array of membrane proteins on the cell surface.

ACKNOWLEDGMENTS

Supported in part by National Institutes of Health grants HL-30496, HL-51538 (TNT), HL-28476 (RHC), and the John A. Hartford Gerontology Fellowship (RPM) and grants from Pfizer Pharmaceutical, Inc. (TNT/RPM).

BIBLIOGRAPHY

Bloch, K. (1983). Sterol structure and membrane function. *Critical Review of Biochemistry 14*, 47–92.
Bretcher, M. S., & Munro, S. (1993). Cholesterol and the Golgi apparatus. *Science, 261*, 1280.

Chen, M., Mason, R. P., & Tulenko, T. N. (1995). Atherosclerosis alters composition, structure and function of arterial smooth muscle plasma membranes. *Biochimica et Biophysica Acta, 1272* (2):101–112.

Gleason, M. M., Medow, M. S., & Tulenko, T. N. (1991). Excess membrane cholesterol alters calcium movements, cytosolic calcium levels, and membrane fluidity in arterial smooth muscle cells. *Circulatory Research, 69,* 216–227.

Lange, Y., Swaisgood, M. H., Ramos, B. V., & Steck, T. L. (1989). Plasma membranes contain half the phospholipid and 90% of the cholesterol and sphingomyelin in cultured human fibroblast. *Journal of Biological Chemistry 264,* 3786–3793.

Ross, R. (1986). The pathogenesis of atherosclerosis—an update. *New England Journal of Medicine, 314,* 488–500.

Roth, G. S., Joseph, J. A., & Mason, R. P. (1995). Membrane alterations as causes of impaired signal transduction in Alzheimer's disease and aging. *Trends in Neurological Sciences, 18,* 203–206.

Stepp, D. S., & Tulenko, T. N. (1994). Alterations in basal and serotonin-stimulated Ca^{2+} movements and vasoconstriction in atherosclerotic aorta. *Arteriosclerosis and Thrombosis, 14,* 1854–1859.

Tulenko, T. N., Bialecki, R., Gleason, M. M., & D'Angelo, J. (1990). Ion channels, membrane lipids and cholesterol: A role for membrane lipid domains in arterial function, In T. N. Tulenko & R. H. Cox (Eds.), *Progress in clinical biological research* New York. A R Liss, (pp. 187–203).

Vance, D. E., & Vance, J. Biochemistry of lipids, lipoproteins and membranes. In A. Neuberger & L. L. M. van Deenen *New comprehensive biochemistry.* (1991). (vol. 20). (Eds.), New York: Elsevier.

Yeagle, P. (1992). *The structure of biological membranes.* Boca Raton, FL: CRC Press.

Yeagle, P. L., (1985). Cholesterol and the cell membrane. *Biochim Biophys Acta, 822,* 267–287.

Yeagle, P. L. (1989). Lipid regulation of cell membrane structure and function. *FASEB Journal, 3,* 1833–1842.

Yeagle, P. L., & Young, J. E. (1986). Factors contributing to the distribution of cholesterol among phospholipid vesicles. *Journal of Biological Chemistry, 261,* 8175–8181.

Cognitive–Behavioral Interventions

Helen M. DeVries

Wheaton College

Cognitive Triad Pattern of dysfunctional thinking characteristic of depressed persons in which they hold negative beliefs about the self, experiences, and the future.

Dysfunctional Thought Record A cognitive–behavioral technique that is used to help individuals identify and monitor cognitive distortions.

Schema Long-standing underlying assumptions or systems of belief from which the basic cognitive distortions and automatic thoughts emerge.

COGNITIVE–BEHAVIORAL therapy is a time-limited and structured approach to treatment that emphasizes the role of cognitive processes in shaping emotions and behavior. The basic premise is that the way an individual cognitively structures his or her experience (i.e., the "meaning" given to the experience) will determine how that person feels and behaves. The approach to treatment is active and directive, with the therapist and patient working collaboratively. The goal of therapy is to teach patients to recognize their dysfunctional and irrational thoughts, and to replace these with more adaptive and functional responses. Cognitive–behavioral therapy emphasizes teaching coping skills for dealing with problems rather than "curing" the problem. The assumption is that by learning coping strategies, individuals will be better prepared to deal with present and future difficulties. Three of the leading figures in the development of general cognitive theory and approaches to intervention are Albert Ellis, Donald Meichenbaum, and Aaron Beck.

I. THEORETICAL ASSUMPTIONS OF COGNITIVE–BEHAVIORAL THERAPY

A. Causes of Problems

Cognitive theory suggests that negative emotions are linked to an individual's capacity to distort reality in dysfunctional ways. Although everyone experiences stressful life events over the course of a lifetime, it is the individual's subjective experience of that stress that determines whether they experience psychological distress. Thus, the interaction between the experience of a stressful event and the individual's perception of that event predicts outcome.

Beck's cognitive model identifies three specific factors that disrupt an individual's capacity to perceive and respond to experiences in a functional way. The first is known as the "negative or cognitive triad," an interactive set of negative or distorted beliefs about the self, experiences, and the future. Depressed persons, for example, often believe themselves to be unworthy or deficient and thus interpret negative life events as their fault or as a result of their own inadequacy. Thus, the person who does not get an expected promotion at work would attribute this to the belief, "I am mediocre," rather than considering alternative explanations (i.e., "The person who got the promotion had more seniority."). In the same way, beliefs about life events and the future will filter the way an individual interprets his or her experience.

The second factor in Beck's model is maladaptive "schema." Schemas are stable organizational patterns of thought that form the basic framework for classifying and evaluating experience. These schemas reflect a kind of worldview represented by a set of underlying beliefs about self and others. Often these beliefs, while automatic, are implicit and out of the conscious awareness of the person. Maladaptive schemas impair the individual's ability to objectively evaluate interactions and events, foster a persistent negative response bias, and frequently result in negative affective and behavioral symptoms. For example, following the death of a spouse, the person who holds the schema, "Unless I am married, I will be miserable," would be likely to endorse such statements as "My life is over," "I will never be loved again," or "I can never be happy again." This schema pushes the individual into an unrealistic appraisal of the situation and to a negative appraisal of self, experience, and the future.

The third factor is that maladaptive schemas lead to errors in cognitive processing and logical thinking. In particular, identifiable patterns in cognitive errors are common and include (a) selective attention (focusing on some details while ignoring other relevant facts of the situation); (b) overgeneralization (assuming that the outcome of one incident will occur in all situations); (c) arbitrary inference (drawing a conclusion in the absence of evidence); (d) magnification or minimization (distorting the importance or significance of a single event); (e) personalization (assuming automatically that external events relate to oneself); (f) "all-or-none" thinking (categorizing continuous experiences as dichotomous extremes, such as good or bad, loved or hated).

B. Goals and Strategies of Therapy

The purpose of cognitive and cognitive–behavioral therapy is to identify the dysfunctional thoughts and beliefs that lead to errors in cognitive processing and to teach individuals the skills that permit a more balanced and accurate view of their situation. The process of therapy includes the following components:

1. Identifying the occurrence of negative thoughts.
2. Establishing the relationship between negative thoughts and feelings.
3. Learning specific cognitive–behavioral techniques for challenging negative or dysfunctional thinking.
4. Developing more adaptive interpretations and responses to specific situations.
5. Identifying and altering general maladaptive schemas that foster development of depression and/or anxiety.

The therapeutic approach is one of active collaboration between client and therapist. Sessions are structured and emphasize targeting problems, skills training, and problem solving. "Homework" requiring practice of new skills is assigned regularly and reviewed in each session. Treatment length is generally brief (10 to 20 sessions). One or two follow-up sessions are sometimes scheduled for relapse prevention and skills maintenance.

II. RATIONALE FOR USE OF COGNITIVE–BEHAVIORAL INTERVENTIONS WITH OLDER ADULTS

A. Normal Problems of Aging

It is generally recognized that, as a group, older adults are subjected to an increasing number of stressful life events associated with the normal process of aging. Many of the developmental tasks of late adulthood, such as the need to adapt to sensory and perceptual losses, to cope with the loss of significant others, to adjust to changes in work and family roles, can occur simultaneously or in close succession, complicating the adjustment process. The success with which older adults adapt to these and similar developmental tasks will predict their vulnerability for decreased mental and physical well-being. [See ADAPTATION.]

For those older adults who experience these tasks as problematic and seek treatment for their emotional distress, cognitive–behavioral therapy has been shown to be helpful. In particular, cognitive–behavioral therapy's problem-focused approach, with its emphasis on the development of coping skills, is ideally suited for helping individuals respond to normal developmental and life-adjustment tasks. In addition, cognitive–behavioral therapy has been used successfully with older adults to alleviate symptoms of specific psychiatric disorders, especially depression. [See DEPRESSION.]

B. Format of Cognitive–Behavioral Therapy

Until recently, mental health providers often assumed that the elderly would not benefit from psychotherapy. The belief was that older adults were inflexible and incapable of change. Some even assumed that depression and deteriorating mental well-being were normal concomitants of old age. This view was challenged by several research groups and new studies have demonstrated the efficacy of psychotherapy for this population. In particular, researchers have found that therapy with the elderly is most helpful if it is (a) not stigmatizing (emphasis on coping skills not psychopathology); (b) structured (so client knows what to expect); (c) time-limited (provides hope that individual will soon see improvement); and (d) goal-oriented (has problem-solving focus). Cognitive–behavioral therapy meets these criteria. In addition, the collaborative stance and present-focused emphasis of cognitive–behavioral therapy generally make it feel more respectful and appealing to an older population.

III. RECOMMENDED ADAPTATIONS AND MODIFICATIONS OF STANDARD COGNITIVE-BEHAVIORAL THERAPY FOR USE WITH OLDER ADULTS

Although the standard techniques of cognitive–behavioral therapy can be used with older adults, certain modifications in the implementation of treatment are recommended to accommodate age-related changes in personality and intellectual functioning.

A. Accommodation to the Unique Experiences of This Population

1. Age Differences
One of the most obvious differences between working with older and younger client groups is the likelihood of an age gap between client and therapist. The thera-

pist must recognize and be sensitive to ways in which age compatibility impacts therapy, particularly in the therapeutic relationship and in the identification of appropriate therapeutic goals. For example, a young therapist may find it difficult to accept treatment goals that might be important for someone who has only 5 or 10 years of life left. The tendency may be to aim for long-term personality change rather than helping the client change or adapt to an immediate situation.

2. Heterogenous Population
Older adults comprise a widely diverse and heterogenous population. Variations in educational level, physical health, intellectual functioning, interests, life circumstances, and social history are often greater than that found in a younger population. Such diversity demands added flexibility and sensitivity on the part of the therapist in obtaining a thorough psychological, social, and medical history. Attention to the multiple factors that may be operating in the situation facing the older adult will enhance the therapist's ability to tailor treatment to the unique needs of a specific individual.

B. Modifications to Process of Therapy

1. Active Role of Therapist
In working with the elderly, the therapist needs to be more active, particularly in maintaining the focus and structure of the session. Older clients sometimes digress from the task at hand to share additional material not related to the therapeutic objectives or to engage in spontaneous life review. The therapist must use clinical judgment to determine when it is necessary to refocus the topic of discussion and redirect the client to the immediate problem under discussion. Taking an active role, however, does not imply an overly directive or "pushy" style of interaction that patronizes or infantilizes the older adult. A strong therapeutic alliance is critical for successful outcome.

2. Slower Pace of Therapy
Several sensory and developmental changes associated with normal aging require some adjustment to the pace of therapy. Sensory deficits, including decreased visual and auditory acuity, can affect the rate and accuracy of information processing. The therapist should inquire about hearing loss, speak more slowly,

and enunciate clearly. Adjustments to the physical environment, including bright lighting and low background noise, will help compensate for many sensory difficulties.

Developmental changes in the elderly also impact their capacity to learn new information and demand a slower pace in therapy. Research indicates that the elderly experience a gradual decline in their ability to absorb and recall new information, learning at a slower rate or in a different way than younger persons. It is helpful to present important information in several different sensory modalities. For example, using handouts and written feedback or having clients frequently repeat major points will enhance encoding of new information. Asking elderly clients to take notes and write down important information during therapy sessions will also improve their capacity to absorb new material. Pretherapy cognitive screening of older clients to assess level of intellectual functioning will ensure that those with gross deficits (i.e., moderate to severe dementia) are excluded from treatment. Clients with only mild deficits can still benefit from treatment if proper adjustments are made in method and rate of presenting new material. [See LEARNING.]

C. Need for Socialization to Therapy

Older adults differ widely in their level of therapeutic sophistication. Many grew up in a culture that viewed psychotherapy as a treatment for "crazy" people. They often hold the belief that it is a "shame" or embarrassment to be in therapy. The therapist should explore the older client's expectations, stereotypes, and fears about the process of therapy in order to elicit potentially obstructive assumptions. For example, many older clients think of therapy as a passive process, like going to the doctor to get "fixed." It is therefore helpful to educate these clients about the active nature of cognitive therapy, which requires their full participation. The therapist should stress the need for a collaborative relationship, the importance of completing "homework," and the structured format of individual sessions. In addition, it is often important to review the special "rules," conditions, and safeguards of therapy that might differ from the normal rules governing social interactions.

IV. TREATMENT APPROACHES

A. Treatment of Common Life-Stage Problems of Older Adults

Most older adults adapt successfully to the multiple developmental and social changes that are common in late life. For those who experience distress or develop psychological symptoms, cognitive therapy offers an ideal treatment modality. The emphasis in cognitive therapy on the acquisition of coping skills provides older adults with concrete strategies for dealing with areas of problematic adjustment.

1. Bereavement

Older adults must adjust to multiple losses associated with aging, including death of spouse, family, and friends. A less obvious form of loss involves the change in relationship quality due to the cognitive or physical impairment of a spouse or friend. These losses, as well as the awareness of one's own mortality, often trigger a review and evaluation of unrealized dreams, lost opportunities, and unresolved relationships. This review may activate negative thoughts and maladaptive schema that impede the recovery process. Cognitive interventions that identify these negative thoughts and challenge their accuracy will facilitate a more positive grief reaction and process. For example, schema like "I can't survive alone," "My life is a total failure," or "I'll never be happy again" lock the person into a negative cognitive set that distorts the ability to interpret experience accurately. Using cognitive techniques, such as "examining the evidence" and "generating alternative thoughts," in combination with behavioral techniques, such as increasing pleasant events, will facilitate a more positive recovery from loss. [See BEREAVEMENT AND LOSS.]

2. Chronic Illness and Disability

A large percentage of the elderly (some estimate as high as 85%) have some type of chronic illness, such as arthritis, diabetes, hypertension, respiratory or cardiac problems. Many older adults also experience a loss or reduction in physical and intellectual abilities that leave them dependent on others for assistance. These physical changes may impose limitations on their lifestyle to accommodate restrictive medical schedules and regimens, cause chronic pain, strain their coping resources, and/or challenge their sense of self-worth, competence, and control. Those who have negative beliefs about themselves and their ability to cope with their illness are at risk for developing psychological symptoms. In addition, changes in physical functioning may cause a person to drop out of meaningful activities, resulting in a reduced sense of well-being and life satisfaction.

Cognitive–behavioral interventions that identify negative beliefs about the illness or disability (such as "Nobody wants to be around a sick person"), that foster more adaptive thinking about the situation (i.e., "My family and friends still enjoy my company"), and that promote continued participation in pleasant and meaningful activities will encourage better adjustment to the illness or disability.

3. Changes in Social and Family Roles and Dynamics

Older adults experience normative transitions associated with aging that result in changes or losses of important roles. If the individual's personal identity or feelings of self-worth were tied up in a particular role, the loss of that role can be devastating. From a cognitive–behavioral perspective, the way an individual perceives these role changes and the beliefs they hold about their own value and importance outside of these roles will determine how well they negotiate the transition. For example, a person who believes that his or her life is only meaningful if they are making money may respond to retirement with thoughts about no longer having worth or not being needed. [See IDENTITY.]

Normative changes in family structure also occur as the family moves through developmental stages. Intergenerational differences and conflicts are bound to emerge as elderly parents and adult children negotiate new roles and relationships. Elderly parents may become depressed if ill health or financial constraints force them to become dependent on children. Conversely, parents may feel hurt or abandoned if they perceive that their children are not available to care for them. Identifying an individual's expectations and assumptions about the nature of late-life parent–child relationships will shed light on why certain family interactions become problematic. [See GENERATIONAL DIFFERENCES.]

Marital conflicts can also erupt as couples in long-standing relationships undergo changes in patterns of functioning due to retirement, illness, loss of parent-

ing role, and so on. Couples tend to carve out areas of responsibility over the course of their marriage that may be threatened by the change in status of one or the other partner. In addition, life changes (particularly the loss of the shared parenting role) may leave the couple feeling that they have little in common or have lost a sense of purpose. Cognitive–behavioral therapy can be very helpful in challenging unhelpful or negative perspectives on role and relationship changes associated with aging.

4. Ageism and Low Self-Esteem

Our youth-oriented culture fosters a stereotype of old age that is less than optimistic. Some older adults accept these stereotypes as inevitable truths and believe that being old means being undesirable, unattractive, and unwanted. These beliefs can lead to a sense of futility about the future and a passive acceptance of problems with no effort to overcome difficulties. Clearly, cognitive approaches that challenge and dispel the myths about aging can help activate the individual into a more positive coping response to age-related changes. [See SELF ESTEEM.]

B. Treatment of Psychiatric Disorders

1. Depression

Depression is the most common mental health problem in the elderly. It has received much attention in the published literature and is probably the best researched of the psychiatric disorders in the elderly. In addition, epidemiological evidence indicates that the elderly have the highest suicide rate of any age group, with about one-fourth of all suicides carried out by persons age 60 or older. There is also growing awareness of "silent" suicides among older adults who determine to die through self-starvation or noncompliance with medical treatment. Because depression is frequently cited as the principal risk factor for suicide, it is particularly critical to diagnose and treat depression in the elderly.

This is not to say, however, that depression is a normative condition of old age. As with a younger population, depression is a treatable psychiatric disorder in the elderly. There is a significant literature suggesting that cognitive therapy is an effective treatment modality for depressive disorders in both younger and older adults. Cognitive–behavioral therapy was specifically developed for the treatment of depression and has been standardized into well-documented treatment protocols. However, cognitive therapy is often not the sole method of treating depression in the elderly. It is frequently combined with pharmacotherapy, supportive, behavioral, or family therapy.

Some caution must be exercised when working with older clients who are depressed. Differentiating symptoms of depression from underlying medical problems is particularly critical in the elderly. In addition, there are several differences in the presentation of symptoms found in depressed older adults. They are more likely to report somatic rather than psychological symptoms and to seek medical services rather than psychiatric services for treatment of depression. The typical symptoms of depression often overlap with normative changes associated with aging, such as alterations in sleep, appetite, and physical health. Thus, older adults may go to their physician complaining of physical symptoms such as weight loss or lack of energy without recognizing an underlying depression. In addition, depressed elderly often tend to withdraw from social activities, confine themselves to bed, neglect bodily functions, and evidence symptoms of apathy and self-deprecation.

Cognitive techniques that have been shown to be helpful in treating depression in older adults include the use of the Dysfunctional Thought Record to monitor the occurrence of negative automatic thoughts, to illustrate the relationship between thoughts and emotions, and to challenge the thoughts related to the patient's negative mood. Behavioral techniques, such as daily monitoring of mood and increased participation in pleasant events, are often helpful early in treatment to break through the depressive inertia, improve mood, and create positive expectations for therapy. Assertiveness training frequently restores a sense of self-efficacy and control for those whose depression is linked to issues of dependency.

Although most cognitive–behavioral interventions for the treatment of depression in the elderly were designed for use in individual therapy, some programs emphasizing group interventions have been developed. In particular, psychoeducational groups designed to alleviate depressive symptoms through the acquisition of cognitive and behavioral skills have shown promising results. Psychoeducational groups that emphasize teaching coping skills for managing anger and depression have also been developed for elderly spouses and adult children who are caregivers of frail or cognitively impaired family members. Group approaches have the added advantage of increasing social interaction and contact for isolated or lonely individuals. However, research suggests that older adults with severe levels of depressive symptoms would probably not benefit from this form of treatment and should be treated individually.

Several recent studies have explored the use of cognitive–behavioral interventions with elderly persons experiencing somatic symptoms (such as late-life insomnia, chronic pain) or chronic illness. Adjustments to standard treatment protocols (such as simplification of therapy techniques, and use of short, frequent sessions) and consideration of the special needs of this population (such as removing barriers to participation) are usually necessary for successful implementation. Preliminary results suggest that cognitive–behavioral therapy offers a promising approach for teaching patients to cope with chronic pain or disability, challenges the perception of being a "burden," alleviates somatic symptoms, and enhances positive mood.

Other studies have examined the effectiveness of cognitive–behavioral therapy to treat depression in Alzheimer's patients. Because depression has been shown to impair cognitive functioning, treatment of depression in Alzheimer patients is warranted and, although not halting the disease progression, can help reduce excess disability in functioning. Specifically, cognitive techniques are used primarily with early-stage Alzheimer patients to reduce cognitive distortions and to help the person generate more adaptive ways of viewing situations and events. Behavioral interventions are helpful with more moderately or severely demented adults and seek to modify the person–environment interactions by increasing positive activities and decreasing negative ones. Clinicians, however, have to be aware of the cognitive capabilities of the patient, adapt interventions appropriately, and be able to communicate clearly with patients and caregivers. [See DEMENTIA.]

In summary, cognitive–behavioral interventions for the treatment of depression in older adults have shown promise and positive results. However, a multilevel approach is recommended to deal with depression in the elderly, with equal attention given to both psychological and physical factors.

2. Anxiety

Survey data indicate that anxiety symptoms are more prevalent in elderly people than in any other age group, occurring at about twice the rate among older adults compared to younger adults. Data suggest that the most common types of anxiety disorders among the elderly are phobias (often with components representing exaggerations of rational concerns), generalized anxiety, and mixed anxious–depressive symptoms. Late-life onset of obsessive–compulsive and panic disorders, on the other hand, appear to be relatively rare. Treating anxiety in the elderly is particularly important due to the negative impact of anxiety on cognitive functioning. Thus, high levels of anxiety can interfere with memory, learning, and attentional capacities in older adults and mimic the symptoms of dementia. Treatment of anxiety is often complicated in a high percentage of older adults by the coexistence of depression with the anxiety.

Currently, pharmacotherapy is the most common form of treatment for symptoms of anxiety, despite increasing evidence that the use of benzodiazepines by older patients is associated with increased risk of morbidity, including excess sedation, cognitive impairment, falls, and vulnerability to withdrawal symptoms. Cognitive or behavioral therapy, on the other hand, is virtually without risk.

Although some studies evaluating the effectiveness of cognitive behavioral interventions in the treatment of depression in older adults have also reported reductions in concurrent symptoms of anxiety, few interventions designed specifically for the treatment of anxiety disorders in the elderly have been developed or evaluated. Of the few programs described in the literature, some have incorporated behavioral approaches to managing anxiety, with an emphasis on instruction in progressive muscle relaxation and controlled breathing techniques. Others emphasize more cognitive interventions that teach clients to reinterpret their anxiety symptoms in a nonthreatening way. For example, an individual who experiences anxiety regarding physical symptoms may have the automatic thought, "I must have cancer." Cognitive therapy would teach them to substitute the more realistic and reassuring thought, "I was just thoroughly examined by my physician and no problems were detected."

Although more work is needed in the development and evaluation of cognitive–behavioral interventions for anxiety in the elderly, preliminary studies suggest that this approach holds promise as a safe and effective treatment.

3. Drug and Alcohol Abuse

Late-life onset of significant problems related to abuse of drugs and alcohol is not uncommon among the elderly. The high rate of prescribed medication use, increased physiological sensitivity to drug effects, and the danger of interaction effects of multiple medications and/or alcohol place older adults at high risk for deliberate or accidental misuse of drugs or alcohol. In addition, some older adults turn to alcohol to help cope with stressful life events, thus increasing the risk of addiction or toxic interactions. Heavy use of drugs or alcohol will increase the risk for depression, illness (including risk for falls and accidents), and cognitive impairment.

Cognitive and behavioral interventions for treating real or potential substance abuse problems might include (a) education regarding the importance of monitoring drug and alcohol consumption, (b) development of strategies for managing complex drug regimens, and (c) acquisition of coping skills for managing negative emotions and stressful life events. Individuals who have a long history of chronic alcohol and drug abuse problems would not be suitable for this treatment approach.

V. EFFECTIVENESS OF COGNITIVE-BEHAVIORAL INTERVENTIONS WITH OLDER ADULTS

As more controlled studies are emerging that seek to evaluate the effectiveness of cognitive–behavioral therapy in treating the psychological problems of the elderly, results are encouraging regarding its efficacy in reducing negative psychological symptoms. Differential effectiveness of cognitive–behavioral therapy compared to other forms of psychotherapy, however, is less certain. Most studies comparing outcomes across different treatment modalities have limitations that make conclusions problematic. In general, data indicate that some form of treatment is better than no treatment, thus supporting the idea that the elderly can benefit from therapy with success rates that are comparable to those with younger patients. A few studies suggest that, although there is little difference across treatment modalities at the conclusion of therapy, long-term maintenance of gains is more likely with cognitive–behavioral therapy. The implication is that the acquisition of coping skills enables older adults to adapt more successfully to ongoing life stressors. More controlled studies are needed to test these assumptions.

Research examining outcome variables in cognitive–behavioral therapy also suggests that certain patient-specific and therapist-specific variables are critical to successful outcome. Patient-specific variables that seem to be related to outcome include (a) initial intensity of depressed mood; (b) presence of a personality disorder in addition to the depression; (c) depth and quality of social and emotional relationships with friends and/or family; and (d) acceptable level of intellectual flexibility and functioning (i.e., absence of severe cognitive decline or rigidity).

A recent study comparing cognitive–behavioral and psychodynamic interventions for older depressed family caregivers is one of the first to document a specific patient-by-treatment interaction in predicting outcome (length of time caregiving × type of therapy). Specifically, the longer the time spent as a caregiver, the more positive the outcome with cognitive–behavioral therapy compared to other treatment modalities. The suggested implication is that early in caregiving, older adults respond best to an intervention that acknowledges and explores the sense of loss associated with the many changes in current and future plans caused by the illness (psychodynamic therapy). On the other hand, long-term caregivers whose social and emotional resources are dwindling may respond better to highly structured, skill-oriented interventions that focus on coping rather than emphasizing their losses (cognitive–behavioral therapy).

Other studies examining the effectiveness of cognitive–behavioral therapy with depressed older adults have identified additional patient-specific variables associated with outcome. Individuals who generally respond well to cognitive–behavioral therapy are those experiencing reactive depression where a clear precipitant can be determined and whose depression can be seen as a response to the specific event or situation. Patients with chronic depression, or with a depressive episode superimposed on dysthymia, can be treated effectively, however, if the goals are modest and the general aim is for improved affective status, rather than complete remission of the disorder. The use of medication in conjunction with cognitive–behavioral therapy and the extension of treatment to 30 or 40 sessions may also facilitate the rate of improvement in the chronically depressed patient.

Therapist-specific variables that are associated with outcome have not been specifically studied. However, anecdotal data and general cognitive therapy outcome studies tend to underscore the importance of establishing a collaborative therapeutic relationship with the client. For a therapist working with older adults, special issues must be addressed in establishing that relationship. In particular, it is important that therapists examine their own attitudes toward the elderly for potential biases that might negatively impact the therapeutic relationship. Respect for the life experiences and accomplishments of the older client rather than a sole focus on the current difficulties will also help establish a strong therapeutic alliance.

In conclusion, cognitive–behavioral therapy appears to be an appropriate and effective intervention for psychological problems in the elderly. Although special modifications to the standard course of treatment may be necessary, particularly the format and pace at which new information is presented, older adults treated with cognitive–behavioral therapy seem to show a similar improvement rate as that of younger adults. More research into specific factors that might contribute uniquely to outcome would be most helpful in developing new and more comprehensive cognitive–behavioral interventions for addressing the emotional problems of older adults. [See MENTAL HEALTH.]

BIBLIOGRAPHY

Gallagher-Thompson, D., & DeVries, H. (1994). "Coping with frustration" classes: Development and preliminary outcomes with women who care for relatives with dementia. *The Gerontologist, 34,* 548–552.

Gallagher-Thompson, D., & Steffen, A. (1994). Comparative effects of cognitive-behavioral and brief psychodynamic psychotherapies for depressed family caregivers. *Journal of Consulting and Clinical Psychology, 62,* 543–549.

Glanz, M. (1989). Cognitive therapy with the elderly. In A. Freeman, K. Simon, L. Beutler, & H. Arkowitz (Eds.), *Comprehensive handbook of cognitive therapy* (pp. 467–490). New York: Plenum Press.

McCarthy, P., Katz, I., & Foa, E. (1991). Cognitive-behavioral treatment of anxiety in the elderly: A proposed model. In C.

Salzman & B. Lebowitz (Eds.), *Anxiety in the elderly: Treatment and research* (pp. 197–214). New York: Springer Publishing Co.

Moberg, P., & Lazarus, L. (1990). *Psychotherapy of depression in the elderly. Psychiatric Annals, 20,* 92–96.

Morris, R., & Morris, L. (1991). Cognitive and behavioural approaches with the depressed elderly. *International Journal of Geriatric Psychiatry, 6,* 407–413.

Rybarczyk, B., Gallagher-Thompson, D., Rodman, J., Zeiss, A., et al. (1992). Applying cognitive-behavioral psychotherapy to the chronically ill elderly: Treatment issues and case illustration. *International Psychogeriatrics, 4,* 127–140.

Teri, L., & Gallagher-Thompson, D. (1991). Cognitive-behavioral interventions for treatment of depression in Alzheimer's patients. *The Gerontologist, 31,* 413–416.

Thompson, L., Gantz, F., Florsheim, M., DelMaestro, S., Rodman, J., & Gallagher-Thompson, D. (1991). Cognitive-behavioral therapy for affective disorders in the elderly. In W. Myers (Ed.), *New techniques in the psychotherapy of older patients* (pp. 3–19). Washington, DC: American Psychiatric Association Press.

Widner, S., & Zeichner, A. (1993). Psychologic interventions for the elderly chronic pain patients. *Clinical Gerontologist, 13,* 3–18.

Cohort Studies

Peter Uhlenberg

University of North Carolina, Chapel Hill

Matilda White Riley

National Institute on Aging

Cohort A set of people born (or entering a particular system such as a hospital, school, or community of scientists) during a specific time period, whose lives may be traced in cohort studies.

Cohort Aging The continuous movement of a cohort from one age stratum to the next, as cohort members grow older physiologically, psychologically, and socially over the life course from birth to death.

Cohort Succession Members of new cohorts are continually born into a society or group and move up through the age strata as they grow older. As members of one cohort age out of a particular stratum, they are replaced by members of oncoming cohorts.

Generation Though popularly used to mean cohort, to avoid confusion the term is best reserved for parent–child and other kin relationships.

Intercohort Differentiation Differences between cohorts in size, composition, patterns of aging, characteristics of members, or experiences associated with the differing historical eras spanning their respective lives.

Subcohorts Segments of people in a cohort who experience differing life-course patterns; defined by characteristics such as gender, race, or class, or by exposure to particular historical trends or events.

COHORT STUDIES map and compare the collective life-course patterns of people born at different periods of time in order to deepen understanding of the aging process and to explore its variations. These studies show how cohorts tie human lives to history and to the social and cultural changes that give them broader meaning. Cohort comparisons were brought into use by public health researchers in the 1930s for studying human lives, and were adapted for broad application in many disciplines during the 1960s and 1970s by Norman Ryder, Matilda Riley, Mervyn Susser, and others. An early study by Wade Hampton Frost in 1939 illustrates the power of cohort analysis in research on aging. By looking at cohort patterns, he uncovered a finding that had been hidden in the usual cross-sectional statistics: that deaths from tuberculosis were consistently highest among people in their twenties. This and related findings led to the public health emphasis on prevention of many diseases and disabilities before people ever reach old age. They also influenced subsequent cohort studies in demography, epidemiology, social and environmental sciences, and other disciplinary and policy arenas. The notion of cohort (often inappropriately called "generation") now pervades both scientific and popular discourse. The studies selected here illustrate for later life how cohorts—and the subgroups within them—are formed and change, how they affect human relationships across all ages, and how they are influenced by and also influence social structures and institutions. [*See* AGE STRATIFICATION.]

I. COHORTS AND THE AGING PROCESS

The behavior, attitudes, and physical and mental functioning of people reaching the later stages of the life course define the nature of aging during particular periods of time. Should successive cohorts simply replicate the life patterns of their predecessors, on the average no change in the aging process would occur. There is, of course, substantial continuity across adjacent cohorts, as members age physiologically, psychologically, and socially in similar ways. However, there are many forces that can produce significant differences in the experience of aging for cohorts that are separated by even a single year. Indeed, studies focusing on only a single cohort often fall into the "fallacy of cohort-centrism," which erroneously assumes that members of all cohorts will age in exactly the same fashion as members of the cohort under scrutiny.

A. Some Sources of Differences in Cohort Aging

Cohort studies examine a variety of forces that shape cohort differences in aging: forces that range from those inherent in the biology of the organism or in the physical environment, to those in the underlying culture or exigencies of history. Five types of forces are commonly identified in actual studies.

1. Historical Change
Foremost among these distinguishing forces is the fact that each cohort lives through a unique period of history. Hence its members cannot follow exactly the same track through old age as that of the cohorts that preceded it. The broad sweep of history encompasses many changes that influence cohort differences, including those listed below.

2. Compositional Differences
The composition and early experience of cohorts arriving at old age at different times are important considerations. Cohorts differ in size and racial and gender composition. Furthermore, members entering old age from successive cohorts differ in educational background, marital and family history, work history, religious commitments, savings and pension acquisition, war experiences, political affiliation, and so on.

3. Structural Changes
Another source of differences is found in changes in the social institutions that provide the milieu for aging, and that shape human lives through age-related opportunities and constraints. The changing role of the state in transferring resources to the elderly and in protecting their rights impacts the aging experience. Changes in the organizations providing care for the health or the disabilities of the elderly alter the pathways that cohorts follow through later life. Changes in the structures of family, work, and retirement alter how successive cohorts experience old age. During periods of rapid social change, marked reconstructions of the shape and meaning of old age can be expected.

4. Technological Development
Technological developments also impact cohorts differentially. Changes in medical and public health technology alter the survival patterns and functional ability levels of aging cohorts. Communication technology affects access to information and contact with others. Advances in equipment and prostheses designed for the physically disabled affect the lifestyles of elderly persons. Technology related to housing features, monitors, and emergency care influence the ability of those in later life to live independently. A moment's consideration of the influences on earlier cohorts wrought by invention of the telephone, the automobile, or radio and television demonstrates that periods of rapid technological development are associated with significant modifications of the experience of aging.

5. Cohort Linkages
Among the most basic forces influencing how a cohort ages are its linkages with other cohorts whose members are at other life stages. Throughout the entire life course a cohort is vitally linked to other cohorts through the family, kinship, economic, political, and social bonds of its members. No cohort stands alone. Thus the size, composition, and behavior of cohorts in young adulthood influence the aging experience of cohorts concurrently moving through later life. The work and family patterns of young adults have implications for the relationships that older persons have

with them. The size and economic productivity of cohorts recently born will influence the economic well-being of cohorts that reach old age before them. Thus intercohort and intergenerational relationships are often given special attention in studies of cohort aging.

B. Heterogeneity within Cohorts

This cohort perspective on aging provides a conceptual schema for studying historical changes in aging and for directing attention to forces likely to shape the course of aging in the future. However, a common limitation in using this perspective must be stated at the outset. Treating cohort patterns as averages that refer to the aggregate or collective lives of individual cohort members facilitates comparison. Yet these average or modal patterns can obscure wide variations that reflect the marked heterogeneity of older people and their positions in society. Accordingly, measures of variability add important insights into differences in the aging of cohort members.

Rather than focusing on the aggregate level, some cohort studies focus on aging processes at the level of individual cohort members or of subcohorts. Here, membership in a particular cohort is treated as a "contextual characteristic" that can be analyzed together with genetic predisposition, cognitive functioning, religious affiliation, and other individual characteristics to investigate how history and other factors affect the heterogeneous ways people grow older.

C. Data for Cohort Studies

Cohort studies vary widely, not only in the forms and methods of analysis (not described here), but also in the data used to describe people's lives. Some studies collect new data for immediate objectives. Others are based on diaries, genealogies, or the content of published material. Most long-term quantitative studies rely on computerized archives that are made widely available to users, such as those housed at the University of Michigan. Although much archived material is designed for use in single disciplines, several cohort studies of older people combine biological, psychological, and social information: as in the Health and Retirement Survey sponsored by the National Institute on Aging, or the Swedish Gothenburg follow-up of three cohorts of 70-year-olds.

II. SELECTED DIMENSIONS OF COHORT AGING

Cohort succession, with its link to the aging process, is marked by differences in the modal patterns of whole cohorts (described in this section), and by changes in the internal patterns within each cohort (see section III). Studies have shown large modal differences on many dimensions between cohorts entering old age in different time periods. For example, members of cohorts now old differ from those who grew old in the past in respect to educational level, family history, work history, diet and exercise, exposure to acute versus chronic diseases, standards of living, number of years in retirement, and—perhaps most significant of all—the number of years they can expect to survive. And members of cohorts who will be old in the future will predictably be still different again. Studies of four selected dimensions of cohort aging will serve as examples: mortality and survival, active life expectancy, retirement, and economic status and pension benefits.

A. Mortality and Survival

Cohort life tables, a statistical device for tracing the attrition due to death that a cohort experiences as it ages over the full life course, are used for understanding both historical and prospective changes in mortality conditions that affect survival.

I. Historical Changes

Mortality declines since the mid-nineteenth century have had profound effects in differentiating the survival experiences of successive birth cohorts. Data in Table I summarize the experiences of cohorts of males and females born in 1840, 1890, and the projected experiences for those born in 1940 and 1990. Only 5 or 6% of the individuals born around the middle of the nineteenth century (1840) survived to age 85, and gender differences in survival to old age were minor. In the cohort born 50 years later (1890), twice as many females as males survived to age 85 (18% versus 9%). The relatively low survival to age 85 for cohorts born around the beginning of this century, reaching age 85 in the 1980s and 1990s, shows that the contemporary "oldest-old" population is a highly select group from the initial birth cohorts.

Table I Percent Distribution of Deaths by Stage of Life for Cohorts Born in 1840, 1890, 1940, and 1990, by Gender

Age category	Gender and birth cohort							
	Males				Females			
	1840	1890	1940	1990	1840	1890	1940	1990
0–19	39	28	8	2	36	26	6	1
20–64	31	29	21	17	31	21	13	10
65–84	26	33	47	46	27	34	38	34
85+	5	9	24	35	6	18	44	55

2. Future Estimates

In contrast, more than half of all females and over a third of all males born in 1990 are expected to survive to at least age 85. The vast change in proportion surviving to the oldest ages contributes to the growing recognition of distinct stages of life within old age. Much recent empirical research divides the population over age 60 into three categories: young-old (60–69), middle-old (70–84), and oldest-old (85+); and a fourth category of 100+ is now being added. This is not to say that chronological age is the most meaningful way to distinguish various phases of old age. Peter Laslett, for example, abandoning years of age altogether, makes a provocative case for distinguishing the Third Age of life (the culmination of the life career that is marked by personal achievement and fulfillment) from the Fourth Age (a period of decline and dependency).

3. Implications of Survival

The expected survival patterns of cohorts currently in the early stages of life is a subject of great interest and debate. The numbers in these cohorts who will survive to old age have important implications for the future of such old age programs as Social Security and Medicare. The size of the population over age 65 in 2050 can be projected by applying appropriate cohort life tables to each cohort born before 1985 (since the 1985 cohort will reach age 65 in 2050). However, projections vary widely because of differing assumptions. The U.S. Census Bureau projects that the most likely number of persons over age 65 in 2050 will be 76 million, but could reach 89 million if a more optimistic mortality scenario prevails. Other researchers regard even the most optimistic Census Bu-

reau projection as far too cautious. Some conclude that under plausible conditions (mortality rates declining at 2% per year) there would be 111 million over age 65 in 2050. Still others suggest a number as high as 128 million. Whatever the particular estimates, the unprecedented survival patterns of contemporary non-old cohorts have extremely significant implications for the future of aging in the United States. [*See* LONGEVITY AND LONG-LIVED POPULATIONS.]

B. Active Life Expectancy

The dramatically rising patterns of cohort survival do not speak to the issue of quality of life. Increasingly, aging researchers are concerned about the quality of the many years added by declining mortality. Are members of cohorts now reaching old age experiencing more years of later life in an active, disability-free state? Or, are more persons being kept alive longer in feeble and dependent states? As the evidence begins to come in, it so far suggests that changes in both directions are occuring, though improved functioning seems to outweigh survival of the least fit. On the one hand, cohorts reaching older ages at the end of the 1980s, when compared to those already old at the beginning of the decade, show improvements in functional status. Moreover, cohorts entering old age more recently are experiencing lower disability rates than did the cohorts that preceded them. On the other hand, life expectancy for disabled persons is increasing. Consequently, it is possible that members of cohorts reaching old age in the future may anticipate both a longer period of old age without functional limitations *and* a longer period at the end of life with limitations. When cohorts are compared age-for-age, the health status of those aging in the future may well surpass that of cohorts already old today. [*See* POSTPONEMENT OF AGING.]

Beyond describing changes in the timing and duration of disabilities in later life, studies of cohort differences provide clues as to why change is occurring. At the individual level it is well established that earlier life history (smoking, diet, health care, exercise) is linked to the timing of later-life disabilities. Cohorts as aggregates also differ on those variables that are related to "healthy" aging, having been differentially affected by antismoking campaigns, information on harmful effects of cholesterol and fat in diets, and health-care insurance coverage. Interestingly too, development of new drugs, rehabilitation therapies, and diagnostic technologies impact cohorts differently depending on their stage of life when innovations occur.

Forecasts of cohort patterns of functional ability provide an important base for projecting future health-care costs and the potential for productive contributions by older persons.

C. Retirement

Studies of changing retirement patterns also show marked intercohort differentiation, although the gender differences are pronounced. Tracking age patterns of labor-force participation for cohorts of men moving through middle and old age during most of the twentieth century shows the emergence of retirement as a social institution. Between World War II and the mid-1980s, retirement had been occurring earlier in life. Across a number of Western countries, including the United States, members of each successive cohort had exited from the labor force at progressively younger ages. When the 1918 U.S. cohort reached age 62 in 1980, over 40% of the men were retired. This is twice the rate of retirement at age 62 for men born just 16 years earlier (in 1904). Since the mid-1980s, however, this trend has not persisted; and questions of a possible reversal in male retirement patterns await the experiences of cohorts reaching old age in the 1990s and beyond.

For women, the patterns of labor-force participation are quite different. In the cohorts entering adulthood early in this century, only a minority of women engaged in paid work outside the home; hence retirement has not been a common experience in later life for these women. Across more recent cohorts, labor-force participation rates have consistently increased at all ages up to 60. For cohorts passing age 60 since 1965, female employment rates at older ages have remained about level—the result of offsetting trends of higher participation rates at younger ages combined with higher retirement rates at older ages. For married women, these changing work histories mean that increasing numbers of couples must grapple with the respective timing of retirement for both husband and wife.

Such comparisons of cohort experiences provide insights into the forces that influence retirement decisions. Historical changes associated with cohort differences in retirement behavior involve the revolution in the social roles of women and alterations in family structures, the organization of work, labor-force conditions, social attitudes toward retirement, and institutional mechanisms that facilitate early withdrawal from the labor force (e.g., pension systems, disability insurance). In cohorts of men and women reaching old age today, the combination of early retirement and prolonged life expectancy means that, on the average, one-third of adult life is spent in retirement. Other changes, such as improved health and increased educational levels, also mark the members of these newly retired cohorts. Given these shifts, it is not surprising that questions are being raised about the meaning of retirement and the possible desirability of extending the worklife for cohorts in the future. Those issues are especially salient on the agenda for cohort studies in view of the great size of the baby-boom cohorts beginning to reach age 65 after 2010. [See AGE STRATIFICATION; RETIREMENT, WORK AND EMPLOYMENT.]

D. Pensions and Economic Status

Employer pensions and their impact on economic status is one further example of historical developments differentiating the aging experience of successive cohorts. The life course stage of cohorts when changes in pension coverage and pension types occur has consequences for retirement income and security in later life.

1. Spread of Private Pensions

Following World War II, encouraged by federal tax policy, the prevalence and value of pension benefits grew for over three decades. In particular, the percentage of nonagricultural workers in the private sector covered by pension plans increased rapidly from 15% in 1940 to 40% in 1960, then slowed, but by 1975 the proportion covered had reached nearly 50%. After 1975 coverage rates stopped increasing, and actually declined slightly in the 1980s. However, the previous growth in coverage has contributed to long-term improvement in the economic status of cohorts entering old age. With the spread of pensions, each more recent cohort has retired earlier, but with higher retirement income than its predecessors.

2. Changing Nature of Pensions

For cohorts retiring in the near future, uncertain as the political climate may be, there are implications not only of the diminishing spread of employer pension systems, but also of the recent shift from defined benefit (DB) to defined contribution (DC) pension systems. Under DB plans, workers know the level of their expected retirement income, whereas under DC plans, the value of benefits at the time of retirement is uncertain. These two types of plans differ in several ways that affect cohorts retiring in the future. First, the growth of DC plans relative to DB plans is likely to reduce incentives for early retirement; whereas DB provide actuarial benefits for retiring early, DC plans do not. DC plans are really savings accounts with tax advantages, and are age-neutral with respect to time of retirement. Second, the growth of DC plans may accentuate the already significant role of pensions in creating income inequality within cohorts in later life. Because many DC plans are funded entirely or in part by employee contributions, lower paid (and younger) workers are less likely to take advantage of such plans when offered by an employer. Also, workers with lower incomes are more likely to interfere with the growth of DC pensions because they can borrow on these accounts or receive lump sum cashouts when they change jobs. In contrast, higher paid employees are more likely to contribute the maximum possible, thereby accruing larger pension benefits over time. Moreover, the growth of DC plans leads to increasing uncertainty about future pension incomes in retirement. Under a DB plan, approximate annual pension income can be anticipated well in advance of retirement; whereas under a DC plan, the amount that will be in the fund at retirement is less predictable. More significantly, because no individual can know how many years of life will remain after retirement, a DC pension fund could be depleted too soon, or drawn on too slowly. Consequently, the shift toward DC pensions is complicating efforts to anticipate how well prepared financially future cohorts of retirees will be. [See ECONOMICS: INDIVIDUAL; ECONOMICS: SOCIETY.]

III. INTRACOHORT VARIATION AND THE LIFE COURSE OF SUBCOHORTS

Despite the importance of modal differences in cohort aging, cohorts are not monolithic entities. In many respects, their individual members become increasingly heterogeneous as they grow older. Some cohort studies examine heterogeneity by comparing "subco-

horts" that experience differing life-course patterns. Subcohorts are commonly defined by enduring characteristics like race, gender, or family background; or by characteristics that develop or change over the life course such as health, marital status, or rural–urban residence. Studies of subcohorts (e.g., lower-class white males vs. upper-class black females) ask such questions as these: What determines cohort composition (division into subcohorts) when arriving at old age? What later-life changes occur in cohort heterogeneity? How do historical events differentially impact subgroups within cohorts? As noted above, the answers are frequently obtained from studies that compare successive cohorts.

A. Cohort Composition When Arriving at Old Age

Accounting for the race, gender, and economic background of cohorts entering old age today is relatively straightforward, because each cohort begins with a particular composition at the time of the birth. Changes in other compositional respects then occur before the members reach the threshold of old age, and are traced to three sets of factors (or a combination of them).

I. Differential Mortality

Differential mortality means that members of certain subcohorts are more likely than others to survive into old age. In twentieth-century United States, differential mortality has favored females over males and Whites over Blacks. Consequently, the proportion of cohort members who are male and/or Black tends to decrease as cohorts age over the life course. Consider, for example, the 1925–1929 birth cohort when it was aged 0–4 (in 1930) compared to when it was aged 60–64 (in 1990). Between these two time periods the male portion of the cohort declined from 50.7% to 46.6% and the black segment declined from 10.7% to 9.1%. Because survival is associated with higher educational status, differential mortality also operates to increase the proportion of highly educated persons within cohorts as they age from young adulthood to old age.

2. Status Transitions

Significant changes within cohorts over the adult years of life occur as a result of transitions in variable characteristics, such as marital, health, and functional status. In particular, cohort composition is affected by differential rates of mobility from one economic class to another prior to old age. Until recently, the long-term growth of the American economy had produced a modal life-course pattern of upward economic mobility. For example, the proportion of the 1925–1929 birth cohort living in poverty dropped from 72% in 1930 to less than 10% when it reached old age in 1990 (based on the current U.S. Census Bureau definition of poverty). This modal upward trend has not, however, prevented increasingly sharp bifurcation of each cohort into subpopulations of the relatively rich and the relatively poor. Given current economic uncertainties throughout the world, there is no guarantee of future directions in these trends.

3. International Migration

International migration in and out of the population alters cohort composition in line with the ages and other characteristics of the migrants. In the United States, for example, cohorts reaching old age in the 1940s and 1950s contained many members from the mass migrations from southern and Eastern Europe that occurred around the turn of the century. Cohorts reaching old age in the future will be distinguished by the large numbers of Hispanics and Asians who entered the United States following changes in immigration laws since 1965. [See MIGRATION.]

B. Later-Life Changes in Cohort Heterogeneity

Once reaching old age, cohorts continue to experience changes in heterogeneity as they move through the later years. Although mortality and biological aging processes operate to enlarge the relative size of subcohorts that are female, widowed, or functionally disabled, many of the other changes in subcohort aging are reflections of social processes. For example, Dale Dannefer notes the operation of a "Matthew effect," where the gap between the advantaged and disadvantaged subcohorts tends to widen in later life. He explains how the organization of work in American society produces different trajectories through old age. Those who enjoy jobs with comparatively higher incomes, greater security, and more generous retirement benefits can anticipate greater increases in late-life economic advantage than those who work in less privileged jobs. Similarly, those with jobs that provide safe and mentally stimulating work environments tend to experience healthier and happier aging than their cohort peers who work in less favorable environments.

Studies examining the differential aging of subcohorts often yield insight into factors contributing to "successful versus unsuccessful" aging. Interventions have been scrutinized that might reduce the proportion of cohort members moving into disadvantaged statuses in old age. Some studies focus on interventions in the structure of education and work throughout life. Other studies seek to counter the ageism in society that restricts access to opportunities and to preventive and rehabilitative services for older people. Still others assess social policies aimed to reduce the excessive risks of adverse changes experienced by elderly women, blacks, Hispanics, and unmarried persons.

C. Differential Impact on Subcohorts of Historical Events

Subcohorts differ not only in composition and experiences, but also in their responses to social trends and historical events. For example, Glen Elder's classic 1979 study of the Great Depression showed that the repercussions on family patterns and resources were more traumatic for children in the subcohort who were young, rather than older, at the time of the Depression. Three examples will illustrate the nature of such studies.

1. Voluntary Association Membership

An event of great importance for African Americans was the Civil Rights Movement in the 1960s and the related legislation intended to end racial discrimination and segregation. As one outcome of this legislation, the African-American (black) subpopulation in each cohort gained access to previously segregated voluntary organizations, such as fraternal organizations and service clubs. But the significance of these new opportunities for Blacks depended heavily on their cohort identification, which determined their age when the change occurred. Among those that had lived through young adulthood prior to 1960, members of the black subcohort have remained much less involved than Whites in fraternal and social organizations. For more recent cohorts, however, difference in membership between black and white subcohorts has been muted. This finding suggests that future cohorts of elderly Blacks, whatever their status in the larger society, may experience greater support from voluntary organizations than Blacks who are already old.

2. Father–Offspring Bonds

The increases in out-of-wedlock births, divorce, and mother-only households in the decades following 1960 have implications for future aging experience. For example, some studies consider men who are absent from the household during the early years of their child. In father-absent households, the bond between father and child tends to be weakened. If these weakened bonds lead to increasingly matrifocal kinship structures in later life, a growing proportion of elderly men will predictably lack access to social and instrumental support from their children. By tracking subcohorts of men who already have weak links to children, it is possible to anticipate when these men will be entering that phase of old age characterized by high risks of dependency.

3. Fetal Development

In order to examine the life-course consequences of prenatal nutrition, a study of the Dutch famine resulting from enemy blockade in 1944–45 was able to distinguish subcohorts of men whose fetal development was, or was not, subjected to the famine. Tracking the lives of these men up to age 50 (made possible through remarkable records for the country as a whole) yielded a wide range of findings: the absence of the expected association between poor prenatal nutrition and cognitive development; an excess of obesity in those exposed early in gestation, in contrast to a deficiency in weight for those exposed late; and a heightened risk of schizophrenia in midlife. This intricately designed and well-known analysis illustrates the ingenuity and effort often required of cohort studies.

IV. CONNECTIONS ACROSS COHORTS

The later lives of members of particular cohorts are shaped not only by earlier life-course experiences and surrounding social structures, but also by relation-ships with the parallel lives of members of other cohorts preceding or following them. Cohort studies give special attention to two types of linkages: generational linkages in families and public transfer of economic resources between cohorts.

A. Intergenerational Bonds

Much earlier research on intergenerational relationships in the United States found that strong bonds between parents and their children typically persist until the end of the parents' lives. These bonds involve not only emotional commitment, but also frequent contact and caregiving in time of need. Because intergenerational bonds are rooted in the life histories of both parents and children, however, they are subject to change as new cohorts replace the currently elderly parents or their adult offspring.

The strength of future parent–child relationships could change if, in old age, a growing proportion of cohort members were childless or did not live near a child. Yet there is no evidence that either of these changes is likely to occur. Rates of childlessness are higher for cohorts already in old age in the 1990s than for any cohort that will enter old age in the foreseeable future. Moreover, because rates of geographic mobility have decreased in recent decades, it is not clear that cohorts entering old age in the future will live farther away from their children.

There are, however, two other changes that could alter family relationships in the future. The first is parental divorce, which often adversely affects parent–child relationships in later life. The proportion of persons entering old age who have experienced a divorce earlier in life will increase significantly for those cohorts arriving at old age after 2010 (cohorts that entered young adulthood after 1970). Consequently, unless the detrimental effects of divorce on intergenerational relationships change, an increasing proportion of elderly cohort members will lack strong linkages with adult children. In the second place, adult children are less likely to support aging parents in the face of competing demands for their own time and energy. Growing female labor-force participation and rising rates of single-parent families among cohorts currently in young and middle adulthood suggest that fewer daughters may be available in the future to care for their aging parents.

B. Public Transfer of Resources

For several decades the U.S. government has managed a large-scale transfer of financial resources across cohorts. Payroll taxes on the working population (mostly members of cohorts who are at ages between 20 and 64) are used to finance the Social Security and Medicare benefits transferred to members of cohorts who are at later ages. Under certain conditions, a cohort might experience an even balance over its lifetime in taxes paid and benefits received. Under other conditions it is possible for certain cohorts to experience either large advantages or disadvantages relative to other cohorts.

Despite the imprecision of accounting procedures, some studies show that cohorts entering old age before 2000 are receiving old age benefits far in excess of the taxes (contributions) they had paid in advance. On average, members of these cohorts are receiving larger old age benefits than their predecessors, and over an extended period of survival. In effect, these privileged cohorts largely avoided paying the higher taxes needed to support their improved retirement benefits. However, when the baby boom cohorts retire in the years following 2010, the ratio of workers to retirees will be much lower than previously, and predictably members of these cohorts will not receive benefits in old age proportionate to the relatively high payroll taxes they paid earlier in life. Such issues affecting cohort inequities in the lifetime balance between taxes paid and benefits received are receiving increasing attention in cohort studies.

V. INTERPLAY BETWEEN COHORTS AND SOCIAL STRUCTURES

Fuller understanding of the patterns of cohort aging depends on studies that examine the interrelationship between people's changing lives and the surrounding social structures in families, schools, offices and factories, communities, nursing homes, and the changing society as a whole. At given historical periods, people of different ages in all the coexisting cohorts are passing through age-related structures, and are thereby encountering the associated role opportunities and norms. The influence of these encounters is two-directional. In one direction, lives of cohort members are influenced *by* such structures and their historical

changes (as in many of the foregoing examples); in the other direction, the collective lives of cohort members also exert influence *on* these structures. Some cohort studies (though many more are needed) focus on this two-directional interplay.

A. Structural Influences on Cohort Patterns

In one direction of the interplay, an early analysis by Peter Uhlenberg in 1969 illustrates structural influences on cohort aging patterns. This study scrutinized five cohorts of women, born in selected years between 1830 and 1920. For each cohort, Uhlenberg calculated the numbers of women who, depending on what path they followed at different life transitions, pursued each of six possible life-course patterns. These patterns ranged between the extremes of Type 1 women, who died before age 20, to Type 6 women, who survived to age 20, married, had children, and were still surviving with their husbands alive to age 55. Of the six patterns, Type 1 was the most frequent in the earliest (1830) cohort, but became consistently less common in each succeeding cohort. By contrast, Type 6 became increasingly more common until, in the most recent (1920) cohort it became so predominant as to be termed the "typical" pattern.

These changes in cohort aging patterns can, in one direction, be viewed as consequences of structural changes: such as social changes in control of infectious diseases, or in marriage and childbearing customs associated with increasingly diverse subcultures of parents. In the other direction, the study began to note how these changes in cohort aging patterns produced such structural consequences as the decline in numbers of roles for orphans or for early widows, or emergence of the new "empty nest" roles in family life.

B. Influence of Cohort Patterns on Social Structures

A few studies illustrate in further detail this reciprocal influence of changing life-course patterns on social structures. In particular they point to resultant changes in cohort norms, and to the structural consequences of shifts in cohort size.

1. Cohort Norms

The opening of the work role to the majority of women in more recent cohorts is described in another set of studies that show how changing lives affect normative expectations in social structures. (Uhlenberg's "typical" pattern of women's lives preceded the trend toward participation in paid work outside the home.) Historical data on the work lives of successive cohorts of U.S. women over an entire century reveal a consistent and striking transformation: in each more recent cohort, larger and larger proportions of women spent much of their adult lives in the labor force. From cohort to cohort, as this wave has mounted, the changes in behaviors began to change structures. As women in those early cohorts demonstrated what they could do, more and more work roles opened up for women at every age up to retirement. Gradually, too, norms changed (illustrating the mechanism called "cohort norm formation"). First it became acceptable for women to work. Now it is often expected, even required, that women at all income levels, even including young mothers, *should* work. Clearly, changing lives in successive cohorts have altered structures. (In turn, further structural changes will be needed in the future to relieve the resultant strain from combined work-and-family roles on those younger women in the more recent cohorts. Each direction of influence ultimately leads to pressures in the opposite direction.)

2. Cohort Size

Changes in cohort size also have powerful effects on social structures. The dramatic consequences are now widely familiar because of the consequences of the "baby boom cohorts." Great increases in cohort size first required that schools expand, but then contract as smaller cohorts followed. This same process was subsequently repeated in colleges, then in work organizations, and it will occur again in retirement communities and nursing homes. For example, the marked rise in total lifetime Medicare expenditures for cohorts turning 65 in 1990, compared with those who will turn 65 in 2020, has been attributed almost entirely to the larger size of the later cohort.

That the effects of cohort size are not limited to current experiences with these exceptional baby boom cohorts, however, is evidenced by Joan Waring's classic 1975 study. Her detailed analysis of the process of "disordered cohort flow" shows the consequences for social structures of alterations between large and small cohorts.

C. Interplay between Cohorts and Social Structures

Studies of very different places and times point to the persistence of these two-directional influences between changing lives and changing structures (called "interdependent dynamisms").

One analysis (by Anne Foner and David Kertzer) of less well-developed societies in Africa specifies features of this dialectical interplay that are potentially universal. In these societies, cohorts or "age sets" are clearly defined, and each moves on a prescribed schedule from the roles in one age stratum to roles in the next (such as warrior or elder). This detailed examination of the processes of role transitions reveals that, despite their explicit organization, tensions and conflicts arise as each new cohort must contend with the earlier cohort it is replacing. These conflicts and tensions correspondingly press to change the structural practices governing transitions. Such internally generated changes in cohort aging processes are further exacerbated by external changes (e.g., in the quality of the soil that can cause famines, or in the impact of surrounding societies). Then, in turn, the transitions in their altered form affect the lives of the people in the succeeding cohorts.

Thus, the dynamic processes of cohort succession and social change continually challenge the existing structures which, in their turn, shape the cohort aging processes described in the studies cited here.

VI. SUMMARY

This review of cohort studies shows that they do the following:

1. They force recognition that aging is a dynamic process that occurs within historical and social contexts; hence members of different cohorts grow old in widely differing ways.
2. They specify how and when particular changes in the aging process occur (through comparison of the experiences of successive cohorts).
3. They point to the heterogeneity in the aging experience, and to biopsychosocial forces operating to produce differential aging for particular individuals and subcohorts.
4. They provide clues to how social changes affect

the way individuals age, and how the succession of cohorts alters the existing structures that shape the aging process.

BIBLIOGRAPHY

Crystal, S., Shea, D., & Krishnaswami, S. (1992). Educational attainment, occupational history, and stratification: Determinants of later-life economic outcomes. *Journal of Gerontology: Social Sciences, 47,* S213–S221.

Easterlin, R. A., Schaeffer, C. M., & Macunovich, D. J. (1993). Will the baby boomers be less well off than their parents? Income, wealth, and family circumstances over the life course in the United States. *Population and Development Review, 19,* 497–522.

Himes, C. L. (1992). Future caregivers: Projected family structures of older persons. *Journal of Gerontology: Social Sciences, 47,* S17–S26.

Manton, K. G., Stallard, E., & Liu, K. (1993). Frailty and forecasts of active life expectancy in the United States. In K. G. Manton, B. H. Singer, & R. M. Suzman (Eds.), *Forecasting the health of elderly populations* (pp. 159–181). New York: Springer-Verlag.

Preston, S. H. (1992). Cohort succession and the future of the oldest old. In R. M. Suzman, D. P. Willis, & K. G. Manton (Eds.), *The oldest old* (pp. 50–57). New York: Oxford University Press.

Riley, M. W. (1994). Aging and society: Past, present, future. *The Gerontologist, 34,* 436–446.

Riley, M. W., Foner, A., & Waring, J. (1988). Sociology of age. In N. Smelser (Ed.), *Handbook of sociology* (pp. 243–290). Newbury Park CA: Sage Publications.

Riley, M. W., Kahn, R. L., & Foner, A. (Eds.). (1994). *Age and structural lag: Society's failure to provide meaningful opportunities in work, family, and leisure.* New York: John Wiley and Sons.

Uhlenberg, P. (1992). Population aging and social policy. *Annual Review of Sociology, 18,* 449–474.

Uhlenberg, P., & Miner, S. (1995). Life course and aging: A cohort perspective. In R. H. Binstock & L. K. George (Eds.), *Handbook of aging and the social sciences* (4th ed.), (pp. 208–228). San Diego: Academic Press.

Comparative and Cross-Cultural Studies

Christine L. Fry

Loyola University of Chicago

I. Importance of Comparative Research
II. Comparative Research Designs
III. Old People
IV. Old Age
V. Needed Research

Cross-Cultural   Research of an open-ended and qualitative nature within a meaningful ethnic group or community of a specific culture.
Cross-National   Research using survey instruments on probability samples to compare the responses of people across nations.
Holocultural   Research using a standard sample of world cultures based on secondary data reported ethnographically and organized within the Human Relations Area files.

Gerontology has always had a healthy respect for **COMPARATIVE RESEARCH**. Elders from one context have been compared with their counterparts elsewhere in order to determine what is universal about growing old and to distinguish that which is specific to a particular population and sociocultural circumstance. Although all research is based on comparison (male–female, young–old, rich–poor), cross-cultural research involves a distinctive research design. At a bare minimum two or more populations with known biological or cultural properties are systematically examined to evaluate hypotheses about how differences shape experiences of aging. Beyond this basic criterion, how comparative re-

search is by necessity quite diverse reflects the problem under investigation and the variety of contexts in which people live.

I. IMPORTANCE OF COMPARATIVE RESEARCH

Why engage in comparative research? Coordinating data collection and analysis from around the globe is expensive and time intensive. What is the payoff? There are a number of very compelling reasons for comparative research. First, curiosity is a property of the human intellect. What is it like in far away places and do they do it (e.g., age) better or worse than we? Second and more importantly, diversity helps us formulate and clarify questions. If everything were uniform, there would be virtually no reason to ask questions. For instance, if everyone had the same skin color, why would one want to know what skin color does? With skin color ranging from dark to light, one may want an explanation to discover the positive functions of dark skin and ultraviolet ray protection. Likewise light skin has positive functions in tanning and vitamin D production for bone metabolism. With cultural phenomena, differences are even more important in challenging accepted worldviews that appear to be the natural and only way of understanding and doing things. Just like conceptions of skin color, traditional approaches to such old-age issues as retirement, pensions, nursing homes, or even Alzheimer's disease are one way of doing or understanding things, not *the only way*. Third, by encompassing the full range of human experience, scientific theories about that experience are enriched and strengthened. For gerontology, if limiting investigations to nations where old age has been declared a problem may perpetuate these myths. By including the full gamut from small-scale foraging societies to the most industrialized societies of Europe and North America, researchers gain diversity and challenge the models generated by one societal type. Furthermore, this strengthens theories by isolating the social and cultural forces that shape the experience of aging in distinct settings. In the end one can separate the universal from the culturally specific in the experience of aging. Finally, cross-cultural research allows one to learn something about his or her own society. The individual's culture is seen as "the alien." By studying other cultures, we better comprehend our own.

Comparative research is not without its pitfalls. What has become known as the "comparative method" can be abused. All data collection and analysis must meet standards of data quality control. The most familiar issues are of validity and reliability. Validity is an assurance that the indicators selected are actually measuring what they should be as suggested by the theory under investigation. Reliability is the confidence placed in procedures to abstract from the data through coding to reduce distortion of the idiosyncracies of the coders on the resulting data. In other words, the coders should have sufficiently explicit understandings of coding categories so that one coder could replicate the work of another coder with minimal variation in results. In addition to validity and reliability, cross-cultural analysis requires guarantees of comparability. With issues of measurement resolved, one still must consider if what one's comparing across sites is even similar in meaning. Can something as fundamental as old age, be defined in a way that is meaningful to corporate executives in New York City and to peasant farmers in rural Mexico? Generally, for primary data, collected first hand by researchers, comparability problems are made explicit through discussion and negotiation. Secondary data from existing records present more challenges because investigators must interpret the meaning of the records.

II. COMPARATIVE RESEARCH DESIGNS

Comparative research designs fall into two broad categories: cross-national and cross-cultural. Distinguishing these types of research are distinctive methodologies and units of analysis.

A. Cross-National

The intent of cross-national research is to compare people living in different political units or nations. Thus the unit of analysis is a country sometimes differentiated into rural or urban settings or into ethnic groups. Researchers select the people who will participate through national probability sampling. These individuals are then asked to either complete a questionnaire or to agree to be interviewed by a survey researcher using a standardized interview guide. Most often the questions are designed to be efficiently answered and recorded in a "closed-ended" format. Here alternative answers to the questions are figured out in advance so they may be checked off on the questionnaire and transferred to electronic form for data analysis. In contrast, "open-ended" questions permit more variability in responses, which in turn present more challenges in categorizing variation. Results from cross-national research are presented using statistical tables to document national differences on a wide variety of issues, including health, family support, and retirement.

B. Cross-Cultural

Comparing entire nations is beyond the intention of cross-cultural research. Instead, the units of analysis are more homogenous cultural units such as ethnic groups, villages, or urban enclaves. Investigators focus on how cultural understandings and context shape the way aging is perceived and experienced. Research strategies are more open ended and involve the use of qualitative methods (as compared to the quantitative designs of survey research). Although quantitative techniques may be used, results are presented in an ethnographic form describing the cultural context along with any statistical information.

Specific designs for cross-cultural research are quite variable. At one extreme are large-scale research projects involving a team of investigators using the same research design and adapting protocols to several cultural settings. On the other extreme are single researchers designing their research to shed further light on an existing problem or to redefine that issue by investigating it in a different cultural context. Because primary data are sometimes expensive and difficult to obtain, secondary data are very attractive. Existing ethnographies are systematically organized and mined for information relevant to a topic. The most comprehensive endeavor to use published reports as comparative data is the Human Relations Area Files (HRAF). A distinctive comparative approach has evolved known as *Holocultural*. This method is based on a sample of 186 cultures that are relatively independent of each other and ethnographically well documented. Alternatively, ethnographic case studies may be selected by a criterion such as region or by societal type to elucidate a topic on a comparative basis.

III. OLD PEOPLE

Comparative studies of older people began, like gerontology itself, with an assumption that old age was a problematic state of affairs. Among the first tasks were to demographically document the percent of older adults in a society and to ascertain how well they were doing. Subsequently, topics of investigation became more diversified once it was understood that old people are among the most heterogenous populations.

A. Demography

Demography is among the most comparative endeavors. The vital statistics and demographic profiles of one nation are interesting, but take on new meaning when contrasted with the population statistics of other nations. Through comparison one can understand the dynamics of fertility, mortality, migration, and the factors shaping population size and structure.

Within the past two centuries, world population has been most impacted by the Industrial Revolution. Increased productivity and demand for workers combined with improved sanitation and medical technology resulted in high fertility and remarkable declines in mortality, especially among infants and children.

The net result was an exponential increase in world population with a doubling every 50 years. Comparative demographics reveal the continuing shock wave of industry. For the nations experiencing industrialization the earliest, populations are now considered to be aging. Initially, populations became young, but with the rewards for large families declining and child-rearing costs increasing, fertility declined. With further reductions in mortality, the formerly youthful population ages because there are fewer children replacing their parents and grandparents. This phenomena has been identified as the "demographic transition." In nations that are experiencing industrialization more recently, the demographic transition has not yet occurred, and populations are youthful and expanding. Projections are that the world population will continue to expand until the twenty-second century when the effect of industry stabilizes with a world population of 14–19 billion.

If advances have been made in extending life and reducing mortality, how long is it possible for a human being to survive? Demographic profiles indicate surviving to over 100 is rare even in industrialized countries, but is increasingly possible. In at least three nonindustrialized village or ethnic groups extreme longevity is reported of up to and possibly over 130 years. This is an enticing prospect given molecular biological evidence that humans potentially could have life spans of 120–160 years. However, research among the Abkhasians in the former Soviet Union state of Georgia, the Ecuadorians in Vilcabamba, and the Hunzakut of the Himalayas reveal that people here grow old, but not as old as they claim. Assuming identities of parents to avoid military conscription or age escalation to claim attention and respect led a few elders to state they are far older than they are. In the absence of birth certificates, evidence of real age is difficult to prove without multiple documentation through baptismal records, marriage certificates, birth histories, and connections to known regional and national history. Thus, in spite of reports of superlongevity, the nations where people are surviving to become centenarians are in the industrialized nations of Europe, North America, and Asia. From this work we are reminded that age is not just a simple biological or demographic fact, but can be manipulated and is a potent factor in the politics of daily life. [See DEMOGRAPHY; LONGEVITY AND LONG–LIVED POPULATIONS.]

B. Well-Being and Successful Aging

As gerontology crystallized into a specialization, researchers accepted a societal definition that saw aging as problematic. Thus one important task was to document how older adults saw their lives. Well-being measures, morale scales, or life satisfaction indices became a major methodological focus and area of inquiry. Cross-cultural research presented immediate challenges to psychometric scales attempting to measure morale because of inherent cultural assumptions about psychological well-being. Comparative research focused on questions of the status of older people, how they are treated, and what is available to them to maintain a position within a community.

It was hypothesized that older people are better off in more small-scale tribal and peasant cultures as compared to their counterparts in the industrialized world. A rather obvious point of difference is that older people in industrial countries are expected to retire, which removes them from production and a major activity of adulthood. In tribal societies, work is subsistence based and largely domestic. Productive activities are familial and lifelong, until one is no longer able. This "paradise lost" hypothesis has not received much substantiation. Retirement has not produced social isolation and a life stage which has limited possibilities. Quite to the contrary, given the medical technology, labor-saving devices, and the economic supports in social security and pension plans, old age is full of opportunity and possibilities. It is a time of freedom from the responsibilities of younger life stages. [See RETIREMENT.]

In small-scale cultures life is less technologically buffered. Where such amenities as indoor plumbing, central heating, or electricity are absent, water must be hauled instead of turning on the tap. Fuel must be collected instead of setting the thermostat higher. Likewise a trip to visit a relative may involve a several kilometer walk instead of a ride in a car. Physical demands are higher for everyone, including older adults. In old age some individuals may unwillingly find themselves physically active through expectations of their families.

Although generally older people are well treated and respected members of their societies, abandonment and killing are not rare. In about half of the technologically simple societies practices exist that result in the hastened deaths of some older people.

Many of these societies are foraging groups who during the harshest seasons may be forced to sacrifice their least productive member for the survival of the group. On the other hand, many of these societies are agriculturalists in temperate climates. Cross-cultural research has revealed that intact, contributing older people are supported and cared for. Once an individual becomes severely impaired and feeble, support is withdrawn. It is a very difficult family decision often effected at the request of the person who will die. Death may occur violently as a son murders his parent or may happen by abandonment or by withholding food and water.

With older adults experiencing considerable support in most societies and especially in technologically advanced societies, what promotes a "good old age?" One obvious factor is the physical condition of one's body. As health declines, it becomes increasingly difficult to work and to do one's daily routine. Another factor is security. To have assurance that the material basis of life (food, shelter, warmth) will continue into the future and at a level one is accustomed to, is a very important component of successful aging. Another ingredient for aging well is a safety net of support, usually from family. Health, security, and support are near universal in their desirability, but how they are actualized and the consequences of deficits are highly variable. I discuss these in the sections that follow.

C. Health

In promoting well-being, health is very important. Declines in health status are universally feared. Yet on a cross-cultural basis, health is not just the physical status of the body. Health and its understanding is culturally mitigated. Body states are interpreted though cultural knowledge as is exemplified by menopause. In their late forties or early fifties all women experience a change in hormones accompanying the cessation of ovulation. However, across cultures we find major differences in the symptoms signaling the change. In Japan, the most frequent complaints are of shoulder stiffness, headaches, backaches, constipation, chilliness, and irritability. Women in North America report problems with hot flashes, palpitations, night sweats, and tiredness. Unless Asian and European women have different physiologies, changing body states are given cultural meaning.

Across cultures declining health means decreased

functionality. Difficulty in moving and loss of strength and perceptual acuity are threats to adult status. If one can no longer do that which is expected of most adults, then full participation in social life is compromised. Comparative research again reveals the impact of culture in at least two ways.

First, functionality is culturally defined. Older Americans have to be able to do certain things because of their technological environment and cultural expectations. Where one must be able to read and where a significant portion of recreation and information comes from television, impaired vision is isolating. Likewise when one can no longer negotiate stairs, cleaning, cooking, shopping, or managing finances, then the ideal of maintaining an independent household is compromised. In other cultures where literacy is rare and where households are jointly organized with extended families, difficulties in vision and in domestic activities are not as threatening.

Second, culture compensates for human frailties through people and technology. Again we find variation. In technologically simpler cultures people are more likely to be mobilized. For instance, if one can no longer haul water, the presence of a grandchild who can resolves the problem. In more complex societies with lots of labor-saving devices, physical frailty is buffered through technology. Not only do machines save time, but the need for physical strength is reduced. Also prothesis such as pacemakers, wheelchairs, glasses, hearing aids, and walkers directly enable people with impairment to continue to do their daily activities. Ironically, even with the ability to reduce the effects of declining functionality with technology, people still fear the frustrations that come with disability. [*See* GERONTECHNOLOGY.]

D. Security

Control over a resource that others value is certainly a very direct way of promoting one's well-being and security. Comparative research has revealed that where older adults are in control of wealth, land, food, the labor of others, and even information, they are elevated in status and face very secure futures. In old age, relatively few can hold on to enough wealth to be able to manipulate kin through the promise of a sizable inheritance. In any culture there are people who are more than comfortable and others in need. Also, some economies work against material accumu-

lation. Under these circumstances old age can become very trying. With physical abilities declining, the very basis of life—food—is at risk. In the abundance of industrialized societies, we find marked wealth differentials, but we also find old age to be economically stabilized through social security and social welfare policies. In North America and Europe older people are less likely to see material issues as threatening their old age.

E. Kinship and Support

Caregiving and support of older people is a major social issue, but it is primarily a family issue. Families look after and when needed care for their older member. Cross-cultural studies of kinship have encountered such tremendous variation in family organization that it is almost impossible to come up with a simple definition of marriage or what constitutes a family. Families reflect the economies in which they are located. In nonindustrial societies, kinship plays a much larger role in people's lives. Families are both political and economic units, anchored in a larger society. Interdependency is reinforced by a domestic division of labor whereby the kin unit manages its affairs for the good of its members, including those who are old.

In contrast, kinship diminishes in industrial economies. Lower fertility reduces the number of kin. But more importantly, occupational structures come to dominate peoples lives. Individuals participate in industry through an extensive division of labor within bureaucratically organized corporations. With increased wealth families no longer maintain and rely on a family fund as households become financially autonomous. Families continue to be very important, but the meaning of kinship is quite different. Kin are cherished for their personalities and friendship, not for how much support they can contribute. Parents invest very heavily in fewer children to encourage them to meet their full potential. Very few parents expect their children to return home in adulthood. In fact, a returning adult child is seen as very problematic.

For caregiving, the above contrast would appear to work against older adults in industrialized society. Families have been the traditional safety nets for older people. In industrialized societies families are smaller. Households are residentially separate and financially autonomous. Solidarity is based on affect, which is not necessarily the best way to mobilize people because sentiments can change very rapidly. Yet the news is not all bad. Families in North America and Europe go to great lengths to care for their older members. Also, as states and economies become more complex a new safety net appears—the market. Virtually everyone in an industrial economy satisfies their basic needs by purchasing food, clothing, and shelter in the marketplace. For older adults, the market is basic and continues to complement what family members contribute. Domestic help, lawn services, or even home care can be hired, which help to reduce the caregiving burden for kin. A rather obvious catch-22 in this is that there must be sufficient financial resources to access the market. [See SOCIAL NETWORKS, SUPPORT, AND INTEGRATION.]

IV. OLD AGE

A. Definitions

One of the most striking aspects of age on a worldwide basis is the limited distribution of its explicit use in organizing social life. Aging is a temporal process. Time is culturally configured. With technological sophistication time can be measured and finely calibrated from milliseconds to millennia. Hours, days, and years are the more meaningful units. For most of human history and the majority of small-scale cultures, time is not an important dimension of life. Only bureaucratically organized industrialized cultures use time to organize daily schedules and age to regulate their populations. Here people need to know their ages and are issued birth certificates. People of specified ages are expected to be in school, serve in the military; be able to drive, drink, and vote; and to be entitled to Social Security. For people living in these contexts, age is very important.

Also on a comparative basis, old age has been difficult to define. Most industrialized societies set their pensionable ages in the early to midsixties. Thus old age has a chronological marker. Gerontologists, however, were quick to point out that in spite of its impartiality, chronological age was a poor predictor of ability. Functional age is far more meaningful in terms of what people can do in their daily lives. In cultures where chronological age is rarely known, functional-

ity is what defines old age. In nations with youthful populations and where vital statistics are kept, chronological thresholds are lowered to the midfifties or even to the forties.

B. Life Course

One of the major theoretical breakthroughs in gerontology has been the emergence of the life span perspective. Initially, gerontology coalesced with a focus on old age. Old age and all its diversity cannot be isolated from the rest of adulthood. Consequently, the life course became a major unit in gerontological research. Cross-cultural research challenges the way we have modeled the life course.

A long-standing problem in social anthropology suggested ways in which age can be formalized into an explicit principle of social organization. Many small-scale societies make relative age a criterion by which the males are organized into age-stratified groups. Cohorts of boys are initiated into an age class. These classes, sometimes called age sets or generation sets, are bounded groups that are opened for recruitment and then closed once they are complete. A more junior set is then opened. All men are members of a set and sets are ranked in seniority—boys, warriors, householders, elders, and so forth. The specifics of how the age classes are organized are quite variable, but in the formality of age organization such concepts as age grading, age stratification, and age norms were documented in simpler social contexts and sharply defined.

Life courses are seen as role courses ordered by age norms and expectations. Cohorts entered adulthood upon completing a finely age-graded system of formal education. Jobs and marriage signal full adult status. Within families, generations become more distinctive because of lower fertility and childbearing occurring most commonly in the twenties or very early thirties. Within jobs we find seniority and for some career ladders. A new stage is entered with retirement and an exit from the labor force. Although individual role courses are variable, life courses are seen as sequenced and staged. The life course is divisible into intervals distinguished by age-sensitive status transitions.

Age class systems and a staged life course appear to be parallels in differing cultural contexts. Beyond defining graded categories, the similarity vanishes.

Age classes are political institutions organizing males in a public arena. For the most part they are the most salient in the junior classes and see diminishing significance for the more senior males. Age classes do not organize all of life and usually only indirectly affect women. The staged life course is a near universal expectation from youth to old age. This view of the life course is also restricted to industrialized societies and especially to the middle classes of those societies. People in small-scale societies do not see life as sequenced through life stages. Age-sensitive roles are not clearly demarcated. Formal education is rare and not universal, thus no finely age-graded classes. Wage labor is intermittent and there is no real job market. No one retires from subsistence activities. Fertility is higher and family are much more generationally continuous with siblings who may be 20 or more years separated by age. Under these circumstances, people have life courses that note youth and old age, but they are more functionally and individually defined. Even in industrialized societies people who are marginalized in poverty, aspire to, but find it difficult to attain a sequenced life course. [See LIFE COURSE.]

V. NEEDED RESEARCH

Gerontology is at a very important juncture as a discipline. In the half century of work, the multidisciplinary effort in gerontology has evolved an ambitious agenda involving research, application, and advocacy. The people who invented gerontology did so working from disciplinary perspectives that set out to define *the* problem of old age and how to improve quality of lives physically and socially. From the current perspective, it is not too surprising that researchers found no modal old person, but an incredible diversity in the experience of growing old. Gerontologists are just now on the thresholds of discovering processes that define age and shape how people experience aging. Comparative research is needed now, more than ever.

A. Research

Comparative research shows that world populations are remarkably diverse biologically and culturally. The mapping of the human genome and break-

throughs in molecular biology show that populations differ genetically. Biological models of aging deal with an intrinsically difficult problem in differentiating genetic from environmental factors. Unfortunately, most models are either based predominantly on animal data or on males in North America of European descent. Given the technology available, more progress can be made by examining human variation and diversity over the life span in genetically diverse populations.

Social and cultural research emphasizing diversity is also required. Our understanding of age and life courses is primarily rooted in one type of social context, urbanized industry. To more fully understand the processes that result in age being such an important aspect of these complex nations, researchers must examine other contexts. Smaller-scale societies, developing nations, ethnic diversity, minority groups, and local-level communities provide a natural laboratory in which to investigate the meaning of age and the role it plays in people's lives. Likewise, researchers should explore the meanings elderly people find in their lives. Because meaning is cultural, diversity will further add to our understanding of the linkage between cultural context and personhood.

B. Societal Transformation

Much of the interpretation of global differences in aging has been couched in a theory of modernization. Underlying most of this thought is the optimism of the 1960s, which spawned economic development programs with the intent of hastening the transformation of underdeveloped countries to become industrialized. By the 1990s this has not happened and probably will not happen. On the other hand, economic change continues, but not as predicted by modernization. Globalization of the world economy is changing life both in the developed and underdeveloped world. Automation has eliminated many jobs in heavy industry and in the service sector. Jobs are being sent overseas to "industrial zones," in Asia and Latin America. In what is becoming a global assembly line, what happens to age? How are these changes affecting people who are now old in both the developed and less developed world? How are altered life chances shaping the lives of those who are entering adulthood and what are the implications for their aging? One must study a phenomenon as it is happening.

BIBLIOGRAPHY

Albert, S. M., & Cattell, M. G. (1994). *Old age in global perspective: Cross-cultural and cross-national views.* New York: G. K. Hall and Co.

Crews, D. E., & Garruto, R. M. (1994). *Biological anthropology and aging: Perspectives on human variation over the life span.* New York: Oxford University Press.

Keith, J., Fry, C., Glascock, A. P., Ikels, C., Dickerson-Putman, J., Harpending, H. C., & Draper, P. (1994). *The aging experience: Diversity and commonality across cultures.* Thousand Oaks, CA: Sage Publications.

Lock, M. (1993). *Encounters with aging: Mythologies of menopause in Japan and North America.* Berkeley: University of California Press.

Schweitzer, M. M. (Ed.). (1991). *Anthropology of aging.* Westport, CT: Greenwood Press.

Sokolovsky, J. (Ed.). (1990). *The cultural context of aging: Worldwide perspectives.* New York: Bergin and Garvey.

Conditioning

Diana S. Woodruff-Pak

Temple University

Richard L. Port

Slippery Rock College

Conditioned Response (CR)   Learned response of organism after repeated pairing of a neutral stimulus such as a tone or light (called the conditioned stimulus) and a reflex-eliciting stimulus such as a shock or corneal airpuff (called the unconditioned stimulus). Once learning has occurred, the CR occurs to the conditioned stimulus, even in the absence of the unconditioned stimulus.

Conditioned Stimulus (CS)   A neutral stimulus such as a tone or light that does not normally elicit a reflexive response. For example, a tone does not normally elicit an eyeblink.

Reinforcement   Stimulation presented after the occurrence of a behavior that increases the occurrence of that behavior. For example, a food pellet presented after a bar press in a rat will increase the incidence of bar pressing. The food pellet is the reinforcement.

Unconditioned Response (UR)   The reflexive response that occurs to an unconditioned stimulus. For example, the eyeblink is a UR to a corneal airpuff.

Unconditioned Stimulus (US)   A stimulus that always elicits a reflexive response. For example, a corneal airpuff elicits an eyeblink. A shock to the paw elicits withdrawal of the paw.

Classical (Pavlovian) and instrumental (Thorndikian) **CONDITIONING** are the two most widely employed paradigms for the investigation of simple associative learning. Both paradigms involve the exposure of the organism to the temporal joining of two or more events. The Nobel laureate physiologist Ivan Petrovich Pavlov discovered the conditioned reflex in the first decade of the twentieth century. His discovery was that the presentation of a neutral stimulus followed shortly thereafter by a reflex-inducing stimulus (e.g., meat powder to elicit salivation) resulted in the elicitation of the reflex by the neutral stimulus after repeated pairings. Instrumental conditioning, wherein reinforcement is contingent upon the occurrence of a given behavioral response, was first systematically studied by Edward Lee Thorndike early in this century. Thus, for most of the twentieth century, techniques for the investigation of simple associative learning have been available, and Pavlov was the first to observe that old dogs condition more slowly than young dogs. This initiated the very fruitful investigation of conditioning and aging.

I. CLASSICAL CONDITIONING

The standard format for the presentation of stimuli in classical conditioning is called the delay paradigm. A neutral stimulus such as a tone or light is called the conditioned stimulus (CS). It is presented for a duration of around half a second. While it is still on, the unconditioned stimulus (US) is presented, and the CS and US coterminate 50–100 msec later. Learning occurs when the organism responds to the CS before the onset of the US. This learned response is called the conditioned response (CR). Three types of classical conditioning paradigms have been used in life span developmental studies, and the delay and trace paradigms are the ones used most often to study aging

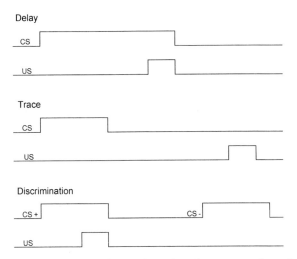

Figure 1 Examples of three classical conditioning paradigms. In the Delay paradigm, the conditioned stimulus (CS) onsets at least 100 ms before the onset of the unconditioned stimulus (US). There is an overlap between the CS and US. In the Trace paradigm, the CS and US do not overlap. The CS onsets and turns off, there is a blank or "trace" period of no stimulus, and then the US onsets. In the Discrimination paradigm there are two CSs. The CS+ is always followed by the US. The CS− is never followed by the US. The subject learns to respond to the CS+ and ignore the CS−.

(see Figure 1). In the delay paradigm the CS precedes the US by a fixed amount of time and is on while the US is presented. The CS and the US do not overlap in the trace paradigm because the CS is turned off, a blank period ensues, and then the US occurs. The term *trace* is used because the subject must form a memory trace of the CS to associate it with the later arriving US. In the discrimination conditioning paradigm, two CSs are presented. The CS+ is paired with the US, but the CS− never occurs with the US. For example, a 500-Hz tone might be the CS+, and a 1000-Hz tone might be a CS−. If the US were an airpuff to the eye, the subject's task would be to blink before the airpuff when the 500-Hz tone onsets and to ignore the 1000-Hz tone. Acquisition of the conditioned discrimination takes more trials and is considered more difficult than delay conditioning.

On no other species is there such a large body of parametric data on classical conditioning as on the classically conditioned eyeblink response on the rabbit. Indeed, much of the general literature on classical conditioning is based on data collected in the rabbit with the nictitating membrane (NM or third eyelid of the rabbit) response and in the human with the

eyeblink. Ernest Hilgard was the first to study eyeblink classical conditioning (EBCC) in animals and did classic studies on human EBCC as well. His work established the close correspondence in properties of the conditioned eyeblink response in humans and other animals, suggesting that the underlying neuronal mechanisms of memory storage and retrieval are the same in all mammals, including humans. Here, perhaps more than in any other form of learning, neuronal mechanisms of memory elucidated in infrahuman mammals apply directly to the human condition. Isadore Gormezano was the first to publish EBCC studies in the rabbit and to introduce measurement of the NM extension response.

Most studies of aging and classical conditioning have used rabbits or humans as subjects. However, there are advantages of other species such as mice and rats for research on aging. In particular, mice and rats with their short gestation period, large litter size, relatively small space requirements, and short life spans make them highly desirable for research on development and aging. Neither the genetic controls nor the breeding environments presently available for rabbits equal those in place of the mouse and rat. However, mice and rats have behavioral characteristics that make them poor candidates for the study of EBCC; for example, their high activity levels and the consequent difficulty of restraint and their high blink rates. Some of our colleagues are overcoming difficulties with EBCC research with rats and mice, particularly in the unrestrained animal. We anticipate that the rat and mouse model of EBCC will provide additional impetus to the study of the neurobiological substrates of classical conditioning over the life span.

A. Eyeblink Conditioning in Aging Animals

EBCC displays natural age-related deficits in all species in which it has been tested. The three nonhuman mammalian species showing age difference in EBCC are rabbits, cats, and rats.

In some laboratories, research on EBCC and aging has occurred long enough so that hundreds of rabbits of various ages have been run. Using a delay paradigm in which the interval between the CS and US was 750 ms, 102 rabbits ranging in age from 3–54 months in Diana Woodruff-Pak's laboratory showed significant age-related impairment in trials to learning criterion between the ages of 21–30 months, with no significant

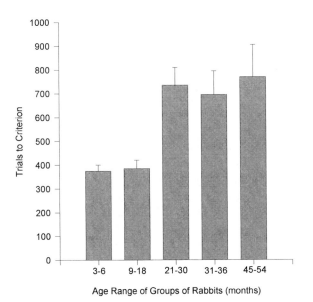

Figure 2 Trials to learning criterion (eight conditioned responses in nine consecutive trials) in the 750-ms eyeblink classical conditioning (EBCC) paradigm in 102 New Zealand white rabbits ranging in age from 3–54 months. Age ranges in months for the five groups of rabbits are 3–6 ($n = 37$), 9–18 ($n = 18$), 21–30 ($n = 27$), 31–36 ($n = 13$), and 45–54 ($n = 7$; Woodruff-Pak, unpublished data).

additional decline in the older groups (see Figure 2). These results were paralleled closely in John Disterhoft's laboratory using the 600-ms short CS trace paradigm. In 180 rabbits over the age range of 2–36 months, age-associated learning impairments were seen by 24 months of age.

Because rabbits have a life expectancy that has been estimated to be about 8 years, these animals may be useful as animal models for studies of brain and behavior relationships in aging. Assuming that human life expectancy is almost 80 years, it is tempting to make a linear extrapolation from the human to the rabbit life expectancy and equate a human decade with a rabbit year. In this scheme, a 60-year-old human would be equivalent to a 6-year-old rabbit. However, there are a number of reasons why a linear interpolation of human to rabbit life expectancy probably is inappropriate. For example, at birth the rabbit is much more mature than the human, and rabbits reach puberty by 6 months. According to the linear extrapolation between human and rabbit age, a 6-month-old rabbit would be the equivalent of a 5-year-old human. However, because 5-year-old children cannot repro-

duce, the linear interpolation between human and rabbit age is inaccurate in early life. Using reproductive capacity as a biomarker, a 6-month-old rabbit is roughly comparable to an adolescent aged 12–14 years. Three years of age in rabbits might compare to humans in their 50s, and humans in their sixth decade might correspond in age to 4-year-old rabbits. Age changes in reproductive capacity appear to be a useful means to parallel human and rabbit age because age differences in learning and memory occur at similar times in the life course of these two species when reproductive capacity is used as a biomarker to assess age.

B. Eyeblink Conditioning in Aging Humans

Differences between EBCC in young and elderly nursing home residents in a single 70- to 90-trial EBCC session were first observed in the early 1950s by the russian scientists, Gakkel and Zinina, and reported in the United States by Jerome in the first *Handbook of the Psychology of Aging* in 1959. These results were replicated and extended to normal, community-residing older adults. The main and striking result was the relative inability of the older subjects to acquire CRs. In Woodruff-Pak's laboratory, data were collected on EBCC in the delay paradigm using a 400-ms CS–US interval in over 100 adults ranging in age from 18–83. Subjects received a series of 108 trials consisting of one unpaired and eight paired tone and airpuff presentations. Neutral instructions designed neither to facilitate nor inhibit eyeblinks were given. Results indicated that age differences in acquisition in EBCC are large. The age differences in EBCC did not appear abruptly in the sixties and older. Rather, subjects in their forties were already demonstrating a lower level of conditioning. Large age differences existed in the delay classical conditioning paradigm, and they first appeared in the forties. These results were replicated almost identically in Paul Solomon's laboratory. Don Powell's laboratory reported age differences in both EBCC and heart rate classical conditioning.

C. Brain Substrates of Eyeblink Classical Conditioning

The neural circuitry underlying EBCC in rabbits has been almost completely identified. The essential site of the plasticity for learning resides in the ipsilateral cerebellum, and the hippocampus, although not essential, can affect the rate of conditioning. Significant changes occur in the cerebellum and in the hippocampus during normal aging. It may now be possible to identify and characterize the critical age-related changes in the brain underlying the age-associated decline in EBCC.

1. Cerebellum

The ipsilateral cerebellum has been identified in rabbits as the critical substrate for EBCC. The role of cerebellum in EBCC in humans has been less thoroughly investigated. Nevertheless, results with patients with damage to cerebellum in Daum's, Hallett's, and Woodruff-Pak's laboratories along with additional published case studies provide suggestive evidence that the ipsilateral cerebellum is essential for EBCC in humans, as it is in rabbits. Furthermore, one positron emission tomography (PET) study reported significant activation in sites in the inferior cerebellar cortex and deep nuclei of adults engaged in EBCC. In another PET study of EBCC in young adult humans, there was deactivation in cerebellum ipsilateral to the conditioned eye that was attributed to decreases in Purkinje cell activity.

Cerebellar Purkinje cells appear to be selectively impaired by processes of aging in rabbits and humans. Evidence suggesting that the cerebellar cortex (where Purkinje cells reside) is involved in EBCC was provided in studies in which acquisition in rabbits is tested after they receive cerebellar cortical aspirations. Lesions of the cerebellar cortex affect how rapidly and how well rabbits developed CRs with the ipsilateral eye, but the lesions did not prevent acquisition. Cortically lesioned rabbits required seven times as many trials to attain learning criterion.

To relate EBCC to Purkinje cell loss, we counted Purkinje cells in rabbits conditioned in the 750-ms trace paradigm and aged 3–50 months (Woodruff-Pak et al., 1990). Comparisons of the total number of Purkinje cells counted for each age group revealed a highly significant difference. Older rabbits had fewer Purkinje cells. Cell counts in the molecular layer of the same animals indicated no age differences. This result suggests that differential tissue shrinkage in young and old brains was not the cause of the age differences in Purkinje cells. There was a correlation of $-.79$ ($p < .005$) between Purkinje cell number and

trials to criterion. The fewer Purkinje cells a rabbit had, the longer it took to learn. The relationship was relatively independent of age. A partial correlation removing the variance due to age yielded an r of $-.61$ ($p < .025$). These results were replicated and extended using immunohistochemical staining techniques.

Cerebellar interpositus nucleus neurons in 25 rabbits aged 3–81 months wre immunostained, and cell counts were related to acquisition and retention of EBCC. In the case of interpositus nucleus neurons, correlations were higher with retention than acquisition. Neuroanatomical data showing correlations between Purkinje cells and acquisition and one-year retention and interpositus neurons and 1-year retention (but not acquisition) support previous work identifying the interpositus nucleus as the site of the essential memory trace and the cerebellar cortex as a system important in establishing that memory trace. Cell loss in Purkinje and interpositus nucleus cells appears to account for some of the age-related differences in acquisition and retention.

2. Hippocampus

Neuronal unit activity in the hippocampus increases markedly within trials early in the EBCC process. Pyramidal cells in the CA1 region in hippocampus develop a neural model of the behavioral eyeblink response as rabbits acquire CRs. Although the hippocampus is engaged during acquisition in EBCC, rabbits acquire CRs normally in the delay paradigm in the absence of a hippocampus. In contrast, lesions of the cerebellar interpositus nucleus in rabbits abolish CRs and eliminate hippocampal CA1 pyramidal cell firing with the behavioral response.

There is some disagreement about the role of the hippocampus in the trace paradigm in rabbits. Several laboratories have reported that the timing of the CR in the trace (but not the delay) paradigm is disrupted with removal of the dorsal hippocampus. Researchers in another laboratory argued that the more complete hippocampal removal prevents acquisition in the trace paradigm.

We demonstrated acquisition and retention of EBCC in the 400-ms delay and 900-ms trace (400-ms CS, 500-ms trace, 900-ms CS–US interval) paradigms in the well-studied, profoundly amnesic human subject, H.M., who had bilateral removal of the medial temporal lobe structures including most of the hippocampus. Other investigators have also reported relatively normal acquisition in the delay paradigm in amnesic patients with medial temporal lobe lesions. These results with humans are consistent with observations in hippocampectomized rabbits in the delay paradigm.

The hippocampus is not essential for acquisition in the delay EBCC paradigm in rabbits or humans, although the trace paradigm in rabbits is affected by hippocampal lesions. In addition, disruption or facilitation of the hippocampus affects the rate of conditioning in the delay paradigm. For this reason the hippocampus is said to play a modulatory role in EBCC. Electrical stimulation of the preforant path establishing long-term potentiation in hippocampus causes more rapid EBCC in a discrimination paradigm. Disruption of muscarinic receptors in the septo-hippocampal cholinergic system with scopolamine injections impairs acquisition of EBCC in animals and humans. Scopolamine injections also eliminate hippocampal pyramidal cell activity in conjunction with the CR and UR. Disruption of nicotinic cholinergic receptors with the nicotinic antagonist mecamylamine profoundly delay acquisition.

An abnormally functioning hippocampus impairs learning, but the absence of a hippocampus does not. The memory trace itself is not in the hippocampus, but the hippocampus can markedly influence the storage process. This modulatory role for the hippocampus may be particularly significant in Alzheimer's disease (AD). In humans, AD appears to profoundly alter hippocampal neuronal function. A major disruption of the brain cholinergic system occurs, impairing cholinergic innervation of cortical and hippocampal neurons. Experimental procedures disrupting hippocampal cholinergic function, such as microinjections of scopolamine to the medial septum and lesions of the medial septum, prolong the rate of acquisition of EBCC in rabbits. These data from the animal model led us to predict that AD patients, having hippocampal dysfunction, would show poorer EBCC than normal adults, and that hypothesis was supported in AD and in older adults with Down's syndrome (DS) who developed AD. [See DEMENTIA; LEARNING; MEMORY.]

3. Eyeblink Conditioning, the Hippocampus, and Alzheimer's Disease

Impaired learning and memory ability are the behavioral hallmarks of AD. AD is a progressive dementia characterized neuropathologically by extensive loss of neurons and the presence of amyloid-containing senile plaques (SPs) as well as neurofibrillary tangles (NFTs). Alzheimer-like neuropathology has been observed in the brains of virtually all adults with DS autopsied over the age of 35 years. These individuals are called DS/AD. Woodruff-Pak's prediction that adults with probable AD, having hippocampal cholinergic disruption, would show impaired EBCC was supported. We have replicated and extended this result, and it has been independently replicated. AD disrupts EBCC beyond the impairment seen in normal aging. Adults with DS/AD like patients with AD perform EBCC poorly. Adults with DS under age 35 condition significantly better than adults with DS/AD. These results suggest that EBCC may be an index of the onset of AD-like neuropathology.

Longitudinal results with normal elderly adults indicate that EBCC may have utility in the *early* detection of dementia. A 3-year longitudinal study of nondemented adults tested on EBCC revealed that three of the seven normal subjects testing in the AD range (below 25% CRs at Time 1) became demented within 2 or 3 years. A fourth "normal" subject who scored just above criterion (26% CRs) also developed dementia within 2 years of the initial testing. A fifth subject in this group died within a year of the initial testing. Thus, of eight nondemented subjects age-matched to probable AD patients who scored on EBCC in the AD range, only three were cognitively normal at the end of a 3-year period (see Figure 3). Age-matched nondemented subjects scoring above criterion remained cognitively intact during the period of the longitudinal investigation. Of the eight "normal" elderly producing 26% CRs or less, a 3-year follow up finds five (62.5%) demented or dead, and only three who were cognitively normal.

The hypothesis that patients with probable AD and DS/AD would perform more poorly than age-matched control subjects on EBCC due to cholinergic system disruption in hippocampus continues to receive support. AD neuropathology in the form of β-amyloid (βA) plaques in DS/AD cerebellum does not appear to impair Purkinje cells or cerebellar cortical function beyond the effects of normal aging. Furthermore, there are only a limited number of plaques in the AD cerebellum (and none in the cerebellum in normal aging). To investigate further the neuropathology that was involved in the disruption of EBCC

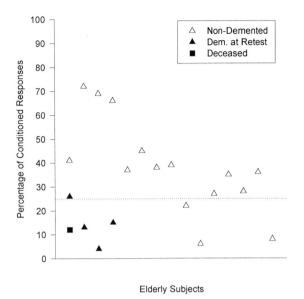

Figure 3 Percentage of conditioned responses (CRs) in one eyeblink classical conditioning (EBCC) session for 20 elderly subjects (mean age = 83) who were normal control subjects. In a longitudinal study lasting 3 years, four subjects scoring below 26% CRs became demented and a fifth subject in that range died (from Ferrante & Woodruff-Pak, 1995).

in AD and DS/AD, we evaluated whether subjects with probable AD could *ever* attain learning criterion.

In rabbits, lesions to cerebellar interpositus nucleus prevent acquisition or retention of EBCC. Rabbits with disrupted septo-hippocampal cholinergic systems condition poorly: they take about five times the normal number of trials to attain learning criterion. However, rabbits with disrupted cholinergic systems (scopolamine injections) eventually acquire CRs. Scopolamine injections in humans have a similar disruptive effect on EBCC, but human subjects with scopolamine injections eventually acquire CRs.

Probable AD patients, adults over 35 with DS/AD, and normal control subjects were tested extensively on EBCC. We tested them for five times as many trials as the normal one-session EBCC test period. It was anticipated that if these subjects were exposed to enough trials, they would eventually acquire CRs. Twelve adults with probable AD, twelve adults with DS/AD, and six nondemented elderly control subjects completed five consecutive daily sessions of EBCC in the 400-ms delay paradigm. Trials to a learning criterion of producing eight CRs in nine consecutive

trials was computed for all subjects. Within the 450 conditioning trials, the percentage of subjects attaining learning criterion was 58% of the probable AD patients, 92% of the patients with DS/AD, and 100% of the normal, elderly subjects. Given enough trials, subjects with AD or DS/AD acquire CRs, although they are severely impaired initially. All subjects eventually exceed the criterion of producing 25% CRs.

Adults with AD and DS/AD were able to produce CRs when given sufficient training. The neural substrate for EBCC was not eliminated in these subjects, although the learning mechanism was disrupted. Results support the interpretation that EBCC impairment in AD and DS/AD resulted from hippocampal cholinergic disruption. These data, along with our results that βA does not appear to damage Purkinje cells and their dendrites suggest that the disrupted hippocampus (and *not* the cerebellum) delays acquisition in AD and DS/AD beyond the impairment in normal aging.

Neuropathology in AD affects the neural circuitry involved in EBCC. Our working hypotheses is that AD disrupts the hippocampal cholinergic system, impairing the rate of acquisition of EBCC in AD patients as the rate in acquisition is impaired in rabbits and humans injected with a cholinergic muscarinic antagonist, scopolamine, or a cholinergic nicotinic antagonist, mecamylamine.

a. Summary The prediction that EBCC would be affected in AD and DS/AD beyond the effect of normal aging was based on results with the rabbit model system of EBCC. Currently, there has been success in defining a substantial portion of the essential neural circuitry underlying EBCC in rabbits. The ipsilateral cerebellum is the essential site of plasticity for learning and memory of the CR. We have demonstrated a relationship between Purkinje cell loss in cerebellum and age-related deficits in EBCC. The additional deficit seen in EBCC in AD may be caused by damage to the hippocampal cholinergic system.

4. Eyeblink Conditioning in Rabbits as a Preclinical Test for Drugs to Treat Alzheimer's Disease

Attempts are underway to ameliorate the cognitive impairment suffered by dementia patients. A number of drugs that affect the cholinergic system or other mechanisms affecting brain function are being tested for their potential as cognition enhancers. It was because of the known involvement of pyramidal cells in the CA1 region of the hippocampus in EBCC in rabbits that this paradigm appeared to be relevant for evaluation of nefiracetam. Nefiracetam promotes the release of diverse neurotransmitters such as acetylcholine (ACh), gamma amino-butyric acid (GABA), and monoamines. The long-lasting N/L-type Ca^{2+} channel currents were more than doubled by nefiracetam with no effect on the transient T-type current. Activation of the long-lasting N/L-type Ca^{2+} channel currents may be the mechanism by which nefiracetam promotes release of a number of neurotransmitters. Following oxygen and glucose deprivation, nefiracetam protected membrane dysfunction in hippocampal CA1 neurons. Because older rabbits show impaired acquisition in EBCC and delayed hippocampal responding in the CR period, and because facilitation in hippocampus can expedite acquisition, it was anticipated that nefiracetam would enhance acquisition of EBCC in older rabbits.

Nefiracetam was established in older rabbits in the 750-ms CS–US interval delay paradigm of EBCC. Rabbits (mean age of 29 months) were assigned in groups of eight to one of six dose levels. Comparing six dose levels, all dependent measures (percentage CRs, CR amplitude, and response latency) indicated significantly better conditioning in rabbits treated with 10 mg/kg nefiracetam, but this dose did not elevate motor responding or responding in the unpaired condition. Nefiracetam facilitated acquisition of EBCC in older rabbits.

Results reported here are behavioral, and we do not have evidence regarding the site of activity of nefiracetam in rabbit brains. Research on the model system of EBCC in rabbits demonstrated that the hippocampus plays a modulatory role in acquisition, and the ipsilateral cerebellum is essential for acquisition and retention. Given nefiracetam's demonstrated role in stimulating the release of ACh via the GABAergic system, it is more likely that the compound is affecting the hippocampus where cholinergic neurons are plentiful than the cerebellum, where they are much fewer. CA1 pyramidal neurons are activated during EBCC, and these cells show a 15–20% loss in old adult animals, including rabbits. Nefiracetam may ameliorate learning deficits in older rabbits by improving the function of the remaining hippocampal pyramidal cells.

If nefiracetam affects EBCC via the hippocampus (such as at the level of improving function in hippocampal pyramidal cells), injection of nefiracetam in rabbits with intact hippocampus should ameliorate EBCC, whereas injection in hippocampectomized rabbits should not. Among groups treated with nefiracetam, trials to learning criterion were significantly greater in hippocampectomized rabbits than in rabbits with intact hippocampus. Rabbits with vehicle had significantly more trials to criterion than those with nefiracetam. Hippocampectomized rabbits with nefiracetam learned more slowly than rabbits with cortical surgery and controls with intact hippocampus. These results suggest that nefiracetam may act to ameliorate EBCC in older rabbits via the hippocampus.

II. INSTRUMENTAL CONDITIONING

Instrumental conditioning refers to the type of learning in which the probability of a response is altered by a change in the consequences for that response. When a rat presses a lever and receives a food pellet, the probability that the rat will press the lever again is increased. Relatively few attempts have been made to create animal models of learning, memory, and aging using instrumental conditioning, and there is a relative paucity of human and animal research on aging and instrumental conditioning. One reason for this scarcity of research is that age is not a variable of interest to investigators whose primary research interest is instrumental conditioning. These investigators study external environmental determinants of behavior rather than intrinsic subject qualities such as age. Despite paradigmatic differences between classical and instrumental conditioning, the existing data indicate that age-related differences in instrumental performance usually parallel those found in classical conditioning.

A. Simple Acquisition and Extinction

The acquisition of an appetitively (positive) reinforced response has been shown to be markedly slower in aged rats. Similar deficits were observed with an aversive reinforcer; older rats show slower acquisition rates in comparison to young subjects. Both of these impairments have been noted in the senescence-accelerated mouse as well. The senescence-accelerated mouse is an animal model in which aging occurs more rapidly than it does in the normal mouse.

The type of instrumental conditioning for which there appears to be the largest age differences is avoidance conditioning. In this kind of learning a response is emitted that enables the organism to avoid receipt of a noxious stimulus event. Age-related deficits in avoidance conditioning have been reported by numerous investigators. Deficits in passive avoidance retention in different strains of aged mice and rats continue to be observed.

Conditional learning, which requires the subjects to learn instrumental responses to discriminative stimuli, also reveals slower acquisition rates in aged animals. In studies of appetitive reinforcement, avoidance conditioning, and discriminative instrumental conditioning, initial acquisition appears to be impaired in aged animals.

Although initial acquisition is impaired in older animals, we recently observed that older rats showed extinction rates that were comparable to young subjects when they are trained to an equivalent criterion. Moreover, after extinction of the response rate to near zero levels, older animals relearned the behavior as quickly and efficiently as young animals. Age-related learning deficits may be restricted to initial acquisition. These initial learning deficits can be alleviated by additional training.

B. Effects of Schedule of Reinforcement

The effect of reinforcement schedule, which contributes to the degree of difficulty in learning the instrumental task, has been studied extensively in aged animals. Conditioning with a variable interval schedule, wherein reinforcement is available only after a variable interval (i.e., every 20, 30, or 40 sec) has elapsed since the previous reinforcement, produces robust age-related differences in acquisition that are exacerbated by changes in environmental conditions such as distracting noise. Thus, attentional variables may contribute to these age-related differences.

Effects of a fixed interval (FI) schedule of reinforcement are less clear. Aged rats show response patterns similar to young subjects after acquisition of an instrumental response using a FI schedule. However, data were not recorded or analyzed for the initial training period, and it is unknown as to whether aged animals

showed early learning rates differing from those of younger subjects. Yet, this is consistent with the view that early learning may be affected by age, whereas later performance is not.

Differential reinforcement of low rates of responding (DRL) reveals a profound learning deficit in rabbits with lesions to the hippocampus. Because the hippocampal formation is a primary site of age-related impairment, it is predicted that aged rats would display significant impairment during acquisition under DRL. As in training with continuous reinforcement, this initial deficit was overcome with additional training.

C. Age-Related Effects on Retention

The passive avoidance task reinforces rodents for remaining on one side of a chamber. The active nature of rodents results in their inclination to explore the entire chamber. As soon as they cross to the opposite side of the chamber, they receive a paw shock. To avoid shock to the paws, the rodent must remain on one side of the chamber and avoid exploring the other side. Retention of this passive response over a 4-hour period shows moderate age differences, and retention over a 24-hour period shows robust age differences. No age differences in retention were observed after 1 hour.

The performance of C57 mice on retention of passive avoidance was compared to performance on a number of other tasks. The performance of the aged mice reflected an impairment in the ability to remember the aversive event for sufficiently long periods of time. Certain operational similarities exist between the passive avoidance retention deficit and impairment of recent memory observed in aged human and nonhuman primates. The event to be remembered is brief and discrete, there is little or no practice or rehearsal, and retention decays rapidly, usually within hours after the event.

To summarize the results on instrumental conditioning in aging animals, it appears that there is a consistent deficit that is restricted to the early association of the response with its consequence, but there is less of a difference once a response is established to a criterion level. This may be analogous to small or nonexistent differences in memory between young and older humans once initial learning is equated.

These observations indicate that only under certain

circumstances are age-related effects on learning significant. These effects may be overcome by additional training, and they appear to reflect quantitative rather than qualitative differences. In many instances there is intact retention and reacquisition of previously learned behaviors by aged animals. This result suggests that recent experience involving activation of the neurological elements contributing to learning and memory may ameliorate age-related differences in learning. This concept is supported by recent findings that prior long-term training in an instrumental conditioning task improves performance of aged rats in subsequent spatial learning and attenuates decrement in synaptic function that is observed in untrained aged rats. Thus, it is possible that much of the impairment observed in aged subjects reflects the effects of use or disuse of significant neurobiological substrates.

BIBLIOGRAPHY

Daum, I., Channon, S., Polkey, C. E., & Gray, J. A. (1991). Classical conditioning after temporal lobe lesions in man: Impairment in conditional discrimination. *Behavioral Neuroscience, 105,* 396–408.

Ferrante, L. S., & Woodruff-Pak, D. S. (1995). Longitudinal investigation of eyeblink classical conditioning in the old-old. *Journal of Gerontology: Psychological Science, 50B,* P42–P50.

Kowalska, M., & Disterhoft, J. F. (1994). Relation of nimodipine dose and serum concentration to learning enhancement in aging rabbits. *Experimental Neurology, 127,* 159–166.

Powell, D. A., Buchanan, S. L., & Hernandez, L. L. (1991). Classical (Pavlovian) conditioning models of age-related changes in associative learning and their neurobiological substrates. *Progress in Neurobiology, 36,* 201–228.

Solomon, P. R., Pomerleau, D., Bennett, L., James, J., & Morse, D. L. (1989). Acquisition of the classically conditioned eyeblink response in humans over the lifespan. *Psychology and Aging, 4,* 34–41.

Topka, H., Valls-Sole, J., Massaquoi, S. G., & Hallett, M. (1993). Deficit in classical conditioning in patients with cerebellar degeneration. *Brain, 116,* 961–969.

Woodruff-Pak, D. S. (1990). Mammalian models of learning, memory, and aging. In J. E. Birren & K. W. Schaie (Eds.), *Handbook of the psychology of aging* (3rd ed., pp. 235–257). San Diego: Academic Press.

Woodruff-Pak, D. S., Finkbiner, R. G., & Sasse, D. K. (1990). Eyeblink conditioning discriminates Alzheimer's patients from non-demented aged. *NeuroReport, 1,* 45–48.

Woodruff-Pak, D. S., & Li, Y.-T. (1994). Nefiracetam (DM-9384): Effect on eyeblink classical conditioning in older rabbits. *Psychopharmacology, 114,* 200–208.

Woodruff-Pak, D. S., Logan, C. G., & Thompson, R. F. (1990). Neurobiological substrates of classical conditioning across the life span. In A. Diamond (Ed.), *The development and neural bases of higher cognitive functions* (pp. 150–178). New York: New York Academy of Sciences Press.

Consumer Behavior

Catherine A. Cole and Nadine N. Castellano

University of Iowa

Baby Boom Generation People who were born between 1946 and 1964 (about 76 million people).
Decision Heuristics Shortcuts, rules of thumb, or simplifying strategies for making decisions.
Marketing Mix Variables that a marketing manager can control; usually includes product, price, promotion, and distribution.
Market Segment Group of consumers with similar needs and wants.
Target Market A specific market segment or segments that an organization attempts to reach with a marketing mix designed for the needs and wants of the segment(s).
Working Memory Where information is stored temporarily and is encoded for transmission into long-term storage.

CONSUMER BEHAVIOR encompasses mental and physical activities that consumers engage in when searching for, evaluating, purchasing, and using products and services. Consumers give up their scarce resources (including money, time, and effort) to receive items of value in market exchanges. For example, researchers studying how consumers buy long-term care insurance might investigate questions such as (a) what kinds of consumers buy this type of insurance (e.g., income, age, gender, lifestyle, etc.); (b) where they buy it (e.g., from an agent that they know vs. from an 800 number on a television program); (c) when they buy it (e.g., prompted by a critical event such as the necessity of putting a parent in long-term care); (d) how they buy it (e.g., through the workplace vs. through independent agents vs. after reading a consumer magazine); (e) why they buy it (e.g., fear of depleting life savings vs. desire for excellent care in old age, etc); and (f) what happens after they buy it (e.g., thoughts concerning the purchase).

I. MOTIVATION FOR STUDYING OLDER ADULTS' CONSUMER BEHAVIOR

Until recently, business and marketing researchers virtually ignored the older market. Perhaps this neglect arose from inaccurate stereotypes about elderly consumers. However, more and more businesses, governmental agencies, and researchers recognize the importance of the rapidly growing older market. The statistics paint an impressive picture. Today, people over the age of 65 head over 18 million households. By the year 2010, one out of every seven Americans will be 65 or older. The over 55 age group is growing twice as fast as the population as a whole. In addition, the mature market contains a very attractive subsegment of affluent older adults who have health, income, and free time. In this article, we first discuss why businesses, policy makers, and researchers are interested in the growing older market. Then, we introduce the reader to the consumer behavior literature, and finally discuss how the aging process affects marketplace behavior.

A. Business

Not only is the size of the elderly population increasing, but the financial well-being of many people in this age group is well-off. For example, seven out of ten older adults own their own home; furthermore, 85% of these homeowners have no mortgages. Older adults control over 50% of the nation's discretionary income and 77% of all financial assets. The elderly segment accounts for over $60 billion in annual consumer spending in the United States. Moreover, this segment is an active one. For example, fewer than one out of twenty people over 65 live in institutions. Census data also suggest that over half the people 65 and over report no activity limitation. In summary, elderly consumers comprise a segment that is generally substantial, identifiable, and accessible—key requirements for targeting segments.

Because this segment is so attractive to business, it is essential to understand how marketing to this group is similar to and different from marketing to younger adults. For example, like the younger market, the older market is sufficiently heterogeneous to warrant being broken down into segments. Some suggest segmenting the mature market on the basis of age: 55–64, 65–74, 75–84, and over 85. Others suggest incorporating income, education, personality, and lifestyle variables into mature market segmentation schemes.

Businesses try to tailor all aspects of the marketing mix to the needs and interests of each market segment within the older market. We are seeing an explosion of new products, as well as repositionings of current products, all designed for the older adult. Accompanying these product offerings are specially designed advertising campaigns, price strategies, and distribution plans. There is considerable debate regarding how business can best take advantage of the marketing opportunities proffered by this segment.

B. Public Policy

From a public policy perspective, two issues emerge as the size of the older market increases. First, popular press and government conferences suggest that older adults are frequently the target for unscrupulous business activities. As a result, public policy makers need to identify appropriate ways to curb the most flagrant business deceptions. Second, public policy makers need to consider whether public information campaigns are effectively reaching the older market.

Consider first the problem of unscrupulous business practices targeted to elderly consumers. Current data suggest that about 34% of the victims of telemarketing fraud are elderly. White House Conferences on Aging have also identified difficulties elderly people encounter when applying for credit, purchasing food, buying insurance or investments, using prescription drugs, and selecting medical services.

Two remedies seem appropriate. First, consumer education efforts might raise the level of knowledge about consumer rights in the older market. An American Association of Retired Persons Survey suggests that the problems older Americans face from dishonest businesses are compounded by older adults' lack of knowledge about their rights as consumers. For example, older consumers (those over the age of 65) are much less likely than consumers under the age of 65 to know that one has several days to cancel purchases made from door-to-door salespeople (36% vs. 53%) and that consumers are not able to cancel purchases made by credit card over the telephone (19% vs. 28%).

Another remedy might entail passing legislation to restrict the more unscrupulous business practices. For example, current legislation is being considered to regulate telemarketing practices. The legislation would restrict activities of telemarketers. Specifically, it would ban some deceptive sales practices and would protect consumers from sales calls early in the morning or late at night.

As mentioned earlier, an additional public policy issue concerns designing effective public information campaigns that reach consumers of all ages. As an example, consider the private, federal, and state agencies attempting to educate Americans regarding good health practices. These agencies use the mass media as an integral part of most health promotion campaigns. Some agencies are beginning to use paid advertising as well as public service announcements in their media efforts.

Evidence indicates the presence of public health campaigns targeted to older Americans. In addition, survey research shows that older adults are interested in maintaining or improving their health. However, many older adults have limited knowledge regarding the relationship between certain lifestyle behaviors and disease incidence. The significance of this low degree of knowledge becomes apparent when one considers the estimate that 40–70% of premature deaths can be prevented through better control of behavioral risk factors. Furthermore, research indicates that much of the health promotion efforts of the 1980s have had little impact on the elderly audience. Specifically, government-sponsored surveys suggest that consumers do not understand why or how controllable risks such as diet, exercise, and weight control are important to disease prevention. Thus, there is a need for additional research identifying how to effectively communicate health and other public information to older consumers.

Both business practitioners and public policy makers, then, are vitally interested in reaching older consumers. Consumer behavior researchers offer insight into how to achieve this through two main avenues: adapting theories of aging from other fields to the marketplace and adapting marketing theories and models (such as consumer decision making) to the elderly. These goals present a wide variety of research areas that researchers have only begun to study.

C. Theoretical

Interest in developing theories and models to explain age differences in consumer behavior is fairly recent. Initially, researchers were content to describe differences between the older and younger markets. However, practitioners would like to predict the behavior of future cohorts of elderly consumers. For example, a practitioner might ask the following question: As the baby boom generation reaches retirement age, will their general consumption patterns change to be similar to the current over 65 market or will their general consumption patterns remain unique to their cohort? Answering this question is difficult, but developing theories about how aging affects consumers makes finding the answer easier.

Social aging theories, as applied in marketing, involve understanding how society assigns people to consumer roles and positions across the life span. These consumer roles and positions change as a person ages because society has perceptions about the capabilities of people at various ages or life stages.

Thus, when an individual retires, he or she may adopt society's expectations of appropriate consumer behavior for someone in this life stage. According to Activity Theory (a social aging theory), entering retirement represents a major transition point when people exit from many social relationships. As a result, older consumers must find compensatory activities to maintain their psychological and social well-being. Businesses might design services that meet these changing needs. For example, travel agencies might design group trips for older adults that involve travel to exotic places and opportunities to meet new people. Disengagement theory (another social aging theory) posits that as people age they voluntarily withdraw from social ties and retreat into isolation. One possible effect of this withdrawal is a greater use of the mass media by elderly consumers to help counteract isolation. Thus, radio and television networks might develop programming to service this market segment. These and other social aging theories are useful because they force marketers to think about how market needs change as people move through different stages in the life course.

An important theoretical emphasis with respect to the elderly consumer has been on cognitive theories of aging. Cognition entails the mental processes that transform, reduce, elaborate, sort, and retrieve sensory input. One mechanism affecting cognition is working memory capacity. The capacity of working memory is limited in all adults, but the elderly may experience either a decline in the capacity or a slowing down of processing speed. Thus, older adults are not able to store as much information or process as much information as younger adults are. Specifically, strategies for encoding information from sources such as advertisements and product labels may take much longer for the elderly to execute than for younger adults. As we describe later in this article, however, there are specific strategies and devices that can assist the elderly consumer in adapting to cognitive change. [See MEMORY.]

Theories developed to understand aging processes help us understand consumer behavior of all age groups. For example, working memory limitations may affect younger consumers when they face tasks involving very demanding memory loads and fast rates of presentation—as is the case with telephone sales presentations. Although young adults use processing strategies efficiently, at some point, memory

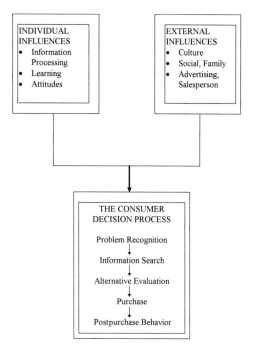

Figure 1   A general model of consumer behavior.

loads and time pressure may combine to interrupt the routines that adults typically use.

II. A GENERAL MODEL OF CONSUMER DECISION MAKING

Before we describe older adults' consumer behavior, it is useful to discuss how consumers of all ages make decisions (Figure 1). The purchase decision process generally consists of five stages: problem recognition, information search, alternative evaluation, purchase decision, and postpurchase behavior. Both individual characteristics, such as personality and information-processing ability, and external events, such as cultural values and exposure to advertising, affect this process. This process is most often applied to actual purchases of products or services, but applies to the adoption of ideas as well. Although the model applies to a variety of products and services it does not apply to every consumer for every purchase. Sometimes, especially under circumstances when the consumer

does not care much about the decision, the consumer may move straight from information search to purchase and postpone evaluation until after consumption. [*See* Decision Making and Everyday Problem Solving.]

A. Problem Recognition

Problem recognition is the first step toward making an actual purchase. Consumers recognize that their ideal situations differ from their actual situations. It can be as simple as noticing that the coffee is running low, or as complicated as realizing that life insurance is needed. Occasionally, marketing itself can trigger problem recognition, such as when a salesperson points out the inferiority of a computer diskette drive to a CD-ROM drive.

B. Information Search

After recognizing that problems exist, consumers begin to search for information about solutions to their problems. The search can be either internal, where consumers scan their memory for previous experiences, or external, where consumers consult a wide variety of informational sources, including advertising. Some would argue that marketing has the greatest capacity to affect consumer behavior during the information search stage.

A great number of factors affect how consumers search. For example, as perceived time pressure increases, the search decreases. Knowledge of the product category may limit search by allowing responses to become routine, as in the case where a family purchases only one cereal because they know that it meets all their requirements. On the other hand, knowledge may lead to an increased amount of search by allowing consumers to have a richer understanding of what they are evaluating. For example, computer experts will read more and speak longer with a salesperson because they understand bytes, ram, and processors. Several consumer behavior researchers have found that prior knowledge is the single most important factor affecting external search. From a consumer's perspective, the perceived payoff from searching affects how much effort the consumer is willing to expend in search. If the closest Infiniti dealer is 100 miles away, consumers may not invest in the effort to drive there if they feel that acceptable alternatives are closer. The outcome of this stage is to suggest criteria for consumers to use during purchase as well as brand names that satisfy these criteria.

C. Alternative Evaluation

Many studies show that consumers consider only a few alternatives when making a purchase. In this stage, consumers evaluate the brands according to the criteria established. A well-known model of how this process occurs is the multiweight–multiattribute method. This model suggests that consumers ascertain the features of the product that are important. They then weigh the features or attributes according to their relative importance. Then consumers evaluate each brand on these features, giving total "scores" to each brand. Consumers, however, will not always be certain about the weights to assign the attributes nor will they always be certain about the values to assign to an alternative on an attribute. One group of researchers found that as uncertainty increases, the willingness of consumers to pay for attributes that bring pleasure increases, even if the attributes are not needed.

In the multiattribute model, a compensatory type model, performance on one attribute can "compensate" for performance on another attribute. Other evaluation models are noncompensatory; performance on one attribute cannot compensate for lack of performance on another. For example, a consumer who is buying a car may find that one brand has excellent gas mileage, which compensates for its less than ideal comfort. On the other hand, air bags may be one attribute that the consumer must have; no matter how good the gas mileage, the car will only be considered if it has air bags.

As one can see, consumers do not always conform to specific models. Often consumers use heuristics to solve their purchase problems. One heuristic might be, "Select the first cereal that is low in sugar and high in fiber." Such a simplifying rule makes the grocery shopping task easier, but means that the consumer does not consider all the available alternatives. In another heuristic, consumers may use reference points to compare various decision alternatives. When consumers see sale prices on items such as furniture, they compare the sale price to the full retail price or reference point. Thus, a furniture retailer when trying to predict how consumers will react to a price reduction must consider both the sale price and the full price (reference point).

D. Purchase

Once consumers evaluate alternatives, they make a purchase decision. The consumer might make the decision before actually purchasing the item. For example, before grocery shopping, the consumer might draw up a grocery list with brand names listed. Alternatively, the consumer might decide on a destination, such as a mall, and then select a branded item once at the mall.

E. Postpurchase Behavior

Once consumers purchase products, they must decide how satisfied they are with their purchases. Often this involves anxiety or stress about the decision, called cognitive dissonance. Because this stress feels uncomfortable, consumers will often take steps to alleviate their dissonance. At this point, consumers may enter the search stage again, looking for information that confirms that they made the right decision. Many advertisers utilize advertising to help alleviate this cognitive dissonance.

III. AGE DIFFERENCES IN CONSUMER DECISION MAKING: EMPIRICAL EVIDENCE AND EXPLANATIONS

Although consumer decision-making research spans a broad range of topics, researchers studying age differences in consumer decision making have tended to focus on just a few topic areas. In this section, and in Table I, we review the empirical evidence for age differences in search for information and alternative evaluation. Generally, the existing literature suggests that elderly consumers are different from younger consumers in important ways. However, it is important to keep in mind that the older market is diverse and that different segments show these characteristics to differing degrees. Furthermore, even within

Table I Research on Age Differences in Consumer Decision Making

Topic	Method	Major findings[a]
Search for information		
• Furse, Punj, & Stewart (1984). *Journal of Consumer Research, 10*(March), 417–431.	Survey	OAs search less than YAs.
• Schaninger & Sciglimpaglia (1981). *Journal of Consumer Research, 8,* 208–216.	Experiment	OAs consider fewer attributes and alternatives than YAs.
• Cole & Balasubramanian (1993). *Journal of Consumer Research, 10,* 417–431.	Experiment / Field study	OAs search as much as YAs when task is familiar; OAs search less when task is unfamiliar.
• Cole & Houston (1987). *Journal of Marketing Research, 24,* 55–63.	Experiment	OAs learn less than YAs from TV and print advertising.
• Gaeth & Heath (1987). *Journal of Consumer Research, 14,* 43–54.	Experiment	OAs less able than YAs to process advertising claims.
• Gorn, Goldberg, Chattopadhyay, & Litvack (1991). *Journal of Advertising Research, 31,* 23–32.	Experiment	OAs recall less from commercials with background music than from commercials without background music.
• Stephens (1982). *Journal of Advertising, 11,* 48–55.	Experiment	OAs recall less than YAs from TV commercials.
Alternative Evaluation		
• Gilly & Zeithaml (1985). *Journal of Consumer Research, 12,* 353–357.	Survey	OAs as likely as YAs to adopt a new technology when the relative advantage is clear.
• Wilkes (1992). *Journal of Consumer Research, 19,* 292–301.	Survey	Nonchronological age influences fashion interest and participation in activities.
• Tepper (1994). *Journal of Consumer Research, 20,* 503–519.	Experiment	Consumers, 50–54, least likely to use senior discounts; consumers, 65+, most likely.

[a]OAs, older adults; YAs, young adults.

a segment, some consumer tasks may exacerbate or minimize these differences.

A. Search for Information

In this section, we first address the problem of general search behavior; next we turn to advertising, a major influence on the information consumers acquire about products and services. Older consumers appear to search less for information than younger consumers prior to making a purchase decision. For example, a survey of automobile buyers found that older consumers searched less but were more satisfied with their previous choices, than other clusters of customers. Another study found that when selecting unfamiliar brands, older homemakers considered fewer attributes and alternatives than younger homemakers.

One recent study investigated age differences in search behavior in a supermarket setting and in a computer laboratory. Two observers watched consumers buying cereal in a supermarket. Shoppers inspected very few packages before making a choice, so no age differences emerged in how much people searched. However, when an observer intercepted shoppers and asked them to purchase a cereal that met certain nutritional criteria, younger adults engaged in more search than older adults, who did not change how much they searched. In the laboratory, using a computerized search program, older adults searched less for information about unfamiliar cereals than younger adults.

What explains this contradictory pattern of results? Whether or not age differences in search emerge may depend on task characteristics. Age differences in search may not emerge when consumers perform such simple, routine tasks as grocery shopping because no one searches very much in such situations. When engaging in familiar, but complex tasks, such as buying a new car, older adults may search less than younger adults because they use their years of shopping experience to design efficient search strategies. However, elderly consumers may restrict search when given a new search problem because of scarce information-processing resources. For example, older consumers with diminished working memory capacity may not easily store information about alternatives in memory. As a result, they may not search for as much information as younger consumers.

This proposition is consistent with results from intelligence testing research. In order to understand developmental patterns, a number of researchers have distinguished between two types of intelligence: fluid and crystallized. Fluid intelligence, reflected in tests of figural relations, memory span, and most processes involved in acquiring new information, decreases with increased age in adulthood. Crystallized intelligence, reflected in tests such as vocabulary, general information, comprehension, arithmetic, and reasoning with familiar material, is stable across adulthood. Given that crystallized intelligence represents an individual's knowledge base, it appears that the aging process does not affect the knowledge base of adults. Instead, age differences probably arise from older adults' difficulties in acquiring and using new information.

General evidence suggests that listening to the radio and watching TV are important as sources of information for older adults. Like younger adults, older adults may acquire information about products and services through the mass media. A number of studies in the marketing literature have shown that recall and comprehension of advertising claims are lower in older consumer groups than in younger consumer groups. However, researchers have shown that specific task conditions that are under the control of the manager can affect the size of these age differences. The studied task conditions, which are as varied as the commercials themselves, include the media vehicle used, whether or not speech is compressed, presence of background noise, and whether or not claims are explicitly stated.

Although gerontologists have focused on recall and comprehension of spoken and written text, marketing researchers have focused on unintentional processing of advertising messages that are embedded in programming. One recent study showed that, although the elderly consistently performed worse on all measures of learning about advertising, the size of age

differences was greater for television than for print. Older adults had problems deeply processing information in print media. Younger adults recalled more in the television medium than they recalled in the print medium. However, older adults did not realize the learning benefits of television. The pattern of results suggests that older adults encounter difficulties encoding information.

In another interesting study, an advertising researcher asked whether the use of compressed speech in advertising affects age differences in recall. Three different age groups of consumers—young (20–29), middle aged (40–49), and older (60–69)—watched five television commercials for five food products. Some subjects saw normal commercials, whereas others saw the same 30-sec commercials that had been compressed into 25 sec. Two days later the participants had to recall the commercials, products, and brands that they had seen. As expected, older adults recalled less than younger adults, but time compression did not affect either group's ability to remember.

Advertising researchers have also tested whether background music in television commercials may impair learning among elderly consumers. It generally appears that recall of product claims is lower for elderly consumers exposed to the commercial with background music than for elderly consumers exposed to the same commercial without background music. Apparently, background music distracts the elderly listener from attending to and processing relevant information. An interesting, but unanswered question is whether the distracting nature of music differentially affects elderly consumers when compared to younger consumers.

Another advertising issue is whether or not there are age differences in ability to judge truthfulness of claims in print advertising. Suppose an ad says "Brimstone tires will increase the safety of your winter driving." Viewers might be asked if the following statement *has* to be true (Brimstone tires will increase the safety of your winter driving). This procedure represents a test of a direct assertion. However, suppose the ad says "Have a safe winter. Drive on Brimstone tires." Viewers could be asked whether the statement (Brimstone tires will increase the safety of your winter driving) *has* to be true. This procedure represents a test of a pragmatic implication. Apparently, when consumers must rely on their memory about the claims there are no age differences in the consumers' abilities to judge statement truthfulness. However, young adults are more likely than older adults to judge correctly the truthfulness of implied claims when the advertisements are available during assessment.

In summary, the presence of age differences in learning and comprehension is not surprising because most of the consumer behavior research is based on extensive work in gerontology. This prior gerontological research demonstrates that age differences frequently emerge when subjects process spoken or written text. Generally, changes in working memory are thought to cause the differences. The marketing literature has contributed to the knowledge by showing that learning and comprehension differences found in laboratory research emerge in real-world settings where stimuli are ordinary commercials. More research is needed on how specific characteristics of advertising stimuli affect age differences and how to measure and test advertising effects on different age groups. [See LEARNING.]

B. Alternative Evaluation

A large body of consumer research shows that a disparate range of individual and external variables influence consumers' evaluations of products. For many years, marketing practitioners thought older adults lagged behind younger adults in adopting new products and services. However, recent data suggest that this belief may be a negative stereotype, rather than a reality.

One recent survey asked younger and older consumers about their acceptance and adoption of several new products. These products included scanner-equipped grocery stores, electronic funds transfer, automated teller machines, and custom telephone calling services. Except for custom telephone calling services, older adults were as knowledgeable about these technologies as younger consumers. Generally, though, a smaller percentage of elderly consumers had tried and adopted these technologies than younger consumers. The one exception was electronic funds transfer services, which the elderly consumers had tried and adopted in greater numbers than younger consumers. Apparently, like other consumers, elderly consumers will purchase product innovations when the product possesses a clear benefit and meets a specific need.

Brand choice research investigates how consumers evaluate and select a brand within a product class.

Work on self-image–product image congruity suggests that consumers will purchase a brand or product with an image that is congruent with their self-image.

One interesting measure of an older consumer's self-image is cognitive age (see Table II). This measure has four dimensions: feel-age (how old a person feels), look-age (how old a person feels she or he looks), do-age (how involved a person is in doing things she or he perceives are favored by a certain age group), and interest-age (how similar a person perceives his or her interests are to members of a certain age group). Cognitive age, not chronological age, affects purchase of personal care products, fashion merchandise, entertainment, and cultural activities.

Discounts from list price, another attribute affecting consumer brand choice, has also been studied in the context of age differences. One common business practice, designed to draw in the older market, offers older consumers a senior citizen's price discount. Do consumers evaluate retailers and service providers who provide such discounts favorably? Some self-report studies indicate that elderly adults say they favor retailers that offer senior citizen discounts, but other surveys show that many older adults will not participate in such programs.

Recently, a consumer behavior researcher conducted a focus group and an experiment in order to determine whether or not older adults respond favorably to age-related discounts. Consumers in the focus group indicated that they thought senior citizen discounts had negative connotations. Focus group participants also raised concerns over how others might evaluate and react to them if they used the discount. In the experiment, consumers' reactions to a 10% discount were studied. Consumers learned that this discount was either a senior citizen discount offered to customers over a certain age or a privileged customer discount offered to special customers. Consumers' reactions to the discount varied by age. Respondents in the youngest age group (50–54) were the least likely to use a discount promoted with an age segmentation cue, and adults over the age of 65 were willing to use either of the 10% discounts. The middle age group (55–64) was willing to use the senior discount even though they believed that others would not give senior citizen discount users much respect.

This research resolves prior inconsistencies about consumers' reactions to senior citizens' discounts. Apparently, mature consumers (those in their 50s) are

Table II Instruction and Format for the Self-Perceived Age Measure[a]

Most people seem to have other "ages" besides their official or "date of birth" age. The questions that follow have been developed to find out about your "unofficial" age. Please specify which age group you FEEL you really belong to: twenties, thirties, forties, fifties, sixties, seventies, or eighties.

I feel as though I am in my—	20s	30s	40s	50s	60s	70s	80s
I look as though I am in my—	20s	30s	40s	50s	60s	70s	80s
I do most things as though I were in my—	20s	30s	40s	50s	60s	70s	80s
My interests are mostly those of a person in her—	20s	30s	40s	50s	60s	70s	80s

[a]From Barak & Schiffman (1981). Cognitive age: A nonchronological age variable. In K. Monroe, (Ed.), *Advances in consumer rersearch* (Vol. 8, pp. 602–608). Ann Arbor: Association for Consumer Research.

reluctant to accept the label of "senior citizen," but by the time consumers reach retirement age, they are willing to accept the label.

In summary, a host of unresolved questions center around the attribute weights and decision rules that adults of all ages use when evaluating alternatives. Do consumers use the same attributes, the same decision weights, and the same decision rules when solving unfamiliar problems like new product adoptions decisions? Consumers facing such problems may have to select a decision strategy by evaluating the costs and benefits of using known strategies. Such construction processes may differ across age groups because older consumers, with fewer cognitive resources than younger consumers, may perceive higher cognitive costs for certain strategies than younger consumers.

In contrast to new product decisions, brand choice decisions are often routine low-involvement decisions. Here, all consumers may use similar well-practiced heuristics. Both the congruence of the brand image with the consumer's self-image and the consumer's past experience may affect brand choice. Future research might examine how the older consumer's considerable knowledge and experience moderates any age differences in judgment and choice processes.

IV. IMPROVING CONSUMER DECISION MAKING

We have described the decision-making process and how elderly adults differ from younger adults with respect to this process. Now we look at intervention programs designed to improve consumer decision making. Specifically, we consider decision aids, training programs, and modified stimuli.

A. Improving Use of Information through Decision Aids

A series of studies have investigated how age differences in selective attention might affect older adult's ability to use nutritional information contained on product labels. Literature from gerontology and psychology suggests that older adults are more susceptible to interference from the irrelevant components of a stimulus (or other environmental noise) than are younger adults. In the experiments, subjects had to select a cereal that met certain criteria. Some subjects learned to circle the relevant information on the nutritional label with a red pen before they made a decision. The decision aid, then, was to highlight the relevant information. Both older and younger adults benefited from the perception aid. However, older consumers remained less able to make good nutritional choices than younger consumers even after being encouraged to focus on the relevant information. In a follow-up experiment, the investigators boxed the relevant information and placed it in a separate location on the label. This time subjects with moderate, but not severe, disembedding deficiencies were helped. (A disembedding deficiency occurs when people are unable to separate relevant from irrelevant information.) People without this deficiency (field-independent subjects) gained little from the aid. Given that the stated aim of nutritional labeling laws is to make nutritional information easy for all consumers to use, this study suggests that such information should be placed in the same spot on all labels.

A different group of investigators tried to aid the use of nutritional information by encouraging older and younger adults to write information down as they acquired it from the computer. Using this decision aid, age differences in search intensity were greatly diminished.

Taken together, these two studies suggest that decision aids may successfully improve consumer decision making. Circling or writing down important information may especially help the elderly consumer focus on relevant information. Thus, in an environment where there is information overload, simple decision aids may help.

B. Facilitating Learning of Advertising Information through Campaign Format

Advertisers have long been concerned with ways of presenting information to all age groups that are easily understood and recalled. By changing specific aspects of a television commercial format, advertisers can alter message comprehension and recall. Quite a bit is known about message format effects on younger audiences. As an illustration, we know that simply varying the execution of an ad increases the amount of information recalled as compared to repeating the same ad. For example, stating a product claim once in a business setting and again in a home setting is better than repeating the product claim twice in a business setting.

Although few investigators in marketing have looked at the question of whether message appeal affects age differences in message comprehension and recall, gerontologists have studied age differences in recall of both expository and narrative texts. They find that narrative texts produce higher recall and smaller age differences than expository texts. Researchers suggest that narrative structure may compensate at least partially for memory limitations in older adults by guiding and constraining text processes at encoding and retrieval. Thus, in a current project, one of the authors is investigating whether certain message formats minimize age differences in recall and comprehension.

By increasing message repetitions, advertisers can increase message comprehension and recall in all audiences. Current research is studying the effects of increasing radio commercial repetitions from one to three to eight on recall and comprehension. Age differences in recall and recall-based comprehension measures emerge at all repetition levels, but both age groups benefit from increasing repetitions.

C. Improving Decision Making through Training

Two investigators have developed an interactive training program to reduce susceptibility to misleading advertising without increasing consumer suspicion of advertising claims. They found that the training (a) reduced susceptibility to misleading statements in both age groups; (b) equated misleadingness between older trained adults and younger untrained adults; and (c) reduced the younger adult's ability to discriminate between nonmisleading and potentially misleading claims.

D. Improving Decision Making

In summary, efforts to eliminate age differences with decision aids have not been entirely successful in equating older adults' performance with that of younger adults. Instead, training, stimulus redesign, and decision aids often help all age groups.

To develop a decision aid that differentially benefits the older consumer, consumer researchers must first closely analyze the consumer's task. They then need to identify the source of age differences in task performance. For example, do age differences emerge at the information acquisition stage or at the alternative evaluation stage? Furthermore, the consumer behavior researcher needs a model about why these age differences emerge. Perhaps age differences at the information acquisition stage arise because of working memory differences. Once researchers understand the source of age differences, they can design effective aids.

However, the consumer behavior researcher needs to evaluate the consequences of "aiding" decision making. For example, when researchers trained subjects to discriminate between directly asserted and implied claims, they worried about increasing younger

Table III Research Questions

Topic	Research question
Market segmentation	• What dimensions should be used to segment the older market? • How stable will emerging segments be across time?
Promotion	• How can advertising campaigns be designed to maximize learning and comprehension in all age groups? • How can advertising campaigns be designed to minimize chances of offending consumers of diverse ages? • Are there age differences in attitudes toward different message appeals? • Does consumer self-confidence mediate deceptive advertising effects? Are older adults less self-confident than younger adults?
Pricing	• Will younger cohorts show reluctance to use senior citizen discounts as they age?
Product	• How can package information be designed so that it is easy for all age groups to use it? • How can instructions for product use be designed so that it is easy for all age groups to comprehend them?
Problem recognition	• Do elderly adults rely more heavily on externally motivated problem recognition than younger adults?
Alternative evaluation	• Are there age differences in methods of evaluating alternatives? In attribute weights? In uncertainty evaluation? • Are there age differences in heuristics used?
Decision aids	• When do decision aids improve decision making of older consumers?

subjects' skepticism of advertising beyond realistic levels. Similarly, an advertiser targeting older adults may increase learning in this audience by increasing the number of message repetitions. However, if younger adults are also part of the target market, increased message repetitions may irritate and alienate these consumers.

In addition, the consumer behavior researcher needs to think about whether the aid is managerially relevant. For example, two researchers suggested that consumers should highlight relevant information before making a decision. However, it is really not realistic to recommend that consumers take pens into the supermarket to highlight relevant information on product packages. Retailers would clearly object to consumers' putting marked packages back on the shelf.

VI. FUTURE RESEARCH DIRECTIONS AND CONCLUDING COMMENTS

Over the life course, consumers build up a repertoire of strategies to solve diverse consumption problems. These problems include routine tasks such as buying cereal at the grocery store and complex tasks such as buying long-term care insurance. Both the consumption problems and the strategies people use to solve the problems evolve over time to reflect a person's changing life experiences and abilities. Decision aids, training, and modified marketing stimuli can make it easier for consumers to use different strategies by reducing the cognitive effort required to execute a particular strategy.

There are a number of unanswered questions about how older consumers adapt their decision-making strategies to changing cognitive abilities, social roles, and to task and context demands (See Table III). Preliminary evidence suggests that older consumers are likely to run into difficulties, because of changed cognitive abilities, in new situations with new products or services. Older adults may, for example, encounter difficulties learning new information through advertising; similarly, they may run into problems using new product information presented on a nutritional label. In new situations, older consumers may limit search for information, rely on previously learned decision strategies, and resist innovations until the benefits are clear.

Because there is considerable heterogeneity in the over 65 market, it is important to bear in mind that age-related changes in cognitive ability are not the same for everyone and in fact may not occur for everyone. An individual's health history and lifestyle may attenuate the timing and size of changes. Much of the consumer behavior literature points out memory deficiencies in older adults in comparison with younger adults. However, the magnitude of memory deficits appears to vary with task conditions and how information is placed into or recovered from memory.

Studying the consumer behavior of older Americans has never been more important than it is now. With the impending maturity of the baby boom generation, the size of the elderly consumer market is a force that businesses, public policy makers, and academic researchers can no longer ignore. The older consumer behaves in ways that are inherently different than the ways of a younger consumers. We have briefly discussed many of these differences in this article. Marketing strategies aimed at affecting older consumers' behavior must then be formulated specifically for the older market.

BIBLIOGRAPHY

American Association of Retired Persons. (1990) *A report on the survey of older consumer behavior.* Washington, DC: Consumer Affairs, American Association of Retired Persons, 1909 K Street NW, Washington, DC 20049.

Cole, C. A., & Balasubramanian, S. K. (1993). Age differences in consumers' search for information: Public policy implications. *Journal of Consumer Research, 20*(June), 157–169.

Cole, C. A., & Gaeth, G. J. (1990). Cognitive and age-related differences in the ability to use nutritional information in a complex environment. *Journal of Marketing Research, 17*(May), 175–184.

Gaeth, G. J., & Heath, T. (1987). The cognitive processing of misleading advertising in young and old adults. *Journal of Consumer Research, 14*(June), 43–54.

John, D. R., & Cole, C. A. (1986). Age differences in information processing: Understanding deficits in young and elderly consumers. *Journal of Consumer Research, 13*(December), 297–315.

Moschis, G. (1992). *Marketing to older consumers.* Westport CT: Quorum Books.

Payne, J. W., Bettman, J. R., & Johnson, E. J. (1993). *The adaptive decision maker.* Cambridge, UK: Press Syndicate of the University of Cambridge.

Tepper, K. (1994). The role of labeling processes in elderly consumers' response to age segmentation cues. *Journal of Consumer Research, 20*(March), 503–519.

Creativity

Dean Keith Simonton

University of California at Davis

Career Age   The number of years a creative individual has been active in a given domain (as contrasted with chronological age).

Cumulative Advantage   The phenomenon where creators who are initially successful gain advantages that help them become even more successful relative to those who are less successful at the outset.

Divergent Thinking   The mental capacity for generating numerous, varied, or original responses to a given conceptual stimulus.

Equal-Odds Rule   The principle that quality of output (creativity) is a positive and constant function of quantity of output (productivity).

Old-Age Style   The distinctive mode of expression that characterizes the final works of great artists.

Swan-Song Phenomenon   The tendency for composers to produce highly distinctive musical masterpieces in the closing years of their life.

CREATIVITY is an elusive concept that is not easily defined. The only statement that can be made with absolute confidence is that creativity has something to do with the production of creative ideas. An idea is said to be creative if it fulfills two conditions. First, the idea must be original in the sense of statistical rarity. Ideas that emerge from only one individual are more original than those that arise in the minds of many individuals. Lots of people have held down a beach blanket with a shoe, but only one person has revolutionized physics by proposing the general theory of relativity. Second, the idea must be adaptive in some meaningful way. For instance, it must solve some important problem or accomplish some significant task. Without this second requirement, one could not discriminate the bizarre mental ramblings of a psychotic from the breakthrough ideas of a scientific genius. Hence, creative ideas are simultaneously original and adaptive.

I. INTRODUCTION

When trying to get more specific, however, the consensus disappears. Different researchers will have contrary conceptions of what creativity entails. There are at least three main viewpoints:

1. Creativity is a mental process, or a set of mental processes, that generates creative ideas. These cognitive operations might include insight, intuition, and imagination. This is the preferred definition of cognitive psychologists who study problem solving in laboratory experiments.

2. Creativity is a characteristic of concrete products, such as a painting, poem, or invention. Those products that satisfy certain standards—such as novelty, elegance, beauty, and technical virtuosity—are called creative. This is the perspective adopted in theoretical and empirical aesthetics.

3. Creativity is a special personality trait, or cluster of traits, on which individuals may vary. For example, individuals who exhibit sufficient intelligence, ambition, determination, independence, and originality

may be identified as creative. This is the definition adopted by personality psychologists who examine the traits that distinguish creative persons from everyday populations.

Hence, creativity may be examined as a process, a product, or a person. Despite this conceptual divergence, the three perspectives can overlap and converge in various forms. For instance, researchers might study individual differences in cognitive styles—or preferred modes of information processing. This variation may then correlate with the production of creative ideas. Other investigators may examine individual differences in the output of creative products. Those persons who are the most prolific may then be said to be the most creative by this criterion. Thus, there exists a tremendous variety of ways that creativity can be examined in the behavioral sciences.

From the standpoint of gerontology, the most crucial issue has always been the relationship between creativity and aging. Does creativity necessarily decline with age? Is the age decrement such that one cannot expect creativity from individuals well advanced in years? What circumstances enable a person to maintain high levels of creativity toward the very end of life? These questions are important for both practical and theoretical reasons. On the practical side, a negative relationship between creativity and old age would provide a strong case for compulsory retirement. At least this argument could apply to those who are employed in positions where creativity is essential to effective performance. Professors at research universities and scientists at industrial laboratories are obvious examples. On the theoretical side, furthermore, an age decrement in creativity would have important consequences for the understanding of the aging process. Indeed, the supposed creative decline in the late years has often been taken as a sign of intellectual impairments in the final decades of life. In contrast, if this commonplace conception can be shown to be very much mistaken, one would have to draw very different conclusions about the nature of aging.

Because there are multiple definitions of creativity, the relationship between aging and creativity can be examined more than one way. Actually, researchers have tended to attack the problem from just two different angles. On the one hand, some investigators have defined creativity in terms of performance on

measures of the mental processes most relevant to the production of creative ideas. These psychometric instruments are often referred to as "creativity tests." On the other hand, other investigators have preferred a more behavioral definition, using counts of creative products as indicators of underlying creativity. The creative achievements in these longitudinal tabulations may include paintings, poems, compositions, patents, books, journal articles, or other discrete items. These alternative research strategies do not always lead to identical conclusions.

II. PSYCHOMETRIC ASSESSMENTS

Many psychometric instruments exist that purport to assess creativity. However, most investigators have relied on those creativity tests that evaluate a person's capacity for "divergent thinking." Measures of divergent thinking examine whether a person can produce a large number of alternative and novel responses to test stimuli. There actually exist several such instruments, each concentrating on a particular process (fluency, flexibility, originality, etc.) or medium (verbal versus visual). Whatever the details, studies using these divergent-thinking tests have often found that creativity tends to exhibit a roughly inverted-U function of age. That is, the scores may peak somewhere in one's thirties or forties, and thereafter decline. Judging from these psychometric inquiries, creativity shows a noticeable and sometimes quite pronounced decrement in the latter half of life. The aging process appears to be antithetical to the demonstration of creative activity.

Nevertheless, these psychometric findings must be interpreted with great caution. These results may not necessarily provide conclusive proof that creativity must decline after an individual reaches middle age. There are three principal difficulties:

1. Most of these psychometric studies rely exclusively on cross-sectional rather than longitudinal data. Instead of actually looking at how test performance changes as an individual gets older, most investigations merely compare the test scores of individuals at different ages. The latter approach is adopted simply for convenience. It obviously takes more time to examine the same subjects for several years in order to gauge the changes more directly. Yet in the absence

of a truly longitudinal analysis, the findings can be extremely misleading. The effects of age can be confounded with the effects of cohort. It is possible, for example, that the older persons in a sample came from a generation that went through schools with quite different educational philosophies than those that predominated when the younger persons in the study were educated. These contrasts alone could account for any observed contrasts in test performance in cross-sectional studies. Hence, it is significant that those few investigations that employ a longitudinal design usually report smaller declines in creativity than normally seen in cross-sectional research.

2. The form of the age curve depends greatly on the specific tests used. It must be emphasized that divergent-thinking measures represent only one possible approach to the assessment of creativity. Consequently, different longitudinal trends can obtain when alternative psychometric instruments are used. For instance, tests that evaluate problem-solving skills in more everyday situations can actually produce scores that increase with age. [See DECISION MAKING AND EVERYDAY PROBLEM SOLVING.] In addition, measures that impose strict time limits during test administration tend to show greater age decrements than those instruments that are untimed. This difference reflects the fact that the speed of thought processes tends to decline in the later years of life. Timed tests thus put older subjects at a comparative disadvantage.

3. Many experts in the area of creativity research seriously question the validity of all so-called creativity tests. Validation studies usually show that such tests display rather modest correlations with direct measures of creative behavior. The main problem is that most of these psychometric measures assess generic mental processes and cognitive styles. Yet investigators have now come to realize that creativity is for the most part domain specific. For instance, an individual might be highly creative in music but exhibit no creativity whatsoever in literature. Part of the reason for this differentiation is that creativity in any field requires the acquisition of a tremendous amount of domain-specific knowledge and skills. Usually creative individuals must devote approximately 10 years to intensive study and training before they have the expertise necessary for the production of ideas that are both original and adaptive. This essential requirement is completely overlooked by tests that

assess mental processes or cognitive styles in domains of general information.

These three difficulties suggest that it may prove more fruitful to adopt an alternative strategy. If one wishes to learn how creativity changes with age, it might be best to scrutinize how the output of creative products changes during the course of a creator's career. Such inquiries would be inherently longitudinal in design, and the indicators of creativity would enjoy the most validity. After all, the production of creative ideas is the primary criterion against which we must evaluate any measure of creativity.

III. PRODUCTIVITY MEASUREMENTS

The scientific study of the relation between age and creative productivity began in 1835, and thus it represents one of the oldest topics in gerontological research. The classic investigations are those conducted by Harvey C. Lehman, especially as summarized in his book *Age and Achievement*. Here he examined the fluctuations in creative output in a wide range of disciplines in the arts, sciences, and humanities. His data show a consistent tendency for creative productivity to follow an approximately inverted-U function of age. Creativity again rose to a peak somewhere in a person's thirties or forties, and then progressively declined. The age decrement was very similar to what is observed in performance on the psychometric measures.

Unfortunately, Lehman's work suffered from many methodological deficiencies that often rendered his results ambiguous. This deficiency caused many behavioral scientists to question the validity of his conclusions. Three problems were especially serious:

1. Lehman's tabulations focused on those products that were the most successful or influential. The total output of works was largely ignored. Critics of his research objected to the value judgment implicit in this methodological decision. The critics argued that a fairer gauge of creativity would require a count of the total output regardless of whether the product attains acclaim or earns appreciation. When this alternative strategy was taken, productivity in the later years of life seemed more substantial than Lehman's statistics appeared to indicate.

2. Lehman did not make any correction for

changes in the number of persons active within a creative discipline. There has been a tendency for this number to increase, sometimes quite dramatically. For instance, the number of scientists has been growing exponentially. As a consequence, the older a creator gets, the more other individuals will be active in the same creative domain. That tendency is tantamount to stating that as creative individuals age, they must face increasingly more competitors. Concert halls can perform only so many compositions, art galleries can exhibit only so many pieces, and journals can publish only so many articles. This puts all creators at an ever-growing disadvantage as they age.

3. Lehman's longitudinal tabulations would often fail to introduce corrections for individual differences in life span. Counts of the number of creative products emerging at different ages will automatically show a decline in output if these counts are summed across large numbers of creative individuals. This must happen because those creators who die at younger ages will be prevented from contributing works at later ages. There are fewer creative products at the hands of 80-year-olds than 40-year-olds in part because octogenarians are relatively rare. Accordingly, those statistics that fail to adjust for this artifact will exaggerate the age decrement in the advanced years.

Fortunately, more recent research has taken advantage of more sophisticated methods to take care of these and other complaints. At the same time, these modern investigations have verified Lehman's central conclusion: The output of creative products tends to first increase with age until a peak is reached, after which productivity declines. The peak may occur a little later in life, and the postpeak decline may be less pronounced, but an age decrement occurs nonetheless. Even so, this same research also suggests that the prospects for creativity in the later years is not so dismal as it first appeared. The relevant findings concern (a) the magnitude of the age decrement, (b) contrasts across creative domains, (c) individual differences in lifetime output, (d) the contrast between career and chronological age, (e) extraneous influences on productivity, (f) the equal-odds rule, and (g) qualitative transformations in creativity.

A. Magnitude of the Age Decrement

Even though an age decrement is commonly observed, the size of this decrease is not as substantial as often

thought. Certainly the predicted level of creative productivity rarely drops to zero. In fact, output in the last decade of life can compare quite favorably to other decades of a creative career. For instance, persons in their seventies will usually be more productive than the same persons were in their twenties. Moreover, this late-life productivity will even look respectable when contrasted with the career peak, when the output rate reaches the maximum. In the typical case, individuals in their seventies will be producing ideas at a pace only 50% below what they accomplished during the high point of their careers. It is trivial to debate whether this percentage means that the creative mind is half-empty or half-full after it enters the traditional retirement age. The conclusion remains that creative individuals do not necessarily "dry up" or "run out of steam."

This fact alone should help us to understand how it is possible for an impressive number of creative achievements to come from individuals who are well advanced in years. To offer some illustrations: Cervantes completed the second part of *Don Quixote* at age 68; Franklin invented bifocal lenses when he was 78 years old; Humboldt wrote his *Cosmos* when he was between 76 and 89 years of age; and Goethe finished the second part of *Faust* when he was in his early eighties. Perhaps the most remarkable example, however, is the case of Henri Chevreul. After a distinguished career as a chemist, Chevreul switched fields in his nineties to become a pioneer in gerontological research. His last publication appeared just a year before his death at age 103.

B. Contrasts across Creative Domains

Any consideration of the age decrement cannot ignore the considerable variation that occurs across domains of creative activity. The specific shape of the age curve, including the location of the peak and the magnitude of the postpeak drop, varies according to the discipline in which the creativity takes place. In some fields the peak will appear much later in life, sometimes around the fifties or sixties. Moreover, the decline will be very gradual, even imperceptible. Accordingly, octogenarians will be as productive as they were when they were in their supposed prime. This longitudinal pattern tends to hold for philosophy, history, and various forms of scholarship. For example, Kant published his first philosophical masterpiece, the *Critique* of *Pure Reason*, when he was 57, and his last notable contribution, the *Critique of Judgment*, when he was 66.

Of course, in other fields the age decrement will be accentuated. The career peak might appear in the late twenties or early thirties, and the postpeak decline may be almost precipitous. Such age curves tend to be seen in the output of lyric poetry, abstract mathematics, and theoretical physics. Nonetheless, the picture of late-life creativity is not totally grim. In the worse-case scenario, productivity in the seventies will fall to around 5% of the output rate attained at the career optimum. Thus, creativity is only slowed, not stopped. Nothing prevents individuals in one of these disciplines from coming out with a masterpiece in the final years. Tennyson was still producing notable poems in his eighties, and the last volume of Laplace's *Celestial Mechanics* appeared when he was in his seventies.

C. Individual Differences in Lifetime Output

There exists extraordinary variation in the lifetime output of various creative individuals. In fact, the distribution of total productivity is far more varied than the distribution of most physical and psychological traits, such as height or intelligence. Typically, the most productive creators in any field are at least 100 times more prolific than their least productive colleagues. So extreme is this contrast that the individuals who are in the top 10% in total output tend to account for about half of all the creative products in a particular domain. For example, only 16 composers account for half of the music regularly performed in the classical repertoire.

This productive elite attains this prodigious output three ways. First, they tend to launch their careers earlier than normal, often in the late teens or early twenties. Second, they tend to maintain high annual output rates throughout the career, often publishing two, three, or four times the rate of their less distinguished colleagues. Third, they tend to continue their prolific output much later in life, most often letting death decide when their careers shall end. These last two components are especially crucial to understanding late-life creativity. Individual differences in creative productivity are so substantial that this variation will largely negate the impact of the age decrement when making comparisons across creators. Hence,

highly prolific contributors in their seventies and eighties often display more creative productivity than much less prolific contributors who are active at their career peaks. Indeed, a Nobel prize-winning scientist will make more contributions after age 60 than most scientists make during their entire careers.

D. Career Age versus Chronological Age

It is a common mistake to conceive the age curves as expressing creative productivity as a function of chronological age. Almost all of the tables and figures published over the past 150 years take this point of view. Along the horizontal axis of the typical graph the researcher will usually mark off consecutive decades or half-decades according to age since birth (e.g., twenties, thirties, forties, etc.). The investigators then count the number of creative products falling within each time interval. This manner of presenting and analyzing the data is straightforward but terribly misleading. The curves expressing the changes in creative output across the life span are not strictly a function of chronological age but rather of career age. What matters most is how long the individual has been engaged in a given creative enterprise. Hence, to be precise one should not say that an individual peaks at age 40, but rather that the peak is attained about 15 years into a career.

Admittedly, if we are counting creative contributions across a large number of individuals, the distinction between chronological and career age will make little difference. If the average person launches the career at age 25, then the average person will attain the optimum at age 40. Furthermore, chronological and career age will correlate very highly with each other. This strong association appears because people usually enter and leave the educational system at about the same ages anyway. Consequently, most beginning creators in a particular field will be in about the same cohort. Nevertheless, circumstances do arise where the correspondence between chronological and career age breaks down. Some individuals might be a "late bloomers" who did not discover their true calling until they were more advanced in years. Some of these persons may have undergone midlife career changes, perhaps even going to college as "reentry students."

Whatever the causes, those who begin their careers later in life will tend to have age curves that are displaced proportionally later as well. If the peak normally comes 15 years after the career onset, and the person does not get started until age 40, then the optimum will appear around age 55 rather than age 40. In addition, the impact of the age decrement would also not be felt until much later in life. The late starter may have to reach the 90th year of life before he or she showed any clear signs of serious decline.

The career of the Austrian composer Anton Bruckner illustrates this possible outcome. Bruckner spent the first part of his life as an obscure and provincial creator of church music. However, an encounter with the operas of Richard Wagner inspired him to become a symphonic composer with a similar sonic landscape. He therefore did not create his first symphony, a student piece given number "00," until he was 39 years old, and he was 50 before his first masterpiece emerged from his pen. Two more successful symphonies appeared when he was 59 and 60 years of age. He died at age 70, before he could write the concluding movement to his last symphony. Yet that piece is still considered a masterwork. Because Bruckner's entire career was shifted over about 20 years, he was in his prime at an age when many other composers were well past theirs.

E. Extraneous Influences on Productivity

A large proportion of the decline in output in the last half of life is by no means inevitable. Rather, much of any age decrement can be attributed to extraneous factors. To the extent that these detrimental influences can be overcome, creative productivity can often continue at higher levels than predicted by the usual age curves. For instance, as a career advances, creative individuals frequently find themselves increasingly engaged in activities that take them away from the studio, laboratory, or writing desk. In academic and industrial settings, these activities often entail time-consuming and stressful administrative responsibilities. Consistent with this adverse impact is the recurrent finding that creative persons will often experience an upsurge in productivity upon retirement. This resuscitation is especially likely in those domains where knowledge or skill does not become quickly obsolete.

Perhaps the most obvious external constraint on productivity in the later years is physical health. Creative individuals, like everyone else, can suffer from debilitating illnesses in old age. Indeed, some creators have had to make heroic efforts to maintain any level of productivity at all. Johann Sebastian Bach was eventually obliged by blindness to compose his works by laborious dictation; Matisse attached crayons to bamboo poles so that he could continue to do art from his wheelchair. Hence, any advances in medicine that lengthen the number of years of sound health will probably prolong and intensify the amount of creativity seen in the closing decades of life.

In contrast, certain environments can operate to sustain creativity well into old age. In the sciences, for example, those individuals who are embedded in a rich disciplinary network of colleagues and students tend to display much longer creative careers. This positive influence evidently operates by stimulating the scientists so that they can rejuvenate their creative potential. Likewise, those individuals who maintain a high level of intellectual activity, and who remain open to outside influences, will be able to keep their creative productivity at higher levels. This is one reason that the greatest artists often display multiple periods, each identified with a distinct style. Once these creators have exhausted one aesthetic framework, they will move on to another, and thereby refresh their creativity.

A fascinating illustration is the composer Stravinsky, who went through several musical styles over the course of his long career. At 70 years of age he quite unexpectedly revitalized his creativity by adopting a compositional style that he had hitherto ignored, the twelve-tone technique of Schoenberg. This dramatic change permitted him to extend his creative life by another 10 years.

F. Equal-Odds Rule

Earlier it was noted that Lehman's studies were criticized for only counting successful works, while ignoring the often much larger output of unsuccessful products. The critics believed that if total output is examined, the outlook for late-life creativity would appear more optimistic. That is, productivity may remain high in the final years of life even if that productivity does not have an impact on contemporaries or posterity. One problem with this argument harks back to the very definition of creativity. A creative product is an entity that is deemed original and adaptive by other individuals. If an individual continues to produce unoriginal and ineffective works toward the end of their career, that does not mean that the person is still being creative. Hence, on analytical grounds, this argument has no relevance to the question of the relation between age and creative productivity.

Yet there is a more important point: The above argument assumed that the age curves for total output were different than those for just creative production. Presumably the postpeak decline is less drastic when all potential contributions are tabulated regardless of merit. Nonetheless, earlier studies making this contention did not use the most appropriate methods. In fact, more recent analyses simply do not support this conclusion. The relation between age and productivity is essentially the same whether we count total output, successful output, or unsuccessful output. The peak occurs at about the same place during the course of the career, and the postpeak decrements are comparable. The ups and downs in the appearance of major products parallels those for minor products. Quality of output is strongly associated with quantity of output.

This concordance might lead to more pessimism about the prospects for creativity in the later years. But such pessimism is unjustified if the longitudinal data are examined from a different angle. The first step is to calculate the ratio of successful works to the total output produced in consecutive age periods. This yields a "quality ratio" or "hit rate." To illustrate, for a sample of scientists this ratio would consist of the proportion of frequently cited articles relative to total articles produced during each age period. The next step is to see how this quality ratio changes as a creative individual gets older. The answer is straightforward: The ratio fluctuates randomly throughout the career. There are good years and bad years, but there is no consistent tendency for the hit rate to increase or decrease, nor display some curvilinear form.

Therefore, the older members of a creative domain boast the same quality ratio as do their younger colleagues. This equal-odds rule has obvious implications for any discussion of the connection between age and creativity. Although these creative elders may be generating fewer masterpieces in their last years, they are also producing fewer neglected pieces. Each product has the same chance of success no matter how old the creator was at the time of production. So if creativity is gauged in terms of success rate, there is no rationale

for even speaking of an age decrement at all. The equal-odds rule thus advises everyone to judge each potential contribution on its merits, for age has no value as a predictor of creative accomplishment at this level.

G. Qualitative Transformations

One obvious limitation of simply counting creative products per age period is that the procedure implicitly treats all works as virtually identical. This hidden assumption is patently invalid. Clearly an epic poem should get more credit than a sonnet, and a monograph should earn more points than a research note. The standard solution to this problem is to assign differential weights to the longitudinal tabulations. For example, musical compositions might be weighted according to the amount of thematic material they contain, the complexity of instrumentation, the number and type of movements, and playing time. This would make Beethoven's *Missa Solemnis* count more than his piano bagatelle *Für Elise*.

What makes the implementation of this solution especially urgent is that individuals tend to change their preferred mode of creative expression as their careers advance. A poet might begin with brief lyrics before attempting more ambitious narrative and epic forms; a scientist might start with journal articles and then write increasingly more books and monographs. Because the number of creative ideas found in each creative product thus increases over time, the output of titles will decrease faster than the production of ideas. The weighting procedures allow us to compensate for this crucial shift of growing creative maturity.

However, this methodological improvement ignores another qualitative change that is even more profound. As creators get older, they may grapple with more difficult themes and issues, and thereby make the content of their works more profound, and even devise much more rich forms. For instance, as authors age their juvenile preoccupations with love won and lost tend to be replaced with deeper ruminations over the meaning of life, over the place of human existence in the larger scheme of things. By thus waxing philosophical, creative individuals will often try to say more with less, to concentrate an intense amount of significance within strikingly elegant expression. These life span transitions require a more complex approach to the measurement of creativity. Even weighted counts will not capture the amount of creativity that may be going into each piece.

This point becomes especially urgent when considering one final empirical finding: Creators entering their last years often dramatically alter the approach they take to their creative activities. For instance, visual artists in their concluding years may exhibit a sudden shift toward what has been called the "old-age style." Similarly, composers will frequently display a "swan-song phenomenon." Rather than betray a decline in creative power, these works often serve as last artistic testaments. Practically a creator's entire life and career is summarized within a single, often brief, but highly concentrated masterpiece that serves as the career's most worthy capstone. It is as if the greatest creative personalities wish to end it all with a bang, not a whimper. The very fact that an old master can still succeed in such an awesome task is ample testimony to the respectable creative powers that can yet remain in advanced old age.

IV. THEORETICAL INTERPRETATIONS

So far the focus has been on the empirical findings that describe the linkage between creativity and aging. Behavioral scientists have proposed a large number of theoretical accounts as well. These theories vary greatly in how well they explain the available data. They also differ with respect to their implications for creativity in the later part of life. These diverse theoretical frameworks fall into four broad categories: psychobiological, sociological, economic, and psychological.

A. Psychobiological Theories

Creativity obviously takes place in the human brain. Therefore, any biological process that impairs brain function as the body ages will naturally have a similarly negative impact on creative thought. For example, as people get older, reaction time usually tends to increase, as the general rate of information processing gradually slows down. If creativity is assessed by time tests, this neurological shift will necessarily cause inferior performance. Older individuals will simply generate fewer responses in a given unit of time. Hence,

only on untimed tests can this inherent disadvantage be minimized. Of course, here I am referring merely to the quantity of ideas produced over a certain period. The quality of those ideas may not necessarily diminish just because the rate of output slows down. Indeed, the equal-odds rule shows that the ratio of good to bad ideas stays more or less constant throughout the life span.

Nevertheless, biological changes may affect the intellect in more subtle ways. Work on IQ tests has established the important distinction between crystallized and fluid intelligence. Where the former concerns relatively permanent knowledge, such as a person's active vocabulary, the latter concerns more flexible skills, such as problem-solving ability. For reasons not completely understood, these two types of intelligence have different trajectories across the life span. Crystallized intelligence will often steadily increase, with a relatively minimal age decrement towards the end, whereas fluid intelligence will normally decline somewhat rapidly in the later years. In fact, the divergent thinking tests discussed earlier may be viewed as measures of fluid intelligence, and their age trends follow the same course. This contrast is important because different kinds of creativity may require a distinctive mix of crystallized and fluid intelligence. The nature of this mix may then decide where the career peak tends to be for a particular field. The differences between mathematicians and geologists or between poets and novelists may be partly explained on this principle.

Even so, psychobiological explanations cannot account for many crucial features of longitudinal changes in creativity. Most conspicuous is the finding that creative productivity is principally a function of career age. By comparison, any psychobiological account must be expressed in terms of chronological age. Consequently, it is difficult to use this perspective to comprehend those individuals who enter a creative enterprise later in life, and yet who still manage to display the expected career trajectories. Perhaps the best conclusion to draw is that various biological factors operate mostly as extraneous influences. Their main effect on late bloomers may be to depress the height of the career peak and steepen the slope of the postpeak decline. Meanwhile the specific shape of the age curve will be largely dictated by other factors that have nothing to do with biology. [*See* THEORIES OF AGING: BIOLOGICAL.]

B. Sociological Theories

Sociologists adopt a totally different approach to explicating how creativity changes across the life span. Their tendency is to concentrate on objective creative behavior, as gauged by the output of actual products. This productivity is then seen to be largely if not entirely the function of the prevailing reward structures of a discipline. These structures reinforce certain forms of creative output while discouraging other forms. Output is maintained across the life span when the social rewards for continued productivity are maintained throughout the career. On the other hand, productivity will diminish and disappear when the disciplinary reinforcements are no longer forthcoming.

This explanatory position is best seen in the principle of "accumulative advantage." According to this principle, creative individuals live in a very competitive world where many are called but few are chosen. Not all papers submitted to professional journals will be accepted for publication; only a subset of the artworks submitted to a show will be selected by the jury for exhibition. Those who have the fortune to achieve success early will have higher odds of attaining further successes, whereas those who experience the misfortune of early rejection will be more prone to endure further failure. Those in the first group are thereby encouraged to increase their productivity, whereas those in the second group will suffer discouragement, and eventually drop out of the race. This difference is accelerated because the initially successful will obtain access to social support—such as paid positions, laboratories, studios, contracts, fellowships, and grants—that will be withheld from those that have not yet proven themselves. The upshot is that the rich get richer and the poor get poorer.

The principle of accumulative advantage can explain many of the details of career trajectories. For instance, those individuals who are successful earlier will obtain the resources that will permit them to maintain their productivity at a higher rate and to continue their output until later in the career. In contrast, those less lucky will never become very prolific, and will end their productive careers earlier. This pattern closely approximates what is actually observed. A remarkable feature of this explanation is that it makes no assumptions whatsoever about individual differences in creativity. Even if all individuals entering the contest are roughly equal in native ability, they will eventually stratify according to the length and productivity of their careers. Moreover, persons who are no longer productive in the later years cannot really be blamed for their fate. They are simply those who got off on the wrong foot at the very outset of their careers. If they had accumulated the same external resources as their most successful colleagues, they too would be just as prolific in old age.

Although the sociological account has many attractive aspects, it also suffers from numerous explanatory inadequacies. For example, it does not do a very good job explaining the appearance of creative late bloomers. More seriously, it has problems accounting for interdisciplinary contrasts in the career trajectories. Why do mathematicians peak early and geologists peak later? In addition, it cannot handle the finer details about individual variation in the career course. For instance, research has shown that the most prolific creators in a discipline attain their productive peaks at the same career age as their less prolific colleagues. The principle of accumulative advantage, in contrast, predicts that the former will peak later than the latter. Hence, the sociological framework may at best only capture a portion of the process underlying age changes in creative output. [See THEORIES OF AGING: SOCIAL.]

C. Economic Theories

Economists have advanced an interpretation that has a certain affinity with that put forward by sociologists. They also posit that creativity is a behavior maintained by extrinsic incentives. Yet the economists focus more on the individual rather than concentrate on the reward structures of a creative domain. Economists begin by assuming that human beings are rational creatures who try to maximize the benefits they receive in life while minimizing the costs. Hence, individuals are always calculating "cost–benefit ratios" or "utility functions" in order to decide on a proper course of action. This calculation process becomes complex when a person has to examine the trade-off between short-term costs and the corresponding long-term benefits. A classic example is education, which consumes much time and money in the short run, but helps ensure a comfortable standard of living in the long run.

Creative individuals face a similar choice. Creativity, according to the economists, requires considerable investment in "human capital." That is, creative individuals must devote much time, energy, and expense to mastering the knowledge and techniques of a field before they can generate a creative product. Yet only the products themselves bring benefits in promotions, prizes, and pay raises. Furthermore, creative individuals must continually reinvest their resources in order to maintain productivity throughout their career. Otherwise their expertise will become obsolete, and they will correspondingly fall behind the leading edge or latest fashion. For a person just starting out in a career, the short-term costs of this investment will pay great dividends in the long term. Yet for a person already well advanced in years, the current losses may outweigh the expected gains. For one thing, death may end the person's career before the opportunity has appeared to reap the benefits. Additionally, the "marginal utility" of a creative product may decline for those individuals who have already made many contributions. One published poem means more to a young poet with no previous publications than does the same achievement to an established poet who has already put out several volumes of poetry. The net result of these economic decisions is a decline in creative output toward the closing years of the career. The age decrement is thus a natural repercussion of a gradual shift in the incentives and disincentives faced by creative individuals as they get older.

This economic model can explicate many other aspects of the relationship between creativity and age. Nonetheless, this model is not capable of explaining all the details. For example, it is not clear how it would account for the upturn in creativity that is often observed in the final years. What material incentives could possibly induce a dying creator to produce a swan song or final artistic testament? It would seem that the short-term costs of such projects would immensely overwhelm any anticipated long-term benefits. As in the case of the sociologists, economic models can probably only account for a portion of the phenomenon.

D. Psychological Theories

Psychologists, naturally, place even more emphasis on what is going on in the individual. Presumably the age changes in creativity are some function of cognitive, motivational, or dispositional variables that undergo transformations over the lifetime. For instance, the results of the psychometric studies may be used to explain the findings of the productivity studies. If divergent thinking represents a process fundamental to creative thought, and if scores on tests of divergent cognition decline in the latter part of life, then this trend may underlie the parallel drop in creative productivity. Furthermore, because different forms of these cognitive measures often exhibit distinct longitudinal trends, it is also possible to use these findings to explain the interdisciplinary contrasts in the age curves for creative output. Perhaps creativity in different disciplines requires a distinct mix of cognitive styles, where each mixture will show an agewise trend that is a weighted average of the separate trends for each mental process entering the mix.

There are three main problems with this particular interpretation, however. First, and as pointed out earlier, the connection between performance on creativity tests and the demonstration of creative behavior is by no means strong. Second, longitudinal and cross-sectional studies of these psychometric measures have focused on chronological rather than career age. Third, this explanation somewhat begs the core question; if productivity changes reflect underlying changes in mental capacities, the latter changes remain to be explained.

Other psychological interpretations do not suffer from these drawbacks. For example, according to one information-processing theory of creative productivity, the longitudinal trends in output emerge from the very process by which creative potential converts into actual creative products. This theory predicts that the age curves will vary across disciplines in a manner that corresponds to the complexity and richness of the concepts and skills needed to generate and develop creative ideas. This theory also holds that the age curves depend on career age rather than chronological age. One distinctive asset of this theoretical account is that it makes very precise predictions about longitudinal changes in output across individuals and disciplines. Even so, this theory cannot explain certain details, such as the occurrence of the swan-song phenomenon. [See THEORIES OF AGING: PSYCHOLOGICAL.]

In fact, at present there is no theory of creativity that can deal successfully with all the empirical findings reviewed in this article. The relation between creativity and aging is perhaps far too complicated to permit simple theoretical interpretations.

BIBLIOGRAPHY

Adams-Price, C. (Ed.). (1996). *Creativity and aging.* New York: Springer.

Kastenbaum, R. (1991). The creative impulse: Why it won't just quit. *Generations 15,* 7.

Perlmutter, M. (Ed.). (1990). *Late life potential.* Washington, DC: Gerontological Society of America.

Simonton, D. K. (1990). Creativity in the later years: Optimistic prospects for achievement. *Gerontologist, 30,* 626.

Simonton, D. K. (1994). *Greatness.* New York: Guilford Press.

Crime and Age

Edith Elisabeth Flynn

Northeastern University

Cohort Group of individuals sharing a statistical factor, such as age, in a demographic study.

Crime Rates The incidence of crime related to the population.

Criminal Careers Concept describing the onset of criminal activity, the types and number of crimes committed, and the termination of law-violating behavior.

Cross-Sectional Research Studies groups of people of different ages at particular points in time.

Incidence of Crime Rate of offending by offenders.

Index Offenses Also known as Part I crimes.

Longitutional Research Studies a particular group of people over a period of time.

Prevalence of Crime Proportion of persons in a population who are offenders.

Property Crimes Include burglary, larceny theft, motor vehicle theft, and arson.

Recidivism Relapse into criminal behavior.

Uniform Crime Reports (UCR) Annual reports on criminal activity collected and published by the Federal Bureau of Investigation (FBI). The reports divide offenses into two major categories: Part I crimes consist of murder, nonnegligent manslaughter, forc- ible rape, robbery, aggravated assault, burglary, larceny, and auto theft. Part II offenses include less serious crimes such as forgery, fraud, embezzlement, sex offenses, and others not meeting the FBI's criteria of seriousness and frequency to qualify for Part I.

Violent Crimes Include murder, forcible rape, robbery, and aggravated assault.

Criminology is the scientific study of **CRIME** and delinquency as social phenomena. This relatively young field of study has three principal divisions: (a) the sociology of law, which examines how laws are made and enforced; (b) criminal etiology, which studies the causes of crime; and (c) penology, which addresses society's response to crime and includes the study of the criminal justice system. Criminologists are social scientists who utilize the research methods of modern science to develop a body of general, verifiable principles regarding law, deviance, and crime. Criminological analysis looks upon crime and deviance not as isolated events but as highly complex forms of social behavior. To fully understand the meaning of deviance and crime, the discipline goes beyond the legal definitions of crime and examines the total social context within which deviance and lawlessness arise. In the process of studying the causes of crime, a vast body of research has identified age, gender, ethnicity, social class, family status, and community environments as major social correlates of crime.

I. INTRODUCTION

This article explores in depth the relationship between age and crime and summarizes current information on this subject. Section II examines in some detail the age–crime curve as it emerges from national crime statistics collected by the Federal Bureau of Investigation (FBI). Section III discusses key statistical properties of the age–crime curve. Section IV probes the significance of the age–crime curve and reviews the ongoing debate in criminology on the true relation between age and crime. Section V explores age as a critical social correlate of crime, along with other key variables. Section VI considers age as a critical variable in the formation and termination of criminal careers. It also explores current criminal justice system responses to chronic offenders and questions the efficacy of these responses in terms of their potential for crime control and crime reduction. Section VII investigates the effects of society's age structure on America's crime rate and tracks the expansion of the nation's juvenile population into the next century. The article concludes by assessing the implications of demographic changes on crime control and criminal justice policies.

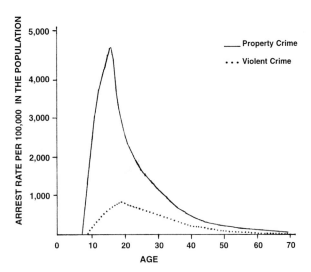

Figure I   The relationship between age and crime. Property crime arrests peak at age 16 and at 18 for violent crime. There were 746.1 violent crimes and 4,736.9 property crimes per 100,000 inhabitants in 1993. (From FBI, 1994. *Crime in the United States, 1993.* Washington, DC: Government Printing Office, pp. 10, 35, 227–228.)

II. THE RELATIONSHIP BETWEEN AGE AND CRIME

One of the few undisputed facts in criminology is the age distribution of crime. Official crime statistics, supported by victim survey research, show clearly that crime is a young man's game, with most serious crimes being committed by young males between the ages of 14 and 24. Beyond this brief vignette, age–crime curves show reliably that age is inversely related to criminal activity, with crime rates rising rapidly from the minimum age of responsibility, peaking during adolescence, and then decreasing quickly. The decline is rapid at first, followed by a more gradual downward curve throughout a person's life cycle. Figure 1 shows the property and violent crime rates for Americans per 100,000 in the population in 1993, as reported by the FBI. Property crime rate peaks at age 16, and the violent crime rate peaks at age 18. The relationship between age and crime is of great interest to criminology and vital to theoretical development in the discipline. Criminologists consider age to be a major correlate

of crime, along with gender, ethnicity, social class, family status, and community environments.

III. STATISTICAL EVIDENCE OF THE AGE–CRIME CURVE

Juveniles and young adults are arrested at disproportionate rates to their numbers in the general population. According to the FBI's Uniform Crime Reporting Index, youngsters between the ages of 10 and 17 represented 11.3% of the total U.S. population in 1993. But they accounted for 18.4% of all violent crime arrests and for over one-third (33.2%) of all property crime arrests for that year. The disproportionate contribution of the young to the nation's crime problem jumps graphically to the fore when looking at the arrest statistics for all persons under the age of 25. That group makes up only 21.2% of the U.S. population but accounts for more than half (58.3%) of all arrests for index property offenses and almost half (47.4%) of violent crime. The peak arrest age for most offenses is between 16 and 19, with property crime peaking at 16 and violent crime cresting at 18. After age 30, arrest rates decline. From age 50 on, arrest rates become marginal (1.3% and below). The decrease in criminal activity with increasing age is known as maturational reform or the "aging-out effect."

IV. SIGNIFICANCE OF THE AGE–CRIME RELATIONSHIP: THE AGE DEBATE

The persistence of a distinct age–crime relationship has been documented by many studies across time, gender, ethnicity, types of offenses, and different cultures. This phenomenon and the consistency of the data have led some criminologists to suggest that the age–crime curve is invariant. They further believe that this distinct relationship between crime and age cannot be accounted for by changes in other factors with age. As a result, they maintain that age exerts a direct causal effect on crime. Given this causal effect, proponents of this school of thought suggest that the study of the age–crime relationship has little relevance for the study of crime, because all persons commit less crime as they age regardless of ethnicity, gender, social class, family, or any other variable.

On the opposite side of this age–crime debate is another school of thought, pointing to inherent weaknesses in aggregate, cross-sectional statistics, such as those featured in the nation's Uniform Crime Reports. It notes that although these data depict variations in the prevalence of crime, they offer little information on the incidence of crime. In fact, aggregate age–crime curves are singularly unyielding about age–crime curves for individual cases. This is because crime incidence varies considerably between the beginning and end of individual criminal careers. It also varies by the types of crimes that are committed. For example, vandalism or motor vehicle theft are clearly crimes of adolescence. They peak early, when youngsters are between the ages of 15 and 16. By contrast, white-collar crimes such as fraud or embezzlement peak relatively late, when perpetrators are in their late twenties and early thirties. Furthermore, just because the aggregate age–crime curve declines precipitously after adolescence, it does not necessarily signify that the number of crimes committed by every offender declines in a similar fashion. In fact, many cross-cultural, longitudinal research studies have demonstrated that although the frequency of criminal offending does follow the dictates of the age–crime curve for a major-

ity of offenders, some very active individuals continue to violate the law unabated.

V. AGE AS AN IMPORTANT DETERMINANT IN THE ETIOLOGY OF CRIME

Questions of why some individuals turn to crime while others do not and why most youthful offenders "age out" of criminal activities while others persist in offending, have prompted a good deal of prospective and retrospective longitudinal research on the causes of crime. The results of these efforts indicate that onset, frequency, and cessation of criminal offending varies, depending on a number of biological, individual, and social factors.

Biological and individual factors help account for the shape of the age–crime curve because many criminal activities are contingent upon certain levels of physical and mental development. For example, rising testosterone levels in young males are consistently linked to aggression and violent behavior during adolescence, when immaturity, the pursuit of immediate gratification, and risk taking behavior are also highly prevalent. As adolescents become adults, physical and mental maturation begin to play key roles in their desistance from crime. In a similar vein, the commission of some types of crimes, such as robbery or rape, is contingent upon certain degrees of strength, force, and agility. With increasing age, these offenders lose their physical power to assault, rob, escape, and avoid apprehension.

Although biology and individual factors do set some of the parameters of the age–crime curve, they fall short of explaining it. Adequate explanations depend on linking the curve to changes in a person's social environment. To that end, criminological research has identified a number of social factors that are of greater importance in explaining the age–crime curve than those focusing exclusively on changes in a person's biological or personal characteristics. The following behavioral factors are consistently associated with very serious, violent, and chronic juvenile crime: (a) dysfunctional families; (b) physical or sexual abuse; (c) delinquent peer groups; (d) poor school performance; and (e) high-crime neighborhoods. As the United States enters the twenty-first century, there is nothing on the horizon in terms of legislation or policy development that effectively responds to any of these factors, which does not bode well for the nation's crime rate or crime control.

A. Dysfunctional Families

Historically, the family has carried the primary responsibility for the socialization of children. Basic personality traits, perceptions of right and wrong, and personal values are formed within this primary social setting at an early age, long before the other socializing institutions, such as religion, education, or the workplace begin to exert their influence. Socialization is an integrative process of moral internalization and informal and formal education. Successful socialization implies civilization and, by definition, law-abiding behavior.

Most criminologists agree that a stable, secure, and mutually supportive family is exceedingly important in delinquency prevention. Conversely, children growing up in a family filled with violence, abuse, and neglect are most likely to embark on a life of delinquency and crime. The simple truth is that children raised in dysfunctional families have difficulty developing the prosocial identities and values needed to become productive, law-abiding citizens. The following are major indicators of the breakdown of the American family.

The number of children raised in homes broken by divorce, separation, desertion, or death is escalating. The nation's divorce rate is among the highest recorded in the world. The birthrate for unmarried women is fast approaching 50 births per 1000. Teenage pregnancy rates are among the highest in developed nations. The number of households headed by women has more than doubled in less than one generation. More than half of all mothers with school-aged children work outside the home, most out of economic necessity. The result is a steadily rising number of children who find themselves under the care of a single parent, a working mother, a day nursery, and too often, a television set. The percentage of children who do not have full-time parental supervision at home is close to 60% and rising.

Research on the effects of rapid social change and family disruption on crime is extensive and discouraging. Strong ties have been established between parental criminality and delinquency in children. Although the precise causes of intergenerational deviance are not yet known, there is some evidence of a genetic, psychological, and social factor linkage. Much family dysfunction is also related to a growing problem with parental alcohol and substance abuse. For example, there is a strong association between substance abuse, child maltreatment, and infants born with fetal alcohol syndrome or congenital drug addiction. Children raised by substance-abusing adults also have a much greater propensity to develop substance-abuse problems themselves, when compared to youths raised in drug-free home environments. Finally, certain child-rearing practices have emerged as primary factors leading to delinquent offspring. They include inadequate or inconsistent parenting, such as disciplinary practices that alternate between harshness and overindulgence; the use of severe corporal punishment; treating children with coldness and distance; and exposing children to an incessant barrage of parental conflict.

B. Physical and Sexual Abuse

The correlation between violent physical or sexual child abuse and delinquency is positive and strong. Although estimates vary, more than one million children are abused and tortured in any given year by their parents or caregivers seriously enough to require hospital treatment. Unreported child abuse may be four to six times higher. The number of children who die as a result of parental maltreatment is estimated at between 2000 and 5000 in any given year. Research evidence has consistently linked physical or sexual abuse to risky sexual behaviors, particularly among girls, and to substance abuse, illegitimacy, and suicide. Furthermore, children already vulnerable with neurological and psychological problems seem to become prime candidates for delinquency not only if they are physically abused, but also if they merely witness habitual violence and brutality in their homes. Serious physical abuse can cause neurological or psychomotor disturbances, and children with such impairments have been found to disproportionately exhibit a tendency toward very serious and sometimes brutal violence.

C. Delinquent Peer Groups

As children mature, the influence and control of parents wanes and peer influence heightens. Crime statistics show that delinquent acts tend to be committed in small groups, rather than by youths acting alone. These statistics coupled with the fact that most children gravitate to forming close-knit peer groups during their early teenage years provide the single best explanation for the rapid escalation of delinquency and crime depicted by the age–crime curve. Although many desist offending, there is ample empirical evidence that youngsters who are involved with delinquent friends, belong to gangs, and otherwise associate with deviant persons are most likely to become involved in delinquency and crime.

D. Poor School Performance

The failure of schools as an agent of socialization is well documented, especially in socioeconomically deprived urban environments. Even though no clear causal relationship has been established between school failure and crime, there is agreement among criminologists that educational institutions lag in fulfilling their primary socialization function in modern society. The rising level of student violence and vandalism during the past two decades is well documented. When considering the amount of time children spend at school, it comes as no surprise that youngsters are at greater risk of violence in and around schools than anywhere else. Pilfering, assaults, robberies, fights, and racial antagonisms are a major part of school life and especially pronounced in urban schools. With the exception of trespassing and breaking and entering, most crimes committed in schools are perpetrated by the students in attendance. Teacher victimization through property crime and assault is frequent. Poor schooling and negative attitudes toward school are strongly related to delinquency and crime, substance abuse, disdain for authority, increased social fears, racism, and reduced productivity. Absenteeism and lack of discipline are major problems. Too many schools have watered-down curricula and reflect an alienated, prisonlike atmosphere. Many teachers, unappreciated by the public and their charges, are also alienated, demoralized, and prone to burnout. The disruptions, crime, and vandalism have taken their toll. Achievement scores are low, with many schools graduating technological illiterates, and more disturbingly, too many functional illiterates, ill equipped to face a job market requiring ever more knowledge and skills.

E. High-Crime Neighborhoods

Many of America's inner-city neighborhoods are characterized by poverty, transience, high population density, neglect, and physical deterioration. They are also marked by exceedingly high crime rates when compared to more affluent residential areas. Inner cities have high levels of unemployment, especially for members of minority groups. Even though there is no direct cause-and-effect relationship between poverty and crime (many single parents living in high-risk areas do not produce delinquent children), there is very strong evidence of structural linkages between family disruption, failing public school systems, economic marginality, declining low-skilled, blue-collar employment opportunities, and crime in high-risk, inner-city neighborhoods. Life in such neighborhoods breeds cynicism and alienation. Devoid of positive social control, such areas amplify criminogenic forces and further destabilize these areas. In that light, social, physical, and material conditions of neighborhoods exert an independent effect on delinquency and crime over which individual residents have little, if any, control.

VI. AGE AND CAREER OFFENDERS

Many studies analyzing delinquency and crime patterns in cohorts show that any given group contains a relatively small number of repeat offenders who commit a disproportionately large number of crimes. This "chronic offender group" (approximately 8%) is responsible for more than half of all the offenses committed, including a large portion of homicides, rapes, robberies, and aggravated assaults. Although the road to a chronic criminal career is highly complex and defies simple explanations, the studies agree on the following points. Most delinquents do not become chronic offenders. A few mischievous and petty delinquencies do not usually lead to an acceleration of serious criminal offending. Compared with conventional delinquent youths, chronic offenders begin their criminal careers at very young ages, often before reaching the age of 10. In fact, age at the onset of offending is the single best predictor of becoming chronic offenders and embarking on adult criminal careers. According to these studies, the younger a person is when first arrested, convicted, or confined for any criminal behavior, the more likely it is for that individual to continue offending. Offense patterns of chronic delinquents are often characterized by excessive violence, destruction, and lack of remorse. Calculations of the average lengths of criminal careers show them to be about 6 years, with career lengths peaking between the ages of 30 and 40. These findings have great potential for crime control and penal policy development. This is because if chronic offenders could be correctly identified and incarcerated for long periods of time, the crime rate should decline considerably.

Responding to these findings, Congress and state governments have passed a wide range of legislative initiatives during the past few years. Rooted in chronic offender research, these efforts are designed to deal more effectively with the nation's mounting crime problem. They do so by targeting high-risk, violent, and persistent offenders for rigorous prosecution. If found guilty in a court of law, such offenders are sentenced to long periods of incarceration, including life without parole. Advocates of longer sentences assume that they will both reduce crime and, ultimately, save taxpayer money. This is because they believe that such sentences will not only decrease the cost of victimization through incapacitation, but will also reduce the substantial costs of rearrest and reprocessing of repeat offenders by the criminal justice system.

Yet in spite of these dramatic legislative changes in sentencing, it is not known whether they will ultimately achieve the desired effect of crime reduction. This is because the research evidence on selective incapacitation is still incomplete. At present, criminologists do not yet have the ability to predict precisely which offenders present unusually high risks for recidivism and violence. Obversely, there is a similar lack of knowledge to correctly predict which offenders represent unusually low risks to society. The result has been legislative overkill. Present sentencing schemes cast too wide a net in their efforts to incapacitate and punish the serious, repeat offender. In the process, too many criminals are incarcerated whose crimes are minor and who do not pose a threat to the community.

The cumulative impact of career offender laws and related harsh sentences for repeat offenders has led this nation to the highest incarceration rate in the world, with over 350 prisoners per 100,000 U.S. residents! To date, prison populations have increased

close to a million persons in state and federal prisons. The cost of maintaining these prisoners has risen concomitantly, and will reach $19 billion in 1995, excluding the costs of holding prisoners in the nation's city and county jails. If current trends continue unabated, the costs of incarceration are destined to rise further. This is because of the unprecedented growth of lifers and elderly in prisons, whose health-care needs double and triple the cost of caring for younger inmates in the general prison population.

Considering what is known about the relationship between age and crime, current developments in criminal justice countervail existing knowledge: statistically speaking, recidivism is known to decline with increases in age. Because offending at an early age is highly predictive of long criminal careers, scarce public resources would be better focused on crime prevention rather than on aging and geriatric inmates, whose criminal careers have peaked and decelerated long ago.

VII. AGE STRUCTURE AND CRIME

Because crime varies with age, changes in the age structure of society exert an important impact on the crime rate independent of the other known factors, such as dysfunctional families, schools, peers, and neighborhoods. The baby boom after World War II is well known and documented. The twin promises of peace and prosperity accelerated the nation's marriage and birth rates with highly predictable consequences. When the baby boom generation reached its most crime-prone years during the 1960s, the country's crime rate rose precipitously. By 1980, the crime rate peaked at 5,950 per 100,000 in the population and declined. A decade later, Index crimes were down, along with the proportion of juveniles in the total population. Since then, Index crimes have been falling, with minor fluctuations. There have been further small decreases in the national crime rate since 1990. However, recent crime rates conceal two highly divergent and troubling trends: although adult crime rates are declining as the baby boom generation ages, juvenile violent crime has increased rapidly. An examination of the nation's homicide rate, calculated per 100,000 inhabitants, illuminates the problem. Since 1985, the homicide rate for adults aged 25 and over has steadily declined from 8 to 5.2% in 1993. During the same time, the homicide rate for young adults aged 18 to 24 has increased from 16 to 26%. Worst of all, for juveniles aged 14 to 17, the homicide rate has more than doubled from 7 to almost 19%. Considering the fact that the nation's adolescent population will expand to 23% by 2005, the problem of rapidly rising serious, violent juvenile crime will only be compounded.

VIII. SUMMARY

In summary, the state of criminological knowledge about the relationship between age and crime indicates that current criminal justice policies are misdirected. If today's unacceptably high crime rates are to be reversed, and more importantly, if a new crime wave is to be averted, the focus should be on primary prevention. This is best accomplished by assisting dysfunctional families, juveniles, and school systems outside the criminal justice system and by early intervention programs for youths within the system.

BIBLIOGRAPHY

Adler, F., Gerhard, O., Mueller, W., & Laufer, W. S. (1991). *Criminology.* New York: McGraw-Hill, Inc.

Farrington, D. P. (1986). Age and crime. In M. Tonry & N. Morris (Ed.), *Crime and justice: An annual review of research* (vol. 7, pp. 189–250). Chicago: University of Chicago Press.

Federal Bureau of Investigation. (1994). *Uniform crime reports, 1993.* Washington, DC: U.S. Government Printing Office.

Greenwood, P. W. (1995). Juvenile crime and juvenile justice. In J. Q. Wilson & J. Petersilia (Eds.), *Crime* (pp. 91–117). San Francisco: ICS Press.

Hirschi, T., & Gottfredson, M. (1983). Age and the explanation of crime. *American Journal of Sociology 89,* N 3:552–584.

Sampson, R. J., & Laub, J. H. (1993). *Crime in the making.* Cambridge, MA: Harvard University Press.

Siegel, L. J., & Senna, J. J. (1994). *Juvenile delinquency: Theory, practice and law.* St. Paul: West Publishing Company.

Wright, K. N., & Wright, K. E. (1994). *Family life, delinquency and crime: A policymaker's guide.* Washington, DC: The Office of Juvenile Justice and Delinquency Prevention.

D

Death and Dying

Robert Kastenbaum

Arizona State University

Advance Directive A document that instructs physicians on the type of treatment a person wishes to receive if unable to express his or her wishes at a later time because of impairment. (The living will is a type of advance directive.)

Brain Death A condition in which vegetative processes of the body may continue, although the capacity for thought, experience, and behavior has been destroyed.

Death Anxiety A turbulent emotional state that may be aroused when people encounter reminders of their mortality.

Deathbed Scenes Interactions between a dying person and his or her family, friends, and care providers shortly before or at the actual time of death.

Death System The practical and symbolic actions taken by a society to mediate the individual's relationship with death.

Dying Process of physical decline that ends in death. This term emphasizes the person who is living through the process, as distinguished from the status of the medical condition itself (*see* Terminal illness).

Hospice An alternative to traditional medical care of dying people that gives highest priority to relief of pain and other symptoms (also known as the palliative care approach).

Life Expectancy Statistical estimate of the number of years of life a person is likely to have remaining; can be calculated from date of birth or from one's present age.

Organ Donation Removal of body parts from a person at death to restore function or save the life of another person.

Patient's Self-Determination Act Federal law that requires health-care facilities to ask patients if they have advanced directives to govern their treatment.

Persistent Vegetative State The continuation of vital body functions over a period of weeks, months, or even years despite the individual's lack of responsiveness (a condition often maintained through the use of a ventilator and/or other lifesupport devices, but that may also exist spontaneously).

Terminal Illness An incurable condition that will lead to a person's death within a year or less. The period immediately preceding death is known as the end phase.

Even the longest life ends in **DEATH**, the irreversible cessation of biological functioning. Despite the universality of death, however, new technologies and new sociopolitical circumstances have generated controversies about precisely what is meant by death, and under precisely what circumstances a person may be viewed as dead. These changes, controversies, and conflicts have increased the need for informed decision-making regarding end-of-life issues.

I. NEW QUESTIONS ABOUT DEATH AND DYING

Philosophers and theologians have long disputed the fundamental nature of *death*, but for practical purposes most people have had little difficulty in defining both this term and its frequent companion, *dying*. Death was considered to be the final cessation of life functions. Generally, this determination was made by observing the lack of respiration, pulse, and response to stimulation as well as by lowered body temperature (hypothermia). Dying referred to the period immediately preceding death when it was obvious that the individual was losing vital functions and was beyond successful medical intervention.

Both terms are now subject to dispute and ambiguity. Three related developments have had much influence on this situation: (a) longer intervals between onset of illness and death, (b) life-support technology, and (c) organ donation.

1. In the past many deaths occurred after a relatively brief episode of acute illness; this pattern still is common in societies with inadequate nutrition, public health programs, and medical resources. For example, a person with a severe case of typhoid or viral infection might show a rapid and obvious decline. It would be clear that this person was "dying." Such trajectories of death are becoming less frequent in technologically advanced societies. People are more likely to live for prolonged periods of time with an illness that will eventually become fatal. Cancer is the model disease of this type. Because a person with an incurable cancer may live for a long time and with a high quality of life, it does not seem appropriate to apply the term *dying* to this situation. There is room for differing opinions as to when a person with a terminal illness has become a dying person—and these differing opinions are consequential, because people tend to change the way they interact with people when they are defined as dying. Nurses and physicians now tend not to use the term *dying* at all, but to speak instead of the "end-phase" period in which vital bodily functions are shutting down. This usage has not yet gained wide circulation with the general public.

2. Life-support technology has become increasingly available in the United States and other technologically advanced nations. The body of a person who would otherwise die very soon can be maintained by devices that feed, hydrate, medicate, and, if necessary, force air in and out of the lungs. This technology has been used with some success for relatively short periods in helping people recover from traumatic injuries and acute medical crises. However, life-support technology has also been used to maintain people who are unresponsive and who seem to have little or no chance of recovery. Some of these people show no electrical activity of the brain; others show activity only in the lower levels of the central nervous system (CNS). There is controversy regarding the nature of brain death. At one extreme is the position that the person is alive as long as any physiological activity can be observed (persistent vegetative state). At the other extreme is the position that the *person* is dead if the higher reaches of the CNS are not functional, even if the body is maintained indefinitely. The practical consequences are obvious: if this person really is dead, then there would not seem to be any point in starting or maintaining life support.

3. Organ donation has become a significant component of the health-care system. This development has further intensified the question of how death should be defined and determined. It should be noted that the ongoing controversies have little to do with the meaning of death in a religious or philosophical sense. The emphasis is on the criteria for certifying "deadness." Those with a stake in successful organ donations are naturally inclined to define "dead" so as to maximize the harvesting of organs at the earliest possible time. Those with a stake in preserving what is left of the life of a nonresponsive patient—and hoping for a miraculous recovery—favor more restrictive criteria. Two competent and well-intentioned physicians, then, may well have different approaches to defining the same person as either alive or dead, depending on their goals and responsibilities.

Two practical concerns also exercise considerable influence in the current debates regarding the definitions of dying and death. Economic issues often dominate the discussion. It is very expensive to maintain a body in a life-support system. Furthermore, in general, it is very expensive to provide care to people in the end phases of their terminal illness. Officials who are charged with controlling the spiraling costs of health care recognize that these two related types of service (extended life support and end-phase management) are major contributors to the problem. "I have a plan for extending the lives of dying people and putting more nonresponsive patients on life-support systems," is a statement that neither the health-care system nor the government would be eager to hear.

The other source of pressure is quite different, but

operates in the same direction. Family members and friends often are distressed when dying is prolonged or death is delayed (whichever interpretation one chooses to make). The familiar phrase "death and dignity" arose from this concern. However, this concern is not only for the person whose suffering seems to be unnecessarily prolonged, but also for those who will be bereaved. The ordeal of grieving and mourning is complicated when the loved one is simultaneously both alive and dead. Furthermore, the emotional stress on family and friends makes it difficult for them to carry out their other responsibilities (e.g., parenting, working). As much as they might cherish the patient, they may also feel the need to get on with their own lives, a need that seems in this situation to have been thwarted by medical technology. [*See* BEREAVEMENT AND LOSS.]

Health-care providers, administrators, and researchers are now having to deal with ambiguity and controversy regarding the most basic elements in their mission: When and what is dead? What and when is dying? Societal forces are exercising an influence over the entire spectrum of responses to dying and death. Moreover, these responses are also closely linked to attitudes about the later adult years.

II. SOCIETAL ATTITUDES TOWARD THE DEATH OF ELDERLY PEOPLE

A. The Death System

It is helpful to look first at the big picture. All societies attempt to cope with universal needs related to mortality. The society may consist of relatively few people who have lived in the same place for many generations, share the same belief system, and meet each other every day in face-to-face interactions. By contrast, the society may consist of millions of people who are highly mobile and who interact with each other through telephone, e-mail, fax, and mass communications. These differences affect every sphere of life. In a traditional face-to-face society, for example, people are likely to end their lives in a familiar setting and in the company of those they have known very well for many years. In the United States, by contrast, it is common to change residence numerous times and to experience the terminal phase of life

far from one's point of origin, some in congregate care facilities.

Furthermore, at the point of death there are often collisions between ways of life. For example, the patriarch of a large Hispanic family was silent, withdrawn, and depressed during hospitalization for his final illness. After the first day he refused to speak in either English or Spanish. Family and hospital staff agreed that the dying man felt intimidated and alienated by the barren, bustling hospital environment. Acting quickly, the family turned to a hospice care program. The patient was brought home and his family instructed and assisted in providing the needed care. The silence and tension immediately dissipated, and his life ended a few days later with all the family and friends who could find a place present around his bed. Here, fortunately, there was an integration of the support of lifelong companions and the symptom relief made possible by medical advances. In our pluralistic society there are encounters every day between the mainstream health-care system and the traditions and values that particular families bring to the end-of-life situation.

Despite their differences, all societies attempt to cope with the same set of death-related issues. These efforts result in a set of implicit rules regarding the way one should think, feel, and behave in death-related situations. The death system has already been defined as "the practical and symbolic actions taken by a society to mediate the individual's relationship with death." A team of paramedics responding promptly to an injury accident provides an example of practical actions; touching the name of a family member of the Vietnam Memorial Wall is an example of a meaningful symbolic action.

The major functions of the death system are as follows:

1. Warnings and predictions. In the United States these take such forms as the cautions printed on cigarette packages, weather advisories, and epidemiological forecasts of emerging threats to life (e.g., the recent increase in the incidence of tuberculosis).

2. Preventing death. The continuing campaign to see that all children receive a full range of immunization shots is one example; another is the limitation on the number of hours a commercial pilot can fly within a particular time frame.

3. Caring for the dying. The establishment of the

hospice movement is providing an alternative to traditional medical management of terminal illness in the United States and many other nations. Elderly adults often constitute between two-thirds and three-fourths of the patients in hospice programs.

4. Disposing of the dead. The tradition of whole body burial and elaborate funeral arrangements has been challenged in recent years by the alternatives of cremation and simple, economical arrangements. Because many elderly adults relocate to sunbelt states there is increased interest in cremation as an economical alternative to shipping remains "back home" for burial.

5. Social consolidation after death. Some deaths shake a society to its roots. The assassination of leaders such as John F. Kennedy, Robert Kennedy, and Martin Luther King elicited strong reactions and still reverberate. The deaths that resulted from the bombing of a federal building in Oklahoma City also had a devastating effect on the nation's sense of security. The need for social consolidation after death exists in private life as well, but, too often, the bereaved person does not receive adequate support. For example, society tends to underestimate the grief experienced either by the parents of a stillborn infant or by the adult child whose elderly parent has died.

6. Making sense of death. Why did this person have to die now and in this way? Why does anybody and everybody have to die? Religious beliefs and practices provide acceptable answers to some but not all people. Both the individual and society experience intensified stress when a death is perceived as meaningless.

7. Killing. All societies kill, and all societies have rules that are intended to limit killing. In the United States the long-standing debate about capital punishment has been joined by the assisted suicide and euthanasia controversy. Who has the right to kill whom and under what circumstances? One of the key issues today is whether or not one person has the right to help another person end his or her life: Is killing an option that must be restricted to society acting through its rule-governed officials, or can it also be a perogative of the individual?

The mainstream death system of the United States has a profound influence on the ways in which elderly adults experience the last phases of their lives. This influence is mediated by a complex and ever-shifting mix of societal attitudes regarding the nature, value, and function of the older person.

B. Attitudes and Their Consequences

Attitudes have consequences. For example, presenting the same message to two people will elicit different responses if one has a trustful and the other a distrustful attitude. Behavior can be predicted (although imperfectly) from a knowledge of a person's *predisposition toward action*, which is another way of saying *attitude*. Attitudes may be held by society at large as well as by individuals. The power of societal attitudes to influence large-scale decisions is demonstrated whenever political or corporate officials change their plans based on opinion surveys or focus groups.

Societal attitudes also influence the lives of individuals across many situations. Perhaps the most significant dimension is the tendency to include or exclude a given set of people from full participation in the society. It has been well established that mainstream American attitudes tend to be exclusionary with respect to elderly men and women. Elders are to have their "place," but off to the side. Blatantly negative attitudes toward elders are usually reserved for those who refuse to stay in their assigned roles and demand a full share of attention, resources, and access to power. Those who slip quietly into the role expected of elders are seen as posing a lesser threat and therefore tend to be spared outright abuse. For those who do conform to expectations, the discriminatory pattern is more subtle and is covered by a veneer of toleration and acceptance. [*See* ABUSE AND NEGLECT OF ELDERS; AGEISM AND DISCRIMINATION.]

Unfortunately, elderly people are subject not only to negative age stereotypes, but also to our society's aversive attitude toward dying and death. Although no time of life is exempt from the possibility of bereavement or terminal illness, these risks increase with advancing adult age, placing us in double jeopardy as potential victims of societal discomfort with both aging and death. Elders who have been recently widowed often experience the consequences of these converging negative attitudes. Already kept at a distance by society because of their age, they may now be shunned even by their peers because they have been touched by death. A member of a widowed persons' support group offered her own explanation of this phenomenon: "First, most people don't know what to say to you, so they get tight and jittery around you. But second, and more important, they look at you and think, 'That could happen to me, too!' You just being there reminds them that death is real and husbands die and this could happen to them, too."

Aging and death are broad concepts that are somewhat remote from everyday experience. By contrast, elderly people are palpable and available for inspection. Vague, conflicted, and unresolved feelings about aging and death often become concretized and projected on elderly people. A companion's response to seeing an elderly couple strolling by a lake provides a clear example of the tendency to use elderly people as externalizations of one's own fears. "I will never be an old woman. I will never let myself become dependent. I will never just sit around and watch the world go by. I will never die slowly and painfully. Let me assure you, I am being serious. One of these days, while I still have my health and independence, I will end my life. And I have it all worked out." This intelligent and robust woman in her early 50s described the specific method she would use to commit suicide. "I have seen plenty of old people," she added for emphasis, "so I don't intend to be one." Meanwhile, the elderly couple who had innocently provided the stimulus for this monologue continued to stroll around the lake, hand in hand. The woman who assumed that aging would be worse than death had not conversed with the couple and had no direct knowledge of their lives: she was a prisoner of the societal stereotype she had imposed on them—and on herself.

There are features common to societal attitudes toward elderly people and toward people who have been touched by death. The most prominent features are as follows:

1. Discomfort with one's own future status. American society encourages the development of a self-concept that emphasizes youth and the early adult years. This self-concept does not encompass the entire life course, nor the coping resources that could help one to deal with new challenges and opportunities in the later adult years. The "I" who will grow old and the "I" who will face bereavement and the prospect of death tend to be excluded from the dominant sense of self. More than neglect is involved: often there is also entrenched resistance to thinking about who one

will become. The person who fully embraces societal attitudes tends to cling to the implicit assumptions that "I will never grow old. And I will not be there when I die, because that person will be a stranger, not my real self."

2. Negative characterization of elderly persons and persons who have been touched by death. Elderly persons are assumed to be frail, lethargic, asexual, senile, incompetent, useless, and burdensome. They are also assumed to be depressed and withdrawn, preoccupied with their own miseries. Dying and bereaved persons are also assumed to be depressed, withdrawn, and preoccupied with their own miseries. The other negative characterizations apply as well, with the exception of "senile." Even here, though, a similar assumption is substituted: the dying person's mind is assumed to have been dulled and disoriented by illness. Research has yielded quite a different picture. There are marked individual differences among elders, among dying persons, and among those who are both elderly and terminally ill. Furthermore, many of the negative features noted above occur in response to socioenvironmental deprivation and stress and can be prevented or remedied by modifications in the circumstances with which the individual must cope.

3. Legitimization of avoidance strategies. Both sets of stereotypes provide justification for avoiding intimate contact. These justifications may be expressed in such statements as, "One should not bring up sensitive topics such as, um, death. This would only make them more depressed." "We should respect their privacy and not wear them out with conversation. What they really want is to be alone with their memories." "You can't really have a meaningful conversation with an old/dying person. It would just be upsetting to both of us." Under the surface of these propositions lies the anxiety of confrontation with those who remind us of our own unresolved problems with aging and death. This avoidant attitude can be observed in nonverbal as well as verbal interactions: many people fear to touch or be touched by either an elderly or a dying person—as though one might "catch" mortality.

4. Communication, when it cannot be avoided, should be governed by special rules. When younger adults converse with elders they tend to use "secondary baby talk," a simplified speech accompanied by exaggerated intonations and facial expressions. This

practice has been observed with professional caregivers as well as the general public. This communicational approach attempts to control what the other person can say. Although the specific implicit rules are somewhat different when communicating with a dying or bereaved person there is the same emphasis on avoiding a free and unpredictable exchange of thoughts and feelings.

Studies have repeatedly shown that most people try to keep a greater physical and social distance between themselves and those who are perceived as dying or grieving. Analysis of the verbal and nonbehavioral components of communicational interactions has found that egalitarian give-and-take is replaced by "down-talking" in which the elderly, bereaved, or dying person is treated as inferior in status, power, and value. The implicit rule here is, "You, aged or dying person, have little value left to society so I do not need to spend much time and effort on your behalf."

The convergence of negative attitudes toward both aging and death has many consequences. For example, it is often assumed that the death of an elderly person is relatively unimportant. Accordingly, it is not considered necessary to make sure that caring people are with the dying elder, to arrange for memorial services, or to provide support to survivors. Until the recent promulgation of the hospice concept, the American death system had given little attention to the psychological, social, and spiritual needs of the dying person. When the dying person is also devalued because of age, there has been even less inclination to gather around. Elders who reside in institutions are still likely to die alone despite the (theoretical) availability of other people.

This dismissive approach to the death of an elderly person has its effects on those who participate in the process. For example, staff members of nursing care facilities report feeling more depressed about their own future because they have seen repeatedly how the deaths—and therefore the lives—of elderly residents have been accorded little respect and value.

This process also ignores the needs of those who did love and value the deceased. Their own grief and mourning experiences may be complicated by the lack of acknowledgment and support for their loss. The elderly dying person often is very important to some

people, including both lifelong companions and those caregivers who have come to admire them. Societal attitudes that legitimize turning away from the dying elderly person can therefore have long-term adverse consequences.

The death of an aged person is still the occasion for elaborate funeral and memorial observations in some societies, and among some ethnic communities in the United States (e.g., the Hmong who have immigrated here from Laos). It is not a simple matter of "body disposal," but an affirmation both of the person whose life has just ended and the group's fundamental values. By contrast, funeral directors continue to report that the general preference among Americans is for services that are quick, streamlined, and restrained. "Let's get it over quickly and with the least fuss" is the rule that often seems to govern the funeral and memorial observances for an aged person.

The differential value placed on younger and older adults also leads to a differential response when death occurs. In the American death system it is expected that most people's lives will be spared until they have reached an advanced age. The death of a young person is therefore much more likely to arouse disturbing questions: "Why did this happen? What is life all about if a person can die so young?" The death system's function of trying to give meaning to death seldom comes into operation when an aged person dies. This differential response not only reveals an imbalance in philosophical values, but also reduces the opportunity to prevent premature deaths among elders. For example, some elder deaths that appeared to be "natural" and "inevitable" have turned out to have resulted from inadequate supervision of medications or outright abuse. Many people still have difficulty in understanding that a death can be premature even in advanced age.

There are also economic consequences of society's attitudes toward aging and death. The assumption that both elders and dying people are hopeless cases without significant value to society or themselves makes it easier to restrict the resources available for their care. An important exception can be observed, however. Physicians and hospital systems have been known to harvest the financial entitlements that are available to elderly and dying people whether or not the services provided are actually beneficial to the patients. Diagnostic tests and invasive treatment procedures that have little or no potential to restore the individual's health may be carried out because they are reimbursable. As the end phase of a terminal illness approaches, patients may not be in a position to express and defend their preference to be spared further procedures, and the family may hesitate to challenge medical authority.

Another turn of events has been known to occur near the very end. Medical expenses usually rise sharply in the last few weeks of life. At this point, the medical care system and third-party insurers are in danger of losing money. A well-known strategy then comes into play: the attempt to reduce services or transfer the elderly dying person to somebody else's budget (e.g., sending a patient who has now become an economic liability to a nursing care facility without explicitly acknowledging that this person is in the end phase of life). The health-care establishment therefore welcomed hospice programs as much for their reduction of expenses as for their substantive benefits to patients and families. This awkward arrangement—moving from overuse of services to withdrawal of services for economic reasons—has been made possible by society's judgment that the elderly dying person has little intrinsic value. [See HEALTH CARE AND SERVICES; HOSPICE.]

Perhaps the most dangerous consequence of these negative societal attitudes is its resistance to change. Stereotyped assumptions about elderly, dying, and widowed people legitimize the avoidance of communicational interactions and therefore reduce opportunities to test these assumptions against reality. Elders are given little opportunity to express themselves when subjected to secondary baby talk; terminally ill people are given little opportunity to express themselves when subjected to special rules of interaction that include physical distancing, avoidance of eye contact, and other nonverbal enforcers. The stereotypes do not persist because they have a firm basis in established fact. On the contrary! Research, enlightened clinical experience, and first-person narratives from elderly and dying people demonstrate a great diversity of personal resources, lifestyles, and experiences. People who have entered the lives of elders in the role of caregiver or researcher often report that they have themselves received something valuable from the relationship. Every elder and every dying person has a unique story to share: it is the active listener who remains in short supply.

III. INDIVIDUAL ORIENTATIONS TOWARD DYING AND DEATH

We turn now to the elderly person's own view of dying and death. This view cannot be completely separated from societal attitudes—the longer a person lives, the longer this person has been influenced by prevailing beliefs and customs. Nevertheless, it is always the individual, not society, who faces death and who therefore has occasion to consider the nature and meaning of this prospect.

A. Death Anxiety

Do people become more or less anxious about death with advancing age? There are three basic hypotheses:

1. We become more anxious with age because death is more closely in prospect.
2. We become less anxious because death is perceived as less of a threat.
3. We develop an orientation toward death early in our lives and therefore bring our characteristic level of anxiety with us into the late adult years.

Each of these hypotheses has its sphere of utility. It would not be sound, however, to overextend any of the hypotheses to cover all the phenomena. Heightened death anxiety with advancing age is most likely to occur under four circumstances: (a) acute symptomatic episodes; (b) perceived lack of social support; (c) failure of coping strategies; and (d) fear of rejection or punishment by God. A person with lung cancer or emphysema, for example, may experience alarming episodes of respiratory distress. It is the increasing vulnerability to these episodes rather than age per se that heightens death anxiety. People who feel alone and abandoned are also likely to experience death anxiety more often and more intensely. This feeling commonly is accompanied by the concern that they will die without the solace of companionship. Multiple and unremitting life stresses can overwhelm the individual's ability to control external events and maintain his or her own internal sense of security. A sudden exacerbation of death anxiety under these circumstances does not necessarily signify that the person's life is actually in acute jeopardy. Rather, death has become the symbol of one's feeling of helplessness and dissolution. Not many examples have been found of terror related to expectations of punishment or rejection after death among elders, but such experiences can be intense when they do occur.

What is common to all of the above circumstances is that their association with age is indirect: not all elders experience frightening symptomatic episodes, believe themselves to be without social support, feel overwhelmed by the stresses and challenges of life, or conceive of God as a severe judge of their lives. Moreover, all of these circumstances can be alleviated to some extent by timely and appropriate interventions. Sensitive and reliable companionship has proven valuable in all of these anxiety-arousing circumstances.

Decreased death anxiety has been reported by many elderly people, although there are no substantial longitudinal studies to confirm that death anxiety varies with adult age. The fact that self-reported death anxiety is relatively low in studies of elderly men and women might be explained as a cohort or generational effect instead of an intraindividual change with age. Nevertheless, both scores on standard questionnaires and reflections on the course of one's life suggest that more people experience a decrease rather than an increase in death anxiety in their later adult years.

The most frequent explanation offered by elderly men and women themselves is that they have had a life. A strong marriage, the nurturing of children and grandchildren, and a sense of having met one's responsibilities in all spheres of life are accomplishments that death cannot invalidate. This explanation takes on additional credibility when it is compared with the orientation toward death that is more characteristic of young adults. Death anxiety scores generally are higher among young adults, and they voice concerns about all the plans and desires that might never come to fruition. People who are still searching for their personal identities and sense of worth are more likely to be anxious about the possibility of a foreshortened future, than those who have a firm sense of self, value, and accomplishment. Again, age is only an indirect variable here. Young adults can achieve a sense of living fully and well, and elderly adults can be burdened by a sense of disappointment, regret, and unfulfillment.

Another major contributing factor to reduced death anxiety in the later adult years is cumulative experience with losses and limitations. A person of 80 is unlikely to retain the 20-year-old's sense of invulnerability. Most people learn how to accommodate themselves to the changes that occur over a long life. A person may at first resent the need to acquire glasses or a hearing aid, but then utilize these devices to maintain quality of life. When an elder remarked, "I still like chili, but chili doesn't like me," this was but one of many examples of accommodation. He later put his orientation toward life and death into this perspective: "I stopped being immortal a long time ago. I am in the flow of life, the flow of aging, we all are. This flow, this river delivers us into the great sea. That's life. That's just the way things are."

Consistency of attitude toward death also can be observed. Studies of personality patterns across the adult years suggest that the individual's basic way of dealing with self and world remain fairly consistent from youth through age. It is not surprising, then, to note that both sources of anxiety and strategies for coping with anxiety show some consistency over the years. People who throughout most of their lives have depended on other people to cope with anxiety-arousing situations are likely to continue to do so when they are faced with death-related situations. Consistency is also likely to hold true for those whose preferred coping technique has been *counterphobic* (seeking out encounters with sources of fear, e.g., by taking extra risks with their lives), avoidance, or intellectualization. Problems arise when a preferred strategy for coping with anxiety is no longer available or effective. For example, a person who has characteristically bolted from situations and relationships that aroused anxiety may discover there is no easy way to escape from a failing body.

People with relatively high levels of general anxiety throughout their lives are likely to maintain this level in their later years. Their feelings of distress, helplessness, and apprehension may seem to be centered on death, but often can be reduced when they are helped to feel more secure and competent in their overall management of situations and relationships.

The consistency hypothesis is less useful in explaining some common changes that occur throughout the adult years in people with differing personalities and lifestyles. Regardless of personality style, people tend to feel more concern about the manner in which they will die rather than the fact of death per se. Elderly men and women often express concerns about becoming helpless, dependent, and subjected to life-support devices. Fears of disfiguration, pain, and clouded consciousness are voiced more frequently and with more intensity than fear of death. By and large, elders seem to come to terms with their mortality, whether through faith in God and survival, or through a philosophical acceptance.

Unfortunately, equanimity in the face of death is sometimes mistaken for a willingness, even an eagerness to exit from life. This erroneous assumption can have significant consequences (e.g., the withholding or withdrawal of vital services to an elderly person who, it is assumed, no longer places much value on his or her own life). The underlying dynamic in this misattribution can take the form "If *I* were that old and if *I* had physical limitations and if *I* felt I had lived a full life—well, I'd certainly be ready to go!" One has but to engage in serious communicational exchanges with elderly people to discover that it is possible to cherish everyday life while at the same time accepting the reality of death.

B. Living through Dying

"A person is either living or dying." This proposition is likely to be rejected when it is expressed so plainly. Nevertheless, our society has long had difficulty in accepting the fact that a dying person is still a living person. As already noted, when a person was defined as terminally ill, others tended to become more tense, unnatural, and remote in their interactions. This shift would be experienced by the dying person as rejection and abandonment. Evading or denying the fact of terminal illness therefore became a common strategy. Those gathered around the bed of a dying person would steadfastly insist that he or she would soon be up and around, and the dying person was supposed to go along with this mutual pretense script. These maneuvers served primarily to reduce the other person's sense of anxiety and helplessness.

Terminally ill people often felt constrained to accommodate to the anxiety-control needs they detected in their companions and visitors. Communicating one's own fears, doubts, and needs would risk the further attentuation of relationships. It was difficult to communicate in an open and honest manner with people who could not accept a person as both living and dying. Ironically, the dying person's hesitancy in sharing his or her thoughts was often interpreted as "denial" when it was actually a strategic maneuver

intended to reduce the anxiety of family and friends who were themselves hesitant to face the facts.

Dying people tended to be deprived of reliable communication and social support not only because they aroused anxiety in others, but also because they represented the failure of the system to prevent death. The American death system, casting its lot with technology and aggressive treatment, had assigned a low priority to care of the dying. A person who was both elderly and terminally ill was an unwelcome reminder that the ability of the medical establishment to work miracles did have its limits. Furthermore, the dying person often was subject to pain and other symptoms that were not well controlled through the prevailing pattern of medical management. Restricted in communicational interactions, rejected as medical failures, and left to their suffering, terminally ill people were hard pressed to find comfort and value in the end phase of life in a positive and meaningful manner.

This negative pattern of avoidance and social isolation is now being transformed by the concurrent emergence of three new developments.

1. Death education and counseling. Academic courses and professional workshops on death and dying started to appear in the middle 1960s. It is now possible to discuss these once-taboo topics openly and in depth. This educational development is being strengthened by a substantial increase in research. Opinions and assumptions are gradually being replaced by the results of well-crafted studies. Counselors willing and able to help people deal with dying, death, and grief have also become more numerous as a result of the death education movement.

2. The hospice movement has grown rapidly and proven to be a viable alternative to traditional medical management of terminal illness. With both grassroot public support and the dedication of some health-care professionals, the hospice movement has raised the care of the dying person to a higher priority in the American death system. Those who select the hospice alternative—especially at a relatively early point in their terminal illness—are likely to benefit from improved techniques for controlling pain and other symptoms, as well as from the opportunity to live at home much of the time. The improved comfort and communication associated with hospice care enables dying people to draw more fully on their own resources and the resources of their most valued companions.

3. The lectures and writings of Elizabeth Kubler-Ross. More effectively than anyone before her, Kubler-Ross demonstrated that dying people are very much living people and are responsive to honest interactions. Both professional caregivers and the general public were encouraged by her example to engage in more frequent and meaningful interactions with dying persons. Much subsequent knowledge and improvement in care can be credited to Kubler-Ross's restoration of the dying person to the heart of the community.

One facet of Kubler-Ross's approach became especially influential: her stage theory of dying. According to this theory, dying people move through a sequence of orientations toward death. The individual's response is said to pass from denial and shock through anger, bargaining, depression, and acceptance. People may spend varying periods of time in a particular stage, and not all people complete the progression. This concept of stages seemed helpful to many people because it was the first to outline a predictable course through the dying process. The anxious family member, friend, or health-care professional now had something to go on. One could understand what was happening with the dying person and thereby be able to respond in an appropriate way be identifying the stage.

Despite its rapid and widespread acceptance, however, the stage theory has not been confirmed by research. For example, elderly people who have lived with a progressive illness over an extended period of time are not likely to respond with denial and shock when they learn that their condition has become terminal. Similarly, "bargaining" may be absent for those who had come to terms with their mortality before the onset of the terminal illness. People have responses other than the five mentioned by Kubler-Ross, and the sequences in which they occur have much to do with the individual's entire life situation.

The problem is not simply with the particular stages, but with all the individual and situational factors that are not well encompassed by the theory. Ignored by stage theory are such significant facets of the dying person's experience as the specific illness and its current status, the mode of treatment, personality style, ethnic and religious beliefs, life situation, and social support network. Reliance on stage theory can reduce attention to the entire spectrum of experiences and forces that influence the dying person, and to the dying person's own distinctive way of interpreting life within the shadow of death.

IV. END-OF-LIFE ISSUES AND CHOICES

It was once assumed that life passes out of the individual's control when death comes into prospect. In recent years, however, the American public has become better informed about end-of-life issues and choices. This development can be seen as a facet of the consumer rights movement (sparked by Ralph Nader) as well as the emergence of hospice care and death education.

Elderly adults are becoming increasingly interested in learning about the issues and choices. As a woman in her late eighties observed, "I am still responsible for my life. I think I should take some responsibility for my death, too, don't you?"

There are often two preliminary problems to solve before an elder can deal effectively with the available choices. First, it may be necessary to overcome the resistance of adult children to discussing end-of-life issues. Many younger adults still assume that talking about death is "morbid" and likely to traumatize an elderly person. They need to be reassured that their parents or grandparents are neither depressed nor fragile. Instead, it just makes sense to discuss death-related issues, come to an understanding within the family, make the choices, and then continue to go on with life. The alternative is to be overtaken by events and not have the opportunity to have one's preferences fulfilled.

Second, it may be useful to review one's priorities for life as well as for death. The person who is making death-related decisions also has important decisions to make about life because there is a continuing trend toward increased life expectancy *during* the later adult years. This increase is illustrated by Table I.

The trend toward increasing life expectancy also includes ages beyond 65. The obvious implication is that elderly people need not choose between thinking about life *or* death. Those who wish to have some influence on death-related circumstances can do so by familiarizing themselves with the options, but there will still remain the even greater challenge of deciding how one wants to utilize the many years of life that may still be ahead.

The end-of-life option that is most germane here

Table I Life Expectancy at Age 65 in the United States (All Races)

Year	Men	Women	Both sexes
1900	11.5	12.2	11.9
1950	12.8	15.0	13.9
1960	12.8	15.8	14.3
1970	13.1	17.0	15.2
1980	14.1	18.3	16.4
1989	15.2	18.8	17.2

Checklist I Advance Directive Options

Yes	No	Options
		1. I want all life-sustaining treatments to be discontinued if I become terminally ill and permanently incompetent.
		2. I want all life-sustaining treatments to be discontinued if I become permanently unconscious, whether terminally ill or not.
		3. I want all life-sustaining treatments to be discontinued if I become unconscious and have very little change of ever recovering consciousness or avoiding permanent brain injury.
		4. I want to be kept alive if I become gravely ill and have only a slight chance of recovery (5% or less), and would probably require weeks or months of further treatment before the outcome became clear.
		5. I want to have fluids and nutrition discontinued if other life-support measures are discontinued.

concerns advance directives for health care. (Other important issues include choice of hospice or traditional care, distribution of personal assets, and funeral or memorial arrangements.) Because this option is still evolving it may be useful to summarize its history. A document known as the living will was introduced in 1968 by a nonprofit organization that was then called The Euthanasia Educational Council (later renamed, Concern for Dying). This was one of the first expressions of the nascent death awareness movement. The living will was intended as an instruction for health-care personnel should the situation arise in which the individual could not communicate directly his or her own preference (e.g., comatose). The document was to be signed by the individual while he or she was mentally competent with witnesses and a notary public present.

Theoretically, this advance directive could have expressed the wish that physicians do everything they can to prolong life, but in practice almost all living wills conformed to the following language as given in the model document:

> If at such time the situation should arise in which there is no reasonable expectation of my recovery from extreme physical or mental disability, I direct that I be allowed to die and not be kept alive by medications, artificial means, or "heroic measures." I do, however, ask that medication be mercifully administered to me to alleviate suffering, even though this may shorten my remaining time.

The living will was received favorably by the American public. There were several drawbacks, however.

- Health-care personnel were under no obligation to act in accordance with living wills. It was not a legally enforceable instrument.
- Many physicians who were in sympathy with the intent of living wills hesitated to act upon them out of concern that they might be accused of malpractice or homicide.
- The language was too vague and the instructions too general to serve as guidelines in many situations (e.g., just what is "artificial" or "heroic"?).

Additionally, there was a large disparity between the approval rate for living wills and their actual utilization. For example, surveys of physicians and nurses find overwhelming agreement with the principle of the living will, but also that relatively few had "gotten around" to doing one for themselves.

These problems were partially remedied in succeeding years as almost all state legislatures around the nation passed bills that established some version of the living will as a legal document. Often called "natural death acts," these laws provided protection for health-care personnel who acted in accordance with living wills. Nevertheless, there was still confusion and frustration because the instructions appeared too vague. Recognition of this problem led to a new generation of advance directives in which the individual is encouraged to be more specific.

The major options are given in Checklist 1. These options may at first appear similar, but the differences can be critical in guiding medical decision making in a crisis situation.

An advance directive that is clear on options such as the above is more likely to be honored by health-care personnel than the more ambiguous language of the original living will. Whether or not an individual intends to authorize an advanced directive it is a useful learning experience to consider these options and become familiar with their implications.

An important new development has now appeared. The Patient Self-Determination Act (PSDA) is part of a measure passed by the United States Congress in 1990 and activated December 1, 1991. The PSDA has the somewhat paradoxical effect of making an option obligatory. Every health-care institution that receives either Medicare or Medicaid reimbursements must ask all clients about their preferences in a terminal illness situation. Patients must be informed of their rights to accept or refuse treatment and to provide the facility with an advance directive if they so desire. The institution must also make federal informational materials available to the patients.

The PSDA would seem to strengthen appreciably the individual's ability to have his or her wishes respected in terminal situations. Unfortunately, this promise has not yet been fulfilled. Undermining the effective utilization of PSDAs are the following factors:

- The federal government did not allocate funds for a public education program, so many individuals entering a health-care facility are not prepared for making a decision.
- Information transfer within and between health-care systems is not yet reliable with respect to advance directives. The people who would need to have that information available to them instantly may not have access to the directives.
- Many health-care systems have shunted the processing of advance directives to personnel with little education in this field and little authority to see that the directives are properly handled.
- There is no penalty for health-care providers who fail to honor advance directives.

The limited evidence now available suggests that many health-care systems are giving only token compliance with advance directives and many people remain unprepared to make a decision on their own behalf.

Elderly adults who make the effort to learn about their end-of-life options are in a position not only to influence future events in their own lives, but also to serve as mentors for younger adults and an insistent voice demanding that health-care systems give the attention that advance directives deserve.

BIBLIOGRAPHY

Callahan, D. (1993). *The troubled dream of life.* New York: Simon & Schuster.

Glaser, B. G., & Strauss, A. (1966). *Awareness of dying.* Chicago: Aldine.

Haas, W. H. III, & Longino, C. F., Jr. (1994). Population growth, distribution, and characteristics. In R. J. Manheimer (Ed.), *Older Americans almanac* (pp. 23–48). Detroit: Gale Research, Inc.

Heatherton, T. F., & Weinberger, J. L. (Eds.). (1994). *Can personality change?* Washington, DC: American Psychological Association.

Hoefler, J. M. (1994). *Deathright: Culture, medicine, politics, and the right to die.* Boulder: Westview Press.

Kastenbaum, R. (1995). *Death, society, and human experience.* (5th ed.). Boston: Allyn & Bacon.

Kastenbaum, R. (1994). End-of-life issues. In R. J. Manheimer (Ed.), *Older Americans almanac* (pp. 595–616). Detroit: Gale Research, Inc.

Kastenbaum, R. (1992). *The psychology of death.* (rev. ed.). New York: Springer Publishing Co., Inc.

Kubler-Ross, E. (1969). *On death and dying.* New York: Macmillan.

President's Commission for the Study of Ethical Problems in Medicine and Biomedical and Behavioral Research (1983). *Deciding to forego life-sustaining treatment.* Washington, DC: U.S. Government Printing Office.

Pugh, D., & West, D. J. (1994–1995). Advance directive and the self-determination act: A patient's perspective. *Omega, Journal of Death and Dying, 30,* 249–256.

Ryan, E. B., Hamilton, J. M., & Kwong See, S. (1994). Patronizing the old: How do younger and older adults respond to baby talk in the nursing home? *International Journal of Aging and Human Development, 39,* 21–32.

Quill, T. E. (1993). *Death and dignity.* New York: W. W. Norton & Co.

Decision Making and Everyday Problem Solving

Fredda Blanchard-Fields

Georgia Institute of Technology

Abstract Problem Solving Problems that involve finding the correct solution to a novel task that incorporate novel stimuli. Examples include concept learning, visuospatial tasks, and search tasks.

Ecological Validity A concern with the investigation of processes used in everyday life.

Emotional Salience The degree to which an individual is emotionally involved in the problem situation presented.

Emotion-Focused Strategy These solutions involve covert behaviors that manage or control emotional reactions such as positively reappraising a situation or passively accepting a situation.

Problem-Focused Strategy These solutions involve self-initiated, overt behaviors that deal directly with a problem and its effects, such as taking direct action to alter a situation or seeking information or advice about it.

Problem-Solving Efficacy The use of effective and adaptive problem-solving strategies.

Empirical evidence based on traditional models of abstract **PROBLEM SOLVING AND DECISION MAKING** demonstrates decline in performance as

adults grow older. However, researchers have become increasingly dissatisfied with this theoretical and methodological approach as the sole means for assessing adult intellectual functioning. In response to these concerns, a growing body of research has emerged, assessing skills and knowledge necessary for successful functioning in an everyday context. In contrast to research demonstrating decline in abstract problem solving, competence in problem-solving ability in adulthood and aging are most evident in socioemotional or everyday types of situations. This is particularly evident when the way the individual perceives and structures the problem situation is taken into consideration. In other words, problem-solving efficacy may not simply be a function of how many more "correct" solutions to problems an individual generates, but is more a function of (a) whether or not the problem reflects situations encountered in daily life, (b) how the individual interprets and restructures the problem space of the everyday situation, and (c) how adaptive the solution is given the individual's goals and context of living.

I. APPROACHES TO THE STUDY OF EVERYDAY PROBLEM SOLVING

A. Concerns about Traditional Approaches to Problem Solving

Research examining age differences in abstract problem solving demonstrates more effective problem solving in college youth as compared to older adults. However, the majority of these studies are grounded in traditional conceptions of cognitive maturity in adulthood and thus, reflect supposedly "context-free" measures of problem solving and overly formalistic youth-oriented criteria of problem-solving competence. Such tasks include concept learning, abstract inferencing, and logical reasoning tasks, all of which opt for more formal operational criteria that lead to only one correct solution. Use of these formalistic or context-free measures of problem solving to assess age differences implies that they are valid indicators of adaptive skills across multiple contexts of functioning in adulthood. Alternatively, they may only represent adaptive skills most appropriate in an academic context.

The question arises as to whether these types of problem-solving tasks adequately reflect a complete picture of adaptive cognitive functioning in adulthood. Effective problem solving on these more traditional tasks may be limited when referring to specific adaptive outcomes in adulthood, for example, in socioemotional, family, work, or health-related domains. In fact, older adults report that their social reasoning about everyday matters has improved over time despite losses in other areas. In addition, some have argued that the skills necessary to perform abstract problem-solving tasks are not well practiced in middle-aged and older adults. Thus, alternative approaches to investigating everyday problem solving have emerged with a common goal: to identify and measure types of problem-solving skills required for effective functioning in an everyday context during adulthood.

B. The Issue of Ecological Validity

In pursuit of this goal, the issue of ecological validity with respect to problem-solving tasks resulted in a movement towards the use of more meaningful and realistic materials in problem-solving studies. Initially, this approach involved changing the content of traditional problem-solving tasks to conform to content more relevant in adulthood (e.g., substituting arithmetic strategies to select best buys in a supermarket for strategies used to solve an abstract numerical problem). By improving the face validity of the tasks it was assumed that the bias inherent in abstract problem-solving tasks would be removed. Studies conducted within this framework resulted in an attenuation of the age difference findings demonstrated in more tra-

ditional problem-solving studies. However, a negative linear relationship between age and problem-solving performance still remained. Does the simple content variation of abstract tasks address the issue of the underlying criteria used to judge problem-solving efficacy? It is argued that these tasks only reflect a cosmetic change to content and are still grounded in traditional abstract problem solving (and youth-oriented) criteria. For example, they still demand a single correct solution and involve the same necessary strategies used to solve abstract problems.

C. Structural Change in the Nature of the Task: Characteristics of Everyday Problem Solving

Another approach to the ecological validity issue is to redirect attention from simple content variation of tasks towards utilizing differential structures of tasks. This means developing completely new types of problems, similar to those that adults encounter in their everyday lives. Attempts to restructure problem-solving tasks involves specifying characteristics unique to problems found in an everyday context. These characteristics may be distinct from those used to assess abstract reasoning skills. Beyond the major characteristic that problems reflect situations frequently encountered in daily living, these distinct properties include the ill-structured nature of problems, interpersonal and social emphasis, and an extended time frame for determining the effectiveness of solutions.

Problem-solving tasks grounded in the more traditional orientation tend to be well-structured in that (a) the experimenter defines the problem and the rules to be followed and (b) a single correct solution to the problem situation is required. An important avenue that has been generally overlooked in such tasks is the examination of goals and strategies used by individuals to solve ill-structured or ambiguous tasks. As a function of the social content inherent in these situations, ill-structured problems are unpredictable and are continually in transformation. The resulting ambiguity as to what defines these types of problems requires individuals to generate their own interpretation of a problem situation rather than to rely on the structure imposed by others. In addition to multiple definitions of a problem space, there are multiple solutions to ill-structured problems, all potentially effective depending upon the trade-offs one is willing to make. Finally, unlike time-constrained traditional abstract problems, whether or not a decision to choose a particular solution strategy (among many potential candidates) for everyday problems proves to be successful may take an extended time period (e.g., it may take months or even years to determine if one has chosen a compatible marital partner).

Past research on problem solving has relied primarily upon problem situations and measures that play down interpersonal features of everyday problem solving (i.e., problems that ignore the social context in which everyday problem solving takes place). In contrast, current research suggests that the nature of everyday problem solving is inherently interpersonal and social. This calls attention to the importance of emotions and other psychosocial factors involved in solving problems. In fact, studies show that as adults grow older, their problem-solving goals become more concerned with other people, intimacy, and generativity. In sum, the ill-structured, time-extended, and social nature of task structures tend to be more representative of those problems encountered in everyday life and stress the importance of taking a contextual perspective for assessing the efficacy of everyday problem solving.

D. A Contextual Perspective on Everyday Problem Solving

A contextual perspective on everyday problem solving stresses the importance of considering how changing contextual demands influence how individuals solve problems. Contextual factors include (a) knowledge brought to a context, (b) situational goals and demands in a particular context, (c) well-instantiated goals reflecting personal traits and accumulation of experience, (d) changing life circumstances, and (e) historical-cultural influences. All of these factors combine to influence the appraisal and interpretation of a problem, and the motivation to employ specific strategies to solve the problem.

Researchers suggest that successful problem solving can be conceived in a context of adaptive cognition where cognitive and affective functioning as well as physical characteristics of the environment interact or are embedded in cultural values, attitudes, and sociocultural institutions. As a result, criteria unique to everyday problem solving in adulthood and aging

as a function of contextual demands need to be specified. For example, well-structured, single-criterion problems may be encountered frequently for youth in academic contexts. Thus, more traditional modes of problem solving are adaptive in this context. However, situations reflecting multiple criteria for potential solutions are more prominent in the problems of everyday living faced by older adults. There are several researchers who have attempted to specify these criteria from various theoretical perspectives.

For example, adaptive problem solving in an everyday context has been purported to entail (a) an awareness that the veracity of the solution to a particular problem is relative to differing perspectives and goals of the individual; (b) an awareness of the role of self in interpreting problems; and (c) a recognition that logical reasoning is embedded in a sociocultural matrix. In other words, in order for an individual to exercise good judgment in problems reflecting uncertainty and ambiguity, she or he needs to take into consideration a contextual perspective. From this framework, effective problem solving in an everyday context involves an "openness" to perspectives and solutions in order to meet the adaptive demands of one's environment in addition to an organizational structure to maintain continuity. It also suggests an "openness" on the part of assessment criteria to take into consideration whether or not a problem-solving strategy is effective as a function of the demands of the environment and the goals of the problem solver in that particular context.

II. ADULT DEVELOPMENTAL DIFFERENCES IN EVERYDAY PROBLEM SOLVING AND DECISION MAKING

A. The Problem-Solving Process

Before selecting the appropriate strategies to solve everyday problem situations, the problem solver must first specify the set of conditions she or he perceives as needing a resolution. This process involves defining and interpreting the nature of the problem and is reflected in specific goals set to achieve a desired outcome. Specific components of this process can include (a) determining what caused the problem, (b) establishing the degree to which the individual has control over the cause and means to solve the problem, and

(c) defining the important aspects of the problem situation (e.g., pleasing others, eliminating obstacles, proving oneself). How the individual defines a problem influences the strategies perceived to be effective, the desirability of these strategies, as well as the strategies actually selected to solve the problem.

The majority of research examining developmental trajectories of problem-solving ability in adulthood have focused on strategy selection and problem-solving efficacy. However, there is a recent increase in studies examining developmental differences in problem interpretations and goals per se, and how they relate to the selection of problem-solving strategies. These will be explored later. In general, the findings from studies examining developmental trajectories of the efficacy of everyday problem-solving strategies are less than consistent. Before reporting these findings, however, it is necessary to specify variations in criteria used to judge problem-solving efficacy.

B. Criteria for Judging Strategy Efficacy

The measures used most often in the problem-solving literature have been primarily quantitative in nature, such as the number of solutions generated, the number of steps to arrive at a solution, or the lack of redundancy in responding. In this case, both responses and criteria for efficacy of the solution have been generated by experimenters. It has been suggested by some that these types of measures may obscure qualitative differences inherent in the solutions themselves.

Another criteria for judging problem-solving efficacy captures the individual's own perspective on problem-solving competence. Individuals rate the efficacy of their own solutions. In this way, the criteria for problem-solving efficacy is determined by what the individual perceives to be effective given that she or he is living in the particular context in question. Along the same lines, researchers have used a criterion group of judges to determine problem-solving efficacy (e.g., individuals' solutions are compared to the ratings provided by adult judges). In essence, this approach provides a prototype (by means of the judges' efficacy ratings) of what is adaptive in a particular context. Solutions generated by participants in the study can be compared to this prototype. However, both self- or judge-perceived scales may be too global

to delineate the qualitatively different form and content of an individual's solutions.

Until recently, relatively little effort has focused on the sensitivity of the dependent measures used to capture possible developmental differences in how the individual structures reality and approaches everyday problems. In this case, it is necessary to use problem-solving tasks requiring individuals to generate their own interpretation of the problem situation. This approach considers qualitative differences in the form and content of solutions. For example, scoring systems may assess the type of problem-solving strategy used in particular situations (e.g., problem-focused strategies, cognitive reevaluations, emotional regulation). By contrast, other scoring systems examine the development of relativistic thinking in problem solving (i.e., the ability to consider and coordinate multiple perspectives in a problem situation). Embedded in these approaches is the assumption that one level of problem solving is invariably better than another. This not only requires further empirical support, it needs to be reconciled with the contextualist notion that superiority of a problem-solving strategy is relative to how adaptive it is given the particular demands of the context.

C. Age Differences in Problem-Solving Efficacy

A research paradigm employing quantitative criteria for assessing age differences in adults' everyday problem solving typically asks young, middle-aged, and older adults to generate solutions for hypothetical practical problems (e.g., When you open the refrigerator up, you notice that it is not cold inside, but rather it is warm. What would you do?). Criteria for effective problem solving included number of "safe and effective" solutions as well as number of "self-initiated" solutions generated. Findings indicate that middle-aged adults outperformed younger and older adults (who did not differ from each other). Although older adults did not outperform younger age groups, these findings are in sharp contrast to the typical age differences found in performance on more abstract, formal problems (i.e., younger adults outperformed both middle-aged and older adults). There has been some corroboration of this finding when decision-making tasks are employed (e.g., deciding which automobile to purchase). For example, research demonstrates negative correlations between age and how well adults rank ordered automobiles in terms of attributes relevant to potential car buyers. However, other research suggests that although there are age differences in the way adults performed the task, young and older adults did not differ in the final choice of car or the time spent making the decision.

The demonstrated decline in problem solving and decision making in older adults has been interpreted by some to reflect a biologically determined decline in the maximum potential of cognitive processing beginning after early adulthood. Although experience may compensate for this deficit during the major portion of adulthood, for example, through practice, it is in the older adult years that the decline is sufficient to interfere with even frequently practiced abilities.

In contrast to decline in everyday problem-solving ability, other researchers find either equivalent performance among younger, middle-aged, and older adults, or progression in problem-solving efficacy and decision making on the part of older adults. However, different criteria for judging problem efficacy are employed in these studies. For example, in a number of studies participants generated a solution to various problem situations (as performed in the above studies). In these studies individuals rated the efficacy of their own solutions. Results indicated no age differences between young, middle-aged, and older adults when self-perceived problem-solving efficacy was assessed.

However, these findings have been shown to be moderated somewhat by the relevance of problems to participants' lives. For example, equivalent self-rated problem-solving efficacy across age groups was found when participants generated their own problems. However, solutions for experimenter-generated problems were perceived as more efficacious (i.e., better) by younger and middle-aged adults than the solutions they had used for problems from their own lives. Interestingly, older adults viewed their solutions to both types of problems as equally efficacious.

In the above study, solutions to experimenter-generated problems were rated also by adult judges as better than solutions to real-world problems. This was true for all age groups. Thus, experimenter ratings were in agreement with the ratings of younger and middle-aged adults for these two types of problems. The self-ratings of older adults did not reflect the pattern of experimenter ratings for solution efficacy across problem types.

Other studies that obtained ratings from adult judges demonstrated an increase in problem-solving efficacy. An Everyday Problem Solving Inventory was developed to assess practical problem solving in everyday situations. The inventory consists of six different content domains in which an adult might experience a problem situation, including consumer issues, home management, interpersonal conflicts with family members, conflicts with friends, conflicts with co-workers, and dealing with technical information. Possible responses were enumerated for each of these situations (including problem-focused action, cognitive problem analysis, passive-dependent behavior, and avoidant thinking and denial) and were evaluated by judges, ranging in age from 24–72, as to their perceived efficacy. The inventory was then administered to adults ranging in age from 20–78 years. Examination of age differences revealed that effective performance on the problem-solving inventory (as defined by the judges) increased with age, whereas performance on more traditional problem-solving tasks declined after middle age.

Other studies examined qualitative differences in problem-solving strategy as indexed by level of cognitive maturity (i.e., flexibility in responding, complexity of problem interpretation, mature vs. defensive strategies). For example, older adults used more mature coping strategies in response to hypothetical stressful problems than adolescents and younger adults. Whereas adolescents were more likely to engage in defensive strategies such as blaming oneself or others in a situation, more mature adults tended to reframe the aspects of the situation through positive reappraisal. Similarly, other studies found that youth placed more importance on consciously controlling their environment through logical problem solving, whereas older adults placed more importance on integrating inner expression (how one feels) with outer presentation (how one acts).

Research also indicates that older adults use a variety of strategies as a function of the type of issues they are addressing (e.g., family, relationship, consumer problems). For example, researchers examined different styles of problem solving in adolescence through older adulthood. Problems representing consumer decisions and home management yielded no age differences in problem-solving style. All age groups tended to use more problem-focused strategies. However, older adults endorsed strategies evincing an awareness of when to avoid or passively accept a situation within interpersonal domains (e.g., conflicts with family or friends) as compared to more instrumental problem domains (e.g., consumer matters). Young adults opted more for a problem-focused or cognitive analytic approach to all problems. They concluded that older adults may be engaging in a more differentiated approach to problem situations in that they use diverse strategies in handling problems as a function of whether the situation was more instrumental or interpersonal in nature. Similarly, in other studies, older adults were more likely to endorse emotion-focused strategies than younger adults, who adopted more problem-focused strategies.

Interestingly, older adults were capable of using problem-focused and cognitive analytical strategies (as evidenced by a lack of age differences or increased use of these strategies). These findings are in contrast with the results of other research that suggests that older adults "lack" the ability to engage in cognitively complex strategies.

Finally, studies examining decision-making strategies also find no age differences in accuracy and effectiveness of decisions in consumer-related domains. For example, older and younger adults did not differ in (a) accuracy of how much money to invest in a retirement account, (b) an analysis of information about Medicare insurance policies, (c) giving advice, and (d) information strategies in making consumer decisions to purchase objects in a variety store. [See CONSUMER BEHAVIOR.]

In sum, it appears that everyday problem-solving measures can be critically influenced by the world from which the problems are derived—that of the experimenter versus that of the participant. What constitutes a good solution to a problem may depend on the criteria used to judge problem-solving efficacy (e.g., who is making such a decision, the experimenter or the individual who tried the solution and had to live with the consequences). Finally, older adults are not necessarily less capable at solving problems than other age groups, though age did influence the types of problems people report.

The majority of studies reported thus far have examined age differences in problem-solution efficacy utilizing different outcome criteria. Another body of research has addressed differential findings for age differences in everyday problem solving as a function of mediating factors such as problem appraisal, personal relevance, and emotional salience.

III. FACTORS MEDIATING AGE DIFFERENCES IN EVERYDAY PROBLEM SOLVING

A. Problem Appraisal

Differences in strategy use for everyday problem solving are shown to be a function of age differences in the underlying interpretations of the problem or decision-making situation. Indeed, effective problem solving depends upon a realistic appraisal of the situation that matches or approximates the unfolding of events. Furthermore, there is a need to examine differences in problem appraisal between younger and older adults in order to understand better strategy use and the potential adaptive nature of such age differences.

For example, one study found that younger and older adults differed in their appraisal of problems as a function of the type of situation and relevance to their everyday functioning (e.g., a visit to the doctor's office and problems arising at a dinner party). On the one hand, older adults interpreted the doctor's office problems as external-social (i.e., something about the social circumstances rather than themselves). On the other hand, older adults viewed the dinner party problem more as internal-cognitive (e.g., something to do with their decision making). Younger adults interpreted both problems as internal-affective (e.g., attributed the problem to their personal emotions). In addition, the way in which both age groups interpreted the problem influenced their subsequent selection of problem-solving strategies.

Other researchers have also found that older adults interpret everyday problems differently than younger adults in that they focus on interpersonal concerns of the problem. Some propose that mature thinking involves the redefinition of the problem space by accepting inherent uncertainties and resolving them. Similarly, other researchers suggest that this interpretive process in adulthood is characterized by increased awareness of self as interpreter or the ability to consider multiple perspectives in reasoning tasks of an interpersonal nature. A number of developmental changes in how individuals structure reality and approach a problem situation (e.g., awareness of self as interpreter, cognitive representations of events, cognitive appraisal) have been identified. However, more research is needed linking these changes in problem appraisal with subsequent selection of problem-solving strategies.

B. Personal Relevance

As noted earlier, personal relevance, whether it takes the form of age relevance (e.g., problems characteristic of the participant's age group) or self-generated problems, appears to affect whether or not age differences in problem-solving efficacy will be observed. In fact, older adults are shown to be more influenced by perceived relevance of individual problems. However, the findings are mixed. First, a number of studies reveal that older adults perform better on tasks reflecting personal relevance and familiarity than on hypothetical tasks. In other words, young and middle-aged adults outperformed older adults on hypothetical problems, whereas there were no age differences when problems were self-generated. In addition, as noted earlier, in contrast to younger adults, older adults rated their solutions for self-generated problems equally as effective as their solutions generated for experimenter-generated (hypothetical) problems.

When age-relevant problems were developed for individuals of varying ages (e.g., problems relevant to young, middle-aged, and older adults) young and middle-aged adults performed best on problems relevant to their own age group, whereas older adults did not vary as a function of the age relevance of the problems. Some argue that experience and familiarity may compensate for deficits in everyday problem solving. However, more research directly examining this variable is needed. At this point it can be argued that familiarity and personal relevance mediates age differences in everyday problem solving. In other words, familiar problems tend to be managed effectively in a similar fashion across age groups.

C. Emotional Salience

In the beginning of this article it was noted that one of the defining characteristics of everyday problem solving was the interpersonal nature of problem situations encountered in everyday life. In addition, a common finding among studies on age differences in prob-

lem-solving strategies is that changes in strategy preference are most evident in interpersonal situations that characteristically embody emotional and psychosocial factors. The apparent role that emotion plays in how an individual construes a problem (particularly in an interpersonal context) and, in turn, adopts a problem-solving strategy has recently been addressed in the problem-solving literature. For example, with increasing age and emotional maturity, individuals engage in more mature social reasoning (e.g., increased relativistic thinking) in emotionally laden situations; older adults with high affective intensity demonstrate more dialectical thinking; higher levels of ego maturity involving emotional regulation and openness to affective experience relate to more mature coping and problem solving; older adults make more complex causal attributions in problem situations that are high in emotional salience; and emotional salience plays an important role in age differences in coping with stress.

In a recent study, emotional salience of problems (ranging from high to low) was found to be a critical determinant of the degree to which individuals reported a particular problem-solving strategy. In low and high emotionally salient situations, there were no age differences in the use of instrumental and proactive problem-solving strategies. However, in high emotionally salient situations, older adults endorsed more passive-dependent and avoidant strategies than either young or middle-aged adults. These findings tend to support the premise that older adults' responses are related to the nature of the problem situation. Older adults, like the other age groups, used more problem-focused strategies in less emotionally salient and more instrumental task situations (e.g., returning defective merchandise). When the situations were more emotionally salient (e.g., moving to a new town, taking care of an older parent) older adults used more emotional regulating strategies (e.g., suppressing emotions, not trying to alter an uncontrollable situation).

Similarly, a number of studies have shown that, in general, older adults use more emotion-focused styles of coping than younger adults. For example, older adults report fewer negative emotions, and appear to be better equipped with cognitive problem-solving skills for negative emotions. Older adults have been shown to use more emotion-focused coping when the problem situation is appraised as uncontrollable when compared to younger adults. Finally, a life span developmental perspective has been proposed with respect to emotional regulation. In the latter half of the life span individuals find emotional aspects of information more salient. In addition, older adults prefer to focus on the emotional potential in interpersonal relationships. In contrast, younger adults are less likely to focus on emotional aspects of information presented. In interpersonal relationships, they focus more on the information- and stimulation-seeking potential. Evidence for adulthood changes in the use of affective appraisal and emotional regulation stress the importance for future research to examine everyday problem solving within an emotional context.

D. Individual-Difference Factors in Everyday Problem Solving

Individual-difference variables such as reasoning ability, cognitive style, personality characteristics, and so on may better index problem-solving differences than age. The current literature suggests that age may not serve as the best marker of developmental differences, given the increased interindividual variability found in adulthood. A number of researchers have found other candidates that are better predictors of developmental differences, such as educational level, ego development, authoritarianism, intolerance for ambiguity, and cognitive-personality style. For example, many studies suggest that individuals with more formal education perform better in problem-solving contexts. Cognitive style has also been shown to influence problem-solving efficacy. For example, intolerance for ambiguity and emotional maturity were shown to be better predictors of problem interpretation (in the form of causal attributions) than age. Similarly, the degree to which an individual endorses authoritarian attitudes has been shown to eliminate age differences found in reasoning about parental problems.

The individual-differences approach recognizes that age is only probabilistically associated with aspects of problem solving and that this association can in fact be influenced and even moderated by a host of relevant variables (e.g., beliefs, attitudes, cognitive style). For example, an individual-differences model could make it possible to evaluate the conditions un-

der which adults of varying ages and of different personological and developmental characteristics are likely to engage in qualitatively different strategies of everyday problem solving.

IV. CONCLUSIONS AND IMPLICATIONS

In conclusion, if one assumes that traditional problem-solving measures have been relatively abstract, with low ecological validity and/or low emotional saliency, then developmental and age differences would only emerge on measures sensitive to information-processing or mechanistic manipulations (e.g., number of solutions generated). In this case, findings demonstrate decreasing problem-solving ability with increasing age. However, when presented with tasks of high emotional salience, ambiguity, and ecological validity, developmental differences have been documented that are related to qualitative changes in the way the individual perceives their problem-solving efficacy and structures everyday problems.

Therefore, in order to attain a more complete picture of developmental variation in problem solving, both research perspectives are needed. Researchers must be able to differentiate when age differences are due to a production deficiency or genuine regression on the part of older adults and when these differences can be attributed to discriminative and volitional choices in problem-solving strategy. Developmental differences can exist concurrently with regard to decline in abstract problem-solving ability and increased sophistication in appraisal and approaches to solving real-world problems. Both types of developmental changes can exist in parallel and may even complement each other.

BIBLIOGRAPHY

Corneilus, S. W. (1990). Aging and everyday cognitive abilities. In T. M. Hess (Ed.), *Aging and cognition: Knowledge organization and utilization* (pp. 411–460). Amsterdam: Elsevier.

Denney, N. W. (1990). Adult age differences in traditional and practical problem solving. In E. Lovelace (Ed.), *Aging and cognition: Mental processes, self awareness, and interventions* (pp. 329–349). Amsterdam: Elsevier.

Dixon, R. (1992). Contextual approaches to adult intellectual development. In R. J. Sternberg & C. A. Berg (Eds.), *Intellec-*

tual development (pp. 350–380). New York: Cambridge University Press.

Perlmutter, M., Kaplan, M., & Nyquist, L. (1990). Development of adaptive competence in adulthood. *Human Development, 33,* 185–197.

Poon, L. W., Rubin, D. C., & Wilson, B. A. (Eds.). (1990). *Everyday cognition in adulthood and later life.* New York: Cambridge University Press.

Sansone, C., & Berg, C. (1993). Adapting to the environment across the life span: Different process or different inputs? *International Journal of Behavioral Development, 16,* 215–241.

Dementia

Ingmar Skoog

Institute of Clinical Neurosciences
Section of Psychiatry, Sahlgrenska Hospital
Göteborg, Sweden

Kaj Blennow

Institute of Clinical Neuroscience
Section of Neurochemistry
Mölndal Hospital, Sweden

Jan Marcusson

Department of Geriatric Medicine
University Hospital
Linköping, Sweden

Alzheimer's Disease A disorder characterized by a clinical picture of slowly progressive dementia and by the histopathological changes of neuronal and synaptic degeneration accompanied by senile plaques and neurofibrillary tangles in certain areas of the brain.

Dementia A syndrome characterized by a global decline in intellectual functioning, affecting, for instance, memory, language, executive functioning, and personality.

Frontal Lobe Dementia Disorders that affect the frontal lobes of the brain. The clinical presentation is mainly characterized by personality changes and language disturbances.

Multi-Infarct Dementia Dementia presumed to be caused by multiple infarcts in the brain.

Vascular Dementia A dementia syndrome presumed to be caused by cerebrovascular disorders.

White Matter Lesions Lesions in the white matter of the brain, mostly affecting the myeline sheaths in subcortical areas. When these changes are revealed by computed tomography of the brain or magnetic resonance imaging the term *leukoaraiosis* is often used. The lesions have been associated with dementia.

DEMENTIA is a syndrome of global intellectual decline. It has become a major health-care problem in the Western world due to the increasing number of elderly people. Dementia may be caused by more than 70 diseases, the most common being Alzheimer's disease (AD) and vascular disorders, often subsumed under the term vascular dementia (VaD). The prevalence of dementia increases with age. AD is characterized clinically by a slowly progressive decline in intellectual functions and histopathologically by large numbers of senile plaques and neurofibrillary tangles in certain brain regions. VaD relates to various cerebrovascular disorders and different types of ischaemic lesions in the brain. The most common forms are probably multi-infarct dementia (MID) and dementia related to subcortical white matter lesions. Frontal lobe dementia is characterized by changes in personality and language, and by atrophy in the frontal lobe. About 10% of all dementias are potentially treatable. It is therefore important to undertake a careful clinical examination in all cases of dementia. During recent years pharmacological treatment of AD has been introduced in the United States. However, most care and pharmacological treatment in cases of dementia are directed against concomitant behavioral disturbances.

I. THE DEMENTIA SYNDROME

A. Background

Dementia is a syndrome characterized by a decline in memory and other intellectual functions (e.g., orientation, visuospatial abilities, language, and thinking) and changes in personality and emotions. The modern concept of dementia does not imply anything about prognosis (i.e., the course may be progressive, static, fluctuating, or even reversible). The disturbance should represent a decline from a previously higher level, give rise to difficulties in everyday life and not occur exclusively during altered consciousness. Around 70 disorders have been associated with dementia, the most common being Alzheimer's disease (AD) and vascular disorders, often subsumed under the term vascular dementia (VaD).

The increasing number and proportion of elderly people in most countries of the world has resulted in increased scientific interest in dementia during the last 20 years. In Medline, 220 articles on dementia were listed in 1973, compared with 652 in 1983 and 2084 in 1993. Nearly 40% of all articles on dementia published between 1965 and 1993 were published from 1990 to 1993.

B. Definition of Dementia

The definition of dementia has varied during the years. A classic study from the early 1950s regarding the mortality in psychiatric inpatients by Sir Martin Roth from England gave rise to the so-called Roth criteria, which were based on severe decline in memory and disorientation for time and place. What Roth described was so-called senile dementia and is an illustration of a previous opinion that based the definition mainly on a decline in memory. The modern concept of dementia emphasizes that dementia is a global decline that affects more areas of intellectual functions than just memory.

During recent years, the dominating scientific definition has been from the *Diagnostic and Statistical Manual of Mental Disorders* (3rd ed. revised) (*DSM-III-R*; 1987), released by the American Psychiatric Association. A new version was released during 1994 (*DSM-IV*) (see Table I). Throughout the world, diseases are registered according to the classification by the World Health Organization (WHO) *International Classification of Diseases* (*ICD*). The previous version, the *ICD-9*, was not detailed regarding dementia. The last version, ICD-10 (1992), however, reflects the increased interest in dementia during the

Table I Definition of Dementia in the Diagnostic and Statistical Manual of Mental Disorders (4th ed.)

A. The development of multiple cognitive deficits manifested by both of the following:
1. Memory impairment,
2. One (or more) of the following cognitive disturbances:
   a. aphasia
   b. apraxia
   c. agnosia
   d. disturbances in executive functioning.
B. The cognitive deficits each cause significant impairment in social or occupational functioning and represent a significant decline from a previous level of functioning.
C. The deficits do not occur exclusively during the course of a delirium.

last decades and is therefore more detailed regarding the description of dementing disorders (see Table II).

These diagnostic systems are based on a global symptomatology as that often seen in a typical case of AD. Disorders with more circumscribed symptoms, focal signs, or an atypical course may therefore not be classified as dementia (e.g., frontal lobe dementia or subcortical dementia).

Another way to classify dementing disorders is according to the location in the brain where the pathological process mainly takes place (see Table III). Dementia with *frontotemporal dominance* (e.g., Pick's disease or non-Alzheimer's frontal lobe dementia) is dominated by the clinical picture of personality

Table II Definition of Dementia in the International Classification of Diseases (10th ed.)

A. There is evidence of each of the following:
1. A decline in memory
2. A decline in other cognitive abilities characterized by deterioration in judgment and thinking, such as planning and organizing, and in general information processing.
3. The decline in 1 and 2 causes impaired abilities in daily living.
B. Awareness of the environment (i.e., absence of clouding of consciousness)
C. There is a decline in emotional control or motivation, or a change in social behavior manifest as at least one of the following: emotional lability, irritability, apathy, or coarsening of social behavior.
D. The symptoms in criterion A should have been present for at least 6 months.

Table III Causes of Dementia Adopted from the Swedish Consensus

Primary degenerative dementias	Vascular dementias	Secondary dementias	Others
Frontotemporal dominance	Cortical	Normal pressure hydro-cephalus	Mixed types
Pick's disease	Multi-infarct dementia	Metabolic disturbances	
Frontotemporal degeneration of non-Alzheimer's type	Strategic infarcts	Nutritional deficiencies	
Amyotrophic lateral sclerosis with dementia	Hypovolemic dementia	Intoxications	
Atypical Alzheimer's disease	Subcortical	Infections	
Familial forms	Status lacunare	Creutzfeldt-Jakob disease	
Temporoparietal dominance	Binswanger's disease	Borrelia	
Early-onset Alzheimer's disease	White-matter lesions	Neurosyphilis	
Senile dementia of Alzheimer's type	Ischemic-hypoxic dementia	AIDS	
Familial Alzheimers disease	Others	Other infections	
Down's syndrome with dementia of Alzheimer's type	Mixed types	Brain tumor	
Traumatic dementia of Alzheimer's type	Arteropathies	Trauma	
Subcortical dominance		Subdural hematoma	
Huntington's disease		Boxing	
Progressive supranuclear palsy		Others	
Shy-Drager's syndrome			
Dementia with multiple sclerosis			
Progressive subcortical gliosis			
Hallervorden-Spatz disease			
Others			
Parkinson's disease with dementia			

changes, decline in initiative, and a mild memory disturbance. Dementia with *temporoparietal dominance* (e.g., AD) is characterized by apraxia, agnosia, and memory disturbance. Dementia with *subcortical dominance* (e.g., Huntington's disease, progressive supranuclear paralysis, Parkinson's disease, subcortical white-matter dementia) is characterized by psychomotor retardation and extrapyramidal symptoms.

The dementia disorder may often start many years before it becomes clinically manifest. Retrospectively, one may often find that the patient had very mild symptoms at a subclinical level, (e.g., memory and language loss and personality change) several years before the disease became clinically manifest. Probably, these subclinical symptoms are manifestations of incipient brain pathology.

Delirium may be difficult to differentiate from dementia. Delirium is a qualitative change in attention (clouded consciousness) with a fragmentation of thinking. The intensity of symptoms may fluctuate during the day or over several days. Episodes of delirium are common during the course of dementia, which

makes the differential diagnosis sometimes difficult. Common causes of delirium include physical illnessess (e.g., urinary tract infections) and drug side effects (e.g., digitalis and anticholinergic agents).

Depression may sometimes be dominated by a decline in intellectual functions (pseudodementia) and may then be difficult to differentiate from a primary dementia. A careful history and observation generally reveals that other symptoms of depression are present, and in these cases the dementia disappears after treatment. Longitudinal studies show, however, that a substantial number of people with pseudodementia develop a primary dementia 2–3 years later.

C. Severity of Dementia

Severity of dementia may be defined in different ways, often based on the patient's ability in activities of daily living (ADLs). According to the *DSM-III-R* criteria, *mild* dementia is accompanied by a definite decline in intellectual ability, where social and occupational abilities are impaired, but the individual is still able to live independently. In *moderate* dementia, the individual needs daily supervision, and in *severe* dementia he or she needs continuous supervision (i.e., institutionalization).

The dimensional rather than categorical character makes mild dementia sometimes difficult to separate from normal aging. Fairly small differences in diagnostic criteria may produce large variations in reported prevalence rates. Mowry and Burvill found a variation in the prevalence of mild dementia ranging from 3–64% when different criteria were used on the same population. Different criteria also diagnosed different individuals. Furthermore, preconceptions about aging may lead to underestimation of the prevalence of dementia, especially among the very old. The concept of mild dementia is therefore uncertain, and the prevalence varies between 2–50% in the ages above 65 years. If a decline from a previously higher level can be shown (by obtaining information from key informants or by following the patients over time) the validity may be higher.

There is thus an overlap between the clinical picture of mild dementia and normal aging. This overlap is also found regarding the brain changes accompanying specific dementia disorders. The typical brain changes seen in AD's (i.e., senile plaques and neurofibrillary tangles) may also be found in high proportions of perfectly normal elderly, especially among the very old. Vascular changes associated with dementia (e.g., multiple infarcts and white-matter changes) also show an overlap with normal aging.

II. CAUSES OF DEMENTIA

Although a syndrome of dementia may evolve in connection with more than 70 diseases, the predominant causes are AD and VaD. However, the etiological diagnosis of dementia is difficult to make from the symptomatology alone, because of the similarities in clinical pictures between different forms of dementia, and because there is still no biological marker for the diagnosis of AD or VaD. Often AD is taken as a diagnosis of exclusion, as in the NINCDS-ADRDA-criteria and the diagnosis of VaD is made if the patient has a history of cerebrovascular disease. From a clinical perspective, mixed types of dementia are common, especially among the oldest-old. Auxiliary investigations, including careful history taking, neurological, psychiatric, and physical examinations, interview of

a close informant, computed tomography (CT scan) of the head, a chest X ray, biochemical screening, including vitamin B_{12} level, a thyroid function test, and cerebrospinal fluid examinations are necessary. These investigations have not been available in some community-based studies, which has made the etiological differentiation of dementia difficult in this type of study. Bearing this in mind, most population studies report that 50–70% of demented cases have a diagnosis of AD and 20–30% a diagnosis of VaD. In a recent Swedish study on 85-year-olds, where the diagnosis was based on a comprehensive examination, including CT scan of the head, VaD was more common than previously supposed, and it is possible that this type of dementia has been underreported during the last decades.

The proportions of different types of dementia have also been studied in autopsy studies and in evaluation units. However, such studies may have selection bias and changes might occur between examination and autopsy. With these potential biases in mind, AD, or "senile dementia," is most often reported to be the commonest type in both autopsy studies and clinical evaluation units. Studies from evaluation units rely on patients having reached the units, which is influenced by the clinical picture of the disorder, including severity, an atypical picture, or disturbed behavior, as well as referral practices and the extent of evaluations performed by primary-care physicians. Patients with an obvious cause for their dementia may not be referred for further evaluations, which may account for the low proportions of VaD and rather high proportions of secondary dementias that are generally reported from such units.

Diseases that cause dementia may thus be classified in different ways. One way is to classify by the dominating location of the disease process (e.g., frontal lobe dementia, subcortical dementia). Another is to classify according to the underlying disease (e.g., AD, VaD, normal pressure hydrocephalus). Most classification systems are a mixture of these approaches.

In Table III, we have classified the dementias as primary degenerative dementias, VaDs, and other types of dementias. We have then further subdivided according to the dominating location of the disease process, according to the Swedish Consensus Conference. Primary degenerative dementias are caused by neurodegeneration that primarily affects the central nervous system (CNS). We will describe in more detail one disease with mainly temporoparietal symptoms. (AD) and one with mainly frontotemporal symptoms (frontal-lobe degeneration of non-Alzheimer's type). These disorders are generally progressive and destroy neurons or other cells in the CNS. VaDs are caused by disorders in the cardiovascular system (e.g., stroke and small vessel disease).

Secondary dementias are caused by disorders with a known etiology, reversible or treatable conditions, and disorders that do not primarily affect the CNS, but may lead to dementia if the brain becomes involved. This means that normal pressure hydrocephalus and Creutzfeldt-Jakob's disease, which primarily engage the CNS, are treated as secondary dementias.

III. EPIDEMIOLOGY

The prevalence of dementia increases with age. The figures from a meta-analyses on moderate to severe dementia based on 47 studies performed up to the mid-1980s and presented by Jorm et al. are shown in Table IV. The figures are uncertain in the oldest ages as the number of persons examined in these ages generally has been low. There is an ongoing debate whether the prevalence reaches a plateau after the age of 90.

The incidence of dementia has not been studied as extensively as the prevalence, but the studies so far performed show an increase with age (Table IV). There is a hypothesis that the incidence may decline after the age of 90 years.

The relationship with increasing age has resulted in the suggestion that dementia is an extreme variant of normal aging. The argument is that if one just

becomes old enough everyone will become demented. In line with this, several cross-sectional studies report a decline in the results on psychometric testings with increasing age. However, cross-sectional studies are not only influenced by age per se, but also by the fact that people in different ages belong to different birth cohorts (i.e., they have lived through different time periods, have different schooling, etc.). Longitudinal studies report that the results on testings do not decline much with age. Some abilities (e.g., language) remain relatively intact, whereas others (e.g., psychomotor speed and visuospatial functions) show a moderate decline. Another finding, which suggests that dementia is not just caused by age per se, is a recent finding from a study of 100-year-olds in Lund, Sweden, which reported a surprisingly low prevalence of dementia.

Dementia is an important cause of institutionalization in the elderly. Generally dementing disorders are associated with an increased mortality, which is true both for AD and VaD, and VaD has a higher mortality than AD. The most common causes for death are pulmonary infections in AD and cardiovascular disorders in VaD.

IV. ALZHEIMER'S DISEASE

AD is regarded to be the major cause of dementia, and is the fourth or fifth most common cause of death in the Western society. Although relatively rare familial forms of AD exist, the majority of patients have no obvious family history and are classified as sporadic AD. The etiology and pathogenesis of sporadic AD are largely unknown.

A. Clinical Characteristics

The symptomatology in AD is best characterized by using a three-stage model. During the first stage, the symptoms are often vague and diffuse and develop insidiously. Memory disturbances are the most prominent symptom, but slight impairment of visuospatial functioning, language, and concentration may occur. In the second stage, the symptomatology is dominated by the cardinal cortical "instrumental" (or "parietal") symptoms (sensory dysphasia, dyspraxia, dysgnosia, and visuospatial disturbance), together with a pro-

Table IV Estimated Prevalence and Incidence of Moderate to Severe Dementia

Age (years)	Prevalence (%)	Incidence (%)
65–70	1	—
70–75	3	1
75–80	6	2
80–85	11	3–4
85–90	21	4–9
90–95	39	—

Table V NINCDS-ADRDA Criteria for "Probable Alzheimer's Disease"

1. Progressive dementia with deficits in two or more areas of cognition
2. No disturbance of consciousness at the time of diagnosis
3. Onset between ages 40 and 90
4. Absence of other disorders that alone could account for the dementia:
   - manic–depressive disorder
   - Parkinson's disease
   - multi-infarct dementia
   - drug intoxication
   - other less common disorders (e.g., thyroid disease)

The diagnosis is supported by:
1. Progressive instrumental symptoms (aphasia, agnosia, and apraxia)
2. Impaired activities of daily living and altered patterns of behavior
3. Family history of similar disorders
4. Laboratory results of
   - normal lumbar puncture
   - normal or nonspecific changes (increased slow-wave activity) on EEG
   - cerebral atrophy on CT, with progression on serial observations

Clinical findings consistent with the diagnosis:
1. Plateaus in the course of progression
2. Associated psychiatric (e.g., depression, delusions) symptoms
3. Associated neurologic (e.g., myoclonus, seizures) symptoms, especially with more advanced disease
4. CT normal for age

Features that make the diagnosis uncertain or unlikely:
1. Sudden, apoplectic onset
2. Focal neurologic findings (e.g., hemiparesis) early in the course of the illness
3. Seizures or gait disturbances very early in the course of the illness

gressive worsening of memory disturbances, whereas the personality and social behavior remain relatively spared. In the third stage, all mental functions, including the emotional ones, are severely impaired, and the disease inevitably leads to death by complications.

B. Clinical Diagnosis

The most commonly used criteria for a clinical diagnosis of AD was developed by the NINCDS-ADRDA work group (Table V). In summary, the clinical diagnosis of "probable AD" is made by exclusion of other causes of dementia, without any positive symptomatological criteria.

In clinical practice, the diagnosis of AD is made on the basis of a thorough clinical examination, the results of which are weighed together with the information gathered from auxiliary investigations, such as EEG, brain imaging (CT, MRI), and laboratory tests.

The first step in the clinical diagnosis of AD is to establish the presence of dementia by evaluation of the medical history and the mental status. By somatic, psychiatric and neurological examinations, features of secondary dementias (e.g., thyroid disorders) and other psychiatric (e.g., depression) and neurological (e.g., Creutzfeldt–Jacob's disease, MID) disorders may be recognized.

For the diagnosis of AD, several authors have stressed the importance of identifying its characteristic symptomatology. Thereby, it may be possible to differentiate AD from other dementias, such as frontal-lobe dementias (e.g., Pick's disease), which is characterized by change in personality, and subcortical dementias (e.g., progressive supranuclear palsy, Parkinson's disease), which are characterized by a slowing of cognition, speech, and comprehension; forgetfulness; and alterations in affect. Neuropsychological tests may support the clinical diagnosis of dementia, but give little aid in the differentiation between AD and other types of dementia.

Brain atrophy may be visualized using CT or magnetic resonance imaging (MRI). AD patients as a group show a higher degree of ventricular and cortical sulcal enlargement than age-matched controls. However, atrophy is not specific of AD, and there is considerable overlap between AD patients and nondemented individuals. Nevertheless, CT should be carried out in every patient because CT and MRI can identify treatable structural diseases, such as subdural haematoma and brain tumor. CT and MRI are also important for the identification of cerebral infarcts, characteristic of MID.

An evaluation of cerebral metabolism and/or cerebral blood flow by regional cerebral blood flow (rCBF) or single photon emission computed tomography (SPECT) may be helpful in the clinical diagnosis of AD and the differentiation from other dementias (e.g., Pick's disease) and normal aging by identifying the reduced whole-hemisphere blood flow or metabolism and the regional temporo-parietal pattern of AD.

The typical electroencephalography (EEG) findings in AD are a decrease in alpha-frequency and increased slow-wave activity. However, diffuse slowing is an EEG pattern seen in almost all dementias and a normal EEG is found in some patients with AD.

Today, there are no specific laboratory tests for AD. Instead, laboratory tests are done to identify secondary causes of the dementia, for example, thyroid disorders and vitamin deficiency (see below). Investigation of the cerebrospinal fluid (CSF) is also essential to identify secondary causes of dementia, preferentially chronic infections (e.g., Borrelia encephalitis).

C. Neuropathology

The neuropathological changes of AD consist of a degeneration of the neurons and their synapses, and an increased number of senile plaques (SP) and neurofibrillary tangles (NFT) compared with that found in nondemented individuals of the same age. However, the overlap in the presence of SP and NFT between normal aging and dementia is considerable at the oldest ages, and such brain changes may be especially abundant also in very old nondemented persons.

It is generally agreed that a definite diagnosis of AD can only be made after neuropathological examination. However, the neuropathological criteria for AD differ in their specific staining procedure, the changes that are to be quantified (SP and/or NFT), and on the vascular exclusion criteria. These variables have a major impact on the sensitivity and specificity. The most commonly used criteria for a neuropathological diagnosis of AD were formulated by the National Institute of Aging (NIA). These criteria are based on age-dependent limits of cortical SP counts (NFT are not a prerequisite).

1. Amyloid Deposition, Senile Plaques, and Cerebral Amyloid Angiopathy

SP are round to ovoid lesions, with a diameter of 15–200 μm, consisting of a central core of amyloid fibers surrounded by numerous dystrophic (swollen), degenerating neurites and reactive microglia. SPs are particularly numerous in the association cortex and in the hippocampal complex, but are also found in subcortical grey matter structures. Cerebral amyloid angiopathy (CAA) consists of amyloid deposits in the leptomeningeal and intracortical arterioles and capillaries.

The amyloid deposited in SP and CAA mainly consists of a specific protein termed Aβ, which is a product from a set of much larger precursors, collectively referred to as the amyloid precursor proteins (APP), which are encoded by a single gene on chromosome 21. There are several different molecular weight forms containing the Aβ amyloid sequence. The most abundant isoforms of APP are termed by their molecular weights as APP695, APP751, and APP770. Of these, APP770 is the dominant isoform in most tissues, whereas APP695 (without a protease inhibitor region) is the dominant isoform in the brain. The reason for this difference between different tissues is not known. There is no clear difference in the proportion between the different APP isoforms between patients with AD and age-matched individuals without dementia.

The physiological function of APP is incompletely known. APP undergoes fast axonal transport to the synaptic region where it interacts with the extracellular matrix (ECM), suggesting that APP may be important for neuronal plasticity. The secretory form of APP is identical to protease nexin-II, suggesting a role in growth regulation or neurite outgrowth.

Several lines of evidence also suggest a role for APP in the tissue damage repair process. Thus, a disturbance in the normal function of APP and its metabolism may be important in the pathogenesis of AD.

APP is found in all cells in the body, and has the structure of a transmembrane protein, with a long extracellular N-terminal segment and a short intracellular C-terminal segment. The Aβ protein part of APP encompasses the first 28 extracellular and the following 11–15 transmembrane amino acids. The normal metabolism of APP is partly known. In one metabolic pathway, nonamyloidogenic secretory forms of APP are generated by cleavage within the Aβ protein region, by an unidentified enzyme, often termed "APP secretase." It has long been assumed that the Aβ fragment is produced by a disturbance in the normal APP metabolism. In another metabolic pathway, Aβ protein is generated continuously as a soluble protein during normal cellular metabolism, by cleavage of APP on each side of the Aβ sequence by two unidentified proteases.

It is now clear how soluble Aβ protein aggregates to insoluble amyloid fibrils. Synthetic Aβ aggregate and form β-sheet structure in vitro, suggesting that Aβ protein alone has the properties for amyloid formation. Other experiments suggest that precipitation of Aβ protein to fibrils may be enhanced by binding to "pathological chaperones" such as apolipoprotein E (ApoE), Apolipoprotein J (ApoJ), and α_1-antichymotrypsin.

Concerning the pathogenic importance of amyloid deposition, there are two schools with different opinions. One school regards amyloid deposition to be the central event in the etiology and pathogenesis of AD, and have proposed the amyloid cascade hypothesis. According to this hypothesis, deposition of Aβ is the central event in the pathogenesis of AD, which is regarded as an amyloid storage disease of the brain. Amyloid deposition is believed to start a cascade of events that finally results in dementia. The essential prediction in the amyloid cascade hypothesis is that Aβ, or aggregates thereof, is neurotoxic. This hypothesis has been both extensively tested (in cell culture systems, and by injecting Aβ protein directly into the brain of animals) and debated but not proven.

The other school agrees that amyloid deposition and SPs accompany AD, but considers that more research is needed before settling the question whether Aβ protein deposition is the factor that causes the neuronal dysfunction and dementia, or whether it is a pathological by-product of the disease, without direct pathogenetic importance. These researchers note that deposition of Aβ protein often occurs in the brains of elderly persons without evidence of dementia or neuronal damage, and that it is an inevitable consequence of aging, found in 100% of centenarians. Furthermore, deposition of Aβ in the brain (more than would be expected for the patient's age) is also found at the periphery of cerebral infarcts, in the perivascular space around arteriovenous malformations, in non-Down's syndrome mentally retarded individuals, after acute cerebral trauma, and in dementia pugilistica. These data do not support the notion that deposition of Aβ protein is a phenomenon specific to AD.

In a minority of AD cases, there is a clear family history. In a small number of these families, the disease segregates with different mutations on the APP gene on chromosome 21, whereas the majority of familial cases show linkage to the recently described S182 gene on the long arm of chromosome 14. A third gene, termed STM2, located on chromosome 1, also segregates with a rare familial form of AD, found in Volga-German ancestors. In all of these families, the disease has an early onset (around 40–60 years of age). In vitro studies have suggested that some mutations in the APP gene may result in an increased production of APP, whereas others may increase the tendency for Aβ protein to aggregate to amyloid fibrils. These findings support the amyloid cascade hypothesis, at least in a small number of cases with familial AD.

Our opinion concerning the amyloid cascade hypothesis is that although experiments in vitro and in rodents may give clues, the hypothesis has to be confirmed in humans. The real challenge for the amyloid cascade hypothesis will come when drugs that prevent amyloid deposition in experimental models can be tested in living patients with AD to see if the disease can be arrested or cured.

2. Neurofibrillary Tangles and Hyperphosphorylation of tau Protein

NFT are intracytoplasmic changes, composed of paired helical filaments (PHF), which are proteinaceous filaments twisted around each other in a helical manner. NFT are primarily found in the anteriomedial temporal lobe and in the association cortex, but also in other areas, such as the nucleus basalis of Meynert.

The principal component of the PHF, neuropil threads and SP neurites, is probably an abnormally hyperphosphorylated form of tau protein (PHFtau). The normal tau protein is located in the axons, where it binds to tubulin in the microtubules, thereby promoting microtubule assembly and stability.

It is hypothesised that tau dissociates from the microtubules as a result of hyperphosphorylation (and conversion to PHFtau). Thereafter, PHFtau redistributes within the neuron, is cleaved to smaller fragments that become ubiquitinated, and finally polymerize into insoluble PHF. However, recent studies have shown that a considerable proportion of the normal tau protein in the brain exists in a highly phosphorylated state, findings that may change the hypothesis of how PHF are formed.

The disease specificity of NFT is low. Besides being present in AD, they inevitably accompany aging, and are also found in a wide range of disorders. This lack of disease specificity may suggest that NFT are nonspecific results of brain damage.

Although knowledge of both APP and Aβ protein and tau and PHFtau has vastly increased, the relationship between the deposition of amyloid (and development of SPs) and the abnormal hyperphosphorylation of tau protein (and development of PHF and NFT) remains obscure.

3. Synaptic Degeneration and Loss

Since synaptic integrity is essential for mental functioning the dementia in AD must be the direct result of a synaptic dysfunction or loss. In AD, evidence of a marked synaptic loss in the hippocampus and in several cortical regions has also been established using different methodology, including electron microscopy, immunohistochemistry, and quantitative Western blotting.

The major part of the synaptic pathology in AD is localized in the neuropil, without clear relation to SP and NFT. The degree of synapse pathology correlates well with clinical measures of the dementia, whereas SPs and NFTs show a weaker correlation. It has been suggested that the central event in the pathogenesis of AD is a synaptic degeneration and loss.

D. Apolipoprotein E

ApoE is a constituent of several plasma lipoproteins, and is essential in the redistribution of lipids in the body. The ApoE gene shows polymorphism with three

			Amino-acid 112	Amino-acid 158
Allele	Apo ε2	5'	----- TGC ---------- **TGC** ----- 3'	
Isoform	Apo E2	NH$_2$	----- Cys ---------- **Cys** ----- COOH	
Allele	Apo ε3	5'	----- TGC ---------- CGC ----- 3'	
Isoform	Apo E3	NH$_2$	----- Cys ---------- Arg ----- COOH	
Allele	Apo ε4	5'	----- **CGC** ---------- CGC ----- 3'	
Isoform	Apo E4	NH$_2$	----- **Arg** ---------- Arg ----- COOH	

Figure 1   Apolipoprotein E alleles and isoforms. Differences in base-pairs between Apoε alleles and in amino acids between ApoE isoforms are marked in bold.

different alleles, $\varepsilon2$, $\varepsilon3$, and $\varepsilon4$, giving rise to three different isoforms (ApoE2, E3, and E4 (Figure 1)). In the general population, ApoE3 is the most common isoform (77–78%), while the ApoE2 frequency is 7–8% and the ApoE4 frequency is 14–16%.

Recently, it was found that ApoE immunoreactivity was present in the SP in AD. Thereafter, several papers reported an increased frequency of the ApoE4 isoform in both familial and sporadic AD, findings that thereafter have been well confirmed. However, the specificity of an increased ApoE4 frequency has to be further studied, as it is controversial whether an increased ApoE4 isoform frequency also is present in VaD, frontal lobe dementia, and in diffuse Lewy body disease.

A major hypothesis concerning the pathogenetic mechanism of ApoE in AD is that ApoE is involved in $A\beta$ protein deposition. The first evidence for this came from the studies showing that ApoE immunoreactivity is found in the SP and in CAA. AD patients homozygous for ApoE4 also have higher average SP density, and more intense $A\beta$ immunoreactivity in SP, than patients without or with only one ApoE4 isoform. ApoE4 has been shown to bind to $A\beta$ in vitro, with ApoE4 having higher affinity to $A\beta$ protein than ApoE3, while other studies have found the reverse. Furthermore, in vitro experiments have shown that incubation of $A\beta$ protein with ApoE give rise to $A\beta$–ApoE complexes that precipitate to amyloid-like fibrils, with ApoE4 giving faster precipitation and a more dense meshwork of fibrils than ApoE3. Therefore, it has been suggested that ApoE may act as a "pathological chaperone," that binds to normally soluble $A\beta$ protein, making it insoluble and thus sequestered in SP and CAA.

Other findings do not support that ApoE is involved in the early stages of fibrillar amyloid formation. First, immunoreactivity to ApoE is markedly more limited than to $A\beta$ protein in brain tissue from AD patients, and is preferentially found in the core of classical SPs (consisting of fibrillar amyloid), while it is not found, or is weak, in diffuse plaques (consisting of nonfibrillar "preamyloid" $A\beta$ protein). Second, the binding between ApoE and $A\beta$ is within the hydrophobic carboxyl-terminal region of ApoE, which has been found to bind to amyloid in virtually any amyloid-associated disease, irrespective of the form amyloid protein (e.g., prion protein, prealbumin, and immunoglobulin light chains). Similarly, the highly hydrophobic $A\beta$ protein attracts a variety of other proteins (e.g., ApoB, ApoJ, α_1-antichymotrypsin, complement factors, heparin sulphate proteoglycans, and serum amyloid P component). Therefore, it is possible that the binding between ApoE and $A\beta$ protein may simply reflect its hydrophobic nature, without primary pathogenetic significance.

ApoE immunoreactivity is also found in neurofibrillary tangles. In vitro experiments have shown that ApoE3 binds more strongly to tau protein than to ApoE4. These findings led to the hypothesis that ApoE3, by binding to tau, slows the degree of phosphorylation and self-assembly into PHFs. However, the number of NFTs, or the level of PHFtau, do not differ between AD patients with and without the ApoE4 isoform, and the ApoE4 isoform frequency is probably also increased in senile dementia of the Lewy body type, a disorder not characterized by NFTs.

It has been suggested that ApoE is involved in the regulation of the mobilization and transport of lipids during neuronal repair and reactive synaptogenesis after injury. After experimental lesions in animals, astrocytes engulf the presynaptic terminals and their axons, which are then stored within the astrocytes, where the accumulation of cholesterol induces a synthesis of ApoE. The cholesterol and other lipids form ApoE–lipoprotein particles, which may then be directed to specific target sites within the CNS, and taken up by specific receptor-mediated endocytosis in the neuronal growth cones, for usage in neuronal and synaptic regeneration. It has been hypothesized that AD patients may be unable to induce the synthesis of ApoE in response to the neuronal degeneration, and that those with ApoE4 have an impaired reactive synaptogenesis to compensate for the age-related neuronal cell loss.

E. Neurotransmitter Disturbances

A disturbance in the cholinergic system was first described in AD in the 1970s, and has been well confirmed. However, we now know that the disturbances in AD involve the disruption of multiple neurotransmitter systems, including noradrenaline, serotonin, the excitatory amino acids, and neuropeptides such as somatostatin. This multiplicity of deficits may explain why neurotransmitter replacement therapy of one of these neurotransmitter systems, such as the use of acetylcholine inhibitors, do not have dramatic effects.

F. Heterogeneity of Alzheimer's Disease

It is now generally accepted that AD is a heterogeneous disorder, with a rare familial and common sporadic form. Within the familial form, different mutations on chromosomes 21, 14 and 1 are found. However, there are also much evidence that sporadic AD is a heterogeneous group. The term AD was originally reserved for dementia in patients with presenile onset (before 65 years of age), whereas the term *senile dementia* was used when the onset was after the age of 65. Since the 1960s, largely based on the observation that NFT and SP were also found in the brains of senile dementia patients, these disorders have been held to represent a single, homogeneous entity.

However, several studies have shown that the characteristic cortical instrumental symptoms are more frequent and more severe in younger than in older AD patients. It is also well established that the cortical neuropathological changes (the neuronal loss and the intensity of NFTs and SPs) and the neurotransmitter disturbances, are more severe in younger than in older AD patients. Recent studies have also revealed that the synaptic degeneration is more pronounced in younger than in older AD patients. These findings have been suggested to reflect a more severe cortical involvement in younger AD patients.

In contrast, white-matter lesions (WMLs), or leukoaraiosis (LA) have been found to be more frequent in older than in younger AD patients. WMLs can be visualized by CT or magnetic resonance imaging (MRI), or neuropathologically, by myelin stains. A vascular pathogenesis—an association with arteriolosclerosis (lipohyalinosis) in the end arteries supplying the periventricular white matter—is probably the most important cause of WMLs.

It has been suggested that two main subgroups of sporadic AD can be delimited. One subgroup, AD type I, or "pure AD" is characterized by relatively young age at onset (most often 55–65 or 70 years of age), symptoms of memory disturbances, marked instrumental symptoms, but absence of hypertension, WMLs, and other vascular changes. The other subgroup, AD type-II, or "senile dementia" is characterized by late age at onset (over 70--75 years), a more generalized symptomatology of memory disturbances, general cognitive and confusional symptoms, but mild instrumental symptoms. Hypertension and WMLs are frequent.

Although this dichotomization is preliminary, it may be used both in scientific studies and in drug trials in an attempt to identify patients with a more pure form of AD. According to the threshold theory, formulated by Roth and Tomlinson in England in the 1970s, both the severity of the pathological process(es), and the size of the reserve capacity are of importance for the production of dementia. In young and middle-aged people, the threshold for dementia is high, and severe pathological changes may be needed to cause dementia. In contrast, in old individuals, the reserve capacity has been reduced by age-related changes. Moreover, many pathological processes become more frequent with increasing age, both degenerative and vascular. Thus, a combination of lowered reserve capacity due to aging, and different combinations of age-related changes, both degenerative (e.g., SP, NFT, Lewy, bodies synaptic and neuronal degeneration) and vascular (e.g., WMLs), may be responsible for the dementia in the individual patient.

V. VASCULAR DEMENTIA

VaD is caused by disorders in the cerebrovascular system (e.g., stroke and small vessel disease). Historically, until the 1960s, dementia was considered a result of chronic ischemia secondary to atherosclerosis of cerebral arteries or "hardening of the arteries." In 1974, Hachinski et al. introduced the term MID. Thereafter the occurrence of multiple small or large infarcts came to be considered almost the only basis of VaD. In the mid-1970s the scientific emphasis in the study of dementia changed from vascular to primary degenerative disorders and AD, and VaD came to be regarded as less common. Current scientific discoveries have again resulted in greater interest in vascular mechanisms. During the last few years the term VaD has been introduced, but it is still used almost synonymously with the concept of MID. However, multiple infarcts are not the only cause of VaD, which may also be caused by subcortical WMLs, hereditary cerebral

Table VI The NINDS-AIREN Criteria for Vascular Dementia

Probable vascular dementia
1. Dementia
2. Cerebrovascular disease
   a. Focal signs consistent with stroke
      and
   b. Relevant CVD by brain imaging
      Multiple large-vessel infarcts
      Single strategically placed infarct
      Multiple lacunae (basal ganglia, white matter)
      Extensive periventricular white-matter lesions
3. Relationship between 1 and 2
   a. Dementia onset within 3 months following stroke
   b. Abrupt deterioration in cognitive functions
      Fluctuating stepwise progression
Possible vascular dementia
1. Dementia
2. Cerebrovascular disease
   Focal signs consistent with stroke
3. Absence of relationship between 1 and 2
   a. Dementia onset more than 3 months following stroke
   b. Subtle onset or variable course
Definite vascular dementia
1. Clinical criteria for probable vascular dementia
2. Histopathologic evidence of cerebrovascular disease
3. Absence of significant neurofibrillary tangles and neuritic plaques
4. Absence of other clinical or pathological disorder capable of producing dementia

hemorrhage with amyloidosis, granular cortical atrophy, hypertensive encephalopathy, cerebral amyloid angiopathy, cerebral vasculitis, and hemodynamic disorders. In many cases there is a combination of changes. The main causes of VaDs are probably thrombo-embolism (e.g., MID) and cerebral small vessel diseases (e.g., white-matter dementia). This new approach to VaD is reflected by the recently published NINDS-AIREN criteria (Table VI).

A. Multi-infarct Dementia

MID is a dementia syndrome related to multiple small or large brain infarcts, often too small individually to produce a major clinical incident. According to Tatemichi, subjects with ischemic stroke have at least a nine times increased risk for dementia. Most cerebral infarcts are due to thrombo-embolism from extracranial arteries and the heart. The typical clinical picture is one of sudden onset, stepwise deterioration, a fluctuating course, history of stroke or transitoric ischemic attacks (TIA), often in relation to the onset of dementia, focal neurological symptoms and signs, and hypertension. In the early course, the cognitive impairment may have a large variability depending on the site of the lesions. However, in a large minority of cases the dementia may have a gradual onset with a slowly progressive course and without focal clinical signs or infarcts on brain imaging (especially when CT scan has been used), which makes it difficult to differentiate from AD. The pathogenesis of MID is not clear. It has been suggested that the dementia may be related to the location or the volume of the infarct. In stroke patients, dementia has been associated with left-sided or bilateral infarcts, and volume of macroscopic infarcts. The risk factors suggested for MID are similar to those in stroke, including advanced age, male sex, hypertension, diabetes mellitus, smoking, and cardiac diseases. MID is reported to be more common in Finland, the former Soviet Union, and Asian countries than in Western Europe and the United States.

B. Hemodynamic Dementia

Hemodynamic dementia (or hypoperfusion dementia) refers to a dementia with onset in connection with an episode of severe systemic hypotension. This may be caused by extracranial disorders (e.g., arrythmias or cardiac failure). At autopsy, patients with a clinical diagnosis of hemodynamic dementia often have a picture of MID.

C. White-Matter Lesions

After the advent of CT, interest has increased in subcortical WMLs as a cause of dementia. First described by Durand-Fardel in 1854, followed by Binswanger in 1894, fewer than 50 autopsied cases were described in the literature up to 1980. Since 1980, when it became possible to discern WMLs on brain imaging, they have been reported in thousands of patients. This "epidemic" gave rise to a question of the validity of WMLs as a diagnostic entity, and it was claimed they were overemphasized. However, before the advent of CT, the level of interest among pathologists in white-matter disorders was low, and the white matter was not routinely evaluated in detail in most patients, which is necessary as the lesions are difficult to detect without whole brain sections, and myelin staining. The true incidence is probably therefore much higher than formerly believed, and it may even be the most common form of VaD. The increased interest is reflected by the fact that more than 300 autopsied cases with the typical histological picture have been described since 1980.

The pathological description includes marked or diffuse demyelination and moderate loss of axons with astrogliosis and incomplete infarction in subcortical structures of both hemispheres and arteriosclerotic changes with hyalinization or fibrosis and thickening of the vessel walls and narrowing of the lumina of the small penetrating arteries and arterioles in the white matter, often accompanied by a reduction of oligodendrocytes. The cortex is generally well preserved, as are the subcortical U fibers and corpus callosum, probably due to a different blood supply. The changes are often associated with lacunar infarcts. In 15 studies or case reports on the clinico-pathological correlations of subjects with WMLs on CT, the histopathological picture described above has been reported in 53 out of 55 autopsied cases.

Many terms have been used for this pathological entity. In 1902 Alzheimer coined the term Binswanger's disease, which has been used extensively. Other terms include subcortical arteriosclerotic encephalopathy, arteriolosclerotic leucoencephalopathy, leukoencephalopathy, senile leucoencephalopathy, subcortical encephalomalacia, or selective incomplete white-matter infarction. For the entity seen on CT or MRI, the above-mentioned terms have been used as well as white-matter low attenuation, WMLs, periventricular white-matter lucencies, and leukoaraiosis. In the following presentation, the term WMLs is used to describe the findings on CT, MRI, and autopsy.

The main hypothesis regarding the cause of WMLs is that long-standing hypertension causes lipohyalinosis and thickening of the vessel walls with narrowing of the lumen of the small perforating arteries and arterioles that nourish the deep WM. Episodes of hypotension, related to aging, drugs, or cardiac failure, may lead to hypoperfusion and hypoxia-ischaemia, leading to loss of myelin in the WM. The deep WM has few collaterals, which makes it more vulnerable to ischaemia than the cortex when a penetrating vessel occludes. Furthermore, myelin is probably more vulnerable to ischemia than axons. In the early stages, remyelination may occur if the underlying cause of hypoperfusion is eliminated. The lesions may also remain stable after a single episode of hypoperfusion. It has been suggested that the arterial changes are due to exposure of vessel walls to increased pressure over time. The greater the pressure or life span, the more likely are these changes to be present. Others consider, however, that no convincing proof of this theory exists.

The dementia associated with WMLs is probably caused by subcortical–cortical or cortico-cortical disconnection. In support of this opinion, delayed central conduction time has been found in patients with WMLs. WMLs have been associated with a spectrum of clinical pictures ranging from no memory disturbances to dementia. As a rule, the dementia has an insidious onset and a slowly progressive course, which makes it difficult to distinguish from AD. The dementia is generally of a subcortical type, with associated symptoms of a frontal lobe syndrome. The typical clinical picture includes extrapyramidal signs with psychomotor retardation, bilateral or unilateral pyramidal tract signs, pseudobulbar palsy, urinary incontinence, gait dysfunction, apathy, loss of drive, and emotional blunting. WMLs have been associated with vascular diseases, especially hypertension. Sometimes it is reported that WMLs are associated with focal neurological deficits. The reason for this may be that stroke and WMLs share the same risk factors, mainly hypertension.

D. Mixed Dementias

The common coincidence of AD and VaD as mixed dementia is becoming increasingly recognized, and this may even be the most common form of dementia. The combination of the two entities may suffice to cause dementia when neither alone is sufficient to do so. On a clinical basis, however, it is difficult to differentiate mixed AD–MID from pure MID. WMLs have been described in both clinical and autopsied cases of AD, and they seem to be more common in late than in early AD and often occur independently of the gray matter processes in AD.

E. Other Vascular Disorders Associated with Dementia

Vasculitis (e.g., temporalis arteritis and lupus erythematosus) may sometimes lead to dementia. However, when the underlying disorder is treated, the dementia may resolve.

VI. FRONTAL LOBE DEMENTIA

Several disease entities are included in the group of frontotemporal dementias. The largest group is frontal lobe degeneration of non-Alzheimer's type. In the following paragraphs this disease is called frontal lobe degeneration (FLD). In clinical work, the term *frontal lobe dementia* is often used. The group of frontotemporal dementias also include Pick's disease, progressive subcortical gliosis, and amyotrophic lateral sclerosis with frontal dementia symptoms and progressive aphasia. The latter is caused by an asymmetric degeneration of the language-dominant part of the frontal and temporal lobes, resulting in more language than behavioral disturbances. Patients with AD, VaD, Huntington's disease, Parkinson's disease, and some other brain disorders may also exhibit symptoms of the frontal lobe type during the course of their diseases.

FLD was extensively described by researchers from Lund, Sweden, in the mid-1980s. In their postmortem material consisting of about 400 dementia cases, frontal lobe degeneration was described in 8% of the total material. Most of those with frontal lobe symptoms exhibited a neuropathological picture that was not previously described and was labeled as frontal lobe degeneration of non-Alzheimer's type. At autopsy only a minority exhibited a picture of Pick's disease, at that time considered the dominant form of FLD (see below). However, it is generally not possible to differentiate clinically frontal lobe degeneration from Pick's disease.

A. Clinical Symptoms

The mean age for the onset of the disease is below the age of 60 with a mean duration of 8 years. Fifty percent of the cases are familial.

Behavioral disturbances and changes in personality occur early in FLD or Pick's disease, whereas memory deficits occur late in these diseases. Lack of insight and judgment, decreased inhibition, impulsiveness, restlessness, and anxiety occur early. These symptoms, together with concentration difficulties, make it difficult for the patient to manage his or her usual activities, even though memory and several higher brain functions initially may be preserved. Early symptoms also include depressed mood and apathy. Aggressiveness and irritability are common as are emotional bluntness and indifference. Sometimes the clinical picture may alternate between apathy and restlessness. Psychotic symptoms (e.g., delusions and hallucinations) and hypochondrical ideas are common. Hyperphagia (bulimia) is also common and may sometimes lead to weight gain.

Typically, these patients have a progressive language disturbance of expressive motor type, with a stereotyped speech, reduced number of words, and sometimes echolalia. By contrast, receptive language is often intact, and initially the patient can act adequately upon instructions, although he has difficulties in making himself understood. As the disease progresses, dementia symptoms with memory deficits and dyspraxia occur. In the more advanced stages, the patient is typically unable to talk (mutism), dyspractic, and unable to interpret the surrounding and his own body signals. In some cases dysphagia makes it impossible to swallow solid food. On clinical examination, one may observe primitive reflexes and hyperflexia. Other patients may be physically preserved and able to walk and thus require specially demanding care and supervision.

In many cases behavioral disturbance makes it impossible for the frontal lobe demented patients to remain with relatives at home, and there are also difficulties in group living with other demented patients.

B. Diagnosis

Frontal lobe degeneration should be suspected when a patient presents with the clinical picture described above. The expressive, motor, and language disturbance is an especially typical symptom. Neuropsychological testing reveals a language disturbance that is more pronounced in the motor functions, while the receptive language functions usually are intact. CT scan or MRI of the brain may show atrophy of the frontal lobe and enlarged anterior horns of the lateral ventricles. Electroencephalogram (EEG) is usually normal during the first stages of the disease. Measurements of the regional cerebral blood flow (rCBF) usually detect reduced activity of the frontal lobes.

Differential diagnostic evaluation must distinguish primary frontal lobe dementia from VaD with frontal symptoms, AD with frontal symptoms, amyotrophic lateral sclerosis (ALS) with frontal symptoms, primary progressive aphasia, Huntington's disease, depression, Creutzfeldt-Jakob disease, frontal lobe tumor alcohol-induced brain damages, and several psychiatric conditions. Pick's disease can be reliably separated from FLD only after neuropathological examination.

C. Neuropathology

At autopsy one observes atrophied gyri and enlargements of the sulci in pronounced cases. Microscopically, the pathological changes are most pronounced in the frontal lobes and, in more advanced cases, at the temporal poles. The pathological changes include loss of neurons in cortical layer 1–3, reactive astrocytosis and white-matter changes that correspond to the cortical atrophy. There are no Alzheimer's-like changes in the histopathological picture.

D. Pick's Disease

In Pick's disease the clinical picture is very similar to the above for FLD. However, the neuropathological picture is more pronounced, spreads to all cortical layers, and there are swollen nerve cell bodies with inclusion (Pick) bodies.

E. Etiology and Pathogenesis

The etiology and pathogenesis of FLD is not known. There is a high frequency of the disease in some families, pointing to a possible genetic factor as being of etiological importance.

Table VII Treatable Conditions That Can Cause Dementia-like Symptoms

Psychiatric origin	Somatic origin
Delirium	Delirium
Depression	Subdural hematoma
Psychosis	Brain tumor
	Normal pressure hydrocephalus
	Hypercalcemia
	Hypothyroidism
	Vitamin B12 deficiency
	CNS infections
	Drug intoxication

F. Treatment

There is no specific pharmacological treatment for the disease. The most important interventions are treatment of psychiatric symptoms, such as depression, anxiety, hallucinations, and behavioral symptoms (see next section).

VII. DIAGNOSIS AND EVALUATION OF DEMENTIA

A. Background

It has been suggested that in 10–20% of the instances, dementia syndromes are caused by potentially treatable conditions, may be worsened by treatable conditions, or may be retarded by treatment (Tables VII and VIII). Furthermore, physical and mental disorders

Table VIII Common Conditions That Secondarily Can Cause Worsening of Cognitive or Behavioral Function in a Patient with a Dementing Disorder

Psychosocial origin	Somatic origin
Sensory deprivation	Infections
• social isolation	Pain
• inadequate living	Anemia
Depression	• gastric ulcer
	Constipation
	Heart insufficiency

Table IX Purposes of Dementia Investigation

A dementia investigation should be performed to:
  Identify dementia-like, many times treatable, conditions (e.g., depression, hypothyreosis) and make adequate actions against these conditions.
  Identify dementing disease and type of dementia disorder.
  Describe the individual brain damages and corresponding symptoms and handicaps.
  Describe the losses of function in daily life.
  Describe the remaining functions and abilities that can be improved and subject to rehabilitation.
  Identify and treat associated somatic and psychic symptoms and diseases.
  Describe the social situation and help psychosocial actions to be made (e.g., day-care centers, change of living situation). Also include support for the relatives.
  Work as a medical base in the future progress of the disease.
  Give adequate information to the patients, relatives, and staff.

in subjects with dementia are often neglected, and these may contribute to the deterioration of function. It is therefore important that all patients with a new diagnosis of dementia and all demented patients with a sudden deterioration in their condition receive a careful medical examination and a further investigation that is basic for adequate medical, psychological, and social care. Without a proper dementia evaluation, possibly treatable conditions may be neglected. When a dementia syndrome is well established, the type of dementia should still be diagnosed. The different dementing diseases have different progression and clinical pictures. It is now possible to treat patients with AD pharmacologically, but the diagnosis must be ascertained before treatment can start. Every demented person exhibits individual symptoms due to particular brain damage and individual background (e.g., influence of education and personality). In order to give adequate care, one must know what brain damages and symptoms exist in each case. The purposes of clinical investigation in dementia are shown in Table IX.

B. Contents of the Dementia Investigation

The dementia investigation can often be performed at an outpatient clinic. A complete dementia evaluation sufficient to fulfill the aims described above and in Table IX should include the following:

1. Medical and social history
2. Complete psychiatric and medical evaluation including neurological and mental state examination
3. Laboratory tests of blood and cerebrospinal fluid
4. Brain imaging
5. Evaluation of activities of daily living (ADL)
6. Social investigations
7. Summary evaluation and planning for the future

C. Mental State Evaluation

There are several different diagnostic criteria for dementia and dementing diseases, as described above. A common but rough method for testing mental status is the Mini-Mental State Examination (MMSE). A result of less than 24 on the MMSE (maximum 30), suggests the presence of dementia. However, several other conditions affecting cognitive functions (e.g., depression or low level of education) can influence the results on the MMSE. Furthermore, persons with high intellectual functions may perform well on MMSE but still have dementia at an early stage.

D. Laboratory Tests

Laboratory tests are primarily performed to detect specific causes for the dementia symptoms. Hypothyroidism, vitamine B-12 deficiency, or drug effects can sometimes completely or partly explain the dementia symptoms. However, there are today no definite biological markers to confirm any of the primary dementing diseases. Examples of laboratory tests that can constitute the laboratory work-up in dementia disorders are given in Table X. It should be noted that determination of apolipoprotein E alleles or isoforms has too low sensitivity and specificity to be included in the routine laboratory investigation.

E. Neuroimaging

CT or MRI should be performed in most cases to exclude potentially treatable conditions (e.g., brain tumor, subdural hematoma, and normal pressure hy-

Table X Laboratory Tests in the Investigation of Dementia Disorders

	Reason for investigation
Blood and serum analyses	
B-Erythrocyte sedimentation rate	Inflammation/infection
B-Hemoglobin	Anaemia
B-White blood cell count	Inflammation/infection
S-albumin, S-calcium	Hyperparathyroidism
S-γ-glutamyl transferase or S-carbohydrate deficient transferrin	Alcoholism/liver disease
B-glucose	Diabetes
S-Thyroid stimulating hormone	Thyroid disease
S-vitamin B12 or S-methyl malonic acid, or S-homocysteine	Vitamin B12 deficiency
S-sodium, S-potassium, S-Creatinin	
S-transaminases	Liver diseases
P-folate	Folate deficiency
Serological tests	Lues, HIV, Borrelia
Toxicological screening	Drug intoxication
Cerebrospinal fluid analyses	
CSF-leukocytes, mononuclear and polynuclear	Inflammation/infection
CSF/S albumin ratio	Blood-brain barrier damage
IgG index, IgM index, and isoelectric focusing	Inflammation/infection
CSF-tau protein	Axonal degeneration (Alzheimer's disease?)
Extended analyses	
PCR analysis	Analysis of APP-mutations
PCR-analysis or isoelectric focusing	Determination of ApoE-alleles/isoforms

drocephalus), unless the patient is too old or too weak to be subject for surgical interventions. The major reason for performing neuroimaging is thus to find secondary (and more often treatable) causes of dementia. Several reports show that 5–20% of the cases exhibit structural pathology on neuroimaging. Neuroimaging can also help in the differentiation between degenerative and VaD, in the latter case showing infarcts or WMLs.

Measurements of the regional cerebral blood flow often using SPECT (single photon emission computerized tomography) is often performed in dementia investigations. This technique may show reduced activity over affected brain areas, even though typical patterns of disease can be difficult to establish in individual cases.

F. Electroencephalography

EEG is a sensitive method for finding an organic brain disorder, because the EEG is often pathological early in the dementia diseases. The EEG adds little, however, to differentiated diagnosis.

G. Lumbar Puncture

Lumbar puncture is often used to exclude CNS infections and to indicate blood–brain barrier damage. Although required in only a minority of instances, lumbar puncture should always be performed when a CNS infection is suspected.

Cerebrospinal fluid (CSF) analyses may detect evidence of blood–brain barrier damage, which is found in cases with tumors and in cerebrovascular disorders, including MID. The blood–brain barrier function is evaluated by determination of the CSF/S albumin ratio [= CSF-albumin (mg/L)/serum-albumin (g/L)]. CSF analyses are also essential to detect cerebral inflammatory disorders (e.g., systemic lupus erythematosus and multiple sclerosis) and infections (e.g., Borrelia encephalitis, syphilis). A mononuclear pleocytosis and signs of intrathecal immunoglobulin production are found in different chronic infections that can mimic, for example, AD. Intrathecal immunoglobulin production can be quantitatively determined by the IgG index and IgM index, or qualitatively detected by the finding of CSF-specific oligoclonal bands on isoelectric focusing. Finally, determination of CSF-tau protein may be used as a marker for chronic axonal degeneration, with high sensitivity for the diagnosis of AD.

H. Neuropsychological Testing

Neuropsychological testing can be used, for example, in early cases when the clinical symptoms are discrete and neuroimaging, EEG, and other tests are close to normal. The neuropsychological testing may detect signs of organic brain disorder in these cases. A skilled interpretation can often provide helpful corroborative evidence for subtle regional brain damage (e.g., subcortical or frontal lobe pathology). It may also identify specific symptom profiles and preserved functions.

I. Final Work-up

Finally the responsible physician makes a summary evaluation of all findings including medical history, physical, psychiatric, neurological, mental status, and laboratory results. These may possibly point to a particular dementing disorder. The physician should also initiate possible treatment and attempt to optimize the psychosocial environments for the patients. The latter may include day-care activities and psychological support for the patient or the relatives at different stages of the disease.

VIII. PHARMACOLOGICAL TREATMENT AND CARE

The pharmacological treatment and care of dementia patients are closely related. Behavioral disturbances may often be adequately managed by the caregiver. But sometimes, in addition, pharmacological treatment is necessary.

During the disease process, the demented person may exhibit a number of different behavioral symptoms, which are susceptible to pharmacological treatment. However, one symptom (e.g., aggressiveness) may be caused by many different factors, underscoring the necessity of an individual evaluation. Therefore it is important to use a holistic view in the treatment of demented persons (Figure 2). The adequate management throughout the disease process requires a competent individual to be close to the demented person. Often special caregiving and psychosocial actions must be initiated.

In other cases a medical condition (e.g., one which causes pain), can result in a behavioral disturbance that requires a professional medical action. Too often demented persons with behavioral disturbances are inadequately evaluated by doctors. The onset or worsening of a behavioral disturbance may be due to progression of the dementia, but may also be due to other concomitant diseases. A demented person who suffers from pain may have difficulties to express what troubles him or her. Instead of describing the symptom (e.g., angina pectoris), the patient may display aggressiveness and behavioral disturbance.

Daily care and nonpharmacological treatment of demented persons requires a broad knowledge about dementia diseases and their different clinical pictures. Such knowledge is also helpful to relatives taking care of the demented person. For professional caregivers it is important to know the personal history of each patient, including the dementia disease and the handicaps it causes, former occupation, special interests, and so forth.

A. Activity Training

The need for activity is highly individual. Many demented persons have a need for physical activity. Some demented persons walk for hours every day. For patients in special group living, the need for physical and mental activity in a structured manner is important. If the demented person does not have a structured day with meaningful activities, disturbing behavioral symptoms like aggressiveness and restlessness may easily occur. These symptoms may result in use of pharmacological treatment, for example anxiolytics. However, pharmacological treatment should never be a substitute for lack in care of the demented person.

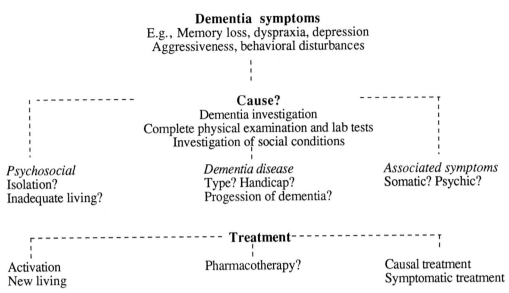

Figure 2 Schematic presentation of the management of the patient with symptoms of possible dementia. Evaluation of the symptoms of dementia demands a comprehensive approach. In addition to dementing diseases, other conditions such as psychosocial disorders or associated somatic conditions may contribute to the clinical picture. Before treatment is chosen, a complete analysis of the different areas for possible underlying causes of the symptoms has to be made.

It is also important for elderly, especially demented persons, to have the opportunity to rest and think. Some special considerations may be needed to enable such relaxation.

There are convincing studies showing that demented persons living in special homes for the demented, where structured activities are performed several days per week with well-educated staff, have a higher level of functioning and fewer psychiatric symptoms than patients living in circumstances where they spend most of the day by themselves.

B. Pharmacological Treatment

I. Specific Treatment

a. Alzheimer's Disease Treatment against AD with tacrine (tetrahydroaminoacridine) has been practiced in the United States since 1993. In 1995 this compound was also registered in some European countries. Tacrine is given to AD patients with mild to moderate dementia. It attempts to improve the cognitive functions by preventing the breakdown of the neurotransmitter acetylcholine. The clinical effect is an improvement in logical thinking and memory but an appreciable clinical benefit is observed in only a minority (perhaps 30–40%) of cases. The treatment may give rise to liver side effects. In Europe the treatment is usually handled by doctors with special experience regarding dementia diseases.

b. Vascular Dementia The strategy in the treatment of MID is to prevent new strokes. Although no formal studies have been performed, the use of anticoagulant agents, for example, low dose treatment with salicylates, may be beneficial. Treatment of cardiac arrhythmias and high blood pressure may also be essential. Regarding white-matter dementia, antihypertensive treatment may potentially prevent the changes in the small vessels. Monitoring of blood pressure is essential during treatment as overtreatment may cause hypotension.

2. Depressive Symptoms

Such symptoms are common in dementing diseases. Several studies support the benefit of selective serotonin reuptake inhibitors (SSRIs) in improving both depressive symptoms and cognitive functions. Many AD patients receive SSRI compounds during disease progression. However, depressive symptoms may often be related to inadequate care and lack of stimulation, which should be managed before pharmacological treatment is started.

3. Anxiety

This is also a common symptom in dementia. In many cases the anxiety symptoms must be treated with benzodiazepines. However, benzodiazepines may often cause sleepiness and fatigue in demented persons.

4. Psychotic Symptoms

Psychosis is common throughout the dementia process. Delusions, paranoid ideas, and hallucinations exist at some point in at least half of dementia cases. Delusions can be difficult to differentiate from perceptional and memory disturbances. Psychotic symptoms should first be treated with low-dose neuroleptics like haloperidol and risperidone. However, the sensitivity to extrapyramidal symptoms must be considered. Despite their well-known anticholinergic and autonomic effects, older agents such as thioridazine (in low doses) are often helpful.

5. Sleep Disturbances

Such problems are also common in dementia. The first step in the treatment should be to optimize psychosocial conditions like physical activity, avoiding daytime napping, assuring the feeling of security at night, and care of possible underlying somatic diseases. Thereafter, pharmacological treatment of sleep disorder may still be needed. Compounds like zolpidem and zopiklon are nonbenzodiazepine compounds with few side effects (like hangover), but with good clinical efficacy. Therefore these new compounds should be used in the first instance. In some cases compounds with longer duration are needed (e.g., in demented individuals with severe sleep disturbance where short-acting compounds like zolpidem or zopihlon are not sufficient to induce sleep over night, that is >6 hours).

6. Aggressiveness and Behavioral Disturbances

These problems must first be evaluated at the psychosocial and somatic level. Inadequate isolation and somatic diseases, perhaps causing pain or other symp-

toms, may explain aggressiveness and behavioral disturbance. When these causes have been excluded, pharmacological treatment can be undertaken. In many cases SSRI compounds with antidepressant effect can have benefit. If these do not have effect, low-dose neuroleptics may be used.

7. Future Compounds

Future compounds against AD are in development in clinical trials all over the world. Several compounds are directed against the pathogenesis of AD with the loss of neurons. In addition, symptomatic treatments at the neurotransmittor level are also tested. However, there are no compounds today in clinical trials, that promise to prevent the onset of dementia.

BIBLIOGRAPHY

American Psychiatric Association. (1994). *Diagnostic and statistical manual of mental disorders*. (4th ed.). Washington, DC: American Psychiatric Association.

Blennow, K., & Wallin, A. (1992). Clinical heterogeneity of probable Alzheimer's disease. *Journal of Geriatric Psychiatry and Neurology, 5,* 106.

Brun, A., Englund, E., Gustafson, L., Passant, U., Mann, D. M. A., Neary, D., & Snowden, J. S. (1994). Clinical and neuropathological criteria for frontotemporal dementia. *Journal of Neurology, Neurosurgery, and Psychiatry 57,* 416.

Burns, A., & Levy, R. (Eds.). (1994). *Dementia*. London: Chapman & Hall.

Erkinjuntti T., & Hachinski, V. (1993). Dementia post stroke. In *Physical medicine and rehabilitation: State of the art reviews* (Vol. 7). Philadelphia: Hanley & Belfus, Inc.

Erkinjuntti, T., & Hachinski, V. (1993). Rethinking vascular dementia. *Cerebrovascular Diseases, 3,* 3.

Haase G. R. (1977). Diseases presenting as dementia. In C. E. Wells (Ed.). *Dementia*. FA Davis Company. USA.

International Classification of Diseases. Tenth version. (1992) WHO.

Jorm, A. (1990). *The epidemiology of Alzheimer's disease and related disorders*. London: Chapman and Hall.

McKhann, G., Drachman, D., Folstein, M., Katzman, R., Price, D., & Stadlan, E. (1984). Clinical diagnosis of Alzheimer's disease: report of the NINCDS-ADRDA Work Group under the auspices of Department of Health and Human Services Task Force on Alzheimer's disease. *Neurology, 34,* 939.

Román, G. C., Tatemichi, T. K., Erkinjuntti, T., et al. (1993). Vascular dementia: Diagnostic criteria for research studies. Report of the NINDS-AIREN international workshop. *Neurology, 43,* 250.

Skoog, I. (1994). Risk factors for vascular dementia. A review. *Dementia, 5,* 137.

Skoog, I., Palmertz, B., Andreasson, L-A. (1994). The prevalence of white matter lesions on computed tomography of the brain in demented and non-demented 85-year-olds. *Journal of Geriatric Psychiatry and Neurology, 7,* 169.

Strittmatter, W. J., & Roses, A. D. (1996). Apolipoprotein E and Alzheimer's disease. *Annual Review of Neuroscience, 19,* 53.

Terry, R. D., Katzman, R., & Bick, K. L. (Eds.). (1994). *Alzheimer's disease.* New York: Raven Press Ltd.

Wallin, A., Brun, A., & Gustafson, L. (Eds.). (1994). Swedish consensus on dementia diseases. *Acta Neurological Scandinavian 90* (suppl. 157), 1–31.

World Health Organization (1992). *International classification of diseases.* (10th ed.). WHO.

Demography

George C. Myers

Duke University

Mitchell L. Eggers

Economic Commission for Europe

Demographic Transition The historical process of change in national populations from high levels to low levels of fertility and mortality.

Demography of the Aged Examination of the changing social, behavioral, economic, demographic, health, and epidemiologic status of older persons, the factors responsible for these changes, and their consequences.

Demography of Population Aging Examination of the causes, mechanisms, and societal consequences of age structural changes in the total population.

Population Aging Changes in the age structure of a population that can be measured by increases in the proportion of total population at older ages and increasing mean or median age of the population. Sometimes also used to reflect the increasing numbers of older persons and high annual rates of growth.

Stable Population A virtually unchanging population age structure that would result inevitably from the application of given constant schedules of age-specific fertility and mortality.

There is growing interest in demographic research directed to various aspects of the field of aging. The term **DEMOGRAPHY OF AGING** has come increasingly to be used to identify studies that adopt demographic perspectives to study aging processes and the changing characteristics of older populations. In gen-

eral, demographers focus on the examination of the size, composition, and spatial distribution of populations and the four main determinants of changes in these population characteristics: namely, fertility, mortality, migration, and changes in status. In addition, demographers are concerned with the measurement, modeling, and policy implications of past, current, and projected levels and age patterns of these determinants. Age, therefore, is a central focus of attention for demographers and provides a natural rationale for examining many gerontological issues.

I. INTRODUCTION

Demography as a field is noted for several distinctive features. Demographers address societal issues of major policy importance, such as rapid population growth associated with high fertility, the effects of large-scale population movements, and more recently changes in population structures marked by global population aging. The conceptual models that they bring to bear include not only the interrelationships among the main demographic factors, but also the social, economic, and behavioral determinants and the consequences of major population trends. This broad perspective involves the description and analysis of major population shifts, with the main goal being to measure and untangle the forces that brought them about historically and how they may shape the future. This entails the construction and specification of mathematical and statistical models—life table approaches, stable population models, hazard models, and structural equation models—to provide an understanding of causal relationships, a necessary condition for forecasting future trends. It is acknowledged that demographers have made important contributions in designing and improving the accuracy of major data-collection efforts, such as censuses, vital registration systems, and broad-based population surveys. In recent years, longitudinal surveys have been undertaken increasingly to provide a means for examining important transitions and behavioral changes that affect individuals and their families over the life course. Thus, demography has developed into an interdisciplinary scientific field with distinctive methodological approaches for the empirical study of comparative population structures and changes over time.

The demography of aging actually comprises two distinct subfields: the *demography of population aging* and the *demography of the aged*. Each of these subfields has a distinct substantive and methodological orientation. The demography of population aging is primarily concerned with the causes, mechanisms, and societal consequences of age structural changes in the total population, whereas the demography of the aged is concerned with the evolving social, economic, demographic, health, and epidemiological status of older persons who exceed some arbitrarily defined age, most frequently ages 60 and 65. Like the major field of demography, the subfields are interdisciplinary in nature, which has precipitated several new areas of concentrated research interest. Two of these, family demography and biodemography, are examined in section IV, New Directions.

II. DEMOGRAPHY OF POPULATION AGING

A. Historical Development

The emergence of concern with population aging initially arose from two distinct developments. First, the recognition in the late nineteenth century that an impressive shift in the age structure was occurring in certain national populations and, second, the subsequent uncovering of several analytical relationships that provided significant insights into the forces and processes of population aging.

Early recognition of population aging occurred in France and Sweden in the late nineteenth century, at a time in which the proportions of the population aged 65 and over in both countries were approaching 8%. In 1900, Gustav Sundbärg, a Swedish researcher, conducted the first rudimentary comparative analyses of the age profiles of national populations. He calculated the proportions of population in three age groups—under age 15, 15 though 49, and 50 and over for several countries. In comparing the results, he found that most European countries had nearly 50% of their population in the age group 15–49, but differed markedly in the proportions at young and old ages. He speculated that countries would retain the same levels at adult ages, but would shift over time from having high proportions of young persons to high proportions of older persons.

This remarkable insight then led him to characterize national populations as gradually shifting from progressive (younger) to stationary and eventually to regressive (older) age structures. Moreover, he indicated that these shifts in the age structure of a population were due primarily to changes in fertility and mortality. Sundbärg can thus be credited with being the first person to conduct quantitative cross-national comparisons of changing levels of vital events and their effects on population structures that would lead inevitably to population aging. Moreover, by stipulating the roles of declining fertility and mortality, he anticipated the notion that came to be known later as the demographic transition.

Although some attention to the possibilities of population aging and accompanying fears of depopulation was manifested in the recession period of the 1930s, especially in France and Great Britain, concerted research into the analytical aspects of the issue only began in the post-World War II period. In the early 1950s, several relationships and mathematical equations of fundamental importance to the demographic dynamics of population aging were introduced by demographers at the Population Division of the United Nations and Princeton University, most notably Jean Bourgeois-Pichat, Frank Lorimer, and Ansley Coale. The discovery of these equations, which unveil precise relationships among several elementary population parameters, put the demography of aging on a sound analytical footing.

B. Models of Population Dynamics

Using stable population equations first expressed by Lotka and co-workers in the early part of the twentieth century, these demographers began with an initial stable age structure, varied the fertility rates while holding mortality constant, and then compared the resulting stable age structures. With this comparative statics approach, they were able to isolate the effects of fertility declines on population age structures. Similar procedures were applied to examine the effects of changing mortality rates while holding fertility schedules constant. Three key findings relevant for the field emerged from these exercises.

One, Coale's research, in particular, showed that changes in fertility (e.g., in the birthrate) cause the entire age distribution to "pivot" about the mean age of the childbearing. The mean age of childbearing is approximately equal to the mean length of generation, which is between ages 25 and 30 for most countries in the world. The pivoting of the age structure about the mean age of childbearing connotes that an increase in the birthrate, *ceteris paribus,* results in an increase in the proportion of the total population below that age and a decrease in the birthrate on the proportion above it. Thus, declines in the fertility rate, which have been observed in most of the world's populations in the past 30 years, lead to population aging.

A second major finding relates to the effects of changing mortality on age structure. Demographers have demonstrated that a mortality change with respect to age (measured by a log linear transformation that expresses the mortality rate decreasing by the same relative amount throughout the age range) has little or no effect on the age structure. Thus, mortality levels can change, albeit in a restricted form, and have no effect on the age distribution. In this specific case, the entire effect of the change is "felt" equally among all age groups resulting in no structural adjustment. The population growth rate may change, but not the age structure. Observed mortality declines in real populations, however, do not occur in such a simple pattern with respect to age. Instead, they are concentrated either between birth and early childhood or at ages 50 or 60 and above. Concentration of a mortality decline between birth and early childhood results in a younger age distribution; the effect of more infants surviving is analogous to an increase in the birthrate. Concentration of a mortality decline at later ages results in an older age distribution. The point at which a mortality improvement leads to an older, rather than a younger, population is marked by a life expectancy at birth of between 60 and 65 years.

A third finding was that fertility changes have far more influence on initial population aging than do mortality changes, a somewhat counterintuitive result now well known to demographers. Fertility changes have more initial impact because they are introduced into the age structure at a single point—age zero. In contrast, age-specific patterns of mortality improvement that are spread throughout the age range have offsetting effects with respect to age structure adjustment. As major declines in mortality levels shift from younger to older ages, as has been historically the case, mortality comes to play a major role in the population aging process. The effects of these transitions on age structure lie at the heart of what has been described as the shift from aging from the base (of the age distribution) to aging at the apex.

Formal demographic investigations carried out by Preston and associates in the mid-1980s on the relationship between intrinsic and actual population growth rates revealed further analytical insights into population aging. They showed that when the fertility rate drops to replacement level in a population closed to migration and remains there indefinitely, a condition corresponding to a total fertility rate slightly over two children per woman and an intrinsic growth rate of zero, the growth rate of the population below the mean age of childbearing is zero. This is an important insight into the forces of population aging because it implies, and in fact necessitates, that all future population growth beyond the time at which fertility achieves replacement level takes place in age groups above the mean age of childbearing.

Thus, after the fertility rate falls to replacement level, all subsequent growth is the result of growth momentum built into the age structure, and it occurs because already-born, large cohorts replace the smaller cohorts above the mean age of childbearing. The inevitable result of this growth of the middle and upper age population segments is rapid population aging. Moreover, in populations experiencing low and falling mortality (life expectancy exceeding 60 years), the growth of upper age segments is enhanced because mortality reductions occur at ever more advanced ages. This results in steady gains in life expectancy and the growth of the oldest old population (85 years and over). The picture is much the same for both sexes, except that the relative survival of women is much greater than that of men, and as a group they usually experience more advanced population aging.

C. Population Aging Trends

I. World

The world's population is aging rapidly and will continue to do so well into the twenty-first century. Table I shows that the world's number of older persons 65 years of age and over more than doubled between 1950 and 1990 and is projected to reach over 809 million by the year 2025. The annual growth rate for the *total* population decreased slightly from 1.8% just after the Second World War to 1.7% in 1985–1990, but is projected to fall to 1.0% by 2020–2025. In contrast, the growth rate of the aged population moves in an opposite direction; it increases from 2.0% in 1950–1955 to 2.4% in 1985–1990, and continues to accelerate to a level of 3.0% annually in 2020–2025. In terms of the two summary measures of population aging reported in the table (the percentage of the population age 65 and over and the median age) both show only a modest rise in the earlier period, but marked increases from 1990 onwards. Within the aged population itself, the numbers of the oldest old, 80 years of age and over, have increased greatly. However, in the period ahead they will only increase marginally as a proportion of the total aged population. This reflects the large influx of the baby boom cohorts into the older ages in the second and third decades of the next century.

Table I Dynamics of World Population Aging, 1950–2025[a]

	1950	1990	2025
Numbers (1000s)			
Total aged	144,380	325,747	809,339
80+	15,853	53,692	135,923
80+ of total aged (%)	11.0	16.5	16.8
Indicators			
Percent 65+	5.1	6.2	9.7
Median age	23.4	24.2	31.0
Rates of growth			
Total	1.8	1.7	1.0
65+	2.2	2.7	3.0
65+ — total	0.4	1.0	2.0
Growth factors			
Total fertility rate	5.0	3.4	2.4
Life expectancy at birth	46.4	63.3	72.5
Infant mortality	155.0	68.0	31.0

[a]From *World Population Reports: The 1992 Revision.* New York: United Nations, 1993.

Population aging, as noted earlier, is the result of dynamic changes that have taken place in fertility and mortality levels. The total fertility rate, life expectancy at birth, and the infant mortality rate are commonly used by demographers to measure these levels. The total fertility rate decreased from five children per woman on average in 1950–1955 to 3.4 in 1985–1990, and is expected to decline further to 2.4 in 2020–2025, according to these United Nations projections. World mortality rates also have improved markedly during most of the twentieth century, in spite of some countertrends in certain geographic regions (e.g., Central and Eastern Europe, and the former Soviet Union). The average life expectancy at birth increased between 1950–1955 and 1985–1990 by nearly 17 years to reach 63.3, and it is projected to reach 72.5 years by 2020–2025. Declines in infant mortality accounted for most of the increase in life expectancy in the earlier period. In accordance with theoretical expectations, the proportion of aged persons was moderated in the period up to 1990 by large reductions in infant mortality, in spite of substantial declines in fertility. However, in the 1990–2025 period the sustained fertility reductions, even at lower levels, acting in concert with mortality reductions concentrated at later ages, will bring about major changes in the median age and percentage of older persons in the world's population.

2. Major Regions

These observations for the world as a whole serve to illustrate the main dimensions of population aging, but they do not capture the major differences that exist between the world's major regions and the countries that they comprise. The demographic transition in vital rates from high levels of fertility and mortality to low levels has already progressed significantly in the more developed countries. The median age of the aggregated, more developed region was 33.6 years in 1990 and is expected to reach 39.8 by 2025. The percentage of population 65 years and over is slightly over 12% currently and will rise to 18.3% by the end of projection period. The current rate of growth of the older population in the more developed region will remain fairly stable at about 1.9% annually.

In contrast, population aging in the less developed region is far less advanced, with a median age of 22.0 years in 1990 and 4.5% of the population aged. These levels will increase to 29.6 years and 8.0% respectively in 2025. The rate of growth of the older population will continue to accelerate from 4.5% currently to 8.0% annually in the period 2020–2025. A majority of the world's aged already live in less developed countries (56.2%), and by 2025 nearly 70% of the 809 million older persons will live in this region. This reflects the enormous population momentum that is built into the age structures and the changing vital rates for the less economically advanced countries. Truly, it is fair to say that population aging has become a worldwide demographic phenomenon.

D. Policy Implications

Demographers and other social scientists increasingly have been called upon to examine the consequences of the broad shifts in overall population structure brought about by population aging. Because of the seemingly irreversible nature of these developments, some observers have referred to them as a "gerontologic revolution" that brings about enduring societal changes in economic, social, and political structures. Forecasts inform us that the effects of population aging are expected to be particularly significant in the second and third decades of the new century, but it is important to emphasize that important changes already have occurred to alter the composition and age structure of the older population.

In the economic realm, attention has been given to the effects of population aging on rates of economic growth, aggregate savings, investments, consumption patterns, and labor supply. There is growing concern over the future capacity of state economies to maintain social security, health, and other entitlement programs at existing levels. Moreover, the labor force in many developed societies is continuing to age, therefore raising questions about potential labor scarcity, productivity, and appropriate retirement ages. These macroeconomic issues arising from population aging require demographic projections and integrated models to examine current trends and future scenarios. [See ECONOMICS: SOCIETY.]

There also are social and political implications of major importance. Many of these relate to changes in kin and family structures and intergenerational relations, a topic considered in a later section. Population aging affects roles, role transitions, and behaviors across the life course, as well as the expectations that individuals hold regarding their future lifetimes. The progressive aging of the voting age population in many countries, along with prevailing patterns of voting behavior, has raised concerns over the extent to which older persons may gain increasing influence in political spheres and the possibility of intergenerational conflict.

III. DEMOGRAPHY OF THE AGED

The second major subfield directs attention primarily to the composition of the older population, how it changes over time, and the major dynamic factors that bring these changes about. The aged can be viewed as a particular subpopulation that has its own age, sex, and other defining characteristics. Like the total population, it is subject to change resulting from entrants (persons reaching the qualifying ages or moving geographically into the population); exits (persons dying or moving out of the population); and changes in the characteristics of the population through either volitional (e.g., persons marrying) or nonvolitional shifts (e.g., becoming widowed).

If is often noted that turnover in the older subpopulation is usually greater than in the younger population because of the frequency of events that take place at these ages. For example, over three-quarters of the deaths occurring in more developed countries occur at ages 65 and above. Similarly, change is common in terms of working behavior, social relationships, onset of multiple chronic diseases, disability, living arrangements, and not infrequently in the economic conditions of later life. Thus, studying the dynamic changes in the composition of the older population and transitions occurring in the lives of older persons presents some challenging conceptual and methodological issues.

Population aging, as noted earlier, brings about increased numbers of older persons and generally increases the proportion they represent of total population. The momentum for the numerical growth emanates from the size of earlier birth cohorts and the survival that they have experienced. Thus, the great surge in the growth of the older population that can be expected in the second and third decades of the next century reflects the succession of large baby boom cohorts from the post-World War II period. Analyses of cohort succession, the dominant characteristics of these cohorts, and their likely effects on the composition of future older populations has been a very fertile field of recent demographic research. [*See* COHORT STUDIES.]

Considerable attention has been given to the increasing demographic diversity found in this subpopulation. Among characteristic features that have been most often noted are the rapid growth of the oldest-old segments of the older population, the declining ratios of older males to females, and the increasing ethnic and racial makeup of the older population. These changes reflect not only cohort succession, but important changes that have occurred in levels of survival for subgroups in the older population. Mortality reductions continue to be experienced at the older ages, thereby raising life expectancies at even the most advanced ages. The trends in survival have been largely responsible for the growth of the oldest-old population, the most rapidly increasing age group in most countries. An increasing number of research studies focus on this segment of the older population, for they are often the most in need of social supports and long-term care.

Finally, it should be noted that demographic studies of the geographic mobility of older persons continue to receive considerable research attention. Although levels of mobility among older persons are substantially below those of the younger population, the nature of the moves and their implications for older persons can be significant. Among the main types of mobility that have been examined are retirement moves, geographic relocations made to be closer to other family members, and moves into institutions and family households necessitated by health and other circumstances. These various types of moves have often proved difficult to measure, and concerted data collection efforts are currently being developed to assess their importance.

IV. NEW DIRECTIONS

A. Family Demography

A flourishing area of demographic research focuses on how population aging affects changing family structures and functions. The more generic term *family* is used to identify this subfield in order to encompass broad family features such as kinship structures and extended family relations, as well as the structure of households and dynamic aspects of intrafamily interactions. Demographers have been concerned with examining major trends and determinants in these dimensions across time and in different societal settings. The determinants of these trends that have been studied include not only demographic factors, such as changes in fertility, mortality, and geographic mobility, but also related social changes in family formation and marital patterns, labor supply, and preferences as they are shaped by cultural values and norms.

The family, as a major social institution, plays a central role in socialization, accumulation and allocation of resources, and provision of support and care for family members. The latter dimensions are particularly important in the case of families that contain older members in need of assistance. These functions are strongly influenced by structural features of the extended and nuclear family, household living arrangements, and interactions among family members.

1. Kinship Structures

Formal demographic analyses, along the lines presented in the earlier discussion, have yielded some important observations about the effect of the main demographic changes on family structures. Declines in fertility naturally bring about smaller families and less extensive lateral kinship ties with siblings, cousins, and eventually with aunts and uncles. Lower mortality, especially concentrated at younger ages as it is initially, may counteract some of these tendencies. However, as mortality declines extend into the older ages, they increase the number of surviving parents for an adult child. Thus, there is greater vertical kinship. The result of changes in these two demographic parameters is the creation of what has been referred to as the "beanpole" family, with greater numbers of generations made up of smaller sized nuclear families.

A corollary of these developments reflects on the numbers, types, and durations spent in various roles over the life course. Because of less time spent in child rearing for a parent, greater durations of one's adult lifetime are spent with parents, and interestingly, a greater number of family membership roles will be experienced in a lifetime. Depending on the generation in question, older persons will have less younger relations, but younger persons will have more older relations. It is this paradoxical situation that contributes to the concern over the future burdens of caring for older persons if mortality continues to decline at advanced ages and fertility remains low or declines further.

These kin structures may differ significantly between rural and urban areas within countries; reflecting variations in the timing of changing vital rates and internal migration. They are also affected by sex differentials in mortality that lead to sex imbalances that favor female over male kin. However, in some Asian societies, such as China and Korea, sex selectivity in fertility favoring males through selective abortion may serve to counteract these imbalances over time.

2. Household Structures

Household composition, which greatly influences the level of emotional, physical, and material support available to elderly persons, is formed from a constellation of kin and unrelated individuals. A trend reported for most countries in the world has been toward smaller household sizes. Lower fertility accounts for some of this decline, but it also can be attributed to shifting living arrangements away from coresidence of older persons with their adult children.

For many elderly persons, living arrangements are the single most important social structure governing their everyday lives. The term living arrangements is interpreted broadly and includes the full set of within-household social relationships, as well as the features and conditions of the dwelling units in which households reside. However, demographers have devoted greater attention to the former considerations.

The most dominant trend in living arrangements among the elderly has been the steady increase in the proportions of older persons living with spouses and those who live alone, especially among widows, and declines in those living with children or other relatives. Trends in independent living by older intact husband–wife families are greatly affected by the improved joint survival of married persons up to and continuing into the later stages of life. For both intact nuclear families that contain older persons and for older unmarried persons, factors that have been found to be related to independent living are improved economic circumstances, better health and disability status, and declines in available kin, most notably children. Underlying these factors has been the implied desire for greater independence and privacy on the part of both older parents and their children. Recent econometric analyses suggest, however, that a downturn in the

proportion of young-old widows (ages 65–74) living alone has occurred in the 1980s in the United States, mainly due to greater numbers of baby boom children who are themselves unmarried and in need of assistance in living accommodations. This suggests that trends in such arrangements as living alone are not unilinear, but are sensitive to cohort fluctuations in the number and demands of children, as well as the conditions of older parents. [See HOUSING.]

Coresidence is only one reflection of the ties that parents can have with their children. Indeed, it is often noted for developed societies that coresidence is much less common than in developing countries, but that close spatial residence may exist and communications and assistance and social support between kin may be very strong. Another feature of living arrangements that has been receiving increased research attention is the role that geographic mobility can play in altering the propinquity of kin. One way that this can be assessed is by the amount of travel-time that it takes for a parent to visit a nearest child or vice versa. Recent examination of changes in these travel time differences among older persons indicate that they tend to decline over time (attributable mainly to geographic shifts) and that increased functional disability is associated with the probability and size of spatial convergence, especially for lower income and ethnic groups.

3. Family Dynamics

These basic analyses of kin and household structure have provided the groundwork for extensive research that has been undertaken on intergenerational flows of resources on both macro- and microlevels. An important feature of recent demographic research in this area has been to examine intergenerational transfers and the decision-making processes underlying the use of resources.

The family plays a major role in the societal allocation of resources through such mechanisms as the creation of human capital, family labor supply, direct in vivo financial transfers, and bequests. But not all of these transfers are monetary or in goods, many are social support services, such as caregiving (either instrumental or expressive). Considerable research is underway that attempts to assess the amount of these transfers among household family members and across generations. Moreover, attention also is being given to larger societal accounting for all transfers including governmental transfers. Formal demographic analyses provide macroparameters for estimating the demand side of these equations.

On the microlevel, there is considerable attention being given to intrafamily decision-making regarding transfers of various types. These social demographic studies are focusing on expectations that individuals have regarding future transfers, especially those relating to potential sources of care and other forms of support. Moreover, attention is being given to the likelihood of future survival, economic conditions, and possible future changes in living arrangements, such as movement into a nursing home. These research efforts directed to expectational data are not unlike those of earlier studies of expectations regarding fertility outcomes (e.g., ideal and expected family size) that demographers have developed. Surveys also have increasingly sought to obtain data from multiple individuals in a household, including spouses and other caregivers, that make it possible to examine the dynamics of the family interactions and decision-making. Moreover, many recent surveys involve longitudinal designs that make it possible to assess transitions in important dimensions of the lives of older persons.

B. Biodemography of Aging

A new direction of research that seeks to integrate more fully demography and the biological sciences has been termed the *biodemography* of aging. The fields of comparative population biology, population genetics, and epidemiology have long shared common perspectives and methodological approaches with the field of demography. For example, the stable population model discussed earlier has been widely used for studies of not only human populations, but those of other species as well. In turn, demographers have examined biological and genetic factors as possible explanations for fertility and mortality trends and differentials (e.g., the effects of fecundity on fertility levels and genetic factors on sex mortality differentials).

Although the term biodemography was first introduced in 1949, the emphasis on the aging process accounts for much of the recent interest in this interdisciplinary perspective. The great gains in life expectancy that have been made in the last half of the twentieth century have raised important questions about the possible biological limits to human longev-

ity, the factors that are involved in the observed deceleration of mortality rates at advanced ages, and how these changes affect the incidence and prevalence of chronic diseases and disabilities, especially among persons at older ages. To probe such questions requires deeper understanding of the complex, interrelated factors that underlie the disease, disability, and death processes.

A focus on aging and the aged population calls attention to a number of distinctive features of current developments: One, a majority of deaths occur at the older ages, with half of the female and one-third of the male deaths occurring at age 80 and above in developed countries. These deaths at older ages are mainly attributable to noncommunicable chronic diseases with extended lifetime trajectories. Two, older persons are more likely to experience comorbidities, sensory deficits, and functional limitations that limit their capacity to fulfill the basic activities of daily life. Three, a broad range of factors can be identified that influence age-related changes in health and functioning, such as senescence, genetic predispositions, physiological states, nutritional status, physical and cognitive functioning, health behaviors, and medical care and other interventions. Thus, there is a rich set of conceptual issues that challenge interdisciplinary researchers in this subfield.

A broad range of data sources is being developed that will enable studies to be undertaken to address these issues. The first, surveys of older persons, including the oldest old, are increasingly being designed to examine multidimensional aspects of the aging process. This includes clinical assessments of anthropometry, physical performance, cognitive status, blood chemistry, and genetic markers. Many of these surveys are longitudinal in design, which enable researchers to identify important transitions in physiological and psychosocial states and, thereby, examine causal relationships more precisely. Data from surveys are being linked to other sources of data (e.g., administrative records, death certificates) that make it possible to enrich analyses of outcomes and intergenerational patterns with more reliable data. Finally, many surveys are now national in scope and include samples of important subgroups in the population, such as minorities, women, and cohorts of persons at important transition points in the later-life course (e.g., preretirement and retirement periods, the advanced ages of life, etc.).

Second, studies of twins are being expanded to provide natural experiments for examining the inheritability of longevity, frailty, and patterns of dementia across the life course and especially at older ages. These studies enable researchers to investigate the relative roles of genetic and environmental factors for measurable outcomes in the aging process. Multigenerational twin registers are being created in a number of countries, which will enable important comparative analyses to be undertaken. [*See* BEHAVIORAL GENETICS.]

Third, animal colonies of mammalian and nonmammalian species already exist to study issues relating to aging, but there is a new emphasis on conducting research to examine age-related mortality, cause of death, and even disability processes using animal models. Understanding the demographic structures and dynamics of nonhuman species may offer important insights into aging processes in humans. There have been renewed calls for a more comparative emphasis in aging research to emphasize the place of humans in a larger mammalian demographic perspective. Animal models also offer the advantages of experimental designs for studying various interventions. An example of the latter is the large-scale programs to examine diet restriction and its effects on life extension. [*See* MODELS OF AGING: VERTEBRATES.] Evidence suggests a deceleration in the rate of increase in mortality at the oldest ages for insect and human populations, perhaps due to heterogeneity at the cohort level, allowing only the heartiest to survive to the most advanced ages. Thus, Gompertz curves, which imply exponentially increasing rates of mortality with age, do not fit actual age mortality patterns at advanced ages for several species.

Demographers and other social scientists have been involved in a broad range of activities relating to the biodemography subfield. An important aspect of this effort involves the use of demographic analytic models for examining population structures and their dynamics. These include stable population models; actuarial procedures, such as the life table, multistate models, and hazard models; and multivariate statistical applications. Many of these tools are now being used to make forecasts of mortality, disease, and disability trends on a national level. Thus, the implications of population aging are being examined not only in terms of compositional changes, but also many dimensions of direct importance in determining appropriate societal responses to the relative health and well-being of older persons. Simulation approaches also are used for examining the potential impact of various interventions on levels of these dimensions and their economic and social implications.

BIBLIOGRAPHY

Bongaarts, J., Burch, T. K., & Wachter, K. (Eds.). (1987). *Family demography: Methods and their applications.* Oxford: Clarendon Press.

Coale, A. J. (1957). How the age distribution of a human population is determined. In *Cold Spring Harbor symposia on quantitative biology* (vol. XXII pp. 83–89). Cold Spring Harbor, New York: The Biological Laboratory.

Kinsella, K., & Taeuber, C. M. (1993). *An aging world II.* U.S. Bureau of the Census International Population Reports P95/92-3. Washington, DC: U.S. Government Printing Office.

Martin, L. D., & Preston, S. H. (Eds.). (1994). *Demography of aging.* Washington, DC: National Academy Press.

Myers, G. C. (1990). Demography of aging. *in* R. H. Binstock & L. K. George (Eds.), *Handbook of aging and the social sciences* (3rd ed.). San Diego: Academic Press.

Preston, S. H., Himes, C., & Eggers, M. (1988). Demographic conditions responsible for population aging. *Demography, 26,* 691–704.

Siegel, J. (1993). *A generation of change: A profile of America's older population.* New York: Russell Sage Foundation.

Suzman, R. M., Willis, D. P., & Manton, K. G. (Eds.). (1992). *The oldest old.* New York: Oxford University Press.

Treas, J. (1995). Older Americans in the 1990s and beyond. *Population Bulletin, 50,* 2. Washington, DC: Population Reference Bureau.

Treas, J., & Torrecilha, R. (1995). The older population. *in* R. Farley (Ed.). *State of the Union: America in the 1990s. Vol. 2, Social Trends.* New York: Russell Sage Foundation.

United Nations. (1994). *Ageing and the family.* New York: United Nations.

United Nations. (1956). *The aging of populations and its economic and social implications.* New York: United Nations.

Depression

Harold G. Koenig and Dan G. Blazer, II

Duke University Medical Center

Depression   A disorder of mood that involves symptoms of sadness, discouragement, and feelings of hopelessness, as well as loss of appetite, difficulty sleeping, and loss of energy. Although depression can be a transient state for some, for others it may last many months, and sometimes, many years.

Mania   A disorder of mood that involves symptoms of euphoria, excess energy, talkativeness, and racing thoughts, and at its extreme, psychotic symptoms like delusions or hallucinations. If a person has one episode of mania in their life, they qualify for the diagnosis of bipolar disorder.

Delusion   A fixed, false belief that the person cannot be dissuaded from. Delusions may be difficult to distinguish from reality in some cases (being watched or followed by someone); in other cases, they can be bizarre and completely unrealistic (a transmitter implanted in one's brain that sends out signals). Delusions are a hallmark of psychotic disorders.

Psychotherapy   A form of mental treatment involving talking or personal interaction with a patient. A variety of psychotherapies exist; the four main types are supportive therapy, cognitive-behavioral therapy, interpersonal psychotherapy, and psychodynamic psychotherapy. This is a common form of treatment for mild to moderate depression.

Psychopharmacology   The study of drugs used to treat mental or psychological disorders. Because many of the emotional disorders involve an imbalance of chemicals in the brain (neurotransmitters), drugs are frequently used to treat conditions like depression and bipolar disorder. With proper drug treatment, 80% of depressed persons will improve.

The importance of **DEPRESSION** in the elderly, its impact on physical health, and current methods of diagnostic classification will be examined. The epidemiology of late-life depression will be reviewed, focusing on older adults living in the community and those seen in medical settings (medical outpatients, inpatients, and nursing homes). Factors that increase vulnerability to depression will be addressed by discussing a comprehensive model of depression etiology in later life. The clinical presentation of affective disorders is examined, with a focus on major depression, minor depression, normal grief, and mood disorders due to medical conditions. A differential diagnosis to distinguish depression from other late-life psychiatric disorders is developed. Depression management is discussed in terms of psychotherapy, psychopharamacology, and electroconvulsive therapy. Prognosis and response to treatment are then reviewed, and a brief discussion of research frontiers concludes the chapter.

I. IMPORTANCE

Depression is one of the most common and treatable psychiatric illnesses in late life. It is also a major cause for cognitive impairment, anxiety, and psychotic symptoms among the elderly. Recognition and differentiation of depression from other late-life psychiatric disorders like schizophrenia, delusional disorder, primary anxiety disorder, and bipolar disorder, is of utmost importance. Besides impairing quality of life and producing severe emotional pain, depression also impacts adversely on other health outcomes and on use of health services. Older persons with major depression and physical illness experience increased mortality when compared to nondepressed peers. Medical hospital stays for depressed elders are nearly double those of matched controls.

Recovery from hip fracture, stroke, and chronic arthritis is delayed among persons suffering from depression, due to a loss of motivation towards recovery and difficulty complying with the rehabilitation program. Depression and anxiety have been related to falling and perceptions of poorer balance, and is a predictor of early nursing home placement of patients with Alzheimer's disease (AD). Depressive disorder in the elderly is a treatable condition, with response rates of up to nearly 80% when combinations of medication and psychotherapy are used.

II. DIAGNOSTIC CLASSIFICATION

Depression is a mood state characterized by sadness, discouragement, or demoralization often in response to a loss or a disappointment. Most persons will experience fluctuations in their mood from one day to another in response to successes or failures at attempts to get their needs met. However, when a depressed mood persists over time, becomes associated with other psychological and physical symptoms, and adversely affects a person's functioning at work, at home, or in other interpersonal settings, then a *disorder* is said to exist. Level of social functioning and role performance are particularly sensitive indices for assessing whether a depressive disorder is present and for monitoring response to treatment. Formal treat-

ment should be initiated when depression becomes a disorder.

Many mental health professionals view depression as a psychiatric disorder with clinical manifestations that exist on a continuum. According to Sir Aubrey Lewis in 1934, the different classifications of depression are "nothing more than attempts to distinguish between acute and chronic, mild and severe." More recently, some mental health specialists have argued that a unitary view of depression on a continuum from mild to severe is a more reasonable way to describe the clinical syndrome. Observer-rated or self-rated depression scales that count numbers of symptoms purport to assess the severity of depression along this continuum.

Nevertheless, a categorical approach to classifying depression is the one chosen by most modern investigators in psychiatry and is the one described in the *Diagnostic and Statistical Manual of Mental Disorders* (4th ed.) (*DSM-IV*). The *DSM-IV* addresses the special presentations of depression and other psychiatric disorders in the elderly. Depression is viewed as a group of distinct syndromes, each mutually exclusive, associated with certain clinical criteria, and linked with different treatment strategies. This is the approach taken in this article. We recognize, however, that other constructs of depression must complement the categorical approach in the diagnosis and treatment of older adults who often experience symptoms that do not fit into the procrustean bed of a given diagnostic category. There must continually be an emphasis on the patient's level of functioning (work, social, and recreational) during the process of assessment, acute treatment, and maintenance of remission.

III. EPIDEMIOLOGY

There are many reasons why one would expect depressive disorders to be especially common among older adults. Late life can be a time of loss and disturbing change in health, activity level, social roles, friendship and family networks, and financial circumstances. Given these psychosocial stressors, in the setting of impaired cerebral functioning due to vascular disease or age-associated degenerative diseases, one would expect high rates of depression among the elderly. In fact, this is precisely what early epidemiologic research seemed to show. Even Erik Erikson, in his description of the psychosocial stages of human development, emphasized that the struggle between integrity and despair was the *primary developmental task* for the older adult.

Despite the above logic and the predictable findings from early epidemiologic research, modern studies have failed to confirm this conventional wisdom. A number of recent, well-designed local and national surveys show that most older adults living in the community do not experience significant depression. The National Institute of Mental Health Epidemiologic Catchment Area studies, which surveyed over 20,000 adults in the early 1980s, reported rates of major depression of less than 1% among persons over age 65, compared with 2–5% for younger adults. A similar trend was found for bipolar disorder, where only 0.1% of over 5,500 elders fulfilled criteria for the diagnosis within the past 1 year, compared to 1% of younger persons. A more recent national survey of 8098 adults led by Ronald Kessler found high rates of affective disorder among younger persons compared to middle-aged or older adults. Mental health experts have at least partly attributed the high rates of mood disorder, alcoholism, and drug abuse among younger cohorts to a deterioration during the past 30 years of social and family values that may have played an instrumental role in protecting the current cohort of older adults from emotional disorders.

Another reason for the relatively low rate of major depression in the elderly is that many depressions in this age group are subsyndromal and do not fit well into the current diagnostic nomenclature. Symptoms like insomnia, fatigue, impaired concentration, anxiety, somatization, and a host of other physical and emotional discomforts are commonly reported by older patients to their physicians. It is difficult to determine whether these "somatic" symptoms should be attributed to physical or psychological causes. Many of these symptoms do not fall into a diagnosable category of psychiatric disorder; nevertheless, they frequently have an adverse effect on physical function. In fact, there is evidence for a high rate of subsyndromal depression in the community-dwelling elderly. Although less than 1% experienced a major depression, at least one-quarter of older persons experience mild but significant depressive symptomatology that impacts on their social or occupational functioning. [*See* Epidemiology.]

IV. MEDICAL ILLNESS AND INSTITUTIONALIZATION

Although major depression among healthy older adults living in the community is relatively infrequent, this is not the case for those who are physically ill, chronically disabled, or institutionalized. Among elderly patients hospitalized with physical illness, approximately 10% fulfill criteria for a major depressive disorder and at least 30% have minor depressions. Once discharged from the hospital, two-thirds of these patients continue to experience significant mood disorder for 3–12 months thereafter, and rates of depression among older medical outpatients is high (7–15%). Finally, institutionalized older adults experience the highest rates of major depression, where between 10 and 16% fulfill the criteria. Depression's adverse effect on the survival of medically ill older adults has been repeatedly documented. Despite these negative consequences, only a small proportion (perhaps only 10–20%) of depressed elderly patients in medical settings are ever diagnosed or treated.

V. BIPOLAR DISORDER

Although this chapter focuses primarily on depressive disorder, brief mention of the epidemiology of bipolar disorder is appropriate. Manic-depressive disorder is much less common in older than younger adults. Younger patients with bipolar disorder frequently demonstrated a pattern of increasing manic episodes in midlife followed by decreasing episodes thereafter. This age difference in the presentation of bipolar disorder may at least partly be attributable to its nonspecific presentation in the elderly. Bipolar disorder frequently presents with a mixture of manic, dysphoric, and cognitive symptoms in older adults. This makes the diagnosis difficult to distinguish from agitated depression, schizophrenia, or dementia. Perhaps the most common symptom in older adults is impaired concentration or distractibility (i.e., manic delirium); euphoria and grandiosity may be less common among older than younger adults. Cerebrovascular and degenerative neurological diseases often play a major role in the etiology of manic episodes that present for the first time in later life.

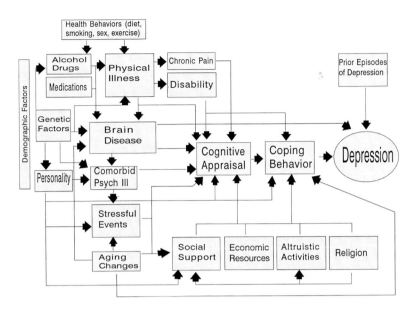

Figure I   Etiological model of depression in later life. (Reprinted with permission from Koenig, H. G., Blazer, D. G., & Hocking, L. B., 1995. Depression, anxiety and other affective disorders. In C. K. Cassel, H. J. Cohen, E. B. Larson, D. E. Meier, N. Resnick, L. Rubenstein, and L. B. Sorensen (Eds.), *Geriatric medicine*, (3rd ed.) New York: Springer-Verlag.)

VI. RISK FACTORS FOR DEPRESSION

Geriatric depression has a wide range of genetic, psychosocial, and acquired biological determinants. These factors interact in a complex manner to increase the older adult's vulnerability to depression. Changes in brain neurotransmitters can profoundly affect mood, just as negative life experiences (such as the stress induced by chronic physical illness, disability, or loss of loved ones) can induce alterations in brain chemistry. [*See* NEUROTRANSMITTERS AND NEUROTROPHIC FACTORS.]

Figure 1 demonstrates the complex interplay of biological and psychosocial factors acting over the lifetime of the individual that lead to depressive illness in later life. According to this hypothetical model, genetic factors provide the basic substrate that underlies temperament. Developmental influences, based on the "fit" of the child to his or her caregivers, contribute to personality in ways that may increase or decrease the person's risk of depression. Based on the person's underlying temperament, early relationships, and later-life experiences, he or she will develop stable patterns of coping with external stressors, including those precipitated by the aging process.

Problems with physical health, ability to care for self, and the changing social environment have greater and greater influence as the person ages. Vulnerability to physical illness is determined by many factors, including past and present health habits (smoking, alcohol consumption, diet, exercise, etc.), accidental injury, and individual susceptibility to illness. Physical disease may compromise brain function, reducing cognitive capacity to implement coping behaviors that facilitate psychosocial adjustment. Disability, associated with loss of independence and control over one's life, has a pivotal influence on the emotional well-being. When associated with chronic pain that disrupts sleep, drains energy, and prevents participation in pleasurable activities, chronic disability often causes deep feelings of shame, humiliation, and helplessness—psychological experiences that provide fertile ground for the development of a depressive disorder.

Nevertheless, physical illness, disability, level of pain, or other negative life circumstances do not themselves directly cause emotional disorder. Two intervening steps, cognitive appraisal and coping behavior, largely determine whether the older person will eventually become depressed. Cognitive appraisal involves how persons perceive and interpret what is happening to them: what their experiences mean in terms of life goals and valued relationships. The older adult who is able to view negative experiences as having meaning and can place them in a larger framework is more likely to adapt successfully. Once meaning is given to the experiences, then adjustment is next influenced by choice of coping behavior. For example, the stressed older adult may choose to numb his or herself with alcohol or tranquilizers; alternatively, he or she may become more involved in volunteer work as a distraction from problems. Supportive family and friends, religious beliefs, and economic resources all contribute to the range of available coping strategies.

A. Specific Risk Factors

A more comprehensive discussion of specific factors that increase vulnerability to depression now follows. Genetic factors contribute less to late-life depressions than to those occurring for the first time earlier in the life cycle, although they do play a role. A history of depression is found in only 5–8% of patients diagnosed with depression for the first time after age 60, compared with 20% of relatives of younger depressives. Sex differences persist into later life, where women continue to experience depression nearly twice as frequently as men. Whether this represents a true genetic susceptibility, a learned psychosocial vulnerability, or simply a greater expression of emotional symptoms by women is unclear.

Personality disorder can interfere with adaptation to the life changes associated with aging. Increased rates of antisocial, borderline, histrionic, narcissistic, avoidant, dependent, obsessive-compulsive, and passive-aggressive traits have been found in depressed compared with nondepressed elders. Compulsive personality disorder is particularly prevalent (50%) among older adults who have both depression and Axis II disorders. Compared to depressed younger adults, however, late-onset depressives are less likely to have a comorbid personality disorder.

The effects of health habits on increasing vulnerability to late-life depression are cumulative over the lifetime of the individual. Unrestrained eating habits,

lack of regular exercise, careless sexual practices, smoking, excess alcohol consumption, and little concern over health maintenance can lead to physical diseases that cause depression directly by their effects on the central nervous system (CNS) or indirectly by inducing disability. Vitamin B deficiencies, smoking, and lack of aerobic exercises have now been linked to depression in various studies.

Specific medical illnesses have been associated with high rates of depression, including hyperthyroidism, hypothyroidism, hyperparathyroidism (with hypercalcemia), myocardial infarction, congestive heart failure, chronic obstructive pulmonary disease, and cancers of the pancreas or lung. In particular, diseases affecting the CNS like stroke, Parkinson's disease, and AD are often associated with depressive illness in older adults. Specific brain diseases or lesions that increase intracranial pressure or interfere with frontal lobe function (infections, cysts, tumors) may also increase the risk of depression. Whether these effects are due to organic changes in the bioamine pathways of the brain that influence mood or to psychosocial maladjustment to the disability that such disorders cause is unclear and hotly debated. In any case, treatment of depression in medically ill older adults often results in significant improvement in psychological as well as physiological symptoms. [*See* Brain and Central Nervous System.]

Prescription and over-the-counter (OTC) drugs can increase the risk of mood disorder by their depressant effects on the CNS. This is particularly true for antihypertensives (reserpine, beta-blockers, clonidine, prazosin, guanethidine), antiparkinsonian drugs, minor and major tranquilizers, alcohol, antitumor drugs (tamoxefin, vincristine, L-asparaginase, interferon), and sterioids (dexamethasone, prednisone, estrogen, progesterone).

Although some have argued for a link between depression and certain diseases or medications, others have suggested that it is not the specific medical condition, but the overall level of physical impairment and illness severity that is more important. Numerous studies, in both community-dwelling and medically ill older populations, have found a strong correlation between illness severity and depression, regardless of the specific disease. This is particularly true for studies of elderly patients hospitalized with a wide range of medical illnesses. When these patients are followed over time, emotional function appears to track closely with physical function, improving when the physical condition improves and worsening as function declines.

As noted earlier, when pain is chronic and inadequately controlled, it is frequently associated with depression and anxiety. Moderate to severe pain has been found in over 70% of the depressed patients compared with only one-third of controls. Many of the symptoms of chronic pain and depression overlap and are almost indistinguishable. The functional disability that chronic pain induces appears to be a major mediating variable between it and depressive illness. [*See* PAIN AND PRESBYALGOS.]

Prior episodes of psychiatric illness, particularly depression, schizophrenia, anxiety disorder, or substance abuse, increase the older person's risk of depression. Each episode of depression or mania increases the risk of having a recurrence in the future (a phenomenon known as "kindling"). This high risk of recurrence, particularly in persons over the age of 50, has prompted some mental health specialists to advocate prolonged maintenance therapy, perhaps lifelong, in older adults with one or more episodes of major depression. [*See* MENTAL HEALTH.]

Schizophrenia and the organic mental disorders increase the risk of depression in late life primarily by their effects on social roles and interpersonal relationships, acting as psychosocial stressors in the same way that bereavement or physical illness does. Alcoholism, particularly when it occurs for the first time in late life, is often associated with depression and psychosocial stress. At least one-third of elderly alcoholics have a primary mood disorder that precedes their problems with alcohol. Even if primary, alcoholism often has destructive effects on occupational, family, and physical functioning that lead to social isolation and depression.

Negative life events (other than physical illness) are known to precede the development of late-life depression in many cases, acting as precipitants in the individual made vulnerable by other factors. Negative events include bereavement, sickness of a close family member, divorce or separation, death of friends, relocation to a different community, and financial or legal troubles. Nearly 15% of adults require treatment for depression following the loss of a spouse. Stressful life experiences may cause physical changes in the brain by activating the proto-oncogene *c-fos* and other transcription factors that

interfere with the production of mood-regulating neurotransmitters.

Factors that decrease older adults' vulnerability to depression include social support, religious beliefs, and economic resources. Adverse social factors often lead to depression in later life. As contacts with friends and family lessen because of death, relocation, or disability, the elder's social network becomes smaller and smaller. Feelings of loneliness and worthlessness lead to depression. Depression itself may then cause a loss of social interest that leads to further withdrawal from others. Thus, a vicious cycle ensues and may lead to a downward spiral of deepening social isolation and depression. Active intervention by family, community groups, or health-care providers may help to break this cycle. A wide range of qualitative and quantitative studies have found that high elder satisfaction with family and community support can buffer against depression. Some investigators, however, have found that social predictors of depression outcome vary by age group, with social support and physical health factors being stronger predictors in the younger age groups.

The older person's social support network may be particularly important in the setting of negative life events. Among older persons experiencing stressful health problems, those with poor social support are much more likely to experience depressive symptoms. Only certain types of social support, however, help to prevent the development of depression. The actual number of persons in the support network or their marital status may be less important than the quality of the social network in terms of homogeneity, the presence of confidants, or high level of intimacy, and perception by the elder of the interaction as satisfying and fulfilling. [*See* SOCIAL NETWORKS, SUPPORT, AND INTEGRATION.]

More and more recent research suggests that religion may be another psychosocial resource that buffers against depression. Judeo-Christian beliefs and behaviors are widely prevalent among older Americans. In 1994, 80% of persons over age 65 were members of a church or synagogue; 52% attended church weekly or more often; 95% prayed; over 90% believed their prayers were heard and answered; and 76% indicated that religion was "very important" to them. Religion can be helpful to older adults in a number of ways. For instance, it may help them to understand, cope with, and adapt to interpersonal and physical health problems. When asked an open-ended question, What enables you to cope? about one-third of older men and two-thirds of women spontaneously give answers like "the Lord," "trust in God," "prayer," and other religious responses. Quantitative studies have examined whether or not religious beliefs and behaviors are actually related to better mental health. These studies have confirmed that higher life satisfaction and well-being, better adjustment, and less frequent depression and anxiety is found in more religiously active subjects.

The associations between mental health and religion are most evident in older adults with physical illness. In hospitalized older persons, religious coping is not only inversely related to depressive symptoms at baseline, but also is one of the few psychosocial variables that predict resolution of depression when patients are followed up over time. Furthermore, there may be an interaction between religiousness and perception of physical health by older adults. At any given level of chronic medical illness, elders who are more religious are less likely to view themselves as disabled. Likewise, if disabled, religious elders are less likely to experience depression. This finding has been reported by several investigators working at different sites. Thus, Judeo-Christian religious beliefs and practices appear to influence how older persons perceive their physical condition and moderate the adverse effects that disability can have on mental health. Within the past 15 years, over 50 published studies have reported associations between religious variables and mental health outcomes, with positive effects most commonly found in older women and in African Americans. [*See* RELIGION AND SPIRITUALITY.]

Although supportive family, concerned friends, and a strong religious faith all help to decrease vulnerability to depression in later life, economic resources also play a role. Low income is commonly associated with higher rates of depression and anxiety. Financial resources expand the elder's range of coping options. After a disabling physical illness or psychological loss, the financially secure older adult may distract him or herself by taking a trip or vacation, by purchasing adaptive devices to help maintain independence, or perhaps, by postponing nursing home placement by hiring 24-hour private-duty nursing staff. Thus, social, religious, and economic resources interact together, often compensating for each other, as they lower the older adult's risk of emotional illness.

VII. CLINICAL PRESENTATION

The symptoms of depression in older adults are similar to those experienced by younger persons, and may be categorized as psychological or somatic. Psychological or affective symptoms include depressed, sad, or irritable mood, loss of interest and pleasure in activities previously enjoyed, decreased motivation, tearfulness, feelings of worthlessness or being a burden, hopelessness, helplessness, social withdrawal, and wanting to die or end one's life. Somatic, endogenous, or biological symptoms of depression include a pervasive sense of fatigue, loss of energy, difficulty concentrating, impaired sleep, and changes in appetite or weight. As noted earlier, when these symptoms interfere with social, occupational, or recreational functioning, intervention is required.

A. Major Depression

This is the most serious form of depressive disorder. The *DSM-IV* defines major depression in terms of symptom type and duration. To fulfill the diagnostic criteria, a person must have experienced depressed mood or marked loss of the ability to experience pleasure nearly every day for at least 2 weeks. Besides the mood criterion, he or she must also have experienced at least four of the following eight symptoms during this period: loss of appetite or weight loss (5% or more of body weight), insomnia or hypersomnia, psychomotor agitation or retardation, fatigue or loss of energy, feelings of worthlessness or guilt, diminished concentration, thoughts of suicide, or loss of interest.

These symptoms cannot be secondary to some other underlying psychiatric disorder (schizoaffective disorder, schizophrenia, or other psychotic disorder) or due to the direct physiological effects of a drug, alcohol, or physical illness; there can be no history of a manic or hypomanic episode; and the symptoms cannot be accounted for by bereavement (within 2 months of loss of a spouse). Symptoms of depression are often difficult to distinguish from those due to medical illness or chronic pain. In a study of hospitalized medically ill older patients, those symptoms that best distinguished patients with depression were (in order of importance) loss of interest, insomnia, suicidal thoughts, and hypochondriasis; in that study, fatigue, weight loss, genital symptoms, and somatic anxiety were weakly related or unrelated to depression.

Four subtypes of major depression—melancholic, psychotic, atypical, and seasonal—are particularly important because of their response to somatic treatment. According to the *DSM-IV*, melancholic depressions are associated with a loss of pleasure in almost all activities (anhedonia) or a lack of mood reactivity (mood does not improve when hearing good news or talking with friends), *plus* at least three or more of the following symptoms: a distinct quality of mood, depression worse in the morning (diurnal variation), early morning awakening (two or more hours before usual), psychomotor retardation or agitation, significant weight loss, or excessive guilt. Melancholic depressions are thought to be particularly responsive to antidepressant drug therapy.

Psychotic depressions, on the other hand, are characterized by delusional thinking (bizarre beliefs or ideas from which the person cannot be dissuaded), marked paranoia or suspiciousness, and sometimes by auditory hallucinations (voices that are mumbled or difficult to understand). Elders with major depression are more likely to experience psychotic symptoms than are depressed younger adults. Delusional symptoms frequently involve some type of persecution or preoccupation with an incurable illness, not uncommonly involving the gastrointestinal system. Psychotic depressions are known to respond rapidly to electroconvulsive therapy (ECT) or to a combination of antidepressants and antipsychotics. Atypical depressions are characterized by mood reactivity and the presence of at least two of the following symptoms: increased appetite or weight gain, hypersomnia, leaden paralysis, and interpersonal sensitivity. These depressions are often responsive to the monoamine oxidase (MAO) inhibitors. Seasonal depressions are major depressive episodes that have their onset in a regular temporal pattern in the fall or winter of the year. These depressions often go into full remission during the spring of the year, and are particularly responsive to light therapy.

B. Minor Depression

Depressive symptoms may not fulfill the severity or duration criteria for major depression, yet still impact adversely on social or occupational functioning. The *DSM-IV* places these primary depressive disorders into the following categories: dysthymia, depression not otherwise specified, and adjustment disorder with depressed mood. Dysthymic disorder is characterized by a chronically depressed mood that is present more days than not during at least a 2-year period. Depressed mood must be associated with at least two of the following: decreased appetite or overeating, insomnia or hypersomnia, low energy or fatigue, low self-esteem, poor concentration or indecision, and hopelessness. Patients with dysthymia periodically fulfill criteria for a major depression; when this occurs, a "double depression" is said to exist. Dysthymic disorder in the elderly is less frequent than in younger persons, but this difference is not as great as for major depression. These chronic depressions are difficult to treat and often associated with stable personality traits; nevertheless, studies have shown that many patients respond to therapeutic doses of tricyclic antidepressants, and many additional patients benefit from psychotherapy.

Adjustment disorder with depressed mood is perhaps one of the most common subsyndromal forms of depression found among older adults. It is defined as a maladaptive reaction to an identifiable stressor; the mood disturbance must occur within 6 months of the stressful experience and must be more prominent than would be expected given the nature of the stressor. Adjustment disorder frequently occurs in the setting of physical illness. Depression not otherwise specified (NOS) is a catchall category of milder forms of depression that adversely affect functioning, but do not fit into any known diagnostic subtype. Two subcategories for depression NOS are particularly common in later life. The first type is similar to dysthymic disorder, but there are intermittent periods of normal mood lasting more than a few months. The second category of depression NOS involves brief episodes of depression that do not meet the criteria for major depression and are not reactive to any known psychosocial stressor.

C. Normal Grief

Many older adults experience significant losses, such as death of a spouse, that are accompanied by depressive symptoms that are understandable and expected. These symptoms are not indicative of psychiatric disorder and, in fact, must be experienced for the person to work through and adapt to the loss.

Symptoms of normal grief may include sensations such as shortness of breath or sighing respirations, tightness in the throat, fatigue, a temporary loss of interest, difficulty sleeping, and loss of appetite. The person may be preoccupied with the lost object. The normal grief process becomes derailed when the usual symptoms are significantly delayed, persist beyond the expected time period (residual symptoms may normally last up to 2 years for some older adults), or are associated with feelings of marked worthlessness, guilt, or suicidal thoughts. The *DSM-IV* suggests that patients who fulfill criteria for major depression 2 months after bereavement should be treated for the disorder. Social support, especially "appraised" or "belonging" support, has been shown to significantly reduce the severity or likelihood of depression following bereavement. [*See* BEREAVEMENT AND LOSS.]

D. Mood Disorder Due to a General Medical Condition or Substance-Induced Mood Disorder

Once called *organic mood disorder*, this depressive condition is a direct physiological result of a physical illness (hypothyroidism, hypercalcemia, etc.), a medication (antihypertensive, steroid preparation, etc.), or a mood-alterning substance (alcohol, minor tranquilizers, withdrawal from amphetamines, etc.). Cognitive impairment is often coexistent with mood disorder, as well as feelings of fear, anxiety, irritability, and excessive somatic concerns. It is difficult to determine whether a depression is a direct physiological effect on the brain of a medical disorder or psychoactive substance, or whether it is an adjustment disorder to the psychosocial consequences of the illness, drug, or substance abuse problem.

VIII. DIFFERENTIAL DIAGNOSIS

Besides medical conditions, a wide range of psychiatric conditions can mimic primary depressive disorder in older adults, including hypochondriasis, anxiety disorder, alcoholism, psychoactive substance use, dementia, delusional disorder, and schizophrenia.

Hypochondriasis may be defined as an unrealistic interpretation of physical sensations as abnormal and

a preoccupation with those sensations. Studies have shown that between 60 and 70% of depressed persons may experience hypochondriacal symptoms. Because of the high likelihood of undetected physical illness, any older adult who presents with what appears to be hypochondriacal complaints deserves a complete and thorough physical examination along with regular follow-up by a medical physician. If after repeated medical evaluation, no apparent physiological cause for the symptoms can be found, then evaluation for depression should occur. Hypochondriasis can be distinguished from depression by how long the symptoms have persisted (hypochondriacal symptoms often persist for years), by the degree of suffering experienced by the patient (depressed patients experience greater suffering), and by the waxing and waning course of depression, which is less common with hypochondriasis where symptoms tend to be more constant.

There is also a heavy overlap between agitated depression, hypochondriasis, generalized anxiety disorder, and panic disorder in later life. Patients with generalized anxiety disorder usually admit to a life-long tendency toward anxiety and worry. Patients with panic disorder and secondary depression can often be differentiated from primary depression by determining which symptoms arose first; patients with panic disorder will report a history of anxiety symptoms that preceded the onset of the depression. The frequent mixture of depressive, anxiety, and hypochondriacal symptoms in older adults makes the identification of the primary illness difficult. Nevertheless, making the correct diagnosis is important because hypochondriacal patients often do not tolerate antidepressants because of their hypersensitivity to drug side effects.

Chronic alcoholism may be present in as many as 10% of older adults, and may either lead to depression or be a consequence of it. Furthermore, many of the physiological symptoms of alcohol intoxication and alcohol withdrawal mimic depressive disorder. It is not possible to diagnose a primary depressive disorder in an alcoholic until he or she has been sober for at least 2 to 4 weeks. On the other hand, almost 30% of elderly alcoholics have a primary mood disorder and another 20% a primary dementia that underlies their drinking behavior. [*See* ALCOHOL AND DRUGS.]

Dementia and depression are likewise difficult to

distinguish because of the cognitive impairment often seen with depression, and the frontal lobe amotivational state that often accompanies dementia. Furthermore, a significant proportion of patients with a progressive dementia experience a reactive depression, and many depressed patients with cognitive impairment go on to develop dementia. Again, the key to diagnosis is sorting out which symptoms began first and the course of the illnesses over time. [See DEMENTIA.]

The sudden appearance of a psychosis in later life, with paranoid or delusional thinking, may indicate the onset of a major depression, an organic dementia, or a major late-life psychosis. Older adults with dementia, late-life schizophrenia, or delusional disorder are not usually as profoundly depressed as elders with psychotic depression. Elderly schizophrenics are usually distressed by delusions that are bizarre and obviously implausible, such as delusions of influence or control; auditory hallucinations may also be present and are less often associated with guilt, punishment, or suicidal content than those of psychotic depression. Furthermore, late-life psychoses and dementia with psychotic features seldom begin suddenly; rather, their onset is characterized by gradual withdrawal and paranoia.

Elders with psychotic depression may also be difficult to distinguish from those with bipolar disorder and mixed or dysphoric mania. A classical manic episode is characterized by a distinct period of elevated or expansive mood associated with three or more of the following symptoms: distractibility, grandiosity, decreased need for sleep, pressured speech that is difficult to interrupt, flight of ideas or racing thoughts, increased goal-directed activity, and excessive spending, sex, or other pleasurable activity. Because irritability and distractibility are the most prominent clinical symptoms in older adults, these can be difficult to distinguish from the irritable mood, decreased concentration, and indecisiveness of the depressed patient. A history of lithium exposure or periods of overactivity, increased energy, or decreased need for sleep are important features that may distinguish bipolar patients from those with unipolar depression. This is an important distinction because treatment with antidepressants may worsen the manic episode or lead to rapid cycling.

IX. MANAGEMENT OF GERIATRIC DEPRESSION

Prior to beginning treatment, careful attention must be paid to differential diagnosis. If it is decided that a depressive disorder is present, a brief laboratory evaluation should be conducted to rule out hypothyroidism, vitamin deficiencies, metabolic disturbances, chronic infections, or brain lesions. A baseline electrocardiogram should be performed if treatment with antidepressants is considered. Management includes psychological support, psychotherapy, pharmacotherapy, and in some cases, electroconvulsive therapy (ECT). To begin with, the clinician must forge a therapeutic alliance with the patient by providing psychological support for acute symptoms; psychological support involves attentive listening, empathy, expression of concern, and active support of the patient's coping behaviors; the dependent patient should be allowed to temporarily depend on the therapist or others in their social network; the paranoid patient should be allowed to control the distance in the relationship. Concurrent with supportive therapy, a social worker or nurse may be enlisted to help the patient deal with practical problems, provide education, or make appropriate referrals. Many patients with minor depression will respond by a decrease in symptoms to these interventions alone.

A. Psychotherapy

Perhaps the most "proven" psychotherapy in older adults is cognitive-behavioral therapy (CBT). CBT is usually administered by a psychologist or specially trained social worker. It can be administered either on an individual basis or, when cost is an issue, in a group format. Elders are trained to identify negative thinking, challenge maladaptive assumptions, avoid catastrophizing, and change dysfunctional attitudes and behaviors. Response rates to CBT are comparable to those obtained from drug treatment. When CBT is administered in a group setting and combined with a psychoeducational and problem-solving approach, it is quite acceptable to older adults, particularly when recommended by their physician. For some patients with minor depression or mild forms of major depression, psychotherapy can be used as the sole treatment modality. [See COGNITIVE–BEHAVIORAL INTERVENTIONS.]

Table I Antidepressant Medication Doses, Side Effects, Therapeutic Levels, and Cost for Older Adults

Drug	Initial (mg/day)	Maintenance (mg/day)	Therapeutic level (ng/dl)[a]	Side effect profile[b]			Cost[e]
				Sedation	Anticholinergic	Hypotension	
Doxepin	25	25–100	>100	3	3	3	$
Nortriptyline	10	10–75	50–150	2	2	2	$$$$
Desipramine	25	50–175	>125	1	1	2	$$
Trazodone	50	150–300	NA	3	+/−	2	$$
Fluoxetine	5	10–20	NA	+/−	+/−	+/−	$$$$$
Sertraline	25	50–100	NA	+/−	+/−	+/−	$$$$$
Paroxetine	10	10–40	NA	+/−	+/−	+/−	$$$$$
Venlafaxine	25	25–75	NA	+/−	+/−	—[d]	$$$$$
Bupropion	75	75–300	NA	+/−	+/−	0	$$$$
Methylphenidate	10	15–30	NA	0	0	—[e]	$
Phenelzine	15	30–60	>80% inhib of MAO	+/−	1	2	$$$
Lithium carbonate	150	150–900	0.4–0.7 mmol/l	1	0	0	$

NA; not applicable
[a]MAO, monoamine oxidase.
[b]3 indicates strong, 2 moderate, 1 mild, +/− negligible; 0, none.
[c]$ low cost, $$$$$ high cost.
[d]May cause sustained increases in blood pressure at doses >200 mg/d.
[e]May increase blood pressure.

B. Psychopharmacology

Often, however, psychotherapy is combined with drug treatment, particularly in patients with melancholic symptomatology. The combination of interpersonal psychotherapy with drug treatment has been associated with response rates near 80%. Five classes of drugs are now commonly used to treat depression in older adults, including (a) second-generation tricyclic antidepressants (nortriptyline and desipramine), (b) trazodone and bupropion, (c) the selective serotonin reuptake inhibitors (SSRIs) (fluoxetine, sertraline, paroxetine), (d) MAO inhibitors (phenelzine and tranylcypromine), and (e) psychostimulants (methylphenidate) (Table I). For years, second-generation tricyclic antidepressants have been the drugs of choice for late-life depressions. Nortriptyline and desipramine are generally effective and safe when used in older adults. They can be used at doses considerably below those prescribed for younger patients, and doses of 20–50 mg/day of nortriptyline or 25–75 mg/day of desipramine often achieve a therapeutic response in frail elders with other health problems. Anticholinergic side effects can often be treated successfully with bethanecol.

In recent times, however, the SSRIs and bupropion are beginning to replace tricyclics as first-line therapy for depressive disorders, particularly those than can be treated on an outpatient basis or those with nonmelancholic symptomatology. This is because of their relative safety in overdose, freedom from anticholinergic and orthostatic effects, ease of administration, and overall patient tolerance. SSRIs, however, have their own drawbacks, including high cost, excessive stimulation or sedation, anorexia and weight loss, and cardiac effects. Recent studies have also demonstrated that tricyclic antidepressants may be more effective than SSRIs for the treatment for elderly patients with severe, recurrent depressions.

MAO inhibitors have been shown to be as effective as tricyclic antidepressants in the treatment of late-life depressions, and are particularly effective in atypical depressions. Because of their side effects (orthostasis and sedation) and interaction with other medications and OTC cold preparations, they can be difficult to use in the elderly. Likewise, methylphenidate may be used to treat depression in older patients with multiple concurrent medical problems to enhance appetite and reduce apathy; however, dependence may occur and require an escalation of dose to maintain an effect. Furthermore, it is unclear whether stimulants have a true antidepressant effect or simply activate psychomotor-retarded, apathetic patients so that they look less depressed. [See PHARMACOLOGY.]

C. Electroconvulsive Therapy

When medications fail to relieve depression, cannot be tolerated, or a more immediate effect is desired, ECT should be considered as a treatment alternative. ECT is a remarkably effective and safe treatment for depression in older patients. Of the 1500 ECT treatments performed each year at Duke University Medical Center, 70% are done in persons over the age of 60. Modern techniques have markedly reduced the side effects of this procedure feared in the past, including effects on memory (unilateral electrode placement has greatly decreased these effects). ECT may be effective in 60–80% of patients who have failed to respond to other treatment modalities. Long-term effects in maintaining remission, however, are less certain; among patients who do not receive maintenance ECT (monthly treatments) or antidepressant drugs after a course of ECT treatment, over 50% will relapse within a 1-year period.

X. PROGNOSIS

Major depressive disorder is a cyclic disorder that follows a pattern of remission and relapse. Without some type of maintenance treatment, 80% of persons will eventually relapse after an episode of major depression. Until recently, follow-up studies of depressed geriatric patients indicated that one-third recovered completely, one-third experienced a partial recovery or relapsed soon after recovery, and one-third remained continuously depressed. This rather dismal prognosis, however, has been challenged by more recent studies that report that almost two-thirds of depressed elders remain either continuously well or have further episodes with complete recovery during 5 to 10 years of follow-up.

Acutely hospitalized, severely depressed geriatric inpatients, while at greater risk for persistent depression than less severely ill outpatients, still experience complete symptom remission about 50% of the time

by the time of hospital discharge. Other studies indicate that almost three-quarters of hospitalized depressed elders have recovered by 1–4 years after discharge, regardless of treatment modality. Depressed elderly *medical* inpatients are more resistent to treatment than are those who are healthy; nevertheless, nearly 60% of these patients have been shown to recover from their depression. Furthermore, treatment reduces mortality in the first 3 months after discharge and improves quality of life as reported by both patients and their relatives. Finally, studies that have examined differences in recovery rate by age group have found no significant differences in outcome between younger, middle-aged, and elderly subjects. In summary, an older depressed person today who is treated with a combination of antidepressant therapy, psychotherapy, and/or ECT has about an 80% chance of complete recovery from that episode of depression. This is about the same prognosis that younger depressed patients can expect. Older adults with depression, however, are at particular risk for suicide. This problem is of greater concern now because rates of suicide among the elderly are increasing.

XI. RESEARCH FRONTIERS

The National Institutes of Health Consensus Development Conference outlined six major areas that future research studies must address:

1. Does depression in late life differ in its clinical presentation from depression that occurs earlier in the life cycle? Do correlates of onset and predictors of outcome differ between early- and late-onset depressions? Recent studies have shown that social factors and physical illness play a stronger role in predicting depression outcomes in younger than older patients. More work in this area is needed.

2. What is the prevalence of depression in different subpopulations of older adults (healthy community dwellers, medically ill, minority groups, very old, nursing home patients, socioeconomically deprived, and so forth)? What factors increase the risk of depression onset, prolong the course, and increase risk of suicide? As noted earlier, there are reports of increasing suicide among older adults in the past 10 years. Information is needed on

what factors in society are changing to cause this increase.

3. What treatments are safe, efficacious, and cost effective for managing late-life depression? Are there specific groups of depressed elders who are most likely to benefit from specific treatments? How effective is ECT as continuation and maintenance therapy? What about specific psychotherapeutic and psychopharmacologic treatments for grief? What about treatments for primary-care patients with depression? Older medical patients whose doctors are given patient-specific recommendations about the evaluation of depression, exacerbating medications, and guidelines about prescribing antidepressants do not show an improvement in depression or disability severity, despite increased diagnosis of depression and prescription of antidepressants. This challenges our current thinking about how to manage depression in the primary-care setting.

4. What are the patterns of mental health service use by depressed older adults and what are the obstacles that prevent access to care? Many older adults, particularly minority elders, wait to seek mental health care until their disorder is far advanced and difficult to treat.

5. What benefits might be accrued by the timely diagnosis and treatment of depression? Alternatively, what are the consequences of not doing so? What are some demonstration projects that could be initiated to enhance service delivery, focusing on effectiveness research? What community resources exist that might help to enhance early detection and treatment?

6. Is there a relationship between subcortical brain changes, cognitive and depressive symptoms, and early versus late-onset depression? What role do biological factors play in the onset and maintenance of geriatric depression? What is their relative importance compared with the influence of psychosocial factors?

These are but a few of the exciting areas where further research is needed. These recommendations have been reviewed and expanded in *Diagnosis and Treatment of Depression in Late Life Depression* by Schneider and colleagues. Given the projections of increasing disability, dementia, and associated rates of depression and other emotional disorders over the next century, it is vital to obtain a better understanding of the onset, course, and treatment of depressive disorders in later life.

ACKNOWLEDGMENTS

This work was supported by Dr. Koenig's National Institute of Mental Health Clinical Mental Health Academic Award (MH01138) and by the Clinical Research Center for the Study of Depression in Late Life (MH40159).

BIBLIOGRAPHY

Baldwin, R. C., & Jolley, D. J. (1986). The prognosis of depression in old age. *British Journal of Psychiatry, 149,* 574.

Benbow, S. M. (1989). The role of electroconvulsive therapy in the treatment of depressive illness in old age. *British Journal of Psychiatry, 155,* 147.

Blazer, D. G. (1993). *Depression in late life* (2nd ed.). St. Louis: C. V. Mosby.

Blazer, D. G., Hughes, D. C., & George, L. K. (1987). The epidemiology of depression in an elderly community population. *Gerontologist, 27,* 281.

Clayton, P. (1990). Bereavement and depression. *Journal of Clinical Psychiatry, 51* (7, suppl), 34.

Frasure-Smith, N., Lesperance, F., & Talajic, M. (1993). Depression following myocardial infarction. *Journal of the American Medical Association, 270,* 1819.

George, L. K. (1992). Social factors and the onset and outcome of depression. In K. W. Schaie, D. Blazer, & J. S. House (Eds.), Hillsdale, NJ: Erlbaum Associates. *Aging, health behaviors, and health outcomes* (p. 137).

Guthrie, S., & Harvey, A. (1994). Motivation and its influence on outcome in rehabilitation. *Reviews in Clinical Gerontology, 4,* 235.

Klerman, G. L., & Weissman, M. M. (1989). Increasing rates of depression. *Journal of the American Medical Association, 261,* 2229.

Koenig, H. G. (1995). *Research on religion and aging.* Westport, CT: Greenwood Press.

Koenig, H. G., Cohen, H. J., Blazer, D. G., Pieper, C., Meador, K. G., Shelp, F., Goli, V., & DiPasquale, R. (1992). Religious coping and depression in elderly hospitalized medically ill men. *American Journal of Psychiatry, 149,* 1693.

Koenig, H. G., Meador, K. G., Cohen, H. J., & Blazer, D. G. (1988). Depression in elderly men hospitalized with medical illness. *Archives of Internal Medicine, 148,* 1929.

Koenig, H. G., Shelp, F., Goli, V., Cohen, H. J., & Blazer, D. G. (1989). Survival and healthcare utilization in elderly medical inpatients with major depression. *Journal of the American Geriatrics Society, 37,* 599.

Meehan, P. J., Saltzman, L. E., & Sattin, R. W. (1991). Suicides among older United States residents: Epidemiologic characteristics and trends. *American Journal of Public Health, 81,* 1198.

Parmelee, P. A., Katz, I. R., & Lawton, M. P. (1989). Depression among institutionalized aged: Assessment and prevalence estimation. *Journal of Gerontology, 44,* M22.

Post, R. M. (1992). Transduction of psychosocial stress into the neurobiology of recurrent affective disorder. *American Journal of Psychiatry, 149,* 999.

Reynolds, C. F., Fran, E., Perel, J. M., Imber, S. D., Cornes, C., Morycz, R. K., Mazumdar, S., Miller, M. D., Pollock, B. G., Rifai, A. H., Stack. J. A., George, C. J., Houck, P. R., & Kupfer, D. J. (1992). Combined pharmacotherapy and pscyhotherapy in the acute and continuation treatment of elderly patients with recurrent major depression: A preliminary report. *American Journal of Psychiatry, 149,* 1687–1692.

Robins, L. N., & Regier, D. A. (Eds.). (1991). *Psychiatric disorders in America: The epidemiologic catchment area study.* New York: Free Press.

Schneider, L. S., Reynolds, C. F., Lebowitz, B., & Friedhoof, A. J. (Eds.). (1994). *Diagnosis and treatment of depression in late life: Results of the NIH Consensus Development Conference.* Washington, DC: American Psychiatric Press.

Scogin, F., & McElreath, L. (1994). Efficacy of psychosocial treatments for geriatric depression: A quantitative review. *Journal of Consulting & Clinical Psychology, 62,* 69.

Williamson, G. M., & Schulz, R. (1992). Pain, activity restriction, and symptoms of depression among community-residing elderly adults. *Journal of Gerontology, 47,* P367.

Diet and Nutrition

Barbara J. Rolls

The Pennsylvania State University

Adam Drewnowski

University of Michigan

Anorexia   A lack of appetite leading to low food intake.

Body Mass Index (BMI = kg/m²)   A ratio of weight (kg) over height (m) that is commonly used as a measure of overweight.

Endogenous Opioid   A naturally occurring peptide with effects similar to morphine.

Preload   A fixed amount of food given before a meal in order to test how well people adjust or compensate for the calories or nutrients in the preload.

Primary Aging   Changes in physiologic or metabolic functioning that are due primarily to age.

Satiety   The reduction of hunger and the termination of eating that mark the end of a meal.

Secondary Aging   Effects due to acute and chronic disease and medication use.

Sensory-Specific Satiety   As a food is eaten it is judged as less pleasant, whereas the pleasantness of other foods is unchanged.

Aging is accompanied by a variety of physiological, behavioral, and socioeconomic changes that may have a negative impact on **DIET AND NUTRITIONAL STATUS**. Energy needs and energy intake decline with age, as do body weight and lean body mass. Poor health, the use of medications, and sedentary lifestyle may all contribute to age-related anorexia and inadequate dietary intakes. Nutrition studies conducted in clinical and in community settings have pointed to an increased risk of nutrient deficiencies among the elderly. Diets of the elderly have also been described as monotonous and bland, and are said to be marked by sharply reduced consumption of nutrient-dense foods.

I. INTRODUCTION

Although the prevalence of malnutrition among the elderly in the United States is reported as low, aging does place individuals at greater nutritional risk. There are many ways in which the aging process can influence diet and nutrition (see Table I). First, primary aging has been associated with altered sensations of hunger, thirst, and satiety and with imperfect compensation for day-to-day variations in the diet. Low fluid intake, for example, is not compensated for by increased thirst. Sensory-specific satiety, which may serve as a variety-seeking mechanism, is also reported to be reduced. Age-related deficits in smell, and possibly taste, may lead to a lowered enjoyment of foods. These age-related physiological changes may account, in part, for the reported poor quality of the diet in older individuals.

Secondary aging is defined as including some of the age-associated chronic disease states, notably hypertension, hyperlipidemia, atherosclerosis, and diabetes. The presence of chronic disease together with the use of medications and medically prescribed diets is likely to have an impact on energy intake and on diet choices. Impaired mobility, inability to feed oneself, poor oral health, or the use of dentures can also affect the amount and types of foods consumed. In addition, nutrient malabsorption can be caused by altered gastric acid secretion or by interaction with medications.

Finally, social and economic factors play a vitally important role. Old age has been associated with lower economic status that may stem from retirement, failing health, living on fixed income, or death of a spouse. Social isolation has been associated with depression and loneliness, which in turn can be linked to significant changes in eating patterns. These factors can influence the type and quality of food consumed. Marital status, for example, has a major impact on the diets of elderly men, and it is generally accepted that socialization at meals can increase energy intakes.

Primary aging, disease states, and social factors can all affect diet and nutrition in the elderly. Describing their respective contributions is the primary focus of this review.

II. THE POPULATION AT RISK

The elderly are the fastest growing segment in the U.S. population. Currently, 25 million Americans are over the age of 65. By the year 2030, 57 million people are expected to be 65 years or older. Yet the elderly are not a homogeneous population with uniform nutritional needs. Although some subgroups may be at greater risk for anorexia and associated nutritional deficiencies, others, especially women, are more likely to be overweight and obese. In general, body weight increases until late middle age, then plateaus and decreases for older persons.

Nutritional surveys of the U.S. population have shown poor correlations between reported dietary intake of nutrients and clinical and biochemical measures of nutritional status. For example, data showing inadequate intake of energy and protein among the elderly are difficult to reconcile with increased prevalence of obesity and increased percentage of body fat. However, many measures of dietary and nutritional assessment may not be applicable to older people. Most of the nutritional standards that have been used were generated from data on young individuals and were then extrapolated to the elderly. Awareness of

Table I Influences on the Nutritional Status of the Elderly

Primary aging
  Changes in the regulation of thirst and fluid intake
  Changes in the regulation of hunger and food intake
    Poor compensation for the energy content of foods
    Changes in satiety possibly related to hormones, neurotransmitters, or gastrointestinal tract
  Decreased energy output
    Lowered physical activity
    Slowed metabolic rate
  Alterations in ability to taste or smell
  Alterations in sensory-specific satiety
Secondary aging
  Chronic disease states
    Cardiovascular (e.g., hypertension, atherosclerosis)
    Endocrine (e.g., hyperlipidemia, diabetes)
    Cancer
    Infections
    Gastrointestinal (e.g., constipation, diarrhea, nausea, malabsorption)
    Swallowing problems
    Pulmonary
    Muscular and neurological (e.g., stroke, immobility)
    Psychiatric (e.g., depression, dementia, anorexia nervosa)
  Medications
  Medically prescribed diets
  Poor oral health and dentures
Socioeconomic influences
  Lower economic status
    Retirement
    Failing health
    Fixed income
    Death of spouse
  Social isolation and loneliness
  Bereavement

the problems this can cause is leading to collection of more data on intake patterns of the elderly. However, the assessment of dietary intake in large-scale epidemiological studies is often based on self-administered food frequency questionnaires or diet records. Such procedures place demands on memory and cognition and their accuracy may be compromised by forgetfulness, fatigue, or dementia. Dietary intake assessments that are shorter and interview based may be more appropriate for use with the elderly populations. The accuracy of body composition measures also changes as a function of age. Although body fat in young people is stored largely in subcutaneous depots and can be easily measured by skinfold thickness, much of the body fat in older people is stored in the trunk, which is harder to measure using readily accessible techniques such as skinfold thickness. These various assessment problems make it difficult to draw firm conclusions about the nutritional status of the elderly, especially because they are a heterogenous group. One thing is clear; there is a need for two sets of age-specific nutritional status standards for older people; one set for the free-living population and one for those that are chronically or acutely ill.

With these problems in mind, we will briefly examine what existing nutritional surveys indicate about changes in body weight (BW) and nutritional status with age. The National Health and Nutrition Examination Survey II (NHANES II, 1976–1980) shows that the prevalence of overweight increased with age. As shown in Figure 1, older people weigh more and many are fatter than are young people. Body mass index (BMI), the principal measure of overweight for adults, is correlated reasonably well with body fatness.

In contrast to BMI, energy intakes decline as a function of age. Based on a single 24-hour diet recall, a more recent NHANES III study (NHANES III phase 1; 1988–1991) shows that median energy intakes for adults aged 70–79 years are 1797 kcal for men and 1382 kcal for women. The reported macronutrient composition of energy in their diet is approximately 50% carbohydrate, 16% protein, and 34% fat. These data are similar to the results reported for the population as a whole. However, the finding that intake of some vitamins and minerals is low has given rise to concerns that some elderly individuals may consume inadequate levels of nutrient-dense foods. For example, low consumption of calcium and vitamin D has been attributed to low intake of dairy products by the elderly.

Anorexia, or low food intake, is a problem in the elderly because it increases the risk of nutrition-related illness. Though nutritional surveys have shown a low-to-moderate prevalence of nutrient deficiencies in free-living populations, elderly persons living in institutional settings may be at greater risk for malnutrition. Although estimates vary, between 30 and 60% of long-term care older institutionalized individuals have some degree of malnutrition. Studies show that poor nutrition and low BW are not simply a result of disease states, but often precede and predispose elderly individuals to disease and death.

Loss of appetite can be caused by age-related psychological and physical factors. Eating patterns can be influenced by mental factors, such as depression or dementia, and physical factors, including immobility, inability to feed oneself, and poor dentition or ill-fitting dentures. Many elderly individuals have problems with their oral cavity. For example, 42% of the geriatric population in the United States has no natural teeth. Of those with their teeth, 60% have tooth decay and 90% have gum disease, which impair their ability to chew. Tooth loss also affects chewing

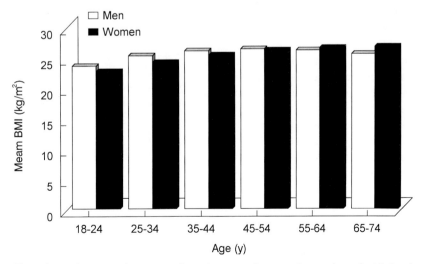

Figure 1 Body mass indices (BMI) for U.S. men and women by age from the National Health and Nutrition Examination Survey II, 1976–1980 (NHANES II).

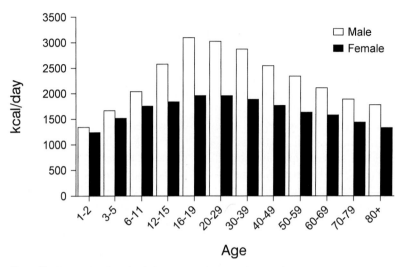

Figure 2 Energy intakes (kcal) for men and women by age from the National Health and Nutrition Examination Survey III, 1988–1991 (NHANES III).

ability, and this is not completely restored by dentures. Impaired chewing can cause changes in food selection, such as decreasing the variety in the diet, which could contribute to nutritional problems.

Decreased physical activity and a slower metabolic rate are part of the explanation for lowered food intake in the elderly. However, decreased energy demands cannot be the explanation for why nutritional problems related to low food intake develop.

III. THIRST AND FLUID INTAKE

Studies on the regulation of fluid intake demonstrate the difficulty experienced by many elderly persons in adjusting to environmental changes and in maintaining their internal state. Salt and water imbalances can lead to illness and death. These difficulties are partly caused by age-associated changes in regulatory systems. Maintenance of sodium and water homeostasis depends on a balance between intake, controlled by thirst and sodium appetite, and output, controlled by the kidneys. Thirst and water intake play a vital role in maintaining fluid and electrolyte balance, because it is only through these intakes that water deficits can be replenished. Conservation of water by the kidneys can only minimize further losses.

Although dehydration is a common cause of fluid

and electrolyte disturbance in the elderly, it is a common clinical observation that the elderly do not seem to get thirsty despite obvious physiologic need. Clinical studies have examined the effects of dehydration on thirst in both healthy young and healthy active elderly men. The men were dehydrated by depriving them of water and were asked to consume a dry diet. After 24 hours without fluids, the elderly men had a reduced ability to experience the sensation of thirst, and they did not drink adequate amounts of water to restore fluid balance. Additional studies have shown that the elderly do not restore fluid losses induced either by exercise or thermal dehydration. The impaired thirst in elderly individuals is due, in part, to changes in the receptors in the central nervous system (CNS) that detect changes in the level of sodium in blood. [See THIRST AND HYDRATION.]

IV. THE REGULATION OF FOOD INTAKE

Several recent investigations have tested the hypothesis that, analogous to the situation for the regulation of fluid intake, aging is associated with a decline in the regulatory mechanisms that influence hunger, appetite, and food intake.

One study demonstrated that elderly men do not adjust their food intake following periods of over- or underfeeding. During a period of ad libitum intake following 21 days of overfeeding, younger men (mean age 24) lost the excess weight gained during overfeeding, whereas the older men (mean age 70) did not. A similar indication of impaired regulatory ability was seen following 21 days of underfeeding in that younger men (mean age 22) regained lost weight and older men (mean age 66) did not. Measurements showed that energy expenditure was unaffected by aging, whereas food intake was not adjusted appropriately to compensate for the over or underfeeding. Although this study shows that the ability to adjust food intake in relation to BW is impaired in older men, it does not touch on whether aging is associated with changes in hunger and satiety or whether the elderly can adjust appropriately to changes in the energy content of foods.

The preloading method has been shown to be a sensitive test of the regulatory capabilities of young study participants. When fixed amounts of a food (preloads) varying in energy content are given 30 min before lunch, the degree to which intake at lunch is adjusted for the energy in the preloads indicates how well food intake regulatory mechanisms are functioning. Thus, healthy elderly (ages 60–84) and young (ages 18–35) men were given either yogurt preloads that varied in energy content, or no yogurt followed by lunch. The elderly males consumed significantly less energy at lunch than the young males in the baseline (no yogurt) condition. Lower intake was concordant with subjective sensations of satiety; ratings of subjective sensations indicated that the older men were less hungry and more full at the start of lunch. This could be part of the explanation for lower intake. The elderly men also showed an impairment in energy intake regulation. Compensation for energy in the preloads was less precise in the elderly than in young males; older men did not appropriately reduce intake at lunch to compensate for the calories in the yogurt.

There are changes in a number of physiological and metabolic systems with age, but the link between these and changes in the regulation of food intake has not been established in humans. Animal studies point to physiological changes that could be involved in changes in food intake regulation with age. For example, it has been shown in young animals that some naturally occurring peptides such as endogenous opioids may be involved in determining the palatability of food and in initiating and terminating eating. Studies indicate that older rats show diminished responses to blockade or stimulation of opioid peptides compared to young rats. Also, older rats have a lower concentration of endogenous opioid peptides in some areas of the brain.

Changes in the gastrointestinal tract with age may affect food intake. The presence of food in the stomach and gut can affect food intake through receptors that detect stretch, or the concentration of nutrients or electrolytes such as sodium. The early onset of satiety sometimes experienced by the elderly could be due to alterations in the hormonal responses that normally accompany eating. For example, cholecystokinin (CCK), a hormone released by the gut in response to eating, has been shown to decrease food intake. Studies in mice show that CCK decreases food intake more in older than in younger animals. CCK also has a prolonged action in older mice. CCK levels have been found to be elevated in older humans. This, combined with an increased sensitivity to CCK, could lead to early satiety in the elderly. Another factor that could affect satiety is the rate at which foods and drinks empty from the stomach. The emptying of solid and liquid foods has been found to be significantly slower in older subjects. Although the difference in stomach emptying is small, it is possible that retaining food in the stomach could affect hunger and satiety and the pattern of meals; that is, the interval between meals might be expected to be longer. This needs to be assessed experimentally by recording food intake. [See GASTROINTESTINAL SYSTEM: FUNCTION AND DYSFUNCTION.]

A number of other possibilities have been suggested to explain the anorexia of the elderly, such as changes in various neurotransmitters and hormones. However, there is no direct evidence to support such speculation. Indeed none of the physiological changes associated with aging have been directly linked to changes in food intake regulation in elderly humans. Clearly, more studies are required to understand changes in physiological systems that impact on the nutritional status of the elderly.

V. DEFICITS OF TASTE AND SMELL

It is commonly believed that age-related deficits in taste and smell are directly responsible for some of the nutritional problems in old age. However, there is very little direct evidence to link diminished sensory functioning with inadequate nutrition and ill health. While there is general agreement that many elderly people suffer from deficits in smell, and possibly taste, the impact of such impairments on nutrition and diet has not always been clear. No study has demonstrated a causal relationship between sensory deficits and altered food choices in the elderly, and there is little evidence to link chemosensory deficits with nutritional status.

There is no doubt that sensory impairments do occur. Studies on taste sensitivity have observed some decline of taste acuity with age, especially after the age of 70 years. Taste sensitivity to water solutions of sweet, sour, salty, and bitter compounds was measured using detection and recognition thresholds. The detection threshold was the minimum concentration of a solution that was perceived as distinct from distilled water, whereas the recognition threshold was the level at which the solution was perceived as salty or sweet. Taste sensitivity was also assessed at solution concentrations above threshold. Studies showed an increase in detection and recognition threshold levels among the elderly and, in some cases, impaired perception of more intense solutions, notably those with bitter and sour tastes.

Although the loss of taste sensitivity with increasing age was initially attributed to degeneration and loss of taste buds, it now appears that the taste system is relatively robust, and that whole-mouth tasting is stable even in late old age. On the other hand, localized taste losses do occur in some elderly subjects, although sometimes they go unnoticed. Taste losses that have been observed among the elderly may be the result of cumulative pathology, including poor oral health, rather than the inevitable outcome of primary or normal aging.

Despite reports of diminished taste acuity for dilute solutions, the perception of sweet, sour, salty, and bitter tastes in foods appears to be resistant to age. Sensory evaluation studies have failed to observe age-related deficits in ratings of saltiness in tomato juice, or a decline in the perception of saltiness in potatoes or broth, or sourness in apple drink. There was no age-related deficit in the intensity ratings for salt and sugar in salted or sweetened dairy products. Only one study reported an age-associated decline in the perception of protein taste in soup.

However, conventional studies on taste acuity do not give an indication of how aging may affect taste preferences. Arguably, not taste perceptions but taste preferences are likely to affect food preferences or food dislikes. Taste preferences have been measured by asking subjects to rate the perceived pleasantness of a stimulus, or through direct ratings of "like" and "dislike." However, hedonic ratings can be influenced by the type of the stimulus, or by the subjects' own concerns with health and dieting. As a result, studies on taste preferences of older subjects have produced no consistent pattern of results. Whereas one early study reported that older subjects preferred less sweet samples of pineapple juice, some later studies showed that the elderly, on the contrary, preferred sweeter and saltier stimuli than did younger subjects. One study reported an increase in liking for higher concentrations of salt with age, but only for water solution and not for chicken soup. Other studies reported no difference in hedonic preferences for sweet solutions between children, young adults, and the oldest adults.

Only one study showed a clear increase in preferences for more intense solutions of sodium chloride, sucrose, and citric acid as a function of age. Four concentrations of each stimulus were presented either in water or in vegetable juice or lemonade. In general, the subjects judged beverages as more pleasant than water solutions. Older subjects preferred higher concentrations of sugar and salt in both water and beverages than did younger subjects. This shift in hedonic preferences toward higher levels of sugar and salt was again thought to be caused by age-related impairments in sensory function.

Though it is generally believed that elevated preferences for salt taste are associated with increased sodium intakes, no study so far has managed to link sensory preferences for salt to dietary sodium intakes at any age. Measures of salt taste preference in the elderly have not been linked to estimated salt intakes. Similarly, no study has linked altered preferences for sweet taste with changes in sugar consumption in the same subject population.

The taste impairments observed in several studies might be the consequence of poor health, including poor oral health, or medication use, and not a direct consequence of normal aging. Whatever the reason, no study has shown a causal link between such impairments and altered patterns of food intake or inadequate nutrition. Research attention has therefore focused on aging and the sense of smell.

The perception and identification of odors is clearly impaired in the elderly. The University of Pennsylvania Smell Identification Test (UPSIT), composed of 40 odors on paper strips, has been used to assess smell functioning in a large number of people including the elderly. In one study, the subjects were 1955 men and women aged 5 to 99 years, including university students and employees, residents of homes for the elderly, and primary and secondary grade-school students. Odor identification data (Figure 3) showed that women were better than men and nonsmokers were better than smokers. Peak performance was seen among subjects aged 20–40 years, with a sharp decline observed after age 60 years. More than half of the people aged 65–80 years had a major olfactory impairment, while three-quarters showed olfactory impairments after the age of 80 years.

Arguably, the selection of real-life foods involves smell rather than taste. Identifying and distinguishing between foods depends on the perception of taste, flavor, and texture. Studies on sensory identification of foods by the elderly showed that food recognition diminished with age. In a pioneering study, young college students (ages 18–22) and elderly residents of

a retirement home (ages 67–93) were presented with 24 different foods to taste and smell. Fresh fruits, vegetables, meats, fish, nuts, grains, and dairy products were steamed, blended and strained, or pureed. Water was added to minimize texture differences. Blindfolded subjects were first presented with a container of food to smell, and then they tasted a teaspoon of the food sample.

The results showed that elderly subjects were sometimes unable to identify blended foods by taste and smell. Out of 24 foods, 21 were more frequently identified by young people than by the elderly. More elderly subjects than younger ones commented on the weakness of taste and smell for the unseasoned, blended foods.

Impaired food identification by the elderly is therefore more likely to involve smell rather than taste deficits. In another study, young (ages 18–26) and older people (ages 65 years and over) attempted to identify pureed foods while blindfolded, using only taste and odor cues. The freshly prepared, steamed, and blended foods were potato, tomato, carrot, broccoli, celery, lemon, pear, banana, beef, coffee, sugar, and salt. Younger people identified more foods on the

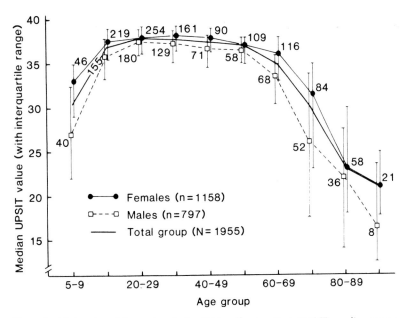

Figure 3 University of Pennsylvania Smell Identification Test (UPSIT) median scores as a function of age and gender (Reproduced with permission from Doty et al., *Science, 226,* 1441–1443. (Copyright 1984 American Association for the Advancement of Science.)

first attempt than did older subjects. Repeating the task with nostrils pinched to eliminate olfactory input removed the age-related differences, suggesting that the foods were identified largely by smell. The key question is whether impairments of smell in the elderly have a measurable impact on food selection.

There is evidence that sensory factors related to the sense of smell play an important role in diet choice. The elderly rated taste, or specifically flavor perception, as a strong influence on their food choices. In a recent survey, 30 elderly individuals ranked the factors that affected their food purchase decisions in three different eating situations (celebration, eating with a friend or spouse, or alone). Familiarity and prior experience with foods and the sensory properties were significantly more important than other factors in all three situations, except when eating alone, when ease of preparation was the most important. Apparently the elderly were often unaware of their sensory loss and reported no decrease in their appreciation of foods or in their ability to smell. It may be that when sensory losses occur gradually over a period of years, the importance of smell in promoting appetite also gradually declines and cognitive compensatory mechanisms take over. In a recent study, smell deficits were observed in a large proportion of elderly women. However, their impact on food consumption patterns and nutritional status appeared minimal.

Still some scientists believe that sensory impairments are the direct cause of reduced pleasure response to foods that may result in a consumption of a monotonous and nutritionally inadequate diet. One intervention approach has been to restore the missing sensation by adding synthetic flavorants to food. These studies reported that flavor amplification increases the intake of nutrient-dense foods in the elderly and may result in improved nutritional as well as immune status. [See SMELL AND TASTE.]

VI. DIETARY VARIETY AND FOOD SELECTION

Age-related sensory impairments are said to result in the consumption of a more monotonous diet. Some studies have reported a decline in dietary variety with age. Analysis of the self-reported dietary intakes of elderly participants in the 1977–1978 National Food Consumption Survey (NFCS) showed that the oldest

participants consumed the least varied diets. These data were based on a sample of adults more than 54 years old ($N = 4{,}983$) drawn from among more than 30,000 people interviewed in the NFCS study. Food consumption data were based on one 24-hour food recall and 2-day food records.

Consumption patterns were analyzed using two separate measures of dietary variety. The first measure, the variety index, was calculated by counting the number of different foods in each of 18 previously defined food groups that were eaten by each individual over 3 days. The elderly respondents ate approximately 35 different foods over 3 days, with men reporting more different foods than did women. The variety index declined slightly from the youngest (age 55–64 years) to the oldest group (>75 years).

The second measure, that of "core" foods, was based on a straight frequency tally of foods consumed over the 3-day period. Foods consumed on at least 1 of the 3 days by approximately 50% of the elderly respondents were whole milk, coffee, white bread, potatoes (other than fried), margarine, and sugar. The authors noted that these items were relatively inexpensive, simple to chew, and easy to prepare. They also noted that a higher proportion of the sample population 75 years and above lived alone and had lower income and educational levels.

An analysis of the most frequently consumed foods in the NHANES II database shows that coffee, white bread, and margarine are the core foods of the American diet. These foods were consumed by more than 50% of the respondents on any given day. The most frequently consumed foods were coffee and tea, white bread, margarine, whole milk, doughnuts, cookies and cake, and sugar. The core foods of the elderly and the core foods of the general public are in fact very similar. Moreover, nutritional trends among the elderly have followed those of the American public. A comparison of 1977–1978 NFCS data with the 1985 Continuing Survey of Food Intakes by Individuals showed that American women ages 19–50 years reduced the consumption of red meat and full-fat milk, but consumed more low-fat milk and low-calorie soft drinks. A similar analysis of intake trends for the elderly showed that they too reduced the consumption of meat, and increased the consumption of low-fat milk, low-calorie beverages, and take-out foods.

The moderate trend toward consumption of a less

varied diet seen in community-dwelling elderly individuals is much more pronounced in long-term care facilities. A survey of 303 institutionalized persons over 65 found that almost two-thirds had changed their diets within the past 5 years. Many of these changes resulted in subjects eating less or restricting their food choices. The effect of limited food choice on the health and nutritional status of the elderly can be serious because consumption of a varied diet is considered the most effective way to assure adequate nutrient intake.

One possible explanation for reduced dietary variety involves altered pleasure responses to food. Normally, as foods are consumed they become less pleasant. This decline, called sensory-specific satiety, is associated with a shift to other food choices during the meal. As a result, people eat more foods when offered a variety of choices than when a single food item is available. Sensory-specific satiety can therefore promote the intake of a more varied and nutritionally balanced diet.

Because sensory-specific satiety encourages consumption of a varied diet and because the elderly have relatively monotonous diets, a reasonable hypothesis is that the elderly have diminished sensory-specific satiety. The effects of age on sensory-specific satiety were investigated in adolescents (ages 12–15), young adults (ages 22–35), older adults (ages 45–60), and the elderly (ages 65–82). Subjects rated the pleasantness of the sensory properties and their desire to eat five foods and then ate either a fixed amount or as much as they wanted of one of the foods (yogurt). They rerated the foods immediately after they finished eating the yogurt. The results showed that sensory-specific satiety differs across age groups (see Figure 4). Subjects over the age of 65 did not show a greater decrease in the rating of the pleasantness of the taste of the food they had consumed compared with ratings of the uneaten foods, that is, they did not show sensory-specific satiety for the taste of the food they had eaten.

It is not clear why the elderly did not show sensory-specific satiety, but it did not appear to be related simply to a loss of sensory function. At the start of the tests, before eating the yogurt, the elderly subjects rated the sensory properties of the test foods as pleasant, as did the other groups. Although the elderly subjects showed the typical decline with age in the ability to identify odors, this did not correlate with

sensory-specific satiety for either taste or odor. This was surprising because it seemed likely that changes in the pleasantness of the taste or odor of a food would depend to some extent upon olfactory function. Further studies relating sensory impairments to the changing hedonic response to foods will be of interest because the mechanisms underlying sensory-specific satiety are not well understood. It is likely that in addition to a sensory component, there is a cognitive component related to the knowledge that a food has just been consumed. It is not clear why the elderly would differ in this respect, but it may be related to a decreased desire for change of all types.

An impairment in sensory-specific satiety would be expected to be associated both with consumption of monotonous diets and with a failure to increase the amount consumed in response to variety in the diet. A recent study showed that the elderly are insensitive to the stimulatory effect of variety on fluid intake. Elderly subjects drank similar amounts following 24 hours of dehydration when they were offered just one beverage (water) and when they were offered four beverages (water, mineral water, cola, orange juice). Although a young control group was not tested, a previous study in young people showed that more fluid was consumed with a variety of drinks than with just one drink. Also, young subjects ate more than a variety of foods was available than when offered just one food, and this increase in intake was related to sensory-specific satiety. Thus, a failure to experience sensory-specific satiety would be expected to be associated not only with a monotonous diet, but also with a lower caloric intake in a varied meal. More studies are needed to examine how age-related changes in sensory-specific satiety influence variety in the diet and food intake, both in experimental situations and in the natural environment. Variety in the diet has been found to be associated with better health in the elderly, and further studies could suggest strategies for increasing the variety in the diets of elderly individuals and in improving their nutritional status.

VII. SOCIOECONOMIC ISSUES

Low food intake in the elderly can be accounted for by multiple factors, ranging from primary aging to changed social and economic circumstances. In several studies of the elderly, a majority indicated a recent

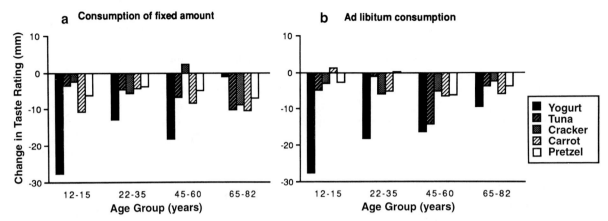

Figure 4 Mean changes in ratings for each of the foods sampled of the pleasantness of the taste of that food from just before to just after eating either 300 g (a) or ad libitum (b) amounts of yogurt by different age groups. This shows that sensory-specific satiety, or the change in pleasantness of the food consumed (yogurt) compared with those not consumed, declines with increasing age. (Reproduced with permission from Rolls and McDermott, *American Journal of Clinical Nutrition, 54*, 988–996, 1991. (Copyright American Society for Clinical Nutrition.)

change in food habits for reasons of health, changes in living status, health beliefs, or simply because of a change in finances. Living arrangements, social isolation, and no socialization at meals may play a role. The living arrangements of older individuals can affect their diet quality. More men living alone consumed a poor quality diet than did men living with a spouse, particularly those 75 years of age or older. The main effect of living alone was to decrease the amount of energy consumed rather than the types of foods chosen. Bereavement was found to be associated with negative effects on nutrient intakes by changing the social environment and altering the social meaning of eating. [*See* BEREAVEMENT AND LOSS.]

Education and other socioeconomic issues appear to play a major role. In a recent study of 152 women aged 85–94 years, old age did not have an adverse effect on food or nutrient intakes. The oldest women reported eating a similar or greater number of weekly servings of fruits, vegetables, dairy products, meats, and sweets as did women aged 64–85 years. On the other hand, education level did have a major impact on nutrient intakes. Women with education beyond high school reported higher intakes of selected vitamins and minerals than did less educated women.

Some of the nutritional problems can be remedied to some extent by providing home-delivered meals and groceries and convenience foods of high nutrient density. Increasing socialization at meals could also have a significant impact, although this has not been

investigated experimentaly in the elderly. Studies in young men and women showed that they ate up to 50% more when eating dinner with three friends than when they ate the same meal alone. The nutrient composition of the diet was not affected. Of interest was the finding that eating with strangers did not increase intake at dinner compared to eating alone. Thus, although socialization at meals could increase intake of the elderly, this may depend on the type of social interactions that take place.

Diet-related attitudes and beliefs may also influence food habits. Some studies have identified taste, health beliefs, familiarity, price, convenience, and prestige as being among the key social determinants of food selection. Older people are generally more concerned with health issues, notably energy and fat consumption, and with food costs. Saving time is not a major issue. Single elderly women are most concerned about food costs.

Pathological concern with BW and dieting has also been observed among elderly women. There have been concerns that age-related anorexia among the elderly resembles the psychiatric syndrome of anorexia nervosa, more commonly reported among young women. Anorexia nervosa is characterized by refusal to maintain a minimum BW, disturbance of body image, morbid fear of fatness, and a preoccupation with food and eating. Endocrine abnormalities are also seen, the most frequent of which is amenorrhea, or cessation of menstruation. A survey of elderly individuals who were below 90% of average BW indicated that pathological responses on a questionnaire used to assess eating-related attitudes were seen in 9% of those tested. Abnormal attitudes included a display of self-control around food, avoiding eating when hungry, enjoying having an empty stomach, engaging in dieting behavior, and being terrified about being overweight. Case reports of anorexia nervosa among elderly women have been described in the literature. The patients were described as having all of the features of the diagnosis except for the amenorrhea. Typically anorexia nervosa is associated with other conditions, particularly depression. Depression in the elderly could exacerbate their anorexia.

VIII. INTERVENTION STRATEGIES

Ideally, diets designed for the elderly should provide nutrient-dense foods. Although energy needs are reduced in old age, dietary requirements for protein, vitamins, and minerals are increased. For example, studies of elderly women in nursing homes reported that calcium intakes were at best marginal in that age group. Women living at home consumed even less calcium than those in nursing homes. As a result, dietary strategies have focused on the consumption of fortified or nutrient-dense foods.

The impaired regulation of food intake seen with aging could influence responses to high-energy nutritional supplements. The elderly are less likely than younger individuals to compensate for the energy in supplements by reducing intake of other foods. This was confirmed in the study in which healthy elderly men did not reduce intake at lunch following high-energy yogurt consumed 30 min earlier. The older men had significantly lower baseline lunch intakes than the younger men, but by preceding the meal with a high-energy supplement the total intake for the meal was increased significantly and to a level comparable to that of the younger men. Thus, dietary supplementation may be an important approach to enhancing the energy intake of the elderly. However, not all of the available data indicate that supplementation is beneficial. In a recent study of frail elderly men and women (mean age 87), daily evening supplementation for 10 weeks with a high-energy multinutrient liquid increased total daily energy intake only when combined with exercise. Participants not exercising decreased intake to compensate for the energy in the supplement. This result differs from that of findings from other laboratories. For example, in one study when elderly patients with poor appetites were given two different nutritionally complete liquid diets to consume freely for 10 days, energy intake was increased significantly. It appeared that there was little compensation for the energy from the supplements. In another study of elderly participants at risk of malnutrition, dietary supplementation was found to increase daily energy intake and weight gain over a 12-week period. Thus, most studies indicate that nutrient-dense supplements can increase energy intake and improve the nutritional status of the elderly. Future studies should systematically determine the critical parameters (type, amount, or energy density of the supplement) associated with supplementation that influence energy intake.

There are a number of other possible strategies for optimizing the diets of the elderly. One strategy involves sensory supplementation. Flavor amplification and flavor enhancement have been mentioned as ways of increasing food palatability to counteract sensory deficits. However, there is little evidence that moderate sensory deficits as opposed to sensory distortions affect nutritional status. Rather, studies indicate that the sensory system in healthy older people is relatively robust and that sensory deficits are not always linked to poor nutrition and weight loss. Although age-related sensory losses undoubtedly detract from the quality of life, no evidence so far has linked them to impaired nutritional status and ill health.

Such narrowing of dietary choices as has been observed may have been due to a deliberate restriction of calories, fat, sugar, and salt. People over the age of 60 are concerned with coronary heart disease, hypertension, and diabetes, and many follow medically prescribed diets that are low in fat, sugar, and salt. Foods containing intense sweeteners and fat substitutes might fulfill a special need. At present, low-calorie foods are used chiefly by people wishing to lose weight. This allows dieters to reduce energy intakes, without narrowing food choices and compromising the hedonic value of food. For elderly individuals who have health problems associated with obesity, such foods can be of benefit. However, many elderly people have energy intakes that are too low to meet energy requirements. Clearly, choosing reduced-calorie products could exacerbate problems of anorexia and low-energy intake in these individuals, especially because they are less likely to compensate for changes in the energy content of foods. Given the growing size of the elderly population, the market for such foods is increasing. A survey by the Calorie Control Council in 1991 indicated that consumers age 60 and over showed the most dramatic increase in the use of low-calorie, sugar-free foods and beverages. Because the elderly are heterogenous in terms of their BW and nutritional requirements, they must be appropriately informed about how energy-modified foods fit into their diets. Regardless of their BW, if they consume reduced-calorie foods these should be of high nutrient density.

A number of strategies for increasing daily energy intakes involve addressing social and economic problems and changing dietary behaviors. Community nutrition programs aimed at the elderly provide subsidized meals both in the home and at congregate sites. Such programs help to overcome some of the problems associated with nutritional difficulties stemming from low income, impaired mobility, loneliness, and lack of socialization at meals. Other strategies involve managing dental and medical problems that affect food intake and encouraging consumption of foods that are readily chewed and digested. Many elderly individuals have swallowing problems that require individualized diets that provide foods of textures that promote consumption. Some elderly individuals, because of low appetite and impaired thirst, must be prompted to eat and drink. Clearly management of the nutritional problems associated with aging requires sensitivity to a wide range of physical, psychological, and environmental influences on food and fluid intake. Future intervention studies should focus on optimal intervention strategies for improving the nutritional status of both community-dwelling and institutionalized elderly individuals.

BIBLIOGRAPHY

Clydesdale, F. M. (Ed.). (1993). Sensory perception in aging workshop. *Critical Reviews in Food Science and Nutrition, 33*, Issue 1.

Garry, P. J., & Chumlea, W. C. (Eds.). (1989). Epidemiologic and methodologic problems in determining nutritional status of older persons. *American Journal of Clinical Nutrition, 50*(suppl. 5).

Jackson, T. M. (Ed.). (1994). Nutrition research and the elderly. *Nutrition Reviews, 52*, No. 8, part 2.

Morley, J. E., Glick, Z., & Rubenstein, L. Z. (Eds.). (1990). *Geriatric nutrition: A comprehensive review.* New York: Raven Press, Ltd.

Murphy, C., Cain, W. S., & Hegsted, D. M. (Eds.). (1989). Nutrition and the chemical senses in aging: Recent advances and current research needs. *Annals of the New York Academy of Sciences, 561.*

DNA and Gene Expression

Jan Vijg

Beth Israel Hospital and Harvard Medical School

Chromatin The complex of DNA and proteins in the nucleus of the interphase cell.

CpG Islands Stretches of DNA, about 1–2 kb long with an average GC content of about 60% as compared to 40% for the genome overall. CpG islands often surround the promoters of constitutively expressed genes.

DNA Conformation DNA higher order structure.

DNA Damage Changes in the DNA chemical structure induced by a variety of different chemical, physical, and biological agents.

DNA Repair The complex of enzymatic systems to remove DNA damage and to restore the original situation.

DNA Replication The process of copying the entire complement of genetic information.

DNA Transcription The process of copying the genetic information encoded in a gene into mRNA.

Gene The segment of DNA encoding a polypeptide chain; it includes regions immediately preceding and following the coding sequence as well as intervening sequences (introns) between individual coding sequences.

Genome The totality of the DNA contained within the diploid chromosome set of an individual or species. The human genome consists of approximately 6 billion base pairs of DNA distributed among 46 chromosomes.

Intron A transcribed but noncoding part of a gene, separating one exon (coding part) from another. Introns are removed from the transcript by splicing together the exons on either side of it.

Mutation Change in the sequence of DNA in a genome that can involve a single base pair position (point mutation) or a rearrangement (deletions, insertions, recombinations). Here, the in vivo mutant frequency is defined as the frequency at which a mutated variant of the gene is found among unmutated copies.

PCR Amplification An in vitro process used as a laboratory tool for copying DNA fragments in an amount sufficient for their analysis.

Promoter The portion of a gene to which RNA polymerase must bind before transcription of the gene can begin.

Proto-oncogenes The normal counterparts in the eukaryotic genome to the oncogenes; products of the latter can transform a cell to become a cancer cell.

Repetitive DNA A collective term for all the DNA sequences that occur more than once in the genome of an organism. Minisatellites are tandem repeats of a short unit occurring all over the genome (clustered at the telomeres). At a given minisatellite locus the copy number can be highly variable and differ between 5 and 50 copies among different chromosomes.

Transgenic Animal Genetically engineered animal, for example, by introducing a foreign DNA fragment into the germ line by microinjection in one of the pronuclei of a fertilized egg. The foreign sequence will integrate in one of the chromosomes and is stably inherited as part of the germ line. From then on the sequence is present in all organs and tissues.

GENES are the units of inheritance. The higher animal genome contains between 50,000 and 100,000 genes. Each gene is a deoxyribonucleic acid (DNA) sequence that carries the information representing a particular polypeptide. A gene is a stable entity, but can suffer a change in sequence. Such a change is called a mutation. The phenotypic results of mutations vary from the undetectable to lethal. Genes are perpetuated (as in cell division or the generation of gametes) by a duplication process of the double-stranded DNA to give identical copies (*replication*). The information encoded in the genes is expressed, first by generating a single-stranded RNA identical in sequence with one of the strands of the duplex DNA (*transcription*), and then by converting the nucleotide sequence of the RNA into the sequence of amino acids comprising a protein (*translation*). Patterns of gene expression can undergo changes with time, as exemplified by the switching on and off of individual genes during development and differentiation. Aging is a process of change with time that is associated with an increased rate of occurrence of pathological lesions, increased susceptibility to disease, and an increased chance of dying. A multitude of physiological, cellular, and molecular changes have been found to occur in aging individuals of various species. The relevance of many of these changes, with respect to possible causal relationships with age-related pathology and/or functional decline, is unclear at present. This is the case for most age-related changes in DNA and gene expression, which have been considered as the basic cause of aging or, alternatively, as merely background noise against a predominantly pathophysiological process. The question to be addressed in molecular gerontology is whether aging can be reduced to a finite number of (molecular) processes based on stochastic damage and/or genetically programmed events.

I. UNDERLYING THEORY

A. Background

Changes in genome organization and expression have long been considered as possible explanations for the general breakdown of structure and function during aging of higher organisms. One rationale behind this concept is that changes in DNA as the ultimate template could lead to qualitative and/or quantitative changes in gene expression. The latter could then give rise to altered cellular phenotypes with loss of function of cells and tissues and multiple forms of pathology as ultimate consequences. Alternatively, age-related changes in gene expression could occur independent of changes in DNA as the consequence of, for example, a genetic program, induction by other changes that occur during aging, long-term pleiotropic effects of other gene functions. Neither of these two concepts rule out the other. The questions to be addressed include (a) what kind of changes in DNA chemical structure, sequence organization, chromatin structure, and gene expression need to be considered; (b) do such changes actually occur and can they be causally related to the aging phenotype; (c) what are the mechanisms by which changes arise; and (d) what are the defense systems minimizing (the effects of) such changes?

B. Evolutionary Basis

According to the present consensus, aging is a non-adaptive process and the inevitable consequence of the declining force of natural selection with age. That is, in view of the very limited survival of individuals of a group or species to advanced age there is no selection against deteriorative processes at old age. Such deteriorative processes could actually represent the adverse actions of multiple genes. The latter are likely to have emerged during evolution by random deleterious mutation and/or as pleiotropic genes with beneficial effects early and adverse effects late in life. In addition, genes controlling aging could involve cellular maintenance and repair. Indeed, the hypothesis that links aging to alterations in cellular macromolecules is supported by observed associations between cellular maintenance and repair and evolutionary variation of life span. For example, evidence has shown that cells from longer lived species have generally more active DNA repair systems than cells from short-lived species. Similar correlations were found for antioxidant defense (e.g., the activity of the enzyme superoxide dismutase [SOD] appeared to be higher in tissues from longer lived species).

Naturally, long-term survival depends on somatic maintenance and/or reserve capacity. However, the evolutionary theory of aging would not predict a maximization of cellular maintenance and repair at the cost of reproduction. This explains why defense systems, such as DNA repair, are inherently imperfect. It has been proposed that a balance exists between somatic maintenance and reproductive efforts, which would differ from species to species as a function of their life-history pattern. This concept of inherently suboptimal molecular preservation implies an age-related accumulation of molecular (and other) defects. Hence, the predicted role of various kinds of damage to DNA and other biological macromolecules, as the ultimate cause of aging.

The type of biological macromolecules that are most important as putative targets of the aging process is still an open question. Some would argue that this is the DNA in view of its unique role in transferring genetic information from cell to cell and from generation to generation. Others, however, would say that changes at the protein level can potentially influence all other macromolecular structures in the cell, including the DNA. In reality, changes have been found at all levels, and the various pathways involved in the cell's macromolecular machinery and its maintenance and repair are so intertwined (illustrated in Fig. 1) that no single molecule, system, or structure can be considered on its own, although a primary or predominant role of one type of molecule cannot be excluded.

From the evolutionary theory of aging it can be deduced that aging is not the result of a genetic program switching genes on and off in an orderly way, like differentiation and development, resulting in con-

sistent changes in gene expression during aging. However, as a response to an initial series of changes that could be stochastic in nature, the cell might react with a number of programmed responses. Such responses include the above-mentioned DNA repair and antioxidant response, and a host of other cellular and molecular defense systems. Other consistent gene expressional changes at old age could have emerged during evolution as delayed pleiotropic effects or even in an adaptive way by group selection, when aged individuals contribute to the likelihood of survival of the group to which they are kin. A speculative example in humans might involve gene expressional changes in the cortex leading to an improved capacity to transfer information to the younger generation.

It follows from the above that both stochastic and programmatic changes can be expected to occur during aging. Age-related changes in DNA can be expected to predominantly be stochastic. That is, each specific alteration or mutation occurs as a relatively rare event, which essentially transforms each organ or tissue into a mosaic of cells. Each cell would have its unique set of "scars" that distinguishes it from all other cells. By contrast, age-related changes in gene expression can represent both programmatic and stochastic events. Indeed, while each aged cell can have its own unique set of up- and/or down-regulated genes, also consistent changes, occurring in each cell of a tissue or organ should be taken into consideration.

II. CHANGES IN DNA

A. DNA Damage

Cellular DNA is continuously damaged by a variety of exogenous and endogenous physical, chemical, and biological agents (Table I). Breaks of the sugar–phosphate backbone are induced (e.g., under the influence of body heat), whereas a variety of cell and tissue-specific exogenous agents such as ultraviolet and polycyclic aromatic hydrocarbons can induce various forms of base damages (e.g., inter- and intrachromosomal cross-links, bulky adducts, methylation, deamination, depurination, and depyrimidination). A major source of spontaneous DNA damage could be free radicals. As a by-product of oxidative phosphory-

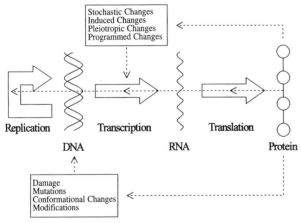

Figure 1 Flow of cellular information from DNA to protein (massive arrows) with the major patterns of influence (dotted lines). It should be noted that although proteins are the endpoints of the flow of information, they influence all cellular processes including their own synthesis.

Table I Major Causes of DNA Damage

A. Endogenous
1. Body heat
2. Oxygen radicals
3. Nonenzymatic glycosylation
4. S-adenosyl-L-methionine (Alkylation)
5. Steroid hormones, excitatory amino acids
B. Exogenous
1. Dietary factors (e.g., benzo[a]pyrene in barbecue)
2. Lifestyle (e.g., smoking, sunbathing)
3. Environmental exposures (e.g., ionizing radiation)

lation and several other biological and physiological processes, oxygen radicals can induce a variety of damages into cellular DNA. Indeed, it has been estimated on the basis of urinary excretion of DNA adducts that oxidative damage to DNA alone occurs at a rate of 10^4 hits per cell per day in the human; in the rat the rate is one order of magnitude higher.

As indicated by the occurrence of DNA adducts in the urine, most of the damage is repaired. However, repair systems may fail during aging, leading to an increased steady state level of DNA damage. Evidence has been obtained that the steady state levels of several forms of DNA damage (e.g., breaks, oxidative damage) increase with age in both humans and rodents. Increases of approximately a factor of two to three in the rat liver have been reported for nuclear and mitochondrial DNA. As demonstrated by Ames and co-workers, the mitochondrial genome appeared to be much more susceptible to oxidative damage than the overall nuclear genome; mtDNA from the rat liver has more than 10 times the level of oxidative DNA damage than does nuclear DNA from the same tissue. The latter is probably explained by a much less efficient DNA repair system to protect mtDNA. However, it is entirely possible that certain areas of the nuclear DNA also accumulate DNA damage much faster than the genome overall. Indeed, DNA repair efficiencies vary considerably between different types of DNA sequences, with actively transcribed genes being repaired best.

Thus, higher levels of DNA (oxidative) damage, especially in mtDNA, appear to be present in at least some organs of older humans and rodents. The question is if this kind of chemical damage can by itself explain some of the age-dependent functional declines that have been reported. The answer is probably no

for at least two reasons. First, at the levels of increase reported for nuclear DNA (from roughly one to two damaged bases per 10,000 bp of nuclear DNA) it is unlikely that there is an important effect. In mtDNA the levels at old age are much higher (almost 20 lesions per 10,000 bp). However, in view of the many mtDNA copies the cell has ample opportunity to compensate for the loss.

Second, it is not always realized that instead of a genuine accumulation of DNA damage it is really the difference between induced and repaired DNA damages that has been measured, that is, steady state levels of DNA damage. It is not possible to know if a particular lesion detected today will still be present tomorrow. Hence, the possibility should be considered that any increase in DNA damage unless it completely overwhelms all defense systems (which at the levels reported is extremely unlikely), has no functional consequences. The situation becomes different when a lesion is fixed in the form of a mutation. That is, when a chemical alteration in DNA structure, recognizable by DNA damage processing systems, is turned into an erroneus base sequence as a permanent part of the genetic heritage. Such DNA sequence changes will be discussed below.

B. DNA Sequence Changes

The present concept of DNA lesions (changes in the DNA chemical structure) that need to be processed in an error-prone way in order to yield mutations (changes in DNA sequence information) is a relatively recent one. Historically, changes in DNA were all considered to be mutations, randomly induced in the chromosomes during aging as a consequence of environmental exposure. The original idea was that such mutations would inactivate genes leading to cell death and/or dysfunctioning. This is essentially a stochastic process. The original hypothesis was experimentally supported by the observation that X rays, even at low doses, reduced the life span of rodents. Since 1958, when a somatic mutation theory of aging was first postulated, there has been tremendous progress in our understanding of the higher animal genome and many of the processes acting upon it. By now it has become clear that somatic mutations do accumulate during aging as the original theory proposed. Indeed, because cellular defense against DNA-damaging agents (including DNA repair) is imperfect, such an accumulation is not surprising (see above).

To accurately measure the rate of mutation accumulation has proven to be more difficult, due to the lack of methodology for measuring low-frequency changes in DNA sequence organization. Genetically engineered mouse model systems, harboring reporter genes that can be rescued from the in vivo situation and subjected to selection in vitro, now allow the detection of all kind of mutations in any organ or tissue. Furthermore, methods like the polymerase chain reaction (PCR) allow the detection of certain mutations directly, that is, without phenotypic selection in vitro. This new methodology has greatly improved the situation and can be expected to lead to great progress in this field, especially in making a connection between mutations and their physiological endpoints.

The first evidence for an increased level of mutations in organs and tissues of old individuals was presented in the 1960s. In looking at mouse liver parenchymal cell metaphase plates after partial hepatectomy, higher numbers of cells with abnormal chromosomes in old as compared to young animals (i.e., from about 10% of the cells in 4–5-month-old mice to 75% in mice older than 12 months) were found. Later, such large structural changes in DNA were observed to increase with donor age in white blood cells of human individuals (i.e., from about 2–4% of the cells being chromosomally aberrated in young individuals to levels that are about six times higher in older persons.

The detection of small DNA sequence changes, like point mutations, has only recently become possible. With the development of tests based on selectable endogenous target genes (e.g., the hypoxanthine phosphoribosyl transferase [HPRT] locus), it became possible to assess the mutant frequency at these loci among T-cells from human and animal donors. These assays suggested that mutant frequencies in humans go up with age from about 1×10^{-6} in young individuals to 1×10^{-5} in middle-aged and old individuals. In mice the mutant frequency appeared to be somewhat higher, that is, from about 5×10^{-6} in young animals to about 3×10^{-5} in middle-aged mice. However, in both mice and men these values could be underestimates, due to the loss of mutants in vivo or in vitro. Also, due to the great individual variation it was not possible with these assays to distinguish between a

linear and an exponential increase of mutations with age. However, most of the increase in mutation rate seems to occur at early age.

As yet, two attempts have been made to find a relationship between HPRT mutant frequency and biological rather than chronological aging. In 1986, researchers demonstrated an age-related increase in HPRT mutant frequency in splenic T cells from BALB/c mice. Interestingly, mutant frequency was the highest in those T-lymphocyte populations with the lowest capacity to produce interleukin-2 or to proliferate in response to mitogenic stimulation. In a more recent study mice were subjected to caloric restriction, the only intervention demonstrated to increase life span. Subsequently, HPRT mutant frequencies were found to increase with age at a significantly slower rate than in the ad libitum fed animals. Both these observations suggest that the level of accumulated somatic mutations reflects biological rather than chronological age.

With the development of transgenic mouse models harboring chromosomally integrated reporter genes, it became possible to directly test the somatic mutation theory of aging by measuring mutations in every organ and tissue in a neutral gene. The first results thus far obtained with some of these models indicate an age-related increase in mutant frequency from about 3×10^{-5} in mice of a few weeks old to $1-2 \times 10^{-4}$ in 24-month-old animals. Several different types of transgenic model systems equipped with reporter genes are now being used and a wealth of new, more accurate information can be expected on both mutation frequencies and spectra in different organs and tissues of these animals during aging. Interestingly, the recently emerged technology of generating mice with germline-inactivated genes (transgenic "knockouts") opens up the possibility to directly assess the influence of cellular and molecular defense systems, e.g., antioxidant defense, DNA repair pathways, on mutation rates and life span.

Other recent findings, made possible by the use of PCR-based techniques, have provided some insight into the possible relationship between somatic mutations and age-related pathophysiology. Using PCR to detect breakpoints, researchers have demonstrated the age-related increase of $t(14;18)(q32;q21)$ translocations in human B-lymphocytes. These translocations involve dysregulation of the *BCL2* gene resulting in a delay of programmed cell death (apoptosis), an important tumor-suppression mechanism. The chromosome 18 *BCL2* locus is the site of oncogenic translocations frequently observed in non-Hodgkin's lymphoma, suggesting a direct causal relationship between somatic mutation accumulation and the increased risk of the elderly for this form of cancer.

C. Mutational Hotspot Regions

By using single molecule PCR amplification, researchers have demonstrated a very high rate of spontaneous (germline and somatic) mutations altering the length of minisatellite loci in the human and mouse genome (10^{-2}–10^{-1} rather than 10^{-6}–10^{-5} at the HPRT locus). Like most of the about 97% noncoding DNA, repeat elements like mini- and microsatellites are often considered as junk without function. However, with the discovery that many gene regulatory elements lie in or among repetitive sequences, this view has been reevaluated. Interestingly, an association has been reported between rare alleles of a minisatellite repeat locus close to the *H-RAS1* proto-oncogene and cancer. This association was explained in terms of a possible interaction of the (mutated) repeat element with transcriptional regulatory factors activating the proto-oncogene. Another example of repeat elements involved in transcriptional regulation is human type-1 diabetes. This form of diabetes appeared to be strongly associated with short alleles of the minisatellite in the 5′-flanking region of the human insulin gene. Recently, the repeat was shown to be capable of transducing transcriptional signals in pancreatic β-cells, with a lower activity for the short alleles.

Clearly, deletional mutations at such hypermutable loci can have profound effects on gene expression. Thusfar, the potential role of minisatellite genetic instability in aging has not been extensively investigated. It should be noted, however, that as early as 1972 a decrease in rRNA gene copy number in the genome of both aging beagle dogs and aging humans was reported. On the basis of similarities in their organization (both minisatellites and rRNA genes are organized in tandem), it is not inconceivable that deletional mutations that result in gene copy loss are generally associated with aging.

A related form of genetic instability is triplet repeat expansion. Expansion of certain trinucleotide repeat sequences has been linked to a number of inherited diseases in humans. These sequences have been shown

to be mitotically and meiotically unstable. The expanded CTG allele, which causes myotonic dystrophy, has been shown to progress toward larger expansion with age with an increased size heterogeneity in peripheral blood leukocytes. As yet it is unknown if triplet repeats, which are undoubtedly present in a large number of genes in the mammalian genome, spontaneously undergo expansion with age, thereby causing some of the adverse effects that have been associated with the diseases in which they were first discovered.

A most interesting region of extremely high mutation rate includes the vasopressin locus in postmitotic neurons of the hypothalamus. It was observed that in the homozygous (di/di; diabetes insipidus) Brattleboro rat the single base deletion that is the cause of the disease was restored with time by deletion mutations restoring the reading frame. These mutations in the vasopressinergic neurons of the rat were shown to be present at the exceptionally high frequency of 10^{-3}–10^{-2} in 20-month-old rats. They appeared to involve a novel mutational event, that is, the deletion of a GA-dinucleotide from two GAGAG motifs. This finding gains extra relevance when it is realized that these mutations occur in postmitotic cells. Most interestingly, the age-related increase in number of mutations was found to be enhanced by the permanent state of hyperactivity of the VP neurons of the di/di rat.

High-frequency mutational events in these cells were also found in PCR-based studies showing intergenic recombination between the vasopressin and the oxytocin gene, which are located on the same chromosome separated by only 10 kbp. These recombinational events were observed in 0.06–0.1% of vasopressinergic neurons and appeared to increase with age.

Studies with the transgenic animal models harboring integrated reporter genes described under B have indicated that in at least one transgenic line, with the lacZ-containing bacteriophage lambda vector integrated near the pseudoautosomal region of the X chromosome, spontaneous mutant frequencies were up to one hundred times higher than in all other lines tested. Clearly this region, which is also meiotically unstable, acts as a mutational hot spot for reasons as yet unknown.

Another unstable DNA region is formed by the telomeres. Telomeres are the tips of the chromosomes, containing an array of tandem repeats. They counter the effect of eukaryotic replication strategy, in which small gaps appear for the RNA primers used to initiate the 5' to 3' DNA strand, by adding telomeric repeats to chromosome ends through the enzyme telomerase. Telomeres also hide the chromosome ends from factors that normally act on DNA termini. Telomere shortening is a well-described phenomenon that occurs during in vitro cell senescence (the loss of proliferative capacity of normal cells during passaging), but also during in vivo aging, for example, in peripheral blood lymphocytes. In this respect, it has been postulated that telomere shortening would act as a molecular clock counting cell divisions and ultimately (because of the inactivation of an essential gene?) limit the replicative potential of primary cells.

Telomere shortening is caused by the absence of the enzyme telomerase in normal diploid cells. Telomerase is present in the germ line, in cell lines with indefinite growth potential and at least in some tumors. With regard to the latter it has been postulated that after some initial telomere shortening (demonstrated in several tumors, including breast cancers) telomerase activity is derepressed. This derepression of telomerase, which could in fact be facilitated by genetic instability (e.g., DNA rearrangements) caused or mediated by the telomere shortening itself, is hypothesized to subsequently lead to a stabilization of the telomeres and the establishment of immortal tumor cells. Telomere shortening, therefore, can be considered as a form of time-dependent genetic instability that can influence gene expression with age.

Finally, a major target for somatic mutations during aging, the mitochondrial genome, could very well turn out to represent the most important one in terms of potential functional consequences. The circular 16.5 kbp mitochondrial genome of mammals specifies 2 rRNAs, 22 tRNAs, and genes encoding 13 mitochondrial protein subunits. These genes are necessary to produce essential enzyme complexes (part of which are encoded in the nuclear genome) involved in oxidative phosphorylation, the ATP generating pathway of the cell. The close physical proximity of the mitochondrial genome to a major source of free radicals has greatly stimulated interest in the possibility that oxidative lesions accumulate rapidly with age in its DNA, resulting in decreased mitochondrial functioning. It was already mentioned that although oxidative damage accumulates much faster in mitochondrial DNA

than in nuclear DNA, a direct role of such chemical lesions in age-related functional decline should be considered unlikely. Fixation of the damage, however, would lead to a genuine and irreversible (except by mitochondrion or cell elimination) accumulation of genetic alteration in the form of point mutations and deletions.

A range of human diseases has been associated with mutations in mtDNA, many of which are deletions. By designing mutant-specific PCRs it was shown that some of these mutations also occur in the absence of disease and greatly increase with age (i.e., by more than 10,000-fold in aging human tissues). The rate of mutation accumulation in the mitochondrial genome seems to increase exponentially. Indeed, certain mtDNA deletions were found at levels of up to 10% of wild-type mtDNA in tissues of very old human individuals. Also nonspecific multiple mtDNA mutations were found to increase with age. This raises the question as to whether all these mutations together could be responsible for mitochondrial functional decline with age, like the decline observed by some investigators in mitochondrial respiratory chain activities in the human heart. As yet this question remains unanswered since it has thus far proved to be impossible to assess the *overall* level of mtDNA mutations in relation to one or more specific functional changes. Indeed, the possibility should be considered that the relatively high copy number in which mitochondria and their genomes are present in any given cell allows ample opportunity for compensation. It is in fact a major challenge to the proponents of somatic mutation theories in general to find ways of demonstrating a direct cause and effect relationship between the molecular events detected at the level of the DNA and specific age-related functional decline in the organ or tissue of interest. In view of its small genome such answers can be expected for the mitochondrial genome first.

D. Epigenetic Changes

In multicellular organisms all cells have the same genotype. Due to activation and/or inactivation of specific genes each cell type acquires a given pattern of gene expression that can be stably maintained during mitosis. The mechanisms to keep the cells locked in a particular regulated state are called epigenetic controls. They involve, first of all, protein–DNA complexes, which can be maintained or modulated in a variety of ways, including sequence-specific transcription factors, histones, and DNA methylation. Chromatin structure, therefore, is involved in transcriptional regulation, from the basic repeat unit, (i.e., the winding of the DNA around the histone octamer to form nucleosomes) to the complex interactions that create looping and bending and unusual DNA structures (e.g., Z-DNA, triplexes). Ultimately, chromatin structure is nucleotide-sequence dependent and it can be expected that random mutations, even at considerable distances away from the gene itself, will influence its regulation. Indeed, DNA regions some distance apart from the actual gene can interact in a cis-configuration to influence the activity of a particular gene.

Very little recent research on aging has been devoted to DNA conformational changes and other alterations in chromatin structure and dynamics. Virtually all studies in the past have addressed changes in the genome overall (e.g., chromatin repeat length, general accessibility to nucleases, histones, nonhistone proteins). The results varied, but overall increases in nucleosome spacing (chromatin repeat length) and a lower sensitivity to nucleases were observed in several tissues and organs of (mainly) rodents. These changes could be caused by changes at the level of the DNA primary structure (e.g., by damage and/or mutations). Age-related changes have also been reported in covalent modifications of histones and nonhistone proteins in mammalian tissues, for example, phosphorylation, acetylation and methylation.

A type of epigenetic mechanism that has drawn some attention is DNA methylation. The level and distribution of 5-methylcytosine may be involved in the regulation of gene expression. In general, hypermethylation has been found to be associated with transcriptional silence and vice versa. This is illustrated by housekeeping genes, transcriptionally active in all cell types and thought not to be regulated by methylation in view of the nonmethylated CpG islands tightly associated with their promoter. By contrast, CpG islands are methylated and nuclease insensitive on inactivated X chromosomes. There is some evidence for a general demethylation during aging, and age-related changes (increases and decreases) in methylation of specific genes have been demonstrated. Since these observations are based on the use of methyl-sensitive restriction enzymes (typically Mspl and Hpall), which screen only a small subset of CpG

doublets no definite conclusion can be drawn. Age-related demethylation could be a factor in age-related reactivation of inactive X-linked genes.

E. Cellular Defense against DNA Changes

To summarize the above, there is abundant evidence for changes in DNA sequence organization during aging. The frequency of such events seems to vary from genomic region to genomic region. Especially the mitochondrial genome, the telomeres, and certain repeat elements seem to undergo mutations at a high rate. In some instances high-frequency mutations have been reported in coding sequences. Defense against such a loss of functional template takes place at various levels (Table II). First, damage can be prevented at an early stage, for example, by the activity of antioxidant enzymes. Then, damage can be repaired through the complex system of DNA repair pathways. Finally, when all other defense systems threaten to be overwhelmed, the cell itself can be removed by programmed cell death or apoptosis. In this sense apoptosis is the ultimate mechanism for the maintenance of phenotypic fidelity in multicellular organisms. The three different lines of defense, prevention, repair and cellular elimination have been proposed to act as a network, and it now becomes clear that pathways are shared by mitosis and apoptosis and possibly also with DNA damage processing. [See CELL DEATH.]

Naturally, cellular defense systems function well at early age. However, as predicted by the evolutionary theory of aging, there is no reason to assume that the preservation of the genetic material in the somatic tissues until long after the reproductive period has a

Table II Molecular and Cellular Defense Systems

1. Free radical scavengers
2. DNA repair
3. The P-450 superfamily
4. Tumor-suppressor genes
5. Heat shock and other stress proteins
6. Regulatory cytokines (e.g., interferon, tumor necrosis factor, interleukins, other growth and regulatory factors)
7. The immunoglobulin superfamily
8. Apoptosis

high priority. The above-described increase in DNA mutations with age is therefore not surprising. Moreover, although there is no evidence at all that repair activities are overwhelmed at old age, causing an error catastrophy as originally hypothesized by Orgel, moderate declines in, for example, the rate of DNA repair have been reported. Suboptimal cellular defense systems that become increasingly less proficient with age can be expected to give rise to three major cellular endpoints: neoplastic transformation, cell death, and cellular senescence. The first two processes have been amply demonstrated to occur at an increasing rate with age. Cellular senescence, defined as the loss of various normal cellular functions without cellular transformation or cell death has thus far only been observed *in vitro* and is known as the "Hayflick" phenomenon. Hayflick made the landmark discovery that normal cells in culture lose the capacity to divide after a fixed number of population doublings, a process which is characterized by a number of other changes indicating functional loss. Interestingly, evidence was recently provided for the emergence of senescent cells in the skin from old human donors.

It is too early at this stage to generate a definitive "damage report" for the aging higher animal genome in terms of the total amount of information loss due to mutations of different types and sizes. For this purpose more data are needed about mutation frequencies and spectra at various loci of the genome in various cell types of humans or animals. On the basis of such data it should be possible to calculate the average amount of functional DNA template that is lost with age. Then it should also be possible to predict if the mutation load of a typical aged genome will influence patterns of gene expression in a way to significantly affect cell and tissue functioning.

III. CHANGES IN GENE EXPRESSION

A. Background

In contrast to the situation with respect to DNA changes, there is not much doubt that changes in gene expression directly reflect many of the deteriorative processes of aging. As mentioned before, age-related changes in gene expression can be due to mutations and other types of stochastic changes in DNA, but they can also be consistent and genetically pro-

grammed. Gene expressional changes can, for example, arise as late pleiotropic effects of differentiation and development, long-term environmental influences (e.g., viruses) and/or occur secondary to other age-related phenomena. Although, as argued before, a genetic program that unfolds to facilitate aging as an adaptive process is not supported by current evolutionary theories of aging, the occurrence of genetically programmed changes in gene expression, for example, in the form of ontogenetically determined pleiotropic cascades, cannot be ruled out. Table III lists some general characteristics of changes in gene expression with age, which will be discussed shortly.

A general age-related decline in transcription, that is, overall RNA synthesis as measured by the incorporation of radiolabeled precursors into RNA, has been observed to occur in a wide variety of organisms. Because the total RNA content does not seem to change, a decline in RNA turnover rate has been proposed. (A comparable decline has been found for protein translation, and because the levels of most proteins seem also to remain constant, a decline in protein turnover was suggested and also found.) The primary cause of such general declines in macromolecular synthesis and their ultimate consequence for the individual to cope with environmental stresses is unknown. In addition, there is no evidence for an increased error rate during transcription and/or translation.

Most attention has been paid to the expression of individual genes with age. Although gene expression can also be controlled post-transcriptionally and post-translationally, the relative concentrations of individual mRNAs primarily determine the cellular phenotype and it would be important to gain insight into the kinds of changes occurring at this level. Different kinds of changes can be envisaged. Genes can become

Table III Changes in Gene Expression with Age: General Characteristics

1. Decline of total transcriptional and translational activity
2. Decrease in total RNA and protein turnover
3. Changes in constitutive levels of many individual mRNAs and proteins (e.g., albumin, α2u-globulin)
4. Decrease in inducibility of various mRNAs and proteins (e.g., immediate early genes, acute phase proteins, P450, c-myc)

over- or underexpressed during aging, previously silent genes can become activated, and previously active genes can be silenced. One can also envisage some kind of qualitative change (i.e., sequence changes). It is important to distinguish nonconsistent from consistent changes in gene expression. Consistent changes are changes that are the same in every cell of a given type or group. They are usually under the control of a genetic program. During aging also nonconsistent changes in gene expression can be expected, for example, due to DNA mutations. Table IV lists some mechanisms that may underly age-related changes in gene expression.

B. Nonconsistent Changes in Gene Expression

Nonconsistent changes in gene expression during aging include the possibility of random gene activation or inactivation, as a direct effect of stochastic gene mutations. Dominant (in proto-oncogenes) and recessive (in tumor suppressor genes) mutations play an important role in cancer initiation and progression, and in that sense are they also indirectly relevant to aging. There is some doubt with respect to the importance of such recessive and dominant gene mutations in aging per se. Assuming a spontaneous mutant frequency of 1×10^{-4} in old cells on average (as illustrated above, there are large differences from locus to locus), one cell in 10,000 will have lost a particular gene. Such defects by themselves are unlikely to influence any given cellular function. In reality, most cellu-

lar functions are based on several genes rather than one, which would increase the DNA functional target size. However, taking into account that the effects of random gene inactivation are likely to be attenuated by complementation of function by different enzymatic pathways, metabolic cooperation between cells, and the ample redundancy at the cellular and tissue level, the possibility should be considered that the original concept of mutations directly influencing organ and tissue functioning does not play an important role in aging processes other than neoplasms.

Relatively recent insight into the regulation of gene expression suggests that mutational changes outside genes could potentially influence gene expression. Comparable effects could be exerted by damaged proteins involved in DNA conformation and the regulation of gene expression. An important consideration in this respect is that gene regulatory effects can be exerted over long distances. Indeed, the DNA and/or protein alterations do not need to be targeted to the gene or its immediate vicinity, but can impair gene functioning by their random accumulation in the transcriptionally competent environment. That is, although targeted mutations have the potential to inactivate a gene, random protein and/or DNA alterations over a distance of up to 10 kb could directly influence the regulation of that gene by causing, for example, local chromatin changes influencing binding of transcription factors, changes in DNA bending and looping, and altered nucleosome positioning.

It is presently not possible to accurately predict the magnitude of transcriptional interference of the above-described stochastic changes. It is reasonable to assume that most stochastic changes will cause a down regulation of the expression of individual genes. A typical example of stochastic down regulation or silencing of a gene is the age-related increase in the number of randomly distributed cardiomyocytes without cytochrome-c-oxidase activity in the human heart.

On the other hand, damage to DNA and/or protein involved in gene expressional control could also switch on rather than inactivate genes. Demethylation (see above) is a candidate mechanism for such events. There is some evidence for derepression of tissue-specific genes. It has been demonstrated that significant amounts of α- and β-globin mRNA were present in mouse brain and liver tissue and increased with age. An age-related derepression was also shown for

Table IV Changes in Gene Expression with Age: Possible Mechanisms

Level of regulation	Possible mechanisms
Chromatin structure	DNA mutation DNA conformation Accessibility of protein-binding sites DNA hyper- or hypomethylation
Transcription factors	Altered binding capacity Altered level of binding protein
mRNA processing and/or mRNA stability	Changes in RNA-binding proteins, e.g., mRNPs
Posttranslational protein alterations; changes in the proteolytic system	Modification, e.g., phosphorylation, oxidation, glycation, etc.

sequences homologous to endogenous murine leukemia virus in brain and liver of mice. This led these authors to propose their dysdifferentiation hypothesis of aging in which a gradual relaxation of gene control leads to derepression of previously nonexpressed genes. The phenomenon, however, does not seem to be universal, and has not been generally confirmed.

A clear case of derepression of a gene as a function of age is the observed reactivation of the X-linked ornithine transcarbamoylase (OTC) gene in aging mice. Histochemical detection showed patches of OTC-producing hepatocytes to occur 50-fold more frequent in old as compared to young mice. The authors suggested that this was due to a reduction in the level of DNA methylation, which has been implicated in the maintenance of X-chromosome inactivation. However, no age-related reactivation was observed for another X-linked gene, the hypoxanthine phosphoribosyltransferase (HPRT) gene, in human fibroblasts.

C. Consistent Changes in Gene Expression

In addition to accidental up or down regulations of gene activity, a number of well-described consistent changes in the expression of individual genes has been reported, mainly in experimental animals. Examples are the hormonally regulated α2U globulin gene, the androgen receptor gene, several acute phase protein genes in the rat and mouse liver, including albumin, P-450 genes, T-kininogen. Of many of these genes the function is incompletely understood. Some others are inducible genes, such as the acute-phase protein genes and the P-450 genes, which have been shown to undergo age-related impairment in the response of their mRNA levels to reach a maximally induced level. Another example of an impaired response is the induction of proto-oncogenes in the heart by hemodynamic stress. Like the rate of somatic mutation accumulation at the DNA level, this kind of consistent gene expressional changes with age were also found to be delayed in calorically restricted animals, suggesting that they are connected to the biological process of aging rather than chronological time. Finally, it should be noted that in addition to altered expression of individual genes, a number of genes have been studied, sometimes at detection limits of one mRNA copy per cell, without any evident aberrant gene expression, that is, changes in steady state mRNA level.

Consistent changes in gene expression could have a number of possible causes. First, the possibility cannot be excluded that they do result from stochastic damage to DNA and/or proteins interfering with proper gene regulation. For example, genes in mutational hot spot regions could undergo down regulation at a high frequency, which would eventually affect all cells in the tissue. Second, many expressional changes could be the result of stress induction, for example by DNA or protein oxidative damage. Then, gene expressional changes occurring at old age may be responses to processes (e.g., hormonal secretion) already determined during development. Such cascades are apparently initiated because they offer some advantage at young age. At later ages they could cause problems and be actually responsible for a number of age-related disorders (e.g., loss of androgen sensitivity due to a decrease in the androgen receptor gene or heart failure due to hemodynamic stress as a consequence of a down regulation of proto-oncogene expression). Finally, as already referred to, viral sequences may also be expressed preferentially at later ages.

To obtain a more complete picture of age-specific patterns of gene expression it is not sufficient to analyze individual genes. As pointed out by one researcher, among the possibly many genes showing quantitative changes with time, only a subset may represent primary determinants of the aging process. To find such genes it is necessary to analyze pleiotropic cascades and interactions between genes. It will be necessary to observe mRNA levels in relation to one another, to identify the genes involved, and to correlate the changes with functional alterations. With the emergence of methods of scale for studying gene expression (e.g., generation of expressed sequence tags [ESTs], differential display of mRNA and RNA arbitrarily primed polymerase chain reaction, the possibility of studying entire cell messages for changes in individual mRNA levels has come within reach.

IV. CHANGES IN GENOME ORGANIZATION AND EXPRESSION: A SYNTHESIS

Aging has been considered both as a programmed series of events and a stochastic process of damage accumulation. The evolutionary theory of aging is a logical explanation of senescent deterioration and death and excludes a genetically programmed series of events that actively cause aging as a purposeful process. Nevertheless, it cannot be denied that aging has programmatic aspects, as indicated by the many observed consistent and reproducible changes in gene expression. It seems important to reconcile the stochastic with the programmatic aspect of aging.

Such a reconciliation has been done before, namely for cancer. Indeed, stochastic somatic mutations are the ultimate cause of a series of events in which the cancer phenotype becomes increasingly more malignant and eventually shows a number of consistent alterations when compared with normal tissue. Many possible pathways that lead from the actual mutational event to the progressed tumor have been unraveled. Thus far this has not been the case for aging. The reason is that an aged individual, much more than a progressed cancer, is essentially a mosaic of cells; each individual cell in a tissue bears a different pattern of "scars." It is more difficult to explain this in terms of consistent patterns of phenotypic changes observed in a typical aged individual, but it is nevertheless possible.

Based on the data presently available it is possible to see the contours of the aging genotype as a prelude to the aging phenotype. Rather than a catalog of useful genes interspersed with functionless DNA, each chromosome is now viewed as a complex information organelle with sophisticated maintenance and control systems. In this concept of a genome, each part has a function, even the noncoding parts of genes, called introns. This would also explain why the introns of some genes show such high conservation between species. Such a holistic view of the genome would assign a variety of functions to noncoding DNA (e.g., structural maintenance, gene regulation).

Having extended the target for age-related changes to the whole genome rather than to a number of individual genes, it is also necessary to address the question of what kind of genetic changes are likely to play a role in determining the aging phenotype. In this context it is important to realize the most striking single characteristic of mammalian genomes: redundancy of genetic information. The most simple form of redundancy is copy number. With many gene copies present the effect of some loss has no immediate adverse effects. This could explain the tolerance of ribosomal RNA gene copy loss, found in tissues of both

beagle dogs and humans during aging, and the increase in inactivated mtDNA. Other forms of redundancy include the fact that more than one gene may specify any given cellular function. Finally, the existence of metabolic and other cellular networks allow the cell to accomplish similar endpoints through multiple overlapping pathways.

On the basis of these recent insights it is unrealistic to interpret the occurrence of changes in DNA and gene expression in the context of unique genes with unique effects, as has been the case in the earlier models of the somatic mutation theory of aging. Instead, as pointed out by Strehler, a more useful background for understanding aging would be in terms of a gradual loss of functional informational redundancy. Rather than the inactivation of unique genes with unique functions, one should think of an initially tolerable loss of genome structural integrity, which would be manifest as a loss of phenotypic flexibility. Indeed, rather than some form of massive loss of essential genes, it is more likely that aging is accompanied by a slow but inexorable loss of genetic redundancy. This would undoubtedly lead to subtle scattered changes in gene expression and in the efficiency of their regulation. Although primarily a stochastic process, this would rapidly take on some programmatic characteristics. The continuous randomization of the genome, by mutations in genes or in regions important in their regulation, unequivocally triggers the cell to respond. This response is programmatic and consists of species-specific stress and repair systems.

Although it would be premature to consider stochastic damage in DNA and/or proteins as a major cause of aging, it is at least a model that accounts for some of the observations that have been made on aged biological macromolecules. Meanwhile, it should be explicitly stated that there is no more evidence for a stochastic basis of aging according to the concept described above, than for a mechanism wholly based on programmatic changes, for example, in the form of delayed adverse effects of early determined processes.

ACKNOWLEDGMENTS

The thoughts expressed in this review were greatly influenced by ideas personally communicated to the author by Drs. Bernard

Strehler, Judith Campisi, and Huber Warner, as well as by the review articles from Franceschi (1989) and Finch (1993) listed in the bibliography. I thank Drs. Michael Boerrigter, Hans-Jorg Martus, and Jeanne Wei for critically reading the manuscript. This work was supported by NIH Grant 1PO1 AG10829-01.

BIBLIOGRAPHY

Ames, B. N., Shigenaga, M. K., & Hagen, T. M. (1993). Oxidants, antioxidants, and the degenerative diseases of aging. *Procedures of the National Academy of Science, USA, 90,* 7915.

Finch, C. E. (1993). Theories of aging. *Aging and Clinical Experimental Research, 5,* 277.

Franceschi, C. (1989). Cell proliferation, cell death, and aging. *Aging and Clinical Experimental Research, 1,* 3.

Kanungo, M. S. (1994). *Genes and aging.* New York: Cambridge University Press.

Mullaart, E., Lohman, P. H. M., Berends, F., & Vijg, J. (1990). DNA damage metabolism and aging. *Mutation Research, 237,* 189.

Rose, M. R. (1991). *Evolutionary biology of aging.* London: Oxford University Press.

Strehler, B. L. (1986). Genetic instability as the primary cause of human aging. *Experimental Gerontology, 21,* 282–319.

van Remmen, H., Ward, W. F., Sabia, R. V., Richardson, A. (1995). Gene Expression and Protein Degradation. In E. Masono (Ed.), *Handbook of Physiology: Aging,* pp. 171–234.

Vijg, J., & Gossen, J. A. (1993). Somatic mutations and cellular aging. *Comparative Biochemical Physiology, 104B,* 429.

Vijg, J. (1995). Somatic mutations and aging: Cause or effect? *Mutation Research* (special issue).

Wolffe, A. P. (1994). Inheritance of chromatin states. *Developmental Genetics, 15,* 463.

E

Economics: Individual

Timothy M. Smeeding

Syracuse University

AFI Adjusted Family Income: after tax cash income from all sources adjusted for differences in family size across the population.

AHEAD Aging Health and Asset Dynamics: a new and continuing longitudinal household panel survey of persons aged 70 and over in 1992 conducted by the University of Michigan's Institute for Social Research.

CBO Congressional Budget Office

GIS Guaranteed Income Supplement: Canada's income tested support program for low-income aged individuals.

GSOEP German Socio-Economic Panel: German continuing longitudinal household panel dataset patterned after the PSID.

HRS Health and Retirement Survey: new and continuing panel dataset for U.S. persons from 51–64 years of age in 1992 conducted by the University of Michigan's Institute for Social Research.

LCH Life Cycle Hypothesis: an economic hypothesis which argues that persons borrow when young, save when in middle age, and spend their savings in retirement such that overall lifetime income roughly equals lifetime consumption spending.

LIS Luxembourg Income Study: 28 country household income survey database spanning the 1970–1995 period and directed by the author at Syracuse University.

OASI Old Age and Survivors Insurance

OECD Organisation for Economic Co-operation and Development

PSID Panel Study of Income Dynamics: America's oldest individual and household panel dataset following the same individuals and their families since 1968, conducted by the University of Michigan's Institute for Social Research.

SCF Survey of Consumer Finances: cross-sectional household survey of income and wealth conducted by the Federal Reserve Bank Board of Governors.

SIPP Survey of Income and Program Participation: household panel survey dataset collected by the U.S. Bureau of the Census.

SSI Supplemental Security Income: America's means-tested support program for low-income aged and disabled.

The **ECONOMICS** of aged individuals deals with their economic resources relative to their economic needs. Resources include income and wealth; needs include outlays for normal living costs and extraordinary outlays such as the health-care costs associated with a significant illness. Household economic survey data is used to compare the aged to the nonaged at a point in time, over time, and across countries. On average, the aged are as well or better off than the nonaged. However, averages are the least interesting descriptors of the aged. Wealth, income, and poverty status differ greatly within the group called the aged.

Unless this heterogeneity is recognized, one cannot understand the economics of the aged.

I. INTRODUCTION

This article reviews the economic status of the aged—and the economics of aging—with economic welfare measured by economic resources available to individuals (income and savings) relative to their needs. Comparisons are made both over time and across countries regarding the poverty and affluence of the aged. In order to present these materials in a comprehensive way, I concentrate on income comparisons that provide the single best widely available measure of economic status at a point in time or over time. As a person ages beyond retirement, reliance on annual income flows is buttressed by reliance on savings. Thus, wealth is also an important factor in the economic well-being of the aged. Other vaid and important measures of economic status, such as consumption, are discussed, but their treatment is more circumscribed because of space and data limitations.

There are a variety of income concepts available to applied researchers, but economists have traditionally relied upon overall disposable personal income as the most important indicator of economic well-being for an individual. Cross-sectional, survey-based money income data are regularly available to researchers. Less readily available, but increasingly useful, are longitudinal "panel" microdata sets that permit researchers to follow individuals and their changing economic circumstances over time. In the United States, the leading examples of the latter are the Health and Retirement Survey (HRS), Panel Study of Income Dynamics (PSID), and the Aging Health and Asset Dynamics (AHEAD) Survey. Data from the Luxembourg Income Study (LIS) project allow for cross-sectional comparisons among several industrial democracies at two points in time (early and middle 1980s). More recent is a project that combines the PSID with the German Socio-Economic Panel (GSOEP), permitting for the first time cross-national comparisons of panel data.

Although money income is a useful measure of economic well-being, it serves largely as a proxy for the variable of ultimate interest: final consumption. To convert income estimates one needs to take account of three factors. First, economic responsibilities and needs can vary substantially among families de-

pending on their characteristics, particularly the number and age of family members. Second, many resources of considerable economic value—for example, homeownership and medical insurance—affect consumption but not money income. Thus, two elderly units with similar money incomes could, in fact, have very different levels of economic well-being; and two families that might generally be judged as having a similar level of economic well-being might have very different levels of money income. Third, current income may rise above or fall below long-run, or permanent, income. Savings or transfers may cushion consumption from these shocks and weaken the relationship between current income and current consumption.

The first two of these limitations can be overcome at least in part by trying to estimate the income value of nonmoney economic resources and by adjusting measures of income to reflect differences in needs based on using adult "equivalence scales." The adjustment is made by dividing the income of a given size and age unit by the relative number of equivalent adults normalized, for example, to a family size of three.

The third can be addressed by annuitizing measures of wealth and estimating their impact on income flows. This is a controversial concept, because decisions about what forms of wealth to include and how to annuitize them make a great difference in the final results, and because the same amount of wealth annuitizes to higher annual income the older the owner. Because there is no fully satisfactory way to combine income and wealth, I stop short of this aggregation and deal with wealth status separately in a later section of the article.

In general, this is a story of both change and variance. Although many Americans anticipate comfortable retirement years, many others age under a significant threat of economic deprivation. There have been dramatic improvements in the average economic well-being of older Americans over the last several decades, but many still subsist near or below the povery line. Using both income and wealth as measures of economic well-being, I present a picture of old age filled with both the bright lights of economic security and the dark tones of economic distress. I then go beyond descriptions of current older Americans to consider the likely economic well-being of next century's older population. Finally, I suggest a set of questions that emerges from our portraits of the current and future aged in America.

There have been and will continue to be major changes in the number, labor-force behavior, and economic well-being of older Americans. At the turn of the century, only 4% of the American population was aged 65 and over. By 1990 it was 13%. Over the next 40 years, the percentage is projected to increase to nearly 22% before leveling off. Perhaps more dramatic are changes in the retirement behavior of this growing population. Nearly one-half of all men aged 65 and over worked in 1950, as did 87% of the men aged 55–64. By 1985, these figures had dropped to 16% and 68%, and they have been steady since then. Older women's labor-force participation has been relatively constant (about 9% in 1992), whereas that of women aged 55–64 has risen from 27% in 1950 to 46% percent in 1992, mirroring the changes in work behavior of women in general. [See RETIREMENT; WORK AND EMPLOYMENT.]

Even while fewer older Americans were working, their economic status, on average, was on the rise, both absolutely and relative to the rest of the population. According to official poverty statistics, 29% of America's elderly were poor in 1966, compared with 13% of those under age 65. By 1993, the 29% dropped to 12%, and the 13% rose to 15%. (The lines crossed in the early 1980s, and there has been relatively little change since then.) Instead of being several times more likely to be poor, the elderly are now less likely than the rest of the population to be living in poverty. But within this encouraging aggregate picture remain many pockets of severe economic distress, especially among elderly minorities and women living alone.

II. INCOME CHANGE: MEANS, MEDIANS, AND INCOME SOURCES

The increased well-being of the elderly as a group over the past 20 years is now a well-documented fact. In 1993, the median income of households with a head aged 65 and over before taxes was $18,702—a gain of over 45% in the purchasing power of this group since 1971. Moreover, the 1993 median income was more than twice the level of the poverty threshold for an elderly couple ($8,740).

Since 1980, the elderly have experienced both a faster increase in average money income and a faster reduction of official (income-based) poverty than have the nonelderly. In large part, the increased relative position of the elderly is due to the slow growth in incomes of working families and the automatic wage indexing of initial benefits and price indexing of existing benefits in Social Security, or better, in the Old Age and Survivors Insurance Program (OASI). Most of this gain took place by 1985. By 1991, real median household money income was below the 1986 value for householders both over and under age 65, though it fell by more for the nonaged (2.7 percentage points) than for the aged (1.3 percentage points). Income gains for the elderly relative to the nonelderly was not a phenomenon unique to the United States. It occurred to an equal or greater extent in Canada and the United Kingdom as well.

In fact, one can now make comparisons between the elderly and the entire population using a broader definition of income, which includes capital gains, plus fringe benefits, in-kind transfers, and implicit rent minus rent paid. Because the income distribution for both elderly and nonelderly is skewed, mean (or average) household income is higher than median household income. For instance, census cash income for all households with members age 65 or over had a mean value of $26,408 in 1991, but a median value of $18,183. Thus, medians allow us to compare the "middle" unit (family or household) in the distribution of elderly to its counterpart among the nonelderly, whereas means measure the average position regardless of the shape of the distribution.

Comparisons of income for the elderly to income for the entire population based on these data indicate that on a broader income basis, adjusting for differences in household size, the mean and median ratios of incomes of households with elders to incomes of all households are 1.05 and 1.02, respectively. In other words, on this basis, the elderly as a group are now as well off as are the nonelderly, as a group.

One of the most comprehensive studies of trends in family incomes since 1970 was completed by the Congressional Budget Office (CBO) in 1988. Using an equivalence adjusted family income (AFI) measure, CBO finds that median incomes for all families (and unrelated individuals) grew by about 20% over the 1970–1986 period. Differences in income growth among various groups are striking. Elderly childless families (largely married couples) and unrelated individuals experienced largely (nearly 50%) increases in real income. Much of the rapid growth in income among the elderly is directly attributable to increased Social Security benefits. Among all retired Social Security recipients, on average, real benefits rose from $3,730 in 1970 to $5,856 in 1986, (in 1986 dollars) an increase of 57%. Families with children did less well, experiencing a 13% increase in incomes, with all of this increase taking place by 1979. Since then real incomes have stagnated for this group. By 1986, childless elderly families had incomes that were substantially higher than that for families with children by their measure.

Over the past 30 years, the American system of income support for the aged has changed in nature and scope (Table I). The traditional "three-legged stool" of Social Security, asset income, and occupational pensions is intact and still well supplemented by earnings (Table I). Social Security grew in the 1970s (due to the 1972 benefit increases noted above) but has leveled off at 40% since 1976. Asset income grew to about a quarter of income by the mid-1980s, but fell to 21% in 1992. Occupational pensions continue to grow and are now about equal to assets as a proportion of income. Earnings continue to slowly decline as current retirement patterns maintain. And there is very little in the way of other incomes for the average American aged person. Other incomes, including private transfers and Supplemental Security Income (SSI), have been only 3% of aged incomes since 1982. [See PENSIONS.]

Table I   Percentage of Shares of Income from Various Sources during Selected Years[a]

| Year | Social Security | Assets income | Occupational | | |
			Pensions	Earnings	Other
1962	31.0	16.0	9.0	28.0	16.0
1967	34.0	15.0	12.0	29.0	10.0
1976	39.0	18.0	16.0	23.0	4.0
1978	38.0	19.0	16.0	23.0	4.0
1980	39.0	22.0	16.0	19.0	4.0
1982	39.0	25.0	15.0	18.0	3.0
1984	38.0	28.0	15.0	16.0	3.0
1986	38.0	26.0	16.0	17.0	3.0
1988	38.0	25.0	17.0	17.0	3.0
1990	36.0	24.0	18.0	18.0	3.0
1992	40.0	21.0	20.0	17.0	3.0

[a] Source: Social Security Administration (1995), p. 22.

III. VARIATION IN WELL-BEING

Despite these impressive gains on average, the key factor to be emphasized in investigations into the economic status of the elderly is their heterogeneity. Joseph Quinn captured the essence of this argument:

> Never begin a sentence with "The elderly are ... or The elderly do ..." No matter what you are discussing, some are, and some are not; some do, and some do not. The most important characteristic of the aged is their diversity. The average can be very deceptive, because it ignores the tremendous dispersion around it. Beware of the mean.

In particular, a major contributor to the rising average economic status for the elderly over time is the very fact that the group is changing. "New entrants" to the elderly group (those persons in households or families headed by a person just turning age 65) arrive with higher average income and wealth than persons leaving that group (those who die in any given year). Although this trend may someday change, over the past two decades, the average household (or family) incomes increased at a faster rate for the elderly as a group than for a specific cohort of elderly household heads over time. Ross et al. also indicated that between 1950 and 1980 successive cohorts of the elderly (families with heads age 65 or over) had increasingly higher ratios of unadjusted money income to needs at age 65. But their data also indicate a decrease in income relative to needs for each of these cohorts in old age.

Using panel data from the PSID to follow a sample of elderly families from 1969 to 1987 (and beyond) indicates that the ratio of income to needs falls after retirement for elderly couples in general, and for widows in particular. For instance, over the period 1969 and 1979, older persons who remained intact as married couples throughout the period experienced a drop of 23% in their ratio of money income to needs between 1 year prior to retirement and 2 years after retirement. The income-to-needs ratio for this same group fell by another 27% during the next 6 years, leaving the average retired couple just 50% as well off 8 years after retirement as they were 1 year prior to retirement. The situation is worse for female survivors (eventual widows) but not for male survivors (widowers) of retiring couples over this period. Seven to eight years after retirement, a widow's income to needs is only 40% as high as that of the preretirement couple. The lesson to be learned here is that when explaining trends in the economic status of the aged, it is important to carefully differentiate across types of studies (panels, cross-section), types of units (widows versus widowers versus couples), and age groupings (cohorts).

IV. POVERTY

Perhaps the most noteworthy accomplishment of the past 30 years is the large and sustained decrease in poverty among the United States elderly. Two useful points of comparison for the elderly in this context are the changing poverty status of children—the other major dependent group in society—and the poverty status of nonelderly adults. Poverty rates for elderly Americans have fallen, whereas those of children (as measured by the incomes of families with children) have increased since 1969. In fact, poverty rates of the elderly have been less than those of children since 1974, and less than the overall national rate since 1983. For the past decade, poverty among the aged has moved in line with poverty among other groups. In 1993, elderly poverty was at 12.2% (up slightly from the 11.4% rate recorded in 1989 and less than half of the 1969 rate of 25.3%), while that of children was 22.7% (the highest poverty rate for this group since 1964). The poverty rate of the aged is now the same as that of nonaged adults (12.4%).

A more detailed picture of poverty among the elderly reveals a diversity of poverty experiences across subgroups (Table II). The overall poverty rates for

the elderly discussed above fail to capture the fact that among the elderly poverty rates run from a low of 5.3% for elderly married males to a high of 21.4% for widowed females aged 65 and older. They also do not convey the fact that the poverty rate for black and/or Hispanic aged (who are 20% of the aged today and will be a much higher fraction next century) is two to three times higher than that for non-Hispanic Whites. For instance, in 1993 poverty among non-Hispanic white females age 65 and over was 13.7%, but 31% for black females and 25.3% for Hispanic females.

In the same way, elderly poverty rates vary tremendously by age. The data in Table II also indicate that, with the exception of widowed men, poverty rates among the elderly increase with age. Because elderly persons aged 85 and over are the fastest growing age group in the nation and these persons are 62% female, this pattern suggests some cause for concern. In any event, the considerable diversity in poverty experience among the elderly needs to be recognized by those who would draw policy implications from comparisons of overall poverty rates alone.

In contrast to income-based measures of economic status, following specific persons in families over a 10-year or longer time period yields a similar picture of economic vulnerability for older women. For instance, 35–41% of elderly women were likely to be poor in at least one year between either 1969 and 1979 or 1983 and 1988 as compared to 20% of women age 25–45. This same body of research suggests that widowhood is a major source of economic insecurity among United States aged women. In fact, using a longer term measure of poverty, these researchers find that a higher proportion of aged women are liable to remain poor over several years than are any other age group in the population. Interestingly, the transition to widow status for women is much less well protected than is the equivalent transition to widowerhood for men. Although these panel data studies are quite suggestive, they are hampered to some extent by relatively small samples of the aged. The new HRS and AHEAD panel data surveys should soon remedy this situation.

Moving to broader measures of economic well-being, for instance those including noncash income, capital gains, imputed rent, and other sources of income, we find lower overall poverty rates—both in absolute terms and relative to the overall poverty rate

Table II Poverty Rates among Subgroups of the Elderly in 1991[a,b]

Category of elderly	Age (%)			
	All 65 and over	65–74	75–84	85 and over
Total	12.2	97	14.9	20.2
Males (Total)	7.6	6.4	9.3	12.6
Male, married	5.3	4.2	7.2	11.4
Male, widowed	13.8	13.2	14.3	13.9
Females (total)	15.4	12.3	18.3	24.1
Female, married	5.7	4.7	8.1	—
Female, widowed	21.4	19.5	22.1	24.4

[a] Source: House Ways and Means Committee (1992).

[b] Estimates show percent of persons poor in each group using the same official United States poverty measures employed in Figure 1.

for the entire population—among the aged. For instance, among those 65 and over, poverty rates can be as low as 6.1% once imputed rent is taken into account. This contrasts with a comparable poverty rate of 10.3% for the population at large.

Although many studies employing expanded income measures find less elderly poverty, none of these studies modify the needs standard to which the expanded income measure is compared. Very little is known about the consumption needs of the elderly. However, we do know that medical care subsidies and medical care needs are highly correlated. To count as "income" a substantial medical care subsidy (e.g., Medicare or Medicaid), while ignoring the additional out-of-pocket costs associated with poor health, may produce an unbalanced view of true economic well-being. We now turn to these issues. [See HEALTH CARE AND SERVICES.]

V. NEAR POVERTY AND NEEDS

The measures of poverty status presented to this point have used various definitions of income, but all have relied on the official United States poverty definition in which the "needs" of the aged (and nonaged) are measured by the Orshansky food multiplier technique developed 30 years ago. "Food times three" adjusted for age and family size differences results in poverty lines for the aged that are 8 to 10% below those of the nonaged, and which exclude several important changes in the consumption bundle of the aged since that time. Although little research has focused on this issue, the initial efforts indicate that health-care expenses of the aged have changed drastically since the 1960s. For instance, the aged now spend a greater share of income on acute health expenses (15%) than they did before the advent of Medicare (11%). Even among poor aged households—who are presumably protected by Medicaid as well as Medicare—acute health-care expenses exceeded 20% of income in 1987.

The income value of homeownership to the aged is also open to some question. Poverty rates among the aged fall by a third or more when one imputes as income the rental value of home equity (defined as market value minus mortgage owed). Because 57% of poor, aged, single women are homeowners, such an imputation produces a fairly large drop in the

poverty rate of this critical group. On the other hand, the United States General Accounting Office calculates that one-half of U.S. aged homeowners spend more than 45% of their incomes on property taxes, utilities, and home maintenance. Of these factors, the Census Bureau adjusts only for property taxes, but not for any additional measure of needs, particularly for health care.

Small differences in "needs" levels for the aged make a large difference in measures of poverty because many of the low-income aged were moved only a short distance beyond the poverty line by changes in average OASI benefit levels and benefit increases over the past 20 years. Near poverty among the elderly (those between 100 and 125% of the poverty line), has decreased only slightly since 1970 as compared to the official poverty rate. Among elderly women householders (largely single women living alone) the percentage who are near poor has actually increased slightly. And, although the aged are less likely to be poor than the population as a whole, they are more likely to have incomes under 125 or 150% of the poverty line than are younger households.

Although average income amounts among the elderly changed only slightly over time (Table I), they belie the fact that incomes vary substantially by type across the income distribution at any point in time (Table III). The bottom quintile in Table III includes both poor and near poor aged. Here Social Security makes up more than 80% of total income. Earnings, asset income, and occupational pensions are negligible. In contrast, the top quintile of elders have a four-legged stool, relying on assets, pensions, and earnings more than Social Security. Here social retirement is only one-fifth of total income.

The high fraction of aged low-income families that rely on Social Security suggests an important reason

Table III Shares of Income among the Aged in the Lowest and Highest Quintile of Money Income, 1992[a]

	Bottom quintile (%)	Top quintile (%)
Social Security	81	20
Asset income	4	29
Occupational pensions	2	22
Earnings	1	27
Other	12	2

[a] Source: Grad (1995).

for additional knowledge that measures needs for single, aged individuals as opposed to aged couples. The Social Security (OASI) benefits of a retired couple are reduced when either the husband or the wife dies. The reduction depends on past earnings and retirement ages for each person. The reduction is usually 33% but, in the case of spouses each claiming their own benefits, it can be 50%. In contrast the poverty line for an aged single person is only 20% less than the poverty line of an aged couple. Owing to the importance of OASI as an income source to low-income widows, a large decrease in OASI can mean a fall into poverty. Research to establish the "correct" equivalence scale is in its infancy but should be pursued vigorously.

VI. INTERNATIONAL COMPARISONS

A. Income and Poverty

Thanks to the research opportunities created by the Luxembourg Income Study (LIS) and by the PSID-GSOEP comparable panel data project, we are able to compare the elderly and other population groups across countries. The data underlying these comparisons consist of national income survey data sets that have been made comparable by rearranging and reclassifying incomes.

The first question these data can answer is how well off the aged are relative to the average household in a society. Comparisons are made on the basis of disposable income, including all forms of cash income (earnings, private pensions, property income, and government transfers net of income and payroll taxes) adjusted for differences in the size and composition of households. Each country's median income for the aged is divided by its counterpart for the entire population.

On this basis the United States elderly had a relative median income in the middle 1980s that exceeds the average relative median income of the aged of the entire group by only 2 percentage points (85 versus 83%). The aged in France, Germany, and The Netherlands had higher relative incomes. In contrast, United States aged couples were the most affluent group by far, owing to their relative youth and to the successively higher real economic status of each generation of United States adults turning 65 (see above). But

United States elderly women living alone have incomes that are far below the "other country" average, with only Australian single women being worse off.

Measures of "permanent" disposable income for German and United States aged over the 1983–1988 period show much the same pattern. Permanent income is estimated as average total income over the 1983–1988 period. Permanent incomes for men in the United States and Germany were 98–101% of the adjusted mean. However, permanent incomes for women in the United States were only 77% of the national average as opposed to 94% for German women.

Poverty rates among the elderly are measured relative to various fractions of adjusted median overall income in each nation in Figure 1A. The United States poverty lines for single persons and couples are about 41% of adjusted median income. And so the 40% poverty line estimates in Figure 1 are close to the official United States government poverty estimates. Different fractions of median income (e.g., the 50% median rate, which is equivalent to the United States 125% "near poverty" figure, and the 60% rate commonly used in Scandinavian countries) produce different poverty rates in each bar. However, with the exception of only Australia using 60% of the median measure, the United States has everywhere the highest elderly poverty rates of the countries studied. The diversity of economic circumstances among the United States aged extends to poverty as well as affluence. Of all the countries studied, the United States does the least adequate job of preventing poverty among the elderly.

The PSID-GSOEP comparisons reveal a similar pattern of cross-national differences. The percentage of elderly women who are ever poor (using a 50% of adjusted median income poverty rate) in Germany is half that in the United States over the 1983–1988 period. In the same vein, the percentage of elderly women who are poor on a permanent income basis is 28.7% in the United States compared to 6.6% in Germany.

The LIS data can be extended to examine further the relative poverty of single women. I noted above the very large difference in the United States between the median adjusted income of elderly married couples and the median adjusted incomes of single aged women living alone. A natural question to ask is

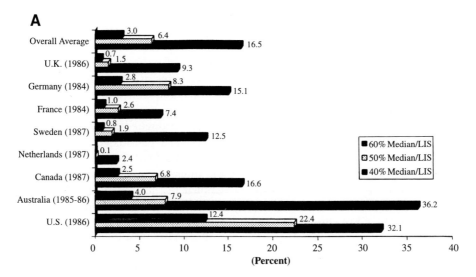

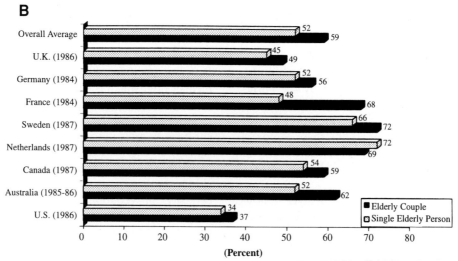

Figure I (A) Poverty rates among elderly persons—percent of persons with incomes below a given fraction of adjusted median income. Income is adjusted by using the simple equivalence sale, which counts the first person in the household as 1.0 and all other persons as 0.5, regardless of age. Elderly households are those with heads aged 65 or older. Hence a single aged person needs 50% of the income of a three-person family household, while an aged couple needs 75% as much to reach the same standard of living. Poverty rates are percentage of persons aged 65 and over whose household disposable after-tax incomes fall below the specified percentage of adjusted median income. The United States poverty line was 40.7% of adjusted income in 1986. (B) Minimum old age benefit as percent adjusted median income. Minimum benefits as published by the Organisation for Economic Co-operation and Development (OECD) were compared to adjusted median income after adjusting for national price changes. For the United States, the figures include the SSI benefit, plus the OASI disregard, plus food stamps as indicated in U.S. Congress (1992). For other nations the combination of benefits was determined by OECD. In the Netherlands and Sweden, benefits are adjusted for income taxation. Simple row averages exclude missing values.

whether the poverty rates for these groups reflect this difference. In the United States, household poverty rates for aged married couples are below those for the nonaged population at large, whereas those for single aged women are above the average. The difference between the two groups' poverty rates was 11.6 percentage points in 1986, with elderly couple rates at 6.0% and elderly single women at 17.6%. In no other country do we find this same pattern. In every country except Germany (where the differences are small) aged poverty rates—for both single women and couples—are below nonaged poverty rates. Hence, elderly single women in the United States are not only the poorest group among the aged, they are also the only group of aged with poverty rates significantly higher than the population as a whole.

Beyond the United States, only in Canada do we find large positive differences in poverty rates between aged women living alone and elderly couples. However, the differences are much smaller in Canada, and the poverty rates for both groups are below the rate for nonaged persons. In Sweden, The Netherlands, France, and the United Kingdom, poverty rates for both groups are very low and nearly equal. In Australia, Germany, and the United Kingdom, aged single women living alone actually have lower poverty rates than do aged couples.

B. The Safety Net for the Elderly

Every modern country fights poverty among the elderly differently. The floor for income of the aged in the United States is determined by a mix of Supplemental Security Income (SSI), OASI, and food stamps, but presumably primary reliance is placed on SSI. The sum of SSI benefits, plus the $20 monthly disregard for OASI or other unearned income, plus the value of food stamps equals 34% of adjusted median income for a single aged person, and 37% for a couple (see Fig. 1B). These figures are far below those found in other nations; the average benefit for all countries is 53% for a single person and 59% for couples. Many have pointed out that we "patch together" the safety net for the aged in the United States. The key point, however, is that in the aggregate it does not compare to the income support in other nations, even when we incorporate the $20 disregard for unearned income and near cash benefits like food stamps.

Countries that rely on a means-tested (welfare) ap-

proach such as Australia and Canada have higher guarantees. In addition, Canada does not have a wealth (or assets or resources) test, so there are no "income eligible" but "asset ineligible" aged. Australia has only a means-tested system with large asset disregards and a high guarantee. Between 1981 and 1987, Canada instituted a number of reforms aimed particularly at aged single women living alone. These reforms include a higher Guaranteed Income Supplement (GIS is the Canadian equivalent to SSI) with several specific types of income disregards (e.g., veteran's pensions, family allowances) and a 50% benefit reduction rate for countable income (which includes Canadian Old Age Social Security benefits, property income, and occupational pensions). As with SSI in the United States, many provinces supplement basic GIS benefits. The net result of these changes was to reduce the poverty rate among Canadian aged women by more than one-half between 1981 and 1987.

European nations are more likely to rely on universal social retirement pensions with a relatively high minimum benefit and only a small earnings- (or contribution) related second tier. Even the lowest benefit European nation, the United Kingdom, has a floor 11 to 12 percentage points of median income above the United States minimum benefit. European elderly rely less on occupational (private or public sector, employment related) pensions, and less on asset income than do the United States aged. Hence, both low-income aged households and high-income aged households are more scarce in these nations than in the United States.

VII. WEALTH

A. Role and Importance

Among the very aged, it can be argued that wealth plays an equal, if not greater, role than income in determining economic status. We have already seen the effect that imputed rent from the major asset of the aged—their home—has on relative economic status and on poverty. Wealth plays other important roles as well. For instance, the stock of financial wealth—or lack thereof—has an important effect on the flow of income; interest and dividends make up 29% of the incomes of the top quintile of aged, but only 4% of the incomes of the bottom quintile which includes the poor and near poor aged (Table III). Financial assets also serve as an eligibility barrier to some programs (e.g., Medicaid). Wealth gains provide the wherewithal for the aged to transfer assets to children, grandchildren, and for other useful purposes (e.g., vacations or medical bills for acute and/or chronic health care). Here I deal with what is known about the distribution and disposition of real assets of the elderly—especially financial, but also nonfinancial assets.

The 1988 SIPP wealth data for the aged present a snapshot of the composition of the net worth of the elderly. Home equity represents about 40% of total net worth among those 65 and over. Interest earning assets are 29% of the total, whereas rental property, real estate, stocks, and mutual funds were another 17% of net worth. The rest (14%) is composed of motor vehicles, boats, and other minor categories. Housing is the most equally distributed asset among the elderly, followed by interest earning assets. Most other assets—rental property, real estate, stocks, bonds, mutual funds—are concentrated among the high income and high wealth households headed by an elderly person.

Economic theory, in the form of the life cycle hypothesis (LCH) pioneered by Modigliani, suggests that the aged will draw down their assets as they age. Cross-sectional evidence indicates that assets decline uniformly with age. If the mean wealth of persons aged 65–69 in 1988 is indexed to equal 100, the mean wealth of those 70–74 was only 66, and that of persons 80 or over was 41.

Studies based on the Survey of Income and Program Participation (SIPP) indicate that the elderly do dissave (in real terms), at a slow average rate of 3.9% per year. These studies also suggested that singles decumulate faster than do couples, and that the older aged decumulate faster than do younger aged. However, the reasons for asset decumulation are not easily identified. Moreover, because assets decumulate at very low rates most aged will have net positive balances at death. It could be that the aged plan to leave bequests to their children or make *inter vivos* gifts. Another very real possibility is that assets are kept to meet large expected expenses (vacation cruise, new car, new roof for the house), or unexpected consumption demands (large medical bills). Finally, it could be that the aged transfer assets in large lumps (i.e.,

voluntarily draw them down) to qualify for Medicaid assistance with nursing home expenses. The exact reasons and means by which the aged draw down assets are still largely a mystery.

B. Joint Distribution of Income and Wealth

Recent panel data based research has shown that the pattern of rising income inequality found in the 1980s is reinforced by changes in wealth inequality among these same persons. By and large, the 1983–1989 SCF, the 1984–1989 PSID joint income and wealth data, and the 1984–1988 SIPP data each yield three major findings for older households:

1. The income distribution among older households is more unequal that among the rest of the population and did not change appreciably over this period.
2. Liquid asset holdings increased in value during the 1980s across the entire size distribution of wealth, but especially so at the top of the distribution.
3. Liquid asset holdings among the bottom 30% of households (ranked by income or wealth) are not large. For example, in the bottom 30% of PSID households (ranked by net worth) they grew from $300 to $500 over the 1984–1989 period.

In fact, one study shows that in the bottom 20% of households ranked by income, heads aged 65 or over (75 or over) had a median net worth of $25,220 ($25,291), of which all but $3,536 ($4,474) was represented by home equity in 1988. In contrast, the elderly aged 65 and over (75 and over) in the top quintile of the income distribution had median total net worth of $343,015 ($390,649) and median financial assets of $208,789 ($252,082). Several studies find that only 10–15% of the aged poor had any significant wealth holdings, and various methods for amortizing wealth reduce aged poverty rates by 20% at most. Wealth holdings also vary dramatically by race, with Blacks having only small fractions of the wealth of Whites. The basic conclusion drawn from these studies is that low-income aged generally have low wealth, and financial wealth is very unequally distributed among the aged by income and by race.

VIII. FUTURE ECONOMIC STATUS OF THE AGED

Evidence from the 1950 through 1980 censuses and from wealth surveys taken between 1962 and 1989 suggest that the elderly turning 65 during the next decade will begin their retirement years better off, on average, than prior cohorts. This age group (aged 22–32 in 1960) had the good fortune to be in their prime working years during the period of rapid wage earnings growth in the 1960s, to have their house values soar during the 1970s and early 1980s, and to profit from the high real interest rates and stock market boom of the 1980s. The SCF indicates that the mean net worth of those aged 55–64 in 1983 was 84% above the national mean net worth. Earlier surveys in 1962 and 1969 indicated that the 55–64-year-olds in those years (whose survivors are among today's elderly) had net worth holdings which ranged only from 39–56% above the average. The generation retiring in the near future will also have more long-term two-earner families and hence will receive more private pension and Social Security benefits than any preceding generation since. Simulation estimates indicate that 57% of aged couples, 41% of unmarried men, and 32% of unmarried women received some form of private pension in 1990. These simulations also forecast large increases in these ratios to 86, 70, and 50%, respectively, by 2010.

On the other hand, forecasts based on averages and trends can be misleading. For instance, recent reductions in pension coverage are not reflected in the projections reported above. Other authors have noted a shift in pension coverage from defined benefit (which still provides about 70% of primary coverage, down from about 90% in 1975) to defined contribution. What this change will mean for future pension coverage at retirement and the economic well-being of the elderly is unknown.

Dynamic simulation models require assumptions about wage growth, pension coverage, and survivors benefits, none of which may turn out to be true. Moreover, the receipt of an occupational pension says nothing of its value or generosity now or in the future. What is known is that private pensions are at best partially indexed and that their distribution is highly skewed. Table III suggests that employer pensions provided 20% or more of aggregate income only for

aged households in the top 20% of the income distribution. The bottom two quintiles of the aged, ranked by household income, received only 2 and 8% of their respective incomes from these sources.

Hence, despite the advantages that the aged of the 21st century are likely to enjoy, they will face many of the same pitfalls that plague the elderly today. The Social Security retirement age for "full" benefits will increase from 65 to 66, and then to 67, early in the next century, and there have been legislative attempts to make similar changes in Medicare eligibility. The aged continue to receive the highest health-care finance subsidies, but they also have the greatest need for health care. Because health care for the aged is quite expensive, both to the individual and to society, the sustainability of the current level of Medicare outlays is open to serious question. Changes must either come in the form of higher payroll taxes on the young and/or higher out-of-pocket outlays among the old.

And, despite the rising economic independence of women, only 38% of new Social Security recipients in 1990 claimed benefits based on their own earnings history, exactly the same fraction as in 1960. Thus, survivor benefits will continue to be an important issue.

Given the uncertainties about future Social Security and pension benefits, I am reluctant to speculate about the future economic status of the aged. In addition, I argue that forecasts for the "elderly" as a group are misleading. The "elderly" at any time can be categorized into roughly four age groups—the 55–64-year-olds (near aged), 65–74-year-olds (young aged), 75–84-year-olds (transition years of "middle age" elderly), and those aged 85 and over (the oldest old). Each of these cohorts has faced and will continue to face distinctly different prospects as they age. Each group had different life cycle income experiences during key periods of their lives. Moreover, within each of these cohorts are highly skewed distributions of income and wealth.

IX. SUMMARY AND RESEARCH NEEDS

A consensus view of those studying incomes among the aged finds them to be on average at par with those of the nonaged, but with a wider variance. Poverty rates among the United States aged are below those found in the population at large, but are high relative to international norms. Although these findings vary slightly depending on data sets and income measures, they seem robust enough to raise the quesiton, How should the system be modified to ensure adequate income support for the remaining low-income old, especially aged single women who are rapidly increasing in number and who have historically been at a higher risk of poverty? Related to this issue, research on the income (and consumption) needs of the aged and how they vary between single individuals and couples living alone is sorely needed.

The skewness of the distribution of wealth among the aged mirrors and reinforces that found in the incomes of this group. However, little is still known about how the aged decumulate assets and why. This is a prime area of interest that needs to be addressed to prevent such declines in the future.

Although there is good reason to believe that the current generation of elderly will be in better shape than previous generations, the retirement income status of the baby boom generation, which will begin to retire in 2005, less than 10 years from now, may be in some doubt. The extent to which researchers can count on the experiences of today's elderly to predict the experience of future cohorts of aged is therefore open to question. The uncertainty about the future of occupational pension entitlements is one example of this issue.

As is evident, the United States can learn much about the economic status of its aged by comparing them to the experiences of other nations. In the process, the question arises, Should researchers continue the traditional categorical approach, or should they strive to develop a more universal program to support the aged? Should efforts address improving existing programs, such as Social Security, SSI, Medicare, Medicaid, food stamps, and housing allowances, and focus policy initiatives on specific subgroups in need, such as the elderly, children, minorities, widows, and the disabled? Or should the focus be on people in need, regardless of their demographic characteristics?

Public policy initiatives concerning the elderly have been a qualified success. Cash programs, such as Social Security and SSI, have lifted many older Americans out of poverty. Employer pensions, subsidized by tax legislation, have lifted some of them far from the poverty line. New financial institutions and favorable tax laws have encouraged private accumulation for retirement years, and there are now serious proposals to "privatize" a portion of Social Security by investing some fraction of contributions in private assets.

The net result of these programs is an income distribution in old age that resembles the distribution earlier in life: those with higher earnings in middle age will have higher Social Security and pension benefits and higher wealth when they retire. The United States tolerates more inequality than other industrialized nations throughout the life cycle. U.S. problems stem not from means or medians but from variance. On average, American elderly are just fine, but to focus on the average misses the most important part of the story.

BIBLIOGRAPHY

Burkhauser, R., & Smeeding, T. (1994). *Social Security reform: A budget neutral approach to reducing older women's disproportionate risk of poverty.* (Policy Brief No. 2). Center for Policy Research, The Maxwell School, Syracuse University, Syracuse, NY.

Grad, S. (1995). Tables provided on August 21. Washington, DC: Social Security Administration.

Holden, K., & Smeeding, T. (1990). The poor, the rich and the insecure elderly caught in-between. *Milbank Quarterly/Health and Society, 68,* 191–219.

Holtz-Eakin, D., & Smeeding, T. (1994). Income, wealth and intergenerational relations. In S. Preston & L. Martin (Eds.), *The demography of aging* (pp. 102–145). Washington, DC: National Academy of Sciences Press.

National Academy of Sciences. (1995). *Measuring poverty: A new approach.* Washington, DC: National Academy of Sciences Press.

OECD. (1988). *Reforming public pensions.* Paris: Organization of Economic Cooperation and Development.

Quinn, J. (1987). The economic status of the elderly: Beware the mean. *Review of Income and Wealth, 33,* 63–82.

Quinn, J., & Smeeding, T. (1993). The present and future economic well-being of the aged. In R. Burkhauser & D. Salisbury (Eds.), *Pensions in a changing economy* (pp. 5–18). Washington, DC: Employee Benefit Research Institute.

Ruggles, P., & Moon, M. (1994). The needy or the greedy? Assessing the income support needs of an aging population. In T. Marmor, V. Greene, & T. Smeeding (Eds.), *Economic security and intergenerational justice: A look at North America* (pp. 207–226). Washington, DC: The Urban Institute Press.

Smeeding, T. (1994). Effects of a changing distribution of income on income security and health care models. In *Proceedings of the Conference on Future Income and Health Care Needs and Resources for the Aged* (pp. 209–238). Washington, DC: Public Trustees of the Social Security Administration.

Smeeding, T., Torrey, B., & Rainwater, L. (1993). *Going to extremes: Income inequality, poverty and the U.S. aged in an international perspective.* Unpublished manuscript, The Maxwell School, Syracuse University, Syracuse, NY.

Social Security Administration. (1995). *Fast foods and figures about Social Security.* Washington, DC: U.S. Government Printing Office.

Taeuber, C. (1992). Sixty-five plus in America. *Current Population Reports,* (series P-23, No. 178, October). Washington, DC: U.S. Bureau of the Census.

U.S. Bureau of the Census. (1995). Income, poverty and valuation of noncash benefits: 1993. *Current Population Reports,* (Series P-60, No. 188), February. Washington, DC: U.S. Government Printing Office.

U.S. Congress House Ways and Means Committee. (1992). *Green book: Background material and data on programs within the jurisdiction of the House Ways and Means Committee.* March. Washington, DC: U.S. Government Printing Office.

Economics: Society

Yung-Ping Chen

University of Massachusetts, Boston

The expansion and contraction of social programs for older people and for the population in general occur periodically. Changes in the direction have often been ascribed to political and ideological movements, but often neglected is the powerful role of **ECONOMICS** in the formulation of social policy.

I. INTRODUCTION

When the direction of social policies changes, people often ascribe it to changes in ideology or politics. Frequently lost in the consideration is the powerful role economics plays in social policy. Since the mid-1970s, the economic growth rate has slowed and, as well, the rate of increase in the financial capability of both private and public sectors. From an economic perspective of demand and supply, one may view the need for funding social programs as the force of demand, and the capacity of government to provide them as the force of supply. When the economy is growing more slowly, it will be more difficult to pay for these programs because resources are becoming scarcer; in other words, demand outruns supply, and it aggravates the problem of scarcity.

Scarcity, with all of its social, political, and economic consequences and implications, is such a persuasive concept that it appears to have been frequently taken for granted or treated as an assumption. Although the competition for and distribution of material and human resources obviously influence human behavior and social policies, the notion of scarcity as such is often ignored during discussions of social policy changes. Frequently, suggestions about policies have been branded as "political." Recognizing that the political and legal forces in society do indeed influence the types of human behavior and the directions of social policies, this article attempts to explain that economic factors greatly influence politics and policies. Politics may be the vehicle for change in policies, but it is the underlying fiscal capacity of government that drives politics and policies, dictating whether legislators support a program's expansion or its contraction. In short, political moves and changes in social policies in one direction or the other are heavily influenced by economic consideration, tempered by social and political philosophies.

Thus, now (1995–1996), both the Republican-dominated Congress and the Democratic President are advocating cuts in Medicare and Medicaid with cuts in taxes. They are prompted by a slowing economy and declining fiscal capacity of government, briefly explained in section II.B.

The United States is not unique in this budgetary quandary. Similar problems exist in Latin America, Eastern Europe, the former Soviet Union, and countries of the Organisation for Economic Cooperation and Development (OECD). Scandinavia, the mecca of social programs for the elderly, has not escaped, either. In 1994, Sweden's opposition Social Democratic Party ran on a platform of raising taxes and cutting both social and defense spending in order to reduce bulging budget deficits and massive national debt. Remarkable is the fact that this center-left political party had been responsible for building one of the world's most advanced welfare states. Even more significant is that it won the national election.

Three decades prior, Great Society programs, which included antipoverty measures and health care benefits, largely resulted from the fiscal capacity to accommodate social needs, as briefly described in Section II.A.

II. FISCAL CAPACITY OF THE GOVERNMENT

A. Fiscal Capacity in the 1960s

During the 25 years between 1940 and 1965, both the young-age and old-age dependency ratios were rising. Whereas the young-age dependency ratio increased from 0.582 (582 persons under the age of 20 per 1000 persons between the ages of 20 and 64) in

1940 to 0.764 in 1965, the old-age dependency ratio rose from 0.116 (116 persons age 65 or over per 1000 persons between the ages of 20 and 64) in 1940 to 0.182 in 1965. As a consequence, the total dependency ratios increased from 0.698 in 1940 to 0.946 in 1965 (see Table I).

The concurrent increase in old-age and young-age dependency ratios implied substantial need for social programs for both the young and old dependents (see Appendix A). In the 1960s when the demand for resources for social programs was rising, the fiscal capacity of the federal government was able to accommodate. From the time the recession of 1960–1961 ended in early 1961, there was an unprecedented, continuous expansion of the economy through the end of 1969. Therefore, it was no accident that the Great Society programs, such as antipoverty measures, Medicare, and Medicaid came into existence and grew during the mid-1960s and mid-1970s.

B. Fiscal Capacity in the 1990s

In the two decades between 1950 and 1970, the productivity of American workers grew at the rate of 3.4% per year. During the next 20 years, 1970–1990,

Table I Dependency Ratios in the United States in Selected Years, 1940–2070[a]

Year	Young-age dependency ratio[b]	Old-age dependency ratio[c]	Total dependency ratio[d]	Year	Young-age dependency ratio[b]	Old-age dependency ratio[c]	Total dependency ratio[d]
1940	58.2	11.6	69.8	2005	46.2	20.6	66.8
1945	55.7	12.4	68.1	2010	44.0	21.3	65.3
1950	58.6	13.8	72.4	2015	42.6	23.8	66.4
1955	65.7	15.7	81.4	2020	42.4	27.4	69.8
1960	73.1	17.3	90.4	2025	42.3	31.8	74.7
1965	76.4	18.2	94.6	2030	43.2	35.4	78.6
1970	71.3	18.5	89.8	2035	42.7	36.8	79.5
1975	63.9	18.9	82.8	2040	42.0	36.7	78.7
1980	55.4	19.5	74.9	2045	41.5	36.4	77.9
1985	50.5	20.1	70.6	2050	41.5	36.9	78.4
1990	49.1	20.9	70.0	2055	41.6	37.9	79.5
1995	49.4	21.4	70.8	2060	41.7	39.4	81.1
2000	48.4	21.0	69.4	2065	41.6	40.3	81.9
				2070	41.5	40.8	82.3

[a]Board of Trustees (1995). Federal Old-Age and Survivors Insurance (OASI) and disability insurance (DI) trust funds. 1995 Annual Report, House Document 104-57, 104th Cong., 1st Sess. (Washington, DC: U.S. Government Printing Office; 1995), p. 147. For 1940, 1945, 1950, and 1955 from special tabulations by the Office of the Actuary, courtesy of Felicitie Bell and Stephen C. Goss.

[b]Young-age dependency ratio compares the population under age 21 to the population between ages 20 and 64.

[c]Old-age dependency ratio compares the population age 65 and over to the population between ages 20 and 64.

[d]Total dependency ratio sums young-age and old-age dependency ratios.

however, the average annual growth rate of productivity was only at 1.3%. The net national savings rate was at an annual average of 8% of the gross domestic product (GDP) in the 1960s. It declined to an average of 3.6% in the 1980s and an average of 2% of GDP per year between 1990 and 1993.

The federal budget has been in continual deficit in all the years since 1969. In 1970, the national debt was $381 billion; in 1981, just under $1 trillion. In the 1980s, annual federal budget deficits averaged approximately $150 billion per year. By 1994, the national debt stood at more than $4.5 trillion (see Table II).

Under these fiscally restrictive circumstances, not only are new social programs virtually precluded from being enacted, existing programs are faced with cutbacks.

C. Balancing the Budget

Public opinion polls show that, in the abstract, 80% of Americans favor balancing the budget. The number falls precipitously if it means cuts in Social Security or Medicare or tax increases.

Strong economic arguments can be made for moving toward a balanced budget. The major reason to lower the deficit is to increase national savings, which in turn, increases national investment in physical and human capital, which in turn, increases productivity growth and raises in the standard of living.

Although lowering the deficit may be a wise course, it is quite another to specify how it should be done. In the current political climate, military expenditures cannot be cut and taxes cannot be raised. That puts almost all the pressure of deficit reduction on Medicare, Medicaid, and other social welfare programs. However, health-care programs are essential for the economic security of older people see Appendix B). [See HEALTH CARE AND SERVICES.]

III. ENTITLEMENT PROGRAMS AND THE BUDGET

Federal outlays may be divided into two categories: mandatory and discretionary. Mandatory spending refers to that which is not directly controlled through the annual appropriations process. Discretionary

Table II Budget Deficit and National Debt, 1970–1994 (in $ Billions)[a]

Year	Annual deficit	Accumulated national debt
1970	−$2.8	−$380.9
1971	−23.0	−408.2
1972	−23.4	−435.9
1973	−14.9	−466.3
1974	−6.1	−483.9
1975	−53.2	−541.9
1976	−73.7	−629.0
1977	−53.7	−706.4
1978	−59.2	−776.6
1979	−40.7	−829.5
1980	−73.8	−909.1
1981	−79.0	−994.8
1982	−128.0	−1,137.3
1983	−207.8	−1,371.7
1984	−185.4	−1,564.7
1985	−212.3	−1,817.5
1986	−221.2	−2,120.6
1987	−149.8	−2,346.1
1988	−155.2	−2,601.3
1989	−152.5	−2,868.0
1990	−221.4	−3,206.6
1991	−269.2	−3,598.5
1992	−290.4	−4,002.1
1993	−255.1	−4,351.4
1994	−203.2	−4,643.7

[a]Source: Economic Report of the President, 1995, p. 365.

spending, on the other hand, results from annual congressional acts of appropriation.

The bulk of mandatory spending consists of entitlement programs. Entitlement programs are federal programs providing benefits to individuals, businesses, or units of government that apply for payments and meet the eligibility requirements established by law. Nonentitlement forms of mandatory spending include net interest on the national debt and deposit insurance.

Interest payments on the national debt have been growing rapidly. Since fiscal year (FY) 1980, net interest payments have risen nearly threefold and in FY 1994, almost 14% of all federal outlays. However, the bulk of mandatory federal spending (86% in FY 1994) was for entitlements.

There are over 400 entitlements and other mandatory spending accounts in the federal budget. The largest 10 programs account for over 90% of entitlement spending, which are listed below for FY 1994:

Program	Entitlement spending (%)
Social Security	39.4
Medicare	20.8
Medicaid (Federal share)	10.6
Civil Service retirement and disability	5.0
Unemployment compensation	2.6
Military retirement	3.3
Supplemental Security Income (SSI)	2.8
Food Stamps	3.1
Veterans compensation and pensions	2.4
Family support payments (Federal share)	2.1
	92.1%

Federal entitlement spending has been rising significantly faster than the overall federal budget or GDP. Some believe that explosive growth in entitlement program is a very recent phenomenon, but entitlement growth was actually most pronounced during the years 1967 and 1976 when Medicare and Medicaid began and grew, the food stamp program became a national program, the SSI program was established, and major increases in Social Security benefits (the most prominent of which was the cost-of-living adjustment) went into effect.

From 1976 to 1990, entitlement spending as a percent of total federal outlays actually declined to approximately 45% from 51%. As a percentage of GDP, entitlement spending rose during the late 1960s and the first half of the 1970s, but has remained relatively constant over the past 15 years or so.

After 1995, however, the position of the federal budget will deteriorate. It will not result from the revenue side, because projected revenue is expected to remain fairly constant at about 19% of GDP. The deterioration will come from the spending side due to entitlement programs.

Social Security would not be a problem. It will grow no faster than the economy thanks to favorable demographics. The problem lies in health-care benefits—Medicare and Medicaid—the costs of which are expected to continue rising at double-digit rates throughout the next decade, absent significant reform measures. In FY 1980, the two health-care programs accounted for 5.8 and 2.4% of total outlays, respectively, but those proportions had risen to 10.9 and 5.6% by FY 1994. According to Congressional Budget Office (CBO) projections, by FY 2004 total expenditures for the two programs could reach 16.9 and 8.7% of federal outlays, respectively.

IV. ECONOMICS AND SOCIAL POLICY

A. Nature of Economics

The point of departure in the study of economics is scarcity. Economists start from the fundamental notion that our ability to satisfy human wants is limited. At any one time, an economy has only a limited command over the human and material resources required to produce goods and services. Human wants for goods and services seem limitless, whereas the resources needed for producing these things are limited. Therefore, how best to satisfy unlimited human wants with the available limited resources is the central issue in economics.

Scarcity, as the basic fact of economic life, pervades all societies, irrespective of their political orientation or levels of economic development. People simply do not have all the resources needed to produce all the things they would want to have. This fundamental constraint is as true in a rich country as it is in a poor country; this same constraint exists in countries with different ideologies. Although it always imposes the ultimate constraint, the scarcity condition is more acute in a poor than in a rich country.

B. Three Invisible Forces

Because society does not have all the material and nonmaterial resources with which to produce all the goods and services wanted, choices must be made. Economic reasoning leads one to recognize the trade-off; if one wants more of one thing, one must be prepared to have less of another thing or a little less of everything. What one must give up in order to get something else is known as the opportunity-cost concept of cost.

The opportunity-cost concept applies to all aspects of life. It embodies economic forces. Economic forces are the forces of scarcity, as earlier explained. In order to allocate scarce resources and scarce commodities, some socially agreed-upon criteria must be established.

When a society allows the economic forces to work through the market relatively freely, it's called market forces. Market forces deal with scarcity of goods and services by means of their relative prices. Market forces have been captured in the symbolism of the "invisible hand," which is the price mechanism in which the rise and fall of prices guide actions in buying and selling.

As explained by David Colander in his economics principles text, societies cannot choose whether or not to allow economic forces to operate, because they are always operating. Societies can only choose whether to allow market forces to predominate. Other forces play a major role in deciding whether to let market forces operate. He goes on to point out that social and historical forces often prevent the invisible hand from working. These other forces are captured by the metaphor, "invisible handshake." He further refers to still other forces, metaphorically labeled as the "invisible foot" by some, that may stop economic forces from becoming market forces. These other forces are political and legal influences.

In short, what happens in society can be understood as a reaction to and interaction of the invisible hand (economic forces), the invisible handshake (social and historical forces), and the invisible foot (political and legal forces). Economics has a role to play in sociology, history, and politics, just as sociology, history, and politics have roles to play in economics.

APPENDIX A: DEPENDENCY RATIOS AND DEPENDENCY COSTS

Because the future financing of the Social Security system depends considerably on the number of workers in relation to retirees, dependency ratios serve as a useful index of costs. The old-age dependency ratio, customarily defined as the population aged 65 and over relative to the population 20–64, is projected to rise in the future. Assuming a 1.9 fertility rate, this ratio will increase from .214 in 1995 to .394 in 2060, or an 84% increase for the 75-year period. Such an increase implies an immense rise in the tax burden on the working population in order to finance public expenditures for the old.

However, in addition to increasing the old-age dependency ratio, low fertility rates will result in fewer young persons and thus in a declining "young-age dependency ratio," customarily defined as the ratio of the population under 20 to the population 20–64. This ratio is projected to decrease from .494 in 1995 to .417 in 2055, a decline of about 15.6%.

Because workers are called on to support both the old and young dependents, the total dependency ratio—defined as the sum of the population under 20 and those over 64 relative to the population 20–64—suggests the total support burden on the working population. The total dependency ratio is projected to rise from .708 in 1995 to .811 in 2060, a 14.5% increase over the 75-year period. A rise or decline in the total dependency ratio tends to increase or decrease the total tax burden, but the extent of change depends on the relative costs of supporting the old versus the young and on the degree to which the old-age and young-age dependency ratios change. Moreover, the ability and willingness of the working population to bear such a burden is also an important consideration.

The relative costs of supporting the old versus supporting the young are crucial factors in determining what effect the changing dependency ratios will have on society's support burden. The average cost of an old dependent is believed by some to be approximately three times that of a young dependent, based on a study in the mid-1970s. It was estimated that $3,701 was spent for each aged person under government programs compared to an estimated $1,215 per young dependent. This three-to-one cost figure was arrived at (1) for the old-age dependents by dividing the population over 64 into the estimated total government program expenditures for the old and, (2) for the young dependents, by dividing the population under 18 into the estimated total government program expenditures for this population.

That procedure for arriving at the average cost per dependent produces what should properly be called the "per assumed-dependent cost" in contrast to the "per actual-recipient cost." The per assumed-dependent cost is a definitional one, because all persons in a given age category are included in the figure that is divided into the program expenditures in the numerator. By contrast, the alternate method—per actual-recipient cost—is a more appropriate measure, because it counts only those in the dependent age group who actually receive program expenditures. The assumed-dependent cost approach conceptually underestimates the support cost for the young who receive benefits under government programs, because relatively more young persons than old persons do not receive benefits, yet in the calculation all persons are included as if they were all recipients. Moreover, the three-to-one cost relationship was based on estimates that define young dependents as being under age 18 and thus leave out most expenditures for higher education.

However, the per actual-recipient cost is difficult to obtain for several reasons. Many government programs do not have published (or in some cases even unpublished) data on age and other characteristics of recipients. Also, calculations as to per recipient cost are more difficult because a number of persons are multiple recipients of several government programs. In addition, in-kind programs such as public housing are not easy to measure. A lack of time-series data on recipient characteristics under various government programs poses yet another impediment to analyzing the historical development in dependency ratios and dependency costs.

As mentioned, the change in the tax burden resulting from the change in the total dependency ratio also depends upon the degree to which the old and young dependency ratios change. In the above discussion of the per assumed-dependent cost as opposed to the per actual-recipient cost, the old dependents were defined as the population over 64 and the young dependents as the population under 18. Obviously, if the old group begins at age 62 or 68, or the young category starts at age 20 or 22, the dependency ratios and the associated dependency costs will change.

As also mentioned, the ability and willingness of the working population to bear the support cost is an important consideration. The taxpaying ability of the working population for supporting the dependents is influenced by such factors as the level of earnings, the labor force participation rates, and the unemployment rate; and these factors are in turn influenced by the level of productivity, the rate of economic growth, the state of demand, and the like. Furthermore, the overall financial ability of the working population to bear the support cost will be affected by private as well as public expenditures in behalf of the old and the young dependents.

Finally, the total support cost for all dependents would have to include dependents in the middle-age group in addition to the old and young dependents. Expenditures for middle-aged dependents include a number of government programs covering unemployment, disability, medical care, public assistance, housing subsidy, and the like.

APPENDIX B: A SUPPLY-AND-DEMAND VIEW OF ECONOMIC SECURITY

Economic well-being is generally discussed in reference to several different criteria, such as income, wealth, or consumption. Over the years, the gap has narrowed between the elderly and nonelderly insofar as income is concerned. Some conclude that the elderly have reached the same level of economic security as the nonelderly. However, even if the elderly have gained income parity with the nonelderly in terms of poverty rates, one may not thereby infer that their economic security levels are the same.

Economic security is a broader concept than income security. A person is concerned not only with the acquisition of income and assets, but also with their retention and disposal. It is well known, for example, that the elderly, when compared to the nonelderly, are at greater risk and must budget more for medical and personal care services despite Medicare and Medicaid. But potentially significant expenditures for health care are not generally given explicit consideration in assessments of the economic status of the elderly versus the nonelderly. A more accurate assessment of economic security, therefore, requires that current income, accumulated wealth, and consumption expenditures be considered from the standpoint of supply and demand. In that light, income and wealth represent the supply of resources and consumption represents the demand on those resources.

A. Income

The income status of the elderly has substantially improved in the last 25 years, but income status often is discussed by reference to the incidence of poverty. In 1966, for example, the poverty rate among the elderly was slightly more than double the poverty rate among the nonelderly. Since then, the elderly poverty rate has fallen, and the nonelderly poverty rate rose, both to approximately 13% in 1992. In terms of per capita income, statistics show that the elderly have reached the relative standing of the nonelderly over the last two decades.

B. Net Worth

Another criterion is ownership of accumulated wealth, or more precisely, net worth, which is the value of assets minus the value of liabilities. In terms of wealth, the elderly also fare well. Wealth holdings by persons 65 and older is the highest among all age groups except those between 55 and 64 years old. Some conclude, therefore, that the elderly are better off than the nonelderly, but a good deal of their net worth is in traditionally illiquid forms. Combining illiquid and liquid assets in order to measure economic capacity implies converting illiquid assets into readily spendable income. Home equity, for example, represents a significant part of net worth, but its financial meaningfulness awaits more prevalent practice of home equity conversions.

Some see the increasing use of home-equity lines of credit among middle-aged homeowners as a harbinger of their future comforture with reverse mortgages. But encumbered home equity in middle age is likely to reduce the equity that may be needed for retirement income. This is an important issue, because home equity can be a resource with which to finance consumption in old age. It is especially significant because home equity is increasingly seen as a viable resource to help finance future long-term care.

C. Consumption

The third criterion uses consumption expenditures to infer economic well-being. Neither income nor wealth is a good measure, some argue. They propose that consumption is a superior measure of economic well-being. For example, in 1986, the ratio of income between the affluent and the poor was 16 to 1. That is, a vast difference existed between the poor and the affluent: if a poor person had $1.00, the affluent person had $16.00. But in terms of per-consumer-unit of spending, they would infer that life at the bottom of the American money–income distribution was only moderately less attractive than at the middle, and about half as attractive as at the top. That is, according to per-consumer-unit spending, for every $1.00 spent by the poor, the middle class spent $1.29, and the affluent spent $2.31. Seen in terms of consumption, therefore, the difference between rich and poor was much narrower than in terms of income.

The difference between poor and rich was even smaller, they point out further, when considering consumer expenditures on four basic necessities—food, shelter, apparel, and medical care—for every $1.00

spent by the poor, the middle class spent $1.14, and the affluent spent $1.82. This view must not be taken lightly.

Of the five income distribution quintiles, only the top two showed an excess of incomes over expenditures; they were dissavers. All three lower quintiles showed expenditures over income; they were not dissavers. Perhaps the humorist Artemus Ward anticipated the consumption measure when he said, "Let us all be happy and live within our means, even if we have to borrow the money to do so." Consumption as a measure of economic well-being can be misleading.

How well-off are the elderly under this measure? The same data source, the Consumer Expenditures Survey for 1986 conducted by the Bureau of Labor Statistics, provided information for seven age groups. Per-person spending on the four basics by the oldest two age groups (65–74, and 75+) was higher than all five younger groups. Were the elderly enjoying a higher measure of economic welfare than the nonelderly?

Per-person spending on food, shelter, and apparel, with minor exceptions, was remarkably similar among all age groups. Health care, however, accounted for about 18% of the four basics for the 65–74 age group, and more than 25% of the four basics for the 75+ group, compared with 9% for the 45–54 age group, and less than 7% for all the younger age groups. That the elderly group spends more of its total budget on health care is not surprising. But the inference from using consumption as a measure is that if the elderly spend less on health care, their economic well-being would be lower. Conversely, the young age groups can improve their economic well-being by spending more on health care. The irony is apparent.

D. Supply of and Demand for Resources

In summary, income, wealth, and consumption may be viewed from the standpoint of supply and demand. As stated earlier, income and wealth represent the supply of resources, and consumption represents demand on those resources. In order to measure economic well-being, therefore, income, wealth, and consumption should be included. Even if the elderly have achieved income and wealth levels on a par with the nonelderly, it does not follow that their economic security is the same as younger groups, because older people are faced with an actual or potential higher demand on resources for health care, including long-term care.

Health-care expenditures represent what could be called a *first claim on income*. When the income and assets of the elderly and nonelderly are equal, then the supply of resources is the same for both groups. After the first claim is deducted from these resources, however, an obvious disparity in resources results between the elderly and nonelderly groups.

It is difficult to exaggerate the importance of health care to older Americans. A pre-Socratic philosopher, Heraclitus, said it well in 500 B.C.: "When health is absent, wisdom cannot reveal itself, culture cannot become manifest, strength cannot fight, wealth becomes useless, and intelligence cannot be applied."

BIBLIOGRAPHY

Advisory Council on Social Security (1980). Dependency Ratios and Costs, in *Social Security Financing and Benefits*, Report of the 1979 Advisory Council on Social Security (Washington: U.S. Government Printing Office) 1980-0-341-185-46, DHHS-SSA, pp. 281–285. Updated by the author, who, as a member of the expert panel, drafted the original statement for the council's deliberation and adoption.

Board of Trustees (1995). Federal Old-Age and Survivors Insurance and disability insurance trust funds. 1995 Annual Report, House Document 104-57, 104th Cong., 1st Sess. (Washington, DC: U.S. Government Printing Office; 1995), p. 147.

Chen, Y.-P. (1996). Introduction to *Encyclopedia of Financial Gerontology*. L. A. Vitt & J. K. Siegenthaler, (Eds.). (Westport, Connecticut: Greenwood Publishing Group), pp. xxvii–xxxi.

Colander, D. (1994). *Economics* (2nd ed.). Chicago: Richard D. Irwin, Inc.

Council of Economic Advisers (1995). *Economic Report of the President* (Washington: U.S. Government Printing Office), p. 365.

Endocrine Function and Dysfunction

Felicia V. Nowak and Arshag D. Mooradian

St. Louis University Medical School

Androgens Adrenal or gonadal hormones that enhance male sexual characteristics. Examples are testosterone, dihydrotestosterone, androstenedione, and dehydroepiandrosterone.

Glucocorticoids Adrenal hormones with predominant effects on glucose homeostasis and cell-mediated immunity, such as cortisol.

Mineralocorticoids Adrenal hormones with predominant effect on serum electrolyte metabolism.

Osteopenia Reduced bone mass.

Releasing Hormones Hormones released by the hypothalamus to stimulate various types of pituitary cells (e.g., TRH, CRF, GnRH, GHRH; see text for definitions).

Thyroid Hormones Refers to thyroxine (T_4) and triiodothyronine T_3.

Trophic Hormones Released by pituitary gland to stimulate various target endocrine tissues eg.: TSH, ACTH, FSH, LH, Growth hormone.

Altered cellular metabolism and intercellular signaling occur with advancing age, resulting in widespread changes in **ENDOCRINE FUNCTION**. Aging is associated with both anatomic and secretory changes in the endocrine glands. Cellular responses within the hormone target organs also may change, including receptor binding, intracellular signaling, and gene expression responses. Hormone clearance rates and transport binding proteins may also be altered. Awareness of these changes is essential to the diagnosis and management of endocrine dysfunction in the elderly.

I. INTRODUCTION

A. Overview of Hormonal Changes with Age

Altered cellular metabolism and intercellular signaling with advancing age result in widespread changes in endocrine function. Several mechanisms interact in most systems to bring about the observed changes. Aging is associated with anatomic changes of the endocrine glands. In addition, changes in hormone secretion also occur with age and include alterations in circadian or seasonal biorhythms, changes in pulsatile frequency or amplitude of hormone secretion, as well as absolute changes in mean serum hormonal levels.

Other changes occur in the cellular responses of target organs. Receptor binding and intracellular signaling reflect age-related alterations in plasma membrane properties, enzyme activities, and calcium mobilization. Gene expression, including translation efficiency and transcription rates, may show marked variation with age. [See DNA AND GENE EXPRESSION.] Finally, changes in hormone clearance rates and binding to transport proteins contribute to the overall widespread changes observed.

The mode and mechanism of change vary with the hormone studied. In addition to intrinsic age-related changes in endocrine response, age-associated diseases, increased use of medications, changes in nutritional status, physical activity, and body composition also contribute to age-related endocrine dysfunction.

B. General Principles of Geriatric Endocrinology

The accurate diagnosis of endocrine dysfunction in the elderly requires a high index of suspicion. Signs and symptoms of hormone deficiency or excess may be absent. When such signs and symptoms are present, coexisting malnutrition or chronic disease may often make their interpretation more difficult.

This also applies to hormone measurements and provocative tests. Some hormones, such as luteinizing hormone (LH) and follicle-stimulating hormone (FSH), have clear gender-specific age-related changes. Others such as thyroid-stimulating hormone (TSH) may show more subtle alterations in what is considered normal with age. Provocative tests may give a blunted or altered response. Measurements of bound hormone may be less reliable due to alterations in serum proteins and hormone binding. Clearance rates are often affected by age due to changes in renal or hepatic metabolism, peripheral utilization, and even posttranslational changes in hormone processing.

Finally, therapy needs to be adjusted for age and coexisting disease. Potential side effects of optional therapies such as testosterone will be increased and will affect the risk to benefit assessment of treatment. Essential replacement, such as with thyroid hormone, should be instituted at a low dose and gradually increased to full dosage with careful monitoring of patient response and potential adverse reactions.

With these precautions in mind, every effort should be made to diagnose and treat endocrine abnormalities even in the elderly debilitated patient, as this will improve quality of life. Generalized aging is intimately coupled with widespread progressive alterations in metabolism, of which changes in endocrine function are an integral part. [*See* METABOLISM: CARBOHYDRATE, LIPID, AND PROTEIN.]

II. AGE-RELATED CHANGES IN ANTERIOR PITUITARY

A. Age-Related Changes in Pituitary Function

Morphological changes are seen in the pituitary gland and fossa with aging. Chromophobe adenomas, especially prolactin producing, increase in incidence with age. They may be more difficult to detect clinically, especially in females, because loss of menstrual cyclicity is the most common complaint of young women with prolactinemia, and this index is lost after menopause. In addition, many drugs commonly prescribed in the elderly, such as antidepressants, can secondarily increase prolactin levels into the range of microadenomas.

Aging is also associated with an increased incidence of anatomic and radiographic alterations in the sella turcica, including increased size and demineralization. Often no biochemical abnormalities are associated.

The peptide hormones of the anterior pituitary also change with age. A number of pituitary hormones exhibit altered patterns of secretion with advancing age, including growth hormone (GH), LH, FSH, adrenocorticotropic hormone (ACTH), and TSH. There is a decrease in sleep-induced GH secretion, in peak amplitude, and in 24-hour plasma levels of GH. This occurs despite the finding that there is no change in pituitary GH content with age. However, growth hormone releasing hormone (GHRH) receptors are reduced, and pituitary sensitivity to inhibition by somatostatin is increased. Both of these findings may lead to decreased release of stored GH. There is also a decrease in the GH mediator, insulin-like growth factor-1 (IGF-1) and in one of its binding proteins, insulin-like growth factor binding protein-3 (IGFBP-3). There is also an increase in IGFBP-1 that inhibits IGF-1 bioactivity. An age-related decrease in basal and GHRH-stimulated GH secretion has been reported in male rhesus monkeys and rats. It has been postulated that in humans the decrease in GH action results in the muscle wasting and bone loss commonly seen with aging. However, studies to date have not been able to demonstrate a clear anabolic effect of replacement of GH in elderly subjects, possibly because GH replacement cannot completely correct the alterations in binding proteins.

Serum prolactin levels have been shown to decrease in females after menopause, whereas LH rises dramatically. Both pituitary content of LH and serum LH increase in intact animals. In human females, LH levels rise after menopause because of decreased gonadal steroid feedback. However, the LH response to gonadotropin-releasing hormone (GnRH) actually decreases. Pituitary sensitivity to the negative feedback by gonadal steroids may decrease. Replacement therapy with physiological doses of estrogen in postmenopausal women fails to restore gonadotropin levels to premenopausal values.

In older female rats the amplitude of FSH secretion on proestrus is less than 50% of the amplitude found in young rats. Aging is also associated with significant changes in LH pulsatile secretion. Age-related decreases in LH pulse frequency have been observed in human males and in male rats. Pulse amplitude is unaltered in humans but decreases in rats. Pituitary gonadotrophs isolated from old ovariectomized rats have a significantly lower LH content than young ovariectomized rats. LH beta mRNA is also decreased.

In men, circulating prolactin levels increase slightly, while LH release decreases despite an increase in stored LH. This may be due in part to an increase in the sensitivity of gonadotropin secreting cells to testosterone and dihydrotestosterone, which has been found in healthy older men and aging male rats. Both stored and secreted FSH levels increase in both sexes. The circadian rhythm of prolactin secretion is maintained, as is the pituitary content.

The sex-specific changes in prolactin release may be secondary to changes in estrogen levels, which decrease with age in women and increase in aging men. They may also be secondary to changes in central nervous system (CNS) neurotransmitters and neuromodulators, including dopamine, β-endorphins, and enkephalins, which influence pituitary hormone secretion. [See NEUROTRANSMITTERS AND NEUROTROPHIC FACTORS.]

TSH levels in the pituitary do not change with age, and circulating TSH is normal or slightly elevated. Diurnal variation is unchanged. Pituitary TSH sensitivity to changes in thyroid hormone concentrations decreases in the elderly. This age-related change in set point of the pituitary, as well as decreased renal clearance of TSH, both contribute to the elevated circulating TSH.

The corticotropin (ACTH) content may be slightly reduced in the pituitary with age, but the basal ACTH

Table I Age-Related Changes in Anterior Pituitary Hormone Response[a]

	Change[b]
ACTH response to CRF	N
ACTH response to insulin-induced hypoglycemia	N
ACTH response to intravenous metyrapone	N
TSH response to TRH in women	N
TSH response to TRH in men	↓
Prolactin response to TRH	↓
GH response to GHRH	N or ↓
GH response to insulin-induced hyperglycemia	↓
GH response to arginine infusion	N
GH response to levodopa	↓
LH and FSH response to GnRH	↓

[a]ACTH, adrenocorticotropic hormone; CRF, corticotropin-releasing factor; TSH, thyroid-stimulating hormone; TRH, thyrotropin-releasing hormone; GH, growth hormone; LH, luteinizing hormone; FSH, follicle-stimulating hormone.

[b]N, no change; ↓, decrease.

secretion does not change. However, pituitary response to glucocorticoids shows a blunting of the negative feedback effects with age.

B. Pituitary Dynamic Testing

Although infrequently used, there are occasional indications for dynamic pituitary testing in the elderly. One should be aware of age-related changes in responsiveness. These are summarized in Table I.

The ACTH response to corticotropin-releasing factor (CRF) or alternate stimuli is unchanged with age. TSH, prolactin, GH, LH, and FSH all show diminished stimulatory responses in dynamic testing in a significant proportion of individuals.

III. THYROID GLAND FUNCTION AND DYSFUNCTION WITH AGE

A. Thyroid Structure

There is an increased incidence of thyroid nodules with age. Some studies have estimated that up to 90% of women over 70 years of age have thyroid nodules. Generalized changes may also occur, including increased fibrosis, flattened follicular epithelium, and

Table II Age-Related Changes in Thyroid Hormone Economy[a]

Parameter[b]	Changes
Radioactive iodine uptake	Decreased
T_4 production	Decreased or unaltered
T_3 production	Decreased or unaltered
T_4 degradation	Decreased or unaltered
T_3 degradation	Decreased or unaltered
Serum T_4 concentration (total or free)	Unaltered
Serum T_3 concentration (total or free)	Unaltered or decreased
Serum thyroid hormone binding capacity (T_3 resin uptake)	Unaltered
Serum TSH	Unaltered or increased
Circadian TSH Variation	Decreased
TSH response to TRH	Unaltered or decreased, especially in men
TSH response to thyroid hormone	Decreased
Thyroid response to TSH	Decreased or unaltered

[a]Reprinted from Mooradian, A. D., & Wong N. C. W. (1994). Age-related changes in thyroid hormone action. *European Journal of Endocrinology, 131,* 451, with permission of the publisher.

[b]T_4, thyroxine; T_3, triiodothyronine; TSH, thyroid-stimulating hormone, TRH, thyrotropin-releasing hormone.

increased colloid as well as an increase in lymphocytic and plasma cell infiltration.

In geographic areas of low iodine intake, the incidence of goiter increases markedly with age; up to 50% of the population may be affected.

B. Thyroid Hormone Economy

Age-related changes in serum thyroid hormone concentrations, hormone stability, and hypothalamic pituitary–thyroid interactions are summarized in Table II.

The metabolic response to thyroid hormones changes with age. Overall, there is a decreased response of the basal metabolic rate (BMR) to triiodothyronine (T_3) stimulation and a decrease in lipid peroxidation when corrected for caloric intake.

Serum TSH levels decrease with age in healthy and hypothyroid subjects. A reduced amplitude of secretory pulses is seen in normal elderly subjects, especially at night. The pulse frequency does not change. TSH bioactivity also decreases with age and may reflect age-related changes in glycation. [*See* GLYCATION.] In aging male Fischer 344 rats, immunoreactive serum TSH also shows no change, but pituitary TSH-β subunit mRNA levels and TSH content decrease with age.

The TSH response to TRH has been shown to be reduced in some groups of elderly men but is normal in others and in elderly women. This is apparently counterbalanced by an increased suppressibility of TSH by thyroid hormones in elderly humans. The ability of dexamethasone to suppress the TSH response to TRH is blunted in elderly men, suggesting that the thyrotrope is also more resistant to glucocorticoids. This is of special interest because of the increased serum levels of glucocorticoids in response to several stimuli, which have been reported in elderly men due to age-related changes in the hypothalamic pituitary adrenal axis.

Thyroid gland responsiveness to TSH is not altered with age in vivo. The elevation in serum T_3 in response to thyrotropin-releasing hormone-(TRH)-induced secretion of endogenous TSH is similar in elderly human subjects and young controls. However, a decrease in thyroid membrane high-affinity binding sites for TSH is observed in 24–26-month-old compared with 3–4-month-old rats. This is reflected in a decrease in TSH-stimulated adenyl cyclase activity in old rat thyroid membranes.

In rats, age-related decreases are seen in both TSH responsiveness to TRH as well as T_3 inhibition of the TSH response. Thyroxine (T_4) declines with age, but this decline may be prevented by lifelong caloric restriction.

Several large studies in human subjects have documented no change in serum total T_4 and free T_4 during advanced aging in both males and females. Serum T_3 shows a more striking decrease whereas reverse triiodothyronine (rT_3) increases with age. Nutritional status may affect these levels. Low caloric and carbohydrate intake correlate with elevations in rT_3.

The metabolic clearance of thyroid hormone has been shown to decrease with age. The serum half-life of T_4 increases from a mean duration of 6.7 days in the third decade of life to a mean of 9.1 days by the seventh decade. Deiodination of both T_4 and T_3 is reduced. Sequential monodeiodination is also reduced. The decline in hepatic 5'-monodeiodinase activity may be partly due to a decrease in availability of reduced cofactor thiol groups, which decrease with maturation and aging.

The transport of thyroid hormone into brain and liver tissues is reduced in aged rats. T_3 transport across the plasma membrane is significantly reduced while nuclear uptake remains unchanged. The metabolic implications of these findings have not been established.

Thyroid hormone action involves binding to specific DNA promoter and enhancer regions attenuating or augmenting the expression of specific genes. The effects of aging on T_3 responsiveness of some thyroid hormone responsive genes is shown in Table III. The encoded gene products include enzymes, transporters, hormones, and structural proteins.

T_3 stimulation of malic enzyme is reduced in aged rats. Malic enzyme mRNA is also reduced, suggesting a decrease in transcription rates or mRNA stability. Another enzyme that is stimulated by thyroid hormone is the Na^+-K^+-ATPase. This enzyme response has been shown to decrease with age in both renal cortex and liver. The enzyme may be partly responsible for the calorigenic effects of thyroid hormone, and the decrease may contribute to the age-related decline in thyroid hormone thermogenesis.

Cardiac relaxation slows with age. Ca^{++}–ATPase activity and sarcoplasmic Ca^{++}–ATPase gene expression are reduced in aged rats. The stimulatory effect of T_3 is also reduced. This may contribute to the age-associated slowing of relaxation. Aging and thyroid hormones also affect α- and β-myosin heavy chain (BMHC) gene expression. Both genes are highly expressed in neonates. The α myosin heavy chain declines steadily with age and is stimulated by T_3. The effect of age on this T_3 response is unknown. BMHC also decreases after birth but rises again with aging. The effect of T_3 on this gene is decreased expression through binding to a negative response element in the gene encoding this isoform. With aging the ability of T_3 to suppress BMHC is lost.

The rat liver S_{14} gene enclodes a small nuclear protein ($m_r 17010$) that may be involved in lipogenesis. S_{14} gene expression increases with age. T_3 induces S_{14} gene expression and this response is blunted in older animals.

C. Thyroid Dysfunction: Clinical Aspects

Many clinical features of hypothyroidism are found commonly in the elderly, despite negligible changes in plasma thyroid hormone levels. These findings are summarized in Table IV.

On the other hand, numerous studies have shown a 3–4% incidence of unsuspected (subclinical) hypothyroidism in the elderly. Primary thyroid failure, usually secondary to chronic autoimmune thyroiditis, has been estimated to occur in 4.4% of the population over the age of 60 years. The prevalence of antithyroglobulin and antimicrosomal antibodies increases with age up to 70 then declines so that prevalence at ages >100 years equals that found in controls <50 years. In one large study, a high percentage (80%) of elderly patients with high antimicrosomal antibody titers developed clinical hypothyroidism during a 4-year follow-up period. In contrast, elevated antithyroglobulin antibody titers do not appear to predict increased risk for hypothyroidism.

Hyperthyroidism is more difficult to diagnose in the elderly due to lack of classical clinical signs. Symptoms of hyperthyroidism, especially those secondary to increased adrenergic activity are frequently blunted in older individuals. The reduced signs of adrenergic hyperactivity in elderly hyperthyroid patients may be the result of age-related desensitization of β-adrenergic receptors. The heart rate response is reduced in elderly subjects regardless of thyroid status. Low serum TSH is more common in the older patient, most often accompanied by a normal serum T_4 concentration. In one large study 6 out of 50 elderly patients

Table III The Effects of Aging on Thyroid Hormone (T_3) Responsiveness of Select Biomarkers of Thyroid Hormone Action[a]

Biomarker[b]	T_3 responsiveness in aging
I. Positively regulated	
1. Malic enzyme	Decreased
2. Na$^+$–K$^+$ ATPase	Decreased
3. Ca^{2+} ATPase	Decreased in humans No change in rats
4. Sarcoplasmic Ca^{2+} ATPase mRNA	Decreased
5. Thymocyte 2-deoxy-glucose transporter	Decreased
6. Spot$_{14}$	Decreased
7. Submandibular gland EGF	Decreased in female mice
8. Isoproterenol-stimulated adenylate cyclase	Decreased
9. S$_{11}$/Apo A-I	Altered[c]
10. α-Myosin heavy chain	Unknown
11. GH	Unknown
12. α-Glycerophosphate dehydrogenase	No change
13. Serum angiotensin-converting enzyme	No Change
II. Negatively regulated	
1. TSH α subunit	Unknown
2. TSH β subunit	Decreased
3. Serum TSH	Decreased
4. β-myosin heavy chain	Decreased

[a]Adapted from Mooradian, A.D. and Wong, N. C. W. (1994). Age-related changes in thyroid hormone action. *European Journal of Endocrinology 131*, 451, with permission of the publisher.

[b]EGF, Epidermal growth factor; GH, growth hormone; TSH, thyroid-stimulating hormone.

[c]No down-regulation in hypothyroid aged rats.

with low TSH became hyperthyroid during 4 years of follow-up.

Some of the effects of hyperthyroidism may actually be totally different in some elderly individuals. Weight loss secondary to hyperthyroid status occurs in both young and aged individuals. However, the etiologic pathway may be different. As many as 36% of elderly patients with hyperthyroidism experience anorexia. Using pair fed rats, weight loss in hyperthyroid older rats has been linked directly to decreased food intake in the aged rats compared with their younger counterparts.

A high index of suspicion, appropriate laboratory testing, and careful slow replacement of thyroid hormone when required, will greatly facilitate the care of the elderly patient with thyroid disease.

IV. ADRENAL GLAND FUNCTION AND DISEASE WITH AGE

A. Adrenal Cortex Structure

Structural changes take place in the human adrenal cortex with age. Adrenal gland weight declines slightly with age, and the adrenal cortex undergoes degenerative changes, including increased fibrosis, accumulation of lipofuchsin, epithelial cell dropout, mitochondrial fragmentation, and vascular dilation and hemorrhages. Cellular depletion is observed in the zona reticularis. An increased incidence of adrenal adenomas has been found on autopsy. Up to 50% of adrenal glands from aged subjects show small cortical nodules.

Table IV Age-Related Changes in the Adrenal Axis[a]

	Change[b]
Hypothalamic pituitary unit	
Basal ACTH level	N
Sensitivity to negative feedback by glucocorticoids	↓
ACTH response to	
CRF[c]	N
Insulin-induced hypoglycemia	N
Intravenous metyrapone	N
Adrenal gland	
Glucocorticoids	
Cortisol response to ACTH	N or prolonged
Basal cortisol level	N
Cortisol levels in response to perioperative stress	↑
Circadian rhythm of cortisol secretion	Phase advance
Androgens	
Dehydroepiandrosterone	↓
Androstenedione	↓
Mineralocorticoids	
Aldosterone[d]	↓

[a]Reproduced from Mooradian, A. D. (1992). Geriatric neuroendocrinology. In C. B. Nemeroff (Ed.), *Neuroendocrinology.* (pp. 451–462). Boca Raton, Fl: CRC Press, with permission of the publisher.
[b]N, no change; ↓, decrease; ↑ increase.
[c]CRF, corticotropin-releasing hormone.
[d]The decrease is mostly secondary to decreased renin activity with age.

B. Adrenal Physiology

Physiological changes that take place in the adrenal axis with age are summarized in Table IV.

Hypothalamic corticotropin-releasing factor (CRF or CRH) content does not change in rats or humans as a function of age, but baseline and stimulated portal CRF levels are increased in the rat. This increased activation may reflect the observed increase with age in a subpopulation of CRF neurons that also contain arginine vasopressin (AVP). This AVP-containing subset of neurons is selectively activated by stress.

I. Glucocorticoids

Aging of the hypothalamic pituitary adrenal (HPA) axis is highly species-dependent. In aged dogs, ACTH and cortisol levels show hyperresponsiveness to CRH or stress. In aging rats the ability to secrete ACTH and corticosterone in response to CRH or stress is reduced, but baseline levels of these two hormones are elevated. In male Fischer 344 rats, the pulse amplitude of pituitary ACTH secretion is decreased. Pituitary CRH receptor concentrations are significantly decreased without alterations in ligand affinity.

In humans the pituitary ACTH response to exogenous CRH or to intravenous metyrapone does not change. However, a diminished sensitivity of pituitary ACTH to negative feedback by cortisol is suggested by several findings. Dexamethasone suppression of ACTH has a higher false positive rate, and this is further exacerbated by coexisting dementia or Alzheimer's disease. Exercise endurance training also alters the suppressive effect of dexamethasone on cortisol and ACTH secretion in response to CRH, making it less effective.

Moreover, the increased cortisol response to CRH with normal levels of ACTH suggests decreased negative feedback with or without increased adrenal stimulation of cortisol secretion by ACTH. Challenges that alter CNS feedback to the HPA axis, such as trauma, physostigmine, or naloxone tend to show a greater cortisol response in older subjects. In addition, older subjects show a delayed recovery to baseline cortisol levels following CRH or an ACTH challenge post-surgery. The elderly do have higher serum cortisol in response to depression or to perioperative stress than do young subjects.

The limbic system modulates the HPA axis. In rats, aging is associated with selective loss of corticosterone-binding neurons and glucocorticoid receptor (GR) mRNA in the CA_3 hippocampal zone. Also with age, hippocampal inhibition of ACTH release is attenuated.

Hippocampal neurons have both mineralocorticoid (MR) and glucocorticoid receptors. It is theorized that unlike kidney MR, which are selective for aldosterone, hippocampal MR bind both cortisol and aldosterone. MR and GR may mediate coordinate but antagonistic effects on excitability by hippocampal neurons. In rats and dogs, limbic system MR-binding capacity is markedly decreased with aging, whereas GRs are unchanged, altering the homeostatic balance and leading to HPA hyperreactivity during senescence.

Age-related losses of adrenal steroid receptors have been hypothesized to result from cumulative exposure to glucocorticoids themselves. Administration of exogenous glucocorticoids or chronic stress accelerate hippocampal pathology, whereas adrenalectomy reduces it.

Glucocorticoid target tissues also show age-related changes. The affinity of hepatic cytosolic steroid receptors to dexamethasone and corticosterone is significantly reduced in aged rats, although receptor number does not change. Stimulation of tyrosine amino transferase, a corticosteroid-induced enzyme, decreases with age. Impaired glucocorticoid-receptor activation may be responsible for the decrease.

Changes in the HPA axis may also lead to altered immune function, including reduced tumor surveillance, with aging. Natural killer cell activity shows an age-related decrement both at baseline and in response to CRH in rats.

Evidence that the adrenal gland may directly mediate the age-related reduction in stress tolerance comes from studies that show that restraint-induced expression of heat shock protein 70 (hsp 70) in rat adrenal cortex declines throughout the life span of the rat. Hypophysectomy negates the hsp 70 response, and ACTH replacement restores it, indicating a role for this protein in the physiologic stress response.

There is evidence that persons exposed to elevated cortisol levels due to Cushing's syndromes or exogenous glucocorticoid therapy show a number of cognitive and physical impairments normally associated with aging. These include memory deficits, atherosclerosis, muscle weakness, osteoporosis, immune dysfunction, and cerebral atrophy. Exposure to chronic stress with its associated elevations in ACTH and cortisol may have similar consequences, and stress and aging may act synergistically to exacerbate each other.

Adrenal disorders are not a common endocrinopathy in the older population. The three most common ones are adrenal mass, glucocorticoid excess, and adrenal insufficiency. As in younger patients, a functioning adrenal mass is most likely a pheochromocytoma or aldosteronoma that can be evaluated by abdominal CT and urinary measurements of catecholamines and their metabolites. A serum potassium should also be checked. Most tumors will be nonfunctioning. Those that are functional and those greater than 6 cm or that are rapidly enlarging should be removed if the patient can tolerate surgery.

For evaluation of cortisol excess the low-dose 2-day dexamethasone suppression test (0.5 mg every 6 hr for 48 hr) should be used, as there may be an increased rate of false positive tests in the elderly using the overnight suppression test. If ACTH is also elevated, a tumor secreting ectopic ACTH is the most likely cause in this age group.

Acute adrenal insufficiency is rare and usually occurs in the setting of severe acute illness. The elderly are more susceptible, especially in the setting of acute myocardial infarction, sepsis, or anticoagulation. Adrenal gland metastatic disease or tuberculosis can also cause adrenal insufficiency. A negative ACTH stimulation test will confirm the diagnosis, but this should be deferred if the patient is in acute adrenal collapse. The decreased clearance rate of cortisol may result in a decreased replacement dosage requirement of hydrocortisone or cortisone in the elderly.

2. Adrenal Androgens

Decreased adrenal androgen secretion occurs with age in both sexes. The dehydroepiandrosterone (DHEA) basal secretion as well as secretion after ACTH stimulation decreases with age. Cellular loss in the zona reticularis may contribute to the reduced DHEA secretion. Postmenopausal women compared with young cycling women have decreased product and precursor ratios for DHEA/17-hydroxypregnenolone and for androstenedione/17-hydroxyprogesterone, suggesting a reduction in 17, 20-desmolase with age. In cows, p450 c17mRNA and induction by ACTH are reduced with aging.

In human males, DHEA secretion declines progressively between 20 and 96 years of age. Older men have serum levels that are 5–30% of levels seen in younger men. The age-related reduction in secretion rate of adrenal androgen in both men and women is reflected in reduced urinary 17-ketosteroid excretion.

The physiological implications of the decline in DHEA with age in humans are unclear. In rodents, DHEA has antihypercholesterolemic, antiatherosclerotic, and antihyperglycemic effects.

3. Mineralocorticoids

Aldosterone secretion decreases with age most likely secondary to a reduction in plasma renin activity (PRA) by about 50%. The reduction in aldosterone secretion is evident both at baseline and after salt restriction or standing or in response to ACTH.

The aldosterone clearance rate also decreases with age, by about 20%. This may partially offset the decreased baseline secretion. However, the elderly are more prone to develop postural hypotension and dehydration. This is at least in part due to the decreased mineralocorticoid homeostatic response. Other contributing mechanisms will be discussed in section VIII on water balance.

C. Adrenal Medulla

In rats the adrenal medulla becomes hyperplastic with hypertrophy of individual chromaffin cells with age.

Secretion rates of epinephrine and norepinephrine (NE) from the adrenal gland under resting conditions in the rat increase after 300 days of age. Levels at 800–900 days are 2–4 times higher than those seen at 100 days. Aging also increases the plasma catecholamine response to stress in aged rats. Serum baseline NE but not epinephrine is elevated in 24-month versus 3-month-old Fischer 344 animals. CRH-stimulated catecholamines are also elevated.

In addition, tyrosine hydroxylase (TH) activity and TH-mRNA are elevated in old rats compared with young ones. Exercise conditioning decreases both TH activity and mRNA in young but not old rats, suggesting that sympathoadrenal plasticity diminishes with age.

In humans, plasma NE may increase with age in the general population. This is accompanied by a decrease in platelet $\alpha2$-adrenergic receptors and cardiac β-adrenergic transmission, implying down-regulation with age in the presence of elevated NE. Dopamine levels do not change. Others have found that NE levels do not increase in nonsmokers between the ages of 25 and 65 years. However, elevated levels of both epinephrine and NE were found in healthy octogenarians compared with healthy 24–28-year-olds. Catecholamine excretion has been shown to decrease between 60 and 80 years of age. Smoking significantly elevates catecholamine levels and excretion.

The NE response to upright posture, tilt-table test, insulin-tolerance test, cold-pressor test, or to glucose ingestion is increased in the elderly, whereas both the epinephrine and NE response to exercise at 75% maximal work load is decreased in healthy elderly male subjects as compared to their younger counterparts.

V. THE REPRODUCTIVE SYSTEM

A. Male Reproductive System

In human males, reproductive system aging occurs at both gonadal and supragonadal levels. Primary changes occur in testicular function with a decrease in sperm production and serum testosterone. Both total and bioavailable testosterone are decreased.

Anatomic changes in the testes include thickening of the basement membrane of seminiferous tubules and thinning of the germinal epithelium, increased peritubular fibrosis, and germ cell arrest. The number of Leydig cells and Sertoli cells is reduced with age and there is a decline in daily sperm production. However, normal areas of spermatogenesis are usually preserved until late in life.

The decrease in serum testosterone may be secondary to both primary testicular failure and to decreased LH secretion from the pituitary.

Compared to young men, in healthy older men LH pulse frequency may be reduced and pulse amplitude is maintained. In older rats, both the frequency and amplitude of LH pulses is reduced. The gonadotropin-suppressing activity of testosterone or dihydrotestosterone is increased in healthy elderly men and in aging male rats.

Some impairment in Leydig cell function occurs with age. There is a decrease in pregnenolone production and thus a decreased supply of substrate for conversion to testosterone, FSH is elevated reflecting decreased testicular functions, including sperm production and inhibin secretion by the Sertoli cells. Treatment with clomiphene citrate stimulates gonadotropin levels in elderly men, but both LH and FSH increase less in elderly men than in young men. Elderly men also show a smaller rise in serum testosterone, bioavailable testosterone, and estradiol, indicative of a significantly diminished testicular response. Sertoli cell function declines earlier than Leydig cell function. Several studies have shown a substantial decrease in Sertoli cell inhibin production by the fifth decade, whereas significant decline in testosterone secretion is seen only after the eighth decade.

Complex changes in steroid metabolism occur with aging. The metabolic clearance rates of both testosterone and dihydrotestosterone are reduced. Testosterone reduction to 5β-metabolites is increased. There is also an increase in conversion of testosterone to estradiol. This, coupled with the fact that estradiol clearance is also reduced, leads to an increase of the estradiol–testosterone (E_2/T) ratio in older men.

Age-related changes also take place in tissue uptake of sex steroids. Androgen receptor concentrations in the hypothalamus and pituitary, the testes, and the ventral and lateral prostate are reduced with age in the rat, and receptor affinity in brain and prostate is also reduced [*See* PROSTATE.]. Expression of hepatic androgen receptors also decreases, leading to a decrease in $\alpha2\mu$-globulin mRNA, a biomarker of androgen action in liver.

The secondary effects of aging of this system include decreased muscle mass, anemia, and decreasing libido.

The male Brown Norway rat shows a similar picture with aging, including decreased sperm production, decreased testicular size, decreased inhibin, and decreased serum testosterone. *In vivo* LH is decreased with age, whereas FSH increases. *In vitro* LH-stimulated and basal testosterone production by isolated Leydig cells shows no change with age. Leydig cell number also does not change. Hypothalamic GnRH secretion also continues. However, pituitary GnRH receptors show a significant decrease in the anterior pituitary of aged male rats. This plus an age-related decrease in pituitary calcium second messenger mobilization may be responsible for the reduced LH.

Testicular tumors in humans are primarily a disease of young and middle-aged men. However, rats show an increase in testicular tumors with age.

B. Female Reproductive System

In contrast to the gradual onset of the male climacteric, menopause in the female is a more dramatic event. Cessation of menses is, however, the result of slowly progressive changes in ovarian and hypothalamic-pituitary function.

Fertility declines with age. The conception rate at age 30–34 is only 73% of that seen between age 20–24 i.e., 63% vs. 86% incidence of pregnancy after 12 months of unprotected intercourse). By age 40 the conception rate is only 50%. The median age for menopause in the United States is currently 51 years.

Age-related changes in the human female reproductive system occur mainly at the ovarian and pituitary levels. There is also a significant age-dependent decrease in embryo survival, which is dependent upon ovarian age.

In the mammalian ovary the number of oocytes is fixed at birth and declines with age. In the human ovary few follicles remain at the time of menopause. Sclerotic changes occur in the medullar portion of the aging ovary. Hypophysectomy or food restriction, which is associated with low gonadotropin levels, prolongs the reproductive potential of animals. This suggests that oocyte loss with age is modulated by an atrotogenic effect of gonadotropins.

There is a gradual reduction in ovarian response to the pituitary gonadotropins beginining at least 2–5 years prior to menopause. Ovarian secretion of estradiol and progesterone decreases gradually, and suppression of LH and FSH by estrogen is reduced. Gonadotropin levels begin to increase. The final cessation of cyclic ovarian function leads to markedly decreased estrogen following menopause. LH and FSH levels increase markedly.

Uterine changes also occur secondary to altered ovarian hormones, as well as altered uterine responsiveness to hypothalamic, pituitary, and ovarian hormones and may contribute to a decrease in fecundity with age. Both estrogen receptor numbers and nuclear binding of estrogen receptors are decreased in the aged rodent uterus. Progesterone receptors do not change.

In contrast to the marked decline in ovarian estrogen secretion, ovarian adrenal androgen secretion and peripheral steroid conversion continue. As a result, the normal premenopausal estrogen to androgen and estrone to estradiol ratios are inverted.

The secondary effects of declining estrogen include genital tract atrophy, impaired autonomic vascular tone, and loss of bone density.

In the rat model of reproductive aging, changes are not seen in the number of GnRH-producing cells with age, and isolated hypothalami do not exhibit altered GnRH secretion. However, in vivo GnRH secretion may be reduced. The basic biochemical phenomena responsible for this change in secretion probably occur both within the GnRH-producing neurons and in response to altered cell–cell interactions. Several changes in gene expression occur within the GnRH neuron. Expression of galanin, a brain–gut peptide that colocalizes to a subpopulation of GnRH neurons, is markedly reduced in these cells in aged animals. Expression is linked to estrogen–progesterone levels, implying that the relative concentrations of these two hormones modulate age-related changes in GnRH neuron physiology.

In the CNS, *c-fos* acts as a transcription factor that activates a number of genes, including GnRH. In middle-aged female rats, expression of this gene in the hypothalamus during proestrus is markedly reduced compared with younger animals. Inputs from higher CNS neuroendocrine responsive centers may be indirectly responsible for the altered GnRH response with age in the intact animal. Widespread changes in dopaminergic and cholinergic neurons are known to occur with aging, including areas such as the amygdala and hippocampus, which are involved in higher CNS regulation of reproductive and sexual function. In addition, pituitary LH release in response to GnRH agonists is significantly reduced in aged female mice, and in older female rats the amplitude of FSH pulses is 50% of that found in younger rats.

Proliferative changes in the ovarian epithelium, such as papillomatous outgrowths, are more common in the postmenopausal ovary. Up to one-third of postmenopausal women have stromal hyperplasia. In a small proportion of these patients, excess androgen production causes virilization. Ovarian thecomas occur most commonly in the sixth decade of life and can secrete estrogen or androgens. Estrogenizing thecomas can be associated with endometrial carcinoma.

Lipid cell tumors of the ovary also typically occur in older women. Androstenedione secretion by these tumors can cause virilization.

VI. CALCIUM AND BONE METABOLISM

A. Age-Related Changes in Physiology

The most common age-related histologic change in the parathyroid glands is an increase in the number of oxyphil cells and an increased incidence of oxyphil cell nodules.

Palathyroid hormone (PTH) secretion increases, without a change in clearance, resulting in increased serum PTH in aged rats and in humans above age 65. This is believed to be a compensatory change in response to reduced production of calcitriol and reduced intestinal calcium absorption.

Up to 90% of long-term care elderly patients have subnormal serum levels of calcitriol, and many have elevated serum PTH levels. However, healthy elderly subjects may have normal levels of serum 25-hydroxyvitamin D and calcitriol.

Serum osteocalin, a marker of osteoblast activity, may be normal or decreased in aged humans in the setting of increased PTH. This suggests osteoblast resistance to PTH resulting in decreased bone formation and turnover. In aged rats serum osteocalin is decreased. Paradoxically, in rats, long-term ovariectomy increases bone osteocalin mRNA. The significance of this finding is unclear.

Elderly women have a higher maximal PTH response to EDTA-induced hypocalcemia compared to young women. They also have a greater nonsuppressible component of PTH secretion without a change in set-point. Therapy with 1, 25-dihydroxyvitamin D reverses the abnormal PTH secretory dynamics. Estrogen therapy will also attenuate the plasma PTH levels in elderly women. PTH levels also rise in aging rats. However, the set point for PTH release increases in aged male Fischer 344 rats.

In aged rabbits the renal response to PTH is blunted. There is a decrease in the stimulatory effect via cAMP on the Ca^{++}–Mg^{++}–ATPase. This may lead to decreased calcium reabsorption and increased urinary calcium loss.

In aged rats there is a failure of ionized calcium and 1, 25-dihydroxyvitamin D levels to increase in response to PTH, indicating that both kidney and skeleton may show reduced response to PTH with aging.

It is note worthy that age-related impairment of renal function may falsely elevate immunoassayable levels of PTH due to decreased clearance of PTH metabolites. This is especially of concern if assays for carboxy-terminal PTH are used. The intact PTH-IRMA (immunoradiometric assay) gives more accurate results than assays that measure carboxyl-terminal PTH.

Serum levels of 1,25-dihydroxyvitamin D, the most active form of vitamin D, have been reported either to decrease or remain unchanged in both men and women. Bone levels in women decrease after the age of 45. A decrease in the synthesis of 1,25-dihydroxyvitamin D occurs with aging. There is a decrease in 1α-hydroxylase in the kidney, which results in decreased conversion of 25-hydroxycholecalciferol to 1,25-dihydroxycholecalciferol. This is probably related to reduced responsiveness of the kidney 1α-hydroxylase to PTH.

Some studies have also shown a decrease in 25-hydroxyvitamin D, the substrate for 1α-hydroxylase. Serum 25-hydroxyvitamin D declines in some elderly subjects as a result of dietary insufficiency and decreased sun exposure.

Aging also reduces intestinal and skeletal receptors for 1,25-dihydroxyvitamin D in rats along with a baseline deficiency of calcitriol with aging. Treatment with 1,25-dehydroxyvitamin D partially reverses the decrease in intestinal receptors. Vitamin D replacement also improves oral calcium absorption.

The intestine's ability to absorb calcium decreases with age, especially after age 70. Intestinal calcium uptake decreases in senescent rats as a result of decreased stimulation by 1,25-dihydroxyvitamin D and a decline in calcium transport proteins. GH and PTH act synergistically to increase intestinal absorption of calcium in aged female rats. IGF-1 increases Ca^{++} transport across human intestinal cells in vitro independent of 1,25-dihydroxyvitamin D and may mediate the effect of GH. Thus this defect in intestinal transport may result at least in part from the decreased GH levels that are seen in aging. In addition, IGF-1 levels in femoral cortical bone have been shown to decrease in both men and women between the third and sixth decade of life. This may affect calcium transport into bone.

Aging also affects calcitonin (CT) secretion in female rats. In old but not young rats ovariectomy causes an increase in basal and Ca-stimulated CT levels. Estradiol reduces the plasma CT in response to hypercalcemia in old ovariectomized rats.

B. Osteopenia

Skeletal development is maximal in healthy individuals at age 25 in women and at age 30–35 in men. Bone changes occur during normal aging in both men and women. These include alterations in the dynamics of bone cell populations, uncoupling bone formation and resorption, changes in bone architecture, accumulation of microfractures, changes in mineralization and in the protein matrix. Aging also induces a decrease in skeletal mass. Osteopenia is defined as clinically significant bone loss. In addition to loss of bone mass, osteoporosis is accompanied by bone pain, spinal deformity, loss of height, and an increased incidence of fractures. In healthy males, radial bone mineral content decreases by 1% per year between 30 and 87 years of age, whereas vertebral bone mineral content decreases by 2.3% per year. Treatment with calcium carbonate and cholecalciferol for 3 years does not prevent the decrease in subjects with a high basal dietary calcium intake (>1100 mg/day). In addition, between the ages of 35 and 70 cortical bone strength in bending is decreased by 15–20%, and cancellous bone strength in compression is reduced by about 50%. Bone becomes increasingly brittle and fractures with less energy. [See BONE AND OSTEOPOROSIS.]

Susceptibility to clinically significant osteopenia is affected by many variables including genetics, nutritional status, body mass, exercise, and peak bone mass. Hormonal deficiency such as GH may contribute to lower than normal peak bone mass. Diabetes may be an additional risk factor for development of osteopenia. In rats both aging and Type I diabetes result in increased collagen-linked fluorescence in bone, a measure of nonenzymatic cross-links, which is correlated with decreased bone density, decreased serum osteocalcin, and increased bone fragility. The degree of osteopenia in the elderly depends partly on peak skeletal mass. Osteopenia can in part be prevented from becoming severe by maintaining good nutritional status (protein, calcium, vitamin D) and adequate physical activity.

Gonadal steroid effects on bone may be sex-specific. During development the bone metabolic response to gonadal hormones becomes gender-dependent on androgens in males and on estrogens in females. Androgen deficiency causes osteopenia in aging male rats. This can be reversed by treatment with testosterone, 5α-dihydrotestosterone, or 17β-estradiol.

In aged ovariectomized rats, treatment with estradiol prevents loss of spinal bone mineral content. Calcitonin is less effective. However N-terminal hPTH alone or in combination with estradiol or calcitonin increases BMC to sham-operated levels and increases mechanical strength. This is of special interest because estradiol treatment in oophorectomized women increases intestinal calcium absorption independent of 1,25-dihydroxyvitamin D, prevents BMC loss, and increases serum calcitonin levels. At least one large study has shown that bone mineral density in postmenopausal women can be maintained by estrogen replacement, into the ninth decade of life.

Treatment with oral calcium and vitamin D is also effective. Treatment with 800 I.U./day of vitamin D_3 decreased the fracture rate in a group of French nursing home patients. Other studies using 1,25-dihydroxyvitamin D have shown improved calcium absorption and BMC with a significant decrease in fracture rates.

VII. CARBOHYDRATE METABOLISM IN THE ELDERLY

A decline in glucose tolerance with age is a common finding that leads to an increased incidence of Type 2 or noninsulin-dependent diabetes (NIDDM) in the elderly. If we define diabetes by an oral glucose tolerance test value greater than 200 mg/dL at 2 hr with at least one additional value also above 200 (National Diabetes Data Group) then the percentage of males affected rises steadily from 5% at age 25 to over 30% at age 85. Nearly 50% of individuals with Type II diabetes are over the age of 65 years.

Elderly persons have reduced insulin sensitivity and impaired insulin-mediated glucose uptake in peripheral tissues, especially skeletal muscle. Impaired insulin action with age is not generally accompanied by changes in insulin membrane receptors in target cells. Impairment in the insulin-sensitive glucose trans-

porter, GLUT-4, may be responsible for the defect. Exercise in middle-aged subjects with NIDDM has been shown to elevate levels of GLUT-4 in skeletal muscle and improve glucose tolerance. Exercise in elderly men has been shown to increase the resting metabolic rate and possibly decrease circulating insulin levels and insulin-to-glucose ratios. These differences are related to the percent body fat composition of subjects.

In addition, the pancreatic islets show an increased sensitivity to inhibition of insulin by somatostatin. In rats the impaired secretion is increased by treatment of islets with somatostatin antibodies. This is compounded by the finding that the insulin-to-glucose ratio is usually decreased, suggesting relative islet cell resistance to glucose-stimulated insulin release. This last phenomenon may be related in part to reduced islet cell adenyl cyclase activity.

The insulin clearance rate decreases modestly from a half-life of 11 min in the young to 13 min in the elderly. Plasma glucagon clearance is not changed.

Plasma levels of glucagon do not change with age. In rats secretion of glucagon from pancreatic islets increases with aging. The age-related change in glucagon secretion may be secondary to altered glucose homeostasis, or to reduced pancreatic α-cell responsiveness to glucose or other paracrine regulatory factors. In the elderly the lipolytic and ketogenic but not the hyperglycemic responses to pulsatile glucagon are significantly reduced.

The prevalence of diabetic complications, including retinopathy, nephropathy, and neuropathy, increases with the duration of diabetes. Aging may accelerate the onset of complications due to synergistic effects of aging and diabetes on cellular metabolism.

Advanced glycation end products (AGEs) form spontaneously from glucose-derived Amadori products and accumulate on long-lived tissue proteins. AGEs have been implicated in the pathophysiology of both aging and diabetes.

Pentosidine, a glycation reaction product found in skin and glomerular basement membrane, increases with age. Levels are further elevated above the 95 confidence limit in 80% of diabetics, both Type I and Type II, when compared with age-related nondiabetic controls.

Vibratory perception and thermal discrimination decrease with both age and diabetes. Autonomic dysfunction is also compromised by both factors. Diabetic patients (both Type I and Type II) develop superior mesenteric ganglioneuronal lesions prematurely and in greater numbers than nondiabetic patients.

A number of age-related coexisting disorders may complicate the management of diabetes in the elderly. These include hypodipsia, anorexia, visual impairment, impaired baroreceptor response, depression, altered renal or hepatic function, and multiple medications. The elderly are more prone to hypoglycemia from use of sulfonylureas but may also have a more varied response to insulin. Variations in response to insulin with exercise are also heightened in the elderly. Dietary management may be more difficult, and exercise regimens should be tailored individually according to coexisting physical limitations, such as organic heart disease. In addition, the reduced thirst perception and use of multiple medications increase the risk of hyperglycemic hyperosmolar coma.

In normal aging the pancreas shows loss of compact structure of islets with hyalinization, increased amyloid deposition, and increased incidence of tumors, especially islet cell tumors. Hyalinization is found in almost 50% of diabetic patients over the age of 60. Amyloid, possibly of insulin β-chain origin, is present in the pancreatic islets of approximately 60% of elderly nondiabetic subjects. Most islet cell tumors, especially glucagonomas and somatostatinomas, are diagnosed in the fifth through seventh decades of life.

VIII. WATER METABOLISM IN THE ELDERLY

Multiple interrelated changes in water and electrolyte homeostasis occur with aging (Table V). Elderly subjects show unusual thirst following dehydration, heat stress, or hypertonic saline infusion. There is a change in perception of thirst, possibly a deficit in the opioid-sensitive drinking drive, mediated through oropharyngeal receptors. Naloxone administration decreases fluid intake in young but not old subjects after overnight fluid deprivation; older subjects have a lower rehydration intake after placebo as well. [See HOMEOSTASIS; THIRST AND HYDRATION.]

AVP secretion from the pituitary gland responds

Table V   Age-Related Changes in Water and Salt Homeostasis[a]

Thirst	↓[b]
AVP, baseline	↑ or no change
AVP, after dehydration	↑ (reduced threshold)
Renal response to AVP	↓
Renin–angiotensin	↓
ANP	↑
Renal response to ANP	↓ or no change
Aldosterone responsiveness	↓ (2° ↓ PRA)
Baroreflex sensitivity	↓

[a] AVP, arginine vasopressin; ANP, atrial natriuretic peptide; PRA, plasma renin activity.
[b] ↓, decrease; ↑, increase.

to salt (osmoreceptor) and fluid states (baroreceptor). Baseline AVP secretion in healthy elderly, both supine and ambulatory, may not differ from healthy young subjects when there is no age-related difference in serum osmolarity. However, some studies have shown an increase in baseline AVP with age. There is a rise in AVP following dehydration in both young and old. However, the lowest level of plasma osmolality that will initiate AVP secretion (osmotic threshold) is reduced in the elderly. In addition, the rehydration fall in AVP found in young subjects is not seen in the elderly.

Older subjects also show a reduced AVP response to volume–pressure change with relative renal assistance to AVP. The decreased response may be due to changes in AVP receptors in the kidney. Decreased cyclic AMP (cAMP) generation in response to AVP is involved in the age-related impairment of urinary concentrating ability. This may predispose the elderly to dehydration when intercurrent illness causes increased water loss or limited access to water.

Another important physiological stimulus of AVP secretion is angiotensin II. With aging, plasma renin activity is decreased along with a reduction in angiotensin-converting enzyme activity. Thus the elderly have a reduced capacity for generating angiotensin II, a potent stimulator of AVP secretion and thirst. Hypoangiotensinemia has been implicated as the pathogenetic mechanism of dehydration in a group of hypernatremic elderly patients.

Aging is associated with a decreased ability to excrete salt and water, thus increasing susceptibility to volume overload in elderly individuals. Atrial natriuretic peptide (ANP) is secreted in response to volume expansion and has both diuretic and natriuretic actions. Baseline ANP has been found to be elevated in elderly humans and aged rats. The normal decrease in ANP following dehydration is blunted in the elderly. The source of increased ANP appears to be increased cardiac peptide synthesis, as mRNA levels and immunoreactive peptide are both increased in the left ventricle of aged rats. Young subjects exhibit a significant circadian rhythm for ANP, which elderly subjects do not have.

The effects of aging on ANP action in the kidney are controversial. A 2-hour low-dose ANP analog infusion in one group of healthy elderly men failed to illicit the expected change in blood pressure or renal salt excretion, despite an increase in urinary cyclic guanosine monophosphate (cGMP). Others have found the natriuretic effect of native ANP to be preserved in aging despite a diminished renal hemodynamic response. Renal blood flow decreases and renal vascular resistance increases in young but not old subjects after a 2-hour peptide infusion.

ANP suppresses vasopressin release and raises the threshold of vasopressin release in response to osmotic stimulation in both young and elderly individuals. High baseline circulating ANP levels may also be in part responsible for the observed decrease in PRA. PRA is decreased up to 50% in the elderly, and this reduction in PRA is probably the main cause of decreased aldosterone responsiveness, which is observed in the elderly.

BIBLIOGRAPHY

Campbell, S., & Mooradian, A. D. (1993). Diabetes mellitus. In R. Bressler, M. D. Katz (Eds.), *Geriatric pharmacology* (pp. 409–425). New York: McGraw Hill.

Cummings, D. C. (1990). Menarche menses and menopause: A brief review. *Cleveland Clinical Journal Medicine 57*, 169–175.

Mooradian, A. D. (1992). Management of diabetes in the elderly. In J. E. Morley, S. G. Korenman (Eds.), *Endocrinology and metabolism in the elderly* (pp. 388–405). Oxford: Blackwell Scientific Publications.

Mooradian, A. D. (1992). Water balance in the elderly. In J. E. Morley, S. G. Korenman (Eds.), *Endocrinology and metabolism in the elderly* (pp. 124–136). Oxford: Blackwell Scientific Publications.

Mooradian, A. D. (1992). Geriatric neuroendocrinology. In C. B. Nemenroff (Ed.), *Neuroendocrinology* (pp. 541–562). Boca Raton: CRC Press.

Mooradian, A. D. (1993). Mechanisms of age-related endocrine alterations. *Drugs and Aging, 3*, Part I, 81–97; Part II, 131–146.

Mooradian, A. D. (1995). Normal age-related changes in thyroid hormone economy. *Clinical Geriatriatric Medicine. 11*, 159–169.

Mooradian, A. D., & Wong, N. C. W. (1994). Age-related changes in thyroid hormone action. *European Journal of Endocrinology 131*, 451–461.

Riggs, B. L., & Melton III, L. J. (1992). The prevention and treatment of osteoporosis. (*New England Journal of Medicine. 327*, 620–627.

Sieman, T. E., & Robbins, R. J. (1994). Aging and hypothalamic-pituitary-adrenal response to challenge in humans. *Endocrinology Review, 15*, 233–260.

Tenover, J. S. (1992). Male hormonal changes with aging. In J. E. Morley, S. G. Korenman (Eds.), *Endocrinology and metabolism in the elderly* (pp. 243–261). Boston, MA: Blackwell Scientific Publications

Epidemiology

Kenneth G. Manton

Duke University

Active Life Expectancy The average number of years a member of a population may expect to live free of chronic disability.

Atherogenesis The physiological process by which atherosclerotic plaques start and grow within an organism's circulatory system.

Carcinogenesis The physiological processes leading to loss of growth control by cells in particular tissue systems that lead to the development of malignant cell clones or tumors.

Censoring The systematic loss of cases in a study due to processes relevant to the study goals.

Compression of Mortality Implies that there is a biologically fixed upper bound to the human life span near enough to a population's current life expectancy that further mortality reductions will be constrained by that limit.

Mortality Selection The systematic loss of persons from a population due to high mortality risks being associated with specific characteristics under study.

Observation Plan The logical structure under which data is collected to describe specific processes or events with particular characteristics.

Oldest-old An extremely elderly population often characterized by high rates of comorbidity and chronic disability. Often defined as persons aged 85+.

Osteoporosis The loss of bone mineral density, usually at later ages, and more often in postmenopausal females, often due to hormonal changes.

Plasticity of Aging The concept that the outcomes of biological processes underlying senescence and age-related health changes may be altered by exogenous factors.

EPIDEMIOLOGY is the study of the causes and manifestations of disease in either free-living or experimentally selected populations. Epidemiological methods, concepts, and data vary greatly with the specific diseases and population groups studied. For example, there are well-established epidemiological methods for the study of tropical diseases due to parasites and very different methods for examining the emergence of chronic diseases in developed country populations. Below I consider a relatively new area of study (i.e., the epidemiology of aging).

I. DEFINITION AND CONCEPTS

Epidemiology is the study of the effects of diseases on populations, their health and longevity, and the factors causing and agents transmitting disease. Classically, epidemiology was the study of diseases caused by infectious organisms (i.e., the study of "epidemics")—the rapid rise in disease incidence in a population due to a common exposure to a pathogen (or environmental toxin). Implicit in the classical concept was that there were "host" factors determining the susceptibility of an organism to an exposure, commonly termed a pathogen (for a biological agent like a parasite, bacteria, or virus), or environmental hazard (for physical agents like lead or asbestos exposure), which were transmitted to susceptible members of a population by an agent (e.g., mosquitos for malaria or yellow fever; infected hypodermic needles for AIDS) termed the disease vector.

These, and other epidemiological concepts are modified in studying aging and chronic disease. Chronic disease epidemiology deals with disease processes, often with lengthy latency periods between exposure and disease manifestation with long natural histories of manifest and evolving health consequence for the host. Many physiological mechanisms determining chronic disease progression involve more complex interactions, over longer periods of times, between the natural history of the disease and the physiological characteristics of the host, than in infectious diseases. For example, both atherogenesis and carcinogenesis, after being triggered by exposures, could be manifest in self-sustaining "pathological" physiological processes in the host.

The interactions of disease, disability, and host characteristics in the epidemiology of aging are more complex than for chronic diseases—in part because boundaries between declines in physiological function with age and age-related chronic disease processes become more difficult to delineate as the host's functional age increases. The need for specialized methods, data, and models also increases as, in many developed countries, more persons survive to historically extreme ages. This is because as life expectancy in the United States, for example, increases at later ages (e.g., above age 65 or 85), there is greater potential for the host physiology and the natural history of the disease to systematically change with age—and in ways not often observed in the past. In U.S. Asian and Pacific Islanders, Census Bureau period life expectancy estimates for 1993 are 86.2 years for females and 80.2 years for males—implying even higher cohort life expectancies of perhaps 89 years for females and 83 years for males. This is even higher than Japan, the country with the highest life expectancy at birth (i.e., in 1992, 83.0 years for females and 76.2 years for males) or in Okinawa, the Japanese prefecture with the highest life expectancy. Not only are the U.S. elderly (65+) and oldest-old (85+) populations growing rapidly, but the fastest growing populations are even older. Kestenbaum found the U.S. centenarian population grew 7% per annum between 1980 and 1987 with that growth rate continuing, perhaps even increasing after 1987. Similar rapid growth rates (i.e., 7–8% per annum) for centenarian populations have been observed for longer periods (i.e., two to three decades) in several European countries. Jeune suggested that no one may have survived to age 100 before 1800 and to age 110 before 1931. Thus, the emergence of large centenarian populations is a recent, novel demographic phenomena. [*See* LONGEVITY AND LONG-LIVED POPULATIONS.]

In addition, there is evidence of declines in the age-specific prevalence of chronic disability and morbidity at late ages. The decline may partly be due to early cohort differences in nutrition. Fogel found chronic morbidity prevalence declined 6% per decade for the 75 years between that for Civil War veterans aged 65+ in 1910 versus World War II veterans aged 65+ in 1985. Manton and colleagues found declines in U.S. chronic morbidity and disability prevalence over age 65 from 1982 to 1989, also possibly due to cohort changes in early health care and socioeconomic status.

Thus, not only are there more very elderly persons, not only is the health of the extreme elderly population systematically changing by cohort, not only is there evidence of the plasticity of aging processes in individuals to extreme ages, but researchers are also beginning to observe types of disease–aging interactions that had been rare. For example, Perls found persons aged 95+ may be, on average, healthier than persons 20 years younger due to mortality selection. Fiatarone and colleagues found physical function could be significantly improved at extreme ages (e.g., ages 90+). The slowing of the age trajectory of morbidity and mortality risks at extreme ages (90+) were predicted by theoretical models of human aging and mortality but, until recently, there have not been sufficiently large numbers of extreme elderly persons to study the trajectory of those processes. They were first examined in intensive longitudinal studies of small (e.g., $N = 273$ in the first Duke Longitudinal Study of Aging; $N = 512$ in the Second Duke Longitudinal Study) select elderly cohorts. Consequently, a major task for epidemiological studies of aging is to discern the physiological consequences of age-related disease processes (e.g., chronic diseases like cancer, whose risk increases as a function of the time exposed) from age-dependent processes (i.e., those relating to physiological processes of senescence, e.g., the role of the teleomere in affecting the fidelity of genetic trait transmission) at extreme ages in more general populations. How these processes operate in the population will have major consequences for U.S. health and long-term care policy because of the high average per capita needs of extreme elderly persons.

Also needed to study health at late ages are specialized longitudinal study designs to distinguish aging effects from age-related disease. Early clinical studies of aging processes found that representative samples of elderly populations give different estimates of the age rate of loss of physiological function than study populations that have been screened, with persons with existing chronic disease selected out, to remove explicit chronic disease effects. Put differently, because the prevalence of chronic diseases increases strongly with age, it must be controlled at selection into a longitudinal study population to determine intrinsic rates of aging—as opposed to rates of change contaminated by the impact of chronic disease. For example, Kasch and colleagues found the age rate of decline of cardiac function in physically active elderly populations increased at half of the prior rate estimate. Kitzman and Edward, examining changes in the myocardium with age, found many changes once attributed to aging, to be caused by specific pathological processes. Likewise, Fiatarone and colleagues found voluntary muscle in very elderly (e.g., aged 86–96) and frail populations could respond significantly (e.g., an average increase of 174% in quadricep strength in one study) to resistance training with weights—a result confirmed in clinical trials where nutrition was supplemented.

Another factor requiring study in the epidemiology of aging is that, along with the aging of the individual, there is a lengthy temporal trajectory, or natural history, of chronic disease processes. In the epidemiology of infectious diseases the natural history of a disease was often the life history of a pathogen as it moved through different stages of development (and degrees of infectivity) in different disease vectors (e.g., the natural history of the malarial plasmodium). This is different than studying either the cause of a chronic disease, or changes in its manifestations, in hosts of different physiological ages. For example, several studies have found a significant prevalence of atherosclerotic plaques in young populations (e.g., in the Pathobiological Determinants of Atherosclerosis in Youth (PDAY) study at ages 15–34). Depending on the interactions of risk factors (e.g., high- and low-density lipoprotein (HDL–LDL) ratio; smoking; diabetes; hypertension; factors affecting fibrinolysis; homocysteine metabolism; factors affecting the pro-

duction of free radicals and lipid oxidation; factors affecting growth of smooth muscles in arterial intima), atherogenesis proceeds at different rates in different persons at different ages. In interaction with stress and neuroendocrinological factors, ischemic disease of the myocardium may cause infarction, further ischemia, and myocyte loss (death of myocardium). Now, surgical procedures and thrombolytic agents applied early in the ischemia infarction process may minimize loss of myocardium—even to extreme ages (e.g., >80). However, even a small loss of myocardium may interact with age-dependent cardiac changes at sufficiently late ages to cause congestive heart failure (CHF). [*See* ATHEROSCLEROSIS.]

In highly industrialized societies like the United States and Germany, the age-related evolution of the natural history of "heart disease" may be quite different. The 1988–1991 National Health and Nutrition Examination Survey (NHANESIII) documented the rapid achievement of many goals of the National Cholesterol Education program—both in reducing the population mean cholesterol level and the proportion of the U.S. population with elevated (>240 mg/dl) cholesterol. This, along with improved drug therapy, may slow, or even cause regression of atherosclerotic plaques. In Germany, Hoffmeister and colleagues found cardiovascular disease (CVD) mortality declined 19% between 1984 and 1989 for persons aged 25–69 because of improved medical interventions and reduced case fatality rates. However, some risk factors (i.e., total cholesterol and body mass index [BMI]) showed adverse trends. This suggests that CHF may be, in the future, more prevalent above age 70 in Germany than the United States. Even in the United States, despite large decreases in stroke and CHD mortality, the mortality and hospitalization rates for CHF increased until recently (i.e., the first decline in CHF mortality was documented in 1989). This may be due to use of angiotensin-converting enzyme II (ACE-II) inhibitors but may also reflect population changes in lipoprotein profiles, the health effects of which require 5 years to become fully manifest. [*See* CARDIOVASCULAR SYSTEM; CHOLESTEROL AND CELL PLASMA MEMBRANES.]

The natural history of certain treatable cancers has also changed in that, with improved surveillance to detect microdisease recurrence, it may be possible to intervene before a recurrence becomes systemic. If a recurrence is detected early enough, therapies effective in treating early-stage disease may also prolong survival in early recurrent disease. This extension of survival for persons with disease seems to have occurred for female breast cancer. Some agents like Tamoxifen (an antiestrogen) in female breast cancer, retinoic acid (a redifferentiating agent) in head and neck cancer, or certain isomers of Vitamin E may delay, or even prevent, disease recurrence. [See Cancer and the Elderly.]

Other types of cancer, such as prostate and multiple myeloma have a strong age dependence and increase in prevalence as the population ages. A predisposing condition for multiple myeloma, monoclonal gammopathies of unknown significance (MGUS) have prevalences as high as 19% in occidental populations aged 95+—though MGUS rates in Asian populations are much lower. Thus, the process triggering these cancers may have a more direct relation to the genetic basis of the senescence of certain organ systems in specific racial groups (i.e., prostate cancer risk). In addition to multiple myeloma, prostate cancer risk rises rapidly with age and is less prevalent in Asian than either white or black populations.

A third factor in the epidemiology of aging is that often instead of studying specific diseases, one studies age changes in the degree and type of disability of the host. This is more significant in the epidemiology of aging because of the longer natural history of chronic disease processes, the greater likelihood of multiple diseases coexisting (and interacting) and because a disease at the same stage may have different effects on the functioning of hosts of different physiological ages. In addition, the loss of functioning may itself trigger lethal chronic disease. Colantonio and colleagues found loss of function a risk factor for stroke. Osteoporosis can lead to hip and vertebral fractures that cause disability and predisposition to diseases related to physical debilitation (e.g., pneumonia, peripheral circulatory disease, heart disease). [See Bone and Osteoporosis.]

Measuring functional loss is difficult in elderly populations in that one is not assessing the presence or absence of a disease but the impact over time of one or more of many predisposing diseases on the host's ability to perform specific basic life sustaining functions (e.g., activities of daily living [ADLs] or Instrumental ADLs [IADLs]). One also needs to assess functional changes over time (e.g., "active" life expectancy) as well as discriminate quantitatively be-

tween different types and intensities of disability. Manton and colleagues showed how multivariate procedures could be used to identify the dimensions of function from batteries of functional and physical performance measures. There are conceptual issues involved in disability measurement that affect measurement technologies. There is no overall "gold standard" to validate the diagnosis of disability. Different researchers may make observations about disability that may have equal validity for their study's goals. For example, self-reports of disability may better reflect the morale of the elderly individual and his or her self-perception of what his or her functional capacity "should be." This may better predict the behavior of an impaired older person than physical performance evaluations. That behavior may translate into further health and functional changes—especially in the very elderly (e.g., persons remaining active at later ages better maintain function and health).

A fourth area in the epidemiology of aging is the need to assess multiple interacting diseases and disabilities. As a person ages the likelihood of manifesting a second disease increases with time. This is complicated by the fact that, to survive to late ages to incur subsequent comorbidities, the initial disease process must not be rapidly lethal. Thus, the presence of multiple comorbidities can be an indication of survival to late ages and possibly the prevalence of less aggressive disease. This also suggests that the threshold for defining disease, or a risk state, changes with age (e.g., changes in the criteria for hypercholesterolemia or systolic hypertension with age). This is an area of potential controversy because, although longitudinal studies may suggest a decline with age in the risk associated with a particular risk factor level (e.g., a total cholesterol of 240 mg/dl) that decline may be the result of increased prevalence of chronic diseases with age. Thus, persons in good health at late ages may have the same risk for a given risk factor level as in a much younger person. This affects decisions about whether treatments of diseases should change with age. The Systolic Hypertension in the Elderly Program (SHEP) trials found significant reductions in stroke were achieved by treating isolated systolic hypertension at late ages. In contrast, mildly "elevated" diastolic blood pressure (BP) at late ages may indicate the ability of the heart to maintain prefusion even with some loss of arterial compliance—low diastolic BP may imply impaired cardiac response (e.g., partial "pump" failure).

A fifth area of study in the epidemiology of aging is that effects of genetic factors may be different at later ages due to mortality selection. In studies of twin populations the maximum risk associated with a genetic predisposition to circulatory disease appears to occur in middle age. The risk of genetic factors tends to decline at late ages. This is likely due to lethal genetic manifestations of chronic diseases selecting out susceptible persons so that survivors to late ages have more complex and subtle genetic predispositions to disease. Marenberg and colleagues showed this in a large Swedish study of CHD mortality risk in monozygotic (MZ) and dyzygotic (DZ) twins. The relative risk of CHD death in MZ twins was about 15:1 in middle age—but declined to 1.0 at ages 85+. Similar age patterns of genetic effects were noted in other twin studies. Selection also appeared to reduce the prevalence of the ApoE-4 genotypes in Finnish centenarians, as well as thyroid autoantibodies in Italian centenarians, and human leukocyte antigens (HLA) markers for adult-onset diabetes in Okinawian nonagenarians and centenarians. Similar effects of mortality selection on genetic risks are noted for specific cancers. Lung cancer associated with a genetic predisposition due to dysfunctions in the cytochrome *P-450* enzyme system had a prevalence of 69% at age 50 but only 22% by age 70. [*See* BEHAVIORAL GENETICS.]

II. CONCEPTUAL FRAMEWORKS

These differences, in sum, suggest that the epidemiology of aging requires specialized data, concepts, and methods to deal with the complex dynamics of multiple interacting disease and aging processes. This is illustrated in Figure 1, by a model based on a generalization of the life table survival function (l_x) where there are "survival" functions for morbidity and disability as well as mortality.

In Figure 1 there are three "survival" curves for a hypothetical cohort. The outermost curve (C) reflects the proportion surviving to age x. The second (B) reflects the proportion of the cohort surviving to age x free of disability. The third (A) reflects the proportion surviving to age x without chronic morbidity. Areas between curves represent the number of person-years expected to be lived in a health state. For example,

the area under curve C reflects the total number of person-years lived. Life expectancy is calculated by dividing the number of person-years lived by the initial cohort size. The area under curve B is the number of person-years lived without disability (but possibly with nondisabling diseases). Dividing this number of person-years by the initial cohort size yields the "active" life expectancy. The area under curve A represents the number of person-years lived free of morbidity. Division of this by the initial cohort size yields the "healthy" life expectancy. [*See* COHORT STUDIES.]

Figure 1 is an idealization of health processes in a birth cohort because there can be many specific chronic diseases examined and because disability may vary considerably in type (e.g., cognitive impairment; lower limb impairment leading to problems with mobility) and intensity. The survival curves in Figure 1 can be calculated in different ways depending on the data available. The most basic computations use life tables estimated from vital statistics data and disease and disability prevalence estimates from cross-sectional health surveys. Such procedures are limited in that the rates of health transitions and improvements in individual functioning are unobserved in cross-sectional data. To estimate more complex models, with bidirectional changes in health and function, true longitudinal data are needed with consideration of how the temporal structure of the observational plan detects health episodes of different durations. Nonetheless, Figure 1 is conceptually useful to emphasize the changing linkage with age of mortality and disease dynamics. Even its implementation with prevalence data gives useful summaries of the population impact of disease and disability at a point in time.

Fundamental to evaluating models like in Figure 1 are the effects of biological life span limits on the age linkages of mortality, disease, and disability. In other areas of epidemiology, life span limits are usually not important because ages that are truly extreme for humans as a species are not often studied (e.g., many chronic diseases are studied in middle-aged populations). Studies of nonagenarians and centenarians are often restricted to small populations. The effects of life span limits are related to the rectangularization, or "squaring," of the human survival curve and to the "compression of mortality." This raises questions about the effects of life span limits on the age-specific linkage of mortality with other health events. Such questions have been termed the "compression of mor-

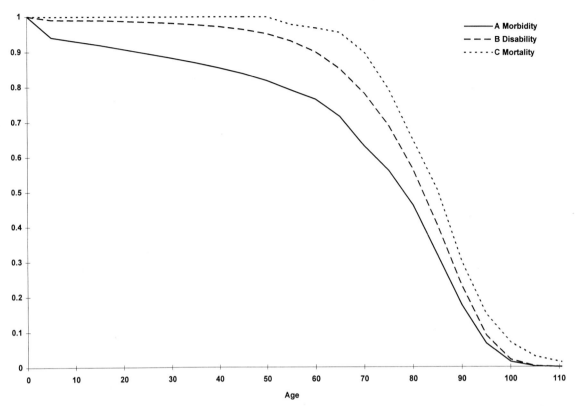

Figure 1 Theoretical relations of morbidity, disability, and mortality outcomes, represented by the change of survival over age.

bidity" (i.e., whether the age at onset of disease or disability can be changed or delayed without increasing life expectancy).

Morbidity and mortality compression pose additional questions:

1. Is there an upper limit to the age to which persons may survive?
2. What is the shape of the survival curve as the life span limit is approached (i.e., how does the variability in the distribution of ages at death decrease)?
3. How are the age structures of morbidity and survival curves affected as that limit is approached?

The maximum life span is difficult to identify analytically because one can only know the lower bound to the life span limit (e.g., a French woman, still living, recently exceeded a documented age of 120.9; a woman living in California reported an age of 126

based on her birth certificate and other documentation). Of more interest is how individual life span potentials are distributed in a population. Manton and colleagues also raised questions about the formalization of concepts of survival curve rectangularization suggesting difficulties in their formalization often prevent a rigorous statistical evaluation.

Many questions about the compression of mortality involve how the genetic heterogeneity in the maximum life span for individuals is distributed. This is important because it determines the degree of irreducible variability in the distribution of those limits. If there is considerable irreducible (e.g., genetic) heterogeneity then the survival curve may never become rectangularized (i.e., its shape will reflect the distribution of the genetic endowment for survival). This is illustrated in Figure 2.

In Figure 2 are plotted the three survival curves from Figure 1 and a "rectangularized" survival curve, C^*. Though life expectancy is roughly the same (i.e.,

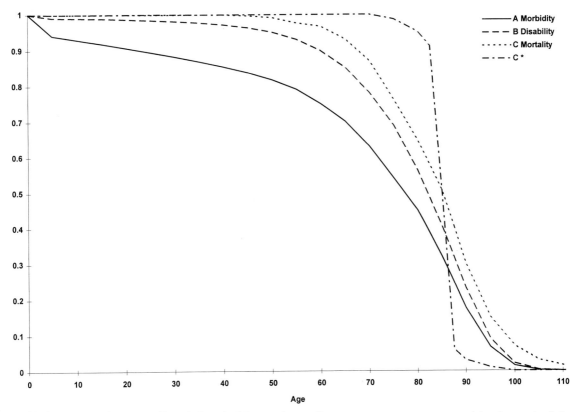

Figure 2 Theoretical relation of morbidity, disability, and mortality outcomes over age represented by changes in their survival curve with the survival curve for mortality drawn to represent (A) a highly rectangularized mortality age pattern (C*), and (B) an age pattern of mortality with significant intrinsic heterogeneity.

the median life span is 90 years for both) for C and C*, survival curve C has more variability (i.e., the standard deviation for C is about 5 years; for C* less than 1 year).

Empirically, as U.S. life expectancy increased so has the variability of ages of death (i.e., the mean and variance of ages at death simultaneously increased so both life expectancy and the highest observed age at death increased). In Social Security life tables for 1990, female life expectancy is 78.7 years and is projected to increase modestly, by 2080, to 84.6 years (+5.9 years). For males the increase is 6.6 years (i.e., from 71.6 to 78.2). The increase in life endurancy (i.e., the age to which 1 in 100,000 persons can expect to survive) is over 12 years for both males and females over the same period. Thus, in those calculations the upper limit of the age at death distribution is expected to increase twice as fast (i.e., to 125 or more years)

as life expectancy. This is different than what occurred from 1900 to 1990, where life expectancy increased 39.2 years for females and 25.2 years for males, whereas life endurancy increased only 7 to 8 years. This is because most life expectancy increases from 1900 to 1990 were due to mortality declines at early ages. After 1990 there is less potential for change at those ages. This again suggests that the epidemiology of aging has to deal with population phenomena that are historically unprecedented; hence, there will necessarily be a need for greater reliance on theory and ancillary data. Of course, a critical issue is how curves B and A will change over age as C changes. Perl suggests that the distance between the disability (B) and mortality (C) curves will be maximum at ages 75–85 and will decline above age 95.

It is likely that there is no simple model for the limiting distribution of ages at death in that, at advanced ages, many genetic effects will interact in complex ways with the environment. Because humans have long life spans and live in heterogeneous environments, it is difficult to isolate genetic and environmental influences on disease risks to assess how health will change at late ages (i.e., age changes in the relation of the three curves above age 95). This is why new observational plans and data are needed.

The shape of the U.S. survival, morbidity, and disability curves have practical implications for various health interventions—both preventative and therapeutic. If either preventative or therapeutic actions are to have significant benefits they must be introduced sufficiently far from the life span-limiting distribution and the associated morbidity and disability curves to produce a sizable effect over time. The effect depends strongly on the relation of the three curves above, say, age 85.

III. STUDY DESIGNS

Resolution of many of the specific issues raised in the first two sections requires special types of longitudinal observational plans.

A problem in designing such plans is that many questions about aging and disease processes may be so detailed that experimental and clinical studies will have to be used to answer specific design issues before population studies of very elderly populations are fielded. For example, the role of antioxidants in preventing disease has been investigated in a number of studies. Vitamin E may have benefit in reducing circulatory disease possibly by slowing atherogenesis and improving glucose metabolism, although the levels of consumption necessary to cause such effects may be considerably higher than the standard recommended daily allowance (RDA) (e.g., 100 vs. 30 international units). Of equal importance is that certain chemical forms (isomers) of specific micronutrients have different physiological effects. Prasad-Edward found that alpha tocopheral succinate (as opposed to alpha tocopheral acetate) may be an even more powerful cellular redifferentiating agent than vitamin A. Other isomers of vitamin E were not as biologically active. Similar issues about the bioactivity of specific chemical forms of a micronutrient have been raised for Vitamin D in treating osteoporosis. It is unlikely that trials and population studies can evaluate all pos-

sible isomers of micronutrients for their degree of biological activity. The selection of the forms of micronutrients evaluated in population studies and the levels of supplementation examined will have to be informed by the consensus of experimental and laboratory results. [See DIET AND NUTRITION.]

As suggested, major issues in study design are the degree of selection in populations of different ages and the temporal structure of the observational plan and its ability to identify disease and disability episodes of different durations. A major area for innovation in study designs of elderly populations is emerging because the quality of U.S. population data is improving. This is due, in part, to the introduction of Social Security in 1937–1938 and Medicare in 1966–1967. Their introduction required improved and more complete registration of the U.S. population and, at the age of entitlement, required relatively rigorous proof of age to receive benefits. In addition, the U.S. vital registration system was completed when Texas entered the system in 1933. Furthermore, the education of elderly cohorts (e.g., aged 85 to 89) has improved since 1980 and will continue to improve to at least 2015—a time when those oldest-old cohorts will have very high proportions educated. Because of these changes, age reporting in U.S. vital registration (i.e., death certificate data) and in Social Security and Medicare records is of similar quality (up to at least age 95 for whites) and will improve further as time passes.

This implies a de facto computerized population registry is developing in the United States, one whose quality of age reporting at late ages is increasing with time since the innovation of its major components. Thus, there are computerized data systems containing lists of all Medicare-eligible persons from which samples of elderly persons can be drawn for health surveys and studies for any specific point in time. This has several advantages over area-probability survey designs based on census data that are employed in many national health surveys. In the list samples, specific elderly individuals are sampled. Because the Medicare list contains data on the age of the person, oversampling of persons at extreme ages can be done from the near complete listing of the U.S. elderly population. Such a person-based sample means that residents in facilities of all types are included. The follow-up of individuals for reinterviewing can be done through Medicare files so that nearly 100% of persons from a prior sample can be tracked and the characteristics of nonrespondents identified. In Medicare files reported ages and dates of death are available as well as information on Medicare-reimbursed use of health services.

In area probability samples, households in an area are sampled so that characteristics of individual elderly nonrespondents are not directly available. The lack of an administrative list sample also means follow-up of individuals, and the identification of decedents is more difficult and likely less complete. Furthermore, because censuses are only done every 10 years, sampling must be based on estimated population characteristics at points in time potentially distant (e.g., 7–8 years) from when the census data are drawn.

Thus, the availability of Medicare-based list samples allows one to draw national samples and to better track them over time. This means that mortality selection and population representativeness can be assessed more completely and on a near real-time basis. This allows for national longitudinal sample survey designs like that of the National Long Term Care Survey (NLTCS) illustrated in Figure 3.

The NLTCS has been conducted in 1982, 1984, 1989, and 1994. Survey records are linked to Medicare service use and mortality files for the entire period. The survey intervals of 2, 5, and 5 years allow for long-term health and functional bidirectional changes to be observed. Because individuals are sampled, persons living in both the community and in institutions of all types are sampled. This was a difficulty in the 1984 Supplement on Aging (SOA) and the 1986, 1988, and 1990 LSOA follow-up (i.e., the

1984 SOA sample was only of community residents so that an institutional sample had to be accumulated over time).

In addition to tracking samples of elderly individuals over time there are two supplementary sampling processes in the NLTCS. The first relied on the fact that because the U.S. prevalence of chronic disability was unknown in 1982, a sample of 35,000 individuals was used (of a total of 55,000 initially drawn from Medicare lists) to get 6000+ detailed community interviews in 1982. There were 26,623 persons who, in 1982, were screened and reported no chronic disability. This sample was larger than needed to meet statistical power requirements for precisely estimating disability incidence rates between 1982 and 1984. Thus, in 1984 only 12,100 persons in the nondisabled sample component were rescreened. The remaining cases define a reservoir of persons, all 65+ in 1982, who could be drawn from for screening at future dates (i.e., 1989, 1994) to maintain the sample size of very elderly (e.g., 85+) persons who have relatively high mortality. Second, to ensure that each cross-sectional sample was representative of all persons 65+, new samples of about 5,000 persons passing age 65 between surveys were drawn from Medicare files and screened for disability. Thus, all NLTCS represent the total U.S. population 65+ at each survey date.

With the 12 years of follow-up (1982–1994) it is possible to make comparisons of very elderly cohorts (e.g., those with residual life expectancies of 5–7 years). Five year intervals are long enough so that significant changes in health and functioning can accumulate in the population. Though a 5-year interval

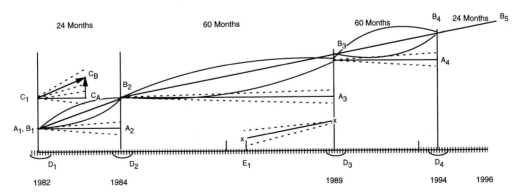

Figure 3 A time line representing the intervals between the 1982, 1984, 1989, and 1994 National Long Term Care Survey and representations of individual sample patterns of disability change, and mortality between those times.

misses shorter health transitions occurring within intersurvey intervals, persons in episodes of all lengths are captured in each sample. However, because the likelihood of sampling a health episode is related to its length, the proportion of short episodes sampled will be small. Furthermore, the weighting of individuals to produce national estimates of health transitions is complex because the interview period is approximately 4 months (areas marked D in Figure 3) so the attrition of sample members within an interview period has to be considered. However, because the exact dates of death are known for periods after 1982, deaths occurring within an interview period can be linked to survey responses at a prior time. This reduces left censoring bias in the 1984, 1989, and 1994 NLTCS.

It is possible to systematically supplement the samples and still make weight calculations because the U.S. population proportions at any point in time are known from the Medicare lists. For census-based samples the population proportions are "known" only every 10 years—between censuses only estimates are available. Thus, in the 1994 NLTCS, a supplementary sample of 540 persons aged 95+ could be drawn to improve the precision of health change estimates at late ages.

The content of core disability and health conditions in the NLTCS was held constant over time so basic health changes could be monitored over time. However, within the time limits to respondent burden in a personal interview of elderly persons it was also possible in the NLTCS to ask supplementary batteries of questions. For example, in the 1994 NLTCS, a series of questions about physical activity and nutrition were asked. Because all disabled persons are interviewed in person, proxy response rules were easier to implement in the NLTCS. An in-person interview is also a better modality to establish the status of a very disabled person than a telephone interview (e.g., for sensory impaired persons).

In the longitudinal survey plan in Figure 3 there is a joint distribution of continuous monitoring of vital status (and Medicare service use) between surveys and detailed assessments at survey times. Can information from this joint distribution be used to improve estimates of mortality risks and health transitions over time? Some estimates can be made directly (e.g., 5-year rates of disability improvements and decrements for specific ages and by gender). However, with ap-

propriate analytic models it is possible to extract more information from the observational plan about complex underlying health processes.

In the NLTCS this was possible because detailed assessments of physical function were made in each detailed interview. With detailed batteries of functional items, multivariate procedures could be used to (a) identify from J items, K reliable dimensions of functioning and (b) calculate scores representing the degree to which a person is characterized by each dimension. With sets of scores calculated for individuals it was possible to examine two different models, both illustrated in Figure 3, to evaluate continuous changes in health. First, the disability scores could be assumed constant for an individual over an interval (i.e., changes occur instantaneously at the time of the next survey). This implies that uncertainty about a person's status increases until the next assessment—then it drops to zero. This is represented by the lines connecting A_2 and A_3. Alternately, a simple model can be assumed to describe changes in an individual's disability scores between two surveys. In Figure 3, between observations B_2 and B_3, scores are assumed to change linearly. This implies, because information at the beginning *and* end of the observation period is used, that uncertainty about the state of the person in the intersurvey period is a maximum in the middle of the interval and then decreases to zero.

Analytic issues remain for "left-" and "right"-censored cases. Left-censored cases are represented by the "age-in" samples (i.e., persons passing age 65 before an interview) (e.g., E_1). Left censoring is less of a problem in a longitudinal survey because prior states of persons are known—an important rationale for continuing longitudinal studies and surveys. Right-censored cases are represented by either persons dying in an intersurvey interval (person C_B)—or the status of persons after the last interview (e.g., B_5). Both problems can be resolved by assuming that persons whose observation at a future (or past) survey were censored had the same rate of change on the K scores as did persons observed at both times—after cases are matched on disability scores (and other demographic—(e.g., age, sex) and social variables at the time when both cases were observed. In this way, a monthly disability trajectory can be imputed up to the time of death for person C_B in Figure 3. The imputed values for the disability scores at the month prior to death can be used to estimate disability-specific mortality functions. Because persons who die (i.e., are right censored) are not observed at two time points, uncertainty about the imputed disability scores increases to the time of death—or other censoring (e.g., end of follow-up; B_5).

This approach uses the 5-year data to make inferences about more short-term health transitions by estimating monthly rates of change for the continuous disability scores. If, in contrast, the survey information is used only to classify persons as disabled or not disabled, then there is no information on the rate of health changes between surveys to determine when an event occurred in the interval. The use of continuous change in scores, assuming that the model of change is reasonable, avoids that problem. For example, for a 95-year-old person starting in good health there is a greater likelihood of a change in disability than for a 65-year-old person in good health. However, health and functional change may be more rapid for a frail 70-year-old than a healthy 95-year-old—with rates different for males and females and for different types of disability.

The combined use of models and mixed data observational plans may be the only practical way of studying health changes in community and other study populations. This is because in a community, the number of extreme elderly may be limited and the rates of changes at late ages (e.g., >90) so rapid that any interview (or assessment) period short enough to capture those changes will be impractical.

Using a model of continuous time changes in health and function also facilitates use of ancillary data from select community and clinical populations. That is, the assumed mathematical structure of underlying health changes allows data across populations and over age and time to be systematically combined with that joint distribution providing more statistical power to resolve questions than using the studies immediately.

IV. SUMMARY

The special data and analytic problems intrinsic to the development of an epidemiology of aging were reviewed (i.e., an epidemiology considering interactions of aging and disease processes up to the biological limits of human survival). These specialized data collection and analytic procedures are needed when exploring health changes at the extreme age limits of human populations. In middle-aged populations the same analytic problems exist, but with smaller effects. For example, at age 50 the effects of selection on disease–risk factor relations on estimates of the heritability of disease traits exist, but will be small for populations with life expectancies over 70 years.

The applicability of such methods also depends on gender because, although age changes in hormonal status tend to be gradual for males, female changes are abrupt because of menopause. For example, the risk of osteoporosis increases rapidly for females postmenopausally. Less well understood are the complex patterns of risk factor–disease interactions that menopause may stimulate in females. Moon and colleagues posited a strong interaction of osteoporotic changes and atherogenesis in postmenopausal females. In addition, changes in female body iron stores may interact with osteoporosis and atherogenesis to affect disease risks. Thus, the need for specialized analytic procedures will occur at younger ages in females due to the rapid hormonal (and associated physiological) changes at menopause. [See ENDOCRINE FUNCTION AND DYSFUNCTION.]

In contrast, in males selection effects may become more rapidly manifest than in females because of female's longer life expectancy. For example, although the incidence of chronic disability may be similar at ages 60 to 80 for males and females, the female prevalence of disability tends to be higher because they survive longer at each disability level at each age. Thus, whether special procedures are required for a specific analysis requires a case-by-case evaluation because the underlying processes they are meant to deal with can initiate at relatively early ages. Thus, there is a continuum of needs for age-specialized epidemiological data collection and analytic methods.

BIBLIOGRAPHY

Colantonio, A., Kasl, S. V., & Ostfeld, A. M. (1992). Level of function predicts first stroke in the elderly. *Stroke, 23,* 1355.

Fiatarone, M., O'Neill, E., Ryan, N., Clements, K., Solares, G., Nelson, M., Roberts, S., Kehayias, J., Lipsitz, L., & Evans, W. (1994). Exercise training and nutritional supplementation for physical frailty in very elderly people. *New England Journal of Medicine, 330,* 1769.

Fogel, R. W. (1994). Economic growth, population theory, and physiology: The bearing of long-term processes on the making of economic policy. *American Economic Review, 84,* 369.

Hoffmeister, H., Mensink, G. B. M., & Stolzenberg, H. (1994). National trends in risk factors for cardiovascular disease in Germany. *Preventive Medicine, 23,* 197.

Jeune, B. (1994). Hundredarige-hale eller hemmelighed? *Gerontologi og Samfund, 10,* 4.

Kasch, F., Boyer, J., Van Camp, S., Verity, L., & Wallace, J. (1993). Effect of exercise on cardiovascular ageing. *Age and Ageing, 22,* 5.

Kestenbaum, B. (1992). A description of the extreme aged population based on improved Medicare enrollment data. *Demography, 29,* 565.

Kitzman, D., & Edwards, W. (1990). Minireview: Age-related changes in the anatomy of the normal human heart. *Journal of Gerontology: Medical Sciences, 45,* M33.

Manton, K. G., Corder, L. S., & Stallard, E. (1993). Estimates of change in chronic disability and institutional incidence and prevalence rates in the U.S. elderly population from the 1982, 1984, and 1989 National Long Term Care Survey. *Journal of Gerontology Social Sciences, 47,* S153.

Manton, K. G., Tolley, H. D. (1991). Rectangularization of the survival curve: Implications of an ill-posed question. *Journal of Aging and Health, 3(2),* 172–193.

Manton, K. G., & Woodbury, M. A. (1992). Grade of Membership analysis in the epidemiology of aging. *In* R. F. Woolson & R. Wallace (Eds.), *Methodologic issues in the epidemiologic study of the elderly* (pp. 333–357). Cambridge: Oxford University Press.

Marenberg, M., Risch, N., Berkman, L., Floderus, B., & de Faire, U. (1994). Genetic susceptibility to death from coronary heart disease in a study of twins. *New England Journal of Medicine, 330,* 1041.

Moon, J., Bandy, B., & Davison, A. J. (1992). Hypothesis: Etiology of atherosclerosis and osteoporosis: Are imbalances in the calciferol endocrine system implicated? *Journal of the American College of Nutrition, 11,* 567.

Perls, T. T. (1994). The oldest old. *Scientific American, 274,* 70.

Prasad, K. N., & Edwards-Prasad, J. (1992). Vitamin E and cancer prevention: Recent advances and future potentials. *Journal of the American College of Nutrition, 11,* 487.

Ethics and Euthanasia

Nancy S. Jecker

University of Washington, Seattle

Active Euthanasia Acting to induce a patient's death.

Assisted Suicide Providing a patient with the means necessary to end his or her life.

Involuntary Euthanasia Ending a patient's life in violation of the patient's wishes.

Nonvoluntary Euthanasia Ending a patient's life without knowledge of the patient's wishes.

Passive Euthanasia Refraining from acting to sustain a patient's life.

Voluntary Euthanasia Ending a patient's life in accordance with the patient's wishes.

EUTHANASIA means a gentle and easy death or the means of bringing about a gentle and easy death. In current usage, euthanasia refers specifically to active euthanasia, defined as performing an action intended to induce a patient's death. For example, a physician who administers a lethal injection for the purpose of ending a patient's life performs an act of euthanasia. Euthanasia as it is currently used can be distinguished from assisted suicide, which involves providing persons with the means necessary to end their own lives. Euthanasia also differs from what has historically been called *passive euthanasia*, which involves refraining from an action, such as cardiopulmonary resuscitation, necessary to sustain a person's life.

Whether active or passive, when an effort is made to end another person's life this effort may either conform to a competent patient's wishes (voluntary euthanasia) or violate a competent patient's wishes (involuntary euthanasia). A third possibility is that the patient's true wishes are not or cannot be known (nonvoluntary euthanasia). This chapter reviews ethical considerations relevant to active voluntary euthanasia; it does not address related issues, such as assisted suicide and withholding and withdrawing life-sustaining treatment, in much detail. Unless otherwise noted, references to euthanasia refer to voluntary active euthanasia.

I. ETHICAL ARGUMENTS SUPPORTING VOLUNTARY ACTIVE EUTHANASIA

A. Autonomy-Based Arguments

Ethical arguments supporting euthanasia often appeal to the ethical principle of autonomy, which requires respect for the voluntary wishes of a competent patient. According to one interpretation, a principle of autonomy requires others *not to interfere* with the autonomous choices of competent individuals. So, for example, a terminally ill patient who wishes to hasten death should not be prevented from doing so. A stronger interpretation of the principle of autonomy holds that we ought to *offer positive assistance* to competent individuals in their efforts to carry out their autonomous choices. According to this stronger interpretation, respect for patient autonomy lends support to taking positive steps to meet a patient's autonomous request for aid in dying, whether in the form of assisted suicide or euthanasia. Yet autonomy-based arguments for assisted suicide or euthanasia apply only to a limited group of persons, namely, persons able to form autonomous and voluntary preferences about terminating their lives.

These remarks make evident that when a principle of autonomy is interpreted as supporting euthanasia, it does not support hastening the death of someone who suffers from depression or other mental impairments that interfere with autonomy. Nor does it sanction terminating the life of a minor child. Arguments invoking autonomy also restrict assisted suicide or euthanasia to persons who are competent at the time assistance is requested, prohibiting such assistance when it is based on the prior request of a now incompetent patient. For instance, advocates of autonomy-based arguments do not generally support meeting a request for euthanasia from a person who is newly diagnosed with Alzheimer's disease and expresses through a living will a preference that his or her life be terminated in the future when mental processes deteriorate to the point that life is no longer worth living. Not only would it be difficult to apply a living will of this kind to specific situations, it has also been argued that in the case of severe dementia, the previously competent person is not the same individual as the later, demented person to whom such a request would be applied.

B. Compassion-Based Arguments

Further support for euthanasia can be found by appealing to ethical considerations of compassion for the suffering of others. This approach calls attention to the fact that despite our best medical efforts, some patients suffer terribly at the end of life. For example, even when health-care providers can prolong life, they may be unable to alleviate a patient's pain and suffering without causing intolerable side effects. Under these circumstances, it has been argued that the only way to respond compassionately to suffering is to hasten a patient's death.

It is important to distinguish between acting for the purpose of relieving suffering, on the one hand, and acting for the purpose of causing death, on the other hand. Actions that *hasten death* do not always qualify as euthanasia, because euthanasia requires acting *for the purpose* of hastening death. Hence, a physi-

cian who administers a morphine drip in order to alleviate a patient's suffering does not perform euthanasia, even if the physician anticipates that morphine will gradually curtail a patient's breathing and cause death. Likewise, a physician who operates on a patient in order to restore function, foreseeing the possibility that complications of surgery may cause death, does not commit an act of euthanasia if the patient dies on the operating table. When supporters of euthanasia invoke compassion-based arguments, they are not claiming that compassion justifies *causing death*, but that compassion justifies acting *in order* to cause death.

Appealing to compassion lends support to euthanasia only in a limited range of cases. Thus, arguments based on compassion do not give ethical warrant to ending the life of people who wish to die but are perfectly healthy and are not experiencing pain or suffering. Nor can compassion-based arguments justify terminating the life of permanently unconscious persons, because such persons do not experience pain or suffering.

II. ETHICAL ARGUMENTS OPPOSING VOLUNTARY ACTIVE EUTHANASIA

A. Slippery-Slope Arguments

In response to the above arguments, opponents of euthanasia hold that permitting one person to terminate another person's life will lead inevitably to various ethical abuses. One form this argument takes is called the psychological slippery slope. According to this line of reasoning, if persons begin to take human life in a certain limited class of cases, this will weaken their psychological inhibition against killing and lead to taking human life in other more troublesome cases. For example, if society permits physicians to end the lives of competent patients who request to have their lives ended, in the future physicians will feel less averse to ending the lives of incompetent patients who are considered a financial or emotional burden on others. The soundness of this argument depends upon the truth or falsity of the empirical prediction it asserts.

Unlike the psychological slippery slope, the logical slippery-slope argument does not rely upon a factual claim about the actual effects of permitting people to end others' lives. Instead, the logical slippery slope holds that persons who conclude that euthanasia is ethically permissible in certain cases are logically committed to holding that it is ethically permissible in other, more troublesome cases. For example, those who defend euthanasia by appealing to the ethical principle of autonomy will find it difficult to refuse to meet a request for euthanasia from a competent person who is perfectly healthy and "tired of life." If such a request expresses an autonomous decision, there appears to be no way to appeal to autonomy to forbid meeting this request.

Although appeals to compassion can justify refusing requests for euthanasia from healthy persons who are not suffering, opponents of euthanasia point out that compassion-based arguments are also vulnerable to slippery-slope objections. This is because an appeal to compassion cannot be used to limit euthanasia to persons who are competent and request death. After all, the pain that an infant or mentally impaired person experiences presumably warrants no less compassion than the pain of a mentally competent adult.

By combining autonomy-based and compassion-based arguments, advocates of euthanasia can justify significant restrictions on euthanasia. However, certain restrictions remain difficult to support. Neither autonomy-based nor compassion-based arguments can justify restricting euthanasia to patients whose deaths are imminent. This is because people may autonomously choose to die even when they have many years ahead to live. And the prospect of suffering for a long time would appear to incite more, not less, compassion than the prospect of suffering for a few weeks or months.

B. Sanctity-of-Life Arguments

Another argument against euthanasia begins with the premise that human life in any form possesses an inherent worth and dignity. Hence, even when a person is suffering terribly or wishes to die, taking that person's life is wrong because it destroys something of immense value. According to this argument, the *intrinsic* value of human life is not contingent on whether a person's life is useful or subjectively valued. So, for example, even when disease renders someone unable to pursue life goals, that person's life continues to be valuable because the value of human life is intrinsic, not contingent on its results or accomplishments. Likewise, even when someone no longer values

life and desires to die, ending that person's life would end something of value.

A principle ascribing intrinsic value to human life gains support from both religious and secular considerations. Whereas religious thinkers may argue that the value of human life stems from the fact that human beings are a divine creation, secular thinkers may argue for the value of human life on the ground that human beings are the highest achievement of an evolutionary process that took millions of years to unfold. Alternatively, rather than appealing to the historical origins of human life, support for the sanctity of human life may be based on comparing a future world with human beings to a future world without human beings. If most people prefer the former world to the latter world, it might be argued that most people implicitly accept the proposition that human life has intrinsic value.

Arguments opposing euthanasia that are based on the sanctity of human life present serious challenges to autonomy- and compassion-based arguments. Against autonomy-based arguments, this approach suggests that even if a competent person prefers to die, ending life causes that person to lose something of value. Against compassion-based arguments, the sanctity-of-human-life principle implies that a life wracked with pain and suffering is still a human life and therefore continues to be of great value.

III. THE PRACTICE OF VOLUNTARY ACTIVE EUTHANASIA

The paucity of empirical data on physician-assisted death makes it difficult to know how widespread the practices of euthanasia and assisted suicide are. Likewise, a dearth of empirical evidence makes it difficult to say how common alleged abuses of ethical guidelines governing these practices might be.

In The Netherlands, physicians practice euthanasia and assisted suicide more openly than physicians in other societies do. Although both euthanasia and assisted suicide are criminal acts in The Netherlands, punishable by a fine or imprisonment, the Dutch penal code allows exceptions to punishment when euthanasia or assisted suicide is driven by a conflict of duties. Dutch courts have interpreted the penal code as allowing leniency in sentencing when certain conditions are met. These include the requirements that the patient suffers from an incurable condition, experiences unbearable suffering, and makes a written request to terminate life. Despite these guidelines, empirical studies show that Dutch physicians sometimes act to end their patients' lives without discussing this decision with a patient, usually because the patient is incompetent and lacks the capacity to participate in such a discussion.

In the United States, the American Medical Association has taken a stand against "the intentional termination of the life of one human being by another." Nonetheless, public debate about physician-assisted death has arguably moved in the direction of greater tolerance for euthanasia. Although in 1950, only 34% of Americans supported euthanasia of incurably ill patients when both patients and families requested it, from the 1970s onward a growing majority of Americans have supported it. In 1991, for example, 63% of people in the United Stated supported euthanasia under these circumstances.

U.S. law may eventually move in the direction of greater tolerance for assisted death. In 1994, for example, Oregon passed an initiative allowing physicians to prescribe, but not administer, lethal medication to competent, terminally ill patients who repeatedly request aid in dying. In the neighboring state of Washington, a U.S. District Court ruled in the same year that a state statute making physician-assisted suicide a felony violates the U.S. Constitution. Although the final determination of the legal status of assisted suicide is unknown, these decisions may mark an important shift of legal and public opinion on this issue.

BIBLIOGRAPHY

Battin, M. P. (1994). *Least worst death*. New York: Oxford University Press.

Blendon, R. J., Szalay, U. S., Knox, R. A. (1992). Should physicians aid their patients in dying?: The public perspective. *Journal of the American Medical Association, 267,* 2658–2662.

Brody, H. (1992). Assisted death: A compassionate response to medical failure. *New England Journal of Medicine, 327,* 1384–1388.

Dworkin, R. (1993). *Life's dominion*. New York: Alfred A. Knopf.

Gomez, C. (1991). *Regulating death*. New York: Free Press.

Jecker, N. S. (1994). Physician-assisted death in the Netherlands and the United States. *Journal of the American Geriatrics Society, 42,* 672–678.

Quill, T. E., Cassel, C. K., Meier, D. E. Proposed criteria for physician-assisted suicide. *New England Journal of Medicine, 327,* 1380–1384.

Evolution and Comparative Biology

Michael R. Rose

University of California, Irvine

Allele   A variant form of a gene.

Antagonistic Pleiotropy   Occurs when multiple effects of a genetic change are opposed in their impact on fitness.

Drosophila   A fly genus commonly used in laboratory research.

Fitness   Net reproductive rate of an organism, weighted according to the growth of the population as a whole.

Fitness Component   A character that numerically defines fitness (e.g., fecundity at a particular age).

Germ Line   The cells that become gametes or offspring.

Malthusian Parameter   The asymptotic growth rate of a population growing without any ecological limitation. Often equal to fitness.

Mutation Accumulation   The increase in frequency of deleterious mutations at later ages due to weak natural selection at those ages.

Soma   That part of the organism that does not produce offspring directly (i.e., that which is not germ-line tissue).

Aging, like all other biological characteristics, evolves. However, the **EVOLUTIONARY MECHANISMS** underlying aging are different from those underlying all other prominent features of organisms. As will be explained, aging evolves through the dereliction of natural selection at later ages, so that normal catego-

ries of biological thought, like "function," "adaptation," and "purpose," cannot be relied on in the study of aging. This idea forms the basis of the evolutionary theory of aging, with which this article begins. Experimental tests of this theory are then discussed. Finally, the **COMPARATIVE BIOLOGY** of aging is reviewed.

I. EVOLUTIONARY THEORY OF AGING

A. Definition of Aging

From the perspective of evolutionary biology, the most important feature of the organism is its fitness: net reproductive output measured from one generation to the next. This variable is usually very hard to measure. Instead, evolutionary biologists commonly study components of fitness, such as viability, fertility, and so on. From the standpoint of aging, the characters of interest to an evolutionary biologist are the two age-specific components of fitness: age-specific survival probabilities and age-specific fertilities. A human example would be the probability of survival from age 20 to age 21. The definition of aging that is normally used in evolutionary biology is a persistent decline in age-specific fitness components, both survival and fertility characters, as a function of age, where this decline is not due to any external factor, such as deteriorating environment, pathogens, and so on.

B. Early Evolutionary Theories of Aging

Evolutionary discussions of aging date back to Alfred Russell Wallace and August Weismann in the nineteenth century. Because these authors were writing before the advent of theoretical population genetics, the core of modern evolutionary theory, their ideas are often incoherent or opaque.

One of the central errors made at that time was the proposal that aging evolved to eliminate elderly individuals, in order to make way for the young. This is an idea that is still cited to this day, at least by authors without training in evolutionary biology. The key mistake in these proposals is that they presume that, without aging, there would be an abundance of elderly, infirm, organisms in natural populations. For the vast majority of species, however, this is not likely to be the case. Most cohorts in natural populations reach very low numbers before significant aging has occurred among them. For such organisms, physiological mechanisms of aging are not needed to remove them from the population. Disease, predation, accident, and bad weather suffice.

By the middle of the twentieth century, R. A. Fisher, J. B. S. Haldane, P. B. Medawar, and G. C. Williams had developed a different kind of evolutionary theory of aging. Their proposals were all based on the idea that natural selection should operate with less effectiveness on later fitness components for the simple reason that these characters would be expressed less often, per lifetime, than early fitness components simply because the probability of survival from birth to any age falls with age. In 1941, Haldane proposed that the human genetic syndrome of Huntington's disease (q.v.) was common relative to many other genetic diseases, despite its lethality, because it was not expressed until middle age, after most of its carriers would have reproduced. Verbal hypotheses like these set the stage for the development of the formal evolutionary theory of aging that was to follow in the last third of the twentieth century.

C. Mathematical Evolutionary Theory of Aging

The mathematical population genetics of aging were developed primarily by W. D. Hamilton and B. Charlesworth in publications that appeared from 1966 to 1980. In this formal analysis, it was shown that Darwinian fitness is often given by the Malthusian parameter associated with a particular genotype. Given the particular age-specific fitness components

for a genotype, its Malthusian parameter is given by r in the following equation:

$$\Sigma e^{-rx}l(x)m(x) = 1, \qquad (1)$$

where the sigma indicates summation, summation proceeding over all positive values of x; x indicates age; $l(x)$ is the probability of survival from birth to age x; $m(x)$ is the fertility at age x; and e is the natural exponential. Effectively, the Malthusian parameter is a sort of averaged net fertility over the life span, allowing for both losses due to mortality and the effects of parallel growth in the entire population.

The mathematical analysis of Hamilton and Charlesworth went on to calculate the impact on fitness, when given by the Malthusian parameter, of age-specific changes in fitness components. They found that, when there is a proportionally uniform change in an age-specific survival probability, such as a 10% reduction, then the impact on fitness was differentially scaled as a function of age according to the expression

$$s(a) = \Sigma_{x=a+1}e^{-rx}l(x)m(x), \qquad (2)$$

where a is the age at which survival probability is changed. Age $a + 1$ is the age at which the summation starts. Note that, after the last age at which offspring are produced, $s(a)$ is zero forever after. Note that, before the first age at which offspring are produced, $s(a)$ is always exactly 1. Before the first and last ages of reproduction, $s(a)$ progressively falls. Figure 1 shows this graphically. This result shows that the *force of natural selection acting on survival falls with adult age*, at least when the assumptions of this analysis are met.

A similar analysis for effects on age-specific fertility gives a comparable "scaling equation," as follows:

$$s'(a) = e^{-ra}l(a) \qquad (3)$$

In this case, if population growth is not negative, then the force of natural selection once again declines with age. But if population growth is strongly negative, then the force of natural selection may indeed increase with age. This corresponds to a situation where a population is declining rapidly toward extinction, so that two offspring produced when the population size is 600 are "worth" less than two offspring produced some time later when the population size is 60. In the latter instance, the offspring are a larger proportion of the population. However, these cases will normally

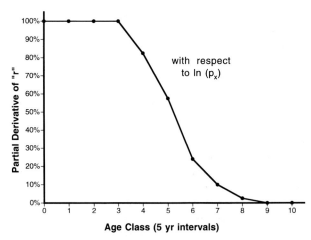

Figure I The force of natural selection, calculated in terms of the impact on fitness (r) of a proportionally uniform change in age-specific survival probability [$P(x)$]. This curve might characterize a species that started reproduction after 20 years of age. The curve plotted shows the force of natural selection relative to its impact before the onset of reproduction, neglecting any absolute scaling effects related to generation time. Qualitatively similar results will arise for any sexually reproducing species, though the width of the initial plateau, the rapidity of the subsequent decline, and the point at which zero is reached will vary.

be rare, because populations declining rapidly to extinction will often become extinct, rendering them unobservable. The typical pattern will remain one in which the force of natural selection acting on fertility will decline with age.

From these results, population geneticists have been able to explain the evolution of declining age-specific fitness components, or aging. These results are very general, among demographies, and have no physiological content. In particular, they do not require or predict the action of any particular mechanism of physiological deterioration. The evolutionary theory of aging accounts for aging in terms of a pervasive failure of adaptation, the particulars of which must be as idiosyncratic to species as the particulars of adaptation for those species are. For this reason, evolutionary biologists have generally been extremely skeptical of proposals that attribute "the cause of aging" to any specific physiological mechanism.

D. Population Genetic Hypotheses

Subordinate to the general evolutionary theory of aging are alternative population genetic theories for

the evolution of aging. These hypotheses presume the validity of the evolutionary theory, particularly the finding that the force of natural selection declines with adult age. These hypotheses are not incompatible with one another; they could all be valid simultaneously. At present, two population genetic hypotheses are considered of primary interest, although others have been proposed. These two are antagonistic pleiotropy and mutation accumulation. Each will be dealt with in turn.

1. Antagonistic Pleiotropy

Antagonistic pleiotropy arises when alleles that have beneficial effects on one set of components of fitness also have deleterious effects on other components of fitness. Both Medawar and Williams argued for the importance of this population-genetic mechanism in the evolution of aging during the 1950s. The underlying concept is one of trade-off; alleles with beneficial effects must in some way "pay" for those benefits in bad side effects.

B. Charlesworth and M. R. Rose analyzed the action of antagonistic pleiotropy mathematically. They showed that the declining force of natural selection would lead to a tendency for selection to fix alleles that have early beneficial effects, but later deleterious effects. This biases evolution toward the production of vigorous young organisms and decrepit old organisms. In addition, antagonistic pleiotropy may lead to the maintenance of genetic variability for aging and related characters, which is of great experimental significance (see next section). At the theoretical level, antagonistic pleiotropy is an important possible mechanism for the evolution of aging. However, the theoretical work does not show that it necessarily arises.

2. Mutation Accumulation

The other cogent population genetic mechanism for the evolution of aging is mutation accumulation. Mutation accumulation arises when the force of natural selection has declined to a point where it has little impact on recurrent deleterious mutations with effects confined to late life. Medawar was the main advocate of the importance of this mechanism in the evolution of aging. Charlesworth analyzed mutation accumulation mathematically, showing that the frequency of deleterious mutations would rise with adult age because of the declining force of natural selection at late ages. This population genetic mechanism also tends to maintain genetic variability for aging, like antagonistic pleiotropy.

II. EXPERIMENTAL STUDIES OF THE EVOLUTION OF AGING

A. Laboratory Evolution of Aging

I. Development of the Experimental Approach

Unlike many parts of biology, the evolutionary theory of aging provides the study of aging with a strong, mathematically developed base on which to plan experiments. One of the most elegant experimental approaches in gerontology is the manipulation of the force of natural selection to shape the evolution of aging patterns. This broad experimental strategy was first proposed by E. B. Edney and R. W. Gill in 1968. Some preliminary experiments of this kind were performed in the 1960s and 1970s by J. M. Wattiaux, R. R. Sokal, and Rose. Properly replicated experiments were not performed until the 1980s, particularly by Rose, L. S. Luckinbill, and R. W. Arking. These experiments are now routine in evolutionary gerontology, almost always using fruit fly species of the genus *Drosophila*.

2. Basic Experimental Design

The design of these experiments depends on the manipulation of the first and last ages of reproduction. Normally these ages are quite close together in the laboratory, so that the experimental organism is given a brief window for reproduction. When the timing of this window is maintained for a number of generations, the force of natural selection will be focused at that age. For example, normal fruit fly culture involves reproduction at 14 days of age, when cultured at 25°, with just a few hours for egg laying allowed. This focuses the force of natural selection on that, relatively early, age. Genetic effects expressed at later ages, much after 14 days, are subject to negligible natural selection. This type of experimental regime allows the evolution of relatively early aging.

An alternative experimental regime is to keep adults alive for some time before they are allowed to contribute offspring to the next generation. In fruit flies, this is done by discarding any eggs that they lay until they have reached the earliest age allowed for reproduction. This can be some weeks later than the 14-day reproduc-

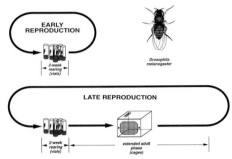

Figure 2 Method of selecting on fruit fly cultures for different times of reproduction. The early-reproduced flies are reared as a cohort in vials, emerging at about 10 days when reared at 25°C. After a few days for mating among the adults, females are allowed to lay eggs in new vials at 14 days of age. These eggs are laid over just a few hours and the adult flies are then discarded, allowing the eggs to start the next generation as a synchronized cohort once more.

Late-reproduced flies are reared in vials as a cohort, like early-reproduced flies, until 14 days of age. The adults are then transferred into large Plexiglas cages, where they are kept as an aging cohort, without replacement, for an additional period of time. During this time, all eggs are discarded shortly after they are laid. After a prolonged adult period, the surviving females from a cage are given the opportunity to lay eggs over one or two days. These eggs are then used to start the next generation as a synchronized cohort.

tive regime. It is common for the age at first reproduction to be as late as 10 weeks of age from emergence of the larva. It should be noted that this procedure does not require that the fruit flies be kept virgin; mating is allowed, just not successful reproduction. The contrast between this procedure and that used with early reproduction is shown in Figure 2.

3. Effects of Changing the Force of Natural Selection

In experiment after experiment, the results of changing the age at which selection is strong have been striking. Figure 3 shows typical data for fruit flies. Mean and maximum life span dramatically increase when the force of natural selection is experimentally strengthened at later ages, as the evolutionary theory predicts. In addition, numerous functions are enhanced at later ages: female fecundity, male virility, flight endurance, locomotion, stress resistance, and so on. This is an extremely important result for our understanding of aging. It reveals that aging is not a by-product, accidental or otherwise, of an unmodifi-

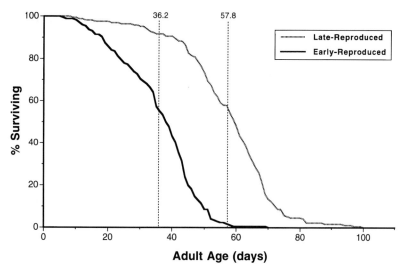

Figure 3 The results obtained with different regimes of culture maintenance are shown for cultures of *Drosophila melanogaster*. Early-reproduced cultures have lower mean and maximum longevities, compared with late-reproduced cultures. About 10 years of selection had been imposed on the different cultures. Both groups of cultures descended from a common ancestor and were replicated fivefold, though the graph aggregates data obtained from each culture regime. (Data from Chippindale, A. K., Leroi, A. M., Kim, S. B., & Rose, M. R. (1993). Phenotypic plasticity and selection in *Drosophila* life-history evolution. I. Nutrition and the cost of reproduction. *Journal of Evolutionary Biology, 6,* 171–193.)

able biochemical process. Rather, aging is an easily modified product of evolution.

B. Experimental Population Genetics of Aging

Given the preeminence of natural selection in determining patterns of aging, the next major experimental question is the population genetic mechanisms that underlie the evolution of aging. As outlined above, there are two main competing hypotheses: antagonistic pleiotropy and mutation accumulation. The evidence that has been brought to bear on these hypotheses has been of two main kinds: (a) correlation between relatives, and (b) indirect responses to selection. In addition to the choice between these hypotheses, there is the issue of the number of genetic loci involved in the evolution of aging. A number of different methods have been used to address this question.

I. Correlation between Relatives
One of the classic techniques in population genetics is the study of the correlations between relatives for char-

acters that are, in part, inherited. This technique can also be used to study the degree to which two or more characters tend to be inherited together. When they are, this usually indicates some degree of pleiotropy among the alleles affecting these characters. In particular, correlated inheritance is indicative of the pattern of pleiotropy, with positive correlations indicating that alleles affect two characters in the same direction, and negative correlations indicating that alleles affect two characters in opposite directions, on average.

The antagonistic pleiotropy mechanism for the evolution of aging requires that some early and late characters exhibit negative genetic correlations with respect to each other. This pattern has been found in a few cases, notably between early fecundity and longevity in fruit flies. However, it has not been found in many more. Artifacts may be responsible for some of these latter results, particularly inbreeding and novel environment effects, both of which bias genetic correlations toward positive values.

Mutation accumulation requires that genetic correlations between early and late characters be approximately zero. The problem for this hypothesis is that these genetic correlations tend to be strongly positive among newly occurring mutations or intermittently negative in long-established genetic variation. Mutation accumulation also requires that heritable genetic variations increases with age. This result has been found in some fruit fly experiments, but not in others.

Both antagonistic pleiotropy and mutation-accumulation mechanisms receive weak and inconsistent experimental support in the literature on genetic correlations. An important factor, however, is that they may act simultaneously and, in so doing, cancel out the predicted effects of *both* mechanisms on correlations between relatives.

2. Indirect Responses to Selection

To some extent, selection experiments are better able to detect the simultaneous action of antagonistic pleiotropy and mutation accumulation. When, for example, postponed aging has evolved as a result of later reproduction in fruit flies, it is expected that antagonistic pleiotropy will cause an immediate reduction in early fecundity, given the results mentioned earlier. This result is often observed. With antagonistic pleiotropy, it is expected that some early, functional characters will be depressed by the laboratory evolution of postponed aging. The observation of this pattern in a number of instances, together with evidence obtained from correlations between relatives, indicates that antagonistic pleiotropy is, in some cases, an important mechanism in the evolution of aging.

The effects of mutation accumulation can also be observed in laboratory evolution experiments. For example, when later reproductive opportunities are denied, it is expected that after many generations later fecundity should be reduced, due to the accumulation of alleles with late-acting deleterious effects. This result was obtained by L. D. Mueller in fruit flies denied later reproduction for more than 100 generations. Other such long-term deteriorations have been obtained by Rose and his colleagues for other characters, especially stress resistance. Mutation accumulation evidently can act over hundreds of generations to undermine functional characters, when the force of selection is reduced, making it an important mechanism for the evolution of aging.

3. The Number of Genes Affecting Aging

An important question concerning the evolutionary genetics of aging is the number of loci affecting it.

Earlier evolutionary theorists argued that an extremely large number of loci are likely to affect aging. This gave rise to some pessimism among evolutionary biologists concerning the feasibility of postponing aging. The success of laboratory evolution experiments in producing organisms with genetically postponed aging, however, forced a reexamination of earlier assumptions.

Other researchers have examined the question in fruit flies using a variety of experimental techniques. Only with one technique, effective factor estimation, has it seemed that the number of loci is small. That result probably arose from arithmetical artifacts. Other estimates have given values in the hundreds of loci for *Drosophila*. At present, the best answer to the question of the number of genes controlling aging is many.

III. COMPARATIVE BIOLOGY OF AGING

A. Presence and Absence of Aging

1. Comparative Predictions of the Evolutionary Theory of Aging

The evolutionary theory of aging is unusual among theories of biology in making some absolute predictions. The experimental corroborations of the prediction that the pattern of aging should evolutionarily respond to manipulation of the force of natural selection have already been mentioned. With even greater strength, the evolutionary theory of aging predicts that all species that exhibit a well-defined separation of germ line from soma must age. Conversely, the evolutionary theory predicts that all species with strictly fissile (splitting in two) reproduction must be free of aging. (This does not mean immortality, because such organisms could still die from disease, predation, or mechanical injury.) These two predictions can be tested extensively using comparative data.

However, many species exhibit neither a well-defined soma nor fissile reproduction. Colonial coelenterates, such as corals, or grasses may have fairly ambiguous delineation of "organisms." Still other forms may combine fissile with sexual reproduction. In these cases, the evolutionary theory does not provide any simple prediction about the pattern of aging. Fully developed population genetics theory could, of course, be formulated to address any of these "hybrid" cases, and some progress along these lines has recently been made. There is no fundamental violation of theory, only some difficult special cases.

2. Aging in Sexual Metazoa

There are very large taxonomic groups in which aging is predicted to be universal. The most common type are probably the metazoa that reproduce only sexually, as well as lacking any sort of vegetative "spreading" such as that exhibited by corals or grasses. In such forms, the life of each organism begins from an egg that develops into an immature animal and ultimately into a sexually mature animal. Sometimes a derivative asexual, typically parthenogenetic, form evolves from such a sexual species, but the essential lifecycle is maintained, with nothing approaching fissile reproduction. Among other prominent examples, both the insects and the vertebrates exhibit this type of life cycle.

Insects and vertebrates are two of the most intensively studied groups of species. There are hundreds of thousands of insect species, many of which have good aging data because of their economic importance. There are far fewer vertebrate species, but they have been studied with even greater zeal than the insects. It is often the case that actuarial or physiological aging is not detected in wild populations of these organisms. For example, several fish species have been studied in which some individuals sampled from the wild appear to have attained great age without signs of physiological aging, notably sturgeon, ocean perch, and rockfish. However, no cohort of fish maintained in the laboratory, until all died free of disease, has failed to exhibit aging. For mammals, the evidence for the ubiquity of aging is best, with respect to both the numbers of species studied and the quality of their care. Among all of these organisms, over the many studies that have been conducted, none have been shown to lack aging. There are no reputable refutations of the prediction of the evolutionary theory of aging that all these species must age. [See MODELS OF AGING: VERTEBRATES.]

3. Aging in Strictly Fissile Forms

At the other end of the evolutionary spectrum with respect to aging are the fissile species. It is important to understand that the concept of fissile here does not mean merely asexual reproduction or budding. It is now well known that budding yeast exhibit aging, as does the asexual protozoan *Tokophyra*. When asexual reproduction is sufficiently asymmetrical, there may be a pseudo "adult" producing "juvenile" offspring. When this occurs in a way that can give rise to differential evolution of such adults and juveniles, then aging can evolve. The cases where, according to the theory, aging cannot evolve are those with strict symmetry between the products of fission, as in the fissile yeast *Saccharomyces pombe* and typical bacteria. In these cases, if aging were to occur, it would extinguish all the descendant lineages, wiping out any such aging lineage, because senescent deterioration would then progress from cell division to cell division. This outcome would be opposed by natural selection acting with full force, which would thus halt such aging among surviving lineages. As required by theory, all such cases of strict fission do not apparently exhibit aging. Once again, however, this does not guarantee immortality; it is not a refutation of the evolutionary theory of aging to show that a particular bacterium eventually dies. [See MODELS OF AGING: INVERTEBRATES, FILAMENTOUS FUNGI, AND YEASTS.]

B. Correlated Evolution of Aging and Other Characters

1. Quantitative Patterns of Aging

One of the most fertile seedbeds for gerontological speculation over the last century or more has been patterns of aging among species that exhibit it. For example, it is usually found that birds live longer in captivity than mammals of a similar size, and this provoked speculation about relationships between the physiology of flight and that of aging. It is also known that larger mammals tend to live longer than smaller mammals. Longer-lived, larger mammals also tend to have lower fertility per brood or per year. Finally, in the 1950s, G. A. Sacher claimed that more cephalized (larger brain weight relative to body weight) mammals tended to live longer. This again led to speculation about the physiological advantages of large brains.

With respect to these patterns, the evolutionary theory of aging makes no absolute predictions. Varied evolutionary mechanisms could generate patterns of this kind. Thus, any particular pattern of aging among aging species does not constitute any kind of test of the evolutionary theory of aging. However, this theory may be helpful in interpreting such findings.

2. Artifacts in Comparative Biology

Although it might be supposed that evolutionary biologists must be strong advocates of the use of between-species comparisons, in fact, evolutionary biologists have developed a number of profound criticisms of the comparative method. One of these is that the statistical degrees of freedom can be greatly overestimated in comparative studies. If one studies 80 species of insects compared with 60 species of mammals, a naive analysis of the data would yield striking correlations between life span, type of skeleton, and number of limbs, given the more than 135 degrees of freedom. But in fact there are no degrees of freedom in this study, because there are only two independent points of data, and no absolute hypotheses with which to compare them. Fortunately, evolutionary biologists have developed methods for correctly calculating the statistical power of any particular comparative analysis. Unfortunately, the corrected values for degrees of freedom are often much less than the initial assumptions.

A second major problem with many comparative analyses is that they are confounded with spurious variables that are already known to have an effect on the characters of interest. The most common of these is body weight, which, in mammals for example, usually increases with (a) the size of most bones, (b) brain size, (c) longevity, (d) brood interval, and so on. If a biological variable that also positively depends on body size is studied for its bivariate correlation with longevity, it may be found to correlate positively with longevity, all other things being equal. However, with enough effort, this problem can be largely obviated using multivariate statistical methods.

Third, comparative correlations between characters can be generated by both (a) pleiotropic effects of genetic variants evolving in response to an unknown selection mechanism, and (b) ecologically correlated selection mechanisms acting on genetically independent characters. Determining which of these two has been involved in the comparative patterns of aging in a particular taxon will be difficult. For example, it has been suggested that the greater longevity of large mammals is due to an unknown physiological advantage of larger size. It has also been suggested by Charlesworth that the greater longevity of large mammals arises because they have lower mortality rates in nature, which is known to be common, thereby preserving a higher intensity of natural selection at later ages and the evolution of relatively delayed aging. Evaluating these two alternative hypotheses across some dozens of mammalian species is a daunting task.

All of these points together suggest that comparative patterns of aging are among the worst possible sources of inference concerning aging. It is easy to obtain findings that are entirely artifactual, whereas it is difficult to distinguish between competing hypotheses.

3. Comparative Natural History of Aging

It is difficult to maintain that much profound information is known about comparative patterns of aging, leaving aside the issue of the presence or absence of aging. In well-studied groups, like mammals, it is generally the case that most species stretch along a continuum from small, fecund, short-lived organisms, like mice, to large, low-fertility, long-lived organisms, like elephants. Within this overall spectrum there are deviations, most dramatically the bats, which live much longer on average than comparable terrestrial mammals. This is an illustration of the general pattern that flightless species age faster than those with flight, even within groups like birds or mammals. It is also the case that species equipped with poison or armor frequently live longer in captivity than comparable species without these adaptations.

The explanation that the evolutionary theory of aging can offer for these patterns is that taxa that have mortality reduction because of a characteristic adaptation, like flight in most birds, may thereby, for purely mathematical reasons derivable from equation (2), have an increased force of natural selection at later ages. This increased force would then lead to the evolution of relatively slower aging, all other things being equal. Such mortality reduction can also arise from poison fangs in snakes, armor in turtles, or great body size in elephants. Moreover, this evolutionary effect could have nothing to do with any immediate physiological benefit arising from poison, bulk, or wings.

BIBLIOGRAPHY

Charlesworth, B. (1994). *Evolution in age-structured populations* (2nd ed.). London: Cambridge University Press.

Finch, C. E. (1990). *Longevity, senescence, and the genome.* Chicago: University of Chicago Press.

Harrison, D. E. (Ed.). (1990). *Genetic effects on aging II.* Caldwell, NJ: Telford Press.

Rose, M. R. (1991). *Evolutionary biology of aging.* New York: Oxford University Press.

Rose, M. R., & Finch, C. E. (Ed.) (1994) *Genetics and evolution of aging.* Dordrecht: Kluwer Academic Publishers.

Extracellular Matrix

Karen M. Reiser

University of California, Davis

Collagen Family of large structural proteins, characterized by triple helix conformation, which provide tensile strength to tissues and organs and serve as a matrix for growth and proliferation of cells.

Elastin Highly insoluble structural protein capable of reversible expansion and contraction, essential for physiological functioning of deformable tissues such as blood vessels, skin, and lung.

Extracellular Matrix Intricate network composed of the structural proteins collagen and elastin in association with proteoglycans that serves as the scaffolding for tissues and organs throughout the body.

Proteoglycan Family of nonfibrillar connective tissue components associated with collagen and elastin in the extracellular space, consisting of a core protein with one or more glycosaminoglycan side chains covalently attached.

The **EXTRACELLULAR MATRIX** serves as the scaffolding for tissues and organs throughout the body, playing an essential role in their structural and functional integrity. Its predominant components are the large, insoluble structural proteins collagen and elastin. Although the matrix was originally thought to be relatively inert, it is now apparent that the matrix undergoes profound structural changes over time. Much progress has been made recently in understanding the molecular basis of these changes, despite formidable technical difficulties in analyzing the matrix proteins. The mechanisms responsible for matrix alterations are also still poorly understood. Although we know that some of these structural changes are under genetic control, many are not, such as the series of reactions between matrix proteins and sugar molecules to form complex colored and fluorescent compounds. As the matrix structure changes over time, so do its physical and chemical properties, such as solubility, flexibility, and mechanical strength. As a result, tissues and organs throughout the body also undergo changes in structure and function. In addition, age-associated changes in matrix affect key properties of the resident cell populations. In summary, many changes we associate with the aging process are attributable either directly or indirectly to cumulative structural changes in the extracellular matrix.

I. INTRODUCTION: WHY IS AGING OF THE EXTRACELLULAR MATRIX IMPORTANT?

Aging is characterized by profound changes in the extracellular matrix, the complex network of long-lived structural proteins and glycosaminoglycans that serves as the scaffolding for virtually every tissue and organ system. It has long been postulated that the process of matrix aging may have more than phenomenological significance, and that within its intertwined pattern of cause and effect may lie the key to understanding fundamental mechanisms of aging in the organism as a whole. One of the earliest unifying hypotheses of aging, advanced almost 50 years ago, proposed that aging was initiated by the development of irreversible cross-links in matrix macromolecules that accumulated over time and led inexorably to the degenerative changes associated with aging. In these early studies, structural changes in matrix macromolecules were inferred from changes in their physicochemical properties. Since then, the tools of modern molecular biology have begun to reveal the molecular basis for many age-associated phenomena previously observed only at the microscopic and macroscopic level. Recent studies suggest that the original concept that the matrix might serve as a kind of "clock" that both regulates and reveals biological age retains considerable validity.

Why is the matrix so suited to the role of biological timekeeper? First, the matrix is truly the "common ground" of an organism, present in all tissues and organs from the earliest developmental stages until death. Second, the two major matrix proteins, collagen and elastin, have extremely long half-lives in vivo. Third, collagen and elastin are subject to extensive post-translational modification, ranging from hydroxylation and glycation of individual residues to the formation of complex cross-links and adducts. Few other proteins besides collagen and elastin possess all three of these qualities: ubiquity, longevity, and plasticity. How are these characteristics related to aging? The long half-life of these proteins means that a given molecule may continue to undergo structural modification over many years. As a consequence, the collagen and elastin molecules in an individual organism accumulate a set of modifications that serve as a kind of "permanent record" of the innumerable interactions between the organism, with its unique genetic endowment, and its uniquely experienced environment. This "record," however, is far from inert. As the matrix changes, so does its effect on proliferation, migration, response to cytokines, and gene expression of resident cell populations. Age-associated changes in matrix also profoundly affect tissue and organ system function. Because of the ubiquity of matrix, these effects on cells and tissues occur throughout the body, ultimately affecting the organism at the systemic level. Thus, the molecular memory of an organism's experience in the world, recorded

in the code of matrix modification, assumes increasing power to direct that experience; it is this transit—from recorder of events to regulator—that lies at the heart of the aging process in matrix. To the extent that we can learn the language of matrix memory, we may find new ways to change the message that has, thus far, been so inexorably determined by the passage of time.

II. ASSESSMENT OF MATRIX AGING: COMMONLY USED METHODOLOGIES

Our conceptual understanding about a phenomenon is often shaped by the tools available for investigation and by the choice of tools used. The investigation of matrix aging provides a particularly apt illustration of the pitfalls that can occur when the limitations of analytic techniques are ignored or, worse, when these very limitations have been mistakenly used to draw inferences about the subject of study. Even a cursory examination of the primary literature on matrix aging reveals a vast number of contradictory reports. Some of the inconsistencies are attributable to differences in study design (particularly differences in the age range of animals studied), whereas some are due to methodological shortcomings, including failure to recognize inherent limitations, failure to recognize implicit assumptions in the assay of choice, and, as a consequence, failure to consider alternative explanations for a particular finding. Thus, before one can attempt to draw any general conclusions from the very large literature, one must have some understanding of the rationale for and the limitations of commonly used analytical techniques used in studying the effects of aging on the matrix.

A. Histochemistry

Light microscopy is one of the oldest techniques for studying the effects of aging on the extracellular matrix proteins. Although qualitative information can be obtained that may be helpful in determining experimental strategies, there are many pitfalls that significantly limit the conclusions that can be drawn from such data. In older studies, histochemical studies using nonspecific stains such as hemotoxylin-eosin were sometimes used to investigate the effects of age on the amount and distribution of collagen in different tissues. Discrepancies between such studies are most likely due to the lack of consensus concerning the definition of "collagen fibers," differences in staining techniques, and differences in tissue preparation. Attempts have also been made to categorize components of the matrix on the basis of their staining properties, giving rise to distinctions between such entities as "reticulin," "collastin," and "basement membrane collagen." Again, there is little consensus as to the definition of such terms. More recently, the discovery that many tissues were composed of more than one genetically distinct collagen aroused interest in the use of "special stains" that were believed to have specificity for a particular collagen type. Mason's trichrome and van Gieson's stain are generally assumed to be specific for type I collagen, whereas Gomori's stain (silver impregnation) has been referred to as type III-specific. However, it is now evident that these stains cannot be used for quantitative assessment of changes in collagen type distribution due to inconsistencies in their ability to stain specific collagen types. For example, silver impregnation is capable of staining newly synthesized type I collagen, but not "mature" fibrils. Furthermore, the staining properties of the more recently discovered collagen types (types V–VI) are unknown. Although there have been attempts to develop more elaborate panels of staining procedures that could be correlated with different collagen types, this approach seems particularly fruitless given the ever-increasing number of genetically distinct collagen types being identified.

Histological assessment of age-associated changes in elastin poses equally difficult problems. Historically, elastic fibers have been characterized by their ability to take up such stains as Verhoeff-hematoxylin, resorcin-fuchsin, and orcein, due to the presence of aldehyde groups and/or strongly hydrophobic regions. However, although some investigators draw inferences about elastin from the use of such stains, it should be emphasized that *elastic fibers are not synonymous with elastin.* Elastic fibers have been shown to be composed of elastin and elastic fiber microfibrils, which in turn comprise several genetically distinct proteins, including fibrillin and the so-called microfibrillar-associated proteins. There is at present little information as to how these microfibrillar components interact with and affect elastin structure. Thus, histochemical studies of age-associated

changes in elastic fibers cannot be construed as providing much structural information as to what happens to elastin during aging.

Finally, there are several general limitations inherent in any type of histological assessment of the effects of aging on matrix. First, it is very likely that the staining properties of collagen and elastin are affected by the profound structural changes that occur with aging, thus making it questionable whether young and old tissue can be directly compared by histochemical techniques. However, no data are available concerning this issue. Second, problems in true random sampling and quantification of staining intensity further reduce the usefulness of histological techniques in assessing age-associated changes in matrix.

B. Mechanical Properties

Histochemical studies are clearly limited by their descriptive nature and by their inability to provide either precise quantitative data or information about events in the matrix occurring at the molecular level. In contrast, mechanical properties can be measured very precisely in collagen. Furthermore, changes in such mechanical properties as thermal contraction force, ultimate load, tensile strength, breaking strength, and strain may be assumed to reflect changes at the molecular level. Thus, the hypothesis that aging resulted from irreversible cross-linking of macromolecules provoked considerable interest in investigating the effects of aging on the mechanical properties of collagen. If indeed progressive cross-linking is a central event in the aging process, then an assay that indirectly reflected degree of cross-linking might have predictive value as a marker of longevity. However, although numerous studies have shown that mechanical properties such as thermal break time are highly correlated with chronological age within a given species, there are no convincing data that these parameters are correlated with longevity. [See LONGEVITY AND LONG-LIVED POPULATIONS.]

One of the major disadvantages of these mechanical assays is the necessity of obtaining collagen in fiber form, as most collagen in the body cannot be isolated as intact fibers, nor can elastin, due to its extreme insolubility. Thus, the lack of correlation between mechanical properties of collagen and longevity may arise from the fact that only fibrillar type I collagen present in tendon is being assessed. It is possible that changes in mechanical properties in this collagen do not accurately reflect age-associated changes occurring in parenchymal tissue containing complex mixtures of fibrillar and nonfibrillar collagen types.

C. Solubility

In part to circumvent the limitations inherent in assays of mechanical properties, several investigators developed methods for precise quantification of collagen solubility, a parameter that has long been observed to increase with age. Urea, neutral salt buffers, and acids of varying strength have all been used to solubilize collagen. Rate of solubilization by enzymatic digestion has also been extensively used, sometimes with enzymes such as pepsin, which are not specific for collagen, but more often with highly purified collagenase. Solubilization is significantly correlated with chronological age within a given species. However, attempts to correlate solubility with longevity have not been as fruitful. Furthermore, studies have also shown that results obtained with one solubilizing agent may not be consistent with results obtained using another. For example, collagenase digestibility of rat collagen decreases very little after rats reach maturity, whereas solubility in urea decreases markedly with age. This discrepancy between effects of different solubilizing agents was not observed in longer lived species such as humans, monkeys, and dogs, raising the possibility that extrapolation from data obtained in a short-lived species to a long-lived species must be done cautiously.

D. Electron Microscopy

Advances in electron microscopy and the development of quantitative morphometric techniques have provided potentially powerful new analytical tools for analyzing the effects of aging. However, this analytical approach suffers from some of the same problems as light microscopy, in that a terminology has developed based upon descriptive features rather than on well-defined chemical entities. The relationship of such terms as *unit collagen fibrils, microfibrils, reticular fibers,* and *primary fibrils* to molecular concepts of collagen structure remains very unclear, despite attempts to correlate fibril diameter with collagen type, degree of glycosylation, and composition of intervening ground substance.

Electron microscopy has perhaps been most fruitful when used in conjunction with X-ray diffraction studies and chemical analyses in elucidating the molecular structure of collagen fibrils. Collagen exists in vivo in the form of fibrils measuring 50–2000 Å. Both low-angle X-ray diffraction and electron microscopy indicate an axial period of about 640 Å, within which characteristic repeating bands can be observed after staining. These striations within a period result from the distribution of charged residues, whereas the periodicity results from the self-assembly of tropocollagen units during fibrillogenesis into 5-stranded helical microfibrils, in which each tropocollagen unit overlaps its neighbors by a multiple of the distance 640 Å (the "quarter-stagger" model). The native fibril consists of aligned microfibrils packed side-to-side; presumably other types of fibrils result from different arrangements of the microfibrils or from interactions with other macromolecular components of the matrix. This type of integrated approach is being used to analyze the changes in molecular packing that result from the posttranslational changes that occur during aging. For example, it has been shown that nonenzymatic glycation leads to expansion of the microfibrillar assembly.

E. Biochemical Studies

During the last 20 years, the explosion of knowledge in biochemistry and molecular biology has resulted in the development of many new methods for studying the effects of aging on synthesis and deposition of matrix proteins. As with other approaches, there are many methodological pitfalls in commonly used biochemical assays that can seriously skew the data, and which have resulted in conflicting reports about the effects of aging on virtually every aspect of matrix biosynthesis.

I. Collagen Content

Early methods for measuring collagen content of tissues such as gelatinization or hot trichloroacetic acid precipitation are not very precise. One of the first specific assays developed for measuring collagen involves quantifying hydroxyproline, an amino acid residue that comprises approximately 15% of the total amino acids present in collagen. Hydroxyproline is, for most purposes, a reasonably specific marker for collagen, as the amount present in elastin and in the Clq component of complement—the only two other

Table I Effects of Aging on Elastin Content of Human Lung

Age (years)	Elastin (% dry wt)	Effect of age	Assay technique
2–80	1–13	↑	Lansing
1–65	8–15	↑	Acetone extraction, Lansing
19–92	35–47	↑	Cold alkali or ether extraction, autoclave
15–83	8	→	Lansing, expressed per unit volume
15–83	8	↑	Lansing, expressed per mg tissue
41–71	18	→	Nitrogen content of insoluble lung

potential sources—is negligible by comparison. Assays based upon oxidation of hydroxyproline to pyrrole, which is quantified colorimetrically, are most often used. Even in this fairly straightforward assay there may be pitfalls, particularly with respect to selecting an appropriate denominator term. If hydroxyproline is expressed as a concentration (per unit tissue weight or unit tissue volume, per gram of total protein or DNA, for example) rather than on a per organ basis, net changes in total collagen may be masked by the effects of age on the denominator term. It may be impossible to compare studies using different denominator terms, as different results may be obtained. Hydroxyproline values may also be significantly affected by tissue preparation; for example, tissues that are either edematous or contaminated with blood may give falsely high values in this assay, as colored impurities from heme absorb light at the same wavelength as the pyrrole chromophore. Gross contamination of a sample with blood, on the other hand, may result in spuriously low values.

2. Elastin Content

Elastin has been less well defined chemically than collagen, in part because, unlike collagen, it is extremely difficult to solubilize in intact form. As a consequence, many approaches have been developed for biochemically measuring elastin, resulting in widely variable estimations of elastin content for several tissues and organs. For example, estimations of lung elastin content vary from 1 to 47%, depending on the assay used, as illustrated in Table I. Probably the most commonly used method for quantitating elastin is the Lansing procedure, in which elastin is isolated on the basis of its insolubility in boiling sodium hydroxide. Several variations of the method exist in which insoluble non-

elastin material is separated from elastin in the final precipitate, including solubilization of elastin with potassium hydroxide (KOH) and elastase digestion. Another approach is to measure nitrogen content of the final precipitate and assume elastin is 16.34% nitrogen. Enzymatic methods for quantitating elastin have also been used, such as digestion of crude tissue preparations with trypsin and collagenase to remove nonelastin proteins. More elaborate versions of this method include sequential treatment of tissue with guanidine, collagenase, guanidine plus a reducing agent, and 6 M urea with sodium dodecylsulfate. All of these methods suffer from the potential loss of elastin during the harsh extraction procedures or the persistence of nonelastin material in the final product. These difficulties are especially pronounced when examining complex tissues and organs containing multiple matrix components. Quantification of elastin by measuring its unique cross-links, desmosine and isodesmodine, have been used as an alternative approach that avoids the problem of including nonelastin material in the final calculation. However, the implicit assumption is that the elastin being quantitated is fully cross-linked, and that the number of desmosines per chain is constant.

3. Collagen Synthesis and Turnover

In addition to serving as a marker for collagen content, hydroxyproline also provides a useful marker for measuring collagen synthesis. The effects of age on collagen synthesis have been studied in vitro using short-term tissue explants. If radiolabeled proline is used as the isotope, the accumulation of labeled hydroxyproline during a defined time period provides a good index of the extent of collagen synthesis. Rate of collagen synthesis (generally expressed as microgram of labeled hydroxyproline per gram of protein per hour) can also be determined using these techniques. Potential sources of trouble in this assay in tissue explants include unexpected effects of age on the precursor proline pool size in a given tissue or organ and failure to distinguish between changes in synthesis and changes in intracellular degradation.

In contrast to the relatively straightforward techniques used to study the effects of aging on collagen synthesis in vitro, studies of collagen biosynthesis in vivo represent one of the most contentious areas of investigation, with wildly divergent conclusions regarding the stability of the matrix. At issue is the question of how collagen ages: Is some or all of the collagen that is synthesized when the animal is young present in old age? Alternatively, is all of the collagen in the body in a state of dynamic equilibrium? Despite decades of investigation, this issue remains far from resolved. Perhaps this is not surprising in view of the difficulties in designing experiments free of artifact, as well as in unambiguously interpreting the data from such experiments. Early studies on collagen metabolism and turnover supported the notion that there might be a pool of "immortal" collagen that is present in the organism throughout life and that becomes increasingly cross-linked over time, thus accounting for the progressive changes associated with aging. Such studies generally involved long-term pulse-decay experiments with labeled amino acids, such as proline, lysine, or glycine. Label reutilization appeared to be minimal, based on plasma-specific activities determined less than 1 week after injection. These conclusions regarding collagen turnover were seriously questioned when studies showed that label recycling, particularly of proline, might be much greater than originally estimated. Several new approaches were developed to circumvent the problem of label recycling, many of which are still in use. One approach involves repeated administration of the labeled precursor during the period of rapid growth, either immediately postnatally or in utero and then waiting until the animal is middle-aged or older to harvest tissue. Variations of pulse-chase techniques have also been used to minimize label recycling, including the administration of very large doses of unlabeled precursor to dilute any recycled label. Some investigators utilizing such "pool expansion" techniques have concluded that the matrix, far from containing immortal pools, seems almost volcanic in its constant activity, with

rapid turnover of collagen throughout adulthood. These conclusions, however, directly contradict studies of turnover utilizing a very different approach: tracking the metabolic fate of collagen labeled with ^{18}O, a radiolabeled precursor that by definition cannot be recycled at all. Studies using ^{18}O labeling in rodents provided definitive proof that some of the collagen molecules that are synthesized during the neonatal period are still present in old age, and are found exclusively in the pool of insoluble collagen, thus suggesting they have undergone progressive cross-linking. How can we reconcile these observations with the data obtained from the "pool expansion" approach? It is possible that "flooding" the animal with unphysiologic doses of the unlabeled precursor amino acids may affect collagen metabolism in some way. However, the simplest explanation is that the pool expansion data have been erroneously interpreted. Because these techniques do not distinguish between intracellular and extracellular collagen, it is likely that the extremely rapid turnover of label does not reflect turnover of matrix collagen, but rather the very rapid *intracellular* breakdown of procollagen (collagen that still has extension peptides attached to it) before it is even secreted from the cell. Rapid intracellular degradation of procollagen has been reported in all connective tissue cells, with levels of breakdown ranging from 10 to 40% of newly synthesized procollagen.

Interestingly, there has been far less disagreement concerning elastin turnover, although presumably some of the concerns regarding label reutilization are similar. Most studies have shown that turnover is extremely slow, and best measured in years.

4. Enzymatically Mediated Cross-links

The elucidation of cross-linking pathways in collagen and elastin and structural characterization of specific cross-links has led to a particularly intriguing area of investigation. The first step in cross-link formation is the oxidative deamination of epsilon amino groups on selected lysine residues (and hydroxylysine residues in collagen) by the extracellular enzyme lysyl oxidase. The resultant aldehydes are then capable of undergoing further reactions with unmodified lysine and hydroxylysine residues to form cross-links characterized by a Schiff base-type double bond. Further stabilization of these cross-links occurs through rearrangement and additional reactions to form tri- and tetrafunctional cross-links. Formation of these cross-links is tightly regulated, as they are synthesized at only one or two sites on the chain. Although collagen and elastin have similar cross-linking pathways, elastin lacks any cross-links derived from hydroxylysine; in addition, elastin contains two "mature" cross-links not found in collagen, desmosine and isodesmosine.

Accurate quantification of cross-links was initially hindered by their scarcity: there may be only one cross-link residue for every 6,000 to 10,000 amino acids. However, the development of high-pressure liquid chromatography led to the development of relatively rapid and accurate techniques for quantifying almost all of the structurally characterized cross-links. Despite these technological advances, there remain many pitfalls in the analysis of cross-links, which most likely account for the conflicting results concerning amounts of cross-links in different tissue and species. Accurate assessment requires rigorous attention to standard preparation, including use of standards to control for variability at all stages of analysis from tissue preparation through hydrolysis; analysis of effective reducing capacity of every isotope batch used for reductive labeling; frequent checks of column efficiency and column regeneration or replacement as soon as performance decrement is noted.

Studies of the effects of aging on enzymatically mediated cross-links led to somewhat surprising results. The reducible cross-links, so called because of their characteristic Schiff base-type double bond, were found to decrease rapidly during the postnatal period in most tissues and species. Known maturational products of these cross-links, the tri- and tetrafunctional cross-links, were found, in many cases, to show a corresponding increase in number during this time. However, these so-called mature cross-links did not continue to increase throughout the life span; in many cases, they leveled off or even declined in number during old age. Thus, although enzymatic cross-linking clearly underwent changes with age, the magnitude of these changes, particularly during the last part of the life span, did not seem to correlate with the progressive changes in physicochemical properties of the matrix. Many attempts were made to discover novel "mature" cross-links that could account for the observed changes in matrix associated with aging. Based on indirect evidence, entities such as "compound M," "poly CB-6," and "the Ehrlich chromogen" have been suggested at various times as possible

candidates. These studies illustrate an important caveat concerning identification of a compound as a cross-link: unless a compound can be directly shown to link two collagen chains (i.e., through sequential digestion, such that one can show that the putative cross-link joins peptide fragments from two separate chains), it cannot be considered a proven cross-link.

5. Sugar-Derived Cross-links

The hypothesis that progressive, irreversible cross-linking was a key feature of aging appeared to be inconsistent with the studies reporting that lysyl oxidase-mediated cross-links showed relatively few changes near the end of the life span. However, cross-links have been identified in collagen that arise from an entirely different pathway, in which the initiating event is the nonenzymatic addition of sugar molecules to lysine and hydroxylysine residues. The sugar adducts then undergo fragmentation to form deoxyglucosones. These highly reactive compounds serve as propagators of a series of reactions that ultimately generate an array of fluorophores and chromophores known collectively as advanced Maillard products or advanced glycation products. Although these reaction pathways have been of considerable interest to food chemists since the turn of the century, it has only been relatively recently that attention has focused on nonenzymatic glycation of proteins *in vivo*. The effects of glycation on long-lived macromolecules such as collagen have been of particular interest, as it has been shown that glycation affects collagen solubility, tensile strength, rupture time, ability to bind to ligands, and conformation. [*See* GLYCATION.]

Early studies of nonenzymatic glycation of matrix reported that aging was associated with increasing levels of glucose adducts on collagen throughout the life span. However, more recent studies by several investigators have not confirmed the earlier reports. These conflicting results are most likely due to differences in the specificity of the analytical techniques used. For example, in many of the earlier studies the investigators used the thiobarbituric acid assay, which is subject to interference by a number of compounds, including free glucose and glycosidically bound carbohydrates. In later studies, more specific techniques have been used for quantification, including the furosine assay and affinity chromatography followed by high-pressure liquid chromatography to isolate the glycated residues. Despite this evidence that the thiobarbituric acid assay is not reliable for quantifying glucose adducts on collagen, it continues to be used for this purpose.

As interest developed in the biological consequences of nonenzymatic glycation of proteins, attention was also focused on maturational products of glycated residues. Although the accumulation of yellow-brown chromophores and fluorophores ("browning products") in aging collagen was first reported over 25 years ago, these compounds were initially thought to arise from oxidative reactions of tyrosine residues. The association between browning products and nonenzymatic glycation of collagen has only been investigated relatively recently. In virtually all tissues and species studied, browning products have been found to increase with age. In these studies, the fluorophores and chromophores are inferred to be Maillard products from indirect evidence, such as spectral similarities to known Maillard products or similarities in chromatographic behavior.

Although attempts have been made to characterize specific browning products, isolation and analysis of such compounds as they exist in vivo has proven very difficult, owing to low yields, difficulties in isolating the desired compounds, and the ease with which artifacts may be generated. For example, the first report of a structurally characterized advanced glycation product present in vivo turned out to be erroneous, for the reported compound was actually in artifact of hydrolysis. In general, unless physiological conditions of temperature and pH are used to isolate putative compounds for analysis, the risk of artifact generation is high; any reports of newly characterized glycation products isolated from tissue should be cautiously evaluated with this caveat in mind. Only one advanced Maillard product has been found in collagen *in vivo* has been isolated and fully characterized, a trifunctional fluorophore known as pentosidine. Pentosidine has been shown to increase throughout the life span in several different tissues and species. Pentosidine, however, is present in very low levels (by comparison, enzymatic cross-links are approximately ten times more numerous), thus making it unlikely that pentosidine itself accounts for age-associated changes in the properties of collagen.

Elastin is characterized by a marked degree of autofluorescence, which increases with age in most tissues studied. Whether or not this fluorescence is due to accumulation of advanced glycation products remains unclear, due in part to the extreme difficulty in preparing elastin for analysis without generating artifacts. This fluorescence has been attributed to various compounds such as dityrosine, lipid peroxidation products, quinones, and reactive carbonyl products.

F. Immunofluorescence

We have seen that one of the major difficulties in correlating histochemical and electron-microscopic analyses of matrix with biochemical analyses has been the discrepancy between *descriptive* definitions of matrix components based on their visual appearance and *structural* definitions based on biochemical analysis. To some extent these difficulties are resolved when immunological identification of matrix components has been combined with light or electron microscopy. Immunological probes have been used to identify specific collagen types, specific collagen chains, and even some of the advanced glycation products.

There are a number of antigenic sites in collagen and procollagen (another name for collagen molecules whose extension peptides have not been cleaved), located in both helical and nonhelical regions. Because there is cross-species reactivity, antibodies for use in human tissue can, for example, be raised against collagen chains purified from bovine tissue. When purified collagen is used as the antigen for preparation of polyclonal antibodies, the antisera produced contain a high titer of antibody for the immunizing antigen. However, moderate levels of antibody reactive with other collagens or procollagens are also present. Thus, purification on immunoadsorbent columns is essential to remove cross-reacting antibodies, following which the specificity should be documented by passive hemagglutination and by radioimmunoassays.

Antibodies have also been prepared that react with advanced glycation products. The so-called AGE (advanced glycation end product) antibody is prepared by injecting rabbits with glycated albumin; the resultant antibodies react with proteins containing advanced glycation products (as assessed by their fluorescence) but not with unmodified proteins. There is serious question as to the interpretation on data utilizing this antibody. A monoclonal antibody is also available for pyrraline, an advanced glycation product that has only been isolated and characterized from proteins incubated with sugar *in vitro*. Although immunohistochemical analysis of tissues with the pyrraline antibody suggest it is widely distributed *in vivo*, it has proved impossible to isolate it from tissues due to its lability.

Although immunological techniques are a powerful addition to routine histochemistry, there are many potential pitfalls. First of all, the anticollagen antibodies must be highly purified, as any cross-reacting antibodies would render a study virtually useless. Even then, interbatch differences in specificity and affinity of anticollagen antibodies and fluorescein-labeled antibodies means that valid comparisons can only be made within a single series. There is no standardized substrate for validating type-specific antibodies. As noted, there is serious question as to what is actually being detected with the AGE-antibody. Another problem may arise when tissues rich in elastic fibers are analyzed. Such fibers have a strong autofluorescence that may interfere with evaluation of immunofluorescence. Finally, making of antigenic determinants in the tissue to be analyzed can seriously interfere with interpretation of results. It is certainly possible that accessibility of antigenic determinants decreases in old tissue due to blocking by proteoglycans, for example, or the accumulation of glycation products. Finally, there is a large degree of subjectivity in interpretation of results as well as potential problems in random sampling.

III. SURVEY OF AGE-ASSOCIATED CHANGES IN THE EXTRACELLULAR MATRIX

Given the discussion of methodological pitfalls described in section II, it is evident that the literature on age-associated changes in the matrix cannot be summarized in a table that restricts itself to a simple listing of species, tissue, parameter, and the effect of aging, although such an approach would make the vase literature seemingly more accessible. Ideally, the validity of each study's conclusions should be considered individually with respect to general pitfalls (age range studied, number of sampling points, adequate sample size for assay variance, particularly if variance increases with age) and pitfalls specific to the assays used, including a careful consideration

Table II Effects of Aging on Collagen Cross-links in Different Tissues in Mice[a]

Tissue	Lung	Skin	Aorta	Tail tendon
DHLNL	↓	nd	↓	nd
HLNL	→	→	↓	↓
OHP	→	nd	↑	nd
gluc-lys	↓	→	→	→
fluorescence	—	↑	↑	↑
pentosidine	—	nd	↑	nd

[a] The crosslink abbreviations are as follows: DHLNL, dihydroxylysinonorleucine (enzyme-mediated difunctional cross-link); HLNL, hydroxylysinonorleucine (enzyme-mediated difunctional cross-link); OHP, hydroxypyridinium (enzyme-mediated fluorescent cross-link; gluc-lys, glucose adduct formed by addition of glucose to lysine residue; fluorescence, collagen-associated fluorescence, assumed to represent advanced glycation products; nd, not detectable; dash, no data reported.

of whether other age-associated changes in the organism may interfere with the assay of interest, thus possibly invalidating a comparison of young and old animals.

Despite these difficulties, particularly in comparing one study with another, we can draw several general conclusions: synthesis and deposition of collagen and elastin occur predominantly during the period of early growth and development; synthesis levels then continue at low levels that change little in old age. Collagen becomes progressively more insoluble with age, and autofluorescence increases in both collagen and elastin. Enzymatically mediated cross-links undergo their most significant changes during the first half of the life span in most tissues and species, "mature" enzymatic cross-links either change little during aging, or sometimes exhibit a biphasic pattern, in which peak levels are reached in middle age, followed by a gradual decrease. In contrast, sugar-derived cross-links accumulate very slowly in most tissues and species during the first half of the life span, with more accelerated accumulation during aging. In some cases significant increases may not occur until the last 10% of the life span. There is considerable species specificity and tissue specificity with respect to both the timing and the magnitude of the changes as illustrated in Tables II–III. Table II provides an example of changes in tissues in a single species, and Table III shows changes in a single tissue among several species.

Table III Effects of Aging on Collagen Cross-links in Skin in Different Species[a]

Species	HLNL	his-HLNL	OHP	HHMD
rat	↓	nd	nd	↓
mouse	→	nd	nd	↓
human	↓	↑	↑	↓
monkey	↓	—	—	↓
cow	↓	↑	nd	—

[a] The cross-link abbreviations are as follows: HLNL, hydroxylysinonorleucine, (enzyme-mediated difunctional cross-link); his-HLNL, histidinohydroxylysinonorleucine (enzyme-mediated trifunctional cross-link, maturational product of HLNL); HHMD, histidinohydroxymerodesmosine (enzyme-mediated tetrafunctional cross-link); dash, no data reported; nd, not detectable.

IV. MODULATION OF MATRIX AGING

There has been no shortage of effort expended on discovering a way to slow or reverse aging of the matrix, given that virtually all of the visible signs of aging are attributable to age-associated changes in its components. Approaches may generally be categorized as either replacement strategies or prevention strategies. For example, there has been considerable interest in attempting to slow aging at the systemic level by administration of growth hormone or insulin-like growth factor. There is evidence that some parameters such as muscle mass may increase, and it is possible that stimulating synthesis of new matrix may improve connective tissue function. Adequate long-term studies of the efficacy or safety of these agents are not available.

Preventive strategies have focused on glycation and oxidation as the primary culprits in degenerative changes of the matrix. From this perspective, agents developed for treatment of diabetes (which is characterized by rapid accumulation of advanced glycation products on connective tissue) may have relevance to aging in the normal population. Several agents have been found to inhibit the initial formation of glucose adducts on collagen, including acetylsalicylic acid, acetic anhydride, ibuprofen, glutathione, and the dibasic amino acids lysine and arginine. However, there have been no long-term trials designed to investigate the effects of these agents in aging. Data suggesting that fructation of collagen may contribute to accumulation of browning products has led to an interest in the use of aldose reductase inhibitors to inhibit biosynthesis of fructose. These agents have met with only limited success in diabetes. Recently there has been interest in aminoguanidine, a hydrazine compound that appears to bind to the reactive deoxyglucosones, thus theoretically preventing their progression into more advanced Maillard products. However, conflicting reports regarding its efficacy in preventing diabetic complications have appeared, and long-term safety has not been adequately studied.

Antioxidant administration has also been enjoying a resurgence of interest as antiaging agents. Although there is some evidence that vitamin E may decrease nonenzymatic glycation of matrix, convincing long-term results are not available. Furthermore, it is unclear that administration of large doses of exogenous antioxidants will alter levels of oxidative stress, due to the tightly regulated homeostatic mechanisms of the antioxidant defense system.

Dietary manipulation is another approach potential for slowing aging. It has long been known that feeding rodents a diet restricted in calories will extend their life span by about 20%. Very recently it has been shown that such lifetime caloric restriction significantly reduces the accumulation of advanced glycation products on matrix in tissues and organs throughout the body. The relationship between life extension and reduction of advanced glycation products remains to be elucidated. Other dietary manipulations may also be beneficial. Very recent studies have shown that the source of carbohydrate in the diet may significantly influence the accumulation of glycation products in matrix as well as the level of oxidative stress. Rats whose sole source of carbohydrate was fructose had significantly more advanced glycation products on their collagen and significantly higher levels of circulating lipid peroxide products than rats whose carbohydrate source was glucose, even after only 6 months on the special diet. Rats fed mixtures of sugars had intermediate values. Whether these dietary manipulations have similar effects in humans remains to be seen. [See DIET AND NUTRITION.]

V. SUMMARY AND CONCLUSIONS

Given the many caveats regarding methodological pitfalls, species specificity and tissue specificity, are there any generalizations we can make about the effects of age on the extracellular matrix? It is perhaps a truism to say that the more we have learned, the more complex the process appears to be, involving a seemingly endless recursive series of feedback loops between different reaction pathways. However, there are a few general patterns we can discern that appear applicable to most tissues and species. During the postnatal period, there is rapid synthesis of matrix molecules, some of which are destined for turnover and replacement, whereas others enter the pool of insoluble matrix, where they remain throughout the animal's life. Enzymatic cross-linking serves as the dominant influence during the first part of the life span, stabilizing and shaping the matrix such that its characteristic properties will best serve the functional needs of the tissue in which it inheres. In middle age, however, the matrix comes increasingly under the sway of stochastic forces that inexorably twist it in unpredictable ways that no longer adhere to the rules of biological design. Recently, the contributions of glycation and oxidation to this process have been the focus of particular interest, and agents designed to intervene in these reactions are being developed. However, perhaps because of the inherent complexity of the process, successful strategies available for attenuating these changes in matrix have not yet been developed. We evidently have much to learn about the intricate mechanisms of this strange clock that keeps unseen time beneath our skin.

BIBLIOGRAPHY

Labuza, T. P., Reineccius, G. A., Monnier, V. M., O'Brien, J., & Baynes, J. W. (Eds.). (1994). *Maillard reactions in chemistry, food and health.* Cambridge, UK: Royal Society of Chemistry.

Reiser, K. M. (1991). Nonenzymatic glycation of collagen in aging and diabetes. *Proceedings of the Society of Experimental Biology and Medicine 196,* 17–29.

Reiser, K. M., McCormick, R. J., & Rucker, R. B. (1992). Enzymatic and nonenzymatic cross-linking of collagen and elastin. *FASEB J. 6,* 2439–2449.

Sell, D. R., & Monnier, V. M. (1995). Aging of long-lived proteins. E. J. Masoro (Ed.). *Handbook of physiology: Volume on aging.* Orlando: CRC Press.

F

Folklore

David Shuldiner

University of Connecticut and Connecticut State Department of Social Services

Applied Folklore The application of concepts, methods, and content of folklore studies to constructive social interventions and problem solving.

Folk Art Works of art or craft using traditional methods, based on shared community aesthetics and in which artistic values are often subordinated to a utilitarian purpose.

Folk Belief Convictions traditionally shared by members of a group, not necessarily based on empirical evidence, but accepted on faith as received wisdom.

Folk Medicine Traditional healing practices employing natural remedies or magico-religious ritual, or both, generally based on naturopathic or homeopathic (versus allopathic) models, and indigenous concepts of disease.

FOLKLORE consists of those traditional forms of expressive behavior that reflect shared identity and experience within social groups whose members have at least one or more traits in common. Common traits include age, gender, sexual orientation, ethnicity, religion, class, occupation, or special interests. Forms of expressive behavior include beliefs, rituals, ceremo-

nies, festivals, stories (such as folktales, legends), personal experience narratives (ranging from anecdotes to oral histories), jargon (special in-group language), proverbs, folk songs, folk dances, traditional or "folk" medicine, and material culture (such as folk art and craft, costume, planting lore, and foodways).

I. FOLKLORE AND AGING: AN OVERVIEW

The field of folklore offers a number of unique perspectives and resources to gerontological research and practice. Forms of expressive behavior are culturally coded sources of information regarding attitudes toward and treatment of the elderly within their respective communities. Some traditional beliefs and practices become associated with old age largely because the elderly members of a given community are the only ones for whom those folk traditions are still a part of their cultural repertoire and identity. In other words, the distinction between the "old ways" and the "old ones" often becomes blurred, particularly as the intensity of shared cultural identity may increase among the aging while it diminishes among younger community members. But the expressive behavior described here is not simply the cultural repository of a community preserved in the memories of its older members. It is also the folklore created and generated by and about elders in settings ranging from village to city to suburbia.

Folklorists conducting field research among diverse groups have commonly sought out older members for the breadth and depth of their cultural knowledge, the result of years of experience living, working, and interacting within social networks of family, community, and workplace. They have drawn attention to the role these elders play in transmitting cultural knowledge to succeeding generations through various forms of expressive behavior. Historically they have tended to treat these elders as the last community members retaining certain traditions. But more recently they have drawn attention to the ongoing process of creating and generating folklore among older adults, providing a two-way cultural bridge to a wider community, with which they may share their cultural wisdom, and from which they may receive recognition and needed services.

II. TRADITIONAL BELIEFS REGARDING AGING AND THE AGED

Attitudes within traditional communities about the aging (and age-related beliefs held by elders themselves) are reflected in the full range of their folklore: proverbs, aphorisms, tales, folk songs, and other forms of expressive behavior. Some of these beliefs relate to social roles, others to attributes of aging. Taken as a whole, they reflect a good deal of ambivalence, both within and across cultures, about the nature of aging and the character of the aged. In fact, such debates within gerontology as that between "disengagement" and "activity" theories mirror an age-old ambiguity within many communities. Paradoxically, traditional conceptions of aging have embraced the wisdom, experience, and sage counsel of elders while recording a litany of derisive notions concerning the forgetfulness, foolishness, and general mental decline of those advanced in years. In like manner, physical signs of aging have been viewed variously as marks of distinction of venerable old age, or as signals of degeneration—negative emblems of the final stage in the human life cycle.

Among positive depictions, the aged have been bestowed with an impressive array of magical attributes in the body of popular belief. Tales and legends abound in which old women or men appear as magical helpers to aid the protagonist in a difficult task. The elderly are often cast in the role of prophet or seer, reflecting a common notion that old people have "second sight."

Among the central figures in many North American Indian creation stories is Grandmother Spider, who brought the People into being and taught them survival skills. A more liminal character is that of Old Man Coyote depicted in trickster tales. Although tricksters may be old or young, they reflect another popular age stereotype, in that they are noteworthy for their capriciousness; on a whim they may choose to rescue or torment the people whose tales have immortalized them.

This duality appears in the depiction of women. Although there is extensive admiration for the miraculous endowments of old wise women, there is also a widespread superstitious fear of an older woman's curse (or evil glance). Old women have, indeed, all too often been cast as loathsome and menacing creatures, or at minimum suspicious characters. The archetypal witch in countless tales is a haggard, wrinkled, often toothless, elderly female.

Folk songs tend to be less ambiguous in their depiction of the aged; the social circumstances they describe commonly reveal a negative valuation of aging and the aged. Within the Anglo-American ballad tradition are numerous such songs with aged characters in the form of satire or lament. In many, discomfort with age is conflated with sexual conflict. "Never Wed an Old Man" is a ribald comment on the sexual shortcomings of an older groom. In "Old Grey Beard" a young woman complains about an arranged marriage with an old man, a common practice in some traditional communities. In another song, "Rocking the Cradle," an old man laments his marriage to a young woman who "roams," bemoaning the fate that has him "rocking the cradle, and the child not his own." Songs such as "The Scolding Wife" play upon the male stereotype of the old married woman as shrew, but single women fare no better: "The Old Maid's Lament," sung as warning to the young not to delay marriage too long, also reflects the marginalization of older unmarried women. A number of ballads are cautionary tales, songs with moral messages composed from the point of view of an older person who recalls the time "when I was a young lad (lass)," and often giving such sage counsel as how to avoid the narrators' follies of youth.

Metaphoric analogs, positive and negative, to old age are abundant in folk imagery. Among the most common of them are the depictions of the spirits of the grain at harvest time. Ceremonies have long been performed in European peasant communities honoring these symbolic emblems of the ripened crops, variously named Old Man or Old Woman (Old Grandmother, Old Rye Woman, the Hag, Old Wife, etc.). Such beliefs and practices have enjoyed wide currency among Native American Indians as well.

Matters meteorological may also bear such metaphoric imagery. In England, as well as many parts of the United States, when it is snowing a child may be told that the Old Woman is shaking her featherbed, or picking geese. Matters psychological may carry the more negative symbolism embodied in the archetypal elderly female ogre, for when nightmares invade one's sleep, such disturbances may be attributed to a visitation by the "Old Hag."

Although the knowledge of sage elders is popularly recognized, proverbial wisdom on the subject is mixed. Biblical verse speaks reverently of the "hoary head" as a "crown of glory" (Proverbs 16:31); Job offered the opinion that "Wisdom is with the aged, and understanding in length of days." Yet Herodes quipped that "white hair blunteth wit"; heralding in the popular imagination countervailing folk belief to that of the "wisdom of age," namely that advancing age is inevitably accompanied by a diminution of the rational faculties.

In fact, a pervasive view persists, both in folk belief and in early gerontological literature, that such signs of degeneration and withdrawal signal a disengagement from the affairs of living and, moreover, a closing of the cycle of life through a return to its earliest stage. That old age is a "second childhood" is a popular, long-standing conception. Aristophanes once observed that "old people are twice children," a sentiment echoed in an early rabbinic commentary: "Once a man, twice a child." The latter aphorism appears verbatim in eighteenth-century American proverbs.

Elders in contemporary society continue to take somewhat of a beating when it comes to folklore relating to aging. Among the slights to age heard by contemporary urban elders are such proverbial phrases as "old hat," for anything outmoded, and the epithet OMH (Old Man with a Hat), usually reserved for capped drivers of slow-moving automobiles. Despite advances in the field of gerontology, positing the continued physical as well as mental vitality and viability of most older adults, the dialectical processes of growth and degeneration that characterize advancing age will continue to condition conflicting views expressed in folk beliefs regarding age and the aging.

III. TRADITIONAL NARRATIVES ABOUT THE AGED

Those tales, legends, and myths found among indigenous peoples throughout the world that feature the aged provide important clues about the role and character of traditional elders in their respective communities. Folklorists have also observed, however, that as much as the setting and characters of a folktale may be culturally coded, the basic themes, and often plot outlines, are so similar across cultural boundaries that they often reveal values that transcend their local settings.

As has been noted, traditional narratives, as with other expressive forms, reveal often conflicting images of aging. Although the heroes in many fairy tales are aided in their quest by a magic helper, often an elderly person, it would not be unlikely for the same hero to be confronted by an elderly antagonist, such as a wizened old witch or evil stepmother.

One instructive body of traditional narratives are those cautionary tales that overtly chasten the listener for harboring prejudices against the aged, while simultaneously revealing those prejudices to be as long-standing as the putative veneration of age. One of the most widespread of these is the story of the abandoned elders, told throughout Asia and among indigenous peoples of the Americas. An Eskimo version relates the adventures of two older women, abandoned as "burdens" by their fellow villagers who felt they could no longer support them. They survive a harsh winter and manage to accumulate a store of food. In one version, community members run into them again, and they share their stores, saving the village from starvation. (In another version, it is two old men who find food while the rest of the village dies of starvation.)

An Arawak tale relates the guidance of an old man who leads the ancestors safely over turbulent waters in a large boat. As long as his advice is followed, all goes well. However, one disaster after another befalls the sojourners as they ignore his warnings: one loses his life when, after being told not to, he shoots a fish in which the old man had recognized a human being; when on land, one who ignores his hunting tips catches nothing; another who steps into a canoe he was told to avoid is lost at sea.

"Mother Holle," a European tale collected by the

brothers Grimm, (with versions found throughout Asia, Africa, and the Americas) carries an analogous admonition to heed the word of elders. A widow has two daughters, one ugly and lazy (the favored "real" daughter), the other, pretty and clever, who does all the work. The latter drops a spindle into a well and is ordered to retrieve it. She jumps in and finds herself in an enchanted place where she compliantly performs several tasks, and meets and works for old Mother Holle. Homesick, she is allowed to leave, and returns to the widow all covered with gold. The mother greedily sends the idle, ugly daughter down the well; this daughter performs no task requested of her, and refuses to work for Mother Holle; she returns home all covered with pitch.

What is particularly telling is that although the aged are depicted favorably, there is a subtext of ambiguity that may be read into these stories. Although consideration for the aged is often the stated or implied moral, the dramatic tension of the narratives rests in whole or part upon mistreatment of elders, or at the least disregard for their advice or abilities. This would tend to reinforce the observation that ambivalence toward aging and the aged is a cross-cultural phenomenon. Moreover, folk and industrial societies apparently share a state of affairs in which respect for elders, though universally valued as an ideal, is observed as much in the breach as in actual practice.

There is a relatively small body of folktales that provide object lessons for the process of aging itself. These offer themes similar to the stories mentioned above, but with a twist: it is the elder characters who themselves are put to the test.

In one Japanese tale, an elderly couple live near a forest. The husband, kind and gentle, keeps a sparrow as a pet; his wife, complains about the bird, as with everything. One day while he is out in the field, she cuts its tongue out. The old man goes into the forest to apologize, meets the bird, who has a new tongue, and is offered a choice of two boxes for his show of concern. He chooses the smaller one; it turns out to be filled with gold coins. His wife greedily sets out to retrieve the larger box from the sparrow, who complies; it is full of demons which torment her until she runs to her husband in the field, who scolds her. The demons eventually vanish, and she vows to mend her ways.

The Jungian analyst Allan Chinen has pointed out that this unique variation on a familiar theme allows an older person to ultimately benefit from the maturity of age by acknowledging her faults and being changed by this awareness, a possibility universally denied to younger counterparts in similar tales. (It is ironic, however, that although ultimately lenient toward the aged, this tale perpetuates the stereotype of the old wife as shrew.)

IV. FOLK WISDOM: ORAL TRADITION AND THE ROLE OF ELDERS

As caretakers of cultural knowledge, a central role of elders in traditional communities has been that of conserving and imparting this folk wisdom. Crucial to performing this role is the memory (in content, style, and structure) of those forms of expressive behavior in which this wisdom is embedded. Principal among these are mythical and legendary narratives, told and retold throughout their lives. These tales of how a people came into being and discovered their place in the scheme of things are also catalogues of important cultural values, often embodied or mirrored in the attributes and actions of specific characters. It is commonly the responsibility of elders to interpret the lessons embedded in traditional narratives, treating them essentially as blueprints for community living.

Another important, if less formal, vehicle for imparting communal knowledge is that of the personal experience narratives of older community members, oral historical accounts (ranging from life stories to anecdotes) that contribute valuable insights into family and community life, while reaffirming the cultural integrity of the teller. A folklorist's perspective on the reminiscences of elders lies somewhere between that of the psychologist and the historian. Whereas the latter treats the life story as data to be corroborated with other historical documents, the former sees it as a vehicle for ego integration.

Taking into account both of these perspectives and integrating them into an aesthetic model, folklorists treat life stories as creative forms of expression reflecting certain traditional values exemplified by narrated events. Embedded in history, they are also vehicles for the (re)construction and affirmation of identity. Therefore, the importance of personal experience narratives may lie not only in the "facts" they relate, but in what they reveal about those values and attitudes held by the narrator that they deem important to convey to the listener, and how narrative devices are employed to that end.

Stories, whether fictional or based on personal experience, are often intended as object lessons. In fact, the line between fiction and nonfiction in storytelling may often be blurred. The presentation of a narrative of personal experience generally conforms to the features of a traditional story. And because the stories of elders are often designed to serve a didactic purpose, the factual information conveyed may often be molded to meet the pedagogical demands of the narrative. It is not that the teller is deliberately lying; it is more the case that the purpose of a story—the lesson, or larger "truth," it conveys—takes precedence, "requiring" embellishments that bring the lessons of life "home," while protecting self-integrity.

What is important here is that the content of folk wisdom is inseparable from the self-identity and communal authority its possession and dispensation conveys. This is a crucial link for elders, for whom, with the cessation of other productive roles, the role of arbiter of traditional knowledge may become central. This role is articulated in a number of ways: not only through storytelling, but also through folk healing, the exercise of ritual authority, and the mastery of traditional arts.

V. TRADITIONAL PRACTICES RELATING TO THE ELDERLY

There are traditional practices, both of long-standing and of recent invention, that have provided elders with ways of making late-life transitions (such as rites of passage into new social roles) and confronting isolation. These would include rituals, ceremonies, and the like, conducted by and for elders.

Some of these are responses to the dialectic of isolation versus incorporation of elderly reflected in other aspects of community life. Although elders may serve as guardians of traditional activities for the community as a whole, occupying important ceremonial offices, they may also find themselves devalued for conditions of age (often conflated with gender, ethnic, and other prejudices); at other times they may simply be rejected for their inability to carry out tasks for which they had been responsible earlier in life. Some

rituals may act, then, as compensatory mechanisms for the alienation of the aging from other community members. [*See* AGEISM AND DISCRIMINATION.]

A. Ritual and Authority

Rituals in which older community members have vested authority are generally those in which positively valued attributes of age, such as breadth and depth of traditional knowledge, experience, and maturity, constitute the very qualifications for office. In most traditional communities, ritual authority and political influence are inseparable, because command of ceremonial knowledge and practice is an essential leadership quality. As caretakers of traditional wisdom, elders are therefore in a position to wield that knowledge in order to oversee and protect community interests. It is for that very reason that elders often suffer compounded effects of cultural displacement.

When a community experiences attrition through out-migration or assimilation, older members not only share the loss of a social foundation for the expression of cultural identity, they also experience the erosion of authority (including recognition and respect) that came with their role as cultural caretakers, including that of arbiter of communal ritual. When ceremonies over which elders have traditionally had control are discontinued, a vital part of their identity ceases to have a viable outlet. Many a folklorist or other field researcher has provided the only remaining opportunity a traditional elder has for the demonstration of his or her command of the knowledge that once conveyed a position of influence, of counsel and guidance, in their respective communities.

Older men may assume leadership in matters ranging from the initiation rites of young males, to the adjudication of civil disputes and criminal cases, the overseeing of healing ceremonies, and other aspects of political leadership. In all of these areas, they are expected to draw upon their mastery of traditional expressive forms, such as traditional oratory, folk medicine, and myths and legends whose narratives not only recount a people's origins, but contain detailed descriptions of the rituals conducted by those elders.

Older women have less commonly attained positions of political leadership within traditional societies, but they have tended to retain ritual authority with respect to all observances concerning women, including all practices relating to the female reproductive cycle, from menarche to menopause. One separate, if not always equal, position has been that of the guardians of folk knowledge passed down within the restricted but protective domain of female secret societies. They have been midwives and herbalists, occasionally shamans, often commanding a specialized knowledge and skill in healing lore, and have also been gifted storytellers. The acrual of ritual authority with age (that is, with the maturation of their knowledge of traditional lore) has not, however, come as readily for older women as it has for men.

B. Rituals of Senescence

Although installation ceremonies may be conducted to honor those traditional elders who have attained positions of ritual authority, there are few rites of passage into the "country of old age" itself. Elevated ritual status is offered to select elders within traditional communities, but the "coming of age" for elders in contemporary society has been accompanied by rituals either designating an exit from a given social role, or a temporary compensation for the liminal identity of the role-disenfranchised.

Contemporary forms of rituals of senescence include celebrations of life transitions, such as retirement ceremonies, and nostalgic public displays such as "old-timers" days, when retired workers or older community members return to the workplace or neighborhood to revisit old social ties and customs and temporarily receive recognition.

One of the most common contemporary forms of celebratory ritual among elders is the observance of birthdays. Often organized by family members, birthday celebrations have become a staple activity among care and service providers at sites where elders gather or reside. Such ceremonies not only provide a pretext for the celebration of age, but also serve as a vehicle for the reinforcement of cultural identity.

Sometimes these celebrations take place within ethnic community centers, where elders may still live within a given folk culture, but may be the only ones left still carrying on certain traditions. In this setting, a ritual such as a birthday celebration may provide an induced setting for certain traditional practices for which there is no longer a consistent community context.

Among a group of Nisei (second-generation Japanese American) elders in a San Francisco senior center,

group birthday parties offer cultural activities, such as *minyo* (folk song), *odori* (dancing), and *shiatsu* (Japanese massage), along with lunch and gift exchanging. Similarly, a Jewish senior center in Venice, California, offers birthday celebrants a luncheon, with folk dancing, the singing of Yiddish folk songs, and a performance by local Jewish musicians.

Many urban senior centers and nursing homes serve elderly who have tenuous or no extant ties with any specific ethnic community. In the absence of communal contexts for other ritual observances, participants in birthday parties at these sites become temporary members of a surrogate folk community, providing an opportunity for the sharing of personal experience and cultural knowledge when other traditional settings are no longer readily available.

Other contemporary ceremonies for the aged have borrowed traditional forms and content to celebrate life transitions for which specific observances have not been previously conducted in traditional communities. Among these are rituals inspired by the feminist critique of negative cultural stereotypes of older women, such as the celebration of the "crone," or wise old woman. Generally speaking, these are postmenopausal observances that have incorporated cross-cultural ritual knowledge traditionally associated with older women, and set, on occasion, within existing religious contexts. There is a deliberate effort here to underscore a positive valuation of aging in general, and menopause in particular, as a cultural construct, rather than a set of medical conditions. Croning ceremonies, then, are contemporary rites of passage that enlist the form and content of folk traditions to signal menopause, and the attending aging process, as signs of growth and wisdom, rather than degeneration.

VI. FOLK MEDICINE

It is generally recognized that effective service and care delivery for the aging depends not only upon a judicious balance of efficiency and compassion, but also upon a knowledge of the specific cultural contexts within which elders live and interact. This includes knowledge about health beliefs and practices held both about the aging, and by older persons themselves. Understanding cultural views on aging and health involves not only gathering information about indigenous health views and customs, but also giving due respect to the often prominent role played by elders in traditional health care.

There are significant differences between folk and conventional (allopathic) medicine that help to explain the often central role that elders play as traditional health-care practitioners. Where allopathic medicine addresses primarily the treatment of specific compartmentalized ailments, folk medicine tends to be more comprehensive, treating the mind–body as a unit, and further viewing the individual within a larger social and environmental context. Folk medicine is not only more holistic in its approach than conventional medicine, it tends not to be the exclusive province of a professional elite.

Most community members tend to accrue, with age, some knowledge of the methods and materia medica of traditional healing. A majority of elders may thus have accumulated the requisite knowledge, but only select individuals are generally recognized who have become, over the years, particularly skilled in the healing arts, and who may continue to provide useful roles in late life as practitioners of folk medicine. In many traditional cultures, therefore, the sage counsel for which elders are sought may often include their knowledge of traditional techniques of therapeutic intervention. Looked at this way, the role of elders as caretakers of traditional culture is inseparable from the role that they have often played in healing the wounds (both physical and psychic, personal and interpersonal) of family and community members, using time-honored natural methods. In the process of treating individual and social ailments, elder folk healers often become mediators between tradition and modernity, bridging cultures in contention.

Ironically, elder folk healers prefigure the very advent of the conventional (scientific) medical establishment that has eclipsed their traditional role and authority. The shaman, or "medicine man" (often a woman), has tended to draw upon a repertoire of techniques and materials that is fairly fixed, but in which competence and authority may increase with the wisdom of age. Among their contemporary counterparts, experience is valued, but technical knowledge is the province of a few specialists whose prominence is based only in part upon their chronological age. Older practitioners of conventional medicine may, in fact, be eventually viewed as out of touch with the latest technical advances.

Another body of traditional health-care practices in folk communities that has been devalued with the advance of modern medicine is one that has historically been the province of older women with special knowledge of healing arts arising from the domestic work over which they have traditionally had dominion. In particular, their knowledge of herbal medicine and practice of midwifery has made them essential partners in traditional health care. Ironically it was their very knowledge of folk medicine that made these traditional healers subject to attack as witches in medieval Europe. Among the central accusations of witchcraft at that time was the possession of medical and obstetrical skills—in effect, practicing the healing arts outside the jurisdiction of the emerging (and exclusively male) conventional medical establishment. Although not all those accused were older women, the association of witchcraft in the popular imagination with the image of an old wizened hag standing over a pot, stirring some concoction of herbs and other exotic materials, to cast spells (often inflicting painful medical conditions) on the unsuspecting, persists to this day.

A common belief among indigenous peoples gives further credence to the powers of elders as healers. The abilities of a healer to treat the ailing are often linked to their connection with spiritual powers. Elders' temporal proximity to death may be seen as an asset, in that they have one foot in the spirit realm where supernatural healing properties may be called upon. Curing ceremonies often involve the "journey" of the healer to the "underworld" to seek the magic that will heal their patient.

Among many Native American Indian groups, there are legends attributing the acquisition of traditional medical knowledge to older persons. Among the Chippewa, it is said that an old man first revealed the healing songs performed by the Medicine Society. A Creek legend relates how knowledge of traditional healing was revealed to the old men by animals of unknown origin. These legends reinforce the role of traditional elders as the guardians and repositories of cultural wisdom. Those who come to practice the healing arts in late life do so precisely at that point when the accumulated knowledge, and the lifetime of experience it represents, conveys authority to the words of a traditional community's senior members. Thus, for those elders who have followed the healer's path, their medical training is inseparable from their lifelong assimilation of the whole body of traditional wisdom.

As indicated earlier, perhaps the most important knowledge traditional elders may possess is the memory of traditional narratives, tales not only of how a people came to be, but also how they acquired the skills and materials to survive, including, as noted, the knowledge of traditional medical practices and materials. The elder healer has heard mythical narratives told and retold throughout a lifetime and has witnessed the specific ceremonies during which they were recited, which are attempts to recapture the healing power embedded in the very story of their origins.

In linking the roles of elders as healers and as storytellers, it is important to consider some general assumptions on illness shared by many traditional societies. Illness, be it psychological or physiological, is often viewed not solely as the ailment of an individual, but as a disruption of the social fabric of a close-knit, interdependent community and its environment. Because mythical narratives describe the natural and cultural foundation upon which the community rests, they may be invoked by the knowledgable to restore a delicate social and ecological balance. Thus elder folk healers may draw as much upon their capacity as interpreters and practitioners of traditional storytelling as upon their medical knowledge to restore the health of individuals and communities.

VII. THE TRADITIONAL ARTS

Another aspect of folklore for which elders have been the cultural repositories are the traditional arts, including not only storytelling, but such expressive forms as folk music, dance, art and craft—guided by, and perpetuating, shared community standards of excellence and beauty, while also bearing the stamp of individual creativity and mastery.

For many elders, their activity as craftspeople, folk artists, musicians, and the like represents both the preservation of folk culture and the mastery of traditional arts over a lifetime of practice. For others, their creative endeavors may reflect late-life efforts, activities that flower after their retirement from wage-earning work and/or raising a family. For these elders, an activity in which they may have initially engaged just to pass the time may represent other important late-life projects, such as a long-delayed cultivation of

latent talent, the reaffirmation of aspects of cultural identity that may have been less demonstrative earlier in their lives, or an exercise in reminiscence—a re-creation of past experience through cultural artifacts (particularly folk art).

Of particular interest to gerontology is the function of folk art as life review. Folklore is often viewed as a community's cultural artifacts preserved from its past. But it may also serve as a vehicle for recalling the past experiences of individual community members. A few examples will illustrate this dual function.

Quilting, like much of folk art, has its origins in a utilitarian purpose. In many communities, words and images have been sewn into quilt patches commemorating family, community, and even historical events. Quilting, although practiced throughout a lifetime for many women, may become a central activity for women (and some men) in late life, when other demands of work are lessened. At this stage, one purpose a quilt has is that of a life record. Not only may sewn images recall past life events, but the materials themselves may evoke specific memories (such as scraps of cloth saved from the making of a wedding gown, or the remnants of a dress worn by a departed family member).

Retired workers, especially loggers, coal miners, sailors, and others whose occupational communities have been known for their folk song repertoires, may sing ballads recalling their working lives. But countless other retirees have turned to folk art that re-creates past work experiences through painting, sculpture, woodworking, or other media, often utilizing the discarded materials of their former workplace.

As with other aspects of expressive behavior, elders are often the last practitioners of those traditional arts that lack a community base to guarantee the continuity of their legacy. Some older craftspeople have themselves faced the consequences of a loss of generativity, having come to maturity when the last exponents of a given craft have died without training any younger apprentices. Taking up an interest later in life in a tradition that by that time is no longer practiced, they fill in a generational gap by reviving this "lost" art, and with the zeal of discovery seek out apprentices to whom they may teach its resurrected lore. Once again, however, they may be faced by another challenge, the lack of people from within their own community interested in or available for training.

The experience of Native American Indians is instructive here. Suffering from years of attrition and cultural dissolution, many local communities have banded together in "pan-Indian" alliances, hosting intertribal activities, such as powwows where, among other things, elders share their folk wisdom cross-culturally, not only among other Indian communities, but with non-Indians invited to learn about native culture. Extending this principle, master basket makers, drummers, and dancers have found ways of perpetuating folklore across cultural boundaries, joining elders from many other traditional communities in a contemporary version of generativity—passing on their legacy to the members of a multiethnic global village.

VIII. APPLIED FOLKLORE AND AGING

In applying concepts, methods, and materials of folklore study to the tackling of practical issues in gerontology, one of the things to be kept in mind is the changing role of folklore among the aging. Having emphasized the importance of elders in traditional societies as teachers of folk wisdom through oral tradition, the most pressing issue has been that of the changing status not only of the elderly in contemporary society, but of one of the vital social roles outlined above, that of providing cultural continuity through leadership, teaching, and healing.

Folklorists conducting field research among the aging have found their relationship to the people they have chosen to study is conditioned by the relationship of these individuals to their respective communities, which has changed, often drastically, over their lifetimes, through attrition, assimilation, migration, dislocation, or a combination of these and other factors. The fieldworker may be assigned the role of student, or "adopted" son or daughter, a willing party to the partial re-creation of the social relations within which folk wisdom has traditionally been imparted. In the absence of an historical community setting, the folklorists are no longer simply researchers, but also surrogate community members. As such, they have, in effect, also become care providers, offering older subjects opportunities for generativity no longer easily available from distant or dissolute communal contexts.

In this respect, those trained in and sensitive to the

social importance—and therapeutic value—of folklore can make an invaluable contribution to gerontological practice. By examining research data, contexts, and methods in terms of their application to the reinforcement of self-worth and cultural identity among elders, they may help to restore the personal and social integrity of an often socially isolated and psychologically alienated population.

A number of care and service providers for the aging have, in fact, developed community-based educational programs on folklore models, such as discussion groups with a content that reflects participants' sense of cultural, geographical, and historical place and their eagerness to share knowledge of local history, lore, and customs. As an example, one volume in a series of popular reading anthologies produced for discussion groups by the National Council on the Aging, based in Washington, D.C., *In the Old Ways*, is devoted to the subject of family and community traditions.

The therapeutic value of folklore among the aging has long been embraced by such service and care professionals as activities coordinators at senior centers and therapeutic recreation directors in nursing homes, who daily take advantage of the creative, as well as healing, properties of the traditional arts, including storytelling, folk art, and music. In recent years, folklorists have played a role in actually documenting the therapeutic effects of folklore. An arthritic folk musician, interviewed about his fiddling skills, is barely able to lift his bow, but once in place, it glides across the strings as the fiddler demonstrates his continued ability to play the tunes he mastered over the years. An Alzheimer's patient, no longer able to construct a complete sentence, recites the entire lyrics to a cherished folk song while singing with his family at the dinner table; a folklorist recording stories of "night doctors" (legends of child abductions for hideous experiments, current among African-Americans in the post-Reconstruction South) in a nursing home meets a resident, diagnosed as senile, who had been unintelligible to staff for years. At the fieldworker's prompting, she proceeds to relate—with halting, but coherent, delivery—several narratives about these night riders.

These and many other instances not only document the restorative and sustaining qualities of creative ("right brain") mental activity, but also they specifically point to the contributions that folklore and folklorists can make to any comprehensive program of wellness directed at older adults.

A growing number of folklorists work as consultants for public health institutions with multicultural client populations, researching and sensitizing staff to indigenous health beliefs and practices, many of these disproportionately maintained by elders. Health-care providers have been encouraged to acknowledge the role of folk medicine by cooperating with elder healers to bridge the gap between ethnic communities and the medical establishment. As examples, physicians in some Indian Health Service hospitals and clinics have found ways in which their practice might complement, rather than compete with, that of traditional medicine men, and mental health workers in Hispanic communities have enlisted *curanderos* to treat psychological maladies rooted in cultural beliefs.

Folklorists may similarly act as catalysts in the empowerment of community elders through projects that highlight the accomplishments of traditional elders. One notable example is "The Grand Generation," sponsored by the Smithsonian Institution in the 1980s, which featured a cross-section of older Americans who were masters of the folk wisdom and material culture of their communities. The Smithsonian, as well as several state arts councils, have folk arts fellowship programs, where older artists are given stipends to teach their craft to younger community members. Initiatives such as these have often revitalized communities by instilling renewed interest in the "old ways" preserved by often isolated older community members.

Another fruitful area for applied folklore is that of intergenerational programs involving the transmission of folk culture, compensating for lost or weak generational ties by restoring the role of elders as teachers of traditional knowledge. In hundreds of schools students have been sent out into local communities to record the life stores and folk wisdom of older adults. Among the most famous of these programs is the Foxfire project, initiated by English teacher Eliot Wigginton in Rabun Gap, Georgia. Since the late 1960s, a school-produced magazine and several books have publicized the folklore, particularly the material culture, of an Appalachian hill community, largely preserved by its older inhabitants.

In Ghana in the early 1980s, the Adult Education Section of UNESCO sponsored a project in which

young people collected folklore of the elders of the Awudome of the Volta region, to be used in developing curriculum materials for a literacy drive.

In the mid-1980s, the U.S. Administration on Aging funded the Laguna Demonstration Project, in which a child-care center was established on the grounds of a nursing home on the Laguna reservation in New Mexico. Residents as well as elders from the local community spent time each day teaching the children the Laguna language, songs, dances, and drumming, and telling them traditional stories.

All of these undertakings illustrate the ways in which the application of concepts, methodology, and content of folklore studies may facilitate communication across boundaries of ethnicity, age, gender, and others, and serve as a vehicle for the enhancement of self-worth and social integration. Moreover, understanding and appreciating the value of traditional expressive behavior among the aging may contribute to positive interventions in care and service providing.

BIBLIOGRAPHY

Bronner, S. J. (1985). *Chain carvers: Old men crafting meaning.* Lexington: University Press of Kentucky.

Chinen, A. B. (1989). *In the ever after: Fairy tales and the second half of life.* Wilmette, IL: Chiron Publications.

Hawes, B. L. (1984). Folk arts and the elderly. In Thomas Vennum (Ed.), *Festival of American folklife program book.* Washington, DC: Smithsonian Institution.

Hufford, M., Hunt, M., & Zeitlin, S. (1987). *The grand generation: Memory, mastery, legacy.* Seattle: University of Washington Press.

Jabbour, A. (1981). Some thoughts from a folk cultural perspective. In P. W. Johnson (Ed.), *Perspectives on aging* (pp. 139–149). Cambridge, MA: Ballinger Publishing.

Kirshenblatt-Gimblett, B. (1989). Objects of memory: Material culture as life review. In E. Oring (Ed.), *Folk groups and folklore genres: A reader* (pp. 329–338). Logan: Utah State University Press.

Mullen, P. (1992). *Listening to old voices: Folklore, life-stories and the elderly.* Urbana: University of Illinois Press.

Myerhoff, B. (1992). *Remembered lives: The work of ritual, storytelling, and growing older.* Ann Arbor: University of Michigan Press.

Shuldiner, D. (1994). Promoting self-worth among the aging. In M. O. Jones (Ed.), *Putting folklore to use* (pp. 214–225). Lexington: University Press of Kentucky.

Wigginton, E. (Ed.). (1971–1990) *Foxfire.* 10 vols. New York: Doubleday.

G

Gastrointestinal System: Function and Dysfunction

David A. Greenwald and Lawrence J. Brandt

Montefiore Medical Center and Albert Einstein College of Medicine

Brush Border The epithelial surface of absorption atop the villi. It bears closely packed hairlike microvilli, each about 2 μm long, and a number of digestive enzymes.

Chylomicron A tiny (billionth of a meter) fat droplet synthesized in the epithelial cells of the small intestine. It contains triglyceride and cholesterol and is covered by a coat of fat and protein.

Cirrhosis A progressive liver disease characterized by diffuse damage to liver cells, with formation of nodules, fibrosis, and permanent disturbance of the normal liver architecture.

Fistula An abnormal connection between an organ and another organ or the skin.

Jaundice An increase in bile pigments, usually because of disease of the liver or biliary system, with resultant yellowish staining of the skin, eyes, deeper tissues, urine, and plasma.

Micelle A submicroscopic aggregation of molecules, such as a droplet, in a gel. Such an aggregation of fat molecules and bile salts are important in the absorption of dietary fats.

Peristalsis A series of muscular contraction waves that propel gastrointestinal contents over short distances.

Stricture A fixed narrowing of the intestine.

Villi Finger-like projections from the inner surface of the intestine that function to increase surface area and thereby absorption capability.

The gastrointestinal (GI) system consists of many interrelated organs. It serves a variety of functions, all of which are crucial to the proper working of the body. The primary function of the GI system is to achieve proper nutrition by the digestion and absorption of ingested nutrients; normal function includes the production of enzymes and hormones as well as the maintenance of proper motility, including excretion of wastes. Dysfunction of the system is common and may be the result of an abnormality of one of the component organs or of a process that is disordered more generally and affects several organs simultaneously. Dysfunction of the GI system is a frequent problem in the elderly, and a major reason for visits to the health-care worker.

I. FUNCTION

A. Anatomy

The GI tract is composed of both hollow and solid organs. The hollow organs are arranged as a continuous tube beginning with the mouth and extending to the anus. The solid organs are connected to the hollow organs by way of ducts. A schematic representation of GI anatomy is depicted in Figure 1.

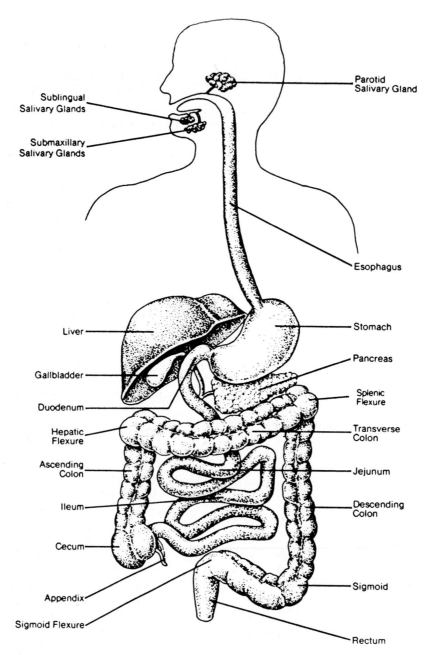

Figure I. A schematic representation of gastrointestinal anatomy. (Figure printed with permission from Solvay Pharmaceuticals, Inc.)

The proximal extent of the GI system is the oral cavity. As a bolus of food is taken into the mouth, the digestive process begins with chewing (or mechanical disruption of the food) and is closely followed by secretion of saliva. Saliva contains enzymes such as amylase that help break down starches into sugars. Openings into the oral cavity exist for secretions from the major salivary glands, including the parotid, sublingual, and submaxillary glands, as well as the minor salivary glands inside the lips. The food bolus is then swallowed as it is propelled backwards by the tongue into the oropharynx, and then into the esophagus.

The esophagus is a tubular structure that measures approximately 10 inches in length and serves as an anatomic conduit between the mouth and the stomach. The point at which the esophagus joins the stomach is termed the gastroesophageal junction. This is an area characterized by a sphincter muscle that functions as a one-way valve, allowing food into the stomach but not allowing gastric contents to "reflux" back up again. The esophagus is lined by layers of flat cells heaped upon one another, collectively known as a stratified squamous epithelium. Mucus-producing glands exist to help the saliva lubricate the passage of food. Food is propelled through the esophagus and past the gastroesophageal junction by peristalsis to enter the stomach.

The stomach is located in the upper and midabdomen and is divided into four distinct regions: fundus, body, antrum, and pylorus. Although the lining of the stomach is composed of a single layer of tall (columnar) cells, each region of the stomach has a distinct microscopic architecture with specialized cells. For example, the fundus and body contain parietal cells, which make acid, and chief cells, which make pepsin, a digestive enzyme that breaks down proteins. G-cells, which produce gastrin, a hormone that stimulates the stomach to produce acid, are located exclusively in the antrum. The pyloric sphincter is the anatomic as well as the functional landmark that separates the stomach from the small intestine.

The small intestine is the longest organ in the body. It measures approximately 22 feet and is divided into the duodenum, the jejunum, and the ileum. The longest segment is the jejunum. Like the stomach, the lining of the small intestine is a single layer of epithelial cells of the columnar type; however, three specialized anatomic modifications exist here to increase the surface area for absorption: the valvulae conniventes, which are bucklings of the lining of the small intestine; the villi, which are fingerlike projections of the mucosa; and the microvilli, which are hairlike modifications of the superficial cell membrane at the brush border, or the barrier between the lumen and the cell. The ileocecal valve separates the small and large intestines and thereby slows the transit of nutrients through the small intestine, thus facilitating digestion. It also protects the small intestine from the bacteria of the large intestine.

The large intestine, or colon, is 4–5 feet long and extends from the ileocecal valve, usually located in the right lower quadrant of the abdomen, to the anus. The appendix is attached to the cecum. Although not important in the digestive process, the appendix may play an important role in the immune system early in life; it atrophies with advancing age. The large intestine is divided anatomically into several regions, including the ascending colon, transverse colon, descending colon, sigmoid colon, and rectum. The colon, like the small intestine, is lined with a columnar epithelium, but the microvilli on the colonic cells are much less prominent than those on the small intestinal cells. The most distal part of the GI tract is the anus, and stool leaves the body after passing the anal sphincter. The lining of the anus consists of a stratified squamous epithelium, similar to that found in the esophagus and the skin, and so all these organs share some diseases because of their common cell type.

The other important structures that are part of the GI system are the liver, pancreas, and gallbladder. The liver is located in the upper abdomen on the right and weighs approximately 4 pounds in men and 3 pounds in women. The liver produces bile, which helps digest fats, and the bile drains into the small intestine by way of the bile ducts. Besides aiding in the digestion of foods, and especially fats, the liver is the most important organ in the detoxification of drugs and medications. The gallbladder is located near the liver, and is connected to the bile ducts via the cystic duct. It stores bile until it is needed for digestion. Finally, the pancreas is found in the midabdomen. It weighs about one-quarter pound, and its secretions drain into the small intestine by way of the pancreatic duct. It functions to help digest all major food classes by secreting a variety of enzymes: amylase to digest starch, lipase for fats, and trypsin and chymotrypsin for proteins. Of course, the pancreas also makes insulin that prevents diabetes.

B. Secretion and Digestion

The regulation of fluid balance is crucial to survival. Approximately 9 L of fluid enter the GI tract per day. Of that amount, about 2 L is ingested by mouth. The remaining 7 L consists of fluids secreted by the various GI organs. Ninety-eight percent of the total amount of fluid that enters the GI tract is reabsorbed in the small intestine and the colon.

Of the secreted fluids, 1 L a day is generated in the mouth as saliva. Saliva contains salivary amylase, an enzyme that is useful in the preliminary breakdown of carbohydrates. Gastric secretion produces about 2 L of fluid per day, consisting primarily of acid and mucus. It has been the classic teaching that as one ages, the capacity to secrete gastric acid also diminishes. Recently this adage has been questioned, and it is now believed that, if a person enjoys good health, the stomach will make a "normal" amount of acid. Sometimes it is difficult to know what "normal" is in an elderly person because the range of normal values that have been established is based on young and not old adults. An additional liter of fluid, bile, is produced by the liver. Bile is a complex fluid made up of electrolytes, bile acids, bilirubin, cholesterol, and lecithin, and functions to help digest fats. Output from the pancreas as "pancreatic juice" accounts for an additional 2 L of fluid per day, and is central to the digestion of already partially degraded nutrients. Finally, an additional 1 L per day is derived from *succus entericus* or the fluids secreted by the gut itself. Only about 1–2 L of the original 9 L of fluid that enters the jejunum is left to pass into the colon, and of that amount, only 200 mL is excreted into the feces. Wet feces are passed as diarrhea, whereas overly dry feces result in constipation.

Many hormones play important roles in normal GI function. These molecules serve to regulate various events in GI physiology. Some hormones oppose the actions of other hormones, thereby leading to exquisite control via a continuous balance of regulatory and counterregulatory forces. Thus, for example, gastrin is a peptide secreted by the stomach and is the major hormonal stimulant to the production of acid by the gastric parietal cells. Gastrin also helps regulate the various muscle sphincters throughout the GI tract and the motility of the digestive organs, their blood flow and fluid balance. Somatostatin is an antagonist to gastrin release, and, therefore, inhibits the production of acid by the stomach as well as some of the other functions of gastrin. Another hormone, cholecystokinin (CCK), is produced by cells in the duodenum and jejunum and regulates the release of bile from the gallbladder. Secretin is produced in the duodenum and stimulates the flow of pancreatic juice. In general, hormones have multiple functions and complex interactions. [*See* ENDOCRINE FUNCTION AND DYSFUNCTION.]

Digestion may be defined as the intraluminal breakdown of food. It proceeds in an orderly way from the mouth through the digestive tract. The purpose of digestion is to reduce complex nutrients into their simplest forms so as to allow for absorption by the small intestine. For example, starches and sugars are sequentially broken down from polysaccharides (many sugars) to oligosaccharides (few sugars), and then ultimately to monosaccharides (one sugar) before they are absorbed and then utilized.

Mastication (chewing) serves to break up large food particles, thereby increasing the total surface area of the food that will be exposed to digestive enzymes. In the mouth, salivary amylase initiates the preliminary digestion of carbohydrates. Once food passes into the stomach, further mechanical and chemical digestion occurs. Churning and grinding of particles in the gastric lumen mechanically reduces their size and is accompanied by chemical digestion in an acid environment.

The most important site of digestion of all dietary intake is the small intestine. The thick, semifluid mass of partly digested food (chyme) is delivered from the stomach to the duodenum at a controlled rate to allow for proper mixing with digestive enzymes. The hormones secretin and CCK stimulate the secretion of pancreatic enzymes and bile. These, in turn, facilitate further breakdown of food particles. In the small intestine, pancreatic enzymes such as amylase, lipase, and proteases, all acting under proper luminal pH, help to digest carbohydrates, fats, and proteins, respectively. [*See* METABOLISM: CARBOHYDRATE, LIPID, AND PROTEIN.] Pancreatic amylase is the primary enzyme involved in carbohydrate digestion. It digests polysaccharides into short oligosaccharides. Protein digestion, which begins with acid and pepsin in the stomach, continues with the pancreatic proteases trypsin and chymotrypsin. Lipase acts within the pH ranges of the intestine to break down fats from triglycerides to glycerol and free fatty acids. In the liver, bile salts are excreted in bile, which then passes into the small intestine. Bile salts help to solubilize fat and fat-soluble vitamins by forming compounds known as micelles. Micelles are critical to the efficient transport of fats across the small intestinal absorptive surface. Finally, brush border enzymes, including disaccharidases (such as lactase, sucrase, and maltase), peptidases, and lipases help to complete the digestion of nutrients into their simplest forms to permit their passage across the small intestinal wall.

Lastly, the process of digestion is enhanced by reabsorption of certain materials central to digestion which, thereby, allows for their reuse. For example, the total amount of bile acids in the body is kept at a steady level, because more than 98% of bile salts produced by the liver are reabsorbed in the terminal ileum and recirculate to the liver by a pathway known as the enterohepatic circulation. The small amount of bile salts lost into the colon each day is replaced by an equal amount synthesized by the liver, thus keeping the total body pool of bile salts constant.

C. Nutrition and Absorption

After appropriate digestion of nutrients, the function of the GI tract is to absorb these nutrients so they may be used for a variety of cellular processes.

Absorption occurs across the cells lining the small intestine, and proceeds via one of several mechanisms. The first is passive absorption, in which material moves along an electrochemical gradient. The second is facilitated transport, in which absorption of one substance is coupled to the transfer of another substance. Finally, there is active transport, in which transport occurs against an electrochemical gradient and requires an expenditure of metabolic energy.

The primary nutrients are fats, carbohydrates, and proteins. All are absorbed in the small intestine. Complex fats are degraded to free fatty acids. Free fatty acids are relatively insoluble in water and require the help of bile salts to solubilize them, a process resulting in the formation of micelles. Micelles can transport fat through the relatively hydrophilic (water-permeable) small intestine into the absorptive cell, where the micelle is disrupted and the now free fatty acid is able to diffuse passively across the cell surface. Once within the cell, the fatty acids are resynthesized into triglycerides by the process of esterification. Then they are packaged for export from the cell in the form of chylomicrons and very low-density lipoproteins, and ultimately are carried to the liver by the lymphatics.

Carbohydrate absorption occurs in the small intestine where monosaccharides are absorbed via facilitated and active transport. Proteins have specific carrier mechanisms allowing for their transport in the form of peptides and single amino acids.

Several other molecules absorbed in the small intes-

tine are critical to the maintenance of normal body function. Calcium is absorbed primarily in the duodenum. Its absorption is regulated by vitamin D through the synthesis of a calcium-binding protein. Iron is absorbed in the duodenum by a carrier-mediated mechanism. Vitamin B_{12}, or cyanocobalamin, is absorbed after being bound to intrinsic factor, another substance that is produced in the stomach. The vitamin B_{12}-intrinsic factor complex actually forms in the upper small intestine with the help of pancreatic juice and protects the vitamin B_{12} until it reaches the ileum, where it is absorbed. Folate is ingested in the form of polyglutamates in many foods. Brush border enzymes hydrolyze polyglutamates to monoglutamates that are transported by passive diffusion and a carrier-mediated process in the duodenum and upper jejunum respectively. Lastly, fat-soluble vitamins such as vitamins A, D, E, and K are transported in micelles in a fashion similar to that of fat molecules.

D. Motility

The motility of the GI tract is complex, and normal motility is critical to proper digestion. In order for GI motility to be effective, it must be coordinated with other intestinal functions such as secretion and absorption, and it must be regulated and integrated in a precise fashion.

Swallowing is an exceedingly complicated process that involves coordinated movements of the tongue, the muscles of the mouth, and the posterior oropharynx, all modulated by multiple cranial nerves. A bolus of food moves down the esophagus in an orderly fashion in a motor pattern known as peristalsis. When a swallow is initiated, a peristaltic wave of contraction proceeds from the proximal esophagus to the distal esophagus, helping to propel the bolus of food downward. In a coordinated fashion, the lower esophageal sphincter relaxes when the peristaltic wave reaches it, thus allowing food to pass into the stomach.

Beyond the gastroesophageal junction, normal GI motility occurs in two patterns: fasting and fed. In the fasting pattern, there are periods of relative rest that alternate with periods of contractile activity. The time of relative rest is known as phase I, and the active period is termed the migrating motor complex (MMC). The MMC consists of phase II, characterized by irregular contractions, and phase III, characterized by a short period of intense contractions. The MMC proceeds in an orderly fashion from the stomach to the distal small intestine. It is often called the "intestinal housekeeper" because of its action to sweep intestinal food contents onward.

The fed pattern is typified by frequent contractions that are somewhat irregular. This pattern starts immediately after a meal is ingested, and replaces the fasting pattern at that point. The fed pattern is dependent on the type of meal ingested. For example, liquid meals produce considerably less prominent contractile activity than do solid meals. The duration of this motility pattern depends on both the quantity and the type of food ingested. Once the stomach has emptied and the intestinal contents have been absorbed, the fasting motility pattern returns. The time it takes for half of a liquid meal to exit the stomach is about 20 minutes, whereas the comparable time for a solid meal is about 90 minutes.

The purposes of GI motility following a meal are to allow for storage, to mix the food, to expose digested nutrients to the absorptive surface, and finally to evacuate the wastes. Toward these ends, different regions of the stomach and upper intestine act differently. The proximal stomach (the fundus) functions primarily as a reservoir for liquids and contracts in a predictable and orderly way to squirt liquids into the distal stomach, through the pylorus, and into the duodenum. A major function of the antrum is to grind and mix solid food. This task is achieved by coordinated contractions and relaxations of the antrum and the pylorus; liquids and very small (<1 mm) solid particles pass the pylorus, while larger particles are "rejected" and subjected to repetitive churning. Once in the small intestine, the partly digested material, or chyme, progresses slowly but steadily as a result of intermittent contractions typical of the "fed" pattern.

The integration of the motor function of the gut is complicated. It is determined by controls at the level of the enteric, autonomic, and central nervous systems. The enteric nervous system is found within the wall of the gut in two plexuses, the myenteric and submucosal. The enteric system is coordinated by a means of cell-to-cell communication known as the paracrine system, as well as by the hormonal system, which has its stimulatory and inhibitory messages carried to its target cells via the bloodstream. The autonomic nervous system includes the sympathetic and parasympathetic nervous systems and mediates responses along reflex pathways. [*See* AUTONOMIC NER-

VOUS SYSTEM.] These systems are connected to the central nervous system. [*See* BRAIN AND CENTRAL NERVOUS SYSTEM.] The brain, then, plays an important part in the coordination of integrated functions of the GI tract. The precise roles of hormones and neuropeptides on the gut-related nervous system, although clearly important, are not yet well defined for many of the substances. GI motility is a complex and well-integrated activity that requires multiple layers of appropriate regulation for the entire system to function properly.

II. DYSFUNCTION

Dysfunction of the GI tract is a broad topic, encompassing a wide range of anatomic and physiologic abnormalities. Dysfunction may be seen at any age, but there are important special considerations that must be made when evaluating an elderly patient. Indeed, the same disease seen at different "phases" of life may appear to be quite dissimilar, and the possibilities for GI dysfunction are significantly more extensive in the elderly as compared with the situation of a younger person (see Table I).

A. The Oral Cavity

The mouth is an often forgotten portion of the GI tract in medical texts, but knowledge of oral cavity dysfunction is important not only for the dentist but also for the gastroenterologist, and may be a clue to the cause of disease elsewhere in the body. Nutritional deficiencies, particularly with respect to the B vitamins (e.g., niacin, riboflavin), may present as glossitis (inflammation of the tongue) or angular stomatitis (inflammation at the corners of the mouth), respectively. Certain skin disorders such as pemphigus and pemphigoid often have coincident oral manifestations. Fungal infection of the mouth (thrush) is not uncommon, especially in elderly patients treated with oral antibiotics; viral diseases such as Herpes simplex infections often are seen in patients who have an underlying malignancy. Finally, epidermal or squamous cell carcinoma of the lip and tongue are seen, especially in elderly men who have a history of heavy tobacco or pipe smoking.

Table I Common Gastrointestinal Complaints in the Elderly and Their Usual Causes

Complaint	Cause
Chest pain[a]	Pill-associated esophagitis
	Tetracycline, quinidine, potassium
	Infections
	Fungus (*Candida*)
	Esophageal dysmotility
	Esophagitis, esophageal ulcers
	Gastroesophageal reflux disease
Constipation	Immobilization, prolonged bed rest
	Low-fiber diet
	Insufficient water intake
	Medications
	Pain medications, laxatives, antidepressants
	Hypothyroidism
	Colorectal malignancy
Diarrhea	Ingestion of poorly absorbed substances
	Magnesium-containing antacids
	Laxatives
	Sugar-free candies
	Infections, food poisonings
	Antibiotic-associated colitis
	"Pseudodiarrhea"
	Watery stool around an obstruction
	Fecal incontinence
	Hyperthyroidism
	Diabetes

[a]Must exclude cardiac sources first.

B. The Esophagus

Gastroesophageal reflux disease (GERD) is the most common esophageal dysfunction. Its chief symptoms are heartburn, dysphagia (difficulty swallowing), and chest pain. Approximately 40% of the population of the United States reports an episode of heartburn at least monthly, and antacids are used frequently. GERD is usually well tolerated but may lead to serious complications including esophagitis, strictures, ulcers, and cancer. The etiology of GERD is thought to involve four components: lower esophageal sphincter incompetence, abnormal esophageal clearance of acid and refluxed material, delayed gastric emptying, and the irritant effect of refluxed gastric contents. Symptoms of GERD may be quite troubling and may be confused with angina (i.e., chest pain of a cardiac origin). A hiatal hernia, or a defect in the anatomic structures that normally confine the stomach within the abdominal cavity, is frequently present in patients with symptomatic GERD.

Motility disorders of the esophagus often are found in patients who complain about chest pain or dysphagia. Achalasia is one such motility disorder and is characterized by the absence of normal esophageal peristalsis, as well as by incomplete or absent relaxation of the sphincteric barrier between the esophagus and stomach. Patients have difficulty swallowing that is progressive over years. An important consideration in the elderly patient is "pseudoachalasia," which is an achalasia-like clinical picture that may be caused by a malignancy infiltrating the nerves at the level of the gastroesophageal junction. Other motility disorders also may produce significant symptoms: diffuse esophageal spasm, a condition in which muscular contractions are simultaneous (i.e., nonperistaltic), and the "nutcracker esophagus," in which high-amplitude simultaneous contractions cause chest pain. Systemic diseases such as thyroid disease, diabetes, and scleroderma also may produce esophageal dysmotility. Some medications, usually when taken without sufficient liquid to wash them out of the esophagus, can stick in and injure the esophagus thereby producing an ulcer or stricture. Most commonly this list includes certain potassium supplements, quinidine, and tetracycline.

Swallowing difficulties may be caused by dysfunction at the level of the oropharynx, as well as by disorders of the esophagus or the gastroesophageal junction discussed above. Oropharyngeal dysphagia is an important cause of such difficulties in the elderly, and may be caused by nervous system diseases (e.g., cerebrovascular accidents, Parkinson's disease, multiple sclerosis, and brain stem tumors), skeletal muscle diseases (e.g., polymyositis—inflammation of the muscles), local anatomic factors (such as bone spurs and arthritis of the cervical vertebrae), and external pressure on the esophagus from the aorta either by an aneurysm or the enlargement and uncoiling of the aorta that occurs with advancing age.

Esophageal tumors are among the most common malignancies in the world, yet they are relatively infrequent in the United States. They are often related to significant alcohol use and cigarette smoking and are more common in males than in females. One type of esophageal cancer, called adenocarcinoma, usually arises from abnormal tissue termed *Barrett's epithelium* near the gastroesophageal junction. Barrett's epithelium is a consequence of GERD, and this condition occurs when the esophagus heals eroded, ulcerated areas with a tissue resembling the normal lining tissue of the stomach. In the esophagus, such gastric tissue has the potential to become malignant over many years. Periodic surveillance with an endoscope detects this premalignant tissue early and therefore permits therapy of such cancers earlier than otherwise would be possible. Unfortunately, however, most esophageal cancers are incurable at the time of diagnosis.

C. Stomach

Peptic ulcer diseases (i.e., gastric and duodenal ulcers) are frequent medical problems. There are approximately 500,000 new cases and 4,000,000 recurrences in the United States each year. Two billion dollars a year is spent on antiulcer medications, and it has been estimated that care for peptic ulcer disease represents about 10% of the total medical costs for all digestive diseases. About one-third of patients with peptic ulcer disease are older than 60 years at the time of diagnosis; its mortality in patients over age 75 is twice that of patients age 65–74, and more than 10 times that of patients age 45–54, although this must be viewed in light of the frequent coexistence of multiple diseases in the elderly individual.

A peptic ulcer may be defined as a defect in the lining of the stomach or duodenum, or less commonly the esophagus (as a result of acid reflux). It is due to a combination of either an excess of aggressive factors that tend to cause ulcers or a decrease of resistance factors that tend to protect against them. Duodenal ulcers are more common than gastric ulcers. Peptic ulcer disease is a significant problem in the elderly, in whom presentations may be atypical, the onset of disease may be severe with hemorrhage or perforation, and the prognosis is not necessarily as favorable as in the young because of misdiagnosis and a hesitation to be aggressive in therapy.

The aggressive factors in excess are acid and pepsin, but it is now felt that most gastric and duodenal ulcers in the elderly (as well as the young) result from infection with a bacterium known as *Helicobacter pylori* or from nonsteroidal anti-inflammatory drugs (NSAIDs); therefore, most ulcers are curable with antibiotics or by stopping the NSAIDs. Decreased resistance of the stomach epithelium is commonly induced by NSAIDs and cigarette smoking.

Disorders associated with reduced gastric secretion also exist. It generally has been believed that gastric secretion diminishes with advancing age, but recently this has been questioned, and it is now believed that the healthy elderly person has a healthy stomach that makes a normal amount of acid. In atrophic gastritis, inflammation of the lining of the stomach is present, probably caused by an autoimmune (self-destructive) mechanism. This leads to destruction of the acid-producing cells of the stomach. When these cells undergo atrophy, besides decreasing their acid production, they become incapable of producing intrinsic factor. The presence of intrinsic factor is crucial to normal vitamin B_{12} absorption, and without it, vitamin B_{12} absorption is disrupted and pernicious anemia develops. Both atrophic gastritis and pernicious anemia are particularly common in the elderly. Moreover, the presence of atrophic gastritis has been linked to the development of gastric malignancies.

Gastric motility may be disordered in the elderly, resulting in a variety of symptoms. When gastric emptying is delayed, bloating, belching, and vomiting can develop as the stomach distends with retained food matter. If the partially digested material remains for a long enough period of time, a concretion known as a bezoar may form; bezoar formation is especially common in edentulous subjects who have had some gastric surgery and who eat foods difficult to digest, such as celery, oranges, and so on. Gastric motility is known to be delayed as a result of certain systemic diseases, most notably diabetes, and as a consequence of some gastric surgery. Medications often affect the movements of the stomach and in the elderly, who frequently are taking multiple medications, motility disturbances are potentially important side effects.

Rates of gastric cancer, particularly involving the distal stomach, have been decreasing over the past several decades but gastric cancer still remains an important cause of cancer death in the world. Success in curing gastric cancer is highly dependent upon the stage at which the cancer is detected. An important association is known between having had prior gastric surgery and the subsequent development, often 20 or more years later, of gastric cancer. This is a significant risk for the elderly patient who may have had surgery in the past for control of peptic ulcer disease. Recently, a sequential connection between chronic *Helicobacter pylori* infection, gastritis, gastric atrophy, and gastric cancer has been theorized, and it is hoped that cure of *Helicobacter pylori* will be followed by a decrease in gastric cancer.

D. The Small Intestine

Small intestinal dysfunction is characterized by maldigestion and malabsorption. Maldigestion may be caused by alterations in the production or function of the usual digestive enzymes, whereas malabsorption generally results from the loss of the normal absorptive surface of the intestine or disruption in the normal absorptive process. Intestinal function is well preserved with aging, and only the ability to absorb calcium and vitamin D may decrease to a clinically significant level. The ability of the small intestine to absorb monosaccharides has been shown to decrease with aging, and the pattern of fat absorption also appears to be different in the elderly, although such relative deficiencies do not lead to significant abnormalities; rather, they are merely curiosities of the aging process.

A variety of conditions lead to maldigestion, including pancreatic insufficiency, in which there is a lack of adequate pancreatic enzyme secretion needed for the normal digestion of fats, starches, and protein. Inadequate amounts of bile salts in the small intestine, as may occur in certain liver or bowel conditions, can lead to problems with fat digestion. Specific carbohydrate enzyme deficiencies may lead to carbohydrate maldigestion. Patients who have had prior gastric surgery may, as a result, have a gastric remnant that produces relatively little acid or that is ineffective in mixing digestive juices and food. Both of these situations may lead to decreased digestion.

Certain conditions lead to a loss of the normal absorptive surface of the small intestine. When the normal villous architecture of the jejunum is disrupted, the surface area becomes inadequate for proper nutrient absorption, and "malabsorption" occurs. This is clinically apparent when it causes chronic diarrhea, often accompanied by evidence of a deficiency state of certain vitamins and minerals usually absorbed in the small intestine. Diseases that affect the small intestine and cause malabsorption include celiac sprue and lymphoma. An important concern in a patient with long-standing celiac sprue is an increased risk of malignancy. Both lymphoma and carcinoma can develop as a complication of sprue and

affect the esophagus, stomach (carcinoma), or the bowel (lymphoma).

Diseases of the intestinal circulation are rare, but nonetheless represent an important cause of GI tract dysfunction, especially in an elderly population. Ischemia occurs when blood flow is insufficient to nourish the tissues, and their dysfunction or death results. Although colonic ischemia is the most common form of intestinal ischemia, ischemia of the small intestine (i.e., acute mesenteric ischemia), is responsible for most of the ischemia-related mortality. In acute mesenteric ischemia, the amount of intestine deprived of blood supply is usually large, the diagnosis is usually made late, and the prognosis is poor, with a mortality rate of approximately 60–80%. This condition has been diagnosed increasingly as the overall population in the country has become "older" and as clinicians have become more familiar with the spectrum of ischemic diseases of the intestine. When a short length of the small intestine is deprived of blood, because of such varied conditions as a strangulated hernia, vasculitis, or trauma, it is termed *focal segmental ischemia* of the small bowel. This condition usually requires surgical intervention but has a good prognosis. Lastly, chronic mesenteric ischemia, or intestinal angina, is a condition caused by atherosclerosis (or narrowing) of the mesenteric vessels. Patients with this problem develop abdominal pain or discomfort after eating, and the pain then slowly abates over several hours. They may develop malabsorption if the ischemic disease is long-standing and damages the absorptive lining of the intestine. This condition can be treated surgically, after which prognosis is good.

E. The Large Intestine

Despite anecdotes to the contrary, most healthy elderly persons move their bowels with normal frequency (i.e., five to seven times weekly). Nonetheless, diarrhea and constipation are common complaints with aging just as they are in the younger years.

Diarrhea may be defined either as an increase in the volume or in the frequency or a decrease in the consistency of stools. Of the 9 L of fluid that passes through the small intestine each day, approximately 1–2 L enter the colon, and only 200 mL passes out of the body in the stool. In the elderly, complaints about increased frequency of bowel movements are actually often related to fecal incontinence due to constipation with run off of liquid stool around a rectal stool mass rather than to diarrhea.

Diarrhea usually is due to changes in the normal fluid regulation by the small and large intestines. Sometimes, diarrhea occurs when there is an accumulation of poorly absorbable substances in the colon. Examples of this in the elderly include intolerance to milk and dairy products caused by various enzyme deficiencies (such as lactase deficiency leading to lactose intolerance) and intake of poorly absorbable substances, such as sorbitol in diet candies or magnesium in antacids or laxatives (e.g., milk of magnesia). Diarrhea may also occur due to the active secretion of fluid, which overwhelms the ability of the colon to reabsorb it. A hormone known as vasoactive intestinal peptide, and certain bacterial toxins, such as cholera toxin, may cause this. Inflammation of the lining of the intestine may lead to increased frequency of loose stools as can occur in inflammatory bowel disease (ulcerative colitis or Crohn's disease) or in severe constipation, where hard masses of dehydrated feces may irritate the intestinal lining and lead to an outpouring of mucus. Laxative use promotes loose stools, and studies have shown that surreptitious laxative abuse increases with aging. Antibiotics often cause GI upset and diarrhea as side effects, and are an important cause of colitis in the elderly. Alterations in intestinal motility may lead to diarrhea and, in the elderly, can occur in the setting of long-standing diabetes as well as in hypo- or hyperthyroidism (an underactive or overactive thyroid gland, respectively).

It generally has been held that people become more constipated as they get older, but there is no scientific evidence to support this. In otherwise healthy old people, no abnormalities have been shown of the motor function of the large intestine. There are, however, alterations in the sensitivity and capacity of the rectum. Constipation is a term used to describe a relative lack or difficulty of bowel movements as compared to an individual's prior bowel pattern, and GI tract "dysfunction" must be considered only when a change has occurred. In the elderly, constipation often is the result of decreased sensation to distension in the rectum, where stool is stored, so that large volumes of stool accumulate before the patient has the urge to defecate; this may even lead to fecal impaction. Immobilization, prolonged bed rest, long-standing laxative use leading to damage to the nerves of the colon, hypothyroidism, and depression all have been associated with constipation in older people, as have disorders of defecation due to abnormalities of the muscles of the pelvic floor. The latter is most common in elderly women whose pelvic muscles have been damaged by multiple childbirths. Complaints of constipation, however, may also be indicative of a structural problem such as cancer, and because the incidence of cancer of the colon increases with age, a change in bowel habits is a key symptom that may help in the early detection of a colon tumor. [See CANCER AND THE ELDERLY.]

Diverticula are outpouchings of the wall of the intestine, usually found in the descending and sigmoid colon, just above the rectum. They are believed to arise in areas of weakness of the intestinal wall where high intraluminal pressures occur because of vigorous muscle contractions. The incidence of diverticular disease increases with advancing age to approximately 50% in the ninth decade of life. Population studies show that diverticula formation can be diminished by eating a high-fiber diet; there is no scientific proof that patients with diverticulosis should avoid fruits, nuts, seeds, and skins. Diverticulosis is progressive and the number of diverticula increase over time. Diverticulosis may be complicated by bleeding and by inflammation called diverticulitis.

Inflammatory bowel disease (i.e., ulcerative colitis and Crohn's disease) afflicts nearly two million people in the United States. Historically, inflammatory bowel disease has been said to have a bimodal age distribution, with a peak incidence in the third and fourth decades and then another smaller peak in the sixth and seventh decades. It is now felt that much of the colitis that appears as a new entity in the population older than 50 is probably infectious or ischemic colitis and not true inflammatory bowel disease.

Ulcerative colitis is a chronic inflammatory disease of the colon that almost always begins in the mucosa of the anorectal junction and extends proximally for a varying length. The disease is limited to the mucosa, or innermost layer, of the colon. Patients usually have bloody diarrhea as their chief complaint. There is an increased risk of cancer in patients with long-standing (i.e., more than 10 years) ulcerative colitis, and that risk is progressive with increasing duration of disease. By contrast, Crohn's disease, the other chronic inflammatory bowel disease, is a chronic transmural disease that can affect any portion of the GI tract from the mouth to the anus. The hallmarks of the disease are strictures and fistulae. Patients frequently present with abdominal pain, diarrhea, fever, or symptoms of bowel obstruction; however, in the elderly, presentations are more subtle and atypical than when disease onset is at a younger age, leading to delays in diagnosis or incorrect diagnoses. Patients who have the onset of either ulcerative colitis or Crohn's disease after the age of 50 may have a worse short-term prognosis than when the disease presents in younger patients; the need for surgical intervention may be more common in older patients with late-onset inflammatory bowel disease.

Colon cancer affects more than 150,000 people in the United States yearly, and is a common malignancy in the elderly. It is usually slow growing and indolent, and may not cause any symptoms or may come to attention only when slow bleeding has resulted in anemia, with consequent weakness, pallor, shortness of breath, angina, or dizziness. Other patients may develop signs and symptoms of large intestinal obstruction. The prognosis for a patient with colon cancer depends largely on the size and extent of spread through the body of the tumor at the time it is detected. Thus, early diagnosis is important; hence the rationale for screening with flexible sigmoidoscopy and yearly tests for occult blood in the stool beginning at age 50.

F. The Liver

Structural and functional changes occur in the liver with aging, and these may affect the manifestations of liver disease in the elderly. There is a progressive decrease in liver weight with senescence; it becomes more fatty; its ability to fight infection and metabolize drugs often diminishes; and blood flow to the liver is decreased. The spectrum and outcome of infectious and inflammatory liver disorders in the elderly appears to be different from that of younger people. For example, acute viral hepatitis due to hepatitis A and chronic viral hepatitis are seen less often in older patients, but have a worse prognosis; disorders related to side effects of drugs are more common.

Liver dysfunction may be acute or chronic. The most common type of hepatitis in the elderly results from toxic agents such as medications, in contrast to hepatitis in the young which is usually viral. Considering the frequency with which medications are prescribed, associated liver dysfunction is surprisingly rare, but nonetheless represents an important problem; medications are estimated to cause up to 20% of cases of jaundice seen in elderly patients and are responsible for 25% of the cases of liver failure reported each year in the United States. Drugs frequently associated with liver inflammation include antibiotics, anesthetics, antihypertensives, and corticosteroids. Viral hepatitis is a more severe disease after the age of 60, with a higher incidence of progression to liver failure and coma, and an increased mortality rate. Alcohol-induced liver damage remains a major problem worldwide, and the elderly are not exempt from the effects of this social toxin. Alcohol causes increased fat in the liver, and may cause hepatitis and ultimately cirrhosis, but the course of alcoholic liver disease appears to be similar for both the young and the old. Liver dysfunction, with resultant jaundice, may occur in the setting of a severe systemic infection, in the postoperative patient, and with obstruction to the flow of bile from the liver to the intestine due to gallstones and tumors of the pancreas, bile ducts, and gallbladder. Finally, the liver may become "swollen," and blood tests of liver function may be abnormal with congestive heart failure: these changes in the liver, even when severe, may show nearly complete reversal if the heart failure is controlled and improved.

Chronic liver disease is characterized by ongoing liver cell degeneration leading to scarring (i.e., fibrosis and cirrhosis). The cirrhotic process appears much the same in the elderly as in the young; it is often clinically silent and progresses without producing symptoms for many years. Once hepatic scarring has occurred, alterations in liver architecture are irreversible, and other systemic changes such as portal hypertension (hypertension within the internal vascular system) may follow. Causes of chronic liver disease include repeated acute insults with toxins such as alcohol, chronic obstruction of the bile ducts as in strictures (narrowings), iron overload, persistence of viral infections such as hepatitis B, C, and D, and autoimmune hepatitis. Sometimes, the etiology of chronic liver disease and cirrhosis is unknown and is referred to as cryptogenic. Cirrhosis from any cause may lead to the development of primary liver cancer; the liver also is the most frequent site of spread of cancer from other parts of the body. Lastly, the liver may be involved in systemic illness, for example the fatty infiltration seen with diabetes mellitus. Such fatty change may result in slightly abnormal blood tests of liver function but rarely is clinically significant.

G. Gallbladder

Over 16 million Americans, or approximately 7% of the U.S. population, have gallstones. Three hundred fifty thousand cholecystectomies are performed annually, and hospital and related expenses total over $1 billion yearly.

The presence of gallstones (cholelithiasis) increases with advancing age such that about 30% of the population older than 65 years has gallstones. There is a female to male preponderance in a ratio of 3 : 1. In general, gallstones are formed primarily of cholesterol, which collects over a small focus of bilirubin, bile acids, or calcium. The stones form when bile, which is produced in the liver and stored in the gallbladder, becomes saturated with cholesterol. This is followed by the formation of a crystal, about which further precipitation of cholesterol occurs, and a gallstone "grows."

Gallstones may be asymptomatic or they may give rise to inflammation in the gallbladder. Such inflammation, termed cholecystitis, may be either acute or chronic. Gallstones also may block the common bile duct, the tube that delivers bile from the liver to the intestine. Such blockage results in jaundice and infection, termed acute cholangitis. A syndrome seen primarily in the elderly, particularly in males, is cholecystitis without gallstones, called acalculous cholecystitis. This tends to occur in the setting of a coexistent serious illness, or perhaps after recent major surgery or severe trauma, when the patient is not allowed food by mouth for a prolonged period and the gallbladder is at rest.

Cancer of the gallbladder, a disease that favors elderly women, is associated with gallstones in 70–90% of cases. Unfortunately, it is rarely curable when diagnosed, even when it is found fortuitously at the time of gallbladder removal for other reasons.

H. Pancreas

Inflammation of the pancreas, or pancreatitis, may be acute or chronic. Acute pancreatitis is usually related to gallstone disease or to alcohol ingestion; gallstones are more likely to be the problem in the elderly. Many commonly prescribed medications, including cortico-steroids, certain antibiotics, and diuretics also cause pancreatitis. Pancreatitis presents with significant abdominal pain and vomiting, and can be diagnosed by blood tests (serum amylase and lipase) or a variety of imaging studies (ultrasound, computed tomography scan). The vast majority of attacks resolve, but some may lead to fulminant disease and death.

Chronic pancreatitis is often the result of repeated insults with a toxin, usually alcohol. In chronic pancreatitis there is ultimately calcification, fibrosis, and atrophy of the pancreas. Pancreatic function may be lost, and since pancreatic enzymes are responsible for a significant portion of nutrient digestion, there may be maldigestion of fats, carbohydrates, and protein. Patients with chronic pancreatitis frequently have severe abdominal pain, greasy foul-smelling stools, and diabetes. Recently, an association has been shown between chronic pancreatitis and pancreatic cancer.

Cancer of the pancreas is unfortunately a common neoplasm. The incidence is higher in males, and there is a strong correlation with advancing age. These tumors usually are found when they obstruct the outflow of bile from the liver and thereby cause jaundice. Weight loss is common. When discovered in a person with jaundice and weight loss, these tumors are usually not suitable for an attempt at a surgical cure, and only palliative and supportive therapy can be offered. Even when found during evaluation for an unrelated

Table II Myths about Gastrointestinal Disease in the Elderly

Myth	Fact
Pills can be swallowed without water.	Adequate liquid is necessary to wash down pills to avoid pill-induced esophageal injury.
With aging, the stomach no longer produces acid.	The healthy elderly person has a healthy stomach which makes a normal amount of acid.
Digestion becomes more difficult with aging.	Intestinal function is well preserved with aging; only absorption of vitamin D and calcium decrease.
Bowels relax with age; old people become constipated.	No evidence of increased constipation or abnormal intestinal motor function in the healthy elderly.

problem, cancer of the pancreas has a dismal prognosis.

III. CONCLUSION

Proper GI function is vital, because it is only through normal digestion, absorption, and motility that adequate nutrition may be maintained. GI dysfunction is frequent in the elderly, however, and often different from that of younger populations. An understanding of the usual changes in function and dysfunction that accompany aging is important (see Table II); the range of dysfunction in the elderly is broad, and making a correct diagnosis is often challenging.

BIBLIOGRAPHY

Brandt, L. J. (1984). *Gastrointestinal disorders of the elderly.* New York: Raven Press.

Friedman, L. S. (Ed.). (1990). Gastrointestinal disorders in the elderly. In *Gastroenterology clinics of North America, 4th ed.* Philadelphia: W.B. Saunders Co.

Greenberger, N. J. (1989). *Gastrointestinal disorders: A pathophysiologic approach, 4th ed.* Chicago: Year Book Medical Publishers, Inc.

Hellemans, J., & Vantrappen, G. (1984). *Gastrointestinal tract disorders in the elderly.* Edinburgh: Churchill Livingstone.

Sleisenger, M. H., & Fordtran, J. S. (Eds.). (1993). *Gastrointestinal disease: Pathophysiology/diagnosis/management, 5th ed.* Philadelphia: W.B. Saunders Co.

Yamada, T. (Ed.). (1995). *Textbook of gastroenterology.* 2nd ed. Philadelphia: J.B. Lippincott Co.

Gender Roles

Sara Arber

University of Surrey

Gender What is recognized as masculine and feminine within a society or cultural group.
Gender Role Behavior that is regarded as appropriate for each gender.
Ideology A pattern of ideas (commonsense knowledge) that purports to explain and legitimate some aspect of the social structure or position of a particular social group.
Sex Biological differences between women and men.

There is both continuity and change in relation to **GENDER ROLES** in later life. Gender roles are affected by both structural and cultural factors. Women predominate among elderly people, especially at the oldest ages. Older women are more likely to be widowed and live alone, whereas older men are likely to be married. Older women are more likely than older men to be disadvantaged by having poorer health and higher levels of functional disability. They have less financial and other material resources, and because of their living arrangements have less access to kin as caregivers. Among older marital partners there is some blurring in gender roles, which occurs particularly if one partner becomes physically or mentally disabled. Older women are advantaged compared to older men in terms of their friendship networks and the social support that they can rely on from friends.

I. GENDER ROLES IN LATER LIFE

A. Sex and Gender

A key distinction is between sex and gender. Sex refers to the biological differences between older men and women, and gender refers to the cultural differences between what is regarded as appropriate behavior for older men compared to older women. Gender is a social construction; in other words, the roles that older men and women occupy in society are not biologically given. What is important is the way that biological sex differences are perceived.

People in society have expectations as to how older women and men should behave. The expected behavior of older women and men is encouraged and reinforced by other adults, by their families, and by role models in the media. To the extent that older people do not conform to appropriate role models they may be chastised or ridiculed by other adults and their peers.

Biological theories about gender role differences are largely disputed, although some writers attribute gender convergence in later life to hormonal changes. However, the weight of evidence suggests that the modest observed gender role convergence relates to a range of demographic and structural changes that will be discussed in this chapter. Some women explain their newfound energy and outgoingness in later life as springing from the diminution of obligatory family roles.

B. Gender Roles

Historical and anthropological research suggests that what are seen as appropriate roles for older men and women are specific to particular societies at particular times. Different societies vary in their images of what is appropriate behavior for older women and men, and these may change over time. For example, it is no longer expected that widows wear black and do not remarry, and in India, the cultural practice of suttee (that widows were burnt on their husband's funeral pyre) has been illegal for over a century.

Younger women's roles are bound up with the private sphere of the household and family, in particular with their roles in reproduction, as housewife and mother. These roles are changing as a higher proportion of women are now in paid employment, but even so, women tend to see their family role as primary and their work role as secondary. However, the current generation of older women spent much less time in the labor market than will be the case for women retiring in the twenty-first century; therefore one may expect differences in their gender role behavior when they enter retirement. Men's roles and identity are primarily bound up with the public sphere of paid employment and the workplace. The breadwinner ideology has had a powerful influence on today's generation of older men, and their primary source of identity has been their occupational work role.

A key issue is to what extent these adult gender roles change once men are no longer engaged in the public sphere of production, and women's role no longer relates to reproduction, in terms of childbearing and child rearing, or supporting their marital partner in his breadwinning role. Do gender roles become more similar in later life, when neither partner is in paid work or centrally engaged in child care?

Gender roles and identities, which have developed in earlier phases of the life course through the institutions of the family, the labor market, and the state, continue to structure women's and men's relation-ships in later life. However, some of these structures become less prominent, particularly those associated with reproduction and the labor market, whereas others may become increasingly important, for example, the gendered nature of state policies in later life, which impact on older women's income and access to health and social care. Thus, there are cross-cutting influences on older women's and men's roles in later life, some tending to diminish gender role differences, others to increase these differences. [*See* LIFE COURSE.]

Section II examines the demography of aging, which makes it clear that traditional gender roles relating to marriage cannot continue unchanged, because half of older women are widowed and over half live alone.

C. Ideologies

Gender roles are supported by ideologies that shape everyday feelings, thoughts, and actions. An ideology is a pattern of ideas (commonsense knowledge), which may be factual or evaluative, which purports to explain and legitimate the social structure and culture of a social group or society. Ideologies serve to justify social actions that are in accordance with that pattern of ideas. They function to construct certain aspects of the social world as natural and universal, and therefore unquestionable and unchallengable. Ideologies underpin societal views about appropriate role behavior of older women and men. However, ideologies have changed and continue to do so.

Societal ideology confirms and reinforces men's dominant status by devaluing women's work and reproductive functions while simultaneously presenting male work as of greater cultural importance. Older people, because they are not in paid work, tend to be devalued by society. They are frequently construed as a burden on the taxpayer, in terms of the high costs of pensions and health care, and on their families, as a burden to be cared for should they become disabled and unable to care for themselves.

What it means to be old is profoundly gendered. The double standard of aging, in which women but not men are expected to retain a youthful appearance, warding off the signs of aging for as long as possible, is widely recognized. Women are still primarily valued for their youth and attractiveness to men, hence it is not surprising that older women are expected to attempt to mask the signs of aging.

D. Gender Relations and Gender Divisions

The term gender relations, by analogy with class relations, refers to the different position of men and women in the social hierarchy of power and status. Gender relations cannot be assumed to be static over the life course, because life transitions, age-based norms, and physiological changes all impact on the way gender roles are constructed and gender identity experienced. Biological differences between the sexes cannot explain gender divisions in later life. Gender divisions must be seen as socially constructed; that is, they are the product of particular cultural definitions and practices that are customary and thus, tend to be accepted without question.

Older women and men interact with one another in their everyday lives; they are not just role players acting out a prepared script. Men are more likely to have power over women, because of ideologies about the primacy of men's over women's roles. In addition, women lack economic power compared with men and are more likely to be economically dependent on their partner, or in advanced old age are customarily economically dependent on the state. Section III examines older women's paucity of independent financial resources relative to men. Older women are also likely to have less physical power, possessing less strength than their partner and younger adults. Older women are more likely than older men to have physical disabilities that limit their ability to accomplish activities of daily living (ADLs), which increases their dependence on others for care, as examined in section IV.

The power of men over women is also collective, because society's sexist assumptions advantage all men. Thus, it is crucial to examine the relationships between individuals and the social structure, between women's everyday experiences and the structure of the society in which they live, including men's power in interpersonal relationships. Only a minority of older women are married, and the extent to which gender roles alter within late-life marriages is examined in section V. Friendships are therefore particularly important for older women. Older women's gender roles facilitate their ability to develop and sustain a wider network of friendship relationships than men (see section VI).

Table I Age Structure of Older Women and Men in England and Wales and the United States[a]

	Women	Men	Sex ratio (women/men)
England and Wales (1993)			
65–74	51	63	1.21
75–84	35	30	1.69
85+	14	7	3.05
	100%	100%	
% 65+ in population	18.6	13.1	
All 65+ (millions)	4.9	3.3	1.48
United States (1990)			
65–74	54	63	1.28
75–84	34	30	1.82
85+	12	7	2.59
	100%	100%	
% 65+ in population	14.6	10.3	
All 65+ (millions)	18.6	12.5	1.49

[a]Sources: Office of Population Censuses and Surveys (1994) *Population Trends, 78,* London: Her Majesty's Stationary Office, Table 6; Taeuber (1992), Table 2.2.

II. DEMOGRAPHIC CHARACTERISTICS

A. Feminization of Later Life

Gender roles in later life are influenced by demographic factors. The proportion of elderly people (over age 65) in the population is increasing, especially the proportion who are age 85 and over. Nineteen percent of women in England and Wales and 13% of men are over age 65 (see Table I). The comparable figures in the United States are 15% of women and 10% of men. In Britain, 14% of elderly women are over age 85 compared with only 7% of elderly men. In the United States, 12% of all elderly women are over 85.

Women's predominance among those over 65 has come to be known as the feminization of later life, which increases with advancing age. In Britain, the gender imbalance is low among the young elderly, with only about 20% more women than men aged 65–74 (Table I). It increases to 70% more women than men among those aged 75–84, and to over three times more women than men aged over 85.

Over age 65, there are nearly 50% more women than men in England and Wales and the United States. The numerical predominance of women in later life is found in all European countries, although the exact

558

Gender Roles

Table II Expectation of Life of Women and Men in England and Wales and the United States[a]

	Women (years)	Men (years)	Sex differential (years)
England and Wales			
1971	75.2	69.0	6.2
1990	78.7	73.2	5.5
United States			
1970	74.8	67.1	7.7
1989	78.6	71.8	6.8

[a]Sources: Office of Population Censuses and Surveys (1994) *Population Trends, 78,* London: Her Majesty's Stationery Office, Table 12; Taeuber (1992), Table 3.1.

proportion varies somewhat, for example, in West Germany there are almost twice as many women as men over age 65, whereas in Greece there are less than a third more women than men. The numerical predominance of older women means that, to the extent that older people are seen as a social problem or a burden on the rest of society, women are disproportionately affected.

The gender imbalance is because male mortality exceeds female at every age. The expectation of life at birth for women in England and Wales is 78.7 and for men is 73.2 (see Table II). In the United States, the female advantage in survival is greater than in the United Kingdom; the expectation of life for women is 78.6 years and for men is 71.8 years. In both countries, the female advantage in survival has diminished slightly over the last 20 years.

B. Marital Status and Living Arrangements

The gender differential in mortality together with the cultural norm for women to marry men older than themselves creates gender differences in marital status and living arrangements in later life. Half of elderly women are widowed in both England and the United States (Table III), whereas for elderly men 72% in England and Wales, and 76% in the United States are married. In both societies, about 40% of women are married. Rather fewer men are widowed in the United States (14%), than in England (17%). The feminization of widowhood is particularly pronounced in the United States, with 4.8 times more elderly widows than widowers, compared with 4.4 times more in England and Wales.

Marital status is associated with living arrangements, and both of these affect gender roles, as well as the availability of informal caregivers and the need for support from personal and welfare services (see section V). Nearly three-quarters of elderly men in both societies live with their wife (Table IV), and so can expect their wife to care for them should they become disabled. The marital role remains a prime one for men throughout their life course (see section VI), but this is not the case for women. Fewer elderly women live with their husband than live alone. More elderly women than men live with other relatives, such as siblings and adult children.

Nearly half of elderly women and a quarter of elderly men in Britain live alone (Table IV). The proportions are somewhat lower in the United States, 42% of women and 16% of men, but the gender differences are striking; there are nearly four times more elderly women than men living alone in the United States. Elderly womens' propensity to live alone has been seen in a negative light, yet solo living does not necessarily imply social vulnerability; it may reflect preference. The high proportion of elderly people currently living alone is an unprecedented situation historically. The reasons for this trend do not lie in the abandonment of kin obligations by younger people, as some have suggested, but rather in changes

Table III Marital Status of Women and Men Aged 65 and over in England and Wales and the United States[a]

	Women (%)	Men (%)	Sex ratio (women/men)
England and Wales (1992)			
Married	38.4	72.3	0.79
Widowed	49.2	16.8	4.36
Divorced	3.8	3.4	1.63
Never married	8.6	7.5	1.70
	100%	100%	
United States (1990)			
Married	41.5	76.5	0.76
Widowed	48.6	14.5	4.77
Divorced	5.1	6.0	1.43
Never married	4.9	4.5	1.63
	100%	100%	

[a]Sources: Office of Population Censuses and Surveys (1994) *Population Trends, 78,* London: Her Majesty's Stationery Office, Table 7; Taeuber (1992), Table 8.6

Table IV Living Arrangements of Women and Men Aged 65 and over in England and Wales and the United States (Noninstitutional Population)[a]

	Women (%)	Men (%)	Sex ratio (women/men)
England and Wales (1991)			
Lives alone	47	23	2.82
Lives with spouse	42	72	0.83
Lives with adult child(ren)	5	2	4.14
Lives with others	5	3	2.23
	100%	100%	
N	(1585)	(2214)	
United States (1990)			
Lives alone	42	16	3.72
Lives with spouse	40	74	0.75
Lives with other relatives	16	8	2.92
Lives with nonrelatives	2	2	1.32
	100%	100%	
N (millions)	17.2	12.3	

[a]Sources: *General Household Survey, 1991* (authors' analysis); Taeuber (1992), Table 6.3.

in marriage and fertility patterns, and in the financial ability, especially since the Second World War, of elderly people to retain their independence. This may be somewhat greater in the United Kingdom than the United States because of the near universal provision of state pensions to elderly people in Britain.

III. GENDER AND INCOME INEQUALITY

An elderly person's roles and opportunities in later life are influenced profoundly by their financial and other material resources, such as income, car ownership, housing, and other assets. In the 1980s American feminists drew attention to the concentration of poverty among elderly women. In Britain, research has uncovered the extent of and the reasons for gender inequality of income in later life. Throughout Europe, elderly women's lower income and living standards compared with men is evident, with the exception of Denmark.

A. Gender and Poverty

One measure of gender inequality of income is the percentage living at or below the level at which means-

tested benefits are payable: the threshold for Income Support in Britain in 1991 was £53 per week (about $80) for a single pensioner or £86 per week (about $130) for a pensioner couple. Fourteen percent of British elderly women received Income Support in 1991, compared with 5% of men. These estimates of the percentages living at Income Support level are conservative because of low take-up; one in five pensioners eligible for means-tested benefit fail to claim it.

In the United States, women constitute nearly three-quarters of the elderly poor, although they represent only 59% of all elderly people. Elderly women are almost twice as likely as elderly men to have an income at or below the poverty threshold, 15% compared with 9%. The racial differential in income is even greater than the gender differential, with over a third of older black women living in poverty. [See ECONOMICS: INDIVIDUAL; ECONOMICS: SOCIETY.]

B. Gender Inequality in Personal Income

Official figures on poverty underestimate the income disadvantage of elderly women when the household, family, or taxation unit is the unit of analysis. The assumption that married couples share money income equally is challenged by a growing body of evidence that within households men have more personal spending money than women. A more accurate picture of gender inequality of income is obtained by comparing the distribution of personal income, that is, income to which an individual has direct, independent access. This includes such income as a person's own state or occupational pension and any survivor's pension, but not their spouse's income.

In Britain there is little difference among elderly people in the amount of personal income they receive from the state pension. However, there are large differences in total income, the median for elderly men was £106 per week in 1991 and for elderly women was £61 per week. This difference is mainly because a much higher percentage of elderly men than women in Britain have income from a nonstate pension (including survivors' pensions), 66% compared with 37%. Few elderly people are in paid employment, but over twice as many men as women had earnings, 8% compared with 4%.

The major source of inequality in personal income among British elderly men and women is occupational pension income, which is closely linked to type of occupation, employment pattern, and lifetime earnings. Elderly British women are far less likely than men to receive any income from an occupational pension, and the amounts are also less, mainly due to the domestic division of labor and the constraints this places on women's employment.

In the United States also, women are less likely than men to have any pension other than the Social Security pension; although half of all employees were covered by private pension schemes, only 20% of women retiring in 1979 had a private pension. In the 1980s, women's likelihood of retiring with a private pension was less than men's, and where women had a pension, the income was on average only 59% of men's.

In spite of formal sex equality and women's increasing employment, the proportion of women belonging to an occupational pension scheme is rising only very slowly. A substantial gender gap in occupational pension income is likely to persist as long as women shoulder the bulk of society's unpaid caring. Women's disadvantage can be alleviated by redistributive state pensions supported from taxation, as in Denmark. However, the trend is in the opposite direction: in Britain and in most other Organization of Economic Cooperation and Development (OECD) countries, concern at the rising cost of public pensions as the population ages has prompted a shift in the balance of pension provision from state to private. In Britain, for example, the basic state pension has been cut since 1979 from 20% of average male earnings to 16% in 1991, and the decline in relative value is projected to continue. Unless the trend towards privatization of pensions is reversed, gender inequality of personal income in later life is likely to increase in the future. [See PENSIONS.]

IV. GENDER, HEALTH, AND DISABILITY

Good health is essential to independence, and the ability to fulfill customary roles, as well as to the maintenance of social relationships. Poor health or disability often means that an elderly person requires help and support, which inevitably will alter their role relationships. Those with higher levels of functional disability or cognitive impairment will require more practical support and personal care from their family, friends, or the state.

Elderly women have been shown in numerous studies to have higher levels of physical incapacity than men. Among those over 75, twice as many British women as men were housebound (22% compared to 11%). Above age 80, elderly women have higher levels of cognitive impairment than men.

Disabilities that hinder mobility and prevent an individual performing basic self-care tasks, such as washing and going to the toilet, are conventionally measured using ADLs. Elderly women within each 5-year age group are nearly twice as likely as men to report impaired mobility, with the sex ratio greatest among the oldest age groups.

In Britain, twice as many elderly women as men have a severe level of disability—14% compared with 7%. They will have difficulty washing and bathing unaided and are unable to walk down the road unaided. This level of disability is likely to require some provision of domestic or personal care and support on a regular basis. Gender differences are particularly striking at the oldest ages; above age 85, 45% of elderly women compared with under a quarter of elderly men are severely disabled.

There are comparable findings in the United States; older women are more likely than men to have difficulty with ADLs because of health or physical problems. In both countries, functionally dependent women are most likely to live alone, whereas the majority of functionally dependent men live with their partner. For example, in the United States by age 85, 36% of functionally dependent men lived with their spouse compared with only 4% of their female counterparts.

Although elderly women have a longer life expectancy than men, they also have a longer period in which they can expect to be functionally disabled or living in an institution. For example, women at 65 living in Massachusetts can expect 10.6 years of nondisabled life, only 1.3 years more than men, despite the fact that women expect to live on average 7.4 years more than men.

Thus, elderly women are disadvantaged compared to men of the same age because they will require a good deal more care and support simply to accomplish the ADLs. The consequence of the gender differential in disability is that elderly women are more likely to require care from their relatives, friends, and neighbors and from state health and welfare services.

V. GENDER ROLES AND CARING

As discussed in the previous section, more elderly women than men need care or support in order to remain living in the community. There are differences between older men and women in their ease of access to people who will provide such care. In Britain elderly disabled women are twice as likely as elderly men with a comparable level of disability to live alone and therefore be reliant on family members living elsewhere, other informal caregivers in the community, and state-provided domiciliary services. This contrasts with the majority of severely disabled elderly men who can rely on support and care provided by their wives. Severely disabled elderly women are twice as likely as equivalent men to live in the home of an adult child (12%) and are more likely than similar men to share their own household with other people. Where elderly disabled people share their household with others, household members perform virtually all of the necessary personal and domestic care tasks for them, and state services are provided at a very low level.

Nearly half of disabled elderly women live alone. Although this promotes independence, it also means they may be reliant on state domiciliary services, mainly home helps and community nurses in the United Kingdom. They are also heavily dependent on the unpaid work of relatives and other unpaid kin who act as caregivers, and they are the group most likely to enter residential care. Elderly women's disadvantage in access to care from family members is compounded by their lower average income (section III); a poor deal for "the caregiver sex," who have spent a lifetime of unpaid work looking after children, husband, and others, often in addition to waged work. [See HOUSING.]

Poor health or disability have implications for relationships between spouses and between parents and their adult children, because of the loss of independence of the person being cared for and the stress that attention to their needs imposes on the caregiver. Because of gender differences in disability and the numerical majority of women in later life, the provision and receipt of informal care are gendered. Older women are more likely than older men to have their ADLs impaired by functional disabilities, yet women are far less likely to have a spouse to provide care and enable them to remain living in the community. Men can largely rely on their wives when care is required, with all the advantages this brings. Women more often have to call upon adult children for help and are twice as likely as men to enter residential care.

VI. MARITAL ROLES IN LATER LIFE

The life course as it evolves invites change in gender roles and relationships, as the material basis of the gender division of labor in employment and child rearing changes. In later life, when these roles have been largely lost, older people could be said to inhabit a "third sphere," which is neither production nor reproduction. The question of whether later life brings greater equality of roles between husbands and wives, and if so, whether this shifts power in marital relationships towards women, is an intriguing one. Some writers have suggested this is so, but it may depend on whether married women have been able to acquire independent pension income. Although the breadwinner role, in terms of wage earning, ends with retirement, husbands' pension income (as discussed in section III) is much higher than women's, which contributes to perpetuating men's relative power in marriage into later life.

Research on how gender roles, attitudes, and expectations develop with aging suggests some gender convergence, or a tendency towards androgyny; gender roles become less sharply defined in the latter half of life, with older men showing more affiliative, nurturant tendencies than younger, while older women are more independent and assertive than younger. The traditional domestic division of labor into "feminine" (especially laundry, cleaning, cooking) and "masculine" tasks (mainly repairs and maintenance of home, garden, and car, where these exist) is reported by some researchers in the United States to diminish with age. However, research on middle-class couples in midlife and later life demonstrated that household tasks were still strongly sex-linked, although retired men and women both had greater involvement in masculine tasks than employed people, and men participated more in feminine tasks after retirement. Taking on cross-sex tasks has been found to be linked with greater well-being for women but not for men, consistent with existing research, which has found that housework is unsatisfying.

Above age 75, gender roles between spouses become more blurred, with men conforming less closely to a masculine stereotype in terms of tasks performed; however, some gender inequality of power persists in the marital relationship. Among older married couples, gender role identity becomes more fluid; for example, the performance of previously gender-related tasks may become more interchangeable between women and men, in response to the functional disability of either partner. Older married couples' are usually determined to maintain their independence as a couple, which tends to override previous gendered roles.

Older couples tend to deal with the shifting balance of health and need for care by the less disabled partner, irrespective of gender, taking on caring tasks and more domestic roles. However, men, whether caregivers or care recipients, are more likely to stay in control. As caregivers, men are willing to set aside gender norms as to appropriate tasks in order to preserve the autonomy and independence of the couple, but in doing so they see themselves and are seen by others as achieving status for performing such cross-gender roles; admired for their competence by all concerned. In contrast, older women, who perform equally heroic tasks to maintain the ideology of the independent and mutually supportive couple, see what they do as obligatory, and this view is shared by those around them, thus giving little social esteem to the care work of older women. Analysis of the meaning and language of caring demonstrates the subtle ways in which gendered power relationships and gender-differentiated esteem may remain despite ostensible gender equivalence in the performance of domestic and caring tasks.

Frailty associated with physiological aging affects not only marital relationships but also wider social support networks, and gender influences the way different types of social networks shift in response to increasing disability and need for assistance. The impact of increasing frailty on support networks is not the same for women and men, the former depending more on their adult children and the latter relying mostly on their wives. [See SOCIAL NETWORKS, SUPPORT, AND INTEGRATION.]

VII. GENDER AND FRIENDSHIP PATTERNS

Friends are especially important for lone elderly people, who may not only have lost the social contacts of work, but also may lack close family in either the geographical or metaphorical sense. For those who live alone, friends are often their primary and most enduring link with society, as well as the main source of emotional support and of help in coping with the loss of previous roles.

From early socialization onwards, gender influences the kind of relationships that are formed. Through their domestic role women develop skills that facilitate intimate friendships. Among lone elderly people, women are more likely than men to be visited and to visit others in their neighborhood, in spite of being on average less physically fit. Structural factors tend to favor women's friendships in later life but work against men's; after men's work-based friendships are weakened by retirement, a void may be left unless they can be maintained through pubs, clubs, and leisure activities.

Women not only have more friends on average than men in later life, but the quality of their friendship tends to differ too; women's friends are often their close confidantes, with whom troubles and joys, anxieties and hopes can be shared, whereas elderly men tend to rely on their wives to fulfill this role. Widowers generally lack the interpersonal resources to make close friends after bereavement, whereas widows are likely to substitute friends for a co-resident companion, and are consequently no more likely to suffer depression than women who live with others. Cross-gender friendships are rare in later life; such a relationship is assumed to have a romantic content, and is subject to normative restraints.

Widowers are more likely to look forward to remarriage than widows, the latter seeing advantages in having friendships with men but often preferring to remain free of women's traditional servicing role in marriage. Thus, although widowhood for women is usually associated with a drop in household income, widows gain the freedom to budget as they choose, and despite losing a lifelong companion, some women may welcome the release from tiresome routine work.

In summary, although elderly women's opportunities for making and maintaining friendships are constrained by lack of material and health resources relative to elderly men's, their relationship skills acquired in earlier life are an asset. They are less likely than their husbands to have placed all their emotional "eggs in one basket" and seem more adaptable to changed circumstances. For lone elderly women, friendships act as a buffer, alleviating some of the effects of their considerable disadvantage in income and poor health.

VIII. COHORT AND AGING CHANGES

The historical period of early socialization has been said to exert a disproportionately powerful influence over attitudes and expectations. Gender relations in different cohorts tend, therefore, to differ according to the gender ideology, military demands, economic climate, and so forth prevailing in their youth. If social change is minimal, gender norms are likely to be reinforced in adulthood by the peer group and by the older generation. However, rapid social change may modify norms established in young adulthood. The far-reaching changes this century in reproductive technology (especially the contraceptive pill), the expansion of women's opportunities in education and employment, changed attitudes to marital relationships and parenthood, the social movements concerned with race and gender equality and citizenship rights for disadvantaged social groups, the shifting needs of capitalism for men's and women's labor, and the backlash against feminism and collectivism have been experienced by different cohorts at varying stages in their life course. How far men and women as they age "move with the times," adapting their gender relationships in response to such changes or adhering to attitudes and behavioral patterns established earlier, is not clear.

The individual's previous biography, in terms of both family and work roles, has a profound influence on their resources, roles, and relationships in later life, as discussed in previous sections. Living through particular secular (or period) changes at different stages of the life course affects individuals' attitudes towards women's and men's roles. The current generation of older people span widely different birth cohorts, those who grew up before the First World War lived through different experiences from those who were children during the interwar depression. The social norms and attitudes extant in the forma-

tive years continue to influence behavior and attitudes throughout the life course. The next generation of older people who grew up in the 1950s and 1960s will have been affected by second-wave feminism and are likely to enter later life with very different employment experiences and gender role expectations.

In relation to research on gender roles in later life, it is important to distinguish the effects of aging, and, for example, long association as a couple, from cohort effects, recognizing the very different historical circumstances in which older and younger people had their most influential socializing experiences. [*See* COHORT STUDIES.]

IX. THE THIRD AGE: A NEW OPPORTUNITY?

Some have argued that in postmodern society, conceptions about age-appropriate behavior are becoming more fluid; norms as to the timing of work and education have become more flexible, and dress and leisure activities are less closely tied to chronological age than in the past. According to these views, normative expectations about appropriate lifestyles among older people are weakening as improved health enables more people to enter a Third Age of active leisure between retirement and the onset of frailty. The idea of the Third Age is discussed by Peter Laslett, who focuses on the positive aspects of population aging, highlighting human agency and stressing the opportunities for personal growth and choice in the Third Age. However, this vision is prescriptive rather than explanatory and is based on elitist assumptions.

It is important to remember that the rosy scenario of a Third Age of self-development, autonomy, consumption, and youthful lifestyles is essentially a bourgeois option, unavailable to those who have low incomes or poor health. It neglects structural inequality, especially inequality between older men and women, and the way material and cultural factors influence the meaning and actual experience of life transitions. Age-based norms may still exert powerful pressure to "act one's age," especially among those with fewer financial resources.

The Third Age appears to offer opportunities for older women to develop other identities than that of wife, mother, or paid worker, through engaging in leisure, social, and other activities. In practice, however, older women continue to be more occupied than men with domestic and family obligations, especially if they are married, so that they have less free time then retired men. But for some women, socialization into gender roles, often barely questioned in young adulthood, may be challenged and resisted as they age. Older women may now feel free to "grow old disgracefully."

X. CONCLUSIONS: GENDER ROLES AND STRUCTURE

A full understanding of gender and aging requires the merging of the microperspective, of gender roles and relationships, with the macroperspective, which takes account of wider societal changes. Macrolevel changes have had major effects on the lives of older women and men. The progressively earlier age of exit from paid employment and improving health of the population has meant that women and men spend many more active years not in paid work, both before and after the state pension age, than in the past. More importantly, state provision in the form of the British state National Insurance pension, which was introduced after the Second World War, has made it possible for older people to live independently of both paid work and of financial support from relatives, a situation that is unprecedented historically. However, there is evidence that current trends in social and economic policy are threatening to reverse these gains, particularly for older women. Although older women have always been poorer than older men, the British state pension has meant that since the 1950s older women have had more independent financial resources than in the past, promoting their opportunities for independent action and social citizenship. However, the signs are that these are under threat.

The greater the movement towards private provision for retirement through occupational and personal pensions as the major source of income in later life, the greater will be the income inequality between older women and men and between those who have had an intermittent, or low paid employment history and those with an advantaged position in the labor market. Thus the opportunities to enjoy a Third Age of

self-development and autonomous action are likely to become increasingly gendered, as well as class-divided, with financial dependency acting as an obstacle to citizenship rights.

Because of the constraints of their earlier domestic roles, women have to rely more heavily than men on household members and the state for financial support. Their higher disability rates, combined with a greater likelihood of living alone, make them more dependent on care-givers in the community and on state services. However, an area in which elderly women are advantaged is that they have wider friendship networks than elderly men, which are particularly valuable in providing social and emotional support.

Despite the structural disadvantages facing older women, later life may be a time when older women are free to construct more individual gender roles, especially if they are freed from the constraints of marriage and conformity within other institutional contexts. They may develop a more authentic identity and orientation, especially following widowhood, when they are no longer constrained to fulfill gendered role obligations expected within marriage. Older widows are more likely than older widowers to reject the idea of remarriage, which is seen as having few benefits for older women and a range of disadvantages. There may be conflicts experienced by older women between pressures to conform to prescribed gender roles and their desire for autonomy in later life.

ACKNOWLEDGMENT

Much of this chapter is based on joint work conducted with Jay Ginn, who has been my research colleague for the last seven years. I am deeply grateful for all her help and support.

BIBLIOGRAPHY

Arber, S., & Evandrou, M. (Ed.). (1993). *Ageing, independence and the life course.* London: Jessica Kingsley.
Arber, S., & Ginn, J. (1991). *Gender and later life: A sociological analysis of resources and constraints.* London: Sage.
Arber, S., & Ginn, J. (Ed.). (1995). *Connecting gender and ageing: A sociological approach.* Buckingham: Open University Press.
Bernard, M., & Meade, K. (Eds.). (1993). *Women come of age: Perspectives on the lives of older women.* London: Edward Arnold.

Glasse, L., & Hendricks, J. (Eds.). (1990). *Gender and aging.* Amityville, NY: Baywood Publishing Company.

Journal of Aging Studies. (1993). Special issue on Women and aging. 7, No. 2.

Laslett, P. (1989). *A fresh map of life: The emergence of the Third Age.* London: George Weidenfeld & Nicholson Limited.

Taeuber, C. M. (1992). *Sixty-five plus in America.* Current Population Reports (Special Studies, P23-178RV). Washington, DC: U.S. Bureau of the Census.

Generational Differences

K. Warner Schaie

The Pennsylvania State University

Cohort   Group of persons entering the environment at the same point or range in time.
Cross-Sectional Sequence   Groups of persons assessed once, where at least two age levels are sampled at a minimum of two different measurement occasions.
Longitudinal Sequence   At least two groups of persons assessed at least Sequence: twice over the same age range.

GENERATIONAL DIFFERENCES will be treated here from a psychological perspective, although attention will be called to the historical context of the concept as it evolved in both sociology and psychology. Moreover, generations will be differentiated from cohorts, and I will discuss the relevance of the literature on cohort differences to an understanding of generational differences. Methodological issues in the psychological study of generational differences and cohort differences will be considered. Examples of findings from the literature will draw largely on the author's Seattle Longitudinal Study (SLS), including findings on generational differences in cognitive performance, selected demographic characteristics, and perceptions of family environments.

I. SOCIOLOGISTS' AND PSYCHOLOGISTS' VIEWS OF GENERATIONS

The concept of generational differences received considerable play in the early part of the century when the sociologist Karl Mannheim called attention to generational conflicts, particularly between adolescents and young adults and their parents. Indeed, much of the literature on generational differences written by sociologists deals with issues of generational conflicts and transmission of values. Similar early concerns in psychology appear in the work of Charlotte Buehler centering on conflicts between adolescents and their parents. Among developmental psychologists, hints of concern about possible effects of generational differences can be found in the work of Raymond Kuhlen, who was the first in psychology to call attention to the fact that individuals age within the context of changing societies, implying the possibility that the timing of behavioral change might be important.

In the more recent literature, generational differences began to resurface in the mid-1960s almost simultaneously in both the sociological and developmental psychology literature. Ryder suggested that the notion of cohort progression was an essential concept for the sociological study of change. This theme was further developed in its implication for social gerontology in a seminal volume by Riley, Johnson, and Foner. The author simultaneously emphasized that aging data obtained from cross-sectional and longitudinal data sets could not correspond with each other. Cross-sectional age differences are confounded with cohort (generational) differences, and longitudinal age changes are confounded with time-of-measurement (period) differences. He specified a general developmental model that examined the formal nature of these relationships, placed them in the framework of quasi-experimental designs in psychology and education, and proposed strategies for collecting and analyzing data that might help obtain better estimates of the age factor.

Attempts to unconfound the age-period-cohort model have been controversial. However, given appropriate limiting assumptions, cohort studies have played an important role in behavioral research not only in controlling for methodological artifacts that might result in the over- or underestimation of aging effects, but also in examining the contextual variables that affect levels of behavior and expression of personality traits over time. There is still a lack of good understanding of the relationship between macrosocietal change and its effects upon age differences and age changes in behavior. The study of generational differences in behavior has provided an initial attempt to identify those variables most prone to shifts across generations. Geropsychologists who began prospective studies of aging from the 1960s on have therefore usually included multiple cohort designs of one kind or other to deal with the issue of possible generational differences.

II. GENERATION AND COHORT

We next distinguish between the terms *generation* and *cohort* by noting that the former term often denotes successive groups in time where the second group could be (but need not necessarily be) the biological offspring of the first group. By contrast, the term *cohort* defines an arbitrary definition of a point in time or range of time during which the members of the group enter the environment (by birth or other temporal entry). Hence the temporal distance between two generations will generally represent a time frame from 20–30 years, whereas cohort differences may and often do cover much shorter periods of time. [*See* Cohort Studies.]

Generational and cohort differences have usually been studied in the context of groups of people (birth cohorts) entering the environment at the same point (or range) of calendar time. It should be stressed nevertheless that the temporal boundaries for generations can also be characterized by noncalendar definitions.

For example, the initial group of workers hired for a new factory or the first faculty of a new educational institution would represent a generation (regardless of the individuals' calendar age), as would the initial membership of a newly formed club, or the first-time purchasers of homes in a new residential subdivision.

III. METHODOLOGICAL ISSUES

A. Research Designs for the Study of Generational Differences

Conventional cross-sectional studies confound age and generational differences, and findings from single-cohort longitudinal studies are often applicable only to the members of the particular generations on which they have been collected. Several alternative sequential strategies have been introduced to deal with this problem, including the behavioral assessment of more than one cohort over a given age range.

The term *sequential* implies that the sampling strategy used to study generational differences must include the acquisition of a sequence of samples taken across several measurement occasions. Perhaps the most widely used sequential strategy is the *cross-sequential* design, in which two or more cohorts are followed during an identical time period. This approach permits the comparison of longitudinal and cross-sectional data (provided that the calendar time ranges are similar for age and cohort). The advantage of this approach is that only two points in time are needed; hence the early appearance in the literature of studies using this design. For purposes of studying generational differences, however, this approach represents a "model misspecification" because it does not allow comparing each cohort over the same age range.

Geropsychologists and other developmental scientists often find the *cohort-sequential* design of greatest interest because it explicitly differentiates intraindividual age changes that occur within a generation from interindividual differences between generations. This design also permits a check of the consistency of age functions over successive generations, thereby offering greater external validity than would be provided by a single-cohort longitudinal design. A cohort-sequential study consists of two or more generations (however defined) being followed over two or more similar age levels. The minimum design for such a

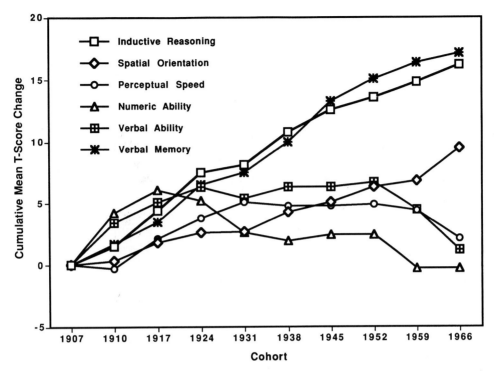

Figure I Cumulative generational differences for six mental abilities for birth cohorts in 7-year intervals from 1907 to 1966. (From Schaie, K. W., 1994. The course of adult intellectual development. *American Psychologist, 49,* 304–313. Reproduced by permission of the American Psychological Association.)

study involves three measurement points, allowing each of two cohorts to be followed over the same age range.

In a typical longitudinal study, *repeated measures* are taken of the same subjects at successive times. But it is also possible to use the same research design but with *independent samples* at each age level being measured. In this alternative one would draw a new (independent) sample from the same cohort initially tested. The independent sampling approach works well when a large sample is drawn from a large population, and when one is primarily interested in the estimation of population parameters. This approach controls for the effects of nonrandom dropout, regression to the mean because of fallible measurement instruments, and effects of practice or inadvertent changes in experimental protocols. If small samples are used it is, of course, necessary to make sure that successive independent samples are matched on factors such as gender, income, and education to avoid

possible differences due to selection biases. [*See* RE-SEARCH DESIGN AND METHODS.]

B. Designs for Specific Issues in the Study of Generational Differences

If the primary interest of an investigator resides in the estimation of magnitudes of generational differences, then the independent samples approach described above will suffice. That is, one needs to obtain data from a minimum of two cohorts at the same age in order to estimate the magnitude of the cohort difference. However, it is probably quite problematic to estimate generational differences at only one age level, because of the possibility of age-by-cohort interactions. Hence, one would recommend for this purpose a cross-sectional sequence of sufficient temporal length that each pair of cohorts can be compared at multiple age levels, even though all cohort pairs cannot be compared at every age level of interest. When

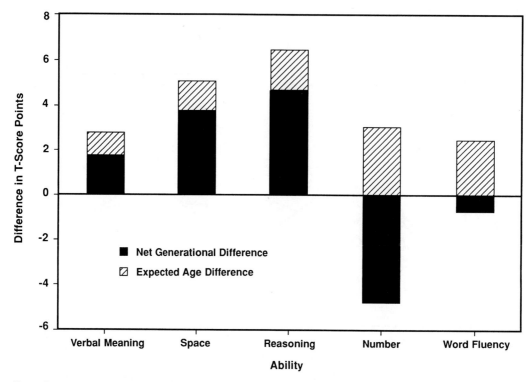

Figure 2 Generational differences in primary mental abilities between parents and their adult offspring. (From Schaie, K. W., Plomin, R., Willis, S. L., Gruber-Baldini, A., & Dutta, R., 1992. Natural cohorts: Family similarity in adult cognition. In T. Sonderegger (Ed.), *Psychology and aging: Nebraska Symposium on Motivation, 1991.* Lincoln, NE: University of Nebraska Press.)

this is done, one can then take the performance of the earliest born cohort as a base and cumulate successive cohort differences, in the same manner as life span psychologists estimate age gradients. This approach permits contrasting generational shifts in performance levels over time for distinct behavioral dimensions.

It should be noted that the above approach will not be applicable to the estimation of generational differences in rates of change. For the latter purpose it is necessary to follow the same individuals over time in the form of a longitudinal sequence that allows contrasting successive cohorts over the same age range. This approach is essential if one wishes to address the question whether there have been any changes in the *rate* of aging for successive generations.

If one wishes to define generational differences as those pertaining to differences in the behavior of successive generations of biologically related individuals, then it is necessary to contrast parents with their adult

offspring. Ideally, data would be required for such parents and offspring at the same ages. Barring the availability of such ideal data, designs of studies involving differences within family units must pay attention to the age at which subjects are assessed, as well as to gender differences, when cross-gender parent–offspring pairs are studied. Adjustments for the confounds of age and gender must often be used in order to get realistic estimates of generational differences within biologically related family units.

IV. SUBSTANTIVE FINDINGS

The remainder of this chapter will outline current knowledge of generational differences in intellectual competence, some selected demographic characteristics, and perceptions of family environments that may

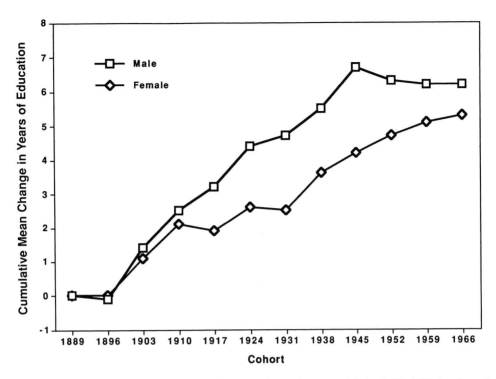

Figure 3 Generational differences in years of education by gender. (From Schaie, K. W., 1995. *Intellectual development in adulthood: The Seattle Longitudinal Study* (p. 157). New York: Cambridge University Press.)

have implications for our understanding of behavioral aging.

A. Generational Differences in Cognitive Abilities

Generational differences were first studied by means of cohort-sequential designs as part of the analyses conducted for the third cycle of the SLS. This study began in 1956 as a cross-sectional inquiry of the primary mental abilities over the age range from the twenties to the seventies. Longitudinal follow-ups have been conducted at five successive time points (7 years apart) in 1963, 1970, 1977, 1984, and 1991. All study participants were community-dwelling members of a health maintenance organization and represent the upper 75% of the socioeconomic spectrum. Figure 1 shows cumulated generational differences for birth cohorts from 1907 to 1966 in 7-year intervals for six primary mental abilities: Verbal Ability (recognition of the meaning of words); Inductive

Reasoning (the ability to abstract rules and principles from reoccurring single instances); Spatial Orientation (mental rotation of objects in two-dimensional space); Numeric Ability (skill in simple mathematical operations such as addition, subtraction, and multiplication); Perceptual Speed (rapid identification or matching of simple objects, or comparison of numbers); and Verbal Memory (immediate and delayed word recall). Each ability was measured by three or four different tests, and Figure 1 shows generational differences on the factor scores estimated for the latent ability constructs.

Substantial positive and linear generational differences were observed for Inductive Reasoning and Verbal Memory. The 60-year gain amounted to approximately 1.5 *SD*. This gain is likely associated with the substantial increase in educational exposure occurring over this time period. The positive gain in Inductive Reasoning across successive generations may also be related to changes in educational practice from rote learning to the encouragement of discovery methods. Of course, the virtual conquest of childhood diseases

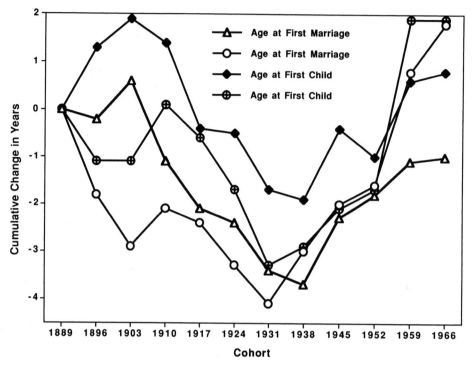

Figure 4 Generational differences in age at first marriage and age at birth of first child, by gender. (From Schaie, K. W., 1995. *Intellectual development in adulthood: The Seattle Longitudinal Study* (p. 157). New York: Cambridge University Press.)

and the adoption of more favorable lifestyles in successive birth cohorts may also be implicated. A similar positive, although less steep, difference pattern occurred for Spatial Orientation. By contrast, Numeric Ability seems to have peaked in the 1920s and has declined somewhat since then. It seems that the same changes in educational practices that have been favorable for Inductive Reasoning have led to some loss in number manipulation skills as well. The decline in Numeric Ability across recent cohorts explains the fact that current cross-sectional studies suggest relatively little decline in Numeric Ability even though substantial decline has been found in longitudinal data. Both Perceptual Speed and Verbal Ability improved somewhat during the earlier part of this century, but have shown modest decline in the baby boom generation. Generational differences of a magnitude similar to the Inductive Reasoning factor have also been observed for a measure of practical intelligence involving common everyday tasks.

Comparisons from family studies of biologically related individuals involving parents and their adult offspring have yielded similar findings on generational differences in cognitive abilities. Figure 2 shows findings on tests of five primary mental abilities for the difference between parents and their adult offspring. The bars show the absolute mean difference in this large set of families. The hatched part of the bar represents an adjustment for the expected age difference between the older parents and their young-adult or middle-aged children. The solid part is the net difference. If there were no differences between generations the solid bar would be zero. As can be seen, there are significant differences favoring the younger (offspring) generation on Inductive Reasoning, Spatial Orientation, and Verbal Ability. On Number ability, it is again the older generation that is at an advantage, although there is little difference on Word Fluency.

B. Generational Differences in Selective Demographic Characteristics

Gerontologists have long been aware that some of the age difference findings reported in the literature are

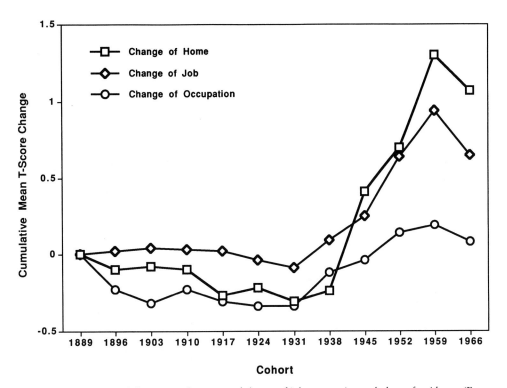

Figure 5 Generational differences in frequency of change of job, occupation and place of residence. (From: Schaie, K. W., 1995. *Intellectual development in adulthood: The Seattle Longitudinal Study* (p. 162). New York: Cambridge University Press.)

clouded by the noncomparability of a variety of demographic characteristics between the young and the old. Often these differences have been interpreted as inevitable products of the aging process, and investigators have failed to correct for them. In studies with my colleagues, we have been able to show that a number of these demographic differences actually have little to do with the aging process but rather must be attributed to generational differences. As examples of substantial generational differences in demographic characteristics I would mention educational level, age at first marriage, and age at birth of first child.

Over the range of birth cohorts represented in the SLS (1889–1966) there has been a steady increase in years of education, amounting to a difference in education of about 5 years between the earliest and latest cohorts studied. As shown in Figure 3, the increase has been approximately 1 year greater for men than for women. Age at first marriage declined by approximately 4 years from the earliest cohort to

those born in the 1930s (the lowest level was reached by men for those born in 1931 and by women for those born in 1938). From then on there has been a steady rise, which is most pronounced for women. As for the age of individuals when their first child was born, there has been a steady increment that leveled off for males for those born in 1952 but has continued to rise for women. On average, parental age at birth of the first child occurs approximately 5 years later for the most recently born than for the earliest cohort. The cumulated generational difference gradients for latter two variables are shown separately by gender in Figure 4.

Other demographic characteristics that may be important in aging studies include measures of mobility (changes in the location of one's home, changes of job, and changes in occupation). Figure 5 shows average changes in the 5 years preceding each reporting date. Note that there is some very modest drop in residential and job mobility from the oldest cohort to that born in 1938; over the same cohort range there are virtually

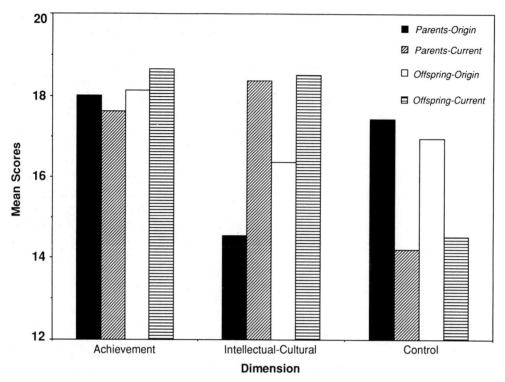

Figure 6 Interaction of perceived family environment by generation and life stage. (From Schaie, K. W., & Willis, S. L., 1995. Perceived family environments across generations. In V. L. Bengtson, K. W. Schaie, & L. Burton (Eds.). *Adult intergenerational relations: Effects of societal change.* New York: Springer.)

no cohort differences in occupational mobility. But, mobility characteristics increase sharply for the baby boomer cohorts for all three measures, residential and job mobility changes showing the most pronounced generational differences.

C. Generational Differences in Perceptions of Family Environments

A final set of findings of generational differences in geropsychology comes from the assessment of perceptions of family environments by older parents and their adult children within their current families and their families of origins (the families in which they were raised). Although one must always be careful in accepting the veracity of subjective data, particularly when it is retrospective in nature, there is substantial evidence of the utility of perceptions of behavioral dimensions.

In addition to comparing such perceptions across

biologically related generations for large populations, it is also instructive to look at shifts in these relationships for successive birth cohorts, similar to those considered above for cognitive and demographic variables. For example, the question may be asked whether there are differences among parent–offspring pairs when offspring are classified into those born prior to World War II, those born during the war years and immediately thereafter, and those who belong to the baby boomer cohorts.

The relevant data inform us that there is a clear differentiation for parents and offspring in the perceived level of all family dimensions between their family of origin and their current families. Obviously the retrospective distance in time is greater for the parents than for the adult offspring. Nevertheless, shifts in the quality of family environments are reported consistently over persons' own life course. The current families are seen as more cohesive and expressive but also characterized by more conflict than was reported for the families of origin. There seems to be a shift towards greater openness and engagement in family interactions. More intensive family interactions are also reflected by intellectual-cultural and active-recreational orientation from the family of origin to the current family. Along with these shifts there is the overall perception of lower levels of perceived control, family organization, and achievement orientation (see Fig. 6). Perhaps these judgments are another way of describing the increasing complexity of modern American families. Combined with continuing reports of ever lower reported levels of social responsibility, this may well mean that the perceived role of the American family is changing from that of a primary socialization agent (operating on behalf of the larger society) to a more effective support system for the needs of the individual family member.

When the two-generation parent–offspring sample is broken down into four distinct cohort groups, it appears that the shifts in perceived family level occurred primarily for perceptions of the family of origin. Perceptions of the current family is much more similar across birth cohorts. This is reasonable because judgments of the current family reflect the current societal climate common to most, whereas perceptions of the family of origin reflect different secular periods for which successive cohorts described their early family experiences.

Substantial correlations between parents' description of their current family environment and their offspring's description of their family of origin provide supporting evidence for the continuity of family values and behaviors. Even though there is a substan-

tial time gap in the period rated, these two ratings do refer to the same parental family unit. This similarity of perceptions across generations was particularly strong for three dimensions most closely reflective of value orientations (achievement, intellectual-cultural, and active-recreational) and for family organization.

It is interesting to note that the magnitude of perceived similarity across generations will differ by gender pairing and by specific family environment dimensions. It is not surprising that the strongest similarity of family environment perceptions occurs within mother–daughter pairings, even though frequency of contact between adult mothers and daughters is only slightly greater than that for other relationship combinations. In fact, the intensity (frequency) of contact between parents and offspring seems to have virtually no impact upon the similarity of reported family environments.

BIBLIOGRAPHY

Bengtson, V. L., Schaie, K. W., & Burton, L. M. (Eds.). (1995). *Adult intergenerational relations: Effects of societal change.* New York: Springer.

Riley, M. W., Johnson, M. J., & Foner, A. (1972). *Aging and society: Vol. 3. A sociology of age stratification.* New York: Sage.

Schaie, K. W. (1994). Developmental designs revisited. In S. H. Cohen & H. W. Reese (Eds.), *Life-span developmental psychology: Theoretical issues revisited.* Hillsdale, NJ: Erlbaum.

Schaie, K. W. (1995). *Intellectual development in adulthood: The Seattle Longitudinal Study.* New York: Cambridge University Press.

Genetics

Thomas E. Johnson, Gordon J. Lithgow, Shin Murakami, and David R. Shook

University of Colorado at Boulder

Allele   One of many particular forms of a gene.

Cellular Senescence   The limited proliferative potential of human somatic cells and of cells of many other species that limits the number of replicative divisions that a cell can undergo; also called replicative senescence.

Gene   The basic unit of inheritance; typically refers to the coding sequence and control regions for a single protein or to a DNA region controlling synthesis of a particular gene product.

Genotype   The entire set of genes and alleles of those genes carried by an individual organism.

Gerontogene   A gene involved in aging; usually refers to genes whose normal function involves a shortening of life.

Heritability   Refers to the fraction of the variability in a phenotype in a population that results from genetic effects rather than from environment or chance.

Longevity Assurance Gene   A gene that normally functions to extend life.

Mutant   An organism carrying a mutation, usually one causing an easily observed change in phenotype.

Mutation   An alteration in the DNA leading to a new allele; typically leads to some observable difference in phenotype.

Phenotype   The visible characteristics of an organism, its appearance.

Segmental Progeroid Diseases   Diseases that mimic aging in that they accelerate some, but not all, physiological processes normally associated with aging.

GENETICS is both a discipline and a research tool. Genetics as a research tool has allowed the identification and reading of the common thread uniting all life on earth, the DNA molecule. Genetics as a discipline has united the biological and biomedical sciences by providing a common framework and tool kit for exploring the multiple processes of life and by providing a common terminology that allows researchers in numerous disparate fields to share information through the identification of genes and the interpretation of their DNA sequence. All of these meanings of the term genetics come into play in this review. Genetics refers to the underlying genetic elements making up living species as well as to the discipline that analyzes these processes. The current state of knowledge of the genetics of aging in humans will first be reviewed. Next studies in model systems that are beginning to reveal the underlying processes associated with aging will be described; much of this work has relied on life span as an end point in the assessment of aging. Finally, we will review the current state of affairs concerning molecular genetic analyses of aging.

I. GENETIC STUDIES IN HUMANS

Genetic studies of aging in humans have proceeded through several distinct routes. First has been the study of an in vitro model of aging: the limited number of cell divisions observed in most, if not all, nontransformed cells in culture, which we will call *cellular senescence.* Second has been the study of rare diseases that have been termed *segmental progeroid diseases* to suggest that in each of these diseases many, but not all, aspects of aging have been accelerated. Examples of these include Hutchinson-Gilford disease and Werner's syndrome. Third, both pedigree analysis and population studies have begun; this work may ultimately reveal genes or, at least chromosomal regions, that are associated with various human diseases and with alterations in length of life. Finally, twin studies and other designs have recently been used to begin to determine what proportion of the variation in age-related function or age at death is genetically determined.

A. Cellular Senescence

Some 35 years ago it was recognized that human cells could not go on dividing forever in tissue culture. This revolutionary observation, cellular senescence, countered classical observations by giants in the field. The acceptance of this fact was quickly followed by the suggestion that the finite proliferative capacity of tissue culture cells might be a model for, or even the basis of, normal human aging. The 1970s saw careful characterization of the aging phenotype of these cells and the finding that the proliferative capacity of these cells declines in parallel with the age of the donor. This fact together with the observations that cell lines derived from certain "segmental progeroid diseases" have a more limited proliferative potential and that proliferative potential correlates with maximum life span potential of a species, have led many to accept that cellular senescence is a valid model of human aging. More recent evidence seems to suggest that cellular senescence may well be cellular differentiation; many similarities between cellular senescence, as studied in the fibroblast, and muscle cell differentiation can be made. Although the dispute cannot be resolved at this time, it seems likely that cellular senescence is a model for terminal differentiation and has relevance to some in vivo cellular aging phenomena.

The analysis of human tissue culture cells is much easier than is the study of intact organisms, and the study of these cells has allowed significant advances in our understanding of cellular processes. The genes responsible for cellular senescence are being identified, and their role in limiting the proliferative capacity of these cells is being elucidated. A surprising result of genetic studies is that in immortalized cell lines, the immortal phenotype is recessive; (i.e., a lack of some essential protein is probably responsible for immortalization rather than the converse). Immortalization seems to result from mutation of any one of four complementation groups; three of these groups have been localized to individual chromosomes. Two recent developments serve to illustrate these points. A gene, variously termed *SDI1*, *WAF1*, or *CIP1*, has been cloned that seems to be one of the players causing cellular senescence. It has been proposed that p21, the protein product of this gene, is involved in regulating the cell cycle by inhibiting cyclin-dependent kinases, thus serving as a checkpoint regulating entry into the S phase of the cell cycle. A second process has also been tentatively identified as a determinant of cellular senescence: the limited proliferative capacity of the telomeres (chromosome ends). Somatic cells lack telomerase—an enzyme that has an RNA cofactor and is used to get around the potentially deadly problem that the 5' ends of the chromosome cannot be replicated without priming—an absolute requirement of DNA polymerase. The telomere model then states that, in the absence of telomerase, telomeres continue to shorten until chromosome instability and other problems occur. Most, perhaps all, human tumors have reactivated the telomerase allowing indefinite replication. It could be that the absence of telomerase in normal somatic cells is an additional assurance preventing oncogenesis and tumor formation. In any case, these findings have major therapeutic implications and have served as an important focus for current research into cellular senescence. [See GROWTH FACTORS AND CELLULAR SENESCENCE.]

B. Segmental Progeroid Mutations

Several human genetic syndromes that accelerate some, but not all, aspects of aging have been described. None of the many syndromes described accelerates all aspects of aging, and thus these are sometimes collectively termed *segmental progeroid* syndromes. Generally, mutations are deleterious because they eliminate or modify functional DNA sequences leading to an alteration at the protein level; thus, it is expected that mutations should shorten the life span. Hutchinson-Gilford and Werner's syndrome are two diseases commonly called *progeria*, but Down's syndrome (Trisomy 21) accelerates more of the various aspects of normal aging. Werner's syndrome, a recessive, adult-onset progeroid disease has been shown to be associated with extensive genomic deletions of 20 kb and greater. Werner's has been mapped to chromosome 8 and cloning of the gene is imminent. Another progeroid syndrome that has received much attention in the popular press is Hutchinson-Gilford disease, also called progeria because it is manifested as rapid aging in children who carry this autosomal dominant disease. It remains in doubt whether these progeroid diseases reflect the normal aging process or only "mimic" it.

C. Markers Associated with Longevity

In an effort to find human gerontogenes, a number of marker association studies have been undertaken. In these studies longevity is shown to be associated with certain alleles and genes within small regions of the human genome by characterizing genetic markers at certain candidate loci. The *HLA* locus has long been a candidate for determining human longevity and at least two studies have suggested that certain *HLA* haplotypes may be associated with increased longevity in at least some populations; the validity of these marker associations at the *HLA* locus remain to be proven. *ACE* and *APOE* have been tested as candidates and both have been found to be associated, although not consistently in the direction predicted. These findings may not be too surprising because of the strong associations between the alleles studied and their effects on health. For example, *APOE-ε4* has recently been associated with frequency of onset and rate of progression of Alzheimer's disease (AD), and certain alleles of the *HLA* locus have long been associated with susceptibility to or more rapid progress of various human diseases. [*See* MARKERS OF AGING.]

D. Diseases Associated with Aging

I. Huntington's Disease

A large number of genetic diseases show age-dependent levels of expression and/or penetrance. These include two diseases that are expressed especially late in life: Huntington's disease (HD) and AD. HD is a disease leading to degeneration of the nervous system. The average age of onset is 35–42 years, and the gene segregates as an autosomal dominant. Despite the fact that HD was the first human gene to be mapped using

restriction fragment-length polymorphism (RFLP) mapping (chromosome 4), it was only cloned in 1993. That cloning was based on the supposition that the phenomenon of "anticipation" (seen in HD as an ever-earlier age of onset in succeeding generations) might result from the expansion of a trinucleotide repeat sequence similar to those that have been implicated in a number of other human neurological diseases. An expanded $(CAG)_n$ longer than the normal range was found in all disease families examined suggesting that this was the HD gene. The coding sequence makes a predicted 348-kD protein of unknown function that shows no homology to any other cloned gene.

2. Alzheimer's Disease

The best example, and certainly the best studied, age-related genetic disease in humans is AD. About 2–6% of people over 65 show symptoms of AD; the prevalence of this disease increases strikingly with age, such that by 85 as many as 40% of the population may show symptoms of AD. Pedigree analysis has allowed the localization of three distinct genes that are involved in the specification of familial AD (FAD). Rare mutations in the gene encoding the precursor protein of Alzheimer-associated amyloid on chromosome 21 are associated with FAD, but these account for only 2–3% of the affected individuals. Genes on 14 and 19 are susceptibility loci associated with late-onset (after age 65) and early-onset forms of the disease, respectively. There are still other pedigrees in which the susceptibility to FAD is unlinked to these three loci, which suggests that there are still other loci to be found. Thus FAD is clearly very heterogeneous in origin. A further complication is that the degree to which FAD is genetic is uncertain, with estimates ranging from 10–100%. A marked association with the *APOE* locus on chromosome 14 has been shown and replicated in many studies, such that individuals homozygous for *APOE-ε4* have an almost eightfold increase in the probability of getting AD at almost any age when compared with people carrying other alleles of *APOE*. [*See* DEMENTIA.]

E. Heritability of Aging and Life Span

From analysis of parent–offspring correlations in life span and differential life spans of identical and fraternal twins, estimates of the fraction of the variation in life span that is under genetic control (the heritability) can be made. Human heritability studies suggest modest amounts of inheritance of longevity, perhaps on the order of 10–30%. Longitudinal studies of various traits suggest that the heritable proportion may change with age in rather surprising ways; unfortunately, little of this material has been published. Another recent area of inquiry is into the genetics of demography. Clearly genetic variation within and between populations plays a major role in affecting demographic predictions of survival.

II. MODEL SYSTEMS

Genetic studies of aging and age-associated effects can be most effectively carried out in species other than humans. The most popular model systems have been mice; however, the long life span and high expenses of maintaining rodents have led a number of investigators to study invertebrate models including *Drosophila melanogaster* (a fruit fly), *Caenorhabditis elegans* (a nematode), and several fungi including *Neurospora crassa, Podospora anserina,* and *Saccharomyces cerevisiae.* Advantages of invertebrates include lower expenses, a life span of weeks or months (instead of years), and much more powerful methods for genetic analysis, including selective breeding and the identification of mutants that have altered aging processes. Because many genetic alterations can shorten life span, most genetic studies have involved the study of longer-lived strains. Only in invertebrates have mutations that lengthen life span been found.

Early studies largely focused on proving that genes play a role in determining longevity or rate of aging and on quantitative estimates of this genetic component through estimations of heritability. Genetic studies have used one of three different approaches (polygenic analyses, identification of mutants, and construction of transgenics). Each approach is based on a different level of background knowledge, the different fields of training of the investigators, and the desired level of understanding. The most powerful approach for understanding biological processes—the identification of mutants and the subsequent cloning and molecular dissection of the underlying molecular mechanisms responsible for the phenotypic alterations—have only been pursued in a few species, and only in *C. elegans* has the approach really been

pursued in any depth. In the last 10 years a number of studies have begun to yield useful information. A molecular understanding of the basis of extended longevity is beginning. [*See* MODELS OF AGING: INVERTEBRATES, FILAMENTOUS FUNGI, AND YEASTS; MODELS OF AGING: VERTEBRATES.]

A. Polygenic Approaches

Many different alleles for many genes can be found in natural populations. Several approaches have taken advantage of this variation: selective breeding, the analysis of recombinant inbred progeny, and the construction of stocks in which single chromosomes from wild populations have been introgressed into a standard stock. These studies are invariably polygenic in that many genes (sometimes hundreds) can contribute to the differences in phenotype, including differences in life span and other life history traits. Such studies have shown significant genetic components for longevity in mice, in fruit flies, and in the nematode. Typical heritability estimates are in the range of 15–30%. These studies also clearly demonstrate that many genes affect this variation in life span.

I. Mice

Smith and Walford observed that strains congenic for the *H-2* locus (part of the mouse major histocompatibility complex [MHC]) showed significant differences in longevity and that certain *H-2* alleles were associated with increased longevity. These strains were also associated with altered levels of phytohemagglutinin response, DNA repair, free radical scavenging enzymes, and cAMP levels. Affects of the *H-2* locus on age of onset of reproductive cyclicity have also been shown. Frequency of cycle time and age of loss of reproductive potential have also been related to *H-2* genotype. Several other genetic studies have shown that the *H-2* locus or genes near to this locus do have an effect on life span, although the effect of this region may be no more than many other regions of the genome. In crosses between C57/DBA F_1 mice and their DBA parents, the largest single-locus effect on average life span was associated with the *B* coat color gene rather than with the *H-2* locus, but if one looked at 90th percentile of survival, the *H-2* locus showed the largest effect. Moreover, there was a small but significant effect of *H-2* heterozygosity, with hybrid strains being slightly longer lived. This study shows that many regions of the genome contain genes with alleles that affect life span and that *H-2* is not unique.

Life spans of 20 BXD (C57BL/6J X DBA/2J) recombinant-inbred strains were determined in an effort to identify the genes (quantitative trait loci—QTLs) that affect length of life. The mean life span of most of these strains were very similar with a few extremes (mean life spans of 479 days vs. 904 days). In a simple regression analysis, 43% of the loci had effects on life span. After more appropriate statistical analyses, there were six genetic regions that were significantly associated with length of survival; the *H-2* region on chromosome 17 was not one of them. Again the MHC region was not detected as having major importance in determining length of life.

Lines of mice have been bred for high or low immune responsiveness. These high and low antibody responder lines have mean life spans that are positively correlated with response to antigen ($r = 0.97$). Further quantitative analysis suggested that high responsiveness is almost dominant over low and that the mode of inheritance is polygenic with 3–7 independent loci being involved in the response. A major problem with these selective breeding studies is that the low line had a mean life span of only 346 days, significantly less than the typical inbred line. Thus, much of the selective response is in the direction of shorter life span, as expected for mice that have a reduced immune response. Therefore, the alleles selected in this study are likely to be ones specifying lower immunity and consequently a reduced life span. Additional confirmatory selective breeding has recently been undertaken to test these earlier findings, but results of these new studies are not yet available.

Another approach to the genetics of aging has been through the study of senescence-accelerated mice (SAM). These mice were identified as spontaneous isolates in a mouse colony in Kyoto and their exact origin is unknown, but they probably resulted from the mating of two or more distinct strains. These mice have shorter than normal life spans and many aspects of the aging processes have been accelerated. They represent a progeroid model of mouse senescence and are being more widely studied despite the lack of knowledge surrounding their origin. Because certain aspects of senescence seem to be differentially accelerated in one or more SAM strains, they may represent

a useful resource, but it remains to be proven that the senescence acceleration reflects normal aging rather than merely mimicing certain aspects of the normal aging processes that have been elicited as a result of one or more mutant alleles in a SAM strain.

2. Drosophila

Despite the failure of selection directly for extended life in fruit flies (*Drosophila melanogaster*), several groups have successfully selected for extended mean and maximum life span by selecting for late age of reproduction. These selections have been performed in outbred populations of fruit flies that had been captured and kept in the laboratory for some time. These selections resulted in an almost twofold increase in longevity and significant increases in late-life reproduction. The increased late fertility was associated with decreased early fertility. Quite surprising is the fact that this increase in life span is not seen in all environments and is dependent on larval density. Under low larval density no differences between selected and control strains were observed. This dependence on growth conditions may explain the earlier negative reports for selection for longer life and also points to the extreme care that must be used in performing selections or other quantitative genetic analyses on life span and probably on other life history traits as well. These environmental effects could also point to important physiological and environmental interactions that could be exploited to determine the molecular basis of this differential longevity.

Longer life is also associated with reduced ovary weight early in life and increased resistance to starvation, desiccation, and other environmental stresses. Indeed, selection for increased desiccation resistance yields longer-lived lines. These responses result from the action of many (even hundreds) of genes or QTLs. Attempts to dissect the process further have revealed regions of the genome that may be especially rich in QTLs, but further dissection has met with little success, perhaps because so many QTLs are involved. Generally, the results are consistent with a trade-off between early fertility and extended life span as might be predicted by the evolutionary theory of aging. However, these are not critical tests of the theory because so many genes are being selected for simultaneously and thus the trade-off may not be at the level of the individual gene. Moreover, it is bothersome that numerous failures to confirm the theory have been discounted by the proponents of this theory. There has been no clear demonstration in *Drosophila* of the pleiotropic action of a single gene on both life span and some other life history trait, such as development or fertility. Moreover, classical studies by Maynard Smith, although frequently cited as showing such pleiotropy, have not been adequately replicated by modern laboratories studying these processes.

The long-lived strains were also resistant to a variety of environmental stresses including free radicals. Indeed at least two different groups have suggested that the physiological basis of the extended life is increased resistance to reactive oxygen species. A variety of other specific physiological alterations have been implicated in these long-lived strains, but none of these alternative models have been critically tested in these selected lines. At least one attempt to critically test the involvement of superoxide dimustase (SOD) in extended life resulted in a failure to detect a significant effect, but this finding was dismissed post hoc because this locus represented only one of hundreds of genes that were segregating in the population. This apparent lack of ability to refute this model suggests that selective breeding for increased life span in *Drosophila* is not likely to yield additional relevant insights into the molecular and physiological basis of life extension; for that other approaches are needed, as described next.

3. Nematodes

Although several species of nematode have been used to study aging, *Caenorhabditis elegans*, a small, free-living soil nematode that was initially chosen by Sydney Brenner to study development and behavior, has proven to be the nematode of choice for all recent studies because of its excellent genetics. Several thousand genes have now been cloned in *C. elegans*, and most of the genome is readily available as an ordered overlapping collection of cosmids and yeast artificial chromosomes (YACs), which greatly facilitates cloning strategies. Procedures for transforming *C. elegans* have been worked out. Hermaphrodites (XX) reproduce by self-fertilization whereas males (XO) occur only rarely but are useful in stock construction. Each hermaphrodite produces about 250 to 300 offspring during her 5-day reproductive period at 20°C. The average life span for an unmated wild-type *C. elegans* hermaphrodite is approximately 3 weeks, which

makes this an attractive model system. All somatic tissue in the adult is post-mitotic.

Because *C. elegans* is an inbreeding species, another approach has been used to identify QTLs that specify longer than normal life spans. Several studies have used recombinant inbred strains, which can be generated very easily due to the self-fertilizing mode of reproduction of *C. elegans*, to ask questions about heritability, genetic trade-offs, and number of genes involved in the specification of life span. Reasonable heritability estimates of 15–30% have been reported; estimates suggest that approximately seven QTLs are involved in determining life span. Some trade-offs between early and late fertility have been identified, but no trade-offs between fertility and life span or rate of development and life span have been found, although more detailed studies are underway.

Two studies have examined crosses between two wild-type strains (N2 and Bergerac) and identified QTLs that are responsible for increased life span. Both studies localized these genes to various chromosomal regions using the Tc1 transposable element to determine map position and strain of origin; polymerase chain reaction (PCR) strategies have been developed that use Tc1 as a molecular marker that can be assayed in individual worms and used to position QTLs. One approach was to examine populations of worms that were segregating these markers and then to see which markers were selectively enriched in older worms, which would indicate that a QTL of interest was nearby. This study found evidence for genes on chromosomes 2, 4, and the X that may be involved in prolonging life and that a number of loci may be selected against in such populations. Nonetheless, this study was not designed in a way that trade-offs between life history traits could be detected. The other study used recombinant-inbred strains and found that QTLs for life span were found on chromosomes 2, 4, and the X and QTLs for fertility on chromosomes 2, 3, and 4. In neither study was there any evidence for the trade-offs between fertility and life span that might be expected from evolutionary theories of aging.

B. Mutants

Mutational analysis represents the most effective means of identifying genes involved in a biological process. Unfortunately, mutational approaches are

Table I Genes Shown to Be Involved in Prolongation of Life

Gene name	Species	Effect of mutation
LAG-1	S. cerevisiae	Overexpression: increased number cell divisions; other mutations: complex effects
LAG-2	S. cerevisiae	Null mutant: decreased number cell divisions; overexpression: increased number cell divisions
SIR-4	S. cerevisiae	Semidominant mutation increase of 50% in cell divisions: altered telomere silencing?
age-1, etc.	N. crassa	Up to 10X increase in conidial longevity
i	P. anserina	Double mutant i viv shows indefinite growth.
gr	P. anserina	Double mutant gr viv shows indefinite growth.
viv	P. anserina	Double mutant i viv or gr viv shows indefinite growth.
age-1	C. elegans	65% increase of mean life span; little effect of fertility; increased resistance to many stresses
spe-26	C. elegans	65% increase of mean life span; > 90% reduction in fertility
daf-2	C. elegans	Twofold increase of mean life span (shift to 20°C); dauer constitutive (25°C)
daf-12	C. elegans	No effect alone; double mutants with daf-2 increases mean life span fourfold (20°C); dauer-constitutive (25°C).
daf-16	C. elegans	Blocks action of daf-2, age-1, and spe-26
clk-1	C. elegans	Extends timing of development, some neurological events, and life span

difficult to apply to aging because of the difficulty of identifying mutant strains with altered aging processes or longer life span. A list of genes that when mutated affect length of life is given in Table I. In fungi several mutations that affect life span have been identified. A series of mutations affect conidial viability in the fungus *Neurosopora crassa* leading to huge extensions of "shelf-life" in these mutants. Clonal viability is affected by mutations in a series of genes in *Podospora anserina*, where either *i viv* or *gr viv* double mutants show indefinite ability to grow. Recently, cellular senescence in the yeast *Saccharomyces cerevisiae* has been used as a model for aging, and mutations in two genes that are differentially expressed over the replicative life span (*LAG-1* or *LAG-2*) can prolong the number of cell divisions. Also mutations in four genes have been found to lengthen the replicative life span of yeast; one of these is *SIR-4*, which plays a role in chromosome silencing.

Although a few studies have been carried out in *Drosophila*, all of the interesting work has been performed in the nematode *C. elegans*. The self-fertilizing nature of this species and the lack of inbreeding depression coupled with the existence of the dauer (an alternative larval stage that can remain immature for months and then resume development to a normal adult with a normal life span) make this species especially attractive for such studies. Screens for long-

lived mutants were carried out some 15 years ago using a replica-plating strategy. These screens produced several long-lived strains, but only one of them could be studied subsequently; all mutations were in the first gene thus identified, which was named *age-1*.

age-1(hx546), the mutant allele most studied, averages a 65% increase in mean life span (25.3 days vs. 15.0 days) and a 110% increase in maximum life span (46.2 days vs. 22.0 days) at 25°C. Long-lived (Age) mutant strains have no change in rate of development, in behavior, or in other life processes and only modest decreases in fertility, if any at all. Some of the most exciting work in *C. elegans* involves the cloning of genes whose protein products are unknown, a process known as "positional cloning," and a great deal of effort has so far failed to reveal a clone for *age-1*, largely because of the difficulty associated with the positional cloning of genes affecting length of life.

There are four other published reports of mutations in *C. elegans* that result in longer life: (a) Mutations in *spe-26* dramatically reduce sperm formation and result in life extensions of about 80% for the hermaphrodite and the mated male. (b) *daf-2* mutants cause dauer formation under temperature-sensitive conditions in which dauers are not usually seen and result in a more than twofold extension of mean life span at the permissive temperature; this extension is blocked by the action of *daf-16*. *daf-2* mutations also affect other life history traits marginally in that reproduction can go on at very low levels for weeks. (c) *rad-8* mutant worms exhibit almost 50% longer mean life span than wild type at 16°C and normal oxygen tension. (d) *clk-1* is a mutation that lengthens life 20–50%, depending on the allele, and also affects many other "timing events" including the length of embryonic and larval development, fertility, and the rate of egg production and behavioral timers such as rate of pumping, food ingestion, and defecation. Recently published reports suggest that several other dauer-constitutive mutants also affect length of life. *daf-23* doubles the length of the normal adult life span, and *daf-12* mutants interact with *daf-2* to cause an enhancement of the life-prolongation phenotype to an almost fourfold increase in mean life span. The dominant, dauer-constitutive mutant, *daf-28*, can also prolong life slightly. Other dauer-formation mutants define a signal-transduction pathway in which homologs to mammalian genes involved in signal transduction can be identified, although the roles of the genes defined above remain unclear. *daf-1* codes for a translational product that has homology to a serine–threonine kinase in the *raf* superfamily and which may be a cell-surface receptor. *daf-4* is the nematode homolog of human bone morphogenetic protein (BMP) receptor with the *daf-7* gene encoding BMP. Finally, *daf-12* encodes a transcription factor of the steroid–thyroid hormone receptor superfamily. Note that none of the cloned genes results in life extension.

Our lab has discovered that most, if not all, long-lived mutants of the nematode are more resistant to many environmental stresses. The bases for this statement are twofold. First, four of the long-lived mutants (*age-1*, *daf-2*, *daf-28*, and *spe-26*) are more resistant to two distinct stressors (thermal stress and UV irradiation). Only *age-1* has been shown to be resistant to reactive oxygen species; the *clk-1* mutation has not been tested for any stressors. Second, induction of thermotolerance via nonlethal heat stress results in a longer life span. *age-1* mutants have higher levels of Cu-Zn SOD and catalase at later ages. *age-1* mutants also respond to thermal stress by expressing heat shock protein 16 (*HSP-16*), an α crystallin homolog, at higher levels than does the wild type. Thus, the *age-1* mutation may be uncovering a common genetic pathway that is involved in the mediation of stress response from a variety of environmental stresses.

C. Transgenics

The ultimate demonstration that a particular process is affected by a particular gene is to show that altering a single gene affects that particular process. The best way to demonstrate this causality is to alter a particular gene and to demonstrate that this affects the phenotype of interest, for instance, life span. Exactly this approach is used in the analysis of transgenic animals (mice, yeast, fruit flies, and nematodes) to demonstrate an effect on aging as a result of alterations in one or a few genes. This approach is just beginning to be applied to a variety of systems to test specific genes for their effects on life span and/or rate of aging.

The best example of the use of transgenics is in *Drosophila*, where transgenic strains that overexpress both Cu-Zn SOD and catalase by 20–50% have been constructed. These transgenic strains had longer life spans and lower rates of mortality than did the wild type. There was also a decrease in the rate of accumulation of oxidized protein and a delay in loss of physical performance. It should be noted that transgenics for both SOD and catalase had life extensions that were much better than the sum of the two single transgenic strains alone. This might be suggested by the involvement of catalase in detoxifying the hydrogen peroxide radical produced by Cu-Zn SOD.

Transgenic strains of *C. elegans* have been produced in an attempt to clone the *age-1* gene by complementation with a normal exogenous gene, but the cloning is still underway. Several transgenic strains of mice have been examined for their effects on aging and life span. Mouse transgenic strains that express the Aβ peptide in neurons show increased neurotoxicity and reduced life spans and probably show an elevation in the level of apoptotic cell death. Mouse strains carrying extra copies of Cu-Zn SOD have shorter life spans and display some of the toxic effects normally associated with Down's syndrome. Other mouse transgenic strains are currently being tested to see what effects loss of different genes might have on life extension and other age-related processes.

III. MOLECULAR STUDIES OF GENES AND GENE ACTION

A. DNA Repair and Somatic Mutation

Almost 50 years ago the suggestion was made that mutations in somatic cells could cause aging. The theory has been extensively tested in several invertebrate metazoans and thoroughly disproved in those short-lived insects. It is unclear whether somatic mutation is a general cause of aging or senescence in most mammalian species, although DNA rearrangements have been implicated in many processes during mammalian aging. Three areas of study continue to be actively pursued as possible causes of aging and senescence in mammals: deletion and rearrangements of the mitochondrial DNA, telomere shortening, and somatic mutation as a cause of cancer.

Convincing evidence has been obtained showing that disruption of the mitochondrial genome specifies senescence in a variety of fungal species. In metazoans there is much less direct evidence for a role of these deletions in causing aging and senescence. Mitochondrial DNA deletions have been found in humans, other mammals, and other higher eukaryotes but at low frequencies, prompting proponents of the theory to suggest that the already characterized deletions represent only "the tip of the iceberg." The prevalence of several well-characterized deletions in older people is unclear and is the subject of active investigation by many groups. Deletions of various portions of the mitochondrial genome have been implicated in a variety of human diseases, but there is no direct support for a causal role for mitochondrial deletions in mammalian senescence.

It is clear that chromosomal rearrangements increase dramatically with increasing age, and several human diseases that cause chromosomal instability have some of the attributes that one might expect for an "accelerated aging" syndrome. For example, Werner's, an adult-onset progeria syndrome, results in a large increase in the frequency of chromosomal aberrations in vivo. Cell cultures from Werner's patients have 10 to 500-fold elevations in the rate of new mutations. Much of the age dependence of cancer has been attributed to new mutations and ionizing radiation both in vitro, and in studies with Hiroshima survivors it has been shown to cause elevated levels of malignant transformation. There is also an age-related increase in mutation frequency in human lymphocytes. Unfortunately the relationship for other age-related diseases (dementia, arthritis, osteoporosis, etc.) are not so simple, and there is little evidence for the involvement of mutations in these processes.

Telomeres (the ends of chromosomes) have particular problems during DNA replication that led to the hypothesis that telomere loss could cause the finite replicative life span of fibroblast cultures. Telomere loss does appear to be causally linked to cellular senescence in mammals, and telomerase (the enzyme that replicates telomeres) seems to be reactivated in most or all immortal cells. On the other hand, there is no direct support for a causal role for telomere loss in causing aging or senescence in mammals.

B. Regulation of Gene Action

Altered gene expression has been put forth as a central mechanism for causing aging and senescence for many years. Even evolutionary models for senescence, which are notoriously free of specific mechanistic predictions, suggest that altered regulation of gene expression might be seen in aged animals. Aging is not development, however. Unlike the situation in development where many genes are being up and down regulated at a variety of different stages in gene expression, aged organisms express almost the same complement of proteins as do young animals. A variety of attempts to find altered patterns of expression at the protein level have resulted in only few or no detectable alterations. At the RNA level some genes are modulated but few are turned on or off completely. However, again, unlike development, there seems to be no large-scale alteration in transcription that is coordinately regulated by the synthesis of new batteries of transcriptional regulatory proteins.

Several systems, including senescent tissue culture cells, tissues, or hepatocytes from aged rats, and invertebrate species (fruit flies and nematodes) are deficient in the synthesis of HSPs after a variety of inductive events. In rat hepatocytes this defect has been traced to altered heat shock factor that is needed to induce transcription from the hsp genes. An exciting hypothesis is that the longer life span of age-1, daf-2, and perhaps other longevity mutants in C. elegans results from an up regulation of genes that respond to a variety of environmental stresses. There are published reports of increased resistance to both oxidative stress and thermal stress, and unpublished work from our lab shows that all of the mutants so far identified as being gerontogenes may extend life by up regulating a variety of different pathways, including resistance to UV irradiation.

By far the most complete understanding for the role of gene regulation in specifying aging and senescence comes from studies on tissue culture cells and may not be a model of aging so much as somatic differentiation. Several genes that are necessary for normal cell cycling are not expressed in senescent tissue culture cells. Several of these genes are regulated at the transcriptional level and are not turned on because of a lack of the E2F transcription factor. Senescent cells also differentially express cyclins and cyclin-dependent protein kinases and overexpress several growth inhibitors. The primary regulator of cell senescence still remains to be identified. [See DNA AND GENE EXPRESSION.]

IV. THE GENETIC FRONTIER IN AGING STUDIES

Effective research strategies are underway, which will allow the identification of key genes and regulatory elements causing aging and senescence or limiting the normal life span. Several key systems, but especially senescent fibroblasts and nematodes, have allowed the identification of crucial genes and processes that limit the normal life span. We can look forward to more and more targeted experiments in mice and clinical experiments in humans that will test our understanding while developing pharmacological interventions into one or more aspects of the aging process. Genetic manipulations and technologies will play a crucial role in the coming era.

BIBLIOGRAPHY

Campisi, J., Dimri, G., & Hara, E. (1996). Control of replicative senescence. In E. L. Schneider & J. W. Rowe (Eds.), *Handbook of the biology of aging*, (4th ed.). San Diego: Academic Press.

Finch, C. E. (1990). *Senescence, longevity, and the genome.* Chicago: University of Chicago Press.

Fleming, J. E., & Rose, M. R. (1996). Genetic analysis of aging in *Drosophila melanogaster.* In E. L. Schneider and J. W. Rowe (Eds.), *Handbook of the biology of aging* (4th ed.). San Diego: Academic Press.

Jazwinski, S. M. (1996). Longevity-assurance genes and mitochondrial DNA alterations: Yeast and filamentous fungi. In E. L. Schneider & J. W. Rowe. (Eds.), *Handbook of the biology of aging* (4th ed.). San Diego: Academic Press.

Johnson, T. E. (1993). Genetic influences on aging in mammals and invertebrates. *Aging: Clinical Experimental Research, 5,* 299.

Lithgow, G. J. (1996). The molecular genetics of *Caenorhabditis elegans.* In E. L. Schneider and J. W. Rowe (Eds.), *Handbook of the biology of aging* (4th ed.). San Diego: Academic Press.

Rose, M. R. (1991). *Evolutionary biology of aging.* New York: Oxford University Press.

Van Remmen, H., Ward, W., Sabia, R. V., & Richardson, A. (1995). Effect of age on gene expression and protein degradation. In E. J. Masoro (Ed.), *Handbook of physiology of aging.* (pp. 171–234). Oxford: Oxford University Press.

Vijg, J. (1990). DNA sequence changes in aging: How frequent, how important?, *Aging, 2,* 105.

Vijg, J., & Papaconstantinou, J. (1990). Aging and longevity genes: Strategies for identifying DNA sequences controlling life span. *Journal of Gerontology: Biological Science, 5,* B179.

Geriatric Assessment: Physical

Laurence Z. Rubenstein

UCLA School of Medicine and Sepulveda Veterans Affairs Medical Center

Comprehensive Geriatric Assessment (CGA) A multidimensional usually interdisciplinary diagnostic process intended to determine a frail elderly person's medical, psychosocial, and function capabilities and problems in order to develop an overall plan for treatment and long-term follow-up.

Geriatric Evaluation and Management (GEM) Program An organized system for performing CGA and follow-up, usually structured around an interdiscipinary team and can be located in a hospital ward (geriatric evaluation unit), an outpatient setting, or be freestanding (consultation service or home-visitation team).

COMPREHENSIVE GERIATRIC ASSESSMENT (CGA) has become one of the fundamental unifying principles of clinical geriatric medicine. It can be defined as a multidimensional usually interdisciplinary diagnostic process intended to determine a frail elderly person's medical, psychosocial, and functional capabilities and problems in order to develop an overall plan for treatment and long-term follow-up. In 1987 CGA was described as the "new technology of geriatrics." As a central part of most geriatric care programs, CGA helps to structure the initial patient evaluation, assists in planning of care, and facilitates

monitoring of patient progress over time. Although CGA includes many components of the standard medical diagnostic evaluation, it focuses on the particular needs of frail elderly persons. In doing so, CGA goes well beyond the routine clinical examination performed under usual "good medical care" in its emphasis on functional status and quality of life, in its comprehensiveness, and in its use of standardized measurement instruments and interdisciplinary teams. By incorporating multidisciplinary perspectives into a systematic assessment, geriatricians attempt to evaluate the "whole patient."

I. OBJECTIVES

Frail elderly people, with their complex clinical presentations and needs, are particularly likely to benefit from this kind of special assessment, which is not ordinarily supplied by care providers in standard settings. The CGA approach, which emphasizes detection and evaluation of distinct geriatric problems and functional impairments, has a number of specific purposes, listed below:

- Improve diagnostic accuracy
- Optimize medical treatment
- Improve medical outcomes
- Improve function and quality of life
- Optimize living location
- Reduce unnecessary service use
- Arrange long-term case management.

The intention is that with CGA, geriatric patients will have more accurate and complete diagnosis, will receive more appropriate care, will have better care outcomes, and will ultimately save money through avoidance of unnecessary services.

CGA can be performed in many locations and health-care contexts. It is often a basic part of care in hospital geriatric units as well as in community senior health centers. It frequently takes place in primary-care settings to supplement the standard medical evaluation. In fact, CGA exists as a continuum, ranging from limited screening assessments and referrals by community health workers, to case-finding assessments by primary-care physicians who can provide some interventions directly and refer their patients for others, to more thorough evaluation of these problems in specialized centers by a geriatrician or interdisciplinary team who plan and initiate therapy and provide limited or complete follow-up. In all cases, the CGA is focused on identifying an older person's functional problems and disabilities, providing or arranging for treatment, and assuring appropriate follow-up.

II. BRIEF HISTORY

The basic concepts of CGA have developed over the past 60 years, combining elements of the traditional medical history and physical examination, the social worker assessment, functional evaluation and treatment methods derived from rehabilitation medicine, and psychometric methods derived from the social sciences. The first published reports of geriatric assessment programs came from the British geriatrician Marjory Warren, who created specialized geriatric assessment units during the 1930s while in charge of a large chronic disease hospital. She found that her patients—most of whom had long been bedridden and relatively neglected while residing in the archaic workhouse infirmary—would often make obvious improvement through a process of systematic evaluation, active mobilization, and selective rehabilitation. As a result of her experiences, Warren advocated that every elderly patient receive what we know today as CGA and an attempt at rehabilitation before being admitted to a long-term care hospital or nursing home.

Since Warren's work, the concepts of CGA have evolved around the world. As geriatric care systems have been initiated, CGA concepts and specific programs have frequently been assigned central roles, usually as focal points for entry into the care systems. In the United States, programs incorporating CGA principles began to appear in the 1970s. The first major U.S. health-care organization to adopt and adapt CGA in a major way was the Department of Veterans Affairs (then the U.S. Veterans Administration [VA] Health Care System), a care system serving military veterans. The VA was challenged relatively early by a disproportionately elderly group of patients, and in the mid-1970s the VA developed an innovative network of special demonstration programs focused on aging—Geriatric Research Education and Clinical Centers (GRECCs)—whose role was to devise creative new clinical care models responding to the special needs of older veterans, as well as to encourage aging-focused research and education programs to train experts in geriatric medicine. Some of these GRECCs started inpatient units based on CGA principles, and several attempted to evaluate the effectiveness of these new clinical programs and them as necessary. Early, noncontrolled evaluations, performed at VAs in California and Arkansas, suggested major beneficial effects, including discovery of previously undetected diagnoses, reduction in medication use, improvement in functional status, and avoidance of some nursing home placements. Larger controlled trials in the VA and elsewhere confirmed these early evaluations, documented additional benefits, and convinced VA policy makers of the value of CGA programs. As a result, the VA founded more CGA units. By 1994, 133 of the 172 VA medical centers had CGA programs, usually called geriatric evaluation and management (GEM) programs, a term coined at a consensus conference in 1989 to better reflect the fact that these programs usually supplement CGA with care and follow-up.

Outside the VA, CGA concepts have become more and more a part of standard care for geriatric patients in the United States. As CGA has evolved, it has not remained restricted to specific geriatric assessment programs (GAPs) or units (GAUs), but has spread throughout the geriatric care system—from nursing homes to community home care. Although there is not yet a national program of health care, principles of CGA are part of virtually every geriatric care program. For example, in many areas, at least a limited geriatric assessment is required by law prior to a person's admission into a rehabilitation program or a nursing home. In a 1989 survey of U.S. hospitals, 9.7% of responding hospitals ($N = 1639$) reported having established a formal GEM unit—a figure higher than might be expected considering the fact that the U.S. health-care system has yet to establish any formal financial incentives to establish or maintain hospital GEMs, which are undoubtedly the most costly of CGA programs to operate. Home care and day treatment programs usually perform a multidimensional assessment prior to initiating treatment. Most experts in geriatric care now agree that a CGA, at least in an abbreviated form, should be performed whenever an elderly person enters the geriatric care system. Certainly, it is imperative to perform CGA on an elderly person prior to any major change in residential setting, such as when nursing home admission is being considered, or following development of a new disability, such as a stroke. In addition, increasing data indicate the value of preventive-outreach screening assessments among populations not yet a part of the geriatric care system, such as through preventive home visits or screening sessions in primary-care settings or senior centers.

In other countries, CGA has been proliferating as well. In Italy, for instance, hospital GEM units have been mandated by law since 1992. In Denmark, CGA occurs widely in hospital, outpatient, and home visitation programs. In the United Kingdom, general practitioners have been mandated since 1990 to offer an annual home visit to their patients for the purposes of CGA. At an international conference on CGA held in 1994 in Florence, Italy, representatives from over 20 countries in 5 continents presented data on formal CGA programs existing and developing in their respective health-care systems.

III. THE BASIC COMPONENTS AND PROCESS OF CGA

The basic components and measurable dimensions of CGA, listed in Table I, include evaluation of medical problems and relevant comorbidity, functional status, psychologic status, social support network and activities, economic needs, and the living environment. Ideally, with the availability of an interdisciplinary team, each component can be assessed by the most appropriate team member(s) and discussed at the interdisciplinary team conference. In more limited settings, such

Table I The Major Components and Measurable Dimensions of Geriatric Assessment

Physical health
  Traditional problem list
  Disease severity indicators
Overall functional ability
  Basic and instrumental activities of daily living (ADL) scales
  Gait and balance measures
  Exercise levels
Psychologic health
  Cognitive (mental status) tests
  Affective (depression) scales
Social and environmental parameters
  Social support resources and needs
  Environmental adequacy and safety
  Advance directives

as a physician's office, the CGA involves fewer specialized disciplines, sometimes the physician alone. This is usually less desirable in terms of both expertise and workload efficiency, because the physician alone cannot ordinarily provide sufficient time to fully deal with the complex needs of frail elderly persons. Yet even abbreviated CGA can provide important benefits if it is well focused on major problems usually excluded from most routine medical care evaluations.

The process of CGA begins following identification of the patient in need—most commonly an elderly person who has experienced deteriorations in health and function. This screening or case-finding function can take place in a number of settings, including within a health-care institution, in a physician's office, or outside the usual health-care system (e.g., screening and referral programs in a senior center). Persons for whom the screening detects no important problem do not need CGA. However, those found to have one or more problems need further assessment. Ordinarily, if health status has worsened but functional level is intact, an elderly person can receive adequate care in usual primary-care settings. However, patients who have new or progressive functional deficits or difficult-to-manage geriatric problems (e.g., incontinence, dementia, frequent falls) should ideally receive CGA in a geriatric care context, since geriatric practitioners are usually more prepared than primary-care providers to deal with these problems.

After reviewing medical information, and perhaps performing a focused physical examination, a CGA evaluates functioning in order to detect whether the patient has problems performing activities necessary for community survival. This is most easily captured using standardized measures of basic activities of daily living (ADLs) and instrumental ADLs (IADLs). Basic ADLs include self-care activities such as eating, dressing, bathing, transferring, and toileting. Patients unable to perform these activities will generally need 12- to 24-hour support by caregivers. IADLs include heavier housework, going on errands, managing finances, and telephoning—activities required for the individual to remain independent in a house or apartment. Ordinarily, these functions are evaluated with self-reports from the patients, although sometimes caregivers or other proxies are asked for the information when the patient is unable to communicate reliably. Proxy information is usually adequate, although caution must be taken in interpreting it, as caregivers have often been shown to somewhat understate a patient's functional abilities. In addition, specific performance tests have been developed to verify self- or proxy-reports of functional data, although in most clinical settings, such performance tests are rarely needed.

To interpret the results of impairments in ADLs and IADLs more fully, physicians will usually need additional information about the patient's environment and social situation. For example, the strength of the patient's social network, the amount and type of caregiver support available, and the level of social activities in which the patient participates will all influence the clinical approach taken in managing detected deficits. This information can perhaps best be obtained by an experienced nurse or social worker. Two other key items of the CGA are at least screening evaluations of cognitive status and depression. In addition, information should be sought from the patient concerning advance directives for health care, which can be of great importance in deciding future treatment plans when the patient no longer is able to communicate lucidly.

Once the CGA has detected and quantified the patient's levels of impairment, disability, and handicap and their causes, appropriate treatment and management strategies must be carefully formulated. This is a crucial step to the effectiveness of CGA, for diagnosis without treatment is rarely of much use! Sometimes a member of the extended assessment team or an outside specialist will need to assist in the final therapeutic formulation. For example, a physical or occupational therapist may need to evaluate a complex patient with difficulty dressing, a condition that could be caused by a number of problems including cognitive impairment, poor finger mobility, or dysfunction of the shoulders, back, or hips. When a reversible cause is found, a specific treatment may eliminate or ameliorate the disability. When the disability is complex or irreversible, rehabilitative or symptom-relief approaches can often provide substantial relief or improvement in function. Knowledge of community or hospital-based resources are essential to formulation of an optimal plan for care and long-term follow-up.

IV. PROGRAM MODELS AND TYPES

CGA can be performed in a wide variety of locations, ranging from the hospital to the office to the home setting. Several factors determine where a CGA should best take place. These factors include the patient's level of disability and cognition, acuity and complexity of illness, social support strength, and access to transportation. In general, more disabled and complex patients with poorer social supports and transportation access will be more likely to need inpatient or in-home CGA services. These patients will be more likely to need prolonged periods of treatment and rehabilitation and be less likely to keep outpatient appointments and comply with recommendations on their own. Hospital programs offer greater opportunities for intensive treatment and rehabilitation under the care of interdisciplinary teams. This can occur on designated inpatient geriatric assessment or special care units, or by receiving a careful geriatric team consultation while on a nongeriatric hospital service.

Most CGAs do not require the full range of technologic capacity nor the intensity of physician and nurse monitoring found in the acute inpatient setting. Yet hospitalization becomes unavoidable when no outpatient setting provides prompt, adequate assessment. A specialized geriatric setting outside an acute hospital ward, such as a day hospital or subacute inpatient geriatric evaluation unit, will provide the easy availability of an interdisciplinary team with the time and expertise to provide needed services efficiently, an adequate level of monitoring, and beds for patients unable to sit or stand for long periods. Inpatient and day hospital assessment programs have the advantage of intensity, speed, and ability to care for particularly frail or acutely ill patients.

Outpatient and in-home assessment programs are generally cheaper because they avoid the need for inpatient stays. Although nonhospital programs cannot provide the level of technologic care possible in the hospital, most elderly persons who are not acutely ill or severely functionally dependent can obtain adequate CGA outside the hospital.

V. BENEFITS OF CGA

A growing literature supports the effectiveness of CGA programs in a variety of settings. As noted above, the early descriptive studies of CGA programs described such benefits as improved diagnostic accuracy, reduced discharges to nursing homes, increased functional status, and reduced medications. Yet, without concurrent control patients, these studies could not distinguish the effects of the programs from simple improvement over time. Nor was it clear how these apparent benefits, most of which affected process of care, would relate to short- or long-term outcome benefits. Beginning in the 1980s, however, controlled studies began to be published that corroborated some of the earlier studies and documented additional benefits, such as improved survival, reduced hospital and nursing home utilization, and in some cases reduced costs. However, these studies were by no means uniform in their results. Some showed a whole series of dramatic and interrelated benefits, whereas others showed few if any benefits.

To resolve some of this discrepancy, and to try to demonstrate particular program elements associated with particular benefits, a systematic meta-analysis was carried out in 1993. This meta-analysis included both published data from the 28 controlled trials as well as substantial amounts of unpublished data systematically retrieved from many of the studies. The meta-analysis identified five CGA program types: hospital units (six studies), hospital consultation teams (eight studies), in-home assessment services (seven studies), outpatient assessment services (four studies), and "hospital–home assessment services" (three studies) the latter of which performed in-home assessments on patients recently discharged from hospitals. The meta-analysis confirmed many of the major reported benefits for many of the program types. Among

these statistically and clinically significant benefits included reduced risk of mortality (by 22% for hospital-based programs at 12 months, and by 14% for all programs combined at 12 months), improved likelihood of living at home (by 47% for hospital-based programs and by 26% for all programs combined at 12 months), reduced hospital (re)admissions (by 12% for all programs at study end), greater chance of cognitive improvement (by 47% for all programs at study end), and greater chance of physical function improvement for patients on hospital units (by 72% for hospital units).

Although not all studies showed equivalent effects, the meta-analysis was able to indicate a number of variables at both the program and patient levels that tended to distinguish trials with large effects from ones with more limited ones. When examined on the program level, hospital CGA units and home-visit assessment teams produced the most dramatic benefits, whereas benefits in office-based programs could not be confirmed. Programs that provided hands-on clinical care or long-term follow-up were generally able to produce greater positive effects than purely consultative programs or ones that lacked follow-up. Another factor associated with greater demonstrated benefits, at least in hospital-based programs, was patient targeting—programs that selected patients who were at high risk for deterioration yet still had "rehabilitation potential" generally had stronger results than less selective programs. Still there are many unanswered questions about which CGA program components are most important and what is most responsible for its effectiveness.

The meta-analysis confirmed the importance of targeting criteria in producing beneficial outcomes. In particular, when use of explicit targeting criteria for patient selection was included as a covariate, increases in some CGA benefits were often found. For example, among the hospital-based CGA studies, positive effects on physical function and likelihood of living at home at 12 months were associated with studies that excluded patients who were relatively "too healthy." A similar effect on physical function was seen in the institutional studies that excluded persons with relatively poor prognoses. The reason for this effect of targeting on outcome size no doubt lies in the ability of careful targeting to concentrate the intervention on patients who can benefit, without diluting the effect size with persons too ill or too well to show a measurable improvement.

VI. POLICY ISSUES AND FUTURE DIRECTIONS

To recapitulate, CGA in a variety of program types is effective in producing a number of important benefits. Not all persons benefit equally, and it is important to target persons most likely to benefit from the programs, using specific criteria geared to the program and population. These criteria include the presence of a "geriatric" condition (e.g., confusion, depression, falls, incontinence, impaired mobility, polypharmacy, pressure sores, sensory impairment) that causes some measurable disability and the absence of end-stage disabling conditions that preclude deriving measurable improvement. Where the intervention is expensive, such as an inpatient unit, careful patient selection is essential to maximize program impact. Where the intervention is cheap, such as a screening clinic, restrictive patient selection is not so important. Thus, choice of patient selection (targeting) criteria should be matched to program goals, size and structure, costs, and population served. Future research is needed to fine-tune these criteria and to better tailor specific criteria to specific programs.

It is likely that as principles of good geriatric care increasingly pervade medical education and the health-care system, standards of care for older people will improve, which may lead to a decreased need for special CGA programs. This potential development is certainly to be welcomed, but it has not yet arrived.

Future research is needed to define better the most effective and efficient methods for performing geriatric assessment and to identify more clearly which individuals are most likely to derive benefit. In the meantime, considerable evidence supports the need for continued growth and expansion of these programs throughout the geriatric care system.

BIBLIOGRAPHY

Applegate, W. B., Miller, S. T., Graney, M. J., Elam, J. T., Burns, R., Akins, D. E. (1990). A randomized controlled trial of a geriatric assessment unit in a community rehabilitation hospital. *New England Journal of Medicine, 322,* 1572–1578.

Deyo, R., Applegate, W. B., Kramer, A., & Meehan, S. (Eds.). (1991). The future of geriatric assessment: Special Issue. *Journal of the American Geriatric Society, 39* (suppl), 1S–59S.

Epstein, A. M., Hall, J. A., Besdine, R., Cumella, E., McNeil, B. J., Rowe, J. W. (1987). The emergence of geriatric assessment units: the "new technology of geriatrics." *Annals of Internal Medicine, 106,* 299–302.

Rubenstein, L. Z., Josephson, K. R., Wieland, G. D., English, P. A., Sayre, J. A., Kane, R. L. (1984). Effectiveness of a geriatric evaluation unit: A randomized clinical trial. *New England Journal of Medicine 311,* 1664–1670.

Rubenstein, L. Z., Wieland, G. D., Bernabei, R. (1995). *Geriatric assessment technology: The state of the art.* Milan: Kurtis Publishers.

Rubenstein, L. Z., Wieland, D., Bernabei, R. (Eds.). (1995). Special issue on comprehensive Geriatric Assessment Research, *Aging: Clinical and Experimental Research.*

Stuck, A. E., Siu A. L., Wieland, G. D., Adams, J., Rubenstein, L. Z. (1993). Comprehensive geriatric assessment: A meta-analysis of controlled trials. *Lancet, 342,* 1032–1036.

Gerontechnology

Max Vercruyssen,[1,2,3] Jan A. M. Graafmans,[1] James L. Fozard,[1,4] Herman Bouma,[1] and Jan Rietsema[1]

[1]Eindhoven University of Technology, Eindhoven, The Netherlands
[2]University of Hawaii
[3]University of Minnesota
[4]National Institute on Aging

Ergonomics (1) The applied science involving the design of human–machine–environment systems with an emphasis on effective use of the strengths and weaknesses of humans in order to optimize system performance (productivity or profit), promote wellness, and minimize risk of injury. (2) The study of work (*ergos*) and its laws and principles (*nomos*). (3) The field of commonsense engineering. The field is vast and contains many subspecializations that might be viewed on a continuum from microergonomics, including the design of machines, tools, and devices for assistance with work and skilled behavior, to macroergonomics that addresses the design of sociotechnical systems and public affairs. The international governing body for this field is the International Ergonomics Association and the primary publications are *Ergonomics* and *Applied Ergonomics*, which are affiliated with the Ergonomics Society (Loughborough, UK), the British national governing body for ergonomics professionals.

Functional Autonomy The ability to function, without assistance from others, in conducting personal and social activities that an individual (or society) wishes to accomplish.

Geriatrics A subspecialty of internal medicine or family practice that is concerned with the health care and psychosocial needs of the elderly. Geriatricians are medical doctors who have been trained in either internal medicine or family practice and have then subspecialized in geriatrics. A certificate of added qualifications in geriatrics is available to eligible physicians who have successfully passed an examination prepared jointly by the American Board of Internal Medicine and the American Board of Family Practice. The American Geriatrics Society and the Clinical Medicine Section of the Gerontological Society of America are the major American professional groups for geriatricians.

Gero-ergonomics The term created among ergonomics professionals for describing concerns of the elderly (*gero*) and the optimal design of products and environment systems for them (*ergonomics*). This term is being replaced in some professional societies with gerontechnology.

Gerontechnology The study of aging and technology for the benefit of preferred living and working environments and adapted medical care for the elderly and caregivers.

Gerontology The scientific study of aging and the aged through integration of disciplines involving both biological and behavioral sciences.

Human Factors The scientific and technological field concerned with optimizing the relationship between human–machine–environment systems (*see ergonomics*). The American national governing body is the Human Factors and Ergonomics Society (Santa Monica, California) and the primary publication is *Human Factors*.

Independent Living Capability of living alone and managing daily physical and mental activities unassisted.

Technology   The research and development of various techniques and products.

Transgenerational Design   The design of products and environment systems for everyone, regardless of age, with a concern for fostering simultaneous usage by individuals across multiple generations (e.g., grandchildren and grandparents).

GERONTECHNOLOGY is the multidisciplinary study of aging and technology for the benefit of preferred living and working environments and adapted medical care for the elderly and caregivers. Gerontechnology is a new professional area or applied discipline that is concerned with development of techniques and products, based on the knowledge of aging processes and preferences of the elderly. Fundamental and applied research activities involve the interaction of the elderly with products and their technical or built environments. Particularly important are the challenges and opportunities of normal and pathological human aging. "Challenges" refer to the age-related changes in physical, physiological, perceptual, cognitive, and motor processes that may become inconvenient. "Opportunities" refer to such positive outcomes as increased time to pursue new activities in self-discovery, work, and relationships with grandchildren and others outside the family. A complementary goal is to understand how age affects the extent and pattern of use of existing technological devices. Essentially, gerontechnology uses available technology to compress years of morbidity (disease conditions) and discomfort while enhancing functional autonomy (extending the years of independent living).

Gerontechnology addresses aging in at least five ways: It provides technology to (a) improve the way in which aging processes themselves are studied; (b) prevent the effects of declines in strength, flexibility, and endurance that are commonly associated with aging; (c) enhance the performance of new roles (opportunities) provided by aging; (d) compensate for declining capabilities (the challenges) associated with aging; and (e) assist caregivers.

I. INTRODUCTION

The average age of the world population is increasing each year, particularly in industrialized nations, due

Figure I   Gerontechnology is the interdisciplinary study involving fundamental and applied research into the interaction of the elderly with products and their technical or built environments. (Logo from Gerontechnology: First International Conference on Technology and Aging, 26–29th August 1991, Eindhoven, The Netherlands, used with permission).

to reduced birth rates, reduced death rates (improved health and survival), and demographic shifts (e.g., baby boomers into later adulthood). This pattern is exaggerated in Europe, the United States, and Japan, causing entire societies to be unprepared for the aging of their citizens (parents, grandparents, and great-grandparents, etc.). However, this problem is compounded by the fact that no two adults age in the same way: Aging is universal, but it expresses itself differently within and between individuals. Genetic variation in tissue composition, repair, and metabolism combines with intrinsic biological aging processes and intrinsic influences—including lifelong differences in patterns of disease, lifestyle, exposure to environmental pollutants, and obstacles of the humanmade environment—to create large individual differences among the elderly. Disabilities and handicaps that occur during life create even greater heterogeneity among coevals. Technology helps compensate for loss of function and provides aid to caregivers, but it also plays a positive role in prevention of disease and disability, enhancement of quality of life, and basic research. The need for the interdisciplinary fields of gerontology and ergonomics increases directly with the degree to which a society is caught unprepared for the dramatic increase in the elder segment (e.g.,

55 years and older) of its population. Never before in human history have so many survived to old age. There are no guidelines for the increasing number of elderly because they have not existed before in such large proportions. Current generations have become pioneers in time and can certainly benefit from recent discoveries in gerontechnology.

Elderly individuals prefer to be integrated into society and function independently; however, most consumer products are manufactured without making allowances for the capabilities and preferences of the elderly. Being able to live and function without assistance partly depends on one's health and abilities, but also on one's social and physical environment. A supportive environment can help maintain functional autonomy even though aging individuals might perhaps see or hear less, move with more difficulty, or have somewhat poorer memories than they did when they were young. The social part of a supportive environment includes family, friends, and sometimes professional caregivers who provide help if needed. [*See* SOCIAL NETWORKS, SUPPORT, AND INTEGRATION.] The physical part includes technology that makes living easier and more enjoyable. Throughout life, technology provides people with products (hardware, software, and services) that help maintain health and wellness, especially perception, communication, information processing, and mobility. Technology is acquired to meet daily needs when it is useful and available at a reasonable cost.

II. BACKGROUND AND HISTORY

The term *gerontechnology* is a composite of two words: *gerontology*, the scientific study of aging and the aged, and *technology*, research and development of various techniques and products. The term was coined by Graafmans and Brouwers at the Technische Universiteit Eindhoven (Technical University of Eindhoven) in The Netherlands. Although formal collaborations of individuals interested in technology and aging dates back to the 1960s, the term *gerontechnology* did not emerge until the late 1980s and only with considerable help from professionals in ergonomics, gerontology, and technology. The following presents some of this historical background.

Ergonomics (the international term, or Human Factors, the American term), the applied science concerned with the laws and principles of work, has developed from physical work and job design studies of the 1800s. However, it was not until the 1940s that ergonomics (human factors) emerged from military, aviation, and engineering psychology as a somewhat independent discipline to consider physical and perceptually demanding tasks in the industrial setting. Ross McFarland brought attention to middle-aged and older workers and became the founder of industrial gerontology. The early pioneers of international ergonomics were McFarland, A. T. Welford, K. F. H. Murrell, and K. U. Smith.

Although military application has always been the strongest part of human factors engineering and ergonomics, in the late 1960s and early 1970s the emphasis of human factors shifted, especially in the United States, from military-aerospace to civilian concerns, including problems confronting the elderly. This was also the period during which the National Institute on Aging was established and the 1971 White House Conference on Aging was held.

In 1981, James L. Fozard was editor of the first special edition of *Human Factors* devoted to aging issues and dedicated to one of the early pioneers in this area—Dr. Ross McFarland. In 1985, American legislators were informed of potential contributions of human factors and ergonomics research and applications for older adults through the *1985 Congressional Office of Technology Report on Technology and Aging*. In 1988, Fozard and A. Dan Fisk provided an overview of potential uses of research in human factors and ergonomics for an elderly population. In 1990, the second special issue on aging was edited by Sara Czaja and included an overview of research needs and application opportunities by David B. D. Smith. In 1990, Dr. Czaja also edited a National Research Council report entitled *Human Factors Research Needs for an Aging Population*, which helped to alert government and other groups concerned with aging of the possibilities of using human factors knowledge and skills to promote and maintain the independence of older persons. Also in 1990, Neal Charness and Elizabeth Bosman prepared the first chapter on human factors and aging in the third edition of the *Handbook of the Psychology of Aging* (J. E. Birren & K. W. Schaie, Eds.).

The Human Factors and Ergonomics Society's Aging Technical Group was founded in the late 1970s by Arnold Small, who served as the first chairman and newsletter editor through 1982. Small almost single-handedly recruited members and personally promoted the technical group and needs of the elderly during these early years.

The International Ergonomics Association (IEA) is the international governing body for the human factors and ergonomics societies in each country. Membership of individuals in any one country means automatic membership in the IEA. One of the subcommittees of the IEA is the Ageing Technical Group, which is concerned with ergonomics research and applications devoted to increasing knowledge and understanding of aging in a wide variety of life settings. Specifically this group provides a professional forum for (a) research related to characteristics, abilities, performance, learning, and needs of the elderly, (b) understanding longitudinal changes with age, (c) applications of research findings and technological assistance, (d) contributing to a greater awareness of aging, and (e) distribution of aging-related ergonomics information. Organized in the 1980s, this technical group has grown with each triennial congress.

In Europe, gerontechnology design and research activities have been strong in Britain, Sweden, Finland, and The Netherlands. Most noteworthy is possibly development of the term *gerontechnology*, the first international conference and a book on this topic in 1991, and a strong network of 17 European countries through the Cooperation on Science and Technology—Ageing and Technology Committee (COST-A5). Recently the DesignAge Network was established by Roger Coleman (Royal College of Arts, UK) with financial support from the European Union. The first postgraduate course and workshop in gerontechnology was offered at the Eindhoven University of Technology (EUT) in 1993. The second postgraduate course was offered in Finland in 1994.

The first academic unit to specialize in this field and the creator of the term gerontechnology was at EUT (Technische Universiteit Eindhoven, TUE, in Dutch) in their Center for Biomedical and Health-Care Technology (Centruum voor Biomedische en Gezondheidstechnologie, BMGT) where the Institute for Gerontechnology (Instituut voor Gerontechnologie) was founded in early 1994. The goal of this institute and BMGT is to support and encourage research and education in gerontechnology throughout the university and in other educational, industrial, and health-care facilities in The Netherlands and other

countries. The institute is also an active interface between EUT and numerous target groups including senior citizens, trade and industry, care professionals, and researchers. The BMGT supports and connects research within a variety of technical programs in human perception, healthy buildings, electrical engineering applications in medicine, biophysics, physiological chemistry, and other areas, all in collaboration with the specific faculties of the university.

The second unit to specialize in gerontechnology was established in Ancona, Italy, by Nicola Fabris. The emphasis of this program is on the continuum of care through support by technology.

The first American academic unit with a curriculum in gerontechnology was created in 1995 at the University of Hawaii's John A. Burns Medical School, Department of Medicine, at the Pacific Islands Geriatric Education Center. The primary objective of this program includes development of research and educational curricula for the training of students and individuals from the community interested in gerontology, but especially geriatric fellows, graduate student researchers, postdoctoral scientists, geriatric residents, and medical students (in their geriatric medicine rotation).

Other academic and professional organizations are currently establishing formal gerontechnology courses and programs, especially in Europe and Japan. Also, training is now provided at numerous locations around the world under such names as human factors and aging (ergonomics and aging), gero-ergonomics, designs for the aged, and so on.

Within human factors and ergonomics societies the technical group specializing in concerns for the elderly have occasionally called themselves gero-ergonomists but the term *gerontechnologists* is becoming more common. Also, *transgenerational design* has been used as a term to advocate the design of products and environment systems for everyone, especially the elderly, in a way that simultaneously satisfies the needs of the young. [*See* HUMAN FACTORS AND ERGONOMICS.]

III. CURRICULA AND FUNDAMENTALS

Fundamental principles and the curricula for research and education are developed over time as various approaches, models, and methods are evaluated for their effectiveness. Because gerontechnology is a new field it lacks the advantage that many fields possess by virtue of their longevity. Nonetheless, there are prototypes and working documents available. Until revised, the following curricula and fundamental concepts are being taught at institutions providing courses, programs, and degrees in gerontechnology.

Common in gerontechnology curricula is a primary purpose to develop an awareness of and interest in the potential of technology for the aging and aged in graduate students from various engineering faculties and in other professionals interested in this field (e.g., from industry, government, and business). Some of the students specialize in gerontechnological research. The educational curriculum is mainly taught through seminars, colloquia, and workshops as a synthetic, interdisciplinary course of study. Collaborations associated with production of the first (1993) and second (1994) postgraduate international courses in gerontechnology have led to development of a European course on gerontechnology. The goals of these courses emphasize practice in thinking about how technology can and should be applied to the aged and the science of gerontology. Accordingly, gerontechnology provides valuable training experience for engineers, designers, architects, and other technologists because the student must learn to use information from a variety of fields, as well as the more specific information from his or her own specialty, in order to develop a solution to a design or system problem. This skill is of use in most professional and personal settings. Research curricula are specific to each institution so are not mentioned here.

A. Systems Approach to Extending Functional Autonomy

Extremely important, now more than ever before in human history, is understanding how person–machine–environment systems can be designed to extend one's years of functional autonomy and independent living. Examining age-related changes in the person, machine, or environment by observing the components independently will result in a different picture of aging and system performance than if one works from the beginning with the assumption that the components are interdependent and that each component must be investigated in relation to its co-components. This is not a new idea, but is a point

that must be emphasized at the onset. Thus an understanding of ergonomics and systems science is essential to effective interactions of people in and with systems or products.

For simplification, ergonomics and human factors may be viewed as the applied science concerned with the design of products, machines, and environments to match the capabilities, limitations, and desires of people thereby enhancing opportunities for optimizing system performance and reducing the risk of injury, illness, and discomfort. Gerontology is concerned with people, specifically research on the biological, psychological, social, and medical aspects of aging. Technology provides products and techniques through research and development, mostly from the fields of chemical, civil, construction, electrical, industrial, information, mechanical, and physical engineering. Ergonomics provides a means for optimizing the relationship of people with products and environments. It is important to consider the psychological, physiological, biomechanical, psychosocial, and economical strengths and limitations of people, especially the elderly and then use the most appropriate technologies available at the time. Regardless of perspective, a systems approach is essential in determining what can be done to extend the number of years that individuals can live and function independently in society.

B. Gap between the Elderly and Technology

There is a two-part gap between the needs for technology by the elderly and the range of suitable products and services available to them. First, many existing technologies have to be adapted for elderly users because perceptual, cognitive, and mobility limitations that often occur with aging make today's technology difficult to use effectively. The problem that must be addressed here is not the function of the technology, but the interface and thus functionality or usability between the technology and its user.

Second, most existing technology is not aimed at solving the unique difficulties (illnesses and limitations of activity) or opportunities (time for new activities and interests) of the elderly of today and in the coming years. The problem that must be addressed here is the challenge of adapting new technology specially oriented towards the aspirations and special characteristics of the elderly in the coming years. Closing the gap between the elderly and technology is a major goal of gerontechnology.

C. Demographic Changes and Increasing Pace of Technology Development

There are two major influences on the gap between the elderly and technology: demographic changes and an increasing pace of technological development. First, there is an ongoing demographic shift in the age distribution of the world population. The relative number of older people will continue to increase into the middle of the next century. At the same time, particularly since the post-World War II baby boom, there has been a relative decrease in the number of teenagers. In many countries, 20% of the population is older than 65 years of age and this proportion is increasing annually.

Second, there is an ever-increasing pace of the density and speed of technology development itself. The current increase in the complexity and speed of information processing and communication technology and the increased sophistication of automobiles and other modes of transportation illustrate these changes. This means that individuals of all ages will be confronted with an ever more rapidly changing technological environment that will continue to develop and change at an often unexpected pace.

D. The Target Population

Gerontechnology is for all ages today and for the life span of each individual regardless of their present age. Sharing a common chronological age does not make for homogeneity among those in an age group. In fact, the opposite is true—many similarities present in childhood vanish in adulthood. Individuals become increasingly dissimilar with age. Differences in life experiences, exposure to diseases, lifestyle, genetic inheritance, and so on, make for relatively greater heterogeneity among elderly persons.

The starting point for gerontechnology is technology made useful for the elderly. Aging may well be accompanied by illness, disease, and injury, so consideration of the health and wellness of the elderly is part of the research needed for gerontechnology, especially when a sickness mostly occurs in the elderly or when it has special effects on them. For example, when a

young and old adult have the same medical problem, such as a broken bone or pneumonia, the recovery period is often longer and the symptoms are usually more severe in the older person.

Even though there is no single elderly group, some age-graded classification of the elderly is useful. One subgroup of the elderly consists of active and healthy persons and contains those from 65 to 75 years of age. This group would benefit from suitable consumer products and services that enhance work and new technology that would improve leisure, work, and family activities that are unique to this period of life. A second subgroup can be distinguished between 75 and 85 years that may need some assisted care to remain independent—a need that might be met by technology. A third subgroup over the age of 85 years would typically need more assisted living and medical care, for which some of the necessary technology could be derived from existing medical resources.

Special attention is given to women in the target group because they become a majority at higher ages and because of the fact that in most cases they have less experience with technology than men and therefore have different attitudes toward the use of technology. In some countries (e.g., Germany), women typically consider themselves less proficient with technical products. As the population base to which gerontechnology is applied expands to include more countries, target-group considerations give increasing importance to culture, ethnicity, religion, occupation, and socioeconomic status.

E. Conceptual Basis of Gerontechnology

Gerontechnology is directed toward a class of people—the aging and the aged—whose needs, interests, and abilities change over time, and their preferred living and working environments. This target population grows heterogeneous with aging. For instance, biological aging processes are universal but not uniform. Genetic differences plus environmental factors ensure that the aging experience of each one of us is unique. Disabilities and diseases are not universal and they occur at any point in the aging of an individual— further contributing to the uniqueness of aging. Environmental factors directly affect one's susceptibility to infectious diseases, carcinogenic agents, and the effects of lifestyle on aging. Variations in the built environment determine one's adaptation to the challenges and opportunities afforded by aging.

Gerontechnology differs from biomedical and environmental technology in the way people's interests are identified and used to shape development of a technology. In biomedical technology, physicians and biomedical scientists identify the needs of patient groups. People have a choice to accept or refuse treatments based on biomedical technology either through ethics committees or directly. In environmental technology, the needs of people are identified partly through public health, science, and public concerns for conservation of natural and human resources. Groups of people may benefit from noise-reducing barriers between highways and residential areas or reduction of air pollution. Working through elected public officials, people limit exploitation of natural resources and increase protection from environmental pollutants. In gerontechnology, the needs of people are identified in two ways. The first is feeedback, the evaluations by people of available technology. Ideally, but not usually, feedback means an evaluation by users of products and environments that goes beyond the success of sales. The second way is feedforward, the identification of needs based on involvement by people in the development and dispersal of technology, which takes two paths: (a) elder persons communicate needs and preferences by serving on focus groups or evaluators of prototypes, and (b) older adults reveal information about their preferences, needs, abilities, and economics through scientific research on the aging process. Both are needed.

Four concepts are central to gerontechnology:

1. Functionality changes when sensory, perceptual, cognitive abilities or skills diminish, when task demands are too high, or when the product characteristics, user interface, or environmental conditions are in conflict with human skills.

2. Age-associated differences in functioning can be altered through technical modifications in the environment. A task that may seem very difficult to an elderly individual in one situation might be easily accomplished with suitable environmental modifications. Therefore, age-grading of abilities should not be considered independently of the technical environment.

3. The level of human abilities, relative to most task demands, changes over the life span: increasing

from childhood to adulthood, remaining stable over most of adult life, and then declining in later life.

4. Greater exposure and hence familiarity with particular display–control configurations that occur over time increases adaptation to those configurations and reduces one's ability to adapt to different configurations. Although such familiarity helps prevent performance declines with age it can also contribute to a mental rigidity that decreases one's adaptive skills in novel situations.

F. Approaches

Two distinctive conceptual approaches have been advanced to guide ergonomics professionals in thinking about aging: (a) the person–environment interaction approach involving persons who physically and psychologically change with increasing age requiring alterations in products and environments so that performance or productivity is optimal, and (b) the life span developmental approach that strives for ergonomics alterations to meet the needs of the individual for aging successfully in a psychosocial, biological, and environmental manner. The first focuses on the disparity between demands of the environment with declining capabilities of the aging individual with the goal of operationally optimizing the match of tasks and task components with assessed performance capabilities of the user population. The latter, however, recommends designing for the elderly (a) to accommodate constancy and growth as well as decline, (b) to be sensitive to social, psychological, and performance needs, and (c) to acknowledge the temporary nature of generalizations about aging because of changes experienced by both people and environments.

Both views share a systems approach toward the accommodation of age-related changes in operator behavior. The ultimate aim of each ergonomics effort is toward the optimal use of human and machine capabilities to achieve the highest degree of effectiveness (performance) of the total system. The implication of this "optimal performance engineering" philosophy is that with regard to performance, aging cannot be defined independently from environment—assessments of human abilities and functions only have meaning in reference to environmental challenges and supports. The interaction of a person with his or her environment may be illustrated in Figure 2 both in terms of the developmental view and the systems approach of human factors and aging. Figure 2 also illustrates a way in which technological change can modify, modulate, or mitigate age-related changes in functioning.

At any point in time, the interaction of people with their environment can be characterized by a two-dimensional diagram: beginning at the center left (outer arrows and boxes) and going clockwise (upward), information is received from the environment (through displays) by the person (through sensation and perception). Evaluation and decision making (cognition) within the operator may result in overt responses (motor actions) that adjust or modify controls of the technical operating system that may be a vehicle or device in the home or work environment. With aging, changes in the internal environment (center box) affect sensitivity to the external environment (e.g., visual, auditory, and climatic) in ways that change significantly over time. The display–control

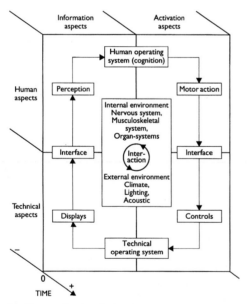

Figure 2 Gerontechnology's person–environment system interactions showing internal and external environments, the human operating system, and the technical operating system all along a third dimension of time ("−" for the past, "0" for the present, and "+" for the future). (Adapted from Graafmans, J. A. M., & Brouwers, T., 1989, Gerontechnology, the modeling of normal aging. *Proceedings of the Human Factors Society 33rd Annual Meeting.* Santa Monica, CA: Human Factors and Ergonomics Society.)

relationship as well as the environment may require changes to accommodate the abilities and needs of older persons. Age adjustments are necessary when changes occur in strength, flexibility, overall fitness, mental functioning, and so on. For instance, visual contrast characteristics depend on differences in sensitivity to ambient light conditions and many other factors.

A time component or "time track" is present along the bottom of the figure, the depth dimension, where "0" designates the present, "−" the past, and "+" the future. Because both the environment and technology change over time as an individual ages, these events are interdependent. Technology introduced today (i.e., "0" on the time axis) may be received differently by young and old users depending on their previous experience ("−" to "0" on the time axis) and is very likely to influence behavior in the future ("0" to "+" on the time axis). Stated another way, the characteristics of the interaction between an individual and the technical environment at present ("0" on the time dimension) is in part determined by past history ("−" to "0"), just as the quality of the past and present person–environment interaction will determine the future interactions ("0" or "+"). The social and educational characteristics of a person as well as health status are part of personal aging and affect the way a person interacts with his or her technical environment.

Ergonomic interventions should emphasize adaptability as a design principle. In housing, for instance, the interface between equipment (e.g., appliances) and their users may change over time, even though the function of these devices does not. Space requirements might also change with time either due to age changes in the needs of the user or because the desire to accommodate to newly introduced technologies or products (e.g., movable and adjustable interior walls and cabinets).

G. Objectives

Gerontechnology addresses aging through at least five objectives in providing technology for (a) improved aging research, (b) prevention, (c) enhancement, (d) compensation, and (e) caregiver assistance. These objectives are presented in at least five delivery modalities and vary according to the age of the reference population (see Figure 3).

Gerontechnology Objectives by Delivery Modality by Age

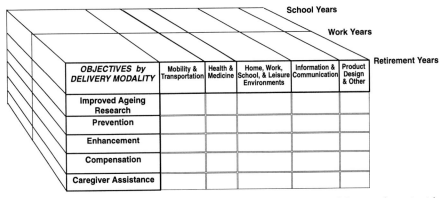

Figure 3 Gerontechnology objectives (rows) according to delivery modalities (columns) with slight modifications made in cells of the two-dimensional matrix throughout the school, work, and retirement years (slices) of the end user.

1. Improved Aging Research

Gerontechnology provides technologies to improve the way in which aging processes themselves are studied. Technological innovations can enhance the depth and breadth of fundamental knowledge and facilitate the application of this information in useful (meaningful) ways. Gerontechnologists can contribute directly to the development of basic (fundamental) aging research capabilities by providing improved technologies and thereby helping to create a richer and more accessible knowledge repository. At the applied level, gerontechnology is a primary agency for the interpretation of fundamental knowledge and the conveyance of this information to lay and professional end users in the form of recommendations, guidelines, and position statements. Examples of the positive contribution of technology includes computer imaging of organs and tissues, signal processing of neurological events and measurements, monitoring of blood flow, and noninvasive acquisition of biochemical measures. Many of these technologies have revolutionized the scientific study of biological and physiological processes of aging.

2. Prevention

Possibly the most effective use of technology for human aging is in prevention, especially age-related declines in strength, flexibility, and endurance and other such capacities or abilities. Technology plays a role in primary prevention (i.e., delaying losses in the first place) and secondary prevention (i.e., avoiding unwanted consequences of the losses). Research has shown that these losses and many other "problems" of the elderly are modifiable through long-range, non-medical interventions involving nutrition, physical activity, strength training, behavior modification, and lifestyle remodeling that avoids exposure to chronically dangerous environmental conditions, such as auditory noise, excessive alcohol and tobacco consumption, and so on. Examples include the benefits of aerobic and strength training in preventing health and wellness problems, and the benefits of noise control throughout a life in reducing the prevalence of impaired hearing in old age. The preventive role of technology includes the design of equipment to facilitate the interventions and the design of monitoring equipment that allows feedback about compliance with interventions and their effectiveness. Examples of this include strength-training equipment that is stimulating and interesting to use, monitoring equipment for physiological functioning, and warning equipment for persons using dangerous tools. Technology plays a role in primary or secondary prevention depending upon the timing of their use. For instance, use of light switches activated by human movement near dangerous stairs or passages prevents problems from occurring. In cases where age-related declines have already occurred, monitoring devices and warning signals may prevent additional consequences caused by the losses (e.g., increased risk of injury caused by sensory of perceptual deficits).

3. Enhancement

Gerontechnology provides technologies to enhance the performance of new roles (opportunities) provided by aging, including changes in work, leisure, living, and social situations. With age comes opportunities in the form of time for new social interactions and activities, time for new learning and leisure activities, and self-fulfillment. This area of development lags behind the others but has great potential. Examples include the design of adaptable housing that meets the differing needs of people during the life cycle of the family or user-friendly communication technologies that remotely connect older users to converse with family and friends in multimedia as well as engage in educational and recreational pursuits. The elderly will acquire new roles as society evolves to make use of the expertise of its older citizens. Technology will influence the way in which young and old alike navigate the information age.

4. Compensation

Gerontechnology provides technologies to compensate for declining capabilities (the challenges) associated with aging. Age-related declines in functional capacities may translate into diminished capabilities that could threaten independent living. Assistive devices and other technological aids for the elderly may compensate for these declines and restore functional autonomy. Most ergonomics applications to aging and the aged are based on this objective, so compensation is the most developed aspect of the five gerontechnological approaches. Examples include products and techniques to offset the consequences of sensory and perceptual losses, task redesign that speeds response time, and devices that can be operated with reduced strength and motor skill. Other examples include adapting lighting conditions to visual task requirements, using mobility aids for locomotion, and nearly any assistive device that permits successful completion of the activities of daily living (ADLs), especially when such activities cannot be completed without compen-

satory assistance. To elaborate, because most falls by the elderly occur at home on the initial step of a flight of stairs and are due to inadequate lighting, it seems appropriate to apply technology to this problem by providing a simple design to increase overall illumination and to provide visual guidance for beginning the step-descending movement sequence. A pressure- or motion-activated two-way switches at the top and bottom of stairways would illuminate the stairs during the short period of time that someone traverses the steps. Such lighting should show both step width for descending and step height for ascending.

5. Caregiver Assistance

Gerontechnology provides technologies to assist those who provide medical and home care for less able elderly persons. For instance, devices have been ergonomically designed to aid in lifting and transfer of individuals who cannot move themselves. One of the most significant recent developments in home-based medical care is the widespread use of complicated medical equipment by family and other nonprofessional caregivers (e.g., respirators, intravenous injection devices, monitoring equipment). The Human Factors and Ergonomics Society has recently created a technical group dedicated to addressing these concerns and providing guidelines for such organizations as the American Institute for Medical Instrumentation.

H. Application Modalities

People of all ages use technology to make it easier to carry out ADLs. Flexibility and adaptability to meet the changing needs of users is very important. Thus, when making design recommendations gerontechnology must consider accessibility and usability by the entire range of generations (youngest to oldest users) and also across the life span of individuals within each generation. The five approaches of gerontechnology can be applied to nearly every aspect of the life of older individuals, particularly in at least five general application modalities: (a) mobility and transportation, (b) health and medicine, (c) home, work, school, and leisure environments, (d) information and communications, and (e) product design. A description of gerontechnology work completed and in progress at EUT and in COST-A5 is available at the EUT's Institute for Gerontechnology.

I. Life Span Changes (Time Dimension)

The third dimension of the matrix in Figure 3 is time (i.e., age of the reference population). One's needs and the use of technologies to meet them change as a function of the priorities in one's life. Although the first two dimensions of the matrix remain the same throughout life, cell contents change considerably during the school years, work years, and retirement years. How one uses and perceives time changes with personal responsibilities to family and friends, marital status, parenting status, elder care provider status, and so on.

Gerontechnology and ergonomics both use the life span developmental view as a theoretical framework in their concern for age changes in the interactions of people with equipment and products, but gerontechnology differs from ergonomics in that ergonomics has not typically included changing person–environment interactions such as training, counseling, or selection of personnel, except for the technology that might be involved in such efforts. Also, gerontechnology is directly concerned with the impact that secular (generational or long-term) changes in technology have on the adaptation of older individuals to those changes.

IV. FINAL COMMENTS

Changes in performance with age varies between and within individuals as a function of the task being performed. Much of the deterioration of physical and mental capacities that accompanies aging can be offset (compensated for) through the development of new strategies for skilled performance. Behavioral training techniques may enhance possibilities for retraining older individuals and maintaining effective skills. And, maintenance of physical fitness through a lifestyle of daily physical activity may prevent age-related deterioration of psychomotor and cognitive performance and thereby maintain high levels of emotional well-being. Gerontechnology strives to enhance wellness of the elderly and those closely associated with older adults.

Loss of performance may be reduced or possibly eliminated through effective design of products, tasks, environments, and systems. Tasks should be designed so that their demands are within the capacity of those who are asked to perform them and within the capacities of as wide an age range of performers as possible. Such designs are likely to enhance performance of all individuals, especially older adults. To obtain optimal person–machine–environment system performance requires practical designs that accommodate subtle individual differences, whether they be named gender or sex; culture, race, or ethnicity; intelligence; age; or other such differences. Thus, a test of effectiveness of a design is to measure the degree to which system performance is maintained regardless of the inter- and intraindividual variations in the human. In other words, the challenge for gerontechnologists, ergonomists, and human factors specialists is to design tasks and systems such that age-related changes have little or no effect on performance, safety, or perceived satisfaction.

BIBLIOGRAPHY

Bouma, H., & Graafmans, J. A. M. (Eds.). (1992). *Gerontechnology.* Amsterdam: IOS Press.

Charness, N., & Bosman, E. A. (1990). Human factors and design for older adults. In J. E. Birren & K. W. Schaie (Eds.), *Handbook of the psychology of aging,* (3rd ed.) (pp. 446–463). San Diego: Academic Press.

Charness, N., & Bosman, E. A. (1992). Age and human factors. In F. I. M. Craik & T. A. Salthouse (Eds.), *The handbook of aging and cognition* (pp. 495–551). Hillsdale, NJ: Erlbaum.

Charness, N., & Bosman, E. A. (1994). Age-related changes in perceptual and psychomotor performance: Implications for engineering design. *Experimental Aging Research, 20,* 45–49.

Coleman, R., & Pullinger, D. J. (Special Issue Eds.). (1993). Designing for our future selves. *Applied Ergonomics, 24*(1), 1–62.

Czaja, S. J. (Special Issue Ed.). (1990). Aging. *Human Factors, 32*(5), 505–623.

Fisk, A. D., & Rogers, W. A. (Eds.) (in press). *Handbook of human factors and the older adult.* San Diego: Academic Press.

Fozard, J. L. (1981). Person–environment relationships in adulthood: Implications for human factors engineering. *Human Factors, 23,* 3–27.

Pirkl, J. J. (1994). *Transgenerational design: Products for an aging population.* New York: Van Nostrand Reinhold.

Small, A. M. (1987). Design for older people. In G. Salvendy (Ed.), *Handbook of human factors* pp. 495–504. New York: Wiley.

Wylde, M. A. (Guest Ed.). (1995). Technology and aging: Developing and marketing new products for older people (Special Issue). *Generations, XIX*(1), 1–62.

Glycation

Annette T. Lee and Anthony Cerami

The Picower Institute for Medical Research

Advanced Glycation End Products (AGEs) Permanent, covalently attached glucose-derived modifications on macromolecules.

Deoxyribonucleic Acid (DNA) Genetic material responsible for transmitting heritable characteristics.

Nonenzymatic Glycation The spontaneous reaction of glucose with biological macromolecules usually involving sugar attachment to a primary amino group.

Reducing Sugars Carbohydrates able to reduce oxidizing agents, typically those possessing an α-hydroxyketone, α-hydroxyaldehyde, hemiketal or hemiacetal group, and including all monosaccharides.

Transgenic Mice Mice containing heritable DNA from another source, which is permanently integrated into the genome of each cell.

Nonenzymatic **GLYCATION** is a term used to describe the permanent posttranslational modification of protein amino groups by reducing sugars. Although initially applied to proteins in the context of food chemistry, nonenzymatic glycation has been shown to occur slowly under physiologic conditions *in vivo* and is now known also to occur with certain nucleic acids and lipid molecules. The nonenzymatic reaction of reducing sugars to form permanent modifications with proteins not only alters their physical characteristics, but also impairs their biological function. These types of sugar-derived modifications have been termed advanced glycation end products (AGEs). During the past two decades, the presence and biological relevance of AGE modification has been evaluated for a number of important proteins. These investigations have led to an increasing body of evidence supporting the pivotal role of nonenzymatic glycation in the pathogenic mechanisms leading to complications associated with normal aging and diabetes mellitus. This review will focus on the current understanding of the chemical pathway and the biological consequences of AGE modification, and possible methods of pharmacological intervention.

I. CHEMISTRY

Nonenzymatic glycation was first described in 1912 by the food chemist Louis C. Maillard to account, in part, for the golden brown color of foods following cooking and for the change in taste and texture of foods during long-term storage. The Maillard reaction, or nonenzymatic glycation, begins with the spontaneous formation of a readily reversible Schiff base between the aldehyde group of a reducing sugar, such as glucose, and a primary amino group of a macromolecule, usually a protein. Within a relatively short time (days), the Schiff base can undergo intramolecular rearrangement and reach equilibrium with a more stable, but still slowly reversible, Amadori product (in the case of glucose). Over several weeks, the Amadori product can undergo a series of further spontaneous reactions including inter- and intramolecular rearrangements, dehydrations, and intermolecular con-

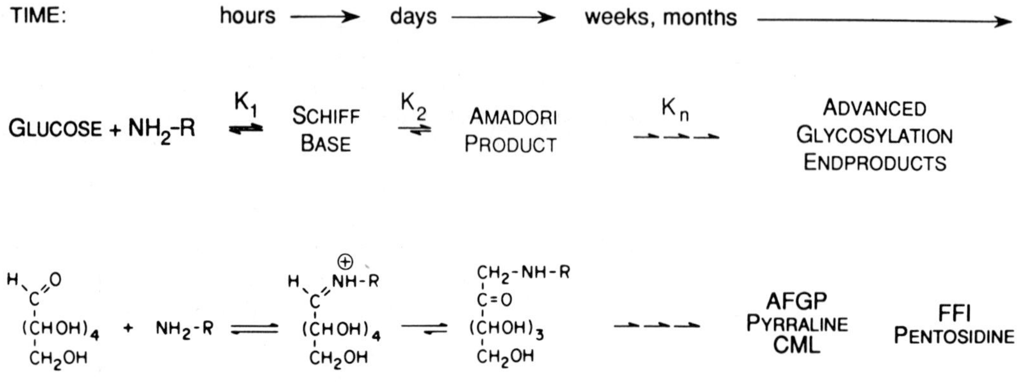

Figure 1 Formation of advanced glycation end products.

densations to form a heterogenous array of irreversible end products that are as a group, fluorescent, yellow-brown in color, and stable inter- and intramolecular cross-links. These end products are collectively referred to as advanced glycation end products (AGEs) (Figure 1). The formation of AGEs is entirely nonenzymatic and is not known to require any cofactors. The extent of AGE formation and accumulation depends on a number of variables such as temperature, pH, protein and glucose concentrations, and substrate turnover. Although temperature, pH, and protein concentration remain relatively constant *in vivo*, variability in mean blood glucose levels (glucose concentration) and protein half-life (incubation time) significantly influences the extent and accumulation of AGE-modified proteins. Proteins with half-lives greater than a few weeks, for instance, have the opportunity to accumulate more nonenzymatic glycation end products than those that have a half-life of only a few days. Proteins that are continuously exposed to circulating glucose, such as extracellular and serum proteins, also have an increased vulnerability to nonenzymatic glycation. In addition, diabetes mellitus, an illness characterized by chronic hyperglycemia, directly influences the rate of accumulation of AGE-modified proteins in proportion to the degree of mean blood glucose elevation.

The characterization and structural identification of specific AGEs has been impeded by the inherent diversity of products formed during the spontaneous chemical reactions and rearrangements of the nonenzymatic glycation pathway. Using model reactions, a limited number of specific AGE structures have been

determined (Figure 2). Because glucose is the major extracellular-reducing sugar in the body, it has been used extensively in model mechanistic studies. However, it is important to note that analogous reactions could occur with other reducing sugars. The first AGE to be isolated was 2-(2-furoyl)-4(5)-(2-furanyl)-1H-imidazole (FFI), which was synthesized by incubating glucose with polylysine or bovine serum albumin. Other AGE structures including pentosidine, carboxymethyl-lysine (CML), and pyrraline have also been identified in model incubations, and their presence has been confirmed *in vivo*. Because the process of AGE formation by nature leads to a markedly heterogeneous spectrum of products, the specific yield of any one product is very limited. For this reason, it

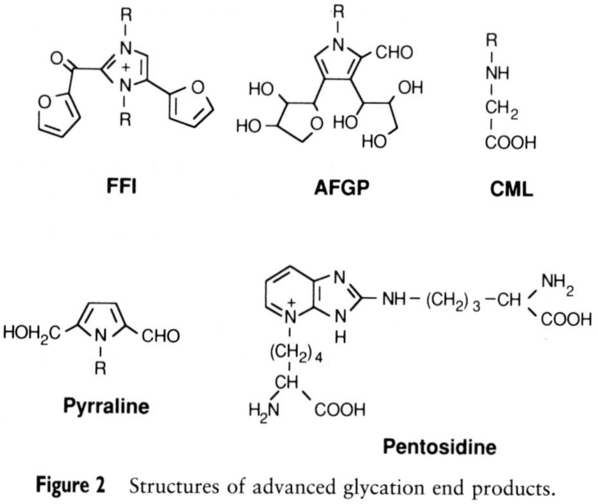

Figure 2 Structures of advanced glycation end products.

was postulated that by inhibiting alternate pathways of the nonenzymatic glycation reaction, one could enrich for specific intermediate compounds. Sulfites have been well recognized by food chemists to inhibit nonenzymatic glycation in foodstuffs and have been used extensively in the food industry as preservatives. The presence of sodium sulfite as an inhibitor in a model reaction of glucose and 6-amino-hexanoic acid led to the identification of an AGE intermediate product, 1-alkyl-2-formyl-3,4-diglycosylpyrrole (AFGP).

II. BIOLOGICAL CONSEQUENCES

The formation of AGEs on biological macromolecules alters their structural and functional properties. This type of slow, progressive modification on biologically relevant macromolecules and the accumulation of these modified macromolecules *in vivo* has been implicated in a number of pathologic abnormalities, most prominently the complications associated with normal aging and long-term diabetes. The similarities in the type and development of such complications suggest that the effects of chronic hyperglycemia resemble accelerated aging.

A. Intracellular Proteins

That nonenzymatic glycation occurred *in vivo* was originally discovered by the presence of a minor hemoglobin species, $A_{1c}(HbA_{1c})$, in erythrocytes. It was later discovered that HbA_{1c} was more prevalent in blood from diabetic individuals compared to nondiabetic. Further biochemical investigations into the origin of HbA_{1c} in blood from diabetic samples demonstrated the presence of a glucose-derived Amadori product covalently linked to the N-terminal valine of the beta-chain of hemoglobin. The clinical measurement of glycosylated hemoglobin in erythrocytes has become an indispensable indicator of circulating mean glucose levels, and is routinely used to assess diabetic control over the 3–4-week period prior to sampling.

Because glucose is found throughout the body, it was hypothesized that other proteins may be sensitive to modification by glucose. Lens proteins were thought to be likely candidates to show the accumulation of AGEs, because these proteins turn over very slowly, if at all. Like hemoglobin in erythrocytes, lens proteins are present in insulin-independent cells; therefore, lens proteins are exposed to glucose levels that directly reflect the extracellular sugar concentrations. In addition, a number of age-related changes in lens proteins, such as increased aggregation, changes in absorption peaks, and the presence of fluorescent chromophores suggested that nonenzymatic glycation occurred prominently within the lens. In particular, the accumulation of lens protein cross-links contributes to the opacification and cataracts so often observed in aged human lens. *In vitro* studies confirmed that lens proteins could react with glucose or glucose-6-phosphate to result in protein cross-links and lead to changes in absorbance and fluorescence spectra similar to those observed in digests of cataractous lens proteins from aged and diabetic individuals. The observed similarities between lens proteins that were nonenzymatically glycated *in vitro* and lens proteins from aged or diabetic individuals provided the first evidence that nonenzymatic glycation was involved in the development and progression of complications related to normal aging and long-term diabetes.

B. Extracellular Proteins

The influence of extracellular glucose on the modification of lens proteins provided further impetus to study the significance of nonenzymatic glycation in the pathogenic mechanisms involving other long-lived proteins. Extracellular proteins were considered to be particularly susceptible because, like proteins within insulin-independent cells, nonenzymatic glycation of extracellular proteins would be directly influenced by the concentration of circulating glucose. Collagen is the predominant extracellular protein in the body and the major component of connective tissues, such as skin, tendons, and cartilage. Given its abundance, long half-life, and accessibility by circulating glucose, collagen appeared to have the necessary characteristics for susceptibility to nonenzymatic glycation. Increased collagen stiffness and rigidity is often ascribed to normal symptoms of aging, and this decreased flexibility might be attributed, in part, to AGE-mediated collagen cross-links. The extent of modification of collagen by nonenzymatic glycation has been measured in a number of different collagen-rich tissues including aorta, dura mater, and skin. In each case, the extent to which collagen has become AGE-modified correlates positively with age. Tissue samples from insulin-dependent diabetics show an increase in AGE-modified collagen as a function of chronological age, but the levels observed were comparable to normal individuals twice as old as the diabetic patients. These results reaffirm that the development of some common consequences of normal aging is accelerated in individuals with long-term diabetes.

The presence of AGEs on collagen not only affects its physical and structural characteristics, but AGE modification of collagen can also contribute to atherosclerosis, nephropathy, and peripheral vascular disorders. Studies have shown that AGE-modified collagen can cross-link not only to other collagen molecules, but also to circulating serum proteins. The covalent attachment and immobilization of circulating proteins such as low-density lipoproteins, serum albumin, and immunoglobulins to tissue collagen is thought to contribute to the development of atherosclerotic lesions, thickening of basement membrane in renal tissue, and peripheral vasculature occlusion.

C. Other Pathologic Consequences

More recent investigations have revealed a potential role of AGE-modified proteins in other age-related pathologies, such as Alzheimer's disease (AD) and brain damage due to stroke. The presence and progressive accumulation of amyloid plaques in brain tissue is a central hallmark of AD, and a great deal of work has centered on the mechanisms leading to the aggregation and deposition of β-amyloid (βA) accumulations in the brain. Recently, amyloid plaques from diseased and normal brain tissues were evaluated for the presence of AGEs. It was found that samples from AD-diseased brains contained almost three times more AGEs per milligram of protein than did age-matched controls. Also, glycation of soluble βA peptides markedly accelerated the formation of insoluble fibrillar βA aggregates in test-tube incubations. These findings suggest that AGEs may be involved in amyloid plaque formation and deposition, and thus contribute to the neuropathologies associated with AD. [See DEMENTIA.]

The exacerbation of another neuropathological disorder by AGEs has recently been observed in a rodent model. Administration of physiological concentrations of AGE-modified proteins to normal rats prior to cerebral artery occlusion caused a significantly larger volume of stroke damage and infarction when compared to nontreated animals. These results suggest that AGEs can initiate potentially neurotoxic processes; however, it is not clear whether AGEs induce damage directly or if they are mediated through one or more secondary pathways.

D. Nucleic Acids

The identification of nonenzymatic modification by glucose of different classes of biologically relevant macromolecules supports the pervasive nature of this reaction in cells and tissues of the body. A number of years ago it was hypothesized that free amino groups on DNA bases could also participate in nonenzymatic reactions with glucose, in a manner similar to that of the Maillard reaction with proteins. The nonenzymatic glycation of DNA may contribute to several well-known age-related genetic dysfunctions, such as decreased RNA and protein synthesis, decreased DNA repair and replication, and increased chromosomal aberrations.

Initial *in vitro* studies demonstrated that amino groups of nucleotides, whether free or polymerized in single- or double-stranded DNA, could react with glucose and glucose-6-phosphate. These nonenzymatic reactions generated glycated DNA with altered absorbance and fluorescence spectra, in a time- and sugar-concentration-dependent manner that were directly comparable to the spectral changes observed to accompany the nonenzymatic glycation of proteins. When plasmid DNA, which had been glycated *in vitro* was used to transform bacteria, the glucose-modified DNA had a significantly lower transformation efficiency than control plasmid DNA. This loss in activity correlated with the length of the incubation period and the glucose concentration present in the reaction. Plasmid DNA isolated from some of the transformed colonies was analyzed and found to contain anomalous sequences. These observations supported, for the first time at the molecular level, the hypothesis that nonenzymatic glycation of DNA could have adverse biological effects. Similar results have been observed in other *in vitro* and *in vivo* prokaryotic and eukaryotic model systems, confirming the mutagenic potential of DNA glycation. The effects of DNA glycation can permanently compromise the integrity of the genome and may result in various degrees of impaired cellular function, in extreme cases inducing cell death.

Transgenic mice containing a specific mutagenesis marker gene, *lacI*, were used to determine whether the effects of nonenzymatic glycation extended to the genome in intact animals. By measuring the accumulation of *lacI* mutants as a function of age, it was determined that mutant frequency increased linearly with time. The types of DNA mutations observed were not limited to simple base substitutions, but included large deletions and insertions, suggesting the activity of complex AGE-dependent DNA repair pathways. Given these results over the short life spans of experimental animals, one can also expect that AGE-induced DNA damage and mutations may account for some of the genetic alterations that are observed in elderly humans.

It has been well documented that there is a significantly higher incidence of birth defects in infants born to insulin-dependent diabetic mothers than in those born to their nondiabetic counterparts. Using the same *lacI* transgenic mice, the mutagenic effects of maternal hyperglycemia on developing embryos could be assessed. In fetuses that developed in diabetic dams versus those developing under normal conditions, there was a two-fold increase in *lacI* mutant frequency. Molecular analysis of these *lacI* mutants showed a pattern of DNA mutations similar to those observed in aged mice. These similarities suggest a common mechanism of DNA damage and subsequent inefficient repair in normal aging and diabetic pregnancies. This study provided the first potential molecular link between maternal hyperglycemia, DNA damage, and congenital malformations.

III. PHARMACOLOGICAL INTERVENTION

Specific knowledge of the chemical pathways involved in AGE formation has allowed potential pharmacological inhibitors to be synthesized. The first compound to show promise in this regard has been the small molecule, aminoguanidine. Aminoguanidine can react with a post-Amadori product to form products that do not go on to form AGEs, and is effective in this regard in test tube reactions and in animals. Although still early in the process of clinical assessment, there is encouraging evidence from animal studies that this drug has the therapeutic potential to pre-

vent the development of AGE-related pathologies. It is hoped that better understandings of the chemistry leading to the formation of AGEs will lead to the development of additional anti-AGE approaches with therapeutic potential.

IV. CONCLUSIONS

The nonenzymatic reactions initiated by the chemical condensations of reducing sugars with proteins and nucleic acids lead to the formation of irreversible structural modifications, AGEs, which have important biological implications. A number of complications associated with diabetes mellitus and chronic hyperglycemia, (e.g., cataracts, collagen stiffening, and atherosclerosis) resemble those characteristics of normal aging, suggesting that the diabetic environment represents a model for accelerated aging. AGEs accumulate slowly in normal aging and more rapidly in the diabetic environment. These molecular modifications appear to account significantly for these similar pathological courses. Therefore, mechanisms that prevent, reduce, or relieve AGE-related diabetic complications can also be expected to improve age-related symptoms. Not only will therapeutic methods of intervention increase the quality of life of millions of individuals affected by diabetes, but they may also benefit the lives of all older individuals.

BIBLIOGRAPHY

Bucala, R., & Cerami, A. (1992). Advanced glycosylation: Chemistry, biology, and implications for diabetes and aging. *Advances in Pharmacology, 23*, 1.

Bucala, R., Vlassara, H., & Cerami, A. (1992). Advanced glycosylation endproducts. In Harding & M. J. C. Crabbe, (Eds.), *Posttranslational modification of proteins*, p. 53–79. Boca Raton: CRC Press.

Lee, A. T., & Cerami, A. (1990). Modifications of proteins and nucleic acids by reducing sugars: Possible role in aging. In E. L. Schneider & J. W. Rowe (Eds.), *Handbook of the biology of aging* (3rd ed.), p. 116–130. San Diego: Academic Press.

Lee, A. T., & Cerami, A. (1992). Role of glycation in aging. *Annals of the New York Academy of Sciences, 663*, 63.

Vlassara, H., Bucala, R., & Striker, L. (1994). Pathogenic effects of advanced glycosylation: Biochemical, biologic, and clinical implications for diabetes and aging. *Laboratory Investigation, 70*, 138.

Grandparenthood

Helen Q. Kivnick and Heather M. Sinclair

University of Minnesota

Affect The feelings, moods, and tones expressed in the family.

Family A basic unit of society, characterized as one whose members are economically and emotionally dependent on one another and are responsible for each other's development, stability, and protection. The family serves as the basic unit of socialization to teach cultural values and adaptation to society. Currently, in our society, the traditional definition of the family is undergoing transition because of the emerging prominence of alternative lifestyles.

Nuclear Family A family consisting of a husband, a wife, and their immediate children.

Extended Family A group of individuals consisting of the nuclear family, as well as individuals related by ties of consanguinity. Extension of ties exists among parents and their children, grandchildren, and between siblings.

Generation A group of individuals constituting a single step in the line of descent from an ancestor.

Intergenerational Pertaining to or involving individuals in different generations.

Role A set of behaviors expected on the basis of a particular status. Roles may be *ascribed* (assigned on the basis of factors over which the individual has no control) or *achieved* (earned on the basis of individual effort).

Instrumental Activity Behavior that is directed toward a goal.

GRANDPARENTHOOD is the family role assigned to an individual whose child produces a child. Grandparenthood is also a dyadic relationship involving a grandparent and a grandchild. Grandparenthood has existed for as long as families have included three or more generations. Its associated rights, responsibilities, behaviors, meanings, and satisfactions have varied with factors that are cultural, demographic, social, economic, psychological, and historical in nature. Grandparenthood has been investigated as a role, status, and relationship. Findings have implications for research and practice.

I. BACKGROUND

A. Anthropological Context

Although grandparents have played a role in family life for as long as families have included three or more generations, the nature of this role has varied with a multiplicity of cultural, demographic, social, economic, psychological, and historical factors. Levels of formality and respect in grandparenthood relationships are directly related to elder power over societal and family structure. In cultures and historical periods where decision making and economic power reside with the old, relations between grandparents and members of other generations are formal and authoritarian, characterized by prerogative and protective care on one side, and by dependence and respect, on the other. Conversely, in cultures and periods in which the old are removed from functional authority, grandparent–grandchild relationships are warmer and more indulgent; they are characterized by a friendly equality that can function to relieve tensions between family generations.

B. Changing Demography of Intergenerational Relations

Over the course of this century, changes in mortality and fertility have led to greater life expectancy and to changing rhythms in the family cycle—both of which have dramatically influenced the nature of intergenerational family relations. Reductions in mortality rates, public health advances, and control over once-fatal childhood diseases have combined to increase life expectancies, over the course of this century, from roughly 46 to nearly 80 years. For the first time in history, human beings can expect to live between one-third and one-half of their lives after they have reproduced. Never before have so many individuals lived long enough (and had their children live long enough) to become grandparents. Demographers report that in 1990, 94% of all older adults with children were grandparents, and nearly 50% were great-grandparents. Reciprocally, birth cohorts of children have never before had so many grandparents and great-grandparents.

Extended life expectancies have increased the number of multigenerational families, and have led to an unprecedented emergence of the long-term intergenerational relationships referred to by one family sociologist as "crescive bonds." Parent–child bonds may be expected to endure for six or more decades, four of which involve parents and their adult children. Americans today typically become grandparents in midlife; they can expect to spend four or more decades—roughly one half of their lives—in this role. One family historian notes that only in this century have grandparents and grandchildren enjoyed a meaningful period of overlap in their lives. Contrary to popular misconception, grandparenting has been a phenomenon of middle age for at least the past century. What makes contemporary grandparenthood demographically unique is its duration through both middle and later life.

Twentieth-century America has seen an overall reduction in the number of children per family, and a corresponding contraction in any given family's period of childbearing. These changes have led to an increasing distinction between parenthood and grandparenthood, both as individual life experiences, and

as statuses within the family. No longer is it common, in mainstream society, for new grandparents to be actively involved in bearing and rearing their own children. Sociologists point out that when a person becomes a grandparent today, he or she is likely to have fewer family roles competing for personal time and attention than would have been the case in previous generations. Today's competing roles are more likely to be located in the workplace and the community than inside the family. (Increasing life expectancies for the frail elderly may come to replace child care with elder care as a major family responsibility of the middle aged and the young old.)

C. Socioeconomic Changes

Family historians describe a shift in the family, dating back to the late 1800s, from a corporate unit whose members were bound by lifelong interdependence, to a largely emotional entity whose members stress individual and nuclear independence. This shift in family structure is closely related to societywide changes in work schedules, retirement, social programs, overall standards of living, transportation, and communication. At the beginning of this period, low wages, unemployment crises, illness, death, and the absence of social welfare programs forced family members to rely on one another for support. Family ties were seen as permanent obligations that took precedence over often transient feelings of affection or its opposite. Over the course of this century wages and general standards of living have risen, the work week has stabilized at roughly 40 hours, and, in many sectors of society, unemployment crises have diminished. Today's average male can expect to spend 15 years of his adult life retired from the labor force. Control over illness and death have increased. Social welfare and insurance programs have transferred basic financial reponsibility for the elderly, the disabled, and the infirm from kin to society as a whole. Improved transportation and communication technologies facilitate frequent contact across great distances. [*See* ECONOMICS: SOCIETY.]

All together, these changes have both permitted and promoted the independence of family generations, nuclear units, and individual members. Obligatory family ties based on need have been replaced with more voluntary bonds based on sentiment and attachment. The family as an institution governed by strict social mores and laws has given way to what has been described as a "companionship," with behavior determined by mutual affection and by membership consensus.

Thus, today's grandparents are likely to have more time and money to spend on their grandchildren than their predecessors did. They are less likely to be raising their own children while actively grandparenting. They are less likely to provide instrumental family services out of need and obligation, and more likely to do so on the basis of desire and affection. Pressures related to work, marriage, education, climate, and security all contribute to the fact that today's grandparents and their grandchildren live at considerable geographic distances from one another. Nonetheless, they are likely to maintain regular telephone contact, and to visit several times a year.

D. Grandparenthood Research

As discussed above, socioeconomic and demographic trends in the first half of this century permitted nuclear families to enact the self-reliance and individual independence that constitute this country's most basic social values. It should therefore not be surprising that family researchers in these years all but ignored the grandparent role, which they saw as either ignominiously dependent or anachronistically controlling. Instead, they drew invidious comparisons between the contemporary American nuclear family, rooted in individualism and democracy, and the historical American family, characterized as multigenerational and patriarchal. During this period grandparents appear in social science research, if at all, almost entirely in the work of anthropologists.

By the late 1950s, family theorists began to challenge their earlier neglect of extended family networks. Over the next fifteen years scholars began to cite evidence for the modern modality of the American "modified extended family," a system of nuclear families bound together by affectional ties, patterns of social activity, and mutual assistance. In addition, family historians of this new period reinterpreted historical data to conclude that harmonious, multigenerational family life had never been common in America. Rather, they asserted, intrafamily cooperation and assistance had always been American

norms; along with parents and children, grandparents had always participated in mutual-help networks of kin.

Grandparenthood research in the 1960s and 1970s focused primarily on such singular qualities as love, authority, esteem, and responsibility. Gradually these unidimensional descriptions gave way to more comprehensive typologies. More recent research has attempted to establish causal links between typological categories and a host of demographic, personality, and family variables.

II. GRANDPARENTHOOD TO GRANDPARENTS

Discussions of the grandparent role often confound the components of behavior, meaning, and satisfaction. Perhaps because all three components are difficult to measure, researchers refer to the grandparent role without systematically differentiating among components or investigating their interrelationships. However, although behavior, meaning, and satisfaction are clearly related, they are, just as clearly, conceptually distinct. In addition to these three components, the grandparent role also involves such elements as role ambiguity, career development, timing, and instrumentality.

A. Behavior

On the basis of interviews with 70 grandparent couples, one study identified five distinct styles of grandparenting: Formal; Fun seeker; Surrogate parent; Reservoir of family wisdom; Distant figure. In a more recent study, 510 grandparents were interviewed to describe three grandparenting styles: Remote; Companionate; Involved.

Research indicates that most contemporary American grandparent relationships may be described as *Companionate* in style. Leisure and pleasure, rather than labor and responsibility, govern these relationships. Grandparents share fun and games with their grandchildren, enjoying affectionate, informal time together. With respect to matters of discipline, values, and socialization, Companionate grandparents say that they hold their tongues and adhere to a widely accepted norm of noninterference across nuclear family boundaries. Some Companionate grandparents express regret at having to withhold what they regard as valuable advice, and others want more interaction with the grandchildren, but know they are powerless to get it. Nonetheless, most reconcile themselves to being both connected to and separate from their grandchildren, and they agree that their lack of authority makes grandparenthood relationships uniquely pleasant and comfortable.

The norm of grandparental noninterference is part of what psychiatrist A. Kornhaber disparages as the *new social contract,* according to which the value of mutual independence supersedes other long-term concerns and short-term needs. Kornhaber reports that after years of heavy family responsibilities, grandparents welcome the opportunity to place their own, individual wishes first. Psychologist D. Gutmann suggests that more than actually wanting to enact freedom, grandparents want to *be seen* as embodying societal values of self-sufficiency and independence. Anthropologist C. Johnson maintains that grandparents acquiesce to noninvolvement largely because they believe they should not interfere in their children's families. According to this view, grandparents actively pursue interests outside the family essentially to distract themselves from intruding.

Remote grandparenthood relationships are characterized by emotional distance and formal, reserved interactions, as experienced by both grandparent and grandchild. This is the behavioral style most often chosen by today's grandparents to describe their own grandparents, two generations ago. *Involved* grandparenting entails spending a good deal of time working and playing together. These relationships are both companionable and instrumental. Their ties are based on exchange, on direct action, and on behaviors, concerns, and responsibilities that many Companionate grandparents would regard as off limits.

Most grandparents and grandchildren can establish only symbolic bonds unless they see each other regularly. However, although amount of contact is often used in research to operationalize importance of the grandparenthood role, this variable is a prerequisite, not a proxy, for the phenomenon researchers seek to measure. Amount and quality of contact may be influenced by geographical proximity and by grandparent health and competing commitments; research suggests that proximity is the most powerful influence. Serving as "lineage bridges," parents can

promote or inhibit relationships between the generations on either side. Parents model relationships with older family members, and they provide children with examples of how to relate to grandparents. Parental attitudes toward older people, in general, and their relations with their own parents, in particular, affect the grandparenthood relationships in their own family. Parents serve as gatekeepers to their children. However, despite this acknowledged power in the middle generation, it seems that only rarely do parents deliberately limit grandparenthood contact.

The grandparent role is enacted by means of specific behaviors that are associated with a multiplicity of variables. Age, gender, and marital status influence grandparent behaviors. Older grandparents tend to be more formal, younger grandparents to be more relaxed and playful. In accord with women's "kin-keeper" role in families, maternal grandmothers tend to be visited more frequently and to be seen as emotionally closer than paternal grandparents. Grandfathers tend to be oriented outside the family, as "ambassadors," whereas grandmothers are oriented inward, as "ministers of the interior." Widows are more likely to be actively involved with their grandchildren than are remarried older men.

As described in research throughout the social sciences, grandparenthood role enactment is also influenced by variables that may be categorized in terms of family structure (e.g., number of grandchildren; importance of family), socioeconomics (e.g., employment status; educational level; economic resources), social resources (e.g., ethnic and subcultural identification; frequency of interaction with friends; community ties; number and nature of nonfamily roles), and personal resources (e.g., health; well-being; personality variables). Perhaps the most outspoken contemporary advocate of grandparenthood as a vital intergenerational connection, Kornhaber identifies a somewhat different set of determinants of grandparent role behavior. He points to societal attitude toward grandparenting, and to personality altruism. He also identifies the following earlier-life, intergenerational determinants of grandparent behavior: (a) the individual's experience as a grandchild; and (b) the individual's parents' grandparenting behaviors. These last determinants remind us that as a relationship in which most people participate for most of their lives, grandparenthood rests on a foundation that is established, inalterably, in childhood. A given adult's grandparenthood is determined both by circumstances that are in effect in adulthood, and also by those that were influential during childhood. For better or worse, the grandchildhood experiences of today's children will influence the grandparenthood they are able to enact two generations hence.

B. Meaning

Attention to behavior, alone, ignores the meaning and importance of the grandparent role to grandparents. Neugarten and Weinstein used their interview data to specify five categories of grandparenthood meaning: source of biological renewal; opportunity to succeed in a new emotional role; teacher–resource person role; vicarious achievement; and remote role). Examining grandparenthood meaning as a product of social and personal forces, V. Wood and J. Robertson designated four grandparenthood role types, representing high versus low dichotomizations of each dimension. These early typologies share the property of categorization (e.g., a grandparent's style is either *formal* or *fun seeker;* the meaning he or she finds in grandparenthood is either *vicarious achievement* or *source of biological renewal.*)

Based on interviews with 286 grandparents, psychologist H. Kivnick deductively derived five different dimensions of grandparenthood meaning: centrality; valued elder; indulgence; immortality through clan; reinvolvement with personal past. Unlike earlier typologies, these dimensions were conceptualized as comprising, all together, the overall meaning a given individual finds in grandparenthood. Rather than being categorized as experiencing grandparenthood in terms of *centrality* or *indulgence,* for example, an individual is assumed to experience grandparenthood in terms of *all five* dimensions; he or she may be scored from high to low on each dimension.

Life cycle theorist E. H. Erikson and his colleagues J. Erikson and H. Kivnick describe the psychosocial theme of *Generativity and Stagnation* as comprising the experiences of caring, nurturing, and maintaining. After middle adulthood's direct "responsibility for the maintenance of the world," generativity comes to involve more indirect nurturing, to promote the robust senses of caring, generational connectedness, and wisdom that are the goals of middle and later adulthood. An integral part of the generational cycle, grandparenthood offers a valuable opportunity for

grandparents to revisit their own capacities to nurture and to care, while, at the same time, enriching the essential generativity received by grandchildren.

Kornhaber and Woodward highlight reciprocity in the ways grandparent and grandchild roles are linked to the developmental needs of both generations. Shared time, shared place, shared activities, commitment to family—all these are crucial in establishing and maintaining a grandparenthood relationship. All are also crucial in accomplishing age-appropriate tasks related to generativity for both grandparent and grandchild. Qualitative exploration of grandparental units provides empirical evidence for the existence of generativity in the grandparenthood relationship. Although interviewed grandparents did not articulate consciously generative goals, enduring positive relations with grandchildren and feelings of success with intergenerational family life were interpreted as indications that grandparenthood facilitates developmental generativity. By maintaining strong affectional ties and mutually acceptable levels of association with grandchildren, grandparents seem to be able to balance their conflicting needs for contact and independence, for family identity and individuality, for personal usefulness and freedom from responsibility.

C. Role Ambiguity and Grandparenthood Career

Failing to find powerful associations between grandparenthood and diverse measures of grandparent well-being, researchers have long described the grandparent role as a relatively unimportant component of later life. Sociologists L. Burton and V. Bengtson note that grandparenthood conforms to Rosow's definition of a tenuous role, (i.e., a definite social position with only vague behavioral guidelines). In the macrosocial structure, grandparenthood cannot be considered a functional role. Its presence or absence is thought to have no definitive effect on whether or not "society is possible." It carries no universal expectations governed by Durkheim's "collective conscience." It assumes a comparably idiosyncratic character within the microstructure; regardless of family expectations, a grandparent may choose to engage or not to engage in any role behavior.

Like that of parent, the role of grandparent follows a career trajectory, and the course of its interactions changes in predictable ways. The career begins with the news of imminent grandparenthood (i.e., of the imminent acquisition of a new status). This anticipatory stage is structured by expectations that are generally vague but enjoyable. The role at this point is titular. Behaviors include telling the news to friends and other family members, and, in some cases, assisting with preparations. Consistent with Kornhaber's new social contract, anticipatory grandparents speak of waiting to see how these new relationships will develop far more often than they describe assuming an active role in creating or structuring them.

Research suggests that once the grandparenthood bond is established in childhood, it remains fairly stable throughout the rest of the life course. Nonetheless, the grandparent career moves through distinct periods. During the grandchild's preschool and elementary years, grandparents typically enjoy their most frequent contact. As grandparent and grandchild spend time together, the grandparent's role broadens and deepens. These are the years Cherlin and Furstenberg refer to as the "fat years," during which grandparents can becoming living ancestors and historians, treasured companions, and role models. During the subsequent "lean years" of the grandchild's adolescence, contact typically decreases and—if a solid bond has been established in the previous stage—the grandparent typically becomes a source of assistance and advice in times of expressed need. The final period of grandparenthood is the longest, beginning when the grandchild enters adulthood and grandparents, like parents, must learn to let go. Great-grandparenthood, with its primarily symbolic significance, may be seen as a separate phase in this long final period.

D. Timing

Neugarten's concept of social time—society's age-grade system for appropriate progression through life's roles—influences the grandparenthood experience. The significance of grandparenthood timing is particularly important in view of the fact that becoming a grandparent is a countertransition (i.e., a role change dependent on a transition initiated by another family member). The timing of grandparenthood hinges both on the age at which the individual became a parent, and also on the age at which his or her children reproduce for the first time. Grandparents have no control over the timing of this countertransition; they must live with the timing forced upon them.

Normative in middle age, first-time grandparenthood is seen as on time when it occurs between the ages of 42 and 57. Research indicates that assuming the grandmother role significantly early (ages 25–38) may result in "crisis accumulation," in which the combined demands of children, grandchildren, work, and other generational family members make a woman vulnerable to "role overload." In addition to concrete behavioral demands, early grandmotherhood may precipitate tension in a young woman's view of herself, and it may trigger conflict in the familywide system of cohesion and social support. Defending against all these tensions, some early grandmothers explicitly refuse to engage in the grandparent role. By contrast, research suggests that on-time grandmothers avoid the strains of off-time transitions and feel good about their grandparenthood timing.

E. Instrumentality

Despite contemporary norms of grandparent noninterference, the role does involve a variety of instrumental expressions. As "family watchdogs," grandparents respond to obvious need in the next generations by providing service. Reciprocally, grandparents often receive essential service from intergenerational family members. The last years of this century are witnessing a dramatic shrinkage of societal economic resources, and a corresponding expansion of the demands placed on extended family members. It is therefore not surprising that the bulk of current grandparenthood research concerns instrumental service provision.

I. Grandparent Caretakers

Grandparents provide care for their grandchildren within a range of structures. Some provide regular day care while the parents are at work. Others provide primary care while coresiding with the grandchildren, and, perhaps, with their parent(s), as well. Still others acquire legal custody of the grandchildren. [See CAREGIVING AND CARING.] Traditionally, the Black community has emphasized support within extended kin networks. Indeed, Black children are much more likely than Whites or Latinos to live in grandparents' homes. However, since 1980 it is White children who have been moving into grandparents' homes at the greatest rates.

Although many grandparents function as their grandchildren's sole caregiver, parents of adolescent mothers often share caregiving responsibilities with coresiding daughters who must now balance the demands of parenthood with the developmental tasks of adolescence. As these families' most consistent providers of care and support, grandparents serve as both role models and caregivers to both mother and grandchild. Grandparents play an important role in assessing the mother's competency to care for her child, often taking over when they judge the mother to be incompetent. For young mothers, grandmothers tend to provide the most and highest quality support when the mother lives with them, and when the grandchild's father is less involved. Young Black mothers are far more likely than Whites to coreside with grandmothers. For older mothers, grandmothers are likely to be most effective caregivers in noncoresidential situations. Grandmothers seem to experience most caregiver satisfaction when they do not have preschool children of their own, and when they, themselves, receive support from a partner or financial assistance such as Aid to Families with Dependent Children (AFDC).

When grandmothers provide daily child care, the grandchild's mother or father or both are usually working full time. Such grandmothers want to help the parent(s) financially, and they would rather not leave their grandchildren in paid day care or at a sitter's house. In such circumstances, grandparents attempt to support the middle-generation nuclear family and help keep it intact.

Under other circumstances (e.g., child abandonment, neglect, or abuse; parental mental or emotional problems; parental death; parental incarceration; parental drug addiction, particularly to crack cocaine), the middle-generation nuclear family is so badly disintegrated that grandparents intervene both to provide care and, when necessary, to assume legal responsibility for the grandchildren. Some of these negative circumstances may arise without warning, such as a young mother's sudden death or incarceration. Others arise as a result of ongoing parent–grandparent negotiation. Still others develop over time, until the grandparent decides that personal intervention is necessary.

Most caregiving grandparents experience emotional, physical, and financial strains associated with their caregiving roles. If their primary caregiving is to be long-term or permanent, grandparents may worry about living long enough to raise their grandchildren to adulthood. Others are concerned about keeping up with the grandchildren's school, social, and physical activities. Still others are anxious about possible psychological harm to grandchildren who have been abused by their parents.

Parental crack cocaine addiction creates unique concerns for grandparent caregivers. Many fear for their own safety and security, as well as their grandchildren's. Some worry that their addicted children will steal their money or property to buy drugs, perhaps using physical violence to do so. Others experience anxiety about the burglaries, drive-by shootings, and dangerous automobile traffic that pervade neighborhoods beset by drug trafficking. In addition, these grandparents anticipate the financial and emotional drains of having to provide care for multiple kin. With respect to the grandchildren, grandparents worry that despite their best caregiving efforts, the children will inherit their parents' addictions.

Grandparents undergo a variety of life changes when they assume parental responsibility for the grandchildren. Most often reported are the negative changes. Grandparents who quit jobs to become full-time caregivers may miss contact with co-workers; most regret decreased opportunities for socializing with friends and confidantes. Many feel cheated of personal space, privacy, and freedom. Others experience moving backward in their lives. Still others find that renewed caregiving responsibilities strain their once postparental marriages. Negative health-related outcomes may include physical conditions such as heart attacks, strokes, diabetes, and arthritis. Alcoholism, increased smoking, and depression and anxiety have all been reported as negative emotional consequences. [See ALCOHOL AND DRUGS: DEPRESSION.]

Not all the changes associated with full-time caregiving are negative. Some caregiving grandparents develop new friendships as they identify with other people who share their current situation. Where some experience marital strain, as noted above, others report enhanced marriages or relationships as the grandchildren foster improved communication and increased time together between partners. Although health problems plague some grandparent caregivers, others experience improved health as they adopt more nutritious diets and engage in physical activity with the grandchildren.

Within the family context, grandparent caregivers may experience a variety of important satisfactions. Those who are displeased with the way they raised their own children may welcome what they regard as a second chance at parenting. Others value the opportunity to nurture their family line. Many treasure the gifts of companionship and love they receive from their grandchildren. Most grandparents who provide caregiving in place of ineffective parents are proud to see themselves as actively creating positive change in an otherwise deteriorating family cycle.

2. Reciprocal Caregiving

The relationship between American elders and their families is characterized by a "generalized reciprocity" across generations. Over the life course, family members exchange affective and instrumental support as needed, effectively making deposits and withdrawals from what T. Antonucci refers to as a lifelong bank of support. Not only do grandparents provide assistance in times of family crises. They receive needed care and support, as well. [*See* SOCIAL NETWORKS, SUPPORT, AND INTEGRATION.]

Although grandparents and their adult grandchildren seem to share expectations of turning to one another for whatever support may be needed, grandparents both expect and receive more emotional than instrumental support from their adult grandchildren. And grandparents generally perceive that they receive more from their adult grandchildren than they currently provide in return. These findings correspond to the literature on relations between adult children and their aging parents. Where instrumental support is provided, it comes most often from female members of the middle generation.

3. Divorce

Middle-generation divorce is one of the major family disruptions against which grandparents are seen as providing continuity. During such times of crisis, older persons' importance to the family may increase significantly. Johnson reports that after a divorce, most grandparents try to provide instrumental assistance (e.g., money, babysitting, and other services) and emotional support to parents and grandchildren. Grandparents may be in a unique position to offer the grandchildren an emotional haven. In some cases,

grandparents assume parental responsibility for a number of years, while the biological parent retains or struggles to regain legal custody.

Divorce can precipitate both increases and decreases in grandparents' contact with their grandchildren. Increases typically result when the grandchildren move to a closer geographic location, when grandmothers provide child care for custodial daughters who reenter the workforce, and when hostile parents are removed from the grandchildren's daily lives. Decreased contact typically results from distant geographic moves and from unresolved grandparent–parent conflict in the wake of the divorce.

Particularly after divorce, parents have the power to facilitate or prevent grandparent access to grandchildren. Although all states (excluding the District of Columbia) have passed grandparent visitation rights statutes, the matter of postdivorce grandparent contact is far from settled. Proponents argue that the grandparent–grandchild bond is uniquely precious, and that it is in the child's best interest for the court to enforce visitation rights. Opponents counter that court-ordered grandparent visitation interferes with appropriate parental authority. Even in the absence of conflict, noncustodial parents may be reluctant to share their child visitation time with grandparents.

In addition to depending on family dynamics, grandparents' roles during and after divorce can vary with grandparent age and lineage. Older grandparents are more likely to experience disabilities that prevent them from offering help and assistance. Even before divorce, younger grandparents tend to be more active and to have more contact with grandchildren. Younger grandparents may also be more tolerant and less judgmental, and they may therefore be more welcome in postdivorce households. Although paternal grandmothers are generally described as having less contact with and providing less assistance to postdivorce grandchildren, many paternal grandmothers make a point of maintaining contact with their former daughters-in-law who, in turn, permit access to the grandchildren.

F. Grandparent Satisfaction and Well-Being

Research finds that grandparents generally report satisfaction, pride, and pleasure in grandparenthood. No one variable emerges as critical in determining level of satisfaction. Rather, chronological age, timing of role entry, religious affiliation, lineage, and frequency of contact all seem to contribute. Despite expressions of role satisfaction, interviewed grandparents frequently mention disappointment and disapproval in connection with particular relationships. They deny wanting to be more involved with their grandchildren, despite psychologist J. Thomas's finding that grandmothers and grandfathers who experience most satisfaction are those who have most responsibility for helping with grandchildren. These contradictions suggest that in circumstances of perceived interpersonal powerlessness, grandparents may be working hard to make the best of existing situations. They feel they can do little to influence particular relationships. What they *can* influence is the satisfaction they allow themselves to experience in grandparenthood, as a whole.

Apart from grandparenthood satisfaction, per se, researchers have tried, with little success, to explore the influence of grandparenthood on grandparents' psychosocial well-being. There appears to be some disagreement about whether higher grandparent involvement with grandchildren's families is associated with increased grandparent morale (as a function of providing essential service) or decreased morale (as a result of being the only available helper when a child's family is in trouble.) The nature of existing research does not permit investigation of the proposition that grandparent involvement may be associated with increased morale among grandparents who might otherwise be even more depressed and despondent.

Psychologist V. Kivett suggests that the grandparent role may provide an important sense of psychological security for both Black and White grandmothers. Kivnick proposes that grandparenthood offers a valuable opportunity for the grandparent to make progress in the essential psychosocial work of middle and later adulthood. As such, the role should be expected to enhance grandparent well-being. Burton identifies psychological rewards experienced by grandmothers who serve as surrogate parents. Psychologist R. Pruchno proposes an elaborate model for evaluating the psychological well-being of grandparent caregivers, as a function of stressors (e.g., child-care demands; competing role demands; life-event demands), resources (personal; family; social; environmental), and perceptions of relative satisfaction and burden.

III. GRANDPARENTHOOD TO YOUNGER GENERATIONS

A. Elusive Influence

Research on grandparent influence generally begins with an impression that grandparents are important in the lives of grandchildren, fails to confirm this importance, and concludes with a perflexed unwillingness to dismiss, altogether, the value of grandparents. Scholars have begun to resolve this contradiction by suggesting that grandparents' importance in families may not reside in observable behaviors or in other easily measurable variables. Rather, their importance may be far more elusive, related to a variety of symbolic meanings and influences that are not easily captured with the tools of quantitative social science.

Perhaps, too, grandparents' major influence may blossom over the life cycle and may be all but undetectable during the "fat years" that are most often studied. For example, research finds little evidence that grandparents' values influence the values of their grandchildren. However, much of this research assesses particular family values, as they exist in grandchildren's minds during childhood. Where do children learn those values that underlie a lifetime of behavior (e.g., commitment to competence at a craft; rootedness in history; commitment to family; understanding generational connectedness)? Perhaps these values are learned in the context of an ongoing relationship with grandparents. It is not unreasonable to expect that meaningful childhood relations with grandparents contribute to positive adjustment and mental health in adulthood, or to lifelong satisfaction in cross-generational relationships. The fact that these influences are not detected by conventional research methodologies neither confirms nor denies their existence.

B. Symbolic Influence

Sociologists identify the following symbolic functions of grandparents within families:

1. Stabilize the next generation by providing a buffer against its mortality;
2. Catalyze family cohesion;
3. Moderate intensity of nuclear family life by providing a sounding board and a mediator for both generations;

4. Serve as "family watchdogs," maintaining a latent observation and protection service that can become active frontline management when necessary;
5. Symbolize family continuity across generational past, present, and future—particularly during times of family disruption.

Family practitioners agree that grandparents can be crucial to the effective functioning of families in the following ways:

1. Reduce intensity of intergenerational conflicts by prompting maneuvering around touchy issues;
2. Mediate and interpret between two generations;
3. Provide emotional and financial support for parenting;
4. Serve as a nexus of family connections;
5. Relate to parents in a way that facilitates marital adjustment;
6. Support parents during times of marital conflict;
7. Modulate family life experiences on the basis of accumulated wisdom;
8. Expand the age range and number of available role models for family members, modeling adulthood and old age for grandchildren, and modeling grandparenthood itself for both children and their parents.

C. Developmental Influence

Despite disappointing empirical results, grandparent researchers remain convinced of the importance of grandparents for grandchildren. Emotional attachments between grandparents and grandchildren have been described as uniquely unconditional because of this relationship's exemption from parent–child intensities and responsibilities. Grandparents can serve as constant objects in the child's life, as "Great Parents" who provide a secure and loving adult–child relationship that is next in emotional power only to the parental bond.

Pastoralists D. Conroy and C. Fahey point out that grandparents have a great deal to do with the initial development of a child's view of life. Kornhaber asserts that children's complete emotional well-being requires a direct, and not merely derived or symbolic, link with their grandparents. In the absence of this relationship children experience a deprivation of nurturance, support, and emotional security. Anthropol-

ogist M. Mead maintains that intergenerational family relationships, exemplified by grandparenthood, are absolutely essential to the child's development of his or her own uniqueness, wholeness, and cultural and historical continuity.

D. Young Adult and Adolescent Grandchildren

If grandchildren's preschool and school years signify grandparenthood's "fat period" to grandparents, the children's adolescent and young adult years signify increasingly lean periods. How do grandchildren experience these distinct relationship periods? Scholars report that the amount of grandparenthood contact during childhood directly affects the type of relationship grandchildren and grandparents later maintain. They further suggest that when close, intimate grandparenthood relationships are formed during childhood, both grandparent and grandchild continue to nurture the attachment throughout life. Nonetheless, literature does not consistently support the view that grandparents remain significant throughout grandchildren's adolescent and young adult years.

Secondary data analysis indicates that adolescent children of single mothers benefit from a grandparent's presence in the home. Because adolescents in single-parent homes are especially independent, they are likely to be in particular need of the supervision and control available in an extended household. Furthermore, a grandparent's presence in a family that otherwise tends to be nonhierarchical may reinforce generational boundaries, thus maintaining the benefits of hierarchical structure.

Based on self-report questionnaires, the overall picture of grandparenthood to adolescents seems to be one of frequent, dynamic intergenerational involvement. High school students report viewing their grandparents as confidantes and companions. They say it is enjoyment of contact, rather than family obligation, that motivates them to maintain these relationships, and they describe brief conversations and important discussions as replacing childhood's largely recreational visits. Young-adult grandchildren describe relationships with grandparents as extremely important; they indicate that contact frequency affects the solidarity, not the importance, of these relationships. However, these findings conflict with longitudinal data indicating that grandchildren's transition from childhood to adolescence prompts a more dramatic change in grandparenthood relationships than any other grandparent or grandchild life transition.

IV. CROSS-CULTURAL GRANDPARENTS

A. Relation to Cultural Values

Mainstream Euro-American culture has long been characterized by its overwhelming emphasis on the principles of autonomy and individualism. Under conditions of economic hardship, individual wishes and aspirations are subordinated to the family obligations that ensure survival. But in times of relative security, behavior is governed by individual independence, self-reliance, and freedom from the constraints of commitment. This underlying value system is absolutely consistent with Cherlin and Furstenberg's description of contemporary American grandparents as paying far more attention to preserving independence (their own, their children's, and their grandchildren's) than to promoting long-term or deep-seated emotional well-being.

Little research is available to describe grandparents in diverse American subcultures that are organized around family commitment, group interdependence, or respect for elders. We might expect Native American grandparents, for example, to be more concerned with a given relationship's impact on a grandchild's long-term development than with its momentary enjoyment value. We might expect Hmong-American grandparenting behaviors to be determined more powerfully by their effect on overall group well-being than by their protection of individual freedom.

B. African-American Grandparents

In view of traditional African emphasis on individual interconnectedness with the group, Kivett's finding that grandparenthood is more salient in the Black community than the White should not be surprising. Black grandparents assume parental responsibility for grandchildren far more often than White grandparents. To a far greater extent than White families, Black families demonstrate regard for older adults, propensities to protect the frail and dependent, and expand-

able household boundaries as dictated by the needs of kin and significant nonkin. Indeed, "fictive" or "pseudo" kin are important members of many Black families. These people are regarded in kinship terms, they are accorded many of kinship's rights and statuses, and they participate fully in informal support networks. Whereas only 8% of Anglos in Bengtson's cross-cultural study report having raised children other than their own biological offspring, nearly half of the Black adults over 60 report having raised fictive children and grandchildren.

Research seems to confirm some stereotypes about Black intergenerational families while failing to confirm others. Burton and Bengtson acknowledge the important tradition represented by Black grandmothers in African-American culture. However, they describe the familiar view that Black women regard children as God's blessing as a holdover from slavery, rather than a cultural tradition. They report that for most of their respondents, off-time grandmotherhood may represent both a symbolic and an instrumental crisis. That is, for these women, too-early accession to this lineage role creates conflicts both in their view of themselves, and also in their family system of cohesion and social support.

African-American scholar R. Taylor notes that aged Blacks have significant and varied family roles, maintaining extensive contact with children and grandchildren. Qualitative studies point to the importance and critical nature of the family for the functioning of elderly African-Americans and, reciprocally, to the importance of these elderly for the survival of African-American families. On many socioeconomic indicators older Blacks represent one of the most severely disadvantaged groups in our society. Their family roles are particularly important, both in view of their special needs for assistance, and also in terms of their unique capacities for contribution.

C. Latino Grandparents

In Latino culture, elders are esteemed for the wisdom that is reserved for them, alone. Within neighborhoods elders act as part of a grapevine of social control. Within households, their presence helps reduce anxiety resulting from such nuclear family stresses as a child's illness, divorce, or overtime work for parents. Hispanic tradition supports the view that elders are teachers who participate in cooperative efforts. Because their wisdom is valued, physical decline does not diminish the family contributions of aged Latinos as it does among Anglos.

Gerontologist C. Garcia points out that extended Latino families must be viewed in terms of function (interaction and exchange) rather than structure (residence). By and large, Latino grandparents live with a child's family. But because a grandparent has many children and because he or she can only live in one household, most middle-generation households do not structurally include grandparents. Functionally, however, Garcia reports that every household views grandparents as active members.

Studies of Chicano grandparents find that grandmothers play several roles:

1. child rearers;
2. participants in family decision making;
3. religious advocates and teachers;
4. participants in a female network of healers.

Both grandmothers and grandfathers value their caregiving activities, considering themselves equally responsible for child rearing. They view their most important task to be teaching the grandchildren Spanish, traditional customs, and morality. Rather than stressing autonomy, they emphasize interdependence and cooperation with their families.

Latino culture does not regard productive work in one's occupation as life's central task. Cultural tradition also values leisure, and it regards extended family relationships as an important source of personal identity. As a result of the family being so highly valued, aged Latinos do not seem to undergo a dramatic role change upon retirement.

V. FUTURE OUTLOOK

A. Research

Grandparenthood has been properly explored within the disciplines of anthropology, sociology, history, family studies, psychology, psychiatry, gerontology, social work, public policy, and cultural studies. Each discipline views the world through its own theoretical lens, focusing on its own issues of concern, utilizing its own research tools, reporting in its own terms. Over the less than 50 years that grandparenthood has

been formally studied, historical trends have influenced not only the role and relationship under investigation, but also the goals, foci, and strategies of research within every involved discipline. Accumulated disparate findings are not easily synthesized into a coherent body of knowledge. Thus, after decades of research, our understanding of grandparenthood—family relationship, ascribed status, social role, psychological object, source of personal meaning, and more—remains fragmented. Attempts to integrate risk confounding description, explanation, prediction, and advocacy.

Quantitative research methods have focused our attention on a wide array of measurable demographic, behavioral, and psychological variables. However, because measurable variables are not necessarily valid operationalizations of the concepts under investigation, descriptive findings too often appear superficial and removed from the lives of the real people who are grandparents. Grandparenthood meaning, importance, and influence remain elusive.

Recent qualitative investigations of cross-cultural grandparents have begun to provide valuable insights into grandparenthood's complexity, and to suggest lines of inquiry for mainstream grandparenthood, as well. This work suggests that the values of particular cultures (concerning family, wisdom, work, aging, and more) are integrally related to grandparenthood and must be explored further. It is to be hoped that qualitative research will continue to make progress in identifying, understanding, operationalizing, and quantifying meaningful variables, and in building theoretical concepts that will be amenable to traditional, quantitative social science research.

As a phenomenon that is both intergenerational and lifelong, grandparenthood must be explored with research strategies that are sensitive both to intergenerational and family systems issues, on the one hand, and to life cycle development issues, on the other. Related to both science and practice, grandparenthood research must be conducted with an eye both to building knowledge and also to improving practice and policy. Areas of special current concern include grandparents as caregivers and as recipients of family care, grandparenthood in the expanding life period of "old-old" age, and grandparents as part of our society's complex system of racial, ethnic, and cultural relations.

B. Practice

Discussions of contemporary American grandparenthood fall on a continuum. At one end we are called to return to the "good old days" of strong family ties. At the other end we are reminded that progress has its costs, and that strong, involved grandparenthood may be one of them. Several important practical issues underlie this entire continuum.

Grandparenthood conflicts and dilemmas may be seen as a metaphor for all family relationships. Every family bond involves a self and an "other," whether that other be an individual or a group. Establishing and maintaining bonds requires a constant balancing and rebalancing of concerns for self with concerns for other. In addition, maintaining family bonds over time requires a balance between perceived well-being now, and anticipated well-being over a life cycle that involves both personal and generational futures. To the extent that we seek to understand or influence grandparenthood, we must do so in the context of these essential balances and their parameters.

American society is constantly evolving. We must remember that just as grandparenthood has changed with past historical shifts, so it will change with the social, economic, and cultural shifts of the present and future. Contemporary grandparenthood may be an understandable reflection of intergenerational affection without interference. But grandparenthood will not necessarily reflect these same values in the future.

Family scholars inform students that maintaining viable intergenerational ties requires considerable care and effort; grandparents have long admonished grandchildren that "You get out of something what you put into it." Grandparenthood as an institution may, indeed, reflect sociohistorical developments. But within any given family, people are free to make of this relationship as much or as little as they choose. American societal norms may encourage individualism and noninterference. But individual families and communities are free to balance these values with cooperation and respectful long-term responsibility. Grandparenthood, as a phenomenon, will continue to reflect large-scale societal currents. But individual people and families need not bob, like dinghies on the waves. The participants in any particular grandparenthood relationship can work to make that relationship meet the needs they decide are important.

BIBLIOGRAPHY

Barranti, C. C. R. (1985). The grandparent/grandchild relationship: Family resource in an era of voluntary bonds. *Family Relations, 34,* 343–352.

Bengtson, V. L., & Robertson, J. F. (1985). *Grandparenthood.* Beverly Hills: Sage.

Cherlin, A. J., & Furstenberg, F. F., Jr. (1986). *The new American grandparent: A place in the family, a life apart.* New York: Basic Books.

Denham, T. E., & Smith, C. W. (1989). The influence of grandparents on grandchildren: A review of the literature and resources. *Family Relations, 38,* 345–350.

George, J. (1988). Children and grandparents: The right to visit. *Children Today,* November–December, 14–18.

Jendrek, M. P. (1994). Grandparents who parent their grandchildren: Circumstances and decisions. *The Gerontologist, 34,* 206–216.

Johnson, C. L. (1992). Divorced and reconstituted families: Effects on the older generations. *Families and Aging, Summer,* 17–20.

Growth Factors and Cellular Senescence

Vincent J. Cristofalo and Christian Sell

Medical College of Pennsylvania

BALBc/3T3 Cells Mouse fibroblast cells that are immortal and will not undergo cellular senescence. These immortal cells display growth characteristics similar to those of nonimmortalized cells. They cease to proliferate upon serum withdrawal, are contact inhibited, and are nontumorigenic in nude mice.

Cell Cycle A term that refers to the process of DNA synthesis and division in a mammalian cell. Typically, cells progress through four well-defined phases: first the cells increase in size during a period known as G_1; second, cells replicate their DNA during S phase; third, the cells prepare for mitosis during a period known as G_2; and finally cells enter mitosis and divide.

Cell Proliferation The process of cellular replication whereby one cell divides into two daughter cells.

Cellular Senescence Refers to the inability of normal cells to proliferate indefinitely when placed into in vitro culture. Typically a population of cells undergoes a defined number of cell divisions and then ceases to divide. Senescence is also characterized by changes in morphology.

Growth Factors Small protein molecules that stimulate nondividing cells to enter the cell cycle and undergo cell division.

Quiescence A term used to describe nonproliferating cells that have been induced to stop dividing by the withdrawal of serum growth factors that are required for replication. Another term that is synonymous with quiescence is G_0. This term refers to a cell that has withdrawn from the cell cycle and is in a nondividing state. The G_0 state is not strictly limited to nonproliferation induced by serum starvation as in quiescence but can refer to a terminally differentiated cell, such as a neuron, that will not divide in the presence of serum.

WI-38 Fetal human lung fibroblast cells that are widely used in studies of proliferative senescence and cell cycle. These are a mortal cell line that undergo characteristic cellular senescence.

CELL PROLIFERATION is controlled by **GROWTH FACTORS** that interact with specific receptors in mammalian cells. In culture, most normal cell types enter a nonproliferating state when the required growth factors are withheld. These nonproliferating cells enter a state that has been termed G_0 or quiesence and can be stimulated to divide by the addition of appropriate growth factors. However, during in vitro senescence cells lose the ability to respond to mitogenic stimuli. Thus a major hallmark of senescent cells is the inability to respond to mitogenic signals that normally stimulate the proliferation of young cells. An understanding of the molecular basis for this attenuated response requires an understanding of the growth requirements of young, proliferating cells.

I. GROWTH FACTOR REQUIREMENTS OF HUMAN FIBROBLAST CELLS

When cells from normal human tissues are taken from the body and placed into tissue culture they can be stimulated to divide and can be maintained for a period of time. Human cells will not divide indefinitely, however. Following a defined number of cell divisions, normal cells cease to divide and are refractory to stimuli which would induce proliferation in "young" cultures. All cells from every tissue studied to date exhibit this pattern of vigorous proliferation followed by a decline in proliferative terminating in nonproliferating cells which are termed senesent. It is of interest to note that cancer cells do not undergo senescence and will proliferate indefinitely in culture. Thus cancer cells are immortal, and this transition to immortality is thought to be a crucial step in the development of cancer.

A major interest in the fields of aging and cancer is to determine what causes senescence and to discover how cells can overcome senescence to become immortal. This article examines what is known concerning the inability of senescent cells to respond to proliferative stimuli.

Phillips and Cristofalo examined systematically the growth factor requirements of WI-38 human fibro-

Table I Classification of Growth Factors for WI-38 Cells

Class 1[a]	Class 2[b]	Class 3[c]
EGF	IGF-1	HC
FGF	IGF-2	DEX
PDGF	INS	
THR		

[a]EGF, epidermal growth factor; FGF, fibroblast growth factor; PDGF, platelet-derived growth factor; THR, thrombine

[b]IGF-1, insulin-like growth factor-1; INS, insulin.

[c]HC, hydrocortisone; DEX, dexamethasone.

blasts. The response to combinations of purified growth factors added to serum-free medium was compared to the proliferative response to medium supplemented with 10% fetal bovine serum. A combination of growth factors was identified that stimulated cell proliferation to the same extent, and at the same rate, as 10% serum. This combination was platelet-derived growth factor (PDGF) at 6 ng/ml, epidermal growth factor (EGF), at 25 ng/ml, insulin (INS) at 5 ug/ml, transferrin (TRS) at 5 ug/ml, and dexamethasone (DEX) at 55 ng/ml.

These growth factors were used in basal serum-free medium MCDB-104. Subsequently, it was found that the addition of $FeSO_4$ abrogated the need for TRS. The addition of INS is functionally equivalent to using insulin-like growth factor-1 (IGF-1), because INS interacts with the IGF-1 receptor on the cell surface at the supraphysiologic concentrations used. In fact, the authors found that INS could be replaced with IGF-1 at a 100-fold lower concentration, roughly the difference in binding affinities of the two growth factors for the IGF-1 receptor. Furthermore, an antibody directed against the IGF-1 receptor, IR-3, blocked the mitogenic effect of INS in these cells.

The studies on the various combinations of growth factors resulted in the recognition of three classes of growth factors that can combine to stimulate WI-38 cells. In Table I these classes of growth factors are listed. The first class of growth factors includes EGF, fibroblast growth factor (FGF), PDGF, and thrombin (THR). The class two growth factors include IGF-1 and 2 as well as INS. All three of these factors exert their mitogenic effects through the IGF-1 receptor.

The third class of growth factors is represented by hydrocortisone (HC) and the synthetic analog DEX. Both of these factors act via the glucocorticoid receptor system. Any one of these "class I" growth factors can be combined with any one "class II" and one "class III" growth factor to stimulate DNA synthesis in WI-38 cells.

Based upon the classification system outlined above, the combination of EGF, IGF-1, and DEX increases the number of cells that enter S phase in a manner similar to the addition of 10% fetal bovine serum-containing medium. In a typical experiment, the actual percentage of cells that enter S phase increases from 9% in serum-free medium to 50–60% in the presence of EGF, IGF-1, and DEX or in the presence of serum. When any of the three required growth factors in excluded the number of cells entering S phase is greatly diminished. The mechanism of this synergy between the classes of growth factors does not seem to be a simple increase in the number of binding sites for factors of separate classes. For example, a study of the number of EGF binding sites following addition of DEX to WI-38 cells shows no increase. Although there is an increase in the number of IGF-1 binding sites upon stimulation with EGF.

II. TEMPORAL REQUIREMENT FOR GROWTH FACTORS

There is a temporal relationship between the three classes of growth factors listed in Table I. If either EGF or IGF-1 are withheld the time of entry into S phase is delayed by approximately the same time interval that the growth factor is withheld. If DEX is withheld for up to 12 hours the cultures will enter S phase with no delay. These results indicate that DEX is required late in G_1 for entry into S phase. Interestingly, the number of binding sites for DEX increases in WI-38 cells upon serum stimulation. Whether this increase is required for mitogenic stimulation by DEX is not known.

As mentioned above, in WI-38 cells, as in BALB C/3T3 mouse fibroblasts, the addition of IGF-1 alone is insufficient to stimulate cells to enter S phase. In BALB 3T3 cells, prior exposure to PDGF is required to sensitize the cells to IGF-1. The number of binding sites for IGF-1 has been found to increase in quiescent

BALB 3T3 cells that have been exposed to PDGF. This is postulated to be a mechanism whereby PDGF renders a cell responsive to stimulation by IGF-1. A similar increase in IGF-1 receptor levels occurs in WI-38 cells. Thus, as in BALB 3T3 cells, the stimulation of quiescent WI-38 cells with either serum or PDGF (a class 1 mitogen) will increase the levels of the IGF-1 receptor that is the point of action for class 2 mitogens. In fact, the increase in IGF-1 receptor levels may be required for the mitogenic action of IGF-1.

III. GROWTH FACTOR STIMULATION OF SENESCENT WI-38 HUMAN FIBROBLASTS

The growth factors discussed previously can stimulate entry into S phase in WI-38 cells at a level similar to serum. However, senescent WI-38 cells do not enter S phase in the presence of either growth factors or serum. This is a hallmark of senescent human fibroblasts. That is, senescent human fibroblasts are unable to proliferate in response to growth factor or serum stimulation. Because the concentrations of growth factors used are sufficient to stimulate the proliferation of young WI-38 cells, the lack of response in senescent cells must be due to an intrinsic change in the cells themselves. A thorough analysis of the dose–response curves of WI-38 cells with increasing population doublings indicates that the dose–response curve does not change for any of the mitogens tested. The maximal proliferative response, however, decreases with age. Thus the aging population of cells shows a progressive loss of responsiveness to mitogens, irrespective of concentration used, over the course of their life span.

To date the only stimulus known to induce DNA synthesis in completely senescent human fibroblasts is the introduction of the simian virus 40 large T antigen. This protein is a potent transforming viral oncogene that has been found to bind two important tumor-suppressor gene products, p53 and Rb, thereby inactivating them. It is thought that this activity is the primary mechanism of action of this viral oncoprotein.

To determine the molecular basis for the lack of response to growth factor stimulation in senescent cells one would logically examine the cellular events that occur upon addition of growth factors. Beginning with the binding of a ligand to a cognate receptor there follows a series of distinct biochemical changes within the cell, some of which have now been described in great detail. To determine at which point in this stimulatory cascade initiated by the growth factor a senescent cell may be unresponsive one must examine each event individually.

Growth factors bind to high-affinity receptors on the cell surface. These receptors are generally membrane-spanning proteins with intrinsic tyrosine kinase activity. The known tyrosine kinase receptors can be grouped into nine classes based upon structural similarities. The differences in these classes reside mainly in the extracellular regions of the receptors. The intracellular regions are all similar in that the major feature is a tyrosine kinase domain that is either continuous or split into two domains.

The first response following the binding of a growth factor to its cognate receptor is an autophosphorylation of that receptor on tyrosine residues. All of the receptors for the class 1 and 2 mitogens listed above contain an intrinsic tyrosine kinase activity that is activated upon ligand binding. These receptors autophosphorylate on specific tyrosine residues. Recently the function of this autophosphorylation has been the subject of intensive research. It has been discovered that the phosphorylated tyrosine residues are sites for protein interactions that are mediated by src homology 2 (SH2) domains. These SH2 domains bind only to phosphorylated tyrosines and are specific for particular motifs. For example, the EGF receptor undergoes autophosphorylation upon ligand binding. One of the sites of autophosphorylation is tyrosine 1068. It has been found that this phosphorylated tyrosine is a binding site for the Grb2 protein. The Grb2 protein contains SH2 and SH3 domains but has no obvious catalytic function and belongs to a family of similar proteins that are thought to be involved in facilitating the association of effector molecules with phosphorylated tyrosine kinase receptors. Other members of this family are Shc and Nck. In the case of Grb2, the protein also binds to a homolog of the *Drosophila* guanine nucleotide exchange factor son of sevenless (SOS). This nucleotide exchange acts downstream of the EGF receptor in *Drosophila* and upstream of ras proteins. In the murine system this receptor complex has been shown to activate ras. This provides a mechanism for the activation of ras by the binding of EGF to the EGF receptor.

IV. GROWTH FACTOR RECEPTORS IN SENESCENT WI-38 CELLS

The first event in growth factor stimulation is binding to the cell surface receptor. In an attempt to determine whether the levels of growth factor receptors are decreased in senescent WI-38 cells, the levels of receptors for some of the first two classes of growth factors in young and senescent fibroblasts have been compared. It was found that the number of PDGF, EGF, and IGF-1 receptors per unit area present on the surface of the senescent cells is similar to the number found on the surface of the young cells. In addition, the affinity of growth factor binding is similar in young and senescent WI-38 cells. Thus a change in the number of binding sites for the class 1 or 2 growth mitogens cannot be the basis for the failure of senescent fibroblasts to respond to growth factors.

The number of binding sites for DEX has been found to decrease significantly over the life span of WI-38 cells. In addition, the ability of these receptors to translocate to the nucleus (a normal response to glucocorticoid binding) has been found to decrease with age.

Interestingly, the addition of DEX to normal serum-containing culture medium of WI-38 cells increases the life span of these cells by up to 40%. Whether this addition prevents the loss of DEX receptors in senescent fibroblasts or extends the life span by some other mechanism is not clear.

V. ACTIVITY OF GROWTH FACTOR RECEPTORS IN SENESCENT WI-38 CELLS

Decreases in the autophosphorylation of growth factor receptors in the senescent cells could provide an explanation for the lack of proliferative response. However, an examination of the autophosphorylation of the PDGF and the EGF receptors in the young and senescent WI-38 cells has revealed no discernable difference in the levels of receptor autophosphorylation. In the case of PDGF and EGF the senescent fibroblasts seem to possess receptors that are activated normally, and there was no difference in tyrosine kinase activity of EGF receptors in vitro between young and senescent WI-38 cells. However, there was a dramatic decrease in the kinase activity of purified EGF receptor in senescent cells. This decrease seems to be due to increased proteolytic activity associated with the EGF receptor in senescent cells. More recently, the IGF-1 receptor was examined in the senescent WI-38 cells and there was no discernable difference in the levels of autophosphorylated receptor.

Recently it has been reported that there is an age-related decrease in the number of EGF receptors in human skin fibroblasts. This decrease in number was accompanied by a decreased internalization of the ligand receptor complex. The authors used only very early passage cells (<3 passages in vitro) and they speculated that the use of very early passage cells may account for differences between these results and previous studies on the EGF receptor in senescent cells.

VI. RESPONSE OF WI-38 CELLS TO INSULIN-LIKE GROWTH FACTOR I

When WI-38 cells are allowed to achieve a high cell density in culture, the proliferating fraction of the population (i.e., that fraction of the culture that synthesizes DNA as measured by thymidine uptake) progressively declines over a period of 6–10 days. At the end of this time the cells become quiescent (G_0). These G_0 cells can be stimulated to divide by the addition of fresh serum-containing medium. During the first 6–8 days, a time prior to entry into the G_0 state, the cells will respond to IGF-1 alone. Fully quiescent cells, however, require two growth factors just as the BALB 3T3 cells. As discussed previously, in the case of WI-38 cells either EGF or PDGF can be used in combination with INS or IGF-1. The levels of the IGF-1 receptor were examined in this system using an autophosphorylation assay (Figure 1). In this assay the tyrosine kinase activity of the receptor is activated by ligand binding and visualized by the presence of phosphorylated tyrosine residues that only appear following ligand binding. The ligand, IGF-1, was added to cultures at intervals following seeding of the culture. The levels of active IGF-1 receptor were measured at each point. As seen in Figure 1, the levels of IGF-1 receptor decrease as the cells lose the ability to respond to IGF-1 alone (shown in the upper panel in Figure 1). It seems that there is a correlation between the levels of the receptor that can be activated and the ability to respond to the ligand. Although this does not prove that the decreased level of the IGF-1 receptor is the

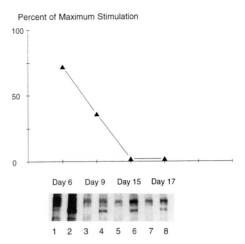

Figure 1 WI-38 human fibroblasts were seeded at $1 \times 10^4/cm^2$. At the days indicated the cells were stimulated by the addition of IGF-1 (50 ng/ml). The percentage of cells entering S phase was determined and is expressed as percent of maximal stimulation by serum in panel A. The levels of the IGF-1 receptor were measured simultaneously. At each point the first lane contains lysate from unstimulated cultures. The second lane contains lysate from cultures stimulated with IGF-1 for 10 min. The autophosphorylated receptor was visualized by staining with an antiphosphotyrosine antibody. The expected size of the autophosphorylated beta subunit of the IGF-1 receptor (95 kD) is indicated by an arrow.

cause of the loss of response to IGF-1, it does indicate the possibility. When fully quiescent young WI-38 cells were exposed to PDGF the levels of the receptor measured by this same assay increase 3–4-fold. The same is true of BALB 3T3 cells as measured by ligand binding. Using antisense oligonucleotides to the receptor this increase in activated receptor was blocked. Thus the levels of the IGF-1 growth factor receptor decrease as fibroblasts become quiescent and increase as the cells are stimulated to divide. This increase occurs in both the young and senescent WI-38 cells, indicating that the point at which the senescent WI-38 stop in G_1 is beyond the increase in the levels of IGF-1 receptor and the activation of this receptor.

VII. ENDOGENOUS PRODUCTION OF GROWTH FACTORS IN WI-38 CELLS

Fibroblasts are known to produce growth factors when cultured in vitro. For example, the production of IGF-1 is induced in human and mouse fibroblast cells when these cells are stimulated with PDGF or

EGF. Although the role of this production in cell proliferation is not clear, it has been reported that the endogenous production of IGF-1 may be required for the proliferation of human fibroblasts. However, this result awaits confirmation by other laboratories.

The production of growth factors by senescent cells has been examined in a number of cell types. In human fibroblasts the levels of IGF-1 decrease as cells become senescent, IGF-1 is only present in proliferating young human fibroblasts, or those that have been conditionally immortalized by a temperature-sensitive simian virus 40 T antigen. The production of hepatocyte growth factor (HGF), in contrast, increases as human lung fibroblasts age in culture. This increased production of HGF is reflected by an increase in the steady state levels of mRNA for the growth factor. In fibroblasts obtained from Hutchinson-Gilford Progeria patients, there is an increased production with age. This increased production was only observed in one strain of progeria fibroblasts and does not seem to represent a change characteristic of this syndrome.

Human fibroblasts also produce interleukin 6 (IL-6). There is both a basal level of production and an increase in the production of this cytokine upon serum stimulation. Other factors, such as activators of protein kinase C, can also cause an increase in the levels of IL-6 produced by these cells. This increase was found to diminish progressively with age. Fibroblasts that had undergone approximately 65% of life span lost the ability to increase the levels of IL-6 mRNA upon stimulation with serum and protein kinase C activators. However, the ability to produce IL-6 in response to forskolin was not diminished, indicating that some signal pathways are impaired in the senescent cells while others remain intact.

Another cytokine produced by human fibroblasts is interleukin 1 (IL-1). Human diploid fibroblasts derived from skin show an age-dependent increase in the expression of IL-1. This change was reflected in vivo. It was found that fibroblasts from donors of increasing age produced increasing amounts of IL-1 at early passage. Presumably the use of early passage cells eliminates changes in gene expression due to culture conditions. In addition, relatively higher levels of IL-1 mRNA are found in cells derived from Werner's Syndrome patients.

At this time it is difficult to determine the relevance of these changes to the loss of proliferative capacity that occurs with senescence. The fact that cells lose the ability to produce certain growth factors seems, at least at first glance, to be extraneous to the loss of proliferative capacity. The factors required for proliferation are presumably contained within the serum and are present in sufficient amounts for optimal cell proliferation. The decreased production of these factors may, however, provide a clue as to which signal pathways are deficient in the senescent cells, and this may ultimately lead to the discovery of the defect that prevents senescent cells from responding to proliferative stimuli.

VIII. PRODUCTION OF INSULIN-LIKE GROWTH FACTOR BINDING PROTEINS BY WI-38 CELLS

Although the production of growth factors may not impinge directly upon the proliferation of cells in culture the cells do have the ability to produce factors that may modify the action of growth factors and thus affect proliferation. These factors are binding proteins that bind growth factors and can either inhibit or augment their activity. One such family of growth factors and binding proteins, which has been studied in senescent fibroblasts, is the IGF-1, IGF-1 binding protein (IGFBP) system. There are currently six IGFBP-1 known. In adult human blood the major IGFBP-1 is IGFBP-3. These binding proteins are postulated to regulate the binding of IGF-1 and 2 to their receptors, control the rate of clearance of the IGFs, control the transport from the vascular compartment, and possibly affect target cell responses.

Although these binding proteins are produced by cells in vitro their role in cell proliferation is unclear. The addition of IGFBP-3 to the culture medium will have inhibitory or stimulatory effects depending upon the experimental conditions. It has been reported that the overexpression of the IGFBP-3 in mouse and human fibroblasts is associated with an inhibition of proliferation.

The levels of IGFBP-3 have been examined in human fibroblasts during senescence. There is an increase in the production of IGFBP-3 in senescent human fibroblast cells compared to young cells. In addition, the senescent cells produce a protease that acts upon the IGF binding proteins. It is possible that these changes may affect the ability of the cell to respond to IGFs and render them less responsive.

IX. INSULIN-LIKE GROWTH FACTOR BINDING PROTEINS IN VIVO

Studies in both rats and humans have found that the levels of IGF-1 in the serum decrease and the relative ratio of IGF-1 to IGFBP-1 changes with age, and this change in the IGF-1 system may play a role in age-related changes in vivo. In addition, the levels of growth hormone, which regulates the production of IGF-1 by the liver, decreases with age.

X. ALTERATIONS IN GENE EXPRESSION IN RESPONSE TO GROWTH FACTORS IN WI-38 CELLS

In addition to the biochemical responses elicited by growth factor stimulation there is an induction of gene expression. These changes act in concert to eventually promote cell division. The list of genes whose expression is induced following growth factor stimulation of quiescent cells is ever increasing. A current estimate of the number of growth factor-induced genes would be in the range of 500. All levels of gene regulation are involved in the increased expression of growth-regulated genes, including transcriptional and posttranscriptional mechanisms. These genes can be classified into three categories based upon their temporal relationship, early, mid G_1, and late.

The early response genes include *c-fos, c-myc, c-jun, Erg-1, Erg-2,* vimentin, Krox-20, and IL-2. This is by no means an exhaustive list of this class of genes. This class of genes shares the general property that new protein synthesis is not required for the increased levels of steady state mRNA that is seen following serum stimulation of quiescent cells. The mRNA levels of the early response genes typically increase rapidly and then decrease as cells progress through G_1. These mRNAs include *c-fos, c-myc,* and *c-jun.* In addition, many of these messages are superinduced when an inhibitor of protein synthesis is added to the cultures. Thus the early-response genes encode for a class of mRNAs with a very short half life, which is postulated to be dependent upon labile proteins.

Genes that are expressed later in G_1 include the mid-G_1 genes, *c-myb, b-myb,* calcyclin, G_1 cyclins, ornithine decarboxylase, and many others.

The final set of genes that are expressed in G_1 in stimulated cells are the G_1/S phase boundary genes. These include the genes that code for the enzymes of DNA replication, for example, DNA polymerase alpha and the proliferating cell nuclear antigen (PCNA). Genes for some of the structural proteins of chromatin, histones, as well as thymidine kinase and ribonucleotide reductase are also expressed at this time. [*See* DNA AND GENE EXPRESSION.]

XI. EXPRESSION OF EARLY G₁ GENES IN SENESCENT CELLS

Many groups have examined the expression of growth-regulated genes in senescent cells. The initial hypothesis was that one could define a point in the cell cycle, presumably in G_1, at which the senescent cells were blocked. This was an analogy to the temperature-sensitive mutants of the cell cycle that had been developed by Claudio Basilico and co-workers. In these mutants the cells progress to well-defined points in G_1. The expression of growth-regulated genes is normal to that point, and subsequent G_1 genes are not expressed.

However, in the case of senescent fibroblasts this expectation was not realized. Expression of many early G_1, mid-G_1, and late G_1 genes increase in senescent cells to the same extent as in early-passage cells. Rittling et al. examined a number of growth-regulated genes in senescent WI-38 cells and observed that all genes examined were expressed in the senescent cells at levels comparable to the early-passage cells. This was in sharp contrast to the initiation of DNA synthesis that was greatly decreased in the senescent population. The early genes examined were *c-myc,* 4F1, JE-3, and 2F1. The mid-G_1 genes examined were *c-Ha-ras,* ornithine decarboxylase, and *p2A9.* The late genes examined were thymidine kinase and histone H3.

Seshadri and Campisi have reported that the expression of one of the early genes, *c-fos,* is decreased in senescent cells. In addition it was reported that the enzyme levels of ornithine decarboxylase was dramatically reduced in senescent cells in spite of a high level of mRNA expression. This indicates that the defects in senescent cells exist at multiple levels. The introduction of *c-fos*, by Phillips and Cristofalo, was later found to increase the number of late-passage cells that could respond to growth factors. This effect was only seen, however, in cells that were approaching the end of life span. Completely senescent cells were refractory to induction of DNA synthesis in the presence of increased levels of *c-fos* expression.

XII. EXPRESSION OF LATE G_1 GENES IN SENESCENT FIBROBLASTS

As discussed above, the majority of the early G_1 genes are expressed at normal levels in senescent fibroblasts. When the late G_1/S phase genes were examined it was found that senescent cells are able to express some late G_1/S phase genes in spite of the fact that they are unable to enter S phase in response to serum. For example, the mRNA for thymidine kinase and histone H3 was found to be induced in senescent cells in a manner similar to early-passage cells. However, the increase in thymidine kinase and histone H3 gene expression has not been observed in all systems. In a recent examination of S phase genes in senescent human fibroblasts, thymidylate synthase, dihydrofolate reductase, and PCNA decreased expression was found. This confirms earlier work that also found that some S phase genes, such as the PCNA and DNA polymerase alpha, are not increased in senescent WI-38 cells. Thus it appears that the senescent fibroblasts may be able to express at least some of the genes associated with S phase, although the cells are incapable of entering S phase.

During recent years a number of cell cycle regulatory proteins have been identified that are synthesized and degraded in a cyclic manner at specific times during the cell cycle. These proteins, named cyclins, are the regulatory subunits of a class of protein kinases termed *cyclin-dependent kinases* (cdks). The function of cdks is required for cell cycle progression during G_1 and G_2 phases. One of the targets of the G_1 cyclins is the tumor-supressor gene product Rb. This gene was originally identified as the locus that displayed loss of heterozygosity in hereditary retinoblastomas. The Rb protein product is phosphorylated in a cell cycle-specific manner late in G_1. Stein and co-workers examined this phosphorylation in senescent human diploid fibroblasts. They found that Rb was not phos-

phorylated in senescent human fibroblasts and postulate that this event may contribute to the G_1 arrest of these cells. It is not clear however, whether this represents a controlling event or is a consequence of a block in prior G_1 events that may be required for Rb phosphorylation.

XIII. GROWTH FACTORS IN VIVO

IGF-1 was initially identified in vitro. It is produced in high concentrations by liver cell cultures and promotes the proliferation of other cell types. When this liver cell factor was purified and identified a high degree of homology with INS was discovered. There are now two similar growth factors in this family, designated IGF-1 and IGF-2. Both of these factors interact with the same cell surface receptor to induce cell proliferation. This receptor is present on a great many cell types including many tumor cells. The requirement for IGF-1 in the proliferation of normal cells has been reviewed by Baserga and Rubin. IGF-1 is present in circulating blood and is postulated to be a major effector of growth hormone (GH) in vivo. In fact, the clinical assessment of acromegaly and dwarfism correlates better with circulating levels of IGF-1 than with circulating levels of GH.

XIV. GROWTH HORMONE IN THE ELDERLY

In vivo the aging process is associated with a diverse set of changes that occur at the cellular, tissue, and organismic levels. It has long been known that the levels of protein synthesis decrease with age in vivo and the loss of function of various tissues may be related to this decrease. It has also been recognized that the process of aging is associated with a decreased level of GH. This has been found to be true in both rats and humans. The mean levels of both GH and IGF-1 decrease with age. When GH treatment is given to elderly individuals the levels of IGF-1 increase. In addition, an alteration in body composition is seen during the course of this therapy. There have been, however, side effects of this GH therapy. These agents are still possible candidates for therapeutic treatment of elderly individuals.

BIBLIOGRAPHY

Baserga, R., & Rubin, R. (1993). Cell cycle and growth control. *Critical Review Eukaryotic Gene Expression, 3,* 47–61.

Carlin, C. R., Phillips, P. D., Knowles, B. B., & Cristofalo, V. J. (1983). Diminished in vitro tyrosine kinase activity of the EGF *Nature, 306,* 617–620.

Cristofalo, V. J., & Pignolo, R. J. (1995). Cell culture as a model. In *Handbook of physiology,* section 11, Aging E. J. Masoro (Ed.), New York: Oxford University Press.

Cristofalo, V. J., Wallace, J. M., & Rosner, B. A. (1979). Glucocorticoid enhancement of proliferative activity in WI-38 cells. *Cold Spring Harbor Conferences on Cell Proliferation, 6,* 875–887.

Ferber, A., Chang, C.-D., Sell, C., Ptaznik, A., Cristofalo, V. J., Hubbard-Smith, K. K., Ozer, H. L., Adamo, M., Roberts, C. T., LeRoith, D., & Baserga, R. (1993). Failure of senescent human fibroblasts to express the IGF-I gene. *Journal of Biological Chemistry, 268,* 17883–17888.

Goldstein, S., Moerman, E. J., Jones, R. A., & Baxter, R. C. (1991). Insulinlike growth factor binding protein 3 accumulates to high levels in culture medium of senescent and quiescent human fibroblasts. *Procedures of the National Academy of Science, 88,* 9680–9684.

Gorman, S. D., & Cristofalo, V. J. (1985). Reinitiation of DNA synthesis in BrdU-selected nondividing senescent WI-38 cells by SV-40 infection. *Journal of Cell Physiology, 1255,* 122–126.

Juul, A., Main, K., Blum, W. F., Lindholm, J., Ranke, M. B., & Skakkeback, N. E. (1994). The ratio between serum levels of IGF-1 and the IGF binding proteins (IGFBP-1, 2 and 3) decreases with age in healthy adults and is increased in acromegalic patients. *Clinical Endocrinology, 41,* 85–93.

Kumar, S., Millis, A. J., & Baglioni, C. (1992). Expression of interleukin 1 inducible genes and production of interleukin 1 by aging fibroblasts., *Procedures of the National Academy of Science, 89,* 4683–4687.

Phillips, P. D., Cristofalo, V. J. (1988). Classification system based on the functional equivalency of mitogens that regulate WI-38 proliferation. *Experimental Cell Research, 175,* 396–403.

Phillips, P. D., Kunle, E., & Cristofalo, V. J. (1983). ^{125}I-EGF binding of ability is stable throughout the replicative lifespan of WI-38 cells. *Journal of Cell Physiology, 114,* 311–316.

Rittling, S. R., Brooks, K. M., Cristofalo, V. J., & Baserga, R. (1986). Expression of cell cycle dependent genes in young and senescent WI-38 fibroblasts. *Procedures of the National Academy of Science, 83,* 3316–3320.

Seshadri, T., & Campisi, J. (1990). Repression of c-fos transcription and an altered genetic program in senescent human fibroblasts. *Science, 247,* 205–209.

Stein, G. H., Besson, M., & Gordon, L. (1990). Failure to phosphorylate the retinoblastoma gene product in senescent human fibroblasts. *Science, 249,* 666–668.

Health Care and Services

Robert L. Kane and Bruce Friedman

University of Minnesota School of Public Health

Adjusted Area Per Capita Cost (AAPCC) Average annual payment to a Medicare beneficiary in a given county, adjusted for demographic factors, used as the basis for rate setting for capitated care under Medicare.

Capitation Payment of a single fee to cover the cost of a specified set of services for a fixed time; the amount of payment is independent of the actual amount of services delivered to a given individual.

Geriatrician A medical specialist who deals specifically with the care of frail older persons.

Geriatric Nurse Practitioner A nurse with advanced training to prepare for providing care to older persons.

Managed Care A system of organizing whereby the responsibility for both the payment and the delivery of care rests within a single organization.

Medicaid A cooperative federal–state program designed to provide health insurance coverage to persons based on their state of poverty. Eligibility and benefit policies are determined by individual states in conjunction with federal guidelines.

Medicare A federally funded and directed program that provides virtual universal entitlement to basic acute health-care insurance coverage to all persons 65 years of age and a small group of those with permanent disability.

Primary Care First contact care, usually typified by the responsibility for coordination, continuity, and comprehensiveness of that care.

HEALTH CARE for older persons includes both acute and chronic care. The majority of acute health-care expenses are borne by a federal program, Medicare. Most long-term care is provided by family and friends. The paid care that is given is paid for either privately or through a welfare program, Medicaid. The coordination between acute and chronic care is poor. Although older persons use a disportionately high amount of health-care services, only recently has a medical specialty been developed to address their care needs. There is strong current interest in using managed care as a means of controlling health-care costs for older persons.

I. HEALTH-CARE COVERAGE

In the United States, persons over age 65 are the only group with ready access to universal health coverage. Partly as a result of such coverage, especially in the context of other age-specific benefits, public opinion has shifted from viewing the older population as a disadvantaged group to one that often portrays them as especially favored.

Since 1965, the Medicare program has provided health insurance protection for virtually all those aged 65 or older. Medicare coverage is divided into two components. Part A, or Hospital Insurance, is available without a premium and covers the costs of hospital care, brief stays in nursing homes for care begun in a hospital, and home health care. Part B of Medicare, called Supplemental Medical Insurance, covers the costs of physician services and related costs such as laboratory tests, specialized services (e.g., physical therapy), and durable medical equipment. Although there is a premium for Part B, it is heavily subsidized with federal funds so that an elderly enrollee pays only about one-quarter of the cost of the insurance.

The Medicare program incorporates devices designed to discourage excessive utilization in the form of deductibles and copayments. For example, beneficiaries must pay the equivalent of the average cost of the first hospital day. There is likewise a deductible payment for ambulatory care and copayment of 20% of the allowable costs. In the case of nursing homes, the copayment is sufficiently large to provide a major disincentive to use. Beginning on day 21, the beneficiary is required to pay daily an amount equal to one-eighth the cost of a hospital day. This payment is generally as much or more than the full cost of a nursing home day. Hence, few Medicare-supported nursing home stays last beyond 20 days, although the program technically can cover up to 100 days after a hospital discharge.

Medicare does not, however, cover some items that are important to adequate health care. Perhaps the most conspicuous omission is coverage for medications provided outside a hospital stay. Likewise, Medicare was designed as an acute-care program; it was not intended to cover long-term care. In fact, Medicare has gradually come to assume the costs for at least some long-term care as well. In part, the line between acute and chronic care has become more diffuse, and in part the high costs of long-term care have encouraged program administrators and care providers to make all possible use of resources financed by third-party payers. Over time, for example, home health care, which was originally intended as only posthospital care to cover the period of recuperation, has become a vehicle for sustained care that may last over half a year.

Although the costs of the Medicare program have grown dramatically since its implementation in 1965, the costs not covered by Medicare have grown each year. In the last few years the point has been reached where, despite this coverage, older persons are spending more out-of-pocket (as a proportion of their income) on health care than they did prior to the passage of Medicare. Additional insurance coverage can come from several sources. Medicare beneficiaries can purchase special insurance that is designed to pay the costs of Medicare's deductibles and copayments. This so-called Medigap insurance, in effect, removes the disincentives created by the co-insurance features of Medicare. Some Medigap plans also cover the costs of physician charges above those permitted under Medicare and some also cover drug costs.

The other major source of third-party coverage comes from Medicaid. Unlike Medicare, which is a federal program of universal entitlement, Medicaid is essentially a federal–state welfare program designed to cover the health costs of those who cannot otherwise afford it. Although the specifics of the program vary from state to state, Medicaid was intended primarily to cover the medical costs of those on categorical welfare programs (i.e., Aid to Families with Dependent Children, Old Age Assistance, Aid to the Blind and Disabled, and Aid to the Totally and Permanently Disabled). The majority of recipients were expected to come from the first group and hence represent largely mothers and children. However, the Medicaid program also contained a provision that extended coverage (at a state's discretion) to those whose medical expenditures represented a disproportionately large share of one's income, such that paying one's medical costs would create a situation of poverty. This so-called *medically needy* is composed largely of older persons in long-term care, especially nursing home residents. As a result, the Medicaid program has emerged, in effect, as two programs—one directed at mothers and children and the other at frail older persons. Although there are more Medicaid recipients in the former group, the cost per recipient is much larger in the latter group, primarily because they become eligible for Medicaid by virtue of high medical expenditures.

With regard to older persons, the benefits of Medicaid have been largely shaped by the coverage under Medicare. Medicaid pays for most services not covered (or not fully covered) under Medicare. Thus, nursing home care and medications become major Medicaid items, along with the deductibles and copayments Medicare demands.

Figure 1 shows the pattern of major sources of medical expenditures for older persons. Moreover, a substantial minority of elderly persons spend a large amount of their income on health-care expenditures. Thirty percent of disabled aged persons have out-of-pocket health-care expenditures that exceed 20% of

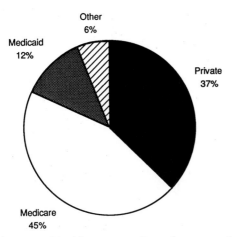

Figure I Personal health-care expenditures for persons 65 years of age or over. (From Waldo et al., 1987.)

their income. These expenses include acute care, drugs, home care, and nursing home care. A much higher proportion of low-income (less than $500 per month in 1982–1984) disabled than high-income (more than $1,000 per month) disabled elderly have health-care expenditures that are greater than 20% of their income, 42% as compared with 11%.

An area poorly covered by Medicare is prevention. Basically, the only direct preventive services paid for under Medicare are influenza immunizations and a limited payment for mammograms to screen for breast cancer. Although there is some feeling that preventive services are better directed at younger groups, there is a strong argument to be made for the need to direct more preventive attention to older persons. Actions such as getting older people to stop smoking or to exercise more have been shown to produce positive health effects. Early detection of problems such as depression or correctable causes of disability can do much to improve the quality of life for older people. Comprehensive geriatric assessments and interventions have been shown to reduce mortality and improve functioning in carefully targeted groups of older patients. There is even some evidence to suggest that the incidence of and complications from falls can be reduced by appropriate exercise and training programs.

II. USE OF SERVICES

In general, older persons use more health care than do younger persons. However, as with other geriatric

phenomena, there is no magic transition point. Persons aged 65 are not automatically different from those aged 64, or even 55. Yet, in the case of health-care utilization there is a sharp transition, because of the influence of Medicare insurance coverage. In examining utilization data, one must try to separate the effects of medical needs from those attributable to access.

Table I shows the differences in utilization rates for selected services for various age groups. Two trends can be noted: (a) in general, utilization increases with age, but (b) the rate of increase is different among the various types of care. Hospital use and physician contacts (telephone or in person) increase with age much more than do physician visits. In contrast, dental care shows a decline with age. As seen in Table II, the sharpest age-linked distinction relates to the use of nursing homes. This pattern is especially interesting because neither dental care nor nursing homes are well covered by Medicare.

The use of services is greatly influenced by the way those services are paid. Greatly concerned that the costs of Medicare, especially hospital costs, were rising even faster than the costs of the rest of medical care (which was itself rising much faster than the rate of inflation), the Medicare program changed the way it paid hospitals beginning in 1984. Instead

Table I Utilization of Hospital, Physician, and Dental Services by Age Group[a]

Service	45–64	65–74	75 and older
Hospital			
Days per person (1993)	8.7	9.9	11.6
Discharges per 100 persons (1993)	12.1	24.3	30.1
Average length of stay (1993)	6.2	7.3	8.1
Physician			
Office visits per person (1993)	3.9	5.4	5.7
Contacts per person (1993)	7.1	9.9	11.6
Dental visits per person (1989)	2.4	2.2	1.8

[a]Sources: Hospital Care: Benson & Marano (1994); Physician Care: Benson & Marano (1994); Dental Care: National Center for Health Statistics (1994).

Table II Utilization of Nursing Home and Home Health Care by Elderly Age Group[a]

Service	65–74	75–84	85 and older
Nursing home residents per 1,000 population (1985)	12.5	57.7	220.3
Home health care discharges per 1,000 population (1992)	41.3	98.8	144.8

[a]Sources: Nursing Home Care: Van Nostrand, Miller, and Furner (1993); Home Health Care: Dey (1995).

of paying them effectively what they claimed it cost to deliver care, a prospective system of payment was introduced, which was fixed at a rate set on the basis of the patient's primary diagnosis and other modifying factors. Nearly 500 different groups were created based on historical hospital lengths of stay. These are known as diagnosis-related groups (DRGs).

The introduction of the Prospective Payment System (PPS) had a dramatic effect on hospital behavior. Whereas hospitals previously had no strong incentives to discharge Medicare patients expeditiously and could justify longer lengths of stay on the basis of the greater levels of complications in their care and the often-encountered difficulty of making arrangements for postdischarge care, the PPS was interpreted as making every patient who stayed over the mean expected length of stay a long-stay patient. Great efforts are now devoted to expediting hospital care and discharging patients as quickly as possible.

Virtually dormant programs provided under Medicare to cover the costs of posthospital care in nursing homes and home health care suddenly blossomed. A whole new industry of postacute care was created.

Another unexpected development was the growth of alternatives to hospitals. Not only was hospital length of stay reduced, many procedures formerly delivered in the hospital setting were now performed in outpatient settings. The press by hospitals to discharge patients "quicker and sicker" raised some concerns. A study done to test the impact of this change in hospital payment failed to reveal any substantial resultant harm in terms of increased mortality or excessive rates of readmissions.

The apparent success of PPS in controlling Medi-

care costs led to interest in expanding this notion of prospective payment to other aspects of care under Medicare. Work was stimulated to develop parallel prospective groupings for ambulatory care, which could cover the costs of episodes of outpatient care. Packages of "bundled" services were proposed, where a fixed fee would cover both hospital and associated medical costs for a given procedure (e.g., a cataract operation).

III. MANAGED CARE

Health services for older people have shared in the general health-care transition to managed care, but less so than for the under 65 population. For more than 20 years, Medicare has been experimenting with the use of health maintenance organizations (HMOs) as vehicles for delivering care to beneficiaries. In essence, HMOs receive a payment equivalent to 95% of the average amount paid by Medicare for persons in each county according to age, sex, welfare status, and institutional status. (Higher rates are paid for persons who are older, female, on welfare, or living in institutions.) This rate is referred to as the adjusted average per capita cost (AAPCC). In return, HMOs are obligated to provide at least the minimum package of benefits available under Medicare. In practice, this coverage is usually offered as at least the equivalent of Medicare services without deductibles or copayments. Thus, it combines Medicare and Medigap insurance.

Depending on the level of the AAPCC, some HMOs can afford to offer beneficiaries this inclusive service at no additional cost beyond what the beneficiaries would otherwise pay for their Part B premium.[1] In some areas, where the AAPCC is quite high, the HMOs can offer much more than the minimum coverage, including such services as drug benefits, preventive care, and eye care. In other areas with lower AAPCC rates, the HMOs must charge an additional premium, usually competitive with the rates charged for Medigap insurance.

From the beneficiaries' perspective, belonging to

[1]The beneficiary saves a considerable amount of money, often $500–$1000 per year, because they do not have to pay a Medigap premium.

an HMO provides a high degree of protection from excess expenditures and a great relief from the sometimes complex paperwork involved in Medicare's fee-for-service payment system. The disadvantages are the need to change physicians if the beneficiary's current physician is not a participant in the HMO, and the potential of encountering the usual problems of managed care: restricted access to specialty services and a sense of depersonalization.

Medicare beneficiaries' participation in HMOs is entirely voluntary. The HMOs are prohibited from refusing enrollment to anyone because of prior health conditions, but marketing strategies are often targeted at attracting the healthy elderly. A study of Medicare HMOs suggested that they indeed had achieved a favorable selection of clients.

The variation in AAPCC rates reflects a large difference in the amount of money Medicare spends for presumably comparable services in different parts of the country, a discrepancy well above anything attributable to wage differentials. For example, the 1995 monthly AAPCC rates in Dade County, Florida (Miami), are $315 for Part A and $300 for Part B. In contrast, the rates for Hennepin County, Minnesota (Minneapolis), are $236 and $126. The difference is almost twofold. Whereas Medicare has moved toward national rates for DRGs, no similar movement has occurred for the AAPCC, primarily because HMOs in high-rate areas would likely not opt to participate if they could do better by staying in fee-for-service practice. In fact, many HMOs have chosen to drop out of the Medicare risk program entirely or have converted to another option that capitates their Part B costs but maintains the Part A costs in the regular Medicare program.

In general, there is little evidence that Medicare HMOs have a special commitment to providing more geriatrically oriented care. Although there are examples of creative use of geriatric approaches, including the extensive use of geriatric nurse practitioners, in some programs many have made no accommodations in their regular care to recognize caring for an older, frailer population.

A particularly noteworthy Medicare HMO project has been developed through the Evercare Corporation that specifically targets nursing home residents. The underlying premise is that providing more intensive primary care (largely through the active use of geriatric nurse practitioners) will lead to reduced hospital care costs that more than offset the investment in primary care.

Managed care principles have been extended to cover a broader range of services that include both acute and chronic care. The two best examples of this expansion are the Social Health Maintenance Organization (S/HMO) and PACE (Program for All-Inclusive Care of the Elderly). The original S/HMO program was developed by Brandeis University on the thesis that combining coverage for acute and chronic care could create sufficient efficiencies to more than pay for itself. Four sites were enrolled and an arrangement negotiated with HCFA whereby the S/HMO sites would receive 100% (instead of 95%) of the AAPCC for a benefit package that would cover a limited amount of long-term care in addition to regular Medicare coverage. Some of the sites charged an additional premium to pay for the long-term care. The four sites were quite varied in their composition. Two were HMOs that expanded their approach to incorporate long-term care; two were long-term care agencies that had to negotiate new affiliations with group practices to provide the acute care. When the programs became operational, they had to find some way to control risk. Rather than introducing a risk-based premium, they opted to charge a fixed amount (subject to some adjustments) and to control the distribution of disability in the enrolled population by establishing quotas for the numbers of severely disabled persons who could be enrolled at any time (equivalent to the proportion in the general population). The evaluation of the first generation of the S/HMOs has suggested that they did not fulfill the mandate their advocates had predicted as strongly as had been hoped. Nonetheless, they did establish the feasibility of merging the two streams of care. The response to their pioneering efforts was sufficient to prompt Congress to renew the waivers that permitted their activity and to mandate additional demonstrations to refine the concept.

The amount of long-term care actually covered by the S/HMOs is limited. A more ambitious synthesis was conducted under the auspices of PACE, which is a program designed to replicate a model originally developed in San Francisco to provide community-based care to frail older persons judged to be eligible for nursing home admission. Unlike the S/HMOs, the PACE projects are designed to cover all acute and long-term care costs. Because the monthly capitated charge is so high, the vast majority of subscribers are covered by Medicaid (as well as by Medicare). In fact, Medicaid usually pays about two-thirds of the overall cost, although the actual rate varies from state to state. The core of the services are based in an adult day health-care setting, where clients can get a combination of social attention, assistance with activities of daily living (eating, bathing, and similar tasks), and regular exposure to primary care. Great efforts are made to keep clients out of institutions, both acute and chronic, by innovative approaches to addressing problems in a timely way.

Other managed care models for the care of older persons are being developed. For example, the state of Minnesota will launch a program also designed to address the needs of those covered by both Medicare and Medicaid. In this instance, the funds will flow to the state, which will in turn contract with managed care providers, to cover the needed care.

IV. POLICY ISSUES

A. Cost

Health-care services for older persons are going through what seems to be a continuous transition. Several issues require active attention even as the system evolves. The cost of Medicare has received repeated attention. In 1992 Medicare spent $3,685 per enrollee. This spending has grown more rapidly than any other component of health care and is the most sensitive to changing demographic patterns. With the aging of the baby boom cohort, Medicare's solvency has been questioned. Part of the problem with Medicare has been the large variation in costs across the country. Although some parts of the program have been standardized to national norms (e.g., DRGs), other components vary greatly, as reflected in the AAPCCs. For example, the average amount spent by Medicare per enrollee ranges from $1,768 for Wyoming to $4,557 for California. It is not at all clear why such variation occurs. More care is not necessarily the same as better care.

One response to the variation has been the promulgation of practice guidelines, which describe the best way to manage various problems. Although it has proven difficult to get physicians to adhere to such standards consistently, the growing shift toward man-

aged care promises to create an environment more conducive to such behavior.

B. Geriatrics

Another pertinent issue addresses the role of geriatrics in modern medical care. Although it has been discussed as a special branch of medicine for over 70 years, geriatrics has begun to make an impression in only the last two decades. Several studies have indicated a substantial need for physicians trained in the care of frail older persons, although estimates of just how many such physicians vary with the study. Most projections acknowledge that it is very unlikely that enough geriatricians will be trained to meet the need for such care. Even the task of adding some geriatric training to the preparation of young primary-care physicians is daunting. It seems far more likely that the principal strategy for introducing more geriatric content will have to rely on "gerontologizing" the education of primary-care physicians.

One alternative solution is to make greater use of geriatric nurse practitioners as primary-care providers. These nurses have been shown to play a useful role in managing the primary care of frail older persons in various settings.

Special geriatric programs may be available in some areas to assist in managing the more complex cases. Since the early reports of great benefit from systematic comprehensive geriatric assessment, there have been a number of studies suggesting that geriatric evaluation and management programs can play a useful role in the overall strategy of caring for older persons, but these programs have not been appreciated by the medical community. Most referrals to such programs still come directly from patients and their families, not from other physicians.

C. Acute and Chronic Links

Geriatric care is characterized by the presence of multiple, interactive problems that span several domains. The management of medical problems, often complex because of the simultaneous occurrence of several problems or atypical presentations, are exacerbated by difficulties in other arenas, such as psychological distress or economic hardship. Conversely, persons needing long-term care are likely to need more, not less, acute care, especially attentive primary care. Successful care cannot be compartmentalized.

Programs are needed to synergize different forms of care, to provide for active coordination and communication. Such an approach requires shared goals and a common sense of accountability. New organizational structures, perhaps built on the framework of managed care, may offer an answer to the question of how to create an environment conducive to such coordinated care. One facet of this new approach may lie in shifting the emphasis of accountability from what is done (the process of care) to what is accomplished (outcomes), leaving more leeway for innovative approaches, including the use of different types of personnel. A greater emphasis on the outcomes of care will require careful analyses to assure that the outcomes used suitably reflect realistic possibilities. It will be necessary to correct for differences in case mix when comparing one group's outcomes to another. In effect, the critical accountability question will be, How do the actual outcomes compare to what can realistically be expected for patients with these characteristics?

D. Demographic Pressures

The demographic forecasts make it imperative to find better, more efficient ways of delivering health-care services to older persons. Although some may question the price of past medical success as creating a situation characterized by "survival of the unfittest," there are some data to suggest that the disability rate among older persons is actually decreasing somewhat. Even under an optimistic scenario, society can anticipate substantial increases in the number of disabled older persons in the coming decades. Better approaches to meeting this demand must be found.

BIBLIOGRAPHY

Brown, R. S., Clement, D. G., Hill, J. W., & Retchin, S. M., et al. (1993). Do health maintenance organizations work for Medicare? *Health Care Financing Review, 15,* 7–23.

Friedman, B., & Kane, R. L. (1993). HMO medical directors' perceptions of geriatric practice in Medicare HMOs. *Journal of the American Geriatrics Society, 41,* 1144–1149.

Gornick, M., & Hall, M. J. (1988). Trends in Medicare utilization of SNFs, HHAs, and rehabilitation hospitals. *Health Care Financing Review,* (ann. suppl.) 27–38.

Harrington, C., Lynch, M., & Newcomer, R. J. (1993). Medical services in social health maintenance organizations. *Gerontologist, 33,* 790–800.

Hayward, R. A., Shapiro, M. F., Freeman, H. E., & Corey, C. R. (1988). Inequities in health services among insured Americans: Do working-age adults have less access to medical care than the elderly? *New England Journal of Medicine, 318,* 1507–1511.

Kosecoff, J., Kahn, K. L., Rogers, W. H., Reinisch, E. J., et al. (1990). Prospective payment system and impairment at discharge. The 'quicker-and-sicker' story revisited. *Journal of the American Medical Association, 264,* 1980–1983.

Leutz, W. N., Greenberg, J. N., Abrahams, R. Prottias, J., et al. (1985). *Changing health care for an aging society.* Lexington, MA: DC Heath.

Manton, K. G., Corder, L. S., & Stallard, E. (1993). Estimates of change in chronic disability and institutional incidence and prevalence rates in the U.S. elderly population from the 1982, 1984, and 1989 National Long Term Care Survey. *Journal of Gerontology: Social Sciences, 48,* S153–S166.

Mundinger, M. O. (1994). Advanced-practice nursing—good medicine for physicians? *New England Journal of Medicine, 330,* 211–214.

Reuben, D. B., & Beck, J. C. (1994). Training physicians to care for older Americans: Progress, obstacles, and future directions. A background paper prepared for the Committee on Strengthening the Geriatric Content of Medical Education, Division of Health Care Services, Institute of Medicine. Washington, DC: National Academy Press.

Russell, L. B., & Manning, C. L. (1989). The effect of prospective payment on Medicare expenditures. *New England Journal of Medicine, 320,* 439–444.

Stuck, A. E., Siu, A. L., Wieland, G. D., Adams, J., et al. (1993). Comprehensive geriatric assessment: A meta-analysis of controlled trials. *The Lancet, 342,* 1032–1036.

Hearing

Sandra Gordon-Salant

University of Maryland

I. Background—Prevalence and Source
of Presbycusis
II. Anatomic and Physiologic Changes in the Auditory
System with Age
III. Age-Related Changes in Auditory Performance
IV. Impact of Age-Related Hearing Loss
V. Remediation
VI. Prevention

Central Auditory Processing Disorder Deficits in processing complex stimuli that are attributed to deterioration of nuclei and tracts of the central auditory nervous system.

Conductive Hearing Loss Hearing loss caused by a pathological condition of the outer ear or middle ear.

Hearing Handicap The impact of a hearing loss on an individual's daily function.

Presbycusis Hearing loss associated with the aging process.

Sensorineural Hearing Loss Hearing loss attributed to deterioration of the cochlea or auditory portion of the eighth cranial nerve (N. VIII).

HEARING declines with advancing age. This is attributed, in part, to age-related changes in the auditory system as well as to exposure to disease processes, ototoxic drugs, and trauma to the auditory system. The consequences of anatomical and physiological deterioration of the auditory mechanism include shifts in hearing sensitivity (hearing loss) and difficulty understanding speech, particularly in noisy or reverberant environments. Feelings of isolation, depression, and anxiety may result from hearing loss and the inability to communicate effectively. Personal hearing aids and assistive listening devices provide benefit to older listeners with hearing loss, although a program of aural rehabilitation may be necessary for the older person to realize the maximum benefit of these devices.

I. BACKGROUND—PREVALENCE AND SOURCE OF PRESBYCUSIS

Hearing loss is the third most commonly reported chronic condition affecting elderly people. It affects approximately 39% of the population aged over 65 years. With the rapid growth in the population over 75 years, it is estimated that there will be approximately 11 million elderly people with hearing loss in the United States by the year 2000.

Presbycusis is the term used traditionally to describe hearing loss associated with the aging process. However, in many older people the apparent hearing loss may be the sum of age-related deterioration of the auditory system (presbycusis), exposure to social and environmental noise encountered in daily life (sociocusis), and disease-related pathological changes of the auditory system (nosocusis). Shifts in hearing sensitivity resulting from exposure to intense noise in industrial or military settings is termed *noise-induced hearing loss* and is distinguished from presbycusis.

Encyclopedia of Gerontology
Volume 1

II. ANATOMIC AND PHYSIOLOGIC CHANGES IN THE AUDITORY SYSTEM WITH AGE

A. Outer and Middle Ear

Figure 1 is a schematic diagram of the outer, middle, and inner ear. The outer ear is composed of the pinna and the external auditory canal. The pinna, a plate of cartilage held in place by six immobile muscles, collects high-frequency energy, directs this energy toward the ear canal, and assists in localizing sounds. The external auditory canal functions as a resonator that amplifies mid- and high-frequency energy (1.5–7 kHz) by approximately 10–15 dB. Changes in these structures observed in elderly people include impacted cerumen (earwax), prolapsed ear canal, enlargement of the pinnae, and atrophy and thinning of the skin that lines the external auditory canal. The effect of these senescent changes on hearing is often not significant, although impacted cerumen can impose a slight high-frequency conductive hearing loss. Structural alterations of the pinna and ear canal theoretically alter the spectral sound localization and resonance properties of the outer ear, but this has not been verified empirically in elderly listeners.

The middle ear is an air-filled cavity that is bounded on its lateral wall by the tympanic membrane. The tympanic membrane and the three ossicles (malleus, incus, stapes) transmit energy to the inner ear via vibrations of the stapes footplate in and out of the oval window. The ossicular chain also amplifies acoustic energy by approximately 30 dB to overcome the impedance mismatch between the air-filled outer and middle ear and the fluid-filled cochlea. The Eustachian tube courses from the anterior wall of the middle ear to the nasopharynx and ventilates the middle ear space with air. The two muscles of the middle ear, the stapedius and tensor tympani, contract in response to loud sound, effectively decreasing transmission of low-frequency energy to the cochlea.

The tympanic membrane becomes stiffer, thinner, and less vascular with increased age. Arthritic changes of the middle ear are observed in individuals over 30 years of age, and increase in prevalence and severity with increasing age. By 70 years of age, thinning and calcification of the cartilaginous incudomalleal and incudostapedial joints of the middle ear are often apparent. Calcification of the cartilage support of the Eustachian tube is also reported in older subjects. Fibers of the two middle ear muscles may atrophy with age. These age-related alterations in middle ear structures frequently do not coincide with significant conductive hearing loss.

B. Labyrinth (Inner Ear) and Nerve of Hearing

The labyrinth is composed of the three semicircular canals, the vestibule, and the cochlea. The semicircular canals and vestibule are part of the vestibular system, which controls the sense of balance, and the cochlea is part of the auditory system. The cochlea in humans has two and three-quarter turns, which are the basal, medial, and apical (incomplete) turns. The vibrations of the stapes footplate in and out of the oval window initiate a characteristic pattern of pressure changes in the perilymphatic fluid that fills the bony cochlea. These pressure changes ultimately cause a mechanical bending of the stereocilia protruding from the tops of inner and outer hair cells, located in the sensory end organ that courses through the cochlea, the organ of Corti. Figure 2 depicts a cross section of the organ of Corti. A transduction process occurs in the organ of Corti, in which mechanical energy (movement of the stereocilia) is converted to neural energy by the hair cells. In inner hair cells, the response to the bending of the stereocilia is the release of neurotransmitter substances at the bottom of the

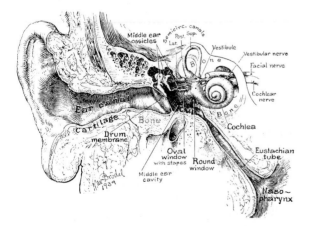

Figure 1   A cross-section of the human outer, middle, and inner ear. (From Brodel, M. (1946). *Three unpublished drawings of the anatomy of the human ear*. Philadelphia: W. B. Saunders Co.)

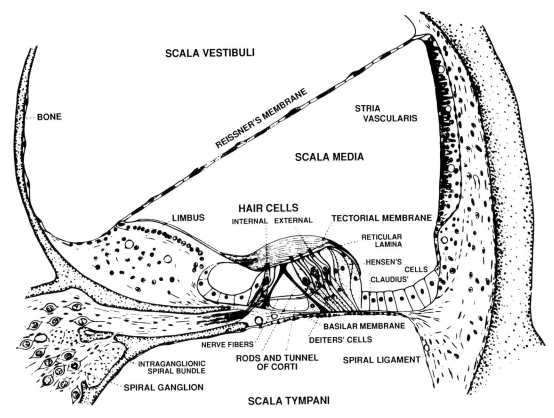

Figure 2 Drawing of a cross-section of one turn of the cochlea showing the organ of Corti. (From Davis, H. *et al.* (1953). Acoustic trauma in the guinea pig. *Journal of the Acoustical Society of America, 25,* 1182.)

hair cell; these are absorbed by neurons of N. VIII, which send nerve impulses to the brain. The bending of the stereocilia in outer hair cells initiates a motor action of outer hair cells that amplifies the response of the cochlea and improves the frequency selectivity of the inner hair cells. The motile action of the outer hair cell membrane and a resulting reverse traveling wave pattern deliver a low-level sound to the outer ear that can be detected as an otoacoustic emission (OAE).

The aging process produces numerous changes in inner ear structures. A prominent change is atrophy and loss of outer hair cells in the basal region of the cochlea, which encodes high-frequency sounds. Deterioration of inner hair cells, supporting cells, and outer hair cells throughout the organ of Corti may occur. Fusion of stereocilia atop the hair cells has also been reported. Hearing loss will occur with a loss of outer hair cells exceeding 20% in the basal turn of the cochlea. The hearing loss attributed to degeneration of the hair cells of the sensory end organ has been termed *sensory presbycusis.* Age-related changes also occur frequently in the vasculature of the cochlea, particularly in the stria vascularis of the cochlear duct. However, a relationship between these vasculature changes and hearing loss has not been established.

Approximately 30,000 neurons collect together to form the afferent auditory portion of N. VIII. The dendrites of these neurons are located primarily under the inner hair cells, the cell bodies are located in the spiral ganglion found in the central core of the cochlea, and the axons course centrally to the cochlear nuclei in the auditory brain stem. The auditory portion of N. VIII codes the spectral, intensive, and temporal attributes of the acoustic signal and transmits this information to the auditory brain stem, where this information is recoded and transmitted centrally.

Age-related degeneration has been reported in the

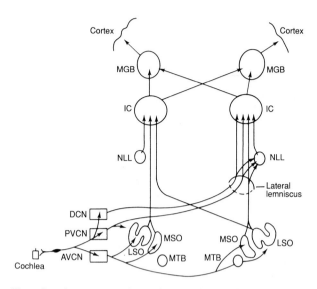

Figure 3 The main ascending auditory pathways of the brain stem. DCN, dorsal cochlear nucleus; PVCN, posteroventral cochlear nucleus; AVCN, anteroventral cochlear nucleus; LSO, lateral superior olive; MSO, medial superior olive; MTB, medial nucleus of the trapezoid body; NLL, nucleus of the lateral lemniscus; IC, inferior colliculus; and MGB, medial geniculate body. (From Pickles, J. O. (1982). *An introduction to the physiology of hearing.* New York: Academic Press.)

spiral ganglion, the neural axons, and the peripheral dendritic processes. Neural degeneration can be coincident with cochlear hair cell loss in elderly people or it can occur independently of atrophy of the organ of Corti. Loss of hearing sensitivity may not result from neural degeneration unless the loss of spiral ganglion cells is severe in the basal turn of the cochlea (exceeding a 50% cell loss). *Neural presbycusis* is the term used to describe age-associated hearing loss of neural origin. Deterioration of neurons comprising N. VIII presumably affects neural coding of the acoustic signal, resulting in distorted signal processing and deficits in speech recognition.

C. Central Auditory Nervous System

The central auditory nervous system (CANS), shown schematically in Fig. 3, consists of aggregates of neurons (nuclei) in the brain stem, midbrain, and cortex, and the neural tracts that interconnect these nuclei. The CANS includes uncrossed tracts and tracts that cross from one side of the brain to the other, making

possible a cross-correlation of signals presented bilaterally. The nuclei of the CANS recode features of acoustic signals and transmit them to the primary auditory cortex for final processing of complex stimuli. Sound localization, auditory attention, pattern discrimination, and absolute recognition of signals are some of the functions attributed to the CANS.

The cochlear nuclei in the auditory brain stem as well as the auditory cortex exhibit the most substantial degeneration with aging. In particular, a widespread loss of neurons in the auditory cortex has been observed. However, the degree of age-related degeneration of the CANS may vary widely among individuals. Evidence for age-related physiological changes in CANS functions in humans is not yet available. Nevertheless, it is possible that age-related degeneration of the CANS has some functional significance for hearing processes. Behavioral measures of central auditory processing (described below) support this hypothesis to some extent.

III. AGE-RELATED CHANGES IN AUDITORY PERFORMANCE

A. Behavioral Measures

1. Auditory Thresholds

Hearing sensitivity declines with increasing age. Cross-sectional and longitudinal studies have assessed pure-tone thresholds in men and women from industrialized societies who are free of otologic disease and significant noise exposure. Results from a recent longitudinal study are shown in Figure 4. The results have shown that, on average, pure-tone air conduction thresholds decrease starting above age 20 years in men and above age 30 years in women. Men show the faster decline in high-frequency hearing sensitivity, with high-frequency thresholds decreasing twice as fast as those of women. Although women also exhibit shifts in hearing sensitivity in the high frequencies, their thresholds in the low frequencies are poorer than those of men of comparable ages. The source of this gender reversal in the low frequencies is not yet known. The average hearing loss in elderly people, aged 70–79 years, can be described as a mild-to-moderately severe, sharply sloping hearing loss in men, and a mild-to-moderate, gradually sloping hearing loss in women.

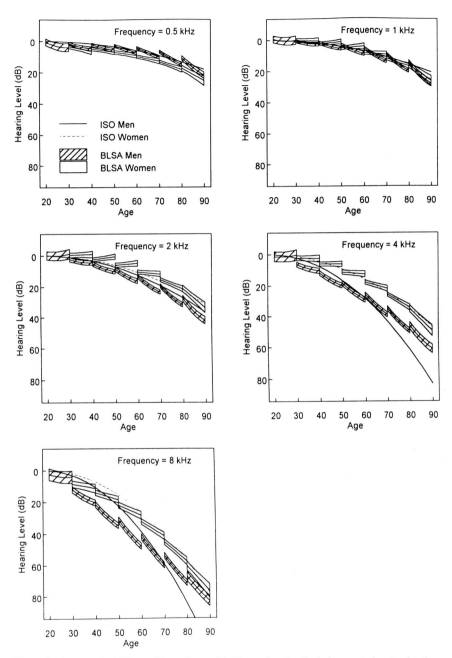

Figure 4 Average (±95% confidence intervals) 10-year longitudinal changes in hearing levels at selected frequencies in men and women in the Baltimore Longitudinal Study on Aging as estimated by mixed-effects regression models. (From Pearson, J. D. *et al.* (1995). Gender differences in age-associated hearing loss. *Journal of the Acoustical Society of America, 97,* 1196–1205.)

Measurement of hearing sensitivity by bone conduction also shows declines in pure-tone thresholds with increasing age. Presentation of a bone conduction stimulus essentially bypasses the outer and middle ear by delivering a vibratory signal more directly to the cochlea. Elderly subjects who have not been screened for middle ear disease or ear canal occlusion frequently exhibit conductive hearing losses, reflected as a gap between air and bone conduction thresholds. However, samples of elderly subjects who have been screened for otologic disorders do not exhibit significant air–bone gaps. This finding suggests that age-related deterioration of the outer and middle ear does not produce a measurable conductive hearing loss in most older subjects. Rather, the shifts in air conduction thresholds noted above are closely matched by shifts in bone conduction thresholds in most elderly people, indicating the presence of a sensorineural hearing loss.

2. Speech Recognition

Elderly people often report difficulty understanding speech. In good acoustic environments, the primary source of this problem in older people is reduced audibility of the speech signal. The level of average conversational speech (65-dB sound pressure level, or SPL) is not sufficiently intense for the listener with a typical age-related hearing loss to receive the weak high-frequency acoustic cues inherent in the speech signal. Speech presented at high levels is perceived well by elderly listeners in quiet environments.

Speech understanding problems of elderly people are exacerbated in noise. This is attributed to the combined effects of direct masking of the noise on the spectral components of speech as well as to reduced audibility of high-frequency speech sounds associated with hearing loss. Young and elderly subjects with comparable hearing sensitivity perform similarly on most speech-in-noise tasks. Thus, the difficulties of speech understanding in noise are not unique to elderly people.

Some speech communication situations are more difficult for older listeners than for younger listeners with comparable hearing sensitivity. Figure 5 presents data on the performance of young and elderly listeners with normal hearing and with hearing loss on reverberant speech tasks and time-compressed speech tasks. As shown in Figure 5, reverberant environments distort the speech signal in a manner that is particularly difficult for elderly listeners. Reverberation refers to a prolongation of sound in an enclosed room. Speech produced in rooms with relatively long reverberation times (such as auditoria) is characterized by overlapping phonetic elements that are difficult to resolve, especially for elderly listeners with hearing loss. Elderly listeners also experience problems understanding rapid speech. Time compression is a laboratory technique that speeds a speech signal without producing spectral distortion. Although younger listeners with hearing loss perform poorly on time-compressed speech tasks, elderly listeners with hearing loss show even more depressed performance. Both reverberant speech and time-compressed speech can be viewed as temporal alterations in the speech waveform. Age effects on these measures, then, may be attributed to deficits in auditory temporal processing that increase with age.

Psychoacoustic measures of auditory duration discrimination in young and elderly listeners support the notion that age-related deficits in temporal processing occur. Moreover, these deficits are correlated with problems in understanding speech distorted by reverberation. Duration discrimination is thought to be mediated by timing mechanisms located in the CANS, thus, the age-associated deficit in duration discrimination may be related to a decline in central auditory processing with age.

Age-related decline in cognitive abilities is also associated with speech understanding problems of elderly listeners. Problems in auditory attention, semantic processing, word retrieval, figure–ground perception, and working memory capacity have been linked to speech recognition deficits in elderly listeners. Studies have shown that performance on speech tasks that increase cognitive demands or increase the number of mental operations is notably poor for elderly listeners. To summarize, problems in speech understanding in difficult listening situations are a major communication complaint of elderly people. These problems are likely the result of a combination of the peripheral hearing loss, deterioration in central auditory mechanisms, and cognitive changes.

B. Electrophysiologic Measures

I. Acoustic Reflexes

Intense sounds activate a reflex that causes contraction of the middle ear muscles, as noted above.

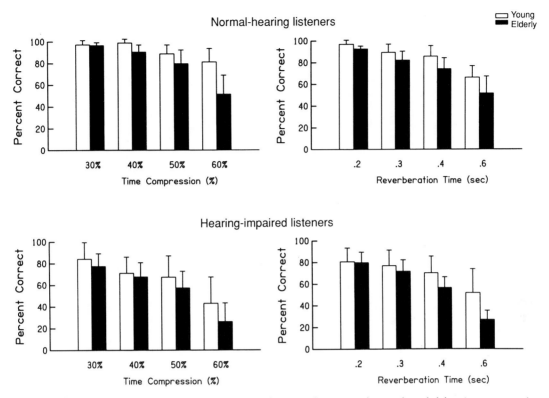

Figure 5 Percent correct recognition of sentences with minimal contextual cues degraded by time compression (left panels) and reverberation (right panels) by young and elderly listeners with normal hearing and with hearing loss.

The acoustic reflex arc is composed of the afferent auditory neurons of N. VIII, the ventral cochlear nucleus, the medial superior olive, the ipsilateral and contralateral nuclei of the facial nerve, and the stapedius muscle. Damage to any structures in the reflex arc affect clinical measures of the acoustic reflex threshold, adaptation, and magnitude. Because anatomical changes associated with the aging process have been observed in many of these structures it is reasonable to expect that age affects measures of the acoustic reflex.

Routine clinical measures of the acoustic reflex, such as acoustic reflex thresholds (ARTs) for tonal activators and acoustic reflex adaptation, are not affected by age. However, aging does have an effect on the growth in amplitude of the acoustic reflex with increasing stimulus level. Elderly subjects show a reduced slope of the growth function compared to younger subjects and a saturation in the growth function. The saturation in the growth function has been attributed to a reduced ability of the aging ear to integrate energy.

2. Auditory Evoked Potentials

The auditory brain stem response (ABR) is a series of seven waves that are evoked and recorded in humans 2–12 ms after onset of a brief acoustic stimulus. The waves reflect the response of N. VIII, the nuclei of the auditory brain stem, and the neural tracts that connect them. The latency, amplitude, and morphology of these waves are affected by pathology of the cochlea, N. VIII, or auditory brain stem.

Assessment of aging effects on the ABR is compromised somewhat by the influence of sensorineural hearing loss. Nevertheless, age appears to exert consistent effects on the ABR, including a small increase in absolute latency of the waves and a decrease in the amplitude of the waves, as shown in Figure 6. Sensory

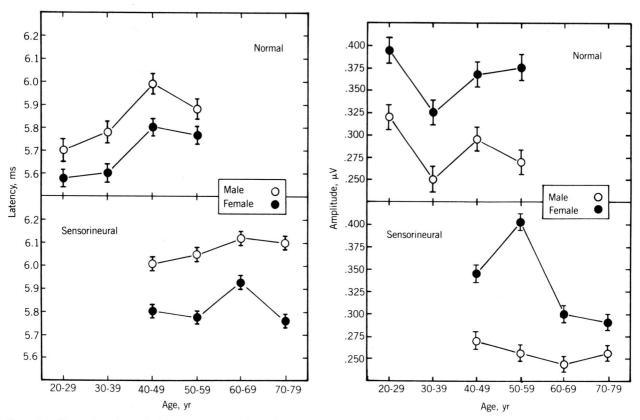

Figure 6 Effects of gender and advancing age on auditory brain stem response (ABR) wave V latency (left graph) and amplitude (right graph), for normal hearing (top panels) and sensorineurally impaired (bottom panels) adult subjects. Vertical bars indicate standard errors of the mean. (From Jerger, J., & Hall, J. (1980). Effects of age and sex on auditory brainstem response (ABR). *Archives of Otolaryngology, 106*, 387–391.)

presbycusis also is associated with an increased Wave V/I amplitude ratio.

Among the other potentials evoked from the auditory system, the P300 holds the most promise for evaluation of the elderly person. The P300 is an event-related potential that is recorded 300 ms after stimulus onset in young adults. It occurs in response to a cognitive task performed by the subject; usually this task is attending to an "oddball" stimulus presented rarely among a sequence of frequent stimuli. Figure 7 shows that the latency of the P300 response increases steadily with increasing age through the life span (10–90 years) at the rate of approximately 1–1.5 ms/year. Researchers have shown that increasing the difficulty of the task by adding background noise affects the latency of this response differentially for elderly people compared

to younger people, possibly reflecting deterioration of central auditory mechanisms.

3. Otoacoustic Emissions

The motile action of cochlear outer hair cells and resulting reverse traveling wave produce a low-level sound that can be recorded in the ear canal. These OAEs can occur spontaneously in about half of healthy ears, or can be evoked by clicks or pure tones in all normal ears. One paradigm, the distortion product OAE, can generate an audiogram that reflects the status of outer hair cells in the region from 1000 Hz through 8000 Hz. The response is absent in people with a mild hearing loss (50-dB hearing level—HL) or greater that is caused by outer hair cell loss.

There is a decrease in the presence of OAEs in subjects who are not screened for normal hearing and

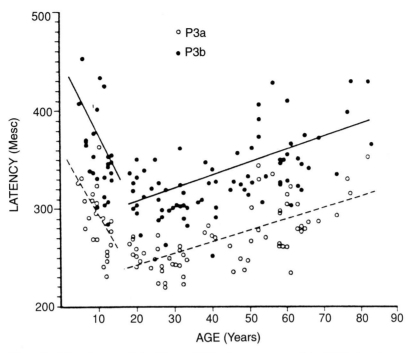

Figure 7 Mean latency of the P3a and P3b subcomponents of the P300 plotted as a function of participant age. Dashed and solid lines represent regression lines computed for the P3a and P3b components, respectively. (From Polich, J., Howard, L., & Starr, A. (1985). Effects of age on the P300 component of the event-related potential from auditory stimuli: Peak definition, variation, and measurement. *Journal of Gerontology, 40,* 721–726.)

are aged 60 years and over compared to younger subjects. However, a linear relationship has been shown between OAE threshold and behavioral threshold. Thus, the age-related change in OAEs among these subjects is attributed primarily to the age-related decline in hearing sensitivity (presumably associated with outer hair cell degeneration). Elderly subjects with clinically normal hearing (20-dB HL or better) also show changes in OAEs compared to younger subjects with normal hearing. These changes include poorer OAE thresholds, reduced amplitude of the OAE response, shallower input–output functions, and lower prevalence of a normal OAE response. At present, the interpretation of these abnormalities in elderly subjects is that they reflect significant shifts in hearing sensitivity with age, even within the range of normal hearing. Therefore, alterations in the OAE response with age reported thus far are confounded with deterioration in high-frequency hearing sensitivity. Nevertheless, assessment of OAEs holds promise

as a method to track early age-related changes in the auditory system that may precede the onset of high-frequency hearing loss.

IV. IMPACT OF AGE-RELATED HEARING LOSS

Age-related hearing impairment has a significant negative impact on daily function and quality of life. Assessment of the consequence of a hearing loss on communication function is often made with a hearing handicap scale. The most popular scale for use with elderly people is the Hearing Handicap Inventory for the Elderly (HHIE). This scale samples the social or situational and emotional effects of hearing loss in various communication situations, as perceived by the respondent. People with a hearing loss of mild degree or greater report significant loss of communication function as measured with this scale. In a random sample of 194 elderly veterans with hearing impairment, 63% reported severe social and emotional handicap due to hearing impairment, and 20% reported mild to moderate handicap. There is a moderate correlation between self-perceived hearing handicap and degree of hearing loss among elderly people. This suggests that older people have different reactions to hearing loss, and that hearing handicap cannot necessarily be predicted from the degree of hearing loss.

Presbycusis is also associated with global functional changes. The Sickness Impact Profile (SIP) has been used to assess sickness-related dysfunction in elderly people with hearing loss. Poor hearing is associated with increased physical and psychosocial dysfunction after adjustments are made for age, race, sex, education, mental status, visual acuity, number of illnesses, and number of medications. The Geriatric Depression Scale has also been applied to elderly people with hearing loss and has revealed the presence of depression in 24% of subjects in a representative sample. Thus, hearing impairment of mild degree or greater may have an adverse effect on physical, emotional, social, and behavioral function among elderly people.

V. REMEDIATION

The most effective means to improve communication and reduce hearing handicap resulting from hearing loss in elderly people is with hearing aids. Hearing aids amplify the speech signal so that it is audible to the listener without being uncomfortably loud. Improvements in hearing aid design and circuitry permit audiologists to select from a wide variety of options for elderly people with age-related hearing loss. For example, the hearing aid's frequency response (gain/frequency) is selected to amplify spectral regions that are least audible for the user and where the user retains some residual hearing. Amplitude compression circuitry is also selected individually to ensure that unusually high-intensity acoustic stimuli are not amplified to uncomfortably loud levels. Digitally controlled analog circuits are now incorporated into many hearing aids. These permit unlimited variations in gain/frequency, compression design, and user control of

hearing aid characteristics in different listening environments. Many hearing aids also include noise-reduction circuitry that attempts to detect the presence of noise and alter the frequency response to reduce amplification of the noise. Unfortunately, there is little empirical evidence at present to verify that these adaptive frequency response designs improve speech recognition in noise.

Nevertheless, elderly people receive significant benefit from hearing aids. Elderly people report significant improvements in social and emotional function, communication function, and cognitive function following hearing aid use. In addition, depression decreases significantly among elderly people who receive hearing aids. [See DEPRESSION.] Despite these benefits of amplification, it is estimated that fewer than 50% of elderly people with hearing loss seek audiological assistance, and only 20% own hearing aids. Some of the more prominent reasons for rejecting hearing aid use among elderly people are cost, appearance, and amplification of background noise.

The chances of successful hearing aid use improve if amplification is offered as part of an aural rehabilitation program. Aural rehabilitation programs include orientation to hearing aid use, counseling the hearing-impaired person and their family about the benefits and limitations of hearing aids, and improving awareness of available contextual cues in reduced cue environments. Some aural rehabilitation programs include formal training in utilizing acoustic cues provided through amplification (auditory training) and speech reading (lipreading) training. Elderly people may also require assistance in overcoming physical disabilities that limit hearing aid use.

Other devices are available to improve communication for elderly people with hearing loss. Assistive listening devices (ALDs) are amplification systems in which the signal is picked up by a microphone located near the source and delivered to the listener via wire, magnetic induction, FM transmission, or infrared transmission. The major advantage of these systems is that the amplified signal is not affected by poor room acoustics (noise and reverberation). ALDs are increasingly popular in theaters, houses of worship, and other large auditoria. ALDs can be adapted for individual use in the home or in assisted care living situations.

Alerting devices are used to promote personal safety in elderly people with hearing loss. These include flashing or vibrating alarms to alert the person that a smoke detector, doorbell, or telephone has been activated. Television caption decoders can be used by elderly people who have reasonably good vision but whose hearing capabilities are limited even with amplification. The ability to watch television has been reported as a high priority for elderly people and is associated with general satisfaction with life. Finally, telephone amplifiers with adjustable volume controls are available on many telephone designs. [*See* GERON-TECHNOLOGY.]

VI. PREVENTION

Numerous risk factors are associated with hearing loss. The most notable of these risk factors is exposure to intense noise, either in industrial or leisure settings. Some of the more prominent sources of noise in daily life include power tools, music, rifle blasts, and various forms of transportation (motorcycles, subways, snowmobiles, etc.). Clearly, exposure to noise in industrialized societies contributes to hearing loss acquired during the life span.

One hypothesis of age-related hearing loss is that it represents the accumulation of exposure to numerous exogenous risk factors during a lifetime, rather than to an endogenous deterioration of the auditory system. Partial support for this theory derives from comparisons of age-related hearing loss among individuals from industrialized versus nonindustrialized societies. Individuals from the Maabans African tribe show much less hearing loss with increasing age than do individuals from industrialized societies. Other support for this notion is that older people exhibit a wide variety of hearing thresholds, and a substantial percentage of the elderly population shows normal hearing. Of course, individuals differ greatly genetically as well, and much of the variance in presbycusis may be genetic in origin. Thus, although hearing loss is prevalent among elderly people, it is not necessarily an inevitable consequence of the aging process.

A search for risk factors that may contribute to apparent age-related hearing loss has been the focus of a hearing protocol conducted by the Baltimore Longitudinal Study of Aging. A recent project examined the relationship between smoking behavior, alcohol consumption, and blood pressure and the development of age-associated hearing loss. The study sample included subjects who had a negative history of otologic disease, no evidence of noise-induced hearing loss, and normal hearing at the onset of the study. Among the risk factors assessed, only systolic blood pressure showed a significant relationship with hearing loss in the mid-frequency range independent of the effects of age. These findings suggest that preventing hypertension might be one method to prevent age-related hearing loss. Other risk factors that continue to be examined include elements in the diet, the use of multiple medications, exposure to moderate noise sources in daily life, and genetic influences on presbycusis. Identification of significant risk factors for apparent age-related hearing loss will make it possible to reduce the prevalence of hearing loss in the elderly population and consequently improve the quality of life for the largest growing segment of the population.

BIBLIOGRAPHY

Committee on Hearing, Bioacoustics, and Biomechanism (CHABA); Working Group on Speech Understanding (1988). Speech understanding and aging. *Journal of the Acoustical Society of America, 83,* 859–895.

Gordon-Salant, S., & Fitzgibbons, P. (1993). Temporal factors and speech recognition performance in young and elderly listeners. *Journal of Speech and Hearing Research, 36,* 1276–1285.

Hall, J. W. III. (1992). *Handbook of auditory evoked responses.* Boston: Allyn and Bacon.

Humes, L., & Christopherson, L. (1991). Speech identification difficulties of hearing-impaired elderly persons: The contributions of auditory processing deficits. *Journal of Speech and Hearing Research, 34,* 686–693.

Mulrow, C. D., Aquilar, C., Endicott, J. E., Tuley, M. R., Velez, R., Charlip, W. S., Rhodes, M. C., Hill, J. A., & DeNino, L. A. (1990). Quality-of-life changes and hearing impairment: A randomized trial. *American College of Physicians, 113,* 188–194.

Pearson, J. D., Morrell, C. H., Gordon-Salant, S., Brant, L. J., Metter, E. J., Klein, L. L., & Fozard, J. L. (1995). Gender differences in a longitudinal study of age-associated hearing loss. *Journal of the Acoustical Society of America, 97,* 1196–1205.

Ripich, D. (Ed.). (1991). *Handbook of geriatric communication disorders.* Austin: Pro-Ed.

Stover, L., & Norton, S. J. (1993). The effects of aging on otoacoustic emissions. *Journal of the Acoustical Society of America, 94,* 2670–2681.

Willott, J. F. (1991). *Aging and the auditory system: Anatomy, physiology, and psychophysics.* San Diego: Singular Publishing Group, Inc.

History of Gerontology

James E. Birren

University of California, Los Angeles

Aging   The process of change or transformation of the young to the old organism. The term refers to the patterns of change that occur with age in genetically representative organisms living under representative environmental conditions.

Apologism   The conviction that the study and manipulation of the body to produce greater longevity is a violation of the natural or cosmic order.

Geriatrics   A branch of medicine specialized in the care and treatment of the diseases and health problems of older persons.

Gerontology   The study of the phenomena of aging from a research and scholarly perspective. It embraces studies from the biological, behavioral, and social sciences.

Senescence   The biological process of growing old associated with an increasing probability of dying and susceptibility to disease.

GERONTOLOGY is an ancient subject but a recent science. In the earliest recorded histories there is evidence that humankind speculated about aging and the association of infirmities and death with advanced age. The processes of aging are complex, and com-

bined with the uncertainties about death, a fertile ground for myth, fantasy, and wishful thinking has always existed. These speculations have given rise to myths about the prolongation of life and the nature of death. Some elements of these myths have been displaced by information provided by scientific research but many still remain as part of our cultural inheritance.

The word *gerontology* was introduced in 1903 by Nobel Laureate, Elie Metchnikoff (1845–1916), professor at the Pasteur Institute of Paris. Although the word gerontology is of relatively recent origin, there were many early scholars who published their observations and thoughts about why the human organism changed in appearance and in function, and the likelihood of death with advancing chronological age. *Gerontology* refers to the study of aging, research, and scholarship in all its aspects. The word is derived from the Greek word for an old man, *geront* or *gerontos* plus the suffix *ology*, which refers to a branch of knowledge or science. The term *geriatrics* refers to a branch of medicine that specializes in the care and treatment of the diseases and health problems of older persons.

From archeological studies of the careful entombment of persons in preliterate times it is apparent that in many cultures a great deal of thought was given to the transition from life to death and to prospects for life after death. In those cultures, care was taken in the manner of burial and in providing accompanying articles that might be useful in a future existence. Although one can only speculate about what our preliterate ancestors thought about old age and aging, their ideas were undoubtedly carried over into many of the earliest written material.

Gerontology and its background may be divided into several periods: (a) the mythic period from prehistory to the Greco-Roman era; (b) the philosophical period, from Greco-Roman days to the Renaissance; (c) the Renaissance; (d) the early scientific period, from about 1600–1800; (e) the expansion of empirical research, from 1800 to about 1930; and (f) modern gerontology. These eras are not sharply demarcated and it might be argued, for example, that the period of modern gerontology begins somewhat later than 1930 when gerontological societies were formed. For example, the Gerontological Society was founded in 1945, later renamed the Gerontological Society of America, and the International Association of Gerontology about 3 years later. Such dates might be used to mark the beginnings of the modern era, although, as will be pointed out later, activities in the 1930s provided the background for this emergence.

I. THE MYTHIC PERIOD

From very early writings it may be concluded that humankind has always speculated about the causes of events and offered explanations that attributed causality to mythical forces. Aging is no exception. Gruman prepared a useful history of thoughts about aging and longevity and compiled an extensive bibliography of the mythology of aging with descriptions of the flow of ideas from ancient times to 1800. One of the earliest writings that discussed aging is the epic of Gilgamesh that Gruman dates to around 3000 B.C. The hero of this Babylonia poem, Gilgamesh, becomes obsessed with the thought of immortal life and of finding the secret to it.

As ancient people saw others grow old and die and observed changes in themselves they wondered how they might avoid death. One mythic explanation is that humans once had the gift of immortality but lost it in a fall from grace by offending the gods or God. This led people to attempt to regain immortality by pleasing the gods, offering sacrifices, praying, or doing heroic deeds in accord with the customs of their culture.

Other myths were that people living in remote parts of the world still retained the secret of very long life or that somewhere there were healing waters, and bathing in them would restore youth if not bestow immortality. Throughout the ages, such myths have led to geographic explorations to find fountains of youth, though these have never yielded the sought-after secret cure or reversal of aging. [*See* MYTHOLOGY.]

Gruman divided the myths about aging and mortality into three main types: (a) antediluvian, which hold that in the past people lived much longer; (b) hyperborean, in which it is believed that people live much longer in some remote part of the world; and (c) the fountain type, in which healing waters or substances are thought to exist somewhere. Gruman also uses the word *prolongevity* to refer to the myths and legends in which longevity is extended by means other than those under human's control.

Myths about longevity have usually been linked with a belief in an "Abode of the Blessed," where the pure have extended life. Elements of this pattern have been widespread, appearing in Persian, Teutonic, Japanese, Hebrew, Hindu, and Chinese myths.

Alexander the Great (356–323 B.C.) is described as having had an encounter with a fountain of life and Ponce de Leon (1460–1521 A.D.) purportedly discovered Florida while looking for a fountain that the North American Indians believed was rejuvenating to those who drank or bathed in its waters. It is surprising how many cultures have passed on legends that describe rejuvenating waters that flowed out of an earthly paradise or described mysterious substances that have the power of prolonging life. Myth and magic and wishful thinking about longevity and death apparently pervaded all societies in prescientific eras.

Today these myths may still underlie the popularity of healing spas, diets, exercise programs, and vitamins of special potency. This comment is not meant to express an evaluation of the validity of ways of modifying the course of aging but to express a link between these high contemporary interests and the underlying fear of old age and dying that must have preoccupied some of our preliterate ancestors and still are important to our contemporaries.

Less available to Western scholars have been the East Indian legends, myths, and perspectives on old age and death. A review of East Indian perspectives on aging and the meaning of life has been provided by Ram-Prasad, in which the ideal life pattern is described as consisting of four stages: studenthood, householder, forest dweller, and renouncer. Codification of what students needed to learn began relatively early, from 1500 to 500 B.C. By the beginning of the Christian era an Indian system of belief that evolved that encouraged conformity to these four stages of the life course. Individuals were expected to fit into a cosmic order, *dharma*. Ram-Prasad describes dharma as being an overall entity that reflects the regulation of all aspects of the cosmos. The law book of ancient India is the Code of Manu. It is of interest that early phases of life include pleasures and increasing wealth, but later phases require detachment or renunciation. Meaningfulness in later life is attained by a transcendental detachment from the requirements of daily living. As an alternative to the transcendent detachment in the later years, one may attempt to derive meaning from world-directed acts; however, in the classical East Indian view of life, in the final stage of life, old age, the individual transcends and renounces the world.

In Hinduism and Buddhism, there is the tenet that the force developed by an individual's actions, *karma*, provides the energy for the series of rebirths and deaths until the individual achieves spiritual liberation. Reincarnation in a different body form represents the transmission or embodiment of the soul into a new structure. The reincarnated form would be an outcome of the individual's actions during previous life.

East Indian thought about old age and death accepts the idea of a preordained cosmic order in which the individual lives through stages en route to some ultimate transcendent state. Thus the background for Indian thought is a mixture of philosophy, religion, and the mythology of a long-existing culture.

There has been some filtration into the West of the idea of reincarnation, though the West has been influenced by the Christian view that the individual is ultimately resurrected for eternal life. Both Hinduism and Christianity regard the conditions of future existence as being a consequence of present moral behavior.

II. GRECO-ROMAN PHILOSOPHERS

The Greek and Roman philosophers dealt with questions about the nature of aging and death. The contributions of philosophy and the beginnings of science derived their strength from the rigor of the reasoning and its logic but not data. Underlying their views is the realization from personal observations that there is a pattern to changes in life marked by stages, cycles, or seasons of a life. Increasingly, in the Greco-Roman views of life there was a separation of the physical or physiological aspects from the moral or religious points of view.

In the fourth century B.C., the Greek philosopher, Epicurus (341?–270 B.C.) thought that if people developed the right attitude about the end of life and death, they lost their fear of them and lived a more peaceful life. According to Gruman, Epicurus thought that a short life could be just as happy as a long one so that prolongation of life was not important. Aristotle (384–322 B.C.) was more interested in the natural phenomena of old age and thought that the old body was cold and dry leading to death. He had a rather fixed view of cosmic relationships and avoided the idea of humankind's rebelling against nature or attempting to ameliorate the course of aging.

Cicero (106–42 B.C.) thought that death was a blessing because it freed our immortal souls from their bodily prisons, and he attempted to rebut major objections to old age, including the one that old age interferes with the enjoyment of sensual pleasures. He expressed the opinion that this is a good loss because it permits the older person to concentrate on the promotion of virtue and reason. According to Cole, the Greco-Roman philosophers' worldview of old age that it was inexorable.

> Beginning at conception, the physiological process of drying out and growing old, continued inexorably until death. The stages of life were nature's milestones, making the diminution of natural heat and increased desecration. Each change dictated its own behavior pattern. This approach to aging and the life cycle took shape in an intellectual world without boundaries between science and philosophy; hence it combined the physical and the moral, interpreting behavioral signs in the light of physiology as well as individual character. (Cole, 1988, p. 49)

In addition to the philosophers of the era, physicians also contributed their observations about the course of life and the afflictions of the body. The most significant of these was Galen (129–199 A.D.), who became a model for physicians and for medicine. He believed, like others of his time, that the body dried out as it grew old. Although this suggests that the adding of moisture to the body might extend life, he did not attempt to interfere with what was regarded as the inevitable changes in the body's balance of heat and cold and the drying out of tissues. Two elements in early thought about aging led to the position attempting to modify the course of life is undesirable. The first of these is that it is against the will of God, the second is that it is against the law of nature. Gruman said that "Galen's writings are dominated by teleological arguments, which emphasize that nature always acts for the best. To the question whether old age is a disease, Galen replied that, 'it is not a disease because it is not contrary to nature,'" (p. 17).

In the late Middle Ages, Galen's interpretation of the biology of life was shared by an Arabic philosopher and physician, Avicenna (980–1037). He believed that the drying-out process began in the embryo and continued as a beneficial influence until growth and development ceased at about the age of 30. It was further thought that as the innate moisture of the body dries up, its innate heat decreases, and the aging body becomes cold and dry. This led to a pessimistic outlook about the capacity of medicine to interfere in the decline of function of an aging body. It was thought that extending the life was not a legitimate medical goal, because each individual had a predetermined fixed term of life.

All societies and cultures have been impressed with cycles of the life span and its conclusion with death, although the interpretations or attributions of the forces behind patterns of change have varied. The Greeks and Romans and the Hindus believed that death was part of a natural cosmic order. In Christianity, a different causal attribution was made, that because of sin humankind had fallen from a state of grace in the Garden of Eden and lost immortality and was destined to live a life on this earth plagued by many problems. Eternal life could come only after death and after a life lived according to religious tenets. For many centuries religion and the practice of medicine shared similar views of the preordained character and length of human life.

The religious and theological underpinnings of Western medieval life encouraged the view that one should not tamper with God's will. This position not only discouraged attempts to modify the course of life but also discouraged science generally because its attempts to understand nature were intrusions into the organization of the cosmos as designed and desired by God. Although both the Old and the New Testaments project the view of the fall of humankind and the loss of immortality due to sinfulness, the res-

urrection of the righteous for eternity is emphasized in Christianity and the New Testament. This views the human body and its afflictions as of little importance in comparison with the soul, which is eternal. Victory over death was achieved by resurrection and eternity by God for the righteous. Translated into the attitudes of educated persons, this discouraged experimentation and explanations cast in terms of natural causes. If one attributes the downfall of humankind from Eden as based on pride, then pride is the paramount sin of the scientist because scientists presume to be able to ascertain causal relationships and thereby God's purposes.

Gruman contrasted apologism and prolongevity. The position of the apologist is essentially that study and manipulation of the body to produce longevity is a violation of the natural order. If humankind became mortal and died because of sin, attempts to modify the course of life are not only likely to be unproductive but they are presumably sinful in and of themselves. By extension, old age and death are beneficial in that it brings us closer to resurrection and eternal life with God. The apologist's position not only deterred the development of science, but it also discouraged the transmission of earlier myths about eternal life that had been passed on in the folklore of many cultures. Just below the surface of medieval society, however, there was evidence that early myths still persisted about eternal life and legendary places in the world where long life was attained. Columbus, for example, in 1498 reported that on his third voyage he located a terrestrial paradise in Venezuela. A relatively recent novel, the *Lost Horizon*, by James Hilton, deals with the myth of Shangri-la. This was the name of a place in the Himalayas where people reportedly lived a very long time.

Medieval theology did not stamp out the desire to believe and perpetuate myths of eternal life on earth or an interest in finding pathways to increase longevity. It did, however, discourage the study and gathering of systematic data on the conditions of life that might lead to life extensions.

In the sixteenth and seventeenth centuries in France and Austria, the Huguenots, a Protestant sect, were expelled and persecuted for their beliefs that encouraged a look at the natural sources of conditions of human life. At that time, the Roman Catholic Church, which dominated Christianity, did not favor the collection and examination of data on the length of human life and its variations in different places and conditions. As recently as the eighteenth and nineteenth centuries, there was evidence that the dominant theology of the West discouraged an empirical approach to demography and epidemiology that could ascribe the length of life to natural phenomena.

Unlike the mythic period, the Greek and later philosophers entered into disputations about their conceptions of aging. Lacking evidence from empirical science, it was the tightness of their logic or elegance of their reasoning that were translated into proof of the validity of their opinions. This was a marked advance in understanding because it brought the circumstances of aging into normal discourse and its causes into disputation rather than leaving them in the hands of temple priests who assigned causes to deistic power or offenses. The philosophers coupled their everyday observations with their abstractions in attempting to weigh evidence before arriving at conclusions. One of the early observations was that in death the body is cold. Hence the loss of heat became an early focus. Aristotle regarded old age as the time when our heat is diminished. Much later this same idea was expressed by Benjamin Franklin (1706–1790), who thought he could rejuvenate a dead chicken by exposing it to a spark of lightening (i.e., heat).

III. THE RENAISSANCE

The fourteenth century was the beginning of a revival of literature, learning, and art in Western Europe. Stimulated by the prosperity of the Italian economy and its culture many new expressions were spawned in art, literature, architecture, and science. In the sixteenth century, the Renaissance was joined by a Reformation movement in which Protestant churches separated from the Roman Catholic church. The Reformation brought with it a new freedom of thought but also new tensions about social controls, religious beliefs, and desirable life activities, though it still carried with it an emphasis on doing good works during one's lifetime.

There are many exceptions to this simple view of the evolution of Western ideas about aging and death. Medieval alchemists thought about prolongevity and apparently had done things to lengthen life. In China, there was no theological resistance to the exploration of natural experiments, and their alchemists also attempted to modify the course of life by using various natural substances.

In the Old Testament of the Bible, there is an account of the attempt to rejuvenate the aging King David (c. 1000–762 B.C.) by placing a young virgin in his bed. There had long been an assumption that inhaling the breath of a young maiden was a stimulus to longevity. This practice called *gerokomy*, was recommended by a seventeenth-century Dutch physician who suggested that an aging burgomeister lie between two young virgins, presumably so that he would obtain maximum benefit, to restore his vitality.

The influence of the Renaissance and the Reformation freed investigators to pursue the gathering of data. Data or information could then be used for sorting out valid from invalid views of the causes of natural events. The use of data probably distinguishes more than anything else the approach to present-day thinking in contrast to that of the Greeks and Romans (i.e., it is not only logic and richness of thought that matters but the availability of data on which to revise thought). It also differs from classical East Indian thought about old age and death, which is based on the assumption that there is a preordained cosmic order in which each individual lives through stages en route to some ultimate transcendent state. Thus, the background for Indian thought is a mixture of philosophy, religion, and the practices of a long-existing culture, although it did not stimulate scientific research on aging.

In Great Britain, the views of Francis Bacon (1561–1626) encouraged the growth of natural sciences and serious inquiry into the processes of aging. In Italy in 1558, Cornaro (1284?–1367) published his *Discourses*, which was very influential in Western Europe. Cornaro believed that longevity could be extended by simple reforms of an individual's life habits. He believed that some very simple hygienic practices would influence the length of life and the condition of a person's health. This view has its counterparts today, that personal dietary habits, exercise, and activity patterns, exposure to noxious environmental influences, and stress influence how long and how well we live. The Renaissance and Reformation permitted a shift in attitudes that supported the growth of natural science and the gathering of systematic data. Although the observations of Galileo (1564–1642) on the organization of the planetary system led to a conflict with the Roman Catholic Church, later observers were able to interpret the organization of the planetary system with impunity and freedom from persecution.

IV. THE SCIENTIFIC ERA

As learned scholars began to make systematic observations in areas other than astronomy, a burgeoning period of science ultimately reached the subject matter of aging. In England, Isaac Newton (1642–1727), a member of then-religiously dominated Trinity College, Cambridge, explored physics and developed laws about the force of gravity. His life exemplified both the quest for understanding in natural terms and the conviction that relationships can be expressed lawfully. Scholars believed that every event or act is the inevitable outcome of its antecedents. The successes of astronomy and the physical sciences in explaining natural phenomena encouraged the growth of science in new directions in biology and medicine. Scientists had the conviction that everything was knowable, all things were deterministic and lawful. This encouraged the growth of new perspectives on the issues of aging, longevity, and death.

The expansion of mathematics and sciences occurred rapidly after the seventeenth century. European universities added many faculty members whose expertise and commitment were to science. This expansion originated in the physical sciences. It was followed by biology and then by psychology and the social sciences, although some remaining unease was experienced in the relationships between philosophy, theology, and by the growth of the behavioral and social sciences. As late as 1937, philosophers at Oxford University stated there could never be a science of the mind and voted down the creation of a department of psychology. Less threatening to the belief structure of organized religion was the study of mathematics, chemistry, and physics than was the study of human behavior. [See PHILOSOPHY.]

The studies of British biologist Charles Darwin (1809–1882) perhaps epitomize the weakening of philosophical and religious presuppositions in characterizing the status of humankind in the universe. Through his observations of various species, Darwin concluded that there had been an evolution of species from simple early forms to later more complex species, including human. Although this did give humans a superior position in the sense that it was a late evolved species, it clearly broke with the creationist tradition, which regarded humankind as a unique and immediate purposive product of a Divine Being. [See EVOLUTION AND COMPARATIVE BIOLOGY.]

The expansive period of science in the nineteenth century was based upon the conviction that all phenomena of nature are lawful and that these laws can be determined through scientific investigation. The first application of this point of view in the study of aging was done by a Belgian scientist, mathematician, statistician, and astronomer Adolphe Quetelet (1796–1874). He published his views with supporting data in Paris in 1835. The translated title of his book is *On Man and the Development of his Faculties*. The determinist point of view is clearly expressed in his provocative opening: "Man is born, grows up, and dies, according to certain laws which have never been properly investigated, either as a whole or in the mode of their mutual reactions," (Quetelet, 1842, Edinburgh translation). Quetelet was a distinguished scientist of his day, and he visited and corresponded widely with other leaders in science in Western Europe. It is of interest to note that it is difficult to classify him in terms of contemporary science. He wrote and studied at a time before there were few formal university departments in many of the disciplines. He could be regarded as one of the earliest quantitative workers in the field of exact social science, but he also dealt with issues of mortality and functional capacities. Trained as a mathematician, he developed the concept of "the average man" around which were distributed measurements according to the law of accidental causes. In this he anticipated the work of Gauss, whose work on the binomial distribution, which is commonly known as the normal or bell-shaped curve. Quetelet reviewed mortality data in relation to age, sex, urban, rural, and national differences. He was convinced that little is beyond knowing if one attends to observation and to describing statistical and mathematical relationships. He clearly adopted a deterministic and organismic perspective about human development and aging. In commenting about previous work he said

But they have neglected to put forward, with sufficient prominence, the study of his physical development, and they have neglected to mark by numbers how individual man increases with respect to weight and height—how, in short, his forces are developed, the sensibility of his organs, and his other physical faculties. They have not determined the age at which his faculties reach their maximum or highest energy, nor the time when they commence to decline. Neither have they determined the relative value of his faculties at different epochs or periods of his life, nor the mode according to which they mutually influence each other, nor the modifying causes. In like manner, the progressive development of moral and intellectual man has scarcely occupied their attention: nor have they noted how the facilities of his mind are at every age influenced by those of the body, nor how his faculties mutually react.

His perspectives on aging as resulting from ecological interactions of heredity, behavior, and the environment are congruent with late twentieth-century thinking.

Quetelet had been in contact with Charles Darwin's cousin Francis Galton (1822–1911), another outstanding intellectual pioneer of the nineteenth century. It is of interest to note that both of them were interested in quantifying the relationship of functional aspects of organisms with the age of the organism. Galton like Quetelet had broad interests. He was originally trained in medicine and mathematics and later studied geography, anthropology, and psychology. He became increasingly interested in anthropometric measurements and, like Quetelet, included measurements of physical and mental functions in his research.

An Englishman, Galton sponsored an exhibition of health in London in the 1880s and gathered considerable data on such things as the upper limits of hearing and changes that occur with advancing age. Galton used the term *human machine*, which undoubtedly reflects his earlier background in physiology. He was interested in fitting the facts of both development and aging in human beings into a broader framework of human evolution and science. One of his major contributions to the study of aging was his gathering of data at the International Health Exhibition of London of 1884. Over 9,337 males and females aged 5–80 years were measured on 17 different functions. Because of his exposure to large masses of data, Galton developed an index of correlation to measure the degree of association of two variables (e.g., age and strength). This was a large step forward because it enabled scholars to separate factors according to the degree to which they were related to age or to some purported causal factor of aging.

Galton was very impressed with the power of biometrics and left his personal fortune to create the first university chair of biometrics. Karl Pearson (1857–

1936) was its first occupant who extended the statistical methods for the analysis of research data, including the development of a quantitative correlation measure whose limits of error could be specified. Galton's interests later turned away from the study of development and aging to the application of Darwin's ideas of evolution. He attempted to develop principles of eugenics for application in the population at large. He wanted to encourage selective breeding of the population so that persons with high intelligence levels would have more offspring. In the nineteenth century, studies of aging were carried out by men like Galton and Quetelet who had high social status and who had the personal funds to finance them. There were no major organized laboratories that conducted research on aging for significant periods of time. Shortly after Galton's work, a physician at Cambridge University, Humphrey, conducted a major survey of the health of older adults. The work, although admirably pioneering and comprehensive, lacked the quantitative synthesis provided by Quetelet and Galton.

In America, the statesman Benjamin Franklin (1706–1790) had earlier stimulated considerable speculation about reviving organisms that were showing no signs of life but might still be resurrected. Because of his involvement with the discovery of the lightning rod and thereby controlling the flow of electrical discharge, he thought that the loss of electricity or the loss of vitality might be the cause of aging. This example underscores many uncertainties in the field of gerontology. That is, it is uncertain whether a particular characteristic of the organism associated with advancing age is the cause of general aging or is a result of it. This dilemma is seen, for example, in the earlier emphasis on heat and the body, which led to the assumption that loss of heat was the cause of aging and if heat were replaced, aging would be stopped or reversed. In a similar way because sexual intercourse seems to decline with age, it was thought that stimulating increased sexual activity might fend off the more general effects of aging.

At the beginning of the twentieth century, a number of biologists began to write prolifically about aging. Their underlying theme was the identification of causes of aging or the transformations that occur with age in the human species. The writing of the day was surrounded by a great deal of optimism about the potency of science. No problem appeared to be beyond its understanding and perhaps even the extension of the human life span was potentially under human's control. There was considerable public interest in prolonging life and even bringing back to life persons who had died.

But serious scholars were becoming more cautious in their expectations that life extension or rejuvenation would be easy or within immediate reach. The Nobel Laureate in physiology, Minot, stated both his optimism and his passion with regard to growing old, which he called senescence.

> We should, indeed, like to have some principle given to us which would retard the rate of senescence and leave us for a longer period the enjoyment of our mature faculties. ... I can venture to suggest to you that in the future deeper insight into these mysteries probably awaits us and there may indeed come a time when we can somewhat regulate these matters. (Minot, 1908, p. 248)

The views of Minot deeply influenced the earliest American psychologist G. S. Hall (1844–1924), president of Clark University. As a developmental psychologist, Hall is credited with initiating research on adolescence. Near the end of his life, Hall (1922) reviewed much of the available information and the then contemporary thinking about aging in his book *Senescence: the Second Half of Life*. Senescence was a term that he adopted from his reading of biologists of his time. He also included his personal psychological interpretations. "As a psychologist I am convinced that the psychic states of old people have great significance. Senescence, like adolescence, has its own feeling, thought, and will, as well as its own psychology and the regime is important, as well as that of the body. Individual differences here are probably greater than in youth" (Hall, 1922, p. 100). In this statement Hall anticipated many later psychologists who also pointed to an increase in individual differences that can occur in many traits with advancing age.

In Russia in the 1920s, the Nobel laureate in physiology, Ivan Pavlov (1849–1936), and his colleagues had observed that older animals learn differently and develop conditioned reflexes differently from young animals. They thought that the process of inhibition was more vulnerable to age than was facilitation. This would be reflected in the fact that old habits would be more difficult to eliminate than recent ones. They anticipated somewhat a later development in interpreting the slowness of speed of behavior with advancing age by pointing out that when a nerve process is slowed or delayed remaining traces of each stimulus

become attracted and overly influence succeeding stimuli, thereby producing chaos.

Pavlov's views about aging were not shared by American researchers. He and his followers believe that the role of the central nervous system (CNS) is important in governing the process of aging of the organism. American physiologists had tended to regard aging of the CNS as resulting from the aging of other organs and the circulatory system rather than its being a primary manifestation of the decline in the regulatory capacity of the CNS itself. More recently the CNS has come to be regarded as an important organ in the aging of primates. [*See* Brain and Central Nervous System.]

V. THE BEGINNING OF THE MODERN PERIOD OF GERONTOLOGY

One of the first laboratories for the systematic study of aging was established in 1928 in the psychology department at Stanford University under the direction of Walter R. Miles (1885–19—); it was supported by the Carnegie Foundation of New York. The motivations behind the establishment of The Stanford Later Maturity Study were many, but an important influence was that in California men over the age of 40 at that time were having difficulties finding work because it was assumed that they were too old. The Stanford laboratory produced about eight doctoral dissertations on various aspects of aging, including such topics as the relations of age to creativity, learning, extinction of learned responses, and motor skills [*See* Creativity; Learning; Motor Control.]

In the 1930s new support for the systematic study of aging came through the activities of the Josiah Macy, Jr. Foundation of New York. The Foundation had supported studies of degenerative diseases related to aging, but the director, Dr. Ludwig Kast, believed that degenerative diseases were part of a manifestation of the process of aging. With this in mind he encouraged scholarship and research on aging. The study of aging was encouraged as a parallel to the already vigorous areas of research on childhood growth and development.

E. V. Cowdry, a cytologist at Washington University in St. Louis, was urged by the Macy Foundation to organize the publication of a major integrative volume of the information on aging. He was encouraged to enlarge his initial conception of the book, which dealt primarily with biomedical aspects of aging, to include environmental influences and social, psychological, and psychiatric issues as well. This encouragement led to a subsequent multidisiciplinary scientific conference and to the collation of the literature on aging from the various sciences in the pioneering volume *Problems of Ageing*, edited by Cowdry in 1939. (It is of interest that the book uses the English spelling of the word *ageing* rather than the standard American *aging*.)

At the time Cowdry's book on aging was published, there was a developing concern about the increased role of chronic diseases as a public health problem. Although earlier, infectious diseases were the major influences on mortality in America, heart disease and cancer were increasing as common causes of death.

The developments in the study of aging that had occurred during the 1930s resulted in the desire to create an organization to promote research on aging. A guest researcher at the Department of Anatomy at Oxford University, Korenchevsky, visited New York and requested that the Macy Foundation sponsor the organization of a Club for Research on Aging. Similar clubs were being organized in Europe. It was thought that such a club would be an organization where men could discuss and dispute aspects of aging as gentleman scholars and researchers. There was established The Club for Research on Aging in New York, which evolved into a conference series on aging supported by the Macy Foundation both before and after 1940.

By 1940 thinking about aging had become more sophisticated and systematic. Both the Public Health Service and the Josiah Macy, Jr. Foundation regarded the processes of aging as multidisciplinary in character. That emphasis has been continued into the present, although many scientists in the various disciplines find it difficult to adopt a multidisciplinary orientation and to regard aging as a multifactorial process having both genetic and environmental basis. Earlier views of aging frequently adopted the medical model, which held that aging is the product of disease. The current view is that manifestations of aging involve many factors that interact to modulate mortality and morbidity.

In 1941 the United States Public Health Service had organized a conference on mental health aspects of aging. At about the same time the Surgeon General of the U.S. Public Health Service negotiated the establishment of a Section on Aging within the National Institutes of Health. In 1941 Dr. Nathan W. Shock was recruited to head the unit. His efforts to initiate research on aging were delayed by America's entry into World War II, which occurred at the same time the research unit was to begin its work.

VI. CONTEMPORARY GERONTOLOGY

Shortly after World War II ended in 1945, activities in gerontology began to accelerate. Medicine's increasing interest in the age-associated degenerative diseases, the increase of an older population which portended an older society, and general scientific advances made new methods of study available to students of aging. One of the leaders in the Macy Foundation's efforts to develop research on aging was Lawrence K. Frank. He was one of five sponsors involved with the founding of the Gerontological Society in New York in 1945. About the same time the American Geriatric Society was founded with both organizations publishing journals. These societies have shown continuing development in their membership and in the scope of annual meetings. The International Association of Gerontology was founded shortly thereafter with its first meeting in Liege, Belgium, in 1948 and its second Congress in St. Louis in 1951. The first Pan American Congress of Gerontology was held in Mexico City in 1956. These organized efforts in gerontology stimulated research, teaching, and service.

The publication rate of scientific articles in aging has been growing exponentially. The various constituent sciences and professions are beginning to create their own specialized divisions and they publish their own specialized journals. Also, the professional or applied aspects of aging are growing in significance, and leaders in these fields are encouraging opportunities to exchange ideas about conditions that will benefit the lives of older people more immediately. Interest in the process of aging is being expressed both within the disciplines and between the disciplines.

In many countries, longitudinal studies of aging are being developed that depend upon the collaboration of scientists from many fields. Understanding the aging of organisms requires the collaboration of many disciplines and needs to be accompanied by a complex orientation that will undoubtedly require new and more sophisticated models. Of great importance to the longevity, health, well-being, and quality of life of older persons is the development of increasingly sophisticated theory and research on aging. An interest has already been expressed in the encouragement of such models. [*See* MODELS OF AGING: INVERTEBRATES, FILAMENTOUS FUNGI, AND YEASTS; MODELS OF AGING: VERTEBRATES.]

In universities, research units on aging are now common and special degree programs in gerontology are offered in at the baccalaureate, master's, and doctoral levels. Assisting in the growth of teaching is the availability of specialized volumes on aging that provide not only current research findings but also historical background in special areas (see bibliography). New works on the humanities, religion, and aging show a trend in collaboration not previously seen, suggesting that there has been initiated a new phase of scholarship and human service in the field of aging.

Because of the importance of knowledge and research on aging for the well-being of present and future generations, there seems little doubt that gerontology will remain a high priority in academic and professional settings.

VII. SUMMARY

Gerontology, the study of aging, has roots that extend far back in history. Humankind has apparently always speculated about the duration of life and the nature of death. In many early cultures myths were created about longevity and death that were passed as legends that explained humankind's mortality. These legends also were presented in religious teachings (e.g., that humankind at one point had immortality but through weakness and sin was reduced to mortal existence).

Gerontology appears to be on an expanding growth course for both scientific and practical reasons. There has been increasing scientific interest in understanding processes of aging from molecular biological processes through behavioral, social, and humanitarian factors. Developing and developed societies show increasingly larger numbers of older persons who have changing interests and needs. Serving older populations brings with it concerns about increasing

standards and efficiency based upon scientific knowledge.

Understanding and explaining the processes of aging has proven to be complex. Aging may be one of the most complex topics undertaken for research in the life sciences. Perhaps in reaction to the complexity of the subject, investigators have increasingly studied limited aspects of aging. Thus, recent gerontology has been characterized as having many aspect studies and aspect theories. It may also be said that gerontology is a field that is data rich and theory poor. Aided by developments in statistical modeling and analysis, subsystems of the organism may be characterized in terms of causal complexes or subgroups of intereacting variables. The interrelationships of these aspects or causal complexes may lead to an interaction with the models developed in physics dealing with chaotic processes and events.

The increase in initiation of longitudinal studies of human populations that embrace genetic, behavioral, social, and other influences may lead to a more organismic approach to aging in place of the present aspect specialization. The duration of humankind's life increasingly seems to be placed in an ecological context that embraces explanations arising from species and unique individual genetic background together with influences from behavioral and social processes and physical and social environments. It is foolhardy to predict the precise character of gerontology in the next century, but it seems highly likely that it will show increasing activity and intellectual and scientific sophistication that will provide the basis for significant advances in humankind's quality of life.

BIBLIOGRAPHY

Binstock, R. H., & George, L. K. (Eds.). (1996). *Handbook of aging and the social sciences* (4th. ed.). San Diego, CA: Academic Press.

Birren, J. E. (1961). A brief history of the psychology of aging. *The Gerontologist, 1,* 69–77, 127–134.

Birren, J. E. (1995). New models of aging: Comment on need and creative efforts. *Canadian Journal on Aging. 14,* 1–3.

Birren, J. E., & Schaie, K. W. (Eds.). (1996). *Handbook of the psychology of aging* (4th ed.). San Diego, CA: Academic Press.

Birren, J. E., Sloane, R. B., & Cohen, G. D. (Eds.). (1992). *Handbook of mental health and aging* (2nd. ed.). San Diego, CA: Academic Press.

Cole, T. R. (1988). Aging, history, and health: Progress and paradox. In, J. J. F. Schroots, J. E. Birren, & A. Svanborg (Eds.), *Health and aging* (pp. 45–63). New York: Springer.

Cowdry, E. V. (Ed.). (1939). *Problems of ageing.* Baltimore, MD: Williams and Wilkins.

Gruman, G. J. (1966). A history of ideas about the prolongation of life: The evolution of prolongevity hypotheses to 1800. Philadelphia: Transactions of the American Philosophical Society.

Hall, G. S. (1922). *Senescence: The second half of life.* New York: Appleton and Co.

Hilton, J. (1933). *Lost Horizon.* New York: W. Morrow & Co.

Kertzer, D. I., & Laslett, P. (Eds.). (1995). *Aging in the past: demography, society, and old age.* Berkeley, CA: The University of California Press.

Kimble, M. A., McFadden, S. H., Ellor, J. W., & Seeber, J. J. (Eds.). (1995). *Aging, spirituality, and religion: A handbook.* Minneapolis, MN: Fortress Press.

Masoro, E. J. (Ed.). (1995). *Handbook of physiology section II: Physiology of aging.* Bethesda, MD: The American Physiological Society.

Metchnikoff, E. (1903). *The nature of man.* New York: G. P. Putnam's and Sons.

Minot, C. S. (1908). *The problem of age, growth, and death.* New York: G. P. Putnam's and Sons.

Quetelet, M. A. (1968). *A treatise on man and the development of his faculties.* (Sur l'homme et le développement de ses facultés, Trans.). New York: Burt Franklin. (Original work published 1835. Paris: Bachelier, Imprimeur-Libraire.)

Ram-Pasad, C. (1995. A classical Indian philosophical perspective on ageing and the meaning of life. *Ageing and Society, 15,* 1–36.

Schneider, E. L., & Rowe, J. W. (Eds.). (1996). *Handbook of the biology of aging* (4th ed.). San Diego, CA: Academic Press.

Home Care and Caregiving

Jennifer M. Kinney

Bowling Green State University

Activities of Daily Living (ADL) Basic self-care activities (e.g., bathing, dressing, grooming). The ability to perform ADLs is frequently used as an indicator of physical health.
Care Recipient An older adult who requires assistance in order to remain independent or semi-independent.
Instrumental Activities of Daily Living (IADL) More complex, higher order self-care activities (e.g., preparing meals, doing laundry, managing money) that permit greater independence. Independence in IADLs is also frequently used as an indicator of physical health.
Later-Life Family Families that have contracted in size, structure, and interaction as a result of launching their adult children.
Longevity Revolution The dramatic increase in the average life expectancy since the beginning of the century that is attributed to the public health movement and advances in medical technology.
Primary Caregiver The one person who is most responsible, on a day-to-day basis, for assisting the care recipient.
Transactional models Widely employed to conceptualize and interpret research on the process of caring for an older family member. These models attempt to gain an understanding of the process

whereby family caregivers confront a potential stressor; assess the extent to which the potential stressor impacts caregivers' personal resources; select coping strategies or mobilize resources to deal with the stressor; and demonstrate certain levels of adaptation.

This chapter discusses **HOME CARE AND CAREGIVING** within the context of later-life families. After reviewing the constellation and configuration of later-life families, health challenges common to later-life families are described, and caregiving is introduced as a normative life event. Caregiving is conceptualized within transactional process models. Three components of the caregiving process are examined: (a) caregiver characteristics, (b) care recipient illness or impairment characteristics, and (c) contextual variables. Following a presentation of the positive and negative consequences of caregiving, the issues of service availability and utilization and the efficacy of interventions designed to assist family caregivers are discussed. Finally, future trends for caregiving in later-life families are proposed.

I. LATER-LIFE FAMILIES

A. Constellation and Configuration

The twentieth century has witnessed what prominent gerontologists characterize as a longevity revolution. That is, the public health movement and advances in medical technology have resulted in a dramatic increase in the average life expectancy since the beginning of the century. Whereas the average life expectancy for Americans in 1900 was 49 years (51 years for women; 48 years for men), the average life expectancy for individuals born in 1990 is approximately 75 years, with estimates of approximately 78 years for women and 71 years for men. As a result of this shift in life expectancy, increasing numbers of individuals are entering later life, and experiencing the chronic conditions and limitations in basic and instrumental activities of daily living (IADLs) that often accompany advanced old age. [*See* LONGEVITY AND LONG-LIVED POPULATIONS.]

The longevity revolution has altered the structure of families in the latter part of the twentieth century. Three- and four-generation families, which at the turn of the century were virtually nonexistent, are now the norm. Today, approximately 40% of all older adults (i.e., those aged 65 and over) are part of a four-generation family. At the turn of the century, prior to the advent of multigenerational families, the major task for families was to raise their children and launch them into adulthood. Today, families are living well into the stage of development that family theorists refer to as the later-life family. Later-life families are not defined by the chronological age of a particular family member. Later-life families are those families who, rather than expanding in size and structure via childbearing, begin the process of constriction as their children enter adulthood, leave home to start families of their own, and limit, at least to some degree, their pattern of interaction with their family of origin.

The "emptying of the nest" that results in a later-life family is often viewed as an opportunity for the original marital dyad to pursue interests and activities that were put on hold during the child-rearing years. During this time, marital satisfaction frequently increases. Depending on the age and social status of the later-life family, retirement may occur in close temporal proximity to the transition to a later-life family, affording the family further opportunity to enjoy the lessening of familial and occupational responsibilities. [*See* RETIREMENT.] Therefore, although later-life families are embedded within multigenerational families, the primary bond within later-life families typically reverts to the original marital dyad. These are the "golden years" for which many couples plan.

B. Health Challenges Facing Later-Life Families

Depending in part on the age at which families enter the stage, many later-life families enjoy protracted periods of relatively good health and well-being. However, a major challenge confronting later-life families as they enter advanced old age is their health status. Health challenges to later-life families can include (a) normal, age-related increases in chronic conditions and limitations in ADLs and IADLs; (b) cognitive impairments that range in severity from mild memory impairment to full-blown dementia; and (c) acute physical health crises and injuries.

Approximately 85% of all older adults (i.e., those aged 65 and older) report at least one chronic illness, and the incidence of chronic illness increases with age. In addition, one-fifth of older adults require some assistance with ADLs (e.g., bathing, dressing, feeding) and one-fifth require assistance with IADLs (e.g., preparing meals, managing money, performing household maintenance). Among old-old adults (i.e., those aged 75 and older), more than one-half suffer from arthritis; approximately four-fifths report at least one ADL limitation; and more than 90% report at least one IADL limitation. Multiple ADL and IADL limitations are common, such that one-fifth of old-old adults report four or more ADL limitations, and one-third report four or more IADL limitations.

Impairments in cognitive functioning, which include orientation to time, place, and person, abstract reasoning, and problem solving, occur with relatively low frequency among older adults. That is, approximately 5% of older adults residing in the community exhibit at least some degree of clinically detectable cognitive impairment. However, this percentage does increase to 20% among adults age 75 and older. Although extreme cognitive impairments such as the dementias (e.g., Alzheimer's disease) occur with even less frequency, it is not atypical for older adults to experience some degree of confusion when they are exposed to unfamiliar environments or situations. [*See* DEMENTIA.]

Older adults experience more chronic conditions than acute health episodes, averaging slightly more than one acute episode annually. Although they occur with relatively low frequency, acute conditions such as pneumonia, influenza, and infection can be quite debilitating for older adults. Many of the chronic conditions experienced by older adults predispose them to such infections. Furthermore, the rates of recovery from acute conditions and injuries are substantially slow for older adults than for younger adults.

C. Caregiving as a Normative Life Event

The onset of ADL and IADL limitations, chronic physical and cognitive impairments, and acute health crises challenge later-life families to make adaptations and accommodations. Many of these adaptations and accommodations center around later-life families' desires to preserve their independence and autonomy. For many later-life families, at the heart of these issues is the ability to continue to reside in the community, in noninstitutional housing.

Of the 95% of older adults who do reside in the community, many reside within a later-life family. That is, approximately three-fourths of all older men, and two-fifths of all older women, live with their spouses. As these families age, structural changes occur, such as the death of a spouse. In addition, although only 5% of all older adults reside in a long-term care facility at any one time, one out of every four older adults experiences at least a brief stay in a long-term care facility in their later years. As these changes occur, most spouses prefer to remain as independent as possible in the community, rather than moving into the homes of other relatives, including their children. Fewer than 10% of all men, and 20% of all older women, reside with relatives other than their spouses. By the age of 85, approximately one-half of all men, and one-tenth of all women, continue to reside within a later-life family. Even in such advanced old age, only one-third of community-dwelling women, and fewer than 20% of community-dwelling men, live with relatives other than their spouses.

For many older adults, the onset of health problems serves as the impetus for their reintegration into their multigenerational family. Although many multigenerational families are geographically dispersed, the suggestion that older family members have been abandoned is a myth. Research amply documents that families are the primary source of assistance to older adults. It is widely cited that more than 80% of all care provided to older adults residing in the community is provided by families and other informal network members. Furthermore, it has been estimated that, for every older adult residing in an institutional environ-

ment, there are at least two or three, if not more, equally impaired older adults who are able to remain in the community, due primarily to the assistance that they receive from family members.

The type, amount, and frequency of assistance provided to older adults by family members is determined, in large part, by the nature and severity of their impairments. For some older adults, assistance with IADLs such as seasonal home maintenance, doing laundry, and shopping for groceries is so infrequent that the family members who provide this assistance do not even consider themselves to be caregivers. In contrast, limitations in ADLs such as bathing, dressing, feeding, and toileting can necessitate weekly, and even daily, assistance. Similarly, depending on the degree of cognitive impairment experienced by older family members, caregiving can range from periodic reminders about doctor visits to the inability to leave the family members in unsupervised conditions. The caregiving demands that result from acute health crises and injuries are comparably diverse.

When health problems and/or functional limitations arise in the life of an older adult, members of the family typically respond in a predictable order. If the older adult requiring assistance (i.e., care recipient) is part of an intact later-life family (i.e., has a spouse), and the spouse is able, the spouse most frequently serves as the primary caregiver (i.e., the one person who is most responsible, on a day-to-day basis, for assisting the older adult). When a spouse is unavailable or unable to serve as the primary caregiver, an adult child most frequently assumes this responsibility.

Regardless of kinship tie, women are far more likely to provide assistance to older family members than are men. This is especially true among adult children who provide assistance to older parents. Thus, although husbands and sons do provide some assistance to older family members, the majority of caregiving responsibilities are assumed by wives and daughters or daughters-in-law. However, in light of the changing roles of women with respect to workforce participation, it is anticipated that increasing numbers of men will assume caregiving responsibilities for older family members.

Much has been written about the "sandwich generation"; that is, those middle-aged women who find themselves sandwiched between the needs of their older parents or parents-in-law and the needs of their own children. Despite some evidence that the risk of being "caught in the middle" is not as high as might be assumed, many gerontologists claim that parent care will become an increasingly common experience, and that more than one-half of adult women who have a surviving parent can expect to provide some form of assistance to that parent in the future. Parent care, combined with potential caregiving responsibilities for parents-in-law and, eventually, a spouse of one's own, increase the probability of providing care to an older adult at some point in one's life. Thus, caregiving is becoming a normative experience for many members, both male and female, of multigenerational families.

II. CAREGIVING AS A PROCESS

A. Transactional Models

The challenge of providing home care to an elderly family member can be best understood in the context of transactional models. Transactional models define stress as the result of an interaction between individuals and their environment, whereby a potential stressor is interpreted in terms of its capacity to do harm. Such models conceptualize individuals' interactions as dynamic, reciprocal, and evolving, with all elements of the system interrelating and changing over time. In this view, individuals interpret interactions, meet the demands of these interactions, and reinterpret these interactions in light of new interactions.

Among transactional models, the model proposed by Richard S. Lazarus and Susan Folkman and that developed by Leonard I. Pearlin and his colleagues are the most comprehensive. Although both models conceptualize stress in terms of specific person–environment transactions and acknowledge the role of individuals' appraisals of these transactions, they differ in the extent to which discrete life events are involved in the stress process. Whereas the emphasis of the model by Lazarus and Folkman is the appraisal process and microlevel aspects of the stress process, Pearlin and colleagues are more concerned with contextual, macrolevel aspects. Lazarus and Folkman describe three steps in the stress process: primary appraisal (identifying a potential stressor as irrelevant, benign-positive, or stressful), secondary appraisal (identifying coping options and their relative effective-

ness), and coping (mobilization of action to confront the threat or challenge). They maintain that appraisal of events as stressful relates to three areas of adaptation: social functioning, morale, and somatic health. [*See* ADAPTATION.]

In contrast to Lazarus and Folkman, Pearlin and his colleagues maintain that chronic life strains are insufficient to predict adaptation. Rather, they believe that the impact of such strains on an individual's social role must be considered, in that different social roles present different challenges, resulting in different coping responses. Additionally, Pearlin and his colleagues propose two categories of circumstances that together result in greater stress than either type does separately. That is, critical life events serve as potential antecedents for creating new strains or increasing the persistent, chronic, day-to-day strains that serve as potential stresses for an individual.

A key mediational process in both transactional models is cognitive interpretation or appraisal; that is, an individual's subjective assessment of a potential stressor. Whether an event is appraised as stressful depends on (i.e., is mediated by) the extent to which it is perceived as a threat or challenge to (a) one's personal resources, in Lazarus and Folkmans' conceptualization; or (b) one's sense of mastery (personal control) and self-esteem in Pearlin and colleagues' conceptualization. Regardless of the specific conceptualization, transactional models emphasize individual variability throughout the process. Furthermore, given the dynamic context in which appraisals are hypothesized to occur, they are subject to reinterpretation over time. Finally, both models distinguish the subjective interpretation process from the adaptational consequences of stress (e.g., health-related and emotional outcomes).

Transactional process models have been widely employed to conceptualize and interpret research on the stresses of caring for an older family member in the community. In general, this research attempts to gain an understanding of the process whereby family caregivers (a) confront a potential stressor (either caregiving in general or discrete stressors within caregiving); (b) assess the extent to which the potential stressor impacts caregivers' personal resources, self-esteem, or mastery; (c) select coping strategies or mobilize resources to deal with the stressor; and (d) demonstrate certain levels of adaptation. Clearly, given the complexity of transactional approaches to caregiving, most researchers limit their focus to the interrelationships among only several of these components. Nonetheless, virtually all research on the process of caregiving examines caregiver characteristics, characteristics of care recipients' illness or impairments, and contextual variables in an attempt to better elucidate the stress–appraisal–coping–adaptation process of providing care to a dependent older relative.

B. Caregiver Characteristics

The variability in older adults' needs and the diversity with which family members respond to these needs does not lend itself to definitive criteria specifying what constitutes a caregiver. That is, being identified as a caregiver is not necessarily based on the type, amount, or frequency of assistance provided to an older family member. The provision of care and assistance to older relatives is embedded within family contexts that have involved the exchange of resources among their members for many years. As such, the expectations and norms within individual families influence the point at which the assistance provided to older relatives is sufficient to designate a family member as a caregiver. Implicit in that designation is the notion that the balance of power between the caregiver and care recipient has shifted, such that, perhaps for the first time in their relationship, the caregiver is in a position of enhanced authority, whereas the care recipient assumes a dependent position. Although demographic characteristics such as age, gender, and ethnic background can be identified as caregiver characteristics, rather than influencing caregiving outcomes directly, they are more appropriately considered as contextual variables, as they establish a context in which caregiving occurs.

1. Motivations for Caregiving

Among the expectations held by families are that family members both care about and, when necessary, care for one another. However, the specific motivations underlying the decision to provide care are not consistent within or across families. Individual caregivers assume responsibility for older family members for a variety of reasons. The reasons are diverse, not mutually exclusive, and can evolve and change over the course of the caregiving process. Motivations for caring for an older family member can be classified

into three general categories: (a) a sense of reciprocity; (b) a sense of obligation; and (c) lack of alternatives.

A sense of reciprocity motivates some family members to care for older relatives. Caregiving can offer family members an opportunity to return the love, affection, and emotional and instrumental support that they received from care recipients at earlier points in their relationships. Caregivers who are motivated by a sense of reciprocity do not believe that they are obligated to care for their relatives. Rather, they welcome and are grateful for the opportunity to provide care. Wives who provide care to husbands frequently indicate that caregiving affords them the opportunity to reciprocate their husbands' earlier efforts to provide for the family financially, whereas husbands frequently view their own caregiving efforts as reciprocating their wives' efforts to maintain their home and raise their children. Similarly, adult children who are motivated by reciprocity view parent care as an opportunity to demonstrate their gratitude for their parents' efforts in raising them into adulthood. [See CAREGIVING AND CARING.]

A second motivation for caregiving is a sense of obligation. Family members who provide care out of a sense of obligation do not do so entirely voluntarily. Rather, they believe that it is their duty to provide care in order to erase a debt that accrued as a result of the care recipients' earlier contributions, such as love, affection, emotional or instrumental support, to the caregivers' earlier development. As such, caregiving is not done selflessly. Instead, it is provided out of the desire to restore equity in the relationship between the caregiver and care recipient. Caregiving for this motivation derives from social expectations and norms that are both externally and internally enforced.

A final motivation for caregiving is necessity. That is, some caregivers have no choice in the assumption of the caregiving role, in that they are the only ones who are available to provide care for the care recipient. Caregivers in this situation, whether spouses or adult children, typically find that no other family members are available or willing to assist with caregiving. In addition, those who care out of necessity frequently lack access to both informal (e.g., friends and neighbors) and formal (e.g., paid caregivers, social services) sources of assistance that could lessen their caregiving responsibilities.

Despite the difficulties inherent in caregiving, when

care is provided out of a sense of reciprocity, caregivers are invested both in caring about and in caring for their older relatives. Caregivers who provide care out of a sense of reciprocity do not do so out of a sense of obligation. Rather, they provide care to older relatives because they want to. When care is provided for motivations other than reciprocity (i.e., out of a sense of obligation and/or necessity), ambivalence frequently results. That is, although many of these caregivers do care about their older relatives, they are not necessarily interested in providing direct care to them. As such, caregivers who are not predisposed toward reciprocity oftentimes question their commitment to their elderly relatives and the larger family, and emotions such as resentment, anger, and guilt are not uncommon. Clearly, the motivation for assuming caregiving responsibilities provides a backdrop against which the caregiving process unfolds.

2. Importance of Appraisals

Research on caregiving typically assesses the degree of stress, or burden, experienced by caregivers, and then relates these measures to caregivers' levels of well-being. In examining the consequences of caregiving, early researchers frequently distinguished between objective burden and subjective burden. Objective burden refers to the events, happenings, and activities in caregivers' lifestyles that arise during caregiving (e.g., dependency associated with care recipients' physical or mental impairments, financial hardships, family relationships, and social and recreational activities), whereas subjective burden refers to caregivers' feelings associated with caregiving (e.g., the stressful, tiring, difficult, or upsetting nature of the caregiving tasks). An advantage of distinguishing objective from subjective burden is that caregiving tasks and caregivers' responses to these tasks can be examined separately. Furthermore, research indicates that, although objective burden is not a strong predictor of caregiver well-being, subjective burden, or a caregiver's appraisal of objective events in caregiving, is.

The finding that caregivers' subjective interpretations (i.e., appraisals) of caregiving tasks are related much more strongly to caregivers' well-being than are objective events themselves helps to explain the single most consistent finding in caregiving research: the great variability in how family members respond to the caregiving role. Research has documented tremendous variability in caregivers' perceptions of their caregiving situations. Consistent with transactional models, caregivers' appraisals of objective events in caregiving differ as a function of individual caregivers' personal resources and the larger social contexts in which they reside.

3. Coping and Self-Concept and Life Orientation

One characteristic of process models is an emphasis on the transactional nature of peoples' experiences. As such, happenings in the environment are interpreted within the context of individuals' previous life experiences. Thus, individuals play an active role in constructing their realities, in identifying potential threats to their well-being, and in formulating solutions to the challenges with which they are confronted. Two resources that individuals bring to these transactions are their coping efforts and their self-concept or life orientation.

Coping includes cognitive and behavioral efforts to manage situations that cause stress and the negative emotions that often accompany stress. Although a variety of taxonomies of coping strategies have been proposed, coping efforts are typically classified as either problem-focused or emotion-focused. Problem-focused strategies are those efforts designed to modify or manage the situation that produces the stress, whereas emotion-focused strategies are those efforts that minimize or eliminate the negative emotions that result from the stress. Coping is hypothesized to have both direct and indirect effects on adaptation to the stress process. Among family caregivers, both problem- and emotion-focused coping have been shown to have beneficial effects when the employed coping strategy is consistent with the nature of the stressor (i.e., use of emotion-focused coping when the source of the stressor is uncontrollable and unchangeable). Conversely, inappropriate use of coping strategies (i.e., use of problem-focused coping with a stressor that cannot be modified) can serve to further exacerbate the stress process.

Just as coping efforts can influence, and be influenced by, the stress process, so too is the case with caregivers' self-concept and orientation to life. Although these latter constructs have received less attention in the literature than have other components of the stress process (e.g., appraisal, coping), there is some evidence that caregivers who report a stronger sense of purpose in life also perceive themselves to be in better health, whereas caregivers who perceive high levels of uncertainty in their lives report poorer perceived health. More specifically, Pearlin and his colleagues have begun to explore both global (i.e., self-esteem and mastery) and context-specific (e.g., role captivity, role engulfment) components of the self-concept that are related to the process of caring for an older family member.

Within transactional process models, caregiver characteristics, including motivations for providing care and self-concept or life orientation, provide a backdrop against which specific caregiving appraisals are made and coping efforts are initiated. These appraisals and coping efforts, in turn, are reappraised and reevaluated by caregivers, and can result in modifications of earlier motivations, orientations to life, and self-concepts. As such, caregiver characteristics are not static predictors of aspects of the caregiving process. Rather, they are evolving elements in caregivers' adaptation to the process of providing care to older family members.

C. Care Recipient Illness and Impairment Characteristics

Early research on in-home caregiving was guided by the assumption that the severity of care recipient impairment defined the caregiving process, with caregivers to more impaired relatives reporting higher levels of distress and lower levels of well-being. With the realization of the importance of caregiver appraisals and other caregiver and contextual variables, the significance of care recipient impairment was reconceptualized. Two of the most salient dimensions of care recipient impairment are (a) whether the nature of the impairment is primarily physical, cognitive, or both, and (b) whether the condition requiring care is acute or chronic.

With respect to the nature of care recipients' impairments, physical and cognitive impairments present different types of challenges to caregivers. Caregiving to relatives with physical impairments requires caregivers to assist with ADLs and IADLs, and caregivers frequently report that these activities result in less time for themselves, disrupt their social relationships with others, and are physically exhausting. In contrast, caregiving to relatives with cognitive impairments requires caregivers to protect the safety and integrity of their relatives from both external threats

and threats that result from care recipients' own inappropriate or dangerous behaviors.

When caregivers' appraisals of the stressfulness of care recipients' physical and cognitive limitations are examined as predictors of caregivers' well-being, the stressfulness associated with cognitive impairments emerges as the stronger predictor of caregiver distress. Thus, it is possible that although caregivers find both physical and cognitive limitations to be stressful, the ADL and IADL assistance necessitated by physical impairments is more predictable and controllable than are the demands necessitated by cognitive impairments. It is also probable that the declines accompanying cognitive impairment are especially symbolic to caregivers, in that they serve as constant reminders of the loss of intellect and the personality of the older family member.

Caregiving demands presented by acute conditions differ from those presented by chronic conditions. When assisting older relatives with needs resulting from acute conditions, many family members do not identify themselves as having adopted the role of caregiver. Rather, they perceive their responsibilities as time-limited and as part of the typical exchange of resources that characterizes many families. In contrast, when caregiving is undertaken in response to chronic conditions, at some point during the process, virtually all family members acknowledge that they have adopted the role of caregiver, regardless of their previous relationship with the care recipient.

Taken together, the nature, severity, and chronicity of care recipient impairment define an impairment trajectory that underlies the caregiving process. The impairment trajectory, combined with the potential for recovery, establishes a context in which caregivers experience the stress–appraisal–coping–adaptation process. Researchers are beginning to follow the process of caregiving as various illness trajectories unfold over time, and the examination of stages and transitions within specific illness trajectories will result in a better understanding of the extent to which care recipient impairment drives the caregiving process.

D. Contextual Variables

Within transactional models of caregiving, a multitude of contextual variables have been examined for their role in the caregiving process and their impact on caregiver well-being. Examples of such contextual variables include demographic characteristics (e.g., caregivers' age, gender, ethnic background, educational attainment), characteristics of caregivers' social and family networks, availability of formal supports and services, and characteristics of the relationship between caregivers and care recipients (e.g., kinship tie, quality of relationship prior to caregiving, duration of the caregiving relationship). Additional variables that Lazarus and Folkman conceptualize as contextual, but that Pearlin and colleagues conceptualize as secondary role strains, are those noncaregiving aspects of caregivers' lives (e.g., family life, employment, social involvements) that are frequently affected in a negative way by the caregiving role. Among these contextual variables and secondary role strains, the quality of the relationship prior to caregiving, the kinship ties between caregivers and care recipients, and the competing responsibilities confronting caregivers are illustrative of the importance of these types of variables in the process of providing care to older family members in the community.

1. Quality of Relationship Prior to Caregiving

Because the provision of care and assistance to an older relative is embedded within a family context, the quality of the relationship between the caregiver and care recipient prior to the onset of caregiving is an important component of the caregiving process. There is some evidence that caregivers who report to have felt closer bonds with their relatives prior to caregiving experience more difficulties during the caregiving process. Among caregivers to spouses with dementia, caregivers who retrospectively report higher levels of marital intimacy both prior to and following the onset of caregiving also report more caregiving strain. In addition, caregivers who report recent losses in marital intimacy are more depressed than those who report more consistent levels of intimacy. However, because these findings do not result from prospective studies, in which relationship quality is assessed prior to the onset of caregiving, these results must be interpreted with caution. That is, caregivers' appraisals of precaregiving relationship quality could be influenced by aspects of the current caregiving relationship, as well as other contextual and motivational factors and the internal and external resources available to caregivers.

2. Kinship Tie between Caregiver and Care Recipient

There is a tendency for spouses and adult children to orient differently to the caregiving role. Spouses tend to enmesh themselves in the caregiving role, abandoning other roles and responsibilities in order to respond to the needs of husbands or wives. In contrast, adult children who are caring for older parents tend to distance themselves, emotionally if not physically, from their caregiving responsibilities. That is, they perform their caregiving responsibilities, yet at the same time, they maintain their precaregiving responsibilities to their own children, spouses, careers, and friends. Thus, whereas caregiving spouses, especially wives, find themselves engulfed in their role as caregiver to the exclusion of previously occupied roles, adult children typically maintain multiple roles (e.g., parenting and work-related roles).

Spouses and adult children also tend to demonstrate differential adaptation to the caregiving role. Upon assumption of the caregiving role, there is a tendency for spouses to demonstrate higher levels of distress, depression, negative affect, psychotropic drug use, and physical health complaints than adult children. However, adult children tend to report more negative feelings about caregiving than do spouses. Upon cessation of the caregiving role, there is some evidence that spouses are less frequently bothered by guilt concerning caregiving efforts that they could have, or should have, made than are adult children.

3. Competing Responsibilities

Despite the emphasis of transactional models on context, early caregiving research did not take into account the numerous noncaregiving roles (e.g., spouse, parent, employee) that are simultaneously occupied by many caregivers. More recently, researchers have conceptualized the caregiving role as one of many roles that comprise caregivers' daily contexts, and provide caregivers with competing responsibilities. Most of the research on these competing responsibilities, or what Pearlin and colleagues refer to as secondary role strains, focus on daughters or daughters-in-law "in the middle" who are also employed outside the home. This research typically investigates the caregiving experience in the context of the other roles that caregivers occupy (e.g., spouse, parent, employee, friend), and examines the extent to which role-specific stresses and satisfactions are associated with levels of well-being. Overall, the results of these investigations indicate that the negative consequences of multiple-role involvement are outweighed by the positive. That is, the satisfactions associated with various noncaregiving roles contribute unique variance in caregivers' well-being after the stresses associated with those roles are removed. Furthermore, there is evidence that when stresses resulting from caregiving responsibilities are high, rewards associated with other roles can have positive effects on well-being.

The importance of contextual variables in the caregiving process cannot be underestimated. However, given the volume, complexity, and interdependency of these contextual variables, definitive statements regarding the impact of any one variable in the caregiving process cannot be made. For example, it is difficult to untangle whether the engulfment in the caregiving role that is typical of spouses is due to (a) the kinship tie between caregiver and care recipient; (b) the fact that more spouse caregivers are female than male (as there is some evidence that women are more likely to exhibit engulfment than are men); or (c) the fact that many older women occupy fewer roles than do caregiving daughters. Such are the complexities inherent in the caregiving process.

E. Consequences of Caregiving

There is no question that providing care to older family members can result in negative outcomes. Comparisons of caregivers to noncaregivers indicate that caregivers report poorer social functioning (e.g., lower levels of satisfaction with, and greater restrictions in, social activities), lower morale (e.g., higher levels of anxiety, hostility, depression, and negative affect; lower levels of life satisfaction), and greater somatic problems (e.g., greater reports of exhaustion, more complaints of physical symptoms, higher levels of psychtropic medication use) than do noncaregivers.

Although the majority of research on the process of caring for an older family member has examined caregiving stress and negative outcomes within transactional process models, these models do allow for the exploration of positive aspects and consequences of caregiving as well. For example, Lazarus and Folkman hypothesize that positive appraisals can buffer individuals from the deleterious consequences of negative appraisals. Similarly, Pearlin and his colleagues propose that personal resources (e.g., mastery, self-esteem, competence, personal gain) are critical components in the adaptation process. In addition, they maintain that mediators, such as coping and social support, can function both directly and indirectly to facilitate caregivers' adaptation to the caregiving process.

Recently, several researchers have begun to examine the positive aspects and consequences of providing care to older family members. Results from these investigations indicate that there is a positive relationship between caregiving stresses and satisfactions, such that caregivers who report high levels of stress also tend to report high levels of satisfaction. Just as rewards associated with noncaregiving roles can contribute to caregivers' well-being, there is some evidence that caregivers whose appraisals are positive (i.e., satisfactions with caregiving outweigh stresses) report better well-being than do caregivers whose net appraisals are negative. Furthermore, results of qualitative investigations suggest that caregivers identify positive, as well as negative, consequences of their caregiving efforts.

The emergence of positive components, within a process that had been traditionally conceptualized as negative, propelled researchers to explore the symbolic meaning that providing care to older relatives holds for family caregivers. Researchers have suggested that the theoretical perspective of existentialism, which deals with finding meaning through suffering, may help to explain the complex process whereby family members identify both enrichment and suffering that arise from their role as caregiver. The importance of finding (or making) meaning is an integral part of the caregiving process for family members. Caregivers must come to terms with their evolving relationship with care recipients; accept their relatives' illness trajectories; and realize the significance of this changing relationship in the context of their own life and the life of the family. The importance of this search for meaning by family caregivers should not be underestimated.

III. THE COURSE OF CAREGIVING: SERVICE AVAILABILITY, UTILIZATION, AND EFFICACY OF INTERVENTIONS

A. Service Availability

A broad range of services are available to help family members who provide care to older relatives. Based on the specific component of the caregiving process that is targeted, most services can be classified into one of two categories. The first category of services includes those that are designed to temporarily relieve caregivers of the instrumental responsibilities of providing care. Examples of such services include homemaker or home health-care services, in-home and on-site respite services, and adult day-care programs. Although the primary goal of these services is to facilitate caregiver adaptation, care recipients as well frequently benefit from the services, either through the receipt of hands-on care or through exposure to structured activity and increased opportunity for social interaction. [*See* HEALTH CARE AND SERVICES.]

The second category of services comprises those that are designed to increase caregivers' knowledge of the caregiving process and to help them better adapt to the role of caregiver. The most common of these services is caregiver support groups. Caregiver support groups vary widely in their relative emphasis on psychoeducational and psychosocial issues; the level of training of the facilitator (i.e., peer, paraprofessional, professional); and structural characteristics (e.g., size, frequency, and duration of meetings; whether the group is limited or open-ended in the number of sessions). Typically, psychoeducational groups (i.e., groups that emphasize caregiver education and training) are offered for a fixed number of sessions and are led by professionals. In contrast, psychosocial groups (i.e., groups in which caregivers discuss their experiences in a supportive environment and learn from one another) are led by peers and/or paraprofessionals, and are open-ended with respect to the number of sessions. Within this category of services, an emerging area involves the use of computer technology to provide caregivers access to other caregivers and professionals through the use of bulletin boards and networks from their own homes.

In addition to services that provide respite and education to caregivers and assist caregivers in managing their emotions and adopting appropriate coping strategies, a third category consists of more individualized services. Such services include interventions aimed at modifying characteristics of care recipients' illnesses. Most typically targeted are those problematic or unsafe behaviors that are secondary to care recipients' cognitive impairments. Examples of such services include medication and the use of behavior modification and behavioral management techniques. Another type of intervention within this category of services is psychotherapy. Such therapeutic interven-

tions can be directed primarily toward caregivers, care recipients, or the family unit.

B. Service Utilization

In light of the broad array of services that are available to assist family members in their efforts to care for older relatives, practitioners are oftentimes puzzled and frustrated by caregivers' claims that services are either unavailable or that barriers prohibit their use. At the same time that caregivers are quick to identify limitations of services (e.g., eligibility criteria, restricted hours, logistical and scheduling problems, quality, cost), practitioners lament that caregivers delay seeking services until the demand is almost too great, and then insist that a combination of services be provided almost immediately. These dynamics suggest an underlying tension between caregiving families and service providers. In part, this tension may derive from family members' previous experiences in seeking services. There is some evidence that the provision of services, especially those that are designed to lessen caregivers' instrumental responsibilities, are not always well matched with caregivers' needs. More importantly, this tension may reflect the fact that service providers do not always appear to be sensitive to family members' perspectives on what it means to request formal assistance.

In actuality, formal services complement, rather than replace, the efforts of family members. Nonetheless, many family members believe that the use of formal services signifies their own inadequacies as caregivers. For many caregivers, the use of formal services is an admission of their own inability to live up to family expectations, and, as such, there exists an uneasy partnership between caregivers and formal service providers. It is oftentimes not made explicit to family caregivers that formal service providers rely on them to serve as advocates and liaisons for their older relatives, and that in order to be successful, formal services require the involvement and participation of family caregivers.

The recruitment of family caregivers into partnership with the formal service delivery system presents a challenge. To the extent that family caregivers interface with the formal system early in the caregiving process, the process is facilitated for everyone: caregivers, care recipients, and the formal system. Early integration permits the development and coordination of a comprehensive plan of service delivery, one that best meets caregivers' and care recipients' current and anticipated needs. In addition, involvement in this process enables caregivers to retain some control over a process that is frequently characterized by uncertainty and change.

C. Efficacy of Interventions Designed to Assist Family Caregivers

Given the ambivalence of family caregivers regarding the use of formal services, perhaps it is not surprising that efforts to evaluate the effectiveness of various caregiving interventions have met with mixed results. Despite a willingness to express complaints concerning the availability and accessibility of various services across a range of investigations, caregivers have reported high levels of satisfaction with adult day-care, in-home and on-site respite services, psychoeducational and psychosocial caregiver support groups, and more intensive interventions (e.g., psychotherapy, behavior modification, behavioral management). However, when assessed by standardized, objective indicators, the efficacy of these interventions is less convincing. Although there is some evidence that the more intensive interventions may result in enhanced caregiver well-being (e.g., lower levels of depression, higher levels of life satisfaction and morale), the other categories of interventions do not consistently produce these effects.

There are several possible explanations for the failure to definitively document the beneficial effects of caregiving interventions. With respect to interventions designed to relieve caregivers' instrumental responsibilities (e.g., respite services, adult day-care programs), delay in institutionalization of care recipients (relative to controls) is frequently employed as an outcome measure. Yet, given the illness trajectories of many care recipients, as well as the competing responsibilities of family caregivers, the appropriateness of delay of institutionalization as an indicator of intervention effectiveness can be questioned. Similarly, the enormity of caregiving and noncaregiving demands, combined with caregivers' efforts to find meaning in their caregiving experiences, are powerful processes that are not easily modified. Thus, it is not surprising that others who have extensively researched the process of family caregiving have cautioned both researchers and practitioners to be

optimistic, albeit realistic, about the potential that interventions hold for family caregivers.

IV. CAREGIVING: THE NEXT GENERATION

There is some indication that the longevity revolution and other demographic trends will challenge upcoming cohorts of baby boomers in advanced old age. As a result of extensions in life expectancy, it is estimated that the need for family caregivers will increase. Demographic trends, however, point to the shrinking availability of such caregivers. The increasing numbers of never married and childless couples, as well as blended families, combined with the smaller family sizes of baby boomers, all serve to decrease the pool of potential family caregivers.

This chapter has discussed the provision of care to older adults in the context of later-life families. Not all older adults, however, are embedded within later-life families. Some older adults who are not and have not been members of later-life families rely on distant relatives and friends to assist them with their dependencies. However, the absence of a spouse and/or children in later life is oftentimes a predictor of premature institutionalization, attesting to the importance of families in the lives of older adults.

The primary challenges for home care and caregiving in the future concern resources and resource allocation. For those older adults for whom family caregivers are not available, alternative sources of care must be developed. Where family care is available, its provision must be made financially viable for families. Both of these challenges require an increased integration of formal and informal helping systems, and more coordinated, comprehensive care planning for older adults and their families. In order for society to adequately care for the estimated 10 to 15 million baby boomers who, in advanced old age, will require long-term care services at home, a true partnership between families and the formal service system is essential. As this partnership is realized, individual families and society alike will be in a position to better understand and appreciate the significance of their mutual efforts to care about, and provide care for, the aging members of our society.

BIBLIOGRAPHY

Biegel, D. E., & Blum, A. (Eds.). (1990). *Aging and caregiving: Theory, research and policy.* Newbury Park, CA: Sage Publications.

Biegel, D. E., Sales, E., & Schulz, R. (Eds.). (1991). *Family caregiving in chronic illness.* Newbury Park, CA: Sage Publications.

Kahana, E., Biegel, D. E., & Wykle, M. (1994). *Family caregiving across the lifespan.* Thousand Oaks, CA: Sage Publications.

Kane, R. A., & Penrod, J. D. (Eds.). (1995). *Family caregiving in an aging society: Policy perspectives.* Thousand Oaks, CA: Sage Publications.

Light, E., Niederehe, G., & Lebowitz, B. (Eds.). (1994). *Stress effects on family caregivers of Alzheimer's patients.* New York: Springer Publishing Company.

Neal, M. B., Chapman, N. L., Ingersoll-Dayton, B., & Emlen, A. C. (1993). *Balancing work and caregiving for children, adults, and elders.* Thousand Oaks, CA: Sage Publications.

Stephens, M. A. P., Crowther, J. H., Hobfoll, S. W., & Tennenbaum, D. L. (1990). *Stress and coping in later-life families.* New York: Hemisphere.

Zarit, S. H., Pearlin, L. I., & Schaie, K. W. (Eds.). (1993). *Caregiving systems: Informal and formal helpers.* Hillsdale, NJ: Erlbaum.

Homeostasis

F. Eugene Yates

University of California, Los Angeles

Control Theory Richard Bellman defined control theory whimsically as "the care and feeding of systems." Formally it is a negative feedback view of arrangements of interacting information and dynamics to guarantee that system performance will be constrained within bounds or to trajectories chosen in advance by the designer. Classical linear control concepts for continuous, linear systems with time-invariant parameters and a single input with single output have been extended in modern optimal control theory. The new approach is far more general, and it emphasizes the state–space description of dynamic systems. It is general enough to encompass time-varying and nonlinear conditions. It is a significant conceptual generalization of the variational theory of classical mechanics to a much wider class of problems and transcends ordinary physical theory. The concepts of control theory can illuminate some biochemical and physiological control processes, but the strengths of modern optimal control theory in technological applications have failed to capture the richness of modern genetic control of protein biosynthesis, self-organization, morphogenesis, and homeodynamic resiliency.

Dynamics The physical science of lawful motion and change under constraints. It has two subdivisions: kinetics, in which forces causing change are ascribed, and kinematics, in which motions are dealt with abstractly without assigning causal forces.

Homeodynamics Homeodynamics advanced by F. E. Yates is an extension or generalization of Cannon's homeostasis, and a rephrasing of homeokinetics, to emphasize that the resiliency of living organisms is achieved without holding internal variables constant. Instead there are many limit-cycle-like, near periodicities and asymptotic orbital stability.

Homeokinetics A physical heuristic to explain behaviors of complex systems according to propositions advanced by A. Iberall and H. Soodak. It is derived from nonlinear mechanics, fluid mechanics, and statistical thermodynamics. It is one foundation of homeodynamics.

Homeorhesis This is C. Waddington's term for stable trajectories in the motions of biological systems or their internal variables. It was developed mathematically as catastrophe theory by René Thom.

Information Information comes in varieties. It is not a classical physical quantity, and it is not conserved. The simplest form is selective, which expresses how surprised one should be if something is observed from a larger set of possibilities. If a transmitter sends only the letter *a*, and one knows that in advance, then the arrival of the 13th letter *a* conveys no surprise and no information. Conversely, if one wins a lottery in which thousands of tickets were sold, the surprise and information content would be extremely large. A more linguistic view of information includes indications, injunctions, or descriptions. Singularities in kinematic flow fields express Gibsonian specificational information of importance in psychophysics. In engineering terms information is often just a number assigned to a measurement.

Resiliency Describes the striking characteristic of complex living systems to withstand a wide (but limited) spectrum of fluctuations without permanently losing their defining structures and functions. It is synonymous with "health" or "vitality."

Senescence The progressive loss of resiliency with age, even in the absence of accidents or disease.

Stability A technical term to be found in engineering, mathematics, and physics that describes the ability of systems of components or equations to behave in a regular, designed, desired, or expected way in spite of a defined range of perturbations.

System Theory System theory is an ill-defined, global perspective that provides a basis for modeling configurations, connections, and behaviors of interacting elements sufficiently complicated to exhibit some counterintuitive activities. It is not a formal theory. It has, however, led to some tactics for the analysis of systems that have proved effective.

HOMEOSTASIS is an ill-defined but powerful, numinous concept reflecting a quasi-vitalistic belief of biologists in the "wisdom of the body." It is also a more technical expression of *stability* in complex, thermodynamically open, nonlinear, dissipative, self-organizing, living systems, usually assumed to be operating "far-from-equilibrium." Between 1926 and 1929 Walter B. Cannon published articles introducing the term and elaborating the "wisdom of the body" perspective, culminating in a truly classical review article. Since then the concept has attracted the notice of control engineers, chemists, physicists, computer scientists, and mathematicians, all of whom address stability in various guises as a technically rich subject. The concept of homeostasis has been enlarged to become *homeodynamics*. Because many multicellular organisms grow old and ultimately become unstable and die, it is evident that senescence must involve progressive and deleterious changes in the conditions supporting homeostasis and homeodynamics.

I. HISTORY OF CONCEPT

A. Bernard, Sechenov, and Cannon

Homeostasis is not a term biologists like to define. Nevertheless, it has irresistible intuitive appeal. Organisms and their subsystems usually seem to act "intentionally" so their operations continue in spite of various threats and perturbations, within wide limits. In the latter half of the nineteenth century, I. Sechenov in Russia and C. Bernard in France called attention to the rich repertoire of physiological and biochemical defenses organisms possessed to assure their continued existence in a vicissitudinal environment. Bernard condensed the matter into what has become perhaps the most famous sentence in the classical physiological literature. Translated into English, the sentence is often reduced to "The ———— of the internal environment is the condition for a free and independent life." The French word in the blank was *fixité*, which is usually translated as *constancy*, and there is the rub. Bernard and Cannon both knew from their own observations that the chemical composition of an organism, even in a steady external environment, was not constant. Yet modern textbooks of physiology typically define homeostasis in terms of constancy (e.g., "One important function of the autonomic nervous system is to assist the body in maintaining a *constant internal environment* [*homeostasis*.] [italics added.]")

In view of large intrasubject variations, homeostasis must be interpreted not as constancy, but as stability, which may be motional, as in limit cycles, tori, or chaotic attractors in topological models. A more appropriate translation of Bernard might read as follows:

> The *stability* of the internal medium is a primary condition for the freedom and independence of certain living bodies in relation to the environment surrounding them. Physiological mechanisms have to function therein assuring the maintenance of conditions necessary for the existence of the cell elements composing them. For we know that there is neither liberty nor independence in the case of the simplest organisms in direct contact with immediate universal circumstances. The possibility of arranging their own internal medium is an exclusive faculty of organisms which have reached a higher stage of complexity and organic differentiation.
>
> Such stability in the internal medium applies to an extremely perfect organism, able continuously to balance outside variations. The greater the freedom of the creature with regard to its external environment, the closer will be, on

the other hand, the connection of its cells with such internal medium, which will necessarily have to maintain ... regularity in its qualities, possible only if it has regulatory processes in operation.

B. Pflüger, Fredericq, and Richet

Cannon opened his 1929 review on homeostasis with this sentence: "Biologists have long been impressed with the ability of living things to maintain their own stability." He then acknowledged the dictum from Pflüger, in 1877, that "the cause of every need of a living being is also the cause of the satisfaction of the need," and he cited Fredericq, who wrote in 1885:

> The living being is an agency of such sort that each disturbing influence induces by itself the calling of compensatory activity to neutralize or repair the disturbance. The higher in the scale of living beings, the more numerous, the more perfect, and the more complicated these regulatory agencies become. They tend to free the organism completely from the unfavorable influences and changes occurring in the environment.

Cannon noted that Richet in 1900 recognized that

> The living being is stable. It must be in order not to be destroyed, dissolved, or disintegrated by the colossal forces, often adverse, which surround it. By an apparent contradiction it maintains its stability only if it is excitable and capable of modifying itself according to external stimuli and adjusting its response to the stimulation. In a sense it is stable because it is modifiable—the slight instability is the necessary condition for the true stability of the organism.

C. Cannon's Term

Cannon emphasized that when changes in surroundings excite reactions in a living system the internal disturbances are normally "kept within narrow limits ... wide oscillations are prevented and the internal conditions are held fairly constant.... The present discussion is concerned with the physiological rather than the physical arrangements for obtaining constancy." He added that "the coordinated physiological reactions which maintain most of the steady states in the body are so complex, and are so peculiar to the living organism, that it has been suggested that a specific designation for these states be employed—homeostasis." Finally, he anticipated the objection that might be offered to the use of the term *stasis*, as implying something set and immobile, a stagnation. As Cannon used it, stasis meant "a condition," and

the prefix "homeo" indicated "like" or "similar" and admits some variation.

II. PREHOMEOSTATIC MODELS FROM CHEMISTRY

A. Le Chatelier's Principle

In 1884 the French chemist Le Chatelier noted that a dynamic (but not a static) equilibrium tends to oppose any change in the conditions. That fact is now referred to as Le Chatelier's principle. A dynamic equilibrium can adjust because forward and reverse processes are active and make the system responsive to changes. In contrast, a column balanced on one end is in a condition of static equilibrium; it has no ability to recover its position when a force pushes it to the side.

B. Law of Mass Action

The Law of Mass Action serves as an example of what might be called "chemical homeostasis." For a reaction of the form $aA + bB \leftrightarrow cC + dD$, the conditions at equilibrium satisfy

$$K = [C]^c [D]^d/[A]^a [B]^b, \qquad (1)$$

where K is a constant, and the molar concentrations $[A]^a$, $[B]^b$, $[C]^c$, and $[D]^d$ are the concentrations at equilibrium. A perturbation of one of the concentrations will lead to adjustments in all of the others so that the equation above is always satisfied (at a given temperature) after adequate time has passed. More generally, thermodynamic systems exhibiting temperature, pressure, and chemical equilibria resist movement away from these equilibrium states. E. D. Schneider and J. J. Kay have extended the concept: When moved away from their local equilibrium state, systems shift their state in a way that opposes applied gradients and moves the system back towards its local equilibrium.

III. HOMEOSTATIC INDEX

Guyton extended the notions of homeostasis to apply to physiological systems in which there were two independent relationships between two physiological variables, one relationship having a positive slope and the other a negative slope. For example,

$$x = f(y) \qquad (dx/dy \text{ positive}) \qquad (2)$$
$$y = g(x) \qquad (dy/dx \text{ negative}) \qquad (3)$$

A physiological example would be that an increase in plasma glucose levels leads to an increase in plasma insulin levels, whereas an increase in plasma insulin levels leads to a decrease in plasma glucose levels. The only way a system can satisfy both functions (which may be linear or nonlinear but must be monotonic) is to live at the intersection of the two functions, which is an equilibrium operating point. If the parameters specifying the functions f and g are unchanging, then the equilibrium operating point will be stable. D. Riggs introduced a "homeostatic index" for the two equations and pointed out that such a relationship could be modeled as a negative feedback loop. When two variables constituting a homeostatic feedback loop are in a steady state, the homeostatic index is the negative product of the first derivatives of the two feedback equations at that steady state:

$$\text{homeostatic index} = -dg(x)/dx \cdot df(y)/dy, \quad (4)$$

where $x = f(y)$ and $y = g(x)$. The homeostatic index will be zero when the homeostatic system is completely ineffective, but will approach infinity as the system approaches perfect compensation for an input perturbation. Homeostatic index is synonymous with the engineering term *open loop gain* for a constant input signal and negative feedback.

IV. UPDATING HOMEOSTASIS: THEMES

Classical homeostasis was conceptually complete by the 1960s. However, advances in physical, mathematical, and engineering views of stability and complexity since then justify attempts to enlarge or update the essence of homeostasis. The new themes include information, cybernetics, control theory, catastrophe theory, chaos theory, and approximate entropy as a regularity statistic. These themes and others constitute the modern "sciences of complexity." (The soundness of some of these largely mathematical and computational views of complexity is now doubted. A different approach seems needed, and homeokinetics and homeodynamics offer a physically based framework for

the purpose.) Some of the newer themes are discussed below.

V. INFORMATION PLUS DYNAMICS: CYBERNETICS

The above homeostatic modeling does not require the concept of information; it relies only on dynamics. However, since 1948 when Norbert Wiener published *Cybernetics*, control and communication in living systems have been likened to technological feedback systems that require a mixture of information with dynamics. From 1948 to 1952 the works of N. Wiener, N. Rashevsky, A. Turing, and J. von Neumann on mathematical biophysics, the chemical basis of morphogenesis, and the general and logical theory of autonomata led to explosive growth in engineering and computation, artificial intelligence, filter theory, and applications of control theory to living systems to account for their homeostatic performance. R. Ashby attempted to make cybernetics more accessible to biologists in 1956, and by 1968 L. von Bertalanffy tried to define a general systems theory for physical, biological, behavioral, and social sciences. W. T. Powers has continued the theme, interpreting animal behavior from the perspective of control. In his work, feedback models of behavior are designed to account for its purposive aspects, and much of behavior is interpreted as being homeostatic. For example, some poikilotherms maintain a more-or-less uniform body temperature by moving back and forth from sun to shade during the day.

VI. PROBLEM OF INTENTIONALITY IN CONTROL THEORY

Applications of control theory and systems analysis to the social, political, and biological sciences drew heavy criticism on both technical and philosophical grounds. But there is an even greater difficulty that presents a central problem in the explication of evolutionary, historical self-organizing systems. The problem can be illustrated by comparing physical organic chemistry with biological chemistry. Both are examples of carbon chemistry; both address the subject of catalysis.

A. Contrast between Organic Chemistry and Biochemistry

Organic chemistry describes catalytic and other reaction mechanisms according to rules reducible in principle to quantum mechanics, but in biochemistry the emphasis is peculiar: reactions are treated as though they had "intentions" other than going to equilibrium. This different flavor of biochemistry can be found in some of the phrases and topic headings in textbooks: communication within a protein molecule; molecular pathology of hemoglobin; the complexity of the replication apparatus may be necessary to assure very high fidelity; lesions in DNA are continually being repaired; cyclic AMP is an ancient hunger signal; information flows through methylated proteins in bacterial chemotaxis. These examples illustrate the teleonomic mind set of the biologist as he or she addresses the phenomena of interest. The apparent intentionality of the biochemistry drives him or her away from simple machine metaphors to information metaphors, and especially to the computer as information-processing machine that can join the two metaphors. But how does carbon chemistry support the concept of error?

B. Setpoints in Control Systems

Standard control theory models require the specification of a reference standard somewhere in the model—in simple cases it appears as a setpoint input—against which the actual performance of the system can be compared, and discrepancies can be used to drive corrective behaviors. For instance, one of the most elaborate models of human thermoregulation, realized as a computer simulation, builds in a reference setpoint of 37°C core temperature at the front end, and then with a 40-compartment model elaborates heat transfers within the body and between the body and the environment, even including hypothalamic algorithms to adjust blood flows to achieve stabilization of the core temperature at the reference value. Such models, however impressive at first glance as mechanistic illustrations of homeostasis, raise the question, What neurons in the hypothalamus "know" 37°C, and how do they hold that as a physical reference value? One begins to suspect that homeostasis is not best accounted for in a control-theoretic sense. Control theory arose out of human intentions about

the performance of machines that humans construct. It is a different matter entirely to account for homeostatic behavior in living systems that evolved spontaneously over evolutionary time scales without incorporating the intentions of a designer. Thus the property of homeostasis reveals deep problems concerning the philosophy of biology itself.

To capture the essence of homeostatic behavior without acting as a deus ex machina injecting information, R. Ashby built a "homeostat" consisting of simple batteries, relays, ammeters, and so on that behaved so as to hold its meter readings at certain values, even when parts of the machine were ripped out! Of course, today there are many other robots that act as if they have purposive behaviors, but these illustrate nothing about biology because programmers are ghosts in those machines, and it is the *designer's intentionality*, not that of a machine, that is observed.

The failure of models based on machines that do work or process information to explain homeostasis has provoked an intellectual crisis in science. Just when many different sciences seem to be converging, and biology is dominated by molecular reductionism, one discovers that machine metaphors for living systems as a means to express reductionism have not only failed, but are fundamentally wrongheaded. A new approach is needed.

VII. HOMEOSTASIS UPDATED

A. Homeorhesis

The term *homeostasis* is hallowed by tradition and so well established that it will not be abandoned. However, in recognition of the fact that the internal environment of complex organisms is not fixed, is not at equilibrium, but is defended by dynamic regulations of trajectories within and across hierarchical organizational levels, the term *homeodynamics* seems more appropriate. The first person to call attention to the need to generalize homeostasis to account for trajectories was Waddington. In 1968 he wrote:

> Phenomena involving the holding constant of some parameters of a physiological situation (e.g., the oxygen tension or pH of the blood) have been well known for a long time. The situation is usually referred to as one of 'homeostasis.' We are here dealing with a similar concept, but of a rather more general nature, in that the thing that is being held constant is not a single parameter, but is a time-ex-

tended course of change, that is to say, a trajectory. The situation can therefore be referred to as one of homeorhesis, i.e., stabilized flow rather than stabilized state (I should like to see some mathematician express the contrast in more precise terms).

B. Catastrophe Theory

René Thom from 1970 to 1983 provided elegant mathematical bases for the extension of homeostasis to homeorhesis. These came to be known as Catastrophe Theory. He showed that systems lose structural stability at bifurcation points in trajectories. Elementary control theories and system theories assumed that systems evolved along trajectories that did not bifurcate, thereby disqualifying themselves as explanations of developmental biology! During autonomous morphogenesis of living systems, such as the creation of a human being from a fertilized egg, one sees that there is some kind of *regular trajectory*, but that no "stage" along the way to the mature adult seems structurally stable; structures and functions both change. Insect metamorphosis presents an even more startling example of structural instability consistent with a regular trajectory. Thus one concludes that life in many important aspects is not structurally stable, but is in some sense dynamically stable.

C. Chaos

Newer developments in nonlinear mechanics have introduced the technical concepts of chaos and strange attractors as stability regimes for many fully deterministic but nonlinear systems, some describable by single equations (in the case of discrete phenomena) or as few as three equations (in the case of continuous phenomena.) Chaotic attractors may have fractal architectures, and the intersection of chaotic dynamics with fractal geometries has generated a new mathematical industry and spectacular computer art.

Chaotic attractors are large-scale aspects of nonlinearly stable dynamic systems that are fully deterministic. However, the behavior of a trajectory attracted to such an attractor is totally unpredictable in the long run. Models of motions within the bounds of chaotic attractors are not periodic, but under certain parameter values they can be nearly so. Extensions of chaotic dynamics now admit the influence of stochastic processes, and the admixture can lead to sur-

prising results for which there is no complete theory. However rich the behavior of models of chaotic dynamics, they fail to encompass living systems because the models are all state-determined in the narrow engineering sense, whereas living systems are not. Again, something different seems to be needed to account for the homeodynamic stability of living systems.

D. Homeodynamics

Homeodynamics has been developed and given a physical basis by A. Iberall and H. Soodak (who called it homeokinetics). Homeodynamics is a construct resting on powerful propositions that extend normal physics heuristically. It develops the view that the important characteristic distinguishing complex entities in a field is that their interactions do not rapidly equipartition energy among the accessible external (translational) and internal degrees of freedom. Instead, very significant time delays appear in the distribution of energy among the internal degrees of freedom of the system—very unlike the more springlike, conservative interactions of simple, idealized, statistical mechanical systems. The net effect of such complexity is to make an account of motion by translational momentum (i.e., by Newton's law of motion) inappropriate. Instead, one must integrate over a time much longer than the relaxational times of translational interactions in order to close the thermodynamic books on energy and entropy changes. This is the process cycle time in which action modes (behaviors) emerge. Certain processes must occur again and again if the system is to persist (i.e., be stable). Otherwise one would observe only relaxational trajectories to equilibrium death. Thus, limit cycle-like, nearly periodic, oscillatory behavior is the signature of energy transformations in open, complex, thermodynamic systems obeying both the First and Second Laws, as all real, complex systems must do. The cyclic processes generate a power spectrum that is discontinuous, with peaks that may be quite broad and nonharmonically related. Quasi-periodicity, or sometimes chaos, characterize the phase-portrait. The persistence is usually secured by asymptotic orbital stability; less common is a definable strange attractor for aperiodic dynamics. In a homeodynamic system the mean levels of most of the state variables are closely determined, but the variances around them can be large. The mean level is kept bounded by dynamic regulation rather than by automatic control or simple self-regulation as in the models described above.

VIII. BEHAVIOR OF PHYSIOLOGICAL VARIABLES—DEGREES OF REGULARITY

A. Variance Structure

The conceptual richness of homeostasis–homeodynamics applies to complex living systems of all kinds, invertebrates as well as vertebrates, plants as well as animals, single- and multicellular. However, Sechenov, Bernard, and Cannon obtained the experimental data supporting the concepts mainly from studies on mammals. If one looks at physicochemical variables inside a human being, for example, nothing observed is fixed or constant. The excursion of data around a mean value in a time history record of a physiological or biochemical variable ranges from very small (for some controlled variables such as plasma hydrogen ion or sodium concentrations, core temperature) to very large (for some manipulated variables such as heart rate.) Many of the variables of both kinds have a circadian (nearly 24-h) rhythm easily identified through spectral analysis. Some variables such as instantaneous heart rate (RR interval on the electrocardiogram) present a very irregular record after the periodic components associated with sleep–wake transitions and respiration are removed. According to some analyses, the structure of the residual variance of heart rate is that of a chaotic attractor.

B. Approximate Entropy

A model-free approach to describing such variability is the new regularity statistic approximate entropy (ApEn) developed by S. Pincus. Applied to the time history of a single variable, ApEn classifies the behavior as regular if the variable holds a constant value or exactly follows simple harmonic motion or a limit cycle. Chaotic dynamics are more irregular (higher ApEn value). For random behavior ApEn is higher still. This measure permits one to ask, How regular should the time history of a homeostatic–homeodynamic variable be under conditions of good health? As noted above, among variables there is a wide range of regularity of behavior associated with, or compatible with, the resiliency of good health. It has been argued that in the case of heart rate an increase in regularity (with aging) may imply a loss of system resiliency through a loss of connectivity, so that internal inputs are increasingly lost.

IX. BEYOND CONSTANCY TO FUNCTIONAL ORDER

To account for the richness of behavior of whole organisms as well as of their internal variables, it is necessary to extend homeostasis beyond simple notions of constancy, equilibria, or steady states, to the homeodynamic concepts of dynamic regulation, moderate regularity, and multiple entailments among internal, cyclic thermodynamic processes, leading to a global resiliency that is good health. These extensions of the concept of homeostasis preserve the original notion that living systems can experience a certain range of perturbations from a fluctuational environment without losing their defining structures and functions and characteristic behaviors after transients have subsided. It is the (mistaken) image of fixity or constancy that has disappeared from the concept. The order shown by biological systems is not particularly high by ordinary physical entropic measures, because it is not primarily structural. Biological order is chiefly *functional*, and that makes all the difference!

X. SENESCENCE OF RESILIENCY

The loss of integration and resiliency with age is senescence. Health equals stability. Poor health is instability. The ultimate instability is the collapse of dynamics of each process to the point equilibrium of death. One sees evidence of the senescent decline in homeostatic–homeodynamic resiliency in the higher death rates per 100,000 of population of elderly people (especially ages 75 years and beyond) compared to middle-aged in flu epidemics, heat waves, winter icy conditions, accidents in crosswalks, automobile accidents at night, and so on. Sudden perturbations, easily accommodated by a homeodynamically resilient organism, are debilitating or lethal in senescence. Various explanations have been offered for the loss of homeostatic–homeodynamic competence with aging, and estimates have been provided for the rate of loss. [*See* Growth Factors and Cellular Senescence.]

BIBLIOGRAPHY

Berlinski, D. (1976). On systems analysis: An essay concerning the limitations of some mathematical methods in the social, political, and biological sciences. Cambridge, MA: MIT Press.

Cannon, W. B. (1929). Organization for physiological homeostasis. *Physiological Reviews 9*, 399–431.

Iberall, A. S., & Soodak, H. (1987). Thermodynamics and complex systems. In F. E. Yates (Ed.), *Self-organizing systems: The emergence of order* (pp. 459–470). New York: Plenum Press.

Pincus, S. M. (1991). Approximate entropy as a measure of system complexity. *Procedures of the National Academy of Science* (USA), 2297–2301.

Rosen, R. (1991). *Life itself: A comprehensive inquiry into the nature, origin, and fabrication of life.* New York: Columbia University Press.

Schneider, E. D., & Kay, J. J. (1994). Life as a manifestation of the Second Law of thermodynamics. *Mathematics and Computer Modelling, 19*, 25–48.

Wiener, N. (1948). *Cybernetics: Control and communication in the animal and the machine.* New York: John Wiley and Sons.

Yates, F. E. (1982). Outline of a physical theory of physiological systems. *Canadian Journal of Physiology and Pharmacology, 60*, 217–248.

Yates, F. E. (1994). Order and complexity in dynamical systems: Homeodynamics as a generalized mechanics for biology. *Mathematics and Computer Modelling, 19*, 49–74.

Yates, F. E., & Benton, L. A. (1995). Loss of integration and resiliency with age: A dissipative destruction. In E. J. Masoro (Ed.), *Handbook of Physiology: Section 11—Aging* (pp. 591–610). New York: Oxford University Press for the American Physiological Society.

Hospice

Bert Hayslip, Jr.

University of North Texas

Euthanasia The withholding of life-extending treatments or the purposeful cutting short of a patient's life, each of which is based on the philosophy that the quality of life is more important than its quality. Euthanasia may or may not occur with the consent of the individual.

Grief The social, emotional, and spiritual response to loss that may or may not be pathological. Grief may be anticipatory in nature or in response to the death of a loved one.

Hospice A concept of caring for the terminally ill and their families emphasizing quality of life, pain control, and the interdisciplinary team as a coordinator of care for dying patients and their families.

Interdisciplinary Team An organized, coordinated effort by professionals and volunteers to provide quality care and case management services to hospice patients and their families.

Palliative Care A central concept of hospice care emphasizing the reduction of pain and the enhancement of quality of life for hospice patients and their families.

HOSPICE is a concept of caring for the terminally ill and their families emphasizing the quality over quantity of life, pain control, and the coordination of care by the interdisciplinary team. Characteristics of hospice care that differentiate it from other forms of health care are (a) the dying person and the family are the unit of care; (b) the interdisciplinary team serves both the patient and the family; (c) care focuses on both the physical, spiritual, and psychosocial aspects of the patient and family unit's functioning; (d) services are available on a 24-hour, seven days per week basis; (e) inpatient and home-care services are available; and (f) bereavement counseling and support are available both prior to and after the patient's death, thereby assuring continuity of care.

I. INTRODUCTION TO CONCEPTS OF HOSPICE CARE

A. The Hospice Philosophy

Hospice is a philosophy of care for people who have terminal illnesses and their families through the use of an interdisciplinary team that develops a coordinated, individualized plan of care. The focus of such care is on pain management and symptom control, within the context of maintaining quality of life for the dying patient and his or her family. Hospice also emphasizes the importance of both physical and spiritual contact between people as death approaches. This "quality of life" however, is very difficult to maintain if the dying person is in pain, is alone, or if he or she is seen as helpless by others. Because dying persons often die a "social death" (i.e., they are treated as if they are dead long before their actual death), hospice care enables the dying person to continue to live until the moment of death. Hospice also offers the family the opportunity to express their feelings about their loss, as well as helping them cope with the reality of living without a loved one. Thus, both the dying person and the family can fully experience dying as a final act of living, and it is because time is precious that hospice emphasizes the nurturing of relationships rather than the curing of an illness that is in reality, beyond cure. Hospice can fill the void that being terminally ill has created for the person in a health-care system that has deemed the patient beyond all hope of cure.

B. Models of Hospice Care

In the United States and Canada, a number of models of hospice care exist: (a) home-based care, usually delivered by community-based professionals and volunteers; (b) home-based care provided by home health-care agencies, or Visiting Nurse Associations (VNA); (c) freestanding, full service, autonomous hospice facilities; (d) separate hospital-based palliative (pain-reducing) care units; and (e) hospital-based, subacute units, emphasizing continuum of care. In addition, some hospices have begun to explore the concept of adult hospice day care. Pediatric hospice programs are also becoming more common.

Approximately half of all hospices are hospital-based, and the remainder are operated by home health-care agenices. A third are freestanding facilities. It is also becoming more common to see nursing homes set aside particular beds or wings for terminally ill residents and their families. Because independent home-care programs are more individualized and can be more innovative, they can offer patients an alternative to institutional-based care. Hospices affiliated with nursing homes and hospitals tend to be more traditional in nature and are more likely to be extensions of those services the institution is currently offering.

The implementation and maintenance of a particular mode of hospice care is affected by the financial, cultural, geographical, psychological, and spiritual factors unique to a given community that influence its ability to support hospice care. The availability of financial support, public and professional attitudes toward health-care delivery, and hospice care in par-

ticular all influence the viability of hospice. Moreover, the availability of institutional care, the rural or urban nature of the geographic area to be served, and available professional resources (e.g., access to technologies for pain control, nearness of large-scale cancer treatment centers, resources for death education) are factors that make some models of hospice care appropriate for some communities and not for others.

Regardless of one's model of hospice care, all hospices share certain characteristics that set them apart from other forms of health care: (a) the dying person and the family are the unit of care; (b) the interdisciplinary team serves both the dying person and the family; (c) care focuses on both the physical and psychosocial aspects of living and dying; (d) Services are continually available on a 24-hour per day, seven days a week basis; (e) both inpatient and home-care services are available to patients and families; and (f) bereavement counseling and support is available to both the dying person and/or the family. Continuity of care, often after death, is assumed in light of the above aspects of hospice.

These characteristics of hospice reflect some basic assumptions about living and dying:

1. Dying is a natural experience; life and death are equally important and meaningful aspects.
2. Dying persons and their families are important in themselves: the dying person's welfare comes first.
3. Dying persons should be able to make decisions for themselves until they are unable or unwilling to do so.
4. Dependence on others and being cared for by them are not shameful.

II. DEVELOPMENT OF HOSPICE CARE IN THE UNITED STATES

A. Death and Dying in American Culture

Hospice is not simply a place where persons go to die, nor is it particular to a certain type of health-care facility. The unique one-on-oneness of hospice care in general stands in contrast to the cure orientation of conventional hospital oncological care or the maintenance mentality of the nursing home. Although in some nursing homes staff are indeed involved and cooperative, patient care is humanized, and respect for human dignity is obvious, many hospitals and nursing homes can be dehumanizing and depersonalizing. As we noted above, dignity or control are particularly important to hospice patients and their families.

The term *institutional dying* stresses the physical care of the body, to reflect the availability of specialized lifesaving, life-extending medical technologies. This emphasis on caring for the body (versus caring for the person), reflects a faith in technology and at the same time a sense of hopelessness in the event that technology fails to cure or reverse the disease process that would otherwise destroy the body. In this light, hospice patients, most of whom have cancer, are less likely to receive intensive medical interventions such as chemotherapy or surgery as well as diagnostic tests (blood tests, X rays) in the weeks prior to death than are those in conventional hospital oncology units. Moreover, although analgesics are also more likely to be regularly prescribed for pain on a fixed schedule in conventional health care, pain medication is prescribed on an individual "as-needed" basis in hospice. A medically aggressive approach near the end of life reflects the "cure" orientation of hospitals versus the "care" orientation of the hospice. Such a perspective on dying also likely contributes to some physicians' reluctance to refer patients to hospice.

Hospice care is often misunderstood as the absence of effort to deal with medical complications that sometimes accompany a terminal illness. In truth, hospice care is very aggressive regarding the dying person's physical or emotional state, with the goal of enhancing the quality of life. Moreover, hospice encourages those persons who desire control over their lives to continue to make decisions about life and death. Consequently, it is inaccurate to think of persons who are healthy as independent, while dying persons are dependent and helpless. Whenever one loves, one acknowledges the essential dependence on others for both physical and emotional nurturance throughout the life span. The care given (or received) at life's end is simply an extension of mutual caring for a spouse, parent, child, or friend.

Many of these values reflect an enhanced awareness and frustration with institutionalized, impersonal dying in this culture, wherein the wholeness and dignity of the person is given lower priority by those who treat diseases, with the hope of cure. A growing awareness of consumer rights, particularly as it relates to changes in the role of funeral and to dying and right-

to-die decisions that have been publicized by the case of Karen Ann Quinlan, has also contributed to the growth of hospice care. Moreover, debates about organ donation, abortion, *in vitro* fertilization, euthanasia, the death penalty, or assisted suicide reflect dissatisfaction with a culture that has taken death out of the home and relocated dying into the hospital or nursing home. In many ways, hospice simply reflects the desire to humanize living and dying and to be able to make decisions about the remainder of one's life, however long that may be.

B. History and Origins of Hospice Care

The concept of hospice dates back to medieval times, where travelers could rest so that they could complete their long and difficult journey. The primary stimulus for hospice in America came from the St. Christopher's hospice in London, founded by Dr. Cicely Saunders in 1967, though hospices clearly had existed for many years in Europe. Since then, initiated by the opening of a home-based care hospice, Hospice, Inc., in New Haven, Connecticut in 1974, nearly 2000 hospices have been founded in North America. Changes in attitudes toward death, legal decisions, legislation affirming the right of the individual to refuse life-sustaining treatment, and the development of the Medicare Hospice Benefit have also encouraged the development of hospice in the United States. Other events important to the hospice movement are the founding of the first hospital-based hospice in North America—the palliative (pain-reducing) care unit at the Royal Victoria Hospital in Montreal, and the formation of the National Hospice Organization (NHO) in 1977. NHO has been important in educating the public about hospice, and in formulating standards for quality hospice care critical to their accreditation, which puts them on par with other health-care alternatives, such as the hospital and nursing homes, as well as making hospice a viable alternative to institutional care for terminally ill persons and their families.

C. Health-Care Delivery in Hospice

Case management ensures that quality hospice care is available to and continuous for each patient and family. Each patient or family unit's needs are seen as unique. Case management matches each unique patient or family unit with whatever services they may need, as well as monitoring changes in their needs for such services. This is especially important because patients and families often know little about caregiving and may have difficulty in dealing with other health care agencies. The coordination of care by the interdisiplinary team as well as with other professionals outside of hospice is an essential component in case management in hospice. Case management also helps patients and families arrange for insurance coverage, plan for emergencies, and if necessary, arrange for services from other agencies. In hospice, case management is often carried out by the primary-care nurse or the social worker.

Many factors must be recognized in developing a workable plan of care. As a given patient's needs vary by age, sex, race, ethnicity, and the nature of one's illness, these factors must be recognized in designing the care plan. Moreover, the patient's previous experiences with illness, death and loss, and the point during the illness at which the individual comes on hospice service are important concerns in case management. Awareness of these influences suggests that case management cannot be carried out in a vacuum. The nature of the dying person's relationships with family, as well as the family's ability to provide physical, social, and emotional support, are also factors that influence the development of the care plan. Even though the care plan is implemented with the patient and family's needs in mind, their values about the involvement of children in the dying process as well as about funeral planning must be repected. Thus, the care plan is likened to a process and as something the patient and family actively participate in.

Information about the patient's needs can be gathered via interactions with patient and family, and is assessed by the interdisciplinary team in formulating a care plan. The team also arranges to coordinate and deliver hospice services, monitors the effectiveness of these services, and if necessary, reevaluates the care plan if the patient's physical or emotional status changes. Numerous decisions regarding everyday changes in the dying person's energy level, emotional state, functional (decision-making, self-care) skills, and needs for pain medication must be made by the team, yet balanced against the quality of the dying person's life as well as against the realities of working, raising children, and running a household.

One should also be prepared for changes in the family's needs for support and information. For exam-

ple, the patient and family may initially ask about insurance coverage, the nature of the illness, its progression and treatment, or what the family can do to help to care for a dying loved one. They may also want to know about the side effects of pain-relieving medications. As the patient's condition worsens, needs for reassurance and support may surface, and concerns about planning a funeral, writing a will, or living without a loved one may be shared. Near death, the family may be less verbal about their needs, and emotional support from a staff member or volunteer may be all that they require. Rather than "doing" something, hospice personnel may meet this need by simply "being there."

D. Mechanisms of Patient Reimbursement

Hospice care became a recognized benefit under Medicare in 1983. Studies had shown that although dying persons represented only a small percentage of all Medicare beneficiaries at any given time, such persons were consuming a disproportionate share of all Medicare expenditures. Three years later, legislation was passed permitting state Medicaid programs the option of covering hospice. At about this time as well, many private health insurance companies also began to seriously consider covering hospice care.

The hospice benefit under Medicare requires that core professional services—physician, nursing, counseling, and medical social work services—be directly provided by the hospice. However, it does not require that hospices directly operate home-care or inpatient care facilities. Rather, Medicare simply requires that the hospice staff maintain responsibility for all services regardless of their location and that they guarantee access to such services on a 24-hour basis.

The same concerns regarding the costs of acute care for dying persons convinced Congress to establish a Medicare benefit that moved private health insurance companies toward hospice coverage. When coverage is available, it appears to be an extension of existing home health benefits, although some plans do explicitly offer hospice benefits. Although the lack of adequate costs, experience, and the lack of accreditation criteria for judging providers have slowed the development of private insurance coverage, the pace of coverage has increased. At present, private insurance seems to favor home-based rather than inpatient-based care. Coverage favors the costs of medical services and less so the psychosocial aspects of care, for example, counseling and bereavement services. Even when covered by Medicare, hospice costs are sometimes paid unnecessarily by patients and families because questions about private health insurance coverage were not asked.

E. Legal and Ethical Aspects of Hospice Care

Legal cases in the 1970s brought to everyone's awareness questions of dying person's ability and right to make decisions regarding the termination of life support, and whether they were legally competent, influencing the extent to which they could make informed health-care decisions. Controversies such as those brought to focus by the Karen Ann Quinlan case prompted states to pass legislation ensuring the individual's right to "die with dignity," and to establish and enforce the use of living wills and other advanced directives. Although many moral and legal issues surrounding such legislation remain to be settled, some precedents have been established. For example, passive euthanasia and the withholding or withdrawal of treatment are legally supported when an informed decision by either the dying person, his or her attending physician, or close family members has been made. NHO does not support either suicide or euthanasia in hospice. While the actual suicide rate among hospice patients is unknown, it is infrequent, as is euthanasia. However, there is the occasional individual for whom "rational" suicide and/or euthanasia may be perceived as an alternative to living in pain or dying an undignified death. Although such statements may mean that the patient's needs are not being met by the hospice, they may also reflect family difficulties, resulting in the dying person's feeling rejected and unloved. Suicidal thoughts may or may not be shared openly. Persons who are depressed and who are contemplating suicide may have a hard time sleeping or eating, refuse medications or visitors, or suddenly change a will. A wish to commit suicide may reflect an individual's particular moral values about the quality versus quantity of life. If such concerns do surface, the staff member should explore whether they are shared by family members, and if they are not, or if family are unaware of them, the caregiver must make a choice regarding whether to discuss them with the family. In most cases it is, however, preferable that

the patient's wishes to discuss suicide or euthanasia with his or her family be respected.

Many hospices have adopted a policy against active euthanasia, as well as the acceptability of suicide. Though no acurate data are available, passive euthanasia is probably routinely practiced by most hospices to that extent that needless pain and suffering take away from the quality of life for most terminally ill individuals. As quality of life is most important in hospice, feelings about life versus death need to be confronted and worked through. Although suicide or euthanasia are personal decisions that should reflect the patient's value system, they are also influenced by the values and behaviors of the caregiver, the hospice itself, and the culture, regarding what an "appropriate death" (see below) is for the dying person. What death and dying mean to each person should also be explored so that the dying patients can understand and clarify their feelings as to why suicide or euthanasia might be preferable to living, and so that the caregiver can more fully understand the dying person. Not discussing such topics or making them seem unimportant suggests communication difficulties that must be remedied quickly. [*See* ETHICS AND EUTHANASIA; SUICIDE.]

There are legal precedents that firmly establish the right of adults to determine what is done with and to their own bodies, recognized as the doctrine of informed consent. Informed consent includes both the simple expression of consent and the obligation to inform (i.e., the provision of adequate and understandable information). Standards regarding understanding are, however, poorly defined and typically rest on the idea of what would be understood by a "reasonable person." Only when information is both adequate and understood is the obligation to inform satisfied. In the event of legal incompetence or the apparent inability to grant informed consent, practitioners turn to the next of kin or to the courts, and many states have statutes that grant family members the legal authority to make health-care decisions if the attending physician believes that the patient cannot make such decisions. Where there are no family-consent laws, staff may either rely on the precedent of family consent or petition a court for the appointment of a guardian.

Increasingly, practitioners are advocating for the use of advance directives. There are two kinds of legally recognized advance directives: living wills and durable powers of attorney for health care. Living wills are written instructions designating the withholding or the withdrawing of life-prolonging treatments in the event of a terminal illness or an irreversible condition. The enforceability of living wills is only possible in states that have passed "natural death act" statutes, which vary from state to state. Most stipulate what constitutes terminal illness and life-prolonging treatments. They also protect the patient by obligating health providers to comply with the patient's desires or transfer the care of the patient to another practitioner who will. Recent court cases, however, have specified that living wills must explicitly state what life-prolonging treatments are to be withheld or withdrawn. The power of attorney gives a designated person the authority to compete a transaction on the behalf of another person. Durable powers of attorney for health care permit an adult to decide who should make medical and health-care decisions should the person become incapacitated. Typically, durable powers of attorney need to be witnessed and notarized.

Defining what death is also raises other legal and ethical concerns. In most states, the determination of death rests on the decision of a licensed physician without additional information. Prior to the availability of life-sustaining technologies and the capability of harvesting organs for transplantation, such decisions posed few problems, as the traditional medical criteria for death emphasized irreversible loss of respiratory and circulatory functioning. For example, although the heart will continue to beat after the brain ceases to function, cardiac death inevitably follows the cessation of brain activity. Likewise, brain death occurs in the prolonged absence of oxygen. However, life-sustaining technologies such as cardiopulmonary resuscitation (CPR), mechanical respiration, artificial nutritional support and hydration can maintain respiration and heartbeat even when there is no brain activity. Many questions can now be raised. Is someone on mechanical respiration technically still alive? If so, withdrawing life supports is now both a moral and a legal issue. Does pulling the plug legally constitute murder? As a body can be artifically ventilated in order to harvest organs for transplant operations, if heartbeat and ventilation are sustained by mechanical means, are organs being removed from bodies still considered to be legally alive?

Even more difficult, and also more common in hospice, is the issue of withholding nutrition or hydra-

tion from a comatose person. Although the body of a comatose person is definitely alive even if there is no higher level cortical activity, withholding food and water will directly cause the body to stop functioning. Legally, does this mean that the practitioner is committing murder? One attempt to solve this problem medically has been to introduce brain death as an additional criteria. Death is now typically defined medically by a set of rules developed by an ad hoc committee of the Harvard Medical School in 1968, wherein four criteria defining brain death must be met: Unreceptivity and unresponsivity, no movements or breathing, no reflexes, and a flat electroencephalogram (EEG). All of the above tests must be repeated at least 24 hours later with no change. Death statutes must include physiological standards for recognizing death, such as those outlined in the Harvard criteria. Without such standards, bodies normally cannot be moved or prepared for burial, organs cannot be harvested, property cannot be transferred to heirs, and the payment of life insurance benefits cannot occur.

III. HOW HOSPICE FUNCTIONS: THE INTERDISCIPLINARY TEAM

A. Hospice Team Philosophy

Hospice uses the interdisciplinary team in tending to the well-being of dying persons and their families. The term *interdisciplinary* suggests that skilled professionals, paraprofessionals, and volunteers all contribute in meeting the many physical and emotional needs of the patient and the family. While the patient's medical needs are given priority, the patient's and family's needs for intimacy, privacy, and support from relatives, friends, or neighbors must also be met. As a critical dimension of hospice, the team functions to evaluate and meet the special requirements of each patient or family unit. Within the plan of care that has been developed for the patient and family, the patient care coordinator, who is often the social worker or nurse, brings together each member of the team to assure continuity of care. This is vitally important during the period of time the patient is actually receiving hospice services, and it is also essential to providing effective bereavement support. The availability of bereavement support is especially critical if the family wishes to disengage from the hospice staff after the death. Family should feel that support from the team is always available to them after a loved one dies.

B. Specific Roles of Team Members

The interdisciplinary team is composed of persons with a mix of professional expertise and background (i.e., nurses, social workers, clergy, physicians, counselors and psychologists, dietitians, physical therapists, pharmacists, and volunteers). As a general rule, direct patient hospice care is managed and carried out by nurses in either inpatient or outpatient settings, under the direction of the hospice medical director in concert with the patient's physician. Important roles are also played by clergy, social workers, and especially by volunteers, who are in many ways the heart and soul of hospice. In most cases, teams meet on a weekly or semiweekly basis to review each case and to discuss problems encountered in carrying out the plan of care, as well as to discuss problems within the family. As noted above, the care plan may need to be modified for any number of reasons.

Physicians have direct input into the delivery of care, and are primarily responsible for the direction of the medical care, which includes both daily, and emergency care. Physicians formulate a medical regimen of pain and symptom control using an array of narcotic and nonnarcotic analgesics (pain-relieving drugs). In hospice however, the physician's role is best defined in relation to the entire team, and often varies a great deal from hospice to hospice. In rare cases, the role of the physician may be minimal, and the physician may not actively function as the medical director or as a participating member of the team. Relative to the more traditional physician, hospice physicians are more likely to play a less authoritarian role in the delivery of care. They are more patient and family oriented and emphasize communication that is both clear and empathic more strongly. Such communication is with both patient and family as well as with other hospice staff. Perhaps the physician's most important roles, other than in prescribing pain medication, are to serve as a community liaison between the hospice and other physicians as well as to coordinate care with the patient's personal physician.

Nurses in hospice often make an initial assessment visit with the family, and because they see the dying person most often, frequently oversee the coordination of direct patient care among the team. In an initial visit, the nurse learns about the history of the illness, and assesses the family's needs to help the hospice care team to design a care plan. In this respect, the nurse is equally attentive to the emotional needs and physical well-being of the patient and family. Promptly relieving pain that often but not always accompanies a terminal illness, as well as keeping the patient as pain-free as possible, is vitally important. Listening and "normalizing" everyday life are also very important aspects of the role that the hospice nurse plays.

Although nurses often carry out most of the hands-on skilled care and assist in case management, the social worker may also serve as a case manager. The social worker often conducts the initial psychosocial assessment of the patient or family unit, dealing with such issues as insurance coverage, pensions, wills, and funeral planning. Although medical social workers may function similarly to the nurse regarding the family's well-being, they usually assume primary responsibility for dealing with the financial and/or legal aspects of terminal care with the family, and in helping the family obtain outside assistance with home care, meal preparation, or in arranging for needed transportation. The social worker also often oversees the follow-up bereavement care of the family.

The volunteer assists the patient and the family in a variety of ways on a continuing as-needed basis. Volunteers can assess the family's physical and emotional status through careful listening and observation so that a crisis of caregiving can be averted. Volunteers an help in the direct hands-on aspects of care: turning patients in bed, bathing, giving haircuts, cleaning house, cooking, picking up children from school, or simply and most importantly, being present. Volunteers should be viewed as an absolutely essential component of the hospice team and should function as such. In most hospices, a volunteer coordinator matches and assigns volunteers to patients and families, and may assist in coordinating and delivering volunteer training. By accompanying the nurse or social worker on an initial visit, the volunteer coordinator can learn about each family's background, interests, and unique needs that influence hospice care, as well as form an impression of each family member as a person.

The role of the clergy is usually more subtle and

often only on "as needed" basis in hospice, though it is difficult to generalize about the extent to which they are involved in the careplan. Clergy assist the team to shed light on the spiritual needs of the patient and, if the patient has no religious affiliation, to minister to the patient and family. Rather than promoting a particular religious philosophy, the chaplain sees to the patient's spiritual well-being by being a link to the religious community. The chaplain often assists in bereavement follow-up, as well as in the training of volunteers. The chaplain can also function as a counselor, or as someone to help the team deal with the stress of caregiving. The hospice administrator, depending on his or her training, can also function in these ways, over and above the overseeing of personnel and reimbursement issues within the hospice. [See Religion and Spirituality.]

Few hospices actually have a psychologist as a paid staff member or a volunteer, although this is changing as the patient or family unit's emotional well-being is being recognized as an even more important influence on the health of the dying person and his or her family. Moreover, hospice staff engage in offering more counseling than any other activity other than providing nursing care. The psychologist or counselor for the most part plays a supportive role in consulting with the team regarding the psychosocial functioning of the patient or family. Counselors' or psychologists' expertise is sought regarding family conflicts associated with the stress of terminal care, or longstanding difficulties that are brought to the surface via the dying of a family member. Such conflicts often interfere with either the delivery of care, or with the patient's or caregiver's well-being.

C. Burnout and Attrition Issues

Stress among hospice workers is unique in that uncertainty about whether one's efforts are effective, the duration of time spent with patients, and the importance attached to one's work are all high. Although individuals vary in their ability to appraise and respond to stress, the unique commitment hospice staff have to their work and the demanding nature of working with dying persons make them especially prone to stress and burnout.

Hospice staff who have little support at work, work long hours, or care for many patients are most likely to be both physically and emotionally overloaded.

Caring deeply for persons who will most certainly die, and not having sufficient time to grieve for each patient after death, may leave some staff feeling hopeless or helpless about their work; they may feel angry, anxious, or depressed. Staff suffering from burnout also report feeling separated or depersonalized from their patients, as well as from fellow team members. Staff with little family support who work in home-care-based hospice situations seem to be at greater risk for job stress and burnout. Younger, or less mature caregivers also seem to be more prone to dysfunctional stress reactions, as do persons who are more anxious about dying or who are trying to cope with the loss of a loved one by working in hospice.

Persons who are stressed also report difficulties in defining their roles as caregivers. It is for these reasons that the turnover rate is high among hospice staff. Most hospices now recognize that some form of regular, timely staff support is critical to lessening stress and minimizing staff turnover, though this has not always been so.

Perhaps most important to minimizing burnout is the selection of hospice staff. Excluding persons who have experienced recent personal losses, those with a great deal of anxiety or concern about their own deaths or about being around dying persons is important. Over and above the selection of team members, the team itself must have time to be alone with one another to discuss technical and creative issues, as well as to express their feelings and provide emotional support regarding their work. Being able to share an office, being aware of other team members' strengths and weaknesses, and being able to talk about one's work are all very important in this respect. Fellow staff should not just listen, but when necessary, be confrontive and forceful to encourage each person's emotional health. Taking care of oneself is central to lessening hospice team stress and burnout. Moreover, opportunities for continued training and cross-disciplinary sharing outside of hospice are essential to minimizing attrition.

IV. HOW HOSPICE FUNCTIONS: WORKING WITH THE PATIENT AND THE FAMILY

A. Appropriate Death in Hospice

Hospice care emphasizes making possible what Avery Weisman has termed an "appropriate death." An appropriate death is defined as dying in the manner that one chooses. For many persons, "appropriate" deaths are pain free and permit one as much personal control and decision-making power as is both possible and desirable. Appropriate death is also defined by the active and loving support of family and friends. By encouraging communication, choice, and the involvement of family in hospice care, appropriate death becomes possible. Four conditions must exist in order for death to be appropriate: (a) awareness, (b) acceptance, (c) propriety, and (d) timeliness.

An awareness of one's terminal illness and its impact on how the remainder of one's life is to be lived is essential to quality hospice care. In addition to a physician-confirmed prognosis of 6 months survival from a terminal illness, the support of a primary caregiver, and the cooperative assistance of one's physician, knowledge of one's terminal illness is almost always an issue in deciding who might be most appropriate for hospice care. In this respect, an appropriate death in hospice is quite possible, as most hospice patients have cancer, are approximately 65 years old, are suffering from a serious functional impairment, are close to death (approximately 3 weeks), and have strong informal family support. Recent findings on the impact of hospice care on place of death suggest that persons served by home-care hospices are more than twice as likely to die at home as are those who are cared for by hospital-based hopsices. Moreover, persons cared for by hospices are three times more likely to die at home than those cared for conventionally. Dying at home, therefore, for many hospice patients, is an appropriate death.

In contrast, persons who are terminally ill may die in a hospital simply because they have little choice, or family members may no longer be able to physically or emotionally handle caring for a dying loved one. Family may falsely feel that pain might be better tolerated or controlled in a hospital setting. Although one's physical condition may dictate that he or she be hospitalized, death at home is possible for most hospice patients. It is for these reasons that a person's awareness of his or her prognosis is highly desirable.

Knowing that one has a terminal illness also makes possible what has been defined as an *open awareness context*. Such a context for the exchange of information allows free and unobtrusive communication, and includes a choice not to talk of death if one wishes. An open awareness context also enables the staff to

provide compassionate care and to gain closure about having supported the patient or family unit throughout (and beyond) the last weeks and months of life. Staff can express themselves as openly and honestly as do patients and their families.

Acceptance of one's death depends upon awareness of it and implies an open examination of whatever problems may arise during the course of hospice care. Propriety is defined as the quality of being proper, and behaving appropriately regarding societal rules or conventions. Propriety first implies dying in terms of both the dying person's and the community's social values, dying in a way that does not conflict with others' expectations (e.g., having tended to one's affairs, being as independent as possible given the circumstances of one's dying, being able to withdraw from others when one desires). The other aspect of propriety deals with having personal values about life and death that are meaningful.

Timeliness reflects the individual's private sense of the "right" or "proper" time to die, though right or proper are difficult to define. Although timeliness does not imply giving up, it does suggest that a longer life would serve no particular end. Interestingly, one indication (over and above the person's physical condition) of the timeliness of death is many persons' ability to clearly state how they might do things differently with their lives, as if they were going to get better. When the dying individual comes to feel that all that can be finished is finished, death is timely or proper for that person. As "unfinished business" interferes with appropriate death, staff should support the dying patient in resolving the unresolved in each person's life. A straightforward question such as, What do you have yet to do?, may be the best approach for those who have unfinished emotional business. They may need to say, I'm sorry, I love you, or simply say good-bye.

B. Patient–Family Dynamics

Although the needs of the dying person are an important focus of hospice, that person is nevertheless embedded in the matrix of relationships and interactions with other family members. Thus, the terminal illness and death of family members affects, and is affected by their position in the system of relationships within the family. For example, death may disrupt patterns of communication, role responsibilities, decision making, and assertions of power or dominance within the family. The very identity of the family and of the individuals in that family may be threatened by death. Each family's reaction to the diagnosis of a terminal illness, its management of a loved one's dying, and its postdeath functioning are all determined by previous family styles and patterns of coping, which have been formed over the years in living together on a daily basis. Through these "transactions" within the family system, the family establishes and reestablishes a distinct style of communicating, tolerating disagreements, resolving conflicts, sharing intimacies, and allocating responsibility. The impact of death also varies by whether a parent or a child dies, interacting with what stage of the family life cycle the family is in.

When hospice care is provided by the family at home, caring for a dying loved one must present a burden the family may see as impossible to cope with. The family must believe that home care is both possible and a desirable, and they must have ready access to nurses, social workers, physicians and morticians, as well as be able to arrange for specialized equipment often essential to quality terminal care (e.g., oxygen, egg crate mattress, hospital bed). The family must also have the nursing skills (e.g., bathing, massage, turning and positioning in bed, giving medications) to make physical care possible. Moreover, knowing when death is imminent, what to do at the moment of death (e.g., attempting to close the eyes, dealing with expulsion of material from the lungs or bowels), and what to do immediately after death (e.g., viewing the body, arranging for pickup by the funeral home, calling the physician, deciding on funeral services, choosing a casket and vault, consideration of embalming or autopsy) are important skills and knowledge that are important in choosing home care. Families report that changes in the dying persons' mental status (inability to communicate, confusion, seizures), and such changes in his or her inability to care for oneself are the most troublesome, as are administering medications, and dealing with the loss of bladder or bowel control. Additionally, managing their time and dealing with well-meaning relatives seems to be difficult for many families caring for a loved one dying at home. Putting personal and career goals on hold, having little "alone time," being isolated from others, feeling guilty, and neglecting one's own health are also sources of stress among caregiving families. Recent

findings suggest that families who have a loved one dying of acquired immunodeficiency syndrome (AIDS) face even greater difficulties. Such families express more difficulty in sharing their feelings, report more stress, are less trusting, and have more illness anxiety than families with other terminal illnesses. Hospice staff can help in the performance of many of these needed tasks through education of the family and through the provision of psychological and spiritual support to them. In most cases, details that seem unmanageable, horrid, or repulsive become less so with a bit of "hands-on" teaching and knowledge.

Families vary in terms of the individual family members' ability to work together. Old conflicts may resurface when a family member is dying. It is for this reason that working with families must be done with an awareness of each family member's needs, wants, strengths, weaknesses, and so on, in relation to the care that hospice provides. In this light, patients' and families' feelings of being overwhelmed directly affect their behavior and willingness to talk. One day, a staff member may be the target of the patient's anger because the patient is in pain or because the person has had a fight with a loved one. Moreover, the individual who is more aware of his or her disease may be more angry or depressed than usual. Such persons may refuse to talk all together. On other days, this same person may be very open or even emotionally dependent on the professional caregiver. Such changes in feeling tone and in communication are to be expected and are characteristic of the ups and downs of the dying process. Despite the vital service hospice staff provide, the patient or family may not always be openly appreciative.

As hospice care extends beyond the death of the patient, it is also important to observe how both the patient and family deal with their grief, as it influences the postdeath adjustment of survivors. Old, unsettled issues may arise; a family member may refuse to discuss the future. Opening up lines of communication may help families face the reality of a loved one's death, particularly if they have had little recent contact with the dying person or where there are longstanding family difficulties. Extended denial of impending death or refusals of help generally suggest problems in grieving for family members, and in such cases, a referral to the counselor or psychologist on the interdisciplinary team may be appropriate. If the quality of the dying person's relationships with loved ones are troubled, coping with the death and adjusting to life after the patient has died become more difficult for the family. [*See* DEATH AND DYING.]

C. Assessment and Treatment of Patient–Family Needs

In evaluating the patient–family unit, one might want to focus on the woman's well-being, health, or extent of support, as female spouses tend to experience more family caregiver burden than do both men and children. It is also helpful to explore the extent to which family caregivers are depressed, whether they have used social services in the past, and their explanations for the dying persons' behavior, as these factors have also been found to predict caregiver burden, and may constitute adjustment difficulties in themselves. These insights may require several visits to achieve, and may require an assessment by more than one hospice staff member. An evaluation of the family's support system is also critical to understanding how they will cope with the illness—do they have extended family, friends, neighbors, or co-workers available? What area support agencies have they contacted (e.g., nursing home, home health-care services)? Do they have savings or private insurance? How much of the cost of care is Medicare likely to cover? Has a will been written? Have funeral arrangements been made? Do they attend or are they members of a church? Would a visit from the hospice clergy be helpful? Through all of this, the family should sense this active support and interest in their welfare and functioning by hospice staff. In cases where significant family dysfunctional patterns are interfering with care, more formal family therapeutic interventions may be necessary. For example, adult children may feel forced to care for a dying parent whom they have resented, and consequently feel guilty if they do not "hold up their end." In this case, reallocating caregiving responsibilities may be necessary.

V. HOW HOSPICE FUNCTIONS: THE COMMUNITY CONTEXT

One very important function that hospice performs is an educational one. Although many may consider the staff or family as the primary recipients of educa-

tion, reaching the public or other professionals is just as important for hospices, as these persons often support hospice in many ways. Death education was first provided by family members or particular knowledgable residents of the community (i.e., clergy). It is only within the last decade or so that death education has become more formalized. What kind of death education a hospice provides depends upon the skills that the staff possess as well as existing expertise in the community. In many communities, the primary source of patient referrals, financial or personal support, and volunteer expertise is local laypersons and professionals. As the hospice is embedded in a community, educating the community at large or professionals can also become an effective publicity or marketing tool by which hospice serves and philosophy are presented to potential consumers of terminal-care services.

A. Education of Professionals

Education and training of its staff is an important form of education that occurs within hospice. As noted above, it is important that staff have regular access to in-service seminars or to local, regional, or national professional conferences and seminars on such topics as grief and bereavement, counseling, or pain control to ensure that each person will feel that he or she is providing quality care. Professional death education may also lessen staff members' feelings of stress and burnout. Professional education encompasses (a) knowing and respecting how other team members function, (b) understanding that caregiving is in the service of the needs of the patient and family, and (c) enhancing the staff's skills in areas that they may not have acquired on their own professionally. Staff education can meld the interdisciplinary team into a cohesive unit and in the process, give each member a greater sense of competence and control that can be communicated to patients and families. Opportunities for staff training should be regularly scheduled, and a portion of the hospice's budget should be allocated to support travel expenses for staff to update their skills as they relate to terminal care. Professional education can also provide a valuable respite from the demands of caregiving on a 24-hour basis.

B. Education of the Family

The above discussion of patient–family dynamics implies that one very important educational function that hospice staff play is training the family to care for a terminally ill loved one, as well as helping the family understand grief and bereavement. Even though hospice care is available on a 24-hour basis, family members nevertheless do spend a substantial amount of time alone with a dying loved one. They need to be educated about many daily tasks that need to be performed to ensure patient comfort and quality of life. For example, preventing skin breakdown (by keeping the skin moist and turning the patient in bed), administering narcotic and nonnarcotic pain medications (orally or by injection, understanding side effects), keeping catheters clean to permit urination, and controlling pain (via the scheduling and dosage of medications) are all necessary daily care skills. Moreover, helping the patient maintain as much activity as his or her limitations will permit, dealing with restrictions in his or her activity, aiding the patient in coughing up mucus (by suctioning), and managing the daily routines of the family are skills that most families can learn. Bathing, massage, using bedpans, managing incontinence or constipation (by meal management and intake of fluids), using oxygen, and becoming familiar with needed medical equipment, local community service agencies, and support groups are also among the skills families may need to acquire. Most hospices provide a written handout to families explaining aspects of daily care that they supplement with a conference with the family. If necessary, these meetings are held again and again as per the family's needs for information and support from staff. Such training also helps the family realize that they must care for themselves physically, psychologically, and spiritually to be able to go on in their caregiving roles. [See CAREGIVING AND CARING.]

Another key educational role staff can play is in helping the family prepare for the death of a loved one at home and in funeral planning. There are many questions to be answered. What will the person look like? Will death be painful? Peaceful? What should be done? Who should be called? What are reasonable funeral costs? Selecting a funeral home, choosing a casket, purchasing a burial plot or a headstone, deciding whether or not to have a loved one embalmed, whether to have an autopsy performed, whether to have an open or closed casket service, the options of memorial services, donations to worthy causes, cremation, body or organ donation, or burial at sea are among the topics that need to be explained and

discussed so that the needs and wishes of the patient and family can be respected. When a loved one actually dies, having the answers to such questions is very comforting to families at a time of intense pain and sadness.

C. Training of Volunteers

Volunteers are vitally important in hospice, and it is for this reason that special attention should be given to hospice volunteer training. The functions of hospice volunteer training are (a) to ensure that individuals reach a specified level of competence, (b) to give participants' insight into their own motives for working with dying patients, and (c) to increase their sense of empathy for and sensitivity to the needs of dying persons and their families. A last, though unintended function of hospice volunteer training is to "weed out" persons who are not suited for hospice work. As volunteer attrition is often high, recruiting and retraining of new volunteers who are typically recruited from the local community is often time-consuming and expensive for most hospices. Volunteers may include family members of former hospice patients or professionals wishing to contribute their expertise or their own interpersonal skills.

Hospice volunteer training programs vary considerably in their content and duration. In some cases they are staffed and led by hospice personnel, and in other cases they utilize outside consultants or experts. In most situations, training deals with a variety of issues pertinent to the volunteer's direct patient contact function: communication skills, knowledge of terminal illness (e.g., cancer, end-stage renal disease, AIDS) and its treatment, family dynamics of caring for a dying loved one, legal aspects of death, grief, and bereavement, funeral planning, volunteer burnout, and spiritual well-being. Encouraging enrollment by interested community laypersons and professionals can facilitate discussion with other persons who have other, more diverse experiences with death and dying. Particularly helpful are presentations by family members about the benefits of hospice care, a discussion by a current active volunteer about his or her role as a volunteer, and presentations by the interdisciplinary team. Requiring each participant to pay an enrollment fee and attend all sessions heightens the credibility of the volunteer's role and ensures that each participant receives competent training. Formalizing the program, moreover, makes each volunteer really feel like a member of the interdisciplinary team, and gives the hospice both credibility and visibility in the eyes of the community.

D. Education of the Public

In many ways, death education is the hospice's primary link to the community and is therefore an important component helping to define the quality of care hospices provide. It must be held to the highest standards, yet not lose its essentially human function of helping individuals cope with death in the process. The benefits to the community are important to both the public and to hospice, as the primary goal of hospice death education and training is to better enable staff to provide one-to-one support for individuals in coping with a terminal illness. Perhaps the most important roles hospice can play educating the community relate to (a) helping persons define their roles as caregivers, (b) educating families regarding the consumer-related aspects of the death and dying industry, (c) assisting families to cope with grief and loss, and (d) helping define interactions with dying persons as persons who are still living. Formats and materials for death education experiences vary tremendously. A didactic, lecturelike format with discussion may work best when increasing factual knowledge and building self-care skills are desired, whereas an experiential-participatory approach may work best when the goals are to increase personal sensitivity, attain insight, or teach everyday caregiving skills. Experience by the author suggests that at the minimum, a reading list (to include popular and scientific works), a lecture–discussion format focusing on the real-life implications, and actively involving participants are essential to quality death education in the community. The use of art, film, role-playing, and a variety of practical exercises is most helpful as well. For example, having participants free associate to the terms *death* or *dying* can sensitize them to their own biases and preconceptions about dying persons. Drawing "death," locating oneself on a "lifeline" beginning with birth and ending with death, writing a mock will, one's own obituary, or an eulogy can also be very beneficial for both professionals and laypersons. Listing one's fears about death, dying, or the afterlife and "stock taking" (if I were to die tomorrow, these are the things I would want to do, people I would

like to say goodbye to, etc.) are also very useful. Again, the value of such exercises and other activities such as field trips, or site visits varies with the resources, skills, and background of the death educator as well as with the intended target audience. At the least, participants should begin to gain insight into their own feelings about death and dying and develop a certain degree of ease in talking about death in honest, yet humane terms.

VI. GRIEF AND BEREAVEMENT IN HOSPICE CARE

Bereavement follow-up is a primary characteristic of hospice and it sets hospice apart from other types of health care for dying persons and their families. In many respects, the job of the formal caregiver has just begun when the patient dies. The family must be sustained and cared for well beyond the death of a loved one. Bereavement care facilitates the expression of grief before death and thereby lessens its severity after death. As the same personnel are encouraged to stay in contact with the family, this ensures continuity of care. Different staff however, may be involved to encourage the family to develop new relationships. [See BEREAVEMENT AND LOSS.]

A. Principles of Grief and Bereavement

Many professionals feel that grief is best understood in terms of a series of discrete stages: (a) initial shock and denial, accompanied by a search for explanations for the death with overlays of anger and hostility; (b) disorganization and reorganization, characterized by a realization that life is not (and will never be) as it once was and an attempt to reorganize one's thoughts and feelings about the death; and (c) recovery, where one forms a new relationship with the deceased as someone who has died, and begins to reestablish a new lifestyle and form new relationships. Although it is clearly the case that grieving takes time, it is probably wise to be cautious about seeing grief in terms of distinct stages, as grief is highly personal. Even in the case of normal grief (referring to the emotional expression of feelings) among bereaved or soon-to-be-bereaved persons, it is best to see grieving as an ongoing process that makes the bereaved person vulnerable in a physical and psychological sense to stress and future losses. It is not surprising that loneliness is the major problem reported by bereaved persons. Regardless of how we see grief however, it is an intensely painful and personal experience that is a necessary part of adapting to loss itself as well as to the role of bereaved person. Although we often grieve anticipatorily (before a person actually dies), some of our grief can also be expressed at a funeral or memorial service. Funerals, as a form of ritual, can therefore serve to structure our emotions at a time when we might feel overwhelmed, or when we require support from others. For many bereaved persons however, their greatest needs for support come in the weeks and months after the death, long after the funeral.

In thinking about grief, what seems crucial is the quality (harmful, self-destructive, unrealistic) of one's behavior, not its quantity (length of time grieving), in deciding about whether a given person needs help or not. Abnormal (maladaptive) grief frequently involves a long-term change in the individual's typical behaviors. Chronic depression, extended denial of the death, self-abusive or self-destructive behavior, and isolation from others are indictors of difficulty in coping with loss. In this light, it is important to separate depression as a normal response to loss from a clinically significant depressive disorder that is part of pathological grief. Although grief and depression are similar in many ways (e.g., dysphoric mood, physical symptoms, withdrawal from social situations), persons who become clinically depressed at bereavement often express feelings of hopelessness, blame themselves for the death, feel excessively guilty, and are sometimes suicidal. They often experience "personal helplessness," believing that no one else has suffered as they have, and that they alone are incapable of coping or going on with their lives. This sense of helplessness both contributes to and is a result of the extended, pervasive social isolation persons who are abnormally grieving often experience. That widowers are more likely to be isolated and less likely to express their feelings may explain why some men may have a more difficult bereavement than women, though there are wide individual differences in grieving among widows and widowers.

Although we typically associate acute grief with unexpected or sudden deaths, families of hospice patients can nevertheless experience many of the physi-cal symptoms of acute grief such as crying, tension, tightness in the throat, intense sighing, muscular weakness, choking and shortness of breath, emptiness in the abdomen, nausea, or intense activity. It is also common to experience feelings of shock, numbness, or denial. For individuals who are experiencing an acute grief reaction, concentration, attention, or decision making is often impaired as they struggle to make sense of what has happened to them. Often, individuals construct a "personal history" of the death in an effort to make sense out of something that does not make sense (e.g., when someone was last seen, what was said, or what they did in the days or weeks preceding death). Even though hospice gives persons the time to grieve anticipatorily, upon learning of a loved one's death, they can nevertheless experience some acute grief.

B. Grief and Bereavement Services Offered to Patients and Families

A variety of very diverse bereavement services are offered by hospices, and some are more obvious in their purpose than are others. These include attending the funeral, providing individual or group counseling, sending postcards, making telephone calls, and holding memorial services and other social events. The intensity of involvement by individual hospice staff or by the interdisciplinary team varies, as does the formality of objective bereavement follow-up. Counseling, companionship, and assessment are the prime reasons reported by staff for bereavement visits, and persons in home-based hospices typically receive more bereavement support and counseling than do those in hospital-based hospices. Related to such bereavement support is the fact that persons in home-based hospices are more emotionally distressed and experience more caregiver burden prior to death than are those in hospital-based hospices. Because hospice care places a special burden on those families caring for a loved one at home, individuals who have suffered more due to the demands of caregiving may fare more poorly after death.

Not all hospice families receive bereavement support. In fact, there is probably a significant proportion of bereaved family members who choose *not* to ask for bereavement support, but nevertheless know that it is available should they need it. It is also possible that many bereaved persons have other sources of support that are effective. Perhaps those who are at greatest risk for difficulties require more formal bereavement support.

There are four major objectives of hospice bereavement care: (a) accepting the reality of the loss of a loved one, (b) experiencing the pain of grief, (c) adjusting to an environment without the deceased, and (d) reinvesting energy into other relationships. At present, reviews and research growing out of the National Hospice Study suggest that although hospice bereavement programs can be very beneficial, objective evidence supporting their efficacy is sparse. Subjective reports do, however, substantiate the value of bereavement follow-up.

Bereavement care is often carried out by social workers, nurses, or volunteers. In many cases, the social worker coordinates both formal (group meetings) and informal (staff and volunteer visits) bereavement efforts. Bereavement care often focuses on those whose grief is pathological, or on the identification of persons who might have later difficulties in coping. *Pathological grief* is most likely in deaths where the relationship with the deceased was an intimate, central one and where the bereaved person feels responsible or feels that the death could have been prevented. Such cases are characterized by profound depression, self-destructive behavior (not eating, sleeplessness, isolation), taking on symptoms of the deceased (e.g., a husband whose wife died of throat cancer develops an extremely bad cough and hoarseness and experiences difficulties in eating or swallowing), extended denial, or adamant refusals of help. These difficulties may coexist with or be exacerbated by other stressors (e.g., financial or work difficulties, illness, drug use, family conflicts, having been recently relocated to a nursing home). For such persons, formal counseling is often necessary. Persons "at risk" for bereavement difficulties might also require active, aggressive bereavement support. Persons who are "at risk" are those who have suffered a "high grief" death (e.g., a sudden death of spouse, an unusually painful death or disfiguring illness, death of a young child or of an adult child), or those who lack adequate social support. Persons who are at risk are also often very angry, have little psychological preparation for death, and seem to be overly dependent on the dying person. The problems of grieving are intensified if the bereaved person experiences several closely spaced deaths that are not able to be worked through. This

inability to grieve is termed *bereavement overload*. For persons whose grief is not problematic, support groups such as the Widow-to-Widow program, sponsored by the American Association of Retired Persons, may be sufficient.

Persons can grow spiritually and emotionally by being with a loved one at a very sad and emotionally difficult time of life. This is vividly expressed by the wife of a hospice patient who died of cancer.

> Knowing that your spouse has a terminal illness is not all bad. It gives you time. Time for all the things you might otherwise not do. Time to talk, mend bridges, get to know each other better, and even time to fight through the things that you need to fight through. This great thing we call time allows us to let go of that loved one without regrets. We can say goodbye and mean goodbye with all our hearts. The time spent preparing for my husband's death is probably the most valuable time of our 17-year marriage. Perhaps in your mind that casts a shadow over our marriage. I think not. I believe that we were very typical of the great percentage of couples. We got caught up in the work of life and often lost contact with each other. We were fortunate to be extremely close and in tune to one another, but we still got caught up in our own personal strives for survival. Had Ray suddenly dropped dead one day we would not have had 6 months to bond and prepare. I am fortunate to be able to say that I have no regrets after Ray's death.

Perhaps being able to say "I have no regrets" is the best bereavement support hospice can offer to a family whose loved one has died.

VII. THE FUTURE OF HOSPICE

The future of hospice can be understood in the context of sociocultural and political forces, wherein the relationship between the public's awareness of death and specific diseases such as cancer (or AIDS), sensitivity to rising health-care costs, and the demand for hospice services are all emphasized. One manner of dealing with unrealistic expectations of what health-care ills hospice can and cannot cure is to educate both the public and professionals about hospice. As demands for hospice services escalate, more professionals and volunteers will need to be trained to meet such needs. In addition, health-care providers need to be educated about hospice so that the hospice concept can be integrated into the existing health-care system. Such changes may be at the expense of independent, privately supported hospices in favor of larger, more established health-care institutions delivering hospice care. In any event, education about death and dying and about hospice care in particular will play a crucial role in the future of hospice care. Of course, future reimbursement of hospice care will hinge on changes in the health-care system that are now being debated. Moreover, clear evidence will be needed to support the contention that hospice is both cost effective and impactful in a psychosocial and psychological sense. As health-care resources become more scarce, this burden of proof will hinge on well-designed research to substantiate the benefits of humane, compassionate care characteristic of hospice.

There are many who feel that hospice may change as hospices become larger, more bureaucratized, and institutional in nature. Moreover, there has been a moderate degree of criticism of for-profit hospices, as many feel that the profit motive undermines the unique nature of hospice staff–patient or family connection. In the future, cost effectiveness, rather than quality of care, may dictate what services hospices provide, to whom such care is directed, as well as determining the locus of this care, as hospice services are now reimbursable under the Medicare benefit. Concomitantly, staff perceptions of hospice care as primarily a philosophy versus being a business will undoubtedly affect the nature of hospice services, particularly for smaller, rural, not-for-profit hospices.

Dealing with these philosophical and ethical conflicts may become a real challenge for many hospices, affecting not only the type of care they provide, but also the types of patients they serve. For smaller, not-for-profit hospices, they may ultimately influence whether a particular hospice will survive in a given community. If hospice changes in these ways, staff turnover may increase, as nurses, for example, find equally high-paying, less stressful jobs elsewhere. In this light, hospices are now forced to compete with other health-care providers for competent staff.

Although increased professionalization and reimbursement may help standardize care and ensure financial viabilty, it remains to be seen whether an emphasis on cost effectiveness and accountability will ultimately undermine the idealistic, voluntary nature of home-based hospice care. Such care has traditionally been provided without regard to the patient's ability to pay. The increased visability of more corporately owned for-profit hospices, where services are increasingly more specialized, with the concomitant use of volunteers for services that do not involve direct patient care, raises many questions. Whether hospice loses its identity as a philosophy of caring for the dying person remains to be seen.

BIBLIOGRAPHY

Corr, C., & Corr, M. (1985). *Hospice approaches to pediatric care.* New York: Springer.

Hayslip, B., & Leon, J. (1992). *Hospice care.* Newbury Park, CA: Sage Publishers.

Hine, V. H. (1979). Dying at home: Can families cope? *Omega, 10,* 175–187.

Lattanzi-Licht, M., & Connor, S. (1995). Care of the dying: The hospice approach. In H. Wass & R. A. Neimeyer (Eds.), *Dying: Facing the facts.* Washington, DC: Taylor and Francis.

Mor, V., Greer, D. S., & Kastenbaum, R. (1988). *The hospice experiment.* Baltimore, MD: Johns Hopkins Press.

Mor, V., & Masterson-Allen, S. (1987). *Hospice care systems: Structure, process, costs and outcome.* New York: Springer.

National Hospice Organization (1994). Standards of a hospice program of care. *The Hospice Journal, 9,* 39–74.

Paradis, L. F. (1985). *Hospice Handbook: A guide for managers and planners.* Rockville, MD: Aspen.

Weisman, A. D. (1988). Appropriate death and the hospice program. *The Hospice Journal, 4,* 65–78.

Housing

Hal Kendig

*La Trobe University
Bundoora, Australia*

Jon Pynoos

*University of
Southern California*

Aging in Place The desire and tendency of older persons to stay in their current dwelling units for as long as possible.

Assisted Living A residential setting that provides private apartments (often efficiencies), a full range of supportive services (e.g., meals, personal care), social activities, continuous protective oversight (24-hour on-site supervision), and is usually licensed.

Congregate Housing Semi-independent multi-unit living arrangement that generally provides group meals to residents.

Continuum of Housing A range of housing options that are differentiated by their complement of services, physically supportive features, and the age or competency level to which they are targeted.

Environmental Press The demands that environmental settings make on residents' physical and mental competencies.

Home Modifications Adaptations to home environments of functionally impaired individuals intended to make it easier and safer to carry out activities such as bathing, cooking, walking, navigating steps, and opening doors.

Household A group of individuals or an individual who live(s) in a dwelling unit.

Naturally Occurring Retirement Communities (NORCS) Housing complexes or neighborhoods that were not planned for the elderly but, due to aging in place and in-movement of new elderly residents, contain high concentrations of older persons.

Supportive Housing Housing complexes in which the owner or manager coordinates a range of supportive services, many of which are provided by third parties, for residents who typically live in their own apartment units. Most do not provide continuous protective oversight and are unlicensed.

The vast majority of older persons live independently in single-family homes or apartments. The importance of their **HOUSING** extends far beyond the shelter provided by "bricks and mortar." The home is the primary base for daily living and it can represent a lifetime of memories and provide a sense of security for the future. For older homeowners, it is usually their most valuable asset. For older renters on a limited and fixed income, housing is often their largest monthly expenditure. The features of the neighborhood in which housing is located are crucial to community life and accessibility of shopping, medical, and recreation.

Especially over the last decade, housing for older persons has been viewed as involving much more than conventional shelter. A larger number of people are reaching the advanced ages where they are likely to have chronic diseases, become frail, and experience losses of family and friends. For these vulnerable individuals, housing and related services can be critical to quality of life. They often are the key factor in enabling a frail older person to stay in a residential setting rather than move to a nursing home.

This overview of housing for older people reviews key concepts, perspectives, living arrangements, and the relationship among housing tenure, income, and wealth. It also discusses housing types and problems followed by an analysis of housing policies and programs that have been developed to improve the housing situation of older persons. Although the major focus of this article is on the United States, it includes references to experiences in other industrialized countries. It covers the features of housing for older people living in general housing, supportive housing, and links between housing and services. Unless otherwise mentioned, the discussion refers to older people as those aged 65 years or over.

I. PERSPECTIVES

Housing and gerontology are multidisciplinary fields that draw on a variety of conceptual perspectives. This section reviews three of the main paradigms that have been applied in developing the present knowledge base about housing the elderly: environmental psychology, the housing market approach, and political anslysis of policies and programs.

A major influence on the field of elderly housing has been environmental psychology. Environmental press, the central concept, refers to the match between individuals' functional capacities and the demands of their environments. A good environmental fit will stimulate and support an individual and enhance his or her functioning and well-being. An overly supportive environment can atrophy an individual's capacities, whereas an overly stressful environment risks a breakdown of capacities and distress. As individuals grow older and their needs and capacities change, it is important to adapt existing environments or ensure appropriate moves to new environments.

The environmental psychology approach is often termed a *microperspective* because it emphasizes how individuals relate to their residential environments. Over the past three decades, the public and private sectors have sponsored research that has applied the microperspective to a wide range of important topics. The emphasis has been on how older people adapt to specially built accommodations, such as homes for the aged, public housing, and nursing homes. This research has shown that sensitive and careful design of building layouts, pedestrian walkways, and other features can assist older persons who would have difficulty in conventional housing settings. The microtradition has devoted little attention to housing for the majority of older people who are capable and live in single-family houses and neighborhoods.

Since the 1980s, increasing attention has been directed to older persons in the broader housing market. Sociological analyses have focused on the household characteristics of the elderly, whereas economic analyses have focused on their housing characteristics. This *macro* work has been greatly stimulated by improved census and survey data on the housing types, conditions, and costs for people of all ages. The information reflects increasing policy attention to identifying the needs of special groups in the housing market and to maintaining the quality and best use of housing resources. The available data provide a picture of the housing of various age groups and the housing of older people by their race, marital status, and income.

An understanding is emerging of how the processes of individual and population aging relate to the changing composition and use of the housing stock. The concept of the life span has been applied to studying housing careers, that is, the succession of dwellings occupied over a lifetime and how these careers interweave with employment and family careers. Housing demography has provided analytical tools that show how the supply and use of housing changes in periods of history, on aging of individuals and cohorts, and with the succession of new cohorts, people, and dwellings. Change in people's use of housing occurs as a result of complex markets for housing, land, and labor as well as public regulations and subsidies.

A final perspective concerns the politics of public intervention in housing markets and the impacts of housing programs. The political economy perspective emphasizes how government policies towards housing are influenced by interest groups, ideological struggles, and economic considerations. Many actions of government—such as subsidies and tax concessions for home ownership—are not age-specific but can have significant impacts when people reach old age. Age-specific policies have risen out of concern for the special needs of older persons, a perception of older persons as the deserving poor, and the growth of older people and the industries that serve them as political constituencies. The political agendas of governments also influence the funding of housing evaluations and studies, which in turn shapes the availability of information and assessments of program and policy effectiveness. In addition, as housing encompasses more than shelter, it inevitably has to cross agency boundaries and must confront sometimes conflicting goals, guidelines, and methods of operation.

Before turning to the present knowledge base, it needs to be acknowledged that research on aging and housing is still at an early stage of development. The complex processes of individual and historical change in housing patterns stand in sharp contrast with available evidence based mainly on cross-sectional surveys and aggregated analyses of trends. It is difficult to compare studies because they can apply different definitions of even basic terms such as households, dwellings, and housing types. Findings differ significantly depending on units of analysis, for example, between individuals or households. Even more problematic are cross-cultural comparisons. Conceptual advances will depend heavily on designing better investigations that take more account of the complexity of the field.

II. LIVING ARRANGEMENTS

A household, the basic unit of housing demand, is made up of an individual who lives alone or a group of people who live together. The composition of households has a major bearing on individuals' cost of living, responsibility for household duties, and proximity of social support. Relatively few older people move immediately after retirement, widowhood, or the onset of disability. The vast majority of them experience personal or household changes while remaining in their established home. Although some older people choose to move to more appropriate housing, most prefer to make housing adjustments through "aging in place."

In the United States in the 1990s, 90% of older people live in conventional housing, consisting primarily of single-family houses and apartments. Approximately 5% of older persons at any one time live in nursing homes and another 5% in other forms of housing that have congregate facilities or services, such as meals. The proportion of older individuals in special housing rises with advancing age yet represents only slightly more than 25% even for those aged 85

years and over. Those who are most likely to live in government-assisted housing are poor, frail, and not presently married. Overall, the proportion of older persons in nonprivate housing in the United States has remained relatively stable over the last few decades. These figures are broadly comparable to those of Australia, the United Kingdom, and other Western countries at similar levels of economic development.

Over the post-war era older people have become much more likely to live alone or live only with their spouse. The explanations are rising real incomes, relief of war housing shortages, and continuing preference for independent living. At present, approximately half of older Americans live only with their spouse, a third live alone, and the remainder live with others (mainly relatives). Living with someone other than a spouse is much more common among older people who are black, Hispanic, poor, or disabled. Particularly vulnerable older people, in terms of income and functional capacities, are overwhelmingly widows who only over recent decades have lived in separate households.

As a result of their generally small households, older people have a disproportionately large presence in the housing stock. Approximately 40% of all American dwellings are headed by a person aged 55 years or older. The head of household is the person who holds the title for an owner-occupied home or who signs the lease for a rented dwelling. The household head is the most common unit for housing analyses relating the characteristic of a dwelling to the personal characteristics of the occupants.

A small proportion of the elderly population can be considered homeless. Homeless people by definition do not live in households and they are virtually invisible in available databases and the housing literature. Other older persons, unable to afford their own homes, live with relatives, unrelated individuals, or in single rooms. The few studies available on these groups highlight their intense difficulties, which can result from a lifelong combination of personal problems and social and economic exclusion.

III. HOUSING TENURE, INCOME, AND WEALTH

Housing tenure is one of the most significant economic divides among people in old age. If the entry costs to home ownership can be met earlier in adult life, savings from the years of peak income are likely to be stored in the home, and this wealth increases through appreciation of house prices. In old age, outright home ownership can provide security of occupancy, relatively low cash outlays for shelter, and the means to buy into other accommodations. Government-subsidized tenants have smaller financial advantages, usually in the form of low rent. Private tenants (in the absence of government protection) face rising market rents and have little security of occupancy.

Older Americans have largely been successful in achieving home ownership. More than three out of every four older household heads either own their own homes outright or they are paying off mortgages. Only 5% of older Americans receive direct housing assistance from the federal government. Those who rent in old age are overwhelmingly in nonsubsidized housing, and they generally have faced lifelong economic disadvantages that restricted capacities to ever buy homes. "Permanent" tenants include disproportionately large numbers of Blacks, Hispanics, residents of large cities, and people who had never married or had divorced (especially women). The vast majority of older Americans with middle or higher incomes are home owners, whereas a small minority of those with low incomes are owners.

Cohorts of older people born at or before the turn of the century have had relatively low lifelong access to home ownership. Those born in the 1920s, who reached old age in the 1980s, have had much higher rates of ownership. People in this cohort were in their prime home-buying years during the economic and housing boom of the 1950s and 1960s, which was assisted by subsidized and regulated housing finance and income tax concessions on interest payments and capital gains. Housing trajectories set during the affluent post-war era are leading to continuing high rates of home ownership for people entering old age during the 1990s.

People who enter old age as home owners generally remain so for nearly all of the remainder of their lives. The relatively small numbers who move out of home ownership for the most part are very old widows who are likely to have experienced economic or health-related functional difficulties. This pattern of stability suggests that age differences found in housing markets at any time reflect strong cohort effects as well as aging effects. They also suggest that housing adjustments in

old age (when they take place at all) usually occur in the last several years of life.

Owning a home outright is very important in enabling older people to maintain an adequate standard of living on a retirement income. Older renters, however, generally live near poverty levels, and their rents are high relative to incomes. Approximately a quarter of all older home owners pay more than a quarter of their income on housing, as compared to two-thirds of all private renters. Excessive housing costs, according to the definition set by the federal government (over 30% of income), are highly concentrated among older persons with low incomes, especially older women and minorities. Such costs make it difficult for older persons to afford other necessities of life such as health care and transportation.

With rising real costs of buying over recent decades, lifelong access to home ownership is likely to be reduced for those reaching old age during the next century. There is likely to be an historic watershed in which fewer older people will have outright home ownership to cushion the effects of low retirement incomes. To sharpen the social divides further, the present cohort of older owners will be bequeathing their housing assets to adult children who also are likely to be owners and who will themselves be on the verge of old age.

The housing tenure of older people and its distributional consequences varies considerably among countries. Although Australia has ownership rates comparable to those in the United States, more people live in public housing in old age and more private tenants have rent assistance. In Britain, only half of older people are home owners, with 40% in public housing and most of the remainder in protected private tenancies. The distributional consequences of housing have followed very different patterns in European and Scandanavian countries that encourage nonprofit housing cooperatives and have fewer policies subsidizing entry to home ownership.

IV. HOUSING TYPES AND PROBLEMS

The vast majority of people enter old age living in homes selected for their appropriateness in midlife when they were in the paid workforce and typically had larger households. For the cohort of people aged 60–69 years in 1960, there were extremely low increases of apartment living over the next 20 years (virtually none among owners and from 11 to 16% among tenants). Thus, with the boom in building detached dwellings in the 1950s and 1960s, four out of every five older people now live in some form of single-family housing. They are no more likely than younger people to live in apartments or medium-density housing.

Residential stability of older persons, combined with declining household size, has raised concerns about underutilization of housing resources. For example, a third of elderly headed households in the United States have an extra bedroom for their household size and two or more nonsleeping rooms. However, studies suggest that very few older people consider their homes too large for them. They report making extensive use of spare rooms for family visits, leisure, and other lifestyle activities centered on the home. Moreover, if older people own their homes outright, there is relatively little financial pressure to change housing. The available evidence suggests that older people are unlikely to be induced into smaller dwellings unless financial and other barriers are lessened and attractive alternatives are available in nearby areas.

The condition of housing occupied by older persons has improved substantially over the post-war era. Fewer than 1% of older people live in overcrowded housing defined as households with more than one person per room. Almost all older persons now live in housing with hot and cold running water, private bathing and toilet facilities, and a sound physical structure. However, almost 8% of older persons live in housing with serious physical deficits such as frequent breakdowns in heating equipment and structure-related problems such as leaky roofs. As with high housing cost, these problems are highly concentrated among older persons with low incomes, especially older women and minorities. Overall, the extent of housing problems by these measures is roughly comparable among younger and older Americans.

These summary statistics on housing problems require careful consideration. On the one hand, many older people, especially those with functional limitations, have minor housing difficulties in the use of their dwelling units even when they are in good condition. The consequences of housing problems can fall particularly severely on a frail older person who is right on the edge of maintaining functional compe-

tency. Furthermore, an apparently small percentage (i.e., 8% in substandard dwellings) still amounts to a very large number of people (more than a million).

On the other hand, the majority of older persons are satisfied with their housing even when it is technically substandard by the above measures. They are unlikely to rate housing as a major area of hardship—certainly less so than younger people. These paradoxes may arise because perceptions are highly specific to individual interpretation. In the case of disadvantaged older persons, apparent satisfaction can reflect low expectations that anything could be done to improve their situation.

A long-standing assumption in the field of housing has been that as persons become more frail, they will have to move from one housing setting to another. While many frail older people eventually move to more supportive accommodations, most wish to continue at home for some time. Of the many needs of frail older people at home, the most common are assistance with gardening, home repairs, supportive features (e.g., grab bars, ramps), and transportation.

The idea of a continuum in the supportiveness of housing is important because it recognizes that housing options can be differentiated by the amount and type of services offered; the supportiveness of the physical setting in terms of accessibility, features, and design; and the age–competency level to which the housing setting is targeted. Figure 1 indicates how different housing options including single-family housing, apartments, board and care homes, and skilled nursing homes generally meet the needs of older persons who are categorized, respectively, as independent, semidependent, and dependent. Although semidependent and even dependent older persons can be found throughout the continuum, independent older persons are very unlikely to be found in housing types such as assisted living specially designed and equipped for frail older persons.

Several housing types exist that serve specific subgroups of the population. For example, several types of purpose-built housing for semi-independent older persons have evolved over the last decade. These options are variously referred to in the United States by such labels as board and care, residential care facilities, and assisted living. In Australia, similar types of housing are called hostels; the Scandinavian versions are generally known as service houses. These types of complexes generally serve persons who are substan-

Housing Options for the Elderly	Independent		Semi-independent				Dependent		
Community Based Single Family Housing	●	●							
Community-Based Apartment Dwelling	●	●							
Granny Flat / Echo Housing		●	●						
Accessory Apartment Dwelling		●	●						
Shared Housing		●	●						
Retirement Community		●	●						
Age Segregated Apartment Dwelling		●	●	●					
Communal Housing			●	●					
Retirement Hotel			●	●					
Congregate House (20-30 units)			●	●	●				
Congregate Housing (100 units +)			●	●	●				
Board and Care Home			●	●	●				
Assisted Living/Personal Care					●	●			
Foster Care					●	●			
Intermediate Nursing Care							●		
Skilled Nursing Care								●	
Continuing Care Retirement Community (CCRC)			●		●		●	●	●

Figure I The continuum of housing. Independent: Living arrangements designed for individuals and couples capable of handling their own housekeeping, cooking, and personal care needs. Semi-independent: Living arrangements designed for those with some chronic limitations. Residents are self-sufficient and capable of self-care, but may rely on the facility for meals, housekeeping, and transportation. Dependent: Living arrangements that provide 24-hour supervision, intermittent services, and nursing care for severely impaired individuals.

tially older than other supportive housing options such as congregate housing which offers only limited services such as meals.

Board and care homes, providing meals, supervision and limited assistance in daily activities number over 30,000, more than double that of nursing homes. However, most of them have only 5 to 20 units and therefore house only about one-fourth the number of residents (about 400,000 persons) as nursing homes; half of their residents are under 62 years of age. Although most board and care homes are privately run, many residents receive state government subsidies as well as Supplemental Security Income (SSI). Most board and care homes are very modest in nature and require that residents share rooms. State governments regulate these homes, but many of the smaller ones are unlicensed and enforcement is lax.

Assisted living, a rapidly growing form of housing in the United States, generally provides independent apartment units (usually including private bathrooms and sometimes kitchens), professional management, and a full range of personal care services including medication monitoring. The attractiveness of assisted living for older persons and their families is attributable to its homelike design, the desire to maximize privacy and autonomy within the dwelling unit, and the availability of more personal care services such as dressing and bathing assistance. Very frail individuals, including those who are incontinent and those with Alzheimer's disease, view assisted living as an alternative to the hospital-like environment of the typical nursing home. Currently, assisted living is primarily available to middle- and upper-income older persons who can afford it.

V. LOCATION

The location of housing can have a major impact on the lives of older persons. It is particularly important for older people to have safe neighborhoods with a range of public and private facilities and good public transportation. Older persons can be especially vulnerable to urban change when they are frail, strongly attached to their homes, and possibly locked in by low house prices or inability to afford higher rents. Older persons report less satisfaction with their neighborhoods compared with their housing. In rural locations, older people can be isolated from essential services and social contact, particularly if they cannot drive a car.

Markets and government policies have substantially restructured American cities over the last generation. As new cohorts of individuals in the middle classes moved outward from the central cities, established home owners have grown old in neighborhoods undergoing major changes in environmental amenities and racial composition. Private tenants have faced rising rents, public or private redevelopment, and conversion of apartments to condominiums. Owners in deteriorating areas may be trapped by falling house prices. In revitalizing areas, owners may be presented with opportunities to cash in on rising property values and move elsewhere.

A recently recognized phenomenon has been the concentration of older persons in areas that attracted but were not intentionally planned for them. In many of these buildings and neighborhoods, older persons have aged in place, having moved into them when they were in their forties, fifties, and sixties. In some situations, the advantages of security and of living with one's age peers have drawn older persons to these settings from other places. Referred to as naturally occurring retirement community (NORCs), these communities do not generally offer the social and health services that older persons need as they age. On the other hand, NORCs provide the opportunity to take advantage of potential economies of scale by clustering services, developing new facilities (e.g., senior centers), and linking housing with services.

Over the last decade increasing numbers of people have been aging in place in single-family homes built in post-war suburban areas. These areas were designed for travel by car and thus have relatively poor public transport and access to private and public facilities. As compared to older inner city areas, the suburbs can present major spatial barriers to people who do not drive cars and may have difficulty walking. They also have a limited range of housing types, sizes, and costs for those who would wish to move to more appropriate housing in a nearby area. These potential difficulties could be minimized greatly by land use policies that ensure a mix of land uses and housing types in new as well as established areas of cities.

VI. HOUSING POLICIES AND PROGRAMS

Since World War II, almost all Western industrialized countries, including the United States, have taken some responsibility to ensure that their citizens have access to decent and affordable housing. Because they are mixed economies and the private sector plays an

important role, many of the policies have attempted to provide a stable economic climate so that the private housing industry, a major sector of the economy, can produce an adequate quantity of housing. In the United States, national housing policy has consisted of federal mortgage guarantee programs, the establishment of a secondary mortgage market and tax incentives for home ownership. These policies have had strong political support, especially among builders and realtors that are powerful interest groups at all levels of government. The elderly, with the highest rates of home ownership, have been major beneficiaries of these overall housing policies.

Governments have also sought to provide housing specifically for vulnerable groups that are not served well by the private sector. In order to stimulate production of housing for the poor, governments have either built complexes themselves or provided subsidies to profit and/or nonprofit developers for the construction of rental housing. Some countries such as the United States and Britain have developed a substantial stock of housing for low- and moderate-income older persons, using supply-type programs. The early supply-oriented programs for the elderly initially emphasized the shelter aspects of housing. In response to the growing number of very frail older persons, more recent approaches have stressed the inclusion of services.

Demand-oriented strategies include programs that provide housing allowances or certificates so consumers can obtain housing beyond what their normal income would purchase. Demand-side approaches tend to be more acceptable to conservative political parties, which resist direct government efforts to increase the supply.

The following discussion will analyze four housing programs that illustrate supply-and-demand strategies governments have used to improve the housing situation of the elderly.

A. Age-Specific Housing for Independent Older Persons

Government-subsidized age-specific housing for independent older persons is of relatively recent origin in all countries. Up until the late 1950s, housing supply programs in the United States, such as public housing, focused on meeting the needs of young families. As home ownership became possible for families with even modest incomes, subsidy programs were viewed as permanent housing for low-income families, many of whom were minorities. In 1956, the eligibility requirements were changed to allow single older persons to live in public housing. Increasing numbers of older people began to be served by these programs for three basic reasons: (a) elderly tenants had lower incomes, fewer assets, and poorer housing conditions than younger renters; (b) long-term residents of subsidized housing programs began to "age in place"; and (c) the elderly were viewed as the deserving poor and were considered less problematic as tenants than younger adults with children.

As older single persons began to move into projects that had previously housed only families, concerns were raised about their safety and potential alienation. At the same time, experts in the emerging field of gerontology began to advocate for age-specific housing for the elderly, which would have specific design features (e.g., emergency call buttons, few or no stairs), common space for socialization, and services such as meals. Psychologists and social scientists were concerned about the adaptability of older persons to such a radical new lifestyle and the potential isolation of large groups of older persons living in age-segregated high-rise buildings. These fears were put to rest, however, by studies finding that residents of age-specific housing, compared with tenants in the community, reported greater morale and life satisfaction, increased friendship formation, increased social interaction, and better perception of health status. By the early 1990s, 37% of public housing units were occupied by the elderly, with over 300,000 older persons residing in projects exclusively for the elderly and disabled and a comparable number of older persons living in family projects.

A step somewhat above public housing in quality is housing for the elderly provided under Section 202 of the National Housing Act of 1959. As originally enacted, Section 202 provided direct, low-interest loans to nonprofit sponsors (mostly religious organizations) to provide housing for moderate-income elderly tenants ineligible for public housing. Although these projects generally had more amenities than public housing (e.g., some provide congregate meals), they were also intended for independent elderly. Early advocates of the program did not want the housing to resemble "homes for the aged." Consequently, the program did not fund services, and it permitted man-

agers to bar applicants who could not live independently. This approach was consistent with the philosophy of the federal housing agency, which considered its responsibility "bricks and mortar" and not services. A total of over 250,000 units of Section 202 housing had been built by 1995.

Other advanced countries have also built government-subsidized housing specifically for older people. For example, in 1962, Peter Townsend, a leading academic, succeeded in urging the British government to develop sheltered housing as a noninstitutional form of care. Great Britain, Denmark, and Sweden have constructed purpose-built dwellings in small clusters with supportive design features and on-site managers. However, most European countries have provided for relatively independent older people mainly through public housing for all age groups.

Various forms of age-specific congregate housing have been sought after by older persons. They have also been popular with government officials who acknowledge that, in contrast to many family projects, housing for the elderly has had few problems and has been well managed. Nevertheless, during the late 1980s, in the United States and other countries, these programs began to experience reduced government funding for new complexes. They have been viewed as relatively costly compared to other housing subsidy approaches, such as vouchers, and have lost favor with conservative governments. There has also been a growing perception that other groups have more pressing needs and that housing for independent older persons has failed to address the problems of very frail older persons. By the mid-1990s, governments in Europe and North America were reducing housing programs for independent older persons or adapting them to serve frail older persons.

B. Supportive Housing and Assisted Living

By the early 1990s, many residents of housing for the elderly had aged in place and were now in their late seventies or eighties with accompanying greater needs for physically supportive features and services. For the most part, these complexes and their managers were ill equipped to meet changing resident needs. At the same time, government concern with housing the elderly was shifting from independent housing to service-enriched housing. This emerging trend has been driven by the search for cost-effective alternatives to expensive nursing homes and the desire of frail older persons to live in residential rather than institutional settings. Consequently, in the last two decades, programs have been created to develop supportive housing that is physically accessible, contains special features, and has a range of services. Two basic strategies have been used to develop housing for very frail older persons: adapting existing housing originally intended for independent elderly and developing new forms of very supportive housing.

One approach to developing supportive housing has been to adapt government-assisted housing for the independent elderly by better equipping it to serve frail older persons. For example, in the mid 1970s, the United States began a 63-site Congregate Housing Services Program (CHSP) demonstration to test the viability of adding a service coordinator and services such as meals, transportation, and homemaking, for tenants with limitations in daily activities. Because of uncertainty related to targeting, questions about the extent to which the program prevented institutionalization, and HUD's reluctance to pay for services, the CHSP remained small.

Although concern about cost-effectiveness has limited programs such as CHSP, such projects have nonetheless demonstrated that existing multi-unit housing complexes can be adapted to improve the quality of life of frail older persons and assist them in aging in place. With these goals in mind, Congress in the early 1990s allocated funds for service coordinators in a wide variety of government-assisted housing complexes for the elderly. However by the mid 1990s, the CHSP and service coordinator programs were threatened by large reductions in federal housing budgets and continuing unresolved issues about responsibility for services.

The difficulties of adapting existing housing, and meeting the needs of very frail older persons for ongoing supervision have led to a very rapid growth in assisted living. Although it can serve very impaired older persons including those with Alzheimer's disease, assisted living has not been generally affordable by low-income persons. Its wider availability requires melding income streams from diverse housing, health, and income programs to pay for costs related to shelter and services, which has been done in several states (e.g., Oregon). Maintaining a residential atmosphere requires appropriate state regulations that stress privacy and autonomy as well as a recognizing that there

may be trade-offs in terms of safety. The enactment of such regulations depends on evaluations concerning quality of life considerations and costs savings relative to nursing home expenditures. The latter benefit has not yet been proven, and some groups have argued that because assisted living serves a population with similar impairments to residents of nursing homes, it should also be strictly regulated.

C. Home Equity Conversion Mortgages

With the erosion of the government safety net, increasing attention has been directed to ways in which older home owners can access the equity in their homes without having to sell and move. There has been increasing interest in reverse mortgages, which allow older persons to draw out money based on their home equity and repay it after they move or die. The complications and risks of these loans, for both lenders and home owners, have been reduced by federal insurance for home equity conversion mortgages (HECMs), which provide increased financial protection and security of occupancy for older persons. With federal support, HECMs have grown over the last 5 years from 2,000 to over 13,000. HECMs have been used for a variety of purposes such as paying off debts to avoid foreclosure, home repairs and modification, medical expenses, and long-term care. Continued expansion of this option for older persons will depend upon ongoing participation by the federal government in providing insurance as well as more active involvement of the secondary mortgage market which in late 1995 was facilitated by a Fannie Mae program to purchase reverse mortgages from lenders.

D. Home Modifications and Repairs

Since the early 1980s, governments have increasingly recognized the preference of older persons to remain in their own homes as long as possible. Policy makers have also begun to examine ways to make more efficient use of existing housing resources with emphasis on single-family homes. Based on the realization that many older persons lived in homes with an extra vacant bedroom, a movement developed to share homes. At the same time, there was increasing evidence that many frail older persons had homes that needed repairs and modifications to help prevent accidents, make caregiving easier, and substitute for costly personal care services. Several studies suggested that home modifications were being held back by inadequate funding, enormous gaps in services, fragmented service delivery, and a low level of awareness concerning the efficacy of home modifications among consumers and professionals.

In the United States, home modification programs are highly reliant on programs such as Community Development Block Grants and the Older Americans Act. Neither of these programs earmark funds for modifications nor necessarily set it as a high priority. In order to enhance the ability to age in place, a number of countries—such as Britain, the Netherlands, and Canada—have launched home-repair and modification programs that focus on upgrading individual units, as well as adding features such as ramps, grab bars, and roll-in showers. Inherent in the design of such programs are policy dilemmas concerning the extent to which payment for such changes should rely on loans, grants, or out-of-pocket expenses.

VII. POLICY AND RESEARCH DIRECTIONS

There are mixed prospects for the adequacy of housing for older people in the future. On the one hand, cohorts entering old age over the next decade will have relatively high rates of home ownership that will cushion the financial adjustments to living on a fixed income. On the other hand, many older people will continue as lifelong tenants with few private options for accommodation or services. Major challenges for meeting housing and related needs include the increasing numbers of people reaching very advanced ages, accessibility difficulties for those growing older in post-war suburbs, and continuing severe restrictions on public expenditure. Although pronounced in the United States, these social and economic trends are also found in other industrialized nations.

The housing of older people in the future will be deeply affected by a wide range of government policies extending to taxation, income, support, and regulation of property and land. While housing situations and policies vary greatly among countries, several broad international directions are apparent. For example, one approach is to provide integrated community care which enables frail older people to remain in their own homes and limits use of costly residential care. A second approach is to encourage older people

who have the money to pay for their own housing and related services whether purchased from the public or the private sector.

Directions in supportive housing for older persons are emphasizing consumer-controlled services and new models of accommodation. Many of these initiatives require increased government flexibility, private public partnerships, and innovative approaches. Their success depends on government involvement through developing and funding housing and services, providing information and technical assistance, and establishing a regulatory framework that protects the rights of frail older persons and other consumers. The new directions aim to break down barriers between programs and to include housing as an integral part of the long-term care system. A number of initiatives have promise to attract public support and yield major benefits for frail older people:

1. *Developing a consumer-controlled voucher system* that would enable older people to choose combinations of housing and services that fit their individual needs and preferences.

2. *Creating new models of housing* such as small scale developments integrated into the community that provide elderly with access to community facilities and intergenerational contact.

3. *Converting nursing homes into more residential settings* that provide very frail older people with increased privacy, autonomy, and choice.

4. *Incorporating new technology* that can make it easier for frail older persons to summon assistance, access information, and carry out tasks independently.

5. *Encouraging universal design and life cycle communities* that ensure that dwellings and neighborhoods provide full access to disabled people of all ages in age-integrated communities.

These directions involve many aspect of housing including financing, regulations, legal rights, modifying and retrofitting environments, and philosophies of management and care. Advances are already being driven by those who can pay themselves for services such as home modifications or moves to a new setting such as assisted living. The choices for low- and moderate-income older persons, however, are much more constrained. Although a new system with greater consumer choice may create flexibility and new solutions, the magnitude of government support remains in doubt in the United States and other countries as housing subsidies are either capped or reduced. Many older persons continue to pay excessive amounts of their income for housing, live in deficient units, and are at risk of moving unnecessarily to more institutional settings.

Action to improve housing for older people needs to be based on sound knowledge. More research can reveal how life experiences, housing markets, and public policies influence people's housing on entry to old age and transitions through the course of old age. The impact of housing on older people's lives needs to be identified in terms of their standards of living, health, independence, and well-being. Rigorous analysis of housing programs can enhance their cost effectiveness and increase their political attractiveness. Such a knowledge base requires a strong emphasis on housing as an important area for applied, multidisciplinary research.

BIBLIOGRAPHY

Golant, S. M. (1992). *Housing America's elderly: Many possibilities, few choices.* Newbury Park, CA: Sage Publications.

Heumann, L. F., & Boldy, D. P., (Eds.). (1993). *Aging in place with dignity: International solutions relating to the low-income and frail elderly.* New York: Praeger.

Kendig, H. (1990). Comparative perspectives on housing, aging and social structure. *In* R. Binstock & L. George (Eds.), *Handbook of aging and the social sciences.* (3rd ed.) San Diego: Academic Press.

Kendig, H. (1990). A life course perspective on housing attainment. In D. Myers (Ed.), *Housing demography: Linking demographic structures and housing choices.* Madison: University of Wisconsin Press.

Lawton, M. P. (1986). *Environment and aging.* Albany, Center for the Study of Aging.

Lawton, M. P. (1991). A future agenda for congregate housing research. In L. W. Kaye & A. Monk (Eds.), *Congregate housing for the elderly: Theoretical, policy, and programmatic perspectives.* New York: Haworth Press.

Pynoos, J. (1992). Linking federally assisted housing with services for frail older people. *Journal of Aging and Social Policy, 4*(3& 4), 157–177.

Pynoos, J., & Liebig, P. (Eds.). (1995). *Housing frail elders: International policies, perspectives, and prospects.* Baltimore: Johns Hopkins University Press.

Pynoos, J., & Golant, S. (1995). Supportive housing and living arrangements. In R. Binstock & L. George (Eds.), *Handbook of aging and the social sciences* (4th ed.) New York: Academic Press.

Regnier, V., Hamilton, J., & Yatabe, S. (1995). *Assisted living for the aged and frail: Innovation in design, management, and finances.* New York: Columbia University Press.

Struyk, R. J., Page, D. B., Newman, S., Carroll, M. Makiko, V., Cohen, B., & Wright, P. (1989). *Providing supportive services to the frail elderly in federally assisted housing.* Washington, DC: U.S. Government Printing Office.

Human Factors and Ergonomics

Joseph H. Goldberg

The Pennsylvania State University

R. Darin Ellis

Wayne State University

Compatibility Relationship of stimuli and responses to human expectations.

Contrast Sensitivity Ability to visually distinguish among varying contrasts, defined by spatial frequency gratings.

Cumulative Trauma Disorder (CTD) Musculoskeletal injury of a joint or limb due to repeated motion, high force, and/or awkward postures.

Functional Anthropometry Measurement and specification of physical body dimensions and limitations related to a task or function.

Physical Work Capacity The amount or rate of work that can be tolerated by a specific population over a period of time.

Psychomotor Skill Coordination ability between sensory perception (vision, hearing) and manual skills to accomplish rapid, accurate movements.

Useful Field of View Usable area of an observer's perceived visual field.

Visual Accommodation Ability to properly focus the eye on a near or far object.

Visual Acuity Ability to resolve very fine visual detail at some observation distance.

Visual Angle Angle subtended by a visual object or target.

HUMAN FACTORS AND ERGONOMICS (HF/E) is a scientific and technological field with the objective of optimizing the relationship between people (individuals, groups, and organizations), technology, and the environment. The area is multidisciplinary, with consideration given to machines, workplaces, and products, as well as the psychological, physiological, and psychosocial aspects of people. Safety, efficiency, and well-being may all be improved in human–machine systems by considering the capabilities and limitations of people in product, process, and environmental design. Aging is an important HF/E consideration in workplace and environmental design, despite a general lack of design and database tools for this segment of the population. In the present context, older adults are considered to be those over 55–65 years of age.

I. MOTIVATION FOR HUMAN FACTORS AND ERGONOMICS

Human factors and ergonomics (HF/E) is rooted in early studies of physical work and job design from the late 1800s. World War II strongly pushed the field, spawning significant developments in military training, cockpit design, and human signal detection. More recently, HF/E has also been driven by industrial safety and efficiency concerns, especially with lifting and other heavy physical tasks. Aging is now an important consideration for many HF/E professionals who specialize in gero-ergonomics. Individuals who currently work in the subfield of Geron-technology are specifically interested in developing aids and devices to mitigate declines in strength, mobility, flexibility, and other areas of age-related loss.

Copyright © 1996 by Academic Press, Inc.
All rights of reproduction in any form reserved.

Several laws have strongly pushed the HF/E field to consider gerontological issues. The Older Americans Act (1965) and Age Discriminaton in Employment Act (1967) attempted to enhance age diversity in the workplace. The Occupational Safety and Health Administration (OSHA) Act (1970) mandated employers' responsibilities for safety in the workplace. The Consumer Product Safety Act (1972) mandated strict liability for manufacturers of consumer products, so that all foreseeable consumers or users of a product are protected. The Equal Employment Opportunity Act (1973) further required employers to justify hiring practices when their workforce was not broadly age or gender-diversified. The Americans with Disabilities Act (1990) also aided the cause of older workers by eliminating many types of discrimination, including age biases. The best motivation for installing an HF/E program into job and product design is simply that it is cost effective. Proactive injury prevention through HF/E design and evaluation has already been shown to significantly reduce both direct and indirect costs of employee injuries.

II. HUMAN FACTORS AND ERGONOMICS IN DAILY LIVING

A. Range of Concerns

The HF/E community is very concerned with design and accommodation of older individuals in the products and processes of daily life. Example concerns include difficulty in interpreting information, loss of visual and hearing capability, balance and coordination problems, lowered stamina, difficulty moving the head and limbs, loss of fine finger and upper-extremity skills, difficulty walking, and postural problems.

I. Anthropometry

Tools, products, systems, and environments should be designed to accommodate the largest proportion of a target population as is economically and technologically feasible. Decisions of what proportion of a population segment are accommodated are based on criteria such as cost, safety, and performance. Some designs intentionally accommodate 5th through 95th population percentiles on some human anthropometric dimension, some up to the 90th percentile, whereas others may design for the 50th percentile. Dimensions

also vary between generations. In the presently aging population, a design that accommodated 95% of the population 25 years ago may no longer be adequate, let alone 10 or 20 years from now. There are many sources of design information on the aging population, including data on functional anthropometry, strength and motor performance, vision, hearing, cognitive abilities, and health concerns.

Functional anthropometry data provide valuable information to tool, product, and workspace designers. Examples include age-related changes in hand-grip characteristics or in seated center of gravity. These data have been extensively compiled from military and civilian populations, from many countries. Traditionally measured from static postures, there is a current trend to study individuals in dynamic postures, such as when determining the necessary reach associated with opening a cupboard for a 62-inch stature female. The average older woman's overhead reach is currently 68 inches. This is marginally adequate to reach the contents of the 68-inch top shelf of most grocery stores, but not for the 73-inch top shelf of most domestic cabinets.

Many anthropometric dimensions (but not all) vary as a function of age. After 30 years of age, stature slowly declines due to slow degeneration of the intervertebral disks. The resulting fluid loss from these disks decreases their ability to support and cushion the spine, resulting in loss of stature of about 1 cm per decade. Hip breadth also increases with age. Despite the fact that anthropometric data are extremely useful in designing for today's older population, a better understanding of the longitudinal intraindividual changes in functional anthropometry is needed to design for the body dimensions of future aging populations.

2. Strength, Balance, and Motor Skills

Maximum strength reaches its peak between 25 and 35 years of age, then slowly declines, especially after age 40. The generalized strength loss, compared with an individual in the early thirties, is 20% at 51–55 years and 40% at 71–75 years of age. Physical exercise can greatly lower these strength losses in older adults. Muscle groups are differentially affected, with knee extension and hand grip showing greater age-related loss than trunk or elbow flexion. Larger muscle groups, as in the legs, are also at great risk of age-related decrements. A substantial proportion of the older population has difficulty with certain physical tasks. In a recent 55 to 74-year-old sample of women, over 40% had trouble kneeling or crouching, 30% had trouble lifting 25 pounds, and 12% could not grip objects with their fingers. Most hand strengths peak at 25–30 years of age, then decline; However, certain pinch grip strengths do not show significant declines until after age 60. [See Motor Control.]

Many older adults have great difficulty with balance and motor performance. Walking difficulties, especially ascending and descending steps, mean that appropriate handholds should be installed wherever possible. This is exemplified by a large number of reported falls while in the bath or shower; railings can greatly aid here. Walking on uneven, moving, or swaying surfaces is also quite hazardous for the elderly. Falls in moving transit buses, for example, are the most prevalent bus-related injury in those over 60 years old. The addition of visual cues to enhance one's postural stability control, such as vertical stripes, may reduce these injuries. These vertical stripes could be applied near moving sidewalks, escalators, subway trains, and airplanes. To lessen the injury potential if a fall occurs, new flooring materials are under investigation that will absorb much of the impact of the body; these may eventually become commonplace in the design of housing for the elderly. [See Balance, Posture, and Gait.]

3. Vision

Both vision and hearing exhibit a similar loss pattern as that shown by physical and physiological characteristics; ability peaks in the twenties, remains fairly constant during early adult life, then slowly declines, accelerating after 60 years of age. Older adults are also more likely to be victims of pathology that afflicts the senses.

Age-related visual function changes include declines in static and dynamic visual acuity, near accommodation, contrast sensitivity, resistance to and recovery from glare, dark adaptation, color discrimination, and stereopsis. Declining dynamic aspects of vision are troublesome in daily life, particularly with visual search, viewing moving objects, and viewing stationary objects while the observer is moving. Older adults' useful visual field of view may be substantially smaller than a younger person's on an equivalent task. This can result in reduced ability to divide visual attention, reduced speed of visual processing, and reduced conspicuity of targets against their backgrounds. These can cause poor recognition of cues in one's peripheral visual field, and increase the detrimental effects of interruption during visual search.

A less pliable lens in older adults can lead to deteriorating near vision and visual accommodation, necessitating purchase of reading glasses to bring one's focal point closer to the eye. In addition to changes in lens pliability, there may be an associated atrophy of muscles controlling the pupil diameter. The pupil size is slightly decreased, as well as the range and speed of its adjustment to differing illumination levels. Both increased lens opacity and decreased pupil size result in a two-thirds reduction in light reaching the retina of the eye at age 60, compared with a 20-year-old. In addition, a slight lens yellowing in older people results in more color-matching errors in the blue-green and red regions of the color spectrum. A 2- to 10-fold increase in scattering of light inside older eyes reduces observed contrast even further.

Visually based tasks for older observers must be designed with sufficiently large targets, illumination, and contrast. Compared with a 20-year-old, a 60-year-old will need a three- to four-fold increase in contrast for the same level of visual performance. The need for greater contrast also produces a higher potential for glare in visual tasks. Older individuals are more sensitive to glare, and require more time to recover from glare, compared with younger individuals. For even moderate glare sources (e.g., 100 lux), older individuals require target luminances that are twice as great as that required by younger individuals, to distinguish a visual target from its bright background. [See Vision.]

4. Hearing

Several changes in hearing are expected with increasing age. The high-frequency hearing threshold level (6–8 kHz) increases continuously at a rate of about 1 dB per year over one's life span. Both aging males and females typically experience at least a 25-dB hearing loss from age 20 to 70. After about 50 years, the threshold level increase may reach the speech communication range (500–2000 Hz), which may motivate an individual to seek hearing amplification aids. This threshold increase typically accelerates with age from about 0.4 dB/year in the forties to about 1.3 dB/year in the eighties. For those (typically males) who have experienced excessive and significant occupational and environmental noise, the above hearing losses may approach 40–50 dB at higher frequencies by age 70. [See HEARING.]

5. Cognition

Age-related declines in cognitive information processing are marked by several specific areas of functional loss. There is a generalized slowing in performance and ability to retrieve information from memory. Information in working memory is more easily disrupted by shifts in attention. Learning and recall may be harder, as it is more difficult to transfer information between short- and long-term memories. Spatial, conceptual, and movement-related incompatibilities cause more difficulty for an older than a younger individual. Objects that are visually or acoustically ambiguous or incomplete may also be more difficult to interpret or encode. [See LEARNING; MEMORY.]

Many activities of daily living (ADLs) have major cognitive requirements, such as attention and problem solving. The temporal changes in characteristics of many of the basic abilities that underlie information processing and cognitive performance are well known. The ability to change, modify, store, and interpret information can help HF/E designers choose the appropriate representation of information such as procedural instructions. For example, instructions for the assembly of consumer products are more effective when represented in graphic rather than narrative format.

6. Health

Pathology may induce additional difficulties with the requirements of an independent lifestyle for an older adult. Chronic health problems such as diabetes, hypertension, and arthritis are much more prevalent in older than younger adults. Recent U.S. Department of Health and Human Services estimates conclude that up to 40% of the population over the age of 65 experiences some limitation due to a chronic health condition, and 25% have a limitation in a major activity. There is also a direct and strong correlation between the number of chronic conditions suffered and the probability of requiring assistance in daily life. [See EPIDEMIOLOGY.]

B. Activities of Daily Living

1. Importance of Activities of Daily Living

Maintenance of independent functioning in later life is of great importance, for two reasons. First, loss of independent functioning forces reliance on outside resources, resulting in costs to the dependent individual, their support mechanisms (e.g., family and friends), and society. Second, older adults assign a great value to independence. Loss of independence can result in lower self-esteem and declines in mental health. To help quantify and standardize the assessment of functioning in older adults, scales have been devised to measure the level of difficulty that an individual has with independent functioning in daily life—the ADLs or the physical ADLs (PADLs). There are many variations of these scales in the wording of questions, specific behaviors of interest, and scoring of results, but all share many characteristics.

Problems in conducting ADL tasks are significant in older individuals. About 23% of those over 65 who live at home have difficulty conducting personal care activities, and about 27% need help with home management tasks. Home accidents also account for 43% of home fatalities in those over 65 years of age. Individuals who cannot adequately perform the ADLs are at a much higher risk for a number of negative outcomes, including placement in a long-term care institution, admission to a hospital, or even death. On the other hand, maintenance or improvement in ADL functioning results in positive outcomes, such as the maintenance of (and discharge to) an independent household. By understanding the component tasks required for the ADLs, and facilitating their performance with better designed tools and environments, HF/E professionals can play a significant role in older individual's lives. [See ACTIVITIES.]

2. Physical Activities of Daily Living

The PADLs are designed to describe basic physical functioning on a personal level. Popular scales include the Katz Index, the Barthel Index, and a section of the Older Adult Research and Service Center Instrument. Most agree on necessary assessment scale items—bathing, dressing, feeding, toileting, and transferring. Some scales also include walking ability and continence. In an ADL assessment, individuals are generally rated as higher functioning when able to perform activities with the assistance of self-help devices or environmental modifications. A recent HF/E research development was faucet levers that require much less force than traditional knobs. Anthropometric and strength databases now allow an estimation of the proportion of individuals in different age groups who can use handles of a given configuration.

Current PADL questionnaires are not specific enough to suggest design modifications for devices or environments. In response to this need, some investigators have broken PADLs down into their constituent task components. Using this approach, an individual can now have multiple PADL impairments from one underlying deficit, such as grip strength. Grip impairments could result in lost independence in tasks ranging from dressing and grooming to toileting. Thus, HF/E interventions can now be designed to address the root causes of the problems, rather than their behavioral symptoms.

3. Instrumental Activities of Daily Living

The instrumental ADLs (IADLs) are categories associated with more complex tasks requiring difficult environmental interactions and significant decision making. Typical IADL scale items include shopping for personal items, preparing meals, managing money, using the telephone, and performing light housework. The multidimensionality of IADLs (compared with ADLs) make HF/E recommendations difficult without a better understanding of the possible root causes of problems. To illustrate, there are a number of dimensions on which an individual could have difficulty when shopping. Transportation could be an issue, as when determining which of several buses to take. Carrying shopping bags could exceed an individual's physical capacity. Similarly, meal preparation has cognitive components (e.g., planning, scheduling, and other problem-solving tasks) as well as motor skill and strength requirements (e.g., cutting, peeling, lifting full pans).

4. Assistive Devices and Interventions

Development of assistive devices for older users is a rapidly expanding HF/E area of interest. These interventions can greatly improve the quality of life and the independence of the older adult. For example using HF/E principles developed from redesign of industrial hand tools, prototype cane handles have been redesigned to optimally distribute a user's weight. Reevaluation of bathroom assist bars has resulted in

better choices for material (rubber rather than metal) and grip pattern (raised rings spaced about an inch apart, rather than an etched crosshatch pattern). Future commercial possibilities in this area are very promising.

5. Other Daily Activities

Physical and instrumental ADLs are well-developed constructs in the gerontological literature, and are strongly linked to important outcome measures. However, there is more to daily life than performance of ADLs. For example, medication adherence is not specifically covered in most implementations of the IADLs. Although investigators are making progress with understanding nonadherence, most research work concentrates on social and psychological factors. HF/E professionals, however, have contributed extensively to the process of designing compliance support mechanisms such as automated telephone reminder systems, better prescription labels, and assistive packaging systems. Contributions have also been made to the design of personal emergency response devices and systems, to ensure that they remain effective and easy to use under stressful circumstances.

C. Driving Activities

Driving is crucial to maintaining the independence of individuals, and age-related changes in driving ability are of great concern to the HF/E community. Driving accident rates are quite stable between about 30 and 70 years of age. Over age 70, there is a sharp increase in accident rates of up to 10 times that of a 30-year-old. As a group, older drivers have more traffic accidents, fatalities, and convictions than others, per mile driven. However, they drive many fewer miles than younger drivers, resulting in smaller absolute numbers of accidents. Reducing the number of annual miles driven, driving only in optimal conditions, and in less crowded areas may all enhance the overall safety of older drivers. [*See* ACCIDENTS: TRAFFIC.]

Driving is a visual-manual tracking and control task, with significant decision making and mental workload demands. Models of accident frequency in older adults show mild correlations with loss of ocular health, visual function, useful field of view, and losses in attention. Declining age-related driving performance is generally not due to a higher incidence of visual acuity problems and eye disease normally associated with older drivers, although those with severe binocular loss of acuity have accident and conviction rates twice as great as those with normal visual fields. Glare recovery and contrast sensitivity are stronger than visual acuity in their relationship to older driver accidents. Older drivers that have been in accidents may show some deficits in attentional performance. Examples include failure to heed signs, yielding the right-of-way, safely turning, and problems at intersections. Psychomotor performance changes may reduce the older driver's ability to maintain a position on a roadway, or maintain a constant velocity. Decisions may be slower, as a result of poorer capability to integrate many sources of information. If driving is infrequent in older individuals, there may be loss of cognitive or motor skill, such as the cues preceding a massive slowdown in traffic, or in the judgment of following distance.

Several current design concepts can enhance the safety of older drivers. Clutter on roadways, via signs and unneeded lights, should be reduced to enhance the distinction between important cues, such as traffic lights, and the visual background. Gradual transitions in lighting, as in ingress to and egress from tunnels, can lessen the glare-sensitivity problem. The contrast of controls for automotive displays should be increased to accommodate older drivers. Street signs and roadway information should be clear, large, and provided far in advance of required actions. The technological development of antilock brakes mean that a loss of ability to sense fine brake pedal pressure will not result in a skid.

D. Communication Activities

Age-related hearing loss, due both to the normal aging process and to chronic noise exposure, can be responsible for difficulties in communication with older adults. Older adults require higher speech-to-noise ratios to equal the performance of their younger counterparts. There is an additional potential of disruption when interpreting rapid speech, speech in poor or missing context, or when discriminating sounds presented over noise. Studies of speech intelligibility have quantified older adults' ability to understand common speech in a variety of situations. Decrements in intelligibility rapidly accelerate after age 60, compared with 20-year-olds. A 70-year-old can expect about a 10% decrement under ideal circumstances (i.e., a quiet

room with clear, 120 word-per-minute speech). The decrement increases to 20% with rapid, 300 word-per-minute speech. The presence of background noises increases the decrement to over 30%. Finally, a room with significant reverberation can produce a speech intelligibility decrement of 50% or more in a 70-year-old, compared with a 20-year-old.

Communication activities with older adults should take place in a quiet environment, at a normal speaking pace of less than 200 words per minute. The optimal group size for speech communications is between four and six persons. Furniture should be arranged to facilitate the use of visual cues, such as a speaker's facial expressions or mouth movements. Background noise should be minimized by eliminating music, adding insulation, or by isolating mechanical systems such as heating, ventilation, and air conditioning. Non-speech signals in the high-frequency range (>4000 Hz) should be avoided. Additionally, reverberation and echoes should be minimized, through the use of carpeting, acoustic ceiling tiles, and window coverings.

E. Summary: The HF/E Approach to Facilitating Independent Function

Due to rapidly growing knowledge on the aging process, the HF/E community is well equipped to consider and solve design issues involving older adults. Their user-centered design approach includes both those who are fully independent and those who require assistance. The application of these principles can dramatically increase the quality of life for many older adults.

Systematic and principled improvements in the ability of older adults to maintain independent functioning requires a four-step process. *First,* there must be continued investigation and discovery of the limitations of the older individual when interacting with the tools, systems, and environments of daily life. Part of this task has already been accomplished, in that many nationally representative data sets can be borrowed from the social sciences to determine the most important ADLs for a situation. Finer resolution of analysis should be achieved through task and protocol analysis techniques, two of the more qualitative evaluation techniques used by HF/E professionals. Task analysis is an organized approach for understanding the required user skills for each element of a complex task. Task analysis has already successfully developed task profiles of ADLs, illustrating shared underlying task components such as grip requirements. Protocol analysis, a technique for understanding users' goals and problems while executing a task, provides rich data that is unobtainable by traditional questionnaires and illustrates the diversity of adaptation and compensation. *Second,* after properly defining the design problem, a design solution is developed. This can evolve in a number of different ways. For example, a biomechanical model of the older hand can suggest the optimal design of cooking utensils or garden tools. A cognitive model can suggest proper arrangement of instructions on a medication label or bus schedule. These models can range in formality from analytical formulas, to computer simulations, to simple conceptual representations of behavior. These models should be based on the scientific gerontological and HF/E literature, and rest on sound theoretical underpinnings. *Third,* given an improved, more optimal design from the model, the designed product should be implemented and evaluated in a controlled manner with a group of users. Due to the complexity of ADLs, the use of appropriate experimental control and a representative user sample are of the utmost importance for the intervention to be fully and objectively evaluated. *Finally,* the evaluation results should be fed back into the design process, ensuring that the database is up-to-date and allows for further iterative development of design-oriented models of older adults engaging in daily life.

III. HUMAN FACTORS AND ERGONOMICS IN WORKING LIFE

A. The Aging Workforce

The workforce is aging, and the design of jobs must accommodate the older worker to avoid a national crisis in working efficiency, safety, health, and job satisfaction. Currently, those 55 and over represent about 18% of the population; by 2010, this will grow to about 27%. Recent estimates suggest there will be over 30 million workers over the age of 85 in the year 2000; 25% of the population will be over 65 years by 2024. As the nation continues its changeover from a heavy industrial to a computer-oriented, service economy, the nature of work capabilities and limitations for the older worker must be considered. In addition to a larger proportion of older workers, there are national trends towards abolishing mandatory retirement, and for raising the eligibility age for Social Security. These will effectively require a workplace that can accommodate larger numbers of older individuals.

There is still much unknown HF/E information about older working populations. Studies conducted in an industrial setting may not generalize well to other industrial populations, and results from studies conducted on nonworking older populations may greatly differ from those of working populations. [*See* WORK AND EMPLOYMENT.]

B. Lifting and Strength-Related Jobs

Despite increases in automation, the current practice in many American industries still requires extensive manual handling of materials. Older workers are especially at risk in these activities. In addition to age-related declines in strength, declining resiliency in body tissues effectively reduces the range of motion of older joints. Awkward body postures are less and less tolerable with age. Furthermore, the size, shape, and biomechanical properties (e.g., stiffness and strength) of the older worker's lower back change, making the back more susceptible to damage, especially from repetitive lifting activity. Recommendations to minimize the risk of lifting-related injury in the older worker are much the same, only more restrictive, than those for younger workers. HF/E professionals recommend that workers over the age of 45 should lift 20% less than their younger counterparts. Static postures, asymmetric postures, repetition, and lifts that require wide ranges of motion should all be avoided. Other activities requiring significant support of the body, such as ladder climbing, should also be avoided by older adults.

C. Repetitive Motion Jobs

Older workers are particularly vulnerable to deleterious effects of repetitive motions in the workplace; many studies have shown that the majority of cumulative trauma disorder (CTD) patients are between 40 and 60 years of age. Additionally, cross-sectional studies generally show that older workers are more symptomatic on a given job. Most studies confound the number of years on the job and age, making it difficult to gain independent estimates of age and time on the job as risk factors. However, the decreases in the resiliency of tissues such as muscles, tendons, and ligaments of older workers logically place them at higher risk, independent of time factors. Recent research has identified overexertion as a major risk factor for CTDs in repetitive tasks. With lower physical work capacities, older workers are more likely to overexert themselves on a given job, thus again increasing their risk. Specific factors that are known to affect CTD incidence include amount of motion repetition, posture of the affected joints and limbs, applied force by the limbs, and other individual factors. Control, keyboard, mouse, and switch devices should not require significant strength, acceleration, or dexterity to operate. Significant wrist deviation or flexion also will especially impair hand strength in older individuals.

A Finnish longitudinal study of ergonomic job design reported that blue-collar workers subjected to continuous muscular stress over their working lifetime suffer a significantly greater risk of muscular disability at age 50 compared with members of the same age cohort in sedentary occupations. No other long-term ergonomic studies have been reported, despite the fact that CTDs that develop after several years of repetitive work now account for over 50% of occupational injuries and illnesses.

Little is known about the long-term effects of work-related CTDs. Workers who experience these problems may also be at risk for later problems such as ADL impairment. Additionally, there is some evidence that older workers are less likely to return to work after experiencing a disability. Thus, study populations may have been contaminated with selection bias. As more older workers remain in the work force for longer periods of time, the prevalence of CTDs will continue to increase. If research confirms these contentions, further efforts will need to be placed by HF/E professionals on redesigning tasks and tools to minimize CTD occurrence.

D. Sustained Monitoring and Information-Processing Jobs

Tasks requiring sustained attention and information processing show severe age-related performance declines. Information-processing ability may show lifelong declines that don't become noticeable until later years. Significant individual differences, however, may greatly alter the onset and magnitude of one's decline in information-processing ability. Decision making is an example where older workers tend to take a cautious approach when responding. There may be deliberation in decision making, with active attempts to reduce one's uncertainty. Older workers may show increased safety concerns, and perhaps greater awareness of the potential for deficiencies in products. The older worker may hold a more balanced view of future trends, as well as appropriate strategies to achieve a solution.

Several guidelines are recommended when designing information-processing jobs. Signal-to-noise ratios should be strengthened, by enhancing signal loudness, brightness, and contrast relative to their background. Noise in controls and displays should be reduced. For example, knobs and computer icons should be designed to reduce irrelevant details. Conceptual, spatial, and movement compatibility should be enhanced, to better utilize existing biases and knowledge bases. For example, a display indicating loudness level should increase by moving up or to the right. Divided attention and time-sharing demands should be reduced between concurrent tasks. This implies separating serial subtasks, and providing appropriate confirmation when each is completed. The time allowed between execution of a response and the signal or stimulus for a subsequent response should be increased, or placed under control of the worker. Machine-paced tasks, in general, should be modified so they are self-paced. Finally, the allowed training or practice time should be increased when learning new material.

E. Visual Inspection Jobs

Visual inspection, a type of sustained monitoring job, requires an individual to repeatedly view products to find one or more types of flaws. There may be hundreds of flaw types to remember, and product flow rates may be very high, allowing the inspector only a fraction of a second to make a decision. The occupational characteristics required for these tasks include excellent visual acuity, sustained periods of concentration, excellent memory, adaptability to daily changes in types of flaws and products, and rapid decision making. Despite large age-related declines in these abilities, the visual inspector continues to be a high seniority job provided to the workers with the most company experience.

Several recommendations may be made to improve the inspection performance of the older worker. Specialized and frequent refresher training on types and sizes of defects should be provided to adequately prepare the individual. Slower memory access means that organizational strategies must be developed to allow the worker to have a well-organized understanding of the most common flaws. An environment should be maintained that has few outside distractions, such as noise or other people talking. In some companies, all inspection is conducted in quiet environments away from manufacturing facilities. Inspection should be self-paced, allowing the older worker to spend more time on a part, if required, to make a decision. Adequate contrast and illumination should be maintained. These should be under the control of each individual inspector, if possible, to avoid glare from uncontrolled lighting sources. Adequate rest periods or job rotation, at least once each hour, should be allowed for visual acuity recovery. Regular (e.g., every 6 months) visual acuity, visual lobe, phoria, stereopsis, and color perception evaluations should be conducted to ensure the older worker can adequately see the flaws. Finally, performance feedback should be provided to allow self-adjustment of decision criteria in defect detection.

F. Fatigue and Shiftwork

Aerobic capacity expresses an individual's maximum ability to use oxygen to produce useful physical work. Increasing aerobic capacity allows an individual to produce more work with less oxygen required, resulting in lowered or delayed fatigue in aerobically demanding tasks. Aerobic capacity generally reaches its peak at about 20 years of age, then gradually declines with increasing age. Without specific training, the aerobic capacity at age 65 is about 70% of that at age 25. Three, 30-minute aerobic exercise periods per week typically result in an average increase in the aerobic capacity by 10–20%, thereby reducing the probability that a given workload will result in fatigue for the older worker. Older individuals may gain significant aerobic training advantage even at lower levels of strenuous exercise. Aerobically demanding work is more hazardous to older than to younger workers, in that older workers have more difficulty

regulating the temperature of their bodies. Those over 40 are more likely to experience heat stroke than those under 25, due to a slowed response of the sweat glands and less overall total body fluid.

The combination of age structure of the current workforce and general trend to make personnel decisions based on seniority result in fewer older employees working off-shifts. Two emerging trends will reverse the current situation and result in more older workers on alternative work schedules. First, industries are attempting to adapt to variation in demand through complex rotating shift schedules for all workers. Second, the workforce of many industries is aging, thus younger workers on less desirable schedules will have a higher average age. In addition to increased susceptibility to fatigue from prolonged work, older workers are more susceptible to the disruptive effects of alternative shift schedules. Particularly harmful are disruptions in circadian rhythms and sleep patterns that occur with much greater severity and prevalence in older shift workers.

Fatigue refers to a diminished capacity for performing useful work. Although there are clearly many factors that can lead to fatigue, HF/E professionals are mainly concerned with the capacity for prolonged activity. In many industries, the opportunity for overtime (additional work) is a benefit of high seniority. Also, many new alternative work schedules use fewer workdays, each with longer hours. Although some field studies show no age by length-of-shift interaction on fatigue, the underlying capacity for work is still reduced. Thus older workers can find themselves in the situation of working longer periods with a reduced capacity, compared to their younger counterparts.

G. Computer Jobs

The computer is the most prevalent workplace of the present, and will continue to be a primary focus of work activity for older workers in the future. Given its prevalence, there are few software and hardware design guidelines tailored specifically for the needs of the older worker.

The input and output interface characteristics between the computer and user are especially important for older workers. Special optical lenses (possibly different from reading glasses) may be prescribed for computer workstation tasks. Bright reds and yellows are easier to distinguish than blues and greens on the screen. Sudden changes of lighting should be avoided, to allow the pupil time to respond, and avoid glare situations. Screen glare should be minimized by appropriate placement of monitors and light sources. The screen should be positioned to allow the user to look somewhat (5–15°) downward, through the lower (near vision) lens of bifocals. Visual search requirements should be minimized through simple menu design, and effective screen organization. Interfaces between programs should be consistent and well organized to minimize the recall requirements by the user. Dark letters on a lighter background (negative screen contrast) produces sharper characters and less visual fatigue, but at the possible expense of more background glare.

There is little age-specific research on computer input devices, but a few general recommendations can be made. A mouse is generally better than the keyboard cursor keys for cursor positioning. However, age-related tremor and loss of fine motor ability (especially with very small targets or icons) could be problematic with a very sensitive trackball or mouse. Touch screens are a good option when the screen density requirements are not large. Spatial locations of screen-based controls should be standardized to eliminate difficult visual search.

Design of software dialogs and structures is an important and developing HF/E area of interest. Little consideration has been given to the needs of older computer users, however. In general, program navigation information should be made very clear, and all controls and action choices should be made very clear to the older user. Problematic color combinations should be avoided, and the speed of the interface should be under the control of the user. Similar-looking icons may be easily confused, so directed user testing of older adults is recommended. Icons should also be compatible with the symbology expectations of an older population.

IV. SUMMARY AND NEED FOR RESEARCH

Capabilities and limitations of aging adults are of great interest to HF/E professionals who design, evaluate, and modify products, processes, and environments to accommodate some proportion of the population. The present review has considered how the changing characteristics of aging adults are manifest in both daily and working lives. The vast and varied research literature on the aging process is currently being distilled by the HF/E community. Knowledge of the losses that tend to follow the aging process have led (and will continue to lead) HF/E professionals to develop design guidelines that are more sensitive to older adults. Implementation of these guidelines in homes, daily activities, and the workplace will contribute greatly to the quality of life for older adults.

The scope of HF/E contributions to gerontology is much broader than assisting in the maintenance of basic physical health, safety, and productivity. Many HF/E professionals are involved in the design of devices and systems that can enhance leisure and recreation. These activities consume a much larger proportion of time in daily life than self-care tasks; in fact, only sleeping exceeds the time spent in recreational and leisure activities. Recent developments have improved the ease of use in consumer products such as gardening tools, VCRs, home computers, and medicine bottles. As the HF/E community begins to more broadly conceptualize the "typical user" to include older adults, product designs will become more inherently transgenerational.

The contribution of HF/E to other fields that support elders in maintaining independence is also of note. As an example, the physical workload requirements on individuals in the caring professions (such as nurses and nurse assistants) have been extensively studied. This research and the work practices derived from it can be directly transferred into informational programs for unpaid caregivers, such as friends and family.

Critical needs have been expressed by prominent investigators in the HF/E field. *First,* continued basic research on the capabilities and limitations of older adults must occur, to create a sizable knowledge database of aging characteristics. Areas of need include better knowledge of age-related attentional changes, and adaptation to physical and physiological repetitive work. *Second,* the findings of basic research must be translated into useful recommendations and design guidelines that can be applied to everyday and working life. These must include cognitive and behavioral considerations, in addition to physical and physiological findings. *Third,* improved mechanisms must be implemented for transferring these guidelines into the hands of designers and those who work with older individuals. Three-dimensional computer simulations of people interacting with a defined environment are now well-accepted design tools. Aging should be added as a factor in these databases and simulations, just as anthropometry can be considered now. The advent of such tools will make gerontological design much more accurate, commonplace, and broadly accepted. *Fourth,* areas of age-related performance and safety declines should be investigated for possible assistive devices or other technology to aid older individuals. These developments could define an exciting area of future commercial growth.

BIBLIOGRAPHY

Chaffin, D. B., & Ashton-Miller, J. A. (1991). Biomechanical aspects of low-back pain in the older worker. *Experimental Aging Research, 17(3),* 734–664.

Charness, N., & Bosman, E. (1992). Human factors and age. In F. I. M. Craik & T. A. Salthouse (Eds.), *The handbook of aging and cognition.* Hillsdale, NJ: Erlbaum.

Coleman, R., & Pullinger, D. J. (1993). Special issue: Designing for our future selves. *Applied Ergonomics, 24*(1).

Czaja, S. J. (Ed.). (1990). *Human factors research needs for an aging population.* Washington, DC: National Academy Press.

Czaja, S. J. (Ed.). (1990). Special issue: Aging. *Human Factors, 32*(5).

Garg, A. (1991). Ergonomics and the older worker: An overview. *Experimental Aging Research, 17(3),* 143–155.

Ilmarinen, J., Tuomi, K., Eskelinen, L., Nygard, C., Huuhtanen, P., & Klockars, M. (1991). Summary and recommendations of a project involving cross-sectional and follow-up studies on the aging worker in Finnish municipal occupations (1981–1985). *Scandanavian Journal of Work, Environment, and Health, 17*(suppl. 1), 135–141.

Small, A. M. (1987). Design for older people. In G. Salvendy (Ed.), *Handbook of human factors* (Chapter 4.4). New York: Wiley-Interscience.

Humor

Ronald J. Manheimer

University of North Carolina at Asheville

Humor A disposition or attitude, expressed through laughter, caused by the painless resolution of a contradiction or synthesis of contraries especially concerning topics capable of provoking anxiety or repression.

The elderly have often been the brunt of jokes, even ones told by age peers. Negative **HUMOR** about aging and the elderly focuses on subjects such as sexual impotence, physical ability, and fear of death. Humor is used as a safety valve for suppressed fears and anxieties about human mortality. But there are positive forms of humor about aging and from the elderly themselves. These reflect humility and acceptance of limitations. Wisdom may also be expressed through humor because many of life's deepest insights concern contradictions and paradoxes of experience. Humor may be thought of as a mood, attitude, disposition or way of looking at the world. Humor shows itself in images of the elderly, as a therapeutic device, and as an aspect of cognitive and affective development.

I. CONCEPTS OF HUMOR

A. The Word *Humor*

The word *humor* has a curious history. It comes from the Latin *humere*, meaning "to be moist." In ancient and medieval physiology, there were four fluids or "humors" that functioned in the body: bile, phlegm, choler, and blood. The relative proportions or balance among these humors would determine a person's health and temperament or disposition. Aging, thought the medieval medical authorities, was characterized by increasing dryness and cooling off of the body. Hence, a lack of humor (moistness) was associated with aging and the elderly. Not surprisingly, the characterization of someone as a "dried-up" old woman or man survives to this day.

Modern views of humor transform the medieval material concept of fluids into metaphorical ones. Good humor, an aspect of happiness, continues to suggest the idea of being well balanced. Ironically, the mechanics of humor are based on an initial imbalance, as when we are thrown off guard, surprised by a joke, witticism, irony, double entendre, sight gag, mime, or pratfall. Humor is the resulting disposition of a specific form of the comical. Hence, to understand humor and its connections to aging and the elderly, one must understand the structure of comedy.

B. Aristotle's Concept of Comedy

In lecture notes collected by his pupils and eventually published as *The Poetics,* Aristotle distinguished comedy from tragedy. Both dramatic forms involve a collision of will—usually that of a prominent aristocrat or warrior—with larger social and cosmic forces such as tribal taboos, family allegiances, wars, and injustice. In tragedy, flaws of human character result in pain: disgrace, downfall, and death. The cosmic realm reveals its dominion over human destiny. But, in comedy, the individual painlessly triumphs through tricks, guile, or subterfuge, surviving humiliation, failure, and degradation. What might have been a flaw of personality (e.g., excessive pride, foolishness, impulsiveness, naïveté) becomes, through inversion, a redeeming quality that turns the tide.

Ancient tragedy and comedy have their roots in religious rituals and, like rituals, have the function of releasing anxieties, repressed desires, anger, and other unruly emotions. The dramas teach moral lessons by producing experiences in the audience that, through sublimation in the form of tears or laughter, bring their lives back into harmony with the social order or produce reflection on the need to adapt to radical changes taking place in that order.

The laugh of humor can express many things but, as Aristotle's delineation of comedy shows, humor depends on both a cognitive and affective process, it concerns topics of great seriousness, contraries or contradictions are involved as deviations from the expected produce both surprise and insight. Humor has both "low" and "high" forms, the former based on making fun at someone else's expense (an individual or group), the latter pointing to features of the shared human plight. Although humor can be revelatory, it can also be escapist.

II. NEGATIVE AND POSITIVE HUMOR ABOUT THE ELDERLY

A. Negative Humor about the Elderly

A gerontologist shared the following joke. An old man, a fellow in his mid-eighties, was walking down the street when he heard a voice saying, "Pick me up, pick me up." He looked around, saw nothing, heard the voice again, and looked down. There was a large green frog calling to him. He picked up the frog and held it on his palm as it explained, "I am a beautiful young woman, turned into a frog by a witch, but if you kiss me I will be restored, and if you do so, I will be yours to fulfill your deepest desires and sexual fantasies." He placed the frog in his pocket and walked on. After a few minutes the frog called out to him, "So why don't you kiss me?" To which he replied, "At my age, I'd rather have a talking frog."

The frog story, a comic variation of the traditional folktale of princes and princesses turned by spells into animals, has a special twist in the context of an older protagonist. The expected action, a kiss bestowed, desire fulfilled, is deflected as the story carries the listener to an opposite moral conclusion, one, perhaps, accompanied by laughter signifying the release of tension. The dramatic twist, going contrary to what might be expected, is what gives the joke its element of surprise: pocketing of the frog and the apparently painless jest of indifference toward sexual desire. The joke pokes fun at growing old as a time of impotence. Akin to the etymological connection of the word humor with moistness, frogs, amphibious creatures of wetlands, have often been associated with dampness (as opposed to toads, which are generally dry-skinned), and hence represent the fecundity of youth.

B. Positive Humor of the Elderly

Now consider a second story, not a joke about older people but an anecdote shared by another aging expert in which an older person expresses a self-effacing type of humor.

Researcher Robert Disch of the Brookdale Center on Aging reports his visit to a clothing store on New York's Lower East Side. Entering the establishment, he's greeted by an elderly Jewish man. Disch begins, "I'm looking for ..." But the tailor, throwing up his hands, stops him midsentence, and with a plaintive voice, sighs, "Yes and I'm looking too." Suddenly, says Disch, a clothing store becomes a sanctuary, a suit of clothes, a call to prayer.

C. Ambivalent Humor about Aging

Jokes and comic literature about aging and older persons have a long, mostly negative tradition, perhaps because humor helps deflect anxious thoughts about death and social oblivion. Humor *about* aging can be quite different from the humor *of* a wise older person. The former is often defensive, distancing; the latter is self-revealing, embracing of others. [*See* AGEISM AND DISCRIMINATION.]

A third form of humor related to aging could be characterized as ambiguous, ambivalent, or even tragicomic. An example can be found again within the camp of gerontologists themselves.

As the theme for its 1992 annual conference, the Gerontological Society of America (GSA) chose

"Health Challenges of an Aging Society." To promote the conference theme, the GSA had an artists design posters and postcards. These showed a bespectacled, dignified, older woman in a beautiful flower-print dress in the act of juggling—lungs, liver, heart, intestines! The image could only be described as macabre, a species of the comical. The comedy lies in the absurdly incongruous combination: a well-dressed, dignified person tossing inner organs into the air. The effect is tragicomedy, the humor and pathos reflecting human mortality and morbidity, the difficulty of "handling" illness and health care, and the serious game of juggling health decisions in which policy makers, researchers, scholars, and the elderly are all engaged. Numerous tragicomic depictions of old age can be found in modern literature, such as Beckett's *Crap's Last Tape* and Coburn's *The Gin Game*.

III. THREE CONTEMPORARY ASPECTS OF HUMOR AND AGING

Three aspects of aging-related humor have emerged in recent years: (a) new images of the elderly in popular culture, (b) humor therapy, and (c) a developmental approach to humor and aging.

A. The Elderly in Popular Media

The humor of older people has gained prominence in feature films (e.g., *Cocoon, Fried Green Tomatoes, Grumpy Old Men*), TV sitcom characters (e.g., *Golden Girls, The Simpsons, Murder, She Wrote*) and characters in newspaper comics (e.g., *Shoe, Family Circus, For Better or Worse*). In many of these elements of popular culture the old are portrayed sympathetically as heroes and heroines, mentors, or as cynical, sometimes ironic, commentators on life and society. They are also portrayed stereotypically as petty, preoccupied, isolated, depressed, and sick. [*See* IMAGES OF AGING.]

B. Humor as Therapy

A recent national movement espousing the therapeutic benefits of laughter caught the attention of gerontologists who discovered how comedy could advance "positive aging," even in a nursing home. Ever since Norman Cousins's 1976 book, *Anatomy of An Illness,* told the story about how "I Love Lucy" TV episodes and film comedies helped him recover from a crippling disease, humor's therapeutic value has climbed the charts of health-care providers. The multiple uses of humor have turned into humor programs, laugh kits, and other techniques for lightening people's lives, enhancing their immune systems, and relieving stress. These techniques have been applied with the elderly.

A 1989 study, the Clemson Humor Project, attempted to prove empirically what had been reported anecdotally, that humor could be used to improve seniors' lives. The study brought humor to the nursing homes through having the residents watch film comedies over a period of months. They, in turn, were compared with a group that watched serious movies, and a control group that watched no movies at all. Researchers findings were mixed: comedy watchers showed increases on happiness and life satisfaction indices compared to the other groups but no effect in areas of adaptation and adjustment. Moreover, although the control groups showed decreased depression, the comedy watchers experienced an increase in depression.

A study reported in 1986 asked patients recovering from cataract surgery to rate a variety of jokes read to them. Faster recovery rates correlated positively with males who ranked high on scores derived from enjoyment of the jokes. Were the jokes a cause of improvement? The study was not definitive.

Although humor as therapy may be beneficial in some situations, it may be inappropriate in others. As Mildred Seltzer pointed out in her article in *The Encyclopedia of Adult Development*: "the attempt to put humor into utilitarian harness does not necessarily either add pleasure or heighten effectiveness."

C. Humor Viewed Developmentally

The eminent twentieth-century philosopher, Ludwig Wittgenstein, asserted that humor was not a mood but "a way of looking at the world." Some experts have asserted that in order to achieve this *weltanschauung*, one's sense of humor may reflect cognitive and moral developmental stages of later life. For example, research has shown the correlation between mastery of advanced levels of cognition and the person's ability to "get the joke."

Could the capacity for humor be an aspect of life-course development, even be a stage of life? Freud and Danish philosopher Søren Kierkegaard thought so. Following Wittgenstein's edict, we begin with a way of looking at the world—a story.

Rising to give his report, a tall, tweed-jacketed senior adjusts his reading glasses, brushes the grey hair from his forehead, and nods at the members of the learning in retirement institute board of directors. Clearing his throat, he begins, "Before giving the long-range planning committee report, I have to preface my remarks." He pauses, smiles knowingly at the expectant faces and continues. "For me, long-range planning means what am I going to do when I get up tomorrow." Everyone laughs. The gentleman goes ahead with his report.

The man in the tweed coat communicates indirectly, through humor, his recognition of the limits of life and expresses a tone of humility shared with fellow time travelers. Laughing at someone and laughing with him is the distinction between humor that sets people apart and that which brings them together. Humor that accepts aging and the contributive role of seniors, can reflect a perspective on life that reveals the smile of wisdom.

Although it might not be possible to convert the humorless of any age, appreciation for humor does seem to deepen and grow more complex as some people age. Greater tolerance of ambiguity and the ability to handle multiple viewpoints and paradoxical life experiences may make one a better humor follower. Those with a great sense of timing may become skilled initiators of humor.

Sigmund Freud recognized humor's positive contribution to mental health. Laughter, Freud asserted, using the early twentieth-century metaphor of the steam engine, is an outlet for psychic or nervous energy. Like a system of pressures, the release valve, laughter, could go off when a person felt that the need to suppress anger or sexual feelings might not be necessary. The energy no longer needed to repress emotion or thought would be discharged in the form of laughter. This could be accomplished, Freud said, in three ways: through jokes or witticisms, by means of the comic, or through humor. Jokes are usually made at someone else's expense. The comic often involves our pleasure at watching someone perceived as inferior, such as the "tramp" Chaplin, the Three Stooges, or the *schlemiel* Woody Allen, to name a few.

But, claimed Freud, the third form, humor, is of another sort. Humor, says Freud, has in it a liberating element that makes it both "fine and elevating." Humor is a way of looking at ourselves that expresses the "triumph of narcissism, the ego's victorious assertion of its own invulnerability." To Freud, humor is not a statement of resignation but a bolt of rebelliousness. Humor rejects the necessity of suffering and, through a shift of perspective, enables one to attain or retain a sense of personal dignity.

Freud's account of jokes or wit, the comic, and humor suggests psychological development: the person moves from a simpler to a more complex expression of laughter. Does capacity for a humorous perspective on life increase with maturation or is it rather a personality trait? Freud doesn't comment, but nineteenth-century Danish philosopher, Søren Kierkegaard, thought humor was an achieved perspective. In fact, he made humor one of his "stages on life's way."

Kierkegaard proposed three "spheres of existence": the aesthetic, the ethical, and the religious. Each "life attitude" is shaped by subjectively different experiences of time. Two additional, transitional stages, irony and humor, completed his theory.

The aesthetic-oriented person delights in sensuous beauty and the enjoyment of what, today, one might call "peak" experiences. But such timeless moments are fleeting and lead to disappointment: peaks are exactly that, they lead to valleys. Sobered by such truths, the ironist steps back from life, adopting an aloof, defensive posture. He or she is not going to be taken in by false hopes and ephemeral thrills. The ironist pretends to be above it all, but it's a lonely place.

The prolonged drama of late adolescence is a learning experience of life's fundamental incongruity: humans are creatures of both the possible and the necessary, the finite and infinite. Our dual nature makes us all part of a human comedy. One can despair about this or choose to belong to the "universally human."

Joining the world of ethical responsibility, the mature adult discovers that marriage, a career, family, and community responsibilities can bring an inner-time sense of enduring and deepening appreciation of life, despite its ups and downs. But, according to Kierkegaard, even the ethical sphere of personal fulfillment based on leading a morally good life has its impediments. Midlife brings with it increased awareness of death, recognition of personal limitations, and the nagging question, Is this all there is? Hence, the quest continues. But now with humility overtaking pride.

Between the ethical and religious sphere is a crucial transitional one—the stage of humor. And it corresponds, roughly, with middle age and later life.

Kierkegaard did not draw a direct parallel between life stages and chronological age. But, in some of his novel-like books, he invented fictional characters who approximate youth, adulthood, and midlife. For several of his seriously philosophical works (e.g., *Philosophical Fragments* and the *Concluding Unscientific Postscript*) he chose the pseudonym Johannes Climacus, one who aspires to climb a ladder of self-knowledge, who calls himself a "humoristic experimenting psychologist."

In these works, Kierkegaard focuses on the paradox of human longing for stability, security and happiness while acknowledging the ways finitude encroaches on these aspirations. The unique disposition of the humor stage is reconciliation with the experience of being a finite creature. Looking back on one's ethical attainments, the individual feels greater humility. Acknowledging the possibilities of further development toward the religious stage, the individual continues to experience the longing for completeness but now knows that it cannot be reached through acts of will, through reason or through feeling.

IV. HUMOR, AGING, AND CREATIVITY

A. Koestler on Humor and Creativity

Adding to the appreciation of humor, Arthur Koestler, in *Act of Creation,* saw remarkable similarities between humor and creativity. Scientific discoveries and jokes both involved holding incongruous facts and ideas together in such a way that a new insight may be born. Koestler termed the common element of humor and creativity *bisociation.* When Einstein climbed aboard a trolley and discovered the analogy he had been seeking for the theory of relativity, one could imagine that Einstein's "aha!" was quickly followed by "ha, ha." Indeed, the laugh of creativity goes back to the bible.

B. Biblical Humor and an Elderly Couple

An ancient laugh reaches us from the chapter of *Genesis.* The primal parents of the Jewish people, Abraham and Sarah, are dwelling in desert tents when three nomadic visitors who are heavenly messengers suddenly show up. Sarah is sitting discretely behind the flap of her tent as one of the messengers tells Abraham that Sarah will soon be with child. This is a remarkable prophecy. Sarah is childless and ninety-years-old and Abraham is close to 100. Even by biblical standards, they are old. Now a divine voice already promised Abraham that not only a child but a whole people would descend from the couple. On that occasion, Abraham had "laughed in his heart." But now, Sarah laughs out loud. The messengers point an accusing finger. How dare she laugh. Sarah denies it though her doubts are certainly reasonable. Nevertheless, it turns out the angels are right. A few sentences later, the proud parents are naming the child Yitzchak (Isaac), from the Hebrew root *to laugh.*

For centuries, biblical scholars have argued over Sarah's laugh. Some hear in it the laugh of sarcasm, others that of doubt, ridicule, or incredulity. These interpretations fail to grasp the mythical quality of the story. Through an imaginative leap, the story links the listener to the story of how God created the world. Sarah and Abraham's laughs echo the creation story: how a world comes forth out of nothing. The birth of Isaac is a human parallel to the surprise of divine creativity. Sarah's becomes the laugh of joy.

V. HUMOR AND WISDOM

From the bible to George Burns, the laughter and humor of older people deal with some of the most serious and difficult of subjects: fertility, sexuality, birth, family, aging, death and wisdom. Seniors' humor can teach us that laughter is a basic human response and humor a natural way of coping.

The first century Jewish historian, Philo, grasped the connection. "If someone has experienced the wisdom that can only be heard from oneself, learned from oneself, and created from oneself, he does not merely participate in laughter: he becomes laughter itself." Achieving enlightened laughter may not be possible for everyone, but when one hears the laugh of the wisely old, one can at least listen and search for smiles of his or her own.

BIBLIOGRAPHY

Aristotle. (1967). *Poetics.* Ann Arbor: University of Michigan Press. (Original work published ca. 335 B.C.)

Cousins, N. (1976). *Anatomy of an illness.* New York: W. W. Norton.

Freud, S. (1959). *Humor: Collected papers.* New York: Basic Books.

Kierkegaard, S. (1941). *Concluding unscientific postscript.* (David F. Swenson, Trans.). Princeton, NJ: Princeton University Press.

Kierkegaard, S. (1962). *Philosophical fragments.* (Howard V. Hong, Trans.). Princeton, NJ: Princeton University Press.

McGuire, F. A., Boyd, R. K., & James, A. (1992). *Therapeutic humor with the elderly.* New York: Haworth Press, Inc.

Monk, R. (1990). *Ludwig Wittgenstein, the duty of genius.* London: Penguin Books.

Morreall, J. (Ed.). (1987). *The philosophy of laughter and humor.* Albany: State University of New York Press.

Morreall, J. (Ed.). (1983). *Taking laughter seriously.* Albany: State University of New York Press.

Scott-Maxwell, F. (1968). *The measure of my day.* New York: Knopf. "When a new disability arrives I look about to see if death has come, and I call quietly, 'Death, is that you? Are you there?' So far the disability has answered, 'Don't be silly, it's me'" (p. 36).

Seltzer, M. (1993). Humor. In R. Kastenbaum (Ed.), *The encyclopedia of adult development* (pp. 222–228). Phoenix: Oryx Press.

Tennant, K. (1986). The Effects of Humor on the Recovery Rate of Cataract Patients: A Pilot Study. In L. Nahemow, K. McCluskey-Fawcett, & P. McGhee (Eds.), *Humor and aging.* Orlando, FL: Academic Press.

I

Identity, Physical

Susan Krauss Whitbourne and Lisa A. Primus

University of Massachusetts at Amherst

Emotion Focused Coping An attempt to change the way one thinks about or appraises a stressful situation rather than changing the situation itself.

Identity Accommodation Changing one's identity in response to identity-relevant experiences.

Identity Assimilation The interpretation of life events relevant to the self in terms of the cognitive and affective schemas that are incorporated in identity.

Multiple Threshold A model predicting intraindividual variation in response to changes associated with the aging process.

Physical Identity The mental representation of one's own body that includes three components: the perception of one's *appearance*, one's *competence*, and one's *health*.

Problem-Focused Coping An attempt to reduce stress by changing the stressful situation.

The construct of **IDENTITY** has been used in the area of adult development and aging to refer to an individual's sense of self over time. Identity is conceptualized as incorporating various content areas, including physical functioning, cognition, social rela-

tionships, and experiences in the world. In this model identity is theorized to form an organizing schema through which the individual's experiences are interpreted. The affective content of identity, for psychologically healthy adults, takes the positive self-referential form encapsulated in the expression "I am a competent, loving, and good person"; competent at work, loving in family life, and morally righteous. Over time, identity is theorized to remain consistent, but also to be responsive to changes in the individual's experiences.

A major focus within gerontological research concerns the effects of the aging process on the body's functioning. In view of the extensive research on physical aspects of the aging process, it is somewhat surprising that the psychological implications of these physical changes are as yet relatively unexplored. Investigations of the relationship between physical health and psychological well-being pertain only very generally to the question of how changes in the body affect the individual's sense of self, self-esteem, and ultimately, subjective well-being. Left unanswered are questions regarding more precise links between physical changes that result from aging and the objective and subjective ways that individuals adapt to these changes. The theoretical perspective stemming from the concept of identity can provide the basis for understanding how the individual's physical sense of self is affected by the aging process. [*See* SELF-ESTEEM.]

The individual's experiences, both past and present, are postulated to relate to identity through processes of assimilation and accommodation. The process of identity assimilation is defined as the interpretation of life events relevant to the self in terms of the cognitive and affective schemas that are incorporated in identity. The events and experiences to which the assimilation function applies can include major life events, cumulative interactions with the environment over time, or minor incidents that can have a potential impact on identity. Each type of experience can have different meanings across individuals depending on the nature of their current self-conceptualizations in identity. The process of identity accommodation, by contrast, involves changing one's identity in response to these identity-relevant experiences.

I. PHYSICAL IDENTITY AND AGING

In previous analyses of identity assimilation and accommodation, the underlying assumption has been that events or experiences serve as stimuli in relation to identity over single points in time. An event that reflects unfavorably on one's identity is likely to be processed first through assimilation, and only after such efforts prove unsatisfactory will identity accommodation follow. As a general principle, it is theorized that a healthy state of adaptation involves a balance or equilibrium between the two identity processes. Overreliance on one or the other identity process can have a number of maladaptive consequences. In terms of the aging body, it seems particularly important that this balance be maintained. If it is not, there can be significant health consequences as well as influences on the individual's well-being.

The aging process presents a particular challenge to the maintenance of a stable physical identity over time. Events caused by the physical aging process are qualitatively different from other experiences in adulthood that are of a more transitory or fleeting nature. An unpleasant encounter in a chance meeting with a stranger that reflects unfavorably upon one's social identity may be dismissed through identity assimilation as not having much personal relevance. If this encounter is of a one-time nature, its potential significance to identity will fade with time. Aging, however, is a process that does not fade with time. The changes that occur as a result of the aging process remain present and may in fact grow with importance as the individual must find ways to integrate them into identity throughout adulthood.

II. THE MULTIPLE THRESHOLD MODEL

A related theoretical concept that can inform the understanding of physical identity in later life is that of the multiple threshold model. According to this model, individuals approach changes in physical and cognitive functioning associated with the aging process as a function of their own unique identities. Each individual has as central to identity a set of physical and cognitive functions that are of particular importance to that individual. For example, the person for whom playing tennis forms a central focus of identity either as a professional endeavor or a valued leisure time activity values the combination of physical agility and mental judgment demanded by the game. The artist values visual and fine motor skills, the gardener relies on being able to dig in the dirt, and the word-game fanatic cherishes the functions of memory and language. For each individual, a particular set of age-related changes will have relevance to this central feature of identity. According to the multiple threshold model, individuals monitor age-related changes in each of these central physical or cognitive functions. These changes are anticipated through a process of vigilance, in which the individual watches and prepares for expected age-related changes in multiple, central functions. Although the aging process brings with it many changes in physical and cognitive functioning, changes in these central functions are the ones that will have maximum salience and impact for the individual. The tennis player remains vigilant for changes in strength or the ability to move around the court; the artist monitors the sense of color perception and the use of fine motor abilities. Changes in these areas will be primarily those that stimulate the identity processes of assimilation and accommodation.

Looking specifically at physical identity in this context, it follows that the aspects of physical functioning most salient to the individual will be the ones that the individual prepares for, tries to prevent, or reacts to when they inevitably occur. Physical identity may further be conceptualized in terms of its subcomponents. Although there is little research and theory on the concept of physical identity per se, it is recognized that the sense of self with regard to physical characteristics is a feature of the self-concept. Furthermore, there is a fairly well-established tradition within psychology regarding the concept of body image. The term body image may be thought of in the narrow sense as the mental representation of one's own body and, for example, may be regarded as a problematic area in certain eating disorders in which the individual has an inaccurate body image. However, recent theorists regard body image more generally as incorporating constructs that may be thought of as synonymous with physical identity. Three components of physical identity can be extrapolated from these investigations. They are the perception of (a) the appearance of one's own body; (b) competence, or the body's ability to perform tasks needed in daily activities; and (c) physical health as a reflection of the individual's risk of mortality. All three of these facets of physical identity can be seen as potential threshold areas. The individual who values appearance will be most sensitive to the effects of aging on outward indicators such as skin texture and hair color. The individual for whom competence in performing physical tasks is most salient will be most reactive to age effects on mobility and strength. Health concerns may be translated into sensitivity to both normal and age-related changes in physical functioning that pertain to the individual's own mortality. Indeed, compared with younger adults, changes in health status are monitored more closely in older adults. There is evidence that concern over negative health changes actually begins earlier than old age and that middle-aged adults anticipate with fear the projected diminution of health and physical abilities.

These experiences in later adulthood that are relevant to physical identity can take place within a number of contexts of adult life, including relationships with family, the performance of job-related duties, leisure involvement, and interactions with friends and acquaintances. Events in the outside world may also have relevance as these influence the individual's ability to function on a daily basis. For example, changes in funding of public transportation can limit the older individual's mobility in an urban setting, further complicating any age-related changes that interfere with self-care and autonomy. [See LEISURE; SOCIAL NETWORKS, SUPPORT, AND INTEGRATION.]

III. CHANGES IN PHYSICAL IDENTITY: APPEARANCE

How individuals react to changes in valued aspects of physical identity may be seen as a function of whether they rely primarily on identity assimilation or identity accommodation. Theoretically, individuals who use identity assimilation would be expected to deny as much as possible the importance of age-related changes in valued aspects of *physical functioning*. Changes in functioning that are related to age are not acknowledged as a result of the aging process, but instead are attributed to transitory states of health or health-related behaviors. This type of denial occurs as an effort, both conscious and unconscious, to preserve and protect the individual's sense of the self as competent and consistent over time. Those older adults who rely more or less exclusively on identity accommodation overreact to small events or experiences and draw overly broad and sweeping conclusions from one instance or situation. With regard to aging, they would be expected to overreact even to small age-related changes, prematurely concluding that they are "over the hill." The individual may start to "feel old" as soon as these external changes begin to occur. It is likely that individuals who rely on accommodation begin to adopt the self-image of being too weak or feeble to continue to maintain their participation in activities that were formerly rewarding to them. A balanced approach to adapting to age-related changes in valued aspects of physical functioning involves taking precautions and attempting to preserve functions for as long as possible, and adapting to them when they occur by finding ways to compensate for losses. The individual may find a compromise between assimilation and accommodation by recognizing that aging is taking place but not letting this knowledge interfere with daily functioning or future plans.

The existing age-relevant research on body image may be examined from the standpoint of the multiple threshold model and, in particular, the three components of bodily identity. The benefits and risks of identity assimilation and accommodation as processes involved in the interaction of physical aging with changes in identity can also be described. With regard to the component of identity involved in appearance, it is clear that the signs of aging are most apparent in the outward features of the individual's face and body. It is a commonplace occurrence for an older adult to reflect on the fact that he or she feels young on the "inside" but appears old on the "outside." Viewing one's white hair and wrinkles in the mirror or having others label one as "elderly" are experiences that become increasingly prevalent with age. Appearance is also relevant to identity because it is tied to a sense of continuity of the self over time and to feelings of self-esteem. The changes associated with aging can lead to increased self-consciousness of one's own age as reflected in the visible appearance of face and body, and in decreased satisfaction with one's appearance. Appearance is also important in interpersonal relationships. It is a well-established finding that people who are attractive are perceived as having favorable psychological qualities and are thus more desirable. A negative focus on appearance is more likely to occur in women, particularly those in their fifties, for whom changes in appearance become the major concern for physical identity. This gender effect may be due to the "uneven" aging of men and women in American culture and the greater value placed on youthful attractiveness in women.

Contributing to the aging of appearance are changes in the individual's skin, hair, facial structures, and body build associated with the aging process. For the most part the effect of these changes is cosmetic, although there are ramifications of the aging of these structures for the individual's overall physical functioning. For example, changes in the texture of the skin can compromise the protective function of the skin against extremes of temperature. Comparisons of present appearance with pictures or memories of early adulthood can be damaging to self-esteem to people who valued their youthful image. At the same time, young people may be repulsed by the wrinkles, discolorations, and white hair of the older person, causing the aged individual to feel rejected and isolated. These changes involve primarily the face, but can also include changes in exposed areas of the body. With regard to body build, changes in body fat and muscle tone that lead to the appearance of a sagging or heavier body shape can result in increased identification of the self as moving away from the figure of youth. The development of "middle-aged spread" is one of the first occurrences to trigger recognition of the self as aging, even before the first gray hairs have become fully evident.

Identity processes can affect the steps that individuals take to slow, compensate for, or correct the changes in appearance caused by aging of the skin. Denial or rejection of the reality of outward changes in appearance through overreliance on identity assimilation may take the form of the individual's continu-

ing to dress in ways that are more characteristic of younger adults. Such individuals continue to think of themselves as "young" even though others see them as "old." The individual who relies overly heavily on accommodation reacts to even small age-related changes such as graying of the hairs in the temple or the first development of noticeable wrinkles by giving up in despair over daily activities that can maintain and promote attractiveness. In such cases, the individual feels that there is no point in attempting to control or monitor facial and bodily appearance. Individuals with a balanced approach to changes in appearance would be expected to acknowledge that these changes are occurring, but not to overreact. They would be expected to adapt gradually, using compensatory or preventative methods when possible. The individual may take advantage of appropriate strategies to maximize his or her attractiveness, stopping short of trying to look like a teenager. The primary method of prevention, which must be started early in life, is for fair-skinned people to avoid direct exposure to the sun and to use sun blocks when exposure cannot be avoided. Cigarette smoke can also be harmful to the skin. Individuals for whom changes in outward appearance are important would be likely to take advantage of these preventative measures. These individuals would also be more likely to compensate for age-related changes in the skin once they have become manifest such as using particular cosmetics to counteract the fragility, sensitivity, and dryness of the skin. When the individual's "threshold" includes changes in bodily build, regular involvement in activities and exercise that maintain muscle tone and reduce fat deposits under the skin can successfully serve as compensatory measures.

IV. CHANGES IN PHYSICAL IDENTITY: COMPETENCE

Bodily competence as a component of identity is more likely to be a function of the individual's mobility and strength, which in turn depend on the strength of muscles and bones, and the flexibility of joints. Competence as a feature of body image is particularly likely to have importance to men in their fifties, but remains of concern throughout old age in terms of the individual's feelings of self-efficacy regarding mobility. Interestingly, in terms of the threshold model, older adults in general seem to be more positive in evaluating their body competence than their appearance.

Changes in the structures that support movement have many pervasive and direct effects on the individual's life, resulting in restrictions in activity and pain, which can interfere with the individual's psychological adaptation and sense of well-being. In part, the effects of mobility loss can be attributed to the enforced reliance on others that is created, leading to other deleterious processes such as being treated like a dependent child. One of the most deleterious outcomes of reduced muscle strength, bone strength, and joint mobility is the heightened susceptibility of older individuals, particularly women, to falls and to serious consequences resulting from falls. Falls that result in a hip fracture are common among the elderly. The seriousness of this problem is evident when one considers that over 250,000 older Americans are hospitalized each year for treatment of a fractured hip. In response to an episode of falling, individuals may overaccommodate to falls by developing a fear of falling or lowered sense of self-efficacy regarding the ability to avoid a fall. Ironically, a result of lowered self-efficacy is a further lowering of postural stability, as they avoid physical activities that might benefit their strength and stability. Understandably, these individuals are vulnerable to feelings of depression and anxiety. Other adults may react to falls in an assimilative manner, repressing their occurrence, and in the process placing themselves at risk for further serious injury as they ignore possible warning signs or indications of danger. [See ACCIDENTS: FALLS.]

With regard to muscle strength, there is a continuous loss of muscle fiber throughout the years of adulthood. However, counteracting the picture of inevitable decline in muscle strength is evidence, accruing from the 1970s, showing that a regular program of exercise can help the middle-aged and older adult compensate substantially for the loss of muscle fibers. Although there is nothing that can be done to stop the loss of muscle cells, the remaining fibers can be strengthened and work efficiency increased through exercise training even in persons as old as 90 years. Individuals who adopt a balance between assimilation and accommodation will be able to recognize the importance of maintaining their fitness without becoming overly discouraged and will take advantage of these measures. Those who deny the importance of

aging changes in bone and muscle, or who feel that there is nothing they can do to alter the aging process, are more likely to fall into patterns of inactivity. [See NEUROMUSCULAR SYSTEM.]

V. CHANGES IN PHYSICAL IDENTITY: HEALTH

The component of bodily identity relating to health can be best understood in terms of available research on cardiovascular (CV) functioning. The adequacy of the CV system is reflected in the individual's ability to engage in a range of physical activities, including walks outside, moving about the house, carrying heavy objects, and engaging in strenuous exercise. Reductions in the CV system's functioning therefore contribute importantly to changes in the structures underlying movement to reduce, potentially, the individual's mobility in the physical environment. In addition, although not as apparent in its effects on identity as appearance, the functioning of the CV system is an important influence on the individual's feelings of well-being and identity. Many individuals interpret changes in this system, whether due to disease or to normal aging changes, as significant for the viability of the body, or its ability to sustain life. Feelings of mortality are perhaps most closely linked to this system. All adults know that the efficiency of the CV system is essential to life so that threats to the integrity of this system are perceived as highly dangerous. Awareness of reduced CV efficiency can therefore serve as reminders of one's own personal mortality.

Given the importance of CV functioning to the overall health and longevity of the individual, there has been a wealth of research pointing to the effectiveness of exercise in slowing or reversing the effects of the aging process on the system. In addition to the benefits that exercise training has for the CV system, it is well established that adults who become involved in aerobic activities experience a variety of positive effects on mood, anxiety levels, and particularly feelings of mastery and control, leading to enhanced feelings of self-esteem. Again, following the logic of the multiple threshold model, it might be expected that individuals who focus particularly on the functioning of this system would be more alert to signs of noticeable changes in capacity or perhaps concomitant health problems. Those who are able to adapt to these changes without becoming despondent and can take advantage of exercise programs should, in turn, be less likely to suffer further detrimental losses. An assimilative approach involving denial of the existence of age changes in CV functioning could cause the individual real bodily harm due to overexertion. Older persons who are not in good shape but who shovel a walk after a snowstorm (ignoring advice not to do so), place themselves at great physical risk. Conversely, those who overaccommodate and believe that exercise or dietary controls cannot stop the inevitable decline of aging will not take advantage of these health-promoting activities. [See CARDIOVASCULAR SYSTEM.]

Maintenance functions of the body relating to patterns of digestion, excretion, and sleeping also have the potential to affect the individual's physical identity and can serve a "threshold" function for those who are particularly sensitive to their schedules of eating and elimination. Both are areas that have tremendous social significance as well and are highly subject to attitudinal influences. Thus, changes in the digestive system at the physiological level due to the aging process itself are minimal in terms of their effect on the individual's adaptation. However, inaccurate conceptions communicated through the media may lead older persons to misuse laxatives, avoid roughage, and become overly preoccupied with minor digestive upsets. What originates as a temporary bout of indigestion or constipation can thereby come to have a more prolonged course. The individual who uses assimilation in approaching the aging of the digestive system may in some ways benefit from this strategy compared to the older person who overreacts to media messages of doom. [See GASTROINTESTINAL SYSTEM: FUNCTION AND DYSFUNCTION.]

Concerns about bladder functioning present a somewhat different challenge. Age-related changes in the bladder may lead the individual to experience reduced ability to control leakage or spillage, and for men changes in the prostate can lead to pain or discomfort when urinating. These changes can be highly disruptive to the older individual's everyday life, causing subjective distress and embarrassment in social situations, and they are difficult to assimilate into identity. The risk the individual faces is that through overaccommodation, the individual develops an exaggerated fear of becoming incontinent that further exacerbates any changes

due to aging. A more balanced approach involves using compensatory strategies that allow the individual to use behavioral methods proven to be effective in controlling continence. [See RENAL AND URINARY TRACT FUNCTION.]

With regard to sleep patterns, interactions between normal aging changes and identity are also of importance. Again, individuals may monitor their sleep patterns as they age, particularly if they have experienced sleep difficulties at any earlier point in life. When they do start to experience changes in sleep patterns, they may take steps that actually worsen their problems. One of the most damaging effects on sleep is anxiety over insomnia, a condition that might well develop in individuals who have believed all their lives that 8 hours of sleep is the normal human need rather than the 7 hours that the average adult actually sleeps. The longer the time spent in bed awake, the harder it will be for the individual to develop a normal nightly rhythm based on this more realistic sleep requirement. It is known that older adults sleep the same number of hours as younger adults, but they spend more time in bed relative to time spent asleep due to longer time taken to fall asleep, more periods of wakefulness during the night, and time spent lying awake before arising in the morning. Yet, if the older person believes that it is necessary to sleep more, or to sleep more continuously, he or she may react to aging changes in sleep patterns by taking inappropriate corrective measures that actually worsen the problem.

Finally, in the area of sexual functioning, all components of bodily identity may be seen as potentially affected by changes due to the aging process. One's appearance is involved to the extent that sexual behavior incorporates aspects of physical attractiveness. The sense of competence also plays a role as the individual may derive feelings of potency from being able to engage in sexual relations. Finally, feelings of health and mortality may also be related to sexual functioning in that individuals may associate the loss of reproductive capacity with the inevitable movement of the body toward death in the postreproductive years. Vigilance regarding the monitoring of these changes may be expected to vary according to the importance attached to sexuality throughout the individual's adult life.

Although there are documented age effects on the

physiological aspects of sexual functioning, these are relatively minimal compared to the psychological associations that individuals have to their own sexual behavior patterns. For women, the impact of loss of reproductive capacity is more obvious due to the disappearance of monthly cycles and the associated loss of ovulation. Women who overaccommodate to this change are likely to take a very dim view of their sexuality, regarding their bodies as wasted and useless. Assimilation of age-related changes in reproductive capacity may, in this regard, have a beneficial effect on identity, as the loss of reproductive capacity in and of itself need not cause age reductions in the enjoyment of sexual relations. Although the aging male is likely to be less preoccupied by his diminished (but not lost) reproductive capacity, he may also find age-related changes to have a negative impact on his enjoyment of sexual relations. He may write himself off as a sexual partner, believing that his masculine prowess has failed. Furthermore, the slowing down that is likely to occur in his sexual functioning may serve as signs that his body is deteriorating and death is around the corner. As is true for any man regardless of age, depression, heavy alcohol use, or late-life career pressures may also interfere with the aging male's ability to enjoy sexual relations. By overaccommodating to age-related changes, the individual may therefore bring about the very changes in sexual enjoyment that he or she has dreaded.

If the aging individual is distressed about changes in the body's appearance, he or she can use cosmetics and creative clothing strategies to disguise or compensate for them. However, changes in the individual's sexual appearance that are visible only to oneself or one's intimate partner may constitute a different set of challenges. It may be embarrassing for the older person to seek the emotional support and reassurance of the partner or even peers about the changing appearance of the body. On the other hand, as the partners in a relationship age together, seeing the changes that both undergo as a result of the aging process may provide a sense of comfort and companionship. A balance between assimilation and accommodation can allow the individual to avoid becoming overly concerned about age changes in sexuality while at the same time recognizing that adaptations must be made if one is to continue to enjoy satisfying sexual relations. [See SEXUALITY, SENSUALITY, AND INTIMACY.]

VI. PHYSICAL IDENTITY AND COPING

The propositions regarding specific areas of physical functioning and their relationship to identity come largely from theoretical analysis and clinical observation, although research in this area is beginning to proceed. Further elaboration of the assimilation and accommodation model should, furthermore, take into account the concept of coping with stress. For the purpose of this discussion, experiences relevant to identity can be considered to represent the *"stressors"* represented in transactional coping models. Two major categories of coping strategies have been identified in the stress literature: emotion-focused and problem-focused coping. In emotion-focused coping, the individual attempts to change the way he or she thinks about or appraises a stressful situation rather than changing the situation itself. Problem-focused coping involves attempts to reduce stress by changing the stressful situation.

As a general statement, it appears that individuals who use problem-focused coping strategies are more likely to maintain higher activity levels and therefore maximize their physical functioning. They are better able to meet their perceived physical needs and tailor their expectations and behavior to fit the changes in their physical identity. Active involvement in sports or exercise, for some elders, not only promotes physical functioning but can serve as an important coping mechanism. Coping style also seems to be related to reactions to a variety of physical health problems. For example, improved levels of coping and the use of social supports (in part, a problem-focused coping measure), were found to be predictive of hospital readmissions for a sample of elderly cardiac patients. Training in problem-focused coping methods has proved helpful in facilitating pain management and reducing anxiety among older individuals with chronic knee pain. The subjective experience of stress, particularly on a daily basis, has been related to prescription drug misuse among elderly individuals. Similarly, in the case of recovering from hip fracture, a condition related to changes in bone strength due to aging or osteoporosis, the use of problem-focused coping may enable individuals to take advantage of rehabilitative methods that can assist in their recovery. As a consequence of more adaptive coping strategies, hip fracture patients are less likely to experience depressive symptoms that would further lower their perceived functional recovery.

As the case of rehabilitation from hip fracture illustrates, the relationship between coping and health can be seen as cyclical. Individuals who successfully use coping strategies to manage stress may actually experience improved physical functioning. In one investigation, individuals reporting high levels of stress were found to have lower ratios of critical immune system markers. Active efforts to reduce stress through seeking social support or physical exercise can have physiological advantages in terms of improved immune system functioning. The aging immune system has been linked to increased vulnerability to influenza, infections, cancer, and certain age-associated autoimmune disorders such as diabetes and possibly atherosclerosis and Alzheimer's disease. Although there are other factors that affect the development of each of these conditions, particularly cancer, a more competent immune system can lower the elderly individual's risk at least to certain forms of cancer and influenza. [See IMMUNE SYSTEM.]

In contrast to the positive effects of problem-focused coping is evidence of the deleterious effects of emotion-focused coping on psychological and physical health outcomes. Individuals who use avoidance as a coping strategy are also likely to report higher levels of physical and psychological symptoms, depression, and psychosocial difficulties even continuing for months after the stressful situation has subsided. However, emotion-focused coping can have positive adaptive value if the situation is completely out of one's control, or if excessive rumination is harmful to improvement. As long as the individual follows prescribed treatment, the outcome may still be positive. When faced with an uncontrollable stressor, direct confrontation is not always necessary for successful coping. In fact, in some cases denial may actually be adaptive. The use of denial as a coping mechanism becomes maladaptive if it prevents the individual from taking action that is beneficial to recovery. In diseases or other health problems that require vigilant attention to bodily signs, such as cancer, kidney failure, or diabetes, coping by denial can lead to the development of life-threatening conditions.

VII. COPING AND ASSIMILATION AND ACCOMMODATION: A MODEL

As helpful as it is to view adaptation to physical changes in terms of coping processes, this approach nevertheless fails to take into account the relevance of these changes to the individual's identity. To gain a more comprehensive view of variations in response to challenges to physical identity associated with the aging process, it is necessary to combine the dimension of problem- versus emotion-focused coping with the dimension of identity assimilation and accommodation. Such an approach produces a fourfold matrix to account for adaptation to the physical aging process. Specific behavioral and adaptive predictions can be made for individuals within each of the four cells created by this matrix.

Individuals who use identity assimilation and emotion-focused coping are likely to deny the relevance of aging to their identities and, at the same time, engage in few behaviors intended to offset or compensate for aging changes. Adverse consequences are more likely to occur for aging individuals who take an assimilative approach to age- or disease-related bodily changes and use emotion focused coping. They may find it more comfortable not to think about the diagnosis or problem and instead go on with life as usual, not changing their identities in response to the knowledge that they are suffering a major change in health or functioning or even have a potentially terminal illness. Consequently, they will not take active efforts to protect and promote their body's ability to fight the condition or disease. Those who use identity assimilation and problem-focused coping, by contrast, would actively become involved in behavioral controls that could serve a preventative or compensatory function. However, they would not integrate into their identities the knowledge that their body has changed in fundamental ways or faces severe health threats. Thus, at the behavioral level, the individual is engaging in appropriate health maintenance and rehabilitative strategies, and is able to take advantage of these strategies in terms of improvements in physical health. However, the individual has chosen not to give particular thought or emphasis to the implications for identity of the problem or disorder.

Identity accommodation may occur in conjunction with either problem- or emotion-focused coping. Individuals who tend to use accommodation to the point that they overreact to a diagnosis or physical disorder may suffer the same adverse consequences as those who deny through assimilation the significance of physical changes or illness. Such individuals believe that what they do in reaction to these changes or diseases will make no difference, and through the emotion-focused strategies of distancing, denial, or avoidance, fail to take the necessary steps to maximize their functioning. Their emotions are likely to be highly dysphoric, and they feel a loss of the ability to control or predict the future course of their physical development or changes in health condition. Individuals who use accommodation but also take steps to confront the changes in physical status or health through problem-focused coping may be likely to take extremely active steps to help reduce their symptoms or the progress of the disease. It is probable that such individuals feel that they are able to control the events in their lives, leading them to be less likely to use palliative coping strategies in favor of ones that address the situation. These individuals would react to disease or physical changes by harnessing their available resources, and they would actively seek further medical treatment as well as less proven alternate treatments. They might be preoccupied with their bodies, but at the same time they would use every opportunity to talk to others and get help, using coping strategies such as confrontation, seeking social support, planful problem solving, and positive reappraisal. If they have a particular disease, they may "become" the disease, which then becomes a major focus of their lives. The risk of this type of coping in combination with identity accommodation is that although the individual adjusts well to the physical identity stressor by taking active steps, he or she may ruminate excessively about the disease.

Healthy adaptation within this model involves the balance between assimilation and accommodation in terms of the impact of age changes or disease on identity. Flexibility of coping style would further promote positive adaptation. When problems arise, such individuals can focus on the physical identity stressor and are open to seeking help from others, but they avoid being preoccupied with the illness when necessary in order to focus on other concerns, such as family or work involvements. This ability to adapt to the challenges of aging reflects what Clark and Anderson described almost three decades ago as char-

acteristic of "successful" aging and, more recently, has been identified as a protective factor against depression in later adulthood.

In this discussion of identity and coping, it is important to emphasize that the individual's use of these processes is not fixed across the span of the aging years. Individuals may use a variety of coping strategies that complement or offset their identity style. Furthermore, assuming that there is a relationship between identity processes and coping, and given the emphasis in the coping literature on the variable nature of coping processes it may be more reasonable to propose that the identity processes are used within the same individual on different occasions, or even within the same individual on the same occasion. As is true for coping strategies, individuals may use one, then another, of the identity processes in their attempts to adapt to changes in the body's appearance, functioning, and health. The theoretically related topics of perceived control, relevance of personal goals, and self-efficacy should also be considered. Individuals who feel that they can control the events in their lives that relate to central aspects of identity, either because they have the personal competence or because the events themselves are controllable, will be more likely to react to aging changes through problem-focused coping. If events themselves are uncontrollable, or they are perceived as such, emotion-focused coping will be more likely to be used. Events that have little personal relevance because they do not have a bearing on central features of identity, however, may not trigger either coping mechanism. Further research is needed to establish the extent to which these related concepts overlap with the proposed mechanisms described here. Interestingly, the prospect that individual differences in identity mediate the relationship between age and personal control beliefs may help to explain the lack of consistency in the literature on age differences in sense of control.

VIII. STEREOTYPES

A final consideration is the role of cultural stereotypes and myths about the aging process. Age-related norms and expectations emphasize the uncontrollable losses that accumulate in the later adult years. The degree to which individuals ascribe to negative stereotypes about the aging process can have a detrimental impact on the motivation to cope actively with age-related changes. To the extent that individuals come to hold these beliefs, they will be more likely to adopt the passive approaches involved in emotion-focused coping strategies. Further reinforcing this passivity are interactions with younger adults in which the older person is treated in a patronizing, infantilizing manner. Such treatment can lower the individual's feelings of personal control and self-efficacy. [*See* AGEISM AND DISCRIMINATION.]

In summary, the construct of physical identity bears central significance to the life of the aging individual. The processes of assimilation and accommodation to the normal changes involved in the aging process are important mechanisms for promoting the individual's ability to adapt to the changes in health and functioning associated with aging. Furthermore, by examining the interaction of identity processes with coping strategies used to manage stress, it is possible to predict and analyze individual variations in adaptation of physical identity to the aging process.

BIBLIOGRAPHY

Baltes, M. M., & Baltes, P. B. (1986). *The psychology of aging and control*. Hillsdale, NJ: Erlbaum.
Brandtstädter, J., & Rothermund, K. (1994). Self-percepts of control in middle and later adulthood: Buffering losses by rescaling goals. *Psychology and Aging, 9*, 265–273.
Cooper, C. C., & Hayslip, B. (November 1994). *Body image as mediated by age, sex, and relationship status*. Paper presented at the Gerontological Society of America's 47th Annual Scientific Meeting, Atlanta, Georgia.
Harter, S. (1988). Causes, correlates, and the functional role of global self-worth: A lifespan perspective. In J. Kolligian & R. Sternberg (Ed.), *Perceptions of competence and incompetence across the lifespan*. New Haven, CT: Yale University Press.
Hennessy, C. H. (1989). Culture in the use, care, and control of the aging body. *Journal of Aging Studies, 3*, 39–54.
Hooker, K., & Kaus, C. R. (1994). Health-related possible selves in young and middle adulthood. *Psychology and Aging, 9*, 126–133.
Janelli, L. M. (1993). Are there body image differences between older men and women? *Western Journal of Nursing Research, 15*, 327–339.
O'Brien, S. J., & Conger, P. R. (1991). No time to look back: Approaching the finish line of life's course. *International Journal of Aging and Human Development, 33*, 75–87.
Pelham, B. W. (1991). On confidence and consequence: The certainty and importance of self-knowledge. *Journal of Personality and Social Psychology, 60*, 518–530.
Ross, M. J., Tait, R. C., Grossberg, G. T., Handal, P. J., Brandeberry, L., & Nakra, R. (1989). Age differences in body consciousness. *Journal of Gerontology: Psychological Sciences, 44*, P23–24.
Whitbourne, S. K. (1986a). *Adult development*. New York: Praeger.
Whitbourne, S. K. (1986b). *The me I know: A study of adult identity*. New York: Springer Verlag.
Whitbourne, S. K. (1996). *The aging individual*. New York: Springer.

Images of Aging

Mike Featherstone

Nottingham Trent University

Mike Hepworth

University of Aberdeen

Ageism Discrimination against individuals or groups because of their age.
Consumer Culture The culture of the consumer society with its images of youth, fitness and beauty.
Images Visual representations of the external appearance of the human body.
Mask of Aging The experience of a disjunction between the aging body and the "ageless" self.
Social Constructionism The view that aging is not a biological given, but is constructed by society.
Stereotypes Over-simplified public images that are often stigmatizing.

Gerontological interest in the analysis of visual **IMAGES OF THE AGING** body and the roie images play in constructing the meaning of the aging process is of comparatively recent origin. It can be traced back to the mid-1960s where it emerged as the result of two major social developments. The first was the belief that one of the most urgent problems facing societies with increasing numbers of older people was that of ageism; a term which refers to the widespread existence of negative attitudes toward people simply because they are biologically older. Analyses of the images of old age in, for example, greetings cards, comic strips, and the movies showed that older people were consistently represented in a negative manner. The second development was the greater awareness of the key role played by visual images in the construction of social life. It is often observed that contemporary western societies are consumer societies and that the construction and dissemination of visual images is a central feature of consumer culture. Technological innovations in the means of producing and communicating visual images have resulted in a massive expansion in the volume and realistic quality of visual images which can be communicated to audiences. Recurrent themes in consumer culture imagery are youthfulness and beauty alongside a negative depiction of ageing and old age.

It is now widely accepted that the quality of life of the increasing population of older people will be considerably enhanced by the elimination of negative images or stereotypes of the aging body as a body in decline and their replacement with positive images of old age as an extended phase of active life. This quest is built on the assumption that the images which circulate in public work in two ways. First, public images are considered to both reflect and shape social attitudes toward older people and the treatment they receive. Second, public images influence individual perceptions of the self and the construction of personal identity in later life. The personal meanings of old age are the result of the reflection by each individual upon the public images of later life with which he or she becomes familiar. Public images are a key resource for making sense of the biological processes of aging which are exposed to public scrutiny because they are evident on the external surfaces of the human body. Wrinkles on the face may, for example, be interpreted either positively—as signs of a life experienced to the full—or negatively—as signs of failure and regret.

It is now, therefore, accepted that images operate

in flexible ways: their meanings exist on several levels and they are always open to a wide variety of interpretations, especially in contemporary Western societies. This perception arises from recent developments in the study of culture and mass communications which have shown that the relationship between image and audience is essentially a dynamic one: audiences can no longer be seen as made up of "cultural dopes" who can be easily manipulated by the image makers. Mass communications may best be understood as "performances," resulting from processes of interaction between image and audience whereby viewers respond to the images (e.g., television or movies) before them according to their specific interests and cultural allegiances. For this reason, gerontologists are becoming aware of the diversity of images of aging that circulate in multicultural societies. They are also becoming aware of the ways in which images of aging are being actively transformed as the result of technological innovations in communication systems (photography, movies, television, video, and computing).

The images of aging now emerging in contemporary Western cultures are, therefore, becoming much more complex and fluid. Good examples of the development of new images alongside older stereotypes can be found in advertisments for goods and services for the expanding section of the population in the fifty plus age group. Advertisers are coming to appreciate the value of associating images of these consumer products (fashions for the over-fifties, cosmetics, retirement homes, vacations, educational opportunities, labor-saving devices) with images of youthful bodies in middle and later life. Biological aging is thus constructed as a period of continuing physical health and activity in opposition to the stereotyped image of middle and later life as a period of diminishing energy and disengagement. Associations between the body in a state of physical decline and rocking chairs, slippers and drowsiness are replaced with images of continuing bodily activity and vigorous social encounters. What is interesting is that these new images, designed to revise and even revolutionize middle and later life, are also images of age-related retirement and leisure and, given this essential ambiguity, open to a more flexible range of interpretations than the comparatively more rigid older representations of life after fifty as inevitably a one-way status passage to old age and death.

I. THE ROLE OF IMAGES IN SOCIAL LIFE

A. Background

From the moment of birth human bodies are biologically programmed to age and die. The effects of this program are visibly displayed on the human face and body. This means that every time one looks at a human being, or an image of a human being in, for example, a painting or a photograph, one perceives an individual who can be identified in terms of his or her age. In biographical accounts of the lives of famous people, paintings or photographs of these individuals when they are older are often identified with the words "in old age" or "as an old man/woman." Because all humans are part of a process of biological growth and decline, and this process is visibly displayed on the face and body, every image of the human face and body is necessarily an image of aging. But human beings do not only exist in a biological lifetime, running from birth to death, they also exist in historical and cultural time. Images of the body are constructed out of the visual images and language available at any particular time in history and in any particular culture. It is because human beings use images, both visual and verbal, to construct social life and give it meaning that they are more than simply biological bodies. But it is also important to note that the relationship between images of the body and the personal experience of the body is complex and is determined by people's lived experience in a variety of cultural contexts. The meanings of images of the aging body, whether they are found in drawings, paintings, photographs, movies, TV programs, or videos, are culturally coded and yet at the same time open to a wide variety of interpretations depending upon the situations in which they are encountered. In some cultures, for example, the wrinkles on an old person's face are viewed with ridicule or disgust, whereas in other cultures they may go unnoticed or even be seen as a sign of higher status. Images of the aging body, therefore, can be used to convey either positive or negative messages, and these messages can powerfully influence the ways in which younger people relate to older people and older people relate to each other.

Although visual images have emerged as the most influential form of mass communication, it must be remembered that they can never be completely separated from language. When looking at a visual image (a caricature of an old person, a photograph of an older man or woman in a biography or in a family photograph album) the understanding of its meaning is necessarily in terms of the categories or typifications made available through language: for example, the language category "old man" or "old woman." Yet at the same time, images are never wholly reducible to language, and it should be recognized that much of social life (and this has been increasingly the case since the development of consumer culture in the nineteenth century) takes place within the visual field. The study of visual images of aging, therefore, requires an acknowledgment of the dynamic relationship between visual representations and language.

B. Definitions

In everyday terminology an image is often regarded as an accurate representation of an object or person. As far as images of human beings are concerned there is a tendency to see the body as something that because of its material (embodied) existence can easily be copied or represented. A photograph of Queen Victoria in later life, for example, is often perceived as an accurate record of the external appearance of that individual "in" old age, an image that is perceived as fixing and framing the essential nature of her embodied selfhood at a particular moment in time. The notion of copying and producing an accurate likeness of an original in a variety of media (the sculpted portrait bust of Benjamin Franklin is another good example) is one of the key meanings of the term image which can be traced back to the original Latin meaning of the term *imago*.

But the term image also has an important second meaning, and this is derived from associations with the role of the *imagination* and the *imaginary*. In this second meaning the emphasis is not on the accurate representation of an independently existing objective reality, but on the power of the imagination to construct and shape an image of reality. There is an interdependency between the image as it is recorded and the imagination of the viewer. From this perspective, images are regarded as playing an active role in the social construction of reality. Reality is understood to be more of an imaginative projection than an object existing independently of the viewer or society. Just as images have an important part to play in the con-

struction of the body, they are also seen as making a significant contribution to the social construction of the self. The self, grounded as it is in the body—or embodied—is thus a product of social interaction. A good example can again be taken from the use of photography. Debates about the accuracy of photographs of family members are a commonplace feature of everyday life, especially those that are prompted by questions about what a certain relative "really looked like" at some point in the past. Similarly, people often have some difficulty in recognizing their own photographs as accurate images of our "real" selves, especially when the photographs were taken several years ago. "Was that how I really looked?" one often asks.

The second meaning of the word image, therefore, refers to the original definition of photography as painting with light. It suggests that an image is essentially produced through an interpretative act whereby the subject's body is clothed and adorned in particular ways and framed in a setting of material objects, all of these carrying a specific symbolic value, emotional tone, and resonance. The image is, then, a social construction that frames a world in order to make sense of a vast array of sensory stimuli. As a photograph relates to a specific point in the lifetime of a person and his or her relations to other persons at that time, it carries hidden significances and emotional charges that are themselves unstable, altering with the changing vicissitudes of the person's subsequent experience. It is also open to changing interpretations of history as in the case of recent analyses of Victorian photography and, in particular, sociological analyses of photographs of older people taken during the closing decades of the nineteenth century. This research shows, for example, how photographs of old people living and working in rural areas of Scotland are not "natural" images but socially constructed compositions deliberately framed to reflect current social beliefs about the simplicity and integrity of country life.

C. Images and Stereotypes

An appreciation of the complexities of images and the theorization of their role in the social construction of reality is now influencing research into the social stereotypes of aging and old age. The word *stereotype* is derived from the Greek *stereos*, meaning form or solid, and *typos* meaning an impression or model.

The process of stereotyping is one in which the subtle differences and nuances that distinguish one individual older person from another are dissolved in order to transform aging into one uniform process. Stereotypes of old men and old women are often regarded as displeasing and offensive by older people because they convey the impression that individual differences and distinctions are somehow dissolved or destroyed by biological age. Moreover the stereotyping of old age as a single uniform process with similar effects on all older people regardless of culture, gender, time, and place, is seen as having a negative effect on the quality of later life precisely because public images of old age in Western culture have tended to focus on its negative aspects. In general, the stereotype *old* is a social category that implies that every old person is not eligible for full acceptance in social life. One of the clearest examples of the stigma of aging is age-discrimination in employment where people over a certain age are barred from applying or are dismissed. Such barriers may, of course, exist only in the form of unwritten rules or understandings that are never explicitly advertised but their ultimate reference point is an image of older age as a social stigma. [*See* AGEISM AND DISCRIMINATION.]

At the same time it must be remembered that the effects of stereotypes of aging are not always as clear cut as is sometimes imagined. Not all stereotypes of old age are negative and stereotypes of aging are often highly ambiguous precisely because old age is not experienced as a single uniform condition. Yet, because the basic social function of stereotypes is to make sense of complex experiences and to reduce tangled patterns of information into an easily communicable set of images, there is a strong possibility that stereotypes may give highly misleading messages to the wider public. A good example is that of the grandfather and grandmother whose popular image is that of gentle, socially disengaged, and desexualized men and women with white hair and ready smiles who dote continuously upon their grandchildren—figures, moreover, who are often white and middle class. The fact that large numbers of grandparents in western societies are in their forties and fifties means that real-life grandparents have an image problem. In this context it is interesting to note that a number of popular magazines have come into existence to cater to a new generation of grandparents who do not identify with this stereotypical image.

Further evidence of the misleading stereotyping of the aging process involves the binary distinction between images of youth, usually represented in Western stereotypes as the most active and desirable phase of life, and images of old age as a period of decline and decay, one that is at best a preparatory stage for death and the afterlife. A typical historical example can be found in an engraving by Jorg Breu the Younger published in Augsburg in 1540. Entitled "The Ten Ages of Man," it displays life as a series of steps leading first of all progressively upward from birth through youth to the high point of middle age (what is often described as "growing up") and then, in the second major phase, stepping inexorably downward through old age toward death, and finally the afterlife (what is often described as "growing old"). In this compelling image, which has for centuries exercised a pervasive influence over the Western imagination, the life course of every individual is structured in terms of series of pre-determined steps which he or she must follow. It is an inflexible image and it does not, therefore, allow any possibility of alternative interpretation.

As a characteristic example of the "ages of man" tradition which continued to stereotype the life cycle well into the nineteenth century, Breu's engraving confirms a clear relationship between old age and decrepitude. The final stage of life in the material world is represented in the image of a bowed and bearded old man, as one of fatigue, invalidity, and preparation for death.

Prior to the seventeenth century Western images of life as a series of ages represented life in masculine terms. The images of the ages of life were images of men. But during the seventeenth century artists began to draw distinctions between the typical stages of the life of man and the stages of life of woman, the "ages of woman" being defined in terms of virtuous domesticity. Prescribed models of the "ages of woman" display the same upward progression to the peak of middle age followed by a series of steps or stages downward to a bedridden old age, death and immortality. In all these images the virtuous—whether male or female—are rewarded with a heavenly afterlife, and the vicious are punished in hell. Such images continue to influence stereotypes of the life course in present-day society, the only significant difference being the absence of an explicitly religious cosmology.

Breu's work is a typical example of the social construction of stereotypes of old age in order to prescribe moral distinctions between virtuous and vicious aging. The boundaries between the ages of life which constitute the life course and the boundaries between positive (moral) and negative (immoral) aging are rigidly defined. This practice has a long history in Western culture and can be traced as far back as classical antiquity with a line of continuity stretching up to the present day. Art historians have shown, for example, in seventeenth-century Holland, how stereotyped images of older men and women were used to depict the moral message of the rewards of the virtuous life for men and women alike. Paintings of avaricious and lewd old men and women stand in deliberate contrast to images of virtuous merchants, craftsmen, and housewives who diligently carry out their gendered duties in expectation of a reward in the next world. The division of labor between men and women is clear but the moral stereotyping of aging as a "journey of life" is the same for both.

Similarly, in nineteenth-century painting, there is a pronounced tendency to represent the idealized form of old age as a final stage of dedicated domestic seclusion, frequently against the backdrop of a rural environment. In addition to framing the potentially threatening physical decline of old age within a comforting domestic setting, such images also reflect nostalgia for a disappearing rural life in a society undergoing rapid modernization with its attendant urbanization and expanding consumer culture. Such nostalgia involves a dual repression of the complexities and often harsh nature of rural life and the realities of growing old in a world where competitive individualism was placing an even higher value on the active physical body. Increasingly in the nineteenth-century, images of old age reflected a moral distinction between those who aged "well," that is, preserved their independence to their last breath, and those who aged "badly" or "gave in" and became dependent on others.

The same process of binary stereotyping occurs in the case of portraiture, an art form whose ostensible purpose since the Renaissance has been the representation of the visible appearance of individual character as revealed in the face and bodily comportment. Yet even when artists set out to paint a portrait of an identifiable individual who has attained old age, their efforts often incorporate elements of stereotypical conventions concerning a "good" (or morally worthy) and a "bad" (or socially deviant) old age.

The more general point to be made, therefore, is that images of old age should often be viewed not so much as descriptions or documentary records of the actual historical conditions of older people but as prescriptive social texts. Art historians often emphasize the distance that can be assumed to exist between, for example, the prolific images of old age in paintings that were produced in The Netherlands during the "Golden Age" of the seventeenth century and the everyday lives of those relatively small numbers of men and women who actually lived long enough to experience old age. These images should be viewed as reflections of the beliefs and traditional conventions governing the pictorial representation of older people as social types. Good examples are the inappropriately amorous old woman in a brothel and the rich old man who foolishly married a young wife and who, for the amusement of the audience, is being conspicuously cuckolded.

The imaging of old age as a symbol of social or political virtue can be traced back to the sculpted portrait busts of prominent figures in classical antiquity. At one period in the history of ancient Rome, from the second century BC to the sixth century AD, portrait busts of elder statesmen were sculpted to give explicit facial expression to idealized political virtues. The signs of aging were carved into these in order to give enduring form to the public virtues of long service and stability as perceived in the faces of their living models. As such they were celebrations of an association between old age and social and political stability, of the perception of a close interrelationship between the virtuously aging individual face and a public life dedicated to duty and self-discipline. This close physiognomic relationship between the public and the private, the inner subjective self and the outer public social identity, was reflected several centuries later in portraits painted by the German artist Albrecht Dürer (1471–1528). The portraits he painted toward the end of his own life of a number of notable converts to the Lutheran religion in Germany have been described as a deliberate attempt to reveal the outward signs of the inner spiritual transformation of men who had been converted to the new religion. It has been argued that Dürer's portrait of Frederick the Wise (1524), who died within two months of its completion, was intended to represent the face of an older man who had been restored through religious conversion to a youthfulness of spirit. In both Roman antiquity and sixteenth-century Lutheran Germany such images of the visible appearance of aging were specifically created as icons of exemplary social qualities. As portraits of recognizable individual persons who were growing older, and therefore in this sense images of aging, they are also expressions of predominant social aspirations concerning forms of spiritual growth and development.

Images of old age continue up to the present day to be constructed as moral images or metaphors of social life, symbolizing the beliefs and values of the age. It is the very conventionality of the belief system underlying traditional images of old age—their stereotypical quality—that has ensured their continued influence up to the present day.

At the same time, there are significant signs that a major transformation in the imaging of aging has been slowly emerging since the mid-nineteenth century. One of the most obvious differences between traditional methods of image production (drawings, paintings, etchings, and so on) and those in use today is the emergence of new techniques of image production and reproduction associated with developments in consumer culture. Also radically different are the means of communicating images and distributing them to a mass audience. Since the nineteenth century, innovations in photography, film, television, and video have vastly increased the number of images in circulation. Moreover, the need to find outlets for mass-produced goods resulted in the proliferation of department stores, shopping malls and arcades, and in the development of visually sophisticated advertising techniques. These processes of mass marketing helped to produce the consumer culture "dream worlds" in which it became possible to attach a whole range of romantic and exotic imagery to mundane goods. Since the mid-nineteenth century, therefore, goods have been increasingly advertised in terms of their value in enhancing the lifestyle of the purchaser. They are no longer bought simply because they satisfy basic human needs such as hunger, warmth, and shelter. Consumer goods should not be regarded as solely material things but as containing a strong symbolic component. In effect they act as "communicators" which engage the admiration, approval, and envy of others. In this context it is the emphasis on the shift from the producing to the consuming body that has a crucial significance for images of aging.

In a world facing for the first time in human history the global prospect of an aging population, the image-saturated consumer culture constantly valorizes bodies that epitomize youthful energy, fitness, and activity. There is a tendency to present bodies, social relationships, and lifestyles as things that need working at, things which can be reshaped and renewed. Indeed the need to combat a fateful sense of bodily fixity and decline is often presented as a moral duty. The result is a foreground of age consciousness and an ageist rejection or denial of the biological decline of later life. Unlike the traditional images of the "ages of man" and of "woman," contemporary images of the life course attempt to eliminate the downhill stages to death and the afterlife and to replace them with an extended plateau of middle life. Ironically enough, the virtuous response to growing older, portrayed as an essentially spiritual acceptance of physical decline and the inevitability of death that we saw in the traditional iconography of aging, is now located in the celebration of resistance to aging and the rejection of old age. In contrast, to age "negatively" is "to let oneself go"—in effect, to abandon the struggle to maintain a youthful appearance and lifestyle.

This rejection of the physical realities of old age in favor of images of a perpetual state of middle age both reflects and gives expression to the ambiguities and uncertainties which increasingly surround old age in contemporary society. As the population of older people expands, particularly the proportion of people aged seventy and over, evidence from empirical research into the everyday lives of older people clearly suggests that the actual experiences of old age are much more varied and often much more positive than ageist stereotypes imply. Even when suffering from ill health or a serious physical disability many older people continue to enjoy independent and fulfilling lives. These findings lend further support to the argument that many of the negative aspects of aging are not biologically or chronologically determined. Rather, they can be shown to be the result of the meanings that individuals give to the aging process in later life. The images they draw upon to construct these positive meanings are therefore of great significance.

It should also be emphasized that the largest proportion of people in the age category seventy-five plus are women. It is now important to construct images of aging which represent the predominance of women in this category and give much greater prominence to positive images of women in later life. This task is seen as particularly important because it is increasingly acknowledged that women suffer from the "double jeopardy" of ageism and sexism.

Interest in images of aging has gradually increased among gerontologists and professional groups working on behalf of older people throughout the Western world. In the United States the Gray Panthers, the National Coalition on Aging, and the American Association of Retired Persons battle to reverse ageist stereotypes of older people as socially dependent and disengaged members of the population. Increasing publicity has also been given in recent years to the positive contribution older people make to social life. The basic assumption here is social constructionist. Older people have unjustly been subjected to the harmful effects of negative stereotypes and those concerned with promoting the interests of older people in the context of an aging world must learn to construct and deploy a new multicultural positive imagery of old age.

At the present time there is a strong tendency for the positive images of aging that have been constructed to counteract negative stereotypes to overemphasize the qualities of youthfulness and as a result to foster a sense of disjunction between the body and the self. Those old people whose bodily appearance does not conform to the youthful stereotype of aging (i.e., whose bodies visibly display the physical signs of aging—wrinkling, hair loss, graying of the hair, reduced flexibility and mobility, impairment of sight and hearing) often express the feeling of being trapped within an aging body. This sense of entrapment has been described as "the mask of aging," a term which refers to the ways in which the aging body can no longer express the subjective experience of the inner self. The biological body grows older but the inner self appears to be "ageless" or fixed at some earlier point in the life course. In its most extreme manifestation, the case of Alzheimer's disease, one of the most distressing experiences of both caregivers and sufferers is that of an essentially youthful inner self relentlessly imprisoned within an old and decaying body. The predominant image here is that of a dualistic contest between two opposing forces: the biological body and the subjective self. [See DEMENTIA.]

II. IMAGES OF AGING IN A MULTICULTURAL WORLD

There are two significant indications of the potential for expanding the range of positive images of aging which are of increasing interest to gerontologists. The first is the growing awareness of a multicultural world. The second is the realization that scientific discoveries and technical innovations have far-reaching consequences for the aging process.

Awareness that we live in a world characterized by multicultural variations is displacing the older sociological view of people bonded together through a common culture with its shared beliefs and values. It is becoming apparent that societies consist of a diversity of cultural groups often engaged in struggles for equality and respect. Among these are ethnic groups and groups of disabled people. Although it is now recognized that biological aging as such is not a unifying force as far as older people are concerned. It is also the case that potentially powerful groups of older people do exist and show signs of becoming increasingly conscious of their social position.

In the not-too-distant past when images of aging were collected for display at conferences and exhibitions, or as illustrations in books and journals there was often a tendency to present oversimplified and sometimes romantic images of old age. The predominant image of aging was very often white and middle class, excluding a wide range of other social groups. References to variations in attitudes to aging according to socio-economic status (SES), ethnic background, and gender tended to be glossed over. Since the late 1980s, however, gerontologists have paid much more attention to class, gender, regional, and ethnic differences.

A useful example is the image of old age as a time of infantilization, as a second childhood. Because Western culture places such a strong emphasis on mature adulthood, there has been an emphasis on the traditional model of the life course for both childhood and old age to be represented as protected and dependent stages of less than full adult status. This continues to be reflected today in the treatment of older people as if they are dependent children, especially by professional caregivers in institutions. Ageism can therefore operate through the dominance of images of dependency that take away the adult status and personhood of the elderly. For many gerontologists and members of interest groups concerned with the rights of older people, infantilizing images of older people must be contested and displaced.

Today, however, the negative image of old age as a second childhood is being reappraised. In Japan, for example, once an individual is past the age of 60, he or she is assumed to have completed the first cycle of life and to have entered another cycle in which childish and mischievous behavior is not only expected but looked upon with affection. In Japan older people may be perceived as "cute," and as such the recipients of affection from young people, an example being the centenarian twins Kin and Gin who became media celebrities. In such a cultural context the wrinkles, graying hair, and slurring speech may be ignored, and even perceived positively as signs that older people have attained a state of grace and are nearer to God and the next world. Respect for the outward physical signs of biological aging, expressed in the form of positive images of the second childhood, is an indication of the filial pietism and paternalism that conditions the treatment of older people in Japan.

Any consideration of multiculturalism and therefore diverse and sometimes competing images of aging alerts us to the danger of pushing the parallel between ageism, racism, and sexism too far. Although race and gender continue to be constituted as "master categories" (relatively unambiguous social categories that entail discrimination and power deficits for the outsider group), such a division is by no means so clearcut with reference to images of older people and their relationships with the young and middle aged. Unlike the social oppositions of race and gender, youth, middle, and old age are essentially transitional statuses within a universal process of biological aging. As transitional statuses they are reshaped by cultural change. The move toward cultural diversity indicates a richer repertoire of images of aging in the forseeable future. There are signs of this already: traditional groups of "elders" whose lives and attitudes toward aging reflect earlier twentieth-century expectations are being displaced by new generations of the "young old," "third agers," aging gays, and many others. A stage in social life has been reached where traditional images, although most certainly of historical and sociological interest, no longer seem relevant.

This view of a rapidly emerging cultural disjunction between even the immediate past, the present, and the future is reinforced by the second significant social transformation. This is the effect of scientific research into the aging process and technological innovations.

The interaction between biology and culture, reflected in studies of the social effects of images of aging, means that human beings are essentially unfinished creatures. Human bodies and experiences of human bodies change with innovations in organ replacement surgery, plastic surgery, and genetic engineering. Such developments are inevitably reflexive: they feed back into the actual experiences of being human. It is now accepted that it is possible to intervene in several of the life processes, including some associated with aging, and to create, so to speak, "new" human bodies from "old." It is therefore possible to identify three developments that will influence images of aging in the future. The first is the capacity to change and modify the external appearance and thus control the image of the aging body. Significantly, plastic surgery now penetrates deeper and deeper below the surface of the skin to sculpt the very structural framework of the body. The second is the ability to reconstruct the inner body by repairing or replacing damaged or decayed body parts. Scientific research is currently on the point of understanding the process of cellular aging so that the "natural" process of decline can be halted or even reversed. The third development entails not so much the repair of the body, but a mode of escape from its confines. Developments in information technology offer the prospect of the construction of cyberspace and virtual reality. This will allow people with sensory impairment and limited mobility the capacity to move freely in highly realistic simulated environments which engage the full range of human senses and offer an enhanced capacity for interaction with others on a more equal basis. A human body damaged or reduced by the aging process may no longer need to represent a prison to the inner self.

The potential of these technological developments coupled with our increasing sensitivity to multiculturalism and global diversity, holds out the prospect of a more complex and differentiated set of images of aging in the future. It is clear that there is not one essential process of aging but many. It is also clear that to make sense of these social transformations in the future, we will need not one gerontology, since the subject of gerontology is becoming so diverse, but many.

BIBLIOGRAPHY

Achenbaum, A. (1995). Images of old age in America 1790–1970: A vision and revision. In (M. Featherstone and A. Wernick Eds.) *Images of aging: Cultural representations of later life.* New York and London: Routledge.

Blaikie, A. (1995). Photographic images of age and generation. *Education and Aging, 10,* 1, 5–15.

Bytheway, B. (1995). *Agism,* Philadelphia and Buckingham: Open University Press.

Cole, T. R. (1992). *The journey of life: A cultural history of aging in America.* Cambridge: Cambridge University Press.

Coupland, N., Coupland, J., & Giles, H. (1991). *Language, society and the elderly: Discourse, Identity and ageing.* Oxford, UK and Cambridge, MA: Blackwell.

Covey, H. C. (1991). *Images of older people in Western art and society.* London: Praeger.

Featherstone, M. (1991). *Consumer culture and postmodernism.* Thousand Oaks, CA: Sage Publications.

Featherstone, M. (1995). Post-bodies, ageing and virtual reality. In M. Featherstone, and A. Wernick (Eds.) *Images of ageing: Cultural representations of later life,* New York and London: Routledge.

Featherstone, M., & Hepworth, M. (1993). Images of ageing. In J. Bond, P. Coleman, & S. Pearce (Eds.), *Ageing in society: An introduction to gerontology, 2nd edition,* Thousand Oaks, CA: Sage Publications.

Featherstone, M., & Hepworth, M. (1991). The mask of aging and the postmodern lifecourse. In M. Featherstone, M. Hepworth & B. S. Turner (Eds.), *The body: Social process and cultural theory,* Thousand Oaks, CA: Sage.

Featherstone, M., & Wernick, A. (Eds) (1995). *Images of ageing: Cultural representations of later life.* New York and London: Routledge.

Hockey, J., & James A. (1993). *Growing up and Growing old: Metaphors of aging in contemporary Britain.* Thousand Oaks CA and London: Sage.

Kuspit, D. B. (1975). Durer and the Lutheran image. *Art in America,* January/February, 56–61.

Nodelman, S. (1975). How to read a Roman portrait. *Art in America,* January/February, 27–29.

Wernick, A. (1995). Selling funerals: Imaging death. In M. Featherstone & A. Wernick (Eds.), *Images of aging: Cultural representations of later life,* New York and London: Routledge.

Immune System

Sharon M. Papciak, Lijun Song, James E. Nagel, and William H. Adler

National Institute on Aging

Apoptosis Active programmed cell death characterized by chromatin condensation, membrane blebbing, cell shrinkage, nuclear fragmentation, and DNA degradation.

B Lymphocyte (B Cell) Lymphocyte that is the precursor of antibody-secreting plasma cell. Can be phenotypically identified by monoclonal antibodies to the CD19, CD20, CD22, and CD23 surface antigens.

Cytokine Secreted polypeptide that affects the function of other cells through local action. Includes lymphokines, monokines, and chemokines.

F_c Receptor Receptors on numerous cell types for the F_c fragment of immunoglobulins. The binding of antibodies to these receptors triggers responses such as phagocytosis, H_2O_2 production, and subprostaglandin synthesis. All lymphoid cells express F_c receptors.

Lipopolysaccharide (LPS) The major component of the outer membrane of gram-negative bacteria. Physiologically, LPS lowers blood pressure, causes fever, blood clotting, and shock through its ability to induce interleukin-1 and tumor necrosis factor production by macrophages.

Mitogens Chemical, plant, or bacterial products that stimulate the mitosis of cells.

T Lymphocyte (T Cell) Lymphocyte that matures in the thymus and is responsible for cell-mediated immunity. Also regulates the growth and differentiation of other immunocompetent cells. They are phenotypically identifiable with monoclonal antibodies to the CD3 (T cells), CD4 (T helper cells), and CD8 (T suppressor/cytotoxic cells) surface antigens.

The **IMMUNE SYSTEM** is a network of cells and organs that provide an organism with host resistance. The system prevents the body's invasion by disease-causing infectious agents, and also supplies it with a means to recognize and destroy mutant cells. The immune system is composed of different cell types (neutrophils, lymphocytes, macrophages, and natural killer cells), soluble factors (cytokines, complement, fibronectin), and tissues (mucosa, lymph nodes, spleen, liver, bone marrow) that are capable of effectively dealing with many diverse threats. In accomplishing these tasks, the immune system may cause allergies and autoimmunity, as well as reject organ transplants.

I. BACKGROUND

It is well established that in the elderly there are changes in the immune system that lead to a decline in lymphocyte function and antibody formation. Overall, these changes contribute to a state of dysfunction in which there is a loss of control and a corresponding decrease in the ability to resist foreign pathogens. The immune system depends on the complex interaction of various cells and cell-free factors to function correctly.

The important subdivisions of the immune system include T lymphocytes (CD3+), B lymphocytes, accessory cells, growth factors, and regulatory factors. There are also subdivisions within each of these classifications, such as helper T cells (CD4+) and suppressor or cytotoxic T cells (CD8+), and pre B cells, B cells, plasma cells, and naive and memory B cells. T-cells demonstrate the greatest adverse effects of age. Because T cells are responsible for control of antibody production, as well as the generation of a cell-mediated immune response, it is easy to see that a loss of T-cell function would be manifest in many different ways. With age there is not a loss of T cells, but rather the development of T cells that have lost their ability to function normally and that undergo apoptosis, rather than clonal expansion, when activated.

The changes seen in the level of immune function in a population of humans or experimental animals is quite variable. Even among inbred animals there is individual variation. Although chronologic age is not a true predictor of the level of immune function in an individual, it is a good predictor of the level of function in a population. With age there is an increase in the number of people or animals who demonstrate a lessening of immune function so that the overall level of function in a population diminishes.

II. LYMPHOID TISSUE

The major areas associated with the presence of lymphocytic tissue are the thymus, spleen, lymph nodes, bone marrow, and the gut- and bronchus-associated tissues. Of these areas, the most important in terms of age-related change is the thymus.

A. Thymus

The thymus is located behind the sternum near the top of the mediastinum. It is roughly bilobate and composed of a medulla and a cortex. In young children the thymus is near the heart and about half as large. The gland increases in size until shortly before the onset of puberty, when it begins to involute. The cellular elements are gradually replaced with fatty tissue, and the production of thymic hormones becomes undetectable after the age of approximately 40 years in humans.

B. Lymph Nodes

The thymus is the only lymphoid tissue that undergoes any significant decrease in healthy adults. Lymph node architecture remains the same with the germinal centers and the reticular elements being present in about the same proportions in both the young and aging host.

C. Spleen and Bone Marrow

Splenic tissue also remains about the same in architecture and degree of cellularity. Bone marrow lymphocytes and plasma cells show an age-related increase in children, but do not show age-related changes in the elderly.

Most of these statements about the lymphoid organs depend heavily on the health status of the individual. In many cases the experimental evidence for a lack of age-related change is based on only a few observations because lymph node biopsies or splenectomies are not performed on healthy people. There is an extensive literature about the immune systems of experimental animals, and in healthy animals there are no major age-related changes in lymphoid tissue other than the thymus.

There are many age-related changes in lymphoid tissue associated with pathological conditions. Lymphomas and many leukemias show an age-related increased incidence. Secondary lymphoid dysfunction can be seen in patients undergoing chemotherapy and radiation therapy, and again this is seen more commonly in the elderly. The time to recover (as well as the extent of lymphocytic recovery) after radiation and chemotherapy for neoplastic disease and the recovery of T cells in the peripheral blood following burn trauma is age-related. These changes occur in relatively "young" individuals. Even in young people in their twenties and thirties, there is a marked delay or inability to fully reconstitute the immune system when compared to teenagers.

At present, there is no treatment to delay the onset of thymic involution, or to restore thymic activity. In inbred strains of mice, transplantation of syngeneic fetal thymus has a restorative effect, but this cannot be sustained even by repeated thymic transplantation procedures. This would suggest that a defect in lymphocyte function seen with aging is due in part to a loss of thymic activity as well as age-related changes in the environment that supports lymphocyte development. These environmental changes have not been identified.

III. T LYMPHOCYTES

The cross-linking of the T-cell receptor (TcR) by an antigen produces a series of biochemical signals. The earliest observable changes are the phosphorylation of tyrosine, the turnover of membrane phospholipids, and a transitory accumulation of high concentrations of intracellular calcium. These events activate several sets of genes that encode transcription factors, lymphokines, and lymphokine receptors that are critical for DNA replication and cell proliferation.

One of the most consistent findings concerning T cells from elderly animals and humans is their decreased proliferation after activation with any of a variety of stimulating agents. Although the defect in the aged T cells could occur at any step in the signaling process between receptor triggering and cell division, a major role can be attributed to a decline in the secretion of interleukin-2 (IL-2) and defects in IL-2 receptor expression and/or function. IL-2 is the major T-cell growth factor. Cells from young individuals produce approximately three times the amount of specific IL-2 mRNA as do the cells from the elderly donors.

Part of the decrease in IL-2 gene expression in the elderly can be attributed to a defect in a set of transcription factors collectively referred to as transcription activator protein (AP-1). AP-1 consists of a 55 kDa c-*fos* protein associated with a c-*jun* and c-*fos* protein to form a DNA-binding complex. AP-1 plays an important role in the initiation of IL-2 mRNA synthesis by binding to the enhancer region of the IL-2 gene. AP-1 activity directly parallels the level of IL-2 mRNA expression. In aged adults, the binding of AP-1 to its consensus DNA sequence is decreased. A component of AP-1, c-*jun*, also exhibits a decreased mRNA expression in T cells from elderly donors compared to young. Other components of AP-1, such as *jun-B* and c-*fos*, do not appear affected by the aging process.

Exogenous IL-2, even in physiologically excessive quantities, does not completely restore the decreased proliferative response observed in T cells from the elderly, suggesting a defect in IL-2R expression or

function or both. The IL-2R is composed of a p55 (α chain), a p75 (β chain), and a recently described additional chain that functions in IL-2-mediated signal transduction. This γ chain, perhaps better named γ_c for common γ chain, is also a component of the physically distinct IL-4, IL-7, IL-9, and IL-15 receptors. The minimal IL-2R complex competent to transduce signals is the $\beta\gamma$ heterodimer. The α subunit is largely responsible for binding IL-2. The relative contributions of each of the three receptor subunits (α, β, γ) in the complete IL-2R signaling pathway remains undetermined.

T cells from elderly donors demonstrate a significantly lower percentage of IL-2Rα-bearing cells compared to young donors. The expression of IL-2Rα mRNA is also decreased in the elderly. Although the number of high-affinity IL-2 receptors per cell and the affinity of these receptors is similar in mitogen-stimulated lymphoblasts from the young and elderly, the cell cultures from elderly individuals produce only half the number of progeny as do lymphoblasts from young donors. Lymphoblasts from young or elderly individuals cultured with and without exogenous IL-2 both demonstrate similar proliferative responsiveness to IL-2 (Figure 1). These data indicate that there are fundamentally two populations of T cells in elderly individuals. One population appears to function the same as T cells from

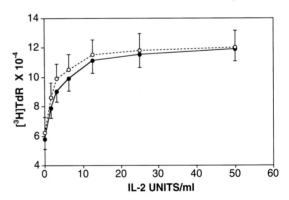

Figure 1 T lymphoblasts were obtained by stimulating T cells from young (open circles) and elderly (closed circles) donors with phorbol myristate acetate (PMA) and A23187 for 55 hr. The activated cells were washed and incubated overnight in complete medium. The viable lymphoblasts were then harvested and cultured in triplicate at 5×10^6 cells per well for 24 hr with various concentrations of rIL-2 and pulsed with [³H]TdR for the final 4 hr of culture.

young individuals, whereas another population does not become activated, does not proliferate, and ultimately undergoes programmed cell death. Although the proportion of nonfunctioning T cells increases with age, attempts to identify them based on cell surface markers have not been successful. Age differences in proliferative capacity are maintained when lymphocytes are separated into helper and suppressor, or naive and memory T-cell subpopulations.

Changes in the composition of the T-cell subpopulations in the elderly do contribute to the age difference in T-cell proliferation following activation by specific stimulants. Although T cells activated through the antigen receptor demonstrate an age-related decline in proliferation and IL-2 synthesis, phorbol myristate acetate (PMA) and calcium ionophore-activated cells show no proliferative differences between cells from young and old donors. PMA activates protein kinase C (PKC) directly and bypasses the transmembrane events that occur when cells are activated through the antigen receptor. Another activation pathway, the CD2 pathway, although not resulting in high levels of IL-2 synthesis, also does not show any age-related decline in IL-2 production. It appears that although some T-cell activation pathways are impaired by the aging process, others are influenced little or not at all. This suggests that different pathways utilize distinctive signaling components, and that different stimulating agents have different preferences for the T-cell subpopulations they activate (e.g., anti-CD2 may preferentially activate memory T cells). Investigation of the pattern of phosphorylated proteins in the cytoplasm of T cells activated by different stimuli shows that different activating agents use different phosphorylated protein messengers. Both increases and decreases in the levels of activation-induced phosphoproteins have been reported in the cells from elderly donors as compared to young.

IV. B LYMPHOCYTES

B lymphocytes and their progeny, plasma cells, mediate humoral immunity by producing various kinds of antibodies. Because many B-cell functions are regulated or controlled by T cells or T-cell products, it is difficult to document clearly age-related changes solely attributable to B lymphocytes.

With age there is a decline in serum antibody heterogeneity as well as a decrease in antibody avidity suggesting defects in B-cell clonal diversity and/or cytokine-induced isotype switching. Studies of B-lymphocyte development generally fail to show any age-specific defects. However, B cells from elderly mice appear to have, at least to some stimuli, altered variable region gene segment utilization and restricted light chain heterogeneity, suggesting that changes may exist in the restriction and maintenance of the working B-cell repertoire.

The amount of synthesized antibody decreases with age. However, the amount and affinity of the antibody produced per responding B cell does not change with age; thus demonstrating a pattern similar to T cells where in the elderly some cells respond normally, whereas others fail to respond. Although not attributable to a primary B-cell defect, the response of B cells to T-cell-dependent antigens such as the bacterial polysaccharides or F_c fragments is defective. Responses to T-cell independent stimuli such as lipopolysaccharide (LPS), tetanus toxoid, and various mitogens also decline. Likely due to inappropriate T-cell regulation, the elderly display an increase in monoclonal serum immunoglobulins and an increased occurrence of autoantibodies that are not associated with an increased incidence of autoimmune disease.

In men, unlike women, there is a significant decrease in the representation of CD19-positive B cells. Because CD19 is involved in the regulation of B-cell proliferation this may, in part, account for the greater incidence of autoimmune diseases in postmenopausal women.

One difference in the response to foreign antigens and self-antigens is the subset of B cells that produce the antibodies. In mice, mature B cells that express CD5 produce many self-reacting antibodies. When compared to the young, CD5-negative B cells from the elderly display poor antibody responses; whereas CD5-positive cells have antibody responses equal to or greater than the young. Present evidence suggests that the B-cell repertoires of old mice exhibit an age-dependent loss of responder cell frequency. The potential repertoire of old mice may be quite different from the repertoire expressed during an immune response.

V. CYTOKINES

Cytokines, which include the categories of lymphokines, monokines, and chemokines, are small molecular weight peptides produced by virtually all nucleated cell types in the body. They differ from hormones that are generally produced by specialized glands and that are present in the circulation. Most cytokines function over short distances as autocrine or paracrine intercellular signals and are present in only picogram to nanogram amounts. In addition to their effects on immune function, cytokines provide the signals that regulate cell growth, inflammation, differentiation, and repair. With the exceptions of macrophage colony-stimulating factor (M-CSF), stem cell factor, erythropoietin, and transforming growth factor β (TGF-β), cytokines are not produced constitutively, but are induced following receptor-mediated cell activation to maintain the integrity of the host.

The major cytokines produced by activated T cells include IL-2, IL-3, IL-4, IL-5, IL-6, IL-9, IL-10, IL-12, interferon-γ (IFN-γ), granulocyte M-CSF (GM-CSF), and the tumor necrosis factors (TNF-α and TNF-β). Activated macrophages and monocytes produce IL-1, TNF, IL-6, IFN-α, IFN-β, the chemotactic cytokines, and the chemokines, including IL-8. Some cytokines are also synthesized by other cells of the immune, circulatory, and neural systems. Although a large number of unique cytokines have been identified, the effects of aging on their production and action are known for only a few.

A. Production

Although the aging process is accompanied by a decline in immune system function, this decline is not mirrored by an overall decrease in cytokine production. Synthesis of some cytokines decreases or remains the same with age, although the synthesis of others (especially those cytokines associated with an inflammatory response) increases with age.

Using cell-surface antigens, T cells can be subdivided into naive or memory cell populations. Memory T cells make up a larger percentage of the T-cell pool in aging populations, whereas naive cells are more prevalent in the young. Memory T cells and naive T cells have different activation requirements and lymphokine secretion patterns. It is presumably the predominance of memory cells in the T-cell pool of the elderly that accounts for the increase in synthesis of some cytokines during the aging process.

B. Interleukin-2

The major function of IL-2, formerly called T-cell growth factor, is the activation of a variety of cells in the immune system, including cytotoxic T cells, helper T cells, B cells, macrophages, and natural killer (NK) cells. The binding of IL-2 to its receptor on these cells results in the proliferation of antigen-activated T cells, increased expression of membrane receptors for other growth factors, and enhanced secretion of lymphokines. Studies with mice and humans demonstrate that the production of IL-2 by T cells decreases with age, but results from studies with rats are less consistent. The type of stimulant used to induce IL-2 production can alter the amount obtained. Although phytohemagglutin (PHA) stimulation of the T cells in humans shows an age-related decline in the synthesis of IL-2 and a decrease in the IL-2 mRNA transcribed, use of PMA and ionophore produces no such age-related difference.

C. Interleukin-3 and 5 and Granulocyte Macrophage Colony Stimulating Factor

IL-3, IL-5, and GM-CSF exert the majority of their biological effects on hemopoietic cells outside of the lymphoid system. These three cytokines act as eosinophil-stimulating factors. IL-3 production has been reported to either increase or decrease with the age of the cell donor. Murine memory CD4-positive and CD8-positive cells produce greater levels of IL-3 and IL-5 than comparable naive cells. There have been reports of age-related declines in the production of GM-CSF by stimulated cell populations from older murine donors.

D. Interleukin-4

IL-4 acts as a B-cell co-stimulatory factor and is involved in many phases of B-cell development. Under certain conditions IL-4 is a potent growth factor for T cells. Old mice display increased IL-4 secretion. Consistent with this murine memory CD4-positive cells produce greater amounts of IL-4 than comparable naive cells.

E. Tumor Necrosis Factor

TNF is produced by activated macrophages and other cells and has a broad range of biological actions on both immune and nonimmune cells. TNF is considered a major inflammatory mediator and can uncouple the metabolism of lipids and sugars from the production of energy. For example, it is responsible for the cachexia (wasting) exhibited by individuals harboring parasitic infections and can induce fever. Murine CD8-positive memory cells produce similar or higher levels of TNF-α and TNF-β than naive CD8-positive cells.

F. Interferon-γ

IFN-γ is a potent activator of macrophages and monocytes, greatly increasing their tumoricidal and microbicidal activities. In addition, IFN-γ has other immunoregulatory properties, including (a) the modulation of expression of class I and II major histocompatibility complex antigens on a variety of cells, (b) the prevention of induction, proliferation, and effector functions of a subset of helper and cytotoxic T cells, and (c) the induction of another subpopulation of helper T cells that regulates cell-mediated immunity. There is an increase in IFN-γ production by the T cells of old mice using bioassay, enzyme-linked immunosorbent assay (ELISA), and mRNA assays. In addition, murine memory CD4-positive and CD8-positive T cells synthesize more IFN-γ than comparable naive cells. The synthesis of IFN-γ mRNA is greater in the T cells of older mice and humans.

VI. CYTOKINE RECEPTORS

Because the intracellular signal transduction process, by which cells become activated, is mediated through the interaction of a cytokine with its receptor, the cell surface expression of the receptors is of crucial importance. Although certain T-cell subsets may "overproduce" some lymphokines in the elderly, the consequent effect of this overproduction may be nullified by the down regulation or uncoupling of their cognate receptors.

Many cytokine receptors have been cloned and can be assigned to one of three major groups: (a) the hematopoietic growth factor receptor (HGFR) family

that includes the majority of cytokine receptors; (b) TNF and nerve growth factor (NGF) receptor superfamily; and (c) the immunoglobulin (Ig)-supergene family. There are, however, a few cytokine receptors (e.g., IL-2Rα chain and IFN-γR) that do not belong to any of these groups.

Information about the mechanisms by which cytokines and their specific receptors transmit signals to the cell nucleus is currently under intense investigation by many laboratories. There appears to be no common signal transduction mechanisms even within a given cytokine family; however, the internalization of the ligand and/or receptor appears important. Additionally, various protein kinases, guanosine triphosphate (GTP)-binding proteins (G proteins), ion fluxes (in particular calcium), and the phosphorylation of cytosolic proteins on serine, threonine, or tyrosine residues all appear important in cytokine signal transduction.

VII. CLINICAL SIGNIFICANCE

There is little doubt that diminished immune responsiveness contributes to an increased susceptibility to infectious disease. There is a higher incidence of pneumonias, cholangitis, diverticulitis, bacteremia, varicella-zoster reexacerbations, asymptomatic bacteriuria, urinary tract infections, and tuberculosis among the elderly. Not only is there a higher incidence of both bacterial and viral illnesses, there is also an increased morbidity and mortality among the elderly from infections. As outlined above, part of this is likely attributable to age-related decreases in the effectiveness of many immune functions, but is also related to commonly occurring age defects in the cardiovascular, genitourinary, and respiratory systems. [See Cardiovascular System; Renal and Urinary Tract Function; Respiratory System.]

Because the incidence of most common cancers increases in the elderly, it seems reasonable to hypothesize that diminished immune function is an important contributing factor in the development of neoplasia. In many elderly, immune surveillance mechanisms that eliminate mutant cells are compromised, which results in an increased risk of cancer. Also, there is an increasing body of evidence indicating that dysregulation within the immune system plays a prominent role in tumor development and/or progression. For example, autocrine production of IL-6 by plasma cells accompanied by a *c-myc* gene rearrangement has been found important in the development of several types of polyclonal plasmacytomas. A similar mechanism appears to occur in myeloma, where the aberrant expression of IL-1 induces the expression of adhesion molecules and paracrine IL-6 synthesis. [*See* CANCER AND THE ELDERLY.]

Apoptosis plays a major role in the differentiation and selection of both T and B lymphocytes. Which cells die and which survive is critical in the discrimination between self and nonself antigens and thus is important in tumor development. Recently, several proteins such as Fas and bcl-2, which are directly involved in inducing or suppressing apoptosis, and the tumor-suppressor genes *RB* and *p53* have been shown to act at various stages of immune cell maturation. The effects these molecules have on tumor development is presently under study by many laboratories.

VIII. SUMMARY

Future research in this area will be concerned less with the documentation of the age-related changes in immune function and more with possible strategies for preserving the integrity of the immune system throughout life. At this time there are no means for doing this, but the testing of cytokines, lymphokines, thymic hormones, and pituitary growth factors will determine if this can be done and eventually will dem-

onstrate if age-related disease patterns can be altered. The variability seen in the levels of immune function in older adults is also providing clues as to the means for preserving function. The development of vaccines with both greater efficacy in the elderly as well as an expanded scope of coverage will also provide better protection from infectious agents. The study of immune function and aging provides an insight as to the process of aging itself, the effects of aging on cellular and tissue function, and provides a promise for being able to alter the patterns of age-related diseases.

BIBLIOGRAPHY

Adler, W. H., & Nagel, J. E. (1994). Clinical immunology and aging. In W. R. Hazzard, E. L. Bierman, J. P. Blass, W. H. Ettinger, Jr., J. B. Halter, & R. Andres (Eds.), *Principles of geriatric medicine and gerontology* (3rd ed.) (pp. 61–75). New York: McGraw-Hill.

Adler, W. H., Song, L., Chopra, R. K., Winchurch, R. A., Waggie, K. S., & Nagel, J. E. (1994). Immunodeficiency of aging. In D. C. Powers, J. E. Morley, & R. M. Coe, (Eds.), *Aging, immunity and infection* (pp. 66–81). New York: Springer.

Möller, G. Ed. (1994). Apoptosis in immunity. *Immunological Review, 142.*

Paul, W. E. (1993). *Fundamental immunology* (3rd ed.). New York: Raven Press.

Song, L., Kim, Y. H., Chopra, R. K., Proust, J. J., Nagel, J. E., Nordin, A. A., & Adler, W. H. (1993). Age-related effects in T cell activation and proliferation. *Experimental Gerontology, 28*, 313–321.

Thompson, A. W. (1994). *The cytokine handbook* (2nd ed.). San Diego: Academic Press.

Inhibition

Joan M. McDowd

University of Kansas Medical Center

Distraction   The state of having been diverted from a previous focus of attention, usually by some other, irrelevant stimuli.

Facilitation   The cognitive process by which relevant information is given priority in the limited-capacity information-processing system.

Inhibition   The cognitive process by which irrelevant information is prevented from gaining access to the limited-capacity information-processing system.

Selective Attention   The interaction of facilitative and inhibitory processes that control the focus of information processing, allowing the individual to concentrate on relevant information and ignore irrelevant information.

Visual Search Paradigms   Any of a variety of tasks that require the individual to locate a target item in a display containing both relevant and irrelevant items.

INHIBITORY PROCESSES play a critical role in the human information-processing system. Because the momentary capacity of the information-processing system is limited, access to the system must be controlled so that relevant information is processed, whereas irrelevant information is not. Selective attention is typically the mechanism that controls access to the processing system. This mechanism involves both the facilitation of relevant information and the inhibition or suppression of irrelevant information (e.g., irrelevant sensory stimuli). Breakdowns in inhibitory function result in distraction and an associated decline in information-processing efficiency. Thus in the domain of cognitive function, inhibitory processes facilitate the selective processing of information to maximize the behavioral efficiency of the individual.

I. INHIBITION IN INFORMATION PROCESSING

In the context of adult development and aging, the notion that altered inhibitory function might underlie many age-related cognitive changes has been considered since the 1950s. Birren stated that the notion of inhibitory decline "has heuristic value for many reported age differences." Pavlov hypothesized that age-related declines in inhibitory function produced the difficulties he observed on the part of older adults in discrimination learning tasks, in extinguishing previously learned responses, and in the control of language functions. In the intervening decades a number of lines of work have been initiated to further examine the role of inhibitory function in age differences in cognitive abilities.

II. PHYSIOLOGICAL INDICES OF INHIBITION: THE ORIENTING RESPONSE

Studies of the autonomic orienting response (OR), a complex pattern of physiological changes elicited by novel and/or significant stimuli, provide one approach to understanding the role of inhibition in information processing. These studies assume that the OR indexes the engagement of attention, and that the magnitude of the OR indexes the extent to which attention is engaged. A further assumption is that inhibitory processes modulate the OR in line with current task demands and behavioral goals. That is, when information is no longer significant or novel, the OR is suppressed. An age-related inhibitory deficit would thus manifest itself as a pattern of ORs that continue to be elicited even after novelty or significance has worn off, or that are elicited in response to stimuli that are irrelevant to the current circumstances.

Studies using the OR to index attention and the suppression of attention in young and old adults have provided some evidence for an age-related decline in the efficiency inhibitory function. For example, in a task requiring individuals to attend to some stimuli and ignore others, young adults showed evidence of differential orienting, but older adults did not. That is, to-be-ignored stimuli elicited the same physiological response in older adults as did the task-relevant information, indicating a failure of inhibitory processes to modulate and suppress responding to the irrelevant information. This pattern of results suggests that older adults are less efficient in the control of attention, and so may be less efficient information processors. [See ATTENTION.]

III. BEHAVIORAL INDICES OF INHIBITION: ATTENTION AND WORKING MEMORY

A. Selective Attention

Selective attention is the mechanism that facilitates the processing of relevant information and suppresses irrelevant information. Failures of selection result in the capture of attention by irrelevant information, commonly called distraction. Many studies in the literature have indicated that older adults are more susceptible to distraction than are young adults, and these studies have been used as evidence to bolster the hypothesis that older adults are less able to inhibit irrelevant information than are young adults.

Patrick Rabbitt's 1965 classic work on age and distraction had young and older adults sorting cards on the basis of prespecified letters printed on the card. Rabbitt observed that the presence of irrelevant letters arranged randomly around the card slowed the sorting times of older adults more than it did young adults. He concluded that the older adults were less able to avoid distraction than were young adults. By implication, therefore, inhibitory processes have been implicated in producing this pattern of results.

Rabbitt's work was followed by other studies designed to explore the parameters that determined the presence and extent of any age-related increase in distractibility. Visual search tasks have frequently been used to assess the efficiency with which individuals can locate and/or identify a target in the presence of distracting, nontarget information. One of the generalizations that emerged from this work is that when selection and suppression can be guided by physical cues such as color, shape, or location, older adults perform comparably to young adults. However, when there is uncertainty about what or where to attend to, older adults are typically at a significant disadvantage relative to young adults.

A similar pattern of results has been observed with the Stroop task. This task requires individuals to name the color in which a color word is printed. For example, if the word *red* printed in green ink is presented, the task is to name the color *green* and inhibit responding to the word *red*. Older adults typically have more difficulty with this task than do young adults, suggesting less efficient inhibitory processes. However, when to-be-named color and color word are separated in space, inhibition of the color word appears to operate comparably in young and older adults. Together, these results suggest that age-related declines in the efficiency of inhibitory function seem to be modulated by task parameters that affect the ease of discriminating between relevant and irrelevant information.

Negative priming is another procedure designed to measure more directly the efficiency of inhibitory function. In this procedure involving targets and distractors, a distractor stimulus that is to be ignored on one trial becomes the to-be-attended stimulus on the subsequent trial. Empirically, it has been observed that responding is slowed in the trial sequence just described relative to a sequence in which there is no relationship between targets and distractors on subsequent trials. This lengthening of reaction time is termed *negative priming*. The theoretical interpretation of this phenomenon is that because the distractor stimulus is inhibited on the initial trial, processing that same stimulus on the subsequent trial will take longer because the effects of the previous inhibition will have to be overcome. The magnitude of the slowing, or negative priming, observed is then taken to index the strength of inhibitory function.

The application of the negative priming procedures to understanding age differences in inhibitory function has produced mixed results. Initial studies involving the naming of words or letters in the presence of distracting words or letters indicated an absence of negative priming among older adults. This pattern of results is in line with the hypothesis of an age-related decline in inhibitory functioning. Subsequent work, however, has indicated that under some circumstances, negative priming, and thus intact inhibitory processes, are observed in older adults. Several studies that involve responding on the basis of target location rather than identity have reported comparable negative priming among old and young adults. These data indicate that age differences in inhibitory function are specific rather than general, and once again when location is available as a cue, inhibitory processes appear to operate similarly for old and young adults.

B. Working Memory

Inhibitory processes have also been hypothesized to play an important role in working memory and related language functions as they change with age. Inhibitory processes are assumed to limit the activation of semantic information to the most relevant information for the task at hand. If inhibitory processes are operating at suboptimal efficiency in older adults, then irrelevant information may be activated and may serve to functionally reduce the capacity of working memory by unnecessarily taking up space there.

Studies using language materials with ambiguous interpretations have been used to test these ideas about inhibition, working memory, and language function. For example, ambiguous prose that might be interpreted in two or more ways is presented, fol-

lowed by disambiguating information. Inhibitory efficiency is indexed by measures of the availability of the incorrect interpretation in working memory. This availability may be measured in priming tasks or implicit memory tasks. Several studies have shown that irrelevant information remains active longer among older adults than young adults, reducing working memory capacity and decreasing the efficiency with which language information can be processed. Declining inhibitory function is cited as responsible for these age-related changes. [*See* MEMORY.]

IV. INHIBITION IN THE SOCIAL ARENA: VERBAL COMMUNICATION

Inhibition not only suppresses selected inputs but also acts to control such outputs as inappropriate behaviors, which might otherwise interfere with normal social interactions. One area in which altered inhibitory function might affect social interactions is in verbal communication. There is some evidence to suggest that older adults are more likely than young adults to exhibit off-target verbosity in conversation or related forms of communication. Older adults appear to be more vulnerable to the intrusion of personal experiences and memories into consciousness. Instead of gating out this information, it may become included in social exchanges regardless of its relevance to the topic at hand. One outcome of this verbosity might be reticence on the part of others to engage a verbose individual in conversation, contributing to some level of social isolation of the verbose person. Thus inhibitory deficits, if truly contributory to this pattern of interactions, can have negative consequences for the social well-being of older individuals.

Studies including measure of both off-target verbosity and psychometric measures of inhibitory processes have indicated a relationship between the two. That is, those individuals who score higher on verbosity measures also do less well on the measures of inhibitory function. Although this relationship is suggestive of a causal role for altered inhibitory efficiency in communication verbosity, other factors may also play a role. An individual's expectations about the constraints of the conversation, the relationship between conversation participants, and lifelong conversation patterns all may influence the direction a conversation may take. Specifying the precise role of inhibitory processes remains for further study. [*See* LANGUAGE AND COMMUNICATION IN AGING AND DEMENTIA.]

V. INHIBITION IN MENTAL HEALTH: SELECTIVE PROCESSING OF INFORMATION

A number of mental health problems have been associated with reduced attention control. For example, in obsessive-compulsive disorder, depression, and schizophrenia it has been suggested that the intrusion of irrelevant or unwanted material into consciousness may contribute to cognitive inefficiency and/or psychological distress. Cognitive theories of depression hold that depressed individuals may be besieged by negative thoughts that overpower normal inhibitory processes. The depressed individual thus perceives or recalls primarily negative information, which in turn perpetuates the depressive episode. Although this view of depression is still controversial, there are a variety of studies using tasks such as the Stroop task that are consistent with the hypothesis that depressed individuals have less efficient inhibitory control. The data on whether this deficit is exacerbated by age-related declines in inhibitory control are also a matter of some controversy. Among the few studies that have addressed this question, some report no greater deficits in older depressed individuals than young depressed individuals, whereas others have suggested that aging and depression have interactive effects to produce the greatest negative impact on behavior. Clearly more work needs to be done to answer this important question regarding the combined effects of aging and depression on inhibitory function. [*See* DEPRESSION.]

Inhibitory dysfunction has also been identified as a fundamental component of the cognitive deficits associated with schizophrenia. Inhibition has been studied in individuals with schizophrenia using similar or identical procedures to those used to assess age effects: physiological orienting and habituation, negative priming, sensory gating, the Stroop task, and continuous performance tasks. The pattern of results indicates that inhibitory deficits in older adults and in individuals with schizophrenia are very similar. Unfortunately, to date very few studies have explicitly examined the combined effects of aging and schizophrenia on inhibitory function. Data from the few studies that have been conducted suggest that the deficits seen in older schizophrenics are greater than those seen in either normal aging or schizophrenia alone. Again, however, more work needs to be done before any strong conclusions can be drawn about the combined effects of aging and schizophrenia on inhibition in cognitive function. [*See* MENTAL HEALTH.]

VI. SUMMARY AND CONCLUSIONS

A variety of studies have provided evidence to suggest that inhibitory function declines with advancing age. However, a number of issues must be considered before any global statement can be made about aging and inhibitory function. For example, inhibitory processes can be observed at many levels of nervous system function, from synaptic connections to overt behavior. Thus there may be multiple types of inhibition and/or multiple inhibitory mechanisms that may play a role in age differences in inhibitory function. A second issue concerns the validity of measures of inhibitory function. In many cases, tasks that are assumed to measure inhibition need to have that assumption tested. And finally, individual differences in inhibitory function across age groups need to be understood and explained. Age does not perfectly predict inhibitory efficiency, and the other relevant factors must be identified in order to better understand the contribution of inhibitory function to cognitive aging.

BIBLIOGRAPHY

Coyne, J. C., & Gotlib, I. H. (1983). The role of cognition in depression: A critical appraisal. *Psychological Bulletin, 94,* 472–505.
Dempster, F. N., & Brainerd, C. J. (1995). *Interference and inhibition in cognition.* San Diego: Academic Press.
Hartley, A. A. (1992). Attention, In F. I. M. Craik & T. A. Salthouse (Eds.), *Handbook of aging and cognition* (pp. 3–49). Hillsdale, NJ: Erlbaum.
McDowd, J. M., Filion, D. L., Harris, M. J., & Braff, D. L. (1993). Sensory gating and inhibitory function in late-life schizophrenia. *Schizophrenia Bulletin, 19,* 733–746.
McDowd, J. M., Oseas-Kreger, D. M., & Filion, D. L. (1995). Inhibitory processes in cognition and aging. In F. N. Dempster & C. J. Brainerd (Eds.), *Interference and inhibition in cognition* (pp. 363–400) San Diego: Academic Press.

ISBN 0-12-226861-X

90018